Y0-BEC-417

# University Casebook Series

# INTERNATIONAL FINANCE

## TRANSACTIONS, POLICY, AND REGULATION

By

HAL S. SCOTT
Nomura Professor of International Financial Systems
Harvard Law School

PHILIP A. WELLONS
Deputy Director
Program on International Financial Systems
Harvard Law School

**Westbury, New York**
**THE FOUNDATION PRESS, INC.**
**1995**

615 Merrick Ave.
Westbury, N.Y. 11590–6607
(516) 832–6950


Printed in the United States of America

**Library of Congress Cataloging-in-Publication Data**

Scott, Hal S.
International finance: transactions, policy, and regulation / by Hal S. Scott, Philip A. Wellons
p. cm.
**ISBN** 1–56662–234–4
1. International finance—Law and legislation—Cases. 2. Banks and banking, International—Law and legislation—Cases. 3. Securities—Cases. I. Wellons, Philip A. II. Title.
K1005.3.S29 1995
341.7'51—dc20 94–40771

# PREFACE

This book is about international finance. The topic includes the international aspects of domestic markets as well as offshore markets. The focus is on government policy, at both national and international levels, because of its dominant role in shaping this field. The introductory chapter explores the basic conceptual and definitional issues concerning the field of international finance.

Domestic financial markets encompass banking and securities activities. The international aspects of these markets involve cross-border transactions. If the domestic markets are in the United States, the international aspects of U.S. banking would involve foreign banks serving U.S. customers and U.S. banks serving foreign customers. For securities, the international aspects involve foreign issuers selling shares to U.S. investors and U.S. issuers selling shares to investors outside the United States.

We concentrate on the major domestic markets of the world, in the United States, Japan, and Europe. They are very important in their own right and one can benefit by looking at their different approaches toward similar problems. Chapters II-III and V-VII of the book, therefore, deal with the international aspects of the U.S., Japanese, and European markets. We focus on the European Union as a unit.

Cross-border finance extends beyond traditional banking and securities activity. The international aspects of domestic markets in newer financial instruments appear in our material on securitization (Chapter XII) and futures and options (Chapter XV). The competition among domestic markets for foreign investors and issuers is explored in Chapter XIII. One of the most dynamic activities in international finance is cross-border investment in emerging markets by foreign institutional investors like pension funds. Much of this investment is in newly privatized companies. Chapter XVII deals with that subject.

Offshore markets are the second key part of international finance. In these markets, the transactors or the currency are foreign. For example, London or Hong Kong are centers for transactions between many non-British or non-Hong Kong institutions. Dollar denominated transactions there are often referred to as eurodollars or asiadollars. The book focuses on the major offshore financial markets: eurodollar deposits and loans (Chapter VIII), eurobonds and global bonds (Chapter XI), and swaps (Chapter XVI). National policies sometimes extend to offshore markets. We look at the effect of asset freezes (Chapter X).

The infrastructure of international finance is important to an understanding of cross-border and offshore markets. Capital adequacy for banks and securities operations (Chapter IV), the payment system (Chapter IX) and clearance and settlement (Chapter XIV) are key elements in this infrastructure.

While our approach is rooted in government policy and regulation, the book introduces the student to basic financial concepts and transactions. Exchange regimes, for example, are necessary background for an understanding of the European Monetary Union (Chapter VI). A student of futures, options, and swaps must understand the basic pricing and functions of these instruments. Only the most basic financial theory is presented.

We believe this approach is new and complements existing texts. Most books about international finance are written for finance or economics courses. They traditionally emphasized exchange rates and have only recently expanded to include offshore financial markets.

HAL S. SCOTT
PHILIP A. WELLONS

Cambridge, Massachusetts
December 1994

# ACKNOWLEDGEMENTS

We gratefully acknowledge permission to publish excerpts from the following material.

"Greenspan Says Japanese Banks' Financial Position Are Undermined by Market Drop," 54 *BNA's Banking Report* 633 (April 9, 1990)

Reprinted with permission from *BNA's Banking Report*, Vol. 54, No. 14 (April 9, 1990), p. 633. Copyright © 1990 by The Bureau of National Affairs, Inc. (800–372–1033).

K. Bradsher, "Banks' Securities Trading Markets Comptroller Fearful," New York Times (April 21, 1994), p. D1

Copyright © 1993/1994 by The New York Times Company. Reprinted by permission.

M. Carter, "The Impact of Pension Investments on the World's Financial Market Structure," a paper given at Harvard Law School, November 15, 1993

Reprinted with permission from M. Carter and Y. Zhou.

P. Cooke, excerpts from Bank Capital Adequacy, Price Waterhouse London (July 1991)

Reprinted with kind permission from Price Waterhouse.

K. Dam, *The Rules of the Game* (1982)

Reprinted with permission from The University of Chicago Press; Copyright © 1982 by The University of Chicago, all rights reserved. Published 1982. Printed in the United States of America.

R. Dayan et al. "Legal Overview of Asset-Backed Securities". From the book: THE HANDBOOK OF ASSET-BACKED SECURITIES By Jess Lederman Copyright © 1990.

Reprinted with permission from Simon & Schuster.

Dufey and Chung, "International Financial Markets: A Survey," in R. L. Kuhn, ed., *International Finance and Investing* (1990)

Reprinted with permission from Dufey and Chung; reprinted with permission from Richard D. Irwin, all rights reserved.

Euroclear, Cross-Border Clearance, Settlement and Custody: Beyond the G30 Recommendations (June 1993)

Reprinted with permission from Morgan Guaranty Trust Company of New York, as operator of the Euroclear System.

T. Friedman, "Soros Gives House Panel Hedge Fund Lesson," New York Times (April 14, 1994)

Copyright © 1993/1994 by The New York Times Company. Reprinted by permission.

D. Gail, J. Norton and M. O'Neal, "The Foreign Bank Supervision Act of 1991: Expanding the Umbrella of Supervisory Regulation" 26 International Lawyer 993 (1992)

Reprinted by permission; Copyright © 1992 American Bar Association.

Goldman, Sachs & Co., Marketing Documents for Roadshow of Telmex ADS Offer (1991)

Copyright © 1991 by Goldman, Sachs & Co.

F. Graaf, *Euromarket Finance: Issues of Euromarket Securities and Syndicated Eurocurrency Loans* (1991)

Reprinted by permission of Kluwer Publishers

E. Greene, A. Beller, G. Cohen, M. Hudson, Jr., and E. Rosen, *U.S. Regulation of the International Securities Markets* (1992)

Reprinted from *U.S. Regulation of the International Securities Markets* with the permission of Prentice Hall Law & Business.

G. Haberman, "Capital requirements of commercial and investment banks: contrasts in regulation," Federal Reserve Bank of New York Quarterly Review, Autumn 1987

Reprinted with permission from G. Haberman; reprinted with permission from Federal Reserve Bank; and reprinted with permission from Federal Reserve Bank of New York Quarterly Review.

Q. Hardy, "Battle to Open Tokyo Markets Heats Up," Wall Street Journal, June 2, 1993, C1

Reprinted by permission of The Wall Street Journal, Copyright © 1993, Dow Jones & Company, Inc. All Rights Reserved Worldwide.

Q. Hardy, "Japan's Big Four Brokerage Firms, Despite Higher Profits, Are Downgraded," Wall Street Journal, January 19, 1994, A15

Reprinted by permission of The Wall Street Journal, Copyright © 1994, Dow Jones & Company, Inc. All Rights Reserved Worldwide.

S. Henderson, "Should Swap Termination Payments Be One-way or Two-way," International Financial Law Review (October 1990), 27-32

This article first appears in the October 1990 issue of International Financial Law Review. Copyright © Euromoney Publications PLC, London, England.

J. Hull, INTRODUCTION TO FUTURES AND OPTIONS MARKETS, copyright © 1991

Reprinted by permission of Prentice-Hall, Inc., Englewood Cliffs, N.J.

U. Koch, "Germany," in Securitization: An International Guide, in International Financial Law Review, Special Supplement (August 1993), 12

This article first appears in the August 1993 issue of International Financial Law Review. Copyright © Euromoney Publications PLC, London, England.

Maurice D. Levi, *International Finance* (1990)

Reproduced with permission of McGraw-Hill, Inc.

R. Litan, "Nightmare in Basle," The International Economy, November/December 1992

Reprinted with permission by The International Economy magazine, November/December 1992, Washington, D.C.

J. May, J. Watson, and H. Thomas, "United Kingdom," in Securitization: An International Guide, in International Financial Law Review, Special Supplement (August 1993), 20

This article first appears in the August 1993 issue of International Financial Law Review. Copyright © Euromoney Publications PLC, London, England.

J. Mullin, "Emerging Equity Markets in the Global Economy," Federal Reserve Bank of New York Quarterly Review (Summer 1993)

Reprinted with permission from J. Mullin; reprinted with permission from Federal Reserve Bank; and reprinted with permission from Federal Reserve Bank of New York Quarterly Review

"The Foreigners Cut Back," The New York Times, May 16, 1993, Sec. 3, 6

Copyright © 1993/1994 by The New York Times Company. Reprinted by permission.

G. Palm and D. Walkovik, United States: A Special Report, in "Issuing Securities: A Guide to Securities Regulation Around the World," International Financial Law Review, Special Supplement (July 1990), 62-84

This article first appears in the July 1990 issue of International Financial Law Review. Copyright © Euromoney Publications PLC, London, England.

T. Prime, *International Bonds and Certificates of Deposit* 45–54 (1991)

Reprinted by permission of Butterworth-Heinemann Ltd.; and reprinted by permission of T. Prime.

D. Rossner and Y. Shimada, "Japan," in Securitization: An International Guide, in International Financial Law Review, Special Supplement (August 1993), 15

This article first appears in the August 1993 issue of International Financial Law Review. Copyright © Euromoney Publications PLC, London, England.

J. Schell, Daimler-Benz Leads Germany to New York Stock Exchange, Int'l Fin. L. Rev. 11 (December 1993)

This article first appears in the December 1993 issue of International Financial Law Review. Copyright © Euromoney Publications PLC, London, England.

H. Scott, Supervision of International Banking Post-BCCI, 8 Ga. St. U. L. Rev. 487 (1992)

Reprinted by permission.

M. Sesit, "Nomura Becomes a Top Program Trader in New York, but Shuns Strategy in Japan," Wall Street Journal, February 7, 1992, C1

Reprinted by permission of The Wall Street Journal, Copyright © 1992, Dow Jones & Company, Inc. All Rights Reserved Worldwide.

M. Sesit and L. Jereski, "Hedge Funds Face Review of Practices," Wall Street Journal (February 28, 1994)

Reprinted by permission of The Wall Street Journal, Copyright © 1994, Dow Jones & Company, Inc. All Rights Reserved Worldwide.

R. Smyth, "Bank of England Blueprint for LSE Settlement System," International Financial Law Review (October 1993), 21–23

This article first appears in the October 1993 issue of International Financial Law Review. Copyright © Euromoney Publications PLC, London, England.

D. Sneider, "Financial Services Reform in Japan," *Int'l Securities Reg. Rept.* 6 (February 6, 1993)

Reprinted with permission from International Securities Regulation Report. Copyright © 1994 by LRP Publications, 580 Village Boulevard, Suite 140, West Palm Beach, FL 33409. All rights reserved. For more information on International Securities Regulation Report, please call 1–407–687–1220, ext. 716.

J. Sterngold, "The $6 Trillion Hole in Japan's Pocket," New York Times, January 21, 1994, D1

*ACKNOWLEDGEMENTS*

Copyright © 1993/1994 by The New York Times Company. Reprinted by permission.

C. A. Stone and A. Zissu, II *Global Risk Based Capital Regulations* (1994)

Reprinted with permission from Stone and Zissu; reprinted with permission from Richard D. Irwin, all rights reserved.

I. Swary and B. Topf, Global Financial Deregulation: Commercial Banking at the Crossroads (1992)

Reprinted by permission of Blackwell Publishers.

E. Symons and J. White, Banking Law, 3rd Edition (1991), 806–9

Reprinted with permission of the West Publishing Corporation.

M. Warren, "The Investment Services Directive: The 'North Sea Alliance' Victory over 'Club Med'," 6 *Int'l Securities Reg. Rept.* 6 (January 12, 1993)

Reprinted with permission from International Securities Regulation Report. Copyright © 1994 by LRP Publications, 580 Village Boulevard, Suite 140, West Palm Beach, FL 33409. All rights reserved. For more information on International Securities Regulation Report, please call 1–407–687–1220, ext. 716.

*

# SUMMARY OF CONTENTS

*

# TABLE OF CONTENTS

# INTERNATIONAL FINANCE

## TRANSACTIONS, POLICY, AND REGULATION

*

# Chapter I

# INTRODUCTION

This book examines international banking and securities transactions and their regulation. It begins with the major national markets of the United States, Europe, and Japan, then turns to the offshore markets. We also consider major areas of international regulation and policy, such as capital adequacy and clearance and settlement.

The first chapter reviews the instruments, long-term market trends, and basic concepts and language of international finance. The readings offer several different perspectives on the subject, that of the scholar (in Dufey and Chung and in Bryant), the practitioner (Maughan), and the regulator (the Bank of England).

Many financial words of art appear in the material often without explanation. The Bank of England article is written for professionals in the field and makes no allowance for the novice. Do not be surprised if many words are new and hard to understand. We recommend two more complete glossaries: G. Munn, F. Garcia and C. Woelfel, *Encyclopedia of Banking and Finance* (9th ed. 1991) and J. Downes and J. Goodman, *Dictionary of Finance and Investment Terms* (3rd ed. 1991).

## A. THE DEFINITION OF AN INTERNATIONAL FINANCIAL TRANSACTION

International financial transactions are the subject of this book. But what makes a transaction international? Dufey and Chung, in the following article, give their definition.

### DUFEY AND CHUNG, "INTERNATIONAL FINANCIAL MARKETS: A SURVEY," IN R.L. KUHN, ED., INTERNATIONAL FINANCE AND INVESTING (1990)

Pp. 3–29.

. . .

#### RELEVANT CONCEPTS AND TERMINOLOGY

We will begin by presenting a conceptual framework to explain the confusing terminology surrounding global financial markets. This framework should also help the reader classify and analyze the value of various instruments and transactions seen in the international marketplace.

. . .

An overview of international financial markets must begin by noting the distinctive qualities of three markets, according to the functions they perform:

1. The market for international payments
2. The market for international credit
3. International markets for real assets

. . .

International Credit Markets

While the essence of the foreign exchange market is the movement of financial claims over space, *credit transactions* involve the exchange of funds over time. Savers, whose income temporarily exceeds their use of funds, make the additional output they have created available to borrowers who have a shortage of funds because they commit resources to real assets (either consumer durables, productive assets in the form of business investment, or government projects) in excess of their current income. Credit markets also aid in distributing risks among participants in this savings and investment process. By generating various types of financial claims, these markets permit savers and borrowers to "fine tune" the combination of risks they are willing to bear.

Such transactions assume various forms. To transform chaos into some semblance of order, it is useful to distinguish first between *fixed income securities* and *equity claims*. The essence of this distinction, of course, is that the former yield returns that are contractually fixed, while the latter provide returns that are dependent upon the success of an enterprise. While this broad characterization is sufficient for most purposes, it is not as sharp as it appears, because the markets have developed many hybrid securities containing elements of both.

. . .

Foreign Real Assets Markets

Finally, there are international markets for claims on real assets. In this context, one usually refers to *Foreign Direct Investment* (FDI). It is important to note that the distinction between FDI and international portfolio investment through equities is not always apparent.

. . .

## A CLASSIFICATION OF INTERNATIONAL CREDIT MARKETS

We begin by introducing a simple conceptual scheme for classifying international credit markets. (See Figure 1.) Essentially it is based on two dimensions: *how* (through which financial channel) and *where* (in which governmental jurisdiction) funds are transferred from savers to borrowers.

Institutional Structure

The first dimension represents the *channel,* or the institutional structure of market participants through which funds are moved.

Resources can be transferred from savers to borrowers through two channels: (1) *financial intermediaries* that attract funds from savers by issuing their own claims and, in turn, lend the funds to those who invest in real assets; and (2) organized *securities markets* in which savers and borrowers can link up directly (savers can purchase securities issued by ultimate borrowers). The organizational pattern of such markets is determined either by convention, the explicit agreement of the participating private entities, by government regulation, or both.

FIGURE 1
International Credit Markets: A Schematic Presentation

| | National | International | |
|---|---|---|---|
| Credit Channel | Domestic | Foreign | "Euro" |
| Financial Intermediaries | | | |
| Securities Markets | | | |
| | "Internal" | | "External" |

. . .

Jurisdictions

The other dimension concerns the *jurisdiction* in which financial resources are transferred. Most credit transactions take place in domestic financial markets. However, many financial markets have extensive links abroad: domestic investors purchase foreign securities and may invest funds in foreign financial institutions. Conversely, domestic banks may lend to foreign residents, and foreign residents may issue securities in the national market or deposit funds with resident financial intermediaries. These are the traditional "foreign" markets for international financial transactions.

The significant aspect of such traditional foreign lending and borrowing is that all transactions are expected to abide by the rules, customs, and institutional arrangements prevailing in the national market concerned. Most important, all these transactions are directly subject to public policy, governing transactions with nonresidents ("foreign transactions") in a particular market. To illustrate, when savers purchase securities in a foreign market, they do so according to the rules, market practices, and regulatory precepts governing such transactions in that particular market. The same applies to those who invest their funds with financial intermediaries abroad.

Likewise, borrowers from abroad who wish to issue securities in a national market must follow the rules and regulations of that market. Here we encounter an important phenomenon that is crucial to understanding international markets: the rules governing the access of foreign borrowers to national markets tend to be discriminatory and restrictive. The same is true with respect to financial intermediaries. The borrower who approaches a foreign financial institution for a loan obtains funds at rates and conditions imposed by the financial institutions of the foreign country, and he is directly affected by the authorities, policy on lending to foreign residents.

During the 1960s, market mechanisms removed international (and to a certain extent even national) borrowing and lending from the jurisdiction of national authorities. This was accomplished by locating the market for credit denominated in a particular currency *outside* the country where that currency is legal tender, i.e., into a jurisdiction offering a more hospitable regulatory climate for such transactions. For example, markets for dollar-denominated loans, deposits, and securities in jurisdictions other than the United States to a large extent avoid U.S. banking and securities regulations. We refer to these markets as *Euromarkets* or more properly as *external* or *offshore markets* to indicate that they are not part of the domestic (or national) financial system. Thus, the essence of this classification is the nature of regulation. Differences in interest rates, practices, and regulations that exist between domestic and external markets arise primarily from the extent to which regulatory constraints are different.

### Structural Summary

Today, virtually all major capital markets, including those of the United States, exhibit the three-tiered structure depicted in Figure 1:

- *Domestic Market.* Usually with unique procedures and institutions stemming from historical and regulatory determinants.
- *Foreign Market.* Attached to the domestic market, where nonresidents supply and take funds, but always under the specific rules established for foreign participants in the national market.
- *External or "Offshore" Market.* Located in a different political jurisdiction and only linked by the currency used to denominate the financial claims to the national market.

The various external markets have more features in common with each other than with their respective national markets. Therefore, they are properly discussed as a common, integrated market where claims denominated in different currencies are exchanged and are referred to as Euromarkets.

. . .

## THE OFFSHORE MARKETS

As pointed out earlier, different national markets are separated by regulation, whereby the regulation and control of the relative money supply (e.g., the currency) represents only a relatively minor aspect of that segmentation. In contrast, the Euromarkets are quite homogeneous, which is why many observers treat them as one market, using the term in singular form. These markets are fairly big and therefore important in and of themselves for both users and providers of funds. In addition, it is largely via the offshore market that national markets have been integrated, which justifies in a fashion the use of the term *global* financial market. Again, however, it is important to distinguish between intermediated markets and securities markets. The first category refers to the Eurocurrency market for bank deposits and bank loans. In contrast, securities include the Eurobond, note, and commercial paper markets.

While similar in principle, the reasons that explain the intermediated Eurocurrency market differ somewhat from those that explain segmented markets for fixed-income securities. Indeed, each could exist without the other. Recognizing these determinants is not only important from the point of view of understanding markets, but also with respect to the analysis of market imperfections that allow arbitrage transactions. Indeed, much of what is known as financial innovation is based on an exploitation of variations in offshore-onshore differences in terms of interest rates and financial contract provisions.

The Catalyst of Regulations

Beginning in the early 1960s, the external market for bank deposits and assets came into existence because banks operating domestically (a category that includes foreign-owned banks) are burdened with costly regulations. These regulations include reserve requirements, the cost of deposit insurance schemes, taxes, and other factors. By the same token, regulations and political pressures that force banks to book assets that are inferior from a risk-return point of view make financial intermediaries in national markets less competitive. Thus, *costs* have forced the shift of deposits and bank assets from national markets to "books" offshore.

Nonresident Convertibility

This basic condition has to be complemented by another: offshore banks must be able to clear payments in the respective national payment system, since at the beginning and end of every offshore deposit, and at the beginning and end of every loan, a payment must be made through the clearing system of the country where the respective currency is legal tender. Technically speaking, this system requires the existence of *nonresident convertibility* as a necessary, but not sufficient, condition for the existence of an offshore banking market. Without it, offshore transactions can only happen on a brokered basis by matching placers and takers of funds. In addition, transactors must have some freedom from exchange controls, because all offshore deposits and loans are international transactions from a legal point of view.

. . .

### Foreign Issuers and Domestic Investors

With respect to the Eurobond market, the set of market imperfections responsible for its existence is based essentially on a regulatory dichotomy: foreign borrowers are prevented from issuing securities in national markets in various ways. (Sometimes these restrictions also pertain to domestic corporate issuers, especially when government preempts the domestic market.) On the other hand, the regulations that might prevent domestic investors from purchasing foreign securities are either less rigid or unenforceable.

### Offshore Investment Accounts

In this context, one must note that investors throughout the world have learned that "country risk" begins at home. High rates of taxation, the existence or threat of exchange controls, political instability, and often an interest rate structure that is kept artificially low have caused people with money to keep a portion of their savings outside their own borders. Often this group comprises the better part of the middle and upper classes in many countries. The havens are well known; they include Switzerland, Luxembourg, London, Singapore, Hong Kong, and the Caribbean. The United States is also an important recipient of "flight capital."

Medium-term, fixed-income obligations of well-known entities denominated in strong currencies (essentially U.S. dollars, the currencies of the DM bloc, and the Japanese yen) represent the ideal vehicle for this investment clientele. Such securities are issued and largely placed *outside* the respective countries where these currencies are means of payment. They are therefore free from withholding taxes and assure anonymity to the holder because they are invariably issued in bearer form. And, while the Eurobond market has attracted a fair share of institutional investors, the market is to a great extent dominated by the behavior of individual investors. Indeed, with the wave of liberalization of major—and even not so major—national markets in the first half of the 1980s, many institutional investors pursuing active portfolio strategies have shifted their purchases back into the national markets, where they find securities with better liquidity.

. . .

## FINANCIAL INNOVATION

Beginning in the 1970s and accelerating in the early 80s, financial markets have seen a wave of new instruments and techniques. One of the motivating factors was advances in information technology, particularly the spread of personal computers throughout the financial industry. Further, increasing interest rate and exchange rate volatility worldwide has fostered the demand for hedge products. Last, but not least, the results of academic financial research were increasingly implemented by financial service providers who offered new products to a receptive market.

It was particularly the development of markets for "derivative" securities, such as futures and options, that led to further developments along these lines. Market participants learned to "unbundle," or "strip," financial contracts into their various components and, by the same token, put them together again into securities that suited the needs of their clients. And this demand was often driven by market imperfections, usually based on regulatory discrepancies.

It was not surprising that the offshore markets generated more than their fair share of financial innovation, with respect to both conceptualization and implementation. This was simply because regulatory discrepancies as well as differences in market perceptions of various investor groups provided fertile soil for financial engineering. This inducement on the demand side was furthered by unique conditions on the supply side. In the offshore markets, which are characterized by almost complete freedom of entry, various financial institutions met head-on in a field open to all comers.

. . .

### *Questions*

1. According to Dufey and Chung, what makes a banking transaction international? If a U.S. bank in New York made a Deutschmark loan to a U.S. company, would that be international? If not, should it be considered international?

2. Citibank is a U.S. bank with a New York headquarters. Suppose its U.K. branch or U.K. subsidiary makes a sterling loan to a resident of the U.K. According to Dufey and Chung, would this be an international banking transaction? If so, would it be a foreign or "euro" transaction?

3. If a Japanese company issued securities in Tokyo, and they were bought in Tokyo by a U.S. investor, would this be an international securities transaction, according to Dufey and Chung? Should it be treated differently than a purely domestic transaction?

4. Various players, such as national governments, regulators, companies, and banks themselves, act in banking markets. How might it matter to them that a banking transaction is international?

Bryant, in his book *International Financial Intermediaries,* argued that conventional measures of banks' international loans were inadequate. His calculations for the year 1982 are given in the following two tables.

## RALPH C. BRYANT, INTERNATIONAL FINANCIAL INTERMEDIATION (1987)

Tables 3–2 and 3–5.

### Table 3–2. *Assets (including Interbank Claims) Reported by Banking Offices in Fifteen Industrial Countries and Eight Offshore Banking Centers, December 31, 1982*

Billions of U.S. dollars at end–1982 exchange rates unless otherwise indicated

| | *Assets with one or more international characteristic* | | | | | *Subtotal of assets with some international characteristic* | |
|---|---|---|---|---|---|---|---|
| *Country or group of countries* | *Claims on foreign residents denominated in foreign currencies* (1) | *Claims on foreign residents denominated in home currency* (2) | *Claims on home residents denominated in foreign currencies* (3) | *Traditional domestic assets (claims on home residents denominated in home currency)* (4) | *Total assets (gross size of banks' balance sheets) (1 ÷ 2 ÷ 3 ÷ 4)* (5) | *Amount (1 ÷ 2 ÷ 3)* (6) | *Percent of total balance sheet [(6 ÷ 5) + 100]* (7) |
| A. Five major European banking centers | 716 | 160 | 242 | 1,957 | 3,075 | 1,118 | 36 |
| United Kingdom | 437 | 26 | 183 | 248 | 893 | 646 | 72 |
| Germany | 19 | 64 | 2 | 1,054 | 1,140 | 86 | 8 |
| France | 124 | 24 | 40 | 466 | 654 | 188 | 29 |
| Switzerland (excluding trustee accounts) | 33 | 38 | 5 | 184 | 260 | 76 | 29 |
| Luxembourg | 102 | 8 | 12 | 6 | 128 | 122 | 96 |
| B. Seven other European countries | 177 | 29 | 69 | 826 | 1,101 | 275 | 25 |
| Austria | 20 | 8 | 8 | 106 | 141 | 35 | 25 |
| Belgium | 61 | 5 | 22 | 42 | 130 | 88 | 68 |
| Denmark | 5 | * | 2 | 25 | 33 | 7 | 22 |
| Ireland | 3 | * | 3 | 14 | 19 | 5 | 28 |
| Italy | 33 | 1 | 18 | 495 | 547 | 53 | 10 |
| Netherlands | 49 | 13 | 8 | 97 | 168 | 72 | 42 |
| Sweden | 6 | 1 | 9 | 48 | 63 | 16 | 25 |
| C. Twelve European countries (BIS reporters) (A + B) | 893 | 188 | 311 | 2,783 | 4,176 | 1,392 | 33 |
| D. Japan | 66 | 25 | 87 | 1,437 | 1,615 | 178 | 11 |
| E. Canada | 37 | 2 | 26 | 171 | 236 | 65 | 27 |
| F. United States | 8 | 356 | * | 1,745 | 2,109 | 363 | 17 |
| G. Fifteen industrial reporting countries (C + D + E + F) | 1,003 | 571 | 425 | 6,136 | 8,135 | 1,999 | 25 |
| H. Eight offshore banking centers | 499 | 9 | 69 | 82 | 660 | 577 | 87 |
| Singapore | 80 | 2 | 28 | 18 | 128 | 109 | 86 |
| Hong Kong | 56 | 2 | 28 | 47 | 133 | 86 | 65 |
| Bahrain | 45 | 5 | 8 | 4 | 62 | 58 | 94 |
| Lebanon | 4 **a** | * | 12 **b** | **b** | 16 | 6 | 60 |
| Bahamas | 132 | * | * | 2 | 134 | 132 | 98 |
| Cayman Islands | 128 | ... | * | ... | 128 | 128 | 100 |
| Panama | 44 | ... | 3 | ... | 47 | 47 | 100 |
| Netherlands Antilles | 11 | **a** | * | 1 | 12 | 11 | 89 |
| I. Swiss trustee accounts | 93 **a** | **a** | ... | ... | 93 | 93 | 100 |
| J. Grand total (G + H + I) | 1,593 | 583 | 494 | 6,218 | 8,887 | 2,669 | 30 |

Table 3–5. *International Assets Reported by Banking Offices in Main BIS Reporting Countries, by Nationality of Ownership, December 1983* [a]

Billions of U.S. dollars at end–1983 exchange rates

| | *Type of international asset* | | | | | |
|---|---|---|---|---|---|---|
| Parent country | *Claims on related offices* [b] | *Claims on other nonaffiliated banks* | *Claims on nonbanks* [c] | *Claims on official monetary institutions* | *CDs* [d] | *Total international assets of offices in all reporting countries* |
| United States [e] | 234 | 213 | 180 | 1 | 2 | 631 |
| Japan | 120 | 194 | 133 | 2 | 3 | 451 |
| France | 24 | 104 | 56 | 5 | * | 190 |
| United Kingdom | 19 | 82 | 65 | 3 | 2 | 171 |
| Germany | 11 | 70 | 62 | 1 | * | 144 |
| Canada | 22 | 29 | 37 | * | 1 | 89 |
| Italy | 2 | 57 | 20 | * | 1 | 80 |
| Switzerland | 13 | 36 | 20 | 2 | 5 | 77 |
| Netherlands | 5 | 36 | 21 | * | n.a. | 62 |
| Belgium | 2 | 18 | 18 | ... | n.a. | 38 |
| Luxembourg | * | 3 | 2 | ... | n.a. | 5 |
| Sweden | 1 | 6 | 11 | * | n.a. | 18 |
| Denmark | 2 | 5 | 2 | ... | n.a. | 9 |
| Other BIS reporting countries | 2 | 4 | 5 | * | * | 12 |
| Consortium banks | 2 | 21 | 19 | 1 | * | 43 |
| Other developed countries | 3 | 9 | 11 | * | * | 23 |
| Middle East | 2 | 11 | 5 | * | * | 18 |
| Latin America | 9 | 3 | 9 | ... | * | 21 |
| Eastern Europe | ... | 3 | 2 | 3 | n.a. | 8 |
| Others | 7 | 19 | 12 | * | 1 | 40 |
| Unallocated | ... | 3 | 4 | ... | ... | 6 |
| Total | 480 | 925 | 695 | 21 | 16 | 2,136 |

## *Questions*

1. How does Bryant's definition of international banking transactions, reflected in Table 3–2, differ from that of Dufey and Chung?

2. For simplicity, focus on Japan, the U.K., and the U.S. in Table 3–2.

   a. What explains the differences in the relative importance of international lending for banks based in the three countries?

   b. Do banks in each country carry on the same kind of international business or does their lending differ by currency and customer in important ways?

   c. What would account for any differences in clientele and currency?

3. Look carefully at the distribution of international assets in Table 3–5. Consider the role of banks headquartered in the Group of Five (G–5) countries: France, Germany, Japan, the U.K., and the U.S.

   a. What do you learn about the international business of the banks in the countries?

   b. Why do banks in the U.K. dominate in the first table but not in the second table?

4. Note that banks are important takers of credit from other banks. What accounts for their role on both sides of the transaction?

## B. CONTEMPORARY INTERNATIONAL FINANCE

In the late 1970s, international bankers based particularly in New York started to forecast the decline of their traditional deposit and loan business. Bankers Trust Company acted on this, selling many of its branches and setting out to become a leader in fee earning rather than asset based services. Its strategy paid off in increased profitability and by the late 1980s it was often cited as a leader in capital market operations worldwide. Many other banks followed.

Trends in banking and securities markets are captured in annual reports of the Bank of England. The following excerpts are from the 1992 report, which focuses on the period since the mid-1980s. Read the article for the activity in the markets, its causes, and an introduction to the various instruments. We examine many later in the book.

### "DEVELOPMENTS IN INTERNATIONAL BANKING AND CAPITAL MARKETS IN 1992"

33 Bank of England Q. Bull. 222–31.
(May 1993).

Overview

Political uncertainties in Europe, interest rate and exchange rate tensions, and subdued growth in the world economy made 1992 a volatile year for financial markets. Despite this, as Table A shows, borrowing in the international financial markets remained resilient.

Table A
Estimated net lending in international markets 1988–92

$ billions: banking flows adjusted to exclude estimated exchange rate effect

| | 1988 | 1989 | 1990 | 1991 | 1992 |
|---|---|---|---|---|---|
| 1 Gross international bank lending | 511 | 807 | 714 | 103 | 152 |
| 2 Net international bank lending | 260 | 410 | 465 | 80 | 195 |
| 3 Gross new bond issues | 227 | 267 | 263 | 320 | 340 |
| 4 *Less* redemptions and repurchases | 79 | 90 | 109 | 149 | 222 |
| 5 Net new bond issues | 148 | 177 | 154 | 170 | 118 |
| 6 Net new euronote placements | 20 | 7 | 32 | 34 | 28 |
| 7 Total international financing (2 + 5 + 6) | 428 | 594 | 651 | 284 | 341 |
| 8 *Less* double counting | 67 | 76 | 79 | 38 | 70 |
| 9 Total net international financing | 361 | 518 | 572 | 246 | 271 |

Source: BIS, Bank of England and Euroclear.

Total borrowing from banks and bond markets more than doubled last year, to $492 billion, around half its record level in 1990. Some market sectors contracted, such as equity-related bonds which were affected by the weakness of the Nikkei. Those that expanded included issues of floating-rate and medium-term notes structured to meet particular interest rate expectations.

Net borrowing from banks and bond markets, as shown in Chart 1, was only slightly higher than last year, at $271 billion, as many borrowers refinanced existing bonds and loans. In particular, much of the debt taken on during the buoyant 1988–90 period has reached, or is approaching, its maturity.

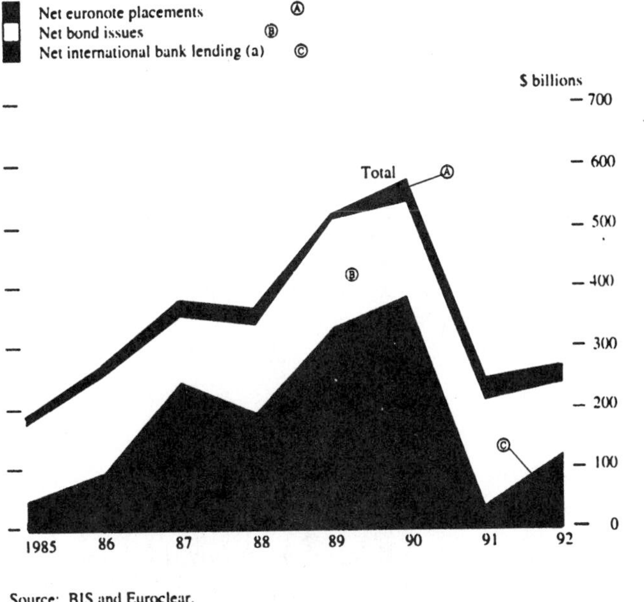


Source: BIS and Euroclear.

(a) Excluding international bonds bought or issued by banks.

Chart 3 gives a breakdown of net bond issues by borrower. A notable feature was the sharp rise in government borrowing, which rose by 40% to account for 34% of net issues. West European governments were prominent borrowers, particularly in the second half of the year, as they funded widening budget deficits, replenished foreign exchange reserves or repaid short-term borrowing extended during the ERM turbulence. Gross borrowing by French, German and Japanese banks was heavy. In net terms, Dutch and German banks borrowed most, in some cases to fund domestic and cross-border expansion. Although corporate borrowing in the international bond market took a smaller share of overall borrowing, ample funds were available to creditworthy borrowers.

. . .

[The Bank of England gives the following percentage breakdown for net international bond issues in Chart 3]:

| | 1992 | 1991 |
|---|---|---|
| Governments | 34.2 | 22.8 |
| International Institutions | 16.7 | 17.4 |
| Banks and Other Financial Institutions | 24.1 | 21.5 |
| Other (mainly industrial and corporate) | 25.0 | 38.3 |
| | 100.0 | 100.0 |

Political uncertainties in Europe, and associated exchange rate and interest rate volatility, affected the currency composition of borrowing from mid-year onwards. As Chart 5 shows, the currency composition of the international bond market shifted: issuance in the Ecu and high-yielding European currency sectors contracted, while the traditional 'safe haven' currency sectors expanded. Early in the year, when the Maastricht Treaty appeared to confirm the path to EMU, investors bought high-yield European bonds in the belief that convergence of European inflation and interest rates would provide capital gains. When Denmark rejected the Treaty in early June, and subsequent realignments demonstrated that exchange rates within the ERM were not immutably fixed, investors switched towards the dollar, the deutschmark and the Swiss franc.

. . .

[The following table reflects in tabular form the data contained in Chart 5 of the Bank of England article]:

**Currency composition of fixed-rate bond issues** [(a)]

Percentage of total issues announced

| Currency denomination | 1991 Year | 1992 Year | Q3 | Q4 | 1993 Q1 |
|---|---|---|---|---|---|
| US dollar | 29 | 33 | 43 | 31 | 30 |
| Ecu | 12 | 7 | — | — | 5 |
| Deutschmark | 4 | 11 | 7 | 18 | 17 |
| Swiss franc | 5 | 5 | 6 | 8 | 3 |
| Sterling | 7 | 7 | 6 | 8 | 9 |
| Canadian dollar | 10 | 6 | 6 | 1 | 11 |
| Yen | 15 | 14 | 14 | 17 | 13 |
| French franc | 7 | 9 | 7 | 10 | 7 |
| Italian lira | 3 | 2 | 1 | — | 1 |
| Other | 8 | 6 | — | 7 | 4 |
| Total | 100 | 100 | 100 | 100 | 100 |

(a) Excluding equity-related issues.

As Chart 7 shows, international interbank lending slowed in 1990, and in both 1991 and 1992 there was a net repayment of interbank loans. One of the reasons for this has been banks' decision in recent years to seek less capital-intensive, and more profitable, ways of managing their balance sheets, principally by using derivatives. Japanese banks continued to reduce their interbank lending—part of their shift from strategies based on market share to return on capital. But European banks' interbank business rose, mostly because of a sharp increase in the third quarter.

**Chart 7**
**Cross-border interbank lending**

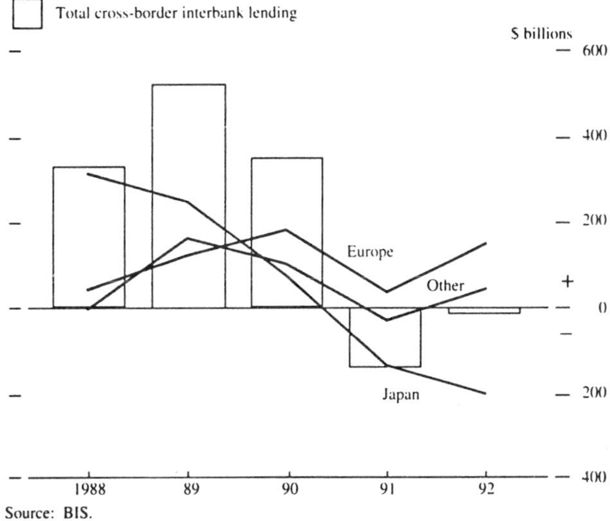

Source: BIS.

The geographical distribution of borrowers in the international financial markets continued to be dominated by entities from OECD countries in 1992. Corporate borrowers from G7 countries contributed to record fixed-rate bond issues as they attempted to lock in to low long-term bond yields in the dollar, yen and Swiss franc sectors. A number of UK and US companies refinanced existing syndicated credit facilities on finer terms. Companies also repaid debt from cash reserves or replaced debt with equity. Corporate 'deleveraging' was particularly prevalent in the United States where the equity market was generally receptive to new issues. Non-bank US companies repaid a net $6.6 billion international bonds last year, after repaying $2.2 billion in 1991. Corporate borrowers from other G7 countries continued to be net borrowers in the international bond market last year. Despite falling in some countries recently, corporate debt: GNP ratios are still high by historical standards; so further deleveraging might be expected.

. . .

International Capital Markets

*International bonds*

Issues in the eurodollar market grew by 25% last year. Borrowing was boosted early in the year as long-term bond yields eased on expectations that the likely pace of recovery was compatible with low inflation and, in the latter part of the year, by the US dollar's safe haven status when confidence in many European currencies was dented. Although borrowing by US corporates (especially lower-rated ones) in the eurobond market remained subdued, US banks and utility companies borrowed heavily in the US domestic market where issuance reached a record. Foreign entities also increased their borrowing in the US public debt market. Canadian and UK borrowers were particularly prominent, although a small number of borrowers from non-OECD countries also issued 'yankee' bonds. Foreign and domestic borrowers also increased their borrowing via 144a private placements. (Rule 144a was introduced in April 1990 and allows borrowers to avoid the costs of an SEC listing needed for a full public issue, provided the securities are sold and traded only among professional investors.)

. . .

Borrowing in the domestic yen bond market rose last year as the gradual easing of issuing and syndication restrictions began to make it more competitive with the euroyen sector.

. . .

The euroyen market was also liberalised slightly: certain euroyen bonds can now be sold to Japanese institutional investors without a 90-day 'seasoning period' and borrowers' net worth requirements for issues of euro and domestic yen bonds were eased.

. . .

Continued issuance of 'global bonds'—securities which can be issued simultaneously in the euro, US and Far East domestic markets, and which can be traded globally through domestic and international clearing systems—was another development last year. Since the first issue by the IBRD in 1989, the issuer base has broadened and the first corporate and sovereign issues took place in 1992. In total, there were fourteen issues in 1992, in US dollars, Canadian dollars and, for the first time, in yen.

As Chart 9 shows, turnover of fixed-income deutschmark bonds far exceeded that for the dollar in 1992 owing to the combined effect of deutschmark liberalisation and a shift from the Ecu sector. In addition, turnover of peseta and French franc bonds doubled and turnover of guilder and Danish kroner bonds rose threefold. Although the value of Ecu turnover was unchanged between the first and second halves of the year, this reflects heavy selling by market-makers attempting to unload unprofitable positions in the second half of the year, rather than genuine 'end-user' investment.

. . .

[The following tabular data comes from Chart 9]:

Fixed Income Bonds
Secondary Market Turnover (Percent)

| | 1992 ($10 trillion) | 1991 ($6 trillion) |
|---|---|---|
| Deutschmark | 31 | 21 |
| U.S. Dollar | 15 | 20 |
| Sterling | 3 | 4 |
| French Franc | 13 | 9 |
| Yen | 5 | 7 |
| ECU | 15 | 18 |
| Other | 18 | 21 |
| | 100 | 100 |

*Floating-rate notes (FRNs)*

Floating-rate note (FRN) issues doubled last year to $43 billion and net FRN borrowing, at $24 billion, compared with $4 billion in 1991. Around three fifths of issues were in US dollars. The rise in FRN issues reflected Tier 2 capital raising by banks and less attractive opportunities to swap fixed-rate dollars into floating-rate, which may have encouraged direct borrowing in the FRN market.

. . .

*Note issuance facilities*

The striking growth of the euromedium-term note (EMTN) market continued last year. The value of new programmes rose by $35 billion to $91 billion, and net new EMTN issues rose 40% to $23 billion. Issuer interest in EMTNs has grown rapidly as they are seen as a cost-effective and flexible complement to eurobonds. Although EMTNs are usually issued on a 'best efforts' basis, in 1992 borrowers made some forty underwritten 'bond' issues under EMTN programmes, after the first such issue in 1991. This trend has further blurred the distinction between EMTNs and traditional eurobonds. Nevertheless, the EMTN market is still far smaller than the international bond market where net issues were $118 billion last year. The range of borrowers in the EMTN market expanded during the year, to include lower-quality non-financial companies in the OECD area and borrowers from non-OECD countries such as Mexico, Korea and Venezuela.

By contrast, borrowing in the eurocommercial paper (ECP) market remained subdued. As the market has matured after a period of growth, so the number of new programmes has fallen: in 1992, borrowers repaid a net $0.6 billion ECP. Corporate downgrades in this traditionally credit-sensitive market and growing competition from recently liberalised domestic CP markets in Europe may both have restrained ECP borrowing last year. The Irish Government established the first sovereign deutschmark commercial paper programme.

*Syndicated credits*

Around a third of announced international syndicated credits may have been for refinancing and restructuring last year. US borrowers were particularly prominent (examples were the $6 billion facilities arranged for Chrysler and Time Warner).

. . .

Outside the OECD area, there was continued demand for syndicated bank loans, particularly from rapidly growing Asian economies in the form of project finance (related to infrastructure) and for aircraft purchase. Asian borrowers announced around $31 billion international syndicated credits last year, compared with $21 billion in 1991.

*International Banking*

During 1992, gross international bank lending recovered to rise by $152 billion, or 2.1% of the outstanding stock, after a net repayment of $103 billion in 1991 (see Table C). This revival reflected business in the third quarter, during and after the foreign exchange turbulence, when gross international bank lending was $287 billion. International interbank lending within the BIS reporting area fell by $4 billion, despite a strong rise of $207 billion in the third quarter, primarily within European centres. The growth in lending to non-banks within the BIS reporting area slowed to 5.0%.

**Table C**

**Growth of international bank lending**

$ billions; *percentage changes in italics*

| | Exchange rate adjusted flows | | | | | Stocks | |
|---|---|---|---|---|---|---|---|
| | 1988 | 1989 | 1990 | 1991 | 1992 | 1992 | |
| Inside reporting area: | | | | | | | |
| Interbank | 336 | 564 | 396 | −205 | −4 | 4,543 | *−0.1* |
| Non-bank | 160 | 230 | 284 | 101 | 89 | 1,878 | *5.0* |
| Outside reporting area | 14 | −2 | −12 | 8 | 63 | 813 | *8.4* |
| Unallocated by country | 1 | 15 | 45 | −7 | 4 | 117 | *3.5* |
| **Gross lending** | **511** | **807** | **714** | **−103** | **152** | **7,350** | ***2.1*** |
| *Less:* Redepositing of funds in the inside area interbank market | 251 | 397 | 249 | −183 | −43 | 3,690 | *−1.2* |
| Net international bank credit | 260 | 410 | 465 | 80 | 195 | 3,660 | *5.6* |
| *Memorandum items:* | | | | | | | |
| Cross-border lending | 436 | 685 | 608 | −55 | 177 | 6,196 | *2.9* |
| Local forex lending | 75 | 122 | 106 | −48 | −25 | 1,154 | *−2.1* |

**Source:** BIS (from data reported to the BIS by banks in the BIS reporting area, i.e., G10 countries, seven other industrialized countries and seven offshore centres).

. . .

*Analysis by centre and currency*

As Table F shows, the United Kingdom, with 16.5% of the total stock of external lending, remains the leading centre for cross-border bank lending ahead of Japan (with 14.2%). In 1992, lending from the United Kingdom increased by $88 billion whereas lending from Japan fell by $59 billion. Large falls in their local foreign currency claims also pushed the share of international business (comprising cross-border and local foreign currency claims) of banks in Japan below that of banks in the United Kingdom. The yen's share of cross-border lending continued to decline in contrast to the share of individual European currencies, nearly all of which rose strongly.

**Table F**

**External lending**

$ billions; *percentage share in italics*

| | Stocks | Exchange rate adjusted flows | | | | | Stocks |
|---|---|---|---|---|---|---|---|
| | 1987 | 1988 | 1989 | 1990 | 1991 | 1992 | 1992 |
| **By centre** | | | | | | | |
| United Kingdom | *20.8* | 34 | 55 | 86 | −52 | 88 | *16.5* |
| Japan | *13.7* | 167 | 153 | 73 | −36 | −59 | *14.2* |
| United States | *12.1* | 47 | 47 | −28 | 7 | −25 | *9.0* |
| France | *6.3* | 23 | 55 | 65 | −15 | 75 | *7.5* |
| Switzerland | *3.5* | — | −6 | 46 | −7 | 6 | *6.1* |
| Germany | *4.9* | 17 | 54 | 73 | 10 | 6 | *5.9* |
| Luxembourg | *4.3* | 19 | 37 | 42 | 18 | 40 | *5.4* |
| Belgium | *3.6* | 1 | 20 | 23 | 2 | 9 | *3.2* |
| Netherlands | *2.7* | 15 | 22 | 22 | 7 | 2 | *2.8* |
| Italy | *1.5* | 3 | 19 | 2 | 5 | 4 | *1.7* |
| Offshore | *22.1* | 97 | 211 | 183 | −1 | −5 | *23.2* |
| Other | *4.5* | −4 | 19 | 21 | 7 | 36 | *4.5* |
| **Total** | **4,208** | **436** | **685** | **608** | **−55** | **177** | **6,196** |
| *Of which:* | | | | | | | |
| Industrial area | 3,278 | 315 | 474 | 425 | −53 | 182 | 4,756 |
| *Of which:* | | | | | | | |
| **By currency:** | | | | | | | |
| US dollar | 51.7 | 123 | 181 | 140 | −76 | 58 | *46.5* |
| Deutschmark | 13.5 | 43 | 64 | 67 | −17 | 72 | *14.5* |
| Yen | 13.3 | 71 | 113 | 43 | −23 | −75 | *12.3* |
| Swiss franc | 6.7 | −6 | −4 | 19 | −7 | −4 | *4.6* |
| Sterling | 3.6 | 30 | 24 | 34 | −29 | 36 | *4.1* |
| ECU | 2.4 | 16 | 21 | 21 | 16 | 13 | *3.5* |
| French franc | 2.2 | 5 | 16 | 38 | 20 | 63 | *4.6* |
| Other | 6.6 | 33 | 60 | 63 | 63 | 19 | *9.9* |

Source: BIS.

*International banking business in London*

London is the leading centre for international bank lending, ahead of Japan. The rise in international bank business in London (see Table G) occurred primarily in the third quarter. British banks accounted for a considerable share of the cross-border business but the strongest growth was generated by other EC banks, particularly French and German. Japanese banks' business in London continued to decline.

**Table G**

**External lending of banks in the United Kingdom**

$ billions

| | Exchange rate adjusted flows | | | | | Stocks |
|---|---|---|---|---|---|---|
| | 1988 | 1989 | 1990 | 1991 | 1992 | 1992 |
| **By country** | | | | | | |
| BIS reporting area | 41 | 57 | 86 | −53 | 79 | 887 |
| Outside reporting area: | | | | | | |
| Developed countries | −2 | −2 | 1 | −1 | 2 | 34 |
| Eastern Europe | 2 | 2 | −5 | −3 | −2 | 11 |
| Oil exporters | 1 | −1 | −2 | −2 | 2 | 17 |
| Non-oil developing countries | −6 | −4 | −3 | 3 | 2 | 47 |
| Other | −2 | 3 | 9 | 4 | 5 | 24 |
| **Total** | **34** | **55** | **86** | **−52** | **88** | **1,020** |
| *Of which:* | | | | | | |
| **By currency** | | | | | | |
| US dollar | 5 | 1 | 18 | −38 | 38 | 508 |
| Deutschmark | 7 | 12 | 18 | 3 | 32 | 156 |
| Sterling | 8 | 5 | 8 | −10 | 25 | 86 |
| Yen | 8 | 18 | 8 | −28 | −31 | 67 |
| ECU | 7 | 6 | 7 | 1 | 4 | 44 |
| **By nationality**[a] | | | | | | |
| Japanese | 19 | 3 | −5 | −57 | −44 | 248 |
| British | −2 | 8 | −1 | −3 | 24 | 156 |
| American | 1 | 9 | 10 | 3 | 4 | 112 |
| German | 2 | 13 | 28 | 5 | 33 | 132 |
| French | 1 | −1 | 5 | 2 | 14 | 48 |
| Italian | 8 | 10 | 19 | 2 | 3 | 80 |

(a) Nationality flows only relate to monthly reporting banks whereas other figures also include quarterly reporting banks and some other financial institutions.

In 1992 banks in the United Kingdom recorded rises in both funds received from, and lent to, countries outside the BIS-reporting area (up by $2.4 billion and $4.2 billion respectively). However, within the rise in funds received, deposits from Saudi Arabia fell by $7.3 billion. Lending to Bahrain saw a rise of $3.8 billion with the remainder well spread.

. . .

## *Notes and Questions*

1. How does the Bank of England's definition of international banking transactions compare with that of Dufey and Chung, or of Bryant?

2. Various undefined terms are used in the Bank of England's market review. Some key definitions, as used by the SEC, taken from U.S. Securities and Exchange Commission, *Report of the Staff of the SEC on the Internationalization of the Securities Markets* (1987), are:

Eurobond—debt security issued multinationally through an international syndicate of banks or securities firms in a currency other than that of the country in which the bond is issued. The all-inclusive term has several derivatives and variations, such as Eurodollar bond, Euroyen bond, Euro–DM bond, etc., that indicate the currency in which the offering is denominated; and Asiadollar bond, etc., which indicates the primary geographic area of the offering (see also Foreign Bond and International Bond).

Eurocommercial Paper—short-term, unsecured debt taking the form of promissory notes and issued in the same manner as Eurobonds.

Eurocurrency Market—the market for deposit liabilities, denominated in a currency other than that of the country of the bank in which the deposit is made.

Euroequity—Euroequities include common and preferred stocks distributed to investors in one or several markets outside the issuer's domestic market by a syndicate of international securities firms and banks.

Euromarket—the generic, all-inclusive term refers to all types of markets other than strictly domestic and foreign markets (see Eurobond, Eurocommercial paper, Eurocurrency market, Euroequity and Euronotes).

Euronotes—the term refers to short-term paper issued in the Euromarket similar in most respects to commercial paper except that it is issued pursuant to a facility of medium-term.

European Currency Unit (ECU)—an artificial currency unit comprising a "basket" of the currencies of nine members of the European Economic Community. The value of an ECU *vis-a-vis* a specific currency is determined according to specific weightings of the participating currencies.

Floating Rate Notes—notes (usually unsecured) paying interest at rates adjusted from time to time to correspond to the yield on a selected money market indicator, such as Treasury bills or LIBOR.

Foreign Bond—debt security issued in a country other than that of the issuer, sold through a syndicate of banks or securities firms located primarily in the country of distribution, and denominated in the currency of that country (see also Eurobond; International Bond).

International Bond—debt security that is issued originally outside the country of the borrower. These usually take the form of Eurobonds or foreign bonds (see also Eurobond; Foreign Bond).

3. Look carefully at Bank of England's Table A, comparing international lending through banks and debt security markets.

a. Analysts of financial markets distinguish between the stock and the flow of funds. "Gross" and "net" mean many different things. Securities market analysts distinguish between primary offerings and trading. What do the numbers in Table A report?

b. Be sure you understand the terms used in the table and the surrounding text: international bonds, euronotes, straight- and floating-rate bonds, equity-related bonds. What do they have in common? How do they differ? What about these securities would make them attractive to issuers and investors?

c. What does Table A reveal about the relative importance of bank loans and securities markets? How do you account for the shift between banking and securities markets?

4. Consider the types of factors the Bank uses to explain international activity in the various markets. What is the role of regulatory factors?

---

The readings describe international bond markets in much greater detail than international equity markets. The Organization for Economic Cooperation and Development (OECD) reports international equity placements since 1987. It tabulates all offerings in which the issuer is based in a country other than that in which it places the offering. So if IBM issued $1 billion in equity, 90% in the United States and 10% in the U.K., the OECD would report $100 million as international.

| International Equity Placements ($ billions) | | | | | | |
|---|---|---|---|---|---|---|
| 1987 | 1988 | 1989 | 1990 | 1991 | 1992 | 1993 |
| $18.2 | $7.7 | $8.1 | $7.3 | $23.6 | $23.5 | $40.7 |

The OECD data do not account for investors based in one country that buy equity issued or traded in another country. In 1991, for example, Baring Securities Company estimated that these flows amounted to $100.6 billion [see R. Waters, "Bad times for global equity flows," *Financial Times,* November 5, 1992].

What do you learn by comparing these data about international equity placements with prior data about international bank loans and debt securities?

## C. COSTS AND BENEFITS OF THE INTERNATIONALIZATION OF FINANCE

In a speech given at Harvard Law School, Deryck Maughan, the president of Salomon Bros., described how securities supplanted banking in international markets over the past few decades, a much longer period than that described by the Bank of England.

DERYCK C. MAUGHAN, "GLOBAL CAPITAL MARKETS AND THE IMPLICATIONS FOR FINANCIAL INSTITUTIONS," EXCERPTS FROM TALK GIVEN AT SEMINAR IN INTERNATIONAL FINANCE, HARVARD LAW SCHOOL

September 20, 1993.

The world's economies, capital markets and financial institutions are connected today as never before.

Was this ordained? Only in part. Are the consequences fully understood? No. How will governments respond to further erosion of their economic sovereignty? Not clear. And how will we, denizens of Wall Street, respond? Variously.

I appear before you the product of two careers (a civil servant and an investment banker) and three continents (Europe, Asia and North America). My observations relate first to the evolution of the international financial system. Second, to the forces that will shape how capital markets develop in the years ahead. And third, to the challenges that societies, regulators, and market participants will face if—as we suspect—global capital becomes more mobile, not less.

**The Evolution of Capital Markets**

National capital markets: For thirty years after the Second World War the international monetary system conceived by Keynes and White held up remarkably well. The key concepts were free trade, fixed but flexible exchange rates, and development finance—promoted in turn by the GATT, the IMF and the World Bank. By and large this was a time of steady growth and low inflation, the era of demand management and the Phillips Curve. Credit markets were highly regulated. Interest rates were subject to government regulation, rather than being set by market forces. Capital markets were poorly developed and essentially national in character and purpose. Exhibit 1 shows the changing relationships among the world's capital markets, with the dots representing the national markets. Prior to 1973, financial markets were independent of one another, ringed by exchange controls and limited by regulations governing financial product innovation and market access.

International capital markets: The strains inherent in this ordered world became apparent in the late 1960s and culminated in President Nixon's devaluation of the dollar in 1971 and declaration that it was no longer convertible into gold. By 1973, the efforts to fix exchange rates between the dollar, the pound, the mark and the yen were abandoned, leading to generalized floating exchange rates, where the demand and supply for currencies established their price. We faced oil shocks, stagflation and interest rates at 20%. The policy consensus fractured, with disagreement on whether it was better to move forward under fixed or floating rates. In this period we also witnessed the rapid development of a large—and largely unregulated—off-shore capital market: the Euromarket. National capital and credit markets were now linked—not directly, but linked nonetheless. There were no reserve requirements for the banks and no SEC for the investment banks. London became the home for literally hundreds of banks and securities companies from all parts of the world, partly due to its favorable location, straddling the time zones of Tokyo and New York, and partly due to regulations which allowed this off-shore market to exist.

Global markets: We have not lacked for drama these ten years past. From the Plaza Accord in 1985 to the rupture of the European monetary system last year; from the bursting of Japan's bubble to the leveraged excesses in our own markets; from the Berlin Wall to Tienanmen Square, and a whole new group of countries looking to the West and its markets for capital. From 1985 on, in country after country, interest rates have been deregulated, capital markets liberated and foreign institutions granted increased access to hitherto protected markets. The essential point for today, however, is that the international system has become a multinational system, a global system where capital flows directly and in growing quantities from one economy to another.

Trends

Let us consider, then, the forces that will shape our future. We have four propositions:

- The first proposition is that there is a fundamental shift from credit markets (in short-hand, "loans") to capital markets (in short-hand, "securities"). The securitization of corporate loans, mortgages and receivables has proceeded apace. We take the United States as a clear case, but this shift applies worldwide.
- Second proposition, that international capital movements have grown rapidly and will continue to do so.
- Third, that derivatives—futures, forwards, options and swaps—have inextricably tied the interests of the world's largest borrowers (governments, banks and corporations) to those of the world's largest investors (pension funds, life insurance companies and mutual funds).
- Fourth, that for asset and liability managers performance is increasingly the name of the game. How can returns be guaranteed for life when asset prices change by the minute? Why limit oneself to a single national capital market?

*Shift to Capital Markets*

Let us take first the shift to capital markets. There has been a dramatic decline in the role of banks and thrifts as financial intermediaries in the United States. Their share of assets has declined from 56% in 1975 to 35% today. (See Exhibit 2.) Pension funds and mutual funds are the big gainers over this period, from 16% to 35%. Deregulation has intensified competition in what has been a highly segmented financial system. Loans have been turned into securities—commercial paper, high-grade bonds, high-yield bonds, collateralized mortgage obligations, and so on. Deposits—the other side of the balance sheet—have migrated to lower cost, performance-oriented asset management vehicles. Ten years ago, Fidelity had $20 billion under management; today $235 billion. Technology will continue to pose a real threat to bricks-and-mortar distribution systems. Banks have responded by diversifying into investment banking, asset management, and, in Europe, insurance. But the point here is simply that loans today are just another financial product. And two-thirds of America's financial assets are now held by institutions that primarily buy securities.

A variation on the same theme is depicted in Exhibit 3: debt securities as a percentage of the total amount of debt and credit in the United States. The graph shows that debt securities now account for

65% of this $15 trillion market, up from 45% of a much smaller market 15 years ago.

*International Capital Movements*

Our second proposition concerns the growth of international capital movements. The Bank for International Settlements, which produced the table in Exhibit 4, estimates that gross inflows and outflows of portfolio capital between countries were close to $100 billion a year in the early 1980s, about $350 billion a year in the late 1980s and some $550 billion last year. Portfolio movements means stocks and bonds, securities. This data does not include direct investments, loans or short-term money movements. These are substantial capital flows running through a global network of securities companies and banks. We cannot show you the central place, the debt or stock exchange where this takes place. Rather, it is a network of dealers connected by modern technology.

Another statistic that makes the same point is that in the United States, gross transactions in securities between domestic and foreign residents amounted to 9% of GNP in 1980 and 90% of GNP in 1990. For Germany the numbers are 7% and 57%; for Japan 7% and 119%. The trend is clear. And if the UK is anything to go by, these countries have some way to go. In the United Kingdom in 1990 international turnover was equivalent to 700% of GNP.

Exhibit 5 shows the growth of international bond issuance in the Euromarket—$28 billion in 1981, $184 billion in 1986 and $285 billion last year. At the same time, American institutions have begun to invest overseas in unprecedented amounts. In 1993 alone, U.S. investment in foreign securities will exceed $100 billion. As foreign demand for capital grows, and as America diversifies its savings, New York's role as an international financial center seems certain to grow.

*Dramatic Growth in Derivatives*

Our third proposition concerns derivatives. The use of derivatives to hedge risk or express a view has grown dramatically in all major markets. "Exchange-traded" derivatives are listed options and futures on interest rates, currencies, and stock indices—organized exchanges, standard contracts. "Over-the-counter" derivatives include interest rate and currency swaps, caps, floors, collars, and options on swaps. Are derivatives stabilizing or de-stabilizing to individual markets? Hotly debated. Do they present an unacceptable level of systemic risk? For those with an interest, we recommend the recent Group of Thirty report on derivatives, chaired by Sir Dennis Weatherstone of J.P. Morgan. It is an industry assessment of market risk, credit risk and other issues. For our present purpose, we should simply note the extraordinary growth of these markets from a national trillion dollars in 1986 to $8 trillion in 1991 and some higher number today. During that time period, "over-the-counter" grew even faster ($500 billion to $4.5 trillion, a 55% compound average annual growth) than exchange traded ($580 billion to

$3.5 trillion, a 43% compound average annual growth), as financial market participants continued to seek custom tailored solutions for their needs.

Let me explain how derivatives are used. A state pension fund wishes to establish an international portfolio of stocks. The fund could go out and buy a lot of stocks, pay commissions, greatly expand its research staff and so on. Or it could call a dealer and say "We want this exposure to these markets" and the dealer will enter into a swap agreement with the state pension fund where we or others will essentially pay directly to the state the returns, positive or negative, on selected stock markets. We will undertake the work of selecting, buying and hedging the stocks, collecting the dividends, paying the taxes and so on. A stock index swap.

Another example might be a U.S. corporation. It likes the absolute level of interest rates, and credit spreads are narrow—say 80 basis points over Treasuries. It does not need to borrow now, but it wants that option, that opportunity for the next six months. We will write an option which locks the spread, guarantees the 80 basis points. And we can guarantee the absolute level of interest rates out for two, three, four years. The client will pay a premium, but he is receiving a service through the derivative market. When the corporation is ready to fund, let us suppose we recommend fixed-rate marks as the lowest cost financing at that time. The company needs dollars, so we swap marks for dollars. It issues fixed-rate but wants floating, so we say "Do you want it off Bills, Labor or Fed funds?" If fixed-rate marks swapped back into floating rate dollars is cheaper than borrowing from the bank, we get the business.

The key point about derivatives today is that they allow market participants to isolate, price and manage risk across the entire maturity spectrum in a variety of markets.

*Performance & Diversification*

Performance is our fourth trend. A lot of people start with government yield curves, what government bonds yield at different maturities. As you can see in Exhibit 6, at 10 years, you can invest in Japan for a 4¼% yield, the United States at 5⅜%, Germany 6⅛%, UK 7⅛%, Italy 9¾%. Which do you select? We have a balance sheet of about $180 billion at Salomon Brothers. About half of that balance sheet is resident outside the United States. So we make this decision every day. We track the correlations between these markets, to assess their degree of independence and whether there is indeed diversification of risk or the risks simply build one on another. Through diversification we seek higher risk-adjusted returns.

It might be argued that as markets continue to be open, the free flow of capital will force convergence of returns across all markets. The graph in Exhibit 7 shows implied yield curves three years from now (derived from the swaps markets). Note that important differences in the yield curves persist. Markets, we have to say, are still significantly domestic. Not everyone is a global investor. Our argument is not that we have a single pool of capital but that markets are now importantly connected, interact, and that the national markets exist within a global system.

In speaking of performance and international diversification, we must also deal with currency exposure. Exhibit 8 tracks the fluctuation in yen and deutsche marks versus the dollar. Spare a thought for those unfortunate foreign investors who helped finance our budget deficits. A Japanese investor who bought Treasuries ten years ago has seen the dollar fall from about 250 yen to the dollar to 108 yen to the dollar. In other words, in yen terms, he receives about 40 cents on the dollar on his principal as his bonds mature. All international investment has to be seen through the currency prism. As difficult and as risky as it may seem, this is what people do. Investors must make a choice as to whether to hedge currency exposure or not. Given volatility, you cannot just buy and hold—and hope the world goes away.

. . .

*Development Finance*

Let us assume for the moment that the system of free trade and global capital prevails. What does it mean for countries that need development finance? Markets are not politically correct. Markets make their own choices. Markets seek the highest risk-adjusted return to capital. Will markets fund the development of sub-Saharan Africa? We doubt it. Markets will sift through the perceived opportunities and make their own choices. Capital is finite. Capital is rationed. More private capital will flow to China in the next five years than Russia. How about Argentina or Poland? Argentina can come to the market right now. Poland does not have the same opportunities. Which would you invest in—India or Brazil? Vietnam is attracting non-American capital; Angola gets very little of anyone's capital. So while we believe in markets as allocators of resources, we have to understand their requirements, and limits. There is still an important role for governments to support countries that do not have access to the capital markets.

*Macroeconomic Management*

What does the development of global capital markets mean for the ability of governments to manage their economies? How effective are fiscal, monetary and exchange rate policies in pursuit of employment and inflation objectives?

**Fiscal policy:** Governments find it difficult to increase tax rates and the majority of their spending is non-discretionary. Health and welfare benefits are largely provided on demand. There is a structural deficit in most developed societies. It is not as easy as was once thought to increase spending or cut taxes and create jobs. So fiscal policy as a tool for national economic managers is severely constrained.

**Exchange rate policy:** It is often said that the prime function of exchange rate policy relates to the balance of payments and specifically the trade account. Aggregate demand includes exports and imports, not just domestic consumption and investment. The exchange rate certainly affects the price of tradable goods and services. But our view is the weight of the argument runs the other way, that is to say capital flows largely determine exchange rates and trade flows adjust accordingly. The numbers: In 1992, $800 billion a day was traded on the foreign exchange market; that is sixty times the volume of world trade in goods.

**Monetary policy:** It seems to us that global capital flows make monetary targeting more problematic because foreign capital is flowing in and out of the national system. We no longer have a closed system as defined by the national money supply. Similarly, interest rates are responding to the total flow of capital, not just the domestic flow of capital. With international capital mobility, attempts to maintain fixed exchange rates and coordinated monetary policies are subject to the ratification of the capital markets. And there lies the tale of monetary union in Europe. The ERM crises of September 1992 and July 1993 demonstrated the limitations faced by national policy makers in their ability to set interest rates and exchange rates in defiance of what markets believed was sustainable.

. . .

*Industry Consolidation*

Another challenge for us is that there will be significant consolidation in our industry in the years ahead. The returns to capital in the financial sector are inadequate. The top firms do well; beyond that there is generally inadequate return. There is still excess capacity in our industry, and regulatory induced fragmentation (especially in the U.S. and Japan). As the industry is further deregulated and exposed to more global competition there will be, in our view, substantial consolidation.

. . .

**EXHIBIT 1:**

## *Capital Markets Evolution*

| | National | International | Global |
|---|---|---|---|
| **Period** | 1945 - 73 | 1973 - 84 | 1985 - ? |
| **System** | Bretton Woods | Generalized Floating | G7/EC |
| **Exchange Rates** | Fixed | Floating | Hybrid |
| **Exchange Controls** | Yes | Hybrid | No |
| **Market Access** | No | Limited | Yes |
| **Derivatives** | No | Limited | Yes |
| **Deregulation** | No | Partial | Yes |

(o04s1405/w) EX1405

***Exhibit 2***

## *Dynamics of U.S. Financial Markets Diminishing Role of Depository Institutions*

### *Assets of US Financial Institutions - 1975 vs 1993*

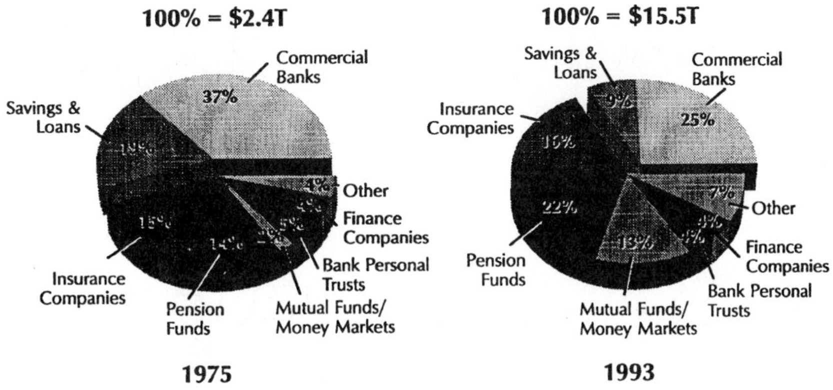

**100% = $2.4T**

Commercial Banks 37%
Savings & Loans 19%
Insurance Companies 15%
Pension Funds 14%
Mutual Funds/ Money Markets 2%
Bank Personal Trusts 5%
Finance Companies 4%
Other 4%

**1975**

**100% = $15.5T**

Savings & Loans 9%
Commercial Banks 25%
Insurance Companies 16%
Pension Funds 22%
Mutual Funds/ Money Markets 13%
Bank Personal Trusts 4%
Finance Companies 4%
Other 7%

**1993**

Source: Federal Reserve
Other: Brokers & Dealers, Credit Unions, Closed-End Funds, Funding Corps., Issuers of Asset-Backed Securities, Mortgage Companies, and REITS.

[G17740]

o06e0811/w

**EXHIBIT 3:**

## *Dynamics of the US Financial Markets*
## *Shift to Debt Securities*

### *US Debt Market*

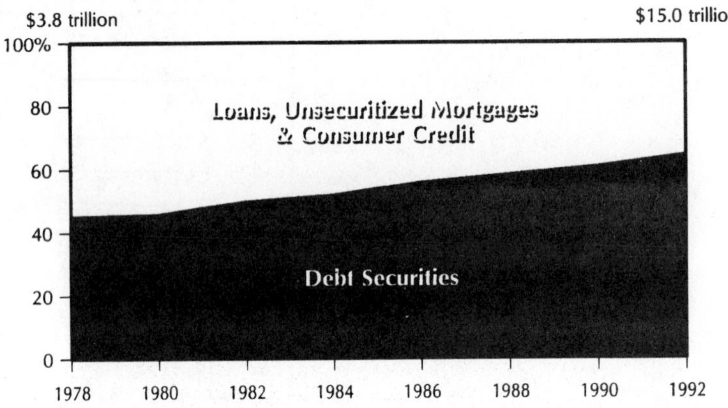


Source: Federal Reserve

(o04s1423/w) EX1423

**EXHIBIT 4**

## *International Portfolio Capital Movements*

*(billions of US dollars)*

| | Avg. 1980-84 | Avg. 1985-89 | 1991 | 1992* |
|---|---|---|---|---|
| **Total Outflows** | 41.8 | 176.8 | 274.0 | 238.0 |
| of which | | | | |
| ▶ U.S. | 5.8 | 9.5 | 45.0 | 48.6 |
| ▶ Japan | 13.8 | 89.9 | 74.3 | 34.4 |
| ▶ E.C. | 18.9 | 62.6 | 120.8 | 139.6 |
| **Total Inflows** | 57.8 | 186.0 | 374.6 | 308.5 |
| of which | | | | |
| ▶ U.S. | 16.7 | 59.2 | 51.2 | 65.0 |
| ▶ Japan | 11.9 | 23.3 | 115.3 | 8.2 |
| ▶ E.C. | 17.7 | 70.4 | 152.3 | 198.5 |

Source: BIS
* Partly estimated.

o04s1416/w

**EXHIBIT 5**

## *International Capital Movements*
## *Eurobonds: New Issuance*

*(US$ in billions)*

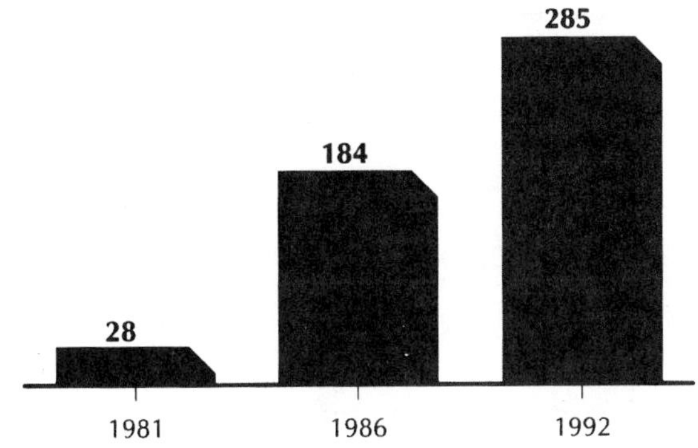


Source: Salomon Economic & Market Analysis

c04e1422/w

**EXHIBIT 6:**

## *Performance & Diversification*
## *Government Yield Curves**

*As of September 16, 1993*

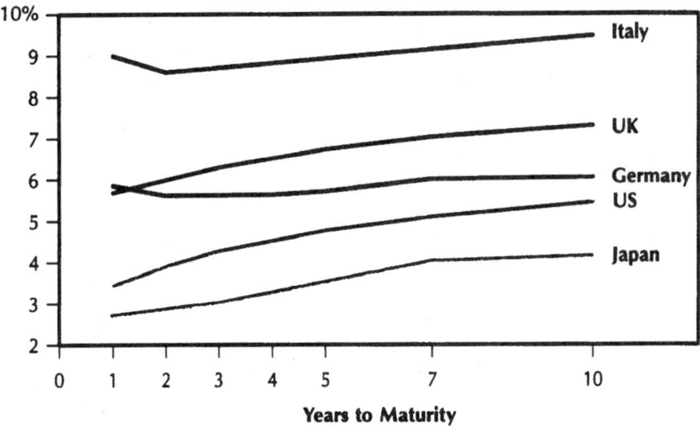


* All yields are quoted on a semiannual bond equivalent basis. Germany and Italy which are typically quoted on an annual basis, have been converted for comparison purposes.

(c04e1418/w) EX1419

**EXHIBIT 7:**

***Performance & Diversification***

## *Implied Yield Curves Three Years Forward**

***As of September 16, 1993***

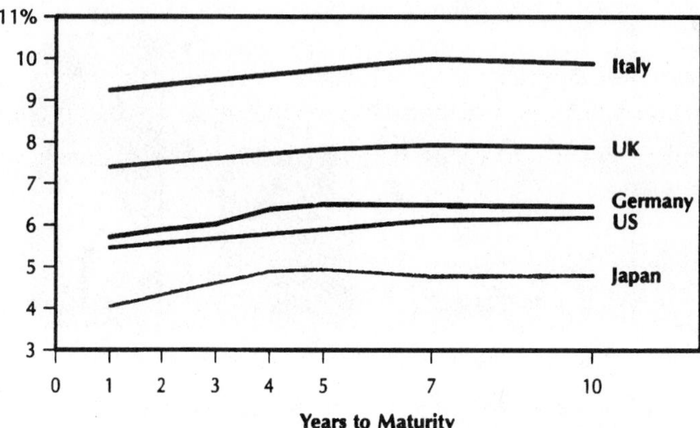


* All yields are quoted on a semiannual bond equivalent basis. Germany and Italy which are typically quoted on an annual basis, have been converted for comparison purposes.

(o04s1424/w) EX1434

**EXHIBIT 8:**

## *Performance & Diversification*
## Currency

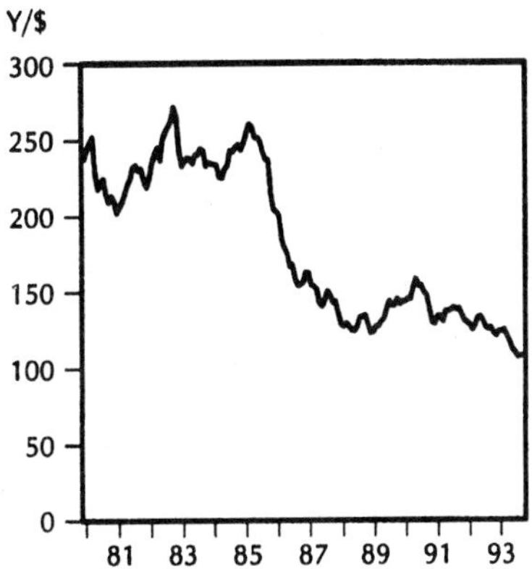


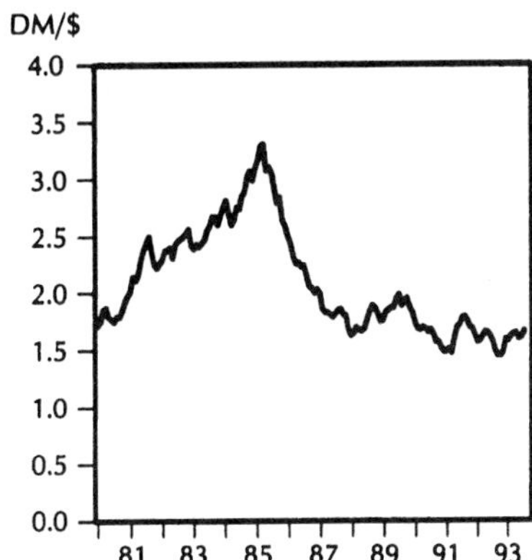


(a04a1417/w) EX1417

### *Questions*

1. Please review Maughan's discussion of the evolution of financial markets. Is there a significant difference between the "international" and "global" phases described in Exhibit 1 and in the text?

2. What are the costs and benefits of the shift from banking to securities in international financial markets?

# Chapter II

# INTERNATIONAL ASPECTS OF U.S. SECURITIES REGULATION

This Chapter begins with some background data on the degree to which the U.S. capital market is internationalized and then examines how the United States regulates (1) the distribution and trading of securities issued by foreign companies in the United States and (2) the distribution outside the United States of securities issued by U.S. companies. This requires some basic understanding of securities regulation in general.

The traditional goal of securities regulation, investor protection, may have to be tempered in a "global market" by (1) the desire of U.S. investors to invest and trade in foreign securities, (2) the reality that they may do so outside the United States, and (3) the importance to the United States of maintaining the world's leading domestic capital market, which requires openness to foreign issuers.

Our focus is on the regulation of the securities markets, primary and secondary, rather than on the firms participating in these markets. Institutional regulation, however, will be the major focus for banking. This difference is driven by the nature of regulatory concerns, investor protection in securities markets and safety and soundness of banks.

## A. INTERNATIONALIZATION OF U.S. SECURITIES MARKETS

In 1987, a major study of the Securities and Exchange Commission examined the internationalization of the U.S. securities markets. Some key excerpts follow.

EXCERPTS FROM U.S. SECURITIES AND EXCHANGE COMMISSION ("SEC")

Report of the Staff of the SEC on the Internationalization of the Securities Markets (1987). Pp. II–11 to II–24, II–62 to II–90.

### C. Unique and Influential Role of U.S. Securities Markets

The U.S. capital markets' influence on other markets—both foreign and international—appears to have been substantial. In general, the U.S. regulatory system has allowed financial innovation to take place—both in the U.S. domestic securities market and in the dollar sector of the Eurobond market. This has facilitated the operational efficiency of our securities markets and international capital mobility. The rapid maturation of the other securities markets, however, presents new challenges and opportunities resulting from increased competition for new issues placement and in secondary market trading in both domestic and international issues.

At the end of 1986 the market capitalization of U.S. equities totaled $2.6 trillion or about 43 percent of the world's stock market capitalization. This is down from 56 percent just two years ago. As seen in Table II–2, the next largest, Japan's, was about two-thirds the size of the U.S. The appreciation of the yen relative to the U.S. dollar and the strong growth of the Japanese stock market have both contributed to the rapid growth in the capitalization of the Japanese equities market. The equity capitalization of most other major markets has been growing faster (measured in U.S. dollars) than the U.S. market. Besides Japan's equity markets which grew at a compound annual rate of 23 percent from 1978 to 1986, the fastest growing equity markets have been Italy's (39 percent), the United Kingdom's (18 percent) and France's (16 percent). By comparison, the U.S. equity market grew 14 percent annually during this period.

. . .

A broader view of the size and depth of the U.S. securities markets is given in Table II–3 which shows the amount of new debt and equity capital raised by governments, private non-financial enterprises, financial institutions and foreign issuers. In 1986, all issuers raised $812 billion in capital through securities issued in the U.S. In Japan, the next largest market, issuers raised slightly more than one-half this amount, $438 billion. Ten years ago the proportions were roughly the same with issuers raising $206 billion in the U.S. and $89 billion in Japan.

. . .

**Table II–2**

**MARKET CAPITALIZATION OF WORLD'S STOCK MARKETS**
(US $ Billions)

| Country | 1978 | 1980 | 1982 | 1984 | 1985 | 1986 |
|---|---|---|---|---|---|---|
| United States | $ 870 | $1,391 | $1,481 | $1,714 | $2,160 | $2,556 |
| Japan | 327 | 357 | 410 | 617 | 909 | 1,746 |
| United Kingdom | 118 | 190 | 182 | 219 | 328 | 440 |
| Germany | 83 | 71 | 69 | 78 | 179 | 246 |
| Canada | 67 | 113 | 105 | 116 | 147 | 166 |
| France | 45 | 53 | 29 | 40 | 79 | 150 |
| Italy | 10 | 25 | 20 | 23 | 65 | 141 |
| Switzerland | 41 | 46 | 41 | 43 | 90 | 132 |
| Australia | 27 | 60 | 41 | 52 | 63 | 78 |
| Netherlands | 22 | 25 | 22 | 31 | 52 | 73 |
| All Others | 75 | 141 | 125 | 133 | 172 | 267 |
| TOTAL | $1,685 | $2,472 | $2,525 | $3,066 | $4,244 | $5,995 |

Note: Data are estimates of exchange-listed stocks with market value of investment companies excluded. U.S. data includes NASDAQ stocks. Data excludes foreign corporations, except for the NASDAQ portion of the U.S. market during the years 1978 to 1982.

Source: SEC Monthly Statistical Review (various issues)
NASDAQ Fact Book (various issues)

## Table II–3

### GROSS NEW ISSUES IN THE CAPITAL MARKETS OF TEN MAJOR COUNTRIES: 1986

| | Total U.S. $ Billions | Percent of Total | | | |
|---|---|---|---|---|---|
| | | Central State Gov't. | Private Enterprises [1] | Financial Institutions [2] | Foreign Issues |
| United States | $812 | 63% | 18% | 18% | 1% |
| Japan | 438 | 43 | 12 | 44 | 1 |
| Italy | 126 | 77 | 13 | 10 | * |
| Germany | 126 | 30 | 5 | 65 | 0 |
| France | 68 | 34 | 31 | 35 | * |
| United Kingdom | 33 | 63 | 23 | 11 | 2 |
| Switzerland | 34 | 4 | 11 | 15 | 69 |
| Canada [3] | 57 | 58 | — | — | * |
| Australia [4] | 28 | 90 | 6 | 4 | 0 |
| Netherlands | 12 | 51 | 6 | 41 | 1 |

* Insignificant (less than 1%)

1. This category includes all non-financial business.
2. This category includes both government and privately-owned institutions.
3. The "Private Enterprises" and "Financial Institutions" figures are combined for Canada totaling 42 percent.
4. Table shows 1985 data for Australia.

Sources: OECD Financial Statistics; Bank of Canada Review, March 1987; Year Book Australia, 1986; Reserve Bank of Australia Bulletin, March 1987; Directorate of Economic and Policy Analysis

The dominant position of the U.S. securities markets can be explained, in part, by the size of our gross national product which is double and even triple that of the other leading economies of the world.

. . .

The U.S. securities markets and its regulation appear to have influenced the shape of other markets. Many securities instruments were first introduced in the U.S. securities market and are now being introduced around the world. U.S. securities firms maintain a sizable presence in most international financial centers.

. . .

A considerable dynamic for change was initiated in the U.S. in the early 1970s with the gradual deregulation of brokerage commission rates on stock exchange transactions. When legislation passed in 1975 completed the process, the U.S. securities industry moved into a much more competitive era. Other countries, such as Canada, started to reduce commission rates on large orders fairly soon thereafter. The process of unfixing commission rates was not completed until 1983 in Canada, 1984 in Australia and 1986 in the United Kingdom.

The quotation and transaction systems which have become an important market medium in the U.S. are being used increasingly in other markets such as Japan, the United Kingdom and Singapore. In addition, automated execution systems for small orders which were introduced in U.S. stock markets in response to the deregulation of commission rates are now being offered in other markets around the world.

. . .

The regulatory climate in the U.S. has permitted our securities markets to become a leader in financial innovation. New financial instruments are now being introduced in foreign markets with increasing frequency. Trading of standardized options began in the U.S. in 1973. In 1975, Canada and in 1976 Australia followed suit with their own programs. The Netherlands started the European Options Exchange in 1978. For seven years this was the second largest market for standardized options. The United Kingdom also introduced standardized options to their markets in 1978 and became the second largest options market in 1985.

. . .

The innovative nature and level of sophistication of the U.S. capital markets is also indicated by the wide range of securities instruments traded actively in the U.S. market. Table II–4 shows the availability of five broad categories of securities instruments in the world's major capital markets. These instruments are important in providing investors, institutions, traders, investment bankers and issuers a broad range of vehicles to manage their assets. Only the U.S. has a highly developed market in all five categories. Japan and the United Kingdom have highly developed markets for three of the five instruments. The other countries have two or fewer.

. . .

The U.S. securities markets are also unique in their regulations governing disclosure, insiders and intermediaries, accompanied by a flexibility that has permitted competition and innovation. The U.S. prohibits insider trading and has vigorous enforcement. U.S. regulation also requires the purchasers of corporate securities to register their ownership (conducted almost entirely by transfer agents and brokers). In many countries the bearer form of securities issuance is practiced, especially for bonds.

## Table II–4

### THE DEVELOPMENT OF CAPITAL MARKET INSTRUMENTS IN THE WORLD'S MAJOR SECURITIES MARKETS

| | Capital Market Instruments | | | | |
|---|---|---|---|---|---|
| Countries | Government Bonds | Corporate Bonds | Corporate Equities | International Bonds [1] | Options and Futures [2] |
| U.S. | H | H | H | H | H |
| Japan | H | I | H | H | L |
| United Kingdom | H | I | H | H | I |
| Germany | H | L | I | H | L |
| Canada | H | I | H | I | I |
| Switzerland | I | I | H | H | L |
| France | I | L | I | L | L |
| Italy | H | L | I | L | L |
| Australia | H | I | H | I | I |
| Netherlands | H | I | I | I | I |

H = A highly developed market exists in which new issues, securities outstanding and trading volume are substantial when compared to the economy's gross national product.

I = The market has developed to an intermediate level where new issues, securities outstanding and trading volume are of moderate size when compared to the economy's gross national product.

L = The market has developed only to a limited extent which may be due to the recent introduction of the product or a market does not yet exist.

1. International bonds include foreign bonds and various currency sectors of the eurobond market.
2. Only four countries have both a market in standardized options and financial futures: Australia, Canada, the United Kingdom and the U.S. The U.S. is the only one with both markets highly developed.

Note: The classification of the government bond, corporate bond, corporate equity and international bond markets is based on a combination of objective factors. The three prime ones are the annualized dollar volume of new issues over several recent years, the dollar amount of issues outstanding, and the rate of turnover in the secondary market. These data are used as a percent of gross national product. For options and financial futures other factors are considered—for example, how recently the market opened, how many different contracts are being traded and the dollar equivalent of the trading volume.

Source: Directorate of Economic and Policy Analysis
U.S. Securities and Exchange Commission

Regulation of new issue and periodic disclosure in the U.S. places considerable emphasis on extensive financial reporting. The disclosure program, including related procedures and potential legal liabilities may, however, serve as a disincentive to the issuance of foreign bonds and equity securities in the U.S. capital market. U.S. regulation emphasizes full disclosure rather than merit regulation which seems to play a much larger role in some other capital markets. Recent modifications to the disclosure program have placed more emphasis on the continuous reporting of corporate issuers. In the U.S. broker-dealers are also closely regulated regarding trading practices, customer protections and financial solvency. The supervision of broker-dealers and trading markets is primarily conducted by self-regulatory organizations ("SROs") such as the exchanges and the NASD under the oversight of the SEC.

The U.S. capital markets are rather flexible and open. New securities products and services are introduced generally without significant regulatory delays. In fact, competition is encouraged by the regulatory framework and, was mandated by the Securities Acts Amendments of 1975. Moreover, foreign securities firms participate in a full range of investment banking and securities activities.

. . .

## I. Foreign Stock Listings and International Stock Trading

Listing on a foreign exchange may broaden an issuer's shareholder base and, in some markets, it is necessary in order for domestic institutions to purchase the company's shares. For example, in France local insurance companies may be prohibited from purchasing shares that are not listed on a French bourse. With respect to certain markets, changes in accounting standards and disclosure requirements have made foreign listings more attractive. This apparently has been a factor in increasing the interest of foreign listings on the Tokyo Stock Exchange.

U.S. exchanges have also undertaken initiatives to increase the number of foreign listed companies. The American and New York Stock Exchanges in June 1987 received approval from the Commission to revise their listing standards. Some foreign corporations apparently had been reluctant to list on U.S. exchanges due to differences in listing standards in the U.S. and their home country. Now certain listing standards may be waived by the American and New York Stock Exchanges if those standards conflict with the laws and practices found in the home market of a foreign corporation. The rule revisions afford U.S. exchanges a better opportunity to compete on an international basis and may provide U.S. investors with greater access to foreign securities.[82]

As of December 1986, 512 foreign corporations had their securities listed on the London Stock Exchange. At the same time 59 foreign companies were listed on the New York Stock Exchange ("NYSE"), approximately one-third of which are Canadian corporations.[83] At the Tokyo Stock Exchange, 52 foreign firms were listed at year-end 1986 compared to only 21 firms at year-end 1985.

. . .

**82.** Securities Exchange Act Release No. 34–24634, June 23, 1987. The American and New York Stock Exchanges identified the following areas in which an exemption or waiver might be provided: quarterly reporting of interim earnings, composition and election of the Board of Directors, voting rights and quorum requirements for shareholder meetings.

**83.** Of these 59 companies, 22 were traded in the form of American Depository Receipts. For a discussion of American Depository Receipts issued and traded in U.S. markets, . . .

On NASDAQ the number of foreign securities equalled 270 at year-end 1986, a slight increase from 266 in 1985. Of these 270 issues, 92 were traded through the use of American Depository Receipts.

## Table II–14

### DOMESTIC AND FOREIGN LISTED COMPANIES ON MAJOR STOCK EXCHANGES
(Year–End)

| Exchange | Domestic Listings 1985 | Domestic Listings 1986 | Foreign Listings 1985 | Foreign Listings 1986 | Total Listings 1985 | Total Listings 1986 |
|---|---|---|---|---|---|---|
| American | 731 | 747 | 51 | 49 | 783 | 796 |
| Amsterdam | 232 | 267 | 242 | 242 | 474 | 509 |
| Australia [1] | 1,069 | 1,162 | 26 | 31 | 1,095 | 1,193 |
| Brussels | 192 | 191 | 144 | 140 | 336 | 331 |
| Copenhagen | 243 | 274 | 6 | 7 | 249 | 281 |
| Germany [1] | 451 | 492 | 177 | 181 | 628 | 673 |
| London | 2,116 | 2,101 | 500 | 512 | 2,616 | 2,613 |
| Luxembourg | N/A | 253 | N/A | 168 | N/A | 421 |
| Milan | 147 | 184 | 0 | 0 | 147 | 184 |
| New York | 1,487 | 1,516 | 54 | 59 | 1,541 | 1,575 |
| Paris | 489 | 874 | 189 | 226 | 687 | 1,100 |
| Singapore | 122 | 122 | 194 | 195 | 316 | 317 |
| Tokyo | 1,476 | 1,499 | 21 | 52 | 1,497 | 1,551 |
| Toronto | 912 | 1,034 | 54 | 51 | 966 | 1,085 |
| Zurich | 131 | 145 | 184 | 194 | 315 | 339 |

1. Reflects data for the Association of Australian and German stock exchanges which include all exchanges in their respective countries.

N.A.—Not available

Source: The London Stock Exchange Quarterly, The London Stock Exchange (various issues)

Even some smaller U.S. firms are tapping foreign markets for capital. At least fourteen U.S. companies have recently floated their initial public offerings in England and subsequently registered their issues on the London Stock Exchange's Unlisted Securities Market (USM). The British financial press opined that these firms raised capital more cheaply than they could have in the U.S. Two other advantages were cited for U.S. companies going public in the United Kingdom: corporations can maintain tighter control by issuing fewer shares to public investors; and U.S. companies may use profit forecasts in their British prospectuses. Issuers cannot use their own forecasts in U.S. prospectuses.

Table II–14 shows the extent of foreign stock listings on fourteen of the world's major stock exchanges at year-end 1986. With the exception of Milan, each of the exchanges had at least one non-domestic listing. The London Stock Exchange has the greatest number of U.S. companies listed on an exchange outside of the U.S. and the highest number of foreign listings of any market. U.S. equity listings on the London Stock Exchange have increased from 73 in 1975 to 199 in 1986. For the three Benelux countries, 44 percent of the listed corporations are foreign companies, while the comparable figure for the Zurich Stock Exchange is 59 percent.

Trading of foreign shares has increased on many exchanges. On the London Stock Exchange, for example, trading activity in foreign equities has averaged approximately $507 million per day since Big–Bang. Prior to October 27, 1986, this figure may have been as low as $24 million per day. At the Tokyo Stock Exchange, between 1973 and 1984, annual trading in foreign equities averaged less than two million shares. In 1985, annual volume in foreign equities increased to 131 million, while trading during the first six months of 1986 equalled 185 million shares.

Trading in foreign equity issues has also increased on the NYSE, from 804 million shares in 1984 to 1.2 billion shares in 1986. As a percent of total NYSE share volume, however, the amount attributable to foreign issues remained fairly constant during this period at approximately 3.5 percent.

. . .

## J. Internationalization of Portfolio Investment Flows

. . .

U.S. investors have increased their purchases of foreign stocks since the elimination of the interest equalization tax. In 1975 U.S. investors bought $1.7 billion in foreign stocks (see Table II–16). By 1986 U.S. purchases of foreign stocks totaled a record $51.7 billion. In a similar dramatic fashion, U.S. investors have increased their purchases of foreign debt securities from $8.7 billion in 1975 to $169.8 billion in 1986. Though U.S. investors sell their holdings of foreign stocks and bonds in adjusting their portfolios, the net capital flow from U.S. transactions in foreign securities has been outbound in every year since 1975. In 1975 U.S. investors purchased $6.3 billion more in foreign securities than they sold. In 1986 net purchases of foreign securities by U.S. investors amounted to $4.5 billion.

. . .

### Table II–16

### INTERNATIONAL TRANSACTIONS IN U.S. AND FOREIGN CORPORATE STOCKS AND DEBT SECURITIES

(U.S. $ Millions)

Corporate Stocks

| | Foreign Activity in U.S. Stocks | | | U.S. Activity in Foreign Stocks | | |
|---|---|---|---|---|---|---|
| Year | Purchases | Sales | Net Capital Flow | Purchases | Sales | Net Capital Flow |
| 1975 | 15,355 | 10,678 | 4,677 | 1,730 | 1,542 | −188 |
| 1980 | 40,298 | 34,870 | 5,428 | 10,044 | 7,897 | −2,147 |
| 1981 | 40,686 | 34,856 | 5,830 | 9,586 | 9,339 | −247 |
| 1982 | 41,881 | 37,981 | 3,900 | 8,504 | 7,163 | −1,341 |
| 1983 | 69,770 | 64,360 | 5,410 | 17,046 | 13,281 | −3,765 |
| 1984 | 59,834 | 62,814 | −2,980 | 15,917 | 14,816 | −1,101 |
| 1985 | 81,995 | 77,054 | 4,941 | 24,803 | 20,861 | −3,942 |
| 1986 | 148,134 | 129,436 | 18,698 | 51,744 | 50,292 | −1,452 |

All Debt Securities[1]

| Year | Foreign Activity in U.S. Debt Securities: Purchases | Sales | Net Capital Flow | U.S. Activity in Foreign Debt Securities: Purchases | Sales | Net Capital Flow |
|---|---|---|---|---|---|---|
| 1975 | 14,306 | 11,545 | 2,761 | 8,720 | 2,383 | −6,337 |
| 1980 | 66,595 | 56,262 | 10,333 | 18,090 | 17,090 | −1,000 |
| 1981 | 85,763 | 65,677 | 20,086 | 23,013 | 17,553 | −5,460 |
| 1982 | 117,632 | 98,863 | 18,769 | 33,809 | 27,167 | −6,642 |
| 1983 | 153,680 | 147,351 | 6,329 | 39,572 | 36,333 | −3,239 |
| 1984 | 275,634 | 241,237 | 34,397 | 59,948 | 56,017 | −3,931 |
| 1985 | 585,174 | 541,042 | 44,132 | 85,214 | 81,216 | −3,998 |
| 1986 | 1,176,027 | 1,100,951 | 75,076 | 169,798 | 166,700 | −3,098 |

1. Data includes both corporate and governmental debt issues.
Source: U.S. Treasury Bulletin (various issues)

Foreign investors' purchases of U.S. stocks and bonds has mirrored the growth of U.S. corporations' presence in overseas markets. Foreigners purchased $15.4 billion of U.S. stocks and $14.3 billion of U.S. debt securities in 1975. In 1986 foreign investors' purchases had increased to $148.1 billion of U.S. stocks and $1.2 trillion of U.S. debt instruments. The net capital flow from their purchases and sales of all U.S. securities has been inbound to the U.S. every year since 1975, increasing from $7.4 billion in 1975 to $93.7 billion in 1986.

Foreign activity in U.S. equity and debt securities reached record highs in 1986. Nevertheless, foreign activity in U.S. debt securities (primarily U.S. Treasury issues) is substantially greater than in U.S. equities. During 1986, 89 percent of the foreign activity in U.S. securities was attributable to transactions in debt securities. The most active foreign participants in the secondary market for U.S. debt securities are investors from Japan and the United Kingdom. Investors from these two countries accounted for 50 percent of the total foreign activity in U.S. debt securities during 1986.

These data, moreover, may underestimate the activity of Japanese investors in U.S. debt markets. This is partly because the recent worldwide expansion of Japanese securities firms, banks, and insurance companies makes it difficult to identify purchases by Japanese institutions that originate (or are held) outside of Japan. For example, according to U.S. sources Japanese net purchases of U.S. debt securities were approximately $14 billion in 1986. But according to Japanese sources, net purchases of U.S. debt securities were over twice this amount, or approximately $32 billion during 1986.

. . .

Total U.S. activity in foreign securities (purchases and sales) also reached a record high in 1986 of $438.5 billion and represents a two-fold increase from 1985's record of $212 billion. As with foreign activity in

U.S. securities, U.S. investors' trading in both foreign stocks and bonds reached record levels in 1986.

U.S. activity in foreign securities has traditionally been concentrated in the debt and equity issues of the United Kingdom and Japan. The equity markets of Japan and the United Kingdom are, respectively, the second and third largest in the world. During 1986, U.S. transactions in the debt and equity securities of these two countries accounted for 67 percent of the total activity by U.S. investors in foreign debt and equity issues.

. . .

### K. Impact of Internationalization on U.S. Markets

There has been an international presence in the U.S. securities markets for at least a century. Strong investment ties have existed among the United Kingdom, Canada, and the U.S. and, more recently, the U.S., Japan and Western Europe. As noted above, there has been a dramatic increase in foreign portfolio investments in the U.S. and in U.S. investments in foreign securities markets. Part of the increase in U.S. portfolio investments in foreign markets reflects the trend in recent years for U.S. investors to purchase mutual funds and closed-end funds investing in foreign securities markets. These funds provide U.S. investors with another avenue into foreign securities markets as well as the diversification typically associated with mutual funds. The number of global mutual funds has increased from 21 in December 1983 to 59 in December 1986 (see Table II–18). The value of international fund sales also grew from $1.5 billion in 1984 to $7.6 billion during 1986. In addition to these global funds, there are about twelve U.S. exchange-listed closed-end country funds investing in the securities of the emerging markets of Korea, Taiwan and Mexico as well as the developed markets such as France, Australia, Germany and Japan.

. . .

**Table II–18**

**OVERVIEW OF GLOBAL MUTUAL FUNDS**
(U.S. $ Billions)

| Year | Number of Funds | Global Fund Assets | Global Fund Sales |
|---|---|---|---|
| 1983 | 21 | $ 3.5 | $ NA |
| 1984 | 30 | 5.2 | 1.5 |
| 1985 | 42 | 7.9 | 1.8 |
| 1986 | 59 | $15.9 | $7.6 |

Source: Investment Company Institute

An increase in U.S. demand for foreign securities is also evidenced by the number of foreign companies with securities traded through NASDAQ or on exchanges in the form of ADRs.

Between 1982 and 1986 the number of ADRs traded through NASDAQ or on a stock exchange increased from 85 to 110. Most ADRs are traded through NASDAQ. In addition, there are several hundred more ADRs traded over-the-counter outside of NASDAQ. There also has been a substantial increase in the total number of ADR shares. Ten years ago there were roughly 150 million such shares outstanding in the U.S. In 1986, there were 2.4 billion shares outstanding; this represents a 16–fold increase over the past decade.

Despite the growth of foreign stocks traded through ADRs there has been a decline in the number of foreign securities listed on U.S. exchanges. In 1976 there were 175 foreign bond issues listed on U.S. exchanges. Ten years later there were 105 issues (see Table II–19). The number of foreign stocks (including ADRs) listed on U.S. exchanges increased only slightly from 115 in 1976 to 123 in 1986. The U.S. stock markets have not kept pace with other stock markets around the world in attracting foreign listings. As noted earlier, the Commission recently approved modifications to the American and NYSE listing standards. This may facilitate foreign listings in the U.S.

The U.S. domestic market has not kept pace with the trend toward internationalization in terms of the amount of capital raised in the U.S. securities market by foreigners. Throughout the last ten years, Yankee securities (foreign issues of stocks and bonds in the U.S.) registered with the SEC have remained generally in the four to six billion dollar range. Also, the number of foreign equity issues traded on U.S. exchanges has remained fairly constant. In 1977 there were 116 such issues. Ten years later there were 123. Foreign bonds traded on the U.S. exchanges have declined from 175 in 1977 to 105 in 1986.

A closer look at the Yankee securities markets shows how U.S. participation in the internationalization process has been uneven. The annual issuance of foreign securities registered with the SEC has not kept pace with the growth in international markets in debt and equity securities. While the issuance of foreign securities in the U.S. has not declined in nominal terms, it has declined in relative terms. In 1977 registered public offerings of foreign issues in the U.S. represented 13 percent of the dollar volume of our public new issues market (see Table II–20). In 1986 that portion dropped to three percent.

It is important to point out that foreign government debt represents by far the largest portion of capital raised by foreign entities in the U.S. securities market. In 1977 foreign governments accounted for 90 percent of capital raised through foreign public offerings registered with the SEC. By 1986 the figure had declined but still represented 64 percent of the total. The remainder of the market has fluctuated between corporate debt and equity. In 1986 equity accounted for 26 percent and corporate debt for 10 percent of total foreign offerings.

. . .

**Table II–19**

**DOMESTIC AND FOREIGN SECURITIES LISTED ON U.S. EXCHANGES**

(Number of Issues)

| | Equity | | Bonds | | Total | |
|---|---|---|---|---|---|---|
| Year | Domestic | Foreign | Domestic | Foreign | Domestic | Foreign |
| 1976 | 3,746 | 116 | 2,923 | 175 | 6,669 | 291 |
| 1977 | 3,559 | 115 | — | — | 3,771 | — |
| 1978 | 3,459 | 106 | 2,961 | 177 | 6,420 | 283 |
| 1979 | 3,377 | 96 | 3,190 | 174 | 6,567 | 270 |
| 1980 | 3,557 | 99 | 3,350 | 157 | 6,907 | 256 |
| 1981 | 3,498 | 103 | 3,405 | 148 | 6,903 | 251 |
| 1982 | 3,530 | 103 | 3,579 | 134 | 7,109 | 237 |
| 1983 | 3,484 | 111 | 3,831 | 128 | 7,315 | 239 |
| 1984 | 3,421 | 114 | 4,043 | 121 | 7,464 | 235 |
| 1985 | 3,374 | 113 | 4,215 | 117 | 7,589 | 230 |
| 1986 | 3,360 | 123 | 4,002 | 105 | 7,362 | 228 |

Source: Directorate of Economic and Policy Analysis
Securities and Exchange Commission

## Table II-20

## DOMESTIC CORPORATE FOREIGN ISSUES REGISTERED AND OFFERED IN THE U.S.

(1977–1986)

| Year | Domestic and Foreign Issues Combined ($billions) | Foreign Issues: Total ($billions) | Foreign Issues: Percent of Domestic and Foreign Combined |
|---|---|---|---|
| 1977 | $ 36.5 | $4.7 | 13% |
| 1978 | 32.9 | 4.4 | 13 |
| 1979 | 40.4 | 5.2 | 13 |
| 1980 | 67.4 | 4.3 | 6 |
| 1981 | 67.7 | 4.4 | 6 |
| 1982 | 74.6 | 2.5 | 3 |
| 1983 | 104.0 | 4.1 | 4 |
| 1984 | 89.2 | 4.3 | 5 |
| 1985 | 132.9 | 5.6 | 4 |
| 1986 | 228.4 | 6.4 | 3 |

Note: The U.S. issues are corporate debt and business equity issues. The foreign issues also include government debt offerings. Cash offerings are included while secondary and exchange offerings are excluded. Also note that the OECD figures on foreign new issues in the U.S. reported in Table 8 differ somewhat from those in this table. The difference is accounted for by the OECD including certain private placements and exempt offerings while under-reporting registered issues in some years.

Source: Directorate of Economic and Policy Analysis
Securities and Exchange Commission

Canada is by far the most frequent user of the Yankee securities market. Canadian disclosure and accounting standards are similar to those of the U.S., making it easier for Canadian entities to raise capital in the U.S. Canadian issuers accounted for roughly half of all foreign debt and equity offerings during the ten-year period ending in 1986 (see Table II–21). With regard to corporate debt offerings, Japan had the next highest number (9) after Canada (36). With regard to equity offerings, Bermuda with 29 was second to Canada with 277. For government debt, Sweden (13 issues) was next after Canada (70 issues) over this ten-year period.

Another aspect of the Yankee securities markets is the extent of secondary market trading in foreign securities. Table II–22 shows the number of ADRs registered for trading in the U.S. The number registered has fluctuated considerably over the last ten years but generally increased in the last three years. In 1981 there were 106 ADRs newly registered with the Commission. In 1982 only 45 were registered. The number rose to 288 registrations in 1985 then dropped to 204 in 1986. Many of these ADRs, however, are the registrations of additional shares of issues already traded in the U.S. Some of the ADR registrations represent the introduction of new foreign issues into the U.S. market. The leading sources of ADRs over the last 10 years have been Australia (308 registrations), the United Kingdom (174), Japan (149), and South Africa (142) (see Table II–21).

. . .

## Table II–21

## FOREIGN SECURITIES REGISTERED IN THE U.S. BY ISSUER'S COUNTRY OF ORIGIN: 1977–1986 COMBINED

(Number of Registrations)

| | Corporate Debt | Corporate/ Business Equity | Government Debt | ADRs | Total |
|---|---|---|---|---|---|
| Africa, Middle East | | | | | |
| South Africa | 1 | 3 | — | 142 | 146 |
| Israel | 3 | 21 | 9 | 3 | 36 |
| All Others | — | — | — | 4 | 4 |
| Asia | | | | | |
| Japan | 9 | 10 | 6 | 149 | 174 |
| Hong Kong | — | 2 | — | 69 | 71 |
| Singapore | — | — | — | 25 | 25 |
| All Others | — | 1 | 3 | 7 | 11 |
| Caribbean, Central and South America | | | | | |
| Bermuda | 1 | 29 | — | 8 | 38 |
| Netherland Antilles | 1 | 11 | — | 2 | 14 |
| Bahamas | — | 11 | — | 1 | 12 |
| All Others | 1 | 21 | 3 | 3 | 28 |
| Europe, Australia | | | | | |
| Australia | 4 | 3 | 4 | 308 | 319 |
| United Kingdom | 2 | 23 | 1 | 174 | 200 |
| Sweden | 1 | 5 | 13 | 19 | 38 |
| W. Germany | — | — | — | 34 | 34 |
| France | — | 4 | 11 | 16 | 31 |
| All Others | 6 | 35 | 41 | 51 | 133 |
| North America | | | | | |
| Canada | 36 | 277 | 70 | 9 | 392 |
| Mexico | 1 | 3 | 2 | 8 | 14 |
| | 66 | 459 | 163 | 1,032 | 1,720 |

Source: Directorate of Economic and Policy Analysis
Securities and Exchange Commission

**Table II–22**

**TYPES OF FOREIGN SECURITIES REGISTERED WITH THE SEC: 1977–1986**

(Number of Issues)

| | Corporate Debt | Corporate/ Business Equity | Government Debt | ADRs | Total |
|---|---|---|---|---|---|
| 1977 | 1 | 22 | 34 | 35 | 92 |
| 1978 | 2 | 21 | 19 | 31 | 73 |
| 1979 | 4 | 29 | 18 | 58 | 109 |
| 1980 | 8 | 49 | 9 | 66 | 132 |
| 1981 | 15 | 48 | 26 | 106 | 195 |
| 1982 | 6 | 32 | 17 | 45 | 100 |
| 1983 | 12 | 84 | 15 | 60 | 171 |
| 1984 | 3 | 44 | 9 | 139 | 195 |
| 1985 | 6 | 80 | 5 | 288 | 379 |
| 1986 | 9 | 50 | 11 | 204 | 274 |

Source: Directorate of Economic and Policy Analysis
Securities and Exchange Commission

Another example of the impact of internationalization on U.S. corporations is the extent to which they now conduct overseas bond financing. U.S. corporations raised $5.8 billion through international bonds and $41.9 billion in registered domestic bond offerings in 1980. The international bonds represented 12 percent of the total $47.7 billion raised in the two markets. By 1986 international bond financing rose to $44 billion while domestic registered bond financing was $157 billion. Thus in 1986 international bonds rose to 22 percent of the total capital raised in these two markets by U.S. issuers.

## L. Future Prospects

The internationalization of the world's securities markets presents new challenges and opportunities for the U.S. securities markets and its regulators. In recent years the international financial landscape has changed in response to economic, institutional, technological, and regulatory forces. While the future cannot be predicted with any degree of certainty, it does appear that the securities markets are likely to maintain their global character in the years ahead.

During the 1980's the world's capital markets became more interdependent. At the same time, the securities markets assumed a larger role in the international capital market. This was due in part to favorable economic conditions and regulatory liberalizations, such as the elimination of exchange controls in Japan and the United Kingdom, that contributed to the expansion of both domestic and international securities markets around the world. Technology also played a role in this process. In a very real sense, the world is getting smaller due to improvements in technology and reduced information costs.

The U.S. markets have played a large role in shaping global trends in securities. In particular, the U.S. markets are highly competitive and innovative. They remain the largest, most sophisticated in the world with the widest range of financial products available to market participants.

The U.S. regulatory structure also appears to have had an impact on other major capital markets around the world. The reductions in transactions costs associated with the deregulation of commission rates in the U.S. exerted pressure on other markets. The benefits that result from vigorous competition have not gone unnoticed in other financial centers. Regulatory restructuring is now occurring in the capital markets of, among others, the United Kingdom, Canada, Japan, and France.

Looking back, the 1960's may be characterized as the decade when the internationalization of the securities markets began its latest phase. The 1970's may be viewed as the decade when the U.S. securities markets entered into a major restructuring, some of which resulted from the Securities Acts Amendments of 1975. This restructuring, the increased competition, and the financial innovation in the U.S. during this decade helped influence the character and pace of regulatory changes in other securities markets.

The 1980's may be viewed as a decade of rapid growth for international transactions in securities and a time when many other financial centers undertook major restructuring of their markets. Regulatory liberalization resulted in increased competition in domestic financial markets and permitted greater foreign participation which accelerated the process of internationalization. The 1990's may present opportunities for further growth and integration of international securities markets and the challenge to develop a global regulatory framework that preserves the efficiencies associated with international capital mobility.

*Updated Information*

The SEC study is somewhat outdated. The following tables give some more current information.

Table A below comes from a new SEC study, *Market 2000, An Examination of Current Equity Market Developments* (January 1994) ("Market 2000"), Exhibit 6. It gives equity market capitalization data from 1986–1992 and should be compared with the data in Table II–2 in the SEC study, supra.

Global Equity Markets Capitalization
In Billions of Dollars

| COUNTRY | 1986 | 1987 | 1988 | 1989 | 1990 | 1991 | 1992 |
|---|---|---|---|---|---|---|---|
| United States | 2,637 | 2,589 | 2,794 | 3,506 | 3,090 | 4,186 | 4,758 |
| Japan | 1,843 | 2,803 | 3,907 | 4,393 | 2,918 | 3,131 | 2,399 |
| United Kingdom | 440 | 681 | 771 | 827 | 868 | 1,003 | 839 |
| Germany | 258 | 213 | 252 | 365 | 379 | 393 | 346 |
| France | 150 | 172 | 245 | 365 | 342 | 374 | 351 |
| Canada | 166 | 219 | 242 | 291 | 242 | 267 | 243 |
| Italy | 140 | 120 | 135 | 169 | 149 | 154 | 115 |
| G–7 Nations | 5,634 | 6,797 | 8,346 | 9,916 | 7,988 | 9,508 | 9,051 |
| All Other Nations | 881 | 1,101 | 1,481 | 1,725 | 1,561 | 1,906 | 2,046 |
| WORLD | 6,515 | 7,898 | 9,827 | 11,641 | 9,549 | 11,414 | 11,097 |

Source: International Finance Corporation

Table B below comes from James L. Cochrane, Assessing and Evaluating the Current Directions of Transnational Listings, NYSE Working Paper 93–03 (January 1993) ("Listings"), Table 1. It gives listing and trading information on foreign companies for the twelve largest stock markets and should be compared with the data in Tables II–14 and II–19 in the SEC study, supra.

**Foreign Companies on the Twelve Largest Stock Markets**

| Market | 1993 Average Daily Turnover (Millions of $U.S.) | Foreign Turnover as a % of Average Daily Turnover | Number of Foreign Companies 1986 | 1990 | 1993 |
|---|---|---|---|---|---|
| NYSE | 9,025 | 8.0% | 59 | 96 | 162 |
| NASDAQ | 5,336 | 5.3% | 244 | 256 | 301 |
| London | 3,389 | 50.6% | 584 | 613 | 485 |
| Tokyo | 3,223 | 0.1% | 52 | 125 | 108 |
| Germany | 2,360 | 2.7% | 181 | 234 | 345 |
| Taiwan | 1,216 | 0.0% | 0 | 0 | 0 |
| Zurich | 833 | 9.0% | 194 | 240 | 249 |
| Korea | 716 | 0.0% | 0 | 0 | 0 |
| Paris | 684 | 2.7% | 195 | 226 | 208 |
| Kuala Lumpur | 584 | 0.9% | 61 | 3 | 3 |
| Osaka | 537 | 0.0% | 0 | 0 | 0 |
| Hong Kong | 531 | 0.2% | 5 | 15 | 27 |

Source: F.I.B.V.

NYSE RESEARCH & PLANNING
October 1994 [G19080]

As a point of comparison, foreign companies have recently been delisting from the Tokyo Stock Exchange due to lack of investor interest and the general fall of activity accompanying the recent plunge of the Nikkei.

Tables C, D and E below from Listings, Tables 2, 5 and 6, gives data on U.S. ownership of foreign equities and should be compared with the data in Table II–16 in the SEC study, supra.

## International Trading of Equities

■ Cross Border ■ Cross Exchange

Billions of U.S. Dollars

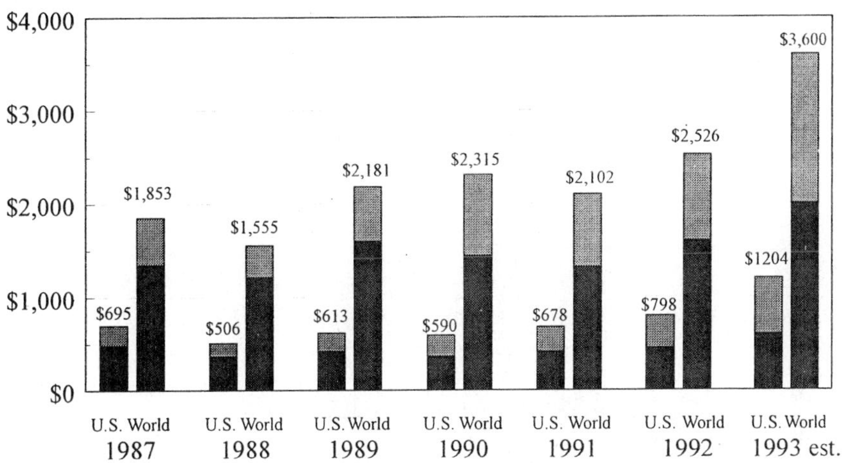


Source: Baring Securities Limited

NYSE RESEARCH & PLANNING
October 1994 [G19081]

## Holdings of Foreign Equities in the United States

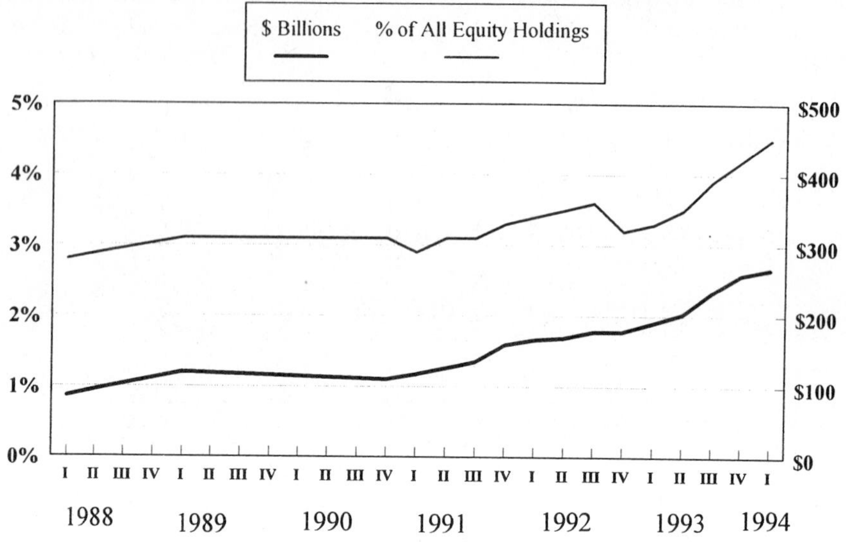


Source: Federal Reserve Board "Flow of Funds"

NYSE RESEARCH & PLANNING
October 1994 [G19082]

## Purchases and Sales of Foreign Stocks in Organized U.S. Markets

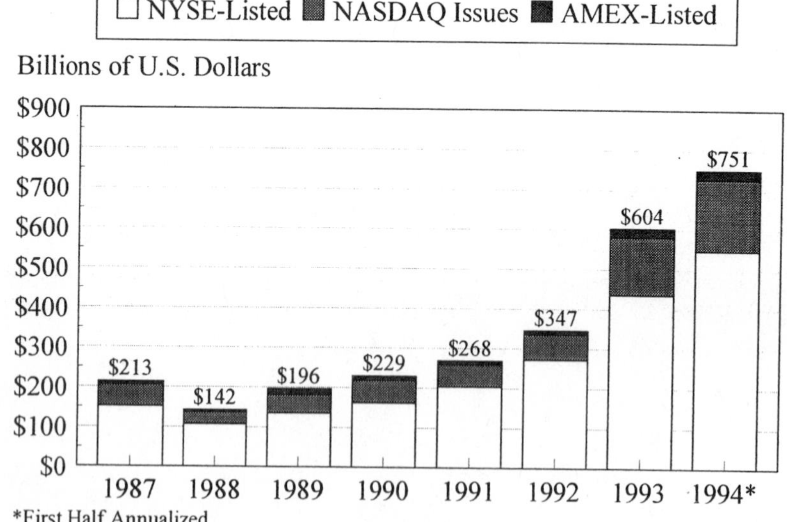


*First Half Annualized

Source: NYSE, Amex, NASD

NYSE RESEARCH & PLANNING
October 1994 [G19083]

Table F below is from Werner Kuehne and J. Michael Schell, Stock Exchange Listings in the U.S.: Disclosure Issues, Daimler–Benz: A Case Study, in American Conference Institute, *Recent Developments in International Securities Law* (October 25–26, 1993), Appendix B. It gives data on primary issuance of securities in the U.S. market and should be compared with data in Table II–20 of the SEC study, supra.

**Table F**

## Foreign Issuer Private Placements and Registered Offerings

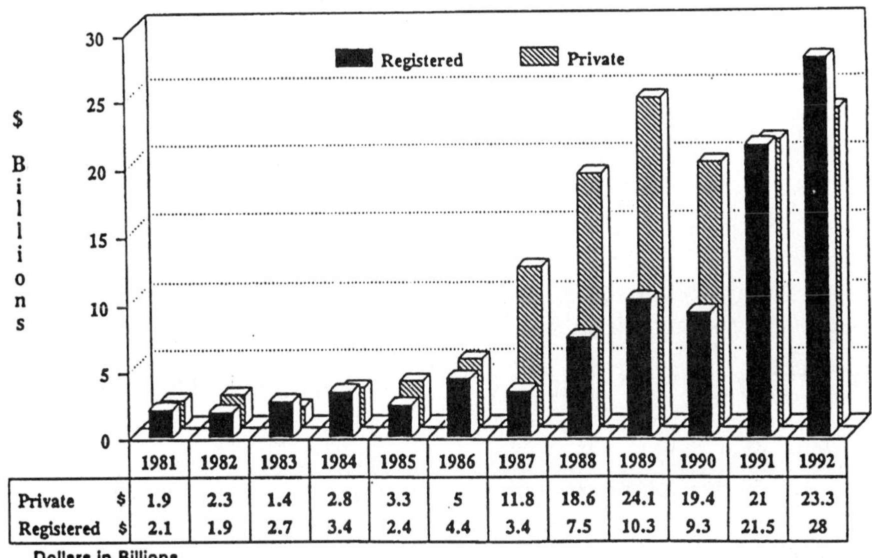


| | 1981 | 1982 | 1983 | 1984 | 1985 | 1986 | 1987 | 1988 | 1989 | 1990 | 1991 | 1992 |
|---|---|---|---|---|---|---|---|---|---|---|---|---|
| Private $ | 1.9 | 2.3 | 1.4 | 2.8 | 3.3 | 5 | 11.8 | 18.6 | 24.1 | 19.4 | 21 | 23.3 |
| Registered $ | 2.1 | 1.9 | 2.7 | 3.4 | 2.4 | 4.4 | 3.4 | 7.5 | 10.3 | 9.3 | 21.5 | 28 |

Dollars in Billions

Source: SEC & Securities Data Corp.

Table G below breaks down U.S. corporate primary distributions, by debt and equity, for all issuers, domestic as well as foreign, and should also be compared with data in Table II–20 of the SEC study.

**Table G**

**U.S. Corporate Primary Distributions ($ Billions)**

| | 1987 | 1988 | 1989 | 1990 | 1991 | 1992 |
|---|---|---|---|---|---|---|
| Domestic | | | | | | |
| Debt | | | | | | |
| Pub. Debt | 219.4 | 237.2 | 274.9 | 290.6 | 508.3 | 744.5 |
| Priv. Placm't | 119.9 | 172.7 | 168.5 | 113.6 | 107.3 | 112.8 |
| Total Debt | 339.3 | 409.9 | 443.4 | 404.2 | 615.6 | 857.3 |
| Equity | | | | | | |
| Pub. Equity | 52.9 | 37.3 | 30.6 | 23.8 | 75.9 | 101.6 |
| Priv. Placm't | 14.5 | 17.9 | 31.5 | 17.5 | 10.8 | 14.9 |
| Total Equity | 67.4 | 55.2 | 62.1 | 41.3 | 86.7 | 116.5 |
| Total | 406.7 | 465.1 | 505.5 | 445.5 | 702.3 | 973.8 |
| Foreign | 15.2 | 26.1 | 34.4 | 28.7 | 42.5 | 51.3 |
| Ratio | | | | | | |
| For./Total | 3.7% | 5.6% | 6.8% | 6.4% | 6.1% | 5.3% |

### *Questions*

1. How internationalized are U.S. securities markets? Have the markets become more internationalized since 1986?

2. Why should the United States care whether or not its securities markets are internationalized?

## B. THE BASIC SECURITIES LAW FRAMEWORK

### G. PALM AND D. WALKOVIK, UNITED STATES: A SPECIAL REPORT, IN "ISSUING SECURITIES: A GUIDE TO SECURITIES REGULATION AROUND THE WORLD"

International Financial Law Review, Special Supplement (July 1990). Pp. 62–84.

In view of its enormous size and comparative stability, the United States capital market has historically been very attractive from a purely financial point of view to non-US issuers of securities. Until recently, however, the perceived complexity of the regulatory system applicable to the US market and, therefore, the perceived cost of attaining and maintaining access to that market, as well as fears (not necessarily supported by fact) about unduly rigorous disclosure requirements, inflexible regulators, and liability exposure, all tended to limit use to a level far below the market's financial capacity and attractiveness.

In recent years, these perceptions have begun to change, in significant part because of the streamlining of the US regulatory scheme applicable to new issuances of securities. Also important has been the recognition by relevant US regulators of the need to harmonise as far as practical US requirements with those applicable in other jurisdictions and to be flexible in applying existing US requirements to non-US issuers, so as not to deprive US investors of the increasingly significant opportunities presented by such investments. This past year, in particular, has witnessed the adoption of an important new rule (Rule 144A) designed to permit unrestricted trading among qualified institutional buyers of certain classes of securities initially issued without compliance with the registration requirements generally applicable to public offerings, and, therefore, without triggering the ongoing registration and reporting requirements arising therefrom. Rule 144A, in conjunction with certain other regulatory developments (Regulation S), is expected significantly to expand access to the US markets for foreign issuers that have avoided such markets because of a reluctance to become subject to the disclosure and reporting requirements of the US federal securities laws.

## OVERVIEW

The US federal securities laws, all of which are administered by the Securities and Exchange Commission (the SEC), consist of six separate, but interrelated, statutes: the Securities Act of 1933, the Securities Exchange Act of 1934, the Public Utility Holding Company Act of 1935, the Trust Indenture Act of 1939, the Investment Advisers Act of 1940, and the Investment Company Act of 1940. These statutes form a comprehensive pattern of federal regulation and, with the exception of the Public Utility Holding Company Act, generally are applicable to those engaged in the distribution of foreign securities in the US.

The two statutes of particular interest to most non-US issuers are the Securities Act relating to the public offering in the US of securities by issuers of those securities or persons in control relationships with those issuers, and the Exchange Act dealing, among other things, with the ownership and trading of securities in the US. In recent years, the regulatory schemes established under these two separate statutes have been increasingly integrated, largely through rules and forms adopted by the SEC.

As background, it will be helpful to note three aspects of the structural approach taken in the Securities Act and the Exchange Act.

First, under the Securities Act, an issuer of securities is required to register with the SEC specific securities to be sold to the public in a particular plan of distribution. A Securities Act registration is, therefore, a one-time event. After the planned distribution of the registered securities has been completed, the registration has no continuing significance except as noted below.

Second, under the Exchange Act, an issuer which has registered securities under the Securities Act or the Exchange Act becomes subject to the continuing reporting requirements created by the Exchange Act, including, for example, in the case of non-Canadian foreign private (i.e. non-governmental) issuers, annual reports on Form 20–F and certain other reports on Form 6–K. A private issuer subject to these reporting requirements is sometimes referred to as a 'reporting company'. An issuer which is a reporting company may qualify for simplified registration requirements under the Securities Act and for other accommodations not available to companies not in the reporting system.

Third, also under the Exchange Act, the non-US private issuer is required to register with the SEC equity securities which are publicly held in the United States (defined in terms of the number of shareholders, but subject to certain exemptions for foreign issuers) and debt or equity securities which are to be listed on a US stock exchange. Exchange Act registration has continuing significance as a basis for securities regulation of the issuer, holders of its securities and certain third parties.

## THE SEC

The SEC is an independent agency of the US Government consisting of five commissioners appointed by the President with a large supporting staff. The commissioners set policy through the adoption of rules and regulations and serve as a quasi-judicial body. Matters relating to the registration of securities by particular issuers and reporting requirements as applied to particular issuers are dealt with exclusively by the SEC staff.

The staff of the SEC has several major line divisions: Corporation Finance, Investment Management, Market Regulation and Enforcement. In addition, there are staff functions such as a Chief Accountant and General Counsel.

Most contacts by non-US issuers with the SEC staff are with the Division of Corporation Finance, which is generally responsible for all Securities Act and Exchange Act filings for the registration of securities and reporting purposes.

The SEC encourages non-US issuers to use the US markets. Over the years, a number of special exemptions and forms have been developed by the staff with the help of bankers, lawyers and accountants who practise in this area. The Division of Corporation Finance has an Office of International Corporate Finance which specialises in dealing with non-US issuers.

The staff encourages foreign issuers to meet with staff members to find solutions to problems which foreign issuers face in the SEC registration and reporting processes. Such meetings are normally attended by high level staff members, who take a particular interest in the problems of non-US issuers.

## REGISTRATION UNDER THE SECURITIES ACT

### Registration requirements and procedures

Generally, no public offering of securities may be made in the US by the issuer of those securities or by a person who controls, is controlled by, or is under common control with, the issuer until a registration statement relating to the offering has been filed under the Securities Act with the SEC. Among the more important exemptions from the registration requirements are certain non-public and other limited offerings, often referred to as 'private placements', and issues of notes maturing in not more than nine months to finance current operational business requirements, generally referred to as 'commercial paper'.

After such a filing has been made, offers of the securities may be made to potential buyers orally or through use of the preliminary prospectus which forms part of the registration statement, but no sales may be made until the registration statement is declared effective by the SEC. A copy of the final form of prospectus must be delivered to each purchaser not later than the time of the confirmation of the sale.

The purpose of the registration and prospectus delivery requirements is to furnish the investor with financial and other information regarding the issuer, the securities and the offering that will enable the investor to make an informed evaluation of the merits of the securities offered.

After a registration statement is filed with the SEC, the SEC staff will determine whether it wishes to review the filing and will advise the issuer of its decision. The review determination generally takes two to five business days. If a review is made, the staff will advise the issuer of any apparent inadequacies in the filing, and, if necessary, the issuer may file an amendment to the registration statement in response to the staff's comments.

As a matter of current staff policy the registration statements of all first-time registrants are reviewed, and the review process generally will take between four and six weeks. After the staff is satisfied with the filing the issuer may request that the SEC declare the registration statement effective. Ordinarily the SEC will declare the registration statement effective promptly after receipt of the request.

**Conventional Offerings.** In a conventional offering the registration statement filed with the SEC relates to a specific offering of securities which is expected to commence soon after filing. In such an offering, the registration statement as initially filed, and related preliminary prospectus, do not contain the offering price and other definitive terms of the offering, such as the underwriting syndicate, discounts and offering commissions, amount of proceeds, and other matters dependent upon the offering price and date. The issuer may elect to include this information in an amendment filed at the same time it asks the SEC to declare the registration statement effective, or it may ask that the registration statement be declared effective with this information (but no other) omitted. In the latter case, a form of prospectus containing this information must be filed with the SEC within two business days after the earlier of the date the offering price of the issue is determined or the date the final prospectus is first used, but in any event within five business days from the date of effectiveness. If such a filing does not occur within the five-day period, an updated post-effective amendment to the registration statement must be filed and declared effective which either contains the offering price and other definitive terms or omits such information and starts a new five-day period running.

**Shelf registration.** The delay inherent in the preparation and filing of a registration statement with the SEC, and the uncertainty as to the length of the further delay resulting from any review period (or even the time necessary to reach a decision not to review) prior to effectiveness of the registration statement is unacceptable to frequent issuers of securities (generally debt). Alternative procedures for certain offerings by qualifying private and governmental issuers which in effect permit instant access to the US capital market are available. These 'shelf' registration procedures (so-called because an amount of securities reasonably expected to be sold within a two-year period is registered in advance of any particular offering, and such securities are sold 'off the shelf' on short notice without any additional action by the SEC) make it possible to bring issues to market on notice of a few hours or less. Under the shelf procedure, the registration statement, with the basic prospectus, is filed, processed and declared effective upon the request of the registrant in the manner referred to in the preceding paragraph, but the time of effectiveness is not co-ordinated with the time of any particular offering, and information as to the specific nature and terms of the securities to be offered and the terms of the offering is not included. Over time, the information contained in the registration statement and basic prospectus generally is updated, either through the filing of amendments or, in the case of private issuers, the incorporation by reference of Exchange Act filings. Securities covered by the shelf registration may be sold using the basic prospectus with a short prospectus supplement which sets out information as to the specific terms of the securities offered, the terms of the offering and any significant recent developments in the issuer's affairs not otherwise reflected in the basic prospectus, either directly or through incorporation by reference. This prospectus supplement simply is subsequently filed with the SEC. No SEC review or declaration of effectiveness is then required. Accordingly, when a shelf registration has been effected, an issuer is in a position to bring an offering to market on very short notice and sell securities immediately upon pricing, thereby increasing its ability to take advantage of particular market opportunities. We would note, however, that under the shelf procedure, a non-US private issuer is required to file interim financial statements (which may be unaudited) as a post-effective amendment to the shelf registration statement as necessary to ensure that at the start of a delayed offering or at all times during a continuous offering not more than six months have elapsed since the date of the latest filed financial statements. This causes significant difficulty for many non-US private issuers, in effect creating 'black out' periods when the shelf is unavailable.

## Registration statement content

**Private Issuers.** The SEC has adopted a series of forms to be used for registration of securities under the Securities Act. For non-Canadian foreign private issuers the principal Securities Act forms are Forms F–1, F–2 and F–3, each used in connection with capital raising, and Form F–4, used in connection with business combinations. Many of the items of the forms incorporate by reference material from the SEC's Regulation S–K, which contains standard instructions for filing forms under the Securities Act and Exchange Act. Significantly, all of the forms include substantially the same information, either by presentation in the prospectus, by delivery of additional disclosure documents with the prospectus, or by incorporation by reference of Exchange Act filings.

A registration statement on any of these forms is signed by the registrant, its principal executive, financial and accounting officers, a majority of its board of directors and its authorised representative in the United States.

**Form F–1.** A first-time, non-Canadian foreign private issuer would register securities under the Securities Act on SEC Form F–1.

The principal requirements of Form F–1 are as follows:

- Information regarding the terms of the securities, the terms of the offering, the plan of distribution of the securities and the use of proceeds.
- A description of the business of the issuer, including (i) a discussion of the general development of the business over the past five years; (ii) principal products produced and services rendered and the principal markets for and methods of distribution of such products and services; (iii) a breakdown of total revenues during the past three years by categories of activity and into geographical markets, with a narrative discussion of material differences between relative contributions to operating profit as compared to relative contributions to revenues; and (iv) special characteristics of the registrant's operations or industry which may have a material impact on future financial performance, and any material country risks unlikely to be known by investors, including dependence upon a few major customers or suppliers, governmental regulation, expiration of material contracts or rights, unusual competitive conditions, cyclicality of the industry and anticipated raw material or energy shortages. Additional disclosures required of electric or gas utilities, companies with oil or gas operations, banks and insurance companies are set out in industry guides adopted by the SEC. Additional information is required of registrants which have not received revenues from operations during each of the three preceding years.
- A brief description of the location and general character of the principal plants, mines and other materially important physical properties of the registrant. In the case of an extractive enterprise, material information as to production, reserves, locations, development and the nature of the registrant's interests is to be given. (Generally, only proven oil or gas reserves and proven or probable other reserves may be disclosed.)
- Selected financial data for each of the last five years, including revenues, income, assets and long-term obligations.

- A management's discussion of the registrant's financial condition, changes in financial condition and results of operations for each year for which financial statements are presented (three years), including information as to trends, commitments and material events and uncertainties relating to liquidity, capital resources and results of operations.

- Prescribed information as to material pending legal proceedings, control of the registrant by a parent or others and 10 per cent shareholders, the nature of any trading market for the securities registered, exchange controls and other governmental, legal or charter limitations affecting non-resident holders of the registrant's securities, withholding or similar taxes to which US holders would be subject under the laws of the country in which the registrant is organised, the directors and executive officers of the registrant and the aggregate compensation paid to them as a group for services in the last year, outstanding options to purchase from the registrant securities of the class being registered, and information otherwise made public as to the interest of management or controlling shareholders and certain associated persons in material transactions with the registrant.

- A description of the securities to be registered.

- Audited balance sheets as of the end of each of the two most recent fiscal years and audited statements of income and changes in financial position for each of the three most recent fiscal years. Regulation S–X sets forth the form and content of and requirements for financial statements required by the US securities laws and SEC rules.

  (i) If the last audited balance sheet is dated more than six months prior to the effective date of the registration statement, interim unaudited financial statements are required. This requirement has had a significant impact on the ability of non-US issuers which publicly release financial statements on a semi-annual basis only. In view of the time required to prepare such financial statements, this requirement has had the effect of creating 'blackout periods' during which the public capital markets in the US have been unavailable to such issuers. Our firm has proposals pending before the SEC to alleviate these problems, in part by adding a grace period to the existing rules which would take into account time necessary to prepare.

  (ii) Generally, the statements must be presented in the currency of the registrant's country.

  (iii) The statements must disclose an informational content substantially similar to statements which comply with US generally accepted accounting principles (GAAP) and Regulation S–X.

(iv) The statements may be prepared according to US GAAP or, alternatively, according to an identified comprehensive body of accounting principles together with a discussion and quantification of material variations from US GAAP and Regulation S–X in the accounting principles, practices and methods used in preparing the financial statements.

(v) In contrast to ongoing Exchange Act reporting requirements, the statements and notes are required to include supplementary information required by US GAAP and Regulation S–X, such as business segment and pension information, unless the securities registered are to be offered only upon exercise of rights granted pro rata to all existing security holders of a class, pursuant to a dividend or interest reinvestment plan or upon the conversion of outstanding convertible securities or the exercise of outstanding warrants (all of which are referred to herein as offerings to existing security holders).

. . .

### Registration statement preparation

The general preparation of the initial Securities Act registration by a non-US private issuer usually requires a significant commitment of management resources to achieve a product which properly presents the issuer to US investors for commercial or marketing purposes and meets SEC requirements and disclosure standards. It will be essential that the issuer have the assistance in that effort of an accounting firm which is expert in US accounting principles and practices, typically one of the international accounting firms which has a substantial US practice. It also will be essential that the issuer have available to it the assistance of US legal advisers who are knowledgeable in SEC requirements, and preferably who are experienced in assisting non-US private issuers in meeting those requirements and approaching US investors and trading markets. The investment bankers who are to underwrite that offering and their legal advisers also will provide advice and assistance in the preparation of the filing and related matters.

As discussed below, the issuer, its directors, certain of its officers, its US agent and underwriters of its registered securities may have liabilities in relation to any Securities Act registration statement for false or misleading statements in or omissions from the filings. This emphasises the importance of careful preparation of the filing, including the importance of conducting a sufficient 'due diligence' investigation of the issuer's affairs, with such professional assistance as is appropriate, to assure that the filing is complete, accurate and otherwise in compliance with the SEC requirements.

Each person referred to in the preceding paragraph (other than the issuer), including any underwriter of a public offering of registered securities, may avoid these Securities Act liabilities if that person can prove that after reasonable investigation he had reasonable ground to believe and did believe that the registration statement was correct and complete. For this reason, as well as for commercial reasons, it is customary for the managing underwriter(s), with the assistance of its legal advisers, to conduct, on behalf of the underwriters, a comprehensive due diligence investigation. Ordinarily this will include a careful review with representatives of the issuer and of the issuer's accountants and legal advisers of successive drafts of the registration statement, interviews with senior officers of the issuer, visits to major facilities and, through the underwriter's legal advisers, review of the issuer's debt instruments, major contracts and other documents of material significance and of the minutes of the issuer's board of directors.

Similar considerations generally are applicable in the case of the preparation of the registration statements of foreign governmental issuers.

### Financial statements and auditors

As noted above, the financial statements required in the Securities Act registration statement of a non-US private issuer must either be prepared according to US GAAP or according to an identified comprehensive body of accounting principles together with a discussion and quantification of material variations from US GAAP in the accounting principles used.

While most non-US private issuers find that they can accommodate these requirements, the preparation of complying financial statements can require considerable work and the time required for completion frequently is the determining factor in establishing the time schedule for the project.

In the case of certain Securities Act registration statement filings, as noted above, the notes to the financial statements must include breakdowns of revenues, operating profits and identifiable assets by industry and geographical segments. This requirement, controversial when first introduced in the United States more than 10 years ago, is now fully accepted by US business enterprises. A requirement for segment disclosure has also been adopted by the International Accounting Standards Committee. In practice most companies have found that they have been able to comply with the segment reporting requirement without disclosing information which would have an adverse effect upon their competitive position.

As discussed above, if the last audited balance sheet is dated more than six months prior to the effectiveness of a registration statement, interim unaudited financial statements are required. This restraint can significantly limit the annual period during which a non-US private issuer can conveniently effect an offering.

The audited financial statements must be audited by accountants who are independent under the SEC's relatively strict standards. In general, it requires that no member or professional employee of the accounting firm may have held any direct or material indirect interest in the securities of the issuer or any affiliate, have served as a promoter, underwriter, voting trustee, director, officer or employee of the issuer or any affiliate or have performed 'services incompatible with the audit function' for the issuer or any affiliate, such as routine accounting or bookkeeping work. In some instances the SEC has insisted that even nominal amounts of the issuer's securities held by accountants be sold.

The audit examination must satisfy US generally accepted auditing standards. Non-US private issuers using a major international accounting firm or a firm applying similar standards usually do not find this requirement to present problems.

### Other matters requiring special attention

**Publicity.** Under the Securities Act no public offering of securities may be made in the US until a Securities Act registration statement is filed; thereafter and until the registration is effective, offers of the securities can be made only orally or with the preliminary prospectus included in the registration statement, and after effectiveness no written material can be used to sell the securities which might fall within the SEC's expansive definition of the term 'prospectus' unless it is preceded or accompanied by a copy of the prospectus which formed part of the registration statement. These rules operate to limit the amount of promotional activity which an issuer may undertake when an offering of its securities is pending or underway. The SEC consistently has taken the position that media advertising, promotional brochures and the like which advertise the company (rather than a product) may be unauthorised offering materials if they are disseminated prior to or during an offering.

Meetings with securities analysts during this period also can raise questions. There are a number of narrowly defined exceptions to these prohibitions, and there have been considerable SEC administrative guidance and practical experience in the area.

**Purchases by an issuer of its own securities during a public offering.** An SEC Rule under the Securities Exchange Act, Rule 10b–6, provides, in substance, that during the period when a public offering of securities is being made in the US on behalf of an issuer or an affiliate of an issuer, neither the issuer nor an affiliated purchaser may purchase or offer to purchase securities of the issuer of the class being offered or certain related securities. This can be of significance where, for example, a foreign issuer or its affiliate ordinarily maintains a market for secondary trading in its shares by purchasing and reselling shares.

In such a case it would be necessary either to suspend these activities during the period of the US public offering or alternatively to seek an exemptive order from the SEC permitting the activities to continue under such conditions as the SEC may permit.

. . .

## STATE SECURITIES AND LEGAL INVESTMENT LAWS

In addition to compliance with the federal securities laws discussed above, the public offering of securities in any State of the US ordinarily will require registration or qualification of the offering under the securities (commonly called 'blue sky') laws of that State. Usually this can be accomplished in a reasonably routine manner, using the Securities Act materials to meet substantive requirements of the State law. Some States require the issuer to file routine periodic reports after the offering is completed. Often this burden can be eliminated by withdrawing the State registration after the securities have been distributed.

Laws of the States of the United States limit the debt securities in which fiduciaries, savings banks and insurance companies may invest. Memoranda sometimes are prepared by US counsel for the underwriters regarding the types of institutions which may invest in the securities being distributed and, in some areas, the kind or amount of funds which they may invest.

## NON-PUBLIC AND OTHER LIMITED OFFERINGS OF SECURITIES IN THE US

While public offerings of securities in the United States by issuers or their affiliates require registration of the securities under the Securities Act, there are exemptions from these registration requirements for certain non-public and other limited offerings. These offerings commonly are referred to as private placements. The exemptions are found in Section 4(2) of the Securities Act and in SEC Regulation D.

Non-US private issuers have increasingly relied upon these exemptions to make a US private placement of a portion of an issue of equity securities being distributed publicly outside the United States. A US private placement may also be useful to raise funds in the US market or for other purposes.

Recently adopted Rule 144A, discussed below, is expected to increase significantly sales of securities of foreign issuers in the US on a private placement basis.

### The Section 4(2) exemption

Section 4(2) exempts from the Securities Act registration statement requirements offers and sales of securities made "in transactions by an issuer not involving any public offering". This phrase generally is construed to refer to transactions by an issuer not involving any public offering in the United States or to US residents or nationals.

The limits of the Section 4(2) exemption have been established only by case law and administrative materials and are not well defined (but see Regulation D below). The underlying principle, which guides interpretation of the exemption, is that the exemption should be available only in those cases in which the offerees and purchasers of the securities do not require the protection of Securities Act registration. The following factors are considered important:

- The number of offerees and purchasers must be limited, although if the securities are of high quality and the offerees and purchasers are large, financially sophisticated institutional investors, a significant number may be permissible. There may be no general solicitation or advertising.

- Information generally comparable to that which would have been provided by a Securities Act registration statement and which is material to investors in the circumstances must be known by or provided to offerees and purchasers. For this reason, as well as for commercial reasons, a private placement memorandum or comparable descriptive material often is prepared for offerees and purchasers. Significantly, however, such materials need not satisfy the SEC registration statement form requirements described above—for example, unless "material" or needed for marketing reasons, US GAAP reconciliation or business segment disclosures may be omitted.

- The offerees and purchasers must be capable of evaluating the merits and risks of the investment (possibly with the help of a qualified adviser).

- There must be understandings or obligations in place reasonably designed to prevent resales by purchasers which, if made, would expand the initial limited offering into a broader distribution in the United States or to US persons that would not qualify for the exemption (such as—pursuant to Rule 144A or Regulation S). Typically each purchaser is required to represent that he is acquiring the securities for his own account and not with a view to resale or distribution. Contractual restrictions, legends on the securities and stop transfer orders to transfer agents may be used to support these limitations upon resales.

Where a US private placement is made concurrently with a public offering of securities outside the United States, the offering materials and distribution arrangements for the public offering must include provisions reasonably designed to prevent any US offering or sales activity outside of the controlled circumstances of the private placement. Regulation S, discussed below, has simplified these procedures.

The limitations upon resales by purchasers in a US private placement referred to above need not extend to resales outside of the United States to non-US persons, provided that the securities so sold are not then resold into the United States or to US persons in a continuing distribution of the securities. Regulation S has created an important safe harbour permitting such resales to be made, for example, in the Eurobond market or on designated overseas stock exchanges, significantly without any inquiry as to the nationality of the purchaser or any restrictions on such purchaser's ability to re-sell the securities—even if back into the United States.

### Regulation D

In addition to the general exemption for private placements found in Securities Act Section 4(2), the SEC has adopted Regulation D which establishes exemptions for non-public and other limited offerings.

A foreign private issuer wishing to effect a US private placement may elect to rely upon one of these exemptions. The observations made above as to controlling the circumstances of and arrangements for a US private placement and as to limitations upon resales by private placement purchasers also apply to transactions effected in reliance upon Regulation D.

Rule 506, a part of Regulation D, is a safe harbour rule which provides that conforming transactions are deemed to qualify for the Section 4(2) exemption. Under Rule 506:

(a) There may be no more than, or the issuer must reasonably believe that there are no more than, 35 US purchasers of the issue other than "accredited investors", a defined term including, in general, a very broad range of institutional investors, directors and executive officers of the issuer and individuals meeting various minimum net worth or net income requirements; and the issuer must reasonably believe that any purchaser who is not an accredited investor, either alone or with his "purchaser representative", has such knowledge and experience in financial and business matters that he is capable of evaluating the merits and risks of the prospective investment. There may be an unlimited number of US purchasers of the issue who are accredited investors.

(b) If any purchaser in an offering is not an accredited investor, then (i) the same kind of information required to be included in a Securities Act registration statement must be furnished to such purchasers (although, in light of the anti-fraud provisions of the federal securities laws, if any such information is furnished consideration should be given to providing the same information to all investors), (ii) the issuer must advise each investor who is not an accredited investor of, and furnish on request, any written information provided by the issuer to accredited investors and (iii) it is necessary for the issuer to provide to each investor an opportunity to ask questions and obtain additional information to verify the accuracy of the information required to be delivered to the purchaser.

(c) No general solicitation or advertising may be used in connection with the offer.

(d) The issuer must use reasonable care to ensure that the purchasers are not acquiring the securities with a view to resale or distribution, including (i) reasonable inquiry to determine if the purchaser is acquiring the security for himself or for others, (ii) written disclosure to the purchaser that the securities have not been registered under the Securities Act and cannot be resold unless so registered or pursuant to an available exemption and (iii) placing legends upon the securities to such effect. These are not exclusive methods to demonstrate such care.

(e) A notice of sale on SEC Form D must be filed with the SEC.

The Rule frequently is used when the investors include natural persons, but most non-public transactions with institutional investors are conducted in reliance upon Section 4(2) itself and not upon Rule 506.

## Rule 144A

On April 19, 1990, the SEC adopted Rule 144A, which establishes an exemption from the registration requirements of the Securities Act for qualifying resales to 'qualified institutional buyers' of securities that were not 'fungible' at the time of issuance with a class of securities publicly traded in the United States. The Rule 144A exemption is a non-exclusive 'safe harbour', which means that if a transaction meets all of the Rule's conditions, it falls into a category defined by the SEC as exempt (a safe harbour).

Perhaps the most significant of the expected effects of Rule 144A will be the increase in the secondary market liquidity of privately placed securities eligible for these resales. Thus, it is expected that the cost of issuing such securities in the US private markets will be reduced. Under certain circumstances, underwritten offerings of newly issued eligible securities to qualified institutions will be treated as exempt transactions not subject to the registration and disclosure requirements of the Securities Act. For non-US private and governmental issuers, the new Rule represents an important liberalisation.

Although Rule 144A undoubtedly will have a significant effect upon the market for privately placed securities of US issuers and distribution practices for such securities, much of the discussion in connection with the proposal of the Rule has centred on its effect on non-US issuers. Most large US companies are already subject to the reporting requirements imposed by the Exchange Act, and accordingly the difficulties of accessing public primary markets which require essentially the same disclosure to which the issuer is already subject have related principally to timing factors. For non-US issuers that have avoided the US private markets because of cost and the US public markets because of a reluctance to become subject to the disclosure and reporting obligations of the US securities laws, the deregulatory impact of the new Rule is more important.

Under Rule 144A, an offer or sale of securities by any person (other than the issuer) is exempt from registration if it meets certain conditions relating principally to the 'non-fungibility' of the securities, the buyer's status as a 'qualified institutional buyer', notice of reliance on the Rule and for certain issuers, information regarding the issuer. Such securities may have been previously issued in a transaction exempt from registration under the Securities Act, or in an offshore transaction not subject to the registration requirements of the Securities Act.

**Non-fungible securities.** The securities must have been 'non-fungible' when issues, i.e. not of the same class as securities listed on a US securities exchange or quoted on NASDAQ. The non-fungibility condition is not applicable in the case of securities for which bid and ask quotations are available in the current 'pink sheets' of the National Quotation Bureau, Inc.

The non-fungibility requirement is intended to inhibit the development of dual markets for the same security—i.e. an active, liquid, private institutional market for a security alongside a public retail market. Whether unregistered securities are non-fungible, and thus eligible for resale under Rule 144A, is determined at the time of their original issuance. Thus, securities that were non-fungible, at the time of their issuance will still be eligible for resale under Rule 144A, even if securities of such class are later listed on a US securities exchange or quoted on the National Association of Securities Dealers Automated Quotation System (NASDAQ).

For purposes of the Rule, common equity securities will be deemed of the same 'class' if the terms are substantially similar and the holders enjoy substantially similar rights and privileges; preferred equity securities will be deemed of the same class if terms relating to dividends, accumulation, voting rights, liquidation preference, participation, convertibility, call, redemption and other similar matters are substantially identical; and debt securities will be deemed of the same class if terms such as interest rate, maturity, redemption, subordination, call and convertibility are substantially identical.

In order to prevent evasion of the Rule's non-fungibility condition, convertible securities are treated as securities of the same class as the underlying security, unless they are subject to a conversion premium of at least 10 per cent at issuance. Similarly, the Rule provides that warrants will be treated as securities of the same class as the underlying securities unless the warrant has a life of at least three years and an exercise premium of at least 10 per cent. The Rule specifies how these premiums are to be calculated.

**Qualified institutional buyer.** The securities must be offered or sold only to 'qualified institutional buyers' (QIBs) (or to offerees and purchasers that the seller and any person acting on behalf of the seller reasonably believe are QIBs) purchasing for their own account or for the account of other QIBs.

In general, a qualified institutional buyer would mean any institution that owns and invests on a discretionary basis at least US$100m in securities of issuers that are not affiliated with the QIB or an entity all the owners of which are QIBs. Banks and thrifts, including foreign banks and their US branches, must not only meet the US$100m test but also have a net worth of US$25m. Broker-dealers need only own and manage an aggregate of US$10m in securities investments, and any broker-dealer qualifies as a QIB if acting as principal in a 'riskless principal transaction' with a QIB. Broker-dealers can also act as agent, on a non-discretionary basis, for sales to QIBs without meeting the US$10m test. A QIB may purchase only for its own account or for the account of another QIB.

The Rule provides that, in determining whether a particular offeree or purchaser is a QIB, the seller may rely on publicly available information regarding the securities investments of the offeree or purchaser appearing in (i) the purchaser's most recent publicly available financial statements, (ii) the most recent publicly available documents filed with the SEC or another United States federal, state or local governmental agency or self-regulatory organisation or with a foreign governmental agency or foreign self-regulatory organisation, (iii) a 'recognised securities manual' or (iv) a certification by an executive officer of the purchaser. Such reliance would not, however, be the exclusive means of satisfying the reasonable belief standard.

**Notice Requirement.** The seller and any person acting on its behalf must take reasonable steps to ensure that the purchaser is aware that the seller may rely on the exemption provided by Rule 144A.

The Rule does not clarify what procedures will constitute 'reasonable steps'. Although there is no express requirement that such notice be given in writing, in some cases a seller that has given such notice orally may also wish to provide written notice so as to avoid questions as to whether the seller is entitled to the Rule's safe harbour. Written notice could be provided in a disclosure document or trade confirmation.

**Information requirement.** In the case of securities of an issuer not subject to the periodic reporting requirements of the Exchange Act, not exempt pursuant to Rule 12g3–2(b) under the Exchange Act, or not of a non-US governmental issuer eligible to register securities under the Securities Act on Schedule B, the issuer or a person acting on its behalf must provide to the holder and prospective buyers upon request certain basic information regarding the issuer. As discussed below, for non-US issuers that furnish to the SEC certain home country reports and other information they otherwise make publicly available, Exchange Act Rule 12g3–2(b) provides an exemption from the US reporting requirements which would otherwise be applicable to non-US issuers whose equity securities are held by 500 or more persons of which 300 or more are US residents.

No information need be disclosed in connection with Rule 144A sales of securities of (i) reporting issuers, (ii) issuers exempt from Exchange Act reporting requirements pursuant to Rule 12g3–2(b) and (iii) non-US governmental issuers eligible to register securities under Schedule B of the Securities Act. The SEC's staff is currently considering whether entities whose securities are backed by a non-US government will be treated as governmental issuers for purposes of the information requirement. For other non-US issuers and non-reporting US issuers, the holder and any prospective purchaser designated by the holder must be able to obtain certain information from the issuer upon request, and such information must have been received. Such right may be created in the terms of the security, by contract or by operation of law or the rules of a self-regulatory organisation.

The required information includes (i) a brief statement of the nature of the issuer's business and its products and services offered and (ii) the issuer's most recent balance sheet, profit and loss and retained earnings statements and other similar financial statements for such part of the previous two fiscal years as the issuer has been in operation (the statements should be audited to the extent possible). The information must be 'reasonably current', which, for non-US private issuers means that the information must meet the timing requirements of the country of domicile or principal trading market.

Although a number of commentators expressed opposition to the information requirement, it is not expected to be burdensome. The SEC emphasised in the release adopting the Rule that:

> 'Many foreign issuers that will be subject to the requirement ... will have securities traded in established offshore markets, and already will have made the required information publicly available in such markets ... The [SEC] expects that the kinds of information commonly furnished under Rule 12g3–2(b) by foreign private issuers almost invariably would satisfy the information requirement and that foreign private issuers who wish their securities to be Rule 144A-eligible will simply obtain a Rule 12g3–2(b) exemption on a voluntary basis.'

**Scope of safe harbour.** Compliance with Rule 144A would not eliminate the need to comply with any applicable requirements of the Exchange Act or the Investment Company Act. For example, most non-US banks and insurance companies fall within the definition of 'investment company' under the Investment Company Act. The registration requirements of the Investment Company Act are sufficiently burdensome that for most non-US issuers an exemption is essential. Thus, unless such an exemption is available or can be obtained, the provisions of the Investment Company Act effectively may preclude non-US banks and insurance companies from offering securities in the United States.

The adoption of Rule 144A and the approval of the NASD's PORTAL rules discussed below will substantially deregulate the market for qualifying transactions in the United States. Although Rule 144A is phrased as an exemption for resales among institutions, its deregulatory impact will also extend to primary offerings of newly issued eligible securities to QIBs. Heretofore, underwritten US offerings of non-exempt securities were generally required to be registered under the Securities Act and were accordingly subject to the disclosure rules and the timing impediments imposed by the registration process. Under Rule 144A, primary offerings may be underwritten provided that the initial sale to the underwriter is entitled to an exemption from Securities Act registration (e.g. by virtue of Section 4(2) or Regulation D). Preliminary Note 7 to the Rule states that the fact that purchasers of securities from the issuer thereof may purchase such securities with a view to reselling such securities pursuant to Rule 144A will not affect the availability to the issuer of an exemption under Section 4(2) or Regulation D. The adopting release provides certain clarifications concerning the issuer's ability to comply with Regulation D in the context of such an underwritten private offering. An issuer that obtains from its purchasers a contractual undertaking not to resell except in accordance with Rule 144A (and otherwise complies with the applicable provisions of Regulation D) should be able to rely on the Regulation D exemption from the Securities Act registration requirements.

Underwritten offerings under Rule 144A should entail reduced transaction costs (including the SEC's registration fee, printing costs, accounting and legal fees and the like) as compared to registered offerings. Qualification of an indenture under the Trust Indenture Act also will not be required in respect of such an underwritten offering of Rule 144A-eligible debt securities. Accordingly, where the potential market for a particular class of securities is primarily or exclusively institutional, as is the case with many debt securities and, with the equity securities of many non-US issuers, Rule 144A may render the registration process unnecessary.

**Secondary Market.** One of the principal effects of Rule 144A should be to increase the liquidity of the secondary market in the US for eligible securities that are not publicly registered. Heretofore, resales of privately placed securities often could be made in further private placements, which frequently involved investment representations, legended securities and opinions of counsel. Resales of securities among QIBs which satisfy the Rule's conditions will now be free of these requirements and will benefit from the certainty of the safe harbour exemption. In addition, the implementation of PORTAL may allow efficient trading of Rule 144A securities by QIBs.

Increased access to the US secondary markets should also result because qualified securities initially offered by issuers (whether domestic or foreign) in offshore transactions that are not subject to the registration requirements of the Securities Act (including those transactions under Regulation S to which the registration requirements would not apply) could be resold immediately to QIBs in the US market in reliance on Rule 144A. In the case of bearer form debt obligations, however, increased access to US markets will be limited by US Federal tax law.

## Portal

In connection with its adoption of Rule 144A, the SEC also approved the rules of the National Association of Securities Dealers, Inc. (the NASD) implementing its PORTAL trading system (the PORTAL Rules). The PORTAL market will provide a means for QIBs under the Securities Act to execute and settle transactions in Rule 144A-eligible US and non-US securities that have been approved by the NASD for deposit into the PORTAL system (PORTAL Securities).

The PORTAL Rules establish a system for secondary trading of unregistered securities in transactions exempt from the registration requirements of the Securities Act pursuant to Rule 144A. Issuers also will be able to introduce qualifying securities into the PORTAL system in primary private placements to PORTAL participants through participating broker-dealers. The PORTAL market will consist of computer and communication facilities that will provide for the dissemination of quotations by participating broker-dealers as well as for the clearance and settlement of domestic and foreign debt and equity securities through designated PORTAL clearing and depository organisations. Participants will access PORTAL through a personal computer or a NASDAQ workstation, and investors will trade through participating brokers and dealers by telephone. Settlements of PORTAL transactions will be on the fifth business day after the trade by book entry through the facilities of the designated depositories (initially The Depository Trust Company for US securities and CEDEL for non-US securities). Transactions may be executed and settled in any currency that is accepted by the applicable depository (at exchange rates negotiated by the parties at the time of the trade). CEDEL accepts 27 currencies, including US dollars; DTC accepts US dollars only.

The PORTAL Rules provide for three classes of participants, designated PORTAL qualified investors, PORTAL brokers and PORTAL dealers. Each PORTAL dealer also must register as a PORTAL qualified investor. Only PORTAL qualified investors and PORTAL dealers may purchase PORTAL Securities, except in the case of Qualified Exit Transactions discussed below. In order to register as a PORTAL qualified investor, an investor or dealer must submit for the NASD's approval an application that demonstrates that it meets the definition of a QIB in Rule 144A. The applicant must also demonstrate that the purchase or sale by it of PORTAL Securities would be exempt from the securities registration and broker-dealer registration requirements of applicable blue sky laws. A PORTAL qualified investor is required to demonstrate annually (or more frequently if required by Rule 144A) that it continues to meet the definition of a QIB. A PORTAL qualified investor also must (i) acknowledge that sellers of PORTAL Securities to it may rely on the exemption from the registration provisions of the Securities Act provided by Rule 144A and (ii) agree to purchase PORTAL Securities only for its own account or for the account of a QIB. All sales and purchases of PORTAL Securities must be effected through a PORTAL broker or PORTAL dealer.

Each PORTAL qualified investor must agree that it will transfer ownership of PORTAL Securities only in transactions or transfers through the PORTAL market or in Qualified Exit Transactions or Qualified Exit Transfers, which are the mechanisms by which a PORTAL Security may be sold or transferred out of the PORTAL system. PORTAL brokers and dealers may not execute a transaction in a PORTAL Security except through the PORTAL market or in a Qualified Exit Transaction.

A 'Qualified Exit Transaction' is a sale to an account outside the PORTAL system either pursuant to an effective registration statement under the Securities Act or in (i) a transaction not subject to registration under the Securities Act by reason of compliance with Securities Act Regulation S, Rule 144A or certain other exemptive rules; (ii) a transfer of the securities to an issuer or an affiliate of the issuer; or (iii) any other transaction which, in the determination of the NASD, is exempt from registration under the Securities Act and results in the purchaser acquiring securities that may be freely resold without registration under the Securities Act. A Qualified Exit Transfer is either a transfer of a participant's securities from its PORTAL account to an account of that participant outside the PORTAL market or a return of securities that have been borrowed from a non-participant for purposes of a short sale.

Securities that have been approved for trading in the PORTAL market may trade on a 'when, as and if issued' basis prior to their deposit in the PORTAL depository. In connection with a primary offering of PORTAL Securities, PORTAL dealers may enter a stabilising bid in the PORTAL market in compliance with the applicable rules under the Exchange Act. Such a bid must be available for all outstanding securities in the PORTAL system of the affected class and may not be entered at the same time that the PORTAL dealer is quoting any other bid or offer for securities of the issue.

Simultaneously with the announcement of the approval of the PORTAL Rules, the Division of Corporation Finance of the SEC also announced that PORTAL will not be considered an automated inter-dealer quotation system for purposes of Rule 12g3–2(b) or any other rule or regulation. Were PORTAL considered to be an automated inter-dealer quotation system, then any foreign private issuer whose securities were traded in PORTAL would be ineligible for the exemption.

## Regulation S

At the time of its adoption of Rule 144A and approval of the PORTAL Rules, the SEC also adopted Regulation S. Regulation S provides generally that offers and sales of securities occurring outside the United States are not subject to the registration requirements of the Securities Act. The Regulation provides non-exclusive safe harbours under which transactions meeting all of the applicable conditions will be deemed to occur outside the United States. The Regulation does not affect the applicability of the antifraud or other provisions of the Federal securities laws.

Regulation S is premised on the general principle that the registration requirements of the Securities Act do not apply to offers and sales of securities that occur outside the United States. This principle is codified in a general statement concerning the applicability of the registration requirements set forth in Rule 901. Regulation S establishes two safe harbour provisions, one applicable to offers and sales by issuers, distributors, their respective affiliates and persons acting on their behalf (the issuer safe harbour), and the other applicable to resales by persons other than the issuer, a distributor, certain of their respective affiliates and persons acting on their behalf (the resale safe harbour). The Regulation defines the term 'distributor' as 'any underwriter, dealer, or other person who participates, pursuant to a contractual arrangement, in the distribution of the securities offered or sold in reliance upon Regulation S.'

If all of the conditions of the relevant safe harbour are satisfied, a transaction involving an offer or sale of securities is deemed to occur outside the United States and, therefore, is not subject to the registration requirements of the Securities Act. Two general conditions must be satisfied in order to rely upon either safe harbour. First, the offer and sale must constitute an "offshore transaction'. Second, no 'directed selling efforts' may be made in the United States in connection with such transaction. In order to qualify for the issuer safe harbour, a transaction may be required to comply with certain additional conditions, depending on the category of securities being offered. With respect to non-US issuers, the categories are organised based on, *inter alia,* whether the issuer is a reporting company under the Exchange Act and the degree of US market interest in the issuer's securities.

The resale safe harbour is available to any person other than the issuer, a distributor, any of their respective affiliates (other than an officer or director who is an 'affiliate' solely by virtue of holding such position, and who is therefore entitled to rely on the resale safe harbour subject to certain conditions) or any person acting on behalf of any of them.

A distributor and its affiliates may rely on the resale safe harbour in connection with secondary transactions in other securities of the same class as those being distributed, provided the securities are not borrowed or replaced with securities from the distribution. Once the distribution has been completed and any applicable restricted period has expired, a distributor will cease to be a 'distributor' for purposes of the Regulation, except with respect to any unsold allotment.

For persons other than dealers, certain other securities professionals and officers and directors of the issuer or a distributor, the availability of the resale safe harbour is subject only to compliance with the offshore transaction requirement and the prohibition on directed selling efforts. When the seller is a dealer or a person receiving a selling concession, fee or other remuneration in respect of the securities offered or sold (a 'securities professional'), and the offer or sale is made prior to the expiration of an applicable restricted period with respect to such securities, then the resale safe harbour is available only if (i) neither the seller nor any person acting on its behalf knows that the offeree or buyer of the securities is a US person and (ii) where the seller or any person acting on its behalf knows that the purchaser is a securities professional, a confirmation containing appropriate restrictive language is sent to the purchaser.

In the case of an offer or sale of securities by an officer or director of the issuer or a distributor, who is deemed to be an 'affiliate' of the issuer or distributor solely by virtue of holding such position, such officer or director may rely on the resale safe harbour, subject only to the offshore transaction requirement and the prohibition on directed selling efforts, provided that no selling concession, fee or other remuneration is paid in connection with such offer or sale other than a usual and customary broker's commission.

The resale safe harbour is available for the resale offshore of any securities, whether or not acquired outside the United States. The SEC has confirmed that resales pursuant to Regulation S of securities originally placed privately will not affect the validity of the private placement exemption relied upon by the issuer. Thus, securities sold in the US in an underwritten offering under Rule 144A could be resold not only in the US pursuant to Rule 144A to QIBs but also outside the US pursuant to the resale safe harbour of Regulation S, thereby further adding to the liquidity of the secondary market for securities of non-US issuers privately placed in the US.

## THE SECURITIES

### Debt

Under US tax regulations currently in effect, securities (including the securities of foreign governments) sold in the US effectively are required to be in fully registered form. If the underwriters and issuer desire to sell a portion of the issue outside the US, securities in bearer form can be provided to non-US persons if certain selling and other restrictions are observed.

As a practical matter, acceptable ratings from the two major statistical rating agencies in the US, Moody's Investors Service, Inc. and Standard & Poor's Corporation, are virtually essential for the successful marketing of investment grade securities in the US public debt market at competitive interest rate levels. The market acceptance of the securities, interest rate and underwriting compensation normally are determined in large part by the ratings assigned.

The rating process typically involves a comprehensive written presentation to the rating agencies by the proposed issuer as well as meetings with the rating agencies and visits by the agencies to the issuer. Rating agency presentations, which are not made public, frequently contain more detail than would be included in a Securities Act registration statement. Issuers and their financial advisers normally prepare the rating agency presentations, although lawyers with experience in the preparation of registration statements for US public offerings often are asked to assist, particularly where a public offering of securities is expected to follow. The rating agencies occasionally require opinions of lawyers on legal issues which they see as particularly relevant to the issuer's credit or the integrity of any complex financing structure to be employed for the issue to be rated.

### Shares

The shares of non-US companies are held and traded in the United States in three forms: (i) as shares issued by the non-US company in its own country; (ii) as shares issued by the non-US company specifically for the US market, referred to as American Shares, which often are similar or identical to the shares issued by the non-US company in its own country except that their dividend distributions are denominated and paid in US dollars; and (iii) as American Depositary Receipts (ADRs).

### American Depositary Receipts

An ADR is a certificate issued by a US bank which represents shares of a non-US company which have been deposited with the bank or its custodian. The certificates typically are denominated in American Depositary Shares. An American Depositary Share may represent a multiple or a fraction of a share of the non-US company deposited in the programme, a relationship designed to cause the American Depositary Shares to trade in a price range which is common in US markets. Persons who hold or acquire shares of the non-US company may deposit them with the bank in exchange for ADRs, and upon request the bank will deliver the underlying shares against the surrender of ADRs. An ADR is transferable upon the books of the US bank, thereby avoiding the delays and costs to US shareholders of transferring shares on foreign registries and, in some cases, the stamp duty or transfer tax imposed upon such transfers. The US bank also performs various shareholder related functions, typically including receiving and disseminating to the ADR holders information relating to shareholder meetings, rights and exchange offers made to shareholders and other similar matters and collecting dividends paid on the underlying shares, converting them to US dollars and distributing them to the ADR holders. The convenience to US shareholders of an ADR facility for shares of a non-US issuer can be expected to encourage US investor interest in those shares, both in connection with public offerings and ongoing trading.

ADR programmes are of two types, unsponsored and sponsored.

**Unsponsored ADR Programmes.** An unsponsored ADR programme may be set up by a US bank on its own initiative, without the sanction of the non-US private issuer, provided that the non-US issuer satisfies the condition mentioned in the following paragraph. The US bank does this in anticipation of the fees it expects to charge to the ADR holders for its services to them. Under this arrangement, no contractual obligations or restrictions are imposed upon the issuer of the underlying shares. The bank, of course, retains total discretion over the conduct of the ADR system, including discretion to terminate it.

The bank establishing an unsponsored ADR programme is considered to be offering the American Depositary Shares to the public in exchange for the shares of the non-US company, and therefore is required to register the American Depositary Shares with the SEC under the Securities Act. The registration is made on SEC Form F–6. Typically, the ADR certificate itself serves as the prospectus which is required by the Securities Act to be delivered to purchasers of securities registered under the Act. Form F–6 does not require any disclosure relating to the non-US issuer or, for an unsponsored programme, any signature on behalf of the non-US issuer or its officers, directors or agents.

Nor does the Securities Act registration give rise to any reporting obligation for the non-US company. However, since 1983 it has been a condition to the registration of ADRs on Form F–6, and thus of the creation of an unsponsored ADR programme, that as of the filing date of the Form F–6, the non-US issuer is either a reporting company or its shares are exempt from Exchange Act registration because the issuer is satisfying the requirements of SEC Rule 12g3–2(b). In order to qualify for this exemption it is necessary for the issuer (or a government official or agency of its country) to furnish to the SEC, on a continuing basis, copies of information which would be material to investors which the issuer (a) makes public in its own country, (b) files with a stock exchange on which its securities are traded and is made public by the exchange or (c) distributes to its security holders. Moreover, the Rule specifies that information so furnished is not deemed 'filed' with the SEC or otherwise subject to the liabilities for false or misleading statements created by the Exchange Act for filed documents.

**Sponsored ADR Programmes.** In a sponsored ADR programme, the facility is established and maintained by the US bank pursuant to a formal agreement between the issuer and the bank, and the issuer generally agrees to pay many of the charges for the bank's services which otherwise would be paid by the ADR holders. The agreement between the issuer and the bank, usually called a Deposit Agreement, in addition to establishing the terms of operation of the facility, may obligate the issuer (i) to maintain its Rule 12g3–2(b) exemption from the Exchange Act Section 12(g) registration requirements, (ii) to deliver to the bank notices and reports to be sent to security holders, and (iii) to indemnify the bank for liabilities arising in connection with its services under the agreement.

The Deposit Agreement will also contain provisions designed to ensure that no shares will be deposited with the bank if they are required to be registered under the Securities Act and have not been so registered.

The American Depositary Shares issued in a sponsored ADR programme, like those in an unsponsored programme, must be registered with the SEC under the Securities Act. The fact that the programme is sponsored does not result in any expansion of the requirements or incidents of such registration except that the Deposit Agreement must be filed as an exhibit to the registration statement and the registration statement must be signed not only by the bank, as in the case of an unsponsored plan, but also in respect of the issuer by the issuer, its principal executive, financial and accounting officers, a majority of its board of directors and its authorised representative in the United States.

## LISTING ON A US STOCK EXCHANGE

Non–US private issuers, which meet the listing qualifications of the New York Stock Exchange (NYSE) or other US stock exchange frequently elect to list their equity securities for trading on that exchange, although in recent years over-the-counter trading in the NASDAQ system has become increasingly important (see below). The US stock exchanges are the NYSE, the American Stock Exchange and several regional exchanges. In 1989 the NYSE accounted for about 48 per cent of all trading in listed stocks in terms of share volume and 65–70 per cent in terms of dollar volume. At December 31, 1989, securities of 98 non-US issuers, including 24 Canadian issuers, were listed on the NYSE and 60 non-US issuers, including 39 Canadian issuers, were listed on the American Stock Exchange.

To list its securities on a US stock exchange a non-US private issuer must (a) meet the minimum qualifications and other requirements for listing established by that exchange, file a listing application with the exchange, sign a listing agreement and listing fee agreement and pay the initial and continuing fees imposed by the exchange and (b) register the securities to be listed under Section 12(b) of the Exchange Act (see below).

A non-US private issuer seeking a listing of its shares on the NYSE would be required to meet either the NYSE Alternate Listing Standards for non-US companies or, at the election of the issuer, the NYSE's listing criteria for US companies. Domestic listing requirements call for minimum distribution of a company's shares within the United States, a major obstacle to many large non-US companies. The Alternate Listing Standards, which focus on worldwide rather than US distribution of a non-US company's shares, are designed to encourage major non-US companies to list their shares.

The Alternate Listing Standards require that the company have at least 5,000 holders of 100 or more shares, at least 2.5 million shares publicly held with a market value of at least US$100m, net tangible assets of at least US$100m and pre-tax income of at least US$100m cumulative for the latest three years with a US$25m minimum for any one of the three years. Where the use of bearer shares outside the US makes it difficult to demonstrate the required number of shareholders, sponsorship by a NYSE member firm as to the liquidity and depth of the market for the company's shares may substitute for documentation concerning the number of shareholders. Ordinarily, the listing would be in the form of American Depositary Shares sponsored by the company.

The NYSE minimum numerical standards for US companies require that the company have at least 2,000 holders of 100 or more shares or total shareholders of at least 2,200 together with an average monthly trading volume for the most recent six months of at least 100,000 shares, at least 1,100,000 shares publicly held, an aggregate market value of publicly held shares of at least US$18m and net tangible assets of at least US$18m. The share distribution requirements relate to public holdings within the US.

In addition to the numerical standards, the NYSE has requirements related to such matters as consolidated financial statements, quarterly reports to shareholders including financial results, outside directors, audit committees, voting rights and the ability of the US holders to participate in rights offerings.

The exchange will work with issuers to establish mutually acceptable periods within which to comply with its requirements, and exemptions from certain of these requirements may be granted by the exchange where the issuer's interim reporting or corporate governance practices are not prohibited by the laws of its country of domicile.

The NYSE encourages prospective applicants for listing to discuss with it on a confidential basis the NYSE's requirements to learn whether the company is eligible for listing and what additional requirements, if any, might first have to be satisfied.

. . .

## CONTINUING REPORTING REQUIREMENTS UNDER THE EXCHANGE ACT

A non-US private issuer which has registered securities under the Securities Act will thereby become subject to the continuing reporting obligations of the Exchange Act (suspended for any fiscal year if at the start of the year the securities of the class registered under the Securities Act are held of record by less than 300 US residents). A non-US private issuer which has registered securities under the Exchange Act (e.g. in connection with listing or quotation on NASDAQ) will also become subject to such reporting obligations.

The required reports for non-Canadian non-US private issuers are annual reports on Form 20–F and other reports on Form 6–K. The Form 20–F is to be filed as an annual report within six months after the end of each fiscal year of the issuer. The business information contained in the Form 20–F is substantially the same as that contained in a Form F–1 registration statement under the Securities Act, except that the financial statements and notes need not include the supplemental information (such as business segment and pension information) referred to above. The Form 20–F may be completed in part by incorporating therein by reference portions of the registrant's annual report to its shareholders.

Form 6–K simply requires that certain information (a) required to be made public by the registrant in its own country, (b) filed by the registrant with a non-US stock exchange and made public by that exchange or (c) distributed to its security holders be furnished to the SEC promptly after it is made public. Material so furnished is not deemed 'filed' with the SEC or otherwise subject to the liabilities for false or misleading statements created by the Exchange Act for filed documents.

A non-US governmental issue will not be subject to any continuous reporting requirements under the federal securities laws unless it lists its securities on a US stock exchange. So long as the securities are so listed, they must be registered under the Exchange Act and the issuer is required to file annual reports with the SEC on Form 18–K, the principal requirements of which are an updating of information on outstanding indebtedness of the issuer and a statement of the receipts and expenditures of the issuer for its most recent fiscal year.

## OVER–THE–COUNTER MARKET TRADING

### NASDAQ

US investor interest in securities traded over-the-counter (that is, otherwise than on a stock exchange) is centered in securities which have been included in the NASDAQ system. NASDAQ is an acronym for National Association of Securities Dealers Automated Quotations and refers to the system operated by the NASD to facilitate inter-dealer trading in the over-the-counter market. This system is an electronic network designed to display continuously updated price quotations (that is, bids and offers) to securities brokers and dealers. The price quotations are provided by 'market makers', defined as broker-dealers that hold themselves out as being willing to buy and sell a security for their own account on a regular or continuous basis. Representative price quotations and daily trading volume for selected NASDAQ securities are published in US financial newspapers and other media.

QUALIFICATION FOR NASDAQ. To qualify for inclusion in the NASDAQ system, the securities of a non-US issuer must be registered under Section 12(g) of the Exchange Act (subject to an exception for a limited period for new issues, and except for certain non-US issuers whose securities were included in the NASDAQ system on October 5, 1983). For initial inclusion there must be two active market makers registered in the security in the NASDAQ system; thereafter there must continue to be at least one active registered market maker. There are also rather modest minimum requirements as to the number of shares publicly held or ADRs issued, the issuer's total assets and total capital and surplus and the number of persons holding the security. Finally, the issuer of a NASDAQ security is required to make prompt disclosure to the public in the United States through international wire services or similar disclosure media of any material information that may affect the value of its securities or influence investors' decisions (with prior notice of such disclosure to the NASD) and to comply with any legal obligation applicable to it regarding the filing or disclosure of information material to the issuer or the security.

At December 31, 1989 approximately 285 non-US equities were included in the NASDAQ system.

NATIONAL MARKET SYSTEM. Securities registered in the NASDAQ system that meet certain additional criteria, described below, may be included in the NASDAQ National Market System. The National Market System is a transaction, as opposed to quotation, reporting system. Participants are required to report most trades within 90 seconds of execution, and the system reports last sale price, daily high and low prices and current volume in addition to the market maker's bid and asked prices. High, low and closing prices for all National Market System securities are generally published daily in the US financial press. Of the 4,965 securities (4,293 issuers) quoted in NASDAQ at December 31, 1989, 2,697 (2,610 issuers) were included in the National Market System.

Upon application to NASDAQ, any NASDAQ security can be included in the NASDAQ National Market System if the issuer had either (a) annual pre-tax income of at least US$750,000 and net income of at least US$400,000 in the most recent fiscal year or in two of the last three fiscal years, at least 500,000 publicly-held shares with a market value of at least US$3m, a price per share prior to application of US$5 or more, net tangible assets of at least US$4m, a minimum of 800 shareholders if the issuer has between 500,000 and 1m publicly-held shares (or a minimum of 400 shareholders if the issuer has either (i) over one million publicly-held shares or (ii) over 500,000 publicly-held shares and average daily trading volume in excess of 2,000 shares per day for the six months preceding the date of application) and at least two NASDAQ market makers or (b) net tangible assets of at least US$12m, at least 1m publicly-held shares with a market value of at least US$15m, at least two NASDAQ market makers, an operating history of three years or more and a minimum of 400 shareholders.

Once designated, continuation as a NASDAQ National Market System security requires that the issuer meet less stringent criteria.

In addition to these quantitative criteria, the issuer of a NASDAQ National Market System security must meet requirements (which are subject to waiver by the NASD in light of business practices or legal requirements in the issuer's country of domicile) as to such matters as the distribution to its shareholders of annual and interim financial statements and reports, outside directors, audit committees and shareholder meetings.

## SECURITIES LAW LIABILITIES

### SECURITIES ACT

If a Securities Act registration statement, when it becomes effective, contains an untrue statement of a material fact or omits to state a material fact required to be stated therein or necessary to make the statements therein not misleading, civil liability is imposed upon the issuer, any person who signs the registration statement (the issuer's chief executive, financial and accounting officers and its authorised representative in the US), every director, every underwriter of the offering and, as to such part, any accountant, engineer or other expert who has with his consent been named as having prepared or certified a part of the registration statement (Securities Act Section 11(a)).

Each of these persons other than the issuer may avoid liability if he can prove that after reasonable investigation he had reasonable ground to believe and did believe that the statements in the registration statement were true and that there was no omission to state a material fact required to be stated therein or necessary to make the statements therein not misleading. Further, to the extent that parts of the registration statement are certified by experts (other than such person), as to those parts he need only prove that he had no reasonable ground to believe and did not believe that there was a misstatement or omission. The standard of reasonableness is that required of a prudent man in the management of his own property (Securities Act Sections 11(b), 11(c)).

The extent of the liability is, in general, the difference between the amount paid for the security (not exceeding the public offering price) and (a) the market price of the security at the time the suit is brought or (b) the price at which the security was disposed of before suit. Damages may be reduced to the extent it is proved that a lower price for the security represents other than depreciation resulting from the misstatement or omission (Securities Act Section 11(e)).

In addition to his rights based upon any material misstatement in or omission from the registration statement at the time it became effective, a purchaser (not knowing that the statement was false or misleading) may recover losses from any person who sold that purchaser the security by means of a prospectus or oral communication which included an untrue statement of a material fact or omitted to state a material fact necessary in order to make the statements therein, in the light of the circumstances under which they were made, not misleading unless the seller can prove that he did not know, and in the exercise of reasonable care could not have known, of the untruth or omission (Securities Act Section 12(2)). Section 12(2) is applicable in the context of any sale of a security by means of a prospectus or oral communication and, therefore, is applicable to Rule 144A offerings and other private placements, as well as public offerings.

A controlling person of any person liable under the provisions mentioned above will be liable jointly and severally with the controlled person unless the controlling person had no knowledge of or reasonable grounds to believe in the existence of the facts by reason of which the liability of the controlled person is alleged (Securities Act Section 15).

Ordinarily there is doubt whether liabilities based upon US securities laws, or judgements obtained in US courts based thereon, would be enforced by courts of other nations.

The issuer usually indemnifies the underwriters or placement agents against any liability arising from a misstatement in or omission from the registration statement or prospectus.

### EXCHANGE ACT

Any person who makes a statement in a filing under the Exchange Act, such as in a Form 20–F, which was at the time and in the light of the circumstances under which it was made false or misleading with respect to any material fact, is liable to any person who, in reliance upon the statement and not knowing that the statement was false or misleading, purchased or sold a security at a price that was affected by the statement, for damages caused by the reliance, unless the person sued can prove that he acted in good faith and did not know that the statement was false or misleading (Exchange Act Section 18(a)).

There also is a possibility that an Exchange Act filing may give rise to liability under other provisions of US securities laws, such as Exchange Act Section 10(b) and Rule 10b–5 thereunder, if it contains any untrue statement of a material fact or omits a material fact necessary to make the statements made, in the light of the circumstances under which they were made, not misleading, at least if such statements or omissions were made knowingly or recklessly.

A controlling person of any person liable under the provisions mentioned in the preceding paragraphs will be liable jointly and severally with the controlled person unless the controlling person acted in good faith and did not directly or indirectly induce the acts constituting the violation or cause of action (Exchange Act Section 20(a)).

In addition, if an Exchange Act filing, such as Form 20–F, is incorporated by reference into a Securities Act registration statement, then for that purpose it will become subject, as a part of the registration statement, to the Securities Act liability standards.

### STATE SECURITIES LAWS

For all practical purposes, liabilities under State securities laws are duplicate of those under the US securities laws.

### *Questions*

1. What are the major problems encountered by foreign companies in issuing securities in the U.S. market through a public offering or through a private placement?

---

## C. OPENING UP U.S. SECURITIES MARKETS

In recent years the SEC has taken various initiatives to make it easier for foreign companies to issue securities in the U.S. market. Rule 144A, as described in the piece by Palm and Walkovik has liberalized private placement rules. The Multijurisdictional Disclosure rules (MJDS) have made it easier for Canadian companies to issue publicly traded securities in the U.S., the ADR system has facilitated issuance and trading in foreign securities, and some flexibility in reporting requirements has been shown in the 1993 case of Daimler–Benz's listing on the New York Stock Exchange.

---

## 1. Rule 144A and Private Placements

The basic Rule 144A framework was set out in the Palm and Walkovik piece. The following material explores the operation and effect of the Rule.

### SIMON BRADY, "EVOLUTION, NOT REVOLUTION"

Euromoney (June 1990), p. 47.

. . .

Two months after the final approvals, much of the initial hype has subsided as bankers, investors and issuers slowly work out exactly what 144a means.

. . .

Optimism is shared to a greater or lesser extent by the houses that matter—the bulge-bracket firms which together underwrite most of the debt and equity securities offered in the US markets.

It is based on an argument which goes something like this: foreign companies seeking debt or equity funding in the US were put off by the SEC registration process. Potential issuers especially disliked converting accounts to conform with US accounting procedures, disclosing sensitive business segment information and reporting the compensation of senior executives.

Registration also made it difficult to time issues to coincide with windows of opportunity and for the separate tranches of multi-jurisdictional offerings to be synchronised.

Consequently, these companies turned either to their domestic markets or to the Euromarkets for funds. It was recognized that many companies from certain countries, especially France, Germany and Switzerland, would never be willing to comply with the registration process. Rule 144a removes the hurdle of registration, allowing issuers easy and efficient access to the US capital markets for the first time.

. . .

"Now there is a whole group that is saying that what 144a is really talking about is the pricing of the true private placement market. Well, what we know about that market is that if you want to sell a private placement, then you can do that. But in fact there is very little trading because, by definition, private buyers buy to hold. The Pru doesn't want to sell its private placements."

Straight corporate debt issues priced in competition with the registered market and the Euromarkets will not be bought by the traditional buyers of private placements—the private desks of insurance companies—whatever the credit rating and whatever the benefits of foreign diversification.

Phil Bennett, director-finance at Salomon Brothers, says: "A triple-A IBM is around 45–50 [basis points] over [Treasuries]. If you go to the private side of an insurance company, and say "IBM, five-year, 45–over, will you buy it?", they say: 'My minimum level is 100,'—minimum level for whatever, the World Bank, IBM, the US government."

These private placement buyers will not reduce their targets in return for the liquidity 144a is supposed to bring, because they have all the liquidity they want already. "The insurance companies who make up 98% of the private placement market didn't ask for this liquidity. They like the incremental yields, the illiquidity premium, the better protection of negotiated covenants. We haven't heard many [investing] institutions clamouring for this liquidity," says Thomas Keaveney, managing director, private finance, at First Boston.

These same investors can buy relatively liquid higher-yielding securities anyway, points out Thaddeus Beczak, managing director of private placements at JP Morgan Securities. "Why should they buy a AA corporate at 80 over when they can buy a AAA mortgage-backed at a much higher spread?"

The issuers will not come to the 144a market if all it offers is what they could have got in the traditional private placement market anyway. They won't use 144a unless they get public-style covenants and documentation and public levels of pricing (which applies as much to equity as to debt—the very small amount of privately-placed foreign equity that exists in the US trades at a substantial discount). "The whole trick here is to get the public side to buy aggressively priced 144a securities," says Phil Bennett.

The logical buyers of this kind of paper will be the public buyers, in particular the money managers and mutual funds. This is where the problems start.

To begin with, while the SEC is clearly happy about allowing large insurance companies to buy 144a securities, it is obviously less comfortable with the idea that mutual funds and money managers buy them. The initial drafts of the rule suggested that investment advisers, such as mutual funds and money managers and broker dealers could only purchase 144a securities if every client in the managed fund for which the security was being bought was considered a qualified buyer.

While the broker-dealers have been exempted from this in the final ruling, the other fiduciaries have not. QIBs may purchase 144a securities for the accounts of other QIBs but not for managed or other fiduciary accounts that are not themselves QIBs.

Mutual funds are not going to be able to buy vast amounts of 144a securities immediately either. Prior to 144a, open-ended registered investment companies and unit investment trusts could only invest 10% of their funds in illiquid (unregistered, privately-placed) securities.

The rule now allows the board of directors or sponsor of these investment companies to delegate to the fund's adviser responsibility for determining whether a particular 144a issue is illiquid. However, the board of directors or sponsor must ensure the liquidity of the 144a securities in the portfolio is consistent with the 10% ceiling on illiquid securities.

. . .

Even the insurance companies are not able to invest in 144a securities without first consulting the rule book. Some state laws and the regulations of bodies such as the National Association of Insurance Commissioners limit the amounts of foreign securities that companies may hold.

. . .

Goldman Sachs acted as agent on a dry-run and brought the first 144a deal to the market—a $100 million placement of 10–year unsecured senior notes for British Aerospace (BAe).

These deals have generated enormous controversy. Firstly, are they really 144a deals? For Goldman's Mark Dash, the answer is yes. "The [BAe] deal was a great success. We have made continuous markets in the issue and the bid is tighter than when we offered the transaction. Also, it was a success *vis-à-vis* covenants—if you call no negotiations and Euro-style covenants a success."

Dash is also adamant that the deal drew in the non-traditional buyers. "The liquidity [which we have provided] has attracted the non-traditional investors, the money managers whose participation will make or break this market in the long term."

Elsewhere, comment ranges from the laudatory to the unprintable. One private debt specialist says: "BAe was marketed at 115 off for a single A, a mid-single A. A mid-single A with name quality [BAe has done a number of leveraged leases incorporating private placements] should have been in the 85, 90, 95 range—I mean some place well through 100. So if that was a 144a offering it was a massive failure because the pricing was so bad—it indicated absolutely no savings versus the old unregistered negotiated covenant structure. No savings whatsoever. So if they insist on calling it a 144a, then call it a failure."

Dash retorts: "That's absurd. Either that guy doesn't know what he is talking about or he is trying to mislead you. Look at [investors'] rate matrices for private placements." But should 144a deals be compared to private placements when the aim is to attract public buyers into a quasi-public market?

British Aerospace was happy with the deal which, they say, saved them five basis points and attracted a wider investor base. They admit, however, that secondary market liquidity is unproven.

Whether or not the documentation represented any advance over previous private placements is also at issue. Debt tests, negative pledges and sale-leaseback restrictions would have been seen as a little excessive in the public markets: "They could have had similar terms a year ago," says JP Morgan's Beczak.

. . .

Philip Krebs, senior vice president at Shearson, thinks that some important elements have been missing from the market so far: "The first 144a issue will be where there is what we could call a syndicate—not just one manager, where there is an offering circular, where prospective buyers can actually read about the issuer in a non-negotiable document which will be the framework for the final prospectus, where there are public style covenants and pricing," he says.

Of these points, the syndicate question is the most important. To attract wavering public buyers, the banks bringing the issues must show a clear commitment to providing an efficient and liquid aftermarket.

The SEC has made this easier to do by relaxing the so-called "haircut" rules, which relate to net capital requirements. Under SEC rules registered broker-dealers must deduct 100% of the carrying-value of non-marketable securities from their net capital calculations. Investment grade securities issued under 144a will be counted as marketable securities which require far less capital to be set against inventories.

By itself this is no guarantee that a secondary market will develop. Goldman was sole agent on the BAe deal and, as one private placement chief says: "If only Goldman trades the deal, why would anybody think there was any additional liquidity?"

. . .

So what will be the effects of 144a on specific markets? The impact upon the existing public and debt markets will be minimal. US and foreign companies already registered with the SEC have little reason to issue much debt under 144a since they already pay registration fees and comply with SEC disclosure requirements.

Public registered issuers do so purely on price. Even the best-case scenarios put forward by the 144a bulls, based on a comparison of spreads between registered and unregistered MTN deals, is that a 144a deal will cost 5–10 basis points more than the public deal. The registration fee and other costs saved would normally be at most 2.5 basis points.

"A small number of US issuers, for example private companies which do not file with the SEC, may use 144a," says JP Morgan's Beczak. "To the best of our knowledge, and both issuers and investors confirm this, there is no reason for listed companies which are already reporting to take advantage of 144a."

Foreign debt issuance will not surge either. Even if investors sort out their legal positions quickly, there is a fairly small universe of companies whose securities they will buy on Euro-terms with home-country disclosure only. These will be the 20–30 largest European and Japanese names such as Toyota, Volkswagen or GEC, which can already get competitive funding in the Euromarkets.

. . .

Wall Street, and First Boston in particular, are most optimistic about the possibilities for equity issuance. Curt Welling, managing director and head of equities at First Boston, says: "We think there is far more of a need for foreign issuers to issue equity than debt in this market. It is far more attractive for that issuer to do that than it is debt. The US markets have not been competitive with either Europe or Japan for a single-A, non-US credit, and 144a is not going to change that a whole lot. However, I do think that there is scope for longer maturity debt issues."

Durkin, vice-president at First Boston, agrees. "I think the equity side offers more opportunities because equity is not valued and priced like fixed-income instruments. Investors are looking more and more at foreign securities and want to invest in them during their own waking hours and with the five-day settlement they are used to.

"Issuers, whose senior executives are paid at least in part in relation to the stock price, want to maximise the valuation of their company by accessing what is arguably the deepest and most secure source of capital in the world".

Multi-tranche issues will be easier to market and synchronise, and most forms of equity placement are eligible.

Large US institutional investors are nowhere near their ceilings for foreign equity holdings and those contacted by Euromoney view foreign equities as more desirable investments than foreign corporate debt. Foreign companies are under-represented on the US exchanges and the private placement market for foreign equities is less than 5% of the private market as a whole. There is clearly room for expansion.

The key to the 144a equity market will be PORTAL, the NASD's system for trading 144a securities. While 144a debt securities will be traded OTC, like the other debt markets, "PORTAL will make or break with the 144a equity market," says one banker. Until it is up and running—which will take at least another two months—issuers and investors may hold off. The Atlas Copco issue will not be traded on PORTAL as too few investors and marketmakers have subscribed. Unless they do, PORTAL and the 144a equity market will fail.

. . .

## PATRICK HARVERSON, "WALL STREET'S QUALIFIED REVOLUTION"

Financial Times (September 8, 1992).

. . .

Mr. Vikram Pandit, head of equity syndicates at Morgan Stanley in New York, says: "Rule 144a has been a success because it has achieved what it set out to do—open up the ability for anyone to come to the US [private placement] market." Yet the liquidity shortage continues to dog the private markets, even with 144a. On the equity side, there are two reasons why.

First, the electronic trading systems that proponents of 144a hoped would provide the foundation for a liquid secondary market have been a failure.

Investors found that the first trading system, Portal, which was set up by the National Association of Securities Dealers (NASD), was user-unfriendly and cumbersome. People quickly stopped using it, and for the past year it has been undergoing an overhaul, and awaits relaunch.

The New York and American stock exchanges, which committed themselves to building a trading system for 144a deals, are both awaiting SEC approval for their systems.

Second, critics of 144a say the SEC was too restrictive in granting its registration exemptions only to qualified institutions, those with at least $100m invested in securities.

Mr. Stephen Cooper, partner with New York law firm Weil, Gotshal & Manges, says the SEC limit "circumscribed a universe of prospective buyers that was too small to achieve true market liquidity".

The drafters of 144a may have aimed the rule at the wrong target. A large segment of the private market is made up of US insurance companies. Insurers invest in private placement issues because, in exchange for illiquidity and complexity, they receive premium rates, which can be locked in for the long term.

Improving liquidity, simplifying the deals and lowering yields, therefore, has no appeal for insurers which run "buy and hold", not trading, accounts. They have not bought 144a securities because they do not fit their particular risk-reward profile.

As for the rest of the private market, it is made up primarily of mutual funds, and they remain reluctant to get involved in 144a deals, especially on the equity side, until secondary market liquidity has been firmly established.

So if liquidity has been a problem, how has nearly $27bn been raised under 144a since its introduction two years ago?

On the equity side, the bulk of the issues have originated abroad. Yet few foreign issuers have come to the US to raise private capital in a stand-alone issue. Those equity issues that have been completed by overseas companies under 144a have generally been arranged alongside offerings in the home market of the issuer. This is because US investors will only buy the securities if they know a secondary market for the stock exists in the home country of the issuer.

On the debt side, investment bankers have overcome the lack of liquidity with some clever financial engineering.

To make private issues more attractive to a wider group of investors, an increasing number of private deals have been designed so that they mimic the qualities of public deals—the idea being to appeal to investors who normally shun private issues because of the lack of a secondary market.

To overcome public investors' fear of illiquidity, deals have been put together that are, in effect, underwritten private issues.

This is not the contradiction it might seem. Broadly defined, an underwritten 144a deal is a private placement in which an investment bank takes on an entire issue of unregistered securities from an issuer on a firm commitment basis (such as in a public deal), and immediately resells the paper to qualified institutional buyers.

Issuers like underwritten private deals because they appeal to a much wider group of investors, the chances of an issue being sold at the right terms are higher, they get their money quicker because the deals can be completed rapidly, and the pricing is generally more favourable than on a traditional private placement.

For their part, public investors go for underwritten private 144a securities because the investment bank that "underwrites" the deal guarantees a liquid secondary market for the securities.

Ironically, these underwritten private deals end up virtually indistinguishable from public deals. Investment bankers even make the documentation in private issues, the "offering circulars", look just like the prospectuses used in public deals.

This may not be what the SEC had in mind when it drew up 144a, but considering that the aim of the rule was to bring the chief quality of the public market, liquidity, to the private market, who is complaining?

## M. CAREY, S. PROWSE AND J. REA, "RECENT DEVELOPMENTS IN THE MARKET FOR PRIVATELY PLACED DEBT"

Fed.Res.Bull. 77, 89–91 (February 1993).

. . .

*Size of the 144A Market*

The 144A market is still developing and consequently is small compared with the traditional private market and, especially, the public bond market. In 1991, the first full year Rule 144A was in place, gross issuance of 144A securities was $17 billion, representing about 20 percent of the volume in the traditional market (table 4). Offerings were up significantly from roughly $2 billion in 1990, but, of course, the rule was in effect only for part of that year, and time was required to bring issues to market after its adoption. Preliminary press reports suggest that the volume of issuance perhaps doubled during the first half of 1992; in contrast, non–144A issuance was down significantly during that period.

4. Gross issuance of debt in public and private markets, 1989–91
Billions of dollars

| Market | 1989 | 1990 | 1991 |
|---|---|---|---|
| Rule 144A private placements | ... | 2 | 17 |
| By foreign issuers | ... | * | 6 |
| Traditional private placements | 135 | 95 | 76 |
| By foreign issuers | 20 | 16 | 13 |
| Public bonds | 189 | 204 | 307 |
| By foreign issuers | 9 | 15 | 20 |

* Less than $500 million.
Source. IDD Information Services.

*Characteristics of 144A Securities*

Underwritten offerings of 144A securities now have many of the features of publicly offered bonds. The terms and documents generally conform to the standards used in the public market; in particular, the bonds have "public style" covenants, which are fewer in number and considerably less restrictive than those found in many traditional private placements. Many components of issuance costs are the same as those in a public offering, although the issuer does avoid the considerable expense associated with public registration. Underwritten 144A securities also have two credit ratings, are not highly structured, and are usually transferred through the book-entry system operated by the Depository Trust Company. In many instances, offering memoranda have been styled to be similar to prospectuses used in public offerings. This procedure has been followed primarily as a part of the underwriters' efforts to market the private placements to traditional public-market investors, such as mutual funds, pension funds, and groups within insurance companies that invest in public bonds. The average size of underwritten private placements has been comparable to that of public offerings. Finally, the terms of the securities are not negotiated with investors but are set before the offering.

Despite the similarity to public bonds, underwritten 144A securities as a group still differ from public bonds, especially with regard to liquidity, and thus their yields on average contain a premium. In the first year of the market, the premium was reported to be about the same as that on traditional private placements. Recent reports suggest, however, that the liquidity of 144A securities has increased and that the premium has decreased as major dealers have allocated capital and traders to making markets for 144A securities.

*Foreign Issuers*

Thus far, foreign issuance has made up a much larger proportion of the 144A market than it has of either the traditional private or public bond markets. Of the $16.7 billion of 144A offerings in 1991, foreign companies or their U.S. subsidiaries were responsible for about one-third (table 4). In contrast, foreign issuers placed only 16 percent of offerings in the traditional private market, and only 7 percent of public offerings were foreign related. Preliminary data for the first half of 1992 suggest that foreign issuance likely made up an even larger share of the 144A market last year.

Several factors appear to lie behind foreign use of the 144A market. One is that the adoption of Rule 144A itself served to publicize the already existing advantages of the private placement market to foreign companies. The effect of the rule has thus been to alter foreigners' perception that all offerings in the United States were subject to excessive regulatory burdens. Moreover, since adoption of the rule, investment banks have devoted more effort to bringing foreign issuers into the private market. A second factor boosting foreign issuance has been the low level of yields in the United States relative to European countries. The 1992 increase in foreign issuance in the public bond market to a record level attests to the yield advantage of U.S. markets. A final factor is that the premium in yields on foreign bonds issued in the private market has reportedly declined.

. . .

### Notes and Questions

1. What are the basic provisions of Rule 144A? What is the role of PORTAL?

2. Will Rule 144A achieve a key objective, to make the private placement market more attractive to foreign issuers and qualified domestic investors?

3. From April 1990—July 1991, $8.35 billion (B) of securities of 95 issuers were sold in Rule 144A placements. $4B was by 69 foreign issuers, $2.3B of which was debt. By 1992, total foreign issues still ran at about 50% of all issues ($10.7B of the $26.6B raised since inception). Private placements by foreign issuers, a very high proportion of which were Rule 144A offerings, were $47B in 1993 compared to total foreign issues of $108B, according to annualized estimates of the Securities Industry Association based on first half data, Report of September 7, 1993.

4. Investment companies, e.g. mutual funds, which have a 10% statutory restriction on investing in illiquid securities, generally regard 144A securities as illiquid—they do, however, have the legal discretion to classify them as liquid. Many Rule 144A offerings are two part transac-

tions where a foreign issuer both issues shares on a foreign public market and through the U.S. private placement market. This suggests that the investor may get liquidity on the foreign market.

5. The SEC has exempted Rule 144A securities issued by foreigners from the anti-manipulation rules, Rules 10b–6, 10b–7, and 10b–8, which are designed to prevent issuers, underwriters and other participants in a securities offering in the United States, from supporting the price of the securities. Securities and Exchange Commission, Securities Releases Nos. 33–7028 and 34–33138, 58 Fed.Reg. 60326 (November 15, 1993).

6. What could be done to make Rule 144A more attractive?

---

## 2. The MJDS Approach

### SECURITIES AND EXCHANGE COMMISSION, MULTIJURISDICTIONAL DISCLOSURE AND MODIFICATIONS TO THE CURRENT REGISTRATION AND REPORTING SYSTEM FOR CANADIAN ISSUERS

58 Fed.Reg. 30036 (July 1, 1991).

### I. Executive Summary

The multijurisdictional disclosure system with Canada ("MJDS") being adopted by the Commission is intended to facilitate the free flow of capital. As a result of the MJDS, a securities offering made in two countries will be regulated in only one. Cross-border offerings in the United States and Canada thus can be made more efficiently and at less expense. Offerings of investment grade securities and offerings of equity securities by certain large issuers, rights offerings, exchange offers and business combinations, all may be conducted under the MJDS. Canadian issuers that meet specified eligibility tests may register securities with the Commission through disclosure documents they have prepared for Canadian regulatory authorities. In addition, specified Canadian issuers may use Canadian disclosure documents to satisfy the Commission's periodic disclosure requirements and tender offer regulations.

. . .

Concurrently with this release, the Canadian Securities Administrators ("CSA") are publishing a National Policy Statement that adopts a multijurisdictional disclosure system for U.S. issuers in Canada. In addition, as a result of coordination by the Commission and Canadian regulators with the North American Securities Administrators Association ("NASAA"), securities regulators at the state level are in the process of adopting rules to accommodate MJDS offerings.

While Canada is the partner of the United States in this inaugural multijurisdictional disclosure initiative, the MJDS is designed with the intention of mitigating on a broader scale the difficulties posed by multinational offerings. Thus, the Commission is continuing its work with securities regulators of other countries with a view toward extending the multijurisdictional disclosure system. In addition, the Commission has proposed rules that would facilitate rights offers and exchange and tender offers relating to foreign securities held in limited amounts in the United States on a similar basis as the MJDS.

## II. Background

In recent years, there has been substantial growth in both U.S. investors' purchases of foreign securities and offerings by U.S. issuers outside the United States. Part of the growth in such transactions has consisted of an increase in the number of offerings made simultaneously in two or more countries, one of which may be the country of the issuer. Such offerings typically are made when the issuer desires to expand the geographic base of its security holders, when the issuer wishes to increase the market for its securities internationally, or when strategic reasons exist (for example, to protect against takeover attempts). In other cases, such offerings are made because the relative cost of financing so dictates, the size of the offering is such that it cannot be absorbed by the issuer's domestic market, or the issuer needs to reach a particular group of securityholders or a broader investor base.

With the increase in U.S. ownership of foreign securities, the unwillingness of foreign issuers to extend rights offers, business combinations, exchange offers or cash tender offers to U.S. shareholders has become increasingly significant. Rather than comply with the requirements of regulators in more than one country, foreign issuers choose at times to exclude jurisdictions such as the United States from their offerings. As a result, U.S. holders are denied the opportunity to realize significant value on their foreign investments.

. . .

On July 24, 1989, the Commission proposed for comment rules, forms, and schedules to provide the foundation for a multijurisdictional disclosure system to facilitate cross-border securities offerings by certain Canadian issuers. Such offerings included rights offerings and exchange offers, as well as offerings of investment grade securities and equity securities by larger issuers. The Ontario Securities Commission ("OSC") and the Commission des valeurs mobilieres du Quebec ("CVMQ") concurrently issued for comment proposals concerning the establishment of a multijurisdictional disclosure system in Canada for certain U.S. issuers.

After reviewing the comments received on the Original Proposal, which were generally supportive but suggested refinements, the Commission proposed for comment on October 22, 1990 a revised multijurisdictional disclosure system.

. . .

The Commission is adopting the MJDS with limited changes from the Reproposal. Canada is the logical first partner for the United States in such an initiative because of the significant presence of Canadian companies in the U.S. trading markets. More than 100 Canadian issuers are listed on the New York Stock Exchange or the American Stock Exchange or are quoted on the National Association of Securities Dealers' Automated Quotation ("NASDAQ") National Market System. Of the 463 foreign issuers filing periodic reports with the Commission under the Exchange Act, more than 240 are Canadian. Canadian companies also are relatively frequent issuers in the U.S. capital markets. In 1989 and 1990 alone, Canadian private issuers made a total of 54 public offerings in the United States, offering approximately $11.9 billion of securities. The Commission's development of the MJDS with Canada is a first step in meeting the needs of issuers making transnational securities offerings.

## III. The Multijurisdictional Disclosure System

### A. *Overview of the MJDS*

To register securities for an offering under the MJDS, a Canadian issuer essentially will take the offering document it prepared under Canadian law and file it with the Commission along with a cover page, certain legends and various exhibits. The Commission finds that permitting certain Canadian issuers to register securities under the MJDS using their home jurisdiction disclosure documents instead of using disclosure documents prepared in accordance with the Securities Act specifications is in the public interest and fully adequate for the protection of U.S. investors.

. . .

For any type of MJDS offering, the Canadian issuer must have at least a three-year history of reporting with a Canadian securities regulatory authority. Except in the case of rights offerings and offerings of certain nonconvertible investment grade securities, an issuer also must satisfy specified size tests of minimum market value and/or public float.

Issuers eligible to rely upon the MJDS include only Canadian "foreign private issuers" [18] and, for specified offerings, Canadian crown corporations. Foreign issuers that do not meet the definition of "foreign private issuer" are in essence U.S. issuers and therefore must use the same forms as U.S. issuers for purposes of registration and reporting under the Securities Act and Exchange Act.[19] Canadian crown corpora-

**18.** "Foreign private issuer" is defined in rule 3b–4 under the Exchange Act (17 CFR 240.3b–4) and rule 405 under the Securities Act (17 CFR 230.405) to include all foreign issuers other than (i) foreign governments, and (ii) foreign issuers that have more than 50 percent of their outstanding voting securities held of record by U.S. residents and that also have: U.S. citizens or residents making up a majority of their executive officers and directors; more than 50 percent of their assets located in the United States; or their business administered principally in the United States.

**19.** Contrary to commenters' concerns, the business of a Canadian issuer that is a subsidiary of a U.S. company will not be deemed automatically to be "principally ad-

tions are those corporations all of whose common shares or comparable equity is owned directly or indirectly by the Government of Canada or a Province or Territory of Canada.

. . .

The issuer's home jurisdiction periodic reports are used under the MJDS to satisfy reporting requirements under the Exchange Act that arise solely by reason of registering securities offerings on the MJDS forms, or when the issuer of the securities meets certain tests of market value, public float and reporting history. Other than requirements relating to English translations, a consent to service of process and, in limited cases, a reconciliation of financial statements, the MJDS disclosure is based on incorporation of the registrant's home jurisdiction documents in their entirety.

. . .

In addition, a newly adopted exemption eliminates the Commission's reporting obligation that otherwise would arise by reason of Securities Act registration under the MJDS in connection with most rights offers, exchange offers and business combinations.

Financial statements included in MJDS disclosure documents may be audited in accordance with generally accepted auditing standards in Canada. Except in rights offerings, compliance with U.S. auditor independence requirements must commence with the audit report on the financial statements for the most recent fiscal year included in the first MJDS filing and continue for each report thereafter. For prior periods, compliance with Canadian independence standards is sufficient.

. . .

Review of a disclosure document submitted under the MJDS will be that customary in Canada. Thus, except in the unusual case where the Commission staff has reason to believe there is a problem with the filing or the offering, the MJDS registration statements generally will be given a "no review" status by the Commission. Further, the MJDS forms for registration under the Securities Act will be made effective automatically upon filing with the Commission except where no contemporaneous offering is being made in Canada and where preliminary materials are being filed. In the case of offerings not made contemporaneously in Canada, such registration statements will be made effective after the Canadian securities regulator has completed its review.

Issuers using the MJDS continue to be subject to provisions imposing civil or criminal liability for fraud in each jurisdiction where the securities are offered. Issuers are subject to the authority of each such

ministered in the United States" (as defined in the foreign private issuer definition) by virtue of such parent-subsidiary relationship. The determination of the location of administration of a business will be made in light of all the facts and circumstances in a particular case.

jurisdiction to halt the offering in the public interest and for the protection of investors.

*B. Securities Act Registration*

1. Offerings by Substantial Issuers

The purpose of the "substantial" designation is to single out issuers whose size is such that there is a large market following for them and the marketplace can be expected to have set a price for their securities based on all publicly available information. The Commission has distinguished for this purpose between investment grade securities and other securities and has provided separate registration forms for each. "Substantial" issuers in the context of convertible investment grade securities are issuers that have a total market value for their equity shares of at least (CN) $180 million and for their public float of at least (CN) $75 million. (For non-convertible investment grade securities, issuers need not meet the "substantial" test.) "Substantial" in the context of registration of all other securities includes those issuers with a market value for their equity shares of at least (CN) $360 million and a public float of (CN) $75 million. The market value of equity shares and public float tests may be measured as of any date within 60 days prior to the date of filing.

. . .

*b. Offerings of Investment Grade Debt and Preferred Stock by Substantial Issuers (Form F–9).* Registration on Form F–9 is permitted for offerings of investment grade debt securities or investment grade preferred stock, if such securities are either non-convertible or are convertible only after one year from the date of issuance.

. . .

The "investment grade" determination has to be made by a nationally recognized statistical rating organization ("NRSRO"). Under the Reproposal, securities would have been deemed "investment grade" if, at the time of effectiveness of the registration statement, at least one NRSRO had rated the security in one of its three highest rating categories that signifies investment grade. The Commission indicated in the Reproposal, however, that to the extent the fourth highest rating category is recognized in the future by Canadian regulatory authorities as signifying investment grade under the MJDS, the Commission would give parallel recognition. In light of such subsequent recognition, Form F–9 as adopted refers to registration of securities with the fourth highest rating.

. . .

4. Disclosure Supplementing Home Jurisdiction Requirements

In light of the absence of requirements for such disclosure under Canadian law, information regarding indemnification provisions relating to directors, officers or controlling persons of the registrant is required to be disclosed in Forms F–8, F–80, F–9 and F–10. A statement regarding the Commission's opinion that indemnification against Securities Act liabilities is against public policy and is therefore unenforceable also is required.

5. Application of Securities Act Rules

The Securities Act rules in Regulation C mandating standards for the preparation and form of prospectuses are inapplicable under the MJDS, unless otherwise specified in the MJDS forms. Other Securities Act rules regarding the offer and sale of securities in the United States generally do apply unless the MJDS form specifies otherwise or the rule, by its terms, is inapplicable. For example, U.S. requirements for prospectus delivery apply to MJDS offerings in the United States, as do safe harbor provisions relating to advertisements and other notices regarding MJDS offerings. In addition, publication of recommendations, opinions or other information with respect to a MJDS registrant or its securities is permitted to the extent provided by Securities Act safe harbor rules. Where appropriate, Securities Act rules have been amended to apply to MJDS forms.

*C. Exchange Act Registration and Reporting*

Canadian issuers that make a registered offering of securities in the United States or have a certain number of shareholders of record resident in the United States and have a threshold amount of assets are subject to registration and reporting requirements under the Exchange Act. Similarly, Canadian issuers listing securities on a national securities exchange or having them quoted on NASDAQ are subject to such Exchange Act requirements. A chart of such reporting obligations and the forms available to Canadians to satisfy them is included as appendix C to this Release.

1. Section 15(d) Obligations

Absent an exemption, section 15(d) of the Exchange Act requires each issuer that has filed a Securities Act registration statement that has become effective to file periodic reports thereafter. While under the Reproposal registration on any of the MJDS Securities Act forms would have resulted in subsequent Exchange Act reporting, the MJDS as adopted provides that securities registered on MJDS Form F–7, F–8 or F–80 are exempt from the section 15(d) requirement to file subsequent reports with the Commission, provided the issuer is furnishing its home country disclosure documents under the rule 12g3–2(b) exemption from the Commission's reporting obligations under section 12(g).

. . .

2. Stock Exchange and NASDAQ–Related Obligations

Section 13(a) of the Exchange Act requires each issuer that has registered securities under that Act to file periodic reports. The Exchange Act requires registration of any class of securities, whether debt or equity, that is listed on a national securities exchange. Exchange Act registration is also required for securities quoted on NASDAQ. Issuers eligible to use MJDS Form F–10, and issuers eligible to use MJDS Form F–9 that are having Form F–9–eligible securities so listed or quoted, may comply with such reporting obligations by filing their home jurisdiction disclosure documents.

. . .

*F. Mechanics of the MJDS*

1. Offerings of Securities

An issuer using the MJDS will prepare a disclosure document according to Canadian requirements and use that document for securities offerings in the United States, subject to minimal additions set forth in the MJDS forms. Of course, if no Canadian takeover bid circular or issuer bid circular (in the case of an exchange offer) or information circular (in the case of a business combination) or prospectus (in all other cases) is prepared with respect to an offering because an exemption from such requirements is being relied upon by the issuer, the offering is not eligible to be made using MJDS forms regardless of whether the eligibility tests are satisfied. Where an offering on Form F–9 or F–10 is being made only in the United States, however, the MJDS is available so long as the home jurisdiction disclosure document is prepared and filed with the Canadian securities regulator in the review jurisdiction.

Review of the disclosure document will be undertaken by Canadian securities authorities and generally will be that customary in Canada. Thus, except in the unusual case where the Commission's staff has reason to believe there is a problem with the filing or the offering, the documents generally will be given a "no review" status by the Commission. For the most part, since the MJDS Securities Act forms become effective upon filing, any Commission review would be undertaken after effectiveness.

The MJDS forms distinguish between the disclosure document required to be given to each investor and the documents to be filed with the Commission. Participating Canadian issuers will provide investors in the United States generally with the same information delivered to investors in Canada. A prospectus used in the United States, however, need not contain any disclosure applicable solely to Canadian offerees or purchasers that is not material to U.S. offerees or purchasers. All the forms and schedules also expressly require that the issuer add to the prospectus or circular legends notifying investors that the investment may have tax consequences in the issuer's jurisdiction, that investors may have to pursue remedies for any securities law violation against persons and assets located in the issuer's jurisdiction, and that any financial statements are prepared in accordance with Canadian accounting standards. Information incorporated by reference into the Canadian registration statement or prospectus that is not required to be delivered to securityholders in the issuer's home jurisdiction is not required to be included in the MJDS prospectus, but must be filed with the Commission as an exhibit to the applicable form. Other documents required by home jurisdiction law to be made publicly available in connection with the transaction, or required to be filed with the Canadian securities regulator concurrently with the Canadian prospectus, also must be filed with the Commission as exhibits to the registration statement or schedule. The rules require the issuer to provide such information to the investor upon request. Such information also will be available in the public files of the Commission. Documents previously filed with the Commission or furnished by the issuer to the Commission pursuant to the rule 12g3-2(b) exemption may be incorporated by reference and need not be filed again.

. . .

## I. Liability

Canadian issuers filing documents with the Commission under the MJDS are subject to civil liability and antifraud provisions of the U.S. securities laws. In addition, MJDS registration statements are subject to the authority of the Commission to suspend their effectiveness.

Commenters have expressed concern that an offering document prepared under applicable Canadian rules in accordance with MJDS forms will be considered misleading solely because information required by other existing Commission forms is omitted. By adopting the MJDS, the Commission in essence is adopting as its own requirements the disclosure requirements of Canadian forms. The effect is the same as if the Commission had set forth each Canadian requirement within the MJDS forms. Moreover, different disclosure is required under Commission registration and reporting forms available to different categories of issuers under present Commission practice. Separate sets of forms for foreign and U.S. issuers have long existed under the Securities Act and the Exchange Act. Accordingly, good faith compliance with the disclosure requirements of the home jurisdiction, as construed by Canadian regulatory authorities, will constitute compliance with the applicable U.S. federal securities disclosure requirements, even if such compliance results in the omission of information which might otherwise have been required as a line item in registration statements filed by U.S. issuers on the Commission's other registration forms.

Further, violation of a home jurisdiction disclosure requirement with respect to an MJDS document will not automatically disqualify the issuer from use of the MJDS with respect to that transaction or report. Instead, the issuer will have violated both a home jurisdiction requirement and an identical Commission disclosure requirement with respect to that document.

. . .

## VI. State Securities Regulation

In addition to complying with the federal securities laws, issuers selling their securities in the United States are subject to state securities laws (including the District of Columbia and Puerto Rico) of those jurisdictions where offers and sales are made. Generally, those laws require registration of securities offered to persons in the state. In most jurisdictions, the registration statement filed with the Commission also will satisfy the state filing requirements. The filings are subject to review by each of the states, as to the adequacy of the disclosure and, in many states, for compliance with additional substantive standards.

. . .

The specific requirements for offering and selling securities in any state are governed by that jurisdiction's statutes, rules and policies. Nevertheless, the North American Securities Administrators Association ("NASAA"), which represents all state securities regulators as well as Canadian provincial regulators and the securities authorities of Mexico, proposes uniform guidelines and procedures which are frequently adopted by many of its member states. In April 1989, NASAA adopted a Statement on Internationalization of the Securities Markets, in which it urged securities regulators to "encourage legitimate capital raising activities across national borders," subject to "minimum rules to ensure investor protection." NASAA also passed a resolution on September 14, 1989 endorsing the MJDS as originally proposed. The NASAA resolution called upon its membership to take any action necessary to accommodate MJDS offerings within state securities laws. NASAA also formed a special task force to work with the Commission and Canadian regulators to determine what accommodations would be appropriate at the state level.

NASAA thereafter conducted a survey of securities administrators in all states, Puerto Rico and the District of Columbia to gather information regarding how such administrators planned to accommodate MJDS offerings in their jurisdictions and the number of state exemptions from registration that may be available to MJDS issuers. Based upon the information obtained from the survey, on August 30, 1990 NASAA adopted four Model Rules to the Uniform Securities Act (1956) and recommended their adoption, where necessary, to the membership. The Model Rules provide, *inter alia,* for: (a) Harmonization of state review periods with Canadian seven-day review periods; (b) acceptance of MJDS Form F–7 in lieu of any state form that may be required to claim an exemption from registration for a rights offering to existing security holders; (c) acceptance of financial information presented in the registration statement in conformity with Canadian generally accepted accounting principles to the extent permitted under the MJDS; and (d) an exemption from registration for secondary trading of securities which are the subject of an MJDS offering and for which a registration statement on Form F–8, F–9 or F–10 has become effective with the Commission. Because Form F–80 was not intended to be part of the Model Rules, some states may not incorporate Form F–80 into their state laws.

Some states already have adopted those rules or similar measures necessary to produce such results. It is anticipated by NASAA that similar action will be taken by substantially all states within the immediate future. Some states are required by their administrative procedures acts to wait for Commission action before formally adopting the changes.

. . .

### *Notes and Questions*

1. How would you compare the objectives of MJDS with those of Rule 144A?

2. In principle, MJDS allows Canadian issuers to comply with U.S. securities laws by filing their home-country disclosure documents. What important qualifications are there to this principle, and are these qualifications justified?

3. In 1993, the SEC made some important changes in MJDS. In April, the Commission required that Canadian financial information be reconciled with U.S. GAAP, 58 Fed.Reg. 35367 (1993). This was based, in part, on the result of a study of the effect of different accounting rules on the statement of income and equity between the U.S. GAAP and foreign GAAP of several countries including Canada, SEC, Division of Corporate Finance, Survey of Financial Statement Reconciliations by Foreign Registrants (May 1, 1993). The following results were found for Canada:

**CANADA**

Number of Registrants

291

**BASIS OF ACCOUNTING PRESENTATION**

Two hundred sixty-nine registrants presented financial statements in accordance with GAAP in their home jurisdiction.

Twenty-two registrants presented financial statements in accordance with U.S. GAAP.

**RECONCILIATION DATA**

Ninety reported no material reconciling differences.[1]

**RECONCILIATION VARIANCES—INCOME**

| Income Under U.S. GAAP Greater Than Income Under Foreign GAAP | Number of Registrants | Variance Range Percent of Foreign GAAP |
|---|---|---|
| More than 100% | 2 | 101.63%, 109.91% |
| 50.01% to 100% | 3 | 57.80%– 62.19% |
| 25.01% to 50% | 4 | 25.78%– 40.08% |

1. Some registrants reported no material reconciling differences in shareholders' equity but provided a reconciliation for material variances in income. Likewise, some registrants reported no material reconciling income statement differences but provided a reconciliation for material variances in balance sheet items. In the following pages, amounts presented under the caption Reconciliation Data represent the number of registrants surveyed that reported no material reconciling differences for either income statement or balance sheet purposes.

| Income Under U.S. GAAP Greater Than Income Under Foreign GAAP | Number of Registrants | Variance Range Percent of Foreign GAAP |
|---|---|---|
| 10.01% to 25% | 8 | 11.49%– 21.92% |
| 0.01% to 10% | 35 | 0.06%– 7.91% |

| Income Under U.S. GAAP Less Than Income Under Foreign GAAP | Number of Registrants | Variance Range Percent of Foreign GAAP |
|---|---|---|
| More than 100% | 22 | (638,900.00)% [2]–(116.39)% |
| 50.01% to 100% | 10 | (82.46)%– (52.32)% |
| 25.01% to 50% | 12 | (50.00)%– (28.09)% |
| 10.01% to 25% | 18 | (24.86)%– (10.01)% |
| 0.01% to 10% | 32 | (7.44)%– (0.03)% |

## RECONCILIATION VARIANCES—EQUITY

| Equity Under U.S. GAAP Greater Than Equity Under Foreign GAAP | Number of Registrants | Variance Range Percent of Foreign GAAP |
|---|---|---|
| More than 100% | 1 | 259.04% |
| 50.01% to 100% | 1 | 59.35% |
| 25.01% to 50% | 1 | 34.57% |
| 10.01% to 25% | 3 | 13.70%–22.14% |
| 0.01% to 10% | 18 | 0.36%– 7.24% |

| Equity Under U.S. GAAP Less Than Equity Under Foreign GAAP | Number of Registrants | Variance Range Percent of Foreign GAAP |
|---|---|---|
| More than 100% | 9 | (1,757.89)%–(101.03)% |
| 50.01% to 100% | 10 | (99.56)%– (51.23)% |
| 25.01% to 50% | 15 | (48.95)%– (25.37)% |
| 10.01% to 25% | 22 | (20.35)%– (10.03)% |
| 0.01% to 10% | 39 | (8.87)%– (0.01)% |

. . .

Did these results justify a U.S. GAAP reconciliation requirement under MJDS?

In November, market capitalization requirements for issuers were eliminated, the public float requirement was changed from $75 million Canadian to $75 million U.S., the reporting history requirement was shortened to 12 from 36 months, and recognition was given to investment grade ratings made by organizations recognized by Canadian securities authorities, 58 Fed.Reg. 62028 (November 23, 1993).

4. Should MJDS be further liberalized and extended to other countries?

---

**2.** Three registrants reported income variances in excess of 1000%, seven reported variances between 500% and 1000% and two reported variances between 200% and 500%. The 638,900% variance is primarily attributable to a large reconciling item compared to an extremely small net income amount. Excluding this variance, the largest percentage would have been 17,835%.

## 3. The Use of ADRs

### SECURITIES AND EXCHANGE COMMISSION, AMERICAN DEPOSITORY RECEIPTS

56 Fed.Reg. 24420 (May 30, 1991).

### I. Introduction

In recent years, investment in foreign securities by United States investors has increased dramatically and, as technological advances and regulatory initiatives bring about more globalized securities markets, such investment can be expected to continue to increase.[1] One of the principal means used by U.S. investors to hold foreign equity securities (other than Canadian issuers' securities) is the American depositary receipt ("ADR").[2] . . .

### II. Background

*A. Description of ADRs*

An ADR [5] represents an ownership interest in a specified number of securities that have been deposited with a depositary by the holder of such securities.[6] The securities that are so deposited ("deposited securities") are typically equity securities of a foreign issuer, and the depositary is typically a U.S. bank or trust company. In exchange for the deposited securities, the depositary issues a negotiable certificate representing the ADRs.

**1.** It is estimated that in 1990, U.S. investors purchased approximately $130.9 billion, and sold approximately $122.5 billion, of foreign equity securities. U.S. Treasury Bulletin p. 93 (Mar. 1991). In 1980, U.S. investors purchased approximately $10.0 billion, and sold approximately $7.9 billion, of foreign equity securities. U.S. Treasury Bulletin (various issues).

**2.** It is estimated that the total dollar volume of ADR trading in 1990 was approximately $125 billion. The Bank of New York, 1990 ADR Market Review and Year End Newsletter (Feb. 1991). The estimated dollar volume in 1963 was approximately $1.8 billion. Kesler, The ADR Weathers the Storm, Euromoney Spec.Supp. 1 (Feb. 1988).

**5.** Since 1983, the Commission's regulations have made a distinction between ADRs and American depositary shares ("ADSs"). Under this distinction, an ADR is the physical certificate that evidences ADSs (in much the same way a stock certificate evidences shares of stock), and an ADS is the security that represents an ownership interest in deposited securities (in much the same way a share of stock represents an ownership interest in a corporation). Although conceptually accurate, some confusion has resulted from this distinction, and it appears that ADR market participants largely do not differentiate between ADRs and ADSs. As a result, it appears appropriate to eliminate the ADR/ADS distinction. In this release, the term "ADS" is not used, and the term "ADR" may, depending on its context, refer to either the physical certificate or the security evidenced by such certificate.

**6.** An ADR may represent one security of a foreign issuer or fractions or multiples of a security of a foreign issuer. The ratio of such securities represented by one ADR (referred to by market participants as the "multiple") is intended to compensate for differences between traditional pricing levels between U.S. and foreign markets. For example, ADRs will often represent two or more securities of a U.K. issuer because sales prices on a per share basis for such securities are generally lower than comparable U.S. securities. Likewise, ADRs will often represent a fraction of one security of a Japanese issuer because sales prices on a per share basis for such securities are generally higher than comparable U.S. securities.

The ADR arrangement provides several benefits to U.S. investors in foreign securities over owning securities directly, including facilitation of share transfers and conversion of dividends paid in a foreign currency. In the past few years, new applications for the ADR arrangement have been developed. ADRs have been used in connection with mergers and acquisitions, restructurings, foreign government debt offerings and funding of employee benefit and compensation plans. In addition, offerings of ADRs have been made under Rule 144A.

Of the approximately 1,550 foreign issuers that as of the end of 1990 were filing or submitting reports under the Exchange Act, there were approximately 502 issuers whose securities were traded through unsponsored ADR facilities registered with the Commission, and 302 issuers whose securities were traded through registered sponsored ADR facilities. These facilities relate to shares of companies in numerous and diverse countries ranging from Australia to Zambia. The preponderance of trading, however, occurs in ADRs for companies incorporated in Western Europe and Japan.

ADRs are not held only by U.S. investors; to some extent non-U.S. investors also hold them. In addition to ADRs, International depositary receipts, Continental depositary receipts and European depositary receipts also trade in the international markets. International depositary receipts are used by non-U.S. traders and investors for investment in non-U.S. markets. European depositary receipts primarily are used to facilitate the trading of Japanese companies' securities in European markets. The Commission requests comment on the development of these instruments, their effect on the ADR market, and the nature of the regulatory scheme applicable to such instruments.

### B. *Unsponsored and Sponsored ADR Facilities*

ADR facilities may be established as either "unsponsored" or "sponsored." While ADRs issued under these two types of facilities are in some respects similar (for example, each ADR represents a fixed number of securities on deposit with a depositary), there are distinctions between them relating to the rights and obligations of ADR holders and the practices of market participants.

#### 1. Unsponsored Facilities

"Unsponsored" ADR facilities generally are created in response to a combination of investor, broker-dealer and depositary interest. Most often, a depositary is the principal initiator of a facility because it perceives U.S. investor interest in a particular foreign security and recognizes the potential income which may be derived from a facility. In other cases, one or more brokers familiar with U.S. investor interest and U.S. trading activity in a foreign issuer's securities may request that a depositary create a facility in order to facilitate trading.

A depositary may establish an unsponsored facility without participation by (or even necessarily the acquiescence of) the issuer of the deposited securities, although typically the depositary, to promote good issuer relations, requests a letter of non-objection from such issuer prior to the establishment of the facility. If the issuer is neither a reporting issuer under the Exchange Act, nor exempt from such reporting pursuant to the "information supplying" exemption provided thereunder, the depositary requests that the issuer establish such exemption. If the issuer does so, thereafter the depositary files a registration statement on Form F–6 for the ADRs. Once the registration statement becomes effective, the depositary begins to accept deposits of securities of the foreign issuer and to issue ADRs against such deposits. Deposited securities are usually held by a custodian appointed by the depositary (often a bank) in the country of incorporation of the foreign issuer.

Holders of unsponsored ADRs generally bear all the costs of such facilities. The depositary usually charges fees upon the deposit and withdrawal of deposited securities, the conversion of dividends into U.S. dollars, the disposition of non-cash distributions, and the performance of other services. The depositary of an unsponsored facility frequently is under no obligation to distribute shareholder communications received from the issuer of the deposited securities or to pass through voting rights to ADR holders in respect of the deposited securities.

2. Sponsored Facilities

A "sponsored" ADR facility is established jointly by an issuer and a depositary.[21] Sponsored ADR facilities are created in generally the same manner as unsponsored facilities, except that the issuer of the deposited securities enters into a deposit agreement with the depositary and signs the Form F–6 registration statement. The deposit agreement sets out the rights and responsibilities of the issuer, the depositary and the ADR holders. Like unsponsored ADR facilities, sponsored ADR facilities usually involve the use of a foreign custodian to hold the deposited securities.

With sponsored facilities, the issuer of the deposited securities generally will bear some of the costs relating to the facility (such as dividend payment fees of the depositary), although ADR holders continue to bear certain other costs (such as deposit and withdrawal fees). Under the terms of most sponsored arrangements, depositaries agree to distribute notices of shareholder meetings and voting instructions, thereby ensuring that ADR holders will be able to exercise voting rights through the depositary with respect to the deposited securities. In

**21.** Certain depositaries describe sponsored facilities in terms of three categories, based on the extent to which the issuer of the deposited securities has accessed the U.S. securities market. A "Level 1 facility" is a sponsored facility the ADRs of which trade in the "Pink Sheets." (See *infra* n. 33 and accompanying text.) Level 2 refers to ADRs quoted on the National Association of Securities Dealers' Automated Quotation system ("NASDAQ") or listed on a national securities exchange when the ADRs have not been offered in a U.S. public offering. Level 3 denotes ADRs quoted on NASDAQ or listed on a national securities exchange after a U.S. public offering of ADRs. Levels 1, 2 and 3 generally indicate lower to higher degrees of issuer involvement with the facility and lower to higher amounts of information made available by the issuer to the public.

addition, the depositary usually agrees to provide shareholder communications and other information to the ADR holders at the request of the issuer of the deposited securities. Although the terms of deposit for sponsored ADR facilities differ from those for unsponsored facilities, sponsorship in and of itself does not result in different reporting or registration requirements with the Commission.

. . .

*C. The ADR Market*

ADRs are traded in the United States in substantially the same manner as domestic issuers' equity securities. Some foreign issuers, seeking to increase visibility, improve liquidity and increase access to U.S. capital markets, choose to list their ADRs on the New York Stock Exchange (the "NYSE"), the American Stock Exchange (the "Amex") or another national securities exchange, or to have their ADRs quoted on NASDAQ.[32] Other foreign issuers choose to have trading in their ADRs conducted in the U.S. over-the-counter ("OTC") market. ADRs are traded in the OTC market through market makers that publish quotations or indications of interest in the "Pink Sheets," a daily listing of market maker quotations operated by the Commerce Clearing House/National Quotation Bureau, or through the OTC Bulletin Board Service ("Bulletin Board"), an electronic service operated by the National Association of Securities Dealers, Inc. ("NASD").

The rules of the NYSE and the Amex require that ADRs listed on those exchanges be sponsored. Similarly, NASDAQ has for several years strongly recommended to issuers of deposited securities that they sponsor an ADR facility before NASDAQ includes their ADRs for quotation. Both sponsored and unsponsored ADRs trade in the OTC market. At the end of 1990, of the 336 sponsored ADR facilities, 66 were listed on NYSE, 4 were listed on Amex, and 55 were quoted on NASDAQ.

The recent trend in the creation of ADR facilities has been away from unsponsored arrangements toward sponsorship. One depositary estimates that the overall percentage of sponsored facilities in the U.S. markets has grown from 12% in 1986 to 38% in June 1990.

. . .

3. Custody, Clearance and Settlement for ADRs

The clearance and settlement process for ADRs generally is the same as for other domestic securities that are traded in U.S. markets. Indeed, one of the chief attractions of ADRs is that investors can own an interest in securities of foreign issuers while holding securities that can trade, clear and settle within automated U.S. systems and within U.S. time periods. If investors directly held foreign securities instead of holding ADRs, their transactions in those securities would be subject to

**32.** In 1989, the dollar volume for ADRs traded on the NYSE was $40.8 billion, representing the trading of 1.2 billion ADRs. NYSE Fact Book, March 1990. NASDAQ reported that in 1989 for 92 ADR issues quoted on NASDAQ, share volume was 1.8 billion shares, with a dollar volume of $17.4 billion. NASDAQ Fact Book, 1990, at 17.

the unfamiliar and sometimes less prompt clearance and settlement processes in the security's foreign trading market.

. . .

*D. Regulatory Treatment*

1. Securities Act Registration

For purposes of the Securities Act, ADRs and deposited securities are considered separate securities, each subject to the registration requirements unless an exemption is available. When a foreign issuer or its affiliate is selling securities to the public in the United States, the securities must be registered with the Commission. While the issuer may choose to sell such securities in ADR form, the use of ADRs to facilitate a public offering does not affect the registration requirement with respect to the foreign issuer's securities. As a result, when there is a public offering of securities in ADR form, both the ADRs and the deposited securities must be registered.

ADRs also may be issued, however, when neither the issuer nor an affiliate is engaging in a public offering of the deposited securities. In that case, registration of the deposited securities is not required. For example, when a person who purchased securities of a foreign issuer in the secondary markets decides to deposit them in an ADR facility, an exemption is ordinarily available for that transaction with respect to the deposited securities. In contrast, the issuance of ADRs upon such a deposit constitutes a public offering of the ADRs which must be registered.

In 1983, the Commission adopted Form F–6 specifically for the registration of ADRs under the Securities Act. Form F–6 provides that the issuer of the ADRs for purposes of the Securities Act is the "legal entity created by the agreement for the issuance of ADRs." Under Form F–6, the depositary signs the registration statement on behalf of that entity, but a depositary signing in that capacity is not deemed to be an issuer, a person signing the registration statement or a person controlling the issuer. If the registration statement relates to a sponsored facility, it must also be signed by the issuer of the deposited securities, its principal officers, a majority of its board of directors and its authorized representative in the United States.

a. *Eligibility requirements for use of Form F–6.* To register ADRs on Form F–6, the deposited securities must be registered or exempt from registration under the Securities Act. In addition, an ADR holder must be able to withdraw the deposited securities evidenced by its ADR at any time, subject only to certain enumerated limitations. Further, Form F–6 may be used for the registration of ADRs only if, as of the filing date of the Form F–6 registration statement, the issuer of the deposited securities either is (or is concurrently becoming) a reporting issuer under the Exchange Act, or is exempt from the reporting requirements of the Exchange Act by virtue of rule 12g3–2(b) thereunder. Rule 12g3–2(b) provides an exemption from the reporting requirements under the Exchange Act for foreign private issuers that furnish to the Commission material information that they publicly file or publish abroad pursuant to law or stock exchange requirements or that they distribute to their security holders.

. . .

b. *Disclosure Required by Form F–6.* Pursuant to Form F–6, the registrant must provide in the prospectus a description of the ADRs being registered. The registrant also must disclose the availability at the Commission's offices of information about the issuer of the deposited securities pursuant to the periodic reporting requirements of the Exchange Act or pursuant to the Rule 12g3–2(b) exemption. In addition, all fees and charges imposed on the ADR holder must be described. The depositary may omit such fee information if it provides a general description of the fees and undertakes to provide a separate fee schedule upon request. The disclosures required by Form F–6 are virtually always set forth in the ADR certificate, and such certificate serves as a prospectus. In addition, certificates for unsponsored ADRs contain the full contractual terms of the ADRs, not just a description of such terms. The ADR certificate is, in essence, a contract between the depositary and each holder of ADRs represented thereby, as well as a prospectus.

. . .

2. Exchange Act Reporting

When a foreign private issuer lists ADRs on a national securities exchange or has ADRs quoted on NASDAQ, it becomes subject to the periodic reporting requirements under the Exchange Act. As a result, such issuer will be required to file annual reports in accordance with the Commission's Form 20–F (which requires financial statements reconciled to U.S. generally accepted accounting principles) and to submit other materials to the extent such materials are required to be prepared pursuant to home market regulations. When a foreign private issuer has ADRs traded in the OTC market, it may either (a) comply with the periodic reporting requirements or (b) establish and maintain an exemption from such requirements by furnishing to the Commission in accordance with rule 12g3–2(b) such annual reports, shareholder communications and other materials as are required to be prepared pursuant to home market regulations. So long as the ADRs are not listed on a U.S. securities exchange or quoted on NASDAQ and so long as an issuer maintains its exemption under rule 12g3–2(b), a sponsored ADR facility will not by itself result in a foreign issuer having to comply with the periodic reporting requirements.

. . .

**III. Request for Comment**

. . .

1. Registration Under the Securities Act

a. *Information about the issuer of the deposited securities.* As presently structured, the prospectus contained in a Form F–6 registration statement need disclose only information regarding the depositary arrangement. No information about the issuer of the deposited securities (other than its identity) need be included in the prospectus. However, as previously noted, Form F–6 requires that the issuer of the deposited securities be reporting under the Exchange Act or furnishing to the Commission certain information it makes public in its home country. Comment is requested as to whether information about the issuer of the deposited securities should continue to be made indirectly available to investors through the Form F–6 eligibility requirement or whether information should be made directly available to investors by a requirement that it be contained in the prospectus itself. If the latter is required, what type of information should be provided, and would incorporation by reference to material available through the Commission be appropriate? What would be the advantage of such incorporation by reference as compared to reliance on the Form F–6 eligibility requirement? Commenters should estimate the cost of provision of information for direct F–6 availability or (if additional cost is involved) for incorporation by reference.

b. *Information about the deposited securities.* Form F–6 does not require prospectus disclosure of information regarding the deposited securities. While procedures for passing through voting and other rights are required to be disclosed, a description of such rights with respect to the deposited securities is not specifically required. For instance, information regarding limitations on foreign ownership of deposited securities, foreign currency exchange controls and other limitations affecting ADR holders are not items of disclosure required by Form F–6. Such disclosure may currently be available from other sources. For example, where the deposited securities are being registered concurrently under the Securities Act, investors would receive a prospectus that includes such disclosure. Such information also may be available through the Commission in a document filed under the Exchange Act.

Comment is requested regarding whether Form F–6 should be amended so that the rights arising from ownership of the deposited securities must be disclosed when such disclosure is not included in other documents filed with or submitted to the Commission. If so, what information about the deposited securities should be required by Form F–6?

. . .

f. *Fees and expenses.* The disclosure required by Form F–6 in connection with the fees and expenses charged by depositaries is usually stated in terms of the maximum fee that could be charged. From discussions with depositaries and others, it appears that in practice the fees for deposit and withdrawal of deposited securities vary widely from no fee at all to the stated maximum fee. Particularly in the case of deposits and withdrawals through brokers, fees are often negotiated on a case-by-case basis. Further, it appears that when dividends or other distributions are paid, there is no disclosure of the currency conversion rate used or the fees and expenses deducted by the depositary or others before payment. As a result of the general nature of the depositaries' fee disclosure or the absence of such disclosure, ADR holders may have limited awareness of both the types and the amounts of charges. Comment is sought as to the extent to which such rates, fees and expenses are not known to ADR holders. Comment also is solicited on whether there is a need for more specific prospectus or other disclosure about fees. If more disclosure is deemed necessary, should the focus be on identification of every event that would result in a fee or expense deduction, or should the disclosure also include more specific estimates of the amount being charged? To the extent that such fees or charges are imposed by persons other than depositaries, should the depositaries be responsible for disclosing them? What consideration should be given to the practice of individual negotiation of fees?

. . .

2. Should Depositaries or Issuers Assume Responsibility for the Registration Statement?

Market participants appear to have accepted the arrangement under which the legal entity created by the agreement for the issuance of ADRs is deemed the "issuer" of the ADRs and the registrant under Form F–6. In essence, no person or entity has the liability of an issuer under Section 11.[82] Does it continue to be appropriate that neither the depositary nor the issuer of the deposited securities assumes responsibility for the content of the registration statement? Should the issuer of the deposited securities expressly assume liability as "issuer" of the ADRs if the issuer of the deposited securities sponsors the ADR program? Should the depositary assume section 11 liability, either as "issuer" or as another signatory to the registration statement, for the entire registration statement or for specified portions of the registration statement? Commenters favoring change should give examples of detriment to ADR holders from the absence of such responsibility. Would full or partial assumption of liability significantly affect the manner in which issuers of deposited securities and depositaries approach the ADR marketplace? Is there a cost associated with such assumption of liability, and how is that cost anticipated to be allocated among participants in the ADR market?

. . .

*B. Should the Exchange Act Treatment of ADRs Be Modified?*

Under current regulations, ADRs that are traded on NASDAQ or in the OTC market are not necessarily subject to a separate reporting requirement under the Exchange Act,[84] but ADRs that are listed on a national securities exchange are subject to such a separate requirement. There appears to be little practical significance in this separate requirement. Although listed ADRs are not the securities of the foreign issuer but rather of the legal entity created by the depositary, it appears to be common practice for the reports of foreign issuers to satisfy the reporting requirements for both the deposited securities and listed ADRs.

The Commission is soliciting comment on whether the reporting exemption applicable to non-listed ADRs should be extended to listed ADRs. Alternatively, the exemption applicable to non-listed ADRs could be eliminated, and the Commission could require periodic reporting with respect to all ADRs. In this connection, comment is requested with respect to whether information other than that currently required to be included in depositaries' semi-annual reports should be required to be included in such reports. If periodic reporting is required, should depositaries, issuers of deposited securities or some other persons be responsible for compliance, and should different reporting requirements be applicable to sponsored and unsponsored facilities?

. . .

### *Questions*

1. In 1992, foreign companies raised $9.1 billion through ADRs, up from $6.8 billion in 1991. Latin America accounted for $4.1 billion, compared with $3.4 billion for european issuers. There were 1050 ADR facilities at year-end 1992. M. Murray, "American Depositary Receipts, Public Issuance Overtakes Private Placements," Euromoney (April 1993).

2. What is an ADR? Compare it to a "normal" security. What is the difference between a sponsored and unsponsored ADR?

3. What is the purpose of an ADR?

4. The F–6 registration statement provides no information about the issuer, only the terms of the ADR arrangement. So the creation of an ADR facility does not trigger the need for a '33 Act issuer registration statement. Exchange listed ADRs, as is the case for other listed securities, are subject to periodic reporting under the '34 Act. If the issue is unlisted, the 12g3–2(b) exemption is available. Is there a registration loophole?

5. Should ADRs which are not publicly issued in the United States be exempted from all reporting requirements under the '34 Act regardless of whether they are listed on an exchange?

## 4. The Daimler–Benz Case: GAAP Reconciliation Compromises

### J. MICHAEL SCHELL, DAIMLER–BENZ LEADS GERMANY TO NEW YORK STOCK EXCHANGE

Int'l Fin.L.Rev. 11 (December 1993).

On October 5, 1993, Daimler–Benz AG became the first German company to list its American Depositary Shares (ADSs) on the New York Stock Exchange (NYSE). This listing was the result of discussions between Daimler–Benz, Germany's largest industrial group, and the Securities and Exchange Commission (SEC). The extensive public disclosure required by the US securities laws has in the past discouraged foreign companies from entering the US capital markets by listing their shares on a national securities exchange or market. German companies, in particular, have avoided the US markets due, in part, to an unwillingness to comply with US accounting standards and reporting requirements. The largest obstacle for German companies has been the requirement that the audited financial statements of a foreign company include a reconciliation to US generally accepted accounting principles (US GAAP). Such a reconciliation from financial statements prepared under German accounting standards has been viewed as too costly and too time consuming by many German companies.

Daimler–Benz, like many other foreign companies, determined that the benefits of entry into the US capital markets outweighed the burdens of the rigorous US disclosure and reporting requirements. In addition to the large size, liquidity and sophistication of the US securities markets, a US stock exchange or market listing offers a foreign company the opportunity for an increased shareholder base in the US, an enhanced relationship with its US customers and greater exposure for the company's name, products and services. In order to obtain these benefits, however, a foreign issuer must comply with the initial and continuing regulatory requirements of the US securities laws. These requirements mandate comprehensive disclosure regarding the issuer's business, operations and financial results.

. . .

**The Daimler–Benz listing**

In the early 1990s, a group of major German companies, including Daimler–Benz, each publicly traded in Germany and each with significant foreign participation in its shareholder base, commenced discussions with the SEC to explore whether the general rule that entry into the US capital markets required quantitative reconciliation of the home country financial statements to US GAAP could be waived. Those discussions continued for over two years without any substantive progress. Key objections of the SEC to German accounting standards included the following:

**Hidden reserves.** German accounting permits a company to manage its earnings by creating 'silent reserves' with undisclosed balances which are increased in good years, thereby lowering the company's reported earnings, and released in bad years, thereby raising the company's reported earnings.

**Segment reporting.** Unlike US GAAP standards, German accounting does not require reporting of operating profit (or loss), identifiable assets and certain other items by business segment.

By the end of 1992 there was little reason to believe that the discussions—which had by then become intermittent at best—would ever produce a resolution that would substantially change the requirements for entry by major German companies into the US capital markets.

Early in 1993 Daimler–Benz and the SEC began a separate discussion on the question of Daimler–Benz' entry into the US capital markets and progress was quite rapid to a resolution of the issues. On March 30, 1993, the SEC and Daimler–Benz conducted a joint press conference at which it was announced that Daimler–Benz would list its ADRs on the NYSE and file a registration statement on Form 20–F with the SEC containing financial information substantially in compliance with the SEC's US GAAP reconciliation requirements. In particular, it was announced that an agreement was reached with respect to the following items.

- **disclosure of reserves.** Daimler–Benz would disclose all "hidden reserves" in its US GAAP reconciliation.
- **provisions for contingencies.** Provisions for contingencies (included in Other provisions) which could not be recorded as liabilities under US GAAP would be reflected as a special category of stockholders' equity (Appropriated retained earnings).
- **segment reporting.** The SEC would recognize Daimler–Benz' four corporate units as the appropriate segments for its segment reporting requirement.
- **presentation of historical financial information.** Daimler–Benz would be required to reconcile its financial information with US GAAP for the last three fiscal years but would not be required to reconcile the first two years reflected in the five-year selected financial information required by Item 8 of Form 20–F.

In the preparation of its Form 20–F Registration Statement, certain disclosure issues arose for Daimler–Benz which were a function of (i) its status as a German company and (ii) the fact that it is a large multinational industrial group. Disclosure regarding "Control of the Registrant" in Item 4 of the Form 20–F requires a tabular presentation of information with respect to (1) any person who is known to the registrant to be the owner of more than 10% of any class of the registrant's voting securities and (2) the total amount of any class of the registrant's voting securities owned by the officers and directors as a group, without naming them. This requirement, however, is qualified by an introductory clause which states "[i]f the registrant's outstanding voting securities are in registered form." The question presented in the context of a foreign issuer, such as Daimler–Benz, is whether the requirement is intended to be wholly inapplicable to any registrant having only bearer shares, as a literal reading of the language would suggest, even though such registrant possesses information which would otherwise be required to be disclosed.

Under German law, most holders of more than 25% of the share capital of a German Aktiengesellschaft are required to promptly notify the company of the level of their holding. As a result of notifications pursuant to this requirement, Daimler–Benz acquired information with regard to two of its shareholders which was responsive to the requirement set forth in Item 4. Daimler–Benz decided to disclose such information, notwithstanding the plausible argument that such disclosure might not be required. In the case of a third shareholder which owned less than 25% of the outstanding share capital of Daimler–Benz, the information was disclosed with regard to its shareholding on the basis of Daimler–Benz' "belief," and for officers and directors it was qualified with "best knowledge," after appropriate inquiry. The basis for the determination to make these disclosures was a recognition that the "registered shares" qualification was intended to relieve the registrant from the responsibility for a 10% shareholder about whom it had no knowledge and no means of obtaining knowledge as well as a recognition that a "Not applicable" response could very well constitute an omission of material information under a general Rule 10b–5 theory.

A second disclosure issue was presented under Item 4 by the fact that Daimler–Benz was in possession of reliable information concerning future events which could have a significant effect on the information presented in this Item. In one case, a large shareholder was to be merged with Daimler–Benz later in the year and the owners of such shareholder were expected to receive Daimler–Benz shares in the merger. Again, although there was no specific form requirement, Daimler–Benz opted to make disclosure of the impending transaction with appropriate explanation and qualification. Similarly, a second large shareholder had indicated a possibility of reducing its position in Daimler–Benz shares. Again, the resolution of the issue was in favor of disclosure based upon the theory that this information was analogous to that required to be described in a Schedule 13D filing by a 5% shareholder regarding "plans or proposals" which relate to or would result in the disposition of securities of the issuer.

Item 9 of Form 20–F, which requires "Management's Discussion and Analysis of Financial Condition and Results of Operations", presents the most difficult and demanding disclosure requirements in the Form, especially for a multinational company operating in multiple business segments which has significant adjustments arising from its quantitative reconciliation to US GAAP. Not surprisingly, apart from the usual attention to trend-indicative information given to changes in pricing and unit sales, special attention must be devoted to the impact on results arising from foreign exchange translation. Moreover, differing contributions to sales and earnings from the various business segments need separate identification and explanation in terms of the component causes and trends which affect them. Finally, if material, a separate discussion of the impact on group results as well as segment results of the quantitative reconciliation to US GAAP is advisable, although it may not be required.

Daimler–Benz addressed these issues as follows. First, with respect to the effects of foreign exchange translation and risk, it developed separate disclosure on the subject which set forth a complete picture of the impact of foreign exchange on its results, a description of the risks associated with that aspect of its business and a description of its activities undertaken to manage that risk. Second, with respect to the US GAAP reconciliation consideration, it once again developed separate textual disclosure to explain the impact of the group adjustments disclosed in the footnotes to the consolidated financial statements on the various business segments in each of the years discussed in the MD & A. Finally, on the subject of relative segment contributions to sales and earnings of the group, Daimler–Benz not only included the relatively customary segment information in tabular form but also included textual disclosure concerning the relative significance of contributions to sales and operating profit (or loss) of each of its four business segments.

**Recent developments**

Since Daimler–Benz listed its ADSs on the NYSE, the SEC has proposed certain rule changes, and adopted others, which would simplify the registration and reporting process for foreign companies entering the US capital markets. One noteworthy proposed rule change, which is similar to an accommodation that allowed Daimler–Benz to list its ADSs on the NYSE, would reduce the US GAAP reconciliation requirement for foreign issuers who are first-time registrants to apply only to the two most recently completed fiscal years and any interim periods required in the registration statement. This requirement would be applicable both to the foreign issuer's financial statements and to the five-year selected financial information required by Item 8 of Form 20–F.

As of November 1993, more than 550 companies from 40 countries file periodic reports with the SEC as a result of having their securities traded in the US capital markets. This list is growing daily, and if the SEC's proposed rule changes are put into effect, it can be expected to grow even more rapidly.

. . .

### *Notes and Questions*

1. What is the importance of the Daimler–Benz listing?

2. The author points to certain changes in GAAP reconciliation requirements since Daimler–Benz. Apart from decreasing the burden of

historical reconciliation for first-time registrants, see Securities and Exchange Commission, Form Requirements Which Govern Age of Financial Statements of Foreign Private Issuers, 58 Fed.Reg. 60304 (November 15, 1993), the Commission also exempted certain foreign issuers from the rules prohibiting market-making during public offerings, 58 Fed.Reg. 60324 (November 15, 1993). A further reform adopted by the Commission permits foreign issuers to prepare a cash flow statement in accordance with a recently amended international standard, International Accounting Standard No. 7, rather than compelling a reconciliation to U.S. GAAP, 58 Fed.Reg. 60307 (November 15, 1993). Is the solution to reconciliation to develop international accounting standards? Is that feasible in the short or medium term?

---

## D. ISSUING SECURITIES ABROAD

The Palm and Wolkovik piece gives some general background on Regulation S which governs the application of U.S. securities laws to securities issued outside the United States. According to the SEC's Office of Economic Analysis, U.S. purchases and sales of foreign securities were $902.9 billion in 1990 compared to $53.1 billion in 1980. Using somewhat different measurement techniques, Salomon (M. Howell and A. Cozzini, Games Without Frontiers, 1991) says U.S. investors purchased $297.4 billion of foreign equities in 1990, compared to $128.5 billion in 1986 (Fig. 18). The general concern is that off-shore distributions to U.S. investors could be used to circumvent U.S. law. The following excerpt from Regulation S, 55 Fed.Reg. 18306 (May 2, 1990) gives some additional background.

. . .

I. EXECUTIVE SUMMARY

On June 10, 1988, the Commission published for comment Regulation S, which was intended to clarify the extraterritorial application of the registration requirements of the Securities Act of 1933 (the "Securities Act"). The proposed Regulation contained both a general statement providing that the registration requirements do not apply to offers and sales that occur outside the United States, and two non-exclusive safe harbors from those requirements for specified offers and sales.

. . .

As with the Proposals, the final Regulation consists of a general statement of applicability of the registration provisions (the "General Statement") and two safe harbors. The General Statement provides that Section 5 of the Securities Act does not apply to offers or sales of securities that occur outside the United States. In order for a transaction to fall within the provisions of the General Statement, both the sale and the offer relating to that sale must be made outside the United

States. The General Statement no longer specifies the factors to be considered in determining the locus of the offer and sale.

As with the Proposals, Regulation S as adopted includes two safe harbors. One safe harbor applies to offers and sales by issuers, securities professionals involved in the distribution process pursuant to contract, their respective affiliates, and persons acting on behalf of any of the foregoing (the "issuer safe harbor"), and the other applies to resales by persons other than the issuer, securities professionals involved in the distribution process pursuant to contract, their respective affiliates (except certain officers and directors), and persons acting on behalf of any of the foregoing (the "resale safe harbor"). An offer, sale or resale of securities that satisfies all conditions of the applicable safe harbor is deemed to be outside the United States within the meaning of the General Statement and thus not subject to the registration requirements of Section 5.

Two general conditions apply to the safe harbors. First, any offer or sale of securities must be made in an "offshore transaction," which requires that no offers be made to persons in the United States and that either: (i) the buyer is (or the seller reasonably believes that the buyer is) offshore at the time of the origination of the buy order, or (ii) for purposes of the issuer safe harbor, the sale is made in, on or through a physical trading floor of an established foreign securities exchange, or (iii) for purposes of the resale safe harbor, the sale is made in, on or through the facilities of a designated offshore securities market, and the transaction is not pre-arranged with a buyer in the United States. Second, in no event could "directed selling efforts" be made in the United States in connection with an offer or sale of securities made under a safe harbor. "Directed selling efforts" are activities undertaken for the purpose of, or that could reasonably be expected to result in, conditioning of the market in the United States for the securities being offered. Exceptions to the general conditions are made with respect to offers and sales to specified institutions not deemed U.S. persons, notwithstanding their presence in the United States.

The issuer safe harbor distinguishes three categories of securities offerings, based upon factors such as the nationality and reporting status of the issuer and the degree of U.S. market interest in the issuer's securities. The first category of offerings has been expanded from the Proposals and includes: securities offered in "overseas directed offerings," securities of foreign issuers in which there is no substantial U.S. market interest, securities backed by the full faith and credit of a foreign government, and securities issued pursuant to certain employee benefit plans. The term "overseas directed offerings" (which replaces "overseas domestic offerings" from the Reproposing Release) includes an offering of a foreign issuer's securities directed to any one foreign country, whether or not the issuer's home country, if such offering is conducted in accordance with local laws, offering practices and documentation. It also includes certain offerings of a domestic issuer's non-convertible debt securities, specified preferred stock and asset-backed securities denominated in the currency of a foreign country, which are directed to a single foreign country, and conducted in accordance with local laws, offering practices and documentation. The second category has been revised to include offerings of securities of U.S. reporting issuers and offerings of debt securities, asset-backed securities and specified preferred stock of foreign issuers with a substantial U.S. market interest. The third, residual category has been adopted substantially as reproposed.

The issuer safe harbor requires implementation of procedural safeguards, which differ for each of the three categories, to ensure that the securities offered come to rest offshore. Offerings under the first category may be made offshore under the issuer safe harbor without any restrictions beyond the general conditions. Offerings made in reliance on the other two categories are subject to additional safeguards, such as restrictions on offer and sale to or for the account or benefit of U.S. persons.

The resale safe harbor has been expanded from the Proposals to allow reliance thereon by certain officers and directors of the issuer or distributors. In such a transaction, no remuneration other than customary broker's commissions may be paid. Otherwise, the resale safe harbor is adopted substantially as reproposed. Under the resale safe harbor, dealers and others receiving selling concessions, fees or other remuneration in connection with the offering (such as sub-underwriters) must comply with requirements designed to reinforce the applicable restriction on directed selling efforts in the United States and the offshore transaction requirement. All other persons eligible to rely on the resale safe harbor need only comply with the general conditions.

The safe harbors are not exclusive and are not intended to create a presumption that any transaction failing to meet their terms is subject to Section 5. Reliance on one of the safe harbors does not affect the availability of any exemption from the Securities Act registration requirements upon which a person may be able to rely.

Regulation S relates solely to the applicability of the registration requirements of Section 5 of the Securities Act. The Regulation does not limit in any way the scope or applicability of the antifraud or other provisions of the federal securities laws or provisions of state law relating to the offer and sale of securities.

. . .

## II. BACKGROUND AND INTRODUCTION

The registration requirements of the Securities Act literally apply to any offer or sale of a security involving interstate commerce or use of the mails, unless an exemption is available. The term "interstate commerce" includes "trade or commerce in securities or any transaction or communication relating thereto ... between any foreign country and any State, Territory or the District of Columbia ...." The Commission, however, historically has recognized that registration of offerings with only incidental jurisdictional contacts should not be required. In Release 4708, the Commission stated that it would not take any enforcement action for failure to register securities of U.S. corporations distributed abroad solely to foreign nationals, even though the means of interstate commerce were used, if the distribution was effected in a manner that would result in the securities coming to rest abroad.

Numerous procedures were employed after the issuance of Release 4708 to ensure that securities sold in reliance upon the Release were sold to non-U.S. persons and "came to rest" abroad. These procedures frequently were the subject of no-action letters issued by the Commission's staff. The staff also construed Release 4708 to permit resales abroad of securities not acquired in reliance on the Release. The staff did not express any view as to when or under what circumstances securities issued pursuant to Release 4708 could be resold in the United States or to U.S. persons. Rather, the staff indicated that resales could only be made in compliance with the registration requirements of the Securities Act or an exemption therefrom.

The development of active international trading markets and the significant increase in offshore offerings of securities, as well as the significant participation by U.S. investors in foreign markets, present numerous questions under the U.S. securities laws. For companies raising capital abroad, a principal issue under the federal securities laws is the reach across national boundaries of the registration requirements under Section 5 of the Securities Act.

The Regulation adopted today is based on a territorial approach to Section 5 of the Securities Act.[19] The registration of securities is intended to protect the U.S. capital markets and investors purchasing in the U.S. market, whether U.S. or foreign nationals. Principles of comity[20] and the reasonable expectations of participants in the global markets justify reliance on laws applicable in jurisdictions outside the United States to define requirements for transactions effected offshore. The territorial approach recognizes the primacy of the laws in which a market is located. As investors choose their markets, they choose the laws and regulations applicable in such markets.

In view of the objectives of Regulation S and the policies underlying the Securities Act, the Regulation is not available for any transaction or

**19.** Territoriality is a fundamental basis for jurisdiction under both international law, D. Greig, *International Law* 210, 214 (2d ed. 1976), and the foreign relations law of the United States. Rest. 3rd, *Restatement of the Foreign Relations Law of the United States* § 402 (1987) ("Revised Restatement"); *Restatement Foreign Relations Law of the United States* § 10 (1965) ("Second Restatement"). See also W. Bishop, International Law 535 (1962); ALI Fed. Sec.Code § 905, Comments 3(b), 4 (1980) ("ALI Code").

**20.** The doctrine of comity emphasizes restraint and tolerance by nations in international affairs. See generally, L. Oppenheim, I *International Law* 34 (H. Lauterpacht ed., 8th ed. 1955). See also I H. Lauterpacht, International Law 44–46 (1970); *Offshore Funds and Rule 10b-5: An International Law Approach to Extraterritorial Jurisdiction Under the Securities Exchange Act of 1934,* 8 Fordham Int'l L.J. 410 (1984–1985), citing Akehurst, *Jurisdiction in International Law,* 1972–1973 Brit. Y.B.Int'l L. 214–215; I. Brownlie, *Principles of Public International Law* 31 (3d ed. 1979).

chain of transactions that, although in technical compliance with the rules, is part of a plan or scheme to evade the registration obligations of the Securities Act. In such cases, registration under the Securities Act would be required.

Regulation S relates solely to the applicability of the registration requirements of Section 5 of the Securities Act, and does not limit the scope or extraterritorial application of the antifraud or other provisions of the federal securities laws or provisions of state law relating to the offer and sale of securities. The antifraud provisions have been broadly applied by the courts to protect U.S. investors and investors in U.S. markets where either significant conduct occurs within the United States (the "conduct" test) or the conduct occurs outside the United States but has a significant effect within the United States or on the interests of U.S. investors (the "effects" test). It is generally accepted that different considerations apply to the extraterritorial application of the antifraud provisions than to the registration provisions of the Securities Act. While it may not be necessary for securities sold in a transaction that occurs outside the United States, but touching this country through conduct or effects, to be registered under United States securities laws, such conduct or effects have been held to provide a basis for jurisdiction under the antifraud provisions of the United States securities laws.

### *Questions*

1. Regulation S defines when securities issued abroad will be exempt from the registration requirements of the '33 Act. What considerations are taken into account in making this determination?

2. What are the general conditions for a Regulation S exemption, and how do they take into account the concerns about granting an exemption?

---

*Links to Other Chapters*

This is our first look at domestic regulation of the international aspects of securities markets. Later, we will be able to compare the U.S. approach with that of the European Union (Chapter V) and Japan (Chapter VII). In addition, we will focus later on how U.S. regulation of U.S. stock markets affects competition between U.S. and foreign markets (Chapter XIII). We will also be able to appreciate in more depth how important clearance and settlement is to the attraction of U.S. markets, a subject we touched upon in this Chapter with respect to ADRs (Chapters XIV and XVII). Finally, bear in mind that one big advantage of investing in U.S. markets is that the securities are dollar denominated. As we shall see, foreign exchange considerations are a big factor in investment decisions (Chapter VI).

# Chapter III

# INTERNATIONAL ASPECTS OF U.S. BANKING REGULATION

This Chapter deals with the international aspects of U.S. banking regulation. It begins with some background on the importance of foreign banks in the United States, and the basic features of U.S. regulation of all banks. The material then examines the two key statutes dealing with foreign banks, the International Banking Act of 1978 (IBA) and the Foreign Bank Supervision Act of 1991 which amended the IBA. The latter statute was in large part prompted by the 1991 failure of the Bank of Commerce and Credit International (BCCI). An Appendix to this Chapter contains the IBA, as amended, together with Regulation K of the Federal Reserve Board that implements its provisions. A major theme throughout is the difficulty of applying a simple "national treatment" standard to foreign banks.

## A. THE IMPORTANCE OF FOREIGN BANKS

As of June 1993, foreign banks maintained 576 U.S. branch and agency offices, 90 U.S. bank subsidiaries and 22 other banking offices. See Table A below. These entities held $867.3 billion in assets, approximately 22% of total U.S. banking assets ($3.9 trillion), and $273.4 billion in commercial loans, approximately 26.9% of the U.S. total. In addition, as of year-end 1992, foreign banks maintained 243 representative offices. Table A below shows the distribution of offices, assets and loans among branches, agencies and subsidiaries.

**Table A**

**Total Assets and Commercial Loans [1] of U.S. Offices of Foreign Banks**

June 30, 1993 and June 30, 1992 ($ Billions)

| | 1993 | | | 1992 | | |
|---|---|---|---|---|---|---|
| | Number of Offices | Assets | Loans | Number of Offices | Assets | Loans |
| Agencies | 200 | 96.4 | 53.5 | 225 | 101.9 | 59.1 |
| Branches | 376 | 596.8 | 155.7 | 390 | 601.5 | 164.8 |
| Total Agencies and Branches | 576 | 693.2 | 209.2 | 615 | 703.4 | 223.9 |
| Bank Subsidiaries [2] | 90 | 174.1 | 63.3 | 94 | 178.3 | 69.0 |
| Other | 22 | 5.4 | .9 | 23 | 5.2 | 1.1 |
| Total Foreign | 688 | 867.3 | 273.4 | 732 | 886.9 | 294.0 |
| Total U.S. | 11,822 | 3,973.0 | 1,017.5 | 12,349 | 3,800.3 | 1,037.8 |
| Ratio of Foreign to All U.S. banks | 5.8% | 21.8% | 26.9% | 5.9% | 23.3% | 28.3% |

1. Commercial, industrial, and commercial real estate loans.
2. Excludes thrifts. Foreign owned thrift subsidiaries only held $13.22 billion in assets in 1993.
Source: American Banker (April 12, 1994)

In 1992, Japanese banks alone had $402.1 billion in assets, or 10.6% of all U.S. banking assets and over 50% of foreign bank assets. Due to the downturn in the Japanese economy, as of June 1993, Japanese banks had fallen to a 9.7% share of all U.S. banking assets, and to a 43.7% share of foreign bank assets.

A recent study of the Federal Reserve Board shows that the foreign bank market share of U.S. banking assets is 30% if one counts the offshore (Caymans, Bahamas) offices of both U.S. and foreign banks that do most of their business in the United States.

As we shall see, branches and agencies of foreign banks can be chartered by the states or federal government. At year-end 1991, 532 of the total 616 branches were state chartered and held 94% of all the assets of branches of foreign banks.

## B. BASIC FEATURES OF U.S. REGULATORY SYSTEM

The U.S. bank regulatory system, like securities regulation, is quite complicated and is an entire field of study by itself. There follows a brief description of the major features of this system.

1. *Safety and soundness regulation.* This type of regulation is intended to prevent banks from failing through controlling risks, and ensuring adequate capital. Failure avoids deposit insurance pay-outs and systemic risk (chain reaction of bank failures through interbank deposit linkage or payment settlement systems, or imitative runs).

2. *Deposit Insurance.* The U.S. insures deposits of up to $100,000. This may minimize bank runs, and be a form of creditor protection, but raises a moral hazard issue: since creditors are insured, they do not police bank risk. The insurance fund (BIF) is normally funded by bank paid premiums, but recently this funding has been insufficient due to thrift and banking failures, and has had to be greatly subsidized (over $200 billion) by federal government expenditures. There is now a system of so-called risk-based insurance premiums where the premiums are determined by capital adequacy and supervisory rating.

3. *Dual Banking System.* Banks are chartered by both states, and the federal government through the Office of the Comptroller of the Currency (OCC). National bank powers are regulated by OCC, while state bank powers are regulated by the states, subject to federal limits. National banks are regulated for safety and soundness by OCC, insured state banks by states and their "primary" federal regulator (the Federal Reserve Board (FRB) if the bank is a Fed member, the Federal Deposit Insurance Corporation (FDIC) if it is not). Uninsured state chartered banks are only regulated by the states, but there are very few. The dual system comes out of a federalist tradition: unwillingness to concentrate too much power in the national government.

4. *Bank Holding Company Regulation.* All large banking organizations operate through bank holding company (BHC) form; public shareholders own the BHC not bank. BHCs are regulated by the FRB. Banks generally have more limited powers than BHCs. BHCs can do activities "closely related to banking," § (4)(c)(8) of the Bank Holding Company Act (BHCA). While BHC powers are more expansive than "banking," neither BHCs nor banks can generally engage in life insurance, commercial activities, or certain securities activities. There is less risk to the bank when activities are done through the BHC (in the BHC itself or in a non-bank subsidiary of the BHC) since BHC losses do not directly hit bank capital. Parallel with BHC power limitations, insurance, commercial and securities firms cannot own banks. BHCs, in the view of the Fed, are supposed to serve as a "source of strength" for banks—be ready to inject capital if bank subsidiaries need it. Thus, they must be adequately capitalized. All formations of BHCs or acquisitions of banks by BHCs are reviewed by FRB.

5. *Limited Securities Powers ("Glass–Steagall").* Banks have limited securities powers. They can only underwrite government debt, but they can do brokerage. Banking affiliates (non-bank subs of BHCs) can do more. They can underwrite corporate debt and equity securities through so-called § 20 subsidiaries, so long as they are not "engaged principally" (more than 10% of gross revenue) in these activities.

6. *Limited Interstate Banking.* Under the Douglas Amendment to the BHCA, BHCs cannot acquire a bank outside their home state (state in which they take most of their deposits) unless the state in which the target bank is located permits the acquisition. Today most states (over 35), and all the large states, allow out-of-state U.S. BHCs from any state to acquire banks within their states. The McFadden Act, however, prohibits interstate branching by national and state member banks (almost all large banks are in these two categories). Most states prohibit out-of-state banks from branching in. The idea is to preserve local banking. The branch ban also avoids supervisory complications, i.e. division of authority between home and host state where a state chartered bank is involved. In 1994, the Congress passed new legislation greatly liberalizing interstate banking restrictions.

## C. REGULATION OF FOREIGN BANKS

The following three readings discuss the regulatory framework for foreign banks in the United States. The important provisions of the key statute, the IBA as amended, and the implementing Regulation K of the Federal Reserve Board are in the Statutory Supplement.

### P. SKIGEN AND J. FITZSIMMONS, "THE IMPACT OF THE INTERNATIONAL BANKING ACT OF 1978 ON FOREIGN BANKS AND THEIR DOMESTIC AND FOREIGN AFFILIATES"

35 Bus. Lawyer 55 (1979).

The International Banking Act of 1978 (the "Act") constitutes the first comprehensive piece of federal legislation designed to regulate the activities of foreign banks which do business in the United States. The Act significantly affects the operations of the existing United States agencies and branches of foreign banks and has far-reaching implications for both the United States and foreign affiliates of foreign banks which now conduct, or are planning to conduct, business in the United States.

. . .

## LEGISLATIVE HISTORY

The Act and certain provisions of FIRICA represent the response of Congress to the increase in foreign banking operations in the United States over recent years. The Report of the Committee on Banking, Housing, and Urban Affairs of the United States Senate which accompanied the Act (the "Senate Report") noted that whereas at the end of 1973 there were approximately 60 foreign banks maintaining offices in the United States with combined assets of approximately $37 billion, by the middle of 1978, 122 foreign banks had facilities in the United States with combined assets of approximately $90 billion. The increase in foreign banking activity in the United States generated a growing concern for the effect of their operations on the domestic banking industry and the monetary policies of the United States.

. . .

Prior to the adoption of the Act, the United States agencies and branches of foreign banks were regulated solely by the states in which they operated. Federal laws restricting domestic banks, including federal limitations on interstate banking and reserve requirements, did not apply to such agencies and branches. In addition, foreign banks and their affiliated companies were free from federal restrictions on non-banking activities unless they acquired a controlling interest in a domestic bank. Many believed that this gave foreign banks a competitive advantage over domestic banks in certain areas of operation. The Act and certain provisions of FIRICA attempt to redress this by extending certain federal regulations applicable to domestic banks and their affiliates to foreign banks and their affiliates and by establishing "the principle of parity of treatment between foreign and domestic banks in like circumstances."

## I. POWERS OF AND RESTRICTIONS ON FOREIGN BANK AGENCIES AND BRANCHES

The Act defines an "agency" as any office or place of business of a foreign bank in the United States at which credit balances are maintained incidental to or arising out of the exercise of banking powers, checks are paid or money is lent, but at which deposits from United States citizens or residents may not be accepted. The Senate Report flatly states that "agencies cannot accept deposits," but the literal provisions of the Act indicate that agencies established pursuant to state authority can accept deposits as long as they are from sources other than citizens or residents of the United States.

A "branch" is defined by the Act as any office or place of business of a foreign bank in the United States at which deposits are received. To the extent that an office of a foreign bank accepts deposits only from sources other than citizens or residents of the United States the definitions of "agency" and "branch" appear to overlap. An office of a foreign bank which accepts deposits only from sources other than citizens or residents of the United States may be considered a branch under the laws of certain states, such as California, even though for purposes of the Act it would fall within the definition of agency.

. . .

The provisions of the Act and FIRICA which affect the United States agencies and branches of foreign banks fall into four general categories:

(i) those which provide for federal licensing of foreign bank agencies and branches as an alternative to licensing by the states;

(ii) those which restrict the right of foreign banks to establish branches and acquire banking subsidiaries in more than one state;

(iii) those which require Federal Deposit Insurance Corporation ("FDIC") insurance for the deposits of foreign bank branches; and

(iv) those which extend to foreign bank agencies and branches and the affiliates of foreign banks certain federal requirements and restrictions formerly applicable only to domestic institutions and their affiliates.

Each of these aspects of the Act is discussed further below.

### A. Federal Licensing

Until now, foreign banks operating agencies or branches in the United States have done so pursuant to state authority. The Act gives foreign banks the option of establishing an agency or branch in the United States pursuant to federal authority. (The Act refers to an agency or branch established pursuant to federal authority as a "federal agency" or "federal branch," respectively, and an agency or branch established pursuant to state authority as a "state agency" or "state branch" respectively.)

More specifically, section 4(a) of the Act provides that a foreign bank which "engages directly in a banking business outside the United States" may establish, with the approval of the Comptroller, one or more federal branches or agencies in any state in which it is not operating a state branch or agency, provided that the laws of such state do not prohibit the establishment of an agency or branch by a foreign bank. In addition, in an effort to further the "federal-state option," section 4(f) of the Act establishes procedures by which a foreign bank may convert an existing state agency or branch into a federal agency or branch.

As noted above, federal agencies and branches may be established by any foreign bank which "engages directly" in a banking business outside the United States. The use of the word "directly" suggests that nonbanking subsidiaries and affiliates of foreign banks may not establish a federal agency or branch even though such nonbanking subsidiaries and affiliates are included in the statutory definition of the term "foreign bank."

By conditioning the right to establish a federal agency or branch on the absence of a state law prohibiting the establishment of a foreign bank agency or branch, the Act appears to allow federal agencies and branches to be licensed in any state whose laws are silent on the issue, as well as in any state which expressly permits such establishment. Consequently, foreign banks which have been unable to find any express statutory authority for establishing an office under a particular state's laws will be able to open an office in such state by seeking a federal, rather than a state, license. In addition, the Senate Report makes it clear that federal agencies and branches can be established in the District of Columbia.

. . .

Except as otherwise specifically provided in the Act or in rules, regulations or orders issued by the Comptroller, the operations of a foreign bank at a federal agency or branch are to be conducted with the same rights and privileges applicable to a national bank at the same location and are subject to the same duties, restrictions, penalties, liabilities, conditions and limitations that would apply under the National Bank Act to a national bank doing business at the same location. Federal agencies are not required to obtain FDIC insurance, however, since the Act prohibits them from accepting deposits. Another exception provides that federal agencies and branches are not required to become members of the Federal Reserve System.

The Act recognizes that federal agencies and branches, unlike national banks, will not be separately incorporated entities and contains several provisions designed to reflect the legal and operational differences created by this. Loan limitations and other restrictions expressed, in the case of a national bank, as a percentage of the bank's capital stock and surplus are deemed, when applied to a federal branch or agency, to refer to the dollar equivalent of the capital stock and surplus of the foreign bank as a whole. In addition, federal agencies and branches are required to satisfy capitalization requirements by means of deposit arrangements.

With regard to the latter, the Act provides that the sum of the deposited assets for each federal agency or branch *may not be less* than the *greater* of (i) "that amount of capital (but not surplus) which would be required" of a national bank being organized at the same location or (ii) 5 percent of the total liabilities of the agency or branch (including acceptances, but excluding accrued expenses and amounts due and other liabilities to offices, branches, agencies, and subsidiaries of the foreign bank). These deposit requirements may be more onerous than comparable requirements under state law with respect to state agencies and branches.

. . .

### B. Interstate Branching

The McFadden Act of 1927 and the Bank Holding Company Act of 1956, as amended (the "BHC Act"), restrict domestic banking organizations from establishing full service banking facilities in more than one state.

Prior to the adoption of the Act, foreign banks were not subject to comparable restrictions and were able to operate full service facilities in more than one state. The Senate Report notes that as of April 1978, there were 63 foreign banks operating banking facilities in more than one state, with 31 of these institutions operating in three or more states through agencies, branches and subsidiaries. Many commentators were of the view that the ability of foreign banks to receive deposits, make loans and pay checks at branches in more than one state gave foreign banks a competitive advantage over domestic banks, particularly in the case of foreign banks which actively competed for domestic commercial and industrial loan business. Others argued that the ability of foreign banks to operate such interstate facilities did not give them a significant competitive advantage, since domestic institutions were able to conduct virtually all of their activities (other than retail deposit-taking activities) on an interstate basis through Edge Act corporations, loan production offices, bank holding companies and correspondent banks. The Senate Report concluded, however, that "the essence of banking is the ability to receive deposits, and it is in this that foreign banks do enjoy a growing significant interstate advantage over domestic banking organizations, which cannot receive deposits outside of their home state."

Section 5 of the Act seeks to remedy the competitive disparity between foreign and domestic banks by prohibiting a foreign bank from directly or indirectly establishing and operating a federal or state branch outside of its "home state" unless the foreign bank enters into an agreement with the Federal Reserve Board to limit the deposits at the proposed branch to those which could be accepted by an Edge Act corporation. In addition, section 5 requires that the operation of the proposed branch be expressly permitted by the state in which it is to be operated, in the case of a federal branch, or approved by the bank regulatory authority of the state in which it is to be operated, in the case of a state branch. The "home state" of a foreign bank that has branches, agencies or subsidiary banks, or any combination thereof, in more than one state is whichever of such states is so determined by election of the foreign bank, or in the absence of such election, by the Federal Reserve Board.

. . .

Section 5 of the Act limits the ability of foreign banks to engage in multi-state banking activity through domestic subsidiaries by extending the restrictions found in section 3(d) of the BHC Act to foreign banks. Section 3(d) of the BHC Act provides that no bank holding company or subsidiary thereof may acquire, directly or indirectly, any voting shares of, interest in, or substantially all of the assets of any bank outside the state in which the operations of the holding company's banking subsidiaries are principally conducted unless the acquisition of such shares or assets of a state bank by an out-of-state bank holding company is specifically authorized by the laws of the state in which the bank is located. The Act provides that for purposes of these restrictions, a foreign bank is deemed to be a bank holding company, the operations of whose banking subsidiaries are principally conducted in the foreign bank's home state. Consequently, a foreign bank may not acquire or establish a subsidiary in a state other than its home state unless the laws of the second state would expressly allow it to do so. Most states do not permit out-of-state banks or bank holding companies to acquire banks in them; consequently, there are very few circumstances under which foreign bank subsidiaries located outside a foreign bank's home state could accept deposits.

In effect, the Act leaves each state free to decide whether and to what extent it wishes to permit foreign banks whose "home" is in another state to establish agencies and branches and to acquire banking subsidiaries within the state and places federal limitations only on that activity—the acceptance of deposits by branches in more than one state—which had given foreign banks a competitive advantage over domestic banks. However, state branches and agencies and subsidiaries which commenced lawful operations outside the home state of a foreign bank (or for which an application to commence business had been lawfully filed with the appropriate authorities) on or before July 27, 1978, are grandfathered.

## C. Federal Deposit Insurance

Prior to the adoption of the Act, the deposits of foreign bank branches were not required to be insured by the FDIC and the FDIC would not insure them. Section 6(a) of the Act now prohibits a foreign bank from establishing a Federal branch which receives "deposits" of less than $100,000 unless the branch obtains FDIC insurance or the Comptroller determines by order or regulation that the branch is not engaged in "domestic retail deposit activities." With regard to state branches, section 6(b) of the Act provides that no foreign bank may establish, and after September 17, 1979 no foreign bank may operate, a state branch in any state in which the deposits of a state bank would be required to be insured unless (i) the branch does not accept deposits of less than $100,000, (ii) the branch has obtained FDIC insurance, or (iii) the FDIC determines by order or regulation that the branch is not engaged in "domestic retail deposit activities."

Although the Act does not define "deposit," the regulations adopted by the FDIC define it broadly, by cross-reference to the definition found in section 3(1) of the Federal Deposit Insurance Act (the "FDI Act").

"Domestic retail deposit activity" is defined, in turn, as the acceptance of an initial deposit of less than $100,000. The FDIC regulations construe the term "initial deposit" to mean the first deposit transaction between a depositor and a branch; for purposes of this definition, simultaneous deposits in different kinds of accounts, such as time, demand or savings, may be aggregated, as may deposit accounts held by a depositor in the same right and capacity.

. . .

A foreign bank with an "insured branch" must pledge assets equal to 10 percent of the average of the insured branch's liabilities for the last 30 days of the most recent calendar quarter. Qualifying assets consist of a variety of interest-bearing obligations issued by banks, corporations, governmental entities and certain international organizations. The FDIC may require a foreign bank to maintain a larger deposit of bonds and assets if, in the judgment of the FDIC, the situation of the bank or any of its branches requires larger deposits in order to protect the insurance fund. If a state licensing authority or the Comptroller requires a foreign bank to pledge assets, the foreign bank may deduct the amount pledged, provided it does not exceed 5 percent of the branch's average liabilities, from the amount of assets required to be pledged to the FDIC.

Although not specifically authorized by the insurance provisions of the Act, the FDIC has adopted regulations imposing an asset maintenance test on insured branches in addition to the pledge of assets requirement. As a result, an insured branch must maintain, on an average daily basis for a weekly computation period, eligible assets payable in United States dollars in an amount at least equal in book value to the amount of the branch's liabilities.

The deposits of an insured branch covered by FDIC insurance are those deposits which (A) are payable in the United States to (i) individuals who are citizens or residents of the United States, (ii) corporations, partnerships, trusts or other legal entities created under the laws of the United States or any state and having their principal place of business within the United States, or (iii) individuals, corporations, partnerships, trusts or other legal entities which are determined by the FDIC, in accordance with its regulations to have such business and financial relationships in the United States as to make the insurance of their deposits consistent with the purposes of the FDI Act, and (B) meet any other criteria prescribed by the FDIC by regulation. The FDIC has taken the position that "there is per se a business or financial nexus to the United States if the depositor places funds in a bank located in the United States." Thus, deposits which of themselves would not trigger the insurance requirement, if placed in an insured branch, would be covered by insurance and counted towards the assessment base.

. . .

## II. PROVISIONS OF THE ACT RELATING TO FOREIGN BANKS WHICH DO BUSINESS IN THE UNITED STATES AND THEIR DOMESTIC AND FOREIGN AFFILIATES

In considering the effect of the Act on the operations of foreign banks, it is essential to recall the definition of "foreign bank" which is very broad and includes the foreign subsidiaries and affiliates of a foreign bank. The Act's restrictions on the activities of a foreign bank can be far-reaching, applying to the domestic and foreign activities of its nonbanking, as well as its banking, affiliates.

### A. Bank Holding Company Act.

The BHC Act requires domestic and foreign companies which directly or indirectly own or control a domestic bank ("bank holding companies") to register with the Federal Reserve Board. It also prohibits such companies from (i) engaging in any activities other than those which the Federal Reserve Board deems to be so closely related to banking as to be a proper incident thereto ("banking activities"), and (ii) directly or indirectly owning or controlling more than 5 percent of the voting shares of a company engaged in any activity which is not a banking activity (a "nonbanking company"). Within two years after a domestic or foreign company becomes a bank holding company, it must divest itself of the ownership and control of the voting shares of any nonbanking company and cease to engage in any nonbanking activity unless the shares or activities in question fall within specified exemptions.

The Act generally extends the BHC Act's registration requirements, restrictions on nonbanking activities and investments in nonbanking companies and restrictions on tie-in, reciprocal and exclusive dealing arrangements to foreign banks which have branches or agencies in the United States and to companies owning or controlling such foreign banks. More specifically, section 8(a) of the Act provides that any foreign bank that maintains a branch or agency in the United States and any company of which any such foreign bank is a subsidiary are subject to the provisions of the BHC Act and sections 105 and 106 of the Bank Holding Company Act Amendments of 1970 (the "BHC Amendments") in the same manner and to the same extent that bank holding companies are subject thereto, except that no such foreign bank or company shall by reason of section 8(a) of the Act be deemed a bank holding company for purposes of section 3 of the BHC Act. As a result of the definition of "subsidiary," any domestic or foreign entity controlling 25 percent or more of the voting shares of a foreign bank with an agency or branch in the United States may be restricted in the activities it may engage in or the investments it may make, either directly or through its affiliates, in the United States and abroad.

At the time Congress passed the Act, many foreign financial institutions owned more than 5 percent of the voting shares of nonbanking companies or were engaging, either directly or through their affiliates, in nonbanking activities in the United States. In order to avoid imposing an undue burden on those institutions, the Act grandfathered certain investments and activities.

(1) "GRANDFATHERED" ACTIVITIES.

Section 8(b) of the Act provides that until December 31, 1985, foreign banks and companies may retain direct or indirect ownership or control of any voting shares of a nonbanking company in the United States if such shares were owned, controlled, or held with power to vote on September 17, 1978, or may engage, until December 31, 1985, in any nonbanking activities in the United States which were engaged in on September 17, 1978. Section 8(c) of the Act further permits such a foreign bank or company to continue, after December 31, 1985, to engage in those nonbanking activities in the United States in which it was lawfully engaged either directly or through an affiliate on July 26, 1978, and to engage directly or through an affiliate in nonbanking activities in the United States which were covered by an application filed on or before July 26, 1978. The Federal Reserve Board, however, after an opportunity for a hearing, may terminate the authority to continue such nonbanking activities after December 31, 1985, if it determines that such action is necessary to prevent undue concentration of resources, decreased or unfair competition, conflicts of interest or unsound banking practices in the United States.

A foreign bank or company may retain ownership or control of any voting shares (and where necessary to prevent dilution of its voting interest, may acquire additional voting shares) of a nonbanking company provided that (i) the foreign bank or company owns, controls or holds with power to vote more than 5 percent of the voting shares of the nonbanking company; (ii) the activities engaged in by the nonbanking company are securities activities; (iii) the majority of the voting shares of the nonbanking company have been owned since July 26, 1978 by a company or group of companies organized under the laws of the United States or any state; and (iv) no foreign bank or group of banks owns or controls, directly or indirectly, 25 percent or more of the voting shares of the nonbanking company. It is unclear whether retention of ownership or control of the voting shares of any such nonbanking company is absolutely "grandfathered" or is also subject to the power of the Federal Reserve Board to terminate the authority to continue "grandfathered" nonbanking activities after December 31, 1985.

Section 105(a) of FIRICA amended section 5 of the BHC Act to authorize the Federal Reserve Board to require a bank holding company to divest itself of a nonbanking subsidiary (other than a nonbanking subsidiary of a bank) or to terminate any activity if the Board has reasonable cause to believe that continued ownership of the nonbanking subsidiary or continued conduct of the activity constitutes a serious risk to the financial safety, soundness or stability of a bank holding company subsidiary bank and is inconsistent with sound banking principles, the purposes of the BHC Act or the Financial Institutions Supervisory Act of 1966. Although not explicitly stated, it appears that this amendment does not apply to any activity the conduct of which, or any nonbanking company the ownership of which, is "grandfathered" by the Act.

. . .

(2) THE FOREIGN BANK HOLDING COMPANY AND SECTION 2(h) EXEMPTION.

In the absence of a grandfather exemption, foreign banks with agencies or branches in the United States and affiliates of those foreign banks must carefully review their activities, both within and without the United States, to determine whether (i) the Federal Reserve Board deems the activities to be banking activities or (ii) their ownership of the nonbanking companies qualifies for certain statutory or regulatory exemptions from the BHC Act's restrictions. In this connection, there are two exemptions which will be of primary interest to foreign institutions and their affiliates. The first exempts investments in foreign corporations which are not "subsidiaries" of the foreign bank or its affiliates if the foreign bank or its affiliates fall within the definition of a "foreign bank holding company" (the "foreign bank holding company exemption"). The second exempts investments in certain foreign corporations principally engaged in business outside the United States (the "2(h) exemption").

. . .

Prior to the Act, the prohibitions of the BHC Act against nonbanking activities and investments did not apply to a bank holding company owning or acquiring shares of a foreign company *if* the foreign company did not do any business in the United States and the bank holding company was principally engaged in the banking business outside the United States. The Act amended this exemption (the 2(h) exemption) to read as follows:

> The prohibitions of section 4 of this Act [on nonbanking activities and direct or indirect ownership or control of the voting shares of nonbanking companies] shall not apply to shares of any company organized under the laws of a foreign country (or to *shares held by such company in any company engaged in the same general line of business as the investor company* or in a business related to the business of the investor company) that is principally engaged in business outside the United States if such shares are held or acquired by a bank holding company organized under the laws of a foreign country that is principally engaged in the banking business outside the United States, except that (1) such exempt foreign company (A) may engage in or hold shares of a company engaged in the business of underwriting, selling or distributing securities in the United States only to the extent that a bank holding company may do so under this Act and under regulations or orders issued by the Board under this Act, and (B) may engage in the United States in any banking or financial operations or types of activities permitted under section 4(c)(8) or in any order or regulation issued by the

Board under such section only with the Board's prior approval under that section, and (2) no domestic office or subsidiary of a bank holding company or subsidiary thereof holding shares of such company may extend credit to a domestic office or subsidiary of such exempt company on terms more favorable than those afforded similar borrowers in the United States. (Emphasis added.)

As amended, the 2(h) exemption applies both to (i) shares of a foreign nonbanking company that does business in the United States if the foreign nonbanking company is principally engaged in business outside the United States, and (ii) shares held by such foreign nonbanking company in any domestic or foreign company engaged in the same general line of business as, or in a business related to, the business of such foreign nonbanking company. Such a foreign nonbanking company, however, (a) may engage in, or hold shares of a company engaged in, the securities business in the United States only to the extent that a bank holding company may do so, and (b) may engage in the United States in any banking activities in the United States or financial operations related thereto only with the prior approval of the Federal Reserve Board. In addition, no United States office or subsidiary of a foreign bank deemed to be a holding company or of any foreign bank holding company subsidiary which holds shares in a foreign nonbanking company may extend credit to a domestic office or subsidiary of such foreign nonbanking company on terms more favorable than those which it affords to similar unrelated borrowers in the United States.

Under the 2(h) exemption, the investments of a foreign holding company and its affiliates in a foreign nonbanking company are exempt from the BHC Act's restrictions on investments in nonbanking companies, regardless of whether or not the nonbanking companies are "subsidiaries," provided, however, that the foreign holding company and its affiliates are "principally engaged in the banking business outside the United States" and the nonbanking companies in which they have invested are "principally engaged in business outside the United States." To qualify for the 2(h) exemption:

(1) The United States activities must be conducted by a foreign company (company Y, in the case of our earlier example) or by a company (the "U.S. Company") owned or controlled by the foreign company (e.g., a subsidiary of company Y) engaged in the same line of business as the foreign company;

(2) The foreign company and the U.S. Company, if applicable, must be principally engaged in business outside the United States; and

(3) The foreign bank and those controlling it must be principally engaged in the banking business outside the United States.

. . .

## D. GAIL, J. NORTON, AND M. O'NEAL, "THE FOREIGN BANK SUPERVISION ACT OF 1991: 'EXPANDING THE UMBRELLA OF SUPERVISORY REGULATION'"

26 International Lawyer 993 (1992).

As 1992 began, the most immediate evidence of Congress's response to the global scandal involving the notorious Bank of Credit and Commerce International (BCCI) and the questionable activities of the Italian Banca Nazionale de Lavorro (BNL) in the United States, other than to schedule still another round of investigatory hearings, were the provisions of the often mischaracterized banking "reform" bill of 1991 (Act) that have greatly heightened U.S. Government scrutiny of and power over foreign banks. Title II of the Act contains the Foreign Bank Supervision Enhancement Act of 1991 (FBSEA), designed to strengthen federal supervision, regulation, and examination of foreign bank operations in the United States. In sum, the new provisions of the FBSEA:

(1) Mandate federal deposit insurance for all deposits under $100,000.

(2) Require foreign banks to obtain the approval of the Board of Governors of the Federal Reserve System (Fed) before opening any branch, agency, or representative office; and permit the Fed to examine and close all such facilities.

(3) Require foreign banks to report loans secured by 25 percent or more of the stock of an insured depository institution.

(4) Impose a criminal penalty for violations of the International Banking Act of 1978 (IBA).

(5) Require U.S. regulators to carry out studies on the capital adequacy and desirability of requiring foreign banks to operate in the United States through subsidiaries rather than branches.

(6) Allow the Fed and Office of the Comptroller of the Currency (OCC) to share information with home country regulators.

(7) Increase civil penalties for filing false and misleading reports.

. . .

### II. The Act

#### A. Deposit Insurance

One of the main regulatory gaps of an overseas bank's regulation (for example, the Bank of England's regulation of BCCI in the United Kingdom) is often the absence of deposit insurance. FBSEA attempts to address this governmental concern of U.S. bank regulators by establishing two conditions to the ability of a foreign bank to accept or maintain deposit accounts having balances of less than $100,000: first, the foreign bank must establish one or more banking subsidiaries in the United States for that purpose; and second, the foreign bank must obtain federal deposit insurance for any such subsidiary in accordance with the

Federal Deposit Insurance Act (FDIA). (An exception to the foregoing requirement is provided for insured branches existing on the date of enactment.) This section of FBSEA was supposed to apply only to retail deposits, as evidenced by the title of the statutory subsection.

. . .

## B. Foreign Bank Offices

### 1. *Establishment of Foreign Bank Offices in the United States*

FBSEA prohibits a foreign bank from establishing a branch or an agency or acquiring ownership or control of a commercial lending company without the prior approval of the Fed, regardless of whether the branch or agency is chartered under state or federal law. This means that a foreign bank may no longer avoid U.S. Government scrutiny by obtaining a state charter for its branch or agency, which is what most foreign banks had done under prior law.

The Fed must not approve a foreign branch, agency, or acquisition of a lending company unless the foreign bank conducts business outside the United States and is "subject to comprehensive supervision and regulation on a consolidated basis" by its home country authorities and the foreign bank furnishes the Fed with information necessary to assess the application. This requirement applies as well to new branches sought to be established by foreign banks operating state-chartered branches as of the date of enactment of FBSEA.

In effect, the Fed is generally trying to upgrade the quality and transparency of international banking supervision and is specifically retaining its own regulatory trigger in the event overseas home country supervision or the information available on a particular foreign bank is deemed inadequate in the view of the Fed. For a number of years the Fed has been supportive of the principles of "consolidated bank supervision" and "home country" supervisory control as employed in the 1983 Revised Concordat on Consolidated Bank Supervision as promulgated by the Basle Committee on Banking Supervision (Basle Committee). However, the BCCI and BNL affairs have made clear that significant gaps in the Concordat's consolidated supervision principles (in terms of conceptual embrace and of practical application) still exist, and the host country regulators need to maintain authority to evaluate the quality (for example, adequate prudential standards such as on capital adequacy, risk asset exposure, and internal audit controls) and effectiveness of the home country's application of consolidated supervisory practices. The host country regulators also need to be aware of the nature and reliability of the information available on the foreign bank and its parent and affiliates before it defers to the supervisory and regulatory authority of the home country. As such, the consolidated supervision and home country principles become conditional, and FBSEA sets a predicate for encouraging close cooperation between the Fed and relevant home country regulators.

FBSEA amends the Bank Holding Company Act of 1956 (BHCA) to designate "managerial resources"—the competence, experience, and integrity of officers, directors, and shareholders—and "financial resources" of the foreign bank as statutory and regulatory factors that the Fed may consider in determining whether to approve an application of a foreign bank or its parent in connection with the establishment of new branches or agencies or the acquisition of control of a commercial lending company. As in most bank failures (including BCCI), the quality and integrity of bank management and bank financial resources are often significant contributing causes. Essentially FBSEA incorporates the existing domestic approval standards under the Fed's Regulation Y.

FBSEA also establishes certain other discretionary, statutory standards that the Fed may take into account in assessing an application. These include the consent of the home country supervisor, the nature of the cooperative relationship of the Fed with this home country regulatory as to sharing of material information, various assurances of the foreign bank, compliance with U.S. laws, needs of the community, and relative size of the bank in its home country. In addition, the Fed may impose such conditions on its approval as it deems necessary (for example, cessation of or restriction on certain activities).

### 2. *Termination*

FBSEA places the ultimate regulatory sanction of an institutional "death sentence" (termination) in the hands of the Fed. The Fed may, after notice and opportunity for a hearing, order a foreign bank operating a state branch, or agency, or commercial lending company to terminate operations. In order to do so, the foreign bank must not be subject to "comprehensive supervision or regulation on a consolidated basis" by its home country authorities. In addition, there must be reason to believe that the foreign bank has violated the law or engaged in "unsafe or unsound banking practice," and thus, continued operation in the United States would not be consistent with public interest or purposes of the IBA, the Bank Holding Company Act of 1956, or the FDICA. The Fed may also recommend to the OCC that the license of any federal branch or federal agency be terminated if the Fed has reason to believe that such foreign bank or any affiliate has engaged in conduct for which the activities of any state branch or agency may be terminated as set forth above.

The Fed has the authority to issue a termination order without a hearing if it determines that expeditious action is necessary in order to protect the public interest. Unless the Fed extends the period, an order becomes effective within a 120-day period beginning on the date the order is issued. Foreign banks ordered to terminate activities in the United States must follow federal and state law regarding closure or dissolution of such offices. Should any office or subsidiary refuse to comply with a termination order, the Fed or the OCC is authorized to invoke the aid of the U.S. district court within the jurisdiction where an office or subsidiary of a foreign bank is located to obtain a judicial mandate requiring compliance with the order.

Within thirty days after an order is issued, a foreign bank can obtain review of a termination order in the United States court of appeals for any circuit in which the bank branch is located or in the United States Court of Appeals for the District of Columbia Circuit. According to the Act, the Fed and the Secretary of the Treasury are responsible for developing criteria to evaluate operations in the United States of foreign banks not subject to "comprehensive supervision or regulation on a consolidated basis."

### 3. *Limitations on Powers of State Branches and Agencies*

As a prime subject area of prudential concern is with the risks inherent in broad bank powers, FBSEA effectively eliminates current competitive advantages that may have inured to state branches and agencies in the power area. New limitations on the activities of foreign state branches and agencies have been imposed. For example, after December 19, 1993, a foreign bank branch may not conduct business that a federal branch is prohibited from conducting unless the activity is within "sound banking practice" and if the foreign bank branch is insured, and the activity does not pose "significant risk" to the FDIC fund.

In addition, for prudential supervisory objectives, state branches and agencies are subject to the same limitations, with respect to loans made to a single borrower, as are applicable to federal branches and federal agencies under the IBA. The limitations that are applicable to federal branches and agencies of foreign banks under the IBA are the national bank lending limits.

The Fed or appropriate state supervisory authority may impose more stringent restrictions on state branches and agencies of foreign banks.

## C. Conduct and Coordination of Examinations

Under prior law (section 7(c) of the original IBA provisions), the Fed had examination powers over foreign bank operations. These powers, however, were viewed largely as ancillary or residual to those of the OCC, the FDIC, or the appropriate state banking authorities. Under FBSEA, the examination authorities of the Fed become (without preempting the examination authority of the other federal and state regulators) central to the statutorily prescribed examination web. Specifically, the Fed is authorized to examine each branch or agency of a foreign bank, each commercial lending company or bank controlled by one or more foreign banks or one or more foreign companies that control a foreign bank, and any other office or affiliate of a foreign bank conducting business in any state. Each branch or agency of a foreign bank must be subject to an on-site examination at least once during each twelve-month period (beginning on the date the most recent examination of such branch or agency ended). The Fed, the OCC, and the FDIC are required to coordinate their examinations with each other and with appropriate state bank supervisors, to the extent such coordination is possible. They should also participate in simultaneous examinations of each office of a foreign bank and each affiliate of such bank operating in the United States when requested to do so.

D. Approval and Supervision of Representative Offices

As with branches and agencies, foreign banks may not establish representative offices without the prior approval of the Fed. The Fed is required to take into account the same standards governing the approval of branches and agencies. And the Fed may impose any additional requirements that it determines are necessary to carry out the purposes of the Act.

The Fed may order the termination of the activities of a representative office on the basis of the same standards, procedures, and requirements applicable to the termination of branches and agencies. The Fed is also authorized to examine each representative office of a foreign bank, the cost of which is assessed against and paid by the foreign bank.

. . .

## H. SCOTT, "SUPERVISION OF INTERNATIONAL BANKING POST–BCCI"

8 Georgia St.Univ.L.Rev. 487 (1992).

. . .

There are three key policy objectives of host countries which affect their supervision of foreign banks: (1) maintaining safety and soundness, (2) avoiding systemic risk, and (3) protecting depositors. I will examine how each of these policies applies when a foreign bank operates in a host country through branches or subsidiaries. Problems of supervision differ depending on which of these two forms one is considering. Of course, branches and subsidiaries are not the only forms in which banks operate abroad. They can also operate purely cross-border without a corporate presence in a host country, as when a bank in London solicits U.S. residents to place funds with the London bank. Banks may also operate abroad through agencies and representative offices. But branches and subsidiaries are the most important forms of operation, and I will concentrate on them.

### I. Safety and Soundness

Host countries generally have less concern with maintaining the safety and soundness of foreign banks operating through subsidiaries than they do in the case of branches.

### A. Subsidiaries

When a foreign bank operates through a subsidiary, the subsidiary is fully subject to the safety and soundness regime of the host country. The host country can ensure the safety and soundness of the foreign subsidiary through the same techniques it applies to domestic banks, such as capital requirements, examinations or audits, and loan limits. The host country will not necessarily be concerned with the safety and soundness of the foreign parent of the host-country subsidiary. The bankruptcy of the parent may result in a transfer of the ownership of the subsidiary, but it will not necessarily affect the safety and soundness of the subsidiary. The subsidiary can continue to operate even though its parent is bankrupt. We have seen this in the Bank of Credit and Commerce International (BCCI) case where alleged subsidiary U.S. banks, like the First American banks, have continued to operate even though the BCCI bank owners are in insolvency proceedings.

But some countries, most notably the United States, are concerned with the safety and soundness of the foreign parents of host-country subsidiaries. This concern is based on the source of strength doctrine. Under this doctrine, the host country looks to the foreign parent to supply capital to the subsidiary if the subsidiary becomes weak. The basic idea is that the strength of the parent determines whether it will be able to save its subsidiary from difficulty by injecting additional capital. In addition, the host country may be concerned that a weak foreign parent may try to loot a local subsidiary through nonmarket value affiliate transactions, for example, purchasing its assets at below market prices.[2]

The safety and soundness of the foreign parent is not, however, within the regulatory control of the host country. For example, the safety and soundness of a U.K. banking parent of a U.S. bank is largely determined by the United Kingdom, not the United States. The United Kingdom determines the capital requirements, auditing and examination standards, and loan limits of its banks. And if one of its banks gets into trouble, the United Kingdom determines whether and how to rescue it. However, if the foreign parent is not a bank, it may be entirely unregulated by the home country.

A key element with respect to safety and soundness is capital. Here we have some international standards. The Group of Ten (G-10) central banks that belong to the Bank for International Settlements in Basle, Switzerland (actually central banks from twelve countries),[3] reached an Accord on capital standards in 1988. Other non-G-10

2. The Hong Kong subsidiary of BCCI was closed on July 8, 1991, shortly after its parent holding company, BCCI Holdings (Luxembourg) SA, was declared insolvent. The Hong Kong subsidiary's insolvency had been largely caused by the discovery of over $268 million in unrecorded liabilities, some of which were due to other failed BCCI entities. A subsidiary may also be imperiled by loans made to failed affiliates.

3. Specifically, Belgium, Canada, France, Germany, Italy, Japan, Luxembourg, the Netherlands, Sweden, Switzerland, the United Kingdom, and the United States.

countries subsequently declared their adherence to the Basle Accord. If the home country of a foreign bank parent subscribes to the Accord, the host country may have some comfort that the parent is safe and sound, but would not have complete assurance.

The Basle Accord deals only with credit risk, making capital adequacy turn on the riskiness of a bank's assets and off balance sheet liabilities; it does not deal with interest rate risk. The standards must be enforced by the home country, and the G–10 and additional subscribers differ in their enforcement capabilities. If assets are worth substantially less than a bank carries them on its books, the bank may have adequate book capital, as prescribed by Basle, but not real capital, which is simply the difference between the real value of assets and liabilities. It is up to the home country to make sure that assets are correctly valued and that loan loss reserves are sufficient. Finally, the Accord only applies to banks, and thus generally cannot protect host countries whose banks are owned by nonbank holding companies rather than banks.

. . .

*B. Branches*

When a foreign bank operates abroad through a branch, the host country is more at the mercy of the home country. The branch is but an office of a bank located in another country. If the foreign bank fails, so do its branches abroad. The viability of the branches is largely determined by the efficacy of supervision by the bank's home country. Host countries again may get some comfort from the fact that the bank's home country subscribes to the Basle Accord, but here the weaknesses of the Basle approach are more serious since the failure of the foreign bank leads directly to the failure of its branches, rather than just depriving the host country of a source of strength as is the case with subsidiaries.

It may be tempting to conclude that host countries would be better off if they forced foreign banks to operate in their countries through subsidiaries rather than branches, but this would be incorrect, principally for two reasons. First, many host countries would prefer that local deposits be backed by the entire capital of the bank, which is the case with branch deposits, rather than the capital of the local subsidiary, the case with subsidiary deposits. Although the host country may have less control over the capital adequacy of the entire bank than it does over the subsidiary, the amount of capital is likely to be much larger. Also, many host countries, particularly smaller or less developed ones, may prefer to rely on home-country supervision rather than their own. Second, and quite important, branches of foreign banks are more competitive than their subsidiaries in host-country markets. This is largely because the loan capacity of the branch in the host country is a function of the bank's worldwide capital; that capacity would be much less if it were a function of the capital of a host-country subsidiary.

. . .

Nonetheless, the United States is moving in the direction of limiting the ability of foreign banks to operate through branches. Section 214 of the Federal Deposit Insurance Corporation (FDIC) Improvement Act of 1991 requires that in the future foreign banks that "accept or maintain" deposits of less than $100,000 (so-called retail deposits) do so through insured subsidiaries rather than through insured branches.

. . .

*C. Determination of the "Home" Country*

Let me turn to another key supervisory issue: How to determine the "home" country of a foreign bank. Since the adequacy of home-country supervision may be an issue for a host country with respect to subsidiaries, and is clearly an issue in the case of branches, identifying the home country for this purpose is essential. This can be done without much difficulty if two conditions hold: (1) there is one foreign bank parent located in one foreign country, and (2) the principal operations of the bank are carried on in that same country. For example, Deutsche Bank, the ultimate parent of all Deutsche Bank foreign subsidiaries, is located in Germany, and the principal operations of Deutsche Bank, as measured by total assets, are in Germany as well. Neither of these conditions was met, however, in the case of BCCI, with somewhat disastrous results.

BCCI was organized as follows. BCCI Holdings, a Luxembourg holding company, was at the top of the corporate pyramid. This entity, in turn, owned two principal banks, BCCI S.A., incorporated in Luxembourg, and BCCI Overseas, incorporated in the Cayman Islands. These banks had subsidiaries and branches in various countries; for example, the Luxembourg bank had over twenty branches in the United Kingdom and a subsidiary in Canada. There were two foreign bank parents rather than one, and neither bank's principal operations were in the country of incorporation, namely Luxembourg or the Cayman Islands.

Why did this cause problems? The fact that there were two foreign bank parents meant that two countries rather than one were responsible for the safety and soundness of the banking organization as a whole; thus, there was no overall consolidated supervision of the banking organization. In principle, this problem might have been cured if Luxembourg had authority to regulate the entire operations of the bank holding company, BCCI Holdings, but this was not the case. The problem might also have been cured if there had been an international agreement that there could only be one ultimate bank parent, that is, that one of the banks had to become a subsidiary of the other, but this was also not the case.

Where two home countries are responsible, neither country is in the position to determine the safety and soundness of the entire operation, and matters can easily fall between the cracks. Where multiple regulators are responsible for the safety and soundness of a bank, no one is really accountable. Further, since the principal operations of the banking organization were in neither country, the supervisors in these countries had a limited ability to make judgments about the safety and soundness of their two banks. Perhaps in such cases the home country should be the country of principal operations, which would probably be the United Kingdom in the case of BCCI. The problem was further compounded by the fact that supervision in the Caymans, and to a lesser extent in Luxembourg, was rather weak.

. . .

*E. Unilateral Measures in the United States*

In the absence of international agreements, host countries will have to protect themselves unilaterally by insisting that foreign banks operating in their countries conform to certain host-country standards. Along these lines, sections 201 to 209 of the FDIC Improvement Act of 1991 strengthened the powers of the Federal Reserve Board to supervise, regulate, and examine foreign bank operations in the United States.

. . .

These unilateral measures may be justified given the risks to host countries signalled by the BCCI affair. Unilateral measures in the name of safety and soundness, however, can easily be used as a subterfuge for protectionism; they have been used by countries to protect domestic banks from increased competition. Various entry limits imposed by foreign countries have been, in fact, a major concern of the United States. One advantage of formulating international standards for safety and soundness would be to limit the protectionist potential that arises from unilateral measures.

## II. SYSTEMIC RISK

The host country needs to protect itself against systemic risk, the risk that the failure of one bank will lead to the failure of other banks. The concern with systemic risk only arises, of course, when one bank fails. But this can occur even with the best supervisory control system. A chain reaction of bank failures can occur through three principal means.

*A. The Chain Reaction Problem*

First, a chain reaction can result from the linkage of interbank deposits. This was a major concern when Continental Illinois Bank almost failed in the mid–1980s. Continental held sizable deposits of other banks; in many cases the amount of the deposits substantially exceeded the capital of the depositor banks. These banks generally held such sizable deposits because they cleared payments, for example, checks or wire transfers, through Continental. If Continental had failed, those banks would have failed as well. Section 308 of the FDIC Improvement Act of 1991 gives the Federal Reserve Board new powers to deal with this problem. It permits the Board to limit the credit extended by an insured depository institution to another depository institution. This may be feasible with respect to placements by one bank with another since the amount of credit extended is fixed for a given term. It will be more difficult with respect to interbank clearing accounts where the amount of credit extended is a function of payments traffic. For example, Bank *A* may be credited by its correspondent Bank *B* for an incoming wire transfer of $10 million. Bank *A* is thus a creditor of Bank *B* for this amount. If Bank *B* were to fail, Bank *A* is seriously exposed. It will be quite difficult, without serious changes in the payment system (for example, forcing banks to make and receive all payments through Federal Reserve rather than correspondent accounts), to limit these types of exposures.

Second, a chain reaction of bank failures can occur through payment system linkage. If one bank fails to settle its position in a net settlement system for large value payments, for example, the Clearing House Interbank Payments System (CHIPS) in the United States, other banks which do not get paid may in turn fail. This risk has been substantially limited by CHIPS credit limits, loss-sharing, and collateral requirements, but could still materialize if two large banks, at the maximum of their permissible net debit positions, were to fail.

Finally, a chain reaction of bank failures can occur through imitative runs. When one bank fails, depositors in other banks, particularly those that are uninsured, may assume that their banks may also fail and so withdraw their funds, exposing these banks to a liquidity crisis and ultimately to failure.

### *B. Subsidiaries*

When a foreign bank operates in a host country through a subsidiary, the host country can protect itself against systemic risk by subjecting the subsidiary to the same rules as other domestic banks. For example, the host country can control the level of deposits the subsidiary takes from other banks or limit the positions it incurs in net settlement payment systems in the same way as it does for domestic banks. Imitative runs could be a major concern to a host country since the failure of any domestic bank, even one that is foreign owned, could cause imitative runs on other domestic banks. For example, there were reportedly imitative runs on other foreign banks in Hong Kong when BCCI's subsidiary in that country was closed. It is much less likely that the failure of the foreign parent will cause a run on host-country banks. While there is some evidence that there was a deposit loss at First American after the failure of BCCI, it is unclear whether this was caused by the BCCI failure or a growing problem with bad loans. In any event, there were no runs on First American or other non-BCCI domestic banks.

If the failure of a foreign-owned bank would likely cause a chain reaction of bank failures, the host country could use its lender-of-last-resort power to keep the bank afloat. The host-country central bank would be lending to a domestic bank in its own currency—the fact of foreign ownership should not be a major obstacle to central bank support.

*C. Branches*

When a foreign bank operates in a host country through a branch, it is more difficult for the host country to deal with the systemic risk problem, particularly as it may manifest itself in the payment system. Branches of foreign banks may be less able than domestic banks to fund settlement obligations quickly in host-country money markets, and their home-country markets could be closed. On the other hand, linkage of interbank deposits should not be a significant problem since domestic banks generally will not clear local currency payments through branches of foreign banks. In addition, imitative runs on domestic banks are less likely to be caused by the failure of a foreign bank; depositors in domestic banks are unlikely to believe their own banks are in trouble just because a foreign bank has failed. The major concern is the payment system.

Unlike the case of the failure of a foreign-owned subsidiary, the failure of the foreign bank itself, along with its host-country branch offices, raises significant lender-of-last-resort issues for the United States. The foreign bank may have to be kept afloat by its own central bank through loans in the home-country currency. But the United States will have no assurance that the home-country central bank will do so. While the Federal Reserve could, in principle, itself extend credit in dollars to the foreign bank, it will be reluctant to do so. Such lending might expose it, and ultimately U.S. taxpayers, to losses. This will be hard to justify when support could have come instead from the home-country central bank.

The host country is likely to take measures to avoid becoming a lender-of-last-resort to a foreign bank. First, it may limit the participation of branches of foreign banks in host-country payment systems. The Banque de France, for example, does not allow foreign banks to participate directly in Sagittaire, its net settlement system for clearing international funds transfers. And it is perhaps not an accident that no foreign banks are settlement participants in the CHIPS system in the United States. Second, the host country may specially limit the settlement positions of branches of foreign banks in their payment systems or require that these positions be fully collateralized.

———

*E. The BCCI Experience*

It appears that the BCCI banks in Luxembourg and the Caymans and their branches, subsidiaries, and agencies (including the U.S. agencies) cleared a significant amount of their dollar payments through Bank of America, but there is no indication that this resulted in any settlement problems for Bank of America or other CHIPS participants. Perhaps this is partly explained by the fact that the Federal Reserve had advance information of the timing of the closure of the BCCI banks. This information was apparently used to help insure that Bank of America and other U.S. banks were not left exposed when the BCCI banks were closed. For example, Bank of America could have managed BCCI payments in a manner that would assure that payments out never exceeded payments in by an amount greater than the collected balances of the BCCI banks. A system for insuring advance warning might be an important way of controlling systemic risk.

The BCCI case has also served to focus renewed attention on another feature of payment system risk, well known since the 1974 Herstatt failure, relating to the settlement of foreign exchange contracts. Since the two legs of currency trades are settled in the payment systems of two different countries, which may operate in different time zones, one party may pay out on one side of the contract before receiving a reciprocal payment in another currency from its counterparty. If the counterparty fails before making the reciprocal payment, the first party has a loss. In fact, it appears that the Industrial Bank of Japan paid out $30 million in Yen to BCCI in Japan before it could receive the reciprocal dollar payment in New York, due to the intervening closure of BCCI on July 5, 1991.

There has been an international initiative to deal with some aspects of payment system risk. The Bank for International Settlements through its Committee on Interbank Netting Schemes has recently set out minimum standards for the design and operation of netting schemes as well as principles for cooperative central bank oversight of such schemes. The major purpose of this effort is to minimize the possibility of settlement failures and thereby to limit systemic risk.

## III. Depositor Protection

One of the principal concerns of a host country is the protection of depositors against losses in the case of bank failure. I will examine this concern as it applies to branches and agencies of foreign banks and then briefly deal with the much simpler case of subsidiaries.

### A. *Branches and Agencies*

Depositors, rightly or wrongly, have come to expect protection, and the failure to honor this expectation carries substantial political risk for incumbent politicians. In my view, depositors are unlikely to differentiate between losing funds in domestic branches of foreign banks and losing funds in domestic banks and will seek to hold politicians responsible in both cases. This political concern mainly involves domestic rather than foreign depositors, although some foreign depositors may be citizens of the host country, for example, a U.S. citizen living abroad, or may have an affiliation with residents in the host country, for example, a foreign subsidiary of a U.S. corporation.

Some countries protect depositors in branches of foreign banks through providing deposit insurance. As previously discussed, until the passage of the FDIC Improvement Act of 1991, the United States required "retail" branches of foreign banks, those taking deposits under $100,000, to be insured; now, such branches are prospectively prohibited. Some other major industrialized countries such as Germany and the United Kingdom insure deposits in branches of foreign banks, while others such as Japan do not. The provision of deposit insurance to depositors in branches of foreign banks creates a major problem for the host-country insurer since its insurance exposure is dependent on the efficacy of home-country regulation and on supervision of the bank. But even if the host country does not insure deposits in branches of foreign banks, it will still be concerned with the potential losses to uninsured branch depositors—particularly domestic depositors—that might arise from the failure of a foreign bank.

One way for the host country to limit insurance fund or depositor losses is to require branches of foreign banks to pledge readily marketable assets and to maintain the value of assets at a certain level in excess of liabilities, a "quasi-capital" requirement. These requirements would help to insure that if the foreign bank failed, sufficient branch assets would be available to the host-country authorities to cover losses. Federally-licensed and many state-licensed branches of foreign banks are subject to such requirements in the United States.

This approach is based on an important but questionable assumption—that the host-country authorities have or should have the legal power to seize branch assets and to control their disposition in the event of the failure of the foreign bank. If the home-country receiver asserts a claim to the assets of the entire bank, including the assets of foreign branches, the host country may not be able to dispose of the assets of the branch, at least not without causing conflict with the home-country receiver. This kind of problem has arisen in the BCCI litigation in the United States and abroad.

While BCCI did not have branches in the United States, the Luxembourg bank operated uninsured state-licensed agencies in New York and Los Angeles at the time of its failure in July 1991. Agencies, like branches, make loans and other investments and are offices of a bank. Both New York and California agencies can take deposits from foreign individuals and companies, and maintain credit balances for any borrower, that is, credit a borrower's account with loan proceeds. In addition, New York agencies can take domestic corporate deposits of $100,000 or greater. While agencies in both states are legally prohibited from taking deposits from individual U.S. citizens or residents, it appears the BCCI agencies did so anyway.

When BCCI failed, its U.S. agencies failed with it. The U.S. assets of the failed BCCI banks, estimated at $550 million, consisted only in minor part of the agencies' assets. Far more important were their alleged stockholdings in several U.S. banks, including First American, and clearing accounts at the Bank of America and some other banks. Claims against U.S. assets included somewhat less than $20 million owed by the agencies to third parties (non-BCCI entities), as well as a $200 million fine which the Federal Reserve Board sought to levy against BCCI for illegally acquiring certain U.S. banks. There was also the prospect of additional fines as a result of criminal prosecutions by federal and state authorities.

In a bankruptcy proceeding in the U.S. District Court, Southern District of New York, which was dealing with BCCI's United States assets, the liquidators of the Luxembourg holding company and the two subsidiary banks obtained, on August 2, 1991, a temporary restraining order (TRO) against any claims to BCCI's U.S. assets, including the assets of the agencies. The TRO was based on section 304 of the U.S. Bankruptcy Code that permits a court to enjoin the pursuit of claims against the U.S. assets of a bankrupt entity on the theory that the claims should be brought as part of a foreign proceeding, in this case, the insolvency proceedings in Luxembourg and the Cayman Islands.

On October 15, 1991, the foreign liquidators agreed to a consent order entered by the bankruptcy court that permitted the California and New York state regulators of the BCCI agencies to remove the agency assets from the bankruptcy court and to take control of them pursuant to ongoing state liquidation proceedings. The consent order further provided that the foreign liquidators would assert no claims to the agency assets in the state proceedings and that any surplus remaining after the liquidation of the assets and satisfaction of estimated claims on the agencies would be remitted to the bankruptcy court.

The consent order also dealt with another group of BCCI assets, deposits in BankAmerica International (BAI), Bank of America's New York Edge Act subsidiary, that served as a clearing bank for the two BCCI banks. BAI had interpleaded these assets, and they had become subject to the jurisdiction of the bankruptcy court. Under the terms of the consent order, the Luxembourg bank's deposits in BAI (SA accounts) were removed from the bankruptcy court's jurisdiction. The foreign liquidators further agreed not to assert claims to the SA accounts unless they failed to become subject to the New York state liquidation proceeding. Other BCCI assets, such as the alleged stock interests in various United States banks, remained subject to the jurisdiction of the bankruptcy court and to the operation of the section 304 TRO.

On December 19, 1991, the BCCI liquidators agreed to plead guilty to various federal and state criminal charges brought against the BCCI banks. These charges included a federal indictment alleging that BCCI secretly acquired control over several U.S. banks. Under the settlement, $275 million in U.S. assets will be used to pay off U.S. creditors of the agencies, to pay part of the outstanding fines, and to increase the capital of U.S. banks illegally owned by BCCI. The $275 million balance of the $550 million in U.S. assets will be turned over to the consolidated bankruptcy proceedings in Luxembourg and the Caymans. On January 23, 1992, the U.S. District Court, Southern District of New York, which had jurisdiction over the bankruptcy proceedings, refused to upset the settlement on the grounds that it could not interfere with the federal prosecution, and on January 24, 1992, the settlement was approved by the U.S. District Court for the District of Columbia over the objections of various creditors.

The net effect of the United States proceedings, pending further appeals, was that $275 million in U.S. assets was not consolidated with the worldwide receivership assets of the BCCI banks in the Luxembourg and Caymans proceedings and thus was not available to creditors of those banks. Also, it appears that the U.S. creditors of the BCCI agencies will receive full payment of their claims.

Certain conclusions can be drawn about these proceedings. As a threshold matter, it is unclear whether assets of agencies or branches of foreign banks are at all subject to the jurisdiction of the U.S. bankruptcy court; assets of failed banks clearly are not. This uncertainty might partly account for the willingness of the BCCI liquidators to have agreed to the bankruptcy consent order of October 15, 1991. In addition, it appears that U.S. assets of failed foreign banks can be cut off from claims by foreign liquidators through the use of host-country criminal prosecutions.

If U.S. or other country assets of failed foreign banks are not fully consolidated in home-country foreign insolvency proceedings—what is called the "ring fence" approach—and such assets are substantial, the ability of a foreign receiver to reorganize a failed bank will be severely limited. While this was not a practical alternative in the BCCI case—earlier efforts to reorganize the bank with an infusion of capital from Abu Dhabi foundered—it could be a problem in future bankruptcies of multinational banks. Indeed, the possible need to reorganize a failed company is a significant rationale for the U.S. Bankruptcy Code's section 304 proceeding. In fact, it was this concern that was behind the decision of U.S. authorities to assert jurisdiction over the London branch assets of Franklin National Bank when that bank was in danger of failing in 1974. The fact that the U.S. authorities had control over all of Franklin's assets was an important factor in their ability to sell the troubled bank to European American Bank.

The failure to consolidate may also result in the inability of non-U.S. creditors to obtain the same pro rata share of all of the bank's assets that they would have obtained if the assets were consolidated. While the creditors of BCCI's U.S. agencies will be fully paid off, creditors in the foreign insolvency proceedings are expected to recover only thirty to forty percent of their claims. This is a somewhat arbitrary result.

Apart from the difficulties of preferring some creditors of a bank at the expense of others, the assets of an agency or branch of a foreign bank may have little to do with their actual business activities. It appears that the BCCI banks shifted assets among branches to avoid detection of insolvency. The difficulty of sorting out assets between various offices of a bank illustrates the need for a consolidated bankruptcy proceeding. A further complication arises insofar as the host country asserts jurisdiction over assets of a failed foreign bank that are within its jurisdiction but are not assets of the entities, an agency or branch, operating in its country. For example, part of the U.S. assets of the BCCI banks reportedly consisted of $85 million of deposits of the Tokyo branch of BCCI Luxembourg. There is no clear rationale for using these assets to satisfy claims of U.S. creditors of U.S. agencies or to make capital infusions into U.S. banks allegedly owned by BCCI, rather than using them to satisfy the claims of Japanese creditors against the Tokyo branch or the claims of worldwide creditors against the Luxembourg bank.

The strongest argument for the host country preserving the assets of a branch or agency of a failed foreign bank for local creditors is that the host country is at risk for the supervisory failures of the home country. This rationale is much stronger when the host country insures local depositors than when it merely seeks to protect their interests as in the case of the U.S. agencies of BCCI. The insurance commitment represents a potential exposure for the taxpayers of the host country. In my view, the claims of uninsured depositors should be fully consolidated with other claims to the worldwide assets of a failed bank. In addition, I do not believe that local assets should be subject to a ring fence just because the host country brings criminal actions against a failed bank. This creates a loophole to consolidation that can be easily exploited by a host country. Moreover, if criminal prosecution is the key to jurisdiction over assets, what if there are prosecutions in several countries? If the Japanese had criminally prosecuted BCCI, why should the United States rather than Japan use all of the U.S. assets (particularly those of the Tokyo branch) to satisfy the criminal fines?

One might consider another approach to the deposit insurance problem: deposits in a branch of a foreign bank could be covered under the deposit protection scheme of its home country and the home country could be given jurisdiction over the worldwide assets of any failed bank. This would have the advantage of having the insuring country bear the risk for its own supervisory shortcomings and preserve the unity of the bankruptcy of the bank. But this approach raises problems of its own.

First and foremost, there is the issue of consumer confusion. Imagine a potential depositor winding his way through Wall Street, or perhaps even Atlanta, past the offices of various banks, including those of branches of foreign banks. A deposit in each domestic bank would be insured similarly under the United States deposit insurance scheme, but a deposit at each of the branches of foreign banks would be insured differently, according to the various schemes in place in the home countries of these banks. Even with full disclosure of the terms of such insurance, as to level of coverage, the degree of risk sharing by depositors, the types of deposits covered, and the speed and convenience of payouts, the consumer may be left with substantial confusion.[14] These

**14.** It could be argued that the rational consumer would also want information about how the deposit insurance "system" works in practice. For example, does the foreign country ever liquidate failed banks, or does it routinely bail them out through capital infusions or central bank loans? But these issues are equally important where deposits in branches of foreign banks are insured by the host country. Deposits

are sophisticated and complicated matters. In theory, this issue might be addressed by some harmonization of deposit insurance schemes through an international agreement, but this is not realistically achievable, in my judgment, in the foreseeable future.

Secondly, there is the ultimate question of whether the home-country insurance fund obligation will actually be honored—this issue has not been free from doubt even in the United States. It would certainly be a major concern for host countries where the bank's home country had a history of economic difficulty.

### B. *The Need for International Solutions*

An international agreement is seriously needed in this area. At the outset, there should be agreement as to what to do when the local entity of the failed foreign bank is not insured. In my view, there is a strong case for home-country bankruptcy jurisdiction for all uninsured claims, including those of government authorities. Also, agreement is needed as to whether host countries should have any claim to jurisdiction over assets other than those of the local entity of the failed bank, for example, clearing accounts of the foreign bank. Again, in my judgment, these assets should be part of the home-country bankruptcy proceeding.

While host countries may be able to ring fence all local assets through brute force, this may be done at the expense of engendering conflict with home-country receivers, as well as foreign creditors, which in some cases may be government authorities. Further, host countries that prefer a ring fence in a case where they are in surplus—host-country assets exceed local claims (the U.S. with respect to BCCI)—may prefer consolidation when they are in deficit. In the context of an international agreement, countries could define their general and long-term interests rather than responding to the exigencies of a particular case.

There are two principal approaches to the deposit insurance issue: (1) host-country deposit insurance and host-country bankruptcy jurisdiction over the assets of insured branches or other insured entities of failed foreign banks, and (2) home-country deposit insurance and home-country bankruptcy jurisdiction over the worldwide assets of failed foreign banks. While each approach has its own problems, I think the former is probably more realistic. However, this choice should be settled by international agreement.

The United States has chosen a third path: not permitting insured retail branches of foreign banks. I think this is ill-advised for the reasons previously stated. It deprives depositors and their insurers of the backing of the worldwide capital of strong foreign banks. These creditors can now only look to the capital of U.S. subsidiaries. Also, this approach limits the competitiveness of foreign banks in U.S. markets. Foreign banks with retail deposit funding will have less lending capacity

in excess of host-country insured amounts may be protected to a greater or lesser degree depending on the bailout policies of the home country.

since they are forced to lend off the capital of subsidiaries rather than worldwide capital. This is not in the interest of potential U.S. borrowers.

*C. Subsidiaries*

Subsidiaries raise no major problems with respect to depositor protection. Subsidiaries are supervised and insured by the host country, and the host country has jurisdiction over the bankruptcy of its own domestic banks whether or not they are owned by foreign banks. As in the BCCI case, various claims may be asserted against the failed bank's interest in its foreign subsidiaries. For example, there are claims against BCCI's interests in various United States banks allegedly owned by BCCI, but these claims only concern ownership of the banks, not their supervision or solvency.

. . .

## *Notes and Questions*

*Subsidiaries*

1. It is useful to distinguish between subsidiaries and branches in considering the issues involved with regulating foreign banks in the United States. Let's start with subsidiaries. The above section on the basic features of the U.S. regulatory system identifies six areas. Which of these do not cause problems in dealing with subsidiaries of foreign banks?

2. What did BCCI teach us about the problems of insuring the safety and soundness of foreign bank owners of U.S. banks? How does effective consolidated supervision, as now required under IBA, work? See § 211.24(c) of Regulation K. Does it solve the safety and soundness problem?

3. Let's turn to activities regulation under the BHCA and Glass–Steagall. If the BHCA were fully applicable to foreign banks with subsidiaries in the U.S., the foreign bank parent, or its affiliates, could only engage in activities that were "closely related to banking," in or *outside* the U.S. Some countries have foreign banks that can engage in almost any activity (universal banks) and other countries permit non-bank affiliates of the bank to engage in these activities. How does IBA and Regulation K handle the problem of the non-U.S. activities of foreign bank holding companies? How does it handle activities within the U.S.? To what extent can a simple national treatment standard be applied to activities of foreign banks?

4. Under § 8 of IBA, a foreign bank can engage in any securities activities that it was engaged in 1978, and even add to them, but it loses this authority if the foreign bank becomes a bank holding company by acquiring a U.S. bank. Thus German and Swiss banks, e.g. Deutsche Bank or Swiss Bank Corporation, which own substantial securities firms, and do banking through branches, have not been able to acquire U.S.

banks without divesting their securities affiliates (17 foreign banks are in this position). What could Deutsche Bank do to get out of this trap?

The following case looks at some issues involved in the use of Section 20 authority by foreign banks.

## BARCLAYS BANK PLC, ORDER APPROVING APPLICATIONS TO ENGAGE, TO A LIMITED EXTENT, IN UNDERWRITING AND DEALING IN DEBT AND EQUITY SECURITIES

76 Fed.Res.Bull. 158 (March 1990).

Canadian Imperial Bank of Commerce, Toronto, Ontario, Canada ("Canadian Imperial"), The Royal Bank of Canada, Montreal, Quebec, Canada ("Royal Bank"), and Barclays PLC and Barclays Bank PLC, London, England ("Barclays") (together referred to as "Applicants"), bank holding companies within the meaning of the Bank Holding Company Act ("BHC Act"), have each applied for the Board's approval under section 4(c)(8) of the BHC Act, 12 U.S.C. § 1843(c)(8), and section 225.23(a)(3) of the Board's Regulation Y, 12 C.F.R. 225.23(a)(3), for their indirect subsidiaries, Wood Gundy Corp., RBC Dominion Securities Corporation, and Barclays de Zoete Wedd Government Securities, Inc., respectively, each located in New York, New York ("Companies"), to underwrite and deal in, on a limited basis, all types of debt securities, including without limitation, sovereign debt securities, corporate debt, debt securities convertible into equity securities, and securities issued by a trust or other vehicle secured by or representing interests in debt obligations.

In addition, Canadian Imperial and Royal Bank have each applied for approval to underwrite and deal in equity securities, including, without limitation, common stock, preferred stock, American Depositary Receipts, and other direct and indirect equity ownership interests in corporations and other entities.

. . .

Canadian Imperial has total consolidated assets equivalent to approximately $82.6 billion. Canadian Imperial owns bank subsidiaries in Los Angeles, California, and New York, New York, and operates agencies in Atlanta, New York City, Los Angeles, and San Francisco.

Royal Bank has total consolidated assets equivalent to approximately $96.0 billion. Royal Bank owns bank subsidiaries in New York, New York, and San Juan, Puerto Rico, and operates branches in Portland, Oregon, New York City, and Puerto Rico and agencies in Miami and San Francisco.

Barclays has total consolidated assets equivalent to approximately $196.1 billion. Barclays owns bank subsidiaries in New York City, Wilmington, Delaware, and Charlotte, North Carolina, and operates branches in New York, Boston, Seattle, and Chicago and agencies in San Francisco and Miami.

I. Glass–Steagall Act

Applicants have previously received Board approval under section 4(c)(8) of the BHC Act for Companies to underwrite and deal in securities that member banks are authorized to underwrite and deal in under the Glass–Steagall Act (hereinafter "eligible securities") and to engage in various other activities permissible for bank holding companies. In order to ensure that Companies would not be engaged principally in underwriting or dealing in securities in violation of section 20 of the Glass–Steagall Act upon commencing the proposed debt and equity securities activities, each Company will limit the gross revenues derived from these activities to no more than 10 percent of its total gross revenues over any two-year period. The Board has previously determined that a company would not be in violation of section 20 of the Glass–Steagall Act if the gross revenue the company derived from underwriting and dealing in ineligible securities does not exceed between 5 and 10 percent of the company's total gross revenues on average over any two-year period. Accordingly, the Board concludes that Applicants' proposals would be consistent with section 20 of the Glass–Steagall Act.

II. Bank Holding Company Act

In order to approve an application under section 4(c)(8) of the BHC Act, the Board must find that the activities to be conducted are "so closely related to banking ... as to be a proper incident thereto." 12 U.S.C. § 1843(c)(8). In January 1989, the Board determined that bank holding companies, through separately incorporated and capitalized subsidiaries ("section 20 subsidiaries" or "underwriting subsidiaries"), may underwrite and deal in ineligible debt and equity securities, subject to the 5 to 10 percent revenue limit established under the Glass–Steagall Act. *J.P. Morgan & Co. Incorporated, et al., 75 Federal Reserve Bulletin* 192 (1989) (the "section 20 Order"). The Board concluded that these activities are closely related to banking and a proper incident thereto, provided that the activities are conducted within a framework of prudential limitations that avoid the potential for conflicts of interest, unsound banking practices, unfair competition and other adverse effects. In reaching this decision, the Board found that the proposals could be expected to result in public benefits such as increased competition, gains in efficiency, greater convenience to users of these services and a strengthened and more competitive banking and financial system.

Applicants have proposed for Companies to conduct the new activities within the prudential framework of limitations established by the Board in the section 20 Order. They have requested, however, certain modifications to that framework, which are discussed below, to account for the fact that each Applicant is a foreign bank that operates predominately outside the United States.

Applicants' requests for modification raise issues under the BHC Act and the framework established in the section 20 Order because, unlike U.S. bank holding companies, Applicants are both banks and bank holding companies. The framework established in the section 20 Order required a separation of federally-insured bank or thrift institutions from an affiliated section 20 subsidiary in order both to insulate U.S.-insured institutions and the federal safety net from the risk of the section 20 subsidiary's activities and for reasons of competitive equity in the United States. Although as banks, Applicants are not supported to any significant extent by the U.S. federal safety net, they have access to any benefits that are associated with their respective home country safety nets, from which they may derive some competitive advantage over U.S. bank holding companies operating under the section 20 framework or other U.S. securities firms. Rigid application of the section 20 framework to Applicants as banks, however, would prevent them generally from being able to establish section 20 subsidiaries in the United States unless they adopted a holding company structure.

The International Banking Act of 1978 ("IBA"), 12 U.S.C. § 3101 *et seq.*, established that foreign banks were to operate in the United States under the principle of national treatment. National treatment in this context calls for parity of treatment between domestic and foreign banking organizations to the extent possible such that one group does not have competitive advantages relative to the other in the United States.

In order to assist in achieving this objective, the IBA provided that any foreign bank that operates a bank, branch or agency in the United States "shall be subject to the provisions of the Bank Holding Company Act ... in the same manner and to the same extent that bank holding companies are subject thereto ..." 12 U.S.C. § 3106(a). The legislative history of the IBA states that this was "to insure competitive equality by allowing foreign financial institutions to expand their U.S. banking-related activities in accordance with the same standards applicable to domestic bank holding companies ... [T]he bill does not affect the type or scope of a foreign bank's nondomestic business." S.Rep. No. 1073, 95th Cong., 2d Sess. 15 (1978).

Applicants have asserted that some of the conditions established in the section 20 Order were imposed on domestic bank holding companies for supervisory reasons and that such conditions should not be applicable to the operations of Applicants. Consequently, they have requested modification of certain conditions, principally those that apply to their non-U.S. operations. Without appropriate modifications, Applicants assert, the conditions of the section 20 Order would be an extraterritorial extension of U.S. regulation and supervision, which would be inconsistent with U.S. policy and international agreements on bank supervision.

The Board has carefully considered Applicants' requests and has determined that, consistent with the IBA and its policy of national treatment, foreign banks must conduct the proposed activities in the United States within the framework of prudential limitations established in the section 20 Order. Giving due regard to the principles of national treatment and the Board's policy not to extend U.S. bank supervisory standards extraterritorially, the Board has determined, as discussed further below, to adjust the funding and certain operational requirements of the section 20 Order where these adjustments would not change the balance of public interest factors that the Board considered in the section 20 Order or cause adverse effects to outweigh public benefits. Consistent with the terms and objectives of the BHC Act and the IBA, the conditions to which the Board believes Applicants should be subject are designed to ensure that the prudential, competitive equity, safety net and prevention of moral hazard objectives of the conditions continue to be met; that U.S. regulation does not interfere with the operations of foreign banks outside the United States; and that foreign bank applicants will not have any significant competitive advantage in the United States over section 20 subsidiaries and non-bank-owned securities firms.

To achieve these ends, the Board has determined that:

(1) the prudential framework of the section 20 Order will apply without modification to the U.S. bank and thrift affiliates of Applicants' underwriting subsidiaries;

(2) the framework will also generally cover U.S. branches and agencies of Applicants;

(3) the Applicants, insofar as their foreign offices and operations are concerned, will be treated as bank holding companies for purposes of the framework consistent with the IBA; and

(4) the responsibility for compliance with the framework will be placed on the section 20 subsidiaries in order to avoid U.S. regulation having an extraterritorial impact.

The Board recognizes that this modified framework raises certain issues of compatibility with that established for U.S.-owned section 20 subsidiaries, principally in the area of bank funding and investment. For example, under the modified framework, a foreign bank may establish and fund a section 20 subsidiary, while a U.S. bank may not.

While there could be potential advantages accruing to Applicants through this differing structure, the Board believes that any advantage would not be significant in light of the effect on them of the overall section 20 framework and the circumstances of these cases, and should not preclude foreign bank ownership of section 20 subsidiaries. The Board notes that the absolute size of the ineligible securities activities of section 20 companies owned by foreign banks will generally be small, as they will necessarily be constrained by the 10 percent revenue limitation established by the Board. The base of eligible securities activities against which to measure ineligible securities activities is derived mainly from U.S. government securities, which do not form as relatively large or as natural an asset base for foreign banks as they do for U.S. banking organizations. In addition, foreign banks in their capacity as bank holding companies will be subject to the provisions of the section 20 Order requiring a bank holding company to deduct from its capital investments in and unsecured lending to a section 20 subsidiary. Finally, the U.S. operations of the foreign bank will be subject to the provisions of the section 20 Order to the same extent as U.S.-owned and section 20 subsidiaries, and, significantly, a foreign-owned section 20 subsidiary may not utilize the credit facilities of its foreign bank parent to gain an advantage over U.S. firms in its securities underwriting and dealing activities. The Board notes that this assessment could change with a significant change in the factors considered by the Board, such as if the size of section 20 companies becomes significant, due to an increase in the revenue limitations, a change in the law governing bank securities activities, or sizeable growth in the base of eligible securities. In such circumstances, the Board may reevaluate its position on these matters from the standpoint of the principles of national treatment.

The modifications adopted by the Board to the section 20 framework as it applies to Applicant foreign banks are discussed below.

*Capital Adequacy Considerations*

In the section 20 Order, the Board stated that it would not permit any impairment in an applicant's financial strength as a result of the provision of capital or liquidity support for the proposed activities. The Board required that each bank holding company deduct from its consolidated primary capital any investments in, or unsecured extensions of credit to, the section 20 subsidiary and exclude from its total consolidated assets the assets of the section 20 subsidiary. This requirement was designed to ensure that the holding company maintains a strong capital position to support its subsidiary banks and that the resources needed for that support would not be put at risk to fund the expanded securities activities.

Applicants have proposed that, in the case of a foreign bank seeking to establish a section 20 company, the proper authority to assess capital adequacy is the home country supervisor, using its own capital guidelines consistent with the standards established by the Basle Committee on Banking Regulations and Supervisory Practices. The Board has adopted guidelines consistent with these standards and considers the Basle Accord an important step toward a more consistent and equitable international standard for assessing capital adequacy.

In 1979, the Board adopted a Policy Statement on Foreign–Based Bank Holding Companies that states a foreign bank with U.S. banking operations is expected to meet the same general standards of financial strength as U.S. bank holding companies. The Board recognized, however, that foreign banks operate outside the United States in accordance with different banking practices and in different legal environments, and that the Board's supervisory responsibilities extend only to the safety and soundness of U.S. banking operations. The Board stated that, consistent with the principles of the BHC Act and the IBA, its policy is not to extend U.S. bank supervisory standards extraterritorially to foreign banks. Rather, the Board would seek to assure itself of the foreign bank's ability to be a source of strength to its U.S. operations.

In light of the Board's policy with respect to foreign bank holding companies and the endorsement and implementation of the Basle Accord by the Applicants' home country regulators, the Board has considered the following in assessing Applicants' capital positions: both before and after deduction of investments in and unsecured loans to the section 20 subsidiary, each Applicant meets the risk-based capital standards established by its home country supervisor under the Basle Accord; each is in good standing with the home country supervisor; the U.S. offices, subsidiary banks, and any subsidiary U.S. holding company of Applicants are in generally satisfactory condition; and all other financial and managerial factors are consistent with the capability of each Applicant to remain a source of strength to its U.S. banking operations.

One of the conditions of the section 20 Order is that the section 20 subsidiary maintain at all times capital adequate to support its activity and cover reasonably expected expenses and losses in accordance with industry norms. The Board has reviewed the capitalization of each of the section 20 subsidiaries and believes that each is adequate in light of its business plan which, at the outside, projects a modest increase in outstanding ineligible securities positions. Barclays notes that additional capitalization of its section 20 subsidiary may be necessary, and has committed to increase capital in the securities subsidiary in early 1991 if, at year end 1990, the subsidiary's assets have grown to the size projected. The section 20 subsidiaries of Canadian Imperial and Royal Bank may also have a need for increased capital if their businesses grow beyond current projections. Accordingly, and subject to any commitments related to capital, approval of these activities is limited to a level consistent with the projections of position size and types of securities contained in each of the applications unless the section 20 subsidiaries receive an appropriate infusion of additional capital.

The Board notes that Applicants have an ongoing responsibility under the Board's regulations to continue to act as a source of financial strength to their U.S. subsidiary banks. 12 C.F.R. 225.-4(a). Under this rule, Applicants are expected to manage their operations, including their section 20 subsidiaries, in such a way as not to compromise or prejudice their ability to continue to act as a source of strength to their U.S. subsidiary banks and thrifts.

*Funding of Section 20 Subsidiaries*

In addition to these capital adequacy considerations, the Board determined in the section 20 Order that the broadening in the scope of permissible securities activities required a prohibition on lending by a bank or thrift affiliate to the section 20 subsidiary, as well as a prohibition on the purchase and sale of financial assets between these institutions for their own account, subject to limited exceptions for clearing U.S. government and agency securities and the purchase and sale of U.S. Treasury securities. The purpose of the prohibitions is to limit the transfer of risk from the securities activities to the federal safety net, both to protect the resources of the federal safety net and to prevent a securities company affiliated with a bank from gaining an unfair competitive advantage over securities companies that are not bank-affiliated. The section 20 Order permitted a bank holding company to provide secured and unsecured credit to an underwriting subsidiary.

In these cases, Applicants are not only bank holding companies within the meaning of the BHC Act but are also banks that have access to deposits in the United States and abroad and have the benefits of the safeguards that most countries afford to their banking systems. Unlike the typical U.S. banking organization structure, foreign banking institutions are not generally organized in a holding company structure. The foreign bank itself is generally the parent organization. Applicants argue that, in light of this organizational structure, the foreign bank parent is the only ultimate source of support for the operations of the section 20 subsidiary. Accordingly, Applicants contend, a determination by the Board that the foreign bank parent could not fund its section 20 subsidiary through loans or investments because it is a bank would have the effect of preventing foreign banks from establishing section 20 subsidiaries in the United States unless they adopted the U.S. holding company structure.

As previously noted, the Board has considered the implications of modifying the section 20 conditions to permit extensions of credit and other support by a foreign bank to its section 20 subsidiary in light of the purposes of the prohibition against such support by a bank affiliate. Because funds of a foreign bank that are generated from abroad are not federally insured, and the foreign bank itself does not have access to the discount window, the provision of support by a foreign bank to its underwriting subsidiary from outside the United States would not directly implicate the federal safety net. In addition, for the reasons discussed above, it does not appear that the ability to provide such support would give securities companies owned by foreign banks a significant competitive advantage over domestically-owned companies.

Moreover, whether or not a funding advantage exists by virtue of Applicants' status as banks, U.S. securities companies, whether or not affiliated with a U.S. bank, may borrow from foreign bank affiliates. The Board notes that certain of the largest U.S. investment banking companies are affiliated with foreign banks from which they may obtain credit. In the case of a U.S. bank holding company that directly owns a foreign bank, the section 20 conditions would not prohibit loans by that foreign bank affiliate to an underwriting subsidiary in the United States, subject to the lending and capital deduction requirements established in the section 20 Order, which are applicable also to the foreign bank Applicants.

Accordingly, in light of these considerations and consistent with the IBA, the Board has determined that Applicant foreign banks should be able to lend to their section 20 subsidiaries in accordance with their status as bank holding companies. The restrictions against lending and purchasing or selling assets will apply, however, to all of Applicants' U.S. banking offices, including their U.S. bank and thrift subsidiaries, branches, and agencies.

Barclays has requested modification of the section 20 conditions in order to lend to its section 20 subsidiary through its U.S. branches. In support of the request, Barclays notes that the deposits in its U.S. branches are not insured by the Federal Deposit Insurance Corporation and Barclays is expected by the Federal Reserve to call on home country resources before seeking credit at the discount window. Therefore, according to Barclays, the U.S. federal safety net would not be exposed even if Barclays' U.S. branches were to lend to its section 20 subsidiary.

The Board has considered this request and has determined that an exception to the section 20 Order to permit U.S. branches of foreign banks to lend to the section 20 subsidiaries would not be appropriate. Although their deposits are not FDIC-insured, these offices are part of the U.S. financial structure and have statutory access to the discount window and payments system. Moreover, in the Board's view, lending to a section 20 subsidiary from a U.S. branch is inconsistent with, and could potentially undermine, the framework that the Board has adopted for the operation of the section 20 companies in the United States.

. . .

*Credit Enhancement and Loans to Customers*

In the section 20 Order, the Board established several limitations on extensions of credit by the applicants or their subsidiaries to customers of the section 20 subsidiaries. The Board provided that bank holding companies and their subsidiaries may not extend credit or issue or enter into any facility that might be viewed as enhancing the creditworthiness or marketability of ineligible securities underwritten or distributed by the section 20 subsidiary, or make loans to issuers of ineligible securities underwritten by the section 20 subsidiaries for the purpose of payment of principal, interest, or dividends on such securities. Affiliates of section 20 subsidiaries also could not knowingly extend credit to a customer secured by, or for the purpose of purchasing, any ineligible security that the section 20 subsidiary underwrites during the period of the underwriting and for 30 days thereafter, or to purchase from the section 20 subsidiary any ineligible security in which the subsidiary makes a market.

These limitations were imposed in order to protect the soundness of U.S. banking institutions by removing improper incentives from the credit granting process. In addition, the limitations protect the federal safety net from the potential for abusive credit practices and prevent bank-affiliated securities companies from obtaining an unfair advantage over companies that are not affiliated with banks.

Applicants argue that because the limitations were imposed primarily to protect the soundness of U.S. banking institutions and the federal safety net, they should not be applied to Applicants' non-U.S. operations in a manner that interferes with those operations or requires them to create costly new compliance systems. Applicants view such requirements not only as entailing substantial costs, but also as amounting to an unwarranted extraterritorial regulation of their non-U.S. operations. Applicants have suggested a number of alternatives to ensure compliance by their non-U.S. operations with the goals of the section 20 conditions.

*Credit Enhancements*

Although Applicants argue generally against the need for limitations on credit enhancements, each has agreed to comply fully with the conditions with respect to their U.S. operations. Barclays also committed to comply with the condition worldwide, while Canadian Imperial and Royal Bank proposed to comply worldwide with the restrictions when the section 20 subsidiary is the sole underwriter or lead or co-lead manager of an underwriting of ineligible securities. Canadian Imperial and Royal Bank contend that a section 20 owned competitors could not without having been examined with respect to their managerial and operational infrastructure and other policies and procedures. Moreover, it has long been the policy of the Board not to grant exemptions under section 4(c)(9) to foreign organizations if the exemption would give the foreign organization a material competitive advantage over U.S. bank holding companies.[13] Accordingly, the Board does not believe Applicants' request for an exemption to be consistent with the policies governing the implementation of section 4(c)(9) of the BHC Act and the request is denied.

5. Let's turn to interstate banking. The general problem in 1978 was that several states permitted foreign banks to acquire banks in their states, but generally prohibited out-of-state domestic BHCs from doing so. This resulted in competitive inequality for domestic BHCs. Barclays Bank U.K. could own banks in several states, but Citicorp could not. Section 5(a)(5) of IBA deals with this problem. What does it mean?

6. Regulation K permits a bank to make a one-time switch of its home state, § 211.22(b). This has given rise to some creative lawyering. In the 1984 Bank of Montreal (BOM) case, BOM had a California and New York subsidiary. New York was its original home state. BOM sought to acquire the Harris Trust Corp., an Illinois bank. Illinois then prohibited any out-of-state bank holding companies from owning Illinois banks.

BOM switched its home state to Illinois. This satisfied the IBA requirement since it was not acquiring a bank in its home state. However, it still had a problem under the Douglas Amendment since, based on the deposits in its California and New York subsidiaries, it was still an out-of-state BHC. It converted these subsidiaries to non-deposit trust companies in order to comply with the Douglas amendment.

Suppose Citicorp's Douglas home state is New York and the Industrial Bank of Japan's (IBJ) IBA home state is New York. Massachusetts allows out-of-state BHCs to acquire Massachusetts banks if Massachusetts BHCs can acquire banks in their states. Can IBJ acquire a bank in Massachusetts? Could Massachusetts pass a law banning all foreign banks from acquiring Massachusetts banks?

In that connection, consider that the Supreme Court in Northeast Bancorp, Inc. v. Board of Governors of the Federal Reserve System, 472 U.S. 159, 105 S.Ct. 2545, 86 L.Ed.2d 112 (1985) held that the Douglas Amendment gave the states authority to permit out-of-state banks from some, but not other, states to acquire banks in their states, thus upholding the regional reciprocity arrangements of six New England states. The Douglas Amendment was introduced on the floor of the Senate, and thus had a slim legislative history. The court relied on a statement by Senator Douglas drawing an analogy between his amendment and the McFadden Act which on an intrastate basis only allows national banks to branch to the extent state banks are permitted to do so under state law. The Court stated "The McFadden Act, did not offer the States an all-or-nothing choice with respect to branch banking," id.,

13. In some cases, this organizational structure is required by the home country's laws governing ownership of banks.

at 172, and thus allowed New England states to permit New England but not other banks into the region.

*Branches*

1. Almost all of the key features of U.S. regulation require some adjustment in dealing with branches of foreign banks. Let's first look at deposit insurance. How was deposit insurance dealt with prior to 1978, by IBA after 1978, and by the amendments to IBA in 1991? Which of the three approaches is preferable? Some countries like Germany insure worldwide deposits. Should the U.S. allow retail or wholesale branches to operate in the U.S. covered by foreign insurance schemes?

2. Is the adequacy of foreign safety and soundness regulation more or less important with respect to branches or subsidiaries of foreign banks? The U.S. has tried to deal with this issue by imposing stricter entry requirements on branches of foreign banks. Do you agree with this approach? Compare U.S. standards with those of the Basle Supervisors' Committee, set forth below.

BASLE COMMITTEE ON BANKING SUPERVISION, MINIMUM STANDARDS FOR THE SUPERVISION OF INTERNATIONAL BANKING GROUPS AND THEIR CROSS-BORDER ESTABLISHMENTS (JUNE 1992).

The following four minimum standards are to be applied by individual supervisory authorities in their own assessment of their relations with supervisory authorities in other countries. In particular, a host-country authority, into whose jurisdiction a bank or banking group is seeking to expand, is called upon to determine whether that bank or banking group's home-country supervisory authority has the necessary capabilities to meet these minimum standards. In making this determination, host-country authorities should review the other authority's statutory powers, past experience in their relations, and the scope of the other authority's administrative practices. Some authorities may initially need to make either statutory or administrative changes in order to comply with these new standards; therefore, in cases where an authority fails to meet one or more of these standards, recognition should be given to the extent to which the authority is actively working to establish the necessary capabilities to permit it to meet all aspects of these minimum standards.

1. *All international banking groups and international banks should be supervised by a home-country authority that capably performs consolidated supervision.*

As a condition for the creation and maintenance of cross-border banking establishments, a host-country authority should assure itself that the relevant bank and, if different, the banking group is subject to the authority of a supervisor with the practical capability of performing consolidated supervision. To meet this minimum standard, the home-country supervisory authority should (a) receive consolidated financial and prudential information on the bank's or banking group's global operations, have the reliability of this information confirmed to its own satisfaction through on-site examination or other means, and assess the information as it may bear on the safety and soundness of the bank or banking group, (b) have the capability to prevent corporate affiliations or structures that either undermine efforts to maintain consolidated financial information or otherwise hinder effective supervision of the bank or banking group, and (c) have the capability to prevent the bank or banking group from creating foreign banking establishments in particular jurisdictions.

2. *The creation of a cross-border banking establishment should receive the prior consent of both the host-country supervisory authority and the bank's and, if different, banking group's home-country supervisory authority*

Consent by a host-country authority for the inward creation of a cross-border banking establishment should only be considered if the appropriate home-country authorities have first given their consent to the bank or banking group's outward expansion. Outward consent by a home-country authority should always be made contingent upon the subsequent receipt of inward consent from the host authority. Thus, in the absence of consent by both the host-country authority and the bank's home-country authority and, if different, the banking group's home-country authority, cross-border expansion will not be permitted. As a matter of procedure, a host-country authority should seek to assure itself that consent has been given by the supervisory authority directly responsible for the entity seeking to create an establishment; this authority, in turn, should assure itself that consent is given by the next higher tier supervisory authority, if any, which may perform consolidated supervision with respect to the entity as part of a banking group.

While the safety and soundness of a bank should be judged by its overall condition, in reviewing proposals for inward and outward expansion, host-country and home-country authorities should, at a minimum, give weight to (a) the strength of the bank's and banking group's capital and (b) the appropriateness of the bank's and banking group's organisation and operating procedures for the effective management of risks, on a local and consolidated basis respectively. In judging these two criteria, a host-country authority should be particularly concerned with the level of support that the parent is capable of providing to the proposed establishment.

The business activities of major international banking groups increasingly cut across traditional supervisory categories. Individual activities or products may be managed on a centralised or decentralised basis, without particular regard to corporate form or the location of a bank's or group's head office. Because of this, before giving consent to the creation of a cross-border establishment, the host-country authority and the bank's and banking group's home-country authorities should each review the allocation of supervisory responsibilities recommended in the Concordat in order to determine whether its application to the proposed establishment is appropriate.

If, as a result of the establishment's proposed activities or the location and structure of the bank's or the banking group's management, either authority concludes that the division of supervisory responsibilities suggested in the Concordat is not appropriate, then that authority has the responsibility to initiate consultations with the other authority so that they reach an explicit understanding on which authority is in the best position to take primary responsibility either generally or in respect of specific activities. A similar review should be undertaken by all authorities if there is a significant change in the bank's or banking group's activities or structure.

Inaction on the part of either authority will be construed as an acceptance of the division of responsibilities established in the Concordat. Thus each authority is responsible for making a deliberate choice between accepting its responsibilities under the Concordat or initiating consultations on an alternative allocation of supervisory responsibilities for the case at hand.

3. *Supervisory authorities should possess the right to gather information from the cross-border banking establishments of the banks or banking groups for which they are the home-country supervisor*

As a condition for giving either inward or outward consent for the creation of a cross-border banking establishment, a supervisory authority should establish an understanding with the other authority that they may each gather information to the extent necessary for effective home-country supervision, either through on-site examination or by other means satisfactory to the recipient, from the cross-border establishments located in one another's jurisdictions of banks or banking groups chartered or incorporated in their respective jurisdictions. Thus, consent for inward expansion by a prospective host-country authority should generally be contingent upon there being such an understanding, with the foreign bank's or banking group's home-country authority, that each authority may gather such information from their respective bank's and banking group's foreign establishments. Similarly, consent for outward expansion by the home-country authority should generally be contingent upon there being such an understanding with the host-country authority. Through such bilateral arrangements, all home-country authorities should be able to improve their ability to review the financial condition of their banks' and banking groups' cross-border banking establishments.

4. *If a host-country authority determines that any one of the foregoing minimum standards is not met to its satisfaction, that authority could impose restrictive measures necessary to satisfy its prudential concerns consistent with these minimum standards, including the prohibition of the creation of banking establishments*

In considering whether to consent to the creation of a banking establishment by a foreign bank or foreign banking group, or in reviewing any other proposal by a foreign bank or banking group which requires its consent, a host-country authority should determine whether the bank or banking group is subject to consolidated supervision by an authority that has—or is actively working to establish—the necessary capabilities to meet these minimum standards. First, the host-country authority should determine whether the bank or banking group is chartered or incorporated in a jurisdiction with which the host-country authority has a mutual understanding for the gathering of information from cross-border establishments. Secondly, the host-country authority should determine whether consent for outward expansion has been given by the appropriate home-country authorities. Thirdly, the host-country authority should determine whether the bank and, if different, the banking group is supervised by a home-country authority which has the practical capability of performing consolidated supervision.

If these minimum standards are not met with respect to a particular bank or banking group, and the relevant home-country authorities are unwilling or unable to initiate the effort to take measures to meet these standards, the host-country authority should prevent the creation in its jurisdiction of any cross-border establishments by that bank or banking group. However, in its sole discretion, the host-country authority may alternatively choose to permit the creation of establishments by such a bank or banking group, subject to whatever prudential restrictions on the scope and nature of the establishment's operations which the host-country authority deems necessary and appropriate to address its prudential concerns, provided that the host-country authority itself also accepts the responsibility to perform adequate supervision of the bank's or banking group's local establishments on a "stand-alone" consolidated basis.

Thus, if a bank or banking group is not subject to the level of supervision and supervisory co-operation required by these minimum standards, and the relevant supervisory authority is not actively working to establish the necessary capabilities, that bank or banking group will only be permitted to expand its operations into jurisdictions whose authorities are adhering to these minimum standards if the host-country authority itself accepts the responsibility to perform supervision of the bank or banking group's local establishments consistent with these minimum standards.

3. The U.S. has also tried to deal with the safety and soundness issue by ring fencing the assets of branches of foreign banks in the event the foreign bank fails (this was done with respect to the agencies of BCCI). Do you agree with this approach?

4. Does the dual banking system exist anymore with respect to branches of foreign banks?

5. As described in the readings, national and state-member banks cannot branch interstate. How does Section 5 of IBA deal with the problem of a foreign bank establishing direct branches of the foreign bank in several states? If the U.S. were to repeal restrictions on interstate branching, would you require a foreign bank to establish interstate branches from a U.S. subsidiary or permit it to have direct branches of the foreign bank in different states? Under the Senate bill to liberalize interstate branching restrictions, pending before the conference committee as of June 1994, foreign banks could only establish interstate branches of a U.S. subsidiary. Under the House bill, foreign banks could have direct branches in different states. The European Union objected to the Senate approach as not providing national treatment.

6. Currently, can a state permit some foreign banks but not others to branch into its state? Consider the following case.

## CONFERENCE OF STATE BANK SUPERVISORS v. CONOVER

715 F.2d 604 (D.C.Cir.1983), cert. denied 466 U.S. 927, 104 S.Ct. 1708, 80 L.Ed.2d 181 (1984).

ROBB, Senior Circuit Judge:

The appellants are state officials responsible for regulation of state-licensed banking institutions. As plaintiffs in the District Court they sued for declaratory and injunctive relief, challenging regulations 12 C.F.R. §§ 28.2(b)-(d), 28.3, & 28.4 (1980) and a portion of an accompanying interpretative statement (44 Fed.Reg. 65381–87 (1979)) adopted by the Comptroller of the Currency pursuant to the International Banking Act of 1978 (IBA). 12 U.S.C. §§ 3101–3108 (Supp. V 1981). Appellants contended that the regulations and statement conflicted with the IBA because they permitted a foreign bank to establish and operate offices where prohibited by state law. In an unreported opinion the District Court granted summary judgment in favor of the Comptroller.

. . .

The IBA sought to provide foreign banks with "national treatment" under which "foreign enterprises ... are treated as competitive equals with their domestic counterparts."

. . .

In this case the controversy centers on the Comptroller's interpretation of certain provisions of sections 4 and 5 of the IBA.

Section 4(a), 12 U.S.C. § 3102(a) (Supp. V 1981), provides that the Comptroller may approve establishment of a foreign bank's federal branch or agency if "establishment of a branch or agency, as the case may be, by a foreign bank is not prohibited by State law." Section 4(d), 12 U.S.C. § 3102(d) (Supp. V 1981), reads: "Notwithstanding any other provision of this section, a foreign bank shall not receive deposits ... at any Federal agency." When a foreign bank opens a federally-chartered branch or agency outside of its home state, section 5(a)(1), 12 U.S.C. § 3103(a)(1) (Supp. V 1981), provides that with certain exceptions "no foreign bank may directly or indirectly establish and operate a Federal branch outside of its home State unless (A) its operation is expressly permitted by the State in which it is to be operated...."

. . .

The appellants complain that the Comptroller erred in interpreting these provisions of the IBA. They say that the Comptroller violated section 4(a) by approving the applications of five Australian banks to convert their state-licensed agencies in New York to home state federal branches although New York law prohibits such banks from opening branches. The appellants say that the Comptroller violated section 5(a) by approving the applications of two of the Australian banks to open interstate federal branches in Illinois in contravention of Illinois law. In the appellants' view, the Comptroller also violated section 5(a) by authorizing a British bank's interstate federal branch located in the State of Washington to conduct business operations that are not permitted to foreign bank branches under Washington law. Finally, the appellants aver that the Comptroller incorrectly interpreted sections 1(b)(5) and 4(d) in permitting federal agencies of foreign banks to accept deposits if the depositors are neither citizens nor residents of the United States.

In discussing the public comments regarding 12 C.F.R. pt. 28 (1980), promulgated pursuant to sections 4 and 13(a) of the IBA, 12 U.S.C. §§ 3102, 3108(a) (Supp. V 1981), the Comptroller noted "that in some states a foreign bank which applies for a state branch or agency must be able to demonstrate that the country under whose laws it was organized permits free or at least equivalent access to U.S. banks." 44 Fed.Reg. 65382 (1979). The Comptroller concluded however that "such a reciprocity approach" is not "binding upon the Comptroller's Office because it is incompatible with the national treatment theme of the IBA, and, further, it is in the nature of a condition or limitation rather than a prohibition on foreign entry." Id. The Comptroller bases this interpretation on his construction of the language of section 4(a) of the IBA, 12 U.S.C. § 3102(a) (Supp. V 1981), which provides:

> Except as provided in section [5] of this [Act], a foreign bank which engages directly in a banking business outside the United States may, with the approval of the Comptroller, establish one

> or more Federal branches or agencies in any State in which (1) it is not operating a branch or agency pursuant to State law and (2) the establishment of a branch or agency, as the case may be, by a foreign bank is not prohibited by State law.

The Comptroller reasons that the words "a foreign bank" in subsection (2) are synonymous with "any foreign bank" so that the Comptroller can license a foreign bank to operate a federal branch in a particular state unless that state prohibits all foreign banks from establishing state-chartered branches. Likewise, the Comptroller contends he can license a foreign bank to operate a federal agency in a particular state unless that state prohibits all foreign banks from establishing state-chartered agencies.

. . .

In short, we find two arguably correct interpretations of an ambiguous statutory provision. The relevant legislative history contains no explicit support for either interpretation. Under these circumstances, we believe section 4(a) can only be interpreted in the light of Congress' overriding objective in enacting the IBA. We find the legislative history replete with references to Congress' intent to accord foreign banks national treatment, under which "foreign enterprises . . . are treated as competitive equals with their domestic counterparts."

. . .

Accordingly, we affirm the Comptroller's interpretation of section 4(a).

Turning now to the second issue in this appeal, we must address the extent to which the Comptroller must defer to state law in licensing a foreign bank's federal interstate office.

. . .

Appellants contend that the Comptroller's interpretation of section 5, as reflected in the above quoted provisions, violates section 5 in two ways. First, the Comptroller's interpretation enables him to license a foreign bank's federal interstate office in a receiving state that does not expressly permit that particular foreign bank to establish a state-chartered interstate office. Second, even if the receiving state permitted a particular foreign bank to establish an interstate office, the Comptroller's interpretation does not require that the bank operations of the federal interstate office be "expressly permitted" by the receiving state.

. . .

The Comptroller contends that a state has essentially the same power to veto the entry of a federal interstate office under section 5(a) as it has to veto the entry of a federal home state office under section 4(a). Thus, the Comptroller contends that he can license a foreign bank's interstate branch unless the receiving state permits *no* foreign bank to operate a state-chartered branch. Similarly, he can license a foreign bank's interstate federal agency unless the receiving state permits *no* foreign bank to operate a state-chartered agency.

. . .

We agree with the District Court's conclusion on this issue. After closely reviewing the language and legislative history of section 5(a) in the light of appellants' arguments, we cannot say that there are "compelling indications" that the Comptroller's interpretation of section 5(a) is wrong.

Thus, we are obliged to defer to the Comptroller's interpretation of the IBA because "the interpretation of an agency charged with the administration of a statute is entitled to substantial deference." Blum v. Bacon, 457 U.S. 132, 141, 102 S.Ct. 2355, 2361, 72 L.Ed.2d 728 (1982).

Section 5(a) provides in relevant part that "no foreign bank may . . . establish and operate a Federal branch [or agency] outside of its home State unless (A) its operation is expressly permitted by the State in which it is to be operated . . . ." 12 U.S.C. § 3103(a)(1), (3) (Supp. V 1981). The dispute in interpreting this section focuses on the words "its operation." The appellants conclude that "its operation" refers to the operation of a particular federal interstate office. Thus, in appellants' view, section 5(a) would prohibit the Comptroller from licensing a federal interstate office if, due to limitations on banking operations or due to banking reciprocity requirements, the receiving state did not expressly permit the "operation" of that federal interstate office. On the other hand, the Comptroller concludes that "its operation" refers only to the interstate office's operation as a branch or as an agency. The Comptroller says that section 5(a) prohibits him from licensing an interstate branch (or agency) unless the receiving state expressly permits foreign banks to operate branches (or agencies). We believe that the language of section 5(a) reasonably supports either party's interpretation of the words "its operation." In addition, unlike the District Court, we do not believe that the precise difference between "expressly permitted" in sections 5(a)(1)(A) and 5(a)(3) and "approved" in sections 5(a)(2)(A) and 5(a)(4) is evident in the language of the statute.

Faced with two arguably reasonable interpretations of one statutory provision, we turn to the legislative history for guidance. Unfortunately, the relevant legislative history does not favor one interpretation over the other. The Senate Report says a foreign bank could "establish branch or agency offices in any State *where this is permissible,*" and "foreign bank branches and agencies would be able, *with appropriate State approval* where necessary, to make both domestic and international commerical [sic] loans at locations throughout the country," and that section 5 allows states "to decide whether *and to what extent* it wishes to permit foreign banks." *1978 Senate Report,* supra, at 10–12, U.S.Code Cong. & Admin.News 1978, pp. 1430–1432 (emphasis added). These general statements are consistent with the interpretation of either party in this appeal.

In short, we do not discern from the language or legislative history of section 5(a) any basis for saying that the Comptroller's interpretation is contrary to law.[18] In so doing, we bear in mind that our task is not to interpret the statute as we think best but rather to determine whether the Comptroller's interpretation was " 'sufficiently reasonable' to be accepted by a reviewing court." FEC v. Democratic Senatorial Campaign Committee, 454 U.S. 27, 39, 102 S.Ct. 38, 46, 70 L.Ed.2d 23 (1981). "To satisfy this standard it is not necessary for a court to find that the agency's construction was the only reasonable one or even the reading the court would have reached if the question initially had arisen in a judicial proceeding." Id. See also Udall v. Tallman, 380 U.S. 1, 16, 85 S.Ct. 792, 801, 13 L.Ed.2d 616 (1965). We hold, therefore, that the Comptroller can license a foreign bank's federal interstate branch in a receiving state if that state permits foreign banks to establish state-chartered interstate branches. Likewise, he can license a foreign bank's federal interstate agency in a receiving state if that state permits foreign banks to establish state-chartered interstate agencies. We also agree with the Comptroller that section 5(a) does not require federal interstate offices to comply with limitations on bank operations imposed by the receiving state.

. . .

---

## D. RECIPROCITY ISSUES

At present, the U.S., in principle, grants unconditional national treatment to foreign banks. The U.S. does not condition access to the U.S. market on the access of U.S. banks to foreign markets (reciprocity). Proposals have been before the Congress, that have come close to passage, to condition access on reciprocity, a conditional national treatment standard. The latest version of this approach is the Fair Trade in Financial Services Act of 1994 (FTFS), H.R. 3248, 103rd Cong., 2nd Sess., reported to the House floor in March 1994. As of June 15, 1994, the House bill, and a similar Senate bill, S. 1527, 103 Cong., 2d Sess., reported to the Senate, had not been voted on by the two chambers. The Clinton Administration backed both bills.

National treatment is defined in H.R. 3248, as receiving "the same competitive opportunities (including effective market access) in such country as are available to the country's domestic banking organizations in like circumstances."

In "determining whether and to what extent a foreign country denies national treatment to United States banking organizations and in determining the effect of any such denial ...," the Secretary of the Treasury must consider certain factors:

"(A) the extent of United States trade with and investment in the foreign country, the size of the foreign country's markets for the financial services involved, and the extent to which United States banking organizations operate or seek to operate in those markets;

"(B) the importance of operations by United States banking organizations in the foreign country to the export of goods and services by United States firms to such country;

"(C) the extent to which the foreign country provides in advance to United States banking organizations a written draft of any measure of general application that the country proposes to adopt, such as regulations, guidelines or other policies regarding new products and services, in order to allow an opportunity for such banking organizations to comment on the measure and for such comments to be taken into account by the foreign country;

"(D) the extent to which the foreign country—

"(i) makes available, in writing, to United States banking organizations the foreign country's requirements for completing any application relating to the provision of financial services;

"(ii) applies published, objective standards and criteria in evaluating any such application from United States banking organizations; and

"(iii) renders administrative decisions relating to any such application within a reasonable period of time;

"(E) the extent to which United States banking organizations may offer foreign exchange services in the foreign country;

"(F) the extent to which United States banking organizations may conduct activities or provide services in the foreign country that banking organizations organized under the laws of the foreign country may not conduct or provide in the foreign country; and

"(G) the extent to which the operations of United States banking organizations, and the ability of such organizations to compete on an equal basis, are affected by—

"(i) the lending or discount policies of the foreign country's central bank;

"(ii) the capital requirements applicable in the foreign country;

"(iii) the regulation of deposit interest rates by the foreign country;

"(iv) any restriction on the operation, establishment, or location of branches in the foreign country; and "(v) any restriction on access to automated teller or banking machine networks in the foreign country."

FTFS requires that the Secretary of the Treasury determine whether the denial of national treatment has had a "significant adverse effect on U.S. banks." U.S. banking regulators, with the concurrence of Treasury, could then deny applications for regulatory approval to banks from offending countries (including new entry and expansion). Existing operations would be grandfathered. The banking regulators would have to comply with the Treasury recommendation unless they reported to Treasury and the Congress that sanctions would seriously impact the U.S. financial or payment systems.

### *Notes and Questions*

1. What do you think of the FTFS national treatment standard as compared with other more traditional definitions, such as de jure national treatment which prohibits formal discriminatory barriers, e.g. prohibiting foreign banks to take retail deposits in a country, or de facto national treatment, which looks at whether there is actual as compared with formal discrimination?

2. How would the U.S. fare if other countries were to apply the FTFS standard to U.S. banks?

3. The GATT negotiations concluded in December 1993 failed to reach any agreement on financial services. The U.S. tried to obtain a so-called two-tier approach to financial services. The U.S. would grant open access to countries that were open to the U.S., but less access for those that were not (so-called second tier countries). This is inconsistent with the normal GATT "most favored nation" approach (MFN) under which a trade concession extended to one country must be extended to all countries. Second-tier countries would not be able to benefit from deregulation of U.S. market (future interstate banking and Glass–Steagall reforms). This was consistent with the conditional national treatment approach. Do you agree with that approach or would you prefer unconditional national treatment?

*Links to Other Chapters*

This Chapter examines U.S. regulation of the international aspects of its banking markets. We will look at how the European Union approaches this matter in Chapter V, and how the Japanese do so in Chapter VII. The idea and importance of capital adequacy for international banks was dealt with in this Chapter, but our next Chapter gets into the details. Much of the concern over bank failure is related to systemic risk. A big area of systemic risk is in the payments system which we examine in depth in Chapter IX. Also, to a great extent, the current concern with the risks of derivatives, dealt with in Chapters XV and XVI, is based on a fear of bank failure, and systemic risk.

## STATUTORY SUPPLEMENT TO CHAPTER III

### International Banking Act of 1978, as amended

### Short title; definitions and rules of construction

SEC. 1(a) This Act may be cited as the "International Banking Act of 1978".

(b) For the purposes of this Act—

(1) "agency" means any office or any place of business of a foreign bank located in any State of the United States at which credit balances are maintained incidental to or arising out of the exercise of banking powers, checks are paid, or money is lent but at which deposits may not be accepted from citizens or residents of the United States;

(2) "Board" means the Board of Governors of the Federal Reserve System;

(3) "branch" means any office or any place of business of a foreign bank located in any State of the United States at which deposits are received;

(4) "Comptroller" means the Comptroller of the Currency;

(5) "Federal agency" means an agency of a foreign bank established and operating under section 4 of this Act;

(6) "Federal branch" means a branch of a foreign bank established and operating under section 4 of this Act;

(7) "foreign bank" means any company organized under the laws of a foreign country, a territory of the United States, Puerto Rico, Guam, American Samoa, or the Virgin Islands, which engages in the business of banking, or any subsidiary or affiliate, organized under such laws, of any such company. For the purposes of this Act the term "foreign bank" includes, without limitation, foreign commercial banks, foreign merchant banks and other foreign institutions that engage in banking activities usual in connection with the business of banking in the countries where such foreign institutions are organized or operating;

(8) "foreign country" means any country other than the United States, and includes any colony, dependency, or possession of any such country;

(9) "commercial lending company" means any institution, other than a bank or an organization operating under section 25 of the Federal Reserve Act, organized under the laws of any State of the United States, or the District of Columbia which maintains credit balances incidental to or arising out of the exercise of banking powers and engages in the business of making commercial loans;

(10) "State" means any State of the United States or the District of Columbia;

(11) "State agency" means an agency of a foreign bank established and operating under the laws of any State;

(12) "State branch" means a branch of a foreign bank established and operating under the laws of any State;

(13) the terms "affiliate," "bank", "bank holding company", "company", "control", and "subsidiary" have the same meanings assigned to those terms in the Bank Holding Company Act of 1956, and the terms "controlled" and "controlling" shall be construed consistently with the term "control" as defined in section 2 of the Bank Holding Company Act of 1956;

(14) "consolidated" means consolidated in accordance with generally accepted accounting principles in the United States consistently applied; and

(15) the term "representative office" means any office of a foreign bank which is located in any State and is not a Federal branch, Federal agency, State branch, State agency, or subsidiary of a foreign bank;

(16) the term "office" means any branch, agency, or representative office; and

(17) the term "State bank supervisor" has the meaning given to such term in section 3 of the Federal Insurance Act.

. . .

### Establishment of Federal branches and agencies by foreign bank Approval of Comptroller

SEC. 4(a) ESTABLISHMENT AND OPERATION OF FEDERAL BRANCHES AND AGENCIES.—

(1) INITIAL FEDERAL BRANCH OR AGENCY.—Except as provided in section 5, a foreign bank which engages directly in a banking business outside the United States may, with the approval of the Comptroller, establish one or more Federal branches or agencies in any State in which (1) it is not operating a branch or agency pursuant to State law and (2) the establishment of a branch or agency, as the case may be, by a foreign bank is not prohibited by State law.

(2) BOARD CONDITIONS REQUIRED TO BE INCLUDED.—In considering any application for approval under this subsection, the Comptroller of the Currency shall include any condition imposed by the Board under section 7(d)(5) as a condition for the approval of such application by the agency.

(b) RULES AND REGULATIONS; RIGHTS AND PRIVILEGES; DUTIES AND LIABILITIES; EXCEPTIONS.—In establishing and operating a Federal branch or agency, a foreign bank shall be subject to such rules, regulations, and orders as the Comptroller considers appropriate to carry out this section, which shall include provisions for service of process and maintenance of branch and agency accounts separate from those of the parent bank. Except as otherwise specifically provided in this Act or in rules, regulations, or orders adopted by the Comptroller under this section, operations of a foreign bank at a Federal branch or agency shall be conducted with the same rights and privileges as a national bank at the same location and shall be subject to all the same duties, restrictions, penalties, liabilities, conditions, and limitations that would apply under the National Bank Act to a national bank doing business at the same location, except that (1) the requirements of section 5240 of the Revised Statutes (12 U.S.C. 481) shall be met with respect to a Federal branch or agency if it is examined at least once in each calendar year; (2) any limitation or restriction based on the capital stock and surplus of a national bank shall be deemed to refer, as applied to a Federal branch or agency, to the dollar equivalent of the capital stock and surplus of the foreign bank, and if the foreign bank has more than one Federal branch or agency the business transacted by all such branches and agencies shall be aggregated in determining compliance with the limitation; (3) a Federal branch or agency shall not be required to become a member bank, as that term is defined in section 1 of the Federal Reserve Act; and (4) a Federal agency shall not be required to become an insured bank as that term is defined in section 3(h) of the Federal Deposit Insurance Act. The Comptroller of the Currency shall coordinate examinations of Federal branches and agencies of foreign banks with examinations conducted by the Board under section 7(c)(1) and, to the extent possible, shall participate in any simultaneous examinations of the United States operations of a foreign bank requested by the Board under such section.

(c) APPLICATION TO ESTABLISH FEDERAL BRANCH OR AGENCY; MATTERS CONSIDERED—In acting on any application to establish a Federal branch or agency, the Comptroller shall take into account the effects of the proposal on competition in the domestic and foreign commerce of the United States, the financial and managerial resources and future prospects of the applicant foreign bank and the branch or agency, and the convenience and needs of the community to be served.

(d) RECEIPT OF DEPOSITS AND EXERCISING OF FIDUCIARY POWERS AT FEDERAL AGENCY PROHIBITED—Notwithstanding any other provision of this section, a foreign bank shall not receive deposits or exercise fiduciary powers at any Federal agency. A foreign bank may, however, maintain at a Federal agency for the account of others credit balances incidental to, or arising out of, the exercise of its lawful powers.

(e) MAINTENANCE OF FEDERAL BRANCH AND FEDERAL AGENCY IN SAME STATE PROHIBITED.—No foreign bank may maintain both a Federal branch and a Federal agency in the same State.

(f) CONVERSION OF FOREIGN BANK BRANCH, AGENCY OR COMMERCIAL LENDING COMPANY INTO FEDERAL BRANCH OR AGENCY; APPROVAL OF COMPTROLLER.—Any branch or agency operated by a foreign bank in a State pursuant to State law and any commercial lending company controlled by a foreign bank may be converted into a Federal branch or agency with the approval of the Comptroller. In the event of any conversion pursuant to this subsection, all of the liabilities of such foreign bank previously payable at the State branch or agency, or all of the liabilities of the commercial lending company, shall thereafter be payable by such foreign bank at the branch or agency established under this subsection.

(g) DEPOSIT REQUIREMENTS; ASSET REQUIREMENTS.—(1) Upon the opening of a Federal branch or agency in any State and thereafter, a foreign bank, in addition to any deposit requirements imposed under section 6 of this Act, shall keep on deposit, in accordance with such rules and regulations as the Comptroller may prescribe, with a member bank designated by such foreign bank, dollar deposits or investment securities of the type that may be held by national banks for their own accounts pursuant to paragraph "Seventh" of section 5136 of the Revised Statutes, as amended, in an amount as hereinafter set forth. Such depository bank shall be located in the State where such branch or agency is located and shall be approved by the Comptroller if it is a national bank and by the Board of Governors of the Federal Reserve System if it is a State Bank.

(2) The aggregate amount of deposited investment securities (calculated on the basis of principal amount or market value, whichever is lower) and dollar deposits for each branch or agency established and operating under this section shall be not less than the greater of (1) that amount of capital (but not surplus) which would be required of a national bank being organized at this location, or (2) 5 per centum of the total liabilities of such branch or agency, including acceptances, but excluding (A) accrued expenses, and (B) amounts due and other liabilities to offices, branches, agencies, and subsidiaries of such foreign bank. The Comptroller may require that the assets deposited pursuant to this subsection shall be maintained in such amounts as he may from time to time deem necessary or desirable, for the maintenance of a sound financial condition, the protection of depositors, and the public interest, but such additional amount shall in no event be greater than would be required to conform to generally accepted banking practices as manifested by banks in the area in which the branch or agency is located.

(3) The deposit shall be maintained with any such member bank pursuant to a deposit agreement in such form and containing such limitations and conditions as the Comptroller may prescribe. So long as it continues business in the ordinary course such foreign bank shall, however, be permitted to collect income on the securities and funds so deposited and from time to time examine and exchange such securities.

(4) Subject to such conditions and requirements as may be prescribed by the Comptroller, each foreign bank shall hold in each State in which it has a Federal branch or agency, assets of such types and in such amount as the Comptroller may prescribe by general or specific regulation or ruling as necessary or desirable for the maintenance of a sound financial condition, the protection of depositors, creditors and the public interest. In determining compliance with any such prescribed asset requirements, the Comptroller shall give credit to (A) assets required to be maintained pursuant to paragraphs (1) and (2) of this subsection, (B) reserves required to be maintained pursuant to section 7(a) of this Act,

and (C) assets pledged, and surety bonds payable, to the Federal Deposit Insurance Corporation to secure the payment of domestic deposits. The Comptroller may prescribe different asset requirements for branches or agencies in different States, in order to ensure competitive equality of Federal branches and agencies with State branches and agencies and domestic banks in those States.

(h) ESTABLISHMENT OF ADDITIONAL BRANCHES OR AGENCIES; APPROVAL OF COMPTROLLER.—ADDITIONAL BRANCHES OR AGENCIES.—

(1) APPROVAL OF AGENCY REQUIRED.—A foreign bank with a Federal branch or agency operating in any State may (A) with the prior approval of the Comptroller establish and operate additional branches or agencies in the State in which such branch or agency is located on the same terms and conditions and subject to the same limitations and restrictions as are applicable to the establishment of branches by a national bank if the principal office of such national bank were located at the same place as the initial branch or agency in such State of such foreign bank and (B) change the designation of its initial branch or agency to any other branch or agency subject to the same limitations and restrictions as are applicable to a change in the designation of the principal office of a national bank if such principal office were located at the same place as such initial branch or agency.

(2) NOTICE TO AND COMMENT BY BOARD.—The Comptroller of the Currency shall provide the Board with notice and an opportunity for comment on any application to establish an additional Federal branch or Federal agency under this subsection.

(i) TERMINATION OF AUTHORITY TO OPERATE FEDERAL BRANCH OR AGENCY.—Authority to operate a Federal branch or agency shall terminate when the parent foreign bank voluntarily relinquishes it or when such parent foreign bank is dissolved or its authority or existence is otherwise terminated or canceled in the country of its organization. If (1) at any time the Comptroller is of the opinion or has reasonable cause to believe that such foreign bank has violated or failed to comply with any of the provisions of this section or any of the rules, regulations, or orders of the Comptroller made pursuant to this section, or (2) a conservator is appointed for such foreign bank or a similar proceeding is initiated in the foreign bank's country of organization, the Comptroller shall have the power, after opportunity for hearing, to revoke the foreign bank's authority to operate a Federal branch or agency. The Comptroller may, in his discretion, deny such opportunity for hearing if he determines such denial to be in the public interest. The Comptroller may restore any such authority upon due proof of compliance with the provisions of this section and the rules, regulations, or orders of the Comptroller made pursuant to this section.

(j) RECEIVERSHIP OVER ASSETS OF FOREIGN BANK IN UNITED STATES.—(1) Whenever the Comptroller revokes a foreign bank's authority to operate a Federal branch or agency or whenever any creditor of any such foreign bank shall have obtained a judgment against it arising out of a transaction with a Federal branch or agency in any court of record of the United States or any State of the United States and made application, accompanied by a certificate from the clerk of the court stating that such judgment has been rendered and has remained unpaid for the space of thirty days, or whenever the Comptroller shall become satisfied that such foreign bank is insolvent, he may, after due consideration of its affairs, in any such case, appoint a receiver who shall take possession of all the property and assets of such foreign bank in the United States and exercise the same rights, privileges, powers, and authority with respect thereto as are now exercised by receivers of national banks appointed by the Comptroller.

(2) In any receivership proceeding ordered pursuant to this subsection (j), whenever there has been paid to each and every depositor and creditor of such foreign bank whose claim or claims shall have been proved or allowed, the full amount of such claims arising out of transactions had by them with any branch or agency of such foreign bank located in any State of the United States, except (A) claims that would not represent an enforceable legal obligation against such branch or agency if such branch or agency were a separate legal entity, and (B) amounts due and other liabilities to other offices or branches or agencies of, and wholly owned (except for a nominal number of directors' shares) subsidiaries of, such foreign bank, and all expenses of the receivership, the Comptroller or the Federal Deposit Insurance Corporation, where that Corporation has been appointed receiver of the foreign bank, shall turn over the remainder, if any, of the assets and proceeds of such foreign bank to the head office of such foreign bank, or to the duly appointed domiciliary liquidator or receiver of such foreign bank.

### Interstate banking by foreign banks

SEC. 5(a) LIMITATIONS.—Except as provided by subsection (b), (1) no foreign bank may directly or indirectly establish and operate a Federal branch outside of its home State unless (A) its operation is expressly permitted by the State in which it is to be operated, and (B) the foreign bank shall enter into an agreement or undertaking with the Board to receive only such deposits at the place of operation of such Federal branch as would be permissible for a corporation organized under section 25(a) of the Federal Reserve Act under rules and regulations administered by the Board; (2) no foreign bank may directly or indirectly establish and operate a State branch outside of its home State unless (A) it is approved by the bank regulatory authority of the State in which such branch is to be operated, and (B) the foreign bank shall enter into an agreement or undertaking with the Board to receive only such deposits at the place of operation of such State branch as would be permissible for a corporation organized under section 25(a) of the Federal Reserve Act under rules and regulations administered by the Board; (3) no foreign bank may directly or indirectly establish and operate a Federal agency outside of its home State unless its operation is expressly permitted by the State in which it is to be operated; (4) no foreign bank may directly or indirectly establish and operate a State agency or commercial lending company subsidiary outside of its home State, unless its establishment and operation is approved by the bank regulatory authority of the State in which it is to be operated; and (5) no foreign bank may directly or indirectly acquire any voting shares of, interest in, or substantially all of the assets of a bank located outside of its home State if such acquisition would be prohibited under section 3(d) of the Bank Holding Company Act of 1956 if the foreign bank were a bank holding company the operations of whose banking subsidiaries were principally conducted in the foreign bank's home State. Notwithstanding any other provisions of Federal or State law, deposits received by any Federal or State branch subject to the limitations of an agreement or undertaking imposed under this subsection shall not be subject to any requirement of mandatory insurance by the Federal Deposit Insurance Corporation.

(b) CONTINUANCE OF LAWFUL INTERSTATE BANKING OPERATIONS PREVIOUSLY COMMENCED.—Unless its authority to do so is lawfully revoked otherwise than pursuant to this section, a foreign bank, notwithstanding any restriction or limitation imposed under subsection (a) of this section, may establish and operate, outside its home State, any State branch, State agency, or bank or commercial lending company subsidiary which commenced lawful operation or for which an application to commence business had been lawfully filed with the appropriate State or Federal authority, as the case may be, on or before July 27, 1978.

(c) DETERMINATION OF HOME STATE OF FOREIGN BANK.—For the purposes of this section, the home State of a foreign bank that has branches, agencies, subsidiary commercial lending companies, or subsidiary banks, or any combination thereof, in more than one State, is whichever of such States is so determined by election of the foreign bank, or, in default of such election, by the Board.

**Insurance of deposits**

SEC. 6(a) No foreign bank may establish or operate a Federal branch which receives deposits of less than $100,000 unless the branch is an insured branch as defined in section 3(s) of the Federal Deposit Insurance Act, or unless the Comptroller determines by order or regulation that the branch is not engaged in domestic retail deposit activities requiring deposit insurance protection, taking account of the size and nature of depositors and deposit accounts.

(b)(1) After the date of enactment of this Act no foreign bank may establish a branch, and after one year following such date no foreign bank may operate a branch, in any State in which the deposits of a bank organized and existing under the laws of that State would be required to be insured, unless the branch is an insured branch as defined in section 3(s) of the Federal Deposit Insurance Act, or unless the branch will not thereafter accept deposits of less than $100,000, or unless the Federal Deposit Insurance Corporation determines by order or regulation that the branch is not engaged in domestic retail deposit activities requiring deposit insurance protection, taking account of the size and nature of depositors and deposit accounts.

[*Time extension* ]

(2) Notwithstanding the previous paragraph, a branch of a foreign bank in operation on the date of enactment of this Act which has applied for Federal deposit insurance pursuant to section 5 of the Federal Deposit Insurance Act by September 17, 1979, and has not had such application denied, may continue to accept domestic retail deposits until January 31, 1980.

(c) RETAIL DEPOSIT-TAKING BY FOREIGN BANKS.—

(1) IN GENERAL.—After the date of enactment of this subsection, notwithstanding any other provision of this Act or any provision of the Federal Deposit Insurance Act, in order to accept or maintain domestic retail deposit accounts having balances of less than $100,000, and requiring deposit insurance protection, a foreign bank shall—

(A) establish 1 or more banking subsidiaries in the United States for that purpose; and

(B) obtain Federal deposit insurance for any such subsidiary in accordance with the Federal Deposit Insurance Act.

(2) EXCEPTION.—Domestic retail deposit accounts with balances of less than $100,000 that require deposit insurance protection may be accepted or maintained in a branch of a foreign bank only if such branch was an insured branch on the date of the enactment of this subsection.

**Authority of Federal Reserve System**

SEC. 7(a) BANK RESERVES.—(1)(A) Except as provided in paragraph (2) of this subsection, subsections (a), (b), (c), (d), (f), (g), (i), (j), (k), and the second sentence of subsection (e) of section 19 of the Federal Reserve Act shall apply to every Federal branch and Federal agency of a foreign bank in the same manner and to the same extent as if the Federal branch or Federal agency were a member bank as that term is defined in section 1 of the Federal Reserve Act; but the Board either by general or specific regulation or ruling may waive the minimum and maximum reserve ratios prescribed under section 19 of the Federal Reserve Act and may prescribe any ratio, not more than 22 per centum, for any obligation of any such Federal branch or Federal agency that the Board may deem reasonable and appropriate, taking into consideration the character of business conducted by such institutions and the need to maintain vigorous and fair competition between and among such institutions and member banks. The Board may impose reserve requirements on Federal branches and Federal agencies in such graduated manner as it deems reasonable and appropriate.

(B) After consultation and in cooperation with the State bank supervisory authorities, the Board may make applicable to any State branch or State agency any requirement made applicable to, or which the Board has authority to impose upon, any Federal branch or agency under subparagraph (A) of this paragraph.

(2) A branch or agency shall be subject to this subsection only if (A) its parent foreign bank has total worldwide consolidated bank assets in excess of $1,000,000,000; (B) its parent foreign bank is controlled by a foreign company which owns or controls foreign banks that in the aggregate have total worldwide consolidated bank assets in excess of $1,000,000,000; or (C) its parent foreign bank is controlled by a group of foreign companies that own or control foreign banks that in the aggregate have total worldwide consolidated bank assets in excess of $1,000,000,000.

(b) EXAMINATION OF BRANCHES AND AGENCIES BY BOARD.—Section 13 of the Federal Reserve Act is amended by adding at the end thereof the following new paragraph:

> "Subject to such restrictions, limitations, and regulations as may be imposed by the Board of Governors of the Federal Reserve System, each Federal Reserve bank may receive deposits from, discount paper endorsed by, and make advances to any branch or agency of a foreign bank in the same manner and to the same extent that it may exercise such powers with respect to a member bank if such branch or agency is maintaining reserves with such Reserve bank pursuant to section 7 of the International Banking Act of 1978. In exercising any such powers with respect to any such branch or agency, each Federal Reserve bank shall give due regard to account balances being maintained by such branch or agency with such Reserve bank and the proportion of the assets of such branch or agency being held as reserves under section 7 of the International Banking Act of 1978. For the purposes of this paragraph, the terms 'branch', 'agency', and 'foreign bank' shall have the same meanings assigned to them in section 1 of the International Banking Act of 1978.".

(c) AUTHORITY OF BOARD TO CONDUCT AND COORDINATE EXAMINATIONS.—

(1) EXAMINATION OF BRANCHES, AGENCIES, AND AFFILIATES.—

(A) IN GENERAL.—The Board may examine each branch or agency of a foreign bank, each commercial lending company or bank controlled by 1 or more foreign banks or 1 or more foreign companies that control a foreign bank, and other office or affiliate of a foreign bank conducting business in any State.

(B) COORDINATION OF EXAMINATIONS.—

(i) IN GENERAL.—The Board shall coordinate examinations under this paragraph with the Comptroller of the Currency, the Federal Deposit Insurance Corporation, and appropriate State bank supervisors to the extent such coordination is possible.

(ii) SIMULTANEOUS EXAMINATIONS.—The Board may request simultaneous examinations of each office of a foreign bank and each affiliate of such bank operating in the United States.

(C) ANNUAL ON-SITE EXAMINATION.—Each branch or agency of a foreign bank shall be examined at least once during each 12-month period (beginning on the date the most recent examination of such branch or agency ended) in an on-site examination.

(D) COST OF EXAMINATIONS.—The cost of any examination under subparagraph (A) shall be assessed against and collected from the foreign bank or the foreign company that controls the foreign bank, as the case may be.

(2) REPORTING REQUIREMENTS.—Each branch or agency of a foreign bank, other than a Federal branch or agency, shall be subject to paragraph 20 and the provision requiring the reports of condition contained in paragraph 6 of section 9 of the Federal Reserve Act (12 U.S.C. 335 and 324) to the same extent and in the same manner as if the branch or agency were a State member bank. In addition to any requirements imposed under section 4 of this Act, each Federal branch and agency shall be subject to subparagraph (a) of section 11 of the Federal Reserve Act (12 U.S.C. 248(a)) and to paragraph 5 of section 21 of the Federal Reserve Act (12 U.S.C. 483) to the same extent and in the same manner as if it were a member bank.

(d) ESTABLISHMENT OF FOREIGN BANK OFFICES IN THE UNITED STATES.—

(1) PRIOR APPROVAL REQUIRED.—No foreign bank may establish a branch or an agency, or acquire ownership or control of a commercial lending company, without the prior approval of the Board.

(2) REQUIRED STANDARDS FOR APPROVAL.—The Board may not approve an application under paragraph (1) unless it determines that—

(A) the foreign bank engages directly in the business of banking outside of the United States and is subject to comprehensive supervision or regulation on a consolidated basis by the appropriate authorities in its home country; and

(B) the foreign bank has furnished to the Board the information it needs to adequately assess the application.

(3) STANDARDS FOR APPROVAL.—In acting on any application under paragraph (1), the Board may take into account—

(A) whether the appropriate authorities in the home country of the foreign bank have consented to the proposed establishment of a branch, agency or commercial lending company in the United States by the foreign bank;

(B) the financial and managerial resources of the foreign bank, including the bank's experience and capacity to engage in international banking;

(C) whether the foreign bank has provided the Board with adequate assurances that the bank will make available to the Board such information on the operations or activities of the foreign bank and any affiliate of the bank that the Board deems necessary to determine and enforce compliance with this Act, the Bank Holding Company Act of 1956, and other applicable Federal law; and

(D) whether the foreign bank and the United States affiliates of the bank are in compliance with applicable United States law.

(4) FACTOR.—In acting on an application under paragraph (1), the Board shall not make the size of the foreign bank the sole determinant factor, and may take into account the needs of the community as well as the length of operation of the foreign bank and its relative size in its home country. Nothing in this paragraph shall affect the ability of the Board to order a State branch, agency, or commercial lending company subsidiary to terminate its activities in the United States pursuant to any standard set forth in this Act.

(5) ESTABLISHMENT OF CONDITIONS.—Consistent with the standards for approval in paragraph (2), the Board may impose such conditions on its approval under this subsection as it deems necessary.

(e) TERMINATION OF FOREIGN BANK OFFICES IN THE UNITED STATES.—

(1) STANDARDS FOR TERMINATION.—The Board, after notice and opportunity for hearing and notice to any appropriate State bank supervisor, may order a foreign bank that operates a State branch or agency or commercial lending company subsidiary in the United States to terminate the activities of such branch, agency, or subsidiary if the Board finds that—

(A) the foreign bank is not subject to comprehensive supervision or regulation on a consolidated basis by the appropriate authorities in its home country; or

(B)(i) there is reasonable cause to believe that such foreign bank, or any affiliate of such foreign bank, has committed a violation of law or engaged in an unsafe or unsound banking practice in the United States; and

(ii) as a result of such violation or practice, the continued operation of the foreign bank's branch, agency or commercial lending company subsidiary in the United States would not be consistent with the public interest or with the purposes of this Act, the Bank Holding Company Act of 1956, or the Federal Deposit Insurance Act.

However, in making findings under this paragraph, the Board shall not make size the sole determinant factor, and may take into account the needs of the community as well as the length of operation of the foreign bank and its relative size in its home country. Nothing in this paragraph shall affect the ability of the Board to order a State branch, agency, or commercial lending company subsidiary to terminate its activities in the United States pursuant to any standard set forth in this Act.

(2) DISCRETION TO DENY HEARING.—The Board may issue an order under paragraph (1) without providing for an opportunity for a hearing

if the Board determines that expeditious action is necessary in order to protect the public interest.

(3) EFFECTIVE DATE OF TERMINATION ORDER.—An order issued under paragraph (1) shall take effect before the end of the 120–day period beginning on the date such order is issued unless the Board extends such period.

(4) COMPLIANCE WITH STATE AND FEDERAL LAW.—Any foreign bank required to terminate activities conducted at offices or subsidiaries in the United States pursuant to this subsection shall comply with the requirements of applicable Federal and State law with respect to procedures for the closure or dissolution of such offices or subsidiaries.

(5) RECOMMENDATION TO AGENCY FOR TERMINATION OF A FEDERAL BRANCH OR AGENCY.—The Board may transmit to the Comptroller of the Currency a recommendation that the license of any Federal branch or Federal agency of a foreign bank be terminated in accordance with section 4(i) if the Board has reasonable cause to believe that such foreign bank or any affiliate of such foreign bank has engaged in conduct for which the activities of any State branch or agency may be terminated under paragraph (1).

(6) ENFORCEMENT OF ORDERS.—

(A) IN GENERAL.—In the case of contumacy of any office or subsidiary of the foreign bank against which—

(i) the Board has issued an order under paragraph (1); or

the Comptroller of the Currency has issued an order under section 4(i),

or a refusal by such office or subsidiary to comply with such order, the Board or the Comptroller of the Currency may invoke the aid of the district court of the United States within the jurisdiction of which the office or subsidiary is located.

(B) COURT ORDER.—any court referred to in subparagraph (A) may issue an order requiring compliance with an order referred to in subparagraph (A).

(7) CRITERIA RELATING TO FOREIGN SUPERVISION.—Not later than 1 year after the date of enactment of this subsection, the Board, in consultation with the Secretary of the Treasury, shall develop and publish criteria to be used in evaluating the operation of any foreign bank in the United States that the board has determined is not subject to comprehensive supervision or regulation on a consolidated basis. In developing such criteria, the Board shall allow reasonable opportunity for public review and comment.

(f) JUDICIAL REVIEW.—

(1) JURISDICTION OF UNITED STATES COURT OF APPEALS.—Any foreign bank—

(A) whose application under subsection (d) or section 10(a) has been disapproved by the Board;

(B) against which the Board has issued an order under subsection (e) or section 10(b); or

(C) against which the Comptroller of the Currency has issued an order under section 4(i) of this Act,

may obtain a review of such order in the United States court of appeals for any circuit in which such foreign bank operates a branch, agency, or commercial lending company that has been required by such order to terminate its activities, or in the United States court of Appeals for the District of Columbia Circuit, by filing a petition for review in the court before the end of the 30–day period beginning on the date the order was issued.

(2) SCOPE OF JUDICIAL REVIEW.—Section 706 of title 5, United States Code (other than paragraph (2)(F) of such section) shall apply with respect to any application or action under subsection (d) or (e).

(g) CONSULTATION WITH STATE BANK SUPERVISOR.—The Board shall request and consider any views of the appropriate State bank supervisor with respect to any application or action under subsection (d) or (e).

(h) LIMITATIONS ON POWERS OF STATE BRANCHES AND AGENCIES.—

(1) IN GENERAL.—After the end of the 1–year period beginning on the date of enactment of the Federal Deposit Insurance Corporation Improvement Act of 1991, a State branch or State agency may not engage in any type of activity that is not permissible for a Federal branch unless—

(A) the Board has determined that such activity is consistent with sound banking practice; and

(B) in the case of an insured branch, the Federal Deposit Insurance Corporation has determined that the activity would pose no significant risk to the deposit insurance fund.

(2) SINGLE BORROWER LENDING LIMIT.—A State branch or State agency shall be subject to the same limitations with respect to loans made to a single borrower as are applicable to a Federal branch or Federal agency under section 4(b).

(3) OTHER AUTHORITY NOT AFFECTED.—This section does not limit the authority of the Board or any State supervisory authority to impose more stringent restrictions.

(i) PROCEEDINGS RELATED TO CONVICTION FOR MONEY LAUNDERING OFFENSES.—

(1) NOTICE OF INTENTION TO ISSUE ORDER.—If the Board finds or receives written notice from the Attorney General that—

(A) any foreign bank which operates a State agency, a State branch which is not an insured branch, or a State commercial lending company subsidiary;

(B) any State agency;

(C) any State branch which is not an insured branch; or

(D) any State commercial lending subsidiary,

has been found guilty of any money laundering offense, the Board shall issue a notice to the agency, branch, or subsidiary of the Board's intention to commence a termination proceeding under subsection (e).

(2) DEFINITIONS.—For purposes of this subsection—

(A) INSURED BRANCH.—The term "insured branch" has the meaning given such term in section 3(s) of the Federal Deposit Insurance Act.

(B) MONEY LAUNDERING OFFENSE DEFINED.—The term "money laundering offense" means any criminal offense under section 1956 or 1957 of title 18, United States Code, or under section 5322 of title 31, United States Code.

(j) STUDY ON EQUIVALENCE OF FOREIGN BANK CAPITAL.—Not later than 180 days after enactment of this subsection, the Board and the Secretary of the Treasury shall jointly submit to the Committee on Banking, Housing, and Urban Affairs of the Senate and the Committee on Banking, Finance and Urban Affairs of the House of Representatives a report—

(1) analyzing the capital standards contained in the framework for measurement of capital adequacy established by the Supervisory Committee of the Bank for International Settlements, foreign regulatory capital standards that apply to foreign banks conducting banking operations in the United States, and the relationship of the Basle and foreign standards to risk-based capital and leverage requirements for United States banks; and

(2) establishing guidelines for the adjustments to be used by the Board in converting data on the capital of such foreign banks to the equivalent risk-based capital and leverage requirements for United States banks for purposes of determining whether a foreign bank's capital level is equivalent to that imposed on United States banks for purposes of determinations under section 7 of the International Banking Act of 1978 and sections 3 and 4 of the Bank Holding Company Act of 1956.

An update shall be prepared annually explaining any changes in the analysis under paragraph (1) and resulting changes in the guidelines pursuant to paragraph (2).

### Nonbanking activities of foreign banks

### Applicability of Bank Holding Company Acts

SEC. 8(a) Except as otherwise provided in this section (1) any foreign bank that maintains a branch or agency in a State, (2) any foreign bank or foreign company controlling a foreign bank that controls a commercial lending company organized under State law, and (3) any company of which any foreign bank or company referred to in (1) and (2) is a subsidiary shall be subject to the provisions of the Bank Holding

Company Act of 1956 [12 U.S.C. 1841 et seq.], and to section 1850 of this title and chapter 22 of this title [12 U.S.C.] [sections 105 and 106 of the Bank Holding Company Act Amendments of 1970] in the same manner and to the same extent that bank holding companies are subject to such provisions.

**Ownership or control of shares of nonbanking companies for certain period**

(b) Until December 31, 1985, a foreign bank or other company to which subsection (a) of this section applies on September 17, 1978, may retain direct or indirect ownership or control of any voting shares of any nonbanking company in the United States that it owned, controlled, or held with power to vote on September 17, 1978, or engage in any nonbanking activities in the United States in which it was engaged on such date.

**Engagement in nonbanking activities after certain period**

(c)(1) After December 31, 1985, a foreign bank or other company to which subsection (a) of this section applies on September 17, 1978, or on the date of the establishment of a branch in a State an application for which was filed on or before July 26, 1978 may continue to engage in nonbanking activities in the United States in which directly or through an affiliate it was lawfully engaged on July 26, 1978 (or on a date subsequent to July 26, 1978, in the case of activities carried on as the result of the direct or indirect acquisition, pursuant to a binding written contract entered into on or before July 26, 1978, of another company engaged in such activities at the time of acquisition), and may engage directly or through an affiliate in nonbanking activities in the United States which are covered by an application to engage in such activities which was filed on or before July 26, 1978; except that the Board by order, after opportunity for hearing, may terminate the authority conferred by this subsection on any such foreign bank or company to engage directly or through an affiliate in any activity otherwise permitted by this subsection if it determines having due regard to the purposes of this chapter [12 U.S.C.] and the Bank Holding Company Act of 1956 [12 U.S.C. 1841 et seq.], that such action is necessary to prevent undue concentration of resources, decreased or unfair competition, conflicts of interest, or unsound banking practices in the United States. Notwithstanding subsection (a) of this section, a foreign bank or company referred to in this subsection may retain ownership or control of any voting shares (or, where necessary to prevent dilution of its voting interest, acquire additional voting shares) of any domestically-controlled affiliate covered in 1978 which since July 26, 1978, has engaged in the business of underwriting, distributing, or otherwise buying or selling stocks, bonds, and other securities in the United States, notwithstanding that such affiliate acquired after July 26, 1978, an interest in, or any or all of the assets of, a going concern, or commences to engage in any new activity or activities. Except in the case of affiliates described in the preceding sentence, nothing in this subsection shall be construed to authorize any foreign bank or company referred to in this subsection, or any affiliate thereof, to engage in activities authorized by this subsection through the acquisition, pursuant to a contract entered into after July 26, 1978, of any interest in or the assets of a going concern engaged in such activities. Any foreign bank or company that is authorized to engage in any activity pursuant to this subsection but, as a result of action of the Board, is required to terminate such activity may retain the ownership or control of shares in any company carrying on such activity for a period of two years from the date on which its authority was so terminated by the Board. As used in this subsection, the term "affiliate" shall mean any company more than 5 per centum of whose voting shares is directly or indirectly owned or controlled or held with power to vote by the specified foreign bank or company, and the term "domestically-controlled affiliate covered in 1978" shall mean an affiliate organized under the laws of the United States or any State thereof if (i) no foreign bank or group of foreign banks acting in concert owns or controls, directly or indirectly, 45 per centum or more of its voting shares, and (ii) no more than 20 per centum of the number of directors as established from time to time to constitute the whole board of directors and 20 per centum of the executive officers of such affiliate are persons affiliated with any such foreign bank. For the purpose of the preceding sentence, the term "persons affiliated with any such foreign bank" shall mean (A) any person who is or was an employee, officer, agent, or director of such foreign bank or who otherwise has or had such a relationship with such foreign bank that would lead such person to represent the interests of such foreign bank, and (B) in the case of any director of such domestically controlled affiliate covered in 1978, any person in favor of whose election as a director votes were cast by less than two-thirds of all shares voting in connection with such election other than shares owned or controlled, directly or indirectly, by any such foreign bank.

### Termination of certain nonbanking activities

(2) The authority conferred by this subsection on a foreign bank or other company shall terminate 2 years after the date on which such foreign bank or other company becomes a "bank holding company" as defined in section 2(a) of the Bank Holding Company Act of 1956 (12 U.S.C. 1841(a)); except that the Board may, upon application of such foreign bank or other company, extend the 2–year period for not more than one year at a time, if, in its judgment, such an extension would not be detrimental to the public interest, but no such extensions shall exceed 3 years in the aggregate.

### Construction of terms

(d) Nothing in this section shall be construed to define a branch or agency of a foreign bank or a commercial lending company controlled by a foreign bank or foreign company that controls a foreign bank as a "bank" for the purposes of any provisions of the Bank Holding Company Act of 1956 [12 U.S.C. 1841 et seq.], or section 1850 of [12 U.S.C.] [section 105 of the Bank Holding Company Act Amendments of 1970], except that any such branch, agency or commercial lending subsidiary shall be deemed a "bank" or "banking subsidiary", as the case may be, for the purposes of applying the prohibitions of chapter 22 of [12 U.S.C.] [section 106 of the Bank Holding Company Act Amendments of 1970] and the exemptions provided in sections 4(c)(1), 4(c)(2), 4(c)(3), and 4(c)(4) of the Bank Holding Company Act of 1956 (12 U.S.C. 1843(c)(1), (2) (3), and (4)) to any foreign bank or other company to which subsection (a) of this section applies.

(e) Section 2(h) of the Bank Holding Company Act of 1956 is amended (1) by striking out "(h) The" and inserting in lieu thereof "(h)(1) Except as provided by paragraph (2), the", (2) by striking out the proviso, and (3) by inserting at the end thereof the following:

> "(2) The prohibitions of section 4 of this Act shall not apply to shares of any company organized under the laws of a foreign country (or to shares held by such company in any company engaged in the same general line of business of the investor company) that is principally engaged in business outside the United States if such shares are held or acquired by a bank holding company organized under the laws of a foreign country that is principally engaged in the banking business outside the United States, except that (1) such exempt foreign company (A) may engage in or hold shares of a company engaged in the business of underwriting, selling or distributing securities in the United States only to the extent that a bank holding company may do so under this Act and under regulations or orders issued by the Board under this Act, and (B) may engage in the United States in any banking or financial operations or types of activities permitted under section 4(c)(8) or in any order or regulation issued by the Board under such section only with the Board's prior approval under that section, and (2) no domestic office or subsidiary of a bank holding company or subsidiary thereof holding shares of such company may extend credit to a domestic office or subsidiary of such exempt company on terms more favorable than those afforded similar borrowers in the United States".

## REGULATION K
## OF THE FEDERAL RESERVE BOARD

### SUBPART A—INTERNATIONAL OPERATIONS OF UNITED STATES BANKING ORGANIZATIONS

### § 211.1 Authority, purpose, and scope.

(a) *Authority.* This subpart is issued by the Board of Governors of the Federal Reserve System ("Board") under the authority of the Federal Reserve Act ("FRA") (12 U.S.C. 221 *et seq.*); the Bank Holding Company Act of 1956 ("BHC Act") (12 U.S.C. 1841 *et seq.*); and the International Banking Act of 1978 ("IBA") (12 U.S.C. 3101 *et seq.*).

Requirements for the collection of information contained in this regulation have been approved by the Office of Management and Budget under the provision of 44 U.S.C. 3501, *et seq.* and have been assigned OMB Nos. 7100–0107; 7100–0109; 7100–0110; 7100–0069; 7100–0086, and 7100–0073.

(b) *Purpose.* This subpart sets out rules governing the international and foreign activities of U.S. banking organizations, including procedures for establishing foreign branches and Edge corporations to engage in international banking and for investments in foreign organizations.

(c) *Scope.* This subpart applies to:

(1) corporations organized under section 25(a) of the FRA (12 U.S.C. 611–631), "Edge corporations";

(2) Corporations having an agreement or undertaking with the Board under section 25 of the FRA (12 U.S.C. 601–604a), "Agreement corporations";

(3) Member banks with respect to their foreign branches and investments in foreign banks under section 25 of the FRA (12 U.S.C. 601–604a);[1] and

(4) Bank holding companies with respect to the exemption from the nonbanking prohibitions of the BHC Act afforded by section 4(c)(13) of the BHC Act (12 U.S.C. 1843(c)(13)).

## § 211.2 Definitions.

Unless otherwise specified, for the purposes of this subpart:

(a) An *affiliate* of an organization means:

(1) Any entity of which the organization is a direct or indirect subsidiary; or

(2) Any direct or indirect subsidiary of the organization or such entity.

(b) *Capital Adequacy Guidelines* means the Capital Adequacy Guidelines for State Member Banks: Risk–Based Measure (12 CFR part 208, app. A).

(c) *Capital and surplus* means paid-in and unimpaired capital and surplus, and includes undivided profits but does not include the proceeds of capital notes or debentures.

(d) *Directly or indirectly,* when used in reference to activities or investments of an organization, means activities or investments of the organization or of any subsidiary of the organization.

(e) *Eligible country* means a country that, since 1980, has restructured its sovereign debt held by foreign creditors, and any other country that the Board deems to be eligible.

1. Section 25 of the FRA, which refers to national banking associations, also applies to state member banks of the Federal Reserve System by virtue of section 9 of the FRA (12 U.S.C. 321).

(f) An Edge corporation is *engaged in banking* if it is ordinarily engaged in the business of accepting deposits in the United States from nonaffiliated persons.

(g) *Engaged in business or engaged in activities* in the United States means maintaining and operating an office (other than a representative office) or subsidiary in the United States.

(h) *Equity* means an ownership interest in an organization, whether through:

(1) Voting or nonvoting shares;

(2) General or limited partnership interests;

(3) Any other form of interest conferring ownership rights, including warrants, debt, or any other interests that are convertible into shares or other ownership rights in the organization; or

(4) Loans that provide rights to participate in the profits of an organization, unless the investor receives a determination that such loans should not be considered equity in the circumstances of the particular investment.

(i) *Foreign or foreign country* refers to one or more foreign nations, and includes the overseas territories, dependencies, and insular possessions of those nations and of the United States, and the Commonwealth of Puerto Rico.

(j) *Foreign bank* means an organization that:

(1) Is organized under the laws of a foreign country;

(2) Engages in the business of banking;

(3) Is recognized as a bank by the bank supervisory or monetary authority of the country of its organization or principal banking operations;

(4) Receives deposits to a substantial extent in the regular course of its business; and

(5) Has the power to accept demand deposits.

(k) *Foreign branch* means an office of an organization (other than a representative office) that is located outside the country under the laws of which the organization is established, at which a banking or financing business is conducted.

(*l*) *Foreign person* means an office or establishment located, or individual residing, outside the United States.

(m) *Investment* means:

(1) The ownership or control of equity;

(2) Binding commitments to acquire equity;

(3) Contributions to the capital and surplus of an organization; and

(4) The holding of an organization's subordinated debt when the investor and the investor's affiliates hold more than 5 percent of the equity of the organization.

(n) *Investor* means an Edge corporation, Agreement corporation, bank holding company, or member bank.

(*o*) *Joint venture* means an organization that has 20 percent or more of its voting shares held directly or indirectly by the investor or by an affiliate of the investor under any authority, but which is not a subsidiary of the investor.

(p) *Loans and extensions of credit* means all direct and indirect advances of funds to a person made on the basis of any obligation of that person to repay funds.

(q) *Organization* means a corporation, government, partnership, association, or any other entity.

(r) *Person* means an individual or an organization.

(s) *Portfolio investment* means an investment in an organization other than a subsidiary or joint venture.

(t) *Representative office* means an office that:

(1) Engages solely in representational and administrative functions, such as soliciting new business or acting as liaison between the organization's head office and customers in the United States; and

(2) Does not have authority to make any business decision (other than decisions relating to the premises or personnel of the representative office) for the account of the organization it represents, including contracting for any deposit or deposit-like liability on behalf of the organization.

(u) *Subsidiary* means an organization more than 50 percent of the voting share of which is held directly or indirectly, or which is otherwise controlled or capable of being controlled, by the investor or an affiliate of the investor under any authority. Among other circumstances, an investor is considered to control an organization if the investor or an affiliate is a general partner of the organization or if the investor and its affiliates directly or indirectly own or control more than 50 percent of the equity of the organization.

(v) *Tier 1 capital* has the same meaning as provided under the Capital Adequacy Guidelines (12 CFR part 208, appendix A).

. . .

### § 211.5 Investments and activities abroad.

(a) *General policy*. Activities abroad, whether conducted directly or indirectly, shall be confined to those of a banking or financial nature and those that are necessary to carry on such activities. In doing so, investors shall at all times act in accordance with high standards of banking or financial prudence, having due regard for diversification of risks, suitable liquidity, and adequacy of capital. Subject to these considerations and the other provisions of this section, it is the Board's policy to allow activities abroad to be organized and operated as best meets corporate policies.

. . .

(d) *Permissible activities.* The Board has determined that the following activities are usual in connection with the transaction of banking or other financial operations abroad:

(1) Commercial and other banking activities;

(2) Financing, including commercial financing, consumer financing, mortgage banking, and factoring;

(3) Leasing real or personal property, or acting as agent, broker, or advisor in leasing real or personal property, if the lease serves as the functional equivalent of an extension of credit to the lessee of the property;

(4) Acting as fiduciary;

(5) Underwriting credit life insurance and credit accident and health insurance;

(6) Performing services for other direct or indirect operations of a U.S. banking organization, including representative functions, sale of long-term debt, name saving, holding assets acquired to prevent loss on a debt previously contracted in good faith, and other activities that are permissible domestically for a bank holding company under section 4(a)(2)(A) and 4(c)(1)(C) of the BHC Act;

(7) Holding the premises of a branch of an Edge corporation or member bank or the premises of a direct or indirect subsidiary, or holding or leasing the residence of an officer or employee of a branch or subsidiary;

(8) Providing investment, financial, or economic advisory services;

(9) General insurance agency and brokerage;

(10) Data processing;

(11) Organizing, sponsoring, and managing a mutual fund if the fund's shares are not sold or distributed in the United States or to U.S. residents and the fund does not exercise managerial control over the firms in which it invests;

(12) Performing management consulting services provided that such services when rendered with respect to the U.S. market shall be restricted to the initial entry;

(13) Underwriting, distributing and dealing in debt securities outside the United States;

(14) Underwriting, distribution, and dealing in equity securities outside the United States as follows:

(i) By an investor, or an affiliate, that had commenced such activities prior to March 27, 1991, and subject to limitations in effect at that time (12 CFR part 211 (1990)); or

(ii) With the approval of the Board, underwriting equity securities if:

(A) Commitments by an investor and its affiliates for the shares of an organization do not in the aggregate exceed the lesser of $60 million or 25 percent of the investor's Tier 1 capital unless the underwriter is covered by binding commitments from subunderwriters or other purchasers obtained by the investor or its affiliates; and

(B) Commitments by an investor and its affiliates for the shares of an organization in excess of those permitted by paragraph (d)(14)(ii)(A) of this section provided that:

(*1*) The underwriting level approved by the Board for the investor and its affiliates in excess of the limitations of paragraph (d)(14)(ii)(A) of this section is fully deducted from the capital of the bank holding company, and from the capital of the bank where the securities activities are conducted by a subsidiary of a U.S. bank; [11] and

(*2*) In the Board's judgment such bank holding company and bank would remain strongly capitalized after such deduction from capital; and

(iii) With the approval of the Board, dealing in the shares of an organization (including the shares of a U.S. organization with respect to foreign persons only and subject to the limitations on owning or controlling shares of a company in section 4 of the BHC Act and the Board's Regulation Y (12 CFR part 225)) where the shares held in the trading or dealing accounts of an investor and its affiliates, when combined with any shares held pursuant to the authority provided under paragraph (b) of this section, do not in the aggregate exceed the lesser of $30 million or 10 percent of the investor's Tier 1 capital, provided however that:

(A) For purposes of determining compliance with the limitations of this paragraph (d)(14)(iii) and paragraph (b)(1)(iii)(A)(2) of this section, long and short positions in the same security may be netted and positions in a security may be offset by futures, forwards, options, and similar instruments referenced to the same security through hedging methods approved by the Board, except that any position in a security shall not be deemed to have been reduced by more than 75 percent;

(B) Any shares held in trading or dealing accounts for longer than 90 days shall be reported to the senior management of the investor;

11. Fifty percent of such capital deductions shall be from Tier 1 capital.

(C) Any shares acquired pursuant to an underwriting commitment for up to 90 days after the payment date for such underwriting shall not be subject to the dollar and percentage limitations of paragraph (d)(14)(iii) of this section or the investment provisions of paragraph (b) of this section, other than the aggregate limits in paragraph (b)(1)(iii)(A)(2) of this section; and

(D) Shares of an organization held in all trading and dealing accounts, when combined with all other equity interests in the organization held by the investor and its affiliates, other than underwriting commitments for shares and shares held pursuant to an underwriting for 90 days following the payment date for such shares, must conform to the permissible limits for investments in an organization under paragraph (b) of this section.[12]

(iv) Underwriting commitments for shares and shares held by an affiliate authorized to underwrite equity securities under section 4(c)(8) of the BHC Act shall not be included in determining compliance with the aggregates limits in paragraph (b)(1)(iii)(A)(2) and the limits of paragraphs (d)(14)(ii)(A) and (iii) of this section, except that shares held by such an affiliate shall be included for purposes of determining compliance with paragraph (d)(14)(iii)(D) of this section.

(15) Operating a travel agency provided that the travel agency is operated in connection with financial services offered abroad by the investor or others;

(16) Underwriting life, annuity, pension fund-related, and other types of insurance, where the associated risks have been previously determined by the Board to be actuarially predictable, provided however that:

(i) Investments in, and loans and extensions of credit (other than loans and extensions of credit fully secured in accordance with the requirements of section 23A of the FRA (12 U.S.C. 371c) or with such other standards as the Board may require) to, the company by the investor or its affiliates are deducted from the capital of the investor; [13] and

(ii) Activities conducted directly or indirectly by a subsidiary of a U.S. insured bank are excluded from the authority of this paragraph.

(17) Acting as a futures commission merchant for financial instruments of the type, and on exchanges, that the Board has previously approved, provided however that:

**12.** Underwriting commitments are combined with shares held by an investor and its affiliates (other than an affiliate authorized to deal in shares under section 4(c)(8) of the BHC Act) in dealing or trading accounts and with portfolio investments for purposes of determining compliance with the aggregate limits in paragraph (b)(1)(iii)(A)(2) of this section.

**13.** Fifty percent of such capital deduction shall be from Tier 1 capital.

(i) Activities are conducted in accordance with the standards set forth in § 225.25(b)(18) of the Board's Regulation Y (12 CFR 225.-25(b)(18)); and

(ii) Prior approval must be obtained for activities conducted on an exchange that requires members to guarantee or otherwise contract to cover losses suffered by other members.

(18) Acting as principal or agent in swap transactions [14] subject to any limitations applicable to state member banks under the Board's Regulation H (12 CFR part 208), except that where such activities involve contracts related to a commodity, such contracts must provide an option for cash settlement and the option must be exercised upon settlement.

(19) Engaging in activities that the Board has determined in Regulation Y (12 CFR 225.25(b)) are closely related to banking under section 4(c)(8) of the BHC Act; and

(20) With the Board's specific approval, engaging in other activities that the Board determines are usual in connection with the transaction of the business of banking or other financial operations abroad and are consistent with the FRA or the BHC Act.

. . .

SUBPART B—FOREIGN BANKING ORGANIZATIONS

### § 211.20 Authority, purpose, and scope.

(a) *Authority.* This subpart is issued by the Board of Governors of the Federal Reserve System ("Board") under the authority of the Bank Holding Company Act of 1956 (12 U.S.C. 1841 *et seq.*) ("BHC Act"); and the International Banking Act of 1978 (12 U.S.C. 3101 *et seq.*) ("IBA").

(b) *Purpose and scope.* This subpart is in furtherance of the purposes of the BHC Act and the IBA. It applies to foreign banks and foreign banking organizations with respect to:

(1) The limitations on interstate banking under section 5 of the IBA (12 U.S.C. 3103);

(2) The exemptions from the nonbanking prohibitions of the BHC Act and the IBA afforded by sections 2(h) and 4(c)(9) of the BHC Act (12 U.S.C. 1841(h) and 1843(c)(9));

(3) Board approval of the establishment of an office of a foreign bank in the United States under sections 7(d) and 10(a) of the IBA (12 U.S.C. 3105(c), 3107(a));

(4) The termination by the Board of a foreign bank's representative office, state branch, state agency, or commercial lending company subsidiary under sections 7(e) and 10(b) of the IBA (12 U.S.C. 3105(e), 3107(b)) and the transmission of a recommendation to the Office of the Comptrol-

14. Swap transactions involving equity instruments are separately authorized under paragraph (d)(14) of this section.

ler of the Currency to terminate a federal branch or federal agency under section 7(e)(5) of the IBA (12 U.S.C. 3105(e)(5));

(5) The examination of an office or affiliate of a foreign bank in the United States as provided in sections 7(c) and 10(c) of the IBA (12 U.S.C. 3105(c), 3107(c));

(6) The disclosure of supervisory information to a foreign supervisor under section 15 of the IBA (12 U.S.C. 3109);

(7) The limitations on loans to one borrower by state branches and state agencies of a foreign bank under section 7(h) of the IBA (12 U.S.C. 3105(g));

(8) The limitation of a state branch and a state agency to conducting only activities that are permissible for a federal branch under section 7(h)(1) of the IBA (12 U.S.C. 3105(h)(1)); and

(9) The deposit insurance requirement for retail deposit taking by a foreign bank under section 6 of the IBA (12 U.S.C. 3104).

(c) *Additional requirements.* Compliance by a foreign bank with the requirements of this subpart and the laws administered and enforced by the Board does not relieve the foreign bank of responsibility to comply with the laws and regulations administered by the licensing authority.

## § 211.21 Definitions.

The definitions of § 211.2 in subpart A of this part apply to this subpart except as a term is otherwise defined in this section:

(a) *Affiliate,* of a foreign bank or of a parent of a foreign bank, means any company that controls, is controlled by, or is under common control with, the foreign bank or the parent of the foreign bank.

(b) *Agency* means any place of business of a foreign bank, located in any state, at which credit balances are maintained, checks are paid, money is lent, or, to the extent not prohibited by state or federal law, deposits are accepted from a person or entity that is not a citizen or resident of the United States. Obligations shall not be considered credit balances unless they are:

(1) Incidental to, or arise out of the exercise of, other lawful banking powers;

(2) To serve a specific purpose;

(3) Not solicited from the general public;

(4) Not used to pay routine operating expenses in the United States such as salaries, rent, or taxes;

(5) Withdrawn within a reasonable period of time after the specific purpose for which they were placed has been accomplished; and

(6) Drawn upon in a manner reasonable in relation to the size and nature of the account.

(c) *Banking subsidiary,* with respect to a specified foreign bank, means a bank that is a subsidiary as the terms *bank* and *subsidiary* are defined in section 2 of the BHC Act (12 U.S.C. 1841).

(d) *Branch* means any place of business of a foreign bank, located in any state, at which deposits are received and that is not an agency, as that term is defined in paragraph (b) of this section.

(e) *Change the status* of an office means convert a representative office into a branch or an agency, an agency into a branch, a federal branch into a state branch, or a federal agency into a state agency, but does not include renewal of the license of an existing office.

(f) *Commercial lending company* means any organization, other than a bank or an organization operating under section 25 of the Federal Reserve Act (FRA) (12 U.S.C. 601–604a), organized under the laws of any state, that maintains credit balances permissible for an agency and engages in the business of making commercial loans. *Commercial lending company* includes any company chartered under Article XII of the banking law of the State of New York.

(g) *Comptroller* means the Office of the Comptroller of the Currency.

(h) *Control* has the same meaning assigned to it in section 2 of the BHC Act (12 U.S.C. 1841), and the terms *controlled* and *controlling* shall be construed consistently with the term *control.*

(i) *Domestic branch* means any place of business of a foreign bank, located in any state that may accept domestic deposits and deposits that are incidental to or for the purpose of carrying out transactions in foreign countries.

(j) A foreign bank *engages directly in the business of banking outside of the United States* if the foreign bank engages directly in banking activities usual in connection with the business of banking in the countries where such foreign bank is organized or operating.

(k) To *establish* means to:

(1) Open and conduct business through an office;

(2) Acquire directly, through merger, consolidation, or similar transaction with another foreign bank, the operations of an office that is open and conducting business;

(3) Acquire an office through the acquisition of a foreign bank subsidiary that will cease to operate in the same corporate form following the acquisition;

(4) Change the status of an office; or

(5) Relocate an office from one state to another.

(*l*) *Federal agency, federal branch, state agency* and *state branch* have the same meanings as in section 1 of the IBA (12 U.S.C. 3101).

(m) *Foreign bank* means an organization that is organized under the laws of a foreign country and that engages directly in the business of banking outside of the United States. The term *foreign bank* does not include a central bank, of a foreign country that does not engage in a commercial banking business in the United States through an office.

(n) *Foreign banking organization* means a foreign bank, (as defined in section 1(b)(7) of the IBA (12 U.S.C. 3101(b)(7)), that operates a branch, agency, or commercial lending company subsidiary in the United States or that controls a bank in the United States, and any company of which such foreign bank is a subsidiary.

(*o*) *Home country,* with respect to a foreign bank, means the country in which the foreign bank is chartered or incorporated.

(p) *Home country supervisor,* with respect to a foreign bank, means the governmental entity or entities in the foreign bank's home country with responsibility for the supervision and regulation of the foreign bank.

(q) *Licensing authority* means:

(1) The relevant state supervisor, with respect to an application to establish a state branch, state agency, commercial lending company or representative office of a foreign bank; or

(2) The Comptroller, with respect to an application to establish a federal branch or federal agency.

(r) *Office or office of a foreign bank* means any branch, agency, representative office, or commercial lending company subsidiary of a foreign bank in the United States.

(s) The *parent* of a foreign bank means any company of which the foreign bank is a subsidiary; the *immediate parent* of a foreign bank is the company of which the foreign bank is a direct subsidiary; and the *ultimate parent* of a foreign bank is the parent of the foreign bank that is not the subsidiary of any other company.

(t) *Regional administrative office* means a representative office that:

(1) Is established by a foreign bank that operates one or more branches, agencies, commercial lending companies, or banks in the United States;

(2) Is located in the same city as one or more of the foreign bank's branches, agencies, commercial lending companies, or banks in the United States; and

(3) Manages, supervises, or coordinates the operations of the foreign bank or its affiliates, if any, in a particular geographic region.

(u) *Relevant state supervisor* means the state entity that is authorized to supervise and regulate a state branch, state agency or commercial lending company or representative office.

(v) *Representative office* means any place of business of a foreign bank, located in any state, that is not a branch, agency, or subsidiary of the foreign bank.

(w) *State* means any state of the United States or the District of Columbia.

(x) *Subsidiary* means any organization 25 percent or more of whose voting shares is directly or indirectly owned, controlled, or held with the power to vote by a company, including a foreign bank or foreign banking organization, or any organization that is otherwise controlled or capable of being controlled by a foreign bank or foreign banking organization.

## § 211.22 Interstate banking operations of foreign banking organizations.

(a) *Determination of home State.* (1) A foreign bank selecting its home State shall do so by filing with the Board a declaration of home State within 180 days of the effective date of this subpart. In the absence of such selection, the Board shall designate a foreign bank's home State. Within one year after the home State of a foreign bank has been determined, unless the Board authorizes a longer period:

(i) The foreign bank shall close domestic branches whose activities are not permissible under section 5(b) of the IBA, convert such domestic branches to agencies, or enter into an agreement with the Board regarding the deposits of such branches as prescribed in section 5(a) of the IBA; and

(ii) The foreign bank shall divest voting shares of interests in, or assets of banks that are not permissible under section 5(b) of the IBA.

(2) A foreign bank that currently does not operate a domestic branch or banking subsidiary shall not be required to select a home State and shall not have its home State designated by the Board.

(3) A foreign bank (except a foreign bank to which paragraph (b)(5) of this section applies) that has any combination of domestic branches, banking subsidiaries, agencies, or commercial lending company subsidiaries that, before July 27, 1978, were established or applies for in more than one State may select its home State only from those States in which the foreign bank has continuously operated such offices.

(4) A foreign bank that established or applied for one domestic branch or one banking subsidiary before July 27, 1978, and that was not otherwise engaged in banking in the United States on that date, shall have as its home State the State in which such domestic branch or banking subsidiary is located.

(5) A foreign bank that before July 27, 1978, had no domestic branches or banking subsidiaries or had only agencies or commercial lending companies, and, after that date, has established or establishes any domestic branch or banking subsidiary shall have as its home State that State in which its initial domestic branch or banking subsidiary is located.

(b) *Change of home State.* A foreign bank may change its home State once if:

(1) 30 days' prior notification of the proposed change is filed with the Board; and

(2) Domestic branches established and investments in banks acquired in reliance on its original home State selection are conformed to those that would have been permissible had the new home State been selected as its home State originally.

(c) *Bank mergers.* (1) A foreign bank with one or more banking subsidiaries that selects as its home State a State other than that in which a banking subsidiary is located, and that proposes to acquire through its subsidiary bank all or substantially all of the assets of a bank larger than its subsidiary bank (in terms of deposits) located outside the foreign bank's home State shall give 60 days' notification to the Board prior to consummation of the proposed transaction.

(2) If, after receiving the notification, the Board makes a preliminary determination within that period that the proposed acquisition would be inconsistent with the foreign bank's home State selection, the foreign bank shall:

(i) Redesignate as its home State the State in which its subsidiary bank is located; or

(ii) Show cause why in the facts and circumstances of its case its home State should not be redesignated (the foreign bank's submission may include a request for a hearing).

(3) On the basis of information available, the Board shall:

(i) Direct the foreign bank redesignate as its home State the State in which its subsidiary bank is located; or

(ii) Take no action with respect to the foreign bank's home State.

(4) Factors to be considered by the Board in making its preliminary and final determinations include the size of the proposed acquisition relative to the foreign bank's other operations in the United States and the ability of the foreign bank to change its home State.

(d) *Attribution of home State.* (1) A foreign bank or organization and the other foreign banks or organizations over which it exercises actual control shall be regarded as one foreign bank and shall be entitled to one home State.

(2) Actual control shall be conclusively presumed to exist in the case of a bank or organization that owns or controls a majority of the voting shares of another bank or organization.

(3) Where it appears to the Board that a foreign bank or organization exercises actual control over the management or policies of another foreign bank or organization, the Board may inform the parties that a preliminary determination of control has been made on the basis of the facts summarized in the communication. In the event of a preliminary determination of control by the Board, the parties shall within 30 days (or such longer period as may be permitted by the Board):

(i) Indicate to the Board a willingness to terminate the control relationship; or

(ii) Set forth such facts and circumstances as may support the contention that actual control does not exist (and may request a hearing to contest the Board's preliminary determination); or

(iii) Accede to the Board's preliminary determination, in which event the parties shall be regarded as one foreign bank and shall be entitled to one home State.

### § 211.23 Nonbanking activities of foreign banking organizations.

(a) [Reserved.]

(b) *Qualifying foreign banking organizations.* Unless specifically made eligible for the exemptions by the Board, a foreign banking organization shall qualify for the exemptions afforded by this section only if, disregarding its United States banking, more than half of its worldwide business is banking; and more than half of its banking business is outside the United States.[1] In order to qualify, a foreign banking organization shall:

(1) Meet at least two of the following requirements:

(i) Banking assets held outside the United States exceed total worldwide nonbanking assets;

(ii) Revenues derived from the business of banking outside the United States exceed total revenues derived from its worldwide nonbanking business; or

(iii) Net income derived from the business of banking outside the United States exceeds total net income derived from its worldwide nonbanking business; and

(2) Meet at least two of the following requirements:

(i) Banking assets held outside the United States exceed banking assets held in the United States;

(ii) Revenues derived from the business of banking outside the United States exceed revenues derived from the business of banking in the United States; or

(iii) Net income derived from the business of banking outside the United States exceeds net income derived from the business of banking in the United States.

(c) *Determining assets, revenues, and net income.* (1) For purposes of paragraph (b) of this section, the total assets, revenues, and net

1. None of the assets, revenues, or net income, whether held or derived directly or indirectly, of a subsidiary bank, branch, agency, commercial lending company, or other company engaged in the business of banking in the United States (including any territory of the United States, Puerto Rico, Guam, American Samoa, or the Virgin Islands) shall be considered held or derived from the business of banking "outside the United States."

income of an organization may be determined on a consolidated or combined basis. Assets, revenues and net income of companies in which the foreign banking organization owns 50 per cent or more of the voting shares shall be included when determining total assets, revenues, and net income. The foreign banking organization may include assets, revenues, and net income of companies in which it owns 25 per cent or more of the voting shares if all such companies within the organization are included;

(2) Assets devoted to, or revenues or net income derived from, activities listed in § 211.5(d) shall be considered banking assets, or revenues or net income derived from the banking business, when conducted within the foreign banking organization by a foreign bank or its subsidiaries.

(d) *Loss of eligibility for exemptions.*

(1) A foreign banking organization that qualified under paragraph (b) of this section shall cease to be eligible for the exemptions of this section if it fails to meet the requirements of paragraph (b) of this section for two consecutive years as reflected in its Annual Reports (F.R. Y–7 filed with the Board.

(2) A foreign banking organization that ceases to be eligible for the exemptions of this section may continue to engage in activities or retain investments commenced or acquired prior to the end of the first fiscal year for which its Annual Report reflects nonconformance with paragraph (b) of this section. Activities commenced or investments made after that date shall be terminated or divested within three months of the filing of the second Annual Report unless the Board grants consent to continue the activity or retain the investment under paragraph (e) of this section.

(3) A foreign banking organization that ceases to qualify under paragraph (b) of this section, or an affiliate of such foreign banking organization, that requests a specific determination of eligibility under paragraph (e) of this section may, prior to the board's determination on eligibility, continue to engage in activities and make investments under the provisions of paragraphs (f)(1), (2) and (4) of this section.

(e) *Specific determination of eligibility for non-qualifying foreign banking organizations.* (1) A foreign banking organization that does not qualify under paragraph (b) of this section for the exemption afforded by this section, or that has lost its eligibility for the exemptions under paragraph (d) of this section, may apply to the Board for a specific determination of eligibility for the exemptions.

(2) A foreign banking organization may apply for a specific determination prior to the time it ceases to be eligible for the exemptions afforded by this section.

(3) In determining whether eligibility for the exemptions would be consistent with the purposes of the BHC Act and in the public interest, the Board shall consider:

(i) The history and the financial and managerial resources of the organization;

(ii) The amount of its business in the United States;

(iii) The amount, type, and location of its non-banking activities, including whether such activities may be conducted by U.S. banks or bank holding companies; and

(iv) Whether eligibility of the foreign banking organization would result in undue concentration of resources, decreased or unfair competition, conflicts of interests, or unsound banking practices.

(4) Such determination shall be subject to any conditions and limitations imposed by the Board, including any requirements to cease activities or dispose of investments.

(5) Determinations of eligibility would generally not be granted where a majority of the business of the foreign banking organization derives from commercial or industrial activities or where the U.S. banking business of the organization is larger than the non-U.S. banking business conducted directly by the foreign bank or banks (as defined in § 211.2(j) of this part) of the organization.

(f) *Permissible activities and investments.* A foreign banking organization that qualifies under paragraph (b) of this section may:

(1) Engage in activities of any kind outside the United States;

(2) Engage directly in activities in the United States that are incidental to its activities outside the United States;

(3) Own or control voting shares of any company that is not engaged, directly or indirectly, in any activities in the United States other than those that are incidental to the international or foreign business of such company;

(4) Own or control voting shares of any company in a fiduciary capacity under circumstances that would entitle such shareholding to an exemption under section 4(c)(4) of the BHC Act if the shares were held or acquired by a bank.

(5) Own or control voting shares of a foreign company that it engaged directly or indirectly in business in the United States other than that which is incidental to its international or foreign business, subject to the following limitations:

(i) More than 50 percent of the foreign company's consolidated assets shall be located, and consolidated revenues derived from, outside the United States; provided however that, if the foreign company fails to meet the requirements of this paragraph for two consecutive years (as reflected in Annual Reports (F.R. Y–7)) filed with the Board by the foreign banking organization, the foreign company shall be divested or its activities terminated within one year of the filing of the second consecutive Annual Report that reflects nonconformance with the requirements of this paragraph, unless the Board grants consent to retain the investment under paragraphs (g) of this section;

(ii) The foreign company shall not directly underwrite, sell, or distribute, nor own or control more than 5 percent of the voting shares of a company that underwrites, sells, or distributes securities in the United States except to the extent permitted bank holding companies;

(iii) If the foreign company is a subsidiary of the foreign banking organization, the foreign company must be, or must control, an operating company, and its direct or indirect activities in the United States shall be subject to the following limitations:

(A) The foreign company's activities in the United States shall be the same kind of activities of related to the activities engaged in directly or indirectly by the foreign company abroad as measured by the "establishment" categories of the Standard Industrial Classification (SIC) (an activity in the United States shall be considered related to an activity outside the United States if it consists of supply, distribution, or sales in furtherance of the activity);

(B) The foreign company may engage in activities in the United States that consist of banking, securities, insurance or other financial operations, or types of activities permitted by regulation or order under section 4(c)(8) of the BHC Act, only under regulations of the Board or with the prior approval of the Board.

(*1*) Activities within Division H (Finance, Insurance, and Real Estate) of the SIC shall be considered banking or financial operations for this purpose, with the exception of acting as operators of nonresidential buildings (SIC 6512), operators of apartment buildings (SIC 6513), operators of dwellings other than apartment buildings (SIC 6514), and operators of residential mobile home sites (SIC 6515); and operating title abstract offices (SIC 6541); and

(*2*) The following activities shall be considered financial activities and may be engaged in only with the approval of the Board under subsection (g): Credit reporting services (SIC 7323); computer and data processing services (SIC 7371, 7372, 7373, 7474, 7375, 7376, 7377, 7378, and 7379); armored car services (SIC 7381); management consulting (SIC 8732, 8741, 8742, and 8748); certain rental and leasing activities (SIC 4741, 7352, 7353, 7359, 7513, 7514, and 7519); accounting, auditing and bookkeeping services (SIC 8721); courier services (SIC 4215 and 4513); and arrangement of passenger transportation (SIC 4724, 4725, and 4729).

(g) *Exemptions under section 4(c)(9) of the BHC Act.* A foreign banking organization that is of the opinion that other activities or investments may, in particular circumstances, meet the conditions for an exemption under section 4(c)(9) of the BHC Act may apply to the Board for such a determination by submitting to the Reserve Bank of the

District in which its banking operations in the United States are principally conducted a letter setting forth the basis for that opinion.

(h) *Reports.* (1) The foreign banking organization shall inform the Board through the organization's Reserve Bank within 30 days after the close of each quarter of all shares of companies engaged, directly or indirectly, in activities in the United States that were acquired during such quarter under the authority of this section.

(2) The foreign banking organization shall also report any direct activities in the United States commenced during such quarter by a foreign subsidiary of the foreign banking organization. This information shall (unless previously furnished) include a brief description of the nature and scope of each company's business in the United States, including the 4–digit SIC numbers of the activities in which the company engages. Such information shall also include the 4–digit SIC numbers of the direct parent of any U.S. company acquired, together with a statement of total assets and revenues of the direct parent.

(i) *Availability of information.* If any information required under this section is unknown and not reasonably available to the foreign banking organization, either because obtaining it would involve unreasonable effort or expense or because it rests peculiarly within the knowledge of a company that is not controlled by the organization, the organization shall:

(1) Give such information on the subject as it possesses or can reasonably acquire together with the sources thereof; and

(2) Include a statement either showing that unreasonable effort or expense would be involved or indicating that the company whose shares were acquired is not controlled by the organization and stating the result of a request for information.

### § 211.24 Approval of offices of foreign banks; procedures for applications; standards for approval; representative office activities and standards for approval; preservation of existing authority.

(a) *Board approval of offices of foreign banks—(1) Prior Board approval of branches, agencies, or commercial lending companies of foreign banks.* (i) Except as otherwise provided in paragraph (a)(3) of this section, a foreign bank shall obtain the approval of the Board before it:

(A) Establishes a branch, agency, or commercial lending company subsidiary in the United States; or

(B) Acquires ownership or control of a commercial lending company subsidiary.

(2) *Prior Board approval of representative offices of foreign banks.* Except as otherwise provided in paragraphs (a)(2) or (a)(3) of this section, a foreign bank shall obtain the approval of the Board before it establishes a representative office in the United States.

(i) *Prior notice for regional administrative offices.* After providing 45 days' prior written notice to the Board, a foreign bank may establish a regional administrative office. The Board may waive the 45–day period if it finds that immediate action is required by the circumstances presented. The notice period shall commence at the time the notice is accepted. The Board may suspend the period or require Board approval prior to the establishment of such an office if the notification raises significant policy, prudential, or supervisory concerns.

(ii) *General consent for representative offices.* The Board grants its general consent for a foreign bank to establish a representative office that solely engages in limited administrative functions that are clearly defined, are performed in connection with the banking activities of the foreign bank, and that do not involve contact or liaison with customers or potential customers (such as separately maintaining back office support systems), provided that the foreign bank notifies the Board in writing within 30 days of the establishment of the representative office.

(3) *After-the-fact Board approval.* Where a foreign bank proposes to establish a branch, agency, representative office, or commercial lending company in the United States through an acquisition of, or merger or consolidation with, a foreign bank with an office in the United States, the Board may, in its discretion, allow the acquisition, merger, or consolidation to proceed before an application to establish the office has been filed or acted upon under this section if:

(i) The foreign bank or banks resulting from the acquisition, merger, or consolidation, will not directly or indirectly own or control more than 5 percent of any class of the voting securities of, or control, a U.S. bank;

(ii) The Board is given reasonable advance notice of the proposed acquisition, merger, or consolidation;

(iii) Prior to consummation of the acquisition, merger, or consolidation, each of the relevant foreign banks commits in writing to comply with the procedures for an application under this section within a reasonable period of time or has already filed an application; and

(iv) Each of the relevant foreign banks commits in writing to abide by the Board's decision on the application, including, if necessary, a decision to terminate the activities of any such U.S. office, as the Board or the Comptroller may require.

(4) *Notice of change in ownership or control or conversion of existing office.* A foreign bank with a U.S. office shall notify the Board in writing within 10 days of either:

(i) A change in the foreign bank's ownership or control where the foreign bank is acquired or controlled by another foreign bank or company and the acquired foreign bank with a U.S. office continues to operate in the same corporate form as prior to the change in ownership or control; or

(ii) The conversion of a branch to an agency or representative office, an agency to a representative office, a state branch to a federal branch, or a state agency to a federal agency.

(5) *Transactions subject to approval under Regulation Y.* Subpart B of the Board's Regulation Y (12 CFR 225.11 through 225.14) governs the acquisition by a foreign banking organization of direct or indirect ownership or control of any voting securities of a bank or bank holding company in the United States if the acquisition results in the foreign banking organization's ownership or control of more than 5 percent of any class of voting securities of a U.S. bank or bank holding company, including through acquisition of a foreign bank or foreign banking organization that owns or controls more than 5 percent of any class of the voting securities of a U.S. bank or bank holding company.

(b) *Procedures for application*—(1) *Filing application.* An application for the Board's prior approval pursuant to this section shall be filed in the manner prescribed by the Board.

(2) *Publication requirement*—(i) *In general.* Except with respect to a proposed transaction where more extensive notice is required by statute or as otherwise provided in paragraphs (b)(2)(ii) and (b)(2)(iii) of this section, the applicant shall publish a notice in a newspaper of general circulation in the community in which the applicant proposes to engage in business. The notice shall state that an application is being filed as of the date of the notice and provide the name of the applicant, the subject matter of the application, the place where comments should be sent, and the date by which comments are due pursuant to paragraph (b)(3) of this section. The applicant shall furnish with its application to the Board a copy of the notice, the date of its publication, and the name and address of the newspaper in which it was published.

(ii) *Exception.* The Board may modify the publication requirement of paragraph (b)(2)(i) of this section in appropriate circumstances.

(iii) *Federal branch or federal agency.* In the case of an application to establish a federal branch or federal agency, compliance with the publication procedures of the Comptroller shall satisfy the publication requirement of this section. Comments regarding the application should be sent to the Board and the Comptroller.

(3) *Written comments.* Within 30 days after publication as required in paragraph (b)(2) of this section, any person may submit to the Board written comments and data on an application. The Board may extend the 30–day comment period if the Board determines that additional relevant information is likely to be provided by interested persons or if other extenuating circumstances exist.

(4) *Board action on application*—(i) *Time limits.* The Board shall act on an application from a foreign bank within 60 calendar days after

the foreign bank has been notified that its application has been accepted, unless the Board determines that the public interest will be served by providing additional time to review the application and notifies the applicant that the 60–day period is being extended.

(ii) *Additional information.* The Board may request any information in addition to that supplied in the application when the Board believes that additional information is necessary for its decision.

(5) *Coordination with other regulators.* Upon receipt of an application by a foreign bank under this section, the Board shall promptly notify, consult with, and consider the views of the licensing authority.

(c) *Standards for approval*—(1) *Mandatory standards*—(i) *General.* As specified in section 7(d) of the IBA (12 U.S.C. 3105(d)), the Board may not approve an application to establish a branch or an agency, or to establish or acquire ownership or control of a commercial lending company, unless it determines that:

(A) Each of the foreign bank and any parent foreign bank engages directly in the business of banking outside the United States and is subject to comprehensive supervision or regulation on a consolidated basis by its home country supervisor; and

(B) The foreign bank has furnished to the Board the information that the Board requires in order to assess the application adequately.

(ii) *Basis for determining comprehensive supervision or regulation on a consolidated basis.* In determining whether a foreign bank and any parent foreign bank is subject to comprehensive supervision or regulation on a consolidated basis, the Board will determine whether the foreign bank is supervised or regulated in such a manner that its home country supervisor receives sufficient information on the worldwide operations of the foreign bank (including the relationships of the bank to any affiliate) to assess the foreign bank's overall financial condition and compliance with law and regulation. In making such a determination, the Board shall assess, among other factors, the extent to which the home country supervisor:

(A) Ensures that the foreign bank has adequate procedures for monitoring and controlling its activities worldwide;

(B) Obtains information on the condition of the foreign bank and its subsidiaries and offices outside the home country through regular reports of examination, audit reports, or otherwise;

(C) Obtains information on the dealings and relationships between the foreign bank and its affiliates, both foreign and domestic;

(D) Receives from the foreign bank financial reports that are consolidated on a worldwide basis, or comparable information that permits analysis of the foreign bank's financial condition on a worldwide, consolidated basis;

(E) Evaluates prudential standards, such as capital adequacy and risk asset exposure, on a worldwide basis.

(2) *Discretionary standards.* In acting on any application under this subpart, the Board may take into account:

(i) *Consent of home country supervisor.* Whether the home country supervisor of the foreign bank has consented to the proposed establishment of a branch, agency or commercial lending company subsidiary;

(ii) *Financial resources.* The financial resources of the foreign bank (including the foreign bank's capital position, projected capital position, profitability, level of indebtedness, and future prospects) and the condition of any U.S. office of the foreign bank;

(iii) *Managerial resources.* The managerial resources of the foreign bank, including the competence, experience, and integrity of the officers and directors; the integrity of its principal shareholders; management's experience and capacity to engage in international banking; and the record of the foreign bank and its management of complying with laws and regulations, and of fulfilling any commitments to, and any conditions imposed by, the Board in connection with any prior application;

(iv) *Sharing information with supervisors.* Whether the foreign bank's home country supervisor and the home country supervisor of any parent of the foreign bank share material information regarding the operations of the foreign bank with other supervisory authorities;

(v) *Assurances to Board.* Whether the foreign bank has provided the Board with adequate assurances that information will be made available to the Board on the operations or activities of the foreign bank and any of its affiliates that the Board deems necessary to determine and enforce compliance with the IBA, the BHC Act, and other applicable federal banking statutes; these assurances shall include a statement from the foreign bank describing any laws that would restrict the bank or any of its parents from providing information to the Board; and

(vi) *Compliance with U.S. law.* Whether the foreign bank and its U.S. affiliates are in compliance with applicable U.S. law, and whether the applicant has established adequate controls and procedures in each of its offices to ensure continuing compliance with U.S. law, including controls directed to detection of money laundering and other unsafe or unsound banking practices.

(3) *Additional factor.* In acting on an application, the Board may consider the needs of the community and the history of operation of the foreign bank and its relative size in its home country, provided, however,

that the size of the foreign bank shall not be the sole factor in determining whether an office of a foreign bank should be approved.

(4) *Board conditions on approval.* The Board may impose such conditions on its approval as it deems necessary, including a condition which may permit future termination of any activities by the Board or, in the case of a federal branch or a federal agency, by the Comptroller, based on the inability of the foreign bank to provide information on its activities or those of its affiliates that the Board deems necessary to determine and enforce compliance with U.S. banking laws.

(d) *Representative offices.*—(1) *Activities.* A representative office may engage in:

(i) Representational and administrative functions in connection with the banking activities of the foreign bank which may include soliciting new business for the foreign bank, conducting research, acting as liaison between the foreign bank's head office and customers in the United States, performing any of the activities described in 12 CFR 250.141(h), or performing back office functions, but shall not include contracting for any deposit or deposit-like liability, lending money, or engaging in any other banking activity for the foreign bank; and

(ii) Other functions for or on behalf of the foreign bank or its affiliates, such as operating as a regional administrative office of the foreign bank, but only to the extent that such other functions are not banking activities and are not prohibited by applicable federal or state law or by ruling or order of the Board.

(2)*Standards for approval of representative offices.* As specified in section 10(a)(2) of the IBA (12 U.S.C. 3107(a)(2)), in acting on the application of a foreign bank to establish a representative office, the Board shall take into account to the extent it deems appropriate the standards for approval set out in paragraph (c) of this section.

(3) *Additional requirements.* The Board may impose any additional requirements that it determines to be necessary to carry out the purposes of the IBA.

(e) *Preservation of existing authority.* Nothing in this subpart shall be construed to relieve any foreign bank or foreign banking organization from any otherwise applicable requirement of federal or state law, including any applicable licensing requirement.

(f) *Reports of crimes and suspected crimes.* Except for a federal branch or a federal agency or a state branch that is insured by the Federal Deposit Insurance Corporation, a branch or agency or a representative office of a foreign bank operating in the United States shall file a criminal referral form, in accordance with the provisions of § 208.20 of the board's Regulation H, 12 CFR 208.20.

### § 211.25 Termination of offices of foreign banks.

(a) *Ground for termination*—(1) *General.* Under sections 7(e) and 10(b) of the IBA (12 U.S.C. 3105(e), 3107(b)), the Board may order a foreign bank to terminate the activities of its representative office, state branch, state agency, or commercial lending company subsidiary if the Board finds that:

(i) The foreign bank is not subject to comprehensive supervision or regulation on a consolidated basis by its home country supervisor in accordance with § 211.24(c)(1) of this subpart; or

(ii)(A) There is reasonable cause to believe that the foreign bank or any of its affiliates has committed a violation of law or engaged in an unsafe or unsound banking practice in the United States; and

(B) As a result of such violation or practice, the continued operation of the foreign bank's representative office, state branch, state agency, or commercial lending company subsidiary would not be consistent with the public interest or with the purposes of the IBA, the BHC Act, or the Federal Deposit Insurance Act (FDIA) (12 U.S.C. 1811 *et seq.*).

(2) *Additional ground.* The Board may also enforce any condition imposed in connection with an order issued under § 211.24 of this subpart.

(b) *Factor.* In making its findings under this section, the Board may take into account the needs of the community as well as the history of operation of the foreign bank and its relative size in its home country, provided, however, that the size of the foreign bank shall not be the sole determining factor in a decision to terminate an office.

(c) *Consultation with relevant state supervisor.* Except in the case of termination pursuant to paragraph (d)(3) of this section, before issuing an order terminating the activities of a state branch, state agency, or commercial lending company subsidiary under this section, the Board shall request and consider the views of the relevant state supervisor.

(d) *Termination procedures.*—(1) *Notice and hearing.* Except as otherwise provided in paragraph (d)(3) of this section, an order issued under paragraph (a)(1) of this section shall be issued only after notice to the relevant state supervisor and the foreign bank and an opportunity for a hearing.

(2) *Procedures for hearing.* Hearings under this section shall be conducted pursuant to the Board's Rules of Practice for Hearings (12 CFR part 263).

(3) *Expedited procedure.* The Board may act without providing an opportunity for a hearing if it determines that expeditious action is necessary in order to protect the public interest. When the Board finds that it is necessary to act without providing an opportunity for a

hearing, the Board may, solely in its discretion, provide the foreign bank that is the subject of the termination order with notice of the intended termination order, grant the foreign bank an opportunity to present a written submission opposing issuance of the order, or take any other action designed to provide the foreign bank with notice and an opportunity to present its views concerning the order.

(e) *Termination of federal branch or federal agency.* The Board may transmit to the Comptroller a recommendation that the license of a federal branch or federal agency be terminated if the Board has reasonable cause to believe that the foreign bank or any affiliate of the foreign bank has engaged in conduct for which the activities of a state branch or state agency may be terminated pursuant to this section.

(f) *Voluntary termination.* A foreign bank shall notify the Board at least 30 days prior to terminating the activities of any office. Notice pursuant to this paragraph is in addition to, and does not satisfy, any other federal or state requirements relating to the termination of an office or the requirement for prior notice of the closing of a branch pursuant to section 39 of the FDIA (12 U.S.C. 1831p).

**§ 211.26 Examination of offices and affiliates of foreign banks.**

(a) *Conduct of examinations.*—(1) *Examination of branches, agencies, commercial lending companies, and affiliates.* The Board may examine any branch or agency of a foreign bank, any commercial lending company or bank controlled by one or more foreign banks or one or more foreign companies that control a foreign bank, and any other office or affiliate of a foreign bank conducting business in any state.

(2) *Examination of representative offices.* The Board may examine any representative office in the manner and with the frequency it deems appropriate.

(b) *Coordination of examinations.* To the extent possible, the Board shall coordinate its examinations of the U.S. offices and U.S. affiliates of a foreign bank with the licensing authority and, in the case of an insured branch, the Federal Deposit Insurance Corporation (FDIC), including through simultaneous examinations of the U.S. offices and U.S. affiliates of a foreign bank.

(c) *Annual on-site examinations.* Each branch, agency, or commercial lending company subsidiary of a foreign bank shall be examined on-site at least once during each 12–month period (beginning on the date the most recent examination of the office ended) by:

(1) The Board;

(2) The FDIC, if the branch of the foreign bank accepts or maintains insured deposits;

(3) The Comptroller, if the branch or agency of the foreign bank is licensed by the Comptroller; or

(4) The state supervisor, if the office of the foreign bank is licensed or chartered by the state.

### § 211.27 Disclosure of supervisory information to foreign supervisors.

(a) *Disclosure by Board.* The Board may disclose information obtained in the course of exercising its supervisory or examination authority to a foreign bank regulatory or supervisory authority if the Board determines that disclosure is appropriate for bank supervisory or regulatory purposes and will not prejudice the interests of the United States.

(b) *Confidentiality requirement.* Before making any disclosure of information pursuant to paragraph (a) of this section, the Board shall obtain, to the extent necessary, the agreement of the foreign bank regulatory or supervisory authority to maintain the confidentiality of such information to the extent possible under applicable law.

### § 211.28 Limitation on loans to one borrower.

(a) *Limitation.* Except as otherwise provided in paragraph (b) of this section, the total loans and extensions of credit by all the state branches and agencies of a foreign bank outstanding to a single borrower at one time shall be aggregated with the total loans and extensions of credit by all federal branches and federal agencies of the same foreign bank outstanding to such borrower at the same time and shall be subject to the limitations and other provisions of section 5200 of the Revised Statutes (12 U.S.C. 84), and the regulations promulgated thereunder, in the same manner that extensions of credit by a federal branch or federal agency are subject to section 4(b) of the IBA (12 U.S.C. 3102(b)) as if such state branches and agencies were federal branches and agencies.

(b) *Preexisting loans and extensions of credit.* Any loans or extensions of credit to a single borrower that were originated prior to December 19, 1991 by a state branch or state agency of the same foreign bank and that, when aggregated with loans and extensions of credit by all other branches and agencies of the foreign bank, exceed the limits set forth in paragraph (a) of this section, may be brought into compliance with such limitations through routine repayment, provided that any new loans or extensions of credit, including renewals of existing unfunded credit lines or extensions of the dates of maturity of existing loans, to the same borrower shall comply with the limits set forth in paragraph (a) of this section.

# Chapter IV

# CAPITAL ADEQUACY

Almost twenty years ago, financial regulators in developed countries started to coordinate their activities. Prompting this effort was a dramatic growth in banks' international and cross-border activities. Banks from many countries were venturing abroad, opening offices and lending to borrowers outside their home country. At about the same time, the oil price rises of the early 1970s catapulted banks into a new job, recycling the deposits of oil surplus countries by lending to developing and industrial countries in deficit. The regulators were concerned.

This chapter reviews the remarkable story of how regulators from many countries cooperated to address those concerns. After devising ways to allocate among themselves responsibility for banks with cross-border operations, regulators turned to substantive policy. Capital adequacy rules were seen as a critical tool. Because rules for the principal activities of commercial banks and securities firms differ so much, we examine them separately.

## PART I. COMMERCIAL BANKS AND CREDIT RISK

This part considers the relevance of capital, the key elements of the Basle Accord, the Accord's performance so far, and the reasons for the remarkable degree of cooperation among the regulators.

## A. THE BACKGROUND TO THE ACCORD

Peter Cooke, the author of the following article about the Basle Accord, chaired the intergovernmental regulatory committee that produced the Accord. After he left the Bank of England for a senior position in Price Waterhouse (London), he evaluated the Accord's performance by survey. His survey, from which we reproduce the introduction, concluded that the Accord largely succeeded in accomplishing its goals.

### PETER COOKE, EXCERPTS FROM BANK CAPITAL ADEQUACY

Price Waterhouse London (July 1991).

### THE BASLE COMMITTEE ON BANKING SUPERVISION

The Basle Committee on Banking Supervision meets under the auspices of the Bank for International Settlements (the BIS) in Basle, Switzerland. It was established in 1976 as the Committee on Banking

Regulations and Supervisory Practices and is a standing committee of the Governors of the Group of Ten major industrialized countries. It consists of representatives of the central banks and supervisory authorities of the G10 countries and Luxembourg.[1] It meets several times a year, usually in Basle and a permanent Secretariat is provided by the BIS. Its task is to promote supervisory cooperation and coordination in the field of banking (and more recently, with other regulatory authorities, in related financial service activities). It makes recommendations to the Committee of Governors and when these recommendations are endorsed it becomes a matter for national authorities to implement them within their national systems of supervision. The Committee has no direct authority other than the weight of its collective opinion and the support of the Central Bank Governors. When the Governors' support is forthcoming its recommendations are implemented in G10 member countries, but increasingly over the years they have also been embraced and adopted by many other countries around the world who also have an interest in promoting the safety and soundness of both the international and their domestic banking systems.

The early work of the Basle Committee was directed to establishing principles for cooperation between banking regulators to cover the activities of banks operating across national frontiers and in a range of national jurisdictions. This led to what has become known as the Basle Concordat which, promulgated in 1976, set out a range of understandings between regulatory authorities about the sharing of supervisory responsibility for multinational banks. The original Concordat was significantly revised in 1983 to embrace the principle of consolidated supervision under which all the arms of international banking businesses are overseen by one authority which has a view of the overall business. The revised Concordat is now accepted as the basis for international cooperation between banking regulators in all countries and was usefully supplemented in 1990 by a paper setting out updated principles for exchanges of information between supervisors.

Also, since the mid–1970's, parallel work to that undertaken by the Basle Committee has been undertaken within the European Commission and by various bodies created within the European Community[2] (notably the Groupe de Contact and the Banking Advisory Committee) working to promote the objectives of the Treaty of Rome and, more recently in particular, the objective of a single market in financial services within the Community by the end of 1992.

## THE GENESIS OF CAPITAL CONVERGENCE

In the early 1980's, increased competition internationally led to concern over deteriorating capital levels in international banks and the

1. Countries represented on the Basle Committee are Belgium, Canada, France, Germany, Italy, Japan, Luxembourg, the Netherlands, Sweden, Switzerland, the United Kingdom, and the United States.

2. Member countries of the European Community are Belgium, Denmark, France, Germany, Greece, the Republic of Ireland, Italy, Luxembourg, the Netherlands, Portugal, Spain and the United Kingdom.

erosion of reasonable risk/reward relationships for banking business. This concern was exacerbated by the emerging debt crisis in the major developing countries. On the recommendation of the Basle Committee, national authorities in many countries began to press their banks to improve their capital ratios. At the same time, it became clear that different approaches in different countries to capital measurement was making comparisons from one banking system to another very difficult and that some more consistent approach would be desirable. From the early 1980's, both the Basle Committee and European Community organizations began to collect information on capital adequacy levels maintained by member country banks as a first step toward devising a more consistent basis for a common approach to capital measurement and capital standards for banks. Furthermore, by the mid–1980's, market developments (particularly the growth of new off-balance sheet instruments and techniques—in part at least themselves the consequence of regulators' pressure to increase capital against on-balance sheet business) were requiring banks and regulators to address a range of risks other than those traditionally arising from a bank's loan portfolio.

THE KEY ELEMENTS OF THE CAPITAL CONVERGENCE FRAMEWORK

- capital definition
  - capital is split between Tier 1 or core elements (equity and disclosed reserves) and Tier 2 or supplementary elements (undisclosed reserves, asset revaluation reserves, general provisions, hybrid debt/equity instruments and subordinated term debt). Some practitioners choose to distinguish between Upper Tier 2 (perpetual debt) and Lower Tier 2 (dated debt). The inclusion of the individual Tier 2 elements is at national discretion.
  - deductions from capital cover goodwill, investments in unconsolidated financial subsidiaries and, at national discretion, holdings of other banks' capital.
  - Tier 2 elements are only eligible up to 100% of Tier 1; subordinated debt must not exceed 50% of Tier 1; and general provisions are limited to 1.25% of risk assets.
- risk asset weightings
  - for on-balance sheet assets five basic scales of risk weightings are applied (0%, 10%, 20%, 50% and 100%). The main categories are central governments, public sector entities, banks and non-bank corporates and for the first three of these certain distinctions are made between OECD and non-OECD counterparties.
  - for off-balance sheet items a system of credit conversion factors is used. These include such categories as commitments and contingencies. The conversion factors are applied to the nominal principal amount of exposure to produce a credit equivalent amount which in turn is weighted according to the category of the counterparty. Interest rate and foreign exchange rate contracts are treated similarly but with adjustments to take into account their particular nature.
- target ratio and timetables
  - the Basle guidelines envisage that banks should build up gradually to the 8% minimum standard by the end of 1992 (of which at least 50% must be in Tier 1 capital). An interim standard of 7.25% was set to be reached by end 1990.
  - in building up from the interim to the full target ratio the balance between Tier 1 and Tier 2 and the amounts of subordinated debt and general provisions allowed in Tier 2 are gradually reduced.

All these factors came together to produce a growing sense among central banks and regulatory authorities that some greater standardization and enhancement of capital measurement and standards was highly desirable in the interests of the system. Efforts were intensified in 1986, particularly through a joint UK/US initiative, to advance a common approach to the measurement of capital through a risk-weighted rather than the more traditional gearing measure, and, through 1987, the Basle Committee hammered out an agreed capital measurement framework and agreed on the 8% minimum standard. After a period of consultation with banks around the world, these were adopted formally in July 1988 and widely endorsed by the supervisory community worldwide at the International Conference of Banking Supervisors in Tokyo in October that year.

By the time of the intense negotiations in 1987, the European Commission's proposals for a capital adequacy regime in the Community



1,2,3

as a cornerstone of its regulatory framework for banks based on the "single passport and home country control" principle were also well advanced, and representatives of the Commission attended the Basle Committee's meetings as observers. This helped to ensure that the EC proposals when introduced (and now implemented) corresponded very closely with the framework agreed in Basle. There is, of course, one major difference between the two sets of measures. The Basle Accord, strictly speaking, was designed to apply particularly to banks operating internationally; it was also a recommendation which, to become effective, had to be adopted and implemented at the national level. The EC directives, on the other hand—one on Own Funds and one on Solvency Ratios—are mandatory on member countries and cover all credit institutions established within the Community. ... The date for the implementation of the two directives in member countries national systems was 1 January 1991.

. . .

The Basle Committee is continuing work on the capital adequacy framework by monitoring national implementation and taking account of the effects of accounting standards and fiscal policy on this implementation. Recently, in February 1991, the Basle Committee published proposals aimed at achieving a more uniform definition of the treatment of provisions in the capital definition. ...

The Committee is also continuing work on the scope of the framework. The existing capital convergence framework essentially addresses only credit risk. Banks are, of course, exposed to a range of other forms of risk such as interest rate risk, foreign exchange risk, position risk, and settlement and operational risks. Since the Basle Accord was promulgated, both the Basle Committee and the European Commission have been pursuing intensively the ways in which these other kinds of risk might most appropriately be incorporated within the regulatory arrangements. In the course of pursuing this work there has been increasing contact between banking regulators and the authorities responsible for the regulation of securities business, particularly the International Organization of Securities Commissions (IOSCO). All three groupings are now coordinating very closely to try to develop a common approach to trading and interest rate risk in particular, although there are still a number of difficult issues to be resolved.

Basle + IOSCO

### *Questions*

1. Why would a government regulate the capital adequacy of its banks? What are the regulators' major concerns?

2. Capital/asset ratios are seen as a very powerful tool of regulation. Consider a simple ratio, such as 1/20. Many regulators applied such a rule before the Basel Accord.

   a. How would it affect a bank's operations?

b. Why would regulators want a certain amount of capital against a known volume of loans?

c. Would banks care about the extent to which they could leverage their capital?

3. What, if anything, is wrong with a simple capital/asset ratio? What would be the impact if banks from country X followed a 1/20 rule and those from country Y a 1/40 rule?

---

## B. THE BASLE ACCORD

Each country that chose to adopt the Accord was to implement it through national regulations. In the United States, the Federal Reserve Board issued one set of regulations for state banks and another for bank holding companies. The Fed had been a leading and early proponent of the Accord, working with the Bank of England to push regulators in other countries to accept it.

The following excerpts from the Fed's guidelines for state banks give some more background about the Accord. You should consider the nature of this Accord. Whose is it? What does it require? How do the parties to the Accord enforce it?

### 1. General Elements and the Definition of Capital

Federal Reserve System, Final Risk-Based Capital Guidelines (selected excerpts).

I. SUPPLEMENTARY INFORMATION AND BACKGROUND

A. *Purpose and History of the Risk–Based Capital Guidelines*

In 1986, and again in 1987 in conjunction with the Bank of England, the Federal banking agencies issued for public comment risk-based capital proposals applicable to U.S. banks and bank holding companies. The principal objectives of these early proposals were: 1) to develop more systematic procedures for factoring on- and off-balance sheet risks into supervisory assessments of capital adequacy; 2) to reduce disincentives to holding liquid, low-risk assets; and 3) to foster coordination among supervisory authorities from major industrial countries, many of which employ risk-sensitive capital measures.

These risk-based capital proposals were consistent with one of the major goals of the International Lending Supervision Act of 1983 ("ILSA"), 12 U.S.C. 3901 *et seq.*, which was to strengthen the bank regulatory framework by encouraging greater coordination among regulatory authorities in different countries. In addition to enhancing the banking agencies' authority to establish and enforce minimum levels of capital for U.S. banking organizations, this Act instructed those agencies to work with governments, central banks, and regulatory authorities of other countries to maintain and, where necessary, strengthen the capital positions of banking institutions involved in international lending.

The Federal Reserve deferred final action on the 1986 and 1987 proposals in order to participate in the development of a more broadly based capital framework that would be applicable to international banking organizations from the major industrial countries. In December 1987, the Basle Committee on Banking Regulations and Supervisory Practices ("Basle Supervisors' Committee") issued a consultative paper (the "Basle Accord") containing proposals for a risk-based capital framework. The principal objectives of the framework were to achieve greater convergence in the measurement and assessment of capital adequacy internationally and to strengthen the capital positions of major international banking organizations. That document served as the basis for consultations and public comment in the Group of Ten ("G–10") countries.

Domestically, the vehicle for consultation and public comment took the form of proposed risk-based capital guidelines, which were based upon the December 1987 Basle Accord, and which the Federal Reserve issued for public comment on March 1, 1988. The comment period on the proposed guidelines formally ended May 13, 1988, although the Board continued to receive and consider comments after that date. Over 180 comment letters were received that addressed various aspects of the proposed guidelines.

A number of changes were made to the December 1987 Basle Accord in light of comments received by both domestic and foreign banking authorities and as a result of consultations among the G–10 countries. The revised July 1988 Basle Accord that was endorsed by the central bank governors of the G–10 countries on July 11, 1988, reflects these changes.

The Board is now issuing in final form its risk-based capital guidelines, revised in light of the public comments received in response to the March 1988 proposal, the ongoing consultative process among the G–10 countries, and discussions with the other U.S. banking agencies. The Board is issuing two sets of guidelines: one is applicable to state member banks and the other is applicable to bank holding companies. The guidelines will be appended to the appropriate supervisory regulations for those organizations—for state member banks, the Board's Regulation H (12 CFR Part 208) and for bank holding companies, Regulation Y (12 CFR Part 225).

These guidelines establish a systematic analytical framework that: 1) makes regulatory capital requirements more sensitive to differences in risk profiles among banking organizations; 2) takes off-balance sheet exposures into explicit account in assessing capital adequacy; and 3) minimizes disincentives to holding liquid, low-risk assets.

The development of a risk-based framework in conjunction with supervisory officials from other industrial countries acknowledges the growing internationalization of major banking and financial markets throughout the world. The harmonization and strengthening of capital standards worldwide should contribute to a more stable and resilient international banking system and help mitigate a source of competitive inequality for international banks stemming from differences in national supervisory capital requirements.

In addition to international banks (to which the Basle Accord is specifically directed), the Federal Reserve is extending the application of the risk-based capital framework to all other U.S. banking organizations under its jurisdiction, regardless of size (as suggested in the March 1988 proposal). The Board believes that the underlying rationale behind the use of a risk-based capital approach applies to small domestic banking institutions as well as large international banking organizations.

The final guidelines contemplate, as did the March 1988 proposal, that the calculation of a risk-based capital ratio is only one step in evaluating capital adequacy. The focus of these guidelines is principally on broad categories of credit risk, although the risk-based framework does take some transfer risk considerations, as well as limited instances of interest rate and market risk, into account in assigning certain assets to risk categories. The measure does not take explicit account of other factors that can affect an organization's financial condition, such as overall interest rate exposure; liquidity, funding and market risks; the quality and level of earnings; investment or loan portfolio concentrations; the quality of loans and investments; the effectiveness of loan and investment policies; and management's overall ability to monitor and control other financial and operating risks. A complete assessment of capital adequacy must take account of each of these considerations including, in particular, the level and severity of problem and classified assets. Thus, the risk-based capital ratio is but one element in the assessment of overall capital adequacy, and the final supervisory judgment of an organization's capital adequacy may differ significantly from conclusions that might be drawn solely from the absolute level of the organization's risk-based capital ratio.

The guidelines, both for state member banks and bank holding companies, consist of a definition of capital, a system for assigning assets and off-balance sheet items to risk categories, a schedule for achieving a *minimum* risk-based capital ratio, and a phase-in period that provides for transitional arrangements. In light of the considerations just discussed, the Board expects that banking organizations will, as a general matter, operate with capital levels well above the minimum risk-based levels. As the Board previously has noted, this is particularly appropriate for banking organizations contemplating significant expansion proposals, as well as for institutions with high or inordinate levels of risk. In all cases, institutions should hold capital commensurate with the level and nature of the risks to which they are exposed.

B. *Overview of the Final Risk-Based Capital Guidelines*

The guidelines comprise four basic elements:

(1) An agreed definition of core or Tier 1 capital, consisting primarily of common stockholders' equity and certain categories of perpetual preferred stock, and a "menu" of internationally accepted items for supplementing core capital (supplementary or Tier 2 capital).

(2) A general framework for assigning assets and off-balance sheet items to broad risk categories and procedures for calculating a risk-based capital ratio.

(3) A schedule for achieving, by no later than the end of 1990, a minimum ratio of total capital-to-risk-weighted assets of 7.25 percent (of which at least 3.25 percentage points should be in the form of core capital elements) and, by no later than the end of 1992, a ratio of 8.0 percent (of which at least 4.0 percentage points should be in the form of core capital elements).

(4) Transitional arrangements and a phase-in period (running through the end of 1992) permitting banking organizations to include some supplementary capital elements in Tier 1 capital on a temporary basis and providing time to bring their capital positions into full conformity with the risk-based capital definitions and minimum supervisory standards.

## ATTACHMENT I

### Sample Calculation of Risk-Based Capital Ratio for State Member Banks

Example of a bank with $6,000 in total capital and the following assets and off-balance sheet items:

| Balance Sheet Assets | |
|---|---|
| Cash | $ 5,000 |
| U.S. Treasuries | 20,000 |
| Balances at domestic banks | 5,000 |
| Loans secured by first liens on 1–4 family residential properties | 5,000 |
| Loans to private corporations | 65,000 |
| Total Balance Sheet Assets | $100,000 |

| Off–Balance Sheet Items | |
|---|---|
| Standby letters of credit ("SLCs") backing general obligation debt issues of U.S. municipalities ("GOs") | $ 10,000 |
| Long-term legally binding commitments to private corporations | 20,000 |
| Total Off–Balance Sheet Items | $ 30,000 |

This bank's total capital to total assets (leverage) ratio would be:

($6,000/$100,000) = 6.00%.

To compute the bank's weighted risk assets:

1. Compute the credit equivalent amount of each off-balance sheet ("OBS") item.

| OBS Item | Face Value | | Conversion Factor | | Credit Equivalent Amount |
|---|---|---|---|---|---|
| SLCs backing municipal GOs | $10,000 | × | 1.00 | = | $10,000 |
| Long-term commitments to private corporations | $20,000 | × | 0.50 | = | $10,000 |

2. Multiply each balance sheet asset and the credit equivalent amount of each OBS item by the appropriate risk weight.

| | | | | | |
|---|---|---|---|---|---|
| 0% Category | | | | | |
| Cash | $ 5,000 | | | | |
| U.S. Treasuries | 20,000 | | | | |
| | $25,000 | × | 0 | = | 0 |
| 20% Category | | | | | |
| Balances at domestic banks | $ 5,000 | | | | |
| Credit equivalent amounts of SLCs backing GOs of U.S. municipalities | 10,000 | | | | |
| | $15,000 | × | 0.20 | = | $ 3,000 |
| 50% Category | | | | | |
| Loans secured by first liens on 1–4 family residential properties | $ 5,000 | × | 0.50 | = | $ 2,500 |
| 100% Category | | | | | |
| Loans to private corporations | $65,000 | | | | |
| Credit equivalent amounts of long-term commitments to private corporations | 10,000 | | | | |
| | $75,000 | × | 1.00 | = | $75,000 |
| Total Risk–Weighted Assets | | | | | $80,500 |

This bank's ratio of total capital to weighted risk assets (risk-based capital ratio) would be:

($6,000/$80,500) = 7.45%

## ATTACHMENT II

### Summary Definition of Qualifying Capital for State Member Banks Using the Year-end 1992 Standards

| Components | Minimum Requirements After Transition Period |
|---|---|
| Core Capital (Tier 1) | Must equal or exceed 4% of weighted risk assets |
| Common stockholders' equity | No limit |
| Qualifying non-cumulative perpetual preferred stock | No limit; banks should avoid undue reliance on preferred stock in Tier 1 |
| Minority interest in equity accounts of consolidated subsidiaries | Banks should avoid using minority interests to introduce elements not otherwise qualifying for Tier 1 capital |
| Less: Goodwill [1] | |
| Supplementary Capital (Tier 2) | Total of Tier 2 is limited to 100% of Tier 2 |
| Allowance for loan and lease losses | Limited to 1.25% of weighted risk assets [2] |
| Perpetual preferred stock | No limit within Tier 2 |
| Hybrid capital instruments and equity contract notes | No limit within Tier 2 |
| Subordinated debt and intermediate-term preferred stock (original weighted average maturity of 5 years or more) | Subordinated debt and intermediate-term preferred stock are limited to 50% of Tier 1; [3] amortized for capital purposes as they approach maturity |
| Revaluation reserves (equity and building) | Not included; banks encouraged to disclose; may be evaluated on a case-by-case basis for international [4] comparisons; and taken into account in making an overall assessment of capital. |
| Deductions (from sum of Tier 1 and Tier 2) | |
| Investments in unconsolidated subsidiaries | |
| Reciprocal holdings of banking organizations' capital securities | |
| Other deductions (such as other subsidiaries or joint ventures) as determined by supervisory authority | On a case-by-case basis or as a matter of policy after formal rulemaking |
| Total Capital (Tier 1 + Tier 2–Deductions) | Must equal or exceed 8% of weighted risk assets |

1. All goodwill, except previously grandfathered goodwill approved in supervisory mergers, is deducted immediately.
2. Amounts in excess of limitations are permitted but do not qualify as capital.
3. Amounts in excess of limitations are permitted but do not qualify as capital.
4. A proportionately greater amount may be deducted from Tier 1 capital if the risks associated with the subsidiary so warrant.

### *Questions*

1. Why was it necessary to define capital? What are the basic ideas that define capital?

2. Consider the components of Tier I capital (in Attachment II). What do they have in common? Why are they included in Tier I rather than Tier II.

a. What is qualifying non-cumulative perpetual preferred stock? Why is it not in Tier II?

b. Goodwill is sometimes included in the book value of stock. Why is it deducted from Tier I capital?

3. What is Tier II capital? How do its components differ from Tier I capital?

a. The inclusion of loan loss reserves in Tier II capital was the subject of a major debate among the countries. Although all eventually agreed to cap the loan loss reserves that could be treated as capital, some governments decided, and were permitted, to accept a higher limit than that adopted by the U.S. Why cannot all loan loss reserves be part of Tier II capital?

b. Revaluation reserves also attracted great debate among the countries. What are they? The Accord permitted regulators to allow as Tier II capital up to 45% of unrealized appreciation of a bank's assets. Some governments, including Japan's, did so. Why would any country permit this? Alternatively, why would any country prohibit this treatment, as the U.S. does?

4. Why is Tier II limited to 100% of Tier I capital?

5. Where do you suppose the 4% + 4% = 8% ratios came from?

6. While the Basle Accord specifies that it applies only to international banks, many countries including the U.S. decided to apply the standards to all banks. Is this appropriate?

7. What is the proper spelling of Basle/Basel?

---

## 2. Risk-weighting

The Accord shifted capital adequacy measures away from the simple ratios (such as 1/20) used in many countries at the time. It introduced risk-weighting. The Fed guidelines set out the risk weights in Attachment III, which follows.

### ATTACHMENT III

### Summary of Risk Weights and Risk Categories for State Member Banks

*Category 1: Zero percent*

1. Cash (domestic and foreign) held in the bank or in transit.
2. Balances due from Federal Reserve Banks (including Federal Reserve Bank stock) and central banks in other OECD countries.

3. Direct claims on, and the portions of claims that are unconditionally guaranteed by, the U.S. Treasury and U.S. Government agencies [1] and the central governments of other OECD countries, and local currency claims on, and the portions of local currency claims that are unconditionally guaranteed by, the central governments of non-OECD countries (including the central banks of non-OECD countries), to the extent that the bank has liabilities booked in that currency.
4. Gold bullion held in the bank's vaults or in another's vaults on an allocated basis, to the extent offset by gold bullion liabilities.

*Category 2: 20 percent*

1. Cash items in the process of collection.
2. All claims (long- or short-term) on, and the portions of claims (long- or short-term) that are guaranteed by, U.S. depository institutions and OECD banks.
3. Short-term claims (remaining maturity of one year or less) on, and the portions of short-term claims that are guaranteed by, non-OECD banks.
4. The portions of claims that are conditionally guaranteed by the central governments of OECD countries and U.S. Government agencies, and the portions of local currency claims that are conditionally guaranteed by the central governments of non-OECD countries, to the extent that the bank has liabilities booked in that currency.
5. Claims on, and the portions of claims that are guaranteed by U.S. Government-sponsored agencies.[2]
6. General obligation claims on, and the portions of claims that are guaranteed by the full faith and credit of, local governments and political subdivisions of the U.S. and other OECD local governments.
7. Claims on, and the portions of claims that are guaranteed by, official multilateral lending institutions or regional development banks.
8. The portions of claims that are collateralized [3] by securities issued or guaranteed by the U.S. Treasury, the central governments of

**1.** For the purpose of calculating the risk-based capital ratio, a U.S. Government agency is defined as an instrumentality of the U.S. Government whose obligations are fully and explicitly guaranteed as to the timely payment of principal and interest by the full faith and credit of the U.S. Government.

**2.** For the purpose of calculating the risk-based capital ratio, a U.S. Government-sponsored agency is defined as an agency originally established or chartered to serve public purposes specified by the U.S. Congress but whose obligations are not *explicitly* guaranteed by the full faith and credit of the U.S. Government.

**3.** The extent of collateralization is determined by current market value.

other OECD countries, U.S. Government agencies, U.S. Government-sponsored agencies, or by cash on deposit in the bank.

9. The portions of claims that are collateralized by securities issued by official multilateral lending institutions or regional development banks.
10. Certain privately-issued securities representing indirect ownership of mortgage-backed U.S. Government agency or U.S. Government-sponsored agency securities.
11. Investments in shares of a fund whose portfolio is permitted to hold only securities that would qualify for the zero or 20 percent risk categories.

*Category 3: 50 Percent*

1. Loans fully secured by first liens on 1–4 family residential properties that have been made in accordance with prudent underwriting standards, that are performing in accordance with their original terms, and are not past due or in nonaccrual status, and certain privately-issued mortgage-backed securities representing indirect ownership of such loans. (Loans made for speculative purposes are excluded.)
2. Revenue bonds or similar claims that are obligations of U.S. state or local governments, or other OECD local governments, but for which the government entity is committed to repay the debt only out of revenues from the facilities financed.
3. Credit equivalent amounts of interest rate and foreign exchange rate related contracts, except for those assigned to a lower risk category.

*Category 4: 100 Percent*

1. All other claims on private obligors.
2. Claims on, or guaranteed by, non-OECD foreign banks with a remaining maturity exceeding one year.
3. Claims on, or guaranteed by, non-OECD central governments that are not included in item 3 of Category 1 or item 4 of Category 2; all claims on non-OECD state or local governments.
4. Obligations issued by U.S. state or local governments, or other OECD local governments (including industrial development authorities and similar entities), repayable solely by a private party or enterprise.
5. Premises, plant, and equipment; other fixed assets; and other real estate owned.
6. Investments in any unconsolidated subsidiaries, joint ventures, or associated companies—if not deducted from capital.
7. Instruments issued by other banking organizations that qualify as capital—if not deducted from capital.

8. Claims on commercial firms owned by a government.
9. All other assets, including any intangible assets that are not deducted from capital.

***Questions***

1. What is the basic idea behind weighting assets by risk?

2. Examine the components of each category. They were the subject of great debate as the Accord was drafted.

a. What is the idea of each of the agreed classifications?

b. Do the items in each component make sense? For example, why do family home mortgages carry one weight and fully collateralized private loans another? Would these weightings distinguish between a U.S. bank's loans to a Greek bank and a Malaysian bank? Should they? What would your opinion be if you discovered that Malaysian banks were as strong or stronger than Greek banks?

3. Overall, how good is this technique of risk weighting?

---

## 3. The Treatment of Off-Balance Sheet Items

Before the Basle Accord, capital adequacy referred to the level of capital relative to loans and other assets carried on the bank's balance sheet. During the early 1980s, however, commercial banks sought more business for which they could charge fees without generating liabilities or assets. See the discussion in Chapter 1. Some of the largest international banks began to grapple with the question of how to measure the risk associated with these non-traditional services.

Regulators agreed on the solution in Attachment IV, which follows. The reading gives the basic elements. To learn about other matters, such as credit conversions for interest rate and foreign exchange contracts, see the guidelines.

Federal Reserve System, Final Risk-Based Capital Guidelines (selected excerpts).

### ATTACHMENT IV

### Credit Conversion Factors for Off-Balance Sheet Items for State Member Banks

*100 Percent Conversion Factor*

1. Direct credit substitutes. (These include general guarantees of indebtedness and all guarantee-type instruments, including standby letters of credit backing the financial obligations of other parties.)
2. Risk participations in bankers acceptances and direct credit substitutes, such as standby letters of credit.

3. Sale and repurchase agreements and assets sold with recourse that are not included on the balance sheet.
4. Forward agreements to purchase assets, including financing facilities, on which drawdown is certain.
5. Securities lent for which the bank is at risk.

*50 Percent Conversion Factor*

1. Transaction-related contingencies. (These include bid bonds, performance bonds, warranties, and standby letters of credit backing the nonfinancial performance of other parties.)
2. Unused portions of commitments with an original maturity[1] exceeding one year, including underwriting commitments and commercial credit lines.
3. Revolving underwriting facilities (RUFs), note issuance facilities (NIFs), and similar arrangements.

*20 Percent Conversion Factor*

1. Short-term, self-liquidating trade-related contingencies, including commercial letters of credit.

*Zero Percent Conversion Factor*

1. Unused portions of commitments with an original maturity[1] of one year or less, or which are unconditionally cancellable at any time, provided a separate credit decision is made before each drawing.

## Questions

1. What is an off-balance sheet item (other than something not on the balance sheet)? What do the items listed in Attachment IV have in common?

2. Would there have been any connection between the pre-Basle treatment of off-balance sheet items and their growth? Banks always had off-balance sheet activity. What might have accounted for the strong growth of these transactions in the early 1980s?

3. Why would regulators be concerned?

4. What is the basic idea behind the treatment of off-balance sheet items?

   a. What is the logic behind each of the conversion factors?

   b. How is risk weighted once the item is converted?

5. Compare the treatment of a $1,000 standby letter of credit and a $1,000 commercial letter of credit given to a private party and to the World Bank.

---

1. Remaining maturity may be used until year-end 1992.

## C. THE PERFORMANCE OF THE BASLE ACCORD

### 1. The Transition to Full Standards

The Accord provided for a phased transition to the new rules. Banks would have to meet a modest standard initially, then a more stringent one by the end of 1990, and finally meet the full test by the end of 1992. Almost immediately, banks began to adjust. By some accounts, such as that which follows, U.S. banks were ready early.

#### K. HOLLAND, "MOST BIG U.S. BANKS ALREADY MEET CAPITAL LEVELS OF THE BASEL ACCORD"

American Banker (April 19, 1990).

. . .

As of yearend 1989, at least 89 of the nation's top 100 bank holding companies reported that they had total capital in excess of the regulatory minimum of 8% of risk-adjusted assets that will be enforced beginning in 1992.

The same number of banking companies said that their Tier 1 capital, which consists mostly of equity, was above the 4% minimum agreed to by international regulators in the Basel accord of 1987.

Leading America's banks in both categories was Republic New York Corp., which had total capital of 21.15% and Tier 1 capital of 12.45%. All together, 42 banks had total capital in excess of 10% of risk-weighted assets, and nine had Tier 1 capital above that level.

At the bottom of the banks reporting was Bank of New England Corp., which reported a total capital ratio of 3.45%. The bank's capital ratio suffered when its real estate portfolio led to massive writeoffs.

On the surface, the largest U.S. banks appear better capitalized today than many of their overseas counterparts. For example, Japanese banks reported an equity-to-assets ratio, roughly equivalent to Tier 1 capital, of 2.59% at the end of September 1989.

But ...

Japanese banks have hidden reserves in the form of securities portfolios that have risen sharply in value in recent years. Even if those portfolios had dropped 45% by the time the Japanese banks reported their interim earnings in September 1989, their equity-to-asset ratios would have averaged 6.05%, according to Thomas E. Gove, a vice president at Thomson Bank Watch.

. . .

---

Hidden reserves brought a mixed blessing to Japanese banks. As Japan's stock market tumbled from 1989 (discussed in a later chapter), the reserves had to be adjusted down. The following events took place in 1990.

## "GREENSPAN SAYS JAPANESE BANKS' FINANCIAL POSITION ARE UNDERMINED BY MARKET DROP"

54 BNA's Banking Report 633 (April 9, 1990).

The recent selloff in Tokyo's financial markets has at least temporarily undermined the competitive position of Japanese banks in global markets, Federal Reserve Board Chairman Alan Greenspan said April 4.

"Clearly the decline in both stocks and bonds has taken some of the momentum out of the Japanese banks' expansion," Greenspan said.

. . .

In Tokyo trading, the 225–share Nikkei index fell 316.78 points, or 1.10 percent, ending the day at 28,442.94. Tokyo shares have plunged about 27 percent since their peak at the end of 1989, wiping out billions of dollars in assets held by individual and institutional investors. Rising interest rates and a falling yen have brought additional losses for bond holders.

Greenspan said even though Japanese financial institutions may have lost some clout in global competition, "the cost of capital is still lower in the Tokyo market than in New York," giving them an advantage compared to U.S. banks. Often, he noted, Japanese banks have large wholesale operations and can compete with loans that offer razor-thin spreads over the cost of funds.

But U.S. banks have fought back by offering an array of off-balance-sheet financing techniques such as interest rate swaps and foreign exchange rate hedges, Greenspan said. According to Fed officials, as of Sept. 30, 1990, the nine U.S. money center banks had $615 billion in assets. In off-balance-sheet activities, they had recorded foreign exchange contracts worth over $2 trillion and interest-rate swaps of $959 billion.

Japan's stock market continued to drop intermittently after that.

As they adjusted their national rules, regulators could set standards higher than those set by Basle. It was a tough call, given competitive pressures, as the following article about Germany shows.

## DAVID WALLER, "GERMAN BANKS WIN MODIFICATION TO CAPITAL RULES"

Financial Times, November 26, 1992.

GERMAN banks have won a partial victory in their long-running battle over new capital adequacy rules which are to be introduced into German law at the beginning of next year.

. . .

At issue is the treatment of unrealised hidden reserves, which consist of extensive portfolios of shares, industrial participations and property, often acquired decades ago and standing at a much lower book value than market value. The German banks want to be able to unlock this value.

. . .

The German government, with the support of the Bundesbank, proposed that German banks should be obliged to accumulate Tier 1 capital—equity, retained earnings and profit-participating certificates—of 5 per cent before being able to count hidden reserves to a maximum of 1 per cent.

Under the compromise proposal, banks will be able to count their unrealised hidden reserves up to a new maximum of 1.4 per cent, once they have built up Tier 1 capital of 4.4 per cent.

Under the new rules, banks will not be allowed to take advantage of the full market value of hidden assets: for prudential reasons banks will only be able to count a certain percentage of the asset value.

In general, the new capital regime will be harder for German banks: at present they are obliged to have core capital of 5.6 per cent.

Under the Brussels-inspired rules, the total required will increase to 8 per cent but for the first time German banks will be able to include not only unrealised hidden reserves but also classes of capital such as subordinated debt.

By the end of 1992, most international banks in major industrial countries reported at least nominal compliance with Basel's 4% + 4% rule, some just barely and other by a large margin. One question was how many could meet the standard in real terms.

### *Questions*

1. Think through the way swings in the market values of a Japanese bank's assets would affect its efforts to meet the Basle ratios. Work through the way hidden reserves affect these efforts. Is the market value of the bank's common stock relevant?

2. What are the banks' options as they adjust to comply with the Accord's standards? How would you expect their responses to affect financial markets?

---

## 2. Amendments to the Accord

After 1988, as the implications of the Accord became apparent, people tried to change the terms of the Accord itself and as it was adopted at the national level. Near the end of 1991, the Committee accepted one amendment to the Accord.

## "BASEL PANEL TIGHTENS RISK-CAPITAL RULE"

American Banker, 11/6/91.

The Basel Committee on Banking Supervision has amended risk-based capital guidelines to make it harder for banks to count loan-loss reserves as capital.

. . .

Until now, the Basel capital guidelines have not clearly identified what sorts of specifically allocated reserves should be excluded from risk-based capital.

But an amendment adopted Tuesday calls for banks to exclude from capital any provisions or reserves specifically created against identified losses—especially losses due to country risk or to depreciating real estate.

. . .

U.S. regulators said they already require U.S. banks to exclude specifically allocated reserves from their capital. "We think this will have no effect on U.S. banks' capital ratios," said one.

American banks report their general loan-loss reserves as a line item on call reports. And they report allocated transfer risk reserves—reserves required by ICERC, an interagency committee assessing country risk—on a separate line.

Regulators already make U.S. banks exclude those allocated reserves from their capital ratios.

. . .

National regulators tried to refine the terms. In the U.S., the Fed proposed in a press release on April 10, 1992 to modify the guidelines as follows:

— lower the risk weight from 100 percent to 50 percent for multi-family housing loans meeting criteria that are specified in the proposal. This change was directed by a provision of the RTC Refunding Act of 1991.

— lower the risk weight from 20 percent to zero for certain transactions that are collateralized by cash and OECD central government securities, including U.S. Government agency securities, provided the transactions meet criteria specified in the proposal. This change is designed to put U.S. banking organizations on a more equal footing with foreign banks with regard to the capital treatment of such transactions.

The Fed issued the first amendment as an interim rule on December 23, 1992.

Others mounted a broad attack on the Accord, arguing that it led to a credit crunch that contributed to recession in the countries that adopted it. Robert Litan, at the Brookings Institution, made the following case:

## ROBERT E. LITAN, "NIGHTMARE IN BASLE"

The International Economy, November/December 1992, p. 7.

. . .

### THE BASLE STANDARDS AND THE "CREDIT CRUNCH"

... The Basle risk weights tilted the incentives of banks heavily toward investing in government bonds rather than making loans. This feature of the risk weights escaped serious criticism most likely because the economies of the industrialized countries were still expanding in the mid-to-late 1980s when the Basle standards were being negotiated.

But times have changed. The economies of Europe, the United States and Japan now are gasping for air. And the Basle risk weights are making it more difficult for them to breathe by discouraging business lending in the United States.

Consider the typical U.S. bank that, at this writing, pays about three percent for deposits and an average of roughly ten percent for long-term (uninsured) debt and equity. With a zero risk weight on government bonds, the cost of funding an investment in such bonds solely with deposits is just three percent. In contrast, the typical bank must fund a 100–percent risk-weighted investment in riskier commercial loans with 8 percent capital and 92 percent deposits, at a weighted cost of 3.56 percent.

In short, to justify making any loan, the bank must more than cover the 56–basis point differential in the costs of funding the loan relative to the costs of funding the purchase of a government. For many banks, the choice has been easy to make. With a steeply upward-sloping yield curve, a bank can earn a margin of roughly three per cent simply by taking short-term deposits and investing them in intermediate-term bonds—and do this with no credit risk! Why, therefore, chase a few more basis points in making a risky loan?

In fact, so many banks have been choosing to play the government bond yield curve that the total volume of bank (commercial and industrial) loans actually fell by nearly $20 billion between December 1991 and July 1992. In contrast, total bank investments in U.S. government bonds grew by more than $50 billion during the same period. As a result, by mid-summer 1992, banks for the first time in nearly three decades had more invested in government securities than in C & I loans.

It is no doubt true that weak demand for commercial loans has contributed to this situation. But the undeniable fact remains that before the Basle Accord, when capital ratios were defined and enforced without assigning different risk weights to different types of assets, the cost of funding both government bonds and loans were the same. Now the funding costs are unequal by a significant margin and the result should not be surprising.

The table provides some further evidence of the distortions created by the risk weights. It compares the growth in both overall bank assets and the total volume of loans and leases during the first fifteen months of the recoveries from the past three recessions. The table highlights two striking differences between the most recent recovery and the two earlier episodes. Bank asset growth this time is sharply lower, as banks have resisted turning the reserves created by the Fed's open market operations into loans and therefore new deposits. And unlike the earlier periods, total loan volume actually has dropped to a significant degree. This experience is in especially sharp contrast to the sharp increase in total loans, much larger even than the growth in bank assets, during the 1983–84 recovery from what then was the deepest U.S. recession (1981–82) since the Great Depression. Clearly, banks this time around are more gun-shy about making loans. The Basle risks weights are a contributing factor.

Responses of the Banking System

*During the First 15 Months of the Past Three Recoveries*

| | % Change in Bank Assets | % Change in Loans and Leases |
|---|---|---|
| March 1975–June 1976 | +7.0 | + 2.6 |
| January 1983–April 1984 | +7.9 | +16.7 |
| March 1991–June 1992 | +1.7 | − 3.7 |

Source: DRI ??

Moreover, by pushing banks into playing the government bond yield curve, the risk weights are impelling banks to take on greater interest rate risk, which may come to haunt them when the yield flattens, as it eventually will. The Federal Reserve has just proposed new rules that would factor interest rate risk into U.S. capital standards. But it is highly ironic that the Fed should now need to plug the leaks in the new capital regime that were largely created by the risk weights in the first place.

---

This analysis prompted members of Congress to seek redress.

## ROBERT M. GARSSON, "KENNEDY SEEKS CUT IN KEY CAPITAL REQUIREMENT"

American Banker, May 4, 1992.

WASHINGTON—In an effort to spur bank lending, Rep. Joseph P. Kennedy 2d., D–Mass., has introduced legislation to reduce a key capital requirement.

The Bank Lending Stimulus Act would cut the leverage capital limit to 3% of assets for up to 18 months. Currently, the minimum stands at 4%, and regulators may require individual banks to meet a higher standard.

### Odds Against Enactment

The Kennedy measure, one of a number of legislative initiatives aimed at easing the credit crunch, faces tough odds and is not expected to be enacted into law this year.

Rep. Kennedy was among the first on Capital Hill to highlight problems from the credit crunch, which has hit his native New England particularly hard. By reducing the leverage limit, more of a bank's assets would be available for commercial loans.

. . .

### *Questions*

1. How easy do you suppose it is to amend the Accord?

2. Are possible macroeconomic effects of the Accord appropriately the concern of those who framed and implement it? How significant should these issues be in decisions to make changes?

## 3. Toward Better Prudential Rules

Improved safety and soundness were the first stated objective of the Accord. We know of no systematic analysis that shows if this objective has been achieved. One's decision should be greatly influenced by one's analysis of the risk-weighting techniques. Robert Litan, in the article cited above, said "Ideally, I would like to see the entire risk weighting system completely scrapped, except to allow for some weighting of off-balance sheet risks in computing the required capital ratio."

## 4. Toward a More Level International Playing Field

A second goal of the Accord was to level the playing field so that no government could give its banks a competitive advantage over other countries' banks by setting low capital adequacy rules. Did it succeed? The early returns raise grave doubts. As you read the following critiques, ask yourself about the implicit standard of performance expected from the Accord. How much can be appropriately asked?

One major complaint was that not all banks had access to the full range of instruments that make up capital. A British banker wrote pseudonymously:

## GALLATIN, "NOTHING TO LOSE BUT THEIR CHAINS"

Euromoney, September 1992.

* * *

Filling lower tier two is easy; filling upper tier two—perpetual subordinated debt—is another matter altogether. Basle permits perpetuals but killed the market because the only buyers of bank perpetuals, in size, were banks themselves, and Basle effectively forbids banks to be buyers themselves. As a result banks have turned to "para-perpetuals" which just scrape into that category: variable-rate notes and step-up perpetuals. The chances are that most of these will be redeemed as soon as banks get a fair shot at raising core capital at a competitive cost.

For the moment, tier one capital is close to impossible to find for most banks, except by issuing ordinary shares, which are expensive and dilutive both to ownership and to earnings. Banks have therefore turned to perpetual preferred stock.

Part of the Basle process was the creation of uniform rules for banks in the developed world, a "level playing-field". Nowhere is the playing-field less level than in the raising of non-cumulative perpetual preferred stock. The only market for this instrument is the U.S. Only the Anglo–Saxon countries, plus a handful of others, provide for preferred stock in their company law. Ironically, the U.K. banks did best from this anomaly because they receive a tax advantage under the U.K.–U.S. double taxation treaty when they issue in the American market. For them, raising tier one capital in the U.S. costs less than it does for American banks issuing in their home market.

Banks from outside the Anglo–Saxon area have gone to great lengths to try to issue tier one preferred shares. Few have succeeded but among them are one Japanese, one French and a few Spanish banks. All of them have had to erect elaborate structures in order to achieve cost-effective tier one capital in a form which U.S. investors will buy.

Other banks have used variants on traditional instruments, for example mandatory convertible subordinated bond issues, to achieve tier one if not now, then in the future.

. . .

---

Analysis of the competitive effect of the Accord across many countries is thwarted by the many factors that shape international competition. Professors Scott and Iwahara compared Japan and the United States. The following is the introduction to their article.

## SCOTT AND IWAHARA, "IN SEARCH OF A LEVEL PLAYING FIELD: THE IMPLEMENTATION OF THE BASLE CAPITAL ACCORD IN JAPAN AND THE UNITED STATES"

Group of Thirty (1994).

... the framers of the Accord sought to establish a framework that was fair and consistent and that would diminish (the Accord's word) competitive inequality. This study focuses on the second objective by examining the implementation of the 1988 Accord in Japan and the United States.

. . .

At the outset, we are extremely skeptical that any accord on capital can have a major impact on competition among banks in different countries. Competitive advantages between banks in two countries are caused primarily not by differences in capital ratios but by differences in comparative advantage, the fundamentals of each economy, and government support in the form of safety net policies. As the "Capital Scorecard" we have devised shows, the stronger safety net in Japan enables that country's banks to obtain cheaper funding than their U.S. competitors can.

**Capital Scorecard**

| **Factor** | **Advantage** | |
|---|---|---|
| | **Japan** | **U.S.** |
| Safety net and other non-Basle policies | ■ | |
| Ratios in addition to Basle | ■ | |
| Scope of application of Basle requirements | | ■ |
| Qualifying capital | | ■ |
| Risk-weighting of assets | | ■ |
| Enforcement | ■ | |

Japanese banks also have an advantage because U.S. banks are subject to capital ratios over and above those imposed by Basle, through leverage ratios, capital required for interest rate risk, and capital required to avoid onerous forms of supervision. On the other hand, U.S. bank holding companies are not strictly subject to the Basle requirements. This enables them to raise capital and downstream it to a bank in the form of equity. Because the Japanese have no bank holding companies, they cannot take advantage of this device.

The heart of the Basle Accord is the definition of capital and the assessment of the risks associated with different kinds of assets (risk-weighting). We believe that the United States has an advantage in these areas, but not because of any fancy footwork in implementing the Accord. Because they can exploit a more sophisticated capital market, U.S. banks can raise capital through cheaper instruments. Moreover, the U.S. tax and accounting rules, and related regulations, give U.S. banks advantages in using gains on appreciated securities as a source of capital.

U.S. banks also have an advantage in risk-weighting because activities that are much more important in the United States than in Japan—residential real estate lending, for example—have low risk-weights. Finally, Japan benefits by significantly less strict enforcement.

We conclude that its limited scope prevents the Basle Accord from making a significant contribution to leveling the playing field between Japanese and U.S. banks. Indeed, by setting a capital floor of 8 percent for risk-weighted assets, the Accord makes the playing field less level, to the disadvantage of U.S. banks, in one important sense. The reason is that Japanese banks do not need to hold 8 percent capital because of the strength of their safety net. Since the Basle Accord mandates that they do, U.S. banks are under some pressure to hold proportionately more, to maintain their competitive standing, and doing so may well drive up U.S. bank costs unnecessarily. In the real world a minimum capital standard may distort rather than improve competitive equality.

We further conclude that only by accident could the Accord diminish competitive inequality between U.S. and Japanese banks. A central point of our study is that even though the capital requirement was implemented in the same way in both countries, it had dramatically different impacts as a result of differences in accounting and tax rules and banking regulations.

The Accord acknowledges that accounting and tax rules could distort the comparability of the capital positions of international banks. Our study shows that such distortion is so massive as to render comparability impossible. The effects cannot be trivialized by a mere disclaimer. We believe the burden is now on the defenders of the Accord to produce credible evidence, beyond rhetoric, that the Accord has made *any* meaningful contribution to leveling the playing field. We guess that the Accord has been of more benefit to U.S. than to Japanese banks because they operate in a more favorable accounting, tax, and regulatory context.

Some claim that, by imposing a minimum 8 percent capital ratio, the Basle Accord helped level the playing field by establishing a common framework that will lead to convergence; in this view our study points only to the need for further harmonization of accounting, regulatory, and tax rules. We agree that the Accord would be more beneficial *if* there were meaningful progress toward harmonization with respect to safety net subsidies and other rules. That we may have a more even playing field in the future does not mean we have one now; and the future, by definition, remains to be seen.

Given the historical propensity of nations to compete for advantage, one might conclude that harmonization is unlikely, and that nations will continue to use safety nets and other rules to their advantage. Our analysis is static in the sense that, by necessity, it is based largely on data and practices in 1992, the first year that the Accord was fully in effect. Still, absent meaningful harmonization outside the Basle framework, we have no reason to believe our conclusions will change.

Finally, how meaningful is it, in the modern world of finance, to even the playing field between banks in different countries? More and more, the traditional business of banking is conducted by nonbanks, such as finance companies and insurance and securities firms, that are entirely outside the Basle framework. Because the Accord does not address this central issue, it can, at best, equalize competition on only part of the playing field. Indeed, the major beneficiaries of the increases in the "equal" costs imposed by the Accord may be firms that compete with banks but are not subject to such costs.

. . .

In short, we believe that the Basle Accord cannot be justified on the grounds that it enhances competition. It must be judged solely on its contribution to strengthening the safety and soundness of international banks—and even that in the light of its possible contribution to credit crunches in periods of economic downturn.

### The Competitive Impact of Capital Ratios

Capital requirements have a significant impact on the competitiveness of banks. A bank that is more highly leveraged than another bank may enjoy a competitive advantage. Take two banks, Bank A and Bank B. They face a 7 percent market rate of interest for marginal increases in the cost of funding; they operate in the same markets and are equally creditworthy. Bank A has a 4 percent capital requirement, that is capital must equal 4 percent of total assets, and Bank B has a 6 percent requirement. Here, capital refers to equity.

The total cost for Bank A in making new loans is

$$.07 \times .96 + .0C \times .04 = .0672 + .0004C,$$

where C is the cost of capital; and the total cost for Bank B in making new loans is

$$.07 \times .94 + .0C \times .06 = .0658 + .0006C.$$

Where the cost of capital exceeds the marginal interest rate (7 percent in the example), Bank A, the more leveraged bank, has a cheaper cost of funds. If, for example, the cost of capital for both banks were 10 percent, the cost of funds for Bank A would be 7.12 percent (6.72 + 0.40), as compared with Bank B's 7.18 percent (6.58 + 0.60). Since equity is almost always costlier than debt because equity is more risky and receives less favorable tax treatment, Bank A will enjoy a competitive advantage over Bank B. Bank A can charge borrowers a lower rate of interest and make the same spread (profit) as Bank B. For example, Bank A can make a 2 percent spread by charging a borrower 9.12 percent, whereas Bank B must charge 9.18 percent to make the same spread. In addition, capital requirements affect the total lending capacity of banks. Bank A, with a 4 percent capital requirement, can lend twenty-five times its capital; Bank B, with a 6 percent requirement, can lend only 16.66 times its capital.

**Competitive Bailout Differential**

In a perfect market, creditors of Bank A might insist on higher rates of interest than would creditors of Bank B because Bank A's higher leverage ratio and smaller capital cushion increase their risk. Government safety nets prevent this from happening in banking. Because deposit insurance, bailout policies, and lender-of-last-resort facilities combine to protect bank creditors against bank failure, creditors may be relatively indifferent to the leverage ratios of their debtors. Although they may not be absolutely certain that they will be repaid, they know that the government will absorb a very significant part of the repayment risk for large international banks. This public absorption of risk means that these banks need not fully compensate their creditors for the risk of increased leverage. From this perspective, the difference between capital/asset ratios for banks in two countries may merely reflect different levels of government subsidy.

Table 1 sets out the Bank for International Settlements (BIS) capital ratios for the ten largest banks (as of 1992) in Japan and the United States. We compare these banks throughout the study since they are likely to be in direct and significant competition with each other in a variety of asset, liability, and off-balance-sheet products.

All of the banks exceed the total minimum capital ratio of 8 percent that BIS requires, but U.S. banks have the higher ratios. The average total ratio of the ten largest U.S. banks is 13.60, compared with 9.67 in Japan. In addition, U.S. banks hold a significantly higher percentage of their total capital in Tier I capital, 67 percent compared with 51 percent for the Japanese. The lower Japanese ratios may merely reflect the recent economic downturn in Japan, particularly the real estate loan losses and the fall of the prices of shares on the Tokyo Stock Exchange. It might also reflect the need for U.S. banks to have more capital than Japanese banks in order to compete with them effectively.

If the de facto guarantee the Japanese government provides against failure is perceived to be stronger than the U.S. government guarantee, U.S. banks would have to be better capitalized than Japanese banks to enjoy the same cost of funds. Of course, U.S. banks would then incur additional costs for capital that Japanese banks did not. U.S. banks could compensate for these additional costs only by being more efficient. The increase in efficiency would then generate the resources necessary for additional capital.

The ratios in Table 1 reflect book rather than real capital. Given more accurate measures of capital, capital ratios for U.S. banks might not be higher. For example, Japanese banks can use only 45 percent of unrealized gains on securities in their investment account as capital, and revaluation reserves alone represent approximately 40 percent of the Tier II capital of the ten largest Japanese banks. Before the 1991–92 fall of the Nikkei index, this percentage would have been considerably

**Table 1. Capital Ratios of Japanese and U.S. Banks**

| Bank | Total | Tier I [1] | Tier II [2] |
|---|---|---|---|
| | **Japanese banks** (September 1993) | | |
| Daiichi | 9.80 | 5.00 | 4.80 |
| Sakura | 9.05 | 4.52 | 4.52 |
| Fuji | 9.82 | 5.11 | 4.71 |
| Mitsubishi | 9.81 | 4.90 | 4.90 |
| Sanwa | 10.20 | 5.18 | 5.02 |
| Sumitomo | 9.91 | 5.45 | 4.45 |
| Tokai | 9.27 | 4.63 | 4.63 |
| Tokyo | 10.41 | 5.44 | 4.97 |
| IBJ | 9.25 | 4.62 | 4.62 |
| LTCB | 9.25 | 4.62 | 4.62 |
| | **U.S. banks** (December 1993) [3] | | |
| BankAmerica | 12.03 | 7.61 | 4.42 |
| Citibank | 11.61 | 6.69 | 4.92 |
| Nations | 11.87 | 7.58 | 4.29 |
| Chemical | 12.40 | 8.30 | 4.10 |
| Chase | 13.68 | 8.81 | 4.87 |
| Bankers | 16.49 | 9.97 | 6.52 |
| Morgan | 14.86 | 10.61 | 4.25 |
| Wells Fargo | 15.59 | 10.62 | 4.97 |
| 1st Interstate | 13.16 | 9.96 | 3.20 |
| Banc One | 14.37 | 10.63 | 3.74 |

1. Basically, equity and earnings.
2. Debt instruments representing residual claims, like preferred stock and subordinated term debt, as well as revaluation and loan loss reserves.
3. The data on U.S. banks are actually for bank holding companies. This is the proper comparison because the nonbanking operations of Japanese banks are conducted in subsidiaries of banks rather than in nonbanking subsidiaries of the parent holding company. Our comparison thus takes into account the consolidated data for nonbanking operations in both countries.

**Source:** Federal Reserve, Japanese Securities Report.

higher. But given Japanese tax rates in excess of 55 percent, revaluation reserves correctly state the maximum after-tax income available from the sale of these securities. And, if securities prices fell from their September 1993 values, the reported capital in Table 1 would be overstated. Even after the fall of Tokyo real estate prices, Japanese banks may have a substantial amount of undisclosed and unrealized gains from real estate holdings, which are not counted at all in Japan as Basle capital. On the other hand, their failure to write off loans or to take adequate loan loss reserves may greatly inflate their book capital.

### Net Subsidies

One might also consider whether Japanese banks actually enjoy a net subsidy, compared with U.S. banks. Roughly speaking, the net subsidy would be the value of the safety net minus the cost of regulation. Under this formulation, regulation would be viewed as a cost banks pay for subsidies, although some regulation would probably exist even without subsidies. The Japanese safety net seems significantly stronger than that of the United States. Japanese bank regulators, the Ministry of Finance (MOF), and the Bank of Japan (BOJ), have been more likely to bail out failing banks than have their American counterparts. Until quite recently, no bank in Japan has failed: regulators have strongly protected banks and have arranged mergers for small troubled banks with big banks. In the few recent cases of bank failure, the MOF arranged the sale of the failed bank's assets to other banks, utilizing the financial aid of the Deposit Insurance Corporation and the BOJ. All deposits in the failed banks, including deposits exceeding the maximum coverage limit of deposit insurance, were transferred to other banks, so no depositor suffered loss. Thus, since World War II, no depositor in a Japanese bank has lost money as a result of bank failure. This record stands in sharp contrast to the current situation in the United States. During 1992, the Federal Deposit Insurance Corporation (FDIC) resolved one-hundred twenty failed banks. In sixty-six of those cases, including the four largest subsidiaries of the $8.8 billion First City Bancorporation, one of the largest failed bank transactions in FDIC history, uninsured depositors lost money.

On the cost side, both U.S. and Japanese banks are subject to considerable regulation. We do not attempt to quantify and compare the costs of regulation, but we would guess that American costs are higher. Many studies have concluded that the cost of U.S. regulation is quite high, but so are the costs of Japanese regulation. Under Japanese banking, corporation, and antitrust laws, and capital market regulations, many restrictions are imposed on Japanese banks. Japanese banks also are subject to nonstatutory public burdens, for instance, the maintenance of the specialized banking system or governmental pressure to bail out failing companies for which they serve as a main bank.

Much of Japanese regulation, however, seems aimed at managing competition, and thus may actually increase Japanese bank profitability (albeit at consumer expense), while the United States emphasizes safety and soundness regulation, a deadweight cost. Indeed, much U.S. regulation, as in the payment system, is intended to decrease the actual public subsidy. Thus, we believe that Japanese banks do have a higher net as well as a higher gross subsidy.

In theory, one might expect the market to arbitrage away competitive advantages for banks. Thus, if Japan had more favorable capital rules, U.S. banks could move there, just as U.S. corporations choose to be organized in the state of Delaware because they prefer Delaware law; or just as banks in the European Union base their operations in the country whose banking regulations they favor. In practice, such moves will not happen. The United States and Japan would not let their major banks shift home countries. Banks might be free to shift particular operations between the two countries, for example, basing certain lending operations in the United States rather than in Japan; but doing so would not materially affect capital regulation, which is imposed on a consolidated basis by the home country.

**The Effect of Higher Minimum Ratios**

Some readers of an earlier version of this paper have suggested that, despite the distorting effect of different levels of government guarantees, the Basle Accord has made the playing field more even because it imposes a minimum 8 percent capital ratio on all banks. Assume that before the Accord state-owned banks in France had a 2 percent capital/asset ratio while U.S. banks had a 7 percent ratio. The French–U.S. differential was 5 percentage points. Some argue that while a minimum 8 percent ratio might require U.S. banks to hold 11 percent to compensate for the stronger French guarantee, its imposition has narrowed the differential to 3 points, thus making the playing field more even. This line of argument is flawed.

To begin with, capital requirements have little meaning for state-owned banks. The state can create whatever equity is required by injecting taxpayer funds, whereas the ability of a privately owned bank to raise equity is subject to market discipline. A state-owned bank can acquire whatever capital it needs even if its earnings prospects are dismal.

But suppose we substituted privately owned Japanese banks for state-owned French banks. Would the argument then have force? Capital requirements deal with nominal not real capital. Real capital is the market value of assets minus the market value of liabilities. If the market (debt suppliers, in particular) believes it is sufficient for Japanese banks to hold 2 percent real capital, it may be inefficient for Japanese banks to hold higher levels, given their put on government capital (the guarantee). They will have a substantial incentive to keep real capital at 2 percent while complying with the nominal 8 percent Basle requirement. This can be done simply by not fully writing off bad loans.

The market and the availability of government guarantees will tend to determine the real capital ratios of banks, as well as the differential in required capital ratios among banks in different countries. Governments may alter this tendency by trying to ensure that real capital ratios are identical to Basle nominal ratios, but different governments may do more or less. Indeed, if the United States were to try to make its banks hold 8 percent real capital, and the Japanese were content to have their banks hold 2 percent real capital, the impact of the 8 percent minimum would be to widen the difference from 5 to 6 points.

Some evidence suggests that the Accord has not by itself narrowed the nominal capital differential between major U.S. and Japanese banks. Table 2 sets out the recent average ratios of tangible equity to total assets for the top ten U.S. and Japanese banks from 1986 to 1992. Equity consists of common and preferred stock plus surplus plus retained earnings. This ratio allows us to compare capital ratios in Japan and the United States before and after the Basle Accord. Risk-based ratios were unavailable for Japanese banks in the pre-Accord period.

While the differential narrowed somewhat in the Basle transition years, 1989–91, it is marginally wider in 1992 than it was in 1986. U.S. and Japanese banks have both increased their capital over the period, but the rates of growth have been about the same. It may be that U.S. regulation requiring ratios higher than Basle's have prevented the differential from narrowing; otherwise, Japanese capital ratios would have increased by more than those of U.S. banks. But the fact remains that Basle has not produced more competitive equality as measured by nominal differentials.

Even a narrowing of the pre-Accord differential would not necessarily improve competitive equality. It is possible that the marginal cost of capital increases as more capital is raised. This outcome would obtain if returns to capital decreased as more capital was raised. The cost to U.S. banks of maintaining a three point differential that requires an 11 percent capital ratio may be higher than the cost of maintaining a five point differential that requires a 7 percent ratio.

**Table 2. Ratio of Tangible Equity to Total Assets, Japanese and U.S. Banks, 1986–92**

| Year | Japanese banks (percent) | U.S. banks (percent) | Difference (percentage points) |
|---|---|---|---|
| 1986 | 1.91 | 5.30 | 3.39 |
| 1987 | 2.20 | 4.98 | 2.78 |
| 1988 | 2.56 | 5.68 | 3.12 |
| 1989 | 2.73 | 5.17 | 2.44 |
| 1990 | 2.94 | 5.34 | 2.40 |
| 1991 | 3.12 | 5.87 | 2.75 |
| 1992 | 3.42 | 6.83 | 3.41 |

**Source:** Federal Reserve, Japanese Securities Report.

In summary, we believe competitive advantages between banks in two countries are caused not by differences in required capital ratios but by differences in comparative advantage, economic fundamentals, or government support levels.

. . .

### *Questions*

1. Be sure you understand the analysis of the bailout differential. What is the nature of the governments' guarantees? If a strong guarantee exists, why have capital at all? Note the distinction between nominal and real capital.

2. Immediately before the Accord, many American and British bankers believed that banks from France and Japan had a great competitive advantage because of their high leverage. Both French and Japa-

nese banks accepted very low rates in international lending, arguably made possible by their low capital requirements. In the section discussing "The Effect of Higher Minimum Ratios," the authors address this. Are they saying that the terms of this Accord failed to erase this difference? Is their conclusion undermined by the relative withdrawal of French and Japanese banks from international markets over the last few years as capital requirements rose?

3. The authors say that "differences in comparative advantage, economic fundamentals or government support levels" determine competitive advantage among banks. What if any conditions would give capital adequacy regulations a significant impact on competition?

4. If the Scott/Iwahara analysis is correct, what is the function of the Accord?

5. Would you advise President Clinton to change the Basle Accord or terminate it?

# PART II. CAPITAL ADEQUACY FOR SECURITIES OPERATIONS

Diversity confounds agreement on capital standards for the non-credit risks of issuing and trading securities. Players, interests, and national approaches are multiple. Banks and securities companies compete, so regulators of both types of firms play a role.

National and multinational rules apply. At the national level, securities regulators setting capital standards include independent agencies such as the U.S. Securities Exchange Commission (SEC), units in finance ministries as in Japan, or even departments of central banks. At the multilateral level, three organizations are trying to draft common standards for their members. For members of the European Union, the European Commission issued the Capital Adequacy Directive (CAD) for investment firms and credit institutions in March 1993. The Basle Committee on Banking Supervision issued its consultative proposal for the prudential supervision of international banks' netting, market risks, and interest rate risk in April 1993. The International Organization of Securities Commissions (IOSCO) tried to issue common capital standards for its members but the effort collapsed in late 1992. Each is alert to the need to cooperate with the others.

This part focuses on the problems of finding a common standard for position risk in equities. It touches on other important risks. One central problem is to agree on the appropriate standard, since countries set very different standards for their broker-dealers and others have relied on the Basle Accord. If one standard is set for securities companies and another for banks, which standard applies to subsidiaries of banks or sister companies of banks through a holding company? What of universal banks that carry out their own securities operations? The CAD resolved these issues for members of the European Union. The rest of the world has not resolved them.

This part first describes the range of risks faced by securities operations, then turns to position risk. Two national approaches to position risk are contrasted to give a base line: the American and the German. The two current multilateral approaches are summarized: CAD and the Basle Committee's proposals. We briefly sketch other risks of securities operations that may call for capital charges. Then we raise two thorny issues that bear directly on the standards for position risk. How should capital be defined for non-credit risks? How specific should the Basle proposals be about consolidating the accounts of banks' affiliates?

As you read the materials, bear in mind that since regulators have not agreed on a common global standard for securities operations, there are many different rules or proposals. For simplicity, we will make some assumptions:

1. The CAD is implemented
2. The Basle Proposals are adopted and implemented
3. When CAD and the Proposals differ, countries adopt the stricter.
4. National securities regulations will continue to govern non-bank securities firms.

While the Accord really addressed only credit risk, CAD and the Proposals address a range of risks, including position risk, counterparty risk, foreign exchange risk, and others. For simplicity, we only address position risk and that only for equity positions.

While Basle applies only to banks, CAD applies to banks and securities companies. The discussion will focus on three types of big players:

a. U.S. securities companies are an example of non-bank securities firms, probably the most important example.

b. Some banks take positions for their own account; German universal banks are among the best known.

c. Finally, at least in the U.S., some position takers may become subject to two very different sets of rules. U.S. banks' bank holding company affiliates could find themselves subject to SEC rules as securities companies and at the same time to the new Basle Proposals. So we look at them too.

## A. RISKS ASSOCIATED WITH SECURITIES OPERATIONS

Regulators now try to tailor their capital standards to the different types of non-credit risk. The U.S. Government Accounting Office explains the common differences and the way a few countries approach them. As you read, consider the ways in which the risks and responses differ from those you encountered in the Basle Accord.

## EXCERPTS FROM U.S. GOVERNMENT ACCOUNTING OFFICE, SECURITIES MARKETS: CHALLENGES TO HARMONIZING INTERNATIONAL CAPITAL STANDARDS REMAIN

(1992).

Securities firms and banks doing securities business risk their capital in complex trading strategies involving securities, futures, currencies, and interest rate swap instruments in the international securities markets. Securities activities are subject to a variety of risks. The type and amount of risk depends on the nature and extent of the securities firms' and banks' activities. The most important of these risks are market risk and counterparty risk. To a lesser extent, securities firms and banks doing a securities business may also face other types of risk, such as the risk of reduced revenues and foreign exchange risk.

Market risk, also called "position risk," is the risk of an adverse movement in a security's price. For example, the market value of a security purchased by a firm may fall before it can be resold.[5] In the case of an equity security, or stock, concerns about the financial performance of the corporate issuer may lead to a decline in the price of the security. In the case of a debt security, or bond, the nonpayment of principal or interest by the issuer, or a change in interest rates, may lead to a subsequent decline in the value of the security.

Counterparty risk, also called "settlement" risk, is the risk that a firm's trading partner will be either unwilling or unable to meet its contractual obligation. For example, a buyer may contract to purchase a security from a second-party seller and then commit to selling the security to a third party. The original buyer would then be exposed to the risk that the original seller may default and not deliver the security.

Other risk may include the risk to a firm associated with such factors as reduced net revenues, an increased administrative burden, or fraud. For example, a decrease in a firm's transaction volume may result in reduced income, while expenses remain constant or increase. Similarly, an unexpected increase in a firm's business may result in a heavier administrative burden that could lead to recordkeeping problems and, in turn, delays in completing transactions, called settlement delays.

Securities activities are also subject to other kinds of risks, such as foreign exchange risk. Foreign exchange risk is the risk that the value of a financial instrument will change due to currency fluctuations.

Systemic risk is the risk that a disturbance could severely impair the workings of the financial system and, at the extreme, cause a complete breakdown in it. For example, the collapse of securities prices could lead to the default of one or more large securities firms. Because of

5. Alternatively, if a securities firm has a "short" position in a security (i.e., it has contracted to sell a security it does not own and must buy it before the contracted sale date), the market risk is that the price of the security may increase.

financial interrelationships, this could lead to further defaults of securities firms and banks. A series of such defaults could extend into the banking system and cause a disruption in the flow of payments in the settlement of financial transactions throughout the world. Shocks could be transmitted from one domestic market to other domestic markets. Such a breakdown in capital markets could disrupt the process of saving and investment, undermine the long-term confidence of private investors, and disrupt the normal course of economic transactions.

### Capital Standards Protect Against Risks

The efficient functioning of financial markets requires that members of the financial community have confidence in each other's ability to transact business. This understanding means that each member of the financial community must have, among other things, adequate capital. Because of the high degree of interdependence among firms in the securities industry—where securities firms often buy and sell securities from one another and have contractual commitments with their counterparts—the failure of one firm to meet its obligation to another could affect the financial viability of other firms.

In general, capital standards are designed to protect customers and to ensure a viable financial system by diminishing the chance of a series of interrelated defaults because of risks in securities markets. Capital standards specify the minimum amount of capital a securities firm or a bank doing securities business should maintain and are often based on the nature and scope of its financial activities. This capital should be sufficient to pay customers, counterparties, and creditors.

In the United States, determining compliance with capital standards requires applying a complex formula to a firm's assets and liabilities to calculate the firm's net capital. Assets, for example, include cash, securities held in proprietary trading accounts, and equipment and buildings. Liabilities include, for example, money owed to customers, banks, and the parent company. Net worth is computed by subtracting liabilities from assets. The value of illiquid assets—such as buildings and furniture—is deducted from net worth calculations. Additional adjustments are made for possible losses in the value of liquid assets by providing that securities positions be adjusted to current market prices and that a discount in the value of securities be taken for possible future market fluctuations.

need for liquidity

### How Capital Is Regulated in Securities Markets

Because of the potential effect on financial markets of the failure of undercapitalized firms, national securities regulators have chosen to enforce "adequate capital levels." Each country has different arrangements for regulating capital. The biggest difference among countries occurs in their treatment of securities and banking activities. In "universal" banking countries, securities business is generally done within banks, and typically one capital standard is applied to both securities and banking activities. In "nonuniversal" banking countries such as the

United States, securities firms and banks are separately regulated and subject to distinctly different capital standards.

Another difference among national capital standards is that the objectives of the standards can differ among countries. For example, in the United States the primary emphasis is on providing sufficient liquid assets to meet liabilities, including customer liabilities, and fostering confidence in the securities industry and the financial system; in Japan the emphasis is on preventing a firm's failure or protecting the financial system.

On an average day, firms and banks doing an international securities business hold billions of dollars in capital. For example, as of July 1991 the 10 largest U.S. securities firms were capitalized at $6.7 billion. Total capitalization of the 10 largest U.K. securities firms, which are lead regulated by the Securities and Futures Association, was 2.4 billion pounds, or about $4.5 billion as of January 1992.

In the United States, SEC is the primary regulator of securities firm capital, but the Federal Reserve System (FRS) and the Department of the Treasury also have a role. SEC oversees capital through a strategy of self-regulation. It creates and revises capital standards as well as oversees self-regulatory organizations, such as NYSE, that have primary responsibility for enforcing the compliance of their member firms with the standards. Although firms created under section 20 of the 1933 Glass–Steagall Act—i.e., securities subsidiaries of bank holding companies—must comply with SEC's capital standards, FRS sets other capital levels and approves capital plans for holding companies that own Section 20 companies. FRS requires that firm capital meet securities industry norms, which in turn are well above SEC minimum capital requirements. The Department of the Treasury has rule-making authority for firms registered as government securities dealers, while the securities regulators carry out oversight and enforcement activities.

In general, the capital levels of large U.S. securities firms exceed minimum requirements. As figure 1.3 indicates, the 10 largest U.S. securities firms have capital levels many times the minimum requirement on any given day.[9] There are a variety of reasons why securities firms operate with capital levels in excess of minimum requirements, including (1) the firm needs to conduct large underwritings or other activities that occur periodically, and (2) the firm uses its capital level as a marketing tool to attract both individual and institutional investors.

9. The capital levels shown are those for the broker-dealer only. They do not necessarily reflect the financial condition of the whole securities firm, which may comprise many parts separate and distinct from the broker-dealer.

**Figure 1.3: Capital Levels of 10 Largest Securities Firms in the United States**
(Dollars in Millions)

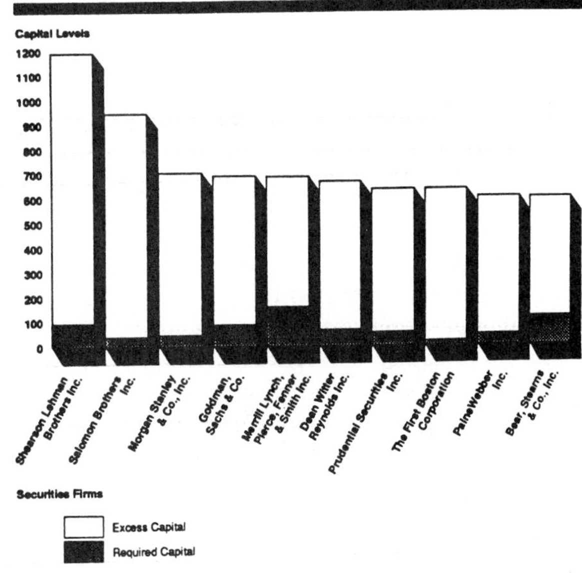


Note: Haircuts and illiquid assets have been deducted from the capital levels.

Source: Securities and Exchange Commission, June 28, 1991.

## Country Capital Standards Differ

International securities market participants are subject to a wide variety of country-specific capital standards. These differing country capital standards have implications for settlement or counterparty risk, systemic risk, and competition among firms, banks, and markets.

For example, some countries value securities at current market prices ("mark to market"), while other countries value them at their original cost. Further, some countries have settlement risk requirements so that the risk of nonperformance in a timely manner is covered within the capital standards, while other countries do not. Also, some countries set differential capital standards according to the type of business done, while other countries use uniform minimum standards for all types of securities businesses.

If securities firms or banks doing securities business fail, any remaining capital can be used to pay off customers, creditors, and counterparties. If securities firms or banks doing securities business fail when their capital falls to minimum capital standards, the failures are more likely to have adverse consequences for customers, creditors, and counterparties in countries with low minimum standards. Firms and banks that fail with higher minimum capital are more likely to meet their obligations. Poorly capitalized firms and banks that cannot meet their obligations may also cause financial difficulty for other securities firms, banks, clearing systems,[10] and hence securities markets. Widespread failure of these firms and banks may thus, in turn, cause other firms and banks to fail in markets with higher capital standards and result in a ripple effect across international financial markets.

Differing country capital standards may also have competitive effects both within a country where securities firms and banks compete for the same securities business or among countries. For example, if banks have more stringent capital standards than those imposed on competing securities firms within the same country, then banks may be at a competitive disadvantage because of the costs associated with holding the higher capital amounts. For the same reason, countries with higher capital standards could be at a competitive disadvantage to countries with lower capital standards. Alternatively, countries with higher standards might be competitively advantaged if they are viewed as safer places to do business than countries with lower capital standards.

### Integrating Securities and Banking Capital Standards

Although securities activities of bank holding companies in the United States, other than government or municipal securities activity, have generally been limited to Section 20 firms—securities subsidiaries of bank holding companies—foreign banks and the foreign operations of U.S. banks, are heavily involved in securities activities. The Basle Committee has already established international capital standards for banks, and these standards differ from the capital standards traditionally applied to securities activities. For example, securities firms are generally required to value their securities at current market values, while banks generally use cost or lower of cost or market. U.S. banks have the option of valuing the securities in their trading portfolios at lower of cost or market, or marking the securities to market. U.S. banks value their investment portfolios at cost. In general, securities firms' standards are designed to provide that the firms have sufficient liquid assets to meet their obligations, while bank standards are designed to ensure that banks remain solvent. Both banks and securities firms are concerned that if securities activities of banks are subject to capital standards different from those of securities firms, the one with the lower standard will have a competitive advantage. Resolving any differences in capital standards is a formidable task, however, because of the differences in operations of banks and securities firms and the resulting variance in the oversight methods securities regulators and bank supervisors use.

Regulators view risks differently for banks and securities firms. Because bank asset turnover is slow and securities firm asset turnover is relatively high, bank risk changes more slowly than securities firm risk. Banks have traditionally invested most of their funds in long-term

10. Clearing systems capture trade data and guarantee that the trade will settle once the data match. Settlement is the final stage of the process when funds and/or financial instruments are exchanged between parties through the clearing organization.

illiquid assets, such as loans to customers. These funds come from highly liquid customer deposits as well as borrowings and the banks' own capital. Banks have traditionally held these assets to maturity. As a result, bank regulators focus on credit risk as the most important and predominant risk.

Because of their high asset turnover, securities firms must be able to absorb the effect of changing market values of their portfolios as they occur. Consequently, securities regulators emphasize valuing securities positions at market prices—and take a deduction on the market value of the securities position—to provide a margin of safety against potential losses that can be incurred as a result of market fluctuations. Securities regulators place little or no value on illiquid assets. Securities firms holding large concentrated securities positions are more vulnerable to sudden market movements than diversified banks because a large portion of securities firms' net worth can be lost quickly.

### *Questions*

1. Why do governments regulate the capital adequacy of firms with securities business?

2. What do securities firms do? How does this compare with the commercial banking business?

3. Evaluate the following assertion that securities firms may not need capital standards at all. It comes from *The Economist,* October 5, 1991, p. 92.

> Securities firms are not banks, whose failure can involve support from central banks or taxpayers. They are, it is sometimes argued, more like manufacturers, whose failure can damage creditors and customers but not enough to justify nannying supervision. Imposing capital standards on securities firms puts costs on both issuers and investors; raising them would reduce the price differential that has led those in search of capital increasingly to prefer securities to bank loans. High mandatory capital ratios might keep some securities firms out of the market.

4. The reading describes the general approach of regulators to the possibility a security company would fail. What are the operational implications of this approach? How does it compare to the approach of bank regulator? Why?

---

## B. CAPITAL ADEQUACY AND POSITION RISK

### 1. National Rules: The American and German Approaches

A study of position risk usefully starts with securities firms and rules at the national level. Some countries, such as Germany, lack special rules. The SEC sets net capital requirements for brokers and dealers. The following summary is from an article written before changes in 1992, which are noted after it.

## GARY HABERMAN, "CAPITAL REQUIREMENTS OF COMMERCIAL AND INVESTMENT BANKS: CONTRASTS IN REGULATION"

Federal Reserve Bank of New York Quarterly Review, Autumn 1987.

### Securities and Exchange Commission Uniform Net Capital Rule for Brokers and Dealers

The SEC first adopted a capital rule in 1944 to establish a standard of financial responsibility for registered brokers and dealers. The most recent comprehensive update of the rule was implemented in 1982. Firms that provide retail brokerage services and that underwrite or deal in corporate or municipal securities must abide by the rule.

The capital rule is a liquidity test in the sense that it seeks to ensure that liquid assets, adjusted for trading risk, exceed senior liabilities by a required margin of safety. A broker-dealer should be able to liquidate quickly and to satisfy the claims of its customers without recourse to formal bankruptcy proceedings. The test is a two-step procedure: first, a determination of the amount of net capital available to meet a firm's capital requirement, and second, a determination of the capital requirement (that is, the margin of safety). Net capital is total capital reduced by various charges and by haircuts that measure trading risk. A firm may choose either the basic or the alternative requirement. (See Figure 1.)

#### Total capital

Total capital equals net worth plus subordinated liabilities and is augmented by allowable credits. It is determined by generally accepted accounting principles on a mark-to-market basis. To be counted as capital, subordinated debt must have a minimum term of one year and may not be prepayable without the prior written approval of the broker-dealer's examining authority (New York Stock Exchange or NASD). Subordinated debt may be in the form of either borrowed cash or borrowed securities, the latter serving as collateral for "secured demand notes." The rule also allows two forms of temporarily borrowed capital. Broker-dealers are permitted to obtain temporary subordinations not exceeding 45 days in maturity as often as three times a year to capitalize underwriting and extraordinary activities. A firm may also have a revolving subordinated loan agreement providing for prepayment within a year.

. . .

Broker-dealers are prohibited from distributing equity capital (for example, through dividends or unsecured loans to owners) if doing so would reduce the firm's net capital below warning levels. Supervisory authorities set warning levels somewhat higher than the minimum requirement; for example, one is 120 percent of the basic requirement.

Figure 1

**SEC Net Capital Computation**

| | |
|---|---|
| Total capital: | Equity<br>Allowable subordinated debt<br>Allowable credits |
| Less deductions: | (Illiquid assets)<br>(Unsecured receivables)<br>(Charges for aged credit exposure)<br>(Market risk haircuts) |
| Net capital | Compared to |
| Requirement: | 6⅔ percent aggregate indebtedness, or 2 percent aggregate debit items |
| Excess capital: | Net capital less the requirement |

*Capital charges:* Total capital is reduced by nonallowable assets and various special charges. An asset is considered nonallowable if it cannot be immediately or quickly converted into cash. This definition applies to fixed and intangible assets, investments and unsecured receivables from affiliates and subsidiaries, most other unsecured receivables, and nonmarketable securities. Special charges include specified types of receivables from other broker-dealers not collected within 30 days and other specified receivables aged beyond 11 or 60 days. Credit exposure is also deducted for purchased securities not received within 30 days and for most sold securities not delivered within 5 days. There are also charges for giving excessive margin on repurchase transactions when a dealer borrows. (If excessive margin is taken when a dealer lends under a resale agreement, the requirement is increased.) Such charges encourage good business practices.

*Haircuts:* The rule recognizes that the prices of marketable assets and liabilities may move adversely during liquidation, thereby reducing net capital available to cover a firm's obligations. The deduction for price risk in the firm's proprietary positions, haircuts, are percentages of the market value of security and forward positions held by the broker-dealer. As a measure of price risk, haircut factors vary in accordance with the type and remaining maturity of securities held or sold short.

For government and high-grade corporate debt, some forms of hedging serve to reduce haircuts. Moreover, within the several maturity subcategories into which government, high-grade corporate and municipal debt securities are grouped, short positions serve to offset long positions fully. Forward contracts receive the haircuts applicable to their underlying securities. Futures and options positions are also explicitly treated. The rule specifies additional haircut charges where the broker-dealer has an undue concentration in securities of a single issuer. For broker-dealers choosing the alternative method of calculating required capital, lower haircut percentages may be taken on certain securities positions, including undue concentration and underwriting commitments. . . .

Figure 2

**Summary of Haircuts Applied to Unhedged Positions**

Government and agency securities:
- 0 to 6 percent in 12 maturity subcategories
- 6 percent applies to 25 year bonds

Municipal securities:
- 0 to 7 percent in 16 maturity categories
- 7 percent applies to 20 year bonds

Commercial paper, bankers acceptances, and certificates of deposits:
- 0 to 0.5 percent in 5 maturity categories
- 0.5 percent applies to 9 month paper

Investment grade corporate debt:
- 2 to 9 percent in 9 maturity categories
- 9 percent applies to 25 year bonds

Preferred stock: 10 percent

Common stock and "all other": [adjusted in 1992—see below]

*Capital requirement:* Net capital must exceed a minimum absolute dollar level and one of two standards that relate to the size of a broker-dealer's business.

The basic method requires that net capital exceed 6⅔ percent of aggregate indebtedness, which includes all liabilities less those specifically exempted. In essence, aggregate indebtedness is any liability not adequately collateralized, secured, or otherwise directly offset by an asset of the broker-dealer. It also includes contingent, off-balance sheet obligations. . . .

The alternative method requires that net capital exceed two percent of aggregate debit items computed in accordance with the Reserve Formula under the Customer Protection Rule. These debit items are the gross debit balances of particular asset accounts and generally represent good quality customer receivables. The rule uses these debit items as a proxy for the size of customer-related business. For small broker-dealers whose business is heavily retail-oriented, these aggregate debit items can represent a majority of a firm's assets. However, for most large broker-dealers who are not heavily retail-oriented, these debit items usually constitute less than 25 percent of total assets.

---

In 1992, the SEC amended the net capital rule (see 57 Federal Register 232, at 56986). Haircuts for "all other" securities (including common stock) would be a deduction of

15 percent of the market value of the greater of the long or short positions and to the extent the market value of the lesser of the long or short positions exceeds 25 percent of the market value of the greater of the long or short positions, the percentage deduction on such excess shall be 15 percent of the market value of such excess.

In sharp contrast to the U.S. is Germany. The GAO summarized elements of its capital rules as follows.

| Framework standard | Germany |
|---|---|
| Does the capital rule set limits on subordinated debt? | YES. Current law does not allow subordinated debt. |
| Does the capital rule provide for recordkeeping, reporting, and examination programs? | YES. A bank has to comply with a wide range of reporting requirements, including a monthly report on on- and off-balance-sheet items, solvency, and liquidity. |
| Does the capital rule cover liquidity and solvency? | YES. As a universal banking country Germany's capital requirements apply only to banks. Their purpose is to protect depositors. The Banking Act requires banks to place their funds so that solvency is always assured. |
| Does the capital rule revalue positions based on current market prices (i.e., mark to market)? | NO. Capital is conservatively defined as reserves. Banks maintain assets and securities at book value or acquisition costs. |
| Does the capital rule have a base requirement? | NO. There is no base requirement for the securities activities of German banks. The intent is to develop an exchange entry requirement. |
| Does the capital rule have a position risk requirement? | YES. Basle credit risk requirements apply with an 8% charge for corporate securities and no charge for government securities. |
| Does the capital rule require that capital should exceed the sum of risk-based requirements? | YES. Assets weighted for their risk cannot exceed 18 times (i.e., 5.5%) liable capital. |

---

The German approach reflects the fact that Germany has universal banks, which both accept deposits like commercial banks and engage in the securities business. The German capital adequacy rules simply say that securities held for trading are subject to the general standard. They are silent on whether long and short positions should be netted.

### *Questions*

1. Be sure you understand how the U.S. sets capital standards for equity held by security companies.

(a) In the abstract, what is the rule? What is its purpose? What is the haircut and the idea behind it? What does it mean that an investor is long or short in a stock?

(b) Suppose a company's assets consist of $100 in long equity positions and $85 in short equity positions and its liabilities are $140. What is its total capital? Its net capital?

2. Every country is trying to protect some groups. Whom are the U.S. regulators trying to protect? What philosophy do the U.S. rules reveal? Is this the same philosophy as Germany?

---

## 2. Position Risk and the Capital Adequacy Directive

After much debate and delay, the European Commission issued its Capital Adequacy Directive ("CAD") for investment companies and other credit institutions in March 1993. This complemented the Investment Services Directive 93/22/EEC of May 10, 1993 discussed in the next chapter of this book. The CAD set capital adequacy rules for several kinds of risk in the firms' trading book, including settlement and counter-party risk (Annex II), foreign exchange risk (Annex III), the risk of a material change in business (Annex IV), and large exposures (Annex VI), as well as position risk (Annex I). Some of these capital requirements are cumulative and supplement capital required for other purposes, such as non-trading business.

The CAD defines key terms, sets rules for initial capital that vary according to the investment firms' services, specifies the "own funds" or capital firms need their own funds to provide against risk, and requires consolidated supervision and reporting. Institutions must mark their trading book to market daily. The CAD requires members to implement its rules by the end of 1996.

Relevant paragraphs of the CAD follow. As you read the annex on position risk, note the general elements for debt instruments and pay special attention to the treatment of equity.

COUNCIL DIRECTIVE 93/6/EEC OF 15 MARCH 1993 ON THE CAPITAL ADEQUACY OF INVESTMENTS FIRMS AND CREDIT INSTITUTIONS, OFFICIAL JOURNAL OF THE EUROPEAN COMMUNITIES

No. L 141/1, 11 June 1993.

DEFINITIONS

*Article 2*

For the purposes of this Directive:

. . .

3. *institutions* shall mean credit institutions and investment firms;

. . .

6. the *trading book* of an institution shall consist of:

(a) its proprietary positions in financial instruments which are held for resale and/or which are taken on by the institution with the intention of benefiting in the short term from actual and/or expected differences between their buying and selling prices, or from other price or interest-rate variations, and positions in financial instruments arising from matched principal broking, or positions taken in order to hedge other elements of the trading book;

. . .

## INITIAL CAPITAL

*Article 3*

1. Investment firms which hold clients' money and/or securities and which offer one or more of the following services shall have initial capital of ECU 125 000:

— the reception and transmission of investors' orders for financial instruments,

— the execution of investors' orders for financial instruments,

— the management of individual portfolios of investments in financial instruments,

provided that they do not deal in any financial instruments for their own account or underwrite issues of financial instruments on a firm commitment basis.

. . .

3. All other investment firms shall have initial capital of ECU 730 000.

. . .

8. The own funds of investment firms may not fall below the level specified in paragraphs 1 to 5 and 7. If they do, however, the competent authorities may, where the circumstances justify it, allow such firms a limited period in which to rectify their situations or cease their activities.

. . .

## ANNEX I

## POSITION RISK

**Netting**

1. The excess of an institution's long (short) positions over its short (long) positions in the same equity, debt and convertible issues and

identical financial futures, options, warrants and covered warrants shall be its net position in each of those different instruments. ...

. . .

3. All net positions, irrespective of their signs, must be converted on a daily basis into the institution's reporting currency at the prevailing spot exchange rate before their aggregation.

. . .

**Specific and general risks**

12. The position risk on a traded debt instrument or equity (or debt or equity derivative) shall be divided into two components in order to calculate the capital required against it. The first shall be its specific-risk component—this is the risk of a price change in the instrument concerned due to factors related to its issuer or, in the case of a derivative, the issuer of the underlying instrument. This second component shall cover its general risk—this is the risk of a price change in the instrument due (in the case of a traded debt instrument or debt derivative) to a change in the level of interest rates or (in the case of an equity or equity derivative) to a broad equity-market movement unrelated to any specific attributes of individual securities.

---

For traded debt instruments, the CAD instructs the institution to classify its net positions by currency and hold capital against general and specific risk. Specific risk is a function of the debtor: central government debt carries zero risk, certain interbank debt has low weights, and the rest requires capital of 8% against net positions. General risk is a function of maturities or duration.

---

EQUITIES

31. The institution shall sum all its net long positions and all its net short positions in accordance with paragraph 1. The sum of the two figures shall be its overall gross position. The differences between them shall be its overall net position.

**Specific risk**

32. It shall multiply its overall gross position by 4% in order to calculate its capital requirement against specific risk.

33. Notwithstanding paragraph 32, the competent authorities may allow the capital requirement against specific risk to be 2% rather than 4% for those portfolios of equities that an institution holds which meet the following conditions:

(i) the equities shall not be those of issuers which have issued traded debt instruments that currently attract an 8% requirement in Table 1 appearing in paragraph 14;

(ii) the equities must be adjudged highly liquid by the competent authorities according to objective criteria;

(iii) no individual position shall comprise more than 5% of the value of the institution's whole equity portfolio. However, the competent authorities may authorize individual positions of up to 10% provided that the total of such positions does not exceed 50% of the portfolio.

**General risk**

34. Its capital requirement against general risk shall be its overall net position multiplied by 8%.

. . .

UNDERWRITING

39. In the case of the underwriting of debt and equity instruments, the competent authorities may allow an institution to use the following procedure in calculating its capital requirements. Firstly, it shall calculate the net positions by deducting the underwriting positions which are subscribed or sub-underwritten by third parties on the basis of formal agreements; secondly, it shall reduce the net positions by the following reduction factors:

| | |
|---|---|
| —working day 0: | 100% |
| —working day 1: | 90% |
| —working days 2 to 3: | 75% |
| —working day 4: | 50% |
| —working day 5: | 25% |
| —after working day 5: | 0%. |

Working day zero shall be the working day on which the institution becomes unconditionally committed to accepting a known quantity of securities at an agreed price.

Thirdly, it shall calculate its capital requirements using the reduced underwriting positions. The competent authorities shall ensure that the institution holds sufficient capital against the risk of loss which exists between the time of the initial commitment and working day 1.

### *Questions*

1. Focus on rules for equity. The distinction between specific and general risks is basic in finance theory and practice. Specific risk refers to the risks associated with the issuer itself. General risks are those not associated with an issuer, such as changes in the market or economy. Why would the CAD distinguish between them to regulate position risk?

2. In the following questions, assume the CAD is in effect and implemented. What are the CAD rules that govern position taking by German universal banks?

(a) Why distinguish between general and specific risk?

(b) How does the CAD calculate general risk for equity? Work through the same example used for a U.S. securities company: assume the bank has 100 long and 85 short in equities. What do we need to know? What are long and short positions? What is an overall net position? Why is it calculated? Does the general offset in CAD have a counterpart in the SEC rule? How would you evaluate the CAD approach, given the statement by Richard Breeden, then chairman of the SEC, that during the 1987 market crash airline equities fell much more than railroad equities?

(c) How does the CAD calculate specific risk for equity? Why does it do so? What do net long and net short mean? What accounts for the treatment of highly liquid positions? Calculate specific risk capital using the hypothetical. Assume the portfolio is highly liquid and diversified. Compare the result to that required by the SEC. What explains the difference?

3. What do you make of the following:

An SEC analysis of a hypothetical portfolio of unrelated buy and sell positions of highly liquid securities suggests that a 2–percent standard is too low because, in contrast to the U.S. standard, it would not have preserved enough capital to cover price moves during the 1987 and 1989 market breaks. U.K. Securities and Investment Board officials [said] that an actual test of portfolios of equities indicated that 2 percent accurately covers the risks in diversified portfolios. SEC officials [said] that no agreement exists on the best model of portfolio diversification .... [GAO, op. cit., chapter 2.]

---

## 3. Position Risk and the Basle Committee's Proposals

During 1993, the initiative for global harmonization shifted from IOSCO to the Basle Committee. IOSCO had actively considered a proposal similar to the CAD approach. When Richard Breeden became chairman of the IOSCO Technical Committee, his implacable opposition to this approach, supported by some other countries like Japan, stopped IOSCO's three-year effort cold in late 1992. Breeden argued that the approach was "highly unsafe" [R. Peston and T. Corrigan, "Breeden opposes IOSCO capital standard," Financial Times, October 28, 1992].

From early 1992, the Basle Committee and the Technical Committee had jointly searched for common rules. The goal was harmony in approach to banks and securities firms. The Technical Committee accepted the CAD's and Basle's building block method, the Basle group agreed to differentiate between specific and general risk. At the end of April 1993, the Basle Committee released a proposal for capital rules to govern netting and market risk and guidelines to supervise interest rate risk (which did not require capital allocation). It would be integrated into the 1988 Basle Accord. The Basle Committee expressed the hope that it could be extended beyond banks to securities firms.

According to the proposal,

["The Supervisory Treatment of Market Risks," Consultative proposal by the Basle Committee on Banking Supervision, Basle, April 1993 (hereafter "Basle Proposals"), p. 1.]

> "market risk is the risk of losses in on- and off-balance-sheet positions arising from movements in market prices, including interest rates, exchange rates and equity values. The basic thrust of the proposals is to require capital ... for open positions in debt securities, equities and foreign exchange."

The Basle Committee favored:

> capital requirements in preference to limits as the appropriate instrument for international convergence in the treatment of market risk. Unlike limits, capital requirements give banks added incentives to use hedging techniques, while ensuring that a prudent capital cushion remains available to cover possible losses. They also enable bank managements to retain flexibility in managing their risks by assessing the risk/reward profile and allocating capital accordingly. [p. 5].

The trading book, against whose current market value capital is charged, includes a "bank's proprietary positions in financial instruments" held to benefit "in the short term from actual or expected differences between their buying and selling prices," to hedge other trading book items, for short-term sale, or "to execute a trade with a customer" [Ibid., p. 6]. The capital charges for debt and equity "would substitute for the credit risk weights" now applied, while charges for foreign exchange risk would be added. Non-trading book items remain subject to the Basle Accord.

The Proposal uses building blocks, although it permits countries to use a "comprehensive approach" like that of the SEC if they demonstrate the effect is at least as stringent as that of the Proposal. The complex capital charges against debt securities are summarized in a study by Price Waterhouse, "The Regulation of Market Risk" (1993) at 45–6.

> [The specific risk requirement] is the sum of individual debt positions each multiplied by a specific risk weighting according to its issuer category and residual maturity ... [long and short positions in the same security may be off-set].
>
> [For general risk, the Committee proposes] two methods very similar to the CAD ...: a 'standard' method based on maturity of debt securities [that is identical to the CAD method] and a 'duration' approach [that differs slightly and would impose] ... a higher capital charge ....

The proposed charges against equities are described in the following section, after which is an illustration prepared by the Committee:

## THE PRUDENTIAL SUPERVISION OF NETTING, MARKET RISKS AND INTEREST RATE RISK

Basle, April 1993, 27–29.

1. This section proposes a minimum capital standard to cover the risk of holding or taking positions in equities in the trading account. Comment on this aspect of the proposals is especially invited in view of the difficulty of structuring common rules that would adequately cover the price risk in different equity markets. This is a matter on which securities regulators have different views according to national perspectives in their own markets. The treatment proposed below represents the Basle Committee's preferred approach, but it could be modified in further discussions with securities regulators.

2. The proposed treatment for equities would be applied to long and short positions in all instruments that exhibit market behaviour similar to equities, but would not apply to non-convertible preferred shares.[24] It is envisaged that long and short positions in the same issue could be netted. Instruments covered would include common stocks, whether voting or non-voting, warrants that give the holder the right to purchase equity securities, those convertible securities that behave like equities, options on equity securities, commitments and other rights to buy or sell equity securities and limited partnership interests. The proposed treatment of derivative products, equity indices and index arbitrage is described in II ....

I. *Specific and general market risk*

3. As with debt securities, it is proposed that the minimum standard for equities should be expressed in terms of the so-called "building-block approach". This means that the overall capital requirement would consist of separately calculated charges for the "specific" risk of holding a long or short position in an individual equity, and for the "general market risk" of holding a long or short position in the market as a whole. Specific risk has some parallels with, but is broader than, credit risk in the sense that it exists whether the position is long or short. General market risk is the risk of a broad market movement unrelated to any specific securities. The long and short position in the market would be calculated on a market-by-market basis, i.e. a separate calculation would have to be carried out for each national market in which the firm held equities.

4. It is proposed that the building-block approach should apply in the following manner. The minimum standard would be expressed in terms of an "x plus y" formula, in which "x", denoting specific risk,

**24.** Non-convertible preferred shares are covered by the debt securities requirements described in section 2.

would apply to the reporting institution's gross equity positions (i.e. the sum of all long equity positions and of all short equity positions) and "y", or general market risk, would apply to the difference between the sum of the longs and the sum of the shorts (i.e. the overall net position in an equity market).

5. If, in the future, wider convergence with securities regulators can be achieved, it is proposed that individual national authorities should have discretion to continue to apply a comprehensive approach, i.e. one that combines specific and general market risks in a single risk charge. To use such an approach, the individual regulator would be required to demonstrate to the satisfaction of his fellow regulators that such an approach would produce, in all circumstances, capital charges equal to or greater than those produced by the minimum "building-block" approach. This demonstration could be made by showing that the authority's rule, by its very nature, required capital charges equal to or greater than the building-block methodology.

6. In setting appropriate charges for the x plus y formula, the Committee proposes that the charge for y (general market risk) should be 8% of the net open position. This number was reached on the basis of analysis in collaboration with securities regulators of the price volatility of the principal equity indices in the major markets.

7. The criteria for determining the x factor for specific risk need to reflect the diversification of the portfolio and the extent to which it contains liquid and marketable stocks. It is important to ensure that a relatively high "x" factor applies *unless* the portfolio is both liquid and well-diversified. It is proposed that an appropriate x factor in the absence of any such assurances should be 8%.

8. Although the Committee accepts that a lower x factor should apply for major institutions whose portfolios are liquid and diversified, it has proved extremely difficult to define liquidity and diversification in a sufficiently tight manner to be used for establishing a common minimum standard. Criteria for liquidity could include turnover, the number of market-makers or belonging to a major index. Diversification could be established by portfolio methodology or by some simple rule requiring concentrations above a certain threshold to carry a higher charge or requiring a minimum number of evenly spread holdings. However, national market characteristics are crucial. Comment is invited on adequate common criteria for liquidity and diversification.

9. In the light of these difficulties, all members of the Basle Committee are content to allow national regulators discretion to determine their own criteria for liquid and diversified portfolios so long as x is not set lower than 4% and on the understanding that a minimum of 8% would apply to portfolios of stocks that fail to meet the liquidity and diversification test. Annex 7 illustrates the capital required for a range of hypothetical portfolios which qualify for 4% (i.e. a 4 plus 8 formula).

. . .

ANNEX 7

## Equities

## Illustration of x plus y methodology

Under the proposed two-part calculation described in Section 3 there would be separate requirements for the position in each individual equity (i.e. the gross position) and for the net position in the market as a whole. The table below illustrates how the system would work for a range of hypothetical portfolios, assuming a capital charge of 4% for the gross positions and 8% for the net positions.

| Sum of long positions | Sum of short positions | Gross position (sum of cols. 1 & 2) | 4% of gross | Net position (difference between cols. 1 & 2) | 8% of net | Capital required (gross + net) |
|---|---|---|---|---|---|---|
| 100 | 0 | 100 | 4 | 100 | 8 | 12 |
| 100 | 25 | 125 | 5 | 75 | 6 | 11 |
| 100 | 50 | 150 | 6 | 50 | 4 | 10 |
| 100 | 75 | 175 | 7 | 25 | 2 | 9 |
| 100 | 100 | 200 | 8 | 0 | 0 | 8 |
| 75 | 100 | 175 | 7 | 25 | 2 | 9 |
| 50 | 100 | 150 | 6 | 50 | 4 | 10 |
| 25 | 100 | 125 | 5 | 75 | 6 | 11 |
| 0 | 100 | 100 | 4 | 100 | 8 | 12 |

. . .

### *Questions*

1. How would the Basle Proposals, if adopted, affect German universal banks? Use the same hypothetical assets.

2. Are the Proposals and CAD basically the same? Do they diverge in any ways that are significant for universal banks? What would account for these divergences?

3. Banks and securities firms responded to the Basle Proposal with less than faint praise. The following article reports the British banks' views. What explains the British banks' response?

### JOHN GAPPER, "BRITISH BANKS CRITICIZE BASLE PROPOSALS"

Financial Times, January 18, 1994, 19.

British banks have become the latest group to criticise proposals from international supervisors to make them set aside extra capital to cover risks in foreign exchange, securities and derivatives trading.

The British Bankers' Association has told the Basle-based committee of international bank supervisors that its proposals are too conservative and will reduce banks' motivation to develop sophisticated risk management.

It describes as "deeply disappointing" and "frankly puzzling" the fact that the proposals do not reward banks which have better monitoring systems with reduced capital charges.

It also criticises the level of capital which the Basle supervisors propose should be set aside to cover equity and equity derivatives positions, and says the proposals may put banks at a competitive disadvantage to securities firms.

The response follows a critical report from the Institute of International Finance, representing 175 international banks, which said that the proposals could undermine the clarity of capital rules covering credit risks.

EU banks, which will have to comply with both the EU capital adequacy directive and Basle rules, will find the regulatory regime "a bit messy" unless the two are harmonised, said the association.

. . .

The association criticises the Basle approach of adding a capital charge for market risk to that of a counterparty credit exposure, arguing that a market movement cannot simultaneously increase both types of risk.

It says there is a danger that trading business will be driven to competitors "by a regime that imposes onerous costs on the banking industry".

## C. OTHER SECURITIES RISKS ADDRESSED BY CAPITAL ADEQUACY RULES

Capital standards exist or are being proposed for risks, other than position risk, in the securities business.

For foreign exchange risk, the CAD "requires that once the firm's overall net foreign exchange position exceeds 2% of its own funds, capital must be provided to cover the excess" [Price Waterhouse, op. cit., 36]. The capital standard, 8% of the excess, applies to almost all of a firm's exposure, including its trading book. The Basle Proposals offer "a measure for the net open position in each currency and two methods for estimating foreign exchange risk in a portfolio of positions" [International Monetary Fund, International Capital Markets Part II: Systemic Issues in International Finance, 36 (IMF) ].

Settlement risks also attract capital standards. We discuss payments and clearance and settlement later in this book. The CAD sets capital standards for settlement risk. The Basle Proposals include capital adequacy standards for bilateral netting if the arrangements can be enforced when a default occurs.

Capital standards are also set by the CAD for underwriting and large positions. Underwriters may very briefly hold many of a firm's shares as a normal part of business; the CAD increases the capital charges against the underwriter's net position in a security as the number of working days the position is held grows. The CAD also sets special capital requirements when the financial institution holds securities issued by one customer that are 25% or more of the institution's own funds. The capital charge rises as the amount rises above 25% and as the number of days in excess grows.

International regulators are also concerned about interest rate risk, which is "the risk that changes in market interest rates might adversely affect an institution's financial condition," according to the Glossary of the Basle Proposals. They propose "a measure of the sensitivity of banks' on- and off-balance-sheet positions to fluctuations in interest rates. Although this risk measure would not attract a capital charge, it is designed to alert regulators of possible excessive exposures to interest rate risk" [IMF, 36]. U.S. bank regulators proposed a similar measure that would carry capital costs.

## D. THE DEFINITION OF CAPITAL FOR NON-CREDIT RISK

National and multilateral capital standards identify the acceptable components of a firm's capital. The CAD, for example, bases its definition on the Council's 1989 Own Funds Directive, which specifies two tiers of capital. Elements include paid up share capital, accumulated reserves, and revaluation reserves. Annex V describes an alternative definition solely for market risk, which the competent authorities may permit. The main component is subordinated debt (in paragraph 2(c)). Illiquid assets are another component, mentioned in paragraph 2(d). The following paragraphs 3, 4, 6, and 7 describe this, which is often called Tier 3.

CAD, ANNEX V
(selected paragraphs)

3. The subordinated loan capital referred to in paragraph 2(c) shall have an initial maturity of at least two years. It shall be fully paid up and the loan agreement shall not include any clause providing that in specified circumstances other than the winding up of the institution the debt will become repayable before the agreed repayment date, unless the competent authorities approve the repayment. Neither the principal nor the interest on such subordinated loan capital may be repaid if such repayment would mean that the own funds of the institution in question would then amount to less than 100% of the institution's overall requirements.

In addition, an institution shall notify the competent authorities of all repayments on such subordinated loan capital as soon as its own funds fall below 120% of its overall requirements.

4. The subordinated loan capital referred to in paragraph 2(c) may not exceed a maximum of 150% of the original own funds left to meet the requirements laid down in Annexes I, II, III, IV and VI and may

approach that maximum only in particular circumstances acceptable to the relevant authorities.

. . .

6. The competent authorities may permit investment firms to exceed the ceiling for subordinated loan capital prescribed in paragraph 4 if they judge it prudentially adequate and provided that the total of such subordinated loan capital ... does not exceed 200% of the original own funds left to meet the requirements imposed in Annexes I, II, III, IV and VI, or 250% of the same amount where investment firms deduct item 2(d) referred to in paragraph 2 when calculating own funds.

7. The competent authorities may permit the ceiling for subordinated loan capital prescribed in paragraph 4 to be exceeded by a credit institution if they judge it prudentially adequate and provided that the total of such subordinated loan capital and the items referred to in paragraph 5 does not exceed 250% of the original own funds left to meet the requirements imposed in Annexes I, II, III and VI.

---

The Basle Proposals acknowledge that the definition "in the 1988 Accord differs from [that] ... commonly used for securities firms and from [that] ... in the" CAD. The authors say that the higher volatility of trading positions demands "a more flexible source of capital" than commercial banks need. Despite their preference to keep the definition in the Basle Accord, they want their proposal to extend to securities firms. The authors recognize that CAD affects European banks already. So they recommend that national supervisors be allowed to permit "an additional form of subordinated debt for the sole purpose of meeting a part of the capital requirements for market risks up to certain limits ...". [These and the following quotes come from 9–12 of the Basle Proposals.]

## BASLE PROPOSALS
(selected paragraphs)

For such instruments to be eligible, they need, if circumstances demand, to be capable of becoming part of an institution's permanent capital and thus be available to absorb losses. They should, therefore, at a minimum:

- be unsecured, subordinated and fully paid up;
- have an original maturity of at least two years;
- not be repayable before the agreed repayment date unless the supervisor agrees;
- be subject to a lock-in clause which stipulates that neither interest nor principal may be paid (even at maturity) if such payment would mean that the capital allotted to the trading

book for debt securities and equities would fall below a threshold 20% above the required capital laid down in these proposals.

20. For banks, any such debt would form a third tier of capital, supplementary to the existing tiers 1 and 2. There are three principal differences between this and the subordinated debt currently permitted as a subset of tier 2 in the 1988 Accord. First, the minimum original maturity is significantly shorter (two years as opposed to five years). Second, the debt is valued at par while in the 1988 Accord it is amortised over the last five years of life. Third, and most important, tier 3 has the lock-in feature which means that, because of the restriction on payment, the debt is effectively available to absorb losses if allotted capital falls below an early-warning level 20% above the minimum. The distinction drawn between tier 2 and tier 3 subordinated debt is not due to judgments about relative quality but to the fact that short-term debt with a lock-in is more appropriate for trading activities whereas longer term debt is more appropriate to normal banking business.

21. The Committee proposes that the following limitations should be applied to the use of tier 3 by banks:

— banks would be entitled to use such debt solely to support the market risks in the trading book for equities and debt securities (including the specific risk in the trading book). This means that any capital requirement arising in respect of banks' foreign exchange risk, or in respect of credit and counterparty risk, would need to be met by the existing definition of capital in the 1988 Accord;

— tier 3 capital would be limited to 250% of tier 1 capital allocated to support securities trading-book risks, which is consistent with the EC's Capital Adequacy Directive applicable to both banks and securities firms. This means that a minimum of about 28½% of trading-book risks would need to be supported by tier 1 capital not required to support risks in the remainder of the book;

— tier 2 elements could be substituted for tier 3 insofar as the overall limits in the 1988 Accord were not breached, that is to say total tier 2 capital could not exceed total tier 1 capital, and long-term subordinated debt could not exceed 50% of tier 1 capital;

— since several members of the Committee do not favour the use of tier 3 capital for banks at all, the Committee is also contemplating, pending further developments in the convergence process more generally, retaining the principle in the present accord that tier 1 capital should represent at least half of total capital, i.e. that the sum total of tier 2 plus tier 3 capital should not exceed total tier 1.

National supervisors would have discretion to refuse the use of short-term subordinated debt for individual banks or for their banking systems generally.

## E. CONSOLIDATION OF AFFILIATES' SECURITIES OPERATIONS

Governments, at least those outside the European Union, may continue to apply different capital standards to banks and securities firms. This raises a question about the level playing field. A similar question may be raised for banks that organize their securities operations in different ways.

Now, at least four types of organizations compete in the international equity market: securities companies, banks that carry out their own securities activities (the German universal banks are an example), banks that operate through subsidiaries (as in France), and the banks with sister companies commonly owned by a holding company (as with U.S. banks).

Assume that the rules for banks' positions were stricter than those for securities companies. Banks would have an incentive to trade through an affiliated securities company if they could. Those banks that could not do so would be at a competitive disadvantage, not only with securities firms but with other banks. In the U.S., the securities subsidiary of a Bank Holding Company is subject to both the Basle Accord and the SEC rules for position risk.

Regulators have tried to come to grips with these competitive issues and with enforcement problems by requiring groups to consolidate their accounts to determine capital adequacy. The CAD, with other directives, requires consolidation when an investment firm or credit institution is the parent of another investment company or credit institution and where a holding company is the parent of an investment company or credit institution. A country's regulators can exempt firms that [Price Waterhouse, 79]:

(i) deduct their holding in subsidiaries from base capital before determining the short-term subordinated debt headroom;

(ii) satisfy the capital requirements on a solo basis;

(iii) have systems in place to monitor and control capital and funding resources; and

(iv) can properly monitor their large exposures on a group basis.

The Basle Proposals took a different tack, for which they were criticized by the Institute for International Finance. The IIF wanted clear rules to govern consolidation. The Basle Committee proposed:

### BASLE PROPOSALS
(selected paragraphs)

III. *Consolidated supervision of market risk*

22. The Committee has for some years strongly supported the concept of consolidated supervision of risk on the grounds that problems in one affiliate could well have a contagion effect on the group as a

whole. Consolidated supervision reduces the scope for risks to escape measurement by being held in unsupervised locations and ensures banking groups have group capital to support all their risks, so preventing excessive gearing up on the same capital base. Consistent with the principle of consolidated supervision, it is proposed that supervisors have discretion to permit banking and financial entities in a group which is running a global consolidated book and whose capital is being assessed on a global basis to report short and long positions in exactly the same instrument (e.g. currencies, equities or bonds), on a net basis, no matter in which location they are booked.[9]

24. The Committee is well aware that banks can reduce positions at the close of business by engaging in a transaction with an affiliate in a later time zone (i.e. "passing" its position). This may be a perfectly legitimate device to enable banks to manage their positions continuously or to reduce intra-group imbalances. If all positions were measured at the same moment in time no problem would arise. In practice, however, reporting is likely to take place on the basis of accounts drawn up at the end of a business day and it is possible, by passing a position continuously west and over the date-line, for an exposure to escape reporting altogether. Supervisors will, therefore, be especially vigilant in ensuring that banks do not pass positions on reporting dates to affiliates whose positions escape measurement or across the international date-line.

## F. OVERALL EVALUATION OF THE MARKET RISK CAPITAL ADEQUACY RULES

How would the SEC, CAD and Basle Proposal position risk rules affect competition among U.S. securities companies, German universal banks, and U.S. Bank Holding Companies' securities subsidiaries? Assume that no other harmonization is possible. What can they do to escape if they are hurt?

*Links To Other Chapters*

Capital rules drive much of international finance. They are very important to the behavior of financial intermediaries in markets for banking (Chapters III and VII), securities (Chapters II and VII), and derivatives (Chapters XV and XVI). Capital adequacy standards have slowed banks' lending activities and increased their off-balance sheet transactions (Chapter XII) in Europe, Japan, and the U.S. and in other offshore markets (Chapter VIII). By so doing, the rules promoted the massive growth in securitization (see Chapter XII). Capital rules limit banks in the payments system (Chapter IX). We return to these issues repeatedly in the book.

9. The positions of less than wholly-owned subsidiaries would be subject to the generally accepted accounting principles in the country where the parent company is supervised.

# Chapter V

# THE EUROPEAN UNION: THE SINGLE MARKET IN FINANCIAL SERVICES

This Chapter examines the operation of the European Union's (EU) internal market in financial services. It begins with some background material on the European Union and its general program to create an internal market free of trading barriers. It then focuses more specifically on securities and banking markets. A key principle underlying the market reforms is mutual recognition.

## A. INTRODUCTION

### S. KEY, "MUTUAL RECOGNITION: INTEGRATION OF THE FINANCIAL SECTOR IN THE EUROPEAN COMMUNITY"

75 Fed.Res.Bull. 591 (September 1989).

#### Development of the Internal Market Program

In the early 1980s, concern was widespread within the European Community that the EC countries were recovering very slowly, compared with the United States and Japan, from the recessions of the late 1970s and were being outstripped by the United States and Japan in new high-technology industries. The conventional wisdom was that, even though tariff barriers among the member states had been dismantled more than a decade earlier, nontariff barriers and market fragmentation within the Community were major impediments to EC economic growth. Partly because of this view, in the first half of the 1980s new initiatives were proposed to reactivate the process of European integration. Perhaps the most far-reaching of these proposals was the draft treaty establishing a European Union that the European Parliament adopted in early 1984. This treaty had no chance of ratification by the member states; but it encouraged the heads of the EC member states, who had previously renewed their commitment in general terms to the goals set forth in the 1957 Treaty of Rome, to take concrete action toward completion of the internal market.[1]

1. The treaty that established the European Economic Community (EEC), which is one of three European Communities established under three separate treaties, is generally known as the Treaty of Rome. The European Coal and Steel Community was established by a 1951 Paris treaty, and the European Atomic Energy Community was established by another Rome treaty in 1957. The term *European Community* is commonly used to refer to all three Europe-

By the mid–1980s, steps toward further integration of the EC market had become easier to take because sustained economic growth had begun in most of the EC countries after the recovery from the 1982 recession. Moreover, the political situation had changed as governments that were more strongly committed to free markets than were their predecessors had come into power in the United Kingdom (in 1979) and in Germany (in 1982).

*The 1985 White Paper*

All of these political and economic developments created an environment in which the Commission that took office at the beginning of 1985, with Jacques Delors as its president, could move forward with proposals for economic integration (see the box "Institutions of the European Community"). By mid–1985, the Commission had prepared a white paper, *Completing the Internal Market,* which the European Council subsequently adopted as the basis for the EC internal market program. The white paper identified 300 pieces of legislation (later revised to 279) that the Community would have to enact to remove restrictions or to harmonize laws of member states. It also set forth a timetable for the enactment of each proposal that called for the entire program to be in place by the end of 1992 (see the box "Forms of EC legislation").

The white paper also announced a new strategy regarding the harmonization of national laws and regulations. In place of the previous, unsuccessful attempt to achieve complete harmonization of standards at the Community level, the Commission adopted an approach involving harmonization of only essential laws and regulations (such as those affecting health and safety) for both goods and services. Under the Commission's new approach, the harmonization of essential standards provides the basis for *mutual recognition* by the member states of the equivalence and validity of each other's laws, regulations, and administrative practices that have not been harmonized at the EC level.

. . .

*The Single European Act*

Both the white paper's goal of implementing the internal market by the end of 1992 and the principle of mutual recognition were included in provisions of the Single European Act, a 1986 agreement among the EC member states that amended the Treaty of Rome.[5] Although the act . . . does not use the term *mutual recognition,* it provides that the Council "may decide that the provisions in force in a Member State must be recognized as being equivalent to those applied by another Member State."

an Communities; the EC institutions are common to all three Communities.

5. The member states of the European Community are Belgium, Denmark, France, Germany, Greece, Ireland, Italy, Luxembourg, the Netherlands, Portugal, Spain, and the United Kingdom.

A major purpose of the Single European Act, which became effective in July 1987, was to make EC decisionmaking more efficient and thereby to facilitate the completion of the internal market. To this end, the Single European Act replaced unanimous voting with "qualified majority voting" for the Council's adoption of most harmonization measures necessary to achieve the internal market. Under qualified majority voting, the number of votes that each member state exercises in the Council is weighted roughly according to its population. Fifty-four votes (out of a total of seventy-six) are required to adopt legislation. Fiscal measures, such as the harmonization of taxes, however, still require unanimous approval of the Council.

Other institutional provisions of the Single European Act were designed to strengthen the role of the European Parliament in EC decisionmaking; however, the Parliament's role remains primarily consultative rather than legislative. Under the new "cooperation procedure," which applies to most measures involving harmonization, the Commission and the Council must take into account amendments that the Parliament proposes. However, the Commission retains considerable power because a parliamentary amendment that the Commission does not support requires the Council's unanimous approval. If the Parliament rejects a measure in its entirety, the Council may enact it only by unanimous vote (see the box "The 'cooperation procedure' ").

. . .

## Creation of a "European Financial Area"

An important part of the EC program to complete the internal market is the creation of a "European Financial Area," which involves eliminating restrictions on the movement of capital among the member states and establishing a framework for a Communitywide market for financial services.

Forms of EC legislation

EC legislation can be in the form of regulations or of directives. A *regulation* is binding in its entirety and is directly applicable throughout the Community without any implementing legislation by the member states. By contrast, a *directive* is addressed to the member states, which are obligated to ensure that the result set forth in the directive is achieved but have discretion as to the details of implementation.

Most of the EC internal market legislation is in the form of directives. Each directive specifies a date by which member states must conform their national laws to the provisions of the directive; typically the states have two years to do so. Therefore, to complete the internal market by the end of 1992, directives would need to be enacted by the Community by the end of 1990.

If a member state does not conform its laws in accordance with an EC directive, not only the EC Commission but also in many cases an individual or a company may take legal action against the member state. An individual or a company may invoke rights under EC law in national courts under the principle of "direct effects," which was developed by the European Court of Justice and has become an important mechanism for ensuring implementation of EC legislation.

Institutions of the European Community

The *Commission* is the executive branch of the European Community and has responsibility for proposing legislation and for ensuring implementation of EC law by the member states. Commissioners are appointed by agreement among the governments of the member states for four-year terms.

The *Council of Ministers*, which consists of representatives of the governments of the member states, is the decisionmaking body and enacts legislation proposed by the Commission. The presidency of the Council rotates among member states every six months. Participants at Council meetings change on the basis of the subject being considered. For example, if banking legislation is being considered, the Council participants are the economic and finance ministers. The "European Council" consists of the heads of state or government and meets semiannually.

The *European Parliament,* which is elected directly by the citizens of the member states, has an extremely limited legislative function. It does, however, have the final approval over the EC budget and over applications for membership in the Community and, with regard to other matters, a consultative role in Council decisions.

The *European Court of Justice* consists of thirteen judges appointed by agreement among the governments of the member states for six-year terms. In general, the Court has original jurisdiction in cases in which the Commission or another Community institution is a party. Other actions are brought in national courts but are referred to the European Court of Justice for preliminary rulings on matters of EC law; such rulings are binding on the national courts. (An EC Court of First Instance was created in 1988 to hear actions brought against Community institutions by EC staff or by private parties in certain technical areas; the European Court of Justice has appellate jurisdiction in such cases.)

The "cooperation procedure"

The cooperation procedure, which is used only for measures that may be adopted by a qualified majority of the Council, involves two readings of the legislation by the European Parliament. When the EC Commission submits a proposal to the Council, the proposal is also sent to the Parliament for a first reading. After obtaining Parliament's opinion and receiving any revisions proposed by the Commission, the Council adopts a "common position." The Council must then submit its common position to Parliament for a second reading.

If the Parliament *accepts* the proposal (or fails to act within three months), the Council must adopt the measure in accordance with its common position.

If the Parliament *rejects* the Council's common position, the Council may adopt the proposal only by a unanimous vote.

If the Parliament *proposes amendments,* within one month the Commission must reexamine the proposal and submit to the Council a revised proposal that either incorporates the Parliament's amendments or justifies their omission. The Council may adopt the Commission's revised proposal by a qualified majority. Unanimity is required for the Council to adopt Parliamentary amendments that were not accepted by the Commission or otherwise to amend the Commission's revised proposal. If the Council does not adopt the revised proposal within three months, the proposal is deemed not to have been adopted.

*Removal of Restrictions on Capital Movements*

Without the free movement of capital, the integration of securities markets and the cross-border provision of financial services would be impossible. At present, four countries—the United Kingdom, Germany, the Netherlands, and Denmark—have fully liberalized capital movements vis-à-vis both other member states and third countries (that is, countries outside the Community). Four other countries—Belgium, Luxembourg, France, and Italy—are already close to doing so.

Under a directive adopted in June 1988, eight EC member states must eliminate any remaining capital controls by July 1, 1990. (Spain and Ireland have extensions until 1992; extensions until 1995 are possible for Portugal and Greece.) This directive was the final step in a lengthy process of liberalization that began in the early 1960s, was set back by restrictions imposed by member states during the economic difficulties of the 1970s, and was reactivated in the early 1980s by a major Commission initiative. With regard to third countries, the 1988 directive states that the EC countries "shall endeavor to attain the same degree of liberalization" of capital movements that applies within the Community to capital movements to and from non-EC countries.

* * *

## The Concept of Mutual Recognition

The goal of the internal market program for the financial sector is to create a single, unified market by removing barriers to the provision of services across borders, to the establishment of branches or subsidiaries of EC financial institutions throughout the Community, and to transactions in securities on Community stock exchanges. In determining the best method of achieving these goals, the Community must decide what principles should be used to establish a regulatory, supervisory, and tax structure that would both facilitate the integration of Community financial markets and satisfy the public policy interests of the member states with regard to safety and soundness, monetary policy, market stability, and consumer and investor protection.

The starting point for the Community was the principle of *nondiscrimination,* a term that in this context refers to the prohibition of discrimination between domestic and foreign residents based on nationality. (By contrast, in the context of trade and capital movements, *nondiscrimination* usually refers to the prohibition of discrimination among foreign residents of different nationalities; the concept is similar to that of a most-favored-nation clause, that is, benefits of any liberalization must be extended to all foreign countries on a nondiscriminatory basis.) Although the right of establishment and the right to provide services in other member states without being subject to any restrictions based on nationality were set forth in the Treaty of Rome, legislative action by the Community and decisions of the European Court of Justice have been necessary to give practical effect to these rights.

Nondiscrimination by an EC member state amounts to offering national treatment to individuals and firms from other member states. Under a policy of national treatment, foreign firms have the same opportunities for establishment and the same powers with respect to their host-country operations that their domestic counterparts have; similarly, foreign firms operating in a host country are subject to the same obligations as their domestic counterparts. The OECD's National Treatment Instrument defines national treatment as treatment under host-country "laws, regulations, and administrative practices ... no less favorable than that accorded in like situations to domestic enterprises." The expression "no less favorable" appears to allow for the possibility that exact national treatment cannot always be achieved and that any adjustments should be resolved in favor of the foreign firm; the wording is not meant to endorse an overall policy of "better than national treatment." The principal purpose of a policy of national treatment is to promote competitive equality between domestic and foreign banking institutions by allowing them to compete on a "level playing field" within the host country.

If the European Community had adopted national treatment as an approach to financial integration, the result would have been a level playing field for foreign and domestic institutions within each national market. But, even though each country's rules would have been applied on a nondiscriminatory basis, twelve separate markets with different rules in each would still have existed. Moreover, although national treatment removes barriers to the provision of services by ensuring fair treatment for entry and operation within a country, it does not by itself address two important issues: the extent to which multinational cooperation or agreement is necessary to regulate and supervise financial activities conducted internationally and the de facto barriers created by the lack of multinational harmonization of regulatory structures. The Community's program attempts to deal with these issues.

One approach, which, as noted previously, the Community originally used with regard to products, is to require member states to modify their differing national laws and regulations in order to implement comprehensive, uniform standards established by the Community. This approach of complete harmonization was abandoned as involving too much detailed legislation at the Community level and as totally impractical to achieve within any reasonable period.

The Community's solution was to adopt the approach of mutual recognition. This approach requires each country to recognize the laws, regulations, and administrative practices of other member states as equivalent to its own and thereby precludes the use of differences in national rules to restrict access. The concept of mutual recognition goes well beyond that of national treatment. Under a policy of mutual recognition, some member states in effect agree to offer treatment that is more favorable than national treatment to firms from other member states.

Mutual recognition cannot simply be decreed among a group of countries with widely divergent legal systems, statutory provisions, and regulatory and supervisory practices. Mutual recognition of rules that differ as to what a country regards as essential elements and characteristics would be politically unacceptable. As a result, a crucial prerequisite for mutual recognition is the harmonization of essential rules. If member states consider certain rules essential but cannot reach agreement on initial harmonization, they may agree explicitly to exclude such rules from mutual recognition and home-country control until agreement can be reached.

In the financial sector, the process of harmonization involves identifying the rules that are essential for ensuring the safety and soundness of financial institutions and the rules that are essential for the protection of depositors, other consumers of financial services, and investors. It also involves determining how detailed the harmonization of these rules must be. For example, one question is whether specifying that the major shareholders of a financial institution must be determined to be "suitable" by home-country authorities is sufficient or whether more specific criteria are needed.

*Home–Country Control*

A corollary of mutual recognition is home-country control. If national laws, regulations, and supervisory practices that have not been harmonized at the EC level are to be accorded mutual recognition, home-country rules and supervisory practices must be accepted as controlling the operations of branches and the cross-border provision of services by financial institutions. However, the principle of home-country control adopted by the Community is not absolute. In accordance with judgments of the European Court of Justice and with EC directives, the host country retains the right to regulate branches or the cross-border provision of services to the extent that doing so is necessary to protect the public interest.

In practice, the division of responsibility between home- and host-country regulators may be rather complicated. In general, the EC directives that have been proposed or adopted in the area of financial services provide for home-country control for initial authorization and for ongoing prudential supervision. However, various aspects of the day-to-day conduct of business could be subject to host-country control on a national treatment basis under, for example, consumer protection laws that are necessary to protect the public interest but have not been harmonized by the Community. In some directives, such host-country control is strictly limited or is prohibited either because the extent of harmonization of investor protection rules at the EC level is considered sufficient (as in the cases of securities prospectuses and unit trusts) or because the wholesale customers covered by the directive are deemed not to require host-country protection (as in the case of cross-border nonlife insurance services). As a result, under the EC directives on securities markets, a company headquartered in Greece and listed on the Greek stock exchange could, for example, be listed on the London stock exchange under Greek rules that satisfied the EC minimum standards but provided prospective British investors with less information than that required of a U.K. firm.

The European Court of Justice has already played a major role in establishing a public interest test for host-country regulation and in determining whether that criterion has been met, and it will undoubtedly continue to do so. In the case of banking, the public interest of the host state appears to be particularly strong because of the role of banks in the credit, monetary, and payments systems and because banks are within the so-called safety net of deposit insurance and of lending of last resort by the monetary authorities. Rather than relying on the overall public interest exception to home-country control, the Second Banking Directive includes explicit exceptions for rules relating to the conduct of host-country monetary policy. In line with the Revised Basle Concordat, an exception to the principle of home-country control is also provided for the supervision of liquidity. In practice, of course, questions are likely to arise as to whether particular restrictions are truly necessary for purposes of monetary policy and whether particular regulations are addressed toward liquidity or solvency.

. . .

*Regulatory Convergence*

The EC approach of mutual recognition could result, at least in the short run, in competitive inequalities and fragmentation of markets. With regard to financial services, however, the Community assumes that over the longer run market forces will create pressure on governments that will lead to a convergence of additional national rules and practices that have not been harmonized at the EC level. Pressures for regulatory convergence within the Community would arise both from the absence of restrictions on capital movements and from the regulatory advantages enjoyed by branches of banks and of investment firms from other member states and also by the head offices of such banks and investment firms in providing services across borders.

In the financial sector, the Community is using the principle of mutual recognition as a pragmatic tool that, together with market forces, is expected to result in a more unified, less restrictive regulatory structure. The process is interactive: Mutual recognition requires initial harmonization, and additional harmonization results from mutual recognition. In adopting the approach of mutual recognition in the financial area, the Community is in effect using trade in financial services as a lever to arbitrage the regulatory policies of the member states.

Regulatory convergence is particularly likely to occur with regard to bank powers because the Community has reached a theoretical consensus on what activities are permissible for banks. In effect, the member states have agreed upon a goal for regulatory convergence. Banks permitted by their home country to engage in any of the activities listed in the Second Banking Directive are specifically permitted to engage in such activities anywhere in the Community through a branch or through cross-border provision of services. As a result, although the Community has not required governments to give their banks the powers on the list, it has created a situation in which regulatory convergence toward the EC list of activities as a result of market forces seems almost inevitable. Other areas, particularly if the model for convergence has not been specified in advance, could be more complicated.

. . .

*Supranational Structure of the Community*

In considering mutual recognition as the approach to financial integration within the Community and its relevance in contexts beyond the Community, one must remember that the member states have agreed to use it as a tool to achieve an integrated market in the context of a structure that, though not a federation, is a rather powerful supranational structure to which the member states have already transferred a significant degree of sovereignty. The customs union with its common external commercial policy is the basis of the internal market, but the internal market is much more than a customs union. It involves a supranational legislative process under which supranational rules ensuring the free movement of goods, persons, services, and capital are adopted and the harmonization of basic laws, regulations, and practices at a supranational level can be achieved. Moreover, a member state is obligated to implement or enforce all EC rules, including those it opposed in the Community legislative process. Community law is accepted as prevailing over national law, and both judgments and preliminary rulings of the European Court of Justice based on Community law are binding and enforceable in the member states. (The principle of supremacy of Community law was not explicitly stated in the Treaty of Rome, but it has been confirmed by the European Court of Justice in judgments interpreting provisions of the treaty.)

The European Community is also more than a single, unified market. Other aspects of the Community addressed either by the original Treaty of Rome or by the Single European Act include social policy, economic and social cohesion, research and development, the environment, and economic and monetary union. The Single European Act also refers to the goal of a "European Union," although there is considerable disagreement within the Community as to what such a union would entail.

These institutional and political characteristics of the European Community are extremely important in considering whether the approach the Community is using for internal financial integration is applicable to removing barriers and achieving a more integrated regulatory structure for financial services and markets beyond the Community. A basic question is how much multinational harmonization would be required and the extent to which sovereignty might need to be surrendered to use the principle of mutual recognition more broadly among nations.

. . .

## B. SECURITIES MARKETS

The EU has focused its efforts in securities markets on facilitating the distribution and trading of securities on a Union wide basis, rather than having twelve separate markets. This has led to Union wide disclosure standards and the removal of prohibitions on the Union wide operation of securities firms.

### 1. Disclosure

M. WARREN, "REGULATORY HARMONY IN THE EUROPEAN COMMUNITIES: THE COMMON MARKET PROSPECTUS"

26 Brooklyn J. Int'l Law 19 (1990).

. . .

The EC has adopted or proposed a number of directives that have contributed to the development of a supranational securities law for the common market. These directives actually include both company law and securities law directives because both classes of directives have embraced a mandatory disclosure philosophy. Accordingly, it is difficult to separate them into discrete categories. Those measures most commonly referred to as securities law directives, include the Admissions Directive, the Listing Particulars Directive, the Interim Reports Directive, the POP Directive, the Mutual Funds Directive, the Investment Services Directive, and the Insider Trading Directive. These seven directives clearly represent the core of an emergent European securities code. Of these, the Listing Particulars Directive, as amended, and the POP Directive are the most significant in the regulation of multijurisdictional securities offerings.

A. *The Listing Particulars Directive*

The Listing Particulars Directive, which was adopted in 1980 and may be referred to as the Information Directive, further develops the EC's "philosophy of disclosure" in the regulation of securities. This directive strongly influenced the United States Securities and Exchange Commission (SEC) in its development of United States disclosure forms for foreign issuers. Unlike national legislation in most of the individual member states, which traditionally required that extensive disclosure be made only to regulatory or self-regulatory bodies, the EC's policy requires disclosure to the general public. The purposes of this directive, as expressed in its preamble, are to provide equivalent protection for investors throughout the common market, to facilitate cross-border exchange listings, and to promote greater interpenetration of national securities markets within the EC. The Listing Particulars Directive requires that an information sheet, termed "listing particulars," in compliance with the directive's disclosure requirements and a prescribed format, be filed and approved in connection with the admission of securities to listing on any securities exchange in the EC. According to the directive, in its implementing legislation each member state must designate a "competent authority" to scrutinize listing particulars to determine whether they satisfy the common disclosure standards imposed by it. Subsequent to approval, the listing particulars must be published for the benefit of investors. For the first time, a multinational disclosure regime, with common disclosure standards and a prescribed format, was to be established by this directive; ultimately it should enable investors and securities analysts, both within and outside the EC, to make investment decisions based on relatively comparable information.

### 1. The Disclosure Scheme

The layout and detailed disclosure requirements of the Listing Particulars Directive are set forth in Schedule A, for equity securities and Schedule B, for debt securities. The areas of disclosure include, *inter alia,* information concerning: 1) those parties responsible for preparing the listing particulars and for auditing the financial statements; 2) the securities and the listing application; 3) the capitalization of the issuer; 4) the issuer's principal business activities, including a breakdown of net turnover by category of activity and geographical markets for the previous three years, its material contracts, patents, and licenses, legal proceedings, employees and investment policies; 5) the issuer's assets and liabilities, financial position, and profits and losses; 6) the issuer's administration management, and supervision, including remuneration, unusual transactions, and equity interests; and 7) recent developments and prospects of the issuer, including recent trends in production, sales, orders, inventories, costs, and selling prices, as well as prospects for the current year. The information is to be presented in an "easily analyzable and comprehensible" form. Competent authorities are permitted to exempt certain required information if it is deemed to be of "minor importance" or if disclosure would be "contrary to the public interest" or "seriously detrimental to the issuer." Significantly, the issuer must also include all other information, based on the particular nature of the issuer and the securities, which "is necessary to enable investors and their investment advisers to make an informed assessment of the assets and liabilities, financial position, profits and losses, and prospects of the issuer and of the rights attaching to such securities." The mandatory disclosure required by this directive is not limited to "filling out a form," but instead extends to all material information relating to the securities to be listed on an EC exchange.

The listing particulars, following their review and approval by the competent authority of the member state, must be published in a widely-distributed newspaper in the member state or in the form of a free brochure made available to the public. Publication must be made within a reasonable period before the effective date on which the securities are officially listed. This directive does not require the delivery of the listing particulars to investors either prior to, at the time of, or subsequent to, their purchase of securities. This regulatory gap is closed in substantial part by the POP Directive, which requires publication of a prospectus prior to a public offering of securities. Civil and criminal sanctions for compliance failures under either directive, however, are left to the discretion of the individual member states. The Listing Particulars Directive does provide for cooperation among competent authorities of the various member states to facilitate simultaneous or roughly contemporaneous listings based on a coordinated text.

### 2. Mutual Recognition

Member states retain considerable flexibility in adopting more stringent or additional disclosure requirements. As previously stated, the first step of the EC's legislative strategy was to establish common minimum standards to ensure a given level of protection for the EC's securities markets. The EC properly recognized that it could not immediately preempt the entire field of securities regulation, despite the primacy of EC law in areas covered by the Treaty of Rome. An important second step was taken by the EC in 1987, when the Council of Ministers approved the Mutual Recognition Directive, which amended the Listing Particulars Directive. The amendment states that once approved by a competent authority in a member state, listing particulars must be recognized as such by all other member states without further approval by their competent authorities and without any additional information generally required by any of those member states. Where more stringent, additional disclosure requirements are applicable to listing particulars in the member state where recognition is sought, these requirements must be disregarded. Consequently, such a member state finds itself in the untenable position of imposing more disclosure requirements and greater regulatory costs on its own domestic issuers, which may pose less of an investment risk than foreign issuers from less-regulated member states. The domestic pressure to reduce this regulatory disequilibrium is likely to result in lowering the stricter state's disclosure regimen to the common denominator established by the directive.

Nevertheless, the Mutual Recognition Directive does undertake to reduce opportunities for forum shopping. It provides that where an issuer seeks to list its securities simultaneously or within a short interval in two or more member states, including the member state where its registered office is located, then the issuer must first secure approval of its home state's competent authority pursuant to its home state's laws. The issuer could still engage in regulatory arbitrage by listing only outside its home state, but this is less likely to occur given the typically wider acceptance and liquidity of its securities in its own domestic market. This course remains possible, however, especially as trading markets centralize and as off-exchange trading volumes increase.

The Mutual Recognition Directive has greater authority than merely extending mutual recognition to listing particulars—as listing particulars—in all member states after approval by a competent authority in any member state. The directive also extends mutual recognition—as listing particulars—to public offer prospectuses used in the sale of listed securities in other member states. Presently, this mutual-recognition requirement is limited to circumstances in which a listing is sought on exchanges in two or more member states and when another member state has approved the prospectus, in accordance with the Listing Particulars Directive, within three months of the further application. A proposed amendment to the Mutual Recognition Directive, however, will extend the mutual recognition requirement to all public offer prospectuses that have been approved by the competent authority in any member state, regardless of whether the securities have been listed previously on a member state's exchange. As amended, the Listing Particulars Directive is designed to integrate the disclosure requirements applicable to the public offer and sale of both listed and unlisted securities. The EC's policy, which is reflected by the directive, is to establish a heretofore nonexistent integrated disclosure system for the listing and distribution of securities in the member states.

. . .

### B. *The Public Offer Prospectus Directive*

The POP Directive was adopted by the Council of Ministers in 1989 after almost a decade of controversial and secretive negotiations. The development of this directive ranks among the EC's most difficult journeys on the path to regulatory harmony. When originally proposed in 1980, the POP Directive faced major opposition. Questions were raised whether 1) a uniform disclosure policy was necessary; 2) the directive should exclude small and medium-sized enterprises; 3) it should exclude Eurobonds and Euroequities; and 4) the POP Directive should incorporate the principle of mutual recognition.[80] In order to

**80.** At the time the *POP Directive* was proposed, the United Kingdom Law Society's Standing Committee on Company Law (Law Society), in response to an inquiry from the United Kingdom Department of Trade and Industry, stated that the directive was not necessary. The Law Society's Standing Committee on Company Law, Memorandum on the Draft Directive on Prospectuses for Unlisted Securities (1981) (unpublished memorandum) [hereinafter Law Society Memorandum].

We do not consider that there is any need for a [d]irective, and indeed we would consider that the introduction of such a directive would be highly detrimental in

secure its adoption, major compromises were reached that have substantially reduced the scope and effect of this directive. Nevertheless, it represents a major achievement by the EC in the establishment of regional regulatory harmony for multijurisdictional securities offerings.

The POP Directive's underlying policies complement those of the Listing Particulars Directive, which was adopted ten years earlier. The POP Directive is intended to protect investors by providing information necessary to assess the risks of investment in securities, to reinforce confidence in securities, to contribute to the correct functioning, and the development of, securities markets, and to establish an equivalent level of securities disclosure among the member states. The directive undertakes to harmonize the disclosure standards of the member states for public offerings of securities, regardless of whether the securities are to be listed on an exchange. By imposing prospectus requirements similar to those required of listing particulars, this directive eliminates disclosure disparities that may have been a disincentive to listing on an exchange. It also further develops the EC's integrated disclosure system in which prospectuses and listing particulars ultimately may be used almost interchangeably throughout the common market.

Before the adoption of the POP Directive, EC law did not require the publication of a prospectus before a public offering of securities. As stated previously, the Listing Particulars Directive requires publication of an information sheet within a reasonable time before the securities are listed on an EC exchange. Currently, if the securities to be listed were also the subject of a public offering, the member state's non-EC law governed whether a prospectus was required, as well as the prospectus' contents and publication. Once the POP Directive is implemented by national legislation in each of the member states, however, this will no

> the United Kingdom in that it would at the least increase the cost to smaller companies of raising money by the issue of securities without a corresponding increase in the protection of investors.

Id. at 5. The Law Society was also opposed to the requirement in the original proposal that all prospectuses be subject to review and approval by a competent authority. Id. at 6.

> This is clearly too great a task for any competent authority [that] does not have the opportunity to be involved throughout the process of the prospectus' preparation. It is hard enough for the most experienced legal and accountancy advisers and merchant banks when engaged actively in the preparation of a prospectus to satisfy themselves that adequate inquiries are made to ensure that there are no material omissions from a prospectus.

Id. at 7. In addition, the committee viewed prior governmental scrutiny or "vetting" as potentially misleading to investors:

> If a system of qualitative vetting [was] introduced, this would cast a heavy responsibility on the persons carrying out the process. While it would be possible to exclude legal liability by appropriate provision in our domestic law, there would still be a tendency for the investing public to believe, even if words of disclaimer were included in the document itself, that the fact that it had been through the vetting process was to some extent a guarantee that there were no material omissions and that the contents of the document were true and based on full enquiry.

Id. at 8–9. The Law Society's position was accepted and, as adopted, the *POP Directive* does not require prior scrutiny of prospectuses for unlisted securities. ... Prospectuses that have not been subjected to prior scrutiny, however, will not be entitled to mutual recognition.

longer be the case. The directive requires that all public offerings of securities within the EC be subject to the publication of a prospectus by the offeror on or before the time the offering is made. Thus, the POP Directive should result in the creation of a "common market prospectus."

## 1. The Disclosure Scheme

The POP Directive establishes a common market prospectus by imposing a prospectus requirement for securities that are to be listed and for those that are not. This is accomplished by the establishment of two regimes. First, to create a regime for public offerings of securities that are to be listed on an exchange, it forces the Listing Particulars Directive to serve two roles. In addition to providing the disclosure format for listing particulars, the Listing Particulars Directive is harnessed by the POP Directive to serve as the disclosure format for a public offer prospectus. The POP Directive simply incorporates by reference the disclosure requirements of the Listing Particulars Directive for public offerings of securities that are to be listed on an EC exchange. With respect to these securities, the directive provides that the contents and procedures for scrutiny and distribution of the prospectus should be determined by the Listing Particulars Directive "subject to adaptations appropriate to the circumstances of a public offer." The POP Directive thus establishes a dual function for listing particulars: they are to serve 1) as an initial information sheet for the secondary market where the securities trade; and 2) as a prospectus for the public offering of those securities.

Second, the POP Directive establishes a prospectus regime of its own for the public offering of securities that will not be listed on an EC exchange. Although the disclosure requirements are less detailed in this instance, they reflect the same basic standards set forth in the Listing Particulars Directive. For securities that are not to be listed, the following categories of disclosure are established for transferable equity-related and debt securities: the persons responsible for the prospectus; the terms of the offer; the nature of the securities; withholding taxes; underwriting arrangements; transfer restrictions and preemptive rights; the issuer's capitalization; the issuer's business activities; the issuer's material contracts, patents, and licenses; legal proceedings; the issuer's annual and interim financial statements; the auditors; management; and the issuer's business trends and prospects for the current year. In addition to specific categories of disclosure, the POP Directive, in a manner similar to that of the Listing Particulars Directive, requires disclosure of all other information, based on the particular nature of the issuer and the securities that may be necessary to enable investors to make an informed assessment of the investment. Prior scrutiny of the prospectus for listed securities is required by reference to the Listing Particulars Directive, but prospectuses for unlisted securities must only be delivered to the appropriate member state authority before its publication. Prior scrutiny and approval by a competent authority, however, is a critical precondition to mutual recognition within the EC.

## 2. The Exclusions From Coverage

The mandatory disclosure regimes imposed by the POP Directive for public offerings of both listed and unlisted securities serve to upgrade and harmonize disclosure standards in the EC. The exclusions set forth in the directive, however, may result in a mandatory disclosure system with very limited application to securities offerings in the common market. The list of exclusions from coverage includes, without limitation, the following:

(a) securities offered to persons in the context of their trades, professions, or occupations (professionals exemption);

(b) securities offered to a restricted circle of people (private placement exemption);

(c) securities the selling price of which does not exceed 40,000 ECU's (small offering exemption);

(d) securities that can be acquired for only consideration of at least 40,000 ECU's (minimum purchase exemption);

(e) securities issued by collective investment undertakings other than closed-end types (mutual fund exemption);

(f) securities offered by or on behalf of governmental entities or public international bodies (government securities exemption);

(g) securities offered in connection with a takeover bid (takeover exchange offers exemption);

(h) securities offered in connection with a merger (merger exchange offers exemption);

(i) securities allotted free of charge to the holders of shares (stock splits and dividend exemption);

(j) securities offered by an issuer in exchange for its own shares if no increase in the issuer's share capital (recapitalization exemption);

(k) securities offered to present or former employees (employee offering exemption);

(*l*) securities resulting from conversion of convertible debt securities and warrants if originally described in a prospectus (conversion exemption);

(m) securities issued to achieve disinterested objectives (nonprofit exemption);

(n) securities representing membership in building societies (building society exemption); and

(*o*) Eurosecurities that are not the subject of a generalized campaign of advertising or canvassing.

The exemptions for private placements, small offerings, minimum purchase offerings, exchange offers, employee offerings, and Eurosecurities come very close to swallowing the disclosure rule. With the exclusion of Eurosecurities, a term that includes both equities and bonds, many regulators are given pause by the question, "what is left?" These exemptions cause one to seriously question the potential for successful implementation of the disclosure goals set forth in the recitals. The POP Directive appears to constitute a mandatory disclosure scheme in search of an issuer.

In fairness to the drafters, it must be conceded that the exigencies of any effort to harmonize the preexisting regulatory policies of twelve sovereign states required considerable compromise. The lobbying efforts of the International Primary Market Association (IPMA), finding its strongest ally in United Kingdom regulators fearful of losing the market that its members control, were difficult to resist. The Commission also proved an ally because of the time pressures of the 1992 deadline and its desire to move on to other equally or more difficult measures, like the proposed Investment Services Directive. The paranoia generated by the IPMA, as well as the general backlash in the United Kingdom to the perceived excesses in the implementation of its Financial Services Act, was more than enough to transform the directive into political rhetoric.

From the beginning, an all-pervasive fear of the Eurobond market taking flight to Zurich or elsewhere outside the EC dictated opposition to the POP Directive. The IPMA line of attack embraced the following tenets:

(a) the marketing techniques of the Eurobond market involve rapid syndication and distribution of securities among financial institutions to take advantage of interest rate and currency fluctuations;

(b) the timing feature, critical to marketing, would be disrupted if prospectus review and delivery requirements were imposed;

(c) the advent of the interest rate and currency swaps market compounded the significance of the timing feature;

(d) the same marketing techniques are increasingly utilized for international equity offerings;

(e) the targeted investors in these "Eurosecurities," as defined by this marketing technique, are sophisticated professionals who do not need or benefit from mandated disclosure;

(f) the Eurosecurities market has experienced no serious defaults or fraudulent offerings; and

(g) if prospectus review and delivery requirements were imposed, the market for Eurosecurities would abandon London, moving "to other capital markets such as those in Switzerland, the Far East, and North America," resulting in the loss of substantial revenues for the EC states.

This "party line" deliberately underestimated the numerous factors that established London as the primary base of operations for the Eurosecurities market. London's preeminent position has largely proved immune from regulatory arbitrage. After all, it has been, and remains, the most highly regulated jurisdiction in the EC in terms of mandated disclosure for public offerings of securities. London's attractiveness as the world's primary international securities market stems from its time zone, language, professional expertise and skilled work force, advanced technological infrastructure, cultural adaptability, quality of life, and political stability. Further, one writer has concluded that London's international market has profited the most from "the globalization of insecurities." Contrary to the IPMA position, it is unlikely that international investment firms, having made huge capital investments to secure positions there, would readily abandon London for another city outside the common market.

Many of the other propositions advanced by those opposed to the POP Directive are also questionable. For example, the propaganda asserting that the Eurosecurities market was a "professionals only market," without a need of mandatory disclosure, was highly misleading. First, the Eurobond market remains substantially retail in nature, with most end investors being individuals seeking both tax avoidance and diversification. Second, most of the other end investors, who, because of the timing feature, must "put up or shut-up" without full disclosure, are institutions managing other people's money. The managers of Eurosecurities syndicates have been forced to "officially list" the securities on the Luxembourg Stock Exchange because of domestic statutory investment restrictions on the investment of funds held in trust for the beneficiaries of these institutional end investors. Accordingly, the Listing Particulars Directive finally provides mandatory disclosure, for a "brass plate" listing, but it comes after the offer and sale pursuant to what has been described as Luxembourg's "nods and winks" review. Nevertheless, the fear of regulatory arbitrage and the drive to meet the 1992 deadline obscured the issues raised by more thoughtful analysis of the "party line."

Once it became clear to the IPMA and other opponents of the POP Directive that a Eurobond exemption could be secured, the goal was expanded to include Euroequities as well. Precisely when this expansion occurred is difficult to determine, but the success achieved in securing the exclusion of Euroequities from the POP Directive was surprising even to the Eurobond industry. The goal and its achievement were predicated largely on the desire for *laissez faire* flexibility, rather than established practice. As one investment banker described it, "we do not want regulation today [that] may hurt us five years from now," despite an acknowledgment that equities involve considerably more investment risk than the investment grade debt typically sold in the Euromarkets. Most experts recognize that a decision to buy equities is much more complex than one to buy bonds given the absence of benchmarks for comparison. Another investment banker described the distinction this way:

> You cannot just say what is the yield, what is the spread to Treasuries, or what is the yield on comparable paper in the secondary market? Is it generous or is it tight? It is much less mathematically mechanical because you need to read each unique story.

In practice Euroequity offerings had initially followed United States disclosure standards, but the relaxed regulatory environment in Europe gradually led to a diminution in the level of disclosure. It now appears that these disclosure practices will not be improved as a result of the POP Directive.

Efforts were made to preserve at least minimal coverage of Eurobonds and Euroequities under the directive. During the working party discussions on the draft directive, informal suggestions were made both for a reduced disclosure scheme for Euroequities and Eurobonds and for a shelf-registration scheme. Another suggestion proffered was to permit prospectuses for these securities to be filed and published after the sale. These proposals received little positive response and, accordingly, were rejected before ever being reduced to print for circulation among regulators and other interested parties.

The POP Directive, as finally adopted, did not exclude Eurobonds and Euroequities altogether. An accord was reached that will require a two-step analysis to determine whether a transactional exemption is available. The first step turns on whether the securities satisfy the terms of the definition provided in the directive. Both Eurobonds and Euroequities are subsumed by the term "Eurosecurities," which is defined by the POP Directive:

> [Eurosecurities] shall mean transferable securities which:
>
> — are to be underwritten and distributed by a syndicate at least two of the members of which have their registered offices in different [s]tates, and
>
> — are offered on a significant scale in one or more [s]tates other than that of the issuer's registered office, and
>
> — may be subscribed for or initially acquired only through a credit institution or other financial institution.

Once the threshold definitional criteria are satisfied, the second step in determination of the exemption must be made. The directive excludes Eurosecurities unless "a generalized campaign of advertising or canvassing was employed." The drafters were unable to reach a consensus as to what is meant by the terms "generalized campaign," "advertising," or "canvassing." Because these terms are undefined in the final version of the directive, numerous questions remain regarding the scope of the exclusion and the degree of regulatory harmony that will be achieved. Even a cursory examination of these terms reveals serious difficulties that are likely to plague the implementation of this directive.

The POP Directive's use of the term "generalized campaign" poses an interesting dilemma. The term must refer to some variant of the term "public offering," because the directive does not apply to securities offerings that are not "public offerings." Unfortunately, the drafters of the POP Directive were unable to reach any agreement on a definition of the term, "public offering." [155] This occasioned their resort to the term, "generalized campaign"; but it is used only in connection with the Eurosecurities exclusion. The exclusion for "[E]urosecurities not subject to a generalized campaign" implies that these offerings actually would constitute public offerings otherwise covered by the directive. If this were not true, the exclusion would have been unnecessary. Accordingly, it would appear that Eurosecurities offerings, as defined by the POP Directive, are public offerings regardless of whether a generalized campaign is employed. Nevertheless, the directive excludes from coverage only those public offerings of Eurosecurities in which no generalized campaign is undertaken. Although this is a plausible construction, the drafters presumably had no answer to the issue of whether Eurosecurities offerings were public or nonpublic offerings. The "party line" discussed above seems to have produced considerable confusion.

. . .

### 3. Mutual Recognition

The mutual recognition provision of the POP Directive complements the mutual recognition amendment to the Listing Particulars Directive, which was previously discussed. A primary policy underlying the mutual recognition doctrine is that investors throughout the common market should be given equivalent protection. Because prospectuses for securities to be listed are subject to the stricter regime under the Listing Particulars Directive, the POP Directive authorizes member states to permit prospectuses for unlisted securities to be prepared in conformity with the Listing Particulars Directive. This facilitates greater equivalence than the widely-variant prospectuses for unlisted securities prepared only on the basis of the general standards set forth in the POP Directive. As a result, all prospectuses, whether for listed or unlisted

**155.**

. . .

Because offerings of securities directly to the general public have occurred only rarely in continental Europe, the public offering concept, as understood in the United States, Canada, and the United Kingdom, is not well developed in the Common Market. Interview with Frank Dangeard, Sullivan & Cromwell, in London (Dec. 20, 1988). For example, it is common practice for financial institutions to acquire substantial blocs of newly-issued securities and immediately resell them to their existing clients. Interview with Andrew Peck, Linklaters & Paines, in London (Nov. 8, 1988). Despite the institution's role as a conduit for the public distribution of securities, this practice is not generally viewed as a public offering requiring prior publication of a prospectus. Id. Issuers and their investment firms apparently turn out the lights following the offer and sale of securities to institutional customers, darkening from view the large volume of immediate resales to those institutions' retail customers. The several steps in the distribution process are separated, rather than integrated, to deny, rather than confirm, the public offering that has been concluded. The end investor is the phantom of Europe's primary market for securities. The public offering concept is poorly developed; the statutory underwriter is virtually unknown.

securities, which are adopted and prepared in conformity with the Listing Particulars Directive, and approved after prior scrutiny by a competent authority, must be given full recognition throughout the EC as public offer prospectuses. Certain limitations are set forth in the POP Directive, but these should not seriously undermine the mutual recognition requirement.

The most important limitation in the POP Directive's mutual recognition provision is the contemporaneity requirement. Public offerings must be conducted either simultaneously or within a short interval of each other. Member states must be given advance notice and may impose translation requirements. Lastly, member states may require additional information specific to its particular market and relating to income tax consequences, paying agents, and notices to investors to be included in the prospectus. Member states, however, cannot require any other additional disclosures and cannot condition use of the prospectus upon first obtaining local approval. After adoption of the proposed revision of the Listing Particulars Directive's mutual recognition amendment, public offer prospectuses and listing particulars approved by a competent authority in a single member state will be entitled to interchangeable mutual recognition in other member states.

. . .

### *Notes and Questions*

1. The general idea behind the Listing Particulars and POP Directives is relatively clear—it is to create a single EU market for multijurisdictional securities offerings. This can be done by having a single set of disclosure documents with which securities can be offered in any EU country.

The Listings Particulars Directive provides that disclosures required for listing on one EU exchange must be accepted by other EU exchanges. Information required by the Directive must be filed and approved before stock can be listed on any exchange. After the disclosures are approved, they are published.

There are also minimum standards that must be observed by any exchange, under the Listing Conditions Directive (not referred to in the Warren article). All listed firms must meet certain minimum requirements with respect to size, earnings, and public float. Why is it necessary to have minimum listing requirements? In the U.S. listing requirements are left to individual exchanges.

The POP provides that any securities offered to the public must have a POP, and that a POP approved in one jurisdiction can be used in another. What does POP add to what was already required under the Listings Particulars Directive?

2. How does mutual recognition work? If you are a French company can you list first on the Luxembourg Exchange and then the French to take advantage of the less rigorous Luxembourg disclosure rules? If a

stock is approved for listing on the Athens Stock Exchange, must it also be approved for listing on the Frankfurt Exchange?

3. Note that there is no common enforcement system; no EU SEC. If a prospectus complying with Luxembourg law is being distributed in France, who is supposed to enforce compliance with Luxembourg law?

4. How would you compare the EU approach to the U.S.'s MJDS initiative?

5. "Eurosecurities" are securities which (1) are underwritten and distributed by a syndicate at least two of the members of which have their registered offices in different states (*multiple state underwriters* ); (2) are offered on a significant scale in one or more states other than that of the issuer's registered office (*distribution in state other than issuer's* ); and (3) may be subscribed for or initially acquired only through a credit institution or other financial institution (*sold to banks* ). Eurosecurities are exempted from the EU disclosure requirements if they are not subject to "a generalized campaign of advertising or canvassing." Does that mean that they are subject to no disclosure requirements?

Suppose a German company wants to issue bonds underwritten by a bank syndicate, including Deutsche Bank and Barclays, to be sold initially to various banks in London. Is this issue exempt from EU disclosure requirements? Would it matter if the bank buyers immediately sold the bonds to individual investors?

Professor Warren obviously disagrees with the exemption. Is he right?

---

## 2. Provision of Services

The EU disclosure requirements deal with securities sold within the EU. Another important element of the single market program is the institutions providing securities services. The Investment Services Directive aims at facilitating the operation of such institutions throughout the Union.

### M. WARREN, "THE INVESTMENT SERVICES DIRECTIVE: THE 'NORTH SEA ALLIANCE' VICTORY OVER 'CLUB MED' "

6 Int'l Securities Reg.Rept. 6 (January 12, 1993).

Last June's breakthrough on the sweeping EC Investment Services Directive marked a decisive victory for the so-called "North Sea Alliance" of free-market oriented European Community countries over the protectionist "Club Med" group (France, Italy, Spain, Portugal, Greece, and Belgium). And among the alliance countries—the United Kingdom, Germany, Ireland, Luxembourg, and the Netherlands—the United Kingdom is the victor with the most spoils.

The breakthrough enabled the EC Council of Ministers to adopt a common position on the ISD on Nov. 24. Its primary purposes are to provide:

- Common minimum authorization (licensing) requirements among the member states.
- Mutual recognition of the license granted in the "home state" by all other member states (or "host states").
- Common minimum financial soundness or "prudential rules."
- Certain guiding principles for adoption of "conduct of business" rules.
- Direct access to domestic stock exchanges for both outside investment firms and banks.
- Investor freedom to trade in either regulated markets or in less-regulated off-exchange markets.
- Minimum transparency rules for regulated exchange markets.

The directive should lead ultimately to a rough equivalency among the 12 member states as to authorization standards, financial soundness rules, and conduct of business principles.

Moreover, the directive's mutual recognition provision, providing in effect a single license, should greatly facilitate EC-wide operations for investment firms and, hence, significant integration of the EC's securities markets. The extent of this integration, while hardly creating a true, single market, should serve as a powerful catalyst for the eventual development of a supranational market system in the EC.

This analysis, however, examines three controversial provisions of the ISD—access to stock exchanges, off-market vs. on-market trading, and transparency rules—and how they will affect European securities markets. It also examines certain competitive advantages that EC banks will enjoy in the securities field as a result of the Council's decision to delay ISD implementation until 1996.

### Access to Stock Exchanges

One of the directive's most contested provisions provides expanded access for both investment firms and banks, with home state authorization, by allowing them to become members of the regulated markets of the host states. If the host state's regulated market has numerical limitations on membership, the host state is required to abolish or to adjust them to meet demand. Investment firms and banks are entitled, through a branch or a host state subsidiary, to become members of, or have access to, regulated markets and clearance and settlement systems of the host state.

The six member states whose laws do not currently allow market membership for banks, but only for their specialized subsidiaries, are allowed to deny access until Dec. 31, 1996, and Spain, Greece, and Portugal are permitted to extend that period until Dec. 31, 1999.

These extensions of time accommodate somewhat the Club Med's understandable opposition to Germany's desire for direct bank access to the domestic stock markets of other member states (which explains why Germany joined the North Sea Alliance in the first place). Prior to the compromise, the Club Med group insisted that member states should be allowed to require all banks to incorporate (and capitalize) separate investment firm subsidiaries as a pre-condition to accessing their domestic stock markets.

### Off–Market vs. On–Market Trading

The Club Med insisted that the directive embody the notion of "concentration," which in its French conception means that shares in French companies held by French residents must be traded in the French stock market. The United Kingdom refused to buy this and, with the backing of the North Sea group, accepted only a watered-down version.

The directive permits a member state to require that securities transactions be carried out on a "regulated market," as opposed to an off-market, assuming four conditions are met: (1) The investor must be a resident of that member state; and (2) must not have exercised the right granted by the directive to opt for an off-exchange market ("explicit authorization" may be required by the host state); (3) the transaction is carried out by the investment firm through its main office or a branch (or under its freedom to provide services) in that member state; and (4) the securities traded are actually listed on a "regulated market" in that member state.

(The ISD defines a "regulated market" as (1) a regularly functioning securities market that is (2) formally designated by its home state and in compliance with home state regulations, (3) with traded securities satisfying certain listing requirements, and is (4) a market that requires compliance with the directive's reporting and transparency requirements.)

The Club Med, led by France, insisted on a concentration requirement as a way to ban lightly regulated, mainly quote-driven and off-exchange markets, including London's SEAQ International and the Eurobond markets, in favor of the more tightly regulated exchange-based, order-driven markets on the Continent.

The Club Med argued that this was necessary to protect widows, orphans, and retail investors, to which one critic replied: "How touching. The simple truth is that southern Europeans want to protect their exchanges from competition." In particular, the Paris bourse has already lost a third of its business in French shares, estimated at $250 million a day, to SEAQ International, which quotes prices in more than 650 international stocks and has cornered roughly 90 percent of international or cross-border securities transactions.

One commentator recently observed that the "reluctance on the part of the Paris market to encourage off-exchange trading at the expense of highly regulated retail exchange markets is related to the apprehension among Europe's exchanges that London's SEAQ International will run them out of business even sooner under the ISD's passport system."

Many have proposed that a two-tier market system would be the best alternative, permitting retail trades to flow through traditional exchange-based markets with their stricter disclosure rules, monitoring functions, and transparency requirements, while permitting wholesale trades by institutional investors and dealers to be handled by more loosely regulated off-exchange markets. The compromise proposed by the Dutch, providing for an investor's right to opt out of a regulated market in favor of an off-market, is likely to harden into a two-tiered system.

Most observers have dreamed about an electronically linked trading system in which the shares of all major EC companies would be listed and traded on all 12 member state exchanges, with equal access and equal protection for all investors. The compromise, at least for the time being, allows SEAQ International to remain as a 13th market for professional traders, co-existing with the exchange-based markets of the member states.

## Transparency

Not unrelated to the concentration notion, and equally controversial, is the directive's creation of minimum transparency rules for the regulated exchange markets of the member states. The Club Med argued that stringent transparency rules were critical to ensuring an adequate level of investor protection and to reducing risks of distortion between competitive markets. The North Sea group, especially the British, argued that limited secrecy regarding trading transactions was essential to the protection of market makers and other financial intermediaries.

The directive now reflects a compromise between the two clubs. It requires (1) publication at the market opening of the weighted average price, the high and low prices, and the volume during the preceding trading day; and (2) after a two-hour calculation period, publication of the weighted average price and the high and low price (not volume) after a one-hour delay, to be updated every 20 minutes to the close. Assuming a 9 a.m. opening, the weighted average traded price, plus the high and low prices, for the period 9 a.m. to 11 a.m. would be published at 12 p.m., and updated every 20 minutes thereafter to cover a two-hour period on a one-hour delayed basis.

Moreover, the directive permits member states to except large blocks and illiquid securities. In stark contrast to the U.S. markets' real-time reporting standards, the directive's market transparency standards are remarkably opaque.

### Banking Industry Inroads

Finally, an analysis of the ISD would not be complete without a note on the impact of the now-effective Second Banking Directive (1989).

This directive seeks to create a single banking market by requiring common standards for authorization and mutual recognition of authorization in the home member state by all host member states where an authorized bank decides to provide services. The scope of activities these banks may engage in, on the basis of home state authorization, includes not only deposit taking and lending, but also trading and underwriting securities, portfolio management, and corporate finance services.

Banks in member states, such as Germany, that authorize universal banking, are now able to provide both commercial banking and investment services throughout the EC pursuant to a single license or "passport." These banks can provide investment services authorized by their home state even though the host state prohibits its own domestic banks from providing these services. (Banks thus authorized to provide investment services do not have to be reauthorized under the ISD.)

As one might imagine, the Second Banking Directive puts non-bank investment firms at a competitive disadvantage. This concern led to the proposal of the ISD to secure a parity position for investment firms. In fact, the EC Commission modeled the ISD after the Second Banking Directive and intended it to take effect at the same time. Unfortunately, the deadline for implementation by the member states has been extended to January 1996.

Even if the member states meet this deadline, more than three years will have elapsed after the Jan. 1, 1993, launching of the EC's single banking market. Banks clearly will have a head start. As a writer for the *Economist* put it, "the field will indeed be single, but still sloping from one end to the other."

### Impact on Markets

Thanks to the directive's new transparency rule—perhaps better described as an "opacity rule"—and the critical "opt-out" escape hatch from its "concentration" requirement, the directive is unlikely to affect London's dominance in the international market.

In fact, the directive may enhance London's position. Although U.K. regulation of professionals remains the most stringent among EC member states, the United Kingdom may dilute those rules as a result of domestic pressure from U.K. firms operating both in the United Kingdom and elsewhere side by side with firms authorized in member states with milder authorization, prudential, and conduct of business rules.

The Investment Services Directive now returns to the European Parliament for a second and final reading. EC officials say it is unlikely that any further changes will be made. They have stated that "the final deal was so finely balanced that anything other than cosmetic alterations would cause the whole directive to collapse."

There follows selected excerpts from Council Directive 93/22/EEC of May 10, 1993 on Investment Services in the Securities Field (O.J. L141/27, June 6, 1993).

TITLE I

Definitions and scope

*Article 1*

For the purposes of this Directive:

1. *investment service* shall mean any of the services listed in Section A of the Annex relating to any of the instruments listed in Section B of the Annex that are provided for a third party;

2. *investment firm* shall mean any legal person the regular occupation or business of which is the provision of investment services for third parties on a professional basis.

For the purposes of this Directive, Member States may include as investment firms undertakings which are not legal persons if:

— their legal status ensures a level of protection for third parties' interests equivalent to that afforded by legal persons, and

— they are subject to equivalent prudential supervision appropriate to their legal form.

. . .

6. *home Member State* shall mean:

(a) where the investment firm is a natural person, the Member State in which his head office is situated;

(b) where the investment firm is a legal person, the Member State in which its registered office is situated or, if under its national law it has no registered office, the Member State in which its head office is situated;

(c) in the case of a market, the Member State in which the registered office of the body which provides trading facilities is situated or, if under its national law it has no registered office, the Member State in which that body's head office is situated;

. . .

13. *regulated market* shall mean a market for the instruments listed in Section B of the Annex which:

— appears on the list provided for in Article 16 drawn up by the Member State which is the home Member State as defined in Article 1(6)(c),

— functions regularly,

— is characterized by the fact that regulations issued or approved by the competent authorities define the conditions for the operation of the market, the conditions for access to the market and, where Directive 79/279/EEC is applicable, the conditions governing admission to listing imposed in that Directive and, where that Directive is not applicable, the conditions that must be satisfied by a financial instrument before it can effectively be dealt in on the market,

— requires compliance with all the reporting and transparency requirements laid down pursuant to Articles 20 and 21;

. . .

*Article 3*

3. Without prejudice to other conditions of general application laid down by national law, the competent authorities shall not grant authorization unless:

— an investment firm has sufficient initial capital in accordance with the rules laid down in Directive 93/6/EEC having regard to the nature of the investment service in question,

— the persons who effectively direct the business of an investment firm are of sufficiently good repute and are sufficiently experienced.

The direction of a firm's business must be decided by at least two persons meeting the above conditions. Where an appropriate arrangement ensures that the same result will be achieved, however, particularly in the cases provided for in the last indent of the third subparagraph of Article 1(2), the competent authorities may grant authorization to investment firms which are natural persons or, taking account of the nature and volume of their activities, to investment firms which are legal persons where such firms are managed by single natural persons in accordance with their articles of association and national laws.

. . .

*Article 6*

The competent authorities of the other Member State involved shall be consulted beforehand on the authorization of any investment firm which is:

— a subsidiary of an investment firm or credit institution authorized in another Member State,

— a subsidiary of the parent undertaking of an investment firm or credit institution authorized in another Member State,

or

— controlled by the same natural or legal persons as control an investment firm or credit institution authorized in another Member State.

## TITLE III

### Relations with third countries

### *Article 7*

. . .

3. Initially no later than six months before this Directive is brought into effect and thereafter periodically the Commission shall draw up a report examining the treatment accorded to Community investment firms in third countries, in the terms referred to in paragraphs 4 and 5, as regards establishment, the carrying on of investment services activities and the acquisition of holdings in third-country investment firms. The Commission shall submit those reports to the Council together with any appropriate proposals.

4. Whenever it appears to the Commission, either on the basis of the reports provided for in paragraph 3 or on the basis of other information, that a third country does not grant Community investment firms effective market access comparable to that granted by the Community to investment firms from that third country; the Commission may submit proposals to the Council for an appropriate mandate for negotiation with a view to obtaining comparable competitive opportunities for Community investment firms. The Council shall act by a qualified majority.

5. Whenever it appears to the Commission, either on the basis of the reports referred to in paragraph 3 or on the basis of other information, that Community investment firms in a third country are not granted national treatment affording the same competitive opportunities as are available to domestic investment firms and that the conditions of effective market access are not fulfilled, the Commission may initiate negotiations in order to remedy the situation.

In the circumstances described in the first subparagraph it may also be decided, at any time and in addition to the initiation of negotiations, in accordance with the procedure to be laid down in the Directive by which the Council will set up the committee referred to in paragraph 1, that the competent authorities of the Member States must limit or suspend their decisions regarding requests pending or future requests for authorization and the acquisition of holdings by direct or indirect parent undertakings governed by the law of the third country in question. The duration of such measures may not exceed three months.

Before the end of that three-month period and in the light of the results of the negotiations the Council may, acting on a proposal from the Commission, decide by a qualified majority whether the measures shall be continued.

Such limitations or suspensions may not be applied to the setting up of subsidiaries by investment firms duly authorized in the Community or by their subsidiaries, or to the acquisition of holdings in Community investment firms by such firms or subsidiaries.

. . .

## TITLE IV

## Operating conditions

. . .

### *Article 10*

Each home Member State shall draw up prudential rules which investment firms shall observe at all times. In particular, such rules shall require that each investment firm:

— have sound administrative and accounting procedures, control and safeguard arrangements for electronic data processing, and adequate internal control mechanisms including, in particular, rules for personal transactions by its employees,

— make adequate arrangements for instruments belonging to investors with a view to safeguarding the latter's ownership rights, especially in the event of the investment firm's instruments for its own account except with the investors' express consent,

— make adequate arrangements for funds belonging to investors with a view to safeguarding the latter's rights and, except in the case of credit institutions, preventing the investment firm's using investors' funds for its own account,

— arrange for records to be kept of transactions executed which shall at least be sufficient to enable the home Member State's authorities to monitor compliance with the prudential rules which they are responsible for applying; such records shall be retained for periods to be laid down by the competent authorities,

— be structured and organized in such a way as to minimize the risk of clients' interests being prejudiced by conflicts of interest between the firm and its clients or between one of its clients and another. Nevertheless, where a branch is set up the organizational arrangements may not conflict with the rules of conduct laid down by the host Member State to cover conflicts of interest.

### *Article 11*

1. Member States shall draw up rules of conduct which investment firms shall observe at all times. Such rules must implement at least the principles set out in the following indents and must be applied in such a way as to take account of the professional nature of the person for whom the service is provided. The Member States shall also apply these rules where appropriate to the non-core services listed in Section C of the Annex. These principles shall ensure that an investment firm:

— acts honestly and fairly in conducting its business activities in the best interests of its clients and the integrity of the market,

— acts with due skill, care and diligence, in the best interests of its clients and the integrity of the market,

— has and employs effectively the resources and procedures that are necessary for the proper performance of its business activities,

— seeks from its clients information regarding their financial situations, investment experience and objectives as regards the services requested,

— makes adequate disclosure of relevant material information in its dealings with its clients,

— tries to avoid conflicts of interests and, when they cannot be avoided, ensures that its clients are fairly treated, and

— complies with all regulatory requirements applicable to the conduct of its business activities so as to promote the best interests of its clients and the integrity of the market.

2. Without prejudice to any decisions to be taken in the context of the harmonization of the rules of conduct, their implementation and the supervision of compliance with them shall remain the responsibility of the Member State in which a service is provided.

3. Where an investment firm executes an order, for the purposes of applying the rules referred to in paragraph 1 the professional nature of the investor shall be assessed with respect to the investor from whom the order originates, regardless of whether the order was placed directly by the investor himself or indirectly through an investment firm providing the service referred to in Section A(1)(a) of the Annex.

. . .

## TITLE V

### The right of establishment and the freedom to provide services

*Article 14*

1. Member States shall ensure that investment services and the other services listed in Section C of the Annex may be provided within their territories ... either by the establishment of a branch or under the freedom to provide services by any investment firm authorized and supervised by the competent authorities of another Member State in accordance with this Directive, provided that such services are covered by the authorization.

. . .

2. Member States may not make the establishment of a branch or the provision of services referred to in paragraph 1 subject to any authorization requirement, to any requirement to provide endowment capital or to any other measure having equivalent effect.

3. A Member State may require that transactions relating to the services referred to in paragraph 1 must, where they satisfy all the following criteria, be carried out on a regulated market:

— the investor must be habitually resident or established in that Member State,

— the investment firm must carry out such transactions through a main establishment, through a branch situated in that Member State or under the freedom to provide services in that Member State,

— the transaction must involve a instrument dealt in on a regulated market in that Member State.

4. Where a Member State applies paragraph 3 it shall give investors habitually resident or established in that Member State the right not to comply with the obligation imposed in paragraph 3 and have the transactions referred to in paragraph 3 carried out away from a regulated market. Member States may make the exercise of this right subject to express authorization, taking into account investors' differing needs for protection and in particular the ability of professional and institutional investors to act in their own best interests. It must in any case be possible for such authorization to be given in conditions that do not jeopardize the prompt execution of investors' orders.

5. The Commission shall report on the operation of paragraphs 3 and 4 not later than 31 December 1998 and shall, if appropriate, propose amendments thereto.

*Article 15*

1. Without prejudice to the exercise of the right of establishment or the freedom to provide services referred to in Article 14, host Member States shall ensure that investment firms which are authorized by the competent authorities of their home Member States to provide the services referred to in Section A(1)(b) and (2) of the Annex can, either directly or indirectly, become members of or have access to the regulated markets in their host Member States where similar services are provided and also become members of or have access to the clearing and settlement systems which are provided for the members of such regulated markets there.

Member States shall abolish any national rules or laws or rules of regulated markets which limit the number of persons allowed access thereto. If, by virtue of its legal structure or its technical capacity, access to a regulated market is limited, the Member State concerned shall ensure that its structure and capacity are regularly adjusted.

2. Membership of or access to a regulated market shall be conditional on investment firms' complying with capital adequacy requirements and home Member States' supervising such compliance in accordance with Directive 93/6/EEC.

Host Member States shall be entitled to impose additional capital requirements only in respect of matters not covered by that Directive.

Access to a regulated market, admission to membership thereof and continued access or membership shall be subject to compliance with the rules of the regulated market in relation to the constitution and administration of the regulated market and to compliance with the rules relating to transactions on the market, with the professional standards imposed on staff operating on and in conjunction with the market, and with the rules and procedures for clearing and settlement. The detailed arrangements for implementing these rules and procedures may be adapted as appropriate, *inter alia* to ensure fulfilment of the ensuing obligations, provided, however, that Article 28 is complied with.

3. In order to meet the obligation imposed in paragraph 1, host Member States shall offer the investment firms referred to in that paragraph the choice of becoming members of or of having access to their regulated markets either:

— directly, by setting up branches in the host Member States, or

— indirectly, by setting up subsidiaries in the host Member States or by acquiring firms in the host Member States that are already members of their regulated markets or already have access thereto.

However, those Member States which, when this Directive is adopted, apply laws which do not permit credit institutions to become members of or have access to regulated markets unless they have specialized subsidiaries may continue until 31 December 1996 to apply the same obligation in a non-discriminatory way to credit institutions from other Member States for purposes of access to those regulated markets.

The Kingdom of Spain, the Hellenic Republic and the Portuguese Republic may extend that period until 31 December 1999. One year before that date the Commission shall draw up a report, taking into account the experience acquired in applying this Article and shall if appropriate, submit a proposal. The Council may, acting by qualified majority on the basis of that proposal, decide to review those arrangements.

4. Subject to paragraphs 1, 2 and 3, where the regulated market of the host Member State operates without any requirement for a physical presence the investment firms referred to in paragraph 1 may become members of or have access to it on the same basis without having to be established in the host Member State. In order to enable their investment firms to become members of or have access to host Member States' regulated markets in accordance with this paragraph home Member States shall allow those host Member States' regulated markets to provide appropriate facilities within the home Member States' territories.

5. This Article shall not affect the Member States' right to authorize or prohibit the creation of new markets within their territories.

. . .

*Article 21*

1. In order to enable investors to assess at any time the terms of a transaction they are considering and to verify afterwards the conditions in which it has been carried out, each competent authority shall, for each of the regulated markets which it has entered on the list provided for in Article 16, take measures to provide investors with the information referred to in paragraph 2. In accordance with the requirements imposed in paragraph 2, the competent authorities shall determine the form in which and the precise time within which the information is to be provided, as well as the means by which it is to be made available, having regard to the nature, size and needs of the market concerned and of the investors operating on that market.

2. The competent authorities shall require for each instrument at least:

(a) publication at the start of each day's trading on the market of the weighted average price, the highest and the lowest prices and the volume dealt in on the regulated market in question for the whole of the preceding day's trading;

(b) in addition, for continuous order-driven and quote-driven markets, publication:

— at the end of each hour's trading on the market, of the weighted average price and the volume dealt in on the regulated market in question for a six-hour trading period ending so as to leave two hours' trading on the market before publication, and

— every 20 minutes, of the weighted average price and the highest and lowest prices on the regulated market in question for a two-hour trading period ending so as to leave one hour's trading on the market before publication.

Where investors have prior access to information on the prices and quantities for which transactions may be undertaken:

(i) such information shall be available at all times during market trading hours;

(ii) the terms announced for a given price and quantity shall be terms on which it is possible for an investor to carry out such a transaction.

The competent authorities may delay or suspend publication where that proves to be justified by exceptional market conditions or, in the case of small markets, to preserve the anonymity of firms and investors. The competent authorities may apply special provisions in the case of exceptional transactions that are very large in scale compared with average transactions in the security in question on that market and in the case of highly illiquid securities defined by means of objective criteria and made public. The competent authorities may also apply more flexible provisions, particularly as regards publication deadlines, for transactions concerning bonds and other forms of securitized debt.

3. In the field governed by this Article each Member State may adopt or maintain more stringent provisions or additional provisions with regard to the substance and form in which information must be made available to investors concerning transactions carried out on regulated markets of which it is the home Member State, provided that those provisions apply regardless of the Member State in which the issuer of the financial instrument is located or of the Member State on the regulated market of which the instrument was listed for the first time.

4. The Commission shall report on the application of this Article no later than 31 December 1997; the Council may, on a proposal from the Commission, decide by a qualified majority to amend this Article.

. . .

*Article 31*

No later than 1 July 1995 Member States shall adopt the laws, regulations and administrative provisions necessary for them to comply with this Directive.

These provisions shall enter into force no later than 31 December 1995. The Member States shall forthwith inform the Commission thereof.

When Member States adopt the provisions referred to in the first paragraph they shall include a reference to this Directive or accompany them with such a reference on the occasion of their official publication. The manner in which such references are to be made shall be laid down by the Member States.

. . .

*ANNEX*

SECTION A

Services

1. (a) Reception and transmission, on behalf of investors, of orders in relation to one or more of the instruments listed in Section B.

(b) Execution of such orders other than for own account.

2. Dealing in any of the instruments listed in Section B for own account.

3. Managing portfolios of investments in accordance with mandates given by investors on a discriminatory, client-by-client basis where such portfolios include one or more of the instruments listed in Section B.

4. Underwriting in respect of issues of any of the instruments listed in Section B and/or the placing of such issues.

## SECTION B

### Instruments

1. (a) Transferable securities.

(b) Units in collective investment undertakings.

2. Money-market instruments.

3. Financial-futures contracts, including equivalent cash-settled instruments.

4. Forward interest-rate agreements (FRAs).

5. Interest-rate, currency and equity swaps.

6. Options to acquire or dispose of any instruments falling within this section of the Annex, including equivalent cash-settled instruments. This category includes in particular options on currency and on interest rates.

## SECTION C

### Non-core services

1. Safekeeping and administration in relation to one or more of the instruments listed in Section B.

2. Safe custody services.

3. Granting credits or loans to an investor to allow him to carry out a transaction in one or more of the instruments listed in Section B, where the firm granting the credit or loan is involved in the transaction.

4. Advice to undertakings on capital structure, industrial strategy and related matters and advice and service relating to mergers and the purchase of undertakings.

5. Services related to underwriting.

6. Investment advice concerning one or more of the instruments listed in Section B.

7. Foreign-exchange service where these are connected with the provision of investment services.

### *Notes and Questions*

1. The main purpose of the Investment Services Directive (ISD) is to authorize a securities firm that offers certain services (on an agreed list) in its home state, to also offer them through branches in any other EU country. In particular, it allows a firm access to stock exchange membership outside of its home country.

As we shall see, banks have already been given the authority to offer securities services on a cross-border basis through branches in the Second Banking Directive (SBD). The delay in implementing the Investment Services Directive has given a theoretical advantage to universal banks; but universal banks must also now meet Basle type capital standards. ISD is due to be implemented, along with CAD, in 1996.

2. Do states have an interest in the safety and soundness of securities firms? If so, how will a host state satisfy itself that an out-of-state firm is safe and sound? *See* ISD, Articles 3 and 10. How can you reconcile Article 11 with a mutual recognition, home country control approach?

3. To what extent can European securities firms choose their home states? Could a German firm faced with heavy regulation in Germany shift its home state to Luxembourg? See Articles 1(6), 3(2) and 6.

4. As Warren observes, the Club Med countries were against allowing banks (as opposed to their affiliates) to have direct membership on exchanges, but they lost out to the North Sea Alliance. See Article 15. Why was Club Med against this? Under Article 15(3), Belgium, France and Italy can wait until December 31, 1996, and Greece, Spain and Portugal until the end of 1999, to implement this change. You should also note a related provision in Article 15(4) which provides that states (home and host) must allow out-of-state investment firms to obtain electronic access (screens) to regulated markets, i.e. French brokers must be given the opportunity to conduct trades on SEAQ. How does this fit within the mutual recognition framework?

5. Club Med took the position that most securities trading should only be allowed on "regulated markets" (defined in Article 1(13)). Is this merely protectionist, or can it be based on investor protection concerns? How does Article 14 solve this problem?

6. Club Med was in favor of market transparency, and would have required that the price and volume of all trades, including large block trades, be reported quickly after completion. This is the trading rule on the Paris Bourse but not on SEAQ, the London Stock Exchange (it is also the rule on the NYSE). What are the pros and cons of this approach? How does Article 21 resolve this issue? Can SEAQ be a regulated market under ISD?

7. What role does CAD play in the development of a single Union-wide securities market?

---

## C. BANKING MARKETS

In the banking area, the EU approach focuses on facilitating the Union wide-operation of banks while at the same time protecting depositors.

## 1. The Second Banking Directive

M. GRUSON AND W. FEURING, "A EUROPEAN COMMUNITY BANKING LAW: THE SECOND BANKING AND RELATED DIRECTIVES," IN THE SINGLE MARKET AND THE LAW OF BANKING

R. Cranston ed. (1991), Ch. 2, pp. 19–34.

The Second Council Directive on the Co-ordination of Laws, Regulations and Administrative Provisions Relating to the Taking-up and Pursuit of the Business of Credit Institutions and Amending Directive 77/780/EEC (the "Second Directive") is the centrepiece of a new banking law unfolding in the European Community. This Directive obliges the Member States of the Community to implement its provisions into their national banking regimes by means of conforming their national banking laws and practices (as to the required results to be achieved) by 1 January 1993. The Second Directive will cause fundamental changes in the legal framework of the banking business in the Community, and will profoundly affect both the way in which banks will be doing business in the Community and the way in which non-Community banks can enter the European market.

. . .

THE SECOND DIRECTIVE

**Institutional coverage**

The Second Directive applies to "credit institutions". A credit institution is defined as an "undertaking whose business is to receive deposits or other repayable funds from the public and to grant credits for its own account". According to the Second Directive, credit institutions that are authorised and supervised as credit institutions by the competent authorities of their Home Member States [10] will benefit from mutual—i.e. Community-wide—recognition of their banking licences with respect to the activities enumerated in the Annex to the Second Directive (the "Annex") and for which they are licensed in the Home Member State. This means that the following entities or activities do not benefit from mutual recognition:

(a) entities that are not authorised and supervised as credit institutions, i.e. a deposit-taking institution, by a Member State, even though they are engaged in some of the activities set forth in the Annex (for example, if a company engages only in financial leasing, and as such is not authorised and supervised by the Home Member State as a credit institution, it is not a credit

10. "Home Member State" of a credit institution as used in this chapter means that Member State of the Community where the credit institution has been licensed as a credit institution. "Host Member State" of a credit institution, as used in this chapter, means the Member State where a credit institution licensed as such in another Member State carries out activities or operates a branch.

institution under the Second Directive, although financial leasing is an activity listed in the Annex); and

(b) entities that engage in activities not included in the Annex, even though they are authorised and supervised as credit institutions by a Member State.

Subsidiaries established in Community countries by non-Community persons under a licence for credit institutions are credit institutions benefiting from the principle of mutual recognition. In other words, non-Community ownership or control of a credit institution does not destroy the mutual recognition of the licence of the credit institution. Community branches of non-Community credit institutions are not authorised as credit institutions by a Member State and therefore do not benefit from mutual recognition.

. . .

**The licence**

The objective of the Second Directive is to create a truly Community-wide internal market for banking services. "Credit institutions" authorised in the Home Member State will be entitled in each of the other Member States: (i) to establish branches; and (ii) to offer their services freely to individuals and businesses, in each case without the need for any further authorisation by the Host Member State. Community credit institutions will be entitled to operate in this way under their Home Member State licences, which will be a Community-wide "single banking licence".

Thus, the Second Directive does not create a "Community" banking licence; but it decrees that each Member State's banking licence shall be valid throughout the Community. The principle proposed by the Second Directive is one of "mutual recognition": each Member State recognises the banking licences of the other Member States. This principle differs radically from the concept of "national treatment", which merely entitles a foreign bank to the same treatment as a domestic bank. The principle of mutual recognition gives credit institutions in one Member State access to all Member States, and creates a Community-wide inter-Member State banking market.

The recognition of the Home Member licence required by the Second Directive is limited to certain specified banking activities or powers: the Home Member State licence is valid in other Member States only with respect to those specified banking activities that are enumerated in the Annex to the Second Directive. The Annex defines the scope of the principle of mutual recognition. Each Member State will have the duty to ensure that at least the activities listed in the Annex may be pursued in its territory by any credit institution authorised and supervised by the authorities of its Home Member State, either through the establishment of a branch or by way of the provision of services across the Member State border. However, the principle of mutual recognition extends only to a branch of a credit institution and not to a subsidiary credit institution, because a subsidiary cannot operate under the parent's licence. A subsidiary, being a separate entity, is required to have its own licence before it can engage in banking activities.

A credit institution licensed in a Member State may provide services throughout the Community with respect to banking activities that meet the following cumulative criteria: (i) the Home Member State licence must permit the pursuit of such activity, or in other words, must give the credit institutions the power to conduct such activity; and (ii) the activity must be set forth in the Annex.

As a consequence, any credit institution authorised as such in its Home Member State may exercise in the Host Member State activities that meet such criteria even if the same activities are not permitted to similar credit institutions of the Host Member State. For instance, if a bank is authorised by its Home Member State licence to participate in securities issues, it is permitted to do so anywhere in the Community, since participation in securities issues is an activity listed in the Annex. On the other hand, if the Home Member State licence does not authorise participation in securities issues, a credit institution may not engage in this activity in a Host Member State even if credit institutions licensed in the Host Member State are entitled to engage in this activity. If the Home Member State licence permits travel agency services, a credit institution still cannot conduct this activity in a Host Member State by virtue of the Second Directive, because travel agency services are not included in the Annex.

The banking powers permitted by the banking licence of a Member State may fall short of the powers enumerated in the Annex. In that case, credit institutions from other Member States may provide services in that Host Member State that credit institutions licensed in that particular Host Member State are not permitted to provide. A probable consequence of the Second Directive is that the powers permitted to banks in all Member States will soon include all the powers set forth in the Annex. The Second Directive will bring about an indirect harmonisation of law, if only by virtue of self-interest of the Member States.

Mutual recognition permits a Community credit institution to provide its services anywhere in the Community, irrespective of where it is licensed. However, the Second Directive forestalls "forum shopping" by obtaining a banking licence in a less restrictive Member State. It states that the principle of mutual recognition requires that Member States do not grant an authorisation or withdraw an existing authorisation where factors such as the credit institution's activities programme and the geographical distribution of activities actually carried on "make it quite clear" that the credit institution has opted for the legal system of one Member State for the purpose of evading the stricter standards in force in another Member State in which it intends to carry on, or if already authorised, where it is actually carrying on, the greater part of its activities.[35] Such power to refuse or withdraw an authorisation is only

35. Second Directive, 8th "whereas" clause. Member States must require that the head office of a credit institution is situated in the same Member State as the

given to *Home* Member States. Host Member States do not have the power to refuse or withdraw an authorisation to operate a branch of a credit institution from another Member State. This provision will prevent the creation of a "banking Delaware" in the Community.

The Annex to the Second Directive sets forth the activities "integral to banking" that currently, in the opinion of the Commission, constitute the core of the traditional banking services in the Community:

1. acceptance of deposits and other repayable funds from the public;
2. lending, including, *inter alia,* consumer and mortgage credit, factoring with or without recourse, and financing of commercial transactions including forfaiting;
3. financial leasing;
4. money transmission services;
5. issuing and administering means of payment (e.g. credit cards, travellers' cheques and bankers' drafts);
6. guarantees and commitments;
7. trading for own account or for account of customers in
   (a) money market instruments (cheques, bills, CDs, etc.),
   (b) foreign exchange,
   (c) financial futures and options,
   (d) exchange and interest rate instruments,
   (e) transferable securities;
8. participation in share issues and the provision of services related to such issues;
9. advice to undertakings on capital structure, industrial strategy and related questions, and advice and services relating to mergers and the purchase of undertakings;
10. money broking;
11. portfolio management and advice;
12. safekeeping and administration of securities;
13. credit reference services;
14. safe custody services.

The Annex is based on the liberal "universal banking" model; it does not distinguish between investment banking and commercial banking, and does not embrace the philosophy of the US Glass–Steagall Act, which in the US prohibits commercial banks from the underwriting of and dealing in corporate debt or equity securities and from being affiliated with companies engaged in such business. Thus, the Annex permits a wide range of securities powers.

The Commission recommends that the Annex be updated under the flexible procedure so that it can respond to the development of new

registered office, and a credit institution is deemed situated in the Member State where it has its registered office. Id.

banking services. The Commission obviously wishes to avoid repeating the experience of US banking law, which does not easily respond to changing market environments.

**Branch establishment**

Under the Second Directive, a Member State may not require a credit institution already authorised in another Member State to obtain a licence before it is permitted to establish a branch in its territory.

A credit institution wishing to establish a branch in another Member State need only inform the authorities of its Home Member State of its intention to set up a branch in the Host Member State. This notification must be accompanied by certain information concerning the credit institution and the branch, in particular the programme of operations and the structural organisation of the branch. The Home Member State authorities must communicate this information, and information on the amount of own funds and the Solvency Ratio of the credit institution, to the authorities of the prospective Host Member State within three months. The only measure that can be taken against the establishment of the branch is a refusal by the Home Member State authorities to inform the Host Member State. This measure may be taken if the Home Member State authorities have reason to doubt the adequacy of the credit institution's organisational structure or its financial situation. The Home Member State must give reasons for such refusal, which is subject to a right of appeal to the courts of the Home Member State.

The Second Directive abolishes the initial endowment capital that is currently required by the majority of Member States for the authorisation of branches of credit institutions already authorised in other Member States.

**Allocation of supervision**

The Second Directive is based on the principle of "home country control", under which each credit institution will generally be supervised by the authorities of its Home Member State, even in regard to activities carried out across the borders of, or through a branch located in, another Member State. There are only a few exceptions to that rule.

As a result of insufficient harmonisation of liquidity standards and insufficient co-ordination in the implementation of monetary policy in the Community within the framework of the European Monetary System, the Second Directive proposes that, as an exception to the principle of home country control, the Host Member State, pending further co-ordination, will retain primary responsibility for the supervision of liquidity of the branches of credit institutions and exclusive responsibility for the implementation of monetary policy. These measures, however, must not embody discriminatory or restrictive treatment based on the fact that the credit institution is authorised in another Member State.

. . .

Although the activities of a credit institution's branches in a Host Member State will generally be supervised by the authorities of the Home Member State according to the rules of the Host Member State, those branches still have to comply with the legal provisions in force in the Host Member State which have been "adopted in the interest of the general good". It remains to be seen whether Member States will use this provision to make inroads against the rule of Home Member State supervision.

. . .

**Investments in the non-bank entities**

In order to control potential risks to the financial stability of credit institutions arising out of investments in non-banking corporations, the Second Directive contains provisions on investments in non-credit and non-financial institutions. These investments ("participations") require particular attention, because they may affect the financial stability of the investing credit institution. Participations in a subsidiary may affect the soundness of the credit institution if the former runs into financial difficulties ("contagion risk") and equity participations constitute a long-term freezing of the assets of the investing credit institution.

The Second Directive requires harmonisation of the differing standards of the Member States regarding equity participations by credit institutions by limiting credit institutions in the following two respects, if they wish to acquire or maintain participations in non-credit or non-financial institutions:

(a) a credit institution may not hold a qualifying (10 per cent or more) holding of an amount greater than 15 per cent of its own funds in an undertaking that is neither a credit institution nor a financial institution; and

(b) the total value of such qualifying holdings may not exceed 60 per cent of own funds of the credit institution.

These limits do not apply to shares held only (i) temporarily during a financial rescue or restructuring operation, (ii) during the normal course of the underwriting process, or (iii) in the institution's own name on behalf of others.

The limits mentioned above may be exceeded in exceptional circumstances. However, in that case the supervisory authorities of the Home Member State of the credit institution exceeding its limits must require such credit institution to increase its own funds or to take other equivalent measures. Compliance with these limits shall be ensured by the authorities of the Home Member State by means of supervision on a consolidated basis in accordance with the Directive on Consolidated Supervision. The authorities of the Home Member State need not apply these limits if they require that 100 per cent of the amounts by which a credit institution's qualifying holdings exceed those limits must be covered by own funds and that the latter shall not be included in the calculation of the solvency ratio.

. . .

### *Notes and Questions*

1. The SBD applies to credit institutions, "undertakings whose business is to receive deposits or other repayable funds from the public and to grant credits for its own account." Why not cover institutions providing either function?

2. The SBD provides that a bank incorporated in one state (home state) can offer in another state (host state) any service it can offer in its home state (that is on an agreed list) and will be supervised by the home state authorities. Does this mean a German bank could offer a type of deposit account or life insurance in France even if French banks were not authorized by French law to do so?

3. What if a Greek bank could not do financial leasing in Greece but wanted to do so in Germany even though German banks could not offer the service in Germany. What could it do? Gruson and Feuring, text at note 35, refer to the 8th "whereas" clause in SBD. It provides:

> Whereas the principles of mutual recognition and of home Member State control require the competent authorities of each Member State not to grant authorization or to withdraw it where factors such as the activities programme, the geographical distribution or the activities actually carried on make it quite clear that a credit institution has opted for the legal system of one Member State for the purpose of evading the stricter standards in force in another Member State in which it intends to carry on or carries on the greater part of its activities; whereas, for the purposes of this Directive, a credit institution shall be deemed to be situated in the Member State in which it has its registered office; whereas the Member States must require that the head office be situated in the same Member State as the registered office;

Also consider a Commission proposal of July 1993 that would require "the head office of a financial undertaking must be in the same Member State as its registered office and that in which the authorization [license] is being required." COM(93) 363 final—SYN 468 (OJ 1993 C229/10) [1993 Proposals].

Could the Greek bank offer the service in Greece through a branch of a Spanish bank subsidiary, employing a "roundtrip" strategy?

4. In 1992, France prohibited a French subsidiary of Barclays from transferring interest on unit trust accounts (mutual funds) to a demand deposit account as an evasion of the French prohibition on paying interest on demand deposit accounts. Under SBD would France be able

to prohibit a branch of Barclays from offering the service? Would this fall into the monetary policy exception to mutual recognition?

5. The SBD leaves supervision to home countries. How would the United Kingdom protect itself against a shaky Luxembourg bank's branch taking U.K. deposits (the BCCI problem)? EU banks are subject to common supervisory standards, such as capital requirements, single exposure limits, limitations on investments in non-financial institutions etc. And EU supervisors are in close touch through a supervisors' committee. Does this solve the potential BCCI problem? The 1993 Proposals require home countries to supervise banking groups. Are these common supervisory standards and new requirements for group supervision sufficient to avoid an EU BCCI? Can host states impose quasi-capital requirements and ring fence branch assets in the event of a bankruptcy?

## H. SCOTT, "RECIPROCITY AND THE SECOND BANKING DIRECTIVE," IN THE SINGLE MARKET AND THE LAW OF BANKING

R. Cranston ed. (1991), Ch. 4, pp. 85–91.

The European Economic Community (EC) adopted its Second Banking Directive on 15 December 1989. Article 9 of this Directive incorporates a reciprocity requirement requiring other countries to give certain specified treatment to EC banks as a condition for banks from these countries taking advantage of the Directive's liberal rules for providing banking services within the EC.

Article 9(3) provides that if the Commission determines "that a third country is not granting Community credit institutions effective market access comparable to that granted by the Community to credit institutions from that third country", the Council may authorise the Commission to open up negotiations to obtain such "comparable competitive opportunities" for EC credit institutions.

Article 9(4) provides that negotiations may also be opened by the Commission on its own, without Council authorisation, whenever it appears to the Commission "that Community credit institutions in a third country do not receive national treatment offering the same competitive opportunities as are available to domestic credit institutions and that the conditions of effective market access are not fulfilled". Furthermore, such a determination may also lead to Member States being required to close their markets to "acquisition of holdings by direct or indirect parent undertakings governed by the laws of the third country in question".

Article 9(4) also provides that such acquisition bans cannot apply to acquisitions that have already been made or to future acquisitions of entities already authorised to operate in the EC. Existing authorised institutions from third countries are thus grandfathered, and are treated on a par with EC institutions.

In short, lack of effective market access for EC institutions can lead to negotiations, whereas lack of national treatment and effective market access can lead to either negotiations or prospective entry bans. There is considerable ambiguity about the use of the word "and". If the "and" is conjunctive, then two findings would be required for an entry ban: lack of national treatment, and effective market access. This holds out the possibility that EC institutions might have effective market access in a country even where there was a lack of national treatment. On the other hand, if the "and" is disjunctive, the EC could impose an entry ban where there was national treatment but no effective market access.

This chapter will look at the following aspects of this reciprocity policy: (1) its lack of application to foreign branches; (2) difficulties in determining the home country of an entering bank; and (3) the operative meaning of the reciprocity tests.

## BRANCH VERSUS SUBSIDIARY

It should be emphasised that the EC reciprocity requirement will not apply to branches, as compared with subsidiaries, of foreign banks. EC branches of foreign banks cannot be used as a base for expansion into the rest of the EC, nor can they offer cross-border services under the liberal provisions of the Second Banking Directive. Unlike subsidiaries, they would be fully subject to the laws and regulations of host countries. Thus, a US bank which sought to establish a branch in the UK would not be subject to an EC reciprocity requirement. This may be a feasible option for a bank wishing to operate in only one or a few EC countries.

Doing business through a branch, rather than a subsidiary, offers certain advantages. The capital of the entire bank serves as a base for the gearing ratio, which determines the size of asset expansion, as well as the base for lending limits applicable to borrowings by a single customer. However, foreign banks may prefer to operate on an EC wide basis through branches of one EC member bank subsidiary ("EC bank strategy") rather than through branches of their home country bank ("home country bank strategy"). The former possibility might be precluded by a determination of lack of reciprocity.

First, the home country bank strategy may subject the operations of the branches to more restrictive regulation than the branches of competitors employing the EC bank strategy. Branches of home country banks will be fully subject to local regulation, while branches of EC banks will be subject to home country regulation. While EC states may deregulate laws in their own countries, so that domestic subsidiaries are not put at a disadvantage in competing with branches of EC banks established in another state, it is far from clear that branches of foreign banks would equally benefit from deregulation aimed at domestic subsidiaries.

Secondly, as the number of states in which the foreign bank wishes to operate through branches increases, the burden of complying with the laws of several states also increases. The EC bank strategy requires compliance with the regulations of one Member State: the EC state in which the bank is established. In contrast, the home country bank strategy requires compliance with the laws of each host state in which a branch is established.

Finally, branches of a foreign bank may be subject to "in lieu of capital" requirements in each of the states in which they operate, while branches of EC banks will not—the sole capital requirement applied to their operations will be those applied by the home state, in accord with the minimum requirements of the Second Directive. This will make the home country bank strategy more expensive and less flexible. The EC bank strategy will require less capital and permit resources to be easily deployed and redeployed among EC Member States.

## DETERMINING THE HOME COUNTRY

The second major issue, that of determining the home country of the entrant, poses substantial problems. It is not self-evident what the home country of a bank, or its holding company, is when it is established in several countries. Truly multinational banks may be seen as having several rather than one home country. If one looked only to the place of incorporation of the entering bank, the reciprocity requirement would be totally ineffective. Suppose, for example, that banks with Switzerland as a home country were barred from entering on reciprocity grounds, but that banks with the US as a home country were not. The strategy would be clear. A Swiss bank would enter into the EC through its US subsidiary. In the US this is called "leapfrogging".

. . .

## WHAT IS RECIPROCITY?

The EC reciprocity requirement embodies two different concepts: (1) national treatment; and (2) competitive opportunities or effective market access comparable to that granted by the EC to banks from third countries. The terms "competitive opportunities" and "effective market access" seem to be used interchangeably.

### National treatment

National treatment is the most widely accepted standard for dealing with trade in banking services, and has been championed by the US. Under this standard, foreign banks are treated, as nearly as possible, like domestic banks. The US has, however, taken the position that countries should offer unconditional national treatment, not reciprocal national treatment. The US has advocated that the EC should treat foreign banks the same as domestic banks without regard to how EC banks are treated by the home countries of the foreign banks. The EC, however, has taken the reciprocal national treatment approach.

The problem with the national treatment standard is that it fails to acknowledge that real differences between domestic and foreign banks may justify treating them differently. Host countries cannot, for example, regulate branches of foreign banks for safety and soundness purposes just like domestic banks. These branches are part and parcel of a bank based in and regulated by another country. Thus, the home and not the host country is the principal examiner of the bank, including its foreign branches. Home country, and not host country, capital requirements and other balance sheet or income statement controls, e.g. liquidity or provisioning requirements, apply to the foreign branch.

The host country might want to ensure that local creditors of the branch are paid off in the event that the foreign bank fails, and might therefore impose "in lieu of capital" or "asset maintenance" requirements on foreign branches. But these requirements respond to the fact that the assets of the foreign bank, unlike those of domestic banks, are generally beyond the reach of the host country.

. . .

**Effective market access**

EC banks may not have "effective market access" even in countries that afford them national treatment. The Commission clearly views US restrictions on inter-state banking and the combination of banking and securities activities as restricting the access of EC banks, even though these restrictions apply to both domestic and foreign banks. The same would be true with respect to Japan's remaining interest rate controls on certain short-term deposits. In this conception, "effective market access" means mirror-image reciprocity. Third countries would be required to give EC banks the same access to third country markets as the EC gives to its own markets. Thus, since the EC allows banking and securities activities to be combined, so should the US.

This standard suffers from the fact that the country imposing the test often assumes that the access it offers to its markets should be the governing standard. Consider the following example. Market I prohibits the combination of banking and securities, and Market II not only permits the combination, but also permits banking and high risk gambling to be combined. The EC is more liberal than the first, but less liberal than the second. If the EC were to keep banks from Market I out of the EC, it should be willing to accept that its banks could be kept out of Market II. It is doubtful, however, that the Commission would accept this as a reasonable result. And if it does not, why should Market I accept the EC market access rules as a benchmark?

Effective market access may also be viewed from a market share point of view. Here, one might compare the market share of EC banks in a particular foreign country—EC banks as a whole, or those from a particular state—with the share of banks of the foreign country in the EC. Mr. De Clercq, for example, has compared the 10 per cent share of Japanese banks of EC deposits with the 0.35 per cent share that EC banks have of Japanese deposits.

The comparison of market shares is a dubious benchmark for reciprocity. There are serious technical problems associated with the proper measurement of market share. More fundamentally, comparative market shares may only measure the relative efficiency of the international banking operations of banks from different countries, the local peculiarities of particular markets, or the legal structure considerations already discussed.

From an economic point of view, there is nothing wrong with a particular country having a high comparative market share of foreign banking markets. Some countries may have a comparative advantage in banking, just as other countries may have a comparative advantage in semi-conductors, steel or armaments.

Some markets, particularly with respect to deposits, may be rationally parochial—depositors may just not trust the solvency of foreign banks, or the dependability of the last-resort lenders, the central banks, that stand behind them.

There is also the political risk of putting money in a foreign bank. If the foreign bank's home state has a serious political dispute with the host state, the depositor's funds may be frozen by the foreign bank's home state. This is a serious problem for US banks given the Iranian, Libyan and Panamanian assets freezes in the last 10 years.

These considerations suggest that reciprocity should not be based on market share comparisons. On the other hand, market share data may be useful as evidence of disparities in legal structure between two states. Perhaps this is what De Clercq had in mind in using the Japanese example.

. . .

---

### *Notes and Questions*

1. Do the SBD reciprocity requirements (there are similar ISD requirements) mean that countries that do not grant national treatment to German banks cannot operate in the EU?

2. Does the SBD require that negotiations be opened with the United States over the issue of reciprocity? How would you compare the reciprocity tests of FTFS and SBD?

---

## 2. Deposit Insurance

### R. DALE, "DEPOSIT INSURANCE: POLICY CLASH OVER EC AND US REFORMS" (PAPER PRESENTED AT LONDON SCHOOL OF ECONOMICS, MAY 1993)

Pp. 13–16.

In 1986 the EC Commission issued a recommendation to the effect that all member states should put in place some form of deposit insurance, although there was no specification of minimum (or maximum) coverage. At this time the EC favoured a territorial approach for national schemes, apparently on the grounds that this would ensure competitive equity for banks operating within any given jurisdiction.

In June 1992 the EC followed its earlier recommendation with a proposal for a Council Directive on deposit guarantee schemes. This was amended in December 1992 and again in March 1993. The stated objectives are to provide some degree of consumer protection while also strengthening systemic stability ("the costs of a run on the banking system may outweigh the costs of imposing a deposit protection check scheme"). The major elements of the proposal can be summarised as follows:

(1) A key principle—representing a reversal of the 1986 recommendation—is that branch depositors should be protected by the home member state, i.e. where the bank has its head office. The stated rationale for this approach is that it locates responsibility for deposit protection in the jurisdiction that also has supervisory responsibility.

(2) The proposal establishes a minimum level of deposit protection in all member states, both with regard to the size of protected deposits and the kinds of deposit to be protected. The minimum size of a protected deposit is set at 15,000 ECU, except that where a member state chooses to adopt a 90% pay-out option (involving an element of coinsurance) the minimum size of the protected deposit is ECU 16,500. Inter-bank deposits and subordinated debt are specifically excluded from insurance coverage, while debt securities and bearer instruments may be excluded.

(3) There is an optional "top-up" provision which allows branches to join a host country deposit insurance scheme. This enables the branch to offer the same level of protection accorded to local banks operating under the host scheme, in cases where the host scheme is more generous than the home scheme. Furthermore, the revised proposal includes a "no export" clause, whereby branches will not be permitted to offer deposit protection in excess of the "host" country, in cases where the home scheme is more generous than the host scheme.

(4) There are no harmonisation requirements relating to the maximum insurance coverage, which is left to the discretion of

member states, nor to funding arrangements or the pricing of deposit insurance. Furthermore, schemes may be administered by either the private or public sector.

When assessed in the light of the previous discussion there appear to be serious problems with the EC's general approach to harmonisation of deposit insurance schemes.

In the first place the proposal represents an awkward compromise between existing national schemes that have quite different objectives. This is most clearly evident in the option accorded to national authorities to incorporate an element of co-insurance, involving depositors in losses of up to 10% of their protected deposits. The co-insurance option appears to be designed to accommodate schemes (such as Germany's) which offer virtually full protection in the interests of systemic stability as well as schemes (notably the UK's) whose main purpose is to protect consumers. However, as pointed out above, co-insurance is unsuited to a deposit protection regime intended to prevent bank runs. The Brussels proposal, instead of establishing clear EC policy priorities, permits the co-existence of rival national schemes with conflicting aims.

To the extent that the EC initiative on deposit insurance is intended to contribute to systemic stability, there is a further difficulty. On the one hand, the EC proposal openly acknowledges the moral hazard dangers of deposit protection and, indeed, cites recent US banking instability as an example of what can happen when deposit protection is excessive. On the other hand, the proposal contains no provisions dealing with the problem of moral hazard—a matter that is by implication left entirely to the discretion of national authorities. In particular, deposit protection can be open-ended (as in Germany) over and above the required minimum level and there are no requirements on the pricing of deposit insurance. Therefore, while the US is responding actively to its own experience of excessive risk-taking associated with 100% de facto deposit protection (above) the EC appears to be largely ignoring these lessons.

In so far as the EC proposal is concerned with eliminating potential competitive distortions, more problems arise. To begin with the key question of funding and pricing of deposit insurance is left largely to the discretion of national authorities. Furthermore, the optional top-up scheme and the "no export" clause ((3) above) are designed to create a level playing field within each national jurisdiction but do so at the cost of creating uneven deposit insurance coverage between member states and between different offices of the same bank. It is paradoxical that in a single European financial market competitive equality should be so overtly sacrificed at the inter-jurisdictional level in an attempt to ensure competitive equality within each Member State's territory.

More generally, the latitude allowed under the harmonisation proposal means that schemes to which banks operating within the EC are subject may vary in the following key respects:

(1) Some schemes will apply the Directive's minimum insurance coverage, others will be more generous.

(2) Some schemes will require insured depositors to absorb up to 10% of deposit losses, others will exclude such coinsurance.

(3) Some bank branches may choose to top up the home country's deposit insurance to the level of the host country's scheme (where higher). Other banks may decline this option.

(4) The coverage of certain categories of wholesale depositor, as well as various categories of financial instrument will vary between schemes.

(5) Branches of banks originating from outside the EC may be subject to the home-country scheme or the host-country scheme.

The authors of the EC proposed Directive are confident that this diversity is workable since a variety of schemes already co-exist within member states. However, the EC proposal makes no allowance for the fact that European regulators have generally preferred to bail out failing banks rather than rely on deposit insurance arrangements. To the extent that this attitude persists, the deposit insurance Directive will be largely redundant. But if there is a change of approach and banks are permitted to fail, then confusion caused by a multiplicity of schemes could prompt calls for full harmonisation of insurance schemes.

Finally, for reasons explained in the previous section, a proposal that focuses exclusively on deposit insurance while neglecting other aspects of the official safety net, cannot be expected to achieve either systemic stability or competitive equity.

The general conclusion, therefore, is that the EC proposal on deposit insurance is either too far-reaching or too limited in scope. It is too far-reaching in that national authorities are being required to adapt their own schemes to a complex common formula which professes to be aimed at financial stabilisation and consumer protection, but which does not appear to make a significant contribution to either. And it is too limited in scope because if these goals are to be achieved a much more radical harmonisation initiative is called for, embracing issues such as moral hazard and procedures for handling failed banks.

---

The following matrix, taken from S. Key, "Deposit Protection Schemes: Issues for an EC Directive," CEPS Research Report No. 11, Table 1, compares the Commission's proposed scheme with some alternatives.

**Table 1**

**Scheme determining level of coverage and assuming financial responsibility under various approaches to deposit insurance for branches**

| | Home-country approach (1) | *Hybrid approaches* | | | | Host-country approach (6) |
|---|---|---|---|---|---|---|
| | | Home-country + Host topping up (2) | Home-country + Host topping up + Host limit on coverage (3) | Host-country + Home reimbursement (4) | Host-country + Home reimbursement not exceeding home level of coverage (5) | |
| A. *Level of coverage*[1] | | | | | | |
| 1. Branches from low-coverage countries | HOME SCHEME | HOST SCHEME[2] | HOST SCHEME[2] | HOST SCHEME | HOST SCHEME | HOST SCHEME |
| 2. Branches from high-coverage countries | HOME SCHEME | HOME SCHEME | HOST SCHEME | HOST SCHEME | HOST SCHEME | HOST SCHEME |
| B. *Financial responsibility* | | | | | | |
| 1. Branches from low-coverage countries | HOME SCHEME | HOME + HOST SCHEMES[2] | HOME + HOST SCHEMES[2] | HOME SCHEME | HOME + HOST SCHEMES | HOST SCHEME |
| 2. Branches from high-coverage countries | HOME SCHEME | HOME SCHEME | HOME SCHEME | HOME SCHEME | HOME SCHEME | HOST SCHEME |

[1] The nonmonetary aspects of coverage are not addressed in this table.
[2] Under the Commission proposal, the host scheme would apply only if a branch exercised the topping-up option.

## *Notes and Questions*

1. The Council of the European Union issued a Common Position On the Proposal For A Directive On Deposit–Guarantee Schemes on October 25, 1993. It is envisioned that the Directive will go into effect

by January 1, 1995. It differs in some respects from the earlier proposal described by Professor Dale. First, the deposit minimum is ECU 20,000 (about $22,400 as of February 17, 1994), although states whose current coverage is below that level, need only provide 15,000 worth of coverage until December 31, 1999. Second, home states are only prohibited until December 31, 1999 from insuring above the host state maximum. The limitation will be reassessed at that time. Also, certain deposits are excluded from the scheme, for example deposits of other banks or large corporations.

2. In the United States, until 1991, depositors in U.S. branches of foreign banks that took retail deposits had to be insured by the United States. After 1991, retail deposit branches are prospectively prohibited—foreign banks must take retail deposits through subsidiaries. The United States abolished retail insured branches of foreign banks largely out of concern that it—the host state—might have to pay for the supervisory failures of a foreign country. Why didn't the EC follow the same approach?

3. The EU scheme prevents home states from providing insurance above the level of host states—the "no export" clause. Do you agree that such a limitation is necessary for an even playing field? The EU scheme permits branches of out-of-state EU banks, whose insurance is below the level of a host state, to join the host state deposit scheme in order to "top-up" their insurance to the level of the host state. Germany currently has unlimited insurance coverage for deposits. How do you think it feels about the no export and top-up provisions? Will out-of-state banks from low insurance countries want to top-up?

---

*Links to Other Chapters*

The EU has adopted an internal mutual recognition approach in the banking and securities areas that goes considerably beyond the U.S.'s and Japan's willingness to defer to the regulatory regimes of other countries (Chapters II, III and VII). This reflects the degree of political union. The EU does not apply the mutual recognition approach to non-EU countries; indeed regulation of financial institutions from non-EU countries is left up to each EU country. Capital adequacy standards for banks and securities firms, CAD, dealt with in the last Chapter, underpins the "single passport" approach. The integration of the internal market is looked upon as part of the greater financial integration contemplated by Maastricht, examined in the next Chapter.

Offshore markets in "eurosecurities" particularly Eurobonds, are looked at extensively in Chapter XI, and the role of European stock exchanges in worldwide competition is covered in Chapter XIII on Stock Exchange Competition. We will also look again in that Chapter at the Club Med proposals whose essential aim was to limit stock market competition.

# Chapter VI

# EUROPEAN MARKETS: MONETARY UNION AND FOREIGN EXCHANGE MARKETS

The European Community's attempts to build a monetary union brought its member governments face to face with the awesome power of the world's foreign exchange markets. The encounters may have seriously damaged economies in Europe and elsewhere. The chapter explores the way the European Monetary System (EMS) has worked and the prospects for the Economic and Monetary Union ("EMU").

To this end, the chapter examines the interplay between exchange rate regimes, government policy, and foreign exchange markets. We present the basics of fixed and floating exchange rate systems, consider the way spot and forward exchange markets work, and examine the logic of interest rate parity. This serves as background to an understanding of the EMS and the EMU.

## A. THE EUROPEAN MONETARY SYSTEM

The European Monetary System "began in 1972 as the snake, which was designed to keep the EEC countries' exchange rates within" a narrow band of each other. In 1979, the snake became the EMS. (See Maurice D. Levi, International Finance 2d ed. (1990).) Not until 1990 did the U.K. join the EMS. At the time, the Bank of England explained how its new membership would work.

### "THE EXCHANGE RATE MECHANISM OF THE EUROPEAN MONETARY SYSTEM"

Bank of England Q. Bull., November 1990, 479.

On Monday 8 October sterling joined the exchange rate mechanism of the European monetary system with a central rate of 0.696904 against the ECU and a bilateral central rate against the deutschemark of £1 = DM 2.95; it will initially operate in the wider 6% band. This article describes the mechanism and sets out the intervention obligations of the participating central banks. The intervention obligations are summarised in the parity grid—a matrix showing the various bilateral central and intervention rates. The matrix which is effective as from 8 October is shown in Table A.

**Table A**
**Bilateral central rates and selling and buying rates in the EMS exchange rate mechanism from 8 October 1990**

| | | B. Fc./L. Fc. 100 = | D. Kr. 100 = | Fr.Fc. 100 = | DM 100 = | I£1 = | Lit 1,000 = | Fl 100 = | Pts 100 = | £1 = |
|---|---|---|---|---|---|---|---|---|---|---|
| **Belgium/ Luxembourg:** | S | — | 553.000 | 628.970 | 2109.50 | 56.5115 | 28.1930 | 1872.15 | 33.6930 | 64.6050 |
| | C | — | 540.723 | 614.977 | 2062.55 | 55.2545 | 27.5661 | 1830.54 | 31.7316 | 60.8451 |
| B.Fc./L.Fc. | B | — | 528.700 | 601.295 | 2016.55 | 54.0250 | 26.9530 | 1789.85 | 29.8850 | 57.3035 |
| **Denmark:** | S | 18.9143 | — | 116.320 | 390.160 | 10.4511 | 5.21400 | 346.240 | 6.23100 | 11.9479 |
| | C | 18.4938 | — | 113.732 | 381.443 | 10.2186 | 5.09803 | 338.537 | 5.86837 | 11.2526 |
| D.Kr. | B | 18.0831 | — | 111.200 | 373.000 | 9.9913 | 4.98500 | 331.020 | 5.52600 | 10.5976 |
| **France:** | S | 16.6310 | 89.9250 | — | 343.050 | 9.18900 | 4.58450 | 304.440 | 5.47850 | 10.50550 |
| | C | 16.2608 | 87.9257 | — | 335.386 | 8.98480 | 4.48247 | 297.661 | 5.15981 | 9.89389 |
| Fr.Fc. | B | 15.8990 | 85.9700 | — | 327.920 | 8.78500 | 4.38300 | 291.040 | 4.85950 | 9.31800 |
| **Germany:** | S | 4.95900 | 26.8100 | 30.4950 | — | 2.74000 | 1.36700 | 90.7700 | 1.63300 | 3.13200 |
| | C | 4.84837 | 26.2162 | 29.8164 | — | 2.67894 | 1.33651 | 88.7526 | 1.53847 | 2.95000 |
| DM | B | 4.74000 | 25.6300 | 29.1500 | — | 2.61900 | 1.30650 | 86.7800 | 1.44900 | 2.77800 |
| **Ireland:** | S | 1.85100 | 10.00870 | 11.3830 | 38.1825 | — | 0.510246 | 33.8868 | 0.609772 | 1.16920 |
| | C | 1.80981 | 9.78604 | 11.1299 | 37.3281 | — | 0.498895 | 33.1293 | 0.574281 | 1.10118 |
| I£ | B | 1.76950 | 9.56830 | 10.8825 | 36.4964 | — | 0.487799 | 32.3939 | 0.540858 | 1.03710 |
| **Italy:** | S | 3710.20 | 20062.0 | 22817.0 | 76540.0 | 2050.03 | — | 67912.0 | 1222.30 | 2343.62 |
| | C | 3627.64 | 19615.4 | 22309.1 | 74821.7 | 2004.43 | — | 66405.3 | 1151.11 | 2207.25 |
| Lit | B | 3546.90 | 19179.0 | 21813.0 | 73157.0 | 1959.84 | — | 64928.0 | 1084.10 | 2078.79 |
| **Netherlands:** | S | 5.58700 | 30.2100 | 34.3600 | 115.2350 | 3.08700 | 1.54000 | — | 1.84050 | 3.52950 |
| | C | 5.46286 | 29.5389 | 33.5953 | 112.6730 | 3.01848 | 1.50590 | — | 1.73345 | 3.32389 |
| Fl | B | 5.34150 | 28.8825 | 32.8475 | 110.1675 | 2.95100 | 1.47250 | — | 1.63250 | 3.13050 |
| **Spain:** | S | 334.619 | 1809.40 | 2057.80 | 6901.70 | 184.892 | 92.2400 | 6125.30 | — | 203.600 |
| | C | 315.143 | 1704.05 | 1938.06 | 6500.00 | 174.131 | 86.8726 | 5768.83 | — | 191.750 |
| Pts | B | 296.802 | 1604.90 | 1825.30 | 6121.70 | 163.997 | 81.8200 | 5433.10 | — | 180.590 |
| **United Kingdom:** | S | 1.74510 | 9.43610 | 10.7320 | 35.9970 | 0.964240 | 0.481050 | 31.9450 | 0.553740 | — |
| | C | 1.64352 | 8.88687 | 10.1073 | 33.8984 | 0.908116 | 0.453053 | 30.0853 | 0.521514 | — |
| £ | B | 1.54790 | 8.36970 | 9.5190 | 31.9280 | 0.855260 | 0.426690 | 28.3340 | 0.491160 | — |

S = Exchange rate at which the central bank of the country in the left hand column will sell the currency identified in the row at the top of the table.

C = Bilateral central rate.

B = Exchange rate at which the central bank of the country in the left hand column will buy the currency identified in the row at the top of the table.

(1) Written by J J Adams in the Bank's Foreign Exchange Division.

(2) The lower and upper bilateral intervention rates (at which central banks are obliged to buy and sell, respectively, the relevant foreign currency in exchange for their own) are derived for the narrow band by multiplying the central rates by factors of 0.977753 for the compulsory buying rates and 1.022753 for the compulsory selling rates. For the wide band currencies, the factors are 0.941798 and 1.061798 respectively. These factors are chosen so as to ensure that central bank A's buying rate for currency B is the same as central bank B's selling rate for currency A. The corresponding margins are -2.2247% and +2.2753% and -5.8202% and +6.1798%. Due to market convention, the intervention rates are normally not exact reciprocals but are rounded to convenient figures. These differences are, however, insignificant in practice.

## Sterling's effective limits in the ERM

(Based on exchange rates on 22 October 1990)

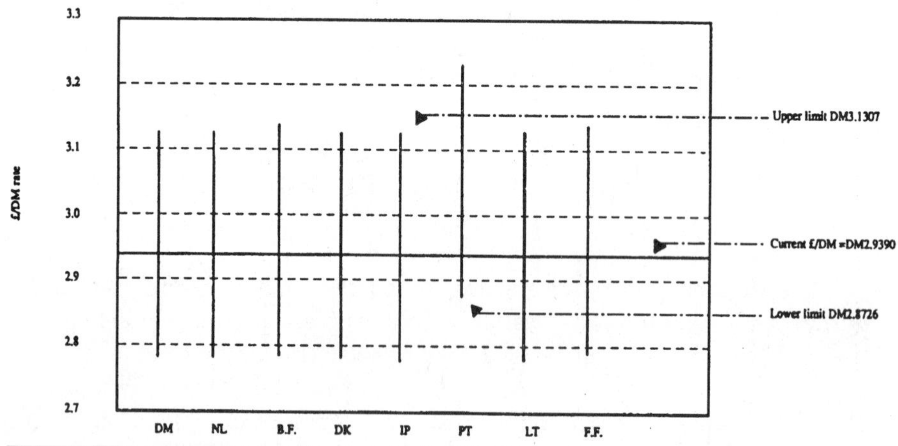


All participating currencies, except the peseta and sterling, must be held within margins of 2¼% on either side of their agreed bilateral central rates against each other participating currency; in the case of the pound and the peseta the scope for movement is 6%.[(2)] If, for example, the Irish punt were to appreciate to I£1 = DFl 3.08700 (the rate shown in the grid as the Dutch central bank's selling rate for Irish punts) against the Dutch guilder, the Nederlandsche Bank would be obliged to buy guilders for punts at that rate in unlimited amounts. At the same time, the Central Bank of Ireland would be obliged to sell punts for guilders at a rate of DFl 100 = I£32.3939 (i.e. its buying rate for guilders, as shown in the grid), the reciprocal of the rate at which the Nederlandsche Bank would be buying guilders for punts.

Narrow band currencies have a maximum possible range of fluctuation against each other of 4½% (= 2 × 2¼%); for those in the wide band the maximum range of fluctuation against all currencies is 12% (= 2 × 6%). Thus sterling could in principle move up within the band from DM 2.7780 (6% below its central rate against the deutschemark) to DM 3.1320 (6% above its central rate). However, such a movement could take place within the band only if, as sterling appreciated, it did not reach its upper limit against any other currency before it reached its upper limit against the deutschemark; in other words, only if sterling moved from being at the bottom of the band at a time when the deutschemark was at the top, to being at the top of the band at a time when the deutschemark was at the bottom. In general, the scope for appreciation is limited by the weakest currency in the band, while the potential for depreciation is limited by the strongest. The chart demonstrates this point. It shows the effective limits on the £/DM rate (using rates observed during the morning of 22 October) implied by the need for sterling to remain within its bilateral limits against all the other currencies in the ERM simultaneously; in the chart all currencies have been translated into £/DM terms. On that morning the effective lower limit was £1 = DM 2.8726: if sterling had fallen below that level, it would have been below its lower limit against the peseta, which at that time was the strongest currency in the system. The effective upper limit at that time, DM 3.1307, was dictated by the position of the Irish punt, which was the weakest currency in the system. Clearly, the effective limits (unlike the formal limits) will fluctuate continuously, as the positions of currencies within the band change.

### Financing intervention

When any two currencies reach their compulsory intervention rates against each other, the two central banks concerned are obliged to meet all bids/offers made to them at the relevant limit rate. This obligation is only binding, however, between the hours of 0800–1500 (GMT). In some cases, this might necessitate a central bank selling a currency not held in its foreign exchange reserves or in an amount which exceeds its current holdings. Operationally this does not cause a problem, however, as the intervening central bank has the right to draw upon the very short term financing facility (VSTF) which is designed primarily to finance intervention at the margin of the ERM band. At the intervention point access to the facility is automatic and the amount of credit available is unlimited. Since November 1987, however, the VSTF has also been available, in certain circumstances and in limited amounts, to finance intervention before a currency reaches a compulsory intervention point, although such intervention may not be undertaken without the prior consent of the central bank whose currency is being used in the intervention. Drawings under the VSTF have to be repaid within approximately three months, although limited amounts may be carried over for up to a further six months.

## The ECU

The ECU was created by the European Community in December 1978 to serve, *inter alia,* as the basis for determining exchange rate parities. It is a composite currency made up of specified amounts of the national currencies of the European Community. The amounts of the component currencies broadly reflect their country's relative economic weight (such as the importance of each country in Community GDP and intra-Community trade) and are normally revised every five years. The amounts were last changed in September 1989, when, among other changes, the ECU basket was enlarged to include the Spanish peseta and the Portuguese escudo. The ECU's composition on 12 October is shown in Table B.

In addition to having bilateral central rates against each other, each currency in the EMS (that is all ERM currencies along with the Greek drachma and the Portuguese escudo) has a central rate against the ECU. These rates were also revised as a consequence of sterling's entry into the mechanism and are shown in Table C.

**Table B**
**Composition of the ECU**

| Currency | Amount[(a)] | Weight[(b)] |
|---|---|---|
| Belgian franc | 3.431 | 8.1 |
| French franc | 1.332 | 19.3 |
| Lira | 151.8 | 9.8 |
| Dutch guilder | 0.2198 | 9.4 |
| Deutschemark | 0.6242 | 30.2 |
| Danish krone | 0.1976 | 2.5 |
| Irish punt | 0.008552 | 1.1 |
| Peseta | 6.885 | 5.3 |
| Drachma | 1.44 | 0.7 |
| Sterling | 0.08784 | 12.8 |
| Escudo | 1.04741 | 0.8 |
| | | **100.0** |

(a) These amounts have applied since September 1989.

(b) Weights based on exchange rates on 12 October 1990. This date has been chosen at random. The weights in the ECU will of course change as the exchange rates for the component currencies are determined by forces of supply and demand.

**Table C**
**Central rates of EMS currencies against the ECU since 8 October 1990**
Units of national currency per ECU

| | |
|---|---|
| Belgian/Luxembourg franc | 42.4032 |
| Danish krone | 7.84195 |
| French franc | 6.89509 |
| Deutschemark | 2.05586 |
| Irish punt | 0.767417 |
| Lira | 1538.24 |
| Dutch guilder | 2.31643 |
| Peseta | 133.631 |
| Sterling | 0.696904 |
| Drachma | 205.311 |
| Escudo | 178.735 |

**The divergence indicator**

The divergence indicator was designed to provide an additional means of identifying currencies in the ERM whose exchange rates are diverging from those of the other currencies, and was intended to create a presumption as to which countries should take corrective action. This indicator compares an ERM currency's market rate against the ECU with its ECU central rate, expressing the percentage difference as a proportion of its Maximum Divergence Spread (MDS). This is the maximum percentage by which a currency's market rate against the ECU can change from its ECU central rate before that currency reaches its bilateral limit against any other participating currency.(1) The ECU is used in the divergence indicator because, as it is a composite currency, it provides a comparison of a national currency's movement against the average of EMS currencies. When a currency's divergence indicator reaches 75% of its maximum divergence ('the divergence threshold') there is a presumption that 'appropriate' action will be taken to contain or reduce the divergence. In practice, however, it is quite common for currencies to reach their compulsory intervention points before reaching or crossing their divergence threshold.

---

[At the time, the Governor of the Bank of England spoke enthusiastically about the benefits membership would give the U.K. These excerpts from his speech are reported in the same Bulletin, 483.]

(1) The MDS for a currency is always less than its percentage range of bilateral fluctuation against any other currency (ie 2¼% or 6%). This is because, as a currency moves the maximum of 2¼% divergence from all other currencies, its own influence will move the ECU down below the average of other currencies: for example, if a currency held a ⅓ weight in the ECU, the maximum divergence (when it was 2¼% away from all other currencies) would be ⅔ × 2¼%. This means that currency/ECU movements will be smaller than bilateral movements.

The ERM's successes did not come overnight, however. During its early years there were a number or realignments which, as you will know, are permitted within the rules. But more recently, the member countries have shown great determination to hold their parities and, where pressures arise, to take the economic measures necessary to deal directly with those pressures, rather than resort to realignment. In fact, there has not been a general realignment since January 1987. The turning point, I think it is generally recognised, came in 1983 when France revised its economic objectives and decided to pursue a rigorous counterinflationary policy within the ERM framework.

This success has not been costless for the member countries. It is generally accepted, for example, that France and Italy have suffered a short-term loss of competitiveness. But in the process they have gained greatly in their battle against inflation and have thus been laying the absolutely necessary foundations for sustained growth in the longer run.

I believe the system can bring similar benefits to the United Kingdom. We have gone in with a central rate of 2.95 against the deutschemark and with 6% bands of fluctuation, rather than the 2¼% bands employed by most members; this has become usual for newly participating currencies as it gives time for markets to adjust and economies to converge more closely. I am confident that these terms are fully consistent with maintaining firm downward pressure on inflation. The immediate reaction of the markets in London and New York on Friday indicates that they too have this confidence.

As elsewhere this process will not be painless. The defeat of inflation never can be. Perhaps the key point is that, by putting an effective floor on sterling's exchange rate, we have introduced an extra discipline—a discipline for policy-makers and for both sides of industry and commerce. Companies will find it more difficult to pass on inflationary wage increases by raising their output prices. They will need to restrain unit costs; if they fail to do so, they will not be able to look to a depreciating currency to given them temporary relief. I should stress that depreciation can only provide just that: temporary relief. And what is worse, it gives the impression of reducing the need to deal with fundamental problems of competitiveness, while in fact only aggravating them and putting them off for a later day.

In terms of how soon and at what short-term cost the benefits of membership come through, a good deal depends on the effect on expectations. I am therefore glad we have been able to join before this winter's pay round gets under way as, although I believe we have quelled the excess demand in the economy, I am concerned about cost-push inflationary pressures.

In sum then, I believe that ERM membership will reinforce our counterinflationary strategy. In addition, it will help our economy to converge with the economies of our Community partners; and will help business by bringing greater exchange rate stability against other European currencies, and possibly more widely, and thus a better environment in which to plan and invest. I hope it will make the United Kingdom an even more attractive place for Japanese investment, which has of course already been strong in recent years.

But, as I have said many times before in anticipation of our joining, the ERM is *not* a panacea. Its benefits will have to be worked for, most of all by maintaining a *firm anti-inflation policy.*

***Questions***

1. The Governor said that membership in EMS gives "an extra discipline." What did he mean?

2. What is the Exchange Rate Mechanism?

3. How is a member's exchange rate set? Look closely at Table C. How does the member's exchange rate fluctuate?

4. What happens when a currency gets to the edge of the band with another currency? Consider what happens as the value of one pound sterling reaches DM 3.132 or DM 2.2778. At both points, what is the obligation of the central bank of each country?

5. As you read the following material, ask yourself if the EMS is a fixed or floating system for exchange rates.

---

## B. EXCHANGE RATE SYSTEMS

An exchange rate gives the prices at which two currencies are sold for each other. Different systems determine these prices. Four types of systems during the last century tended toward either flexible rates set by supply and demand or rates fixed by governments.

### 1. Fixed Rate Systems: The Gold Standard

KENNETH W. DAM, THE RULES OF THE GAME

(1982), 6.

... The first period, whose beginning can be disputed but which ended suddenly and unexpectedly with the beginning of the First World War, demarcates the life of the international gold standard. The second period covers the twenty-odd years between the two wars and can be thought of in connection with the gold exchange standard, though that system actually operated only from roughly 1925 to 1931. The third period, following World War II, spans the quarter century in which the Bretton Woods system was in effect. Thereafter, the years beginning not later than 1973 are usually characterized as a floating exchange rate period. ...

---

In theory, the gold standard system required very little government intervention. Levi described it:

## MAURICE D. LEVI; INTERNATIONAL FINANCE

476–80, (1990) ("Levi").

Under a gold standard each country stands ready to convert its paper or fiat money into gold at a fixed price. This fixing of the price of gold fixes exchange rates between paper monies. For example, if the U.S. Federal Reserve (the "Fed") agrees to buy and sell gold at $40 per ounce, and the Bank of England agrees to £20 per ounce, the exchange rate between the pound and dollar in the form of paper currency or commercial bank deposits will be $2/£. If the exchange rate is not $2/£, the foreign exchange market will not balance because it will be used for converting one currency into the other, but not vice versa. For example, if the exchange rate in the foreign exchange market is $1.60/£, the market will be used for converting dollars into pounds, but not for converting pounds into dollars. This is because it is cheaper for people buying dollars with pounds to buy gold from the Bank of England, ship the gold to the U.S., and sell it to the Federal Reserve for dollars.

. . .

### Price Adjustment under the Gold Standard

The price-level adjustment mechanism under the gold standard is known as the price-specie adjustment mechanism, where "specie" is just another word for precious metal. This mechanism was explained as early as 1752. ... In order to explain the mechanism, let us continue to assume that gold is $40/oz. in the U.S. and £20/oz. in Britain and that at the resulting exchange rate of $2/£, Britain is buying more from the U.S. than the U.S. is buying from Britain. That is, let us assume that Britain has a balance-of-payments deficit with the U.S. The price-specie adjustment mechanism explains how the British deficit and the U.S. surplus are corrected in the following manner.

With Britain buying more from the U.S. than the U.S. is buying from Britain, there is an excess supply of pounds. With flexible exchange rates this will reduce the value of the pound below $2/£, but with a gold standard this will not happen because nobody will sell pounds in the foreign exchange market for less than $2. Rather, as soon as the pound dips even slightly below $2, people will sell pounds to the Bank of England in return for gold, ship the gold to the U.S., and sell the gold to the Federal Reserve for dollars. This gives people $2 for each pound. Therefore, the result of the British balance-of-payments deficit is the movement of gold from the Bank of England to the U.S. Federal Reserve.

The movement of gold from Britain, the deficit country, to the U.S., the surplus country, has effects on both countries' money supplies. This is because in standing ready to exchange gold for paper money at a fixed price, central banks have to make sure they have sufficient gold on hand for those occasions when many people wish to return paper money for gold. Prudent banking requires that a minimum ratio of gold reserves to paper money be held, and indeed, this used to be mandated in many countries, including the U.S., which required that the dollar be backed by at least 25 percent in gold reserves. The maintenance of a minimum reserve ratio means that as the Bank of England loses gold it is forced to reduce the amount of its paper money in circulation. At the same time, the increase in the Federal Reserve gold reserves allows it to put more paper money into circulation.

In the minds of the eighteenth-century classical economists who described the working of the gold standard, the fall in the money supply in the deficit country would cause a general fall in prices. At the same time, the increase in the money supply in the surplus country (in the world we are describing, one country's deficit in the other country's surplus) would cause a general increase in prices.[7] With prices falling in the deficit country, Britain, and increasing in the surplus country, the U.S., there is a decline in British prices versus U.S. prices. This makes British exports more competitive in the U.S., helping them increase. At the same time, U.S. goods in Britain become less competitive than Britain's own import substitutes, so that British imports decline. With British exports increasing and imports decreasing, Britain's deficit declines. Indeed, until the deficit has been completely eliminated there will be an excess supply of pounds, the sale of pounds to the Bank of England, the shipment of gold to the U.S., a decrease in the British money supply, an increase in the U.S. money supply, increasing competitiveness of British products at home and abroad, and a continued reduction in the British deficit.

The price-specie adjustment mechanism works not only via changes in relative prices *between* countries, but also via changes in relative prices *within* each country. In the deficit country, for example, the prices of nontraded goods will decline, but the prices of goods which enter international trade will remain unchanged. . . .

Unfortunately for the effectiveness of the price-specie adjustment mechanism of the gold standard, governments were often tempted to abandon the required reserve ratio between gold and paper money when the maintenance of that ratio ran counter to other objectives. . . .

The policy of not allowing a change in reserves to change the supply of money is known as sterilization or neutralization policy. As goals of full employment became common in the twentieth century, many countries abandoned their effort to maintain the required reserve ratio and focused on their local economic ills. . . .

---

7. The link between the money supply and prices the classical economists had in mind was the quantity theory of money. This theory predicts that prices increase and decrease in proportion to increases and decreases in the money supply.

So in practice, limited government intervention was a myth. According to Dam,

> Looking backward through the telescope of received mythology, the gold standard was an essentially automatic self-adjusting system that functioned without the aid of human hands, particularly those of central bankers and finance ministers. Taking a closer and more direct view, one can see the gold standard in idealized form as a sterling standard in which the Bank of England was central banker to the world, keeping all in equilibrium. On still closer inspection—which to be sure concentrates on the trees of individual country behavior, missing the beauty of the sylvan ensemble—one can see many features of the gold standard that we normally think of as recent developments: floating exchange rates, intervention in exchange markets, central bank foreign lending and borrowing, and the like. *Plus ça change!*

Dam reports that during this period central banks countered the automatic forces in more years than they permitted them to work.

The question remains whether the gold standard could have worked. Levi points out (479–80) that:

... Some economists, most notably Robert Triffin, have said that it could not work. Central to this view is the notion that prices are rigid downward (a feature of Keynesian economics) and that therefore deficits from gold outflows cannot be self-correcting, because prices cannot fall. ...

A number of twentieth-century economists and politicians have favored a return to the gold standard. What appeals to the proponents of this system is the discipline that the gold standard placed on the expansion of the money supply and the check that this therefore placed on that creeping evil, inflation. The economists who prefer a return to the gold standard include Jacques Rueff and Michael Heilperin. The politicians include the late French President Charles de Gaulle and New York Congressman Jack Kemp. ...

---

No treaty fixed the rules of the gold standard. Dam states (p. 24) that:

> The international monetary system of the gold standard period rested fundamentally upon domestic law in each of the principal trading nations. These domestic legal rules were similar, though not identical, in the various countries. The rules generally provided for free import and export of gold bullion and coins by residents and nonresidents alike. In addition, national mints stood ready to accept gold bullion and to turn it into gold coins as well as to reverse the process upon demand. But there were many small differences in national

rules, and even the general principles were not unfailingly followed.

## 2. Fixed Rate Standards: The Bretton Woods Dollar Standard

As World War II was ending, financial leaders from many Allied countries met in Bretton Woods, New Hampshire, where they agreed to a new regime. The U.S. dollar, then the world's strongest currency, would be fixed to gold. The U.S. government promised to give any holder of dollars gold at the rate of $35 for an ounce of gold. Other countries tied their exchange rates to the U.S. dollar at agreed rates that could fluctuate around it in a narrow band. To maintain these par values, the countries agreed to sell their currency if it approached the upper limit or to buy their currency at the lower limit with their foreign exchange reserves (mainly gold and dollars at first).

The International Monetary Fund, a multilateral institution controlled by the U.S. and other industrial countries, was set up to help member countries maintain the agreed exchange rates. The IMF could make funds available to a deficit country if the country adopted agreed policies to improve their economic situation. Devaluation was discouraged but not outlawed.

The new system of fixed rates was a gold exchange and U.S. dollar standard embodied in the IMF treaty, which took effect in 1944. The U.S. was not obligated to maintain a one-to-one ratio of dollars to gold, however; it held reserves at a level that gave people confidence it could meet any demand for gold. Since the dollar was used for international transactions and since governments held dollars as reserves, demand for gold in exchange for dollars was relatively low. But by the time the system broke down in the early 1970s, U.S. reserves were so low that confidence had evaporated. By then, most non-communist countries had signed the treaty.

The dollar standard assumes a price adjustment mechanism. Levi describes this, assuming that private demand sets the dollar/pound exchange rate within the allowed range. If private demand for pounds increases, the Bank of England will supply more by buying dollars and the U.K. money supply will rise. The competitiveness of British goods will fall and imports will rise. As demand for pounds falls, the dollar/pound rate is restored within the allowed range. He continues (480–5):

> ... For example, a balance-of-payments surplus raises the supply of money and hence prices; as a result of this, exports are reduced, imports are increased, and the surplus is thereby eliminated. Of course, if there is sterilization of the balance-of-payments surplus and the money supply is not allowed to increase, the price-level adjustment mechanism will not work. Sterilization will eventually result in a continued growth in foreign exchange reserves and a need to revise the parity exchange rate. This makes exchange-rate forecasting a potentially highly rewarding

activity for the financial executive, since the bank's need to change the parity value becomes clearly apparent in the foreign exchange reserve statistics.

> ... By keeping track of gold reserves, a financial executive could see that the central bank might be forced to raise the price of gold, that is, to devalue. The exact date would be difficult to predict, but actions based on such an assumption are unlikely to result in losses. A country that is losing reserves might manage not to devalue, but it certainly would not revalue, that is, raise the value of its currency by reducing the price of gold set by the central bank. This means that the financial manager would discover either that she or he was correct and a devaluation did occur or that the exchange rate remained as before. Thus there is an opportunity for a one-way bet, and the worst that is likely to happen is that no speculative gain will be made.

The "par" or middle exchange rate in a gold-exchange or dollar standard will respond to changes in reserve positions in a way that is similar to the response in a gold standard. The reserves held to defend the currency in a gold-exchange or dollar standard are made up of U.S. dollars, assets readily convertible to dollars, and gold. When these reserves are getting low, chances are that a devaluation, that is, a reduction in par value, will eventually take place. Indeed, speculation that a devaluation will occur is likely to make it occur. For example, prior to the 1980 devaluation of the Mexican peso, speculators had decided that a peso devaluation was imminent. They therefore sold pesos, and the Mexican authorities were required to purchase them at the lower support point. The pesos were purchased with U.S. dollars and hence the Mexican reserves were lowered. Eventually, reserves were so much reduced that the Mexicans were forced to devalue. The speculators' beliefs were vindicated. In a sense, their expectations were self-fulfilling.

The need to reduce the value of a currency in a country experiencing deficits and declining reserves depends on the ability of the central bank to borrow additional reserves. There are arrangements between central banks for exchanging currency reserves, and there are many lines for borrowing from international institutions such as the International Monetary Fund.

The borrowing arrangements include central-bank swaps. Central-bank swaps involve, for example, the U.S. government making U.S. dollars available to the Bank of Canada when Canadian foreign exchange reserves are low. The Bank of Canada will temporarily swap these U.S. dollars for Canadian dollars. The swap will be reversed later, according to the original agreement. Often the swap will be reversed only after a number of years to allow the borrowing country to correct its balance of payments. Central banks also frequently borrow from private banks. The Bank of Canada, for example, borrowed heavily from both Canadian and U.S. commercial banks during the early and mid 1980s despite the fact that the exchange rate was supposed to be flexible. The ability of central banks to borrow from other central banks and from private banks and international institutions makes the forecasting of exchange rates more difficult. Revisions of par values can be delayed many years by countries with good credit ratings.

Another factor making exchange-rate forecasting under fixed rates difficult is the difference in the need to react to surpluses and deficits. Countries that are facing a deficit and losing reserves will eventually be forced into a devaluation because their reserves and ability to borrow will eventually be gone. On the other hand, the countries enjoying surpluses will be under no pressure to revalue their currencies and may instead allow reserves to keep growing. This represents one of the major problems with the gold-exchange and dollar standards, namely that the responsibility for adjustment, whether this be via a change in the exchange rate or via an automatic change in money supplies and prices, falls on deficit countries more heavily than on surplus countries. . . .

---

There are other "automatic" ways economies can adjust to imbalances that threaten to disrupt the fixed exchange rates. Levi describes two:

**National Income.** The price-level adjustment mechanism requires flexibility of prices in order to operate. The macroeconomic revolution marked by the publication of *The General Theory of Employment, Interest and Money* by John Maynard Keynes, while focusing on a closed economy, spilled over into international finance and introduced an alternative adjustment mechanism that works if price flexibility does not exist. This mechanism, popularized by the followers of Keynes, involves automatic adjustment via changes in national income. Like the price-level adjustment mechanism, the income adjustment system operates on the current account. . . .

**Interest Rates.** The automatic interest-rate adjustment mechanism relies on the effect of the balance of payments on the money supply. We have seen that if the effects are not sterilized, a balance-of-payments deficit will reduce the supply of money, and a surplus will increase it. With a gold standard this occurs because a deficit means a gold outflow and a shrinking money supply, and a surplus means a gold inflow and an increasing money supply. In the gold-exchange and dollar standards; . . . the money supply also declines after deficits and increases after surpluses. In these cases the money supply declines because of intervention in the foreign exchange market. A deficit requires the local monetary authority to purchase its currency to keep the value up. Thus money is withdrawn from circulation. Similarly, a surplus requires the central bank to sell its currency and hence increase the supply of money. With this we can explain the interest-rate adjustment mechanism.

The interest-rate adjustment mechanism via the capital account involves the following. If a deficit occurs, it will reduce the money supply and raise the interest rate. The deficit means surpluses elsewhere. Therefore the money supplies of other countries will be rising. This will reduce their interest rates. For both reasons there is a rise in interest differentials in favor of the deficit country. This will make investment (in securities, and so on) in that country appear relatively more attractive. The resultant inflows on the capital account should improve the balance of payments, thereby correcting the original deficit.

Because capital flows are highly responsive to interest-rate differentials when capital can flow without restriction, the interest-rate adjustment mechanism working via the capital account is likely to be the most effective mechanism in the short run. However, it is necessary that adjustment eventually occur via prices or national income and the current account. This is because capital inflows must be serviced. That is, there will be payments of interest which will appear as a debit in the invisible or service part of the current account. This means that in the future, the current-account deficit will increase.

### *Questions*

1. What is the function of an exchange rate system or regime? What is a regime such as the gold standard supposed to do? Are these functions important?

2. What is a fixed rate system? How is it supposed to work? Pay careful attention to the ways in which countries are supposed to adjust when trade flows between them are not in balance.

3. Kenneth Dam entitled his book "The Rules of the Game," suggesting that exchange regimes have a regulatory role. But no treaties bound the members of the classical gold standard. What are the rules of a fixed rate regime? Who would enforce them? Distinguish between the classical gold standard and the Bretton Woods system.

4. How would you compare the EMS with the fixed rate regimes described in the readings? Are there any important differences? Why would they exist?

---

## 3. Floating Rate Regimes

The Bretton Woods regime expired in 1974 when major industrial countries finally said they would let foreign exchange markets determine the value of their currencies. The U.S. government said it would no longer support the dollar's value. The EC decided to float members' currencies together against the dollar. Dam observed that the EC float could be seen as "merely a decision by Germany to float against the dollar, with the other countries pegging their currencies on the German mark to form a mark area. However, the dictates of European integration required that the decision be presented as a European Economic Community initiative" [191].

While supply and demand were supposed to set currency prices, each country could intervene in the market for its own currency to maintain order. During the early Reagan years, the U.S. remained passive while Japan and Europe set targets. By the mid–1980s, the U.S. had decided to intervene in markets so as to devalue the dollar against other currencies, notably the Yen. The willingness to manage the float has persisted since then.

Over the next two decades there evolved a mixed exchange rate regime. Major trading countries try to manage the value of their currency. They intervene in the currency markets, buying or selling their currency to change its price. They use macroeconomic fiscal and monetary policies, as we shall see in the ERM. They jawbone, making public announcements to encourage market players to act differently. Finance ministers meet periodically in efforts to coordinate or realign their currencies.

Many smaller or non-industrial countries fix their exchange rates against the currency of one or more major trading partners, then adjust as their costs change relative to the partners' costs. An Indonesia, for example, might fix the Rupiah against a basket of other currencies, dominated by the U.S. dollar and the Japanese Yen. If inflation in Indonesia outstrips that in its partner countries, the Government might devalue by announcing a lower fixed rate of exchange for the Rupiah. The central bank would intervene in financial markets to maintain the new rates or use direct rules.

Some countries set official rates largely unrelated to the supply and demand for their currency. A Central American country reportedly wrote the exchange rate into its constitution. People use their official markets when they have no choice; for example, they must convert their investment officially in order to repatriate earnings. Some countries set different rates for different types of transactions; perhaps one high rate for currency to buy consumer goods and another lower rate to buy capital goods. These official rates promptly generate black or grey markets in the currency that operate parallel to the official market and the government loses more leverage over exchange rates.

### *Questions*

1. How does the floating rate system work? What economic factors would you expect to shape supply and demand for a currency?

2. How would countries adjust if their trade is not in balance? Suppose that Germany exports more to Britain than it imports from Britain and that there are no other offsetting flows. What happens next? How does this compare with adjustment in the fixed rate regime?

3. What are the rules for the floating rate regimes described? Is there an appropriate role for government intervention if market forces are supposed to dominate?

4. Why would any government want to interfere with the process of adjustment? Suppose Germany, exporting more to Britain, or the UK, in deficit, wanted to interfere with the adjustment process. What could they do? What enforcement mechanisms might not cause interference?

---

## C. FOREIGN EXCHANGE MARKETS

Foreign exchange markets include cash, spot, forward, swap, futures, and options. Here we focus on the spot and forward markets. Elsewhere in the book we treat derivatives markets. The cash market transfers bank notes at both a retail level, for users such as travellers, and a wholesale level among banks. It is relatively small.

The IMF estimated that daily worldwide net turnover of foreign exchange was $1 trillion in 1992. The market had grown almost 40% since 1989. Transactions in the U.K. accounted for about 30%, followed by the U.S. (19%), Japan (13%), Singapore (7%), and Switzerland (7%). Most transactions involve the U.S. dollar: over 75% of net turnover in the U.K., Singapore, and Switzerland, for example. (Goldstein et al., International Capital Markets, Part I," International Monetary Fund (1993) 24–5) ("Goldstein" hereafter). The relative importance of these markets is described in the following table:

Goldstein, p. 30.

**Table 9. Distribution of Net Turnover by Type of Transaction**
*(In percent of total turnover)*

| | Spot | | | Forward | | | Swaps[1] | | | Futures and Options | | |
|---|---|---|---|---|---|---|---|---|---|---|---|---|
| Country | 1986 | 1989 | 1992 | 1986 | 1989 | 1992 | 1986 | 1989 | 1992 | 1986 | 1989 | 1992 |
| United Kingdom[2] | 73 | 64 | 50 | ... | ... | 6 | 27 | 35 | 41 | ... | 1 | 3 |
| United States[2] | 61 | 62 | 51 | 5 | 5 | 6 | 29 | 25 | 31 | 5 | 8 | 12 |
| Japan[2,3] | 40 | 40 | ... | ... | 6 | ... | ... | 51 | ... | ... | 4 | 6 |
| Singapore[2,3] | ... | 54 | ... | ... | 5 | ... | ... | 38 | ... | ... | 1 | ... |
| Switzerland | ... | 53 | 54 | ... | 5 | 9 | ... | 40 | 33 | ... | 2 | 4 |
| Hong Kong | ... | 61 | 52 | ... | ... | 3 | ... | 39 | 44 | ... | ... | 1 |
| France[2] | ... | 58 | 52 | ... | ... | 4 | ... | 36 | 38 | ... | 6 | 6 |
| Australia | ... | 61 | 42 | ... | 5 | 4 | ... | 32 | 51 | ... | 3 | 3 |
| Canada | 43 | 41 | 35 | 5 | 5 | 4 | 52 | 54 | 61 | ... | ... | ... |

Sources: Bank of Canada; Bank of England; Bank of Japan; Bank for International Settlements (BIS); Banque de France; Federal Reserve Bank of New York; Monetary Affairs Branch, Hong Kong; Monetary Authority of Singapore; Reserve Bank of Australia; and Swiss National Bank.

[1] Some entries in 1986 and 1989 combine outright forwards and swaps.

[2] Data give percentages of total gross turnover by types of transaction except for futures and options in Japan.

[3] Figures reported by the BIS, except for futures and options in Japan.

The IMF sketched the market structure:

Goldstein, p. 25–6.

Foreign exchange transactions are organized at two levels: the wholesale (often called "interbank") market in which dealers trade with each other and with the central banks, and the retail market, which comprises customer transactions. Brokers and dealers participate in both markets, as do some central banks. The distinction between the retail and wholesale markets has become further blurred as some of the larger customers have gained access to the wholesale market through automated trading systems and direct communication links with a large number of dealing banks and financial institutions. The essential difference between dealers and customers is that the latter generally initiate most of their trades whereas dealers also buy and sell foreign currencies in response to orders received from their clients.

The wholesale market is an over-the-counter (OTC) market with no central clearinghouse or exchange. Foreign exchange market activity is dominated by transactions among dealers ...

... But the share of wholesale transactions in total net turnover is decreasing. In the United Kingdom, the share of wholesale trade declined from 91 percent in 1986 to 77 percent in 1992.

The dominance of wholesale transactions reflects dealers' position-taking activity; however, most banks have internal controls ... limiting the size of their open positions. In addition, each retail transaction gives rise to a greater number of wholesale transactions. The limits on open positions, especially overnight positions, mean that dealers will generally try to offset the exposures that result from retail trades. If the bank cannot find another customer interested in undertaking exactly the reverse of the original transaction on the same day, it generally tries to close the position by trading on the wholesale market. If another bank is willing to undertake the reverse transaction, this generates a 1:1 ratio between wholesale orders and retail orders; otherwise, offsetting the original trade would require two or more wholesale transactions. More wholesale transactions are often required to cover an exposure involving forward, swap, or derivatives contracts, particularly if the bank is exposed to changes in a nondollar exchange rate.

The foreign exchange market is dominated by the dealing banks, many of which specialize in making markets in particular currencies—that is, posting public bid and ask prices. For example, the 1993 survey of activity in the United States found that 83 percent of total gross turnover was accounted for by market makers .... Similarly, ... the ten largest dealing banks accounted for 41 percent of total activity ....

... [T]he broker's role in the wholesale market is to match buyers and sellers of foreign exchange, in return for a commission that is usually specified as a percentage of the volume of the transaction. This role is important, owing to the large number of dealing banks .... Larger banks ... dispense with brokers and maintain close working relationships directly with the market-makers in order to have access to timely quotes. ... [B]rokers' share of trading ... has declined [with the] introduction and increased use of automated dealing systems ....

## 1. The Spot Foreign Exchange Market

Levi, 29–37.

### Organization of the Interbank Market

The interbank foreign exchange market is the largest financial market on earth, with a daily volume in excess of $100 billion. It is an informal arrangement of the larger commercial banks and a number of foreign exchange brokers for buying and selling foreign currencies. The banks and brokers are linked together by telephone, Telex, and a satellite communications network called the Society for Worldwide International Financial Telecommunications, SWIFT. This computer-based communications system, based in Brussels, links banks and brokers in just about every financial center. The banks and brokers are in almost constant contact, with activity in some financial center or other 24 hours a day.[3] Because of the speed of communications, significant events have virtually instantaneous impacts everywhere in the world despite the huge distances separating market participants. This is what makes the foreign exchange market just as efficient as a conventional stock or commodity market housed under a common roof.

The efficiency of the foreign exchange market is revealed in the extremely narrow spreads between buying and selling prices. These spreads can be smaller than a tenth of a percent of the value of a contract, and are therefore about one-fortieth or less of the spread faced on bank notes by international travelers. The efficiency of the market is also manifest in the electrifying speed with which exchange rates respond to the continuous flow of information that bombards the market. Participants cannot afford to miss a beat in the frantic pulse of this dynamic, global market. Indeed, the bankers and brokers that constitute the foreign exchange market can scarcely detach themselves from the video screens that provide the latest news and prices as fast as the information can travel via the telephone lines and satellites of the business news wire services.

The banks and foreign exchange brokers, in all countries, collectively determine exchange rates. Each dealer gets "a feel for where the market is going" and takes positions to buy or sell on the basis of this feeling and according to orders received from clients. The feel for the market in each currency, as well as a desire to balance the books, is what determines the position the banker is prepared to take. If it is decided that the bank's pound position should be balanced and, further, customers wish to sell pounds, the bank will enter the market to sell these pounds.

Once the desired amount of buying or selling of a currency has been determined, the banker will call foreign exchange dealers at other banks and "ask for the market." The caller does not say whether he or she wants to buy or sell or state the amount to be traded. The caller might say, "What's your market in sterling?" This means, "At what price are

3. Indeed, in the principal centers like New York, London, Tokyo and Toronto, some banks maintain 24-hour operations to keep up with developments elsewhere during other centers' normal working hours.

you willing to buy and at what price are you willing to sell British pounds for U.S. dollars?" . . .

A difference in quotation of the fourth decimal place can mean thousands of dollars on a large order. It is rather like massive-stakes poker.

If the banker who has been called wants to sell pounds, he or she will quote on the side that is felt to be cheap for pounds, given this banker's feel of the market. For example, if the banker feels that other banks are selling pounds at $1.6120/£ he or she might quote $1.6118/£ as the selling price. In fact, the banker will quote the buying price and the selling price. Having considered the two-way price, the caller will state whether he or she wishes to buy or sell and the amount. Once the rate has been quoted, convention determines that it must be honored whatever the decision of the caller and the amount involved. The caller has about 1 minute to decide and it is fair game to change the rate after this time. Good judgment of the counterparty and good judgment of the direction of the market are essential in this billion-dollar game. It is important to be accurate and constantly in touch with events.

. . .

### Market Clearing and Exchange Brokers

With so many participating banks it may seem remarkable that the market for each currency clears, that is, supply equals demand. Of course, it must be the case that the markets clear, since currencies that banks want to sell are sold, and currencies banks want to buy are bought. However, the markets do not always clear by the banks making direct agreements between themselves. Rather, banks sometimes find it necessary to call in the services of foreign exchange brokers. The brokers find sellers when banks want to buy currencies, and buyers when banks want to sell currencies.

The procedure for dealing with brokers is different from that of banks dealing with each other. A bank will call a broker and state how much foreign exchange it wants to buy or to sell and the rate at which it is willing to buy or sell. This means that it will not ask for a two-way market but will offer to buy or sell a given amount. The broker will communicate to other banks what rates and amounts are available, always showing the best quotes to the potential counterparties. If the two sides of the market are consistent so that a bank will meet the exchange rate demanded by another bank, a trade will be made. Until an agreement has been struck, neither of the two parties knows the identity of the other. When the contract is made, the broker provides the names of the two parties and receives a fee from each of them. It is this fee which makes dealing via brokers more expensive than direct exchange and which therefore explains why larger banks try to make a market between themselves before engaging a broker's services.

The informal nature of the U.S. foreign exchange market, with direct bank dealing coexisting with brokered transactions, is similar to that of markets in Canada, Britain, and many other countries. In France, Germany, and some other countries, including those in Scandinavia, the procedure is rather more formal, with bank representatives, including a representative of the central bank, meeting daily in the same room. Contracts are exchanged directly, although an informal market coexists in which many of the transactions occur. The formal meeting place provides official settlement exchange rates for certain transactions.

**Retail versus Interbank Spot Rates**

While it is only exchange rates between banks that are determined in the interbank market, exchange rates faced by banks' clients are based on these interbank rates. Banks charge their customers slightly more than the going interbank selling or ask rate, and pay their customers slightly less than the interbank buying or bid rate. ...

***Questions***

1. Assume you are advising a U.S. multinational company. The company regularly and in large volumes exports goods to France and buys French products. It holds at least $1 million in French bank accounts and liquid French securities. The company also trades with and invests in Germany. It is a time when the franc is under pressure in the EMS, having been pushed to its lower limit against the Deutsche mark. The French economy does not seem strong. So it seems likely that the franc will devalue.

a. How can the company use the spot market to protect itself?

b. Does this make it a speculator? What would differentiate hedging and speculation in the spot market by this company?

c. How would the company's actions affect the spot FF/DM rate?

---

## 2. The Forward Market

In the forward market the parties contract today to deliver "currency at a specified date in the future, at a price agreed upon today." (Levi, 50). Levi explains market practices:

> Forward exchange quotations are common in a limited number of currencies—those that are most heavily traded. ... [A 1986 survey found] over 94% of the turnover activities ... in the six currencies in which most international trade is conducted .... [T]he forward exchange quotations ... are provided only for specific and rather short periods. ... The 30–day, 90–day, and 180–day quotations are for interbank transactions .... [W]hen dealing with their customers, banks will draw up contracts for periods of a couple of days up to a number of years and these periods do not have to be in even multiples of 30 or anything. ... Since for most currencies the spot

market value date is already 2 business days in the future, the shortest forward contracts are for a period of 3 days. ... [S]preads increase with maturity [because of] the increasing thinness of the market as forward maturity increases ... [making it harder for banks to offset] positions in the interbank forward market after taking orders to buy or sell forward ....

Two types of forward contracts prevail, according to the IMF:

Forward contracts are concluded either in isolation (so-called outright forward purchases or sales) or in combination with a spot or another forward contract in what is referred to as a swap. An outright forward contract is an agreement to exchange specified amounts of one currency for another at some date beyond the spot value date and at an exchange rate specified in the contract. Forward contracts generally come in standard maturities of one month, two months, and so on. Outright forward contracts are not generally concluded between dealers but are common transactions in retail business: they can be closely matched to the customer's needs by being written with nonstandardized quantities and with customer-specific value dates and delivery locations.

Most forward contracts are written as part of a swap arrangement, the simplest form of which matches an exchange of one currency for another on the current spot value date and a reverse exchange on a forward basis. Since the two foreign exchange transactions are made at preset exchange rates, there is no exchange risk in this transaction, but considerable counterparty risk can be involved as one transaction is not made until the contract matures. Swaps are highly flexible instruments that provide a means of hedging against specific maturity exposures in foreign countries or of moving an exposure forward or back in time. ...

Swaps are most commonly entered into by banks and other financial institutions. For example, in the United Kingdom in 1992, only 12 percent of retail business was accounted for by swaps involving nonfinancial customers. Swaps accounted for 41 percent of the total gross market turnover but only 34 percent of retail turnover. On the other hand, outright forward contracts are more often entered into by customers than dealers. For the United Kingdom, 12 percent of customer business (about evenly split between financial customers and nonfinancial customers) was in outright forward contracts compared with only 6 percent for the market as a whole.

The maturity structure of swaps and forwards activity is concentrated in the shorter terms. In April 1992, 70 percent of the U.K. contracts matured in seven days or less, while 63 percent of the contracts in the United States and 66 percent of Canadian contracts fell in the same category. ...

### *Questions*

1. Be sure you understand the basic terms and players. What is forward exchange? Who are the major intermediaries?

2. To say that one currency (such as the DM) is at a forward premium against another (the franc) means that the DM spot rate for francs is below the DM forward rate. Markets expect the DM to increase in value against the dollar. The franc is at a forward discount.

3. Return to the hypothetical in Question 1 about the spot market.

a. How could the MNC use the outright forward market to protect itself?

b. Do these activities make it a speculator?

c. How would the company's actions affect the FF/DM rate and the ERM?

---

## D. INTEREST RATE PARITY CONDITIONS

Among the economic forces shaping foreign exchange movements, one of the most well known is interest rate parity.

Purchasing power parity applies to markets for goods and derives from the law of one price, which holds that "goods priced in different currencies should have the same price when one currency is translated into the other using the spot exchange rate prevailing at the time ...." (Carl Kester and Timothy Luehrman, Case Problems in International Finance (1993) 38.) If the prices differ, arbitragers will buy the cheaper to sell elsewhere until the price differential is erased or else demand for the more expensive good drops, forcing its price down.

Purchasing power parity extends "the law of one price to prices of a basket of goods. In its absolute form, PPP says that the dollar price of a basket of goods in the U.S. is the pound price of the basket in Britain, multiplied by the exchange rate of dollars per pound" (Levi 121). The spot rate equates national price levels. "In its relative form, PPP says that the rate of change of the exchange rate is equal to the difference between inflation rates" (Levi ibid.).

Economists testing this theorem empirically achieved only weak results.

Interest rate parity extends PPP to financial securities. Kester and Luehrman explain below.

### KESTER AND LUERHMAN, 39–40.

#### INTEREST RATE PARITY

The *interest rate parity* (IRP) condition stipulates that the forward premium or discount for one currency relative to another should be equal to the ratio of nominal interest rates on securities of equal risk denominated in the two currencies in question. Notationally, the relationship can be expressed as [3]:

$$\frac{F}{S} = \frac{(1 + R_F)}{(1 + R_D)} \quad \text{or alternatively} \quad F = S\,\frac{(1 + R_F)}{(1 + R_D)}$$

where F = the forward exchange rate for a given time interval

S = the current spot exchange rate

$R_F$ = the nominal interest rate on a security with a maturity equal to that of the forward exchange rate and denominated in a foreign currency, expressed as a decimal fraction

$R_D$ = the nominal interest rate on a security of equivalent maturity and denominated in the domestic currency, also expressed as a decimal fraction

If this condition does not hold, then it will be possible to engage in covered interest arbitrage: a series of transactions that will provide a riskless profit. For example, if the yield on 1-year deutsche mark government bonds is 4 percent and the yield on 1-year U.S. Treasury notes is 8 percent, the deutsche mark should be trading at a 1-year forward premium to the dollar of 3.7% = [ (1.04/1.08) − 1] × 100. Suppose the deutsche mark/dollar spot exchange rate was 1.8000. IRP would imply a 1-year forward rate of 1.8(1.04/1.08) = 1.7333. If, instead, the deutsche mark were trading in the 1-year forward market at 1.75, a riskless profit could be earned by buying what was cheap and selling what was dear, all the time remaining in a "square" position (i.e., being neither long nor short of deutsche marks or dollars). The arbitrage would work as follows:

1. Borrow deutsche marks today for 1 year at 4 percent.

2. Convert the borrowed deutsche marks to dollars in the spot market at an exchange rate of DM 1.8/$.

3. Invest the dollars for 1 year at 8 percent.

4. Buy deutsche marks forward 1 year at DM1.75/$.

If an arbitrageur borrowed, say, DM10 million in step 1, received $5,555,556 upon immediate conversion in the spot market, and received $6,000,000 after investing the dollars for one year at 8%, his or her future profit would be $57,143, regardless of what happened to the deutsche mark/dollar exchange rate during the intervening year. This can be determined by calculating the dollar size of the forward contract the arbitrageur would have to execute in order to repay the borrowed deutsche mark principal plus interest 1 year later: DM10,400,000/1.75 = $5,942,857. The difference between this sized forward contract and the $6 million proceeds from the dollar investment yields the riskless profit of $57,143. Note that the arbitrageur could achieve this without any

**3.**

If interest rates are expressed on a continuously compounding basis, IRP can be approximated as $\frac{(F - S)}{S} = R_F - R_D$. This says that the forward premium or discount on a currency should equal the difference between interest rates.

equity commitment of his or her own. As many arbitrageurs acted to exploit this opportunity, exchange rates and interest rates would be modified through the forces of supply and demand until they conformed to the IRP condition shown above.

---

Empirical tests of interest rate parity support the theorem. Kester and Leuhrman, for example, identified "potential covered interest arbitrage opportunities between the yen and the dollar from January 1976 to November 1985." They plotted "forward premia and discounts on the yen against the national differences in interest rates" and found "close conformity" after accounting for transaction costs. They found few opportunities for riskless profit, suggesting interest rate parity between the yen and the dollar. But they noted that currencies with less active markets might not have arbitragers able to borrow, lend, or cover forward in sufficient volume to achieve interest parity.

### *Questions*

1. Work through the illustrations of the interest parity condition to be sure you understand the principles. In the abstract, what is the relation between domestic and interest rates and the value of a currency? What are the key relative cost elements that determine returns on securities?

2. Using the hypothetical in question 1 for the spot market:

(a) Assume the MNC described above faces these market conditions: exchange rates are FF 2.28 = DM 1 three month spot and FF 3.15 = DM 1 three months forward; domestic interest rates (annualized) are 11% in France and 9% in Germany. Applying the interest rate parity theorem, should the MNC do nothing, borrow DM 10 million to invest in French securities, or borrow FF 30 million to invest in DM securities?

(b) Assume most private market players expect the franc to devalue 10% against the DM within 6 months. How would their behavior in the forward markets affect the spot rates?

(c) How would your answer be affected by the following statement by Levi (157)?

"The amount of adjustment in the interest rates vis-a-vis spot or forward exchange rates depends on the 'thinness' of the markets. The spot exchange market and the securities markets are generally more active than the forward market. It is likely, therefore, that a large part of the adjustment toward interest parity will take place in the forward rate. ... We can therefore think of the forward premium as being determined by the interest differential.

---

# E. ATTACKS ON THE ERM AND THE RESPONSE

## 1. Black Wednesday: September 16, 1992

Britain withdrew from the EMS on September 16, 1992, the victim of a market whose participants believed, despite repeated assertions of commitment by the British government, that the U.K. could do nothing to prevent an inevitable devaluation of the pound. An underlying question is whether devaluation was due to massive speculation or to fundamental economics. In either case, the events underscored the fragility of the EMS.

The following excerpts give both a market perspective and a quasi-official view of the events. References to Maastricht concern the treaty for economic and monetary union of EC members, signed in December 1992. The treaty, which EC members each had to ratify, set a timetable and criteria for economic convergence that would permit monetary union. We turn to Maastricht later in this chapter.

### SAUL HANSELL, "TAMING THE TRILLION-DOLLAR MONSTER," INSTITUTIONAL INVESTOR

December 1992, 47–53 ("Hansell").

Sunday, September 13, dawned as a perfect day for the annual retreat of a large U.S. investment bank's foreign exchange unit. The Florida sun shone brightly as the traders hit the golf course. Then across the links came a bearer of bad tidings, a messenger in a golf cart searching for the firm's head forex trader: The Italian lira had just been devalued by 7 percent. The 35 traders were ordered to return to New York. There was a silver lining, however: The firm had been short lira.

It was a lucky break, the head trader recalls. Against his better judgment, he had sold lira on Friday, going along with many dealers who sold the currency at the end of the trading week for fear of just such a weekend devaluation. At the time, he had not been happy with his lira position; the firm had made lots of money betting that European central banks would stand behind their commitment to keep their currencies within the ranges specified under the Exchange Rate Mechanism. "If people didn't get immediate gratification [from shorting a currency in anticipation of a devaluation], they got out," he said. "We made money this way all the time, and I always said I'd never bet on an ERM realignment."

Back in New York he worked through Sunday night, taking his profit in lira, then dragging himself home for a shower and some sleep as the sun rose. "Then it came to me, a big believer in the ERM," he says emphatically. "They'd devalued the lira, which they'd said they would not do. That told the market the emperor has no clothes. So we prepared for a second wave and sold sterling."

Tidal wave was more like it, as investors and corporations around the world suddenly lost faith in the willingness of Europe's governments to allow the ERM to determine exchange rates; soon they were frantically bailing out of weaker currencies, such as sterling. By Wednesday, September 16, the Bank of England had spent a reported $15 billion—nearly half of Britain's foreign-currency reserves—buying pounds, and it raised interest rates from 10 to 12 percent, then to 15 percent. When it became clear that none of these actions was going to stop the selling pressure, Britain pulled out of the ERM.

**Market quakes**

September 16 has now been dubbed Black Wednesday—an implicit comparison to Black Monday, the 508–point decline in the U.S. stock market on October 19, 1987. The pound closed on Black Wednesday at 2.71 deutsche marks, down only 3 percent. Yet for the traders, investors and central bankers, the sheer violence of the selling still generates the sort of bewildered disbelief that hung over Wall Street at the end of 1987.

. . .

In the long run, however, the central lesson is that the normally benign, long-term capital of institutional investors can, when provoked by external factors, turn into an unstoppable monster that can ransack markets and terrorize economies.

By September 16, hundreds of companies with factories and offices in Britain and thousands of pension funds, insurance companies and other investors that owned sterling-denominated stocks and bonds tried to hedge their exposures, leading to the deluge of sterling for sale. Both market makers and central bankers were fully aware of the growth of world trade and the explosion of global investing. And yet they were shocked by the inability of the central banks to tame the selling. ...

## INTERNATIONAL MONETARY FUND, WORLD ECONOMIC OUTLOOK: INTERIM ASSESSMENT

January 1993, 1–6.

Tensions had been growing in the summer, following the Danish referendum rejecting the Maastricht treaty in early June and the subsequent strengthening of the deutsche mark within the ERM. The lira and sterling experienced particularly strong downward pressures. For the lira, market concern over the country's high level of public debt and its excessive budget deficit contributed to these pressures, especially in view of the risk that progress toward economic and monetary union (EMU), with its convergence requirements, would now be more difficult. In the United Kingdom, the continued recession and a weak current account position influenced market perceptions that the pound sterling might be devalued within the ERM, given the apparent constraints on interest rate policy in that country. The rise in the Bundesbank discount rate on July 16 and further declines in short-term interest rates in the United States added to the tensions by putting upward pressure on the deutsche mark relative to other EMS currencies.

Strains in the ERM during the summer were partially countered by intervention, particularly in support of the lira by the Bank of Italy. Tensions were also partially absorbed by increases in interest rates outside Germany (Chart 1) and by a strengthening of the deutsche mark against other ERM currencies (Chart 3).

From the end of August, anticipation of the French referendum on the Maastricht treaty on September 20 led to a further intensification of pressures within the ERM as opinion polls began to show a significant risk of rejection. At the same time, other developments added to tensions and triggered market speculation that some currencies might be devalued. The dollar declined to a historic low against the deutsche mark early in September as the U.S. Federal Reserve moved to lower interest rates further in response to weak domestic activity. Later, after a decision by Finland to float the markka, the Swedish krona came under intense pressure, leading the authorities to raise official rates on excess drawings on the central bank in steps up to 500 percent to defend the peg to the European currency unit (ECU).

**Chart 1. Major Industrial Countries: Short-Term Interest Rates**
*(In percent a year)*

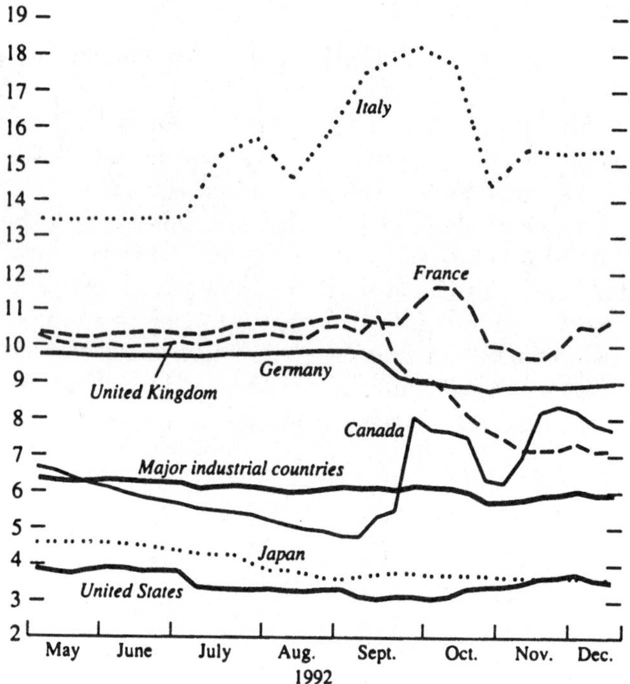


By the second week of September, massive intervention by European central banks was required to prevent the Italian lira from falling below its ERM floor, despite a substantial increase in short-term interest rates. On September 12 the lira was devalued within the ERM, by 7 percent, and the Bundesbank agreed to lower its official interest rates, albeit only marginally. In the following week, however, the lira remained under pressure, and the Spanish peseta fell from the top to the bottom of the wide band. On September 16 the pound sterling became the focus of market attention, and massive intervention was required to keep it from falling below its ERM floor. . . .

**Chart 3. European Monetary System: Positions in the ERM**

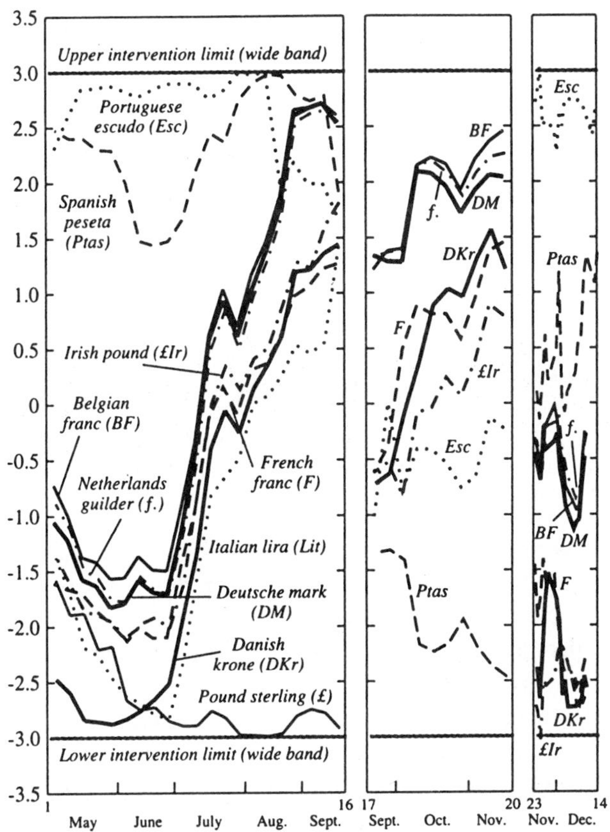


---

Hansell gives some of the political shadings deliberately omitted by the IMF:

> . . . Sterling had been under severe pressure since the Bundesbank raised German interest rates in July, which provided incentives to sell lower-yielding currencies to buy deutsche marks. While the U.S. dollar simply traded down in the market, the terms of the ERM forced the British government to keep sterling's value at no less than 2.80 deutsche marks. The two most direct ways to do that would be to raise U.K.

interest rates or to devalue the pound. Both were politically unpalatable.

The French vote on Maastricht seemed to offer a way out. If French voters said no, or narrowly yes, which officials believed likely, the U.K. authorities thought they could use it as political cover to raise rates or devalue the currency. "If we had raised rates to defend sterling in August, we would have fueled the anti-Maastricht sentiments and the anti-ERM sentiments," says one government official. U.K. authorities also feared that such a move might even bring down the shaky new government of Prime Minister John Major. "If we raised rates in August, and needed to raise them again after the French vote, the political consequences would have been dire," the official admits.

Instead they attempted to support the pound through market intervention. Using intervention to fight against the mark for nearly six weeks had rarely occurred since the Bretton Woods era ended in 1971. Yet the U.K. did have $40 billion in currency reserves, recently bolstered by an ECU10 billion bond issue and unlimited ability to borrow under the ERM.

The intervention held through mid-September. Then, the weekend before the French vote, the Italian lira was devalued within the ERM, and Germany cut rates by a quarter point on the following Monday. The Bank of England was forced to abandon its covert intervention, by which it bought sterling in such a manner as to appear to the market that there was a surge of natural activity. Instead, it was very visibly defending the pound at the bottom of its range. To the Bank of England's traders on Tuesday, it seemed feasible to survive until Friday.

They were wrong. Early Wednesday the bank intervened publicly, buying sterling at around Dm2.78 in conjunction with the Bundesbank and the Banque de France. Within two hours of the opening on that day, however, sterling was at its Dm2.7780 limit against the deutsche mark. Calls came in to dealers from all over the world, from corporations, investors and speculators, all trying to sell sterling and buy deutsche marks.

By 11:00 a.m. the government realized that intervention alone wouldn't work, and announced it would raise short-term rates from 10 to 12 percent. The pound recovered a bit, then fell back to the floor. Just after 2:00 p.m. the government said it would hike rates to 15 percent. The selling pressure only increased.

"It was ludicrous," recalls Barclays' Bate. "You can't take a country in a recession and raise rates by 50 percent." By that point, he notes, "it was one-way traffic. It was apparent that you had a structure in place that wasn't going to survive." The government finally recognized that reality. At 4:00 p.m., after spending an estimated $15 billion, the bank stopped buying pounds and at 7:45 p.m. Chancellor of the

Exchequer Norman Lamont announced that Britain would pull out of the ERM.

---

The IMF has the last word here explaining how underlying economic performance convinced the market a devaluation must occur.

... The French referendum provided a specific focus for the intensification of speculative pressures, but there were more fundamental economic forces at work, stemming from divergences in economic policies and performances across Europe.

In particular, notwithstanding considerable progress toward economic convergence, several countries still had relatively large inflation differentials vis-á-vis the best inflation performers in the ERM, and in some cases the resulting cumulative losses of competitiveness suggested that a realignment of exchange rates would be necessary at some point. In addition, there was a growing conflict between monetary policy objectives in Germany and those in many other European countries because of cyclical divergences. These intra-European tensions were aggravated by the weakness of the U.S. economy, the marked decline in U.S. interest rates, and the associated shift of funds into assets denominated in the stronger European currencies, especially the deutsche mark.

A high degree of economic convergence has been recognized as a condition for exchange rate stability in the EC since the breakdown of the Bretton Woods system of fixed rates in the early 1970s. Early attempts to peg exchange rates ran into difficulties because the participating economies diverged significantly in terms of growth and inflation and because oil price disturbances and different interpretations of the causes of the stagflation of the 1970s provided a poor basis for effective policy coordination. From the early 1980s, however, the new consensus that emerged on the need to pursue medium-term policy objectives, together with the discipline imposed by the ERM, contributed to greater economic convergence. This led to a reduction in the frequency of currency realignments,[7] and all EC currencies with the exception of the Greek drachma eventually joined the ERM. These achievements encouraged the Community to put forward ambitious plans for a gradual transition to EMU.

... From the time the pound sterling joined the ERM in 1990—at an exchange rate that was thought to strike a reasonable balance between the goal of reducing inflation and the need to maintain competitiveness—up to the recent crisis, sterling had appreciated by 10 percent in real terms against the deutsche mark. Compared with its low of 1987, the pound's real appreciation against the mark had been close to

7. Before the September 1992 crisis, the most recent previous realignment took place in January 1987, which was the eleventh realignment since the inception of the EMS in 1979.

20 percent. Similarly, the lira was last realigned in 1987, but from that time to mid–1992 the relatively large increase in Italian labor costs had resulted in a real appreciation of some 18 percent against the deutsche mark. The peseta and the escudo had also appreciated in real terms vis-á-vis the deutsche mark in recent years.

... The pressures for an exchange rate realignment, which had been building for some years as a result of divergent price and cost developments, could reasonably have been expected to persist—or in some cases to intensify—in the future. The deterioration of cost competitiveness was probably smaller for tradable goods industries subject to external market discipline. Nevertheless, there was a clear signal to financial markets of the growing overvaluation of several currencies.

It seems likely that inadequate budgetary convergence reinforced perceptions that some currencies were vulnerable, since experience points to the risk that large fiscal imbalances sooner or later will add to inflationary pressures. Moreover, the introduction of restrictive measures to eliminate excessive fiscal deficits may contribute to downward pressure on the exchange rate during the initial stages of the adjustment process. Apart from Greece, where the large fiscal deficit and high inflation rate have precluded membership in the ERM, the lack of fiscal convergence is serious in Portugal, Spain, and especially Italy, which are expected to have general government deficits amounting to 5¼, 5, and 10½ percent of GDP in 1992, respectively, even though the margin of slack, and hence the impact of automatic stabilizers, is small.[13] In Italy, the unsustainable nature of the budgetary situation was, and remains, particularly evident. Italy has had deficits close to, or greater than, 10 percent of GDP for some years, and the public debt-GDP ratio is expected to approach 110 percent in early 1993. In the absence of stringent fiscal consolidation, moreover, deficits are projected to rise substantially.

Evidence that market participants did not regard the exchange rates that prevailed in mid–1992 as sustainable over the medium term can be found in the evolution of interest rate differentials vis-á-vis Germany. These had narrowed substantially over the past decade for those countries that achieved a high degree of convergence, but relatively large differentials persisted for Italy, Portugal, and Spain even before the recent turbulence (Chart 13). Although short-term interest differentials have generally narrowed in recent years, long-term differentials remained fairly large for these countries. This suggests that markets saw a significant probability of substantial depreciations of the lira, the peseta, and the escudo over the medium term, even though the perceived risk of realignment in the near term was small; such expectations were

**13.** The recent increase in the U.K. budget deficit may also have influenced market perceptions of the sustainability of sterling's position in the ERM. The U.K. general government deficit is expected to exceed 6 percent of GDP in 1992, but since the deficit has widened, mainly because of the deep recession, it can be expected to fall as the economy recovers. Belgium is also expected to have a deficit of about 6 percent of GDP in 1992, but Belgium's inflation rate has been quite low in recent years.

consistent with the relatively strong positions of the escudo and the peseta in the exchange rate band during the first half of 1992. After the Danish referendum in June, however, short-term differentials for these three countries began to widen, and their currencies weakened significantly in the exchange rate band over the course of the summer (Chart 13).

**Chart 13. Interest Rate Differentials vis-à-vis Germany**

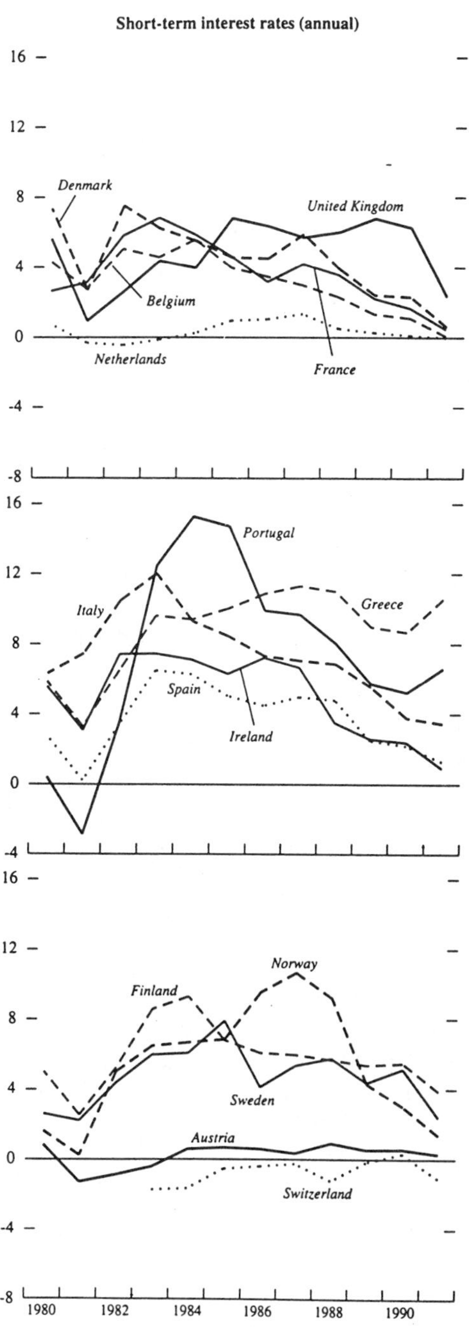

As exchange market tensions subsided somewhat after the September crisis, short-term interest differentials generally declined to the levels prevailing before the crisis. Only in the United Kingdom, however, have short-term rates been reduced significantly below those in Germany—a development that has contributed to the relatively large depreciation of the pound sterling. In contrast, long-term rates remain higher in the United Kingdom than in Germany, although the differential has narrowed slightly. The persistence of relatively large long-term interest differentials for Italy, Spain, and Portugal even after the depreciation of their currencies suggests continued uncertainty about the medium-term inflation outlook as a result of large fiscal imbalances, particularly in Italy.

**Cyclical Divergences and German Unification**

Cyclical divergences have developed since 1990 between Germany, where rising fiscal deficits in the wake of unification led to overheating, and other European countries, where output has fallen or growth has been insufficient to prevent further increases in unemployment. In these circumstances, the need for Germany to pursue a tight monetary policy posed a difficult dilemma for many other European countries, since the high level of interest rates necessary to defend the commitment to stable exchange rates increasingly appeared to be inappropriate in light of domestic macroeconomic conditions. This dilemma between external and domestic objectives affected not only the ERM countries but also those European countries that directly or indirectly had been shadowing the deutsche mark through unilateral pegs, including Finland, Norway, and Sweden.

The conflict with domestic requirements was particularly sharp in the United Kingdom and Finland, which have both been in protracted recession since 1990.

. . .

But the intensity of the speculative pressures that developed against the French franc, in particular, is difficult to explain in view of the high degree of convergence of the French economy since the mid–1980s and its relatively strong external competitive position in recent years. There may have been a perception that the franc was vulnerable because the high unemployment rate in France would limit the scope for significant interest rate increases, as had been the case in the United Kingdom. Perhaps more important, after the exit of the lira and the pound from the ERM, markets appear to have felt that the EMS might break down completely, in which case speculation could have forced the deutsche mark to appreciate against most other European currencies, including the French franc.

. . .

It is unclear, even in retrospect, if the political events would have triggered a crisis had the underlying economic forces been less divergent. However, an exchange rate realignment at an appropriate moment to adjust for divergent fundamentals—with adequate support from strengthened convergence policies together with an intensification of efforts to contain the budget deficit in Germany—could undoubtedly have reduced the strains on the system.

The smaller crisis in November, which led to another realignment of the peseta and to a realignment of the escudo, appears to have reflected market perceptions that these two currencies were vulnerable because of the large inflation differentials in the past and the relatively small realignment of the peseta in September. The decision to float the Swedish krona, which preceded the latest ERM realignment, was related to a failure to reach a new agreement to reduce the excessive fiscal deficit. In addition, notwithstanding the successful defense of the krona in September, the country's deepening economic and financial crisis left the currency vulnerable to renewed pressures. The decision to float the Norwegian krone in early December reflected mounting pressures in the wake of the depreciation of the Swedish krona.

Several important lessons can be drawn from these episodes of exchange market turmoil. The suspension from the ERM of the lira and sterling has left the reputation of the EMS as a zone of monetary stability badly shaken and the system itself potentially vulnerable in the future—not least in view of the fixed timetable for the EMU process and the continued uncertainty about the ratification of the Maastricht treaty. To reduce the risk of a repetition of the crisis, progress toward convergence will need to be reinforced considerably. ... Moreover, although participation in the ERM can be an important element in countries' convergence strategies, recent experience underscores that a fixed exchange rate is likely to be challenged sooner or later unless it is backed by forceful and successful adjustment efforts. To the extent that convergence is achieved only gradually, it will be necessary to undertake small realignments from time to time to avoid the buildup of pressures for larger, more disruptive adjustments.

The crises have confirmed that fully sterilized intervention has only limited effectiveness in influencing exchange rates. Even where parities were successfully defended, as in the case of France and Sweden (in September), substantial adjustments of interest rates were required to support intervention. The episodes also suggest that defense of fixed exchange rates is most successful when it is closely coordinated by the central banks on opposite sides of exchange market pressures. In addition, the pressures against some currencies such as the French franc and the Danish krone, for which the fundamentals did not justify expectations of a realignment, have underlined both the desirability of ensuring rapid progress toward EMU and the crucial importance of the credibility of countries' commitment to converge. The events since September have also underscored the need to strengthen the functioning of the EMS during the transition period.

Finally, the recent episodes have illustrated the extent to which the private sector is willing to take positions when a currency is felt to be overvalued. Indeed, both the size of the market and the number of private operators able to inject very large sums into currency markets are clearly much greater now than in the past, and both have probably been underestimated.

### *Questions*

1. What is the connection between interest rate policy and the evolution of the ERM?

a. Take German interest rate policy as an example. What accounts for the policy? What was its effect on the German economy and on other currencies?

b. In early 1992, when the U.K. was still in EMS, the pound was very near the lower edge of the band. Aside from pulling out, what were Prime Minister Major's options? Some observers have referred to the "tension between realignment and recession." What do they mean? Evaluate the options from Major's point of view. Was membership in the EMS a good move for Britain?

---

## 2. The ERM Crisis of 1993

The markets were not mollified by the 1992 changes in the EMS. Spain and Portugal were forced to devalue their currencies further within the ERM during May 1993. In July, the French franc came under attack again, having withstood attacks in January and February. Denmark and Belgium were also under pressure. By the end of July, the EMS seemed seriously threatened. On July 30, the French franc fell below its ERM floor rate several times but returned as central banks intervened. Defending their own currencies were the central banks of Spain, Portugal, Denmark, and Belgium.

Since Germany's inflation exceeded 4%, the Bundesbank only gradually and slightly lowered German interest rates during July. This failed to reverse the market pressure. The market read into Germany's policy an unwillingness to make decisive cuts in the discount rate even to save the EMS.

On August 2, the eight countries in the EMS agreed to widen the margins for currency fluctuations to 15% from 2.25% or 6%. Germany and the Netherlands agreed to maintain the 2.25% band for their two currencies.

In response, "the founding fathers of the EMS, former French president Valery Giscard d'Estaing and former West German chancellor Helmut Schmidt issued a joint statement saying the agreement was tantamount to suspending the EMS." (A. Fisher et al., "EC governments strive to contain ERM differences," Financial Times, August 3, 1993, 1.)

By October 1993, EC officials were saying "a formal tightening of the bands could not take place in the near future . . . " ("Brussels rules out return to ERM bands," Financial Times, October 15, 1993, 3). They urged instead informal arrangements, like the German/Dutch one. Indeed, by late December 1993, "most currencies . . . [had] crept back into the fluctuation bands they were forced to abandon when the system blew up last August" ("Bands returning to a tighter tune," Financial Times, December 20, 1993, 19). Within the 2.25% band were France, Denmark, Belgium, and Ireland and within the 6% band were Spain and Portugal. One explanation was that Germany now needed lower interest rates too.

While Germany and France were in recession, the U.K. economy began to grow after it withdrew from EMS. Wages actually fell and inflation was relatively low. The trade balance improved. Sterling began to recover on exchange markets. A British financial specialist opined that "Leaving the ERM was unquestionably a good thing . . . It freed us from being dragged further down by the continent's recession and allowed growth to begin."

## 3. An American Call for an End to EMS

In July 1993, a group of six American economists who teach at the Massachusetts Institute of Technology and whose numbers include several Nobel laureates, argued that it was time to end the EMS.

OLIVIER BLANCHARD, RUDIGER DORNBUSCH, STANLEY FISCHER, FRANCO MODIGLIANI, PAUL A. SAMUELSON, AND ROBERT SOLOW, "WHY THE EMS DESERVES AN EARLY BURIAL"

Financial Times. July 29, 1993, p. 9.

The current turmoil in the currency markets and the broader crisis of rising unemployment in Europe is the most striking evidence yet that European monetary policies and exchange rate arrangements are profoundly counterproductive.

By far the most important factor responsible for this debacle is the Bundesbank's policy of high interest rates, combined with certain features of the European Monetary System which have forced other member countries to follow suit: these include the mobility of capital across member countries and the fact that central banks have interpreted the rules of the exchange rate mechanism to require not only the maintenance of fixed exchange rates but also the avoidance of parity adjustments.

The result of high interest rates across Europe has been that unemployment has risen to record levels. Governments have done little but seek a variety of excuses for the loss of jobs. It looks as if the 1930s are being re-enacted. Then, it was felt to be imperative to hang on to gold at any price: today the feeling is to hang on to the D–Mark.

It is not useful to spend too much time allocating blame—on a Bundesbank that fights inflation of "only" 4 per cent, on EMS member countries such as France, which opts for a hard currency at the price of an entirely unwarranted recession, or on a country like Spain, which believes that being in Europe means being a member of the ERM.

In our view, the essential issue is for the EMS countries to shift priorities, putting unemployment at the top of the list and recognising that much labour can be reabsorbed through reflationary policies, beginning with a sharp cut in interest rates.

Of course, countries would have to accept the depressing implications that such a move would have on their exchange rate with the D–Mark, without committing their reserves in an attempt to support the current parity. This means they must be prepared to see their exchange rates fall below their lower limits, and hence face ejection from the ERM.

Ideally it might be hoped that France would take the initiative by slashing interest rates and letting the franc float. Other European countries, including Belgium and Spain, would follow. At this point two possible scenarios are conceivable: the first is that, faced with the prospect of a sharp loss in competitiveness, Germany would limit the damage by cutting interest rates. Within just a few weeks the long-awaited cut in European interest rates would have materialised.

Second, the Bundesbank would refuse to cut rates beyond another token amount, and then Germany would be left alone in the ERM (thereby floating too). This would mean the end of the EMS as presently constituted. But this should not be a cause for regret.

To be sure, there was a time when the ERM, with fixed parities and Bundesbank leadership, performed a very useful function. But in their quest for moderate inflation, countries adopted an unwavering D–Mark peg, which is now becoming a problem.

There is no reason to equate yielding on existing ERM parities with sacrificing the entire anti-inflationary effort of the 1980s. France has no inflation problem—unlike Germany. France can, therefore, afford to do without the recession which the Bundesbank feels it must impose on Germany. Spain has a phenomenal unemployment problem which should be the immediate focus of attention, not a currency peg that is killing growth and prosperity.

Some might bemoan the ensuing incapacitation of the EMS as a rude shock to the dream of European unity. But such a concern is unwarranted.

First, the central element of the European Community is the set of common market institutions, and these should and would remain in place even if the EMS were temporarily impaired. Second, plans for European monetary union are already in tatters. Thus, leaving the present system would only acknowledge a truth that many in Europe refuse to face. Forsaking the present arrangements is the only way to move quickly towards a new European monetary system in which a crisis such as the current one cannot be repeated.

### *Questions*

1. Was the early August widening of the ERM band a fundamental change in the ERM? How would the move have affected speculators?

2. How effective has the EMS been as an exchange regime?

3. Evaluate the British solution. Could the other members have done the same with the same results? Did they effectively do it in August 1993?

---

## F. THE EUROPEAN MONETARY UNION

### 1. The Expected Benefits of a Monetary Union

As early as 1969, EC heads of state wanted to coordinate monetary policy. Twenty years later, a committee chaired by Jacques Delors proposed an Economic and Monetary Union (EMU). The committee described the expected costs and benefits of EMU.

### HERVE CARRE AND KAREN JOHNSON, "PROGRESS TOWARD A EUROPEAN MONETARY UNION"

Federal Reserve Bulletin, October 1991, 769–76.

. . .

According to Robert A. Mundell's seminal contribution to the literature on "optimum currency areas," the judgment on the formation of a monetary area depends on balancing two factors:

1. Monetary union, especially with a single currency, provides benefits by eliminating transaction costs and the uncertainty associated with exchange rate variability.

2. If labor and capital cannot move freely among the regions of the union, adjustment to some kinds of economic shocks, without changes in the nominal exchange rates of the regions, will lead to unemployment and lost output.

On this basis, the overall cost-benefit balance of EMU may be uncertain because labor mobility in the Community is limited and is bound to remain limited at least for a time. Direct examination of the criteria for an optimum currency area for the EC member countries suggests that regional problems are likely. Compared with the U.S. economy, the EC member states show significantly lower labor mobility; have experienced to a greater degree economic shocks that have affected the constituent regions asymmetrically; and, as a result, have relied far more on adjustment of real exchange rates across regions.

The analysis of the costs and benefits of monetary union has been extended to include other considerations. In particular, some analysts have argued that the openness and the industrial diversification of the economies concerned are important criteria that need to be taken into account. The larger the volume of interregional trade, the greater are the cost savings stemming from a monetary union that links the regions. Changes in exchange rates to help sustain economic performance are less critical in a diversified industrial economy, with more intra-industry trade, than in a more specialized economy. In addition, recent developments in the theory of economic growth point to dynamic gains, potentially much greater than the direct gains associated with the elimination of transaction costs and more stable exchange rates. These gains would result from an improvement in the business climate that leads to a self-reinforcing cycle of stronger growth.

In 1990, the EC Commission staff published its evaluation of the potential benefits and costs of forming an economic and monetary union. On balance, the Commission staff found that EMU benefits are likely to outweigh the costs (see box 2).

---

### 2. The Main Benefits and Costs of EMU

The Commission of the European Communities recently completed an analysis of the main benefits and costs of forming EMU. The following statement, which is quoted from that study, groups the benefits and costs under five headings.

(i) *Efficiency and Growth.* Elimination of exchange rate uncertainty and transaction costs, and further refinements to the single market are sure to yield gains in efficiency. Through improving the risk-adjusted rate of return on capital and the business climate more generally there are good chances that a credible commitment to achieving EMU in the not-too-distant future will help further strengthen the trend of investment and growth.

(ii) *Price Stability.* This is a generally accepted objective, and beneficial economically in its own right. The problem is that of attaining price stability at least cost, and then maintaining it. The Community has the opportunity of being able to build its monetary union on the basis of the reputation for monetary stability of its least inflationary Member States. Given the paramount importance of credibility and expectations in winning the continuous fight against inflation at least cost, this is a great advantage.

(iii) *Public Finance.* A new framework of incentives and constraints will condition national budgetary policies, for which the key-words will be autonomy (to respond to country-specific problems), discipline (to avoid excessive deficits) and coordination (to assure an appropriate overall policy-mix in the Community). EMU will also bring valuable gains for many countries' national budgets through reductions in interest rates, as inflation and exchange risk premiums are eliminated. These benefits will very probably outweigh the loss of seigniorage revenue to be experienced by some countries.

(iv) *Adjusting to Economic Shocks.* The main potential cost of EMU is that represented by the loss of monetary and exchange rate policy as an instrument of economic adjustment at the national level. This loss should not be exaggerated since exchange rate changes by the Community in relation to the rest of the world will remain possible, whereas within the EMS the nominal exchange rate instrument is already largely abandoned, and EMU will reduce the incidence of country-specific shocks. Relative real labour costs will still be able to change; budgetary policies at national and Community levels will also absorb shocks and aid adjustment, and the external current account constraint will disappear.

Moreover, model simulations suggest that with EMU, compared to other regimes, the Community would have been able to absorb the major economic shocks of the last two decades with less disturbance in terms of the rate of inflation and, to some extent also, the level of real activity. This is of renewed relevance, given that the Gulf crisis of summer 1990 once again subjects the Community to a potentially damaging economic shock.

(v) *The International System.* With the ECU becoming a major international currency, there will be advantages for the Community as banks and enterprises conduct more of their international business in their own currency; moreover the monetary authorities will be able to economize in external reserves and achieve some international seigniorage gains. EMU will also mean that the Community will be better placed, through its unity, to secure its interests in international coordination processes and negotiate for a balanced multipolar system.

---

## 2. The Maastricht Treaty

At their December 1992 meeting in Maastricht, Holland, EC member governments agreed to a treaty that would carry them to economic and monetary union by January 1, 1999. As you read the summary of the treaty by The Bank of England, compare it to the plan outlined by the Delors Committee. What has changed? Why?

### "THE MAASTRICHT AGREEMENT ON ECONOMIC AND MONETARY UNION"

Bank of England Q. Bull., February 1992.

#### Introduction

The agreement on the draft Treaty on European Union by EC Heads of State or Government at Maastricht last December, which included amendments to the Treaty of Rome on economic and monetary union, marked an important step in the process of European monetary integration that has come to the fore in the past few years. That process was given added momentum by the recommendations of the Delors Committee, accepted at the Madrid Summit in June 1989 as a basis for further work.[1] Stage 1 comprises closer economic and monetary co-operation between member states within the existing institutional framework, aimed at greater convergence of economic performance. It also involves the completion of the Single Market and the strengthening of Community competition policy.

The Strasbourg Summit in December 1989 agreed to hold an early Intergovernmental Conference on EMU, which was convened in December 1990. The IGC held intensive discussions involving finance ministers of all member states, which led to Presidency recommendations last December for Treaty amendments deemed necessary to implement full-scale EMU, with permanently locked exchange rates and a single monetary policy, leading to the adoption of a single currency in due course. The proposed amendments included, in a protocol to the Treaty, a detailed Statute for a European System of Central Banks (ESCB), embracing the existing national central banks and headed by a new monetary institution, the European Central Bank (ECB), based largely on specifications drawn up by the Committee of EC Central Bank Governors. The EMU IGC was accompanied by a parallel conference on political union.

It was agreed at Maastricht that full EMU—known as Stage 3—should begin, for those member states judged eligible to participate, no later than 1 January 1999. But if the Heads of State or Government decide, by qualified majority,[2] on the basis of recommendations by the Finance Ministers' Council (ECOFIN), and after consulting the European Parliament, that a majority of member states fulfil the necessary conditions, they may set an earlier date for the start of Stage 3. Stage 3 could then start as early as 1997, or earlier if the necessary conditions are met. It was also agreed that there should be an early transitional phase—Stage 2—which will reinforce economic convergence beyond Stage 1, including the necessary institutional developments: principally, a European Monetary Institute (EMI), with an advisory and consultative role, taking over the functions of the Committee of Governors of EC Central Banks. It will aim to strengthen the co-ordination of member states' monetary policies, while still leaving ultimate responsibility for policy with national authorities. Stage 2 will also involve technical preparations for Stage 3, and will commence on 1 January 1994.

The British Government played an active part in the IGCs, subject to its general reserve that it could not accept any commitment by the United Kingdom to move to a single currency and monetary policy

1. *Report on Economic and Monetary Union in the European Community* (1989).

2. When the Council of the EC acts by qualified majority, members' votes are weighted as follows: France, Germany, Italy and the United Kingdom, 10 each; Spain & Belgium, Greece, Netherlands and Portugal, 5 each; Denmark and Ireland, 3 each and Luxembourg, 2. For an act to be adopted on a proposal from the Commission, 64 votes in favour are needed. In other cases, as here, 54 votes cast by at least 8 members are needed.

without a separate decision by government and Parliament at the appropriate time. In the event the Government, while being generally satisfied with the technical arrangements proposed for the next two stages of EMU, and in particular their emphasis on free market principles, did not commit the United Kingdom to joining Stage 3, but instead obtained provisions which allow this country an option to join that Stage, subject to a final decision by government and Parliament nearer the time. This option is contained in a protocol that has the legal force of the Treaty. Denmark also reserved the right, in a separate protocol, not to move automatically to Stage 3. The United Kingdom will participate fully in Stage 2 (assuming ratification of the amended Treaty) and firmly expects to meet the convergence conditions that have been set—which will allow it to move to Stage 3 if Parliament so decides. Because of the convergence criteria (described below), no member state can be certain for several years yet that it will be in Stage 3.

The text of the amended Treaty was completed and signed on 7 February, and will be subject to ratification by member states later this year, which would allow the amended Treaty to come into force on 1 January 1993.

**Key features of Stage 3**

Stage 3 will start with the irrevocable locking of exchange rates between participating currencies and with the assumption by the ECB and ESCB of their full powers under the Treaty. They will be responsible for issuing and managing the single currency—the ECU—that will replace national currencies in due course. The basket definition of the ECU will cease to apply when the locking of exchange rates takes place, but the single currency is unlikely to replace national currencies until some time, possibly up to several years, after that. At that time, the national central banks will issue the single currency, subject to ECB authorisation.

The primary objectives and basic tasks of the ESCB and ECB are laid down in Article 105 of the Treaty and Chapter 2 of the ESCB Statute; and the System's structure, operations, governance, and accountability in Articles 106–8 and 109a and b of the Treaty and Chapters III–VI of the Statute. Their primary objective will be to maintain price stability. They will also be required to support the 'general economic policies in the Community', without prejudice to the price stability objective. Their actions will be required to be in accordance with the principles of an open market economy, favouring an efficient allocation of resources.

The ESCB will have as its main tasks the formulation and execution of the single monetary policy, the holding and management of participating member states' official foreign exchange reserves, promotion of the smooth operation of payments systems, and contribution to 'the smooth conduct of policies pursued by the competent authorities relating to the prudential supervision of credit institutions and the stability of the financial system.' This mandate will imply pooling of national responsibility for monetary policy through participation in the Governing Council of the ECB. National central bank governors from participating states will be members of that Council, along with a full time Executive Board appointed by the Heads of State or Government of member states. Members of the Executive Board will have non-renewable eight-year terms. The terms of office of national central bank governors will be at least five years.

No specific *operational* role in prudential supervision is given to the ECB, but the ECOFIN Council will have power to confer specific tasks relating to policies on prudential supervision on the ECB in due course. Such a step would need to be based on a proposal from the Commission, and would require the assent of the European Parliament, and unanimity of all member states in the ECOFIN Council. Furthermore, the ECB and national central banks are empowered to provide clearing and payments facilities, and the ECB will be able to issue regulations on those activities within the Community and with third countries (Statute Article 22). Although the Treaty does not give the ECB an operational role in supervision, the ECB will inevitably be involved in major policy decisions in that area, as in other areas affecting monetary policy, and it would be able to supply liquidity to the banking system through its power 'to conduct credit operations with credit institutions and other market participants, with the lending being based on adequate collateral', subject to its other objectives and responsibilities (Statute Article 18.1, 2nd tiret). National central banks can maintain their existing role in prudential supervision, where they have one.

In the pursuit of their objectives and tasks under the Treaty, the ECB and national central banks are required to be free from all outside interference. Staff of the institutions and members of their decision-making bodies will be required not to seek or take instructions from any outside body, including Community bodies and national governments, and these bodies will undertake not to seek to influence the ECB or national central banks in the performance of their tasks.

Careful thought was given to the question how as powerful an institution as the ECB could be made accountable without detracting unduly from its policy independence. It was recognised that severe organisational and procedural difficulties would be encountered if the ECB were to be made directly accountable to twelve national governments and twelve parliaments individually. Accountability to governments is therefore to be secured through the ECOFIN Council, whose President can participate (but not vote) in meetings of the ECB's Governing Council and submit motions for its consideration; and which may invite the President of the ECB to discuss with it matters relating to ECB tasks and objectives. The ECOFIN Council will also be empowered to amend certain parts of the ESCB Statute, although not those relating to its independence or principal objectives and tasks. The ECB must address an annual report on monetary policy to the European Parliament, the ECOFIN Council, the Commission and the European Council (of Heads of State or Government); and the ECB's President will be required to present the report to the ECOFIN Council and the European Parliament, which may debate it. The ECB President and other members of its Executive Board can be requested to attend hearings of competent committees of the European Parliament. Central bank governors will be free to attend national parliamentary committees in their national capacity or as a representative of the Governing Council of the ECB, although it is possible that they could not be required to do so in the latter capacity.

Another key area of discussion was the allocation of responsibility for external exchange rate policy between the ECOFIN Council and the ECB. It was agreed that responsibility for the choice of exchange rate system (or regime) for the ECU (the single currency) against non-EC currencies in Stage 3, and the central ECU rate within the system, should remain essentially with the ECOFIN Council (Article 109 paragraph 1). It was also agreed that Ministers may, in the absence of a formal system for the exchange rate, 'formulate general orientations' for exchange rate policy *vis-á-vis* non-EC currencies (Article 109, paragraph 2). But the choice of system and central rates would have to be after consultation with the ECB, in an endeavour to reach consensus consistent with the price stability objective: any policy orientations would have to be without prejudice to that objective. Only experience can show how these arrangements will turn out in practice, but the agreed provisions clearly require that exchange rate policy is consistent with the non-inflationary monetary policy of EMU, and that the ECB will have a strong consultative role in this process. Day-to-day exchange rate operations will be the responsibility of the ECB, exercised in a manner consistent with the provisions on exchange rate policy. The ECB will be provided with a strategic sum—initially up to ECU50 billion—of foreign currency reserves for the conduct of exchange-market intervention (Statute Article 30.1).

Some key aspects of the role and operations of the ESCB were left mainly open for later decision. The precise division of labour between the ECB and national central banks in the execution of monetary policy will be for decision nearer the time, but it was agreed that the ECB would 'to the extent deemed possible and appropriate' conduct its operations through the national central banks (Statute Article 12.1, third paragraph), it being accepted that 'the national central banks are an integral part of the ESCB and shall act in accordance with the guidelines and instructions of the ECB' (Statute Article 14.3).

Acceptable solutions were found for several specific UK concerns in Stage 3—for example, agreement to respect as far as possible existing note-issuing practices, which should allow continuation of Scottish and Northern Irish banks' note issues, subject to ECB authorisation; and to respect existing practices in the design of bank-notes, for example, the retention of the Sovereign's portrait on notes issued by the Bank of England.

**Fiscal policy provisions**

The draft Treaty contains a number of provisions that strengthen the process of fiscal surveillance begun in Stage 1 and introduce constraints in the size of fiscal deficits and their financing. From an early stage there was agreement on the three basic fiscal principles of 'no excessive fiscal deficits', 'no monetary financing' and 'no bailouts', but considerable debate developed about how these should be defined, and how they might be implemented in practice. In the event, agreement was reached on provisions that prohibit the ECB or national central banks from providing credit facilities to government or to Community institutions or other public sector bodies, and from purchasing debt instruments *directly* from them (Article 104). There are also provisions that will prevent the Community and governments of member states assuming the financial commitments of other governments or public authorities in the Community (Article 104b), as a necessary condition for the exercise of effective market discipline on national fiscal policy; and to set up more formal procedures of surveillance over fiscal policy, including numerical triggers designed to prompt a Commission investigation into the fiscal policy of member states (Article 104c). In extreme cases, if the ECOFIN Council concludes that policy is grossly in error, there is provision for sanctions on member states failing to correct excessive deficits (Article 104c, paragraph 11), including the imposition of fines.

Other aspects of macroeconomic policy in Stage 3 were left for decision by national governments, subject only to some extension of the kind of general consultation which is already practised as part of economic surveillance under Stage 1 arrangements.

**Key features of Stage 2**

Although UK negotiators agreed on the importance of having a clear picture of what a single currency and monetary policy would entail and contributed positively to that aspect, as to others, they also believed that it was important to focus carefully on what should lie immediately beyond Stage 1. They supported approaches to Stage 2 that saw it as a means of reinforcing convergence by all member states towards a sustainable low inflation performance, thus creating the necessary conditions for eventual monetary union at a later date.

The principal new institutional development in Stage 2 will be the creation of the European Monetary Institute to build on the established policy-consultative activities of the EC Governors' Committee, while still leaving responsibility during Stage 2 clearly in national hands, hence avoiding confusion about where responsibility for policy lies and risks that the credibility of the eventual central institution would be damaged. These arrangements are set out in a protocol containing the EMI Statute. The EMI will, among its other key functions, take over the administration of the European Monetary Co-operation Fund and the accompanying financing mechanisms and monitor the running of the EMS, facilitate the use of the private ECU and oversee the development of the ECU clearing system, be consulted by the national authorities on monetary policy and, within the rules set by ECOFIN, on draft legislation in its field of competence, offer opinions and recommendations to them on these matters, and report annually to the Council on convergence and on the preparation of technical procedures for Stage 3, both the latter by December 1996 at the latest (EMI Statute, Articles 4–7). The EMI will also be entitled to act as agent to manage foreign exchange reserves of member states wishing to hold some of them with the new institution. However, the EMI will not intervene in foreign exchange markets on its own account, and members will not be obliged to hold reserves with it.

All EC central bank governors will be members of the Institute, but there will also be a full-time president who will not be simultaneously a governor (EMI Statute, Article 9). It was agreed that in exercising their responsibilities under the EMI Statute, governors should be independent, but that national central banks themselves need not be independent in Stage 2, before the establishment of the ESCB. National central banks should contribute resources sufficient to enable the EMI to meet its administrative costs. The seat of the EMI (and that of the ECB) was left to be decided by consensus of Heads of State or Government before the end of 1992.

**Convergence criteria**

The Treaty sets out clear and quantified convergence criteria for participation in Stage 3, relating to inflation, government deficits and debt ratios, interest rate differentials, and ERM participation. ... Additional factors, including the extent of integration of markets and developments in unit labour costs and other price indices, are also to be taken into account. These criteria probably cannot be applied purely mechanically, but the UK authorities have frequently urged that judgements on convergence must be based on economic grounds.

Assessment of eligibility to participate in Stage 3 will also include an examination of the compatibility between a member state's legislation affecting the status and role of its central bank and the provisions of the Treaty relating to ECB and national central bank independence. Eligibility will therefore imply important changes in the statutory position of central banks in some member states before the commencement of Stage 3.

**Transition to Stage 3**

The key judgements, both about whether a majority of member states meet the conditions for Stage 3 (if the decision is made in 1996) and about the starting date of that Stage, will be made by the Council meeting in the composition of Heads of State or Government, by qualified majority, acting on reports by the Commission and the EMI, and on the advice of finance ministers and after consultation with the European Parliament. Performance against the convergence criteria will determine which countries may join Stage 3. A majority of member states must be judged to have met the criteria if the decision on commencement is to be taken by 31 December 1996. If a decision to move is not taken then, Stage 3 will start on 1 January 1999; no such majority will be needed then, but whenever the move to Stage 3 occurs only eligible States may join. Those found not eligible will receive a derogation, which will be revoked later if and when a member state is found eligible according to the same criteria.

This raises the possibility that Stage 3 could be formed in 1999 by a smaller group of countries—in theory even as few as two. A reasonable inference would be that, assuming no major unforeseen disruptions, Stage 3 seems fairly likely to begin in January 1999 if not before, although quite possibly with fewer than all the other eleven member states participating (leaving the United Kingdom aside for the moment), and conceivably with less than a majority.

The British Government is fully committed to Stage 2, and the United Kingdom will therefore move to that stage with the rest of the Community (assuming the EMU amendments are ratified). According to the UK Protocol, the United Kingdom would not be required to discontinue overnight (Ways and Means) lending to the Government, unless it moved to Stage 3. Member states are required as appropriate to start the process leading to the independence of the Central Bank. This would not require any action, in the United Kingdom, before a commitment was made to move to Stage 3. The United Kingdom will need to notify the ECOFIN Council of its intention regarding Stage 3 before the end of 1996, depending on the timing of the Council's assessment of convergence. In the event of not joining, it would be able to change its notification and join later, assuming that it satisfied the convergence criteria. The central bank governors of countries not joining Stage 3 would become members of an ECB *General* Council, which would take over the residual functions of the EMI, including in particular the administration of the EMCF and the monitoring of the EMS or a successor exchange rate arrangement governing relations between the single currency and the currencies of member states that do not join Stage 3. It is envisaged that there will be a continuation of arrangements for stabilising exchange rates within the Community in the event that some countries do not join Stage 3.

## Conclusion

The Maastricht agreement on EMU was an important step in the process of European monetary integration, and the culmination of twelve months of complex negotiations to which the United Kingdom contributed positively. The agreement, if ratified, commits the other eleven member states of the Community (subject to Denmark's protocol) to moving to full monetary union by January 1999 at the latest, but participation will depend on meeting the convergence criteria. However, no critical mass of eligible countries will be needed to form monetary union then, and even if convergence proves less good than hoped, it seems probable that at least several countries will be able to satisfy the criteria, given the way in which they have been framed.

The British Government took the view that a final assessment of the costs and benefits of a move to a single monetary policy and single currency could not be made until the time of the Council decision on the appropriateness of such a move. The Government, therefore, did not commit the United Kingdom at Maastricht to joining full monetary union, but instead obtained an option to join which may be exercised nearer the time. There will be a need for government and Parliament to come to a decision on that option a little before the end of 1996. In the meantime, the UK authorities fully expect to meet the convergence conditions. Ratification of the Treaty amendments by Parliament would, moreover, commit the United Kingdom to joining Stage 2 when it starts in January 1994, and to playing a full part in that Stage.

## THE MAIN CONVERGENCE CRITERIA

Four economic criteria for eligibility to join Stage 3 are made explicit in the draft Treaty. These criteria will be used when the Commission and the EMI report to the Council on 'the achievement of a high degree of sustainable convergence' by reference to the individual performance of each member state (Article 109j):

- the achievement of a high degree of price stability; this will be apparent from a rate of inflation which is close to that of, at most, the three best performing Member States in terms of price stability;
- the sustainability of the government financial position; this will be apparent from having achieved a government budgetary position without a deficit that is excessive as determined in accordance with Article 104c(6);
- the observance of the normal fluctuation margins provided for by the Exchange Rate Mechanism of the European Monetary System, for at least two years, without devaluing against the currency of any other Member State;
- the durability of convergence achieved by the Member State and of its participation in the Exchange Rate Mechanism of the European Monetary System being reflected in the long-term interest rate levels.

These are elaborated in the *Protocol on the Convergence Criteria* annexed to the Treaty. There the *inflation* criterion is said to mean that:

- a Member State has a price performance that is sustainable and an average rate of inflation, observed over a period of one year before the examination, that does not exceed that of at most the three best performing Member States in terms of price stability by more than 1½ percentage points. Inflation shall be measured by means of the consumer price index (CPI) on a comparable basis, taking into account differences in national definitions.

The criterion on the *government budgetary position* means that at the time of examination the Member State is not subject to a Council decision, as referred to in Article 104c of the Treaty, that an excessive deficit exists. Article 104c(2) lays down two criteria for the judgment of budgetary performance:

(a) whether the ratio of the planned or actual government deficit to gross domestic product exceeds a reference value, unless

- either the ratio has declined substantially and continuously and reached a level that comes close to the reference value;
- or, alternatively, the excess over the reference value is only exceptional and temporary and the ratio remains close to the reference value;

(b) whether the ratio of government debt to gross domestic product exceeds a reference value, unless the ratio is sufficiently diminishing and approaching the reference value at a satisfactory pace.

The reference values are specified in the Protocol on the Excessive Deficit Procedure:

- 3% for the ratio of the planned or actual government deficit to gross domestic product at market prices.
- 60% for the ratio of government debt to gross domestic product at market prices.

The criterion on *participation in the ERM* means that:

- a Member State has respected the normal fluctuation margins provided for by the Exchange Rate Mechanism of the European Monetary System without severe tensions for at least the last two years before the examination. In particular, the Member State shall not have devalued its currency's bilateral central rate against any other Member State's currency on its own initiative for the same period.

The criterion on *interest rates* means that:

- observed over a period of one year before the examination a Member State has an average nominal long-term interest rate that does not exceed that of at most the three best performing Member States in terms of price stability by more than 2 percentage points. Interest rates shall be measured on the basis of long-term government bonds or comparable securities, taking into account differences in national definitions.

Assessments will also make reference to other economic criteria (relating to integration of markets, balances of payments on current account, and 'unit labour costs and other price indices'). Compatibility between national legislation and the Treaty and Statute provisions relating to the independence of the ECB and national central banks will also be examined (Article 109j).

## 3. The Transition: Will EMU Happen?

The difficult question is whether members of what recently became the European Union will be able to shift by 1999 to the EMU envisioned by the Maastricht treaty.

### a. Ratification

By mid–1993, all but one of the members' national legislatures had ratified the Maastricht treaty. The Danes voted in favor of the treaty in a second referendum. The U.K. ratified the treaty after the government opted out of the social chapter of the treaty. (Since the opt out would allow firms to fire employees more easily, one result of the opt out, bankers predicted, was to make London more competitive in the financial sector. Poor traders could be fired.)

Several governments won against challenges in court that argued the treaty sapped national sovereignty. The most serious suit was in Germany, where the constitutional court ruled in October 1993 that the treaty did not violate the constitution. The German legislature then ratified it and the treaty came into force November 1, 1993.

### b. Convergence

The IMF reported that by 1992 few countries could boast having met the treaty's economic goals (see the following table). Circumstances worsened during 1993. In February 1994, the Bundesbank warned that Germany's gross government debt reached 56% of GDP at the end of 1993 and was likely to pass 60% late in 1994. The general government balance was 3.4% of GDP in 1993. The Bundesbank attributed much of this "mountain of debt" to the cost of reunification. Indeed, by the end of 1993, no country met both debt/GDP ratios of Maastricht.

## IMF, WORLD ECONOMIC OUTLOOK, INTERIM ASSESSMENT

January 1993, 36 ("IMF Interim Assessment").

**Table 7. European Countries: Convergence Indicators for 1991 and 1992**
*(In percent)*

| | 1991 GDP Weights | | Consumer Price Inflation | | General Government Balance/GDP | | Gross Government Debt/GDP [1] | | Long–Term Interest Rates | |
|---|---|---|---|---|---|---|---|---|---|---|
| | In EC | In world | 1991 | 1992 | 1991 | 1992 | 1991 | 1992 | 1991 | 1992 |
| EC countries | | | | | | | | | | |
| France | 19.7 | 5.1 | 3.1 | 2.8 | −2.1 | −2.9 | 47.1 | 47.7 | 9.2 | 8.7 |
| Germany | 25.5 | 6.5 | 4.8 | 5.0 | −3.2 | −3.2 | 41.7 | 42.5 | 8.5 | 7.8 |
| Italy | 17.7 | 4.5 | 6.3 | 5.5 | −10.2 | −10.4 | 103.5 | 108.5 | 13.0 | 13.5 |
| United Kingdom [2] | 16.8 | 4.3 | 5.9 | 3.7 | −2.7 | −6.3 | 34.4 | 35.9 | 9.9 | 9.0 |
| Largest four countries [3] | 79.5 | 20.4 | 4.9 | 4.3 | −4.4 | −5.4 | 55.2 | 56.9 | 10.0 | 9.6 |
| Belgium | 3.2 | 0.8 | 3.2 | 2.4 | −7.6 | −6.8 | 134.4 | 133.4 | 9.3 | 8.8 |
| Denmark [4] | 2.2 | 0.6 | 2.4 | 2.1 | −2.3 | −2.3 | 66.7 | 71.3 | 9.6 | 8.9 |
| Greece [5] | 1.1 | 0.3 | 19.5 | 16.0 | −17.4 | −13.8 | 115.5 | 114.8 | 23.3 | 21.5 |
| Ireland | 0.7 | 0.2 | 3.2 | 3.3 | −2.8 | −1.8 | 98.0 | 100.0 | 9.2 | 10.0 |
| Luxembourg | 0.1 | — | 3.1 | 2.8 | 1.5 | 1.0 | 6.2 | 5.8 | 8.2 | 7.8 |
| Netherlands | 4.6 | 1.2 | 3.9 | 3.3 | −3.9 | −4.0 | 79.6 | 80.0 | 8.7 | 8.0 |
| Portugal | 0.9 | 0.2 | 11.4 | 9.2 | −6.7 | −5.7 | 65.3 | 69.5 | 18.5 | 16.5 |
| Spain | 7.7 | 2.0 | 5.9 | 5.9 | −4.9 | −5.1 | 44.7 | 46.0 | 12.6 | 12.6 |

| | 1991 GDP Weights | | Consumer Price Inflation | | General Government Balance/GDP | | Gross Government Debt/GDP [1] | | Long-Term Interest Rates | |
|---|---|---|---|---|---|---|---|---|---|---|
| | In EC | In world | 1991 | 1992 | 1991 | 1992 | 1991 | 1992 | 1991 | 1992 |
| Smallest eight countries [3] | 20.5 | 5.3 | 5.5 | 5.0 | −5.5 | −5.2 | 75.5 | 77.4 | 11.6 | 11.1 |
| All EC [3] | 100.0 | 25.7 | 5.1 | 4.5 | −4.6 | −5.3 | 59.4 | 61.3 | 10.3 | 9.9 |
| Maastricht convergence criteria [6] | ... | ... | 4.4 | 4.0 | −3.0 | −3.0 | 60.0 | 60.0 | 11.0 | 10.7 |
| Non-EC countries | | | | | | | | | | |
| Austria | ... | 0.7 | 3.3 | 3.8 | −2.2 | −1.9 | 56.5 | 55.8 | 8.6 | 7.9 |
| Finland | ... | 0.6 | 4.2 | 2.7 | −6.0 | −8.8 | 21.7 | 33.0 | 12.2 | 12.8 |
| Norway | ... | 0.5 | 3.2 | 2.3 | −1.1 | −4.3 | 43.3 | 50.0 | 9.9 | 9.6 |
| Sweden | ... | 1.0 | 9.3 | 2.2 | −1.5 | −6.4 | 44.8 | 50.0 | 10.7 | 10.3 |
| Switzerland | ... | 1.0 | 5.9 | 4.0 | −1.7 | −1.7 | 32.1 | 34.3 | 6.4 | 6.6 |
| Five non-EC countries | ... | 3.8 | 5.7 | 3.1 | −2.4 | −4.4 | 38.6 | 43.7 | 9.3 | 9.1 |

Sources: National sources and staff projections.

[1] Debt data are from national sources. They relate to the general government but may not be consistent with the definition agreed at Maastricht.

[2] Debt on fiscal year basis.

[3] Average weighted by 1991 GDP shares.

[4] The debt–GDP ratio would be below 60 percent if adjusted in line with the definition agreed at Maastricht.

[5] Long-term interest rate is twelve-month treasury bill rate.

[6] Unweighted averages.

## Questions

1. What does convergence mean? Are the measures adequate? Is an important test missing?

2. Evaluate trends in convergence and the extent of convergence. Note how markets would react to these trends. What does your analysis say about the likelihood that Stage III will occur on schedule?

---

### c. The Pressure for Stronger Control of Foreign Exchange Markets

The Economists' editors argued in their October 23, 1993 magazine that

> The ERM's failure was ... basic .... Germany's need for high interest rates to combat the inflationary effects of unification conflicted with other members' need for low rates to combat unemployment. The system's piece-meal development, from one that allowed currency realignments to one that resisted them, exposed it to enormous pressures; its ability to withstand them did not increase commensurately. The mechanism lost credibility in the foreign-exchange markets. In the end it did not matter whether the single currency was a good idea or not. The manner of getting to it was unstable.

Not everyone accepted this view. During the summer of 1993, European central bankers considered ways to prevent speculators from overwhelming ERM policy. An article in Euromoney in September 1993 reported that the regulators singled out hedge funds that borrow mainly from investment banks, using margin accounts rather than their own cash to bet against central banks. These funds were largely unregulated. Central bankers believed these funds took positions that were open or not covered adequately. While the regulators' views varied, they seemed to want more stringent prudential rules for the funds as well as banks and securities firms. The article reported the following "proposals to beat the speculators":

## DAVID SHIRREFF, CAN ANYONE TAME THE CURRENCY MARKET?

Euromoney, September 1993, 60.

1. Capital controls as provided for in a 1988 EC directive and in the Maastricht Treaty. According to Article 73c, the European Commission can consider "special measures relating to capital transactions with non–EC countries". Article 73f allows "precautionary measures" if there is an extraordinary threat to the "normal operation of economic and monetary union". Article 73g allows members to take "unilateral action to regulate the movement of capital and payments to and from non–EC countries".

**Objection:** This is anathema to the major EC members, although the Belgian finance minister briefly suggested use of such controls in August.

2. A transaction tax on all foreign exchange deals in as many OECD countries as possible.

**Objection:** Very complicated to apply. If too high (Eichengreen and Wyplosz propose 1% and, for a round trip, 2%), it would hit trade and investment. It would also widen the bid/offer spread on all transactions. Richard Cooper, a Harvard economics professor, suggests ⅛% to ¼% ("to deter sloshing about") but it is "no panacea for governments stuck on particular exchange rates", and no solution to the problems of September 1992.

3. A non-interest-bearing deposit at the central bank equal to a bank's purchase of foreign exchange with domestic currency. Italy used a variation in the 1970s and Spain last year.

**Objection:** There is a loophole, in the currency swap market. The measure also frightens foreign investors. In Spain it hit the bond and equity markets.

4. A capital charge of 8% on the net open foreign exchange position of all institutions where prudential supervision is possible. This is one proposal, for banks, in a paper circulated by the Basle Committee on Bank Supervision.

**Objection:** Impossible to apply beyond the sphere of supervised banks and investment institutions. It is a prudential measure and should not be used for market volume control.

5. Instant economic and monetary union. European exchange-rate mechanism currencies move immediately to fixed exchange rates or a single currency.

**Objection:** There is not sufficient convergence of any European economies, except perhaps the Netherlands, Germany and Austria.

6. **The hard Ecu.** Turning the Ecu into Europe's hardest currency, backed by dedicated reserves at central banks. A country that devalues would have to top up its quota of hard Ecu proportionately.

**Objection:** This was an idea cooked up by the UK treasury to play for time in negotiations on EMU. It expects too much monetary discipline by member countries—including paying penalties for cash creation.

---

Many rules of course, already affect operations in the foreign exchange markets. Although the high barriers erected by exchange controls and limits on capital movements have fallen in many countries and in particular in industrial countries, many governments continue to restrict transactions to or from their country's currency. Many continue to limit cross-border capital movements.

Banks, the major players, are highly regulated. The IMF reports these rules in the major industrial countries. Elsewhere we discuss capital adequacy rules for position risk, limits on institutional investors' ability to hold securities denominated in foreign currency, and margin requirements imposed by exchanges on currency futures and options contracts. Many companies have internal limits on their own foreign exchange operations.

GOLDSTEIN, 36–37.

The regulatory constraints on banks' net open foreign exchange positions (spot and forward) vary considerably across the Group of Ten countries.... Many of the prudential regulations directed specifically at banks' open foreign exchange positions were adopted in response to the failures (stemming largely from foreign exchange trading losses) of Bankhaus Herstatt and Franklin National Bank in 1974.

Belgium, Canada, Luxembourg, Switzerland, and the United States require periodic reporting of foreign exchange exposures and monitor banks' internal risk management practices during routine examinations. These countries emphasize the appropriateness of actual foreign exchange positions relative to the adequacy of internal risk management systems. No common standard or ceiling is imposed.

In the Netherlands and the United Kingdom, guidelines limit net open positions to working balances that typically arise from market-making activities. Compliance with the guidelines is monitored through periodic reporting by banks. In the United Kingdom, the guidelines state that net open dealing positions in any one currency should not exceed 10 percent of capital and that the net short open dealing position of all currencies taken together should not exceed 15 percent of capital. More conservative guidelines apply to institutions with only limited experience in foreign exchange markets. U.K. banks file monthly reports on their net foreign exchange positions with the Bank of England.

In the other Group of Ten countries (France, Germany, Japan, and Sweden), daily net open foreign exchange positions are subject to limits expressed in terms of net positions relative to capital, and compliance with these limits is monitored through periodic reporting. In Germany, for example, banks' net open foreign exchange positions (spot and forward combined) at the end of each business day cannot exceed 30 percent of their capital. German banks file monthly reports on their day-by-day foreign exchange positions.

The Basle Committee on Banking Supervision is currently seeking to broaden the coverage of the accord on international capital adequacy standards to include net open foreign exchange positions (spot and forward) and thereby to treat foreign exchange risk more uniformly. One of the thorny issues in this area is the measurement of foreign exchange risk within a portfolio of currency positions. Here, some allowance needs to be made for correlation among currency movements. To this end, the Committee has developed a proxy measure that tracks the foreign exchange risk of international banks and has proposed an adequate capital charge for that risk measure.

Although foreign exchange risk per se does not yet fall within the domain of the Basle capital adequacy framework, OTC exchange rate contracts do. They are subject to the credit conversion factors for off-balance-sheet items and the credit-risk weights established by the accord. These contracts include cross-currency interest rate swaps, forward foreign exchange contracts, OTC currency options purchased, and similar instruments. Because capital charges are intended to reflect only the risk of counterparty default, exchange-traded derivative instruments (such as foreign currency futures)—which are subject to daily margin requirements—are excluded.

The primary method for converting OTC exchange rate contracts to their credit equivalents involves two steps. First, a bank calculates the total replacement cost of all contracts with positive value by marking them to their current market values. Second, factors are added to reflect potential future exposures over the remaining life of the contracts; a 1 percent factor is used for those contracts with less than one year of residual maturity, and a 5 percent factor for all other contracts.

These credit equivalents (of exchange rate contracts) attract a 50 percent risk weight for calculating a bank's total risk-adjusted assets. Thus, the effective capital requirements for these contracts are 2 percent of their credit equivalents for tier 1 capital and 4 percent for total capital. However, contracts with an original maturity of 14 calendar days or less are excluded from these capital requirements.

The EC directive on capital adequacy for banks and securities firms calls for an 8 percent capital requirement on net open foreign exchange positions in excess of 2 percent of own funds (capital). Unlike the Basle capital requirements for OTC exchange rate contracts, the EC proposal is intended to capture the market risk of foreign exchange positions. The measurement of open positions involves three steps: first, add the net spot position in each currency, the net forward position (i.e., all amounts to be received less all amounts to be paid under outright forward, futures, and currency swap transactions), and a fraction of the total book of foreign currency options; second, the net short or long position in each currency would then be converted to the reporting currency and then summed separately to form the total of the net short and net long positions; and third, take the higher of the two totals as the net foreign exchange position subject to a capital requirement.

***Questions***

1. Evaluate the "proposals to beat speculators." What do they tell you about the ability of countries to affect the foreign exchange markets?

---

## d. The Transition to a European Central Bank: The EMI and the ESCB

In the debate leading to the treaty, two views emerged about where to lodge responsibility for exchange rate policy.

Carre, 779–80.

One side argues that since the exchange rate is an important instrument of economic policy, it should be managed by the political authorities. Those who take this view underline the fact that, after monetary union, the exchange rate policy of the Community will have important consequences for other countries and, therefore, cannot be separated from broader political issues. The other side holds that, because an exchange rate policy may conflict with a domestic monetary policy geared to price stability, it should be the responsibility of the central bank; they consider that all decisions on intervention should be assigned to the ESCB, because full responsibility in this field is a necessary condition for the conduct of a monetary policy oriented toward stability.

In an attempt to reconcile these conflicting views, the Commission has suggested a distinction among three levels of decisionmaking, and an allocation of responsibilities for each level:

1. At the highest level, policymakers choose the exchange rate regime and negotiate international monetary agreements. These activities should clearly be a matter for political authorities, assisted by the ESCB—as is the case now in all countries.

2. At the lowest level, interventions are transacted in the foreign exchange markets, and the daily management of foreign exchange reserves occurs. These activities should be a matter for the ESCB.

3. At the intermediate level, policymakers must decide upon exchange rate and intervention policy—decisionmaking that is the core of the problem. Acknowledging that the exchange rate is an important element of both monetary policy and external economic policy, the Commission has suggested a structure for organizing the dialogue necessary for resolving potential conflicts. It has proposed that exchange rate policy should be defined in a framework of close cooperation between the monetary authority and the economic policymakers and should follow some basic principles, especially that foreign exchange interventions vis-á-vis third currencies should not conflict with the overriding objective of monetary policy. This "cooperative solution" is the basis of the present negotiations.

---

In late October 1993, the EC named the chief of the European Monetary Institute (EMI) and decided on its location. It chose Mr. Alexandre Lamfalussy, an economist who was then general manager of the Bank for International Settlements. He was a Belgian citizen, born in Hungary. As an outside expert to the Delors Committee in 1988 and 1989, he had proposed a transitional agency like the EMI with a strong role.

Member states did not agree about the role of the EMI. The Belgian government wanted the EMI to coordinate monetary policy among EC countries with low inflation. The U.K. government wanted EMI simply to advise. Germany consistently opposed giving EMI operational powers to make or implement monetary policy. In early 1994, the Bundesbank said it would not give the EMI control over any German reserves.

The EC decided to put the EMI in Frankfurt, Germany despite strong competition from the U.K. The French government "knew from the start that basing the central bank in Germany was the price to be paid for monetary union" (Quentin Peel, "European Bank a boost for Frankfurt," Financial Times, October 30–31, 1993, 3).

The EMI officially opened January 1, 1994 with the start of the EMU's second stage.

### e. The Political Will to Make the Transition

As early as February 1993, EC finance ministers agreed "to prolong member states' economic 'convergence' programmes beyond the end of 1995. . . . Several delegations had voiced disquiet about rising unemployment in the EC and poor growth prospects in the Community." Indeed, Denmark, France, Greece, and the U.K. had not even presented their programs to converge. (Lionel Barber, "EC ministers allow for Emu delay," Financial Times, February 16, 1993).

Events over the next months did nothing to increase optimism in several major countries. In May 1993, the U.K. foreign secretary argued that the key problem for the EC was how to absorb 4 to 8 new members from Northern and Eastern Europe. The larger community would force the EC to permit flexible relations among members. Presumably this would complicate the move to EMU because of the need for convergence. In September 1993, the prime minister rejected a return by Britain to the ERM and said his government would search for an alternative that was more flexible, particularly on inflation goals.

Germany emphasized rigorous application of the convergence criteria over meeting the timetable precisely, according to the finance minister (Quentin Peel, "EC moves to repair damage of ERM crisis," Financial Times, August 12, 1993, 1). A few months later, the president of the Bundesbank said "he did not believe lasting monetary union could be achieved without a parallel political union of EU countries." Political differences affected monetary policy. Now the members' central banks aimed at different targets: the Bundesbank used money supply targets, the Bank of England looked to price stability, and other central banks sought stable exchange rates. (Ian Rodger, "Bundesbank will not pass reserves to EMI," Financial Times, January 31, 1994, 2.)

France continued to press for a 1999 EMU.

Four policy options for Europe's monetary arrangements were set out by Andrew Crockett, then executive director of the Bank of England and Lamfalussy's successor-designate at the Bank for International Settlements.

## ANDREW CROCKETT, "THE FUTURE OF MONETARY RELATIONS IN EUROPE," A PAPER DELIVERED AT A SEMINAR IN INTERNATIONAL FINANCE AT HARVARD LAW SCHOOL

November 29, 1993.

. . .

(a) *Do nothing*. It would, of course be possible to leave monetary arrangements exactly as they are now. Each member of the ERM would be able to pursue its own monetary policy, subject only to the loose constraint of not moving outside the broad band. Those currencies whose ERM membership is suspended (sterling and the lira) and non-EC currencies whose link to the ECU has been severed (The Swedish and Norwegian crowns and the Finnish Mark) would continue to float.

This arrangement has seemed to work well in the period since it was adopted. It is tempting therefore to continue it. But there are important risks. First, although the members of the ERM have reaffirmed their belief in the appropriateness of the pre-existing central rates, and have not allowed their currencies to move too far away from them, the risk of more substantial exchange rate volatility remains. This risk would become greater if one or more members of the system became impatient with the inflation/output trade-off implied by keeping close to their central rates. Exchange rate volatility that came anywhere near to using the 15% margins would undermine the single market, and would put in question economic co-operation over a range of issues. I conclude that it is neither desirable nor sustainable to leave exchange rate margins of ± 15 percent as the *only* constraint on economic policy. More precise understandings (explicit or implicit) are needed to provide an effective framework for policy co-operation.

(b) *A return to narrow margins.* This remains the formal objective of ERM members. (The 2 August communique referred to the "temporary" widening of bands). As a practical matter, however, few observers official or private, regarded as feasible to return to narrow margins of ± 2¼ percent in the foreseeable future. All of the underlying features that led to the crises of 1992–93 are still in place. Even in the longer term, it seems unlikely that further shocks can be wholly discounted (albeit not of comparable magnitude to that of German reunification). The memories of market participants are apt to prove quite long, and with ever-greater volumes of internationally mobile funds, narrow margins will only be defensible when markets are convinced that the possibility of exchange rate adjustment has almost completely disappeared. In such conditions, there would be nothing to prevent a rapid movement to stage 3.

I conclude, therefore, that a return to narrow margins is not practicable in the short-run, and may not be a necessary step towards EMU in the long-run. This need not, of course, preclude some narrowing of margins from the present exceptionally wide range. However, to avoid destablishing capital flows, margins should probably be wider than would be necessary to accommodate *actual* exchange rate fluctuations.

(c) *A rapid move to a single currency.* This has been canvassed by some observers as a means of counteracting speculative disturbances. Since it is the possibility of exchange rate changes that gives rise to capital movements, this source of disturbance could be eliminated by moving immediately to irrevocably locked parities (and, soon afterwards, to a single currency). This option might have some attraction if the participants in the system were convinced that existing parities were an appropriate basis for monetary union and they were able to agree on the conditions for a common monetary policy. They would also have to be confident that they could overcome market pressures in the two phases of the transition: the gap between declaring their intention to lock parities and putting in place the technical features of a common monetary policy; and the gap between locking parities between their separate currencies, and introducing a single currency.

The "fast forward" approach to monetary union cannot be completely ruled out on economic grounds. For several reasons, however, it appears unlikely. It would be unwise in circumstances such as the present, when convergence is far from complete. The adjustment pressures placed on domestic economies would be hard to predict, but quite possibly large. However, it also appears that few countries would be prepared to accept the implications for a common monetary policy. With locked parities or a single currency, there can be only one monetary policy and one monetary authority. If that is to be at the sole discretion of the anchor country (i.e. Germany), it is hard to see how it could be made acceptable to others, whose economic circumstances and requirements may be quite different. But if monetary policy is *not* at the sole discretion of the Bundesbank, it is hard to see how this could be acceptable to the German authorities, before Stage 3 of the Maastricht process is reached.

(d) *Intensified Policy Co-ordination.* The fourth approach, which I believe is the one Europe has to move towards, is to accept the continuation of relatively broad bands within the ERM, but to complement these loose exchange rate constraints with a framework for intensified policy coordination.

Such a framework is necessary both for domestic and external reasons. Domestically, countries need a guide for the formulation of monetary policy to replace the exchange rate anchor that has been taken away. Externally, Europe needs some means of distinguishing cooperative from competitive policies, and for exerting peer pressure towards consistent out-turns.

So far, it is not possible to do more than distinguish the broad outline of what such a framework might be. It should certainly embrace an intensified pursuit of policy convergence—meaning by that not just *similar,* but *satisfactory* performance with respect to variables such as inflation and budget deficits. It also requires attention to policy mix, so that divergences in policy mix do not lead to sudden or unsustainable shifts in exchange rates. And, as noted above, it will require attention to be given to the structural as well as to the macroeconomic aspects of convergence.

### *Questions*

1. Could the support for EMU change? What would make Germany or France less interested?

2. What are the implications of Britain's reluctance to join?

3. Evaluate the four options described by Andrew Crockett. Do you agree with his assessment of each?

---

## 4. Stage III: Would it Work?

Some challenged the idea that EMU was a worthwhile goal. Harvard economics professor Martin Feldstein, who chaired President Reagan's council of economic advisers, was one. As you read his critique and a reply by leading European economists, consider which points are most telling.

## MARTIN FELDSTEIN, "THE CASE AGAINST EMU"

The Economist, June 13, 1992, 19.

Government officials and opinion leaders throughout Europe are beginning to ask questions about EMU that might better have been raised before the Maastricht conference. Those who question the advisability of adopting a single currency and a federal structure for Europe are asking: "Are the economic benefits great enough to outweigh the political disadvantages of the federal structure for Europe that would follow the adoption of a single currency?"

That gets the key question exactly backwards. As an economist who watches the debate from across the ocean, my judgment is that a single currency for Europe would be an economic liability. The proper question therefore is: "Would the political advantages of adopting a single currency outweigh the economic disadvantages?"

. . .

### One Market, One Money?

Advocates of a monetary union imply that the adoption of a single currency is necessary to perfect the single market's free trade in goods and services. The European Commission has summarised this official view in the title of its publication. "One Market, One Money".

I am an enthusiastic supporter of the current attempt to achieve a single European market for goods and services. Although such a free-trade zone, even if it involves no increases in external tariffs, could in theory have trade-diverting effects that decrease world welfare, I believe that the weight of the evidence points clearly to a net positive effect from trade creation and from decreased government intervention in domestic markets.

But the creation of a single market for goods and services does not require a monetary union. It is possible to have all the benefits of free trade without a common currency. Indeed, the shift to a common currency could actually diminish trade within Europe. It is also likely to reduce economic well-being by raising future unemployment and increasing the cyclical volatility of activity within individual countries. And it could cause a higher rate of inflation than the current monetary arrangements.

Events in North America are instructive. The United States recently established a free-trade agreement with Canada that will soon include Mexico. Yet nobody seriously suggests that the United States, Canada and Mexico should form a currency union.

. . .

The case for linking monetary union to the creation of the single market is based on the notion that eliminating currency fluctuations within Europe would increase trade among members of the Community. Those who hold this view argue that currency fluctuations inhibit businessmen from expanding their sales in other countries and from buying from foreign producers, because fluctuations in exchange rates can more than wipe out the normal profits from individual transactions.

It is not clear, however, whether this matters in practice. Statistical studies that measured the effect of exchange-rate volatility on trade in Europe have failed to find any impact. Moreover, if businesses really care about exchange-rate risk, they can hedge in the market for foreign-exchange futures. Medium- and long-term futures markets have become much deeper and more efficient in recent years. It is true that businessmen often complain that such hedging is "expensive", but I suspect that they are confusing the very low cost of avoiding uncertainty by buying or selling currency futures with the discount or premium that prevails when the market expects the currency's value to change.

Further evidence that currency volatility does not inhibit trade is the sharp increase in the volume of American imports during the 1980s when the dollar gyrated sharply (see chart 1). And certainly the Japanese have not found that the fluctuations of the yen relative to the dollar and the European currencies have been a serious barrier to their ability to increase exports.

A fixed exchange rate may in some cases even be an obstacle to expanded trade. Consider a manufacturer in Britain who contemplates expanding his marketing efforts in France, where he will compete with producers from the United States. If the dollar falls relative to the franc, the American producers will gain an advantage. If the pound were free to adjust, it might fall in line with the dollar, thus helping to maintain British exports. But if the exchange rate of the British pound is fixed vis-á-vis the French franc and other EC currencies, such devaluation would not be possible. For such a British manufacturer, developing a market in France is less attractive when the sterling-franc exchange rate is fixed.

Fewer resources may therefore go into the manufacture of tradable goods and more into the production of services and goods for the local market. In short, although a world in which all exchange rates were fixed might increase trade, fixing exchange rates for a subset of currencies might actually discourage trade.

A single currency may reduce intra-European trade for another reason. A single tariff-free market should encourage nations to specialise in producing those products for which they have a comparative advantage. But such specialisation makes a country more vulnerable to fluctuations in demand caused by temporary changes in tastes or market conditions. Domestic monetary policy can offset these fluctuations if the country maintains its own currency but not otherwise. The use of a single currency therefore makes product specialisation less attractive: a single currency would reduce the potential gains from trade.

Proponents of monetary union also claim that a single currency can in principle help to create a larger financial market by lowering the transactions costs. This may be a reason for very small countries to tie their currencies to a larger currency, but it is irrelevant for countries as large as Britain, France, Germany and Italy. Sophisticated hedging can now eliminate the currency risks associated with international portfolio investments and other financial transactions among the European markets.

**Chart 1**

## Farewell, monetary policy

Against the uncertain advantages of a currency union must be set the disadvantage of losing an independent national monetary policy. If the demand for the products of a country falls, it will suffer lower employment and output unless wages and prices fall immediately. In practice, wages and prices adjust only slowly, so output and employment suffer.

This could be mitigated with lower domestic interest rates—but that will be impossible if the country shares a single currency with a larger economic area. Moreover, when the exchange rate is flexible the favourable expansionary effect of low domestic interest rates is reinforced by the induced decline of the currency's value. This too is lost when a country no longer has its own currency.

It is worthwhile for a group of independent countries to adopt a single currency when (a) the economic shocks that hit the individual countries are similar and (b) labour is highly mobile among the countries. If the shocks are similar, the appropriate monetary policy is generally the same everywhere; little is to be gained by changing real exchange rates within the proposed currency area. A highly mobile labour force means that, to the extent that there are different shocks in different parts of the currency area, workers will move from regions of declining demand to regions of stronger demand, making different local monetary policies unnecessary.

Just how similar the shocks, and how mobile the labour force must be to justify a currency union depends on the potential gains from such a union. A move to a single currency is economically justified if the gains (lower transactions costs and an expanded financial market) are large enough to outweigh the losses (the loss of domestic interest rates and the nominal exchange rate as policy instruments).

It is hard to argue that the European Community satisfies the two requirements of an optimal currency area. Individual countries suffer substantially different shocks because of differences in the mix of the products they produce, in their dependence on imported oil, and in the foreign markets to which they sell.

The greater specialisation of production that should result from the completion of the single market should increase these differences. Labour mobility among European nations will inevitably remain limited by differences in language and by a culture that, unlike that of the United States, regards geographic mobility with suspicion. Expanding the current group of 12 countries to include the EFTA nations and the countries of Eastern Europe would further exacerbate both of these problems.

**Staying competitive**

The case for maintaining an independent currency goes beyond the ability of a nation to have a countercyclical domestic monetary policy. Equally important is that an independent currency can shift the real exchange rate without a corresponding change in the level of domestic prices.

Changes in equilibrium real exchange rates are inevitable, an important part of the economic environment. For example, a substantial increase in the world price of energy calls for a currency appreciation in the energy-exporting countries and a decline in the real exchange rate of countries that import energy. Alternatively, the equilibrium exchange rate of a country may shift gradually over time because of trends in productivity or tastes.

The Japanese yen appreciated in real terms in the 1960s and 1970s to offset rapid productivity growth in Japan's export sector. Big structural changes in equilibrium real exchange rates can be expected, especially for some of Europe's poorer countries, during the next two decades.

A currency union means, of course, that nominal exchange rates cannot adjust to achieve a needed change in the real exchange rate. The local price level must, therefore, adjust to bring about the change in the real exchange rate. Thus a 10% fall in the real value of a currency can be achieved either by a 10% fall in the nominal exchange rate or by a 10% fall in local wages and prices.

Either form of adjustment can bring the real exchange rate to its equilibrium value, but a decline in domestic prices is likely to require a period of increased unemployment. It would therefore certainly be better to have a decline in the nominal exchange rate. The shift to a single currency in Europe would preclude such nominal exchange-rate adjustments and force real exchange-rate reductions to be achieved through lower local wages and prices.

Not everyone appears to understand this. Proponents of the shift to a single currency sometimes argue incorrectly that the issue of changes in exchange rates among regions is meaningless once a single currency is accepted for the entire area. Once a single market and a single currency are established, the argument goes, no one ever looks at the balance of trade among the component regions. Who, they ask, even knows what happens to the balance of payments between New England and the rest of the United States?

### Lessons from New England

To see why that argument is specious we need only look at what has actually been happening recently in New England. During the 1980s the New England economy benefited from a strong national demand for the products and services in which it specialises, particularly computers, military equipment and financial services. The increased demand for these "exports" from New England to the rest of the United States caused a rise in their prices and in the relative level of New England wages and salaries. During the decade of the 1980s, real incomes per head grew twice as fast in Massachusetts as in the rest of the country.

But now the demand for computers, for military equipment and for financial services has declined. Until there is a relative decline in New England wages and in the prices of New England's "exports" to the rest of the country, the level of unemployment in New England will be abnormally high. Massachusetts has the second-highest unemployment rate among the industrial states, topped only by Michigan. To shrink that unemployment, Massachusetts wages will have to decline relative to wages elsewhere in the nation (see chart 2).

**Chart 2**

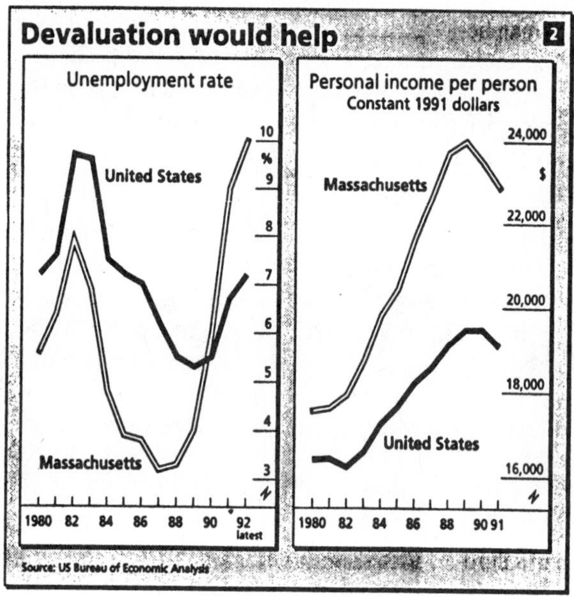


Slowing the growth of wages is a painful process, accompanied by a high level of unemployment, declining property values and the widespread failure of New England banks. New England could deal with the transition in a much less painful way if there were a flexible "New England dollar" that could be allowed to decline in value relative to the currencies of America's other regions.

Although this experience within the American economy shows one of the high costs of having a single currency, nobody seriously suggests that the dollar should be abandoned for a set of regional currencies. Why not? What is so special about the dollar that does not apply equally to the proposed European currency?

One important difference is that the dollar has already existed as a currency for more than 200 years. Although there have been periods of inflation and deflation, the dollar has acquired a reputation as a relatively reliable store of value and stable unit of account.

The proposed European currency has none of the virtues as a store of value and unit of account that only experience can bring. It would start with no reputation and with an untried European central bank. Shifting to it would involve abandoning some currencies that have acquired a reputation for stability and soundness, like the D-mark, as well as other currencies with a less solid but nevertheless positive reputation.

A further reason for a single United States currency is that the American fiscal system provides an alternative source of regional stabilisation, making regional monetary policy less important. Each dollar decline in America's real GNP reduces taxes by about 30 cents and increases transfer payments by about 5 cents. These national fiscal responses are paralleled at the state and regional levels.

When the Massachusetts economy turns down, the residents of Massachusetts send fewer tax dollars to Washington and receive more in transfers from the federal government. To the extent that the Massachusetts downturn is greater than the downturn in the nation as a whole, the result of this fiscal structure is a permanent transfer to Massachusetts. Thus even though Massachusetts lacks an independent monetary policy, a decline in the state's economy automatically triggers a stabilising shift in fiscal policy.

Nothing comparable to America's fiscal system exists in Europe, where virtually all taxes are paid to national and local governments. There is no fiscal transfer from the EC as a whole to countries that experience a relative cyclical decline. Without such a centralised fiscal system, shocks to aggregate demand that are geographically focused, or shifts in the real equilibrium values of national exchange rates, have a bigger impact on regional income and employment.

If a single currency is accepted, national governments might soon have to decide whether to accept the greater volatility of employment and incomes that comes from abandoning an independent monetary policy and flexible exchange rate, or accept instead the loss of national sovereignty over taxes and spending.

**The politics of inflation**

I think it is clear that economic analysis does not provide support for a shift to a single European currency: it is not necessary to facilitate trade and, by eliminating the possibility of independent monetary policies and adjustments of nominal exchange rates, it is likely to add to the cyclical instability of incomes and employment. Why then are so many in Europe calling for EMU? There are, I think, several distinct political reasons.

First, some see a single currency and a European central bank as a way to restrict the ability of national governments to pursue inflationary monetary policies. In particular, those European central bankers who must now answer to their finance ministers see the move to a single currency and a European central bank as a chance to make monetary policy with much less political interference.

In effect, they argue that although each government could by itself pursue a non-inflationary monetary policy, it is politically easier for Europe to do so collectively. Although a European central bank would still be accountable to some political body like the European parliament, distance from national capitals and national parliaments is assumed to reduce the pressure of domestic electoral politics on monetary policy.

They and others who make this argument would in principle accept a much restricted scope for good monetary policy by each national central bank in order to reduce the political temptations for bad national policy. Quite apart from the question that this raises about the making of monetary policy in a democratic society, it implies a potentially very large sacrifice of potentially good monetary policy.

The practical significance of this argument is, however, put in doubt by the Maastricht treaty's ideas about a European central bank. Those proposals raise doubts about the independence of its decisions from the political influence of national capitals. The voting members of the central bank's governing board would be appointed by the member governments and would be eligible for subsequent political appointments by their own governments.

Equally worrying is the decision to have national finance ministers and the European central bank share responsibility for the exchange-rate policy of the EC as a whole. Recent experience and many studies confirm that exchange-rate policy cannot be separated from monetary policy. The only way to change the exchange rate between the new European currency and the dollar or yen would be to change European monetary policy. The designers of the Maastricht treaty either do not understand the role of monetary policy in determining the EC's exchange rate or they want to undermine any possible independence of the central bank.

Of course it might in principle be desirable to establish an independent central bank that is capable of pursuing a sound monetary policy (if it were not for the adverse aspects of losing control of the national interest rate and no longer having flexible nominal exchange rates). But, as a practical matter, the anti-inflation argument for a European central bank is very much weakened by the success of the current European monetary system (EMS).

Under these arrangements, German hegemony has induced other countries over the past decade to pursue a German-style anti-inflationary policy. Inflation in countries like France and Italy has come down sharply during the past ten years, converging towards the low inflation rate in Germany. Why accept a monetary union that would force every country to give up the possibility of countercyclical domestic monetary adjustments and flexible nominal exchange rates in order to prevent inflationary policies by their own central banks that may in any case be only hypothetical?

But it is the very success of the German hegemony that creates the second of the political motivations for European monetary union. Put simply, nobody but the Germans is fully in favour of letting the Bundesbank make monetary policy for all of Europe. For many non-Germans, the creation of a European central bank that manages a European currency is a matter of national pride. For non-German central bankers, it is an opportunity to play an active role in the making of monetary policy.

The reasons for wanting to replace the Bundesbank with a European central bank go beyond national pride and the wishes of European central bankers to have a more active role in the shaping of monetary policy. Not everyone shares Germany's strong anti-inflationary preferences. A European central bank might today adopt a more expansionary monetary policy that accepts permanently higher inflation to avoid a period of slow growth in the 1990s. French officials in particular have frequently emphasised that they regard monetary policy as currently too tight but are constrained by the EMS to follow Germany's lead.

It is ironic that while some advocates of a single currency and a European central bank argue that they want these things in order to reduce the risk of inflation, others see it as a way of relaxing the tough German anti-inflationary policy now implicitly imposed on others by the Bundesbank.

All of which reinforces my belief that the strong advocacy of monetary union does not reflect the political economy of monetary policy any more than it does a technical belief in the ability of monetary union to enhance trade within the European Community. Those who most fervently advocate monetary union do so for a third reason—because they see it as a means to a political union, and a particular type of political union, at that.

A single currency would undoubtedly give the people of Europe more of a sense that they are part of a single country even though they speak different languages and remember different national histories. A single currency and European central bank would transfer substantial power away from national governments and to the nascent European central government. Many would expect that limits on national fiscal policies and enhanced centralised taxation would follow quickly.

Although there are examples of small countries that use a foreign currency as legal tender and provide no currency of their own, there is no sizeable country that does not have its own currency. Perhaps this is the most obvious explanation of the enthusiasm for monetary union among its most ardent supporters. Monetary union and a single currency would be the strongest possible signal that the European Community is on its way to becoming a single state.

**Think again**

Let me conclude by reiterating my principal point. Monetary union is not needed to achieve the advantages of a free-trade zone. On the contrary, an artificially contrived economic and monetary union might actually reduce the volume of trade among the member countries, and would almost certainly increase the average level of unemployment over time.

I can understand, however, that there are those who are willing to accept these adverse economic effects in order to achieve a federalist political union that they favour for other non-economic reasons. What I cannot understand are those who advocate monetary union but reject any movement towards a federalist political structure for Europe. That is a formula for economic costs without any of the supposed political benefits.

Moreover, although monetary union in Europe would almost certainly accelerate the formation of a federalist political union among its members, those countries that are not part of the monetary union would be political outsiders. The consequences of this for the future peace and stability of Europe, while difficult to contemplate with any certainty, may well be unfavourable.

**What does Europe say to you?**

THE ECONOMIST JUNE 13TH 1992

## PAUL DE GRAUWE ET AL., "IN REPLY TO FELDSTEIN"

The Economist, July 4, 1992, 67.

In The Economist of June 13th, Martin Feldstein argued that Europe should abandon its plans for economic and monetary union. In this letter four European economists say he is wrong.

Sir—Martin Feldstein's arguments against EMU are flawed. Take his first claim that the creation of a single market does not require a single currency. The damaging effects of movements in exchange rates on trade may sometimes be exaggerated, but it is quite another matter to argue, as Mr. Feldstein does, that a single currency is likely to reduce intra-European trade. Is he seriously suggesting that internal American trade would be promoted by introducing separate currencies in each state?

Mr. Feldstein ignores the fact that the elimination of exchange-rate variability will reduce transaction costs. These savings could be biggest for smaller firms and for the smaller countries which, he claims, would be adversely affected by EMU.

Mr. Feldstein argues that Europe is not an optimum currency area. This is true, but it is equally true of America. The heart of Mr. Feldstein's argument is that, in the absence of wage flexibility and labour mobility, exchange-rate changes can be useful policy instruments. For example, if one country experiences a decline in demand for its products, a devaluation will increase foreign demand and thereby soften the blow. In a monetary union, the country experiencing such discomfort loses the option to devalue. But this traditional analysis came under increasing criticism during the 1980s. It is now recognised that devaluation is often ineffective in correcting economic shocks, being more likely to generate inflation.

Remember, too, that economic regions are not the same thing as countries. If Europe's textile industry, say, were centred on Milan and the car industry on Turin and Stuttgart, then Milan should ideally have one currency, and Turin and Stuttgart jointly another. Mr. Feldstein's logic points to Europe having more currencies than it does at present. In the absence of such a currency patchwork, replacing the lira and D-mark with the ECU would not, however, make the current mismatch between currencies and economic regions any worse.

## ECONOMIC FOCUS

Moreover, Mr. Feldstein's prediction that integration will necessarily lead to divergence is questionable. Economic integration leads mostly to intra-industry specialisation, where all countries buy and sell similar products, not inter-industry specialisation. This makes countries more alike, and so reduces the chance that shocks will hit one country only.

Mr. Feldstein claims that EMU will lead to stagnation in poorer member countries. But fixed exchange rates during the 1960s did not constrain growth in southern Europe (see table). Growth in output per worker was then much higher in Greece and Portugal than in Germany, and inflation no higher. By contrast, in the 1970s and the early 1980s, when exchange-rate adjustments were more frequent, inflation rose and growth fell sharply in the Mediterranean countries.

**How Southern Europe compares**

| | Inflation (GDP deflator) % annual change | | | Output per worker % annual change | | |
|---|---|---|---|---|---|---|
| | 1961–73 | 1974–83 | 1984–92 | 1961–73 | 1974–83 | 1984–92 |
| Germany | 4.4 | 4.5 | 2.9 | 4.1 | 1.9 | 1.5 |
| Portugal | 3.9 | 20.3 | 15.7 | 6.7 | 3.0 | 3.2 |
| Spain | 7.7 | 16.2 | 7.7 | 6.5 | 3.1 | 2.1 |
| Greece | 4.5 | 17.4 | 16.4 | 8.1 | 1.4 | 1.9 |
| Italy | 5.5 | 17.3 | 7.4 | 5.5 | 1.9 | 1.9 |

What about the danger that, with EMU, real wages in southern Europe will increase faster than productivity—as those in eastern Germany have done recently—and so push up unemployment? One big difference is that the labour markets in the EC are much less integrated than those of united Germany. Cultural and linguistic barriers will continue to exist, limiting labour mobility between countries. Indeed, Europe's low degree of labour mobility turns Mr. Feldstein's argument on its head. America needs a strong federal tax authority because differing regional tax rates can be evaded through migration. Europe has less need for a central tax authority precisely because labour mobility is low, and so national fiscal policies have more effect.

One cannot rule out the possibility of wage increases that outstrip productivity increases in Southern Europe. This has already been happening in recent years, eroding the external competitiveness of Italy, Portugal and Spain. But these losses cannot possibly be blamed on the European monetary system (EMS), as the countries concerned either were not members (Portugal joined only in 1991) or participated in a wide band (Italy, Spain).

An unrealistic convergence in real wages is a problem in any closely integrated economic area, even with separate currencies. But, with a single currency, rising unemployment in southern Europe as a result of deteriorating competitiveness could put serious political pressure on the European Central Bank (ECB). Therefore it may well be true that some of the poorer countries will not be ready and should not join EMU right from the beginning. This, however, is allowed for in the Maastricht treaty.

Mr. Feldstein questions whether the ECB can deliver price stability. He argues that public support for an anti-inflationary policy may be lacking in some countries. The recent convergence of inflation rates suggests, however, that politicians and trade-union leaders everywhere in Europe have come to understand that inflation does not pay. This is surely one important reason why the 12 governments had no difficulty in accepting the primary objective of price stability in the Maastricht treaty.

Moreover, the independence of the ECB will be more toughly ordained than that of the Bundesbank, whose law can be changed by a simple majority in the German parliament, unlike an international treaty. And the ECB will be obliged to aim directly at price stability, whereas the Bundesbank's statutes have the fuzzier aim of preserving the "value of the currency".

EMU sceptics are so fond of the status quo that they forget that the EMS is close to a *de facto* monetary union, defined as an area of fixed exchange rates plus capital mobility. There has been no realignment of exchange rates over the past five years, and general capital mobility was achieved in 1990. EMU will simply consolidate this, adding the appropriate institutional structure and unlocking the benefits of a single currency.

EMU is full of calculated risk. But so is the status quo, which was achieved only through the creation of the EMS—another calculated risk, which was shunned by many of EMU's current critics. We are convinced that EMU is a risk worth taking.

PAUL DE GRAUWE
University of Leuven

DANIEL GROS
Centre for European Policy Studies

ALFRED STEINHERR
European Investment Bank

NIELS THYGESEN
University of Copenhagen

### *Questions*

1. Assume that EMU takes effect as the treaty envisions by 1999. Will it work? Identify the main substantive elements and evaluate the strengths and weaknesses of each. Take into account the views of Feldstein and others. For example, do you agree with Feldstein's argument that a monetary union cannot succeed if the fiscal and monetary policy makers are separated as much as in EMU and if the central bank must rely on other authorities to set foreign exchange policy?

---

*Links to Other Chapters*

Foreign exchange is a basic unit in international finance. The reader has already encountered foreign exchange issues in earlier chapters. In U.S. markets, the American Depository Receipt is used to eliminate or at least minimize foreign exchange risk. For American financial intermediaries, a major accounting problem is how to convert accounts in one currency to another. GAAP reconciliation rules address this. Capital adequacy rules have been proposed to mitigate foreign exchange risk. The lowering of foreign exchange controls was a prerequisite for the European internal market.

We encounter foreign exchange issues throughout the rest of this book. The internationalization of the Yen and the development of offshore Yen currency accounts has been a major concern of Japan's government. Foreign exchange trading and settlements in different time zones gives rise to Herstatt risk in the payments system. Multicurrency clearance and settlement present very complex problems. Foreign exchange risk is at the heart of attempts to enforce or prevent the asset freeze described in Chapter X. Stock exchanges have begun to offer for trade securities denominated in foreign currencies. Futures, options, and swap markets are supposed to reduce foreign exchange risk, although they have been accused of the opposite. Even the final chapter, on emerging markets, presents a security listed in two currencies.

# Chapter VII

# JAPANESE BANKING AND SECURITIES MARKETS: INTERNATIONAL ASPECTS

For decades after World War II, Japan's financial system mobilized savings to fuel the country's remarkable economic recovery and then miracle growth. Guided by the Ministry of Finance (MOF) and the Bank of Japan (BOJ), its central bank, financial firms channelled funds at low rates to high value-added manufacturers, whose exports contributed to the country's ever stronger trade balance. Savers, consumers, and workers bore the cost of this system. To Western observers, the system looked very different from those they knew.

Today, even Japanese officials accept this as a fair picture of the financial system into the mid–1970s. Now the debate rages about the extent to which it still accurately describes the role and operations of the financial firms and their regulators. In the mid–1970s, fiscal deficits forced the government to borrow heavily from banks and others. Some observers argue that the balance of power shifted then from the government to the financial firms and that with that shift came freer markets.

In the early 1980s, the government of Japan announced it would free up its financial system. Since then, it gradually relaxed many formal and informal rules. With time, Japanese savers, users of funds, and financial firms found new opportunities at home and abroad. But change was too slow for many. Among the most outspoken were Americans, who consistently pressed the Japanese government to dismantle what they saw as official and other barriers to free trade in financial services.

The early 1990s brought the collapse of Japan's stock market, a weak domestic economy, a mountain of bad debts held by the banks, and the end of the almost 40 years of Liberal Democratic government, replaced by a loose coalition amid strong public dissatisfaction with the country's political economy. The question seemed to be whether the Japanese financial system could survive without fundamental change. The access of foreigners and the foreign activities of Japanese financial firms might be very different in the future.

Part I of this chapter concerns banks. It sketches the structure and regulation of Japan's financial system, lists the American grievances as stated in the most recent report of the U.S. Department of Treasury, and describes government policy in the financial inversion. Part II concerns securities companies.

As you read this chapter, compare the dominant issues for Japanese cross-border operations with those in the U.S. materials. What is the relative importance of concerns about the safety and soundness of those cross-border operations and concerns about competition? What would account for the differences you observe?

# PART I. JAPANESE BANKS

## A. THE STRUCTURE AND REGULATION OF JAPANESE BANKING

The readings identify as major features of Japanese banking at least the following factors:

- the banks
  - specialize by function and region
  - are very big on an international scale
  - benefit from Japan's current account surplus
  - benefit from keiretsu relationships
- banking has dominated securities markets traditionally
- finance ministry and central bank controls are extensive
  - administrative guidance is preferred to formal rules
  - policy changes very slowly
- bank failures are extremely rare

As you read the materials, consider several questions. How would these features and others you may find affect the international activities of Japanese banks and foreigners who want access to Japanese markets? To what extent would these features be due to government policy? Where government policy plays a role, how readily would you expect the government to be able to change the policies and behavior?

### 1. The Structure of Japan's Financial System

ITZHAK SWARY AND BARRY TOPF, GLOBAL FINANCIAL DEREGULATION: COMMERCIAL BANKING AT THE CROSSROADS

180–92 (1992).

*6.1.1 Introduction*

As might be expected, Japan's financial system reflects to a great degree the characteristics of the Japanese economy and society. Compared with other major industrialized economies, Japan's financial markets display considerable segmentation and specialization, supported by an extensive structure of regulation and constraints, both formal and informal. Financial markets in Japan, moreover, have never been seen as independent mechanisms for the allocation of resources; rather, they have been a means of allocating resources as determined by policy makers. The well-known Japanese emphasis on collective and group achievement applies to the financial sector as well. Thus, outright conflict and confrontational tactics are avoided—although competition, where permissible, can be fierce. This cooperative spirit is facilitated by the widespread movement of individuals between the public and private sectors. Government officials frequently expect to begin a second career working for the very firms they previously regulated.

The Japanese emphasis on loyalty and tradition also influences the structure of Japan's financial system. Given the clearly perceived hierarchical ranking of banks in Japan, the prestige associated with a business deal can be an important factor influencing decisions. These characteristic features of loyalty, tradition, and hierarchy have resulted, until recently, in a slower pace of change and adaptation in Japan than in any of the other major economies. Stability is often seen as a goal in and of itself, and has been achieved to a great degree. Thus, while the United States has experienced an ever increasing number of bank failures—200 in 1988 alone—Japan has had only one bank failure since World War Two. Recently, the well-protected banking industry—which had benefited from clientele and profit margins virtually guaranteed by the Ministry of Finance (MOF)—has been exposed to increased risk and declining profit because of continuous deregulation. The regulatory response to new risks and potential bank failures is still unknown.

Table 6.1 Japan—major economic indicators and the banking system

| | 1980 | 1984 | 1989 |
|---|---|---|---|
| Gross domestic product, (US$ bil.) | 1,062 | 1,256 | 2,830 |
| Current account, (US$ bil.) | −10.8 | +35.0 | +56.8 |
| Consumer inflation (percent) | 4.9 | 2.1 | 2.3 |
| Exchange rate, (yen–US$) (year-end) | 203 | 251 | 138 |
| Interest rate [a] per annum (percent) | 2.25 | 5.0 | 4.3 |
| Population (mil.) | 116.8 | 120.02 | 123.1 |
| Number of depository institutions | 7,456 | 7,263 | 6,744 |
| Number of offices | 40,697 | 42,527 | 45,314 |
| Population per office | 2,870 | 2,822 | 2,717 |
| Number of ATMs | n/a | 58,000 | 68,200 |
| Population per ATM | n/a | 2,069 | 1,805 |

n/a not available
[a] Central bank discount rate.

### *6.1.2 Financial Markets and Institutions*

#### *Financial markets*

Until recently, Japan's financial markets were characterized by a fairly rigid structure, with a large number of highly specialized institutions in well-defined (and usually well-protected) roles. The resultant structural barriers, combined with the considerable power and influence of official policy makers, have produced a financial market that lags behind other major nations in terms of innovation, completeness, and efficiency. This is clearly the result of two critical periods in Japan's recent history: the rapid industrialization of the country following the Meiji restoration of 1866, and the reconstruction and rebuilding of the

Japanese economy following the Second World War. The period of industrialization was characterized by the concentration of power and control in interlocking corporate groupings (called Zaibatsu prior to the Second World War, and Keiretsu in their somewhat weakened post-war form). This form of corporate structure encouraged a strong tradition of binding loyalty in business relationships, including financial activities. The post-war period saw the coordination and concentration of resources on behalf of national goals, an effort achieved through the almost total identification of official and private institutions and the general population with such goals.

### *Direct finance*

Indirect finance remains the main vehicle of financial market flows, especially in smaller business. As a result, financial intermediaries rather than markets have played the crucial role. During the period 1980–84, 89 percent of all financial market activity was indirect finance, with only 11 percent representing direct financial flows (Suzuki, 1987, 13). Thus, for example, the securities markets have been until recently rather unimportant as a source of financing. Instead, Japanese companies have relied heavily on debt (usually loans provided by banks) in their balance sheets, reaching a debt to equity ratio as high as 4:1 (compared with an average 1:1 in the United States; Viner 1987, p. 49).

Moreover, approximately 65 percent of equity in companies listed on the Tokyo Stock Exchange is held in an interlocking fashion by firms in the same Keiretsu, or with a similar close relationship (Viner, p. 46). One of the characteristics of Japanese indirect finance is the "main bank" system, whereby a special single bank represents a banking syndicate.

The stock exchanges had been relegated to a marginal role by frequent speculative cycles and suggestions of unsound practices (such as insider trading and manipulation). However, in the past decade the volume and extent of trading have grown tremendously, undoubtedly marking a turning point in the role of the exchanges both as a source of funding for companies and as a venue for investment by the public. Indeed, the Tokyo Stock Exchange is presently the world's largest. . . .

The privatization of government firms through flotations on the exchange has contributed to this rapid growth. In fact, the market value of one such firm, Nippon Telephone and Telegraph (in 1988, the largest firm in the world by market value), was greater than that of *all* listed West German industrials combined. Clearly, the TSE has become a major factor in Japanese financial markets, both as a venue for raising capital and as an investment alternative for individuals and institutional fund managers. It now presents increased competition for Japan's banks.

The bond market in Japan, including the huge government bond market, while enormous in size, ($1,980 billion at year-end 1989, 19 percent of the global bond market) is overwhelmingly dominated by public sector debt, 64 percent of the total. Bonds issued by private non-financial corporations constitute a marginal part of the bond market (7.7 percent).

Direct financing by Japanese banks has been virtually prohibited by Article 65 of the Securities and Exchange Law (sometimes called the "Japanese Glass–Steagall"), which rigidly defines the roles of financial institutions. Since banks are banned from the securities markets, security companies have filled this vacuum. There are 224 such firms in Japan, with an overwhelming concentration of influence and market share in the so called "big four"—Nomura, Daiwa, Nikko and Yamaichi. While dominating the securities industry in Japan, these firms have also acquired considerable worldwide influence. And as the barriers among financial institutions in Japan are reduced, they will undoubtedly come into more direct competition with the banking industry. For example, in January 1980, security companies began selling small denomination certificates of participation in bond trusts. The trusts, known as Chukoku funds since they invest primarily in medium term government bonds, are essentially similar to Money Market Mutual Funds in the United States. The ability of security firms to offer a close substitute to a bank deposit represented a significant blurring of the line between the security business and banking. In fact, the volume of such funds grew rapidly until 1987, when the deregulation of deposit interest rates slowed and eventually reversed their growth.

The short-term money market in Japan is extremely underdeveloped compared with those of other major industrialized countries. Whereas the volume of outstanding short-term debt in the United States in 1985 was equivalent to 40 percent of GNP, in Japan the figure was only 8 percent. Moreover, the market continues to be highly regulated and controlled, and most reforms enacted in recent years have been largely the result of foreign pressure.

Until 1980, the short-term market consisted of just two instruments: call money (available in maturities of up to seven days and used for settling bank reserve positions); and the bill discount market (in maturities from one to four months and used for transferring liquidity among financial institutions). Access to both instruments is extremely curtailed by the Bank of Japan (BOJ), which also controls the interest rates according to its monetary objectives. The first "free" short-term market, in which interest rates were able to respond to supply and demand, was the Gensaki or collateralized loan market (security repurchase agreement) established in 1970. In addition to having market-sensitive rates, the Gensaki is open to a wider range of participants. Individuals, however, cannot enter the market, and city bank activities are subject to various restrictions. Since 1984, three short-term market instruments have been created: short-term government bonds with a maturity of six months were introduced in February 1986; bonds with a three-month maturity began to be issued in September 1989; and yen-denominated bankers' acceptances were brought forth in June 1985.

Moreover, the combination of domestic demand and foreign pressure has resulted in a number of financial innovations in recent years, including yen CDs in 1984, and the introduction of foreign commercial paper in 1987. Nevertheless, the market is still encumbered by a wide range of restrictions due to both pressure from special interest groups and characteristic Japanese conservatism and caution in introducing change. The BOJ influences the money market by its leverage over the brokers, known as Tanshi, through whom many money market transactions must be channelled. These brokers are traditionally ex-BOJ officials, and as a matter of course consult the BOJ as to the calibration of crucial money market interest rates. Nevertheless, present trends clearly indicate that a freer, more integrated market is evolving.

### *The banking industry*

The rigid structure of Japanese financial markets is apparent in the banking sector, composed of a number of distinct types of institutions with clear functional divisions. Financial institutions have had their roles clearly defined by the triple segmentation of financial activity: the separation of direct and indirect finance (Article 65); the separation of banking and trust business; and the separation between short- and long-term finance. In Japan, both wholesale and retail banking operations are performed together as an integrated unit.

#### Commercial banks

The most important commercial banks are the so-called city banks, roughly equivalent to American money center banks. These 13 institutions (12 following the merger of Mitsui and Taiyo Kobe banks) some direct descendants of Zaibatsu banks, function on a nationwide level and have traditionally been the primary suppliers of funds to Japanese corporations. They have often enjoyed close, nearly exclusive relations with large concerns and other firms. The city banks, usually cash poor, depend heavily on the interbank market for funds and have extremely limited access to long-term funding. At the same time, the growing access of Japanese firms to less expensive direct funding (e.g., commercial paper) has led these banks to search for new areas of activity to maintain growth and profitability. BIS capital rules, and the 1990 declines in the TSE, further encouraged city banks to reduce their size. Moreover, most city banks have huge exposure to US LBOs, construction developers, and real estate lending.

The 64 regional banks, whose activities are usually limited to a specific locality, are major institutions. Indeed, most regional banks are ranked within the largest 500 banks in the world. However, unlike the city banks, regional banks have an abundant base of funds supplied by their retail depositors, and they are large net suppliers of funds in the interbank market. Local firms and borrowers, rather than the large nationwide concerns, are their principal customers for credit.

Foreign banks in Japan play a relatively limited role. With no natural customer base, restricted access to yen funding, and handicapped by cultural differences, the bulk of their business is in foreign exchange and other related areas. While the number of foreign banks has grown from 16 in 1968 to 82 in 1989, their collective share of the market has actually declined in recent years, and a few foreign firms have withdrawn from banking activity in Japan.

Specialized financial institutions

Alongside the commercial banks there exists a variety of special purpose institutions, created and nurtured to fulfil specific functions. Specialization and segmentation imply that access to designated areas is prohibited or restricted, so that only special institutions are allowed to enter. However, as the highly regulated environment in which special purpose banks function gradually becomes more competitive, they will be forced to adapt to a less protected environment.

. . .

### *6.1.3 Banking Product and Bank Competition*

Until recently, there was a strict correspondence between the type of banking institution and its product and range of activities, usually mandated by statute. Because of this strictly segmented financial system, competition within each grouping was intense, while competition between the groups was almost nonexistent. Thus, commercial banks, banned from both the securities business and long-term credit markets, collected deposits and extended short-term credit. Within the commercial bank group, the city banks focused on wholesale banking by maintaining a close relationship with the larger blue chip companies and serving their needs both domestically and abroad. By contrast, the regional banks served small and regional firms, obtained funding through a large natural deposit base, and often lent those funds through the interbank market to the liquidity-starved city banks. Foreign banks, with little access to domestic business, were relegated to the margins of the system and concentrated on foreign exchange and on serving subsidiaries of foreign firms.

The specialized banks had even more distinctly defined products and roles. The long-term credit banks, given their monopoly in obtaining long-term funding, dominated long-term lending. The trust banks, while providing some commercial banking products, concentrated on managing funds they were entrusted with. The various mutual savings and loans banks, credit cooperatives, and credit associations had clearly defined customer bases and roles. The cohesive nature of each of these groupings is highlighted by the role played by the various central banking institutions serving each category.

Under this system, not only were banks limited in their activities, they were also protected from non-bank competition by Article 65 and other regulations and statutes. These administrative guidelines were based on the separation between financial intermediation and direct financing, long- and short-term lending, deposit based and trust based activities, and the maintenance of specialized institutions for specific purposes.

As a result of both basic changes in the Japanese economy and the worldwide movement toward deregulation and liberalization, the rigid structure of the Japanese banking system has begun to change, but at a very measured pace. These changes are designed to force institutions enjoying a protected existence to adapt to competition in both their original markets and in new areas. One of the basic characteristics of the Japanese economy after World War Two was a tremendous shortage of capital. This meant that bankers enjoyed a lender's market for many years. In fact, the power of Japanese bankers had been so great that Japan was long known as "the banker's kingdom."

Today, however, Japanese firms and the nation as a whole generate tremendous capital surpluses. Thus, Japan has now become a borrower's market, and as Japanese firms have become cash rich and less dependent on their bankers, the importance of long-term relationships and corporate loyalty has diminished. In its place a more transaction and performance focused orientation has developed, similar to that in other industrial nations. Greater use of direct finance, seen in both equity (the booming stock exchange) and debt (spreading securitization), has further reduced the dominance of the banks. The regulatory authorities, both to develop more efficient markets and in response to increasing foreign pressure, have slowly and steadily reduced their involvement in the financial markets. For example, in recent years new financial instruments have been permitted, tax distortions reduced, interest rate and deposit regulations removed, and foreign exchange controls relaxed. Euro-yen CDs were introduced in December 1984, a Euro-yen commercial paper market was launched in November 1987, and Euro-yen lending has been deregulated. The ongoing reform of the financial process and the resultant increased competition (together with the BIS capital requirements and a poorly performing capital market) have increased banking risk. The MOF policy, so far, is to encourage strong institutions to assist weaker ones (Sender, 1990).

In response, Japanese banks have widened the scope of their activities. Commercial banks, faced with decreased loan demand and reduced interest margins, are increasingly seeking fee generating activities such as foreign exchange and securities trading, the issuing of mortgage loans, credit card companies, international operations, and even investment banking activities (security underwriting, mergers and acquisition business). Legislative weakening of Article 65 will eventually enable commercial banks to compete with securities houses. As a result, competition from the "big four" security houses in areas close to commercial banking activities, such as money market mutual funds and foreign exchange, is expected to be fierce.

The long-term credit banks, facing declining demand for long-term bank loans, are transforming themselves into investment banks while maintaining their emphasis on long-term financing. They have been very aggressive in courting international business and have become important players in the Euromarkets. The regional banks, notwithstanding their appellation, have increasingly entered national and even international markets. They have established a nationwide automatic teller machine (ATM) network and have established ties with the large, blue chip concerns that were once the exclusive preserve of the city banks.

. . .

While its pace may be uncertain and irregular, it seems clear that the trend toward less regulated and more liberalized financial markets in Japan will continue. There is no doubt that this will result in increased risks, due to the reduction of protective segmentation and the intensified competition.

. . .

*Notes*

1. Specialized financial institutions include three long-term credit banks whose unique role is eroding; 18 trust banks; hundreds of banks and credit associations for small business; a network of agricultural credit cooperatives under the umbrella of a central cooperative bank that invests their very large surplus in money markets; government financial institutions, such as an export-import bank; and a postal savings system that until recently held a very large share of private savings because of an exemption from withholding tax (lost in 1988).

---

## 2. Regulation of Japanese Banks

Swary and Topf, 197–9.

*6.2.1 The Regulatory Framework*

The regulation and supervision of banks in Japan is probably the most extensive and comprehensive of any developed nation. While the overt manifestations of such regulation can sometimes be subtle and indirect, the regulatory influence is in fact pervasive and decisive, affecting bank policy and activity in virtually every area and at almost every level.

Formally, the Bank of Japan, the nation's central bank, presides over the banking system in Japan in a manner somewhat analogous to that of the Bank of England in the United Kingdom. To a great extent, the Bank of Japan's relationship with other banks is contractual rather than statutory; in fact, BOJ decisions do not necessarily carry the weight of law, which has led to some lack of clarity concerning the Bank of Japan's role in bank supervision. This lack of clarity has been overcome by the Japanese inclination to seek accommodation and cooperation, enabling the Bank of Japan to, in fact, have extensive control.

Where the central bank does have statutory authority—in the issuing of currency and the control of the credit system—it has not hesitated to closely dictate the behavior of banks in such matters as the level of interest rates and the volume of credit. Additionally, the Bank of Japan is accorded the role of provider of liquidity to the banking system (lender of last resort), is widely perceived to be the guarantor of solvency for the Japanese banking system, and conducts monetary policy.

Japanese banking law gives actual supervisory authority over banks to the seemingly all-powerful Ministry of Finance. The MOF, in addition to being able to regulate interest rates on bank liabilities, can require banks to divulge virtually any information it deems necessary. It can enforce policy using either non-binding voluntary directives (so-called administrative guidance), or through the issuance of binding rules based on its authority under the banking law. The MOF is responsible for approving the business operations and merger of banks, as well as the opening of new branches.

The regulatory structure of banks in Japan is currently in a state of considerable flux. At present, regulations concerning capital adequacy, liquidity, and loans to single borrowers are formulated and enforced by the Ministry of Finance. The ministry has also devised a set of guidelines concerning international lending by Japanese banks, including a set of "administrative guidelines"—for country-risk evaluation systems. The supervision of overseas branches and subsidiaries is done on a fully consolidated basis, and has been considerably tightened in recent years.

Formally, foreign banks operating in Japan operate under the same laws and guidelines as domestic banks. In practice, however, the treatment of foreign banks is determined by the treatment accorded Japan's banks in the country of origin.

### *Scope of business—capital market activities*

The banking industry is regulated by Article 65 of the Security and Exchange Law, a Glass–Steagall type barrier between banking and the securities (investment banking) business. According to this article, banks are permitted to invest and participate in the underwriting of Japanese National, Municipal and Government guaranteed bonds. In Japan, commercial paper is not considered a security but a bill discounted. As a result of compromise, both banks and securities firms are allowed to handle commercial paper. Overseas affiliates of Japanese banks are permitted to underwrite Eurobond issues by non-Japanese firms. Significantly, most city banks place a high priority on overseas expansion by focusing on securities-related activities. It is expected that progressive liberalization will gradually take place over the next few years. In terms of bank performance, the contribution of non-interest income is currently relatively modest.

These are a number of principal securities powers available to Japanese banks and their subsidiaries:

- Japanese banks may underwrite and deal in government bonds (as of the beginning of the 1980s)
- they may underwrite and deal in commercial paper
- they may serve as the private placement agent of corporate and other debt securities
- they may render investment advice; under the 1986 investment advisory business law, bank subsidiaries may provide investment advisory services
- Japanese banks may buy and sell securities for their own portfolio investment account
- the banks may engage in futures activities both for their own account and for customers.

However, Japanese banks may not engage in insurance activities or in real estate.

Another important regulation that has segmented the banking industry is the provision that only long-term credit banks can issue long-term obligations in the underdeveloped capital market. Consequently, these banks have become an important supplier of long-term funds (especially for foreign borrowing).

### *Notes and Questions*

1. Administrative guidance also restricts banks from dealing in national government bonds, although no statute prohibits this.

2. To what extent are the main structural features of Japanese banking due to government policy? What other factors could explain these features? Consider how significant is the role played by the government.

---

## B. FOREIGN BANKS' ACCESS TO JAPAN'S DOMESTIC BANKING MARKETS

The access of foreign banks to Japan's financial markets is politically charged, particularly with the United States. After the sections describing foreign banks' market penetration and their regulation in Japan, we give the most recent analysis of the U.S. Department of Treasury. The Treasury is critical of barriers to entry facing U.S. banks. Use the material in the first two sections to help you evaluate Treasury's critique. As you read, consider the following questions:

(i) Do any government policies limit foreign banks' entry into Japan's domestic banking markets?

(ii) Do government policies discriminate against foreign banks competing in Japanese markets once they are in? For example, do regulated interest rates have an unfair impact? Is access to the

Bank of Japan's credit window discriminatory? Does administrative guidance discriminate against foreign banks? What is the function of law in a system relying on administrative guidance?

(iii) Overall, which government policies most seriously affect foreign banks' entry and operations in Japan, independent of policies toward the special features of Japanese banking?

(iv) What special features of Japanese banking affect foreign banks operating in Japan? Specifically, what is the effect of the keiretsu relationships on foreign banks operating in Japan?

## 1. Market penetration

During the 1980s, the number of foreign banks in Japan grew from 64 to 82, but their share of all banks' assets fell from 1.9% to 1.4%.

Swary and Topf, 192–5.

The growing importance of Japan as a financial center is illustrated by the increased presence of foreign banks. Only eight banks were represented in Japan before World War Two; by 1968 the number had only grown to sixteen. In that year international pressure on Japan to liberalize the licensing of foreign banks began to bear fruit, resulting in the number of foreign banks with branches in Japan increasing to 50 by 1978, and 82 by 1989.

An additional 124 banks maintained representative offices in Japan by 1987. In July 1985, permission was granted to foreign banks to open trust banks and by 1986 eight such autonomous trust banks were established. Foreign interest extended also to the capital markets; by late 1988, 47 securities firms from ten foreign countries had branches and/or subsidiaries operating in Tokyo.

Foreign banks in Japan lack a natural yen deposit base, because foreign institutions lack branch networks. As foreign banks engage to a certain degree in wholesale banking, they tend to depend on corporate bonds and short-term financial markets. However, foreign banks are prevented from issuing bank bonds, and therefore have been dependent on the money market and yen swap market for yen funds, and on borrowed funds (primarily from their head offices and the Euromarkets) for foreign currency denominated funds. During periods of capital shortage in Japan, foreign banks do have access to imported capital, and their ability to lend this capital to Japanese corporations has generated sizable profits in the past. However, such activity has become much less profitable in recent years, due to the declining demand for loans by the corporate customers, increased access to foreign funds on the part of Japanese banks, and easier access to foreign capital markets as a result of the integration and internationalization of financial markets. In June 1985 foreign banks were allowed to set up trust banking subsidiaries in Japan. In November 1984, they were allowed to deal in government bonds.

Foreign banks in Japan have always been very active in the Tokyo foreign exchange market, in trade financing, and letters of credit. To offset declining corporate lending, foreign banks are seeking to increase their investment in areas such as consumer and housing finance, factoring, and leasing. They emphasize their ability to provide Japanese firms with consultation and data on international markets and operations; information vital to the Japanese effort to maintain growth in overseas trade. These services have probably been the main reason that many Japanese corporations have maintained a relationship with foreign banks.

The entry of foreign banks into the trust banking business is seen as potentially very profitable. With the development of a freer market in asset management, many foreign banks believe that their experience in overseas funds management will enable them to capture a significant market share. Given the vast pool of assets in Japan, such potential fees would be very attractive. So far, the foreign bank presence in Japan has been marginal, representing about 1.4 percent of total assets of the banking system.

Access of foreign financial institutions to the securities markets has also improved, after the issue was raised by a number of foreign governments, including the UK and US. Foreign banks were allowed into the government bond underwriting syndicate in April 1984, and in October 1988 the share per foreign institution was raised from 0.07 percent to 1 percent, with the aggregate foreign share in the syndicate rising from 2.5 percent to 8 percent. Access to the market was further eased in April 1989 when four foreign security firms were appointed lead managers of the syndicate, and the auctioned share of the ten year government bond was increased from 20 percent to 40 percent. As of 1989, 18 foreign banks and 48 foreign security firms were permitted to deal in public bonds, and 25 foreign security firms were regular members of the Tokyo Stock Exchange. The number of foreign security firms in Japan grew from 12 in 1984 to 48 at the end of 1989.

## 2. The Regulation of Foreign Banks in Japan

EDWARD L. SYMONS, JR. AND JAMES J. WHITE, BANKING LAW

3rd Edition, 806–9 (1991).

. . .

The Bank Law of 1981 took effect on April 1, 1982. The Law includes a chapter entitled "Foreign Bank Branch" (Chapter 7). The chapter's six provisions are founded upon the stated principles that foreign bank branches are to be treated equally to domestic commercial banks and that as much "administrative guidance" as possible is to be expressly spelled out in the statute.

So far, the Bank Law has not changed the fact that branching is the only viable means of entry into Japan beyond a representative office.

The Law requires that each foreign bank branch receive an individual license from the Finance Minister. Therefore, a foreign bank cannot be granted one license which, without more, comprehensively permits the bank to establish two or more branches. [Art. 47, para. 1]. The Law treats each branch established as an independent "bank." [Art. 47, para. 2]. A license is granted to an applicant bank after the examination of its application by the M.O.F. in light of criteria set forth in the statute. They [include]:

. . .

(3) the commencement by the applicant of the business of banking shall be proper, such that it shall have no possibility of disturbing order in the financial market, in the light of the conditions of demand and supply of funds in the area where the business of the bank concerned is to be performed, the state of operations of banks and other financial institutions, and other economic and financial circumstances [Art. 4, para. 2, item 3].

... There has never been a "bank" created under the new Bank Law. In fact, no new Japanese commercial bank has been created since World War II, and a foreign "bank," as opposed to "branch," has never been created in Japan. The reason is the view that Japan is overbanked. Consistent with this view, "the promotion of financing efficiency" (one of the long-standing policies of the M.O.F.), is frequently explained by commentators to have the same meaning as "promotion of mergers between banks." Consequently, establishing a subsidiary is not a realistic way for a foreign bank to enter the Japanese banking market.

Acquisition of part or even all of the shares of a presently licensed and operating bank is another logical alternative to de novo entry. However, this method does not have many of the advantages of branching. First, Japanese corporate law allows the use of bylaws to prohibit cumulative voting. (The Commercial Code: Art. 256–3, para. 1). Consequently, acquisition of a small percentage of voting shares cannot guarantee a voice in management. Second, the Anti–Monopoly Law requires the permission of the Fair Trade Commission before a financial institution can acquire more than a 5 percent interest in any domestic corporation (Art. 11). Third, a foreign investor that wishes to obtain more than 10 percent of the outstanding shares of a domestic company must give advance notice to the pertinent authorities and sometimes must procure special approval. (The Foreign Exchange Law: Art. 26, para. 3). Fourth, and most important, is the "interlocking stockholding" phenomenon, wherein bank shareholders usually maintain a business relationship with a bank. Should the bank become the target of a takeover, these so-called "stable shareholders" would show a marked inclination not to dispose of their shares.

Another consideration in entering the banking business in Japan is that the "business of banking" does not cover the broad area of activities in which foreign bankers might wish to engage. (The Bank Law: Art. 10). The business of banking is a much narrower concept in Japan than in the United Kingdom or West Germany, or even than in the United States. For example trust business is in principle reserved exclusively to trust banks. As a legal entity trust banks are identical to commercial banks. They are both "banks" under the Bank Law. As a matter of form trust banks have obtained special approval to operate both trust business and traditional banking business at the same time. What has divided "banks" into two categories—those whose business is orthodox banking and those who devote themselves to trust operations and long-term lending—has been "administrative guidance." Whether foreign banks can enter the trust business is a controversial issue raised by several joint ventures of American commercial banks and large Japanese securities firms. These joint ventures have given birth to another issue—whether securities firms may engage in trust operations. Since both issues are related to the long established "fences," responses to these questions may reshape significantly the Japanese financial system.

Full participation in the domestic market requires access to the savings deposits of Japanese households. For personal savings, consumers primarily use time deposits, which are the main source of funds of the Japanese commercial banks. Most individuals use ordinary savings deposits and make frequent withdrawals from local branches to meet daily needs. Generally, checks are not widely accepted in Japan and most consumer transactions are in cash. The absence of restraints with respect to a bank's branching area, and nation-wide computerized withdrawal and deposit systems, enable a customer who has an account in one branch to withdraw his money from any other branch of the bank, and even sometimes from branches of other banks. Withdrawals can be made instantaneously from automatic tellers machines widely available throughout the country. Public utility charges can be paid from customer's account automatically.

. . .

Relative scarcity of Japanese depository funds for foreign bank branches is mainly due to the lack of branches. As noted above, each branch must acquire an additional license. The result is that 90 percent of foreign bank branches are located in the central business districts of Tokyo and Osaka. Foreign bank branches are not present in any form in the neighborhoods where most retail banking is done.

Additional foreign banks' funds come from the conversion of dollars to Yen on the foreign exchange market. The net conversion into Yen is limited within a certain prescribed amount (swap limit). Although this regulation applies to all authorized foreign exchange banks, considerably larger limits are allocated to foreign bank branches than to domestic banks because, for foreign bank branches, deposits are insufficient to meet their needs for Yen funds. Foreign banks also rely on Yen credits (borrowings) from Japanese financial institutions as a source of funds. There is no restriction today on these credits.

Other means used by foreign banks to raise Yen funds are issuance of negotiable certificates of deposit (NCD), and participation in the "call market," "bills discount market" and "Gensaki market." In each case foreign banks are treated more favorably than domestic banks. NCD's may be issued up to 30 percent of the Yen loan balance of a foreign bank, consisting of loan and securities assets, while a Japanese bank's limit is 50 percent of *its net worth.* Foreign banks also can freely participate in both the "call market" and the "bills discount market." They can raise Yen funds there without any limit, whereas domestic banks are often "guided" by the Bank of Japan which regards excessive dependence on these markets as unsound.... The "Gensaki market," where swap transactions of securities take place, is also completely open to foreign banks. On the other hand domestic city banks are given "guidance" from the B.O.J. on the maximum amount of securities selling used to raise funds. The B.O.J.'s lending facility is also available on favorable terms, although in general its use is strictly limited.

The majority of the Yen funds raised by foreign banks are allocated to commercial loans. Loans are subject to "regulation of large lot loans" and "window guidance." Under the "regulation of large lot loans," credit extension to one debtor may not exceed certain prescribed limits. (The Bank Law: Art. 13, para. 1). The limit for a commercial bank is 20 percent of its net worth (capital plus reserve funds). Foreign banks are exempt from this regulation for the five year period following the effective date of the Bank Law of 1981. "Window guidance," on the other hand, is not based upon a statutory or an administrative power. It is conducted by persuasion through the private business relationship between the B.O.J. and the Japanese financial institutions. The main function of the guidance is to control increases in bank lendings, particularly at a time of monetary restraint. The Japanese domestic banks are subject to detailed guidance and required to maintain strict compliance. Except for the period from 1973 to 1974 when the worldwide oil crisis occurred, foreign banks have never come under this guidance system.

. . .

***Questions***

1. Evaluate the criteria and procedures for entry of foreign banks.

2. Evaluate the limited operations of foreign banks. To what extent are the limits due to government policy? What other factors account for the limits?

---

## 3. The Treasury Department's Critique

Every four years, the Treasury Department gathers information about the openness of the banking and securities markets in many countries. The last study was published in 1990.

The Treasury acknowledged that "new opportunities" had opened for U.S. banks in Japan since discussions between the U.S. and Japanese governments began in the early 1980s. During the decade, the number of foreign branches rose from 38 to 122. Japan generally accorded foreign banks de jure national treatment. Better than national treatment was given when Japan allowed foreign banks to operate in local securities markets through an up to 50% interest in "offshore securities subsidiaries." Japanese banks lacked this vehicle. In 1989, foreign banks' loans grew faster than those of Japanese banks, which were subject to government limits to reduce real estate lending. On the other hand, from 1982 to 1989, Japanese banks' lending grew 145% and foreign banks lending grew only 18%. Finally, Treasury noted that Japanese banks earned a return on total assets of barely .40, well below an acceptable rate for a U.S. bank.

The following excerpts from the portion about Japan give some of the Treasury's major criticisms. The source is Department of the Treasury, "Japan," National Treatment Study 207–41 (1990) (hereafter Treasury Study).

In each case, be sure you understand the argument, then evaluate it.

1. Is the criticism sound?

2. Would change help the foreign banks?

3. What sort of standard is the Treasury applying: de jure national treatment, de facto national treatment, limited market access, or limited competitive opportunity?

## a. Limited Opportunities to Open Branches

U.S. banks can establish a presence in Japan via either branches, subsidiaries or representative offices. Physical expansion of branches in Japan is time-consuming because each branch opening requires issuance of a new license. However, Japanese authorities have made efforts to expedite this process. ... Certain provisions of Japanese laws pertaining to antimonopoly, banking, foreign exchange and foreign trade would also have to be met for acquisition to occur. Up to this point, no existing Japanese bank has been acquired by a foreign entity. Article 4.3 of the banking law provides that a reciprocity standard may be applied to foreign banks operating in Japan, relative to what their home governments allow for Japanese banks. The MOF advises, however, that this provision is applied only to the threshold question of establishment, i.e., banks from a country which totally bars entry to Japanese banks would not be allowed to establish in Japan.

As was the case in 1986, foreign banks, including those from the U.S., have a very small presence in Japan, despite the numerous changes in regulations in recent years. In December 1989, their share of total lending dropped to 1.7 percent, down from earlier years. In March 1983, for example, foreign banks accounted for 3.5 percent of total bank lending. In part, the decline in share reflects the relatively rapid growth of domestic lending in the latter 1980s. It also indicates a conscious judgment by the foreign banking community that the highly competitive environment, characterized by low margins on many types of lending, was not potentially profitable enough to justify a significant expenditure of resources in traditional banking areas. Liberalization in the financial area has continued to provide borrowers with increasing choices of alternative means of raising funds, such as commercial paper. This has contributed to heightened pressure on loan margins. Japanese domestic banks have also generally had a base of regulated deposits, on which generally lower than prevailing market interest is paid. This gives them a competitive advantage over foreign firms, which for reasons cited above, do not have a significant domestic branch presence. Loan charges are based in part on the blended costs of funds to domestic institutions, which continue to be below those of foreign banks. Foreign banks have been more successful in foreign exchange dealing and fee-based transactions. (According to one estimate, foreign banks command a 35 percent share of foreign exchange dealing activity in Japan.)

---

Note that during 1982–89 deposits in foreign banks grew at only half the rate of deposits in Japanese banks.

## b. The Unfair Impact of Regulated Interest Rates

Interest rate controls in Japan, in general, have provided an effective subsidy to Japanese banks and borrowers at the expense of Japanese depositors and foreign banks. To the extent Japanese banks fund themselves with regulated deposits, this subsidy has lowered their average cost of funds, giving Japanese banks a competitive advantage in their home market and, on a consolidated worldwide basis, in markets overseas. This is particularly true since foreign banks, in practice, have not had the option of acquiring a Japanese bank with a large deposit base.

It should be noted that, as controls have been partially relaxed in recent years, the amount of subsidy has lessened; however, it still exists and is considerable. (Japanese depositors lose a substantial sum due to the continued existence of controls on interest payments on deposits which keep rates below what they would be if freely determined; some of this lost interest also benefits borrowers.) While access to deposits at regulated rates has been a factor behind the rapid expansion of Japanese banks' international lending over the past several years, it has not been the only factor. (Others include the large Japanese current account surplus and substantial appreciation of the yen, relatively attractive markets overseas, and a persistent focus on market share.) Nevertheless, domestic interest rate ceilings still reduce the average cost of funds to Japanese banks, which gives them a significant advantage over foreign competitors, enabling them to tolerate narrower margins across a broad range of financial services and transactions.

Since the 1986 Update a series of regulatory changes has reduced the share of bank time deposits still earning low (regulated) interest, but has still not touched more than 40 percent of total bank deposits, including all "non-time" deposits. Until Japanese banks fully compete for all deposits by paying a market rate, Japanese banks will continue to enjoy a government-enforced subsidy at the expense of foreign banks and Japanese depositors. This remains an important factor for foreign banks and other firms, and will continue so until MOF completes deregulation of interest rates by introducing directly market-determined (rather than market-related) interest rates on all deposits, including time, "non-time" and money market certificates.

---

As you evaluate this, note that in Japan branches of foreign banks have no deposit insurance.

### c. Access to the Bank of Japan's Credit Window

Domestic banking institutions also benefit from the ability to make more extensive use of the Bank of Japan's credit facilities. This is especially true for city banks, credit lines for nine of which account for over 70 percent, about yen 5 trillion ($33 billion), of total credit lines under BOJ's direct lending program. Since the loans are made at the discount rate, which is below market rates, they provide a relatively cheap source of funds for banks. A ceiling is set on each individual institution's overall access to direct lending. The Bank of Japan has indicated that, in determining a bank's borrowing ceiling, it considers the firm's "business performance and market presence," based in part on the amount of yen lending and reserve requirements. However, foreign institutions have indicated that the basis for the ceiling determination remains vague and, despite the expansion for them in December 1989, appears to favor Japanese city banks.

---

### d. Keiretsu and Competition

Keiretsu are groups of Japanese companies, in various lines of business, that hold each others' shares, coordinate their business strategies, and share staff. Keiretsu come in many different combinations and degrees of cohesion. While many banks may lend to keiretsu firms, the main bank is the largest creditor and plays a pivotal role. Main banks have great power even though the Anti–Monopoly Law permits them to hold no more than 5% of any commercial firm's shares and prohibits Bank Holding Companies.

The Treasury's concern follows:

One of the major problems affecting foreign banking institutions' customer bases in Japan is the difficulty in penetrating group affiliations. Relationships between the banks and borrowers tend to be much closer than in the U.S., and city banks frequently provide the nucleus around which a group relationship is centered. In addition to providing loans to other group members, the banks are frequently assumed to back other group members with an unofficial guarantee. This enhances the credit standing of group members and lowers their cost of capital. While these relationships may provide benefits to all group members, they can also influence purchasing patterns of goods and services in favor of group members, to the disadvantage of nonmembers—including foreign firms.

### e. Keiretsu and Entry into Japan

... Acquiring an existing Japanese bank is legally possible but extremely difficult because of the cost and pattern of cross-shareholding, which tends to limit the number of shares available for purchase in the market. High stock prices have also acted as a deterrent to even friendly acquisition efforts.

### f. Administrative Guidance

According to one source, administrative guidance makes it "foolish to venture into the Japanese banking market without a resident expert as a guide." Symons and White continue:

> Any foreigner attempting to do business in Japan has, almost without exception, encountered a wall of ambiguity with respect to the laws governing the market. The reason lies in the complex way the Japanese government and commerce interact to create the commercial regulatory scheme. Japanese laws grant a great deal of discretion to the authorities who regulate commerce. As a result, actual regulatory policies and practice develop "flexibly" and are embodied in a complicated web of regulations, guidelines, interpretations and decisions, both published and unpublished. This complex web is called "administrative guidance" ("Gyosei-shido").
>
> This style of administration has often caused substantial difficulties for foreign banks, even those that have long engaged in banking activities in Japan. For example, a bank's main office may issue an order to its Tokyo branch based upon the published rules but its Tokyo branch may find it impermissible to carry out the order after holding lengthy person-to-person negotiations with an official of the Ministry of Finance (M.O.F.). This makes it difficult for foreign banks to plan accurately and with assurance. This ambiguity of rules accompanied by an "administrative guidance" system has recently become a main issue in negotiations between the United States and Japan concerning international commerce. Although under the policy of "internationalization of the Japanese financial market" the M.O.F. has tried to spell out some of the specifics of administrative guidance as clearly as possible, it is unlikely that this can suffice to westernize the Japanese way of governing commerce. This is largely because of the legal and social ethos that underlies all of Japanese business.

. . .

The Treasury said:

A continuing concern of foreign banks operating in Japan is the lack of transparency (see also discussion in Securities Chapter). While there is a body of published laws governing the operation of the banking industry, many important regulations or guidances continue to be given orally. This may disproportionately impact foreign firms, which are both less familiar with the unique Japanese environment and more used to dealing with a clear set of written regulations. Although there has been some improvement in their ability to transmit their views to responsible officials since 1986, foreign firms still experience difficulty on occasion in gaining access to Ministry of Finance and industry consultations influencing their operations. This was a particular problem in the formation of the Tokyo International Financial Futures Exchange, where foreign firms had little input in the decision process and were only informed of important specifics on the eve of the exchange's formation. Foreign participants are not included in the official advisory councils, which advise the Ministry of Finance on proposed structural and regulatory changes of central interest to both domestic and foreign financial firms. There are occasionally, however, informal Ministry of Finance study groups where a foreign firm may be included. One of these is the MOF/BOJ study group on money markets, operating since 1989, with three foreign firm members on it.

### g. Slow Process of Liberalization

[The Treasury said that] while Japan continues to liberalize domestic financial markets, the slow pace of reform has failed to keep up with developments in international financial markets. Foreign banks rely more heavily than their domestic counterparts on the domestic money markets for raising funds. While reforms have been made, money markets remain underdeveloped and unattractive due to restrictive regulations, a limited range of permitted instruments, and an array of taxes which encumber virtually every instrument.

Regulated interest rates (affecting roughly 40 percent of total bank deposits) reduce the average cost of funds to Japanese banks, in effect creating a subsidy which, on a consolidated basis, gives them an advantage over foreign banks in the Japanese market and allows them to tolerate narrower profit margins overseas, thus facilitating their expansion in these markets. The substantial amount of BOJ lending to Japanese commercial banks contributes to this funding advantage. Finally, foreign firms have experienced a lack of transparency in the GOJ regulatory process; participation in the rule making process for new products, services and markets is limited and foreign firms are not systematically allowed early opportunity to comment on proposed rules.

---

### h. Overall Low Foreign Share of Market

As you read the following, what do you learn from the large market share of Japanese banks in America and the small share of U.S. banks in Japan? What hypotheses could explain the difference?

The Treasury simply makes the following contrast:

As of year-end 1989, 18 U.S. banks in Japan operated 31 branches with assets of $16.6 billion and 21 subsidiaries with assets of $2.2 billion. Among the 21 subsidiaries are eight offshore securities subsidiaries, six trust companies, three leasing companies and four information/financial services companies. In contrast, U.S. banks operated 30 branches with assets of $17.9 billion and 14 banking subsidiaries with assets of $722 million in Japan as of year-end 1985. Eleven U.S. banks also maintain representative offices in Japan.

At the end of 1989, 41 Japanese banks in the U.S. operated 35 agencies with assets of $54.8 billion, 66 branches with assets of $306.3 billion, and 25 subsidiaries with assets of $59.4 billion. Japanese banks or individuals controlled five Edge corporations with assets of $236.7 million and one New York State Investment Corporation with assets of $15.5 million. Japanese banks maintain 88 representative offices in the United States. Excluding Edge corporations and the New York State Investment Corporation, this presence represents a net increase of 31 operating offices with an increase of $242.6 billion in assets since year-end 1985. At that time, 27 Japanese banks were operating in the United States, through 25 subsidiaries, 70 branches, and 51 representative offices. Their total assets were $177.9 billion.

*Questions*

1. Please note the questions at the beginning of this part of the text for each of the Treasury's concerns.

2. Compare the relative market share of U.S. banks in Japan and Japanese banks in the U.S.A. What do the different presences tell you? What hypotheses could explain the numbers?

3. Overall, how compelling is Treasury's argument?

4. How have the market liberalization policies affected foreign banks in Japan?

---

## C. THE INTERNATIONAL OPERATIONS OF JAPANESE BANKS

Japanese banks, already a factor for other banks to contend with in the 1970s, emerged as a driving force in international markets outside Japan in the 1980s. Their sheer size, the growing strength of the yen, and the country's burgeoning foreign reserves gave them a clout in foreign and offshore markets matched by few others. By the mid–1980s, the ten largest banks in the world were Japanese. Japanese banks accounted for over 50% of the growth in banks' international assets, and they held almost 40% of international bank assets (Swary and Topf).

Swary and Topf, 196–7.

... Japanese banks are major participants in syndicated loans, sovereign lending, interbank lending, and related markets such as the Euro floating-rate note market. This development is the result of the enormous increase of liquidity in Japan and the relative decline in domestic demand for funds. ...

Japanese banks abroad have also profited from strategies similar to those used by other Japanese industries in penetrating foreign markets: they have concentrated on market share rather than profit margins, and have focused on long-term plans rather than short-term results. Japanese financial institutions also enjoy the added advantage of open markets abroad and protected markets at home. Foreign firms have had considerable difficulty establishing themselves in Japan. This difficulty is due not only to the inaccessibility of Japan's protected markets, but also to such objective difficulties as language, cultural differences and the general force of tradition.

By the end of 1989, 41 Japanese banks had established 272 branches abroad, as well as 194 subsidiaries (by 1988), and 396 representative offices—a massive overseas presence. While located throughout the world, the largest share (about 70 percent) was in the United States, with an especially strong presence in California. In fact, five of the eleven largest banks in California are Japanese-owned. In addition to domestic business, they serve more than 1,000 subsidiaries of Japanese firms and the sizable Japanese population located in California. By year-end 1988, commercial and industrial loans to US residents reached $60 billion. Also, US offices of Japanese banks are large net borrowers in the domestic interbank market. In most UK branches of Japanese banks, assets and liabilities are denominated in currencies other than Sterling. Branches of Japanese banks in the UK, unlike their US offices, deal mainly in foreign currency with non-UK residents. UK branches of Japanese banks are large net borrowers in the interbank Eurocurrency market and are the largest issuer of Euro–CDs. These funds are used to finance related offices in other countries, including head offices in Japan.

Japanese banks have also been aggressive in pursuing every form of business in the Euromarkets. All the city banks have London branches, and an increasing number are opening operations in the Federal Republic of Germany, Switzerland, and other continental centers. By so doing, they have acquired experience in securities dealing, experience that will be invaluable once Article 65 is relaxed. Such involvement was most dramatically illustrated by the Sumitomo bank investment of US$ 500m to obtain a limited interest in Goldman Sachs, the US investment banking partnership. As a condition for approval of the deal, Sumitomo bank received no voting rights in return for its investment.

---

Japanese banks moving abroad seized the chance to broaden their operations into securities outside of Japan. This raised several regulatory problems. Masaaki Tanaka, lecturing at Harvard Law School, May 5, 1992, explained how Japanese regulations affect the operations of Japanese banks in foreign countries:

## MASAAKI TANAKA, "JAPANESE REGULATIONS CONCERNING JAPANESE BANK OPERATIONS IN FOREIGN COUNTRIES"

Excerpts From Talk Delivered at Harvard Law School, May 5, 1992, 15–18.

A major debate occurred during the early 1980's with regard to applicability of Article 65 of the Securities and Exchange Law, which separates banking and securities businesses, to European subsidiaries of Japanese banks and securities companies. The background of this debate was competitive disadvantage allegedly incurred by those subsidiaries against European financial institutions which engage in "universal banking." Eventually permission was granted for those European subsidiaries of the banks to conduct securities business, but no written official document can be found to this effect.

While the foreign subsidiaries of the banks started securities business, it remains essentially unknown to what extent they may expand the scope of their securities business. As there is no definitive Japanese legal authority which prohibits such companies from conducting a full range of securities business, it has been the position of the banks that those subsidiaries should be allowed to engage in the type of securities businesses permitted under the local laws and regulations.

On the other hand, the Ministry, being under the pressure from the Japanese securities industry, has been citing the *spirit* of Article 65 in issuing oral administrative guidances.

One example of such a guidance is called "Three Bureaus' Agreement." It is simply an agreement reached among the Banking Bureau, the International Banking Bureau and the Securities Bureau of the Ministry of Finance with regard to the business of underwriting securities by foreign local companies owned by Japanese banks. Even no circular exists on this issue. What is believed to contain the contents of the agreement is an internal memorandum of the MOF's Banking Bureau, although no seal, an equivalent of a signature, is placed on the memo. The memo reads as follows:

"1. In cases where a foreign local company of a Japanese bank participates in a syndicate of underwriting managers, on the occasion of issuance of a foreign bond by a Japanese company, the Japanese bank shall pay high respect to the experience and the role of the securities companies to date, and be cautious so that no violation arises with respect to the provisions of Article 65 of the Securities and Exchange Law."

"2. In order to implement the purpose of the above thoroughly, an arrangement, an order and so on of the names of companies in a prospectus and tombstone ad shall be given a careful attention."

This is interpreted to mean essentially that a foreign securities subsidiary of a Japanese bank is not allowed to become a lead manager when a Japanese company issues a bond overseas. Currently a regulatory action named "Review of Various Regulations and Practices" is underway, and the Three Bureaus' Agreement is the subject of the review. But, the review process seems to be proceeding not from a legal standpoint, but in search for compromise among interested parties.

The MOF supervises banks' subsidiaries indirectly via reports from the banks. The "Ordinance On Reports Of Foreign Exchange Transactions Etc." requires banks to submit a certain form of report concerning a foreign subsidiary's management condition on an annual basis.

The MOF inspectors also conduct indirect supervision by grading the bank's investment in a foreign subsidiary. The financial position of a subsidiary is examined and discussions take place between the inspector and the bank's official during the examination period.

An on-site examination of a foreign subsidiary is not conducted, but informal hearings from senior management of those subsidiaries are frequently conducted by MOF officials traveling abroad.

During the 1980's, the Japanese banks rapidly expanded their foreign franchise. It may not be too far from the truth to say that the Japanese Banking Law, when enacted in 1981, did not expect such a wave of rapid internationalization of Japanese banks. As a result, the Ministry of Finance was placed in the awkward situation of having to regulate banks' international activities without evident legal authorities. The MOF turned to the objectives of the Banking Law and strived to attain its mission making full use of traditional regulatory process of administrative guidance.

Now comes a new trend where foreign countries criticize such a method of regulation as lacking transparency, as Japanese banks' presence in foreign countries increases and the businesses of foreign financial institutions in Japan become active.

The critical point seems to be the extent to which participants in the Japanese financial market, as opposed to Japanese banks abroad, become aware of and take action to respond to high expectations with regard to Japan's role in the international community. "Internationalization of the Japanese financial market" now is dependent upon "internationalization of domestic participants in the Japanese financial market." Although Japan will achieve this goal, it will take some time before then.

### *Notes and Questions*

1. For many years until the mid–1980s, MOF allowed Japanese banks to open only one or two foreign branches or subsidiaries each year.

The quantitative limit forced banks to think carefully about the strategy behind their overseas expansion over a long period of time. The limit fell as Japan's balance of payments improved dramatically in the 1980s.

2. How significant is MOF's control of the foreign and offshore operations of Japanese banks? Evaluate the "Three Bureaus Agreement." What do you learn from it about the process by which the government framed and applied policy to the offshore operations of its banks?

3. Does the home base of Japanese banks confer a competitive advantage in foreign and international markets? How would the following elements of the Japanese financial system affect the Japanese banks' international operations? How important would these elements be compared to other factors, such as the performance of the economy?

a. Specialization

b. Large size

c. MOF controls over domestic interest rates

d. The no-failures policy toward banks

4. How would you expect the foreign operations of Japan's banks to affect these elements of the financial system?

---

## D. THE IMPACT OF THE FINANCIAL CRISIS IN THE EARLY 1990s

### 1. The Crisis

In 1992, Japan's finance minister acknowledged publicly that the nation's banks carried a dangerously high level of nonperforming loans. The immediate cause was the steep collapse of stock and real property values, whose spectacular price rises the banks had helped to finance in the 1980s. The stock market collapse is discussed in more detail in Part II. The ensuing recession pushed more borrowers into bankruptcy, so that the value of bankruptcies in both 1991 and 1992 was eight times the 1989 value (Robert Thomson, "Property is still the problem for Japanese banks," Financial Times, 21).

Estimates varied about the extent of problem loans. In early 1993, some observers guessed that bad loans held by the 21 largest banks were probably Yen 30 trillion, twice as high as the publicly announced figure of 4.1% of all loans. (Robert Thomson, "Japan's banks under heavy pressure," Financial Times, March 24, 1993, 6.)

By late 1993, the major banks announced of drops of roughly 20% in their net profits. Declining interest rates, which had increased their profitability since 1992, were not dropping as much and so were no longer a good source of profit. A well known rating agency for international banks reported that if loan loss provisions were "at the right level" the Japanese banks would lose all existing capital except their hidden reserves on securities. Japan's banks placed as the least profitable in the world (John Gapper, "Japanese banks' loan woes," Financial Times, December 20, 1993). Not surprisingly, credit rating agencies like Moody's lowered the ratings of Japan's largest banks.

***Question***

1. How would the steep decline in stock prices affect Japanese banks' capital and capacity to lend?

---

## 2. Solving the Bad Loan Problems

Japan's government, rather than force a rapid write-off of the bad debts, initially encouraged banks to help ailing companies and promoted a cooperative agency that would buy problem loans from the banks.

The LDP Government took steps that would disguise the extent of the problem at individual banks and for banks as a group. It allowed banks not to classify as non-performing any loans which they had "restructured" by substantially reducing the interest rate. Banks were permitted to deduct from taxes the lost interest. (Robert Thomson, "Japan's banks under heavy pressure," Financial Times, March 24, 1993, 6.) Trust banks, previously obliged to report only interest actually received, were allowed to book as received unpaid interest not more than six months overdue (Robert Thomson, "Japanese banks put off facing up to bad loans," Financial Times, May 14, 1993, 21).

The Cooperative Credit Purchasing Company (CCPC) was established in 1992 by Japanese banks acting jointly. The banks cannot deduct provisions for their bad loans from income for tax purposes, but they can deduct losses. A bank sells the CCPC bad loans, along with the collateral, usually worth no more than 70% of the loan principal when the loan is made. CCPC values the collateral and pays the bank that value, financed by a loan from the bank. The bank continues to manage the loan and the collateral. If the collateral is sold for less than its transfer price to CCPC, the bank makes up the difference. But in fact, CCPC has sold very little of the collateral it holds.

CCPC made its first big loan purchases, with face values of Yen 683 billion, in the weeks before the end of the banks' fiscal year in 1993. BOJ announced the transfers. By October 1993, just before the end of the semi-annual reporting period, it had paid Yen 602 billion for loans with face values of Yen 1.2 trillion. CCPC has a 10 year life expectancy.

The Bank of Japan let its rediscount rate fall to 1.75% by late 1993. This dropped the cost of funds to the banks which, because their lending rates did not fall proportionately, became more profitable.

BOJ and the Ministry of Finance proposed different ways to solve the bad debt problem. BOJ urged more liberal policies to allow banks to securitize their bad loans, writing off the losses. The governor reportedly wanted stronger banks to write off as much as possible, but the finance minister wanted all banks to follow the ministry's guidelines for gradual write-offs and refrain from securitization. (Robert Thomson, "Japan learns the American way," Financial Times, December 9, 1993, 21.)

MOF allowed banks to enter lines of business previously closed to them, at home and abroad. The reforms are described below. Abroad, for example, commercial banks led underwritings of 29 straight international bonds issued by Japanese companies from April to September 1993; Japanese securities companies led only 17 ("One mountain conquered," The Economist, October 23, 1993, 93).

### *Questions*

1. Why would the government offer banks incentives to restructure their bad loans rather than encourage them to write them off?

2. Evaluate the CCPC solution to the bad debt problem. What is solved? What are the implications for Japanese banks?

3. What does this set of solutions tell you about the likelihood that the barriers to foreign banks will fall? Is the financial system changing fundamentally?

---

## 3. Liberalization and the Financial Reform Act of 1992

In 1989, the government identified five options for reforming the structure of the financial system:

Swary and Topf, 191.

- The piecemeal approach, maintaining the present system while allowing gradual blurring of lines;
- Separate subsidiaries, allowing financial firms to establish single purpose subsidiaries in different areas of finance;
- Multi-functional subsidiaries, allowing firms to set up a subsidiary which would engage in a variety of activities;
- Holding companies, to allow banks and securities firms to establish holding companies which would in turn own various financial subsidiaries;
- A universal banking system, which would introduce a European style fully universal banking system permitting all activities in a single entity.

Three years later, the new law appeared. A summary follows.

## DAVID A. SNEIDER, "FINANCIAL SERVICES REFORM IN JAPAN"

International Securities Regulation Report 6 (February 6, 1993).

In June 1992, Japan's Diet enacted sweeping legislation aimed at increasing competition among different segments of the financial services industry. The Financial Reform Act, which will take effect after implementing regulations are issued in April, amended the Securities and Exchange Law, the Banking Law, and other statutes. The two most significant reforms give banks permission to establish securities subsidiaries similar in function to the so-called "Section 20 affiliates" in the United States and give securities companies and other financial institutions permission to establish trust bank subsidiaries.

The basic approach of the Financial Reform Act is to impose relatively few statutory restrictions on the newly permitted subsidiaries while granting broad regulatory discretion to the Ministry of Finance (MOF) to apply additional limitations. This should enable the MOF to carefully adjust the pace and scope of change according to how quickly affected financial institutions are able to adjust to the new competitive environment. Indeed, while the Financial Reform Act has transformed the landscape of Japan's financial services industry, it is likely to be implemented in such a gradual manner that the impact of the reform will not be felt fully for many years to come.

### Securities Activities by Banks

The Financial Reform Act establishes for the Japanese securities industry a framework similar to that now existing in the United States: Bank groups will be able to compete with securities firms in most lines of business by continuing to conduct certain securities activities in the bank itself and by engaging in other activities through newly permitted securities subsidiaries.

At the same time, however, banks will be handicapped in several important respects: The licenses granted initially to the new subsidiaries will limit their activities primarily to corporate bond underwriting and dealing as well as activities that banks can currently engage in directly; firewall restrictions will be imposed between banks and their securities subsidiaries; and new securities licenses will be issued only on a selective basis. The MOF has stated that it will not consider easing its initial regulations for at least two to three years.

The statutory basis for the new subsidiaries is an amendment to the Securities and Exchange Law's Article 65—often referred to as Japan's Glass–Steagall Act—that allows the MOF to grant securities business licenses to majority-owned subsidiaries of banks and other financial institutions to be specified by ordinance ("securities subsidiaries"). Although acquiring an existing securities firm is a theoretical option, the

MOF has made it clear that acquisitions will not be approved except in a "rescue" context.

*1. Scope of Activities.* Banks in Japan may directly engage in underwriting and dealing of government bonds as well as instruments newly designated as securities under the Securities and Exchange Law as a result of the Financial Reform Act. The latter include such instruments as commercial paper and asset-backed securities. Banks also will be permitted to handle private placements of any security.

Although the Financial Reform Act formally expanded the securities powers of banks—for example, by making commercial paper a "security"—in practice it did little to expand the scope of their direct securities activities.

The only explicit statutory restriction on the scope of activities of securities subsidiaries relates to equity brokerage. Here, the Financial Reform Act provides that "for the time being" the MOF shall not grant to any securities subsidiary a license to engage in that activity and that, if an existing securities firm is acquired by a bank, the MOF may terminate the firm's stock brokerage license. This provision is intended to protect medium- and small-size brokers in particular, which are largely dependent on stock brokerage commissions for their revenue.

In addition to the restriction on equity brokerage, the MOF announced in a Dec. 17 release that it will exercise its licensing authority to exclude securities subsidiaries from engaging initially in the following activities: underwriting, dealing, and brokerage of stocks; brokerage of stock index futures and options; and dealing and brokerage of equity-related products such as convertible bonds and bonds with warrants. In effect, the principal initial reward to the banking industry is access to the straight corporate bond market.

Within this regulatory framework, Japanese banks are expected to allocate their securities activities among different entities:

- Equity brokerage and underwriting and perhaps other retail activities will continue to be conducted by securities firms affiliated with the bank through its industrial group (while direct bank ownership of such affiliates is limited to 5 percent, actual influence arising from group ownership of up to 50 percent and employee exchanges is often very significant).

- Most securities subsidiaries will focus initially on corporate bond underwriting and dealing as well as perhaps private placements, commercial paper, and asset-backed securities, and some may conduct government securities activities.

- In most cases, government securities underwriting and dealing will be kept in the bank, possibly along with optional activities such as asset-backed securities.

*2. Firewall Restrictions.* As with the restrictions on the scope of activities, firewall restrictions will be implemented primarily through regulation. As a matter of statute, the Securities and Exchange Law and the Banking Law expressly prohibit the following with respect to banks and their securities subsidiaries (as well as with respect to new banks and their securities company parents):

- Dual employment of officers or employees in the bank and securities affiliate.

- Transactions between the bank and the securities affiliate that are not entered into on an arm's-length basis.

- Transactions by the securities affiliate with a customer of the bank that are tied to an extension of credit to the customer by the bank.

The Financial Reform Act authorized the MOF to stipulate by ordinance more detailed restrictions deemed necessary to implement the foregoing principles or to otherwise protect investors or the soundness of banks. In its Dec. 17 release, the MOF announced that forthcoming regulations will include the following firewall restrictions:

(a) "Main Bank" Firewall. A securities subsidiary will not be allowed to act as lead manager in a securities offering by any issuer with which its parent bank has a "main bank" relationship unless the issuer has net assets of ¥500 billion ($4 billion) or more. Such a relationship will be deemed to exist if the bank is acting as the issuer's bond trustee (or so-called commissioned company) for the issue or so acted in a majority of the issuer's recent bond offerings. The ¥500 billion net asset test leaves unrestricted underwriting for approximately the 34 largest issuers whose outstanding debt securities currently constitute more than 40 percent, by volume, of the bond market.

In a related move, the MOF announced the five-year phase-out of the so-called Three Bureaus' Guidance, which prevents offshore securities subsidiaries of Japanese banks from lead managing foreign bond offerings by Japanese issuers.

(b) Joint Visits. Joint visits to customers by representatives of a bank and its securities subsidiary will be prohibited in principle unless requested by the customer.

(c) Confidential Information. Exchanges of non-public information concerning a customer or an issuer between a bank and its securities subsidiary will be prohibited unless consented to in writing.

(d) Exchange of Personnel. A securities subsidiary will be expected to raise to 50 percent within five years the ratio of directly recruited employees, as opposed to transferees from its parent bank. Additional restrictions will limit the ability of persons who have served as officers or directors of the securities subsidiary to return to positions of responsibility at its parent bank.

(e) Shared Facilities. The headquarters offices of a bank and its securities subsidiary may not be in the same building. Other restrictions will be imposed on sharing branches, dealing rooms, and computer facilities.

(f) Additional Restrictions. The following will also be subject to restrictions: the percentage of revenues that a securities subsidiary may derive from transactions with its parent bank; underwriting by a securities subsidiary of securities issued by its parent bank; tie-in sales; sales to a bank of securities underwritten by its securities subsidiary; and bank financing of customer purchases of securities underwritten by its securities subsidiary. In addition, the use of proceeds must be disclosed if an offering underwritten by a securities subsidiary is intended to refinance a debt to its parent bank.

3. *Selective Licensing.* Consistent with a Diet resolution attached to the Financial Reform Act, the MOF has stated its intention to control the number and timing of licenses granted to securities subsidiaries in order to maintain an appropriate competitive balance between the securities and banking industries and among different segments of the banking industry. Japan's three long-term credit banks, seven trust banks, and two central cooperative banks are being given a head start of at least one year on the 10 city banks whose extensive retail branch networks are thought to provide an advantage. The MOF is also expected to grant securities licenses only to a limited number of the eligible institutions in any segment, such as to the stronger two of the three long-term credit banks.

## New Trust Banks

The Financial Reform Act, for the first time, permits securities firms to establish commercial bank or trust bank subsidiaries and also permits other financial institutions to set up trust banks. Since Japan's major securities firms are not thought to have an interest in retail banking, they are expected to establish only trust bank subsidiaries which, in addition to trust banking activities, may conduct commercial banking activities such as foreign exchange, swaps, and lending. It is likely that only two or three securities firms will be permitted to establish trust banks initially. Similar to the case of securities subsidiaries, at first only the long-term credit banks, the central cooperative banks, and the Bank of Tokyo will be eligible to establish trust bank subsidiaries, and only several of them will in fact obtain permission.

Like securities subsidiaries, the new trust banks will be restricted both in terms of scope of activity and firewalls. Most significantly, the new firms will be excluded initially from engaging in the most profitable segments of the trust banking business, including loan trusts (a form of savings instrument) and pension trusts (which manage corporate pension funds). Permitted activities include property trusts, such as land trusts, and certain designated money trusts, such as securities investment trusts and fund trusts, which are expected to be a strategic focus of securities firms' subsidiaries.

## Options for Foreign Financial Institutions

The Financial Reform Act offers relatively few benefits to foreign financial institutions because special dispensation previously enabled them to operate both securities and banking entities, and in some cases trust banks, in Japan. The MOF allowed foreign banks to establish 50 percent-owned securities affiliates in the 1980s and foreign securities firms to establish bank branches of 50 percent-owned bank affiliates beginning in 1991.

Under the new law, foreign banks seeking to enter the Japanese securities industry will have three options: apply as in the past for a securities license for the Japanese branch of a non-Japanese securities affiliate, but limit the affiliation to 50 percent; do the same, but increase the affiliation to more than 50 percent; or establish a domestic Japanese securities subsidiary.

In the past, the second and third options were not available because the law required foreign firms to enter the Japanese market through Japanese branches of 50 percent or less foreign affiliates licensed under the Foreign Securities Companies Law. Despite the change in law, the advantages of majority ownership or of entering through a domestic subsidiary rather than an offshore company are unclear.

For foreign financial institutions that already operate securities and banking operations in Japan, the Financial Reform Act offers the option of increasing the affiliation of the two entities from 50 percent. However, because it is highly unlikely that new firewall restrictions will be imposed between the two entities so long as their affiliation is limited to 50 percent, there may be a significant advantage to maintaining the status quo. Some firewall restrictions currently exist between the banking and securities affiliates of foreign institutions, but they are far more limited than the new rules proposed.

### *Questions*

1. Compare the Financial Services Act with the five options considered by the government in 1989. What was chosen? What does this tell you about the prospects for change in Japan's financial system?

2. Does the decision to end the Three Bureaus Agreement indicate that MOF is losing control over offshore activities of banks?

3. How would the Treasury evaluate the Financial Services Act? Do you see signs that the Japanese banking system is fundamentally changed from what Treasury found in earlier studies? Bear in mind that the Clinton Treasury clearly announced its intention to open Japan's financial markets. Will the 1992 law be a useful counterweight to the likely U.S. initiative?

4. What is the role of offshore markets in this restructuring?

---

# PART II. JAPANESE SECURITIES MARKETS

From 1986 to 1990, total equity and bond issues by Japanese firms, at home and abroad, grew more than 4.5 times to Yen 28 trillion, of which 41% was external. In 1991, the volume fell 65%. The late 1989 crash of the Tokyo Stock Exchange "led to a virtual closing of the markets ... from March through June, 1990" and a stagnant market after that, according to Kunio Hamada. He offered the following table showing the major types of domestic and foreign financing over the six years.

## KUNIO HAMADA, "EXTERNAL ISSUES OF SECURITIES BY JAPANESE COMPANIES," IN JAPAN SECURITIES RESEARCH INSTITUTE, CAPITAL MARKETS AND FINANCIAL SERVICES IN JAPAN: REGULATION AND PRACTICE 246 (1992).

Table 1 Internal and External Financing Activities by Japanese Companies

| Year ended March 31, | 1986 | 1987 | 1988 | 1989 | 1990 | 1991 |
|---|---|---|---|---|---|---|
| | | | In billion of Yen | | | |
| Straight Bonds | | | | | | |
| Domestic | 943.5 | 980.0 | 915.0 | 749.0 | 729.0 | 206.6 |
| External | 1,439.3 | 1,639.2 | 824.0 | 842.6 | 1,119.9 | 2,298.2 |
| (Euro-yen) | (235.0) | (472.0) | (312.0) | (154.5) | (334.1) | (1,648.3) |
| Convertible Bonds | | | | | | |
| Domestic | 1,585.5 | 3,468.0 | 5,055.0 | 6,994.5 | 7,639.5 | 911.0 |
| External | 948.0 | 485.3 | 1,076.6 | 1,066.5 | 1,738.9 | 513.8 |
| Bonds w/Equity Warrants | | | | | | |
| Domestic | 55.0 | 104.0 | — | — | 915.0 | 395.0 |
| External | 866.2 | 1,993.2 | 3,439.0 | 4,982.1 | 8,269.8 | 2,624.5 |
| Stock | | | | | | |
| Domestic | 651.3 | 631.5 | 2,083.9 | 4,563.8 | 7,560.0 | 664.3 |
| External | 10.7 | 0.6 | 39.0 | 16.5 | 336.4 | — |
| Domestic Total | 3,235.3 | 5,183.5 | 8,053.9 | 12,307.3 | 16,843.5 | 4,036.3 |
| (%) | (49.8) | (55.7) | (60.0) | (64.1) | (59.5) | (42.6) |
| External Total | 3,264.2 | 4,118.2 | 5,378.7 | 6,907.7 | 11,465.0 | 5,436.5 |
| (%) | (50.2) | (44.3) | (40.0) | (35.9) | (40.5) | (57.4) |
| Grand Total | 6,499.5 | 9,301.7 | 13,432.6 | 19,215.0 | 28,308.5 | 9,472.8 |
| (%) | (100.0) | (100.0) | (100.0) | (100.0) | (100.0) | (100.0) |

Notes: 1. Exclusive of issues of straight bonds by banks, but inclusive of issues by overseas financing subsidiaries of industrial companies.

2. "External" is inclusive of private placements, but "Domestic" is exclusive of private placements.

Source: Bond Review, The Bond Underwriters Association of Japan.

The Ministry of Finance, through its Securities Bureau, regulates Japanese securities markets. It supervises securities companies, securities finance companies, stock exchanges, central depository and delivery organizations, investment trust management companies, foreign securities firms, and banks doing securities business. The Securities Bureau administers primary and secondary markets in stocks, yen and foreign currency bonds. (See Japan Securities Research Institute, Securities Market in Japan (1992).)

Japanese investors, issuers, and financial firms played an increasingly important role in foreign and international markets during the 1980s.

Their activities and the government's policy is the subject of the next section. The following section presents foreigners' efforts to enter and participate in domestic securities markets. Finally, we take a closer look at the crisis in the securities markets since the late 1980s and government policy toward it.

# A. FOREIGN ACCESS TO SECURITIES MARKETS IN JAPAN

As a country running a substantial trade surplus, Japan naturally exports capital. Kinoshita reported the volumes of bond issues by non-residents and the rules governing those issues in the following tables.

**Bond Issuance in Japan by Non-residents**

| Calendar Year | Samurai Bonds[1] | | Reverse Dual Bonds[2] | | Shogun Bonds | | Private Placement of Yen-Denominated Foreign Bonds (Shibosai) | | Samurai CB | | Shogun CB | | Euroven Bonds | |
|---|---|---|---|---|---|---|---|---|---|---|---|---|---|---|
| | No. of issues | Issue amount (million yen) | No. of issues | Issue amount (million yen) | No. of issues | Issue amount (million yen) | No. of issues | Issue amount (million yen) | No. of issues | Issue amount (million yen) | No. of issues | Issue amount (million yen) | No. of issues | Issue amount (million yen) |
| 1970 | 1 | 6,000 | | | | | | | | | | | | |
| 1971 | 3 | 33,000 | | | | | | | | | | | | |
| 1972 | 6 | 85,000 | | | | | 1 | 10,690 | | | | | | |
| 1973 | 3 | 40,000 | | | | | 6 | 40,050 | | | | | | |
| 1974 | 0 | 0 | | | | | | | | | | | | |
| 1975 | 2 | 20,000 | | | | | | | | | | | | |
| 1976 | 6 | 65,000 | | | | | | | | | | | | |
| 1977 | 15 | 296,000 | | | | | 3 | 30,000 | | | | | 2 | 30,000 |
| 1978 | 29 | 722,000 | | | | | 11 | 105,000 | | | | | 1 | 15,000 |
| 1979 | 16 | 333,000 | | | | | 6 | 67,200 | | | | | 2 | 25,000 |
| 1980 | 14 | 261,000 | | | | | | | | | | | 4 | 55,000 |
| 1981 | 27 | 495,000 | | | | | 13 | 117,500 | | | | | 5 | 80,000 |
| 1982 | 37 | 633,000 | | | | | 30 | 193,000 | | | | | 6 | 95,000 |
| 1983 | 41 | 720,000 | | | | | 32 | 179,000 | | | | | 4 | 70,000 |
| 1984 | 37 | 915,000 | | | | | 34 | 199,500 | | | | | 13 | 227,000 |
| 1985 | 35 | 1,115,000 | | | 8 | US$850,A$60 ECU100 | 24 | 157,500 | | | | | 61 | 1,340,700 |
| 1986 | 21 | 590,000 | | | 7 | US$400 Can$415 | 21 | 195,000 | | | | | 139 | 2,731,200 |
| 1987 | 15 | 420,00 | | | 6 | US$600 Can$100 | 10 | 77,500 | | | | | 157 | 3,301,30 |
| 1988 | 22 | 635,000 | | | | | 19 | 162,200 | | | | | 196 | 1,861,200 |
| 1989 | 46 | 1,100,500 | 5 | 175,000 | | | 10 | 73,500 | | | 1 | US$175 | 277 | 2,003,500 |
| | (15) | (319,000) | | | | | | | | | | | | |
| 1990 | 66 | 1,203,000 | 38 | 653,000 | | | 4 | 33,000 | | | | | 219 | 2,120,600 |
| | (24) | (335,000) | | | | | | | | | | | | |
| 1991 (until July 31) | 28 | 536,000 | 15 | 171,000 | | | 2 | 13,500 | 1 | 20,000 | | | 41 | 717,200[3] |
| | (12) | (143,000) | | | | | | | | | | | | |

Notes: 1. The *parenthesized* figures are the number of issues and the issue amount of Samurai Bonds have been issued through the issue registrations, which are included in the figures above for each.
2. The number of issues and the issue amount of Samurai Bonds include those of Reverse Dual Bonds.
3. The number of issues and the issue amount of *Euroven* bonds in 1991 are of issue which has been launched.

Source: *Komei Kinoshita*, "Foreign Issue in Japan," in Japan Securities Research Institute, *Capital Markets and Financial Services in Japan: Regulation and Practice*, 1992, 258, 267.

Types of Issues Permitted in Japan, by Issuer's Residence

| Type of Market | Issuer | Type of Bond | | | | | | | | |
|---|---|---|---|---|---|---|---|---|---|---|
| | | Straight | F.R.N. | Zero CPN. Deep Dsct. | C.B. | Equity Warrant | Debt Warrant | Yen Link | Currency Option | Dual Currency |
| Domestic (Yen) | Japanese | ● | × | ×[1] | ● | ● | × | × | × | × |
| | Non-Japanese | ● | ●[2] | × | ● | ▲ | × | × | × | ● |
| Euromarket (Yen) | Japanese | ● | ● | × | ● | ● | × | | ● | ● |
| | Non-Japanese | ● | ● | ● | ● | ● | ● | | ● | ● |
| Euromarket (Others) | Japanese | ● | ● | × | ● | ● | × | ● | ● | ● |
| | Non-Japanese | — | — | — | — | — | — | ● | — | — |

Notes: 1. Except for discount JGB and discount bank debentures.
2. Permitted on a case-by-case basis.

●: Permitted
×: Not permitted
▲: Under consideration
—: Not regulated by Japanese laws

**Source:** Kinoshita, 269

## 1. Regulation of Non-resident Issuers in Japan

As you read the following portion of Shimada's article comparing the U.S. and Japan, consider the nature of the government's involvement. In what ways does this differ from the U.S.?

### YOSHIKI SHIMADA, "A COMPARISON OF SECURITIES REGULATION IN JAPAN AND THE UNITED STATES"

29 Columbia Journal of Transnational Law 319, 354–7 (hereafter Shimada).

In Japan, any non-resident issuer is required to file an official notification with the MOF before issuing or offering for subscription its securities in Japan. This requirement arises regardless of the securities' currency of denomination or whether an exemption from registration is available under the 1948 Act.

Accordingly, the FECL requires non-resident issuers of Samurai and Shogun bonds in Japan to notify the MOF and to undergo a twenty-day waiting period during which the MOF, and sometimes The Bank of Japan at the MOF's direction, review the offering.[230] The decision to issue Samurai and Shogun bonds is normally made during discussions held between the MOF and the participating underwriters [231] on behalf

**230.** A concern of the MOF and The Bank of Japan is that substantial proceeds arising from issues of Samurai bonds may affect the exchange rate of the yen. Because Samurai proceeds flow overseas when they are converted to the national currency of the issuer, an oversupply of yen abroad in conjunction with increased demand for foreign currencies in Japan would, according to standard economic theory, weaken the yen on world foreign currency markets.

**231.** Lead or co-lead managers of Samurai offerings must be licensed to do securities business in Japan. There are no restrictions, regulations or requirements on the choice of lead or co-lead managers, the composition of underwriting or selling groups or the distribution or allocation of Samurai offerings.

of the issuers.[232] Only non-resident issuers in Japan that have met certain eligibility criteria are considered during these discussions. Only after the MOF and the issuer have agreed to the terms of the offering does the issuer file an official notification with the MOF. Because the official notification is filed after the MOF has already informally approved the offering, the filing of the official notification is generally a procedural formality.

For offerings in Japan by non-resident issuers, the MOF's basic policy has been to disapprove securities offerings if the securities involved are not of a type that Japanese resident issuers may generally issue. For example, if a Japanese resident issuer is barred from privately placing four-year floating rate, U.S. dollar-denominated bonds in Japan, a non-resident issuer will likewise be barred from issuing such securities in Japan, even if that issuance forms only a small percentage of a larger global offering. However, this basic policy has been subject to modification on a case-by-case basis.

The MOF generally will not approve an offering of Samurai or Shogun bonds unless the issuer has met certain eligibility criteria. Separate criteria exist for corporate and sovereign issuers. Corporate issuers with net assets totalling less than ¥600 billion must either have an A rating or better from one of the rating companies or satisfy other financial criteria.[242] Corporate issuers with net assets totalling more

**232.** The four largest securities companies in Japan dominate the Samurai bond market, and typically, each submits to the MOF a list ranking, in order or preference, those clients who wish to issue Samurai bonds.

If any particular offering is opposed by the MOF, the securities companies eliminate it from the list.

Each fiscal quarter, these securities companies engage in discussions amongst themselves to arrive at a joint master list compiled on the basis of the various eligibility criteria. If the securities companies cannot reach agreement, the MOF intervenes to arbitrate.

This interplay between the MOF and the underwriter(s) eliminates the issuer as an active participant in the approval process and delegates its role to an observer awaiting the outcome of stricter domestic negotiations.

When the first Samurai bond was issued in December 1970, the Samurai bond market was limited to supernational banking institutions.

Sears was the first private corporation to raise capital in the Samurai market. In March 1979, Sears issued ¥20 billion in 6.5% five-year bonds.

In July 1984, issuing criteria were further relaxed. As a result, AAA-rated issuers were permitted to issue an unlimited number of Samurai bonds.

Again in December 1984, the eligibility criteria were once again eased to permit AA- and AAA-rated corporations with net assets (defined to equal shareholders' equity) greater that ¥900 million and a shareholders' equity-to-total assets ratio of over forty percent to issue these bonds. After November 1985, all corporations and certain international institutions in which Japan is a member country (such as the Asia Development Bank) that were rated AAA or AA, were rated A or were non-rated, were permitted to issue Samurai and Shogun bonds with maturities up to fifteen, twelve and seven years, respectively.

**242.** Corporate issuers of Samurai and Shogun bonds which have not obtained an A rating or better must satisfy certain financial criteria. Corporate issuers with net assets totalling between ¥110 billion and ¥300 billion must have a shareholders' equity-to-total assets ratio of more than 45% and meet three out of the following four requirements:

(a) a long-term debt-to-capitalization ratio of less than 30%;

(b) an operating profit-to-total assets ratio of more than 8.5%;

(c) an interest coverage of more than 3.5 times; and

than ¥600 billion need not meet any financial criteria nor have obtained any minimum rating. Ineligible corporate issuers are permitted to issue Samurai or Shogun bonds if guaranteed by an eligible parent company. Sovereign issuers engaged in a public offering that have previously issued bonds need not meet any rating or financial criteria, while those that have not previously issued any bonds must have an A rating or better in order to be eligible.[245]

In Japan, any non-resident issuer of yen-denominated securities is required to obtain a license from the MOF before issuing and selling the securities abroad. In addition, these issuers are required to file reports with the MOF on a monthly basis disclosing the specific terms of any yen-denominated securities issued during each month. These requirements apply to issuers issuing or offering for subscription Euroyen bonds in the Euromarkets [268] and Yankee bonds denominated in yen and issued in the United States. The MOF typically grants this license on the condition that the yen-denominated securities issued outside Japan not be sold to Japanese resident investors for a ninety-day period following the date on which the securities were originally issued abroad.[269]

(d) a long-term debt-to-cash flow ratio of less than 250%.

Corporate issuers with net assets totalling between ¥300 billion and ¥600 billion must have a shareholders' equity-to-total assets ratio of more than 40% and satisfy two out of the following four requirements:

(a) a long-term debt-to-capitalization ratio of less than 35%;

(b) operating profit-to-total assets ratio of more than 8.0%;

(c) interest coverage of more than 3.0 times; and

(d) long-term debt-to-cash flow ratio of less than 300%.

**245.** In the case of sovereign issuers engaged in a private offering, the eligibility requirements are as follows: if a sovereign issuer has previously issued bonds in Japan or has borrowed funds in Japan within the last three years in connection with a syndicated commercial loan, it need not satisfy any eligibility criteria; otherwise, a government institution must be rated AA or better while a sovereign issuer other than a government institution must be rated A or better. Private offerings by sovereign issuers are limited to certain aggregate amounts. AAA-rated issuers, AA-rated issuers, and A-rated or non-rated issuers have been permitted to issue only up to maximum aggregate amounts of ¥30 billion, ¥20 billion, and ¥10 billion, respectively.

**268.** Non-resident issuers of Euroyen bonds in Japan used to be required to satisfy eligibility criteria. With the opening of Euroyen bond market in April 1977, the MOF limited the number of issuers permitted to offer Euroyen bonds. The MOF justified this limitation on the ground that increased yen holdings outside of Japan would lessen control over monetary policy and render the Japanese economy more susceptible to adverse economic events and conditions in other countries. "[T]oo rapid establishment of a free Euroyen market may have adverse effects on Japanese fiscal and monetary policies, exchange rates, and Japan's domestic financial systems."

* * *

[Gradually the rules were relaxed.]

After June 1985 the MOF permitted the issuance of the following types of Euroyen bonds by Japanese resident and non-resident issuers as well as straight Euroyen bonds: dual currency bonds; floating rate notes; zero coupon bonds; deep discount bonds; and currency conversion bonds. For example, U.S. resident issuers have raised yen in the Euroyen market and converted their yen proceeds into U.S. dollars via currency swaps ....

**269.** Bonds whose interest payments are made in yen and whose principal payments are made in a foreign currency or bonds whose principal payments are made in yen and whose interest payments are made in a foreign currency ("dual currency bonds") may not be offered or sold to Japanese resident investors for a period of one hundred eighty days after the date of the original issuance of the bonds.

The MOF will generally not grant licenses unless the issuer or the yen-denominated securities themselves have been assigned a specific rating by at least one rating agency recognized by the MOF. Thus, any non-resident issuer is eligible to issue Euroyen bonds and yen-denominated Yankee bonds, so long as either the issuer or the bonds have been assigned a rating from a recognized rating agency.

. . .

When any non-resident issuer raises capital by offering securities in Japan or by issuing yen-denominated securities outside of Japan, not only must the issuer either notify or obtain a license from the MOF, but it must also meet certain eligibility criteria specified by the MOF. In addition, when a securities offering takes place in Japan, the MOF requires registration under the 1948 Act unless an exemption from registration is available. The result of this regulatory framework is that the MOF is able to exercise greater control than the SEC over the capital markets and the flow of capital in and out of Japan and the United States, respectively.

---

Yen denominated foreign bonds were dominated historically by multilateral institutions like the Asian Development Bank. The number of issues was 461 from 1970–90, growing precipitously from only 18 in 1986 to 76 in 1990. Foreign issues listed on the Tokyo Stock Exchange reached 124 in 1990, but about 10% delisted after the market soured:

## EMIKO TERAZONO, MORE FOREIGN COMPANIES TO DELIST FROM TOKYO SE

Financial Times July 23, 1993.

Three foreign companies yesterday applied to delist from the Tokyo Stock Exchange's foreign section. The move is scheduled for October 30.

The three are Warner–Lambert and Bellsouth of the US, and Dixons of the UK. They will take the number of delistings since 1992 to 13, including General Motors of the US, Philips of the Netherlands and Royal Bank of Canada.

The three companies said high costs and administrative burdens were the main reason for ending their Tokyo presence.

The fall in trading activity has also become a concern for foreign companies, which have primarily listed in Tokyo to enhance their international profile.

Shares traded in Tokyo peaked in 1987 with a daily average of 2.76m shares traded: daily volume fell to some 200,000 shares this year.

Tokyo trading in foreign stocks started in 1973. The latest delistings will reduce the number of listed companies to 111, down from a peak of 127 in late 1991.

## 2. The 1990 Treasury Department Report

Comparing the openness of Japan's markets in 1990 with the situation four years earlier, Treasury reported substantial progress.

*Progress Since 1986:* A series of significant measures have been taken since 1986 to open and expand markets. Existing access has been broadened and regulatory practices streamlined. In the Japanese Government bond (JGB) market, foreign firms' shares in the 10–year JGB syndicate were expanded threefold (up to 8 percent) in October 1988. A true price auction for 40 percent of each regular offering of 10–year JGBs was inaugurated in April 1989 (and was increased to 60 percent in October 1990). The Tokyo Stock Exchange admitted 32 new members in 1988 and 1990, including 19 additional foreign firms of which six were American. In the domestic corporate bond market, the list of eligible issuers was expanded, maturities were diversified, private placements were enhanced, bond ratings were introduced and shelf registration for new issues was permitted in October 1988. Risk weighted capital adequacy requirements for securities firms (along the lines of U.S. and U.K. rules) were introduced by MOF in April 1990.

In addition, a variety of new financial instruments were created. These included: a publicly offered 20–year Japanese Government bond in September 1987; domestic and nonresident Euroyen commercial paper (CP) in November 1987; and numerous financial futures and options contracts. Detached yen bond warrants were allowed to be issued domestically in spring 1989. On the other hand, the yen-denominated bankers acceptance (BA), created in 1985, virtually disappeared due to lack of market interest, despite the reduction of the BA stamp tax.

---

Establishing a presence was not a problem. The number of foreign securities companies in Japan doubled to 52 by 1990, of which 22 were U.S.-owned. Twenty-eight foreign banks had set up 50%–controlled offshore subsidiaries; eight were U.S.–owned. Representative offices existed for 128 firms.

The result was a shift in the foreign firms' business. Earlier, they intermediated cross-border flows like sales of securities issued in Japan to foreigners. Now they were competing in domestic markets. According to the Treasury,

> . . . American firms have become particularly active in the Japanese Government securities market, expanding their clients to include domestic institutional investors. In the first year since the initiation of the partial price auction for 10–year JGBs, one American securities firm was the leading successful bidder among all foreign and domestic firms. Three American firms were among the top 13. U.S. firms have also facilitated Japanese investors' access to the U.S. Treasury securities market.

Foreign firms have become especially active in equities trading. American firms have 10 of the 25 foreign-owned seats on the 124–seat Tokyo Stock Exchange. In 1989, the foreign share of secondary market turnover in equities approached 6 percent, contrasting sharply with the small shares that major foreign firms are allocated in domestic equity underwriting syndicates. U.S. firms have also been especially active in derivative markets, particularly those for bond and stock index futures. Eight U.S. securities branches and four U.S. bank branches have also joined the Tokyo International Financial Futures Exchange.

---

But all was not well. The Treasury summarized the continuing problems for U.S. securities firms. Following the Treasury's summary of the problems are its brief descriptions of the most serious ones. As you read this, in each case:

1. Be sure you understand the argument.
2. Evaluate the argument. How would you expect MOF to reply?
3. What standard does Treasury use: de jure national treatment, de facto national treatment, limited market access, limited competitive opportunity?
4. Would change help foreign securities firms?

## a. The Treasury's Summary

Despite these changes, various factors have prevented foreign firms from enjoying a comparable degree of success achieved in other markets. For example, foreign firms have had limited freedom to innovate and offer new products in Japanese markets. Restrictions have prevented securities firms from offering foreign exchange products and services central to their business. Access to domestic underwriting business has been difficult. Japanese investors' direct access to foreign markets and products has also been constrained. In other areas where foreign securities firms have considerable talent, such as pension fund and investment trust management, foreign firms are effectively kept on the sidelines despite limited liberalization. In addition, the regulatory system lacks transparency. Despite some improvement, supervisory procedures, regulations and changes in policy are not always accessible in a timely fashion, and foreign firms are frequently left out of informal consultations.

## b. Policy Toward Financial Innovation in Japan

As reported in earlier national treatment studies, and regularly in discussions between Treasury and the MOF over the past six years, a combination of statutory, regulatory and informal guidance measures frustrates and sometimes prevents the introduction of new products and services. The highly segmented nature of business lines and the regulatory structure can compound these problems. The relatively narrow definition of a "security" under the Securities and Exchange Law in particular has contributed to the difficulties and lengthy delays some securities firms have encountered, as has the reporting and/or approval framework of the Foreign Exchange Law, when the product or service has a non-yen component. Foreign firms have questioned the need for multiple personal visits to various MOF bureaus and the extensive informal guidance which must be carefully interpreted. In May 1990, MOF announced that it would expedite the approval process and approve several pending applications which could help rectify this problem. Subsequently, in mid-June, MOF formally approved several new products for foreign securities firms, which incorporated foreign exchange transactions such as currency options. In addition, in June, MOF gave the green light to dollar denominated money market funds. In September, MOF approved a foreign securities firm's application to offer credit card asset-backed securities in Japan. At the May meeting, MOF also announced its intention to approve the introduction of the Chicago-based GLOBEX electronic futures and options trading system.

. . .

American firms, in particular, feel that their competitive advantage lies in their ability to offer new innovative financial products and a wide range of financial services. Some are frustrated, however, because they feel unable to exploit this strength in Japan due to their inability to offer many of these products and services there. On the other hand, Japanese firms are seen as having the ability to experiment, innovate and imitate in open and competitive markets outside Japan. These U.S. firms feel that by the time new products and techniques are permitted in Japan, Japanese firms have caught up with their foreign counterparts and the foreign firm no longer has any advantage over a Japanese firm. Meanwhile, Japanese firms have been able to compete aggressively for market share internationally, supported financially by their dominance of the Japanese market. MOF states that it admits new products when satisfied that there are no problems from the viewpoint of investor protection and that it has no intention of seeking advantage for Japanese firms.

---

Treasury noted that in the past four years, Japan had made important changes to accommodate innovation:

> In June 1989, two comprehensive regulatory frameworks were established to govern domestic financial futures and options, one each for "banking" and "securities" products. MOF also made regulatory changes to broaden Japanese investor access to foreign futures and options markets: on June 30, 1989, it allowed licensed banks, securities firms and foreign specialized financial futures/options firms to begin brokering foreign futures and options for Japanese clients. (In 1987 and

1988, some designated Japanese financial institutions were permitted access to listed foreign futures and options for their own account but not for their clients.) In May 1989, a bond lending market was established and short selling of bonds, previously prohibited, was allowed. These changes were aimed at improving the secondary market for Japanese Government bonds. The size of the repurchase ("repo") market has increased but remains constrained by taxation impediments.

### c. Foreign Exchange Services

For years, foreign securities firms have been frustrated by Japanese laws (primarily the Foreign Exchange Law) which prohibit them from offering the full range of foreign exchange services in Japan that they can offer elsewhere. They have argued that such restrictions are anachronistic and illogical: Japan is the only major international market where firms encounter such restrictions. Even though such restrictions apply to domestic and foreign firms, they disproportionately affect foreign securities firms by denying them the opportunity to provide products and services at which they excel worldwide. These restrictions may be partially alleviated by MOF's announcement at the May 1990 Working Group Meeting that MOF intends to permit offshore, 50 percent-owned qualified bank subsidiaries of foreign securities firms to establish branches in Tokyo. These banking branches will be able to engage in a wide range of foreign exchange business—an approach MOF is not yet ready to offer domestic Japanese securities firms. Even with such an affiliate bank, however, some firms question whether existing foreign exchange restrictions could still bar foreign securities firms themselves from conducting a full range of competitive securities-related activities, such as the execution of swaps. Moreover, the measure, while welcomed, is viewed as second best to the removal of restrictions preventing securities firms from offering foreign exchange services outright.

### d. Access by Japanese Investors to Foreign Financial Markets

The Foreign Exchange Law and the Foreign Securities Company Law limit the ability of Japanese investors, both individual and institutional, to access overseas markets and products directly. The effect of such regulations has been to force the bulk of Japanese portfolio investment overseas through Ministry of Finance "licensed securities firms" and "authorized foreign exchange banks in Japan." Not only do these restrictions funnel Japanese investor activity primarily through Japanese institutions, but they have provided a regulatory means by which MOF can moderate and direct this activity. MOF's July 1990 actions, announced at the May 1990 meeting of the U.S.–Japan Working Group on Financial Markets, to broaden direct access to overseas markets by raising the ceilings on overseas accounts for individuals, permitting corporations to have such accounts, and allowing these accounts to be used for portfolio investment, should redress some of these concerns.

Also in response to May commitments, the Finance Ministry introduced changes to the Foreign Securities Companies Law, which became effective November 26, to permit foreign securities firms not licensed in Japan to offer securities on a "non-solicitation" basis to individual and corporate investors resident in Japan. Although all of these changes are positive, they leave intact the basic regulatory structure.

### e. Pension Funds

Pension fund management is another example of step-by-step liberalization that impedes foreign entry. Legislation effective April 1, 1990, authorized a new group of firms, licensed discretionary investment advisors, to manage corporate pension funds. While this move could potentially increase foreign firms' access to the management of pension funds, existing and new regulations will limit foreign firms' ability to exploit areas of competitive advantage and may place them at a disadvantage with respect to Japanese firms. Implementing regulations specify the distribution of the assets of a fund (including restrictions on investment in equities, real estate and foreign currency-denominated assets, and a requirement that at least 50 percent of assets for all practical purposes be invested domestically). Portfolio specialization is restricted by requiring that individual managers follow a specified asset distribution scheme. Further regulations will effectively limit the number of new contracts available to investment advisors: management is limited to new money accumulated after a pension fund obtains a license, and regulations establish a minimum contract floor of one billion yen ($6.6 million). These restrictions and the failure to require fund managers to publish their performance record will minimize the role foreign firms can play in offering asset management skills which are performance driven and renowned in other markets.

### f. Investment Trusts

For example, foreign firms have been excluded from the $400 billion investment trust (mutual funds) market, due to MOF's licensing policy. The mutual fund market in Japan is monopolized by 15 licensed investment trust management companies, all of which are affiliated with one of the major Japanese securities firms. December 1989 changes in the official licensing policy will potentially permit additional domestic and, for the first time, foreign firms. Although some changes treat foreign firms better than potential new domestic entrants, the rigorous standards implied by new criteria, which are based on the profile of existing firms in the industry, effectively form a substantial barrier to entry. As a result, new entry will probably be minimal. Only four foreign firms applied for licenses by the February 1990 deadline for the first round of annual licensing (one U.S. firm, two U.K. firms and one U.S./U.K. firm). No Japanese firms applied. (In October 1990, MOF granted preliminary investment trust management to the two U.K. firms. The other two foreign firms are still awaiting licenses.) Even if all four firms are granted licenses, the number of participants in the market will remain minuscule compared to other industrial countries where the number of participants can approach the thousands.

### g. Practices in Domestic Underwriting

Despite persistent efforts and growing domestic client bases, foreign firms can rarely secure more than a minimal share in underwriting syndicates. They allege that this is anomalous when viewed against their share of secondary market trading in Japan, their leading positions in overseas underwritings, and the significant positions accorded Japanese firms in such underwritings. Although the issue is not a regulatory matter, it reflects the market power of the major Japanese firms who lead manage the offerings and is reinforced by the "1000–share rule" for initial public offerings (IPOs) which is enforced by the stock exchanges and the Securities Dealers Association. This rule impedes a foreign firm's ability to place substantial IPO equity shares with its (mainly institutional) clients by limiting each client's maximum to 1000 shares. Foreign firms' participation is also curbed by the securities industry's "30 percent rule," a "voluntary" measure limiting the proportion of each underwriter's shares in a public offering which may be placed with: (a) financial institutions (banks and insurance companies); and (b) listed nonfinancial companies.

### h. Profitability

Foreign firms have also broadened their activities and deepened their commitment. Profitability has been slow, but generally growing. By mid–1989, U.S. firms were among the largest foreign firms: 11 out of the 19 U.S. firms had more than 100 staff members, and six had more than 200. In the first two quarters of 1989, 10 of the 19 showed pre-tax profits compared to 11 of the 28 non-U.S. firms. By mid–1989, the 47 foreign firms had an average capitalization of ¥5.0 billion ($39.4 million); U.S. firms had a higher average of ¥7.7 billion ($60.7 million) (although these figures are skewed by two U.S. firms with considerably above-average capital). Some U.S. firms have added substantial capital since March 1989.

By comparison, the top 42 domestic Japanese securities firms in the same six-month period ending March 1989 were all substantially profitable, averaged 2,645 staff per firm, and had ¥19.6 billion ($154.5 million) in average capital. For the biggest Japanese firms, those figures were roughly five times larger.

#### *Questions*

1. Do any government policies limit foreign securities firms' entry into Japan's domestic markets? What explains the policies? How serious a barrier are they?

   a. Foreign exchange services by securities firms are limited. Why? Is this unique to Japan? Would changing the policy help foreign firms?

b. Access to the investment trust business is limited. What would account for this rule, other than simply a desire to protect firms in the industry?

2. Do government policies discriminate against foreign securities firms competing in Japanese markets once they are in?

a. Suppose MOF delays. Is this inappropriate? Could MOF have any other goal, unrelated to foreign securities companies?

b. Assume MOF does not delay. Is the difference in Japanese and U.S. approaches appropriate for governments to resolve between themselves?

3. What special features of Japanese financial markets would affect foreign firms operating in Japan?

a. What is the effect of keiretsu relationships on foreign securities firms operating in Japan?

b. Do you agree that domestic underwriting practices harm foreign firms competing in Japan? Is this an appropriate topic for intergovernmental discussion, given the fact that this is market practice rather than government policy?

c. How do the other special features affect cross-border access and competition in Japan?

4. Is anything that you might have expected missing from Treasury's critique?

---

## 3. The Clinton Administration's Initiative

In June 1993, the new administration of President Clinton announced that it would "be much more aggressive" opening Japan's financial system. Leading the assault was the Treasury under-secretary for international affairs, Lawrence Summers.

### QUENTIN HARDY, "BATTLE TO OPEN TOKYO MARKETS HEATS UP"

Wall Street Journal, June 2, 1993, C1.

The Clinton administration now is lobbying for greater access to potentially lucrative markets such as pension fund management, insurance and corporate finance underwriting.

The potential payoff is huge. Japan's insurance industry, for example, has about 155 trillion yen ($1.44 trillion) in assets, and pension funds are estimated at $728 billion. Non-Japanese firms now have, at best, 1% of each market.

The new team of negotiators also wants Japan to permit greater use of equity "derivatives" such as futures and options.

U.S. firms dominate trading technology in those areas, and the local arms of Goldman, Sachs & Co., Morgan Stanley Group Inc. and Salomon Inc. have profited in trading the derivatives that are already allowed. They're now pleading for greater freedom.

. . . .

Japanese regulators don't like derivatives, in part, because many of the products can be used to circumvent the rules: A right to buy a stock, which some kinds of derivatives offer, can get a company around stock-ownership regulations, for example. That leaves the regulators with less control over the market.

Financial analysts argue, though, that Japanese companies could benefit from a bigger derivatives market.

"This is something Japanese companies need," says Alicia Ogawa, analyst at Salomon Brothers Asia Ltd. Deregulation is only half-done in Japan, she argues. Therefore, while markets are more lively because of earlier steps to liberalize, companies don't have access to certain benefits, such as the financial protection derivatives can provide. "The volatility is there; the protection isn't," says Ms. Ogawa.

---

At the same time, the Treasury was preparing for its 1994 study of access to foreign financial markets, including those of Japan. The access of U.S. mutual funds to the Japanese market was expected to be one major issue. Robert Pozen, general counsel of Fidelity Investments, wrote critically of Japanese policy in mid–1992. He argued that "no American firm is licensed to offer mutual funds in Japan, although several Japanese firms sell mutual funds to the American public." He said the application process for a license in Japan takes years and is vague, while a Japanese firm could get a U.S. license within six months. Japan requires an initial investment of $7 million, against $100,000 in the U.S. Japan caps the total management fee at 0.35%, while the U.S. set no limit. U.S. firms had to hire at least 30 Japanese citizens, though many fewer could run the business. To distribute their shares in Japan, U.S. firms had to go through another slow, costly administrative review, while Japanese firms in the U.S. could simply file papers and pay $25,000. (Robert Pozen, "Japan's Restricted Mutual Funds," The New York Times, April 12, 1992, 15.)

Corporate bond underwriting in Japan was likely to be another major pressure point. The market was now opening, according to Brian Wallace Semkow, "Foreign Financial Institutions in Japan: Legal and Financial Barriers and Opportunities, Part 2", Butterworths Journal of International Banking and Financial Law 127 (March 1993).

> Foreign securities firms are beginning to make inroads into the underwriting market for corporate bonds. In December 1991, Morgan Stanley was appointed as the first securities firm

to co-lead a domestic bond issue for a Japanese borrower, Nippon Telegraph and Telephone, the shares of which were not permitted to be owned by foreigners until August 1992. NTT chose Morgan Stanley in part because the bond issue was the first in Japan under which the underwriters would use a negotiated fixed-price offering method common in North America and Europe, whereby the issuer and the underwriter determine the terms of the offering in light of market conditions. It is hoped that this approach would become more prevalent in Japan, as it would encourage transparency and stimulate the secondary market for corporate bonds; the prevailing practice of corporate bond underwriters is to offer the highest prices to the issuer, and sell the bonds at varying discounts on the secondary market, making up the difference with high commission rates of 1.2 percent of the face value of the bond.

The Securities Industry Association, a U.S. trade group, said that in 1992 four U.S. securities firms were among the top 20 highest capitalized firms in Japan and three U.S. firms "took the top three spots in operating income generated in Japan." The SIA pointed out that U.S. securities firms lead managed barely 3% of Japanese corporate bond issues worth $36 billion that year. The reasons, according to the SIA, were:

> lack of transparency in securities regulation, which reinforces the monopoly position of the "Big Four" Japanese securities firms;
>
> administrative guidance and outdated regulations [such as "unnecessary involvement of a commission bank, stringent eligibility standards," and costly procedures] which govern the issuance process; and
>
> impediments to issuing and placing new and innovative products ["of the 25 financial products typically available in New York and London, only 12 are allowed in Tokyo"] which address the needs of issuers and investors.

The "long-standing relationship between Japanese issuers and underwriters shut out foreign firms." (Securities Industry Association Position Paper, "Accessing the Japanese Corporate Bond Market, November 1993).

The corporate pension fund market was also likely to be a target. According to the U.S. Investment Fund Institute, Matthew P. Fink, President Investment Company Institute, statement before the U.S. Senate Committee on Banking, Housing, and Urban Affairs, October 26, 1993.

> Although the 17 U.S. firms that are registered under Japan's Investment Advisory Law as discretionary managers receive nominal national treatment, they have little meaningful access to the Japanese pension management market. For ex-

ample, current Japanese law limits a U.S. firm to managing only ⅓ of the assets of a Japanese *corporate pension plan*. Further, as a practical matter U.S. advisers have no access to the Japanese *government pension plan* market.

After several years in which a number of foreign securities firms made record profits in Japan, while their Japanese counterparts reported serious problems, the foreign firms became less interested in operating in Japan. A study by the Japan Center for International Finance reported that foreign financial firms did not expect Tokyo to displace London or New York to become the world's pre-eminent financial center. Ten percent of foreign brokers were leaving or cutting back.

### "THE FOREIGNERS CUT BACK"

The New York Times, May 16, 1993, Sections 3, 6.

With the financial atmosphere getting tougher in Japan, many foreign banks and brokers have responded with their first cuts here and have even moved some operations out of Japan.

Salomon Brothers Asia, for instance, had a staff of 600 at its peak a couple of years ago, but now is trying to whittle that to 510. Prudential Securities has reduced its staff to 90 from 275 three years ago, and has closed one of its two branches. Merrill Lynch Japan has said it remains committed to Japan, but it is closing three of its six retail branches in the country and the head of its Asian operations has moved to Hong Kong from Tokyo.

County Natwest Securities, an arm of Britain's National Westminster Bank, sold its Tokyo Stock Exchange membership recently, the first foreign firm here to do so. Foreign brokers, permitted to join the exchange only since 1986, were clamoring for seats a few years ago.

Disappointment over the pace at which the financial markets are opening here is not the only problem cited. The enormous costs of doing business in Japan—commercial rents are astronomical despite a recent property market slump, and senior foreign executives routinely live in homes that rent for $15,000 to $60,000 a month—were ignored when the markets were perceived to be opening. But now those costs are regarded as a burden.

"The expense level in Tokyo is just too high, and being in Hong Kong puts us closer to our big thrust into China," said Larry Greenberg, formerly the head of the Japanese operations of the Bank of America and now the Hong Kong-based head of Asian commercial banking. "When you're in Hong Kong you're a part of everything that's happening in this part of the world."

### *Questions*

1. What trends do you see in the U.S. complaints over a period of time? What accounts for these trends?

2. What response would you expect from the Japanese government?

---

## B. THE JAPANESE ROLE IN FOREIGN AND INTERNATIONAL SECURITIES MARKETS

Over half of all bonds issued abroad by Japanese companies in 1990 were denominated in Eurodollars. Swiss franc bonds accounted for almost 25% more and Euro-yen bonds another 17%. Small amounts in DM, ECU, and other currencies made up the rest. Over half had equity warrants (which we discuss later in this book), 30% were convertible bonds, and the rest straight, according to Hamada. Since then, the share of equity warrants has declined.

Answering his own question why Japanese firms would borrow abroad given Japan's balance of payments surplus, Hamada said the major reason was the lower total issue cost, even with the expense of currency swaps. He noted these factors:

Hamada, 249–50.

(1) in respect of issue costs,
   a. bond issue expenses, such as fees for commissioned companies (quasi-trustees under the Commercial Code of Japan) and paying agents, are more expensive domestically, and
   b. issue proceeds are available to the issuers on the closing date in international capital markets, while in Japan such are only made available by the commissioned companies to the issuers three days after the closing date; and

(2) in respect of the preparation for and terms and conditions of issues,
   a. financial covenants are severer domestically (usually in international markets only a negative pledge clause being required while in Japan restrictions on dividend payouts and covenants to maintain certain levels of retained earnings being required in addition),
   b. a longer time period is required to prepare for issues in Japan because of the registration requirement under the Securities and Exchange Law (Law No. 25 of 1948, as amended; the "SEL"), and
   c. a greater variety of debt instruments are available in international markets than in Japan, where certain newly-developed instruments such as medium term notes, floating rate notes and foreign currency bonds are not permitted to be issued by Japanese companies.

In recent years, it appears that lower total issue costs, even accounting for currency swap expenses, have been by far the largest factor influencing Japanese corporate issuers to select foreign markets for their external issues.

---

## 1. The Regulation of Offshore Securities Operations

The regulatory framework is no less complex and illusive for securities than for banking abroad. The following description of written law and practice sheds some light. As you read, amalgamate the major rules affecting Japanese issuers and securities companies outside Japan. Identify the policies embodied in these rules.

Shimada, 319, 350–4, 357–60, 363.

The growth of multinational corporations and the dramatic increase in the number of cross-border financings have resulted in the internationalization of securities markets around the world. The large number and size of international securities offerings by American and Japanese multinationals in recent years are evidence of this internationalization.

### A. *Japan's Foreign Exchange and Foreign Trade Control Law*

In the United States, international securities offerings are regulated under the statutory framework of the Securities Act. In Japan, international securities offerings are regulated under the statutory framework of not only the 1948 Act, but also the Foreign Exchange and Foreign Trade Control Law (the FECL), a statute that has no counterpart in the United States. Because of the dual statutory frameworks of the 1948 Act and the FECL, legal issues frequently arise in Japan as to whether international securities offerings are subject to the 1948 Act's registration and prospectus delivery requirements, in addition to the FECL's notification or licensing requirements.[204] In addition, issuers of certain international securities offerings are required to satisfy certain eligibility criteria.[205] By contrast, in the United States, securities offerings, including international securities offerings, are subject to the Securities Act's registration and prospectus delivery requirements only to the extent that they fall within the extraterritorial scope of the Securities Act.

International securities fall into primarily two categories: (1) Eurosecurities, which are offered in Europe usually through an international syndicate of banks and securities companies and sold mostly, and sometimes exclusively, in countries other than the home country of the issuer, and (2) foreign securities, which are offered in a country other than the home country of the issuer primarily through banks and securities companies located in the country where the offering is to be made, distributed in ways that are similar to offerings by domestic issuers in such country and usually denominated in the currency of such country. Because the international new issue market for debt securities is larger than that for equity securities, this part focuses on two types of Euro-

**204.** The FECL requires that issuers of certain international securities offerings notify or obtain a license from the MOF.

**205.** These eligibility criteria are for the most part adopted by the securities industry and are acknowledged by the MOF. These eligibility criteria change quite frequently. The eligibility criteria discussed in this article are those that were in effect as of Nov. 30, 1990.

bonds (Euroyen and Eurodollar bonds[211]) and three types of foreign bonds (Yankee,[212] Samurai and Shogun bonds[213]). The FECL requires MOF notification for issuance by Japanese resident issuers of Euroyen, Eurodollar and Yankee bonds even though these generally fall outside the extraterritorial scope of the 1948 Act and are thereby exempt from the registration and prospectus delivery requirements thereof. Such issuers must also satisfy certain eligibility requirements. Samurai and Shogun bond offerings, on the other hand, trigger both the MOF notification requirements of the FECL and the registration and prospectus delivery requirements of the 1948 Act. In addition, non-resident issuers of Samurai, Shogun and Euroyen bonds in Japan must meet certain eligibility requirements.

In the United States, Samurai, Shogun, Euroyen and Eurodollar securities offerings are usually exempt from the registration and prospectus delivery requirements of the Securities Act because such offerings are usually conducted outside the United States and therefore fall outside the extraterritorial reach of the Securities Act. Yankee securities offerings, on the other hand, require registration with the SEC unless an exemption from registration is available. This contrast between the Japanese and American regulatory scheme reflects a significant difference in regulatory approach.

### B. *Official Notification Under the FECL*

The FECL regulates securities offerings in Japan by non-resident issuers, securities offerings outside Japan by Japanese resident issuers, and offerings in Japan by Japanese resident issuers of securities payable outside Japan or denominated in a currency other than the yen by requiring issuers to file an official notification with the MOF through The Bank of Japan. Any issuer required to file official notifications with the MOF under the FECL is prohibited from issuing or offering for subscription its securities until the expiration of a twenty-day period[222] commencing from the date on which the MOF formally accepts the notification. If the MOF does not formally accept the notification filing, the issuer cannot commence the offering. In practice, the MOF does not accept official notification filings unless the issuer has met certain eligibility requirements.[224]

**211.** Euroyen and Eurodollar bonds are Eurobonds, denominated in Japanese yen and U.S. dollars, respectively.

**212.** In this article, Yankee bonds refer to foreign bonds offered in the United States by non-resident issuers in the United States, distributed typically in the same way as offerings by U.S. domestic issuers and usually denominated in U.S. dollars.

**213.** Samurai and Shogun bonds refer to foreign bonds offered by a non-resident issuer in Japan and denominated in Japanese yen and U.S. dollars, respectively.

**222.** The MOF is granted discretion to shorten the twenty-day waiting period.

**224.** The MOF generally will not accept the filing of an official notification unless the issuer has engaged in discussions with it prior to the filing. During these discussions, the terms and conditions of the filing and any restrictions placed thereon are modified if necessary to meet the MOF's recommendations for changes. After the MOF informally approves the offering, the official notification is formally filed. At this stage, the filing is almost always accepted. On the other hand, if the MOF has

In addition, the MOF has formal authority under the FECL to intervene and order a change in the terms and arrangements of an offering or a suspension of the offering itself if the MOF deems that one of four outcomes would result without its intervention. These four outcomes are: (1) negative effects on international money markets; (2) negative effects on Japan's money or capital markets; (3) negative effects on certain industrial sectors of Japan; or (4) an interference in the performance of Japan's duties under its treaties or other international agreements or a disruption of international peace and security.

. . .

2. Japanese Resident Issuers Offering Securities Outside of Japan

Under the FECL, Japanese resident issuers are required to file official notifications with the MOF before issuing or offering for subscription securities outside of Japan, regardless of the securities' currency of denomination or whether an exemption from registration is available under the 1948 Act.[246] Accordingly, the FECL requires Japanese resident issuers of Yankee bonds[247] and Eurobonds (including both Euroyen[248] and Eurodollar[249] bonds) to file official notifications with the

not informally approved the offering, the filing of the official notification will probably not be accepted, thereby effectively prohibiting the issuer from issuing or offering for subscription its securities.

A period of time preceding formal acceptance, the "prescreening process," is therefore essential for international securities offerings which trigger the FECL's notification requirements. During the prescreening process, the International Finance Section of the MOF, which administers the FECL, may consult with the Securities and Banking Bureaus of the MOF, and with various banking and securities trade associations whose members may be affected by the approved offering. The objective of such discussions is to ensure that no portion of the Japanese financial system will be adversely affected by the proposed offering. The prescreening process is also essential for international securities offerings that trigger the licensing requirements of the FECL.

**246.** According to the FECL, an "[i]ssuance or offer[ing] for subscription abroad of securities" by a Japanese resident issuer constitutes a "capital transaction," requiring that the issuer make an official notification with the MOF.

**247.** Since the opening of the Eurobond market, relatively few Japanese corporations have issued U.S.-registered Yankee bonds. Instead, they have tended to offer Eurobonds because registration is usually not required under the Securities Act and offerings can therefore be flexibly timed and completed quickly. The flexibility and timing advantages of Eurobonds have attracted many Japanese borrowers away from the Yankee Bond market even though Japanese resident issuers have been permitted since 1984 to swap their dollar proceeds raised in a Yankee bond offering into yen without limitation using currency swap techniques.

**248.** In April 1984, for the first time the MOF permitted Japanese resident issuers to issue Euroyen bonds. At that time, approximately thirty Japanese corporations became qualified to issue straight Euroyen bonds, and approximately one hundred corporations became qualified to issue convertible Euroyen bonds. Issue by these corporations represented approximately seventy to eighty percent of the aggregate amount of all straight bonds and forty to sixty percent of the total principal amount of all convertible bonds available of the Japanese domestic market at that time.

In July 1985, the MOF further eased its criteria, rendering approximately sixty additional Japanese resident corporations eligible to have straight Euroyen bonds. Three months later, in October 1985, the MOF further relaxed requirements, making approximately one hundred eighty additional Japanese resident issuers eligible to have convertible Euroyen bonds.

Shortly thereafter, the MOF removed restrictions on the size or number of offerings of Euroyen bonds permitted. For Euroyen offerings by both Japanese resident and

**249.** See note 249 on page 454.

MOF before issuing or offering such bonds. The MOF generally will not accept the filing of official notifications unless Japanese resident issuers of these bonds have satisfied certain eligibility requirements.[250]

The particular eligibility criteria to which a Japanese resident issuer is subject depend upon the type of securities being offered, whether the securities being offered are denominated in yen, and whether the securities being offered are guaranteed by either a bank or the issuer's parent company. For offerings outside Japan of yen-denominated securities by Japanese resident issuers, the issuers must have: (1) either (a) an AA rating or better or (b) an A rating or better and net assets of at least ¥33 billion in the case of a straight bond offering or an offering of bonds coupled with equity warrants and (2) either (a) an A rating or better or (b) a BBB rating or better and net assets of at least ¥33 billion in the case of a convertible bond offering.[252]

Japanese resident issuers seeking to issue or offer for subscription securities denominated in currencies other than yen outside Japan (e.g., Eurodollar bonds) generally must meet the same requirements as for yen-denominated offerings.[253] However, if the securities being issued or offered for subscription are convertible bonds, the issuer need only have a BB rating or better.

If the securities being issued or offered for subscription are denominated in a currency other than yen and are guaranteed by the issuer's

non-resident issuers, there is no longer a requirement that Euroyen bonds be secured by collateral or security, an indenture trust be designated, or that Euroyen bonds be issued in registered form.

The MOF no longer restricts: (1) interest rates; (2) currency or interest rate exchange swaps, whether with Japanese residents or non-residents; (3) underwriting fees or commissions; (4) maturity of the bonds; (5) transferability of the bonds; or (6) the allocation or distribution of the securities outside of Japan. Furthermore, no maximum or minimum limitations are placed on the denominations of individual securities nor on the countries in which the securities can be sold (other than that country's own regulations). Lastly, no restrictions are imposed upon the issuer's choice of lead or co-lead managers or the composition of the underwriting or selling group of Euroyen bond offerings. Both Japanese resident and non-resident underwriters are not required to have a branch or representative office in Japan.

**249.** Japanese resident issuers are permitted to swap their U.S. dollar proceeds of Eurodollar bond offerings into yen without limitation either by selling their dollars for yen in the foreign exchange markets or by entering into currency exchange swaps. Typically, in a currency exchange swap, one party agrees with the other to exchange foreign currencies in accordance with mutually acceptable terms and conditions over a period of time.

Accordingly, many Japanese resident issuers have raised U.S. dollars in the Eurodollar market and converted these dollar proceeds into yen using currency swaps. As in the case of Euroyen offerings, the MOF places no restrictions or requirements on the choice of lead or co-lead managers or on the composition of underwriting or selling groups for Eurodollar bond offerings by Japanese resident issuers.

**250.** Market participants have suggested that the MOF's policy has been to promote the establishment of eligibility criteria comparable to those which Japanese resident issuers must meet when issuing bonds in the Japanese markets in order to avoid encouraging them to offer bonds overseas. Interview with a Japanese attorney.

**252.** In the case of offerings of straight bonds, convertible bonds and bonds coupled with equity warrants, the issuer is also subject to the eligibility criteria for domestic securities offerings.

**253.** Offerings of straight bonds, convertible bonds and bonds coupled with equity warrants subject the issuer to the eligibility criteria applicable to domestic securities offerings.

parent company, the issuer must have (1) net assets of at least ¥10 billion in the case of a straight bond offering and (2) net assets of at least ¥55 billion in the case of an offering of bonds coupled with equity warrants.[255] The issuer is not subject to any eligibility criteria in the case of convertible bond offerings.

A parent company whose guarantee is necessary for an issuer of securities to meet eligibility requirements is required to satisfy the same minimum rating requirements and financial criteria that it would have to satisfy if it were, in fact, the issuer. However, once again, in the case of a convertible bond offering, the parent company is not subject to any minimum rating requirement or financial criterion.

If the foreign currency-denominated securities being issued or offered for subscription are straight bonds which are supported by a bank letter of credit, the issuer must have a BBB rating or better and the letter of credit bank must have an A rating or better. In the case of foreign currency-denominated bonds coupled with equity warrants which are supported by a bank letter of credit, the issuer must have a BBB rating or better and the bank must be rated by at least one rating agency recognized by the MOF.[261] In the case of foreign currency-denominated convertible bonds which are supported by a bank letter of credit, neither the issuer nor the letter of credit bank is subject to any minimum rating requirement or financial criterion.

. . .

## IV. Conclusion

The securities statutes and the regulations promulgated thereunder in both Japan and the United States are similar. However, the manner in which international securities offerings are regulated and the extent to which regulatory control is exercised are quite different. Although the Japanese system of securities regulation was borrowed from the United States, the spirit of the U.S. regulatory system was not. To a certain extent, the differences between the two countries result from the unique Japanese system of administrative guidance. Unlike the SEC, the MOF informally pressures issuers and securities companies involved in international securities offerings to act in ways that further the administrative goals of the MOF.

In the United States, when either a resident or non-resident issuer raises capital by offering securities in the United States or abroad, the SEC requires registration under the Securities Act if the offering falls within the extraterritorial reach of the Securities Act and an exemption

**255.** In the case of offerings of straight bonds and bonds coupled with equity warrants, the issuer and the parent company are also subject to eligibility criteria beyond those applicable to domestic securities offerings.

**261.** When issuing bonds coupled with equity warrants, the issuer is also subject to the eligibility criteria applicable to domestic securities offerings. For straight bond offerings, the issuer and the bank issuing the letter of credit are also subject to eligibility criteria which differ from those eligibility criteria applicable to domestic securities offerings.

from registration is not available under the Securities Act. SEC "approval" is never required. On the other hand, in Japan, issuers and securities companies often engage in informal discussions with the MOF before the start of any international securities offering to ensure MOF approval under the FECL and the 1948 Act. Whenever any Japanese resident issuer raises capital by offering securities abroad, MOF notification and MOF acceptance of such notification is required. ...

## 2. A Case Study: Euroyen Bonds

The Euroyen bond market gives a glimpse of how government policies affect offshore fundraising by Japanese and other issuers. As you read this, relate the policies that emerge to those described more generally in the last section.

### DAIWA EUROPE LTD., "EUROYEN BONDS"

In Euromoney Guide to Financing (1991) 15.

**Market Background**

The Euroyen bond market has grown steadily since the European Investment Bank (EIB) launched the first issue in May 1977. The market has proved itself to be a versatile source of funding for high quality borrowers.

There are two main reasons for the market's expansion. The Japanese Ministry of Finance (MoF) has progressively lifted restrictions on the type of deals permitted as well as the classes of borrowers allowed to tap the market. Added to that, the strength of the yen on the foreign exchange markets has fuelled investor demand for yen-denominated securities.

In the first half of 1991, Euroyen was one of the largest sectors of the Euromarkets, making up 10% of the total volume of new issues. The market has applications for a wide variety of borrowers. It offers them an ideal way to borrow yen. Through a liquid swap market, borrowers can also raise funds in other currencies at attractive rates, either through listed public issues or structured private placements.

The increased activity of foreign banks in Tokyo, and the entry of Japanese banks into the swaps business has proved a positive influence, adding to the swap market's overall liquidity.

**Access**

The issuers of Euroyen bonds fall into four main categories. The Japanese MoF requires all issues to be rated by at least one of six recognized credit rating agencies.

- Supranational, sovereign and sovereign-related issuers. These borrowers bring the largest and most widely-accepted issues, which account for the bulk of secondary market trading. In recent months the majority of these issues have been placed in

Europe. The main buyers have been central banks and institutional investors.

- Japanese corporates are coming to the market more and more. The size of these issues varies as does the credit quality of the issuers. Investor demand is largely Japanese and there tends to be little secondary market liquidity.
- Non–Japanese corporates. These are usually blue-chip issuers, with credit ratings of double-A or better. These deals typically have maturities of up to five years.
- Banks. Non–Japanese banks have in recent years found Euroyen issues targeted at Japanese investors a neat way to reduce their cost of funds. Such issues are often tailored to the requirements of a few investors and are highly structured using options or forwards. These deals are effectively private placements and illiquid in the secondary market. For instance, European banks were big issuers of Nikkei-linked bonds in 1989. These bond issues contained embedded options on the Nikkei–225 index of Japanese stocks.

### New Issues—Procedure and Pricing

The Japanese MoF must give its permission for all new issues in the Euroyen market. The potential borrower can obtain permission by filing a mandate letter and power of attorney through the lead manager of the issue. The approval process requires a minimum of one working day between release of the mandate letter and launch.

. . .

### Investor Base—Japan

By far the largest volume of demand for yen-denominated securities is, inevitably, Japanese. But the MoF bans Japanese investors from buying Euroyen bonds until 90 days after payment date and so non-Japanese investors dominate the primary market. Euroyen issues targeted at Japanese investors often have a short first coupon linked to Libor (London Interbank Offered Rate), so that a European-based financial institution can park the securities; when the 90 days are up, the institution will sell the bonds to a pre-chosen investor in Japan.

Japanese investors tend to hold Euroyen bonds until maturity and use JGBs for short-term position taking. Most Japanese investors require a double-A long-term debt rating for non-Japanese issuers, but they accept lower quality credits if the issuer is a well-known Japanese company.

Within the Japanese sector, the regional banks, the smaller financial institutions and the public sector institutions are important investor groups.

- The regional banks, looking primarily for yield enhancement have a particular interest in lower-rated issuers.

- The public sector bodies prefer longer maturities, normally in the seven to 10–year range.
- Japanese trust banks are a major source of Euroyen buying at the short end of the yield curve, at maturities of three to five years.
- The public and privately controlled pension funds are also big buyers, usually in longer maturities.
- The insurance companies, which used to invest significantly, are now less active.

. . .

**Deregulation of the Euroyen bond market**

| | |
|---|---|
| May 1977 | Daiwa launches first Euroyen issue, a ¥10 bn deal with a seven-year maturity. |
| Dec 1984 | Issuance of unsecured bonds by foreign corporates, state and local governments and government agencies allowed. |
| | Foreign securities companies allowed to act as lead managers |
| | Lead management and co-management restrictions lifted for foreign dealers |
| | Resident corporates allowed to issue Euroyen bonds |
| April 1985 | Abolition of 20% withholding tax payable by foreign investors on bonds issued by Japanese companies |
| June 1985 | Zero coupon and dual currency issues allowed |
| | Non–Japanese borrowers permitted to issue floating rate notes |
| April 1986 | 180–day lock-up period reduced to 90–days |
| June 1986 | Foreign banks allowed to issue Euroyen bonds |
| April 1987 | Issues with four-year maturities allowed |
| June 1989 | Most other restrictions lifted |
| | Issuance in yen permitted under Euro-medium term note programmes |

### *Questions*

1. How would MOF policies affect the foreign and offshore operations of Japanese securities firms? Would their impact be significant?

a. What is the impact of restrictions on domestic securities markets?

b. Does government policy help or hurt the competitive position of Japanese securities firms abroad? For example, recall the discussion of Article 65 and the Three Bureaus guidance in the first part of this chapter. What was the purpose of this policy and how would it affect the securities companies abroad? What are the implications of its abolition? The government regulates commissions at home. What would be the effect of these rules on securities companies' operations abroad? What other competitive effects would you expect from the government's policies?

c. On balance, does their Japanese base help or hinder Japanese securities companies competing in international markets? Consider regulatory and other factors.

d. Rules of this sort often protect one group or another. Whom do these rules protect?

2. How do MOF's policies affect operations abroad by others than securities firms?

a. What is the impact of rules governing investment flows out of Japan? Why should MOF control all this? Do these rules discriminate against foreign securities companies that want to bring Japanese investors to financial markets outside Japan?

b. What is the impact of policy toward pension funds' investment abroad? Does the policy seriously limit outward portfolio investment? Does the pension fund policy discriminate against foreign securities companies? Would change help foreign securities companies? How would an increase from 50% to 75% for offshore investment of pension funds help U.S. securities firms?

---

## 3. Policy Toward Innovation in Offshore Derivatives Markets

One partial explanation for the long deep fall in the Tokyo stock market was that program trading and other derivatives exacerbated the collapse. U.S. securities companies in Japan were condemned for their role. The first article describes the strategy of Nomura Securities Company, the largest in Japan.

## MICHAEL R. SESIT, "NOMURA BECOMES A TOP PROGRAM TRADER IN NEW YORK, BUT SHUNS STRATEGY IN JAPAN"

Wall Street Journal, February 7, 1992, Cl.

NEW YORK—In roughly 18 months, the U.S. subsidiary of Japan's **Nomura Securities** Co. has leaped into the front ranks of American program traders.

But on Nomura's home turf in Tokyo, ironically, U.S. firms such as Salomon Brothers Inc. and Morgan Stanley & Co. continue to run rings around the giant brokerage firm in program trading. Nomura resists using the trading strategies developed by its New York employees in the Japanese market.

That's because program trading is politically unpopular in Japan, where the vulnerable stock market has been rocked more than once by U.S. firms using these strategies. Some Japanese even blame program trading for much of the Tokyo market's 43% decline since late 1989. Corporate culture also comes into play, retarding the U.S. unit's growth by such restrictions as not allowing it to pitch program-trading and other strategies to Nomura customers in other parts of the world.

**Big Market Swings**

Program trading is a catch-all phrase that amounts to sophisticated, computer-driven stock-trading strategies. As defined by the New York Stock Exchange, program trading involves the simultaneous purchase or sale of at least 15 different stocks with a total value of $1 million or more.

The most controversial strategy is stock-index arbitrage—buying or selling large baskets of stocks and simultaneously taking offsetting positions in stock-index futures to capture profits from fleeting price differences. On some occasions, index arbitrage can send a stock market zooming or plunging unexpectedly. Such moves anger some U.S. investors—though many fewer now than several years ago—but have traumatized many Japanese investors.

Nomura has been at or near the top of the Big Board's weekly listing of most-active program traders for months. In the latest listing, for the week ended Jan. 24, Nomura traded 16 million shares in program-trading strategies.

This climb began with the appointment in October 1989 of Max C. Chapman Jr. as co-chairman of Nomura Securities International Inc., the New York unit's formal name. His strategy calls for expansion into program trading and "derivatives," which are instruments such as options and warrants that are based on underlying securities or security indexes. To implement this plan, he hired Joseph R. Schmuckler away from Kidder, Peabody & Co. in March 1990.

**No Money From Home**

The unit's success has come in a market where Nomura itself is an insignificant player and without being allowed to use any of the parent firm's money. Nomura's U.S. unit currently has about $700 million in capital and a balance sheet in excess of $30 billion. So far, Mr. Schmuckler says, the sophisticated stock-trading effort is "consistently and solidly profitable."

Even so, Nomura U.S. has run into resistance at Tokyo headquarters, which helps explain why Nomura isn't a major program trader in its home market. Until last year, Nomura made so much money from selling stock to individual investors that Tokyo executives saw little need for using program trading techniques or derivative securities.

In addition, says a U.S. securities-firm executive, the Japanese style of seeking consensus and of collectively accepting the rewards of success or consequences of failure doesn't produce individuals willing to assume the responsibilities of capital commitment—which program trading requires.

In stock trading, "ultimately, you've got to give a young kid at a desk the power to push the button," says the executive. "If you need five people to make that decision, it won't be made, and the kid will leave."

Also, many of Nomura's senior managers didn't understand the strategies being developed by high-priced American talent in New York. Because they didn't understand, they ridiculed. One Nomura executive in Tokyo once described program trading as a Wall Street disease. More recently, Atsushi Saito, a Nomura executive managing director based in Tokyo, criticized "speculation" in Tokyo's futures markets.

**Troubles With 'Swaps'**

In the U.S., Nomura wouldn't allow its unit to use its credit rating (Triple-A by Moody's Investors Service Inc. and Double-A plus by Standard & Poor's) in backing trading commitments. As a result, the U.S. unit has been significantly limited in expanding into "swap" trading, in which two or more parties exchange financial obligations, and other sophisticated products and techniques.

A separate operation in New York deals in swaps, but it reports directly to Tokyo and has suffered morale and management upheavals. Two departing executives are suing Nomura for, among other things, allegedly violating their contracts and inhibiting their earning potential by limiting their use of the parent company guarantee.

### *Questions*

1. Given Japanese policy toward program trading and off-shore operations at home, what would be the rationale for allowing Nomura to take such an important role abroad?

---

## C. THE STOCK MARKET CRISIS AND THE GOVERNMENT'S RESPONSE

The serious problems in Japan's stock market began in 1989. Japan was not alone, but its problems persisted.

## JAMES STERNGOLD, "THE $6 TRILLION HOLE IN JAPAN'S POCKET"

New York Times, January 21, 1994, D1.

TOKYO, Jan. 20—Many of the world's financial markets have recovered from a decade of excess in which problems were often measured in billions, or even hundreds of billions of dollars. But Japan is now coping with an even more awesome debacle: the loss of at least $6 trillion from one of the steepest plunges in stock and property values of this century.

And it is not over yet: the markets are just marking the anniversary of a crash that has sent stock and real estate prices down more than 50 percent with no clear signs yet of a recovery.

The decline offers both insights into the Japanese financial system and puzzles that add to the uncertainty over Japan's troubled economic future. When the markets first began their tumble in early 1990, some analysts predicted that the decline could ripple through financial systems around the globe. Yet with Wall Street and some European markets reaching new highs, those fears have proved overblown. Even in Japan there has rarely been even a whiff of panic in the air.

### Delayed Agony

Nevertheless, analysts say, while the Japanese Government has taken a series of steps to dampen the effects of the crash, those efforts may have only stretched out the problems. To give a sense of the dimensions of the crash, the American savings and loan crisis may end up costing about $350 billion. The third-world debt crisis appears to have cost banks less than $150 billion.

Some economists argue that the heavy-handed means the Japanese Government has used—such as pouring cash from Government pension funds into the market, pressuring big investors not to sell shares and concealing the full impact of the debacle on banks from the public—may have staved off an abrupt collapse, but at a huge cost that may undermine the financial system.

Japan's huge commercial banks have been unable to lift the economy out of its recession because they have been so battered by a mounting toll of bad loans. And many companies that poured their extra cash into securities investments in the boom years are now finding it difficult to revive their core industrial businesses because of their weakened financial condition. In addition, the reputation of Japan's respected economic planners has been badly damaged.

"The Government and the Bank of Japan thought we could have a soft landing," said Mikio Wakatsuki, chairman of the Japan Research Institute's board of counselors and until recently the deputy governor for international affairs at the Bank of Japan. "We thought we could make it a painless decline. It was maybe a misjudgment."

Takaaki Wakasugi, a professor of finance at Tokyo University and the University of Michigan said: "In the late 1980's, people were living in a dream. They did not understand reality. Right now, in a sense, we're in a state of chaos because of that."

While things have been surprisingly calm on the surface, the biggest victims of the crash, commercial banks, are likely to be impaired for years, analysts say. ...

## Tending the Home Fires

Companies, too, have had to adjust to the new reality of deflation in the financial markets. Many companies, for instance, were lured into making huge investments in stocks, property and golf courses; they have now refocused on their core businesses.

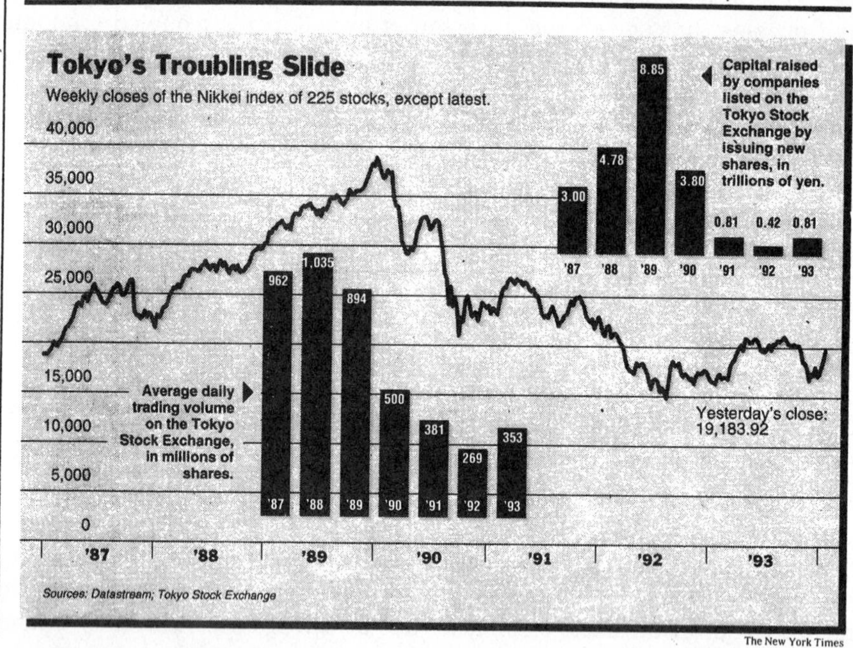


Corporate treasurers, who had spent freely, because raising capital in the stock market was so cheap in the boom years, are being more tight-fisted about investments in research and new operations.

The property market has been even more severely affected. Not only have commercial property prices plunged more than 50 percent in big cities like Tokyo and Osaka, but almost no transactions are taking place.

To sell land is to realize the loss, so companies are sitting on land or transferring it to affiliated companies at prices that bear little relation to real market conditions.

The result has been a sort of slow-motion crash, defying the expectations of many analysts and economists.

"I thought the stock market had gone too high and that it would adjust, but I never thought it would go this low or last this long," said Yoshihiko Miyauchi, chief executive of the Orix Corporation, Japan's largest leasing and diversified financing company. "This is deflation. We haven't had to deal with this kind of thing before."

## Pushing the Yen Up

It all began with the growth of Japan's the so-called bubble economy during the 1980's. Behind the rise had principally been low interest rates and the booming economy of the United States, where Japan sends a large portion of its exports. In September 1985, the Reagan Administration and Japanese officials agreed to send the value of yen soaring against the dollar to make Japanese products more expensive for foreigners, crimping exports. Foreign-made goods became cheaper in Japan, lifting imports.

In fact, there was a temporary reduction in Japan's surpluses, but the shock was a catastrophe for Japanese exporters. They could adjust to a stronger yen, but they needed time, and they needed to make huge investments to improve their efficiency.

The solution was steep reductions in interest rates by the Bank of Japan. Companies did make productive investments—in fact, they overinvested, building more factory capacity than either the domestic or foreign markets could absorb. But the policy also set off a speculative orgy by flooding the markets with cash.

As investors bid stock prices higher, companies raised record sums by selling new shares: 8.85 trillion yen, or $62 billion worth, in 1989 alone.

The Government finally recognized the artificial nature of the market's rise and the possibility of an uncontrolled collapse, and began trying to ratchet down the market by the second half of 1989. The Bank of Japan began to raise its discount rate, and in the first week of 1990 investors got the message.

In the first two years of the market plunge, stock and property prices lost 611.7 trillion yen in value, or nearly $4.9 trillion, according to the Economic Planning Agency.

## Market Is Down 51%

But prices did not drop in a chaotic fury, for the most part. They just went into a sickeningly steep slide as trading volume dried up.

Since then, it has gradually become impossible for companies to raise fresh capital by selling new shares on the Tokyo Stock Exchange. The Nikkei stock market index has fallen 51 percent from its peak of 38,915.87, on the last trading day of 1989, to today's close of 19,183.92.

Publicly, Government officials pledged fidelity to the principles of free-market economics. But it soon became clear that the Finance

Ministry had ordered various Government pension funds to pour money into the stock market starting in 1992. Still, the market fell.

"Officially, of course, the Ministry of Finance denies their intervention, but now they have a very big problem on their hands," said Nobuhiko Matsuno, the former head of the ministry's securities bureau and now senior executive director of the Japan Development Bank. "The financial system is very fragile."

## EMIKO TERAZONO, "TOKYO PREOCCUPIED BY ECONOMY AND POLITICS"

Financial Times, December 11/12, 1993, 23.

Uncertainty over the ability of the Japanese prime minister, Mr Morihiro Hosokawa, to resolve mounting political and economic issues has kept investors away from the Tokyo stock market in spite of low long-term yields and falling money market rates.

Political developments have preoccupied investors as the government's decision to open the rice market and the passage of the political reform bill have become crucial issues, alongside government-mooted additional fiscal measures to prop up the sagging economy.

Mr Hosokawa is currently trying to juggle these issues. However, last week's plunge in the Nikkei index to a year's low of 16,078.71, wiping out the market's local currency gains for the year, has unnerved government officials. It has forced them to turn more of their attention to the economy, and prompted cabinet members to pledge support for share prices through economic stimulus.

Analysts point out that an income tax cut, designed to lift sluggish consumption, is already discounted into share prices. Ms Tomoko Fujii, economist at Salomon Brothers in Tokyo, says that the chances of a market plunge are high if the government fails to announce an income tax cut of around Y5,000bn-Y6,000bn soon.

However, the income tax cuts are expected to form part of an overall tax reform package. Mr Hosokawa will need to twist the arms of bureaucrats at the ministry of finance, which is staunchly insisting that a tax cut be coupled with a consumption tax hike to maintain fiscal soundness.

The prime minister does not have time on his side. He still needs to push political reform through parliament during the current session. If he fails to implement reform, the cabinet is likely to resign, followed by a lower house election, causing a delay in the implementation of economic measures.

Meanwhile, some investors point out that even if additional stimuli are announced, their implementation will take time. "The underlying fundamentals won't change in a short term," says a fund manager at Nippon Life, the country's largest life insurer. However, he says that the company is ready to bargain hunt shares around the 16,000 level.

Pessimism over the economy is increasing. Nomura Research Institute, the research arm of Nomura Securities recently announced that the economy would contract by 0.4 per cent in the next business year. The NRI forecast presumes that the government will introduce another economic stimulus package and an income tax cut, and that the official discount rate will be reduced from the present record low of 1.75 per cent to 1 per cent.

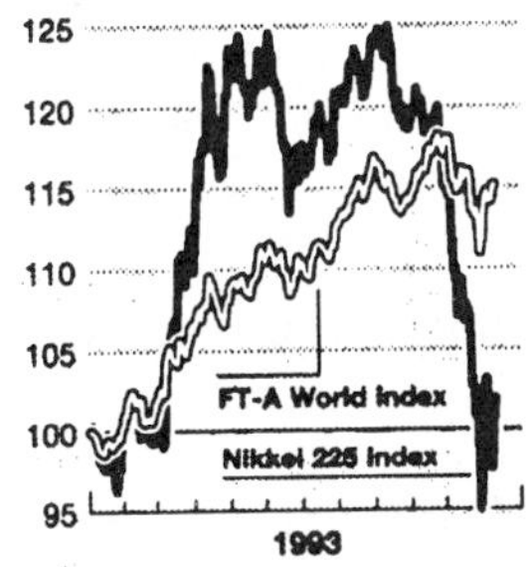

**Japan**

Rebased

125
120
115
110
105
100
95

FT-A World Index

Nikkei 225 Index

1993

Source: Datastream

Concerns over the country's labour market are also heightening as unemployment is rising and the number of job offers are falling. Unemployment in October rose to 2.7 per cent, a six-year high, while the ratio of job offers to job seekers fell to a six-year low of 0.67, or 67 jobs for 100 seekers.

And while the July-September quarter gross domestic product grew 0.5 per cent from the preceding three months, economists attribute the growth to last minute output by companies and aggressive discounts by retailers ahead of the half year book closing.

Most market participants hope that trading will fluctuate around the 17,000 level for the rest of this year. However, the new year may see increased liquidation of stock holdings by companies ahead of the March book closing. Mr Yasuo Ueki at Nikko Securities says that companies have already sold some Y1,900bn worth of shares this year, and are potential sellers of another Y1,000bn.

Banks, which still need to write off mounting bad loans are also expected to continue to realise profits on their long term holdings.

Many brokers hope that a declining trend in the yen will support export oriented high-technology stocks, whose weakness this year has reflected sharp falls in profits, due to sluggish consumer confidence and foreign exchange losses. "The trading cycle points to electronic stocks," says Mr Ueki at Nikko.

Some institutional investors, especially life insurers, which have low exposure to equities, are looking for higher yielding investments. Many shifted into the bond market at the start of the year, and total investments in bonds rose by 42 per cent in the year to June, accounting for almost half of their net cash flow.

Most investors hope that the government will deliver a boost to share prices eventually, and that public insurance and postal funds will come in to buy shares as they did during the first half of this year.

While purchases by public funds have evaporated since the flotation of East Japan Railway in October, weakness in equities ahead of the March year end book closing of their books might bring government influence to bear.

Meanwhile, some analysts take comfort in a traditional approach. Mr Geoffrey Barker, an economist at Baring Securities in Tokyo, points out that stock markets tend to be strong during the first four months of the year. "Investors come in at the start of the year with a determination to make money," he explains.

The effect on Japanese securities companies was severe, although by mid–1993 they were reporting recovery.

## QUENTIN HARDY, "JAPAN'S BIG FOUR BROKERAGE FIRMS, DESPITE HIGHER PROFITS, ARE DOWNGRADED"

Wall Street Journal, January 19, 1994, A15.

TOKYO—These are sweet times for Japan's giant securities companies. After four years of sagging earnings and bruised share prices, profits are up and business is growing.

The Big Four brokerage firms are among the best performers in Tokyo, out-pacing a market that is off to a strong 1994.

Don't bet on the luck lasting.

The brokerage firms still are hamstrung by excessive costs and vulnerable to a new market downturn, analysts say. In the midst of this year's mini-bull run, Standard & Poor's Asia delivered another blow, lowering its ratings of Japan's four brokerage-firm giants: Nomura Securities Co., Daiwa Securities Co., Nikko Securities Co. and Yamaichi Securities Co.

"The securities industry in Japan will continue to be negatively affected by low market turnover and limited new equity offerings," S & P said. "In this kind of environment, it will be difficult for them to recover much of their past earnings power." S & P last downgraded Nomura in 1991, and the other three in 1992.

The Tokyo market has been unusually buoyant lately. Even with a second straight day of losses Tuesday, the Nikkei 225–stock index closed at 18514.55, up 6.3% in the past two weeks. The brokers have done even better: Nikko is up 8.3%, Nomura is up 9.7%, Daiwa has gained 12.7%, and Yamaichi has advanced a whopping 22.7%. The Nihon Keizai Shimbun newspaper this week sharply boosted its projections for the Big Four's profits in the fiscal year ending in March.

The brokerage firms' sunnier outlook reflects a surge in trading volume as well as the price rally—turnover was more than 450 million shares a day last week, compared with about 200 million shares a day at the end of 1993. That makes an enormous difference to the profits of these commission-dependent firms.

But it isn't sustainable, the bears say. Volume already has been lower this week. Over the longer term, the government's artificial support for the market will continue to damp trading, says Yoshio Shima, assistant director of S & P Asia. The market "is being kept at quite high valuations," he says, "and that will restrict market activity."

Another demon: corporate bloat. "The biggest problem is that their expenses are way too high," says Betsy Daniels, an analyst at Morgan Stanley in Tokyo. "Nomura, one of the strongest, has a return-on-equity target of 5%; the average target of a U.S. investment bank is

20%." For the year ended March 31, 1993, she notes, Nomura's return on equity was just 0.15%.

Of course, Tokyo has its bulls these days, particularly among the foreign investors who have led the recent buying. They see a market overdue for a rise after four bad years. They think the Japanese government's multitrillion yen public works splurge will spark a broader economic recovery.

"Corporate profits will double over two years," predicts Chris Mitchinson, a long-time Japan strategist for Salomon Brothers Asia Ltd., who is now a private Japanese investment consultant in London. "We think [the Nikkei] will be between 25,000 and 30,000 by the end of the year." He says Japanese investors will join the foreign stock buyers later this year and recommends loading up on shares of Nomura and Daiwa.

Even such a rally, however, may not benefit the brokerage firms. Financial-market deregulation, Mr. Shima notes, already has Japan's beleaguered banks encroaching on the brokers' turf. "Corporate-bond underwriting fees have fallen by two-thirds in the past year" because of competition, he says. "We expect the negative impact of deregulation to continue—if it's in bond underwriting now, why not equity-linked underwriting in the future?"

The brokers themselves, of course, are more optimistic. "Our consolidated earnings have started to improve," a Nomura spokesman says. "We don't think financial liberalization and increased competition will affect our earnings." Says a Nikko official: "We have no negative forecasts."

Besides, even after the bad years, Japan's brokerage firms are still rich. "Nomura still has a ton of cash," Ms. Daniels says, adding that the companies can continue to weather a bear market. The capital they built up in the late 1980s rally means that, even with yesterday's downgrades, the Japanese brokerage firms still have higher ratings than many of their more profitable U.S. counterparts.

S & P lowered its ratings of debt issued by guaranteed subsidiaries of Daiwa to single-A1 from single–A1–plus. Nikko was lowered to single-A from single-A-plus. Nomura's rating was dropped to double-A from double-A-plus. Yamaichi fell to single-A-minus from single-A.

## *Questions*

1. The government has proposed a range of solutions to the crisis, from macroeconomic policy to efforts to make the markets more efficient. What do its proposals reveal about the extent to which fundamental policy is changing?

2. Compare the relative market share of U.S. securities firms in Japan and Japanese firms in the U.S.A. How have U.S. securities firms performed in Japan? Compare the relative market shares of banks and securities companies in the U.S. and Japan. What does it tell you?

3. Compare the relative weight given competition and prudential issues by government policy in Japan and the U.S. Is the weight the same for banking and securities markets? What explains the differences?

---

*Links To Other Chapters*

Japan's government and financial institutions are very important players in international finance. They and many of the issues raised in this chapter surface throughout this book.

In foreign exchange markets, the government's role extends beyond the policies described in this chapter. In the 1980s, the US and Japanese governments tried to raise the Yen/$ exchange rate and the Bank of Japan tried to offset the deflationary effects by easing the money supply with lower interest rates. This added to liquidity that fueled the bubble. See Chapter VI.

Japanese policies affect the capital adequacy of its financial institutions (see Chapter IV), which in turn affect their performance in international markets and the growth of those markets. The bailout policy in Japan appears to affect its banks' need for capital profoundly, even after the Basle Accord. This policy, and the resulting low capital ratios in the late 1970s and early 1980s encouraged Japanese banks to lend substantially to developing countries through syndicated eurocredits (Chapter VII).

The Japanese and U.S. approaches to financial policy contrast sharply (see Chapters II and III).

Japan's approach to innovation has a significant effect on the growth of international financial markets. It affected the eurobond market's performance (Chapter XI), securitization (Chapter XII), and the futures and options markets (Chapter XV).

The offshore markets offer a way for Japanese financial institutions to escape from stringent domestic regulation. But it is not clear the escape is very far. Japanese influence over its firms' activities in markets outside Japan seems broader than the U.S. government's; see its policy toward Yen eurobonds. Japanese policy is possibly more effective than the U.S. government's; see the reading on asset freezes (Chapter X).

The performance of Japan's financial system affects its banks and securities companies in international markets. In the mid–1980s, they seemed omnipresent. In the 1990s, they withdrew. One sees their limited role in the Telmex global ADR offering (Chapter XVII).

# Chapter VIII

# EURODOLLAR DEPOSITS AND SYNDICATED LOANS

Mystery shrouds the origins of the eurocurrency markets, the major part of the offshore markets. One story, set in the period immediately after World War II, has Soviet firms holding dollars propose to banks based outside the U.S. that they hold the dollars as deposits to avoid the risk that the U.S. might confiscate the funds.

For over twenty years, the euromarkets have played a significant part in international finance. This chapter begins with an explanation of what a eurodollar is, given when the market's role first became apparent. For recent information about the interbank market that makes up much of the eurocurrency market, see the article by the Bank of England in the first chapter.

We then turn to the loan syndication market. It is a market for medium-term loans by groups of banks who fund their loans from deposits in the eurocurrency market. This is the first opportunity to examine the key elements of a sample contract.

## A. INTRODUCTION TO THE EUROCURRENCY MARKET

### M. FRIEDMAN, "THE EURO-DOLLAR MARKET: SOME FIRST PRINCIPLES"

The Morgan Guaranty Survey (October 1969) 4–14.

The Euro-dollar market is the latest example of the mystifying quality of money creation to even the most sophisticated bankers, let alone other businessmen. Recently, I heard a high official of an international financial organization discuss the Euro-dollar market before a collection of high-powered international bankers. He estimated that Euro-dollar deposits totaled some $30 billion. He was then asked: "What is the source of these deposits?" His answer was: partly, U.S. balance-of-payments deficits; partly, dollar reserves of non-U.S. central banks; partly, the proceeds from the sale of Euro-dollar bonds.

This answer is almost complete nonsense. Balance-of-payments deficits do provide foreigners with claims on U.S. dollars. But there is nothing to assure that such claims will be held in the form of Euro-dollars. In any event, U.S. deficits, worldwide, have totaled less than $9 billion for the past five years, on a liquidity basis. Dollar holdings of non-U.S. central banks have fallen during the period of rapid rise in

Euro-dollar deposits but by less than $5 billion. The dollars paid for Euro-bonds had themselves to come from somewhere and do not constitute an independent source. No matter how you try, you cannot get $30 billion from these sources. The answer given is precisely parallel to saying that the source of the $400 billion of deposits in U.S. banks (or for that matter the much larger total of all outstanding short-term claims) is the $60 billion of Federal Reserve credit outstanding.

The correct answer for both Euro-dollars and liabilities of U.S. banks is that their major source is a bookkeeper's pen.[1] The purpose of this article is to explain this statement. The purpose is purely expository. I shall restrict myself essentially to principle and shall not attempt either an empirical evaluation of the Euro-dollar market or a normative judgment of its desirability.

Another striking example of the confusion about Euro-dollars is the discussion, in even the most sophisticated financial papers, of the use of the Euro-dollar market by U.S. commercial banks "to evade tight money," as it is generally phrased. U.S. banks, one reads in a leading financial paper, "have been willing to pay extremely high interest rates . . . to borrow back huge sums of U.S. dollars that have piled up abroad." The image conveyed is that of piles of dollar bills being bundled up and shipped across the ocean on planes and ships—the way New York literally did drain gold from Europe in the bad—or good—old days at times of financial panic. Yet, the more dollars U.S. banks "borrow back" the more Euro-dollar deposits go up! How come? The answer is that it is purely figurative language to speak of "piled up" dollars being "borrowed back." Again, the bookkeeper's pen is at work.

*What are Euro-dollars?*

Just what are Euro-dollars? They are deposit liabilities, denominated in dollars, of banks outside the United States. Engaged in Euro-dollar business, for example, are foreign commercial banks such as the Bank of London and South America, Ltd., merchant banks such as Morgan Grenfell and Co., Ltd., and many of the foreign branches of U.S. commercial banks. Funds placed with these institutions may be owned by anyone—U.S. or foreign residents or citizens, individuals or corporations or governments. Euro-dollars have two basic characteristics: first, they are short-term obligations to pay dollars; second, they are obligations of banking offices located outside the U.S. In principle, there is no hard and fast line between Euro-dollars and other dollar-denominated claims on non-U.S. institutions—just as there is none between claims in the U.S. that we call "money" and other short-term claims. The precise line drawn in practice depends on the exact interpretation given to "short-term" and to "banks." Nothing essential in this article is affected by the precise point at which the line is drawn.

1. The similarity between credit creation in the U.S. fractional reserve banking system and in the Euro-dollar market has of course often been noted.

A homely parallel to Euro-dollars is to be found in the dollar deposit liabilities of bank offices located in the city of Chicago—which could similarly be called "Chicago dollars." Like Euro-dollars, "Chicago dollars" consist of obligations to pay dollars by a collection of banking offices located in a particular geographic area. Again, like Euro-dollars, they may be owned by anyone—residents or nonresidents of the geographic area in question.

The location of the banks is important primarily because it affects the regulations under which the banks operate and hence the way that they can do business. Those Chicago banks that are members of the Federal Reserve System must comply with the System's requirements about reserves, maximum interest rates payable on deposits, and so on; and in addition, of course, with the requirements of the Comptroller of the Currency if they are national banks, and of the Illinois State Banking Commission if they are state banks.

Euro-dollar banks are subject to the regulations of the relevant banking authorities in the country in which they operate. In practice, however, such banks have been subject neither to required reserves on Euro-dollar deposits nor to maximum ceilings on the rates of interest they are permitted to pay on such deposits.

*Regulation and Euro-dollars*

The difference in regulation has played a key role in the development of the Euro-dollar market. No doubt there were minor precursors, but the initial substantial Euro-dollar deposits in the post-World War II period originated with the Russians, who wanted dollar balances but recalled that their dollar holdings in the U.S. had been impounded by the Alien Property Custodian in World War II. Hence they wanted dollar claims not subject to U.S. governmental control.

The most important regulation that has stimulated the development of the Euro-dollar market has been Regulation Q, under which the Federal Reserve has fixed maximum interest rates that member banks could pay on time deposits. Whenever these ceilings become effective, Euro-dollar deposits, paying a higher interest rate, became more attractive than U.S. deposits, and the Euro-dollar market expanded. U.S. banks then borrowed from the Euro-dollar market to replace the withdrawn time deposits.

A third major force has been the direct and indirect exchange controls imposed by the U.S. for "balance-of-payments" purposes the interest-equalization tax, the "voluntary" controls on bank lending abroad and on foreign investment, and, finally, the compulsory controls instituted by President Johnson in January 1968. Without Regulation Q and the exchange controls—all of which, in my opinion, are both unnecessary and undesirable—the Euro-dollar market, though it might still have existed, would not have reached anything like its present dimensions.

*Fractional reserves*

Euro-dollar deposits like "Chicago deposits" are in principle obligations to pay literal dollars—i.e., currency (or coin), all of which consists, at present, of government-issued fiat (Federal Reserve notes, U.S. notes, a few other similar issues, and fractional coinage). In practice, even Chicago banks are called on to discharge only an insignificant part of their deposit obligations by paying out currency. Euro-dollar banks are called on to discharge a negligible part in this form. Deposit obligations are typically discharged by providing a credit or deposit at another bank—as when you draw a check on your bank which the recipient "deposits" in his.

To meet their obligations to pay cash, banks keep a "reserve" of cash on hand. But, of course, since they are continuously receiving as well as paying cash and since in any interval they will be called on to redeem only a small fraction of their obligations in cash, they need on the average keep only a very small part of their assets in cash for this purpose. For Chicago banks, this cash serves also to meet legal reserve requirements. For Euro-dollar banks, the amount of literal cash they hold is negligible.

To meet their obligations to provide a credit at another bank, when a check or similar instrument is used, banks keep deposits at other banks. For Chicago banks, these deposits (which in addition to facilitating the transfer of funds between banks serve to meet legal reserve requirements) are held primarily at Federal Reserve banks. In addition, however, Chicago banks may also keep balances at correspondent banks in other cities.

Like cash, deposits at other banks need be only a small fraction of assets. Banks are continuously receiving funds from other banks, as well as transferring funds to them, so they need reserves only to provide for temporary discrepancies between payments and receipts or sudden unanticipated demands. For Chicago banks, such "prudential" reserves are clearly far smaller than the reserves that they are legally required to keep.

Euro-dollar banks are not subject to legal reserve requirements, but, like Chicago banks, they must keep a prudential reserve in order to be prepared to meet withdrawals of deposits when they are demanded or when they mature. An individual bank will regard as a prudential reserve readily realizable funds both in the Euro-dollar market itself (e.g., Euro-dollar call money) and in the U.S. But for the Euro-dollar system as a whole, Euro-dollar funds cancel, and the prudential reserves available to meet demands for U.S. dollars consist entirely of deposits at banks in New York or other cities in the U.S. and U.S. money market assets that can be liquidated promptly without loss.

The amount of prudential reserves that a Euro-dollar bank will wish to hold—like the amount that a Chicago bank will wish to hold—will depend on its particular mix of demand and time obligations. Time deposits generally require smaller reserves than demand deposits—and in some instances almost zero reserves if the bank can match closely the maturities of its dollar-denominated liabilities and its dollar-denominated loans and investments. Although a precise estimate is difficult to make because of the incompleteness and ambiguity of the available data, prudential reserves of Euro-dollar institutions are clearly a small fraction of total dollar-denominated obligations.

This point—that Euro-dollar institutions, like Chicago banks, are part of a fractional reserve banking system—is the key to understanding the Euro-dollar market. The failure to recognize it is the chief source of misunderstanding about the Euro-dollar market. Most journalistic discussions of the Euro-dollar market proceed as if a Euro-dollar bank held a dollar in the form of cash or of deposits at a U.S. bank corresponding to each dollar of deposit liability. That is the source of such images as "piling up," "borrowing back," "withdrawing," etc. But of course this is not the case. If it were, a Euro-dollar bank could hardly afford to pay 10% or more on its deposit liabilities.

*A hypothetical example*

A Euro-dollar bank typically has total dollar assets roughly equal to its dollar liabilities. But these assets are not in currency or bank deposits. In highly simplified form, the balance sheet of such a bank—or the part of the balance sheet corresponding to its Euro-dollar operations—must look something like that shown in the adjoining column (the numbers in this and later balance sheets are solely for illustrative purposes).

It is the earnings on the $9,500,000 of loans and investments that enable it to pay interest on the $10,000,000 of deposits.

Where did the $10,000,000 of deposits come from? One can say that $700,000 (cash assets minus due to other banks) came from "primary deposits," i.e., is the counterpart to a literal deposit of cash or transfer of funds from other banks. The other $9,300,000 is "created" by the magic of fractional reserve banking—this is the bookkeeper's pen at work.

EURO–DOLLAR BANK H OF LONDON

| **Assets** | | **Liabilities** | |
|---|---|---|---|
| Cash Assets* | $1,000,000 | Deposits | $10,000,000 |
| Dollar-denominated loans | 7,000,000 | Due to other banks | 300,000 |
| Dollar-denominated bonds | 2,500,000 | Capital accounts | 200,000 |
| Total assets | $10,500,000 | Total liabilities | $10,500,000 |

* Includes U.S. currency, deposits in N.Y. and other banks, and other assets immediately realizable in U.S. funds.

Let us look at the process more closely. Suppose an Arab Sheik opens up a new deposit account in London at Bank H (H for hypothetical) by depositing a check for $1,000,000 drawn on the Sheik's demand deposit account at the head office of, say, Morgan Guaranty Trust Company. Let us suppose that Bank H also keeps its N.Y. account at Morgan Guaranty and also as demand deposits. At the first stage, this will add $1,000,000 to the deposit liabilities of Bank H, and the same amount to its assets in the form of deposits due from New York banks. At Morgan Guaranty, the transfer of deposits from the Sheik to Bank H will cause no change in total deposit liabilities.

But Bank H now has excess funds available to lend. It has been keeping cash assets equal to 10% of deposits—not because it was required to do so but because it deemed it prudent to do so. It now has cash equal to 18% (2/11) of deposits. Because of the $1,000,000 of new deposits from the Sheik, it will want to add, say, $100,000 to its balance in New York. This leaves Bank H with $900,000 available to add to its loans and investments. Assume that it makes a loan of $900,000 to, say, UK Ltd., a British corporation engaged in trade with the U.S., giving corporation UK Ltd. a check on Morgan Guaranty. Bank H's balance sheet will now look as follows after the check has cleared:

| **Assets** | | **Liabilities** | |
|---|---|---|---|
| Cash assets | $1,100,000 | Deposits | $11,000,000 |
| Dollar-denominated loans | 7,900,000 | Due to other banks | 300,000 |
| Dollar-denominated bonds | 2,500,000 | Capital accounts | 200,000 |
| Total assets | $11,500,000 | Total liabilities | $11,500,000 |

We now must ask what UK Ltd. does with the $900,000 check. To cut short and simplify the process, let us assume that UK Ltd. incurred the loan because it had been repeatedly troubled by a shortage of funds in New York and wanted to maintain a higher average level of bank balances in New York. Further assume that it also keeps its account at Morgan Guaranty, so that it simply deposits the check in its demand deposit account.

This particular cycle is therefore terminated and we can examine its effect. First, the position of Morgan Guaranty is fundamentally unchanged; it had a deposit liability of $1,000,000 to the Sheik. It now has a deposit liability of $100,000 to Bank H and one of $900,000 to UK Ltd.

Second, the calculated money supply of the U.S. and the demand deposit component thereof are unchanged. That money supply excludes from "adjusted demand deposits" the deposits of U.S. commercial banks at other U.S. commercial banks but it includes deposits of both foreign banks and other foreigners. Therefore, the Sheik's deposit was included before. The deposits of Bank H and UK Ltd. are included now.

Third, the example was set up so that the money supply owned by residents of the U.S. is also unchanged. As a practical matter, the financial statistics gathered and published by the Federal Reserve do not contain sufficient data to permit calculation of the U.S.-owned money supply—a total which would exclude from the money supply as now calculated currency and deposits at U.S. banks owned by nonresidents and include dollar deposits at non-U.S. banks owned by residents. But the hypothetical transactions clearly leave this total unaffected.

Fourth, Euro-dollar deposits are $1,000,000 higher.

However, fifth, the total world supply of dollars held by nonbanks—dollars in the U.S. plus dollars outside the U.S.—is $900,000 not $1,000,000 higher. The reason is that interbank deposits are now higher by $100,000, thanks to the additional deposits of Bank H at Morgan Guaranty. This amount of deposits was formerly an asset of a nonbank (the Arab Sheik); now it is an asset of Bank H. In this way, Bank H has created $900,000 of Euro-dollar deposits. The other $100,000 of Euro-dollar deposits has been transferred from the U.S. to the Euro-dollar area.

Sixth, the balance of payments of the U.S. is unaffected, whether calculated on a liquidity basis or on an official settlements basis. On a liquidity basis, the Arab Sheik's transfer is recorded as a reduction of $1,000,000 in short-term liquid claims on the U.S. but the increased deposits of Bank H and UK Ltd. at Morgan Guaranty are a precisely offsetting increase. On an official settlements basis, the series of transactions has not affected the dollar holdings of any central bank or official institution.[4]

**4.** It is interesting to contrast these effects with those that would have occurred if we substitute a Chicago bank for Bank H of London, i.e., suppose that the Arab Sheik had transferred his funds to a Chicago Bank, say, Continental Illinois, and Continental Illinois had made the loan to UK Ltd., which UK Ltd. again added to its balances at Morgan Guaranty. To simplify matters, assume that the reserve requirements for Continental Illinois and Morgan Guaranty are the same flat 10% that we assumed Bank H of London kept in the form of cash assets (because, let us say, all deposit changes consist of the appropriate mix of demand and time deposits).

First, the position of Morgan Guaranty is now fundamentally changed. Continental Illinois keeps its reserves as deposits at the Federal Reserve Bank of Chicago, not at Morgan Guaranty. Hence it will deposit its net claim of $100,000 on Morgan Guaranty at the Chicago Fed to meet the reserves required for the Sheik's deposit. This will result in a reduction of $100,000 in Morgan Guaranty's reserve balance at the New York Fed. Its deposits have gone down only $100,000 (thanks to the $900,000 deposit by UK Ltd.) so that if it had no excess reserves before it now has deficient reserves. This will set in train a multiple contraction of deposits at Morgan Guaranty and other banks which will end when the $1,000,000 gain in deposits by Continental Illinois is completely offset by a $1,000,000 decline in deposits at Morgan Guaranty and other banks.

Second, the calculated money supply of the U.S. and the demand deposit component thereof are still unchanged.

However, third, the money supply owned by the residents of the U.S. is reduced by the $900,000 increase in the deposits of UK Ltd.

Fourth, there is no change in Euro-dollar deposits.

Fifth, there is no change in the total world supply of dollars.

Sixth, the balance of payments of the U.S. is affected if it is calculated on a liquidity basis but not if it is calculated on an official settlements basis. On a liquidity basis, the deficit would be increased by $900,000 because the loan by Continental Illinois to UK Ltd. would be recorded as a capital outflow but UK Ltd.'s deposit at Morgan Guaranty would be regarded as an increase in U.S. liquid liabilities to foreigners, which are treated as financing the deficit. This enlargement of the deficit on a liquidity basis is highly misleading. It suggests, of course, a worsening of the U.S. payments problem, whereas in fact all that is involved is a worsening of the statistics. The additional dollars that UK Ltd. has in its demand deposit account cannot mean-

Clearly, there is no meaningful sense in which we can say that the $900,000 of created Euro-dollar deposits is derived from a U.S. balance-of-payments deficit, or from dollars held by central banks, or from the proceeds of Euro-dollar bond sales.

*Some complications*

Many complications of this example are possible. They will change the numbers but not in any way the essential principles. But it may help to consider one or two.

(a) Suppose UK Ltd. used the dollar loan to purchase timber from Russia, and Russia wished to hold the proceeds as a dollar deposit at, say, Bank R in London. Then, another round is started—precisely like the one that began when the Sheik transferred funds from Morgan Guaranty to Bank H. Bank R now has $900,000 extra deposit liabilities, matched by $900,000 extra deposits in New York. If it also follows the practice of maintaining cash assets equal to 10% of deposits, it can make a dollar loan of $810,000. If the recipient of the loan keeps it as a demand deposit at Morgan Guaranty, or transfers it to someone who does, the process comes to an end. The result is that total Euro-dollar deposits are up by $1,900,000. Of that total, $1,710,000 is held by nonbanks, with the other $190,000 being additional deposits of banks (the $100,000 extra of Bank H at Morgan Guaranty plus the $90,000 extra of Bank R at Morgan Guaranty).

If the recipient of the loan transfers it to someone who wants to hold it as a Euro-dollar deposit at a third bank, the process continues on its merry way. If, in the extreme, at every stage, the whole of the proceeds of the loan were to end up as Euro-dollar deposits, it is obvious that the total increase in Euro-dollar deposits would be: 1,000,000 + 900,000 + 810,000 + 729,000 + .......... = 10,000,000. At the end of the process, Euro-dollar deposits would be $10,000,000 higher; deposits of Euro-dollar banks at N.Y. banks, $1,000,000 higher; and the total world supply of dollars held by nonbanks, $9,000,000 higher.

This example perhaps makes it clear why bankers in the Euro-dollar market keep insisting that they do not "create" dollars but only transfer them, and why they sincerely believe that all Euro-dollars come from the U.S. *To each banker separately in the chain described, his additional Euro-dollar deposit came in the form of a check on Morgan Guaranty Trust Company of New York!* How are the bankers to know that the $10,000,000 of checks on Morgan Guaranty all constitute repeated claims on the same initial $1,000,000 of deposits? Appearances are deceiving.

This example (involving successive loan extensions by a series of banks) brings out the difference between two concepts that have pro-

ingfully be regarded as a potential claim on U.S. reserve assets. UK Ltd. not only needs them for transactions purposes; it must regard them as tied or matched to its own dollar indebtedness. On an official settlements basis, the series of transactions does not affect the dollar holdings of any central bank or official institution.

duced much confusion: Euro-dollar creation and the Euro-dollar multiplier. In both the simple example and the example involving successive loan extensions, the fraction of Euro-dollars outstanding that has been created is nine-tenths, or, put differently, 10 Euro-dollars exist for every U.S. dollar held as a cash asset in New York by Euro-dollar banks. However, in the simple example, the Euro-dollar multiplier (the ratio of the increase in Euro-dollar deposits to the initial "primary" deposit) is unity; in the second example, it is 10. That is, in the simple example, the total amount of Euro-dollars goes up by $1 for every $1 of U.S. deposits initially transferred to Euro-dollar banks; in the second example, it goes up by $10 for every $1 of U.S. deposits initially transferred. The difference is that in the simple example there is maximum "leakage" from the Euro-dollar system; in the second example, zero "leakage."

The distinction between Euro-dollar creation and the Euro-dollar multiplier makes it clear why there is a definite limit to the amount of Euro-dollars that can be created no matter how low are the prudential reserves that banks hold. For example, if Euro-dollar banks held zero prudential reserves—as it is sometimes claimed that they do against time deposits—100% of the outstanding deposits would be created deposits and the potential multiplier would be infinite. Yet the actual multiplier would be close to unity because only a small part of the funds acquired by borrowers from Euro-dollar banks would end up as additional time deposits in such banks.[5]

(b) Suppose Bank H does not have sufficient demand for dollar loans to use profitably the whole $900,000 of excess dollar funds. Suppose, simultaneously, it is experiencing a heavy demand for sterling loans. It might go to the Bank of England and use the $900,000 to buy sterling. Bank of England deposits at Morgan Guaranty would now go up. But since the Bank of England typically holds its deposits at the New York Federal Reserve Bank, the funds would fairly quickly disappear from Morgan Guaranty's books and show up instead on the Fed's. This, in the first instance, would reduce the reserves of Morgan Guaranty and thus threaten to produce much more extensive monetary effects than any of our other examples. However, the Bank of England typically holds most of its dollar reserves as Treasury bills or the equivalent, not as noninterest earning deposits at the Fed. It would therefore instruct the Fed to buy, say, bills for its account. This would restore the reserves to the banking system and, except for details, we would be back to where we were in the other examples.

### *The key points*

Needless to say, this is far from a comprehensive survey of all the possible complications. But perhaps it suffices to show that the compli-

**5.** This is precisely comparable to the situation of savings and loan associations and mutual savings banks in the U.S.

cations do not affect the fundamental points brought out by the simple example, namely:

1. Euro-dollars, like "Chicago dollars," are mostly the product of the bookkeeper's pen—that is, the result of fractional reserve banking.

2. The amount of Euro-dollars outstanding, like the amount of "Chicago dollars," depends on the desire of owners of wealth to hold the liabilities of the corresponding group of banks.

3. The ultimate increase in the amount of Euro-dollars from an initial transfer of deposits from other banks to Euro-dollar banks depends on:

(a) The amount of their dollar assets Euro-dollar banks choose to hold in the form of cash assets in the U.S., and

(b) The "leakages" from the system—i.e., the final disposition of the funds borrowed from Euro-dollar banks (or acquired by the sale of bonds or other investments to them). The larger the fraction of such funds held as Euro-dollar deposits, the larger the increase in Euro-dollars in total.

4. The existence of the Euro-dollar market increases the total amount of dollar balances available to be held by nonbanks throughout the world for any given amount of money (currency plus deposits at Federal Reserve Banks) created by the Federal Reserve System. It does so by permitting a greater pyramiding on this base by the use of deposits at U.S. banks as prudential reserves for Euro-dollar deposits.

5. The existence of the Euro-dollar market may also create a greater demand for dollars to be held by making dollar balances available in a more convenient form. The net effect of the Euro-dollar market on our balance-of-payments problem (as distinct from our statistical position) depends on whether demand is raised more or less than supply.

My own conjecture—which is based on much too little evidence for me to have much confidence in it—is that demand is raised less than supply and hence that the growth of the Euro-dollar market has on the whole made our balance-of-payments problem more difficult.

6. Whether my conjecture on this score is right or wrong, the Euro-dollar market has almost surely raised the world's nominal money supply (expressed in dollar equivalents) and has thus made the world price level (expressed in dollar equivalents) higher than it would otherwise be. Alternatively, if it is desired to define the money supply exclusive of Euro-dollar deposits, the same effect can be described in terms of a rise in the velocity of the world's money supply. However, this effect, while clear in direction, must be extremely small in magnitude.

*Use of Euro-dollars by U.S. banks*

Let us now turn from this general question of the source of Euro-dollars to the special issue raised at the outset: the effect of Regulation

O and "tight money" on the use of the Euro-dollar market by U.S. banks.

To set the stage, let us suppose, in the framework of our simple example, that Euro-dollar Bank H of London loans the $900,000 excess funds that it has as a result of the initial deposit by the Arab Sheik to the head office of Morgan Guaranty, i.e., gives Morgan Guaranty (New York) a check for $900,000 on itself in return for an I.O.U. from Morgan Guaranty. This kind of borrowing from foreign banks is one of the means by which American banks have blunted the impact of CD losses. The combined effect will be to leave total liabilities of Morgan Guaranty unchanged but to alter their composition: deposit liabilities are now down $900,000 (instead of the $1,000,000 deposit liability it formerly had to the Sheik it now has a deposit liability of $100,000 to Bank H) and other liabilities ("funds borrowed from foreign banks") are up $900,000.

Until very recently, such a change in the form of a bank's liabilities—from deposits to borrowings—had an important effect on its reserve position. Specifically, it freed reserves. With $1,000,000 of demand deposit liabilities to the Arab Sheik, Morgan Guaranty was required to keep in cash or as deposits at the Federal Reserve Bank of New York $175,000 (or $60,000 if, as is more realistic, the Sheik kept his $1,000,000 in the form of a time deposit). With the shift of the funds to Bank H, however, and completion of the $900,000 loan by Bank H to Morgan Guaranty, Morgan Guaranty's reserve requirements at the Fed fell appreciably. Before the issuance of new regulations that became effective on September 4 of this year, Morgan Guaranty was not required to keep any reserve for the liability in the form of the I.O.U. Its only obligation was to keep $17,500 corresponding to the demand deposit of Bank H. The change in the form of its liabilities would therefore have reduced its reserve requirements by $157,500 (or by $42,500 for a time deposit) without any change in its total liabilities or its total assets, or in the composition of its assets; hence it would have had this much more available to lend.

What the Fed did effective September 4 was to make borrowings subject to reserve requirements as well. Morgan Guaranty must now keep a reserve against the I.O.U., the exact percentage depending on the total amount of borrowings by Morgan Guaranty from foreign banks.[6] The new regulations make it impossible to generalize about reserve effects. A U.S. bank losing deposits to a Euro-bank and then recouping funds by giving its I.O.U. may or may not have additional amounts available to lend as a result of transactions of the kind described.

If Bank H made the loan to Chase instead of to Morgan Guaranty, the latter would lose reserves and Chase would gain them. To Chase, it would look as if it were getting additional funds from abroad, but to both

6. The required reserve is 3% of such borrowings so long as they do not exceed 4% of total deposits subject to reserves. On borrowings in excess of that level the required reserve is 10%.

together, the effect would be the same as before—the possible release of required reserves with no change in available reserves.

The bookkeeping character of these transactions, and how they can be stimulated, can perhaps be seen more clearly if we introduce an additional feature of the actual Euro-dollar market, which was not essential heretofore, namely, the role of overseas branches of U.S. banks. In addition, for realism, we shall express our example in terms of time deposits.

Let us start from scratch and consider the head office of Morgan Guaranty in New York and its London branch. Let us look at hypothetical initial balance sheets of both. We shall treat the London branch as if it had just started and had neither assets nor liabilities, and shall restrict the balance sheet for the head office to the part relevant to its CD operations. This set of circumstances gives us the following situation:

**NEW YORK HEAD OFFICE**

| Assets | | Liabilities | |
|---|---|---|---|
| Deposits at F.R. Bank of NY | $ 6,000,000 | Time certificates of deposit | $100,000,000 |
| Other cash assets | 4,000,000 | | |
| Loans | 76,000,000 | | |
| Bonds | 14,000,000 | | |
| Total assets | $100,000,000 | Total liabilities | $100,000,000 |

(Note: Required reserves, $6,000,000)

**LONDON OFFICE**

| Assets | | Liabilities | |
|---|---|---|---|
| | % 0 | | $ 0 |

Now suppose a foreign corporation (perhaps the Arab Sheik's oil company) which holds a long-term maturing CD of $10,000,000 at Morgan Guaranty refuses to renew it because the 6¼% interest it is receiving seems too low. Morgan Guaranty agrees that the return should be greater, but explains it is prohibited by law from paying more. It notes, however, that its London branch is not. Accordingly, the corporation acquires a time deposit at the London office for $10,000,000 "by depositing" the check for $10,000,000 on the New York office it receives in return for the maturing CD—or, more realistically, by transfers on the books in New York and London. Let us look at the balance sheets:

**NEW YORK HEAD OFFICE**

| Assets | | Liabilities | |
|---|---|---|---|
| Deposits at F.R. Bank of NY | $ 6,000,000 | Time certificates of deposit | $ 90,000,000 |
| Other cash assets | 4,000,000 | | |
| Loans | 76,000,000 | Due to London branch | 10,000,000 |
| Bonds | 14,000,000 | | |
| Total assets | $100,000,000 | Total liabilities | $100,000,000 |

**LONDON OFFICE**

| Assets | | Liabilities | |
|---|---|---|---|
| Due from N.Y. office | $10,000,000 | Time certificates of deposit | $10,000,000 |

Clearly, if we consolidate the branch and the head office, the books are completely unchanged. Yet these bookkeeping transactions: (1) enabled Morgan Guaranty to pay a rate in London higher than 6¼% on some certificates of deposit; and (2) reduced its required reserves by $600,000 prior to the recent modification of Regulation M. The reduction in required reserves arose because until recently U.S. banks were not required to keep a reserve against liabilities to their foreign branches. With the amendment of Regulation M, any further reduction of reserves by this route has been eliminated since the Fed now requires a reserve of 10% on the amount due to branch offices in excess of the amount due on average during May.

*Hypocrisy and window dressing*

This example has been expressed in terms of a *foreign* corporation because the story is a bit more complicated for a U.S. corporation, though the end result is the same. First, a U.S. corporation that transfers its funds from a certificate of deposit at a U.S. bank to a deposit at a bank abroad—whether a foreign bank or an overseas branch of a U.S. bank—is deemed by the Department of Commerce to have made a foreign investment. It may do so only if it is within its quota under the direct control over foreign investment with which we are still unfortunately saddled. Second, under pressure from the Fed, commercial banks will not facilitate direct transfers by U.S. corporations—indeed, many will not accept time deposits from U.S. corporations at their overseas branches, whether their own customers or not, unless the corporation can demonstrate that the deposit is being made for an "international" purpose. However, precisely the same results can be accomplished by a U.S. holder of a CD making a deposit in a foreign bank and the foreign bank in turn making a deposit in, or a loan to, the overseas branch of a U.S. bank. As always, this kind of moral suasion does not prevent profitable transactions. It simply produces hypocrisy and window dressing—in this case, by unnecessarily giving business to competitors of U.S. banks!

The final effect is precisely the same as in the simple example of the foreign corporation. That example shows, in highly simplified form, the main way U.S. banks have used the Euro-dollar market and explains why it is that the more they "borrow" or "bring back" from the Euro-dollar market, the higher Euro-dollar deposits mount. In our example, borrowing went up $10,000,000 and so did deposits.

From January 1, 1969 to July 31, 1969 CD deposit liabilities of U.S. banks went down $9.3 billion, and U.S. banks' indebtedness to their own overseas branches went up $8.6 billion. The closeness of these two numbers is not coincidental.

These bookkeeping operations have affected the statistics far more than the realities. The run-off in CD's in the U.S., and the accompanying decline in total commercial bank deposits (which the Fed uses as its "bank credit proxy") have been interpreted as signs of extreme monetary tightness. Money has been tight, but these figures greatly overstate the degree of tightness. The holders of CD's on U.S. banks who replaced them by Euro-dollar deposits did not have their liquidity squeezed. The banks that substituted "due to branches" for "due to depositors on time certificates of deposit" did not have their lending power reduced. The Fed's insistence on keeping Regulation Q ceilings at levels below market rates has simply imposed enormous structural adjustments and shifts of funds on the commercial banking system for no social gain whatsoever.

*Correcting a misunderstanding*

A column that appeared in a leading financial paper just prior to the Fed's revision of reserve requirements encapsules the widespread misunderstanding about the Euro-dollar market. The Euro-dollar market, the column noted, has: " ... ballooned as U.S. banks have discovered that they can ease the squeeze placed on them by the Federal Reserve Board by borrowing back these foreign-deposited dollars that were pumped out largely through U.S. balance-of-payments deficits. Of this pool of $30 billion, U.S. banks as of last week had soaked up $1.3 billion ...

"Thanks to this system, it takes only seconds to transmit money—and money troubles between the U.S. and Europe ... The Federal Reserve's pending proposal to make Euro-dollar borrowing more costly to U.S. banks might make their future demands a shade less voracious, but this doesn't reduce concern about whether there will be strains in repaying the massive amounts already borrowed."

Strains there may be, but they will reflect features of the Euro-dollar market other than those stressed by this newspaper comment. The use of the Euro-dollar market by commercial banks to offset the decline in CD's was primarily a bookkeeping operation. The reverse process a rise in CD's and a matching decline in Euro-dollar borrowings will also require little more than a bookkeeping operation.

### Notes and Questions

1. Be sure you understand the definition of a eurodollar. How is a eurodollar different from a domestic dollar?

2. Would you expect that a bank would have to book and manage offshore accounts in the same place?

3. Consider the relation between interest rates in the eurodollar and domestic deposit markets. The following chart compares the two rates in on deposits in U.S. dollars and Deutsche Marks during the mid–1980s.

DOMESTIC RATES COMPARED TO EURORATES

| | 1983 | 1984 | 1985 | 1986 | 1987 | 1988 |
|---|---|---|---|---|---|---|
| **U.S. DOLLARS RATES** | | | | | | |
| BASE RATES | | | | | | |
| a. DOMESTIC LENDING | 10.79 | 12.04 | 9.93 | 8.35 | 8.25 | 9.32 |
| b. 3 MONTHS' LIBOR | 9.72 | 10.94 | 8.40 | 6.86 | 7.18 | 7.98 |
| c. DOMESTIC DEPOSIT | 9.09 | 10.37 | 8.05 | 6.52 | 6.86 | 7.73 |
| SPREADS | | | | | | |
| d. LENDING—LIBOR (a)—(b) | 1.07 | 1.10 | 1.53 | 1.49 | 1.07 | 1.34 |
| e. LIBOR—DEPOSIT (b)—(c) | .63 | .57 | .35 | .33 | .22 | .25 |
| **DEUTSCHE MARK RATE** | | | | | | |
| BASE RATES | | | | | | |
| a. DOMESTIC LENDING | 10.05 | 9.82 | 9.53 | 8.75 | 8.36 | 8.33 |
| b. 3 MONTHS' LIBOR | 5.60 | 5.83 | 5.37 | 4.64 | 4.06 | 4.33 |
| c. DOMESTIC DEPOSIT | 4.56 | 4.86 | 4.44 | 3.71 | 3.20 | 3.29 |
| SPREADS | | | | | | |
| d. LIBOR—DEPOSIT (b)—(c) | 1.04 | .97 | .93 | .93 | .86 | 1.04 |

**Source:** J. Andersen, *Euromarket Instruments* (1990), p. 13.

a. What relation would you expect to see between the London Interbank Deposit Rate (LIBOR) and domestic deposit rates. What accounts for this relationship?

b. What trends do you see in the Dollar rates and in the DM rates? What might explain these trends?

c. Since the eurocurrency markets are unregulated, why are not the interest rates on the various eurocurrencies closely correlated?

d. Why would a bank raise eurodollars rather than U.S. dollars, which cost less?

4. Milton Friedman described how various U.S. regulations contributed to the growth of the eurodollar market. Many of these regulations are of historical interest only, including Regulation Q, which put a ceiling on interest payable on deposits, and the foreign exchange controls

(the voluntary foreign credit restraint program and the limits on overseas foreign direct investment). Why would the eurodollar market for banking persist after the regulations ended?

5. Various countries have established special arrangements that allow banks to accept deposits from foreigners without making them subject to at least some domestic banking regulations. The U.S. permits U.S. banks to operate international banking facilities that do not impose reserve requirements on foreign depositors. The goal was to allow banks in the U.S. to compete with financial centers. In fact, however, the IBFs have not seriously challenged offshore financial centers like London or Singapore. The U.S. feared that domestic funds might move to the IBFs, so it imposed complex rules to prevent such a shift. The rules muted demand.

6. In the first decades of the euromarkets' existence, national governments were very concerned about their existence and rapid growth. What reasons might account for their concern?

---

## B. THE GROWTH OF THE MARKET FOR SYNDICATED EURODOLLAR LOANS

### "DEVELOPMENTS IN THE INTERNATIONAL SYNDICATED LOAN MARKET IN THE 1980s"

Bank of England Quarterly Bulletin (February 1990) 71.

#### General overview

At the beginning of the 1980s, the market for international syndicated loans was already well established and business was buoyant. New credit facilities worth almost $83 billion were announced in 1980, and a further $101 billion were announced in the following year. Many major international banks were heavily involved in extending loans to borrowers from the less developed countries (LDCs) and newly industrialising economies (NIEs) in the period 1976–82. Some of the assumptions which underlay the banks' policy of portfolio diversification through more overseas lending were, however, increasingly being questioned, particularly in relation to loans extended to state entities in the LDCs. With the intensification of the debt crisis resulting from the decision by Mexico to suspend interest payments to its creditors in August 1982, the euroloan market entered a phrase of sharp contraction. Activity reached a nadir in 1985, when the value of new international syndicated loans amounted to only $19 billion. In contrast, in the capital markets, gross eurobond issues increased from $74 billion in 1982 to $163 billion in 1985. Thus the decline in the use of the syndicated loan as a vehicle for international financial flows was very clearly associated with the process of securitisation which was then having a major impact on financial markets. This phenomenon was related to an increased investor preference for tradable claims and the desire of some borrowers—notably major industrial companies—to exploit the fact that their creditworthiness relative to the banking sector had improved markedly, so giving them an incentive to issue securities directly to end investors.

Since the last quarter of 1986, however, the market for syndicated loans, both international and domestic, has once more experienced high levels of activity, although the composition of borrowers has changed significantly from that at the beginning of the decade. This resurgence has been attributable to three salient factors:

- the desire of corporate institutions in the developed countries to restructure their existing lines of credit into more flexible financing arrangements, such as multiple-option facilities (see below);
- the growth in debt-financed takeovers and management buyouts, reflecting, in part, the reduction in the cost of debt finance resulting from the decline in inflation from the early 1980s; and
- more generally, the competitive funding opportunities that this sector offers to second-tier corporate borrowers which do not possess a sufficiently high credit rating to obtain access to the eurobond market and utilise interest rate swaps at favourable rates.

The relative importance of multiple-option facilities and merger-related loans is illustrated in Chart 1. The syndicated loan market, together with its fixed-income competitors, has also benefited from the extended period of growth that the major OECD economies experienced after the economic slowdown of the early 1980s. In particular, investment expenditure has been strong over the past three years, increasing the demand for funds. During 1989, there also appears to have been a recovery in the value of commitments raised on behalf of developing countries. This increase was partly associated with project finance opportunities and lending relating to commodity earnings, rather than reflecting new money packages to borrowers from heavily indebted countries requiring funds for general or unspecified purposes.

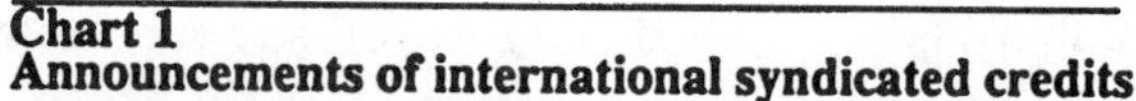
**Chart 1**
**Announcements of international syndicated credits**

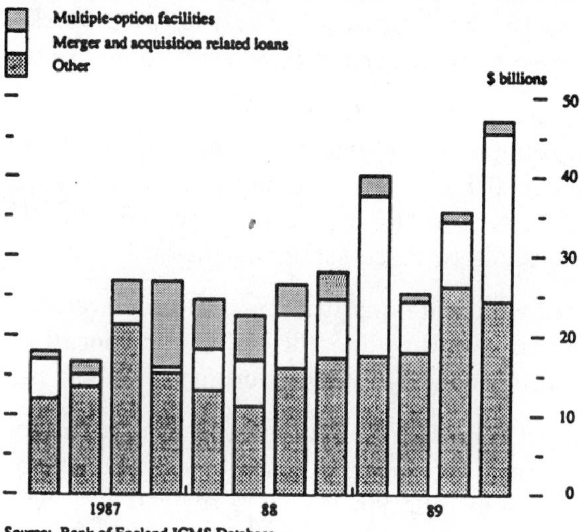


Source: Bank of England ICMS Database.

## Conditions in the syndicated loan market, 1980–89

Until 1985, borrowers from the LDCs and the NIEs generally accounted for a more substantial share of the international syndicated loan market than did borrowers from the major OECD countries (see Chart 2 and Table A). The recovery in volumes which has taken place since the end of 1986, however, almost entirely reflects greater activity by borrowers from the major industrial economies. In recent years there has also been a change in the importance of industrial borrowers generally relative to sovereign borrowers, although the former has always represented the single most important group of borrowers since 1980. Borrowing by central governments and other government departments accounted for approximately 20% of all credits in the early 1980s. After 1982, this proportion declined significantly and is now around 5% of the overall market: governments of LDCs have, in many cases, been excluded from the market altogether, and those of the industrial countries have increasingly turned their attention to bond financing and the euronote sector, where they have been able to obtain finer rates and pursue more precise debt management policies. For example, the Kingdoms of Belgium, Spain and Sweden developed large commercial paper or medium-term note programmes either in the US domestic market or in the euromarket. In contrast, credit facilities arranged on behalf of industrial borrowers have represented over 45% of all syndicated loans in every year since 1982, reaching 88% of all announcements in 1988 and 81% in 1989. US dollar denominated credits have always formed the most significant component of the total market; in every year since 1980 dollar facilities accounted for more than 60% of all international syndicated loans.

**Chart 2**
**Announcements of international syndicated loans, 1972-89**

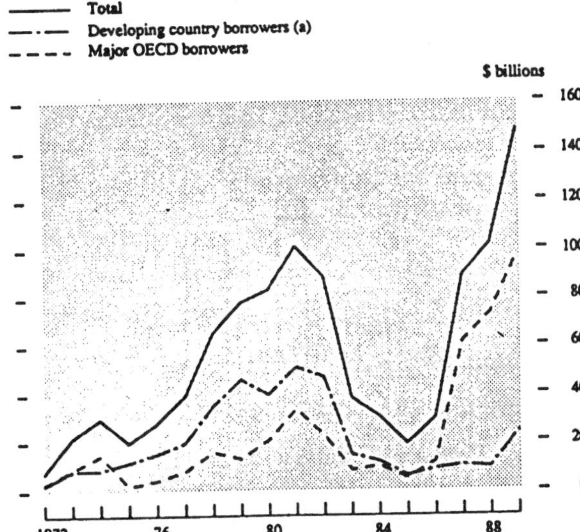


Source: Bank of England ICMS Database.

(a) Includes less developed countries, newly industrialising economies and oil producing countries.

## Table A

### International syndicated credits: borrowers, by region

S billions

| | 1980 | 1981 | 1982 | 1983 | 1984 | 1985 | 1986 | 1987 | 1988 | 1989(x) |
|---|---|---|---|---|---|---|---|---|---|---|
| Major OECD countries | 20.5 | 33.2 | 22.6 | 8.2 | 9.9 | 5.1 | 11.6 | 61.4 | 72.8 | 98.7 |
| Minor OECD countries | 19.4 | 15.7 | 18.4 | 13.6 | 6.2 | 4.4 | 6.5 | 14.9 | 18.3 | 23.9 |
| Eastern Europe | 2.8 | 1.1 | 0.5 | 0.5 | 2.2 | 3.6 | 2.3 | 1.9 | 1.2 | 2.2 |
| International institutions | 0.6 | 0.4 | — | 1.2 | 0.1 | — | 0.4 | 0.4 | 0.1 | 0.1 |
| Less developed countries | 15.0 | 22.5 | 19.7 | 5.1 | 4.0 | 1.5 | 3.7 | 6.5 | 6.2 | 15.0 |
| Newly industrializing economies | 11.1 | 14.7 | 11.8 | 3.5 | 3.5 | 3.0 | 1.1 | 1.1 | 1.5 | 3.7 |
| Oil producing countries | 13.0 | 12.9 | 13.8 | 5.5 | 3.8 | 1.2 | 3.3 | 2.0 | 1.6 | 5.3 |
| Other | 0.4 | 0.4 | 1.4 | 0.4 | 0.4 | 0.2 | 0.7 | 0.5 | 0.1 | 0.1 |
| Total | 82.8 | 100.9 | 88.2 | 38.0 | 30.1 | 19.0 | 29.6 | 88.7 | 101.8 | 149.0 |

**Source:** Bank of England ICMS database.

(x) Provisional

## Table B

### International syndicated credits: breakdown by type of borrower

$ billions

| | 1980 | 1981 | 1982 | 1983 | 1984 | 1985 | 1986 | 1987 | 1988 | 1989(a) |
|---|---|---|---|---|---|---|---|---|---|---|
| Industrial borrowers | 48.5 | 65.1 | 53.3 | 22.0 | 17.1 | 8.5 | 15.2 | 67.8 | 89.4 | 120.6 |
| Banks and financial institutions | 16.9 | 18.9 | 16.9 | 5.0 | 9.0 | 8.2 | 9.0 | 15.0 | 8.9 | 21.1 |
| Central banks | — | — | 1.1 | 1.9 | 0.3 | 0.5 | 1.5 | 1.0 | 1.1 | 1.2 |
| Central government | 14.2 | 14.4 | 16.0 | 8.8 | 3.6 | 1.6 | 3.7 | 4.0 | 1.5 | 4.5 |
| Other government | 3.2 | 2.5 | 0.9 | 0.3 | 0.1 | 0.2 | 0.2 | 0.9 | 0.9 | 1.6 |
| Total | 82.8 | 100.9 | 88.2 | 38.0 | 30.1 | 19.0 | 29.6 | 88.7 | 101.8 | 149.0 |

**Source:** Bank of England ICMS database.

(a) Provisional.

Margins[1] on international syndicated loans for major OECD borrowers underwent a general but not continuous decline from 1982 to the first half of 1988 (see Chart 3). The fall in average margins which took place after 1983 can be attributed to two main factors. First, with the onset of the debt crisis many prime corporate borrowers turned to the various securities markets to service their financing requirements. In particular, the growth of the eurocommercial paper and floating-rate note markets provided borrowers with alternative sources of short-term and floating-rate funding. The banks were therefore obliged to compete more aggressively for international and wholesale business as well as turning their attention to off-balance-sheet financing. Second, the major international banks became involved in arranging standby credit facilities designed to support the commercial paper activities of industrial companies or provide short-term cash advances for working capital purposes. As such loan facilities are not intended to be fully drawn upon in normal circumstances, the margins attached to them are comparatively low and the facility fee represents a more important element in the overall pricing. For almost all of the period from 1982 to 1988, the average margin on loans for borrowers from the major OECD countries was below that incurred by borrowers from the LDCs.

**Chart 3**
**Spreads[(a)] on major OECD and less developed country loans**

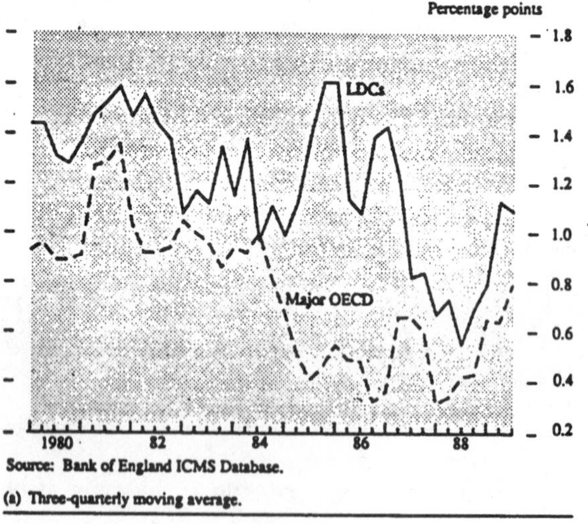


Source: Bank of England ICMS Database.

(a) Three-quarterly moving average.

(1) International syndicated loans are generally priced with reference to the Labor benchmark, although other bases such as the Paris Interbank offered rate (Pibor), the US prime rate or various CD rates are also used. As well as being influenced by market corporation, the margin that is charged above that will essentially be a function of country and credit risk.

More recently, however, average margins have increased for both borrowers from the major OECD countries and those from LDCs, although they remain below the levels seen at the beginning of the decade. The new capital adequacy rules introduced under the auspices of the Bank for International Settlements represent one factor that should cause banks to negotiate higher margins. The increase in spreads may also be attributed to a change in the composition of loan facilities which have been arranged in recent quarters. For example, high margin business in the form of loans to finance acquisitions has become a greater component of the total market. The strength of potential competition among banks in the syndicated loan market, however, acts as a countervailing force, limiting the extent to which spreads may rise.

### Market attributes

The demand for international syndicated credit facilities, which predominantly reflects private sector funding requirements, results from the fact that the syndicated loan market, or more generally the banking sector, is able to perform certain essential functions more satisfactorily than securities-based capital markets. The main advantages of a syndicated loan facility are:

- a credit facility provides the borrower with a stable source of funds—of particular value in the event that other capital markets are subject to some form of disruption;
- the syndicated loan sector generally allows borrowers to raise larger sums than they would be able to obtain through either the eurobond or the equity markets in the short term;
- the ability to arrange deals quickly and discreetly, which may be of value with certain transactions such as takeovers;
- the capacity to provide commitments to lend which can be cancelled relatively easily; it would be difficult to cancel borrowing in the securities markets without reducing investor confidence.

To some extent these advantages are relative rather than absolute. For example, the US domestic commercial paper market and the ECP market can offer a wide range of borrowers access to short-term funds, albeit on an uncommitted basis, and the medium-term note market can be regarded as a form of contingent bond financing. As dealers in these markets will only place notes on a 'best efforts' basis, such programmes do not offer the certainty of committed bank lines. For prime industrial corporate borrowers and well-regarded sovereign borrowers, this does not present a major problem as they will be able to place their paper and bonds at more competitive rates than they could obtain funding in the bank market under normal circumstances. But for a wide spectrum of companies, particularly in Western Europe where the domestic CP markets are less well developed than in the United States and an established 'below investment grade' bond market has not as yet emerged, the stability and certainty of banking relationships continue to be attractive.

**Multiple-option facilities**

A multiple-option facility (MOF) is the general name for a number of credit and money-market fund-raising mechanisms which are documented in a single agreement and are administered by a single agent on behalf of a syndicate of banks. The MOF is typically based upon a committed revolving credit and incorporates other arrangements which allow the borrower to obtain finance on an uncommitted basis, such as tender panels for multicurrency cash advances and bankers' acceptances or facilities allowing for the issue of commercial paper or some other form of note. Such facilities therefore represent a more convenient packaging of existing banking services rather than a fundamental innovation; instead of managing a series of bilateral banking relationships, the corporate treasurer can arrange a significant part of his company's funding through one agent. Under normal circumstances borrowers will obtain funding through a tender panel mechanism or by issuing short-term promissory notes, and will achieve finer rates than they would have to pay if they were to make drawings upon the committed credit component of their MOF. For many major companies the MOF has represented a rationalisation of existing banking services, rather than a net increase in bank intermediation. Moreover, available evidence suggests that drawings made under these facilities are generally modest when compared with the total value of funds that could potentially be obtained under the uncommitted portions.

During 1987 and the first half of 1988 there was a trend among many major industrial companies to consolidate their existing bilateral credit lines into more flexible arrangements such as MOFs, while refinancing debt at favourable rates at the same time. This tendency was particularly evident in the United Kingdom and France, where borrowers took advantage of the greater flexibility provided by MOFs. The development of other banking products such as the revolving underwriting facility and the note issuance facility had already established the concept of competitive bidding mechanisms such as tender panels and the MOF sought to combine this feature with a standard credit. Banks decided to bid aggressively for mandates to arrange such transactions and strongly marketed the product, particularly as such arrangements gave them the opportunity to establish new business relationships after a period in which volumes in the syndicated loan market had been low. The fees and margins attached to these arrangements have generally been regarded as being fine—a number of well-regarded UK companies have been able to obtain MOFs where the annual facility fee was less than 10 basis points and the spread no more than 12.5 basis points over Libor.

As many major companies, both in the United Kingdom and elsewhere, have now acquired MOFs, the demand for such arrangements will increasingly come from second-tier corporate borrowers, for whom various eurocurrency options are less relevant. The implementation of the Basle capital convergence agreement by the United Kingdom and other countries should make banks more reluctant to participate in MOFs at the aggressively-priced margins which were common in the early part of 1988. Some banks may, however, choose to participate in this lower return business in order to establish or retain long-term relationships with customers. Moreover, the more cautious attitude which some bankers have adopted towards high yield mezzanine debt and leveraged transactions could result in a desire to reweight portfolios more towards lower-geared companies wishing to have access to funds for general corporate purposes.

**The syndication process**

The syndicated loan market is able to provide a broad spectrum of borrowers with funding for a wide range of projects. Loans can vary in size from small club deals, where three or four relationship banks can participate in transactions for as little as £10 million, to very large acquisition or project-related credits worth in excess of a billion pounds. For example, Eurotunnel obtained two syndicated loans in the third quarter of 1987 with a combined value of £5 billion, where the syndicate comprised approximately 160 banks. More recently, RJR Acquisition Corp obtained a package of loan facilities worth $13.6 billion in order to provide a consortium headed by Kohlberg Kravis Roberts with the necessary finance to complete the leveraged buyout of RJR Nabisco.

The syndication process commences when either a borrower approaches a bank and invites it to become a syndicate arranger or when the bank itself approaches a corporate borrower which it believes to be seeking funds. The arranger, or in some cases the arrangers, once mandated will then set about co-ordinating a consortium of banks who are prepared to lend money given an initial set of terms. The borrower's relationship banks will usually form the basis of the syndicate and further invitations may be extended according to the size, complexity and the pricing of the loan as well as the desire of the borrower to increase the range of its banking relationships.

Eventually, the arranger or lead-manager may find itself at the apex of a whole hierarchy of institutions, who may accept positions as co-lead managers, managers, co-managers or just participant banks, depending on the amount of money that they are prepared to lend or commit and the input that they have in the syndication process. The larger the credit, the more complex the structure. The lead-management role itself is occasionally undertaken by the treasury department of the company seeking to raise the loan.

The arranger may either undertake the syndication on a 'best efforts basis' or, if the borrower is prepared to pay an appropriate fee, put together an underwriting group to give the borrower a guarantee of committed finance. If the latter route is adopted, the syndication process will take place in two phases. The underwriting group will come together in the primary syndication and then subsequently their commitments may be reduced during a secondary syndication, when new banks will be invited into the consortium. If the terms of the loan are considered attractive or the borrower is well-regarded by the market, the loan may well be oversubscribed. In this case the arranger may either invite the borrower to increase the size of the total credit or the banks may find that the amounts they have committed are scaled down *pro rata.* The completion of a transaction is often evidenced by the publication of a notice, generally referred to as a 'tombstone', in the financial press.

As well as earning a margin over Libor (or any other benchmark) when the loan is drawn, banks in the syndicate will receive various fees. The arranger and other banks in the lead management team, who may be responsible for various aspects of documentation, will generally receive some form of front-end management fee. Other participants will usually expect to receive a participation fee for agreeing to join the facility; the actual size of the fee will vary with the size of the commitment. Once the credit is established, members of the syndicate will often receive an annual facility or commitment fee, again proportional to their commitments. Loan documents may sometimes incorporate a penalty clause, whereby the borrower agrees to pay a fee or give some consideration to the lenders in the event that it pre-pays its debts prior to the specified term.

**Merger and acquisition related lending**

The stock market crash of October 1987 led to speculation that new merger and acquisition activity would decline significantly, reflecting the perceived difficulties of raising new equity finance. The continued buoyancy of company profits within the major industrial economies during 1988, together with the depressed state of many companies' stock market valuations, however, provided a considerable stimulus to new acquisitions. In many cases the syndicated loan has been the vehicle through which such takeovers have been financed. As mentioned above, the banking sector, through consortium loans, allows borrowers to raise larger sums than they are able to obtain through either the eurobond or the equity market over the short term, and to do so quickly. Moreover, borrowers may subsequently refinance such debt by utilising other markets.

The value of international credits arranged to finance acquisitions or mergers increased from $8.8 billion in 1987 to $24.6 billion in 1988 and then expanded to $55.8 billion during 1989 (see Table C). UK companies together with their subsidiaries were the most important national group of borrowers in both 1987 and 1988. To a large extent, this reflected the arrangement of a small number of very large facilities for major UK companies. For example, three financings, arranged for Grand Metropolitan Finance ($6 billion), the Tate and Lyle Group ($1.3 billion) and BAT Industries ($3.2 billion), accounted for almost three quarters of the UK total in 1988. Many of the credits arranged in the period 1987–89 were intended to finance acquisitions of US companies.

Consequently, merger-related syndicated loans have been overwhelmingly dollar-denominated—82% during 1989.

Table C

Merger and acquisition related international syndicated loans

US$ millions

| Country of borrower | 1987 | 1988 | 1989[(a)] |
|---|---|---|---|
| Australia | 641 | 2,311 | 1,247 |
| Canada | 750 | 150 | 2,100 |
| France | — | 2,447 | 789 |
| Japan | — | 1,472 | — |
| United Kingdom | 5,794 | 14,141 | 10,059 |
| United States | 900 | 1,705 | 33,703 |
| Other | 710 | 2,367 | 7,946 |
| Total | 8,795 | 24,593 | 55,844 |
| *of which:* | | | |
| *Sterling* | *457* | *515* | *8,335* |
| *US dollar* | *7,788* | *22,898* | *46,292* |
| *Other* | *550* | *1,180* | *1,217* |

**Source:** Bank of England ICMS database.

(a) Provisional.

Merger-related business can provide banks with two major forms of income: fees from giving advice on the mechanics of mounting a takeover (or defence) and interest charges and other fees from participating in any financing package arranged on behalf of the acquirer. While there is some debate on the subject of exactly how generous are the returns on merger and acquisition business, the greater emphasis which many banks have placed on this type of activity since the beginning of 1988 indicates that it has been perceived as a welcome source of income. While a prime corporate borrower might pay 12.5 basis points or less over Libor on drawings obtained under the committed portion of a MOF, the average margin attached to merger-related eurocurrency loans during the first three quarters of 1989 was 112 basis points; such returns do, however, involve banks assuming a higher risk/return profile. The spread of perceived risk is illustrated by the range of margins from which that average is calculated, which stretches from 15 to 600 basis points. Recently, a number of well-regarded borrowers who were not highly geared nor likely to become so after making their acquisitions were able to obtain large merger-related syndicated credits in the London market at relatively fine rates. There is perhaps a tendency for pricing on merger-related loans for major companies with limited debt levels to move closer to the rates that such companies could obtain on facilities intended to finance working capital.

### Mezzanine debt

Another development which has received considerable attention during the last two years has been the growing use of mezzanine or subordinated debt. This instrument has generally been associated with the current wave of corporate restructuring that is taking place in Western Europe and North America, particularly in connection with leveraged buyouts, where companies are acquired with borrowed funds which result in the acquirer assuming a relatively high gearing ratio. Mezzanine funding can take a number of different forms and refers to the issue of any form of subordinated debt claim. In the United States, mezzanine debt often takes the form of 'below investment grade' bonds, while in Europe it is generally some form of bank debt with equity warrants attached. Although mezzanine debt is usually associated with financing acquisitions and buyouts, it could have other applications, such as certain forms of project finance, where the actual project involved is particularly cash-generative.

Announcements of international syndicated credits and international banking flows

Data on announcements of syndicated loans can yield useful information on a number of issues, such as the degree of competition within particular sectors of the banking market, the extent to which companies in certain countries are restructuring their financial commitments and the growth of new loan products (mezzanine finance, multiple-option facilities). It has also been suggested that announcements of new international syndicated credits could be used as a leading indicator of bank lending to non-banks. The arrangement of credit facilities, however, represents the establishment of commitments to lend and, therefore, it is not always possible to make direct inferences about the value of actual drawings; trends evident in the international syndicated loan market are not necessarily reflected in cross-border flows. A recent study at the Bank using univariate time series techniques came to the conclusion that there was only a weak statistical relationship between announcements of new international syndicated credits and international banking flows. The difficulty in relating the two data sets also arises from the fact that the Bank of England's data on international syndicated loans do not include facilities with a maturity of less than one year; moreover, data on international banking flows will also incorporate drawings upon bilateral lines of credit.

The subordinated debt packages arranged for European buyouts have generally been domestic transactions with relatively little intermediation taking place outside the capital market of the country in which the acquired company is located. This situation could change in the future. The completion of the leveraged buyout of RJR Nabisco at the beginning of 1989 demonstrated that even the very largest companies can be subject to a takeover. Mezzanine financings may also be structured to include layers of debt which possess varying degrees of subordination; the interest rate or the value of the equity warrants attached to more junior claims will be correspondingly higher. The mezzanine market has grown quickly in a comparatively short time and the potential returns from this type of lending are attractive to many banks who have been used to standard corporate credits carrying narrow margins over Libor in recent years. Banks are not the only participants in this market. A number of special-purpose funds have been set up since the beginning of 1988 to provide subordinated finance for buyouts. The reduced creditor protection attached to these loans means that the margin over Libor may be 3% or more, somewhat higher than the margins which might be charged on the senior loan component of a LBO financing. At present, however, the current pattern of European short-term interest rates is having an adverse impact upon new lending opportunities. Nevertheless, if the market in leveraged buyouts were to develop further in Europe, as a result of prominent companies being subject to takeovers or management buyouts, the local markets in mezzanine debt might become insufficient to accommodate the demand for funds, resulting in greater cross-border activity.

**Secondary market**

Another major development since the early 1980s has been the increasing tendency for banks to trade credit participations in the secondary market. While there are few statistics on the total size of the secondary market, the LDC debt problem and more recently the growth in LBOs have encouraged banks to adjust the balance of their loan portfolios. The recent Basle agreement on capital adequacy has presented many banks with the choice of increasing capital or removing assets from their balance sheets; many appear to have chosen to adopt the latter option to some degree, using loan transfers or securitisation to effect the reduction. There are three main methods by which loan participations may be transferred: novation, assignment and subparticipation. Novation involves the replacement of one legal agreement with another, thus extinguishing the contractual relationship between the original creditor and the debtor; assignment and subparticipation are non-recourse funding arrangements which do not normally involve the borrower as they operate in parallel with, rather than instead of, the original loan. This heightened emphasis on marketability could result in the syndicated loan market assuming some of the characteristics of the FRN market. The existence of a well-developed market in participations in syndicated loans results in banks developing many of the same skills that are required to operate successfully in the bond market, namely the ability to market debt claims and to establish a major network of potential investors. This could be regarded as part of a more general process in the euromarkets, where in recent years innovation and securitisation have led to the gradual dissolving of the boundaries between money, credit and capital markets. The existence of an established market in loans or loan participations also raises some interesting issues for bank supervisors. After consultation with the markets, the Bank issued a Notice in February 1989 (BSD/1989/1) which sets out the Bank's supervisory policy on the treatment of loan transfers involving banks.

**Conclusion**

Over the last three years, the international syndicated loan market has clearly demonstrated its ability to mobilise substantial volumes of funds on behalf of a variety of different borrowers. The strength of investment spending over the past three years and the buoyant levels of merger and acquisition activity in recent years have generally provided international financial markets with a major stimulus on the demand side. In particular, acquisition-related lending has come to represent a major component of the overall market for international syndicated credits. More recently, there have been some indications that borrowers from the less developed countries are making greater use of the market in specific contexts. The market has also shown its ability to meet the increasingly complex needs of major corporate borrowers. While the demand for syndicated loans may fluctuate over time, this sector is likely to remain a significant and durable component of international financing.

---

The league tables for banks that arrange syndicates vary every year. As you read the following article, you should consider what factors contribute to a bank's success arranging syndicates.

JOHN EVANS, "U.S. BANKS REMAIN TOPS IN SYNDICATION"

American Banker (January 9, 1992).

LONDON—Bucking the conventional wisdom that American banks are a spent force in global finance, U.S. institutions continue to dominate international syndicated lending, a recent survey found.

Of the top 10 banks that arranged globally distributed loans last year, six were American, according to *International Financing Review,* a British magazine affiliated with the *American Banker.*

In 1990, seven American banks were among the leading 10.

Citicorp ranked as the leader in loan originations, syndicating nearly a third more than its nearest competitor, J.P. Morgan & Co.

Citicorp's grand total was 91 loan syndications during 1991, or $70.1 billion in aggregate. In 1990, it notched up 100 loans, for a total $68.5 billion, and also ranked first.

Last year Morgan handled 72 transactions, including the $5.5 billion reconstruction loan for Kuwait, for a total $47.1 billion, according to the magazine.

Chemical Banking Corp. placed third, with 32 loans totalling $35.5 billion.

**A Core Business**

Syndicated lending is a priority in Citicorp's allocation of capital and resources, despite the institution's current drive for cost reductions, said executive director Brian Woolley.

"Syndicated loans are a very important franchise for us," said Mr. Woolley, who heads international lending. "It's one of the bank's core businesses that are being given the investment, under our new strategy."

Among other highly ranked U.S. banks, First Chicago Corp., BankAmerica Corp., and Manufacturers Hanover Corp. were positioned fifth, sixth, and seventh in the *International Financing Review* rankings. Manufacturers Hanover and Chemical merged on Jan. 1, and taken together, their international loan syndications would have placed them a close second to Citicorp.

Outside the top 10, Chase Manhattan Corp. took 11th place and Bankers Trust New York Corp. 13th.

**Difficult Year**

Bankers said 1991 was exceptionally difficult for loan syndications, with Citicorp's Mr. Woolley identifying the Gulf War, recession, and corporate loan defaults among factors that made lenders nervous worldwide.

"It was probably the toughest year since the Latin American debt reschedulings of the 1980s," said Mr. Woolley, a veteran of the lending business.

Nonetheless, U.S. banking stayed the course when other lending groups, particularly the Japanese, fled the market because of pressure on their capital under the Basel accords, bankers said.

Only one Tokyo institution, Fuji Bank Ltd., was among the top 10 syndicators.

Peter Nightingale, managing director for loan syndication at Manufacturers Hanover, attributed continued U.S. muscle power in global lending to its expertise and pricing skills.

"We've all been in the marketplace a long time and have extensive knowledge and know the right price for a loan," he said. "We continue to have appeal to borrowers, right around the world."

On the borrowing side, the U.S. was the largest single nation seeking loan funds overseas last year. American businesses borrowed a total of $154 billion from overseas sources, virtually unchanged from 1990.

Much U.S. activity was due to major bank loans and refinancings by American corporations. Facilities obtained by Philip Morris Inc., at $15 billion; American Telephone & Telegraph, $7.6 billion; and RJR Nabisco Inc., $6.5 billion, were the largest syndicated globally.

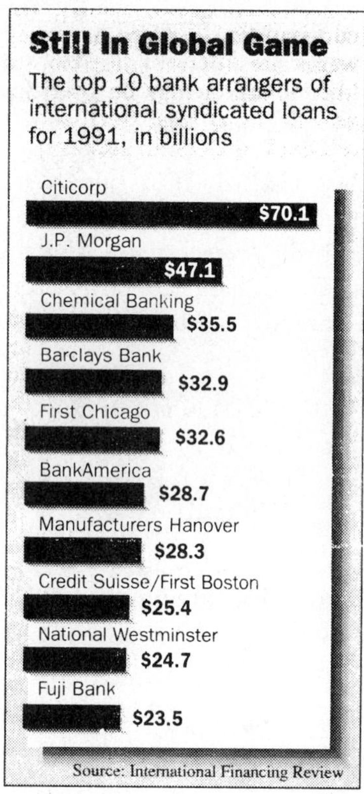


## Loans for Reconstruction

Their nearest rivals were the 4.5 billion loan by Saudi Arabia and the $5.5 billion from Kuwait, fundings aimed at reconstruction and development following the Gulf War.

In contrast, borrowing from European nations slackened last year, to $75 billion from $109 billion in 1990.

Overall, worldwide borrowing rose modestly to $318 billion from $303 billion in 1990.

Mr. Nightingale of Hanover said that, in international lending, credit continued to be freely available from banks to customers as long as the transaction carried the correct interest rate.

"The well-priced deal will sell well," he said, stating that firming interest rate spreads in the course of 1991 "brought some banks back to the game" in the final quarter of the year.

Bankers have said that, with international capital standards on the way, they require a return of about 50 basis points over the benchmark London interbank offered rate to produce sufficient profitability.

### *Questions*

1. Be sure you understand the definition of a syndicated eurocurrency loan ("eurocredit").

2. Who are the parties to a eurocredit? Note that this market expanded during an era of strong lending to borrowers based in developing countries.

3. Compared to a standard bank loan, what are the special features of a eurocredit? How do they work? Why are they possible? How do these features help the parties?

---

## C. THE ALLOCATION OF RISK AMONG THE PARTIES TO A EUROCREDIT

The standard contract for a eurocredit describes who will bear various risks. Some clauses are common to many types of loans. Others, more peculiar to a eurocredit, are the subject of this section.

The clauses come from a sample Revolving Credit Agreement in Anthony Gooch and Linda Klein, Loan Documentation, 2d ed. (1991). The authors, whose practice includes this field, wrote a hypothetical agreement for State–Owned Company to borrow U.S. $250 million for 5 years. The agreement is dated April 15, 1991. The funds are for working capital. The guarantor is the borrower's home government, the Republic of Somewhere. The managers are Big Bank. S.A. (a French bank), Bigger Bank PLC (a British bank), and Biggest Bank, N.A. (a U.S. bank). The eurodollar agent is Infallible Agent Bank and the swing-line agent is Biggest Bank, N.A. The lenders are The Banks Named Herein, often called participating banks in the market.

This is a multi-option revolving credit facility. Within the $250 million limit, the borrower can draw funds priced either as a eurocurrency loan based on LIBOR or as the swing-line loan based on the U.S. prime rate, which is the rate the banks charge their best customers. The authors explain:

> When a borrower may require funds on short notice, the swing-line option is a common alternative in Eurodollar facilities, under which LIBOR-based advances generally require at least three business days' advance notice so that the lenders can make their funding arrangements in the London interbank market. The swing-line option also serves as a stop gap if the lenders cannot fund a desired advance in the London market.

For these services, the borrower agrees to pay interest described below and several fees. A 1% commitment fee is paid annually on the unused part of each commitment. A ¼% facility fee is paid annually on the full commitment, used or not. The management fee, paid at signing, is 1% of the total commitments (in this case, $250 million). Each year both the agents receive $10,000. All payments are made by either to the eurodollar agent or the swing-line agent, as appropriate.

Sovereign immunity is waived. New York law governs this agreement, although many eurocredits are governed by U.K. law.

These agreements are normally quite long, suggesting the drafters are paid by the weight of the document. Here we excerpt parts of the agreement that are specially relevant for eurodollar loans. Some clauses concern the relation between the borrowers and the lenders, others the relation between managers, agents, and the participating banks.

As you read the clauses, ask how each allocates risk and responsibility among the parties. Consider also the consequences of this allocation for the parties and the financial system. Are there some aspects of these agreements that should concern national regulators?

## 1. The Basic Terms of the Loan

### a. Advances and Repayment

*"Advance"* means any Eurodollar Advance or Swing–Line Advance.

*"Commitment,"* with respect to any Bank at any time means the amount designated as such and set forth opposite the name of that Bank on the signature pages hereof, subject to reduction as provided herein.

2.1. *Commitment to Lend.* (a) On the terms and subject to the conditions set forth herein, each Bank shall make Advances hereunder through its Lending Branch to the Borrower from time to time in an aggregate principal amount at any one time outstanding not exceeding that Bank's Commitment. Failure by any Bank to make an Advance to the Borrower shall not relieve any other Bank of its obligations hereunder. No Bank shall have any responsibility for any failure by any other Bank to fulfill its obligations hereunder.

2.2. *Term.* The *"Term"* of each Advance shall mean the period beginning with the applicable Disbursement Date and, (i) in the case of a Eurodollar Advance, ending on the day numerically corresponding to that Disbursement Date in the first, third or sixth month thereafter (subject to Subsection 7.1(b)), and (ii) in the case of a Swing–Line Advance, ending on a day not later than the seventh day after that Disbursement Date (subject to Subsection 7.1(c)), in each case as specified by the Borrower in accordance with Section 2.3.

2.3. *Notice of Intention and Commitment to Borrow.* (a) The Borrower may request Eurodollar Advances hereunder by delivering to the Eurodollar Agent a notice substantially in the form set forth in Exhibit D, with all blank spaces appropriately completed in compliance with Subsection 2.3(d), not later than 1:00 p.m. (London time) on the third Banking Day before the day on which the Borrower wishes to make the borrowing.

(b) The Borrower may request Swing–Line Advances hereunder by giving the Swing–Line Agent notice by telephone and confirming it immediately by a written notice substantially in the form set forth in Exhibit E, with all blank spaces appropriately completed in compliance with Subsection 2.3(d), hand-delivered or sent by telex or facsimile transmission and received not later than 9:30 a.m. (New York City time) on the day on which the Borrower wishes to make the borrowing.

... The aggregate principal amount of Eurodollar Advances to be made on a Disbursement Date must be $50,000,000 or a higher integral multiple of $5,000,000. The aggregate principal amount of all Advances to be made on a Disbursement Date shall be an amount which, when taken together with all other Advances outstanding on that Disbursement Date (excluding any Advances to be repaid from the proceeds of Advances to be made on that date), does not exceed the Total Commitment.

2.4. *Disbursements.* (a) The Eurodollar Agent shall promptly advise each Bank by telex or facsimile transmission of the contents of each request for Eurodollar Advances hereunder, and the amount of the Eurodollar Advance to be made by that Bank on that date, which shall be that Bank's Pro Rata Share of the aggregate principal amount of all the Eurodollar Advances to be made on that date determined on the basis of the respective Commitments of the Banks, subject to such rounding as the Eurodollar Agent may determine. Except as otherwise expressly provided in Subsection 2.4(b), by 10:00 a.m. (New York City time) on each Disbursement Date, each Bank shall, subject to the conditions set forth herein, make available to the Eurodollar Agent the amount so specified, in funds settled through the New York Clearing House Interbank Payments System or such other same-day funds as the Eurodollar Agent may at the time determine to be customary for the settlement in New York City of international banking transactions denominated in Dollars, by deposit to the Eurodollar Agent's account specified in or pursuant to Section 7.1. Subject to the conditions set forth herein, and except as otherwise expressly provided in Subsection 2.4(b), the Eurodollar Agent shall, on that Disbursement Date, credit the funds so received to the account specified by the Borrower pursuant to Subsection 2.3(d).

(b) Any Bank that is obligated to make a new Advance hereunder on a day on which the Borrower is obligated to repay an outstanding Advance of that Bank shall apply the proceeds of its new Advance to make the repayment, and only an amount equal to the excess (if any) of the amount being so borrowed from that Bank over the amount being so repaid to that Bank shall be made available by that Bank to the relevant Agent and remitted by that Agent to the Borrower.

(c) The Swing–Line Agent shall, by 10:30 a.m. (New York City time) on each Disbursement Date for Swing–Line Advances, advise each Bank by telephone of the contents of the request for the Advances and the amount of the Swing–Line Advance to be made by that Bank on that date, which shall be that Bank's Pro Rata Share of the aggregate principal amount of all the Swing–Line Advances to be made on that date determined on the basis of the respective Commitments of the Banks, subject to such rounding as the Swing–Line Agent may determine, and shall confirm such advice immediately by written notice. By 12:30 p.m. (New York City time) on the Disbursement Date, each Bank shall, subject to the conditions set forth herein, make available to the Swing–Line Agent the amount so specified, in immediately available funds, by deposit to the Swing–Line Agent's account specified in or pursuant to Section 7.1. Subject to the conditions set forth herein, and except as otherwise expressly provided in Subsection 2.4(b), the Swing–Line Agent shall, on the Disbursement Date, credit the funds so received to the account specified by the Borrower pursuant to Subsection 2.3(d).

3.1. *Repayment.* Except as otherwise expressly provided herein, the Borrower shall repay each Advance on the last day of its Term.

3.2. *No Prepayment of Eurodollar Advances.* Except as provided in Section 3.4 and Section 3.5, the Borrower may not prepay Eurodollar Advances.

16.3. *Currency.* (a) If any expense required to be reimbursed pursuant to Article 15 is originally incurred in a currency other than Dollars, the Borrower shall nonetheless make reimbursement of that expense in Dollars, in an amount equal to the amount in Dollars that would have been required for the person that incurred that expense to have purchased, in accordance with normal banking procedures, the sum paid in that other currency (after any premium and costs of exchange) on the day that expense was originally incurred. Any interest accruing thereon pursuant to Section 4.2 shall be computed on the basis of the Dollar amount.

(b) Each reference in this Agreement to Dollars is of the essence. The obligation of the Borrower in respect of any amount due under this Agreement or the Notes shall, notwithstanding any payment in any other currency (whether pursuant to a judgment or otherwise), be discharged only to the extent of the amount in Dollars that the person entitled to receive that payment may, in accordance with normal banking procedures, purchase with the sum paid in the other currency (after any premium and costs of exchange) on the Banking Day immediately following the day on which that person receives that payment. If the amount in Dollars that may be so purchased for any reason falls short of the amount originally due, the Borrower shall pay such additional amount, in Dollars, as is necessary to compensate for the shortfall. Any obligation of the Borrower not discharged by that payment shall, to the fullest extent permitted by applicable law, be due as a separate and independent obligation and until discharged as provided herein, shall continue in full force and effect.

## *Questions*

1. Work through the procedure for making the loans. Why is this called a revolving credit agreement?

2. Who bears the risk of exchange rate fluctuations between the dollar and the currency of Somewhere? How would you determine who is best able to bear this risk?

---

## b. Interest Rate Determination

*"Federal Funds Rate,"* for any day, means the rate of interest (expressed as an annual rate) set forth for that day (or, if that day is not a New York Banking Day, the next preceding New York Banking Day) (i) in the daily statistical release of the Federal Reserve Bank of New York entitled "Composite 3:30 p.m. Quotations for U.S. Government Securities" opposite the heading "Federal Funds/Effective Rate" or (ii) if that publication ceases to be published, in any successor to that publication or, if neither that publication nor any successor publication is available, in another publication selected by the Swing–Line Agent reasonably and in good faith for the purpose of giving effect to the intent of the parties, as the rate for overnight borrowing between banks in Dollars in immediately available funds.

*"LIBOR,"* with respect to any Eurodollar Advance, means the rate of interest (expressed as an annual rate) determined by the Eurodollar Agent to be the arithmetic mean (rounded up to the nearest one sixteenth of one percent (1/16%)) of the respective rates of interest communicated to the Eurodollar Agent by the several Reference Banks as the rates at which each of them would offer a deposit in Dollars for a period coextensive with the Term of the Advance in the amount of $5,000,000 (or, if that amount is not representative of the normal amount for a single deposit transaction in that currency in that market at the time, such other amount as is representative thereof), to major banks in the London interbank market at approximately 11:00 a.m. (London time) on the second London Banking Day before the commencement of the Term of that Advance; *provided, however,* that if any of the Reference Banks fails so to communicate a rate, LIBOR shall be determined on the basis of the rate or rates communicated to the Eurodollar Agent by the remaining Reference Bank or Reference Banks.

*"Margin"* means one and one eighth percent (1⅛%).

*"Reference Bank"* means each of the respective principal London offices of Biggest Bank, N.A., Average Quoter Bank Plc and Small & Obscure Banking Company, and *"Reference Banks"* means those offices collectively.

*"Swing–Line Rate"* means, for any day, the greater of (i) the rate of interest publicly announced by the Swing–Line Agent in New York City as its prime or base rate in effect for that day and (ii) the sum of one eighth of one percent (⅛%) and the Federal Funds Rate for that day.

4.1. *Basic Rate.* (a) Except as otherwise expressly provided in Section 4.2, interest shall accrue on each Advance during its Term, from and including the first day of that Term, to but excluding the last day thereof, at a rate per annum equal, (i) in the case of Eurodollar Advances, to the sum of the Margin and LIBOR for that Advance and, (ii) in the case of Swing–Line Advances, to the Swing–Line Rate as in effect on each day during that period.

### *Questions*

1. Be sure you understand the difference between interest rate determination for the eurodollar advances and the swing-line advances.

2. Who bears the risk that the lender's cost of funds will change? Why is this done?

3. Borrowers in many developing countries defaulted on their eurocredit payments when LIBOR rose to about 20% in the early 1980s. Many had borrowed years earlier when LIBOR was 6%. The countries' foreign exchange earnings were a function of international commodity prices, which did not rise with the interest rate.

   a. Since both lenders and borrowers knew the source of the countries' hard currency at the time of the loan, was this a credible allocation of risk?

   b. What alternatives would there be to allocating risk this way?

---

## c. Events of Default: the Cross Default Clause

12.1 *Events of Default.* If one or more of the following events of default (each an "*Event of Default*") occurs and is continuing, the Eurodollar Agent and the Banks shall be entitled to the remedies set forth in Section 12.2.

(d) The Borrower or any Subsidiary (i) fails to pay any of its Indebtedness as and when it becomes payable or (ii) fails to perform or observe any covenant or agreement to be performed or observed by it contained in any other agreement or in any instrument evidencing any of its Indebtedness and, as a result of that failure, any other party to that agreement or instrument is entitled to exercise, and has not irrevocably waived, the right to accelerate the maturity of any amount owing thereunder.

(e) The Guarantor (i) fails to pay any of its External Indebtedness as and when it becomes payable or (ii) fails to perform or observe any covenant or agreement to be performed or observed by it contained in any agreement or instrument evidencing any of its External Indebtedness if, as a result of that failure, any other party to that agreement or instrument is entitled to exercise, and has not irrevocably waived, the right to accelerate the maturity of any amount owing thereunder; *provided, however,* that a failure to pay External Indebtedness shall not constitute an Event of Default under this Subsection if (i) the overdue amounts in the aggregate do not exceed $10,000,000 or the equivalent of that amount in another currency or currencies, (ii) the obligation to pay the overdue amounts has not resulted from acceleration and (iii) the failure is remedied on or before the thirtieth day after it occurs; and *provided further, however,* that a failure to perform any such other covenant or agreement shall not constitute an Event of Default under this Subsection if (i) the aggregate principal amount of External Indebtedness subject to acceleration as a result of all such failures at the time does not exceed $250,000,000 or the equivalent of that amount in another currency or currencies and (ii) the failure is remedied on or before the thirtieth day after it occurs.

12.2. *Default Remedies.* (a) If any Event of Default occurs and is continuing, the Eurodollar Agent shall, upon the request of Majority Banks, by notice to the Borrower and the Guarantor, (i) declare the obligations of each Bank hereunder to be terminated, whereupon those obligations shall terminate, and (ii) declare all amounts payable hereunder or under the Notes by the Borrower that would otherwise be due after the date of termination to be immediately due and payable, whereupon all those amounts shall become immediately due and payable, all without diligence, presentment, demand of payment, protest or notice of any kind, which are expressly waived by the Borrower and the Guarantor;

(b) Each Bank is acting hereunder individually. Nothing herein, and no action taken by any Agent, Bank or Manager, shall be construed to constitute them or any of them a partnership, an association, any other entity or a joint venture. Without limiting the generality of the foregoing, each Agent, Bank and Manager shall be entitled to act independently, whether by court action or otherwise, to enforce or protect its rights under this Agreement and the Notes, subject, in the case of each Bank, to the provisions of Section 12.2(a) regarding any declaration that any unmatured obligations of the Borrower hereunder or under the Notes shall be immediately due and payable upon the occurrence of an Event of Default.

12.3. *Right of Setoff.* If any amount payable by the Borrower or the Guarantor hereunder is not paid as and when due, each of the Borrower and the Guarantor authorizes each Bank and each Affiliate of each Bank to proceed, to the fullest extent permitted by applicable law, without prior notice, by right of setoff, banker's lien, counterclaim or otherwise, against any assets of the Borrower or the Guarantor in any currency that may at any time be in the possession of that Bank or Affiliate, at any branch or office, to the full extent of all amounts payable to the Banks hereunder. Any Bank that so proceeds or that has an Affiliate that so proceeds shall forthwith give notice to the Agents of any action taken by that Bank or Affiliate pursuant to this Section.

*"External Indebtedness,"* with respect to any Person, means any Indebtedness of that Person (i) that is or may by its terms become payable in any currency other than the lawful currency of the Republic of Somewhere or (ii) that is payable to any Person resident in, organized under the laws of or having its principal office outside the Republic of Somewhere.

### *Questions*

1. What is the cross-default clause? How does it work? Why have it?

2. Under what circumstances would the cross-default clause be effectively unavailable to the lenders? What happens if the lenders disagree?

---

## d. Adverse Change

(c) If the Eurodollar Agent, after consultation with the Banks to the extent practicable, determines at any time that (i) it would not be possible to determine LIBOR for a period of one, three or six months as provided herein or (ii) LIBOR as so determined would not adequately reflect the costs to Majority Banks of funding Eurodollar Advances for that period in the London interbank market, the Eurodollar Agent shall forthwith give notice of that determination to the Borrower and the Banks, whereupon the obligations of the Banks to make Eurodollar Advances to the Borrower for a Term equal to the period or periods specified in that notice shall be suspended until the Eurodollar Agent gives notice to the Borrower and the Banks that the circumstances that gave rise to that determination no longer exist.

3.4. *Special Prepayment.* (a) If the Borrower gives notice to the Agents pursuant to Subsection 6.1(a) that it will be required to withhold or deduct Indemnifiable Taxes from a payment to any Bank under this Agreement, the Borrower may elect to terminate the Commitment of that Bank and prepay all outstanding Advances of that Bank on any Banking Day selected by the Borrower by giving notice to the Eurodollar Agent (which shall promptly advise each Bank thereof) not later than the fifth Banking Day before the Banking Day so selected; *provided, however,* that the prepayment date may not be more than five Banking Days before the effective date of the requirement to so withhold or deduct Indemnifiable Taxes; and *provided further, however,* that the Borrower shall not prepay Advances or terminate any Commitment pursuant to this Section if, more than ten Banking Days before the scheduled prepayment date, the withholding or deduction of Indemnifiable Taxes ceases to be required.

6.1. *Withholding; Gross–Up.* (a) Each payment by the Borrower or the Guarantor under this Agreement or the Notes shall be made without withholding on account of any Taxes; *provided, however,* that, if any Taxes are required so to be withheld, the Borrower or the Guarantor (as the case may be) shall give notice to that effect to the Agents, make the necessary withholding and make timely payment of the amount withheld to the appropriate governmental authority. If any Taxes so withheld are Indemnifiable Taxes, the Borrower or the Guarantor (as the case may be) shall forthwith pay any additional amount that may be necessary to ensure that the net amount actually received by each Agent, Bank or Manager (as the case may be) free and clear of Indemnifiable Taxes is equal to the amount that the Agent, Bank or Manager would have received had no Indemnifiable Taxes been withheld. All Taxes so withheld shall be paid before penalties attach thereto or interest accrues thereon. If any such penalties or interest nonetheless become due, the Borrower or the Guarantor (as the case may be) shall make prompt payment thereof to the appropriate governmental authority. If any Agent, Bank or Manager pays any amount in respect of Indemnifiable Taxes on any payment due from the Borrower or the Guarantor hereunder, or penalties or interest thereon, the Borrower or the Guarantor (as the case may be) shall reimburse that Agent, Bank or Manager in Dollars for that payment on demand. If the Borrower or the Guarantor pays any such Taxes or penalties or interest thereon, it shall deliver official tax receipts evidencing the payment or certified copies thereof to the Eurodollar Agent not later than the thirtieth day after payment.

(b) If any Bank gives notice to the Agents of increased costs pursuant to Section 15.4, the Borrower may elect to terminate the Commitment of that Bank and prepay all outstanding Advances of that Bank on any Banking Day by giving notice to the Eurodollar Agent (which shall promptly advise each Bank thereof) not later than the fifth Banking Day before the Banking Day so specified.

15.4. *Increased Costs.* The Borrower shall reimburse each Bank in Dollars on demand for all costs incurred and reductions in amounts received or receivable, as determined by that Bank, that are attributable to that Bank's Advances or the performance by that Bank of its obligations under this Agreement and that occur by reason of the promulgation of any law, regulation or treaty or any change therein or in the application or interpretation thereof or by reason of compliance by that Bank with any direction, requirement or request (whether or not having the force of law) of any governmental authority, including, without limitation, any such cost or reduction resulting from (i) the imposition or amendment of any tax other than (A) any tax measured by the net income of that Bank or its Lending Branch and imposed by the jurisdiction in which that Bank's principal office or Lending Branch is situated and (B) any Taxes (any such cost or reduction occurring by reason of the imposition or amendment of any tax referred to in clauses (A) and (B) of this Section being expressly excluded from the coverage of this Section), (ii) the imposition or amendment of any reserve, special deposit or similar requirement against assets of, liabilities of, deposits with or for the account of, or loans by, that Bank or (iii) the imposition or amendment of any capital requirements or provisions relating to capital adequacy that have the effect of reducing the rate of return on such Bank's or the relevant Lending Branch's capital as a consequence of its Advances or its obligations hereunder to a level below that which it could have achieved but for such adoption, change or compliance. If a Bank has sold one or more participations in its Advances, costs incurred and reductions in amounts receivable by the participants shall be deemed to be attributable to the relevant Advances for purposes of this Section; *provided, however,* that the Borrower shall not be required to reimburse any Bank for an amount greater than the amount that would have been due if that Bank had not sold participations in its Advances.

3.5. *Illegality.* If any Bank determines at any time that any law, regulation or treaty or any change therein or in the interpretation or application thereof makes or will make it unlawful for the Bank to fulfill its commitment in accordance with Section 2.1, to maintain an Advance or to claim or receive any amount payable to it hereunder, the Bank shall give notice of that determination to the Borrower, with copies to the Agents, whereupon the obligations of that Bank hereunder shall terminate and the Bank's Commitment shall be reduced to zero. The Borrower shall repay the Advances of that Bank in full at the end of their respective Terms; *provided, however,* that, if the affected Bank certifies to the Borrower that earlier repayment is necessary in order to enable that Bank to comply with the relevant law, regulation or treaty and specifies an earlier date for repayment, the Borrower shall make repayment on the earlier date so specified. Repayment pursuant to this Section shall be made without premium but together with interest accrued on the Advances being repaid to the date of repayment and all other amounts then payable to the relevant Bank by the Borrower hereunder.

### *Questions*

1. Why make the borrower liable for these changes?
2. Are these credible allocations of risk?

## 2. Allocation of Risk Among Managers, Agents, and Participating Banks

Since many banks lend but only a few deal directly with the borrower and guarantor, the banks provide in the eurocredit agreement for their own responsibilities and risks, on the one hand, and for circumstances in which they must act jointly. The following clauses describe a standard solution. As you read them, consider the balance that is achieved between individual and joint responsibility. What would account for this?

*WHEREAS* the Borrower proposes to borrow from the Banks, and the Banks, severally but not jointly, propose to lend to the Borrower, an aggregate amount of up to $250,000,000 at any one time outstanding, the parties agree as follows.

14.2. *Exculpation.* The Agents and the Managers and their respective directors, officers, employees and agents shall have no responsibility for (i) the truth of any representation or warranty made by the Borrower or the Guarantor in this Agreement or any other document delivered in connection with this Agreement, (ii) the validity or enforceability of this Agreement or any such document, (iii) any failure of the Borrower or the Guarantor to fulfill any of its respective obligations under this Agreement or any such document or (iv) any action taken or omitted to be taken in connection with this Agreement or the Notes, absent gross negligence or willful misconduct. Each Agent shall be entitled to rely in good faith on any communication or document believed by it to be genuine and to have been sent or signed by the proper person or persons and on the opinions and statements of any legal counsel or other professional advisors selected by it and shall not be liable to any other person for any consequence of any such reliance.

14.3. *Information about the Borrower and the Guarantor.* (a) Each Bank has investigated and evaluated, and shall continue to investigate and evaluate, the creditworthiness of the Borrower and the Guarantor and such other issues and information as it has judged appropriate and prudent in connection with its commitment to lend hereunder and the making of its Advances. Except as expressly provided herein, neither Agent shall have any duty to provide any Bank with any credit or other information with respect to the Borrower or the Guarantor, whether that information comes into its possession before or after the disbursement of any Advance.

(b) The Eurodollar Agent shall promptly (i) advise each Bank upon receipt of all the documents referred to in Section 8.1, (ii) advise each Bank upon its receipt of any documents requested in accordance with Section 8.2, (iii) forward to each Bank all Notes received by it for that Bank and (iv) forward to each Bank copies of any documents delivered to the Eurodollar Agent in accordance with Section 6.1. The Eurodollar Agent shall, as soon as practicable, forward to each Bank copies of the documents received pursuant to Section 8.1 and Section 8.2. Each Agent shall promptly transmit to each Bank each notice or other document received by that Agent from the Borrower or the Guarantor addressed to, or calling for action by, that Bank.

14.4. *Duties in Respect of Events of Default.* Neither Agent shall be under any obligation to inquire as to the performance by the Borrower or the Guarantor of its respective obligations under this Agreement or the Notes; *provided, however,* that each Agent shall give prompt notice to each Bank of any Default or Event of Default of which it receives actual notice in its capacity as an Agent hereunder.

14.5. *Other Dealings with the Borrower and the Guarantor.* The Agents and the Managers and their respective Affiliates may, without liability to account to any Bank therefor, make loans to, accept deposits from, and generally engage in any kind of business with, the Borrower and the Guarantor as though the Agents were not the Agents and the Managers were not the Managers hereunder.

14.7. *Covenant to Reimburse.* Each Bank shall reimburse each Agent (to the extent not reimbursed by the Borrower or the Guarantor) on demand for that Bank's Pro Rata Share of all expenses incurred by that Agent in the exercise of its responsibilities hereunder, including, without limitation, the reasonable fees and expenses of legal and other professional advisors.

*"Majority Banks"* means, at any time when no Advance is outstanding, Banks whose Commitments total more than fifty percent (50%) of the Total Commitment and, at any time when any Advance is outstanding, Banks maintaining Advances representing more than fifty percent

(50%) of the aggregate principal amount of the Advances outstanding at that time.

13.2. *Sharing of Payments.* (a) Except as provided in Subsection 13.2(b), if any Bank obtains payment of any amount payable hereunder from the Borrower or the Guarantor other than pursuant to Section 3.3, Section 3.4 or Section 3.5 or by distribution by an Agent pursuant to Section 13.1, whether by exercising a right of setoff or counterclaim or otherwise, with the result that it receives a greater proportion of the interest on or principal of its Advances than any other Bank receives in respect of its Advances, the Bank receiving such proportionately greater share shall promptly purchase from the other Banks such participations in the Eurodollar Advances or Swing–Line Advances, as the case may be, maintained by those other Banks as may be necessary to cause the purchasing Bank to share the excess amount obtained by it ratably with the other Banks; *provided, however,* that, if all or any portion of the amount so obtained by the purchasing Bank is thereafter recovered from that Bank, the related participating purchases under this Subsection shall be rescinded and the purchase price restored to the extent of the recovery, with such adjustments of interest as shall be equitable.

(b) If a Bank obtains a payment of the kind described in Subsection 13.2(a) as a result of a judgment in or settlement of any action or proceeding maintained by that Bank in any court, that Bank shall not be required to share the amount so obtained with any Bank which had a legal right to, but did not, join in that action or proceeding.

### *Questions*

1. What do the managers do for the participating banks? Could any bank do this?

2. What standard of care to participating banks does the agreement set for the managers? Should the standard be one of arm's length or fiduciary relations? Should it vary by function? For example, what standard should apply to the information about the borrower that the managers give participating banks before the agreement is signed?

---

### *Links to Other Chapters*

The eurocredit market illustrates the difficulty national governments face when they try to regulate the activities of their financial institutions in global markets. The different national responses emerge in the readings on the U.S. and Japanese banking markets (Chapters III and VII). One source of difficulty is the existence of financial centers (Chapter I). One result is the reliance by financial intermediaries on private contracts to resolve many issues that the law of any one nation might resolve.

This is the first chapter to examine a market for a specific financial instrument. We also encounter markets for eurobonds and global bonds

(Chapter XI), mortgage backed securities (Chapter XII), euro-Yen interest rate futures and options on those futures (Chapter XV), diff swaps (Chapter XVI), and ADRs for equity (Chapter XVII). Several of these chapters permit analysis at the level of the contract itself.

Syndication, the organizing mechanism for eurocredits, reappears in somewhat different form in bond underwriting (Chapter XI) and global equity offerings (Chapter XVII).

The development of secondary markets for eurocredit participations was an early step toward international securitization (Chapter XII).

Developing countries, which played such an important role in the eurocredit market, do so again in the global market for ADRs (Chapter XVII).

# Chapter IX

# THE PAYMENT SYSTEM

Broadly speaking, the payment system is comprised of the institutions and technologies used for one party to transfer value to another. In modern economies, value is transferred by cash or through claims on banks. Claims on banks may be transferred by a variety of devices, including checks, credit cards and wire transfers. Our focus in this Chapter is on large value transfers through wire transfers, as these are the most important payments in international financial transactions. Each major country has its own large value systems, but the dollar systems have a significant international as well as domestic importance, due to the importance of the use of the dollar as a reserve currency and the size of the eurodollar market. Thus, the U.S. large value transfer systems play a key role in international financial transactions.

This Chapter first examines the operation of the U.S. large value transfer systems, FedWire and CHIPS, in terms of how they operate, the risks they pose, and current efforts to control those risks. It then looks at "Herstatt risk" and some aspects of cross-border and offshore payment systems.

## A. THE USE OF THE U.S. PAYMENT SYSTEM FOR INTERNATIONAL TRANSACTIONS

### H. SCOTT, "WHERE ARE THE DOLLARS?—OFFSHORE FUNDS TRANSFERS"

3 Banking and Finance L.Rev. 243, 252–263 (1989).

. . .

There are numerous methods of making dollar payments in the United States, such as by cash, credit card, paper (cheque or draft), or electronic means (wire transfer). I shall concentrate on wire transfers, the form of payment used for large dollar transfers. Payments by "wire transfer" are transmitted through banks or other depository institutions. "Wire transfer" is a generic term to describe a transaction in which the drawer, which may be an individual, corporation or a bank, instructs his bank (by telephone, computer, or written instruction) to debit his account and transfer funds to the account of a payee. The payee receives payment in the form of a credit to his account.

There are three means by which wire transfers can be made: (1) in-house or correspondent transfer; (2) Fedwire; or (3) CHIPS. This section discusses the use of these methods for purely domestic transactions, and then shows how they may be used to transfer dollars from and to parties holding accounts with banks located outside the United States.

### (i) *In–House and Correspondent Transfers*

If the drawer (the party originating the transfer) and the payee (the beneficiary of the transfer) hold accounts at the same bank, the bank of account merely makes a book transfer by debiting the account of the drawer and crediting the account of the payee. The entire transaction is handled on the books of one bank and is therefore referred to as an in-house transfer.

**IN-HOUSE WIRE TRANSFER**

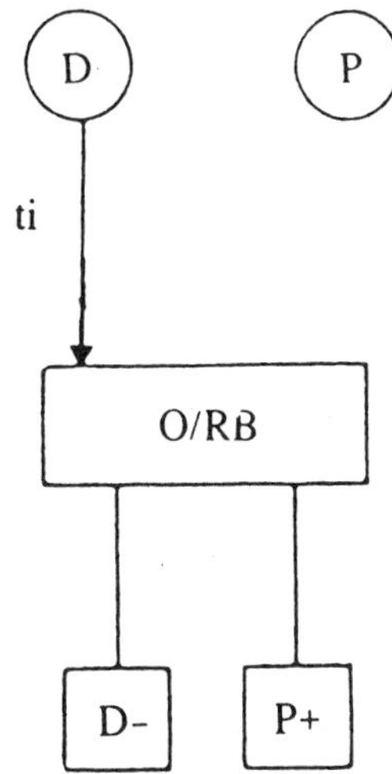


D = Drawer
P = Payee
O/RB = Originating/Receiving Bank
ti = Transfer Instruction

*Note:* Payees generally receive advices from their banks of credits entered on transfer instructions.

If the accounts of the parties are with different banks, correspondent transfers may be used to effect the payment and settle accounts between the originating bank (the bank holding the drawer's account) and the receiving bank (the bank holding the payee's account).

The originating bank, having debited the drawer's account on a payment instruction, may use a communication system, such as a telex, to instruct the receiving bank to credit the account of the payee. Settlement between the banks can be effected by the receiving bank charging the correspondent account of the originating bank held at the receiving bank. This requires the originating bank to hold a balance sufficient to cover the payment with the receiving bank.

**CORRESPONDENT WIRE TRANSFER - I**

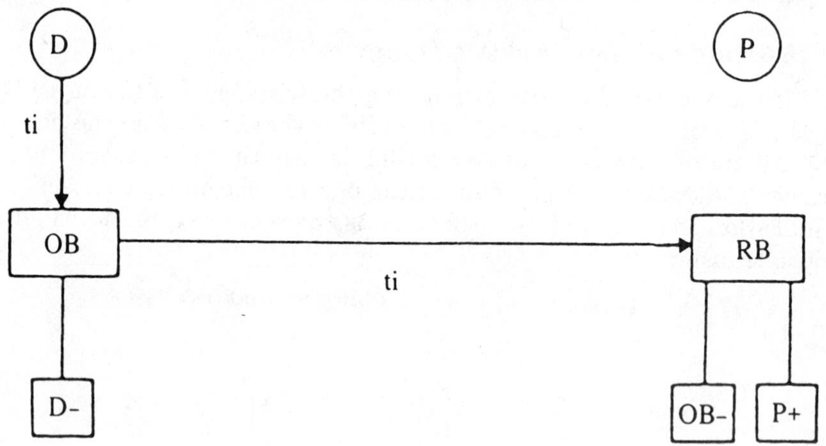


D = Drawer
P = Payee
OB = Originating Bank
RB = Receiving Bank
ti = Transfer Instruction

Alternatively, the receiving bank ("RB") may hold an account with the originating bank ("OB"). In that event, a rolling settlement takes place. OB debits its customer and credits the RB account, a type of in-house transfer. RB, in turn, credits its customer's account. No balances need to be maintained by RB with OB.

**CORRESPONDENT WIRE TRANSFER - II**

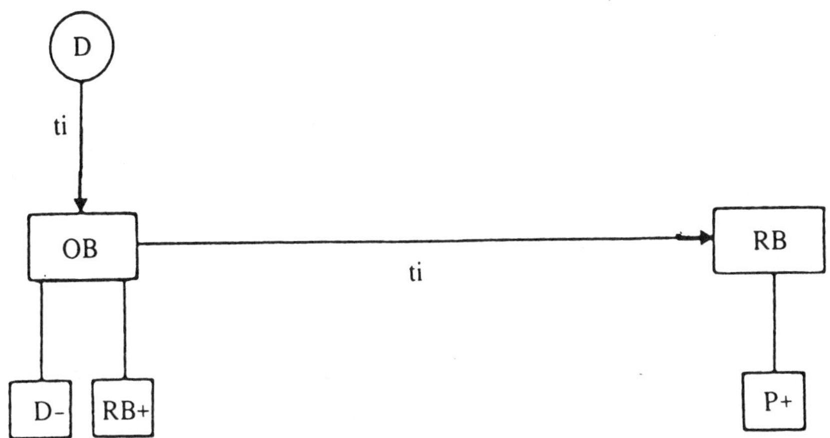


D = Drawer
P = Payee
OB = Originating Bank
RB = Receiving Bank
ti = Transfer Instruction

In the event that OB and RB do not hold accounts with each other, OB may make use of a correspondent to transfer the funds to RB. One possibility is to use an intermediary bank ("IB") which holds an account of both OB and RB. In this case, OB debits the drawer's account, IB debits the OB account and credits the RB account, and RB, having been notified by IB of its credit for the benefit of the payee, credits the payee's account. This transaction would require OB to hold a sufficient balance at IB to cover the payment.

**CORRESPONDENT WIRE TRANSFER - III**
**WITH INTERMEDIARY**

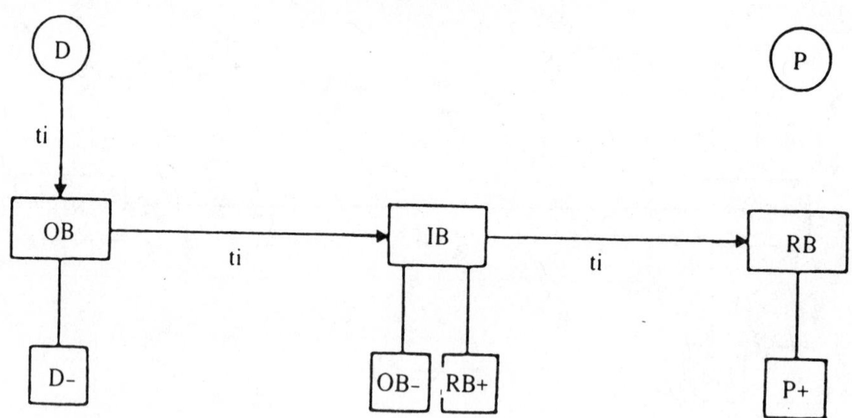


D = Drawer
P = Payee
OB = Originating Bank
RB = Receiving Bank
IB = Intermediary Bank
ti = Transfer Instruction

There are many variations on the theme of correspondent transfers. Another possibility is that IB–X holds an account with OB and also holds the account of RB. In that event, a rolling settlement can take place through account entries. OB debits the drawer and credits IB–X, IB–X credits RB, and RB credits the payee. In this case, there is no need for banks to maintain balances with each other.

CORRESPONDENT WIRE TRANSFER - IV
WITH INTERMEDIARY

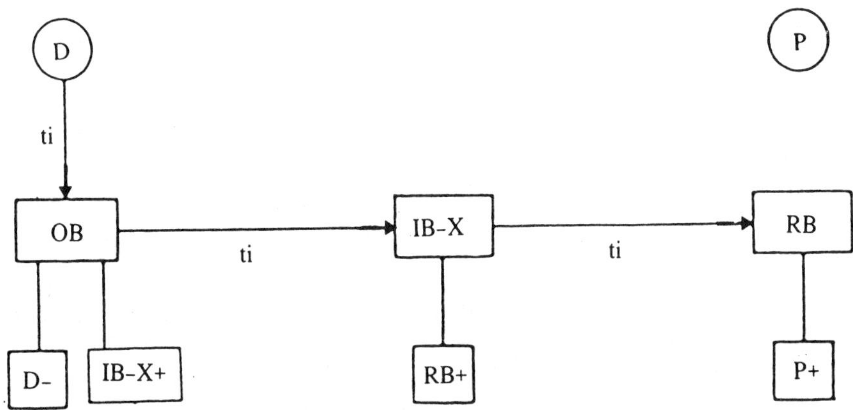


D = Drawer
P = Payee
OB = Originating Bank
RB = Receiving Bank
IB-X = Intermediary Bank
ti = Transfer Instruction

In-house and correspondent transfers in the United States may be used by foreigners to transfer dollars to United States or foreign payees. Suppose a London drawer ("LD") wants to transfer dollars from his London bank ("LOB") to a payee ("NYP") which holds an account at a New York bank ("NYRB"). If LOB and NYRB both hold dollar accounts at the same New York bank ("NYIB"), LOB debits LD, NYIB debits LOB and credits NYRB, and NYRB credits NYP. This is an in-house transfer at NYIB, which is a correspondent of both LOB and NYRB.

Now suppose LD wants to transfer dollars from its LOB account to a London payee ("LP") who banks with another London bank ("LRB"). If LOB and LRB both hold dollar accounts with NYIB, the transaction is the same as above, except that LRB, after receiving the credit from NYIB, credits LP on its books in London. Again, there may be many variations on this theme, but as long as interlinked accounts exist between LOB and LRB, provided by correspondents, a correspondent transfer may be used. No data is collected on the overall use of in-house or correspondent transfers in the United States payment system, but the dollar amounts and number of transactions must be substantial given the fact that correspondent balances at United States banks exceed $31 billion.[35]

**35.** 74 Fed.Res.Bull. A 19 (1988), lines 49 and 50. This aggregates demand balances held by domestic banks, $24.4 billion, and foreign banks, $7.2 billion, at large weekly reporting United States commercial banks, as of October 28, 1987.

(ii) *Fedwire*

Fedwire is a communication and settlement system owned by the twelve United States Federal Reserve Banks. ... Fedwire is used as follows. Having debited the drawer on the payment instruction, the originating bank instructs its Federal Reserve Bank ("FRB") to transfer the funds to the account of the payee at the receiving bank. If FRB holds the accounts of both the originating and receiving banks, it debits the former and credits the latter, and notifies the receiving bank of the credit. The receiving bank then credits the account of the payee.

**FEDWIRE TRANSFER**

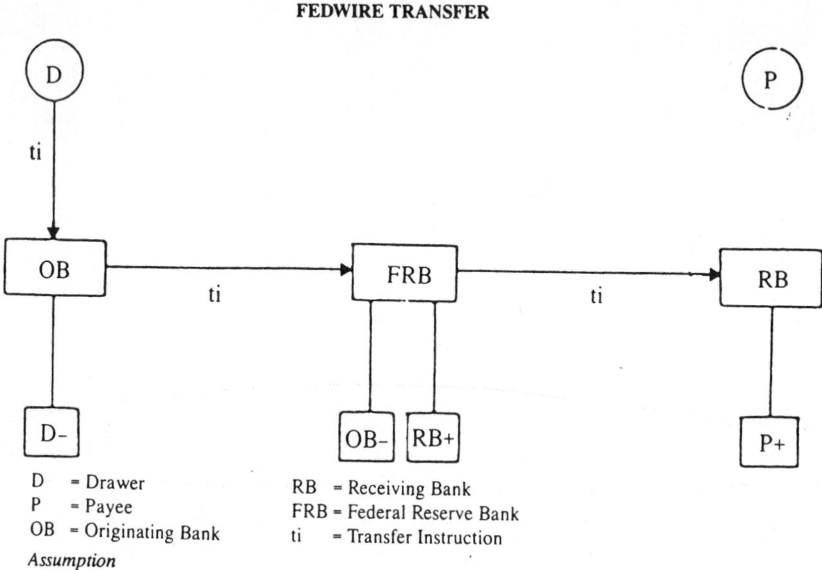


D = Drawer
P = Payee
OB = Originating Bank
RB = Receiving Bank
FRB = Federal Reserve Bank
ti = Transfer Instruction

*Assumption*
OB and RB are located in the same Federal Reserve District.

If the receiving bank holds its account with a different Reserve Bank, FRB–R (the receiving bank's reserve bank), FRB–O (the originating bank's Reserve Bank) debits the originating bank and communicates the instruction to FRB–R. FRB–R credits the account of the receiving bank and notifies the receiving bank of the credit. The receiving bank then credits the account of the payee. The two Reserve Banks then settle their own accounts.

Fedwires are often more convenient than correspondent transfers because a large number of United States banks maintain Federal Reserve accounts. In 1986, there were approximately 8000 reserve accounts. The Federal Reserve Banks, taken together, serve the IB role. Since in most cases the Fed will hold both the OB and RB accounts, there is no need to look for private intermediaries in each transaction. Fedwire can be used in connection with correspondent transfers. If the receiving bank does not hold a Fedwire account, the originating bank can send a Fedwire to the receiving bank's correspondent, that holds a Fed account, for further credit to the receiving bank and its customer.

Fedwire can also be used for transactions involving overseas customers. If LD wants to transfer funds from LOB to NYP at NYRB, and LOB holds an account with its New York correspondent bank ("NYCB1"), LOB debits LD, NYCBI debits LOB and sends a Fedwire to NYRB for NYP. The Fed debits NYCB1 and credits NYRB, and NYRB credits NYP. If the transfer were for LP at LRB, and LRB held an account with its New York correspondent ("NYCB2"), NYCB1 would send the Fedwire to NYCB2. NYCB2 would credit LRB, and LRB would credit LP on its books in London. Thus, New York correspondents serve as intermediaries between the two London banks and use Fedwire as a means for communicating the funds transfer and settling their accounts.

(iii) *CHIPS*

The Clearing House Interbank Payments System ("CHIPS") is owned and operated by the New York Clearing House Association, an organization composed of the major New York City banks.

. . .

CHIPS is a communications and net settlement system for payments by and to two classes of participant banks located in New York City: "settling" and "non-settling" participants. All participants, of which there are about 136, can send payment instructions during the day to each other through a central CHIPS switch linked to their own terminals and computers. Only 21 of the participants are settling participants; these banks settle their own positions, as well as those of other participants on whose behalf they act, through entries to their accounts at the Federal Reserve Bank of New York.

A CHIPS transfer works as follows. Bank OB, a CHIPS participant, sends a payment instruction, on behalf of Customer D, through the CHIPS computer and switching system to Bank RSB (a "settling" receiving bank). The instruction tells Bank RSB to credit the account of Customer P.

**CHIPS**

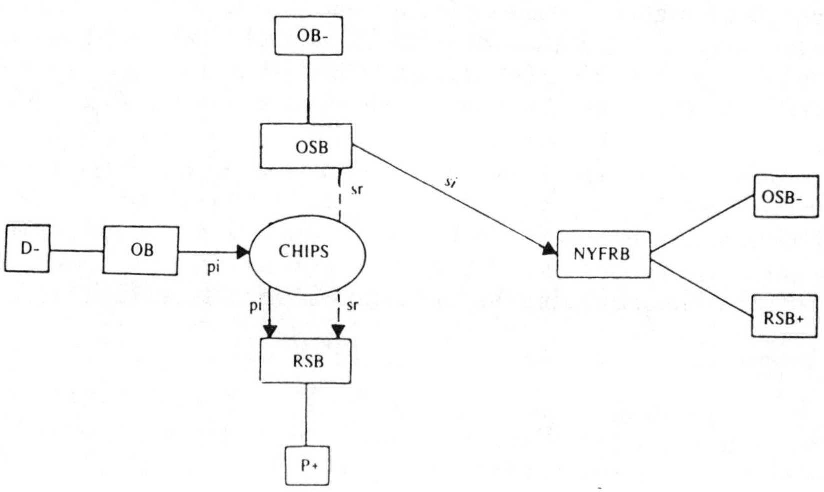


D = Drawer
P = Payee
OB = Originating Bank
OSB = Originator's Settling Bank (CHIPS Settling Participant that settles for Participant OB)
CHIPS = The Clearing House Interbank Payment System's Central Switch
RSB = Receiving Settling Bank (CHIPS Settling Participant that is the RB)
NRFRB = New York Federal Reserve Bank
si = Settlement Instruction via Fedwire
sr = Settlement Report sent at end of day
pi = Payment Instruction

*Assumption*
OSB is in a net debit position.

Settlement, as between OSB, Bank OB's settling participant, and RSB, is made through the CHIPS net settlement procedure. At 4:45 p.m. on a normal business day, the settling participants of CHIPS are given a settlement report by CHIPS that indicates whether they have a net debit or net credit position. A net debit position indicates that payments made by the bank to all other CHIPS participants, together with payments made by the banks for which it settles to all other CHIPS participants, exceed payments received by the bank from all other CHIPS participants, including payments received by banks for which it settles. A net credit position indicates the contrary, *i.e.*, that payments received exceed payments sent.

A net debit position is settled by the net debtor settling participant's sending a Fedwire to the New York Federal Reserve Bank ("NYFRB") instructing NYFRB to debit its Federal Reserve account for the amount of its net debit. The CHIPS chart assumes OSB, one of the settling participants, is in a net debit position. If the net debtor does not have sufficient funds in its reserve account to cover the settlement, it can draw down balances or lines of credit held at other banks by requesting such banks to send a Fedwire to its account at the NYFRB. Once the NYFRB has sufficient funds in the accounts of the net debtors, it debits those accounts and credits the accounts of the net creditors. A bank which is not a settling participant in CHIPS can settle its own net debit position with its settling participant by a correspondent transfer (*e.g.*, the settling participant debits its account) or Fedwire transfer.

CHIPS is regularly used for transactions involving foreign banks. Rather than use Fedwire, LOB's New York correspondent NYCBI can send a CHIPS transfer to NYRB for NYP or to the New York correspondent of LRB, NYCB2, for credit to LRB, and ultimately LP. It is estimated that 90 per cent of CHIPS payment instructions are in connection with foreign transactions.

CHIPS is often used in connection with correspondent transfers to effect payments, particularly where foreign banks are involved. An originating bank may telex its correspondent to transfer funds to a payee at a receiving bank. The originating bank and its correspondent will settle through a debit to the account of the originating bank with the correspondent. But the correspondent then uses CHIPS to transfer funds to the payee at the receiving bank.

. . .

## G. JUNCKER, B. SUMMERS AND F. YOUNG, "A PRIMER ON THE SETTLEMENT OF PAYMENTS IN THE UNITED STATES"

77 Fed.Res.Bull. 847 (November 1991).

In recent years, the soundness of the U.S. payment system, which can be measured by the certainty that payments will settle on schedule, has become a key public policy issue. Payment, or the transmission of an instruction to transfer value that results from a transaction in the economy, and settlement, or the final and unconditional transfer of the value specified in a payment instruction, need not, and in fact generally do not, occur simultaneously. Therefore, the recipient of a payment may face some uncertainty about receiving value even though a payment has been made to him or her. Efforts to reduce the gap of time between payment and settlement, or to ensure ultimate settlement of the payment, contribute to the integrity of the payment system and the efficiency of a market economy.

Four developments have led to the increased public policy attention to payment system integrity and settlement in the United States. First, the daily value of payments has increased significantly because of increased economic activity, growing sophistication and turnover of financial products, and opportunity costs associated with holding non-interest-earning demand deposits. Second, participants in the payment system have become increasingly aware of the credit and liquidity risks associated with clearing and settling payments. Third, the payment process has become more complex because of technological advances and increased emphasis on the efficient processing of payments and their underlying transactions. Finally, new settlement techniques involving netting are being increasingly employed to reduce liquidity requirements and to control risk.

* * *

PAYMENT AND SETTLEMENT

In a modern economy, payment obligations are discharged through the transfer of an accepted monetary asset. In earlier times, the monetary asset could take the form of a commodity, such as gold or silver. Today, most sovereign nations issue fiat money denominated in a national currency unit. Fiat money serves as a store of value and a medium of exchange because it has the public's confidence.

In the United States, the deposits held with banks by their customers, along with bank deposits held with the Federal Reserve, are the monetary assets most frequently used to discharge payment obligations. Accordingly, banks and the banking system are integral to the payment process. In important ways, the safety of the banking system is itself tied to the integrity of the payment system.

A large proportion of economic obligations are discharged primarily through the transfer of demand deposit claims on banks' books. Because a bank can fail, its depositors may bear some default and liquidity risk as a result of their decision to hold bank balances. Banks face no risk in holding deposits directly with the Federal Reserve, however, since a central bank—reflecting its governmental status—is immune from liquidity or credit problems. Thus, balances held with the Federal Reserve, which are referred to as "central bank money," have special significance when used by commercial banks to settle their payments. Settlement in central bank money is universally acceptable because the resulting deposit claim is free of default and liquidity risk.

Banks and the Federal Reserve together provide the settlement infrastructure for the nation's payment system. Commercial banks hold accounts through which the general public's payments are recorded and settled. The many thousands of payments that bank customers make each day result in transfers of balances between banks and therefore affect banks' positions with each other and with the central bank. Of course, banks also make their own payments in connection with carrying out the business of banking. These add to, and are often major sources of, large daily payment flows among banks. Banks can settle these interbank payments through accounts that they hold with each other or through accounts that they hold with a correspondent bank. However, many interbank payments, especially large-value payments, are made through the transfer of balances on the books of the Federal Reserve.

When a bank receives a payment on behalf of its customer, the account holder obtains a deposit claim. If the bank receiving the payment is satisfied that the payment will settle, the bank may make funds available to its customer, that is, it will allow the customer to withdraw, or typically to retransfer, the funds. When a bank makes funds available to its customers before settlement, it is exposed to credit risk because an account holder may withdraw funds and, if settlement does not occur, the bank may not be able to recover the funds. Banks sometimes guarantee the unconditional use of funds to their customers based on the receipt of payments before settlement. In this case, the bank is providing a credit service as well as a payment service to its customer by assuming the risk that settlement may not occur as scheduled. When settlement occurs at the same time the payment is made, however, settlement risk is eliminated for the bank and its customer.

THE WAY PAYMENTS ARE MADE

. . .

Two electronic funds transfer systems—Fedwire, operated by the Federal Reserve Banks, and the Clearing House Interbank Payment System (CHIPS), operated by the New York Clearing House—account for less than 0.1 percent of the number of all payments in the United States; however, they account for more than 80 percent of the value of payments. When a Fedwire payment is processed, the Federal Reserve debits the account of the sending bank and credits the account of the receiving bank. Payment instructions are for the immediate delivery of "central bank money," and Fedwire payments are settled when the amount of the payment is credited to the receiving bank's account with the Federal Reserve or when the receiving bank is notified of the payment. The Federal Reserve "guarantees" the payment to the bank receiving the Fedwire and assumes any credit risk if there are insufficient funds in the Federal Reserve account of the bank sending the payment.

Payments processed over CHIPS, however, are settled only when CHIPS participants fund their net obligations resulting from the day's payment instructions over CHIPS at the close of the business day. Settlement of CHIPS obligations occurs by Fedwire transfers initiated by those in a net debit position for the day's CHIPS activity. If the bank receiving a CHIPS payment makes funds available to its customers before settlement occurs at the end of the day, it is exposed to some risk of loss if CHIPS settlement cannot occur. To ensure that settlement occurs, the New York Clearing House has put in place risk control mechanisms (see description below).

. . .

As indicated, the Federal Reserve Banks extend intraday credit to banks in conjunction with the payment services they provide. Similarly, banks often extend intraday credit when they make payments on behalf of their customers. Thus, both the Federal Reserve and private banks are exposed to credit risk in processing payment transactions. Private banks are also exposed to liquidity risk.

Banks typically control their risk by establishing intraday credit limits for their customers and by monitoring their customers' use of such credit. In some cases, banks require their customers to pledge collateral to cover daylight credit exposures. The Federal Reserve Banks have also adopted risk control procedures: They use "net debit caps" (or ceilings for net debits) to limit the amount of credit extended to individual banks that use Federal Reserve payment services. The Reserve Banks monitor the use of intraday Federal Reserve credit for healthy banks, in most cases, by examining historical data through an ex post monitoring system. On-line, real-time account monitoring is used for the continuous control of intraday credit for certain institutions, especially those under financial stress. Real-time monitoring enables the Federal Reserve to reject or hold funds transfer requests pending the availability of funds to cover them. In some cases, the Reserve Banks may also require banks to pledge collateral to secure the intraday credit they use.

### Gross versus Net Settlement

The settlement of payments occurs on either a gross or a net basis. When payments are settled on a gross basis, each transaction is settled individually. For example, Fedwire is a gross settlement system. When payments are settled on a net basis, the parties to the payments offset the amounts they are due to pay and receive with each other (or with a central party, or clearing-house) and maintain a running balance of the netted amounts. The offsetting of payable and receivable amounts can occur between two parties (bilateral netting) or among many parties (multilateral netting).

In markets characterized by a high volume or high value of transactions among a fixed group of participants, net settlement typically improves the efficiency of payment processing; reduces liquidity needs; and, depending on the type of legal foundation and risk controls used, can help control credit exposures. Netting may be applied in many real and financial markets. For example, petroleum companies active in trading crude oil have bilaterally netted their oil trades for many years and have also participated in a multilateral netting arrangement. Many organized exchanges for commodities and securities also employ forms of netting, usually through formal clearinghouses. Banks themselves actively participate in clearing-houses through which they exchange and net payment transactions.

#### *Bilateral Netting*

Interbank payments are often cleared and settled in bilateral arrangements. For example, two banks that exchange large volumes of payments may agree to exchange certain types of payments, such as checks . . ., and settle the net value of the payments between themselves at a specific time. This type of agreement reduces the value of settlement between the two banks participating in the exchange because they can total the net value of customer transactions payable to and receivable from each other and substitute a single, smaller, net settlement (see box 1). Two banks may also enter into an agreement to net financial contracts, such as those involving foreign exchange, and settle the net amount resulting from the trading.

*Multilateral Netting*

. . .

Box 2 shows a simple numerical example of a funds transfer netting arrangement involving four participants; it illustrates settlement from the perspective of the clearinghouse. In this example, if the four banks did not participate in the clearinghouse, they would collectively need to make a total of ten interbank settlement payments with an aggregate value of $800 in connection with the underlying customer payments. As a result of multilateral netting, only one participant (Bank D) has an obligation to transfer money to the clearinghouse, and the clearinghouse must transfer money to three participants. Multilateral netting and the use of a clearinghouse have allowed these efficiencies to occur.

. . .

1. Effects of the Netting of Payments

The following example illustrates the differences between the exchange of a series of gross payments and the bilateral and multilateral netting of the series of payments from the standpoint of one organization. The assumptions in the example are that Bank A makes payments to and receives payments from nine other banks on a given day. It makes ten $100 payments to and receives ten $95 payments from each of five banks. It also makes ten $95 payments to and receives ten $100 payments from each of four banks. The settlement activity in each of the three cases is as follows:

*Gross Settlement*

Bank A makes ninety payments worth $8,800 and receives ninety payments worth $8,750.

| | |
|---|---|
| Total number of payments made or received by Bank A | 180 |
| Total value of payments made or received by Bank A that must be settled | $17,550 |
| Day's settlement effect on Bank A | – $50 |

*Bilateral Netting*

Bank A nets payments with each of the nine counterparties throughout the day and settles at the end of the day with each. Bank A pays each of five banks $50 for a total of $250 and receives $50 from each of four banks for a total of $200.

| | |
|---|---|
| Total number of settlement payments made or received by Bank A | 9 |

| | |
|---|---|
| Total value of settlement payments made or received by Bank A | $50 |
| Day's settlement effect on Bank A | – $50 |

*Multilateral Netting*

Bank A nets payments with all nine counterparties as a group throughout the day and settles at the end of the day through a common agent for the multilateral netting arrangement. It makes a single payment of $50 for its obligation to this agent.

| | |
|---|---|
| Total number of settlement payments made by Bank A | 1 |
| Total value of settlement payments made by Bank A | $50 |
| Day's settlement effect on Bank A | – $50 |

In each case, the settlement result at the end of the day for Bank A is the same (as long as net settlement occurs normally); however, the number and the value of settlement payments drop dramatically with netting. In bilateral netting, the number of payments to Bank A's counterparties is reduced to just 9 from 180 in gross settlement. In multilateral netting, Bank A need make only a single payment to satisfy its obligation to the group. Because a much smaller amount of money actually changes hands, liquidity needs are also dramatically reduced.

2. Transactions among Four Participants in a Funds Transfer Clearinghouse

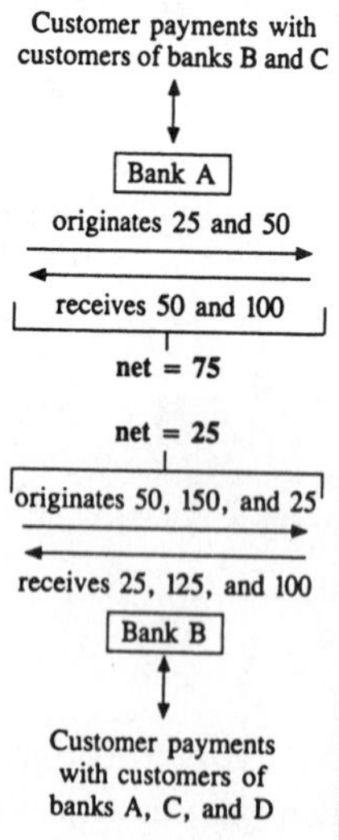

Customer payments with customers of banks B and C

Bank A

originates 25 and 50

receives 50 and 100

net = 75

net = 25

originates 50, 150, and 25

receives 25, 125, and 100

Bank B

Customer payments with customers of banks A, C, and D

**I. Gross payments among banks before netting**

| Bank receiving payment | Bank originating payment | | | | Sum of claims |
|---|---|---|---|---|---|
| | A | B | C | D | |
| A | . . . | 50 | 100 | . . . | 150 |
| B | 25 | . . . | 125 | 100 | 250 |
| C | 50 | 150 | . . . | 125 | 325 |
| D | . . . | 25 | 50 | . . . | 75 |
| Sum of obligations | 75 | 225 | 275 | 225 | 800 |

**II. Net claim or obligation of each bank with the clearinghouse**

| | A | B | C | D | Net |
|---|---|---|---|---|---|
| Total | 75 | 25 | 50 | –150 | 0 |

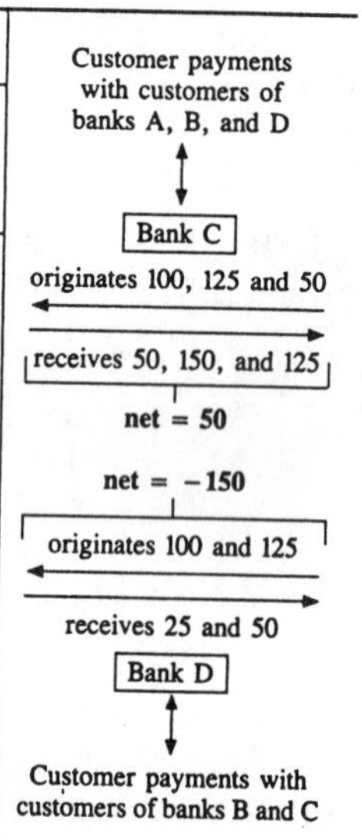

Customer payments with customers of banks A, B, and D

Bank C

originates 100, 125 and 50

receives 50, 150, and 125

net = 50

net = –150

originates 100 and 125

receives 25 and 50

Bank D

Customer payments with customers of banks B and C

*Risks in Netting Arrangements*

Two types of risk arise in bilateral and multilateral netting arrangements: namely, credit and liquidity risk. A third type of risk, systemic risk, may also be present in multilateral netting arrangements. These three types of risk are described in box 3.

In the case of bilateral netting arrangements, banks must evaluate the credit and liquidity risk assumed with the bank on the other side of the bilateral netting arrangement—the "counter-party." If there is doubt about a counterparty, a bank receiving payments from the counterparty on behalf of a customer may choose not to allow the customer access to the funds until settlement has occurred.

A mutualization of the credit risk occurs when more than two banks participate in a netting arrangement. In particular, the timely completion of all the underlying gross transactions that are included in a multilateral netting depends on the ability of each party to meet its single net settlement obligation arising from the netting. If even one participant fails to meet its net settlement obligation, then settlement for all the underlying transactions could be delayed or otherwise disrupted, creating credit and liquidity risks for the participants. Indeed, even a bank that has no dealings with the participant in a multilateral netting that does not settle may be exposed to risk. For example, in the situation described in box 2, participant A has no direct dealings whatsoever with participant D: A does not make payments to D, nor does it receive payments from D. Nonetheless, participant D has a net obligation to the clearinghouse of $150, and participant A's net credit of $75 would be funded from participant D's settlement. Accordingly, participant A depends on participant D to meet its settlement obligation, even though the two have exchanged no payments.

The risks created by privately operated netting arrangements cannot be eliminated, but they can be effectively controlled and limited. The risks cannot be eliminated because extensions of credit between privately owned institutions are an inherent part of such arrangements, and these extensions of credit are subject to some degree of default risk. Two types of risk control systems are used—decentralized and centralized. In netting arrangements based on a system of decentralized controls, the individual participants are responsible for controlling their risk vis-à-vis the other participants with whom they deal as counterparties in the individual transactions (CHIPS is an example of a decentralized risk control arrangement).[4] In contrast, systems with centralized controls typically rely on a central body that becomes the counterparty—usually a clearinghouse—to every transaction cleared through the system: The central counterparty becomes a "buyer" to every seller and a "seller" to every buyer (clearing bodies in the futures and options markets are examples of centralized risk control arrangements).

4. Controls, typically credit limits, are set on a decentralized basis, but they may be enforced through a central computer facility.

### 3. Risks in Netting Arrangements

*Liquidity risk* involves the possibility that a participant in a clearing arrangement will have insufficient funds at settlement to cover its obligation. If this situation occurs, other participants may be negatively affected if they have planned to use the proceeds from the settlement to cover other obligations or, in anticipation of settlement, have already permitted their customers to use such funds. Thus, other participants may have to find alternative sources of funding to cover their obligations while they wait for the "defaulting" participant's ultimate payment to meet its obligation.

*Credit risk* involves the possibility that a participant in a clearing arrangement will be unable to meet its settlement obligation, either in whole or in part, because of its insolvency. In this case, other participants not only face a liquidity problem but also may incur actual losses.

*Systemic risk* involves the possibility that one participant's inability to settle in a clearing arrangement will cause other participants in that clearing group to be unable to meet their obligations either to their customers or to other banks. The value of the transactions exchanged among participants in a clearing arrangement directly affects the degree of systemic risk associated with the arrangement. When high-value payments are exchanged and the turnover of funds within the arrangement is also high, the degree of systemic risk is generally high as well. Consequently, high systemic risk is usually associated with private large-value funds and securities transfer systems.

Clearing arrangements that use either decentralized or centralized risk controls use combinations of the following techniques. To protect participants against credit risk, many clearing organizations establish membership standards, which are used to screen participants when they apply to participate in the arrangement and which are monitored on an ongoing basis. Some clearing organizations require each participant to establish bilateral credit limits with every other participant whereby the volume of payments received from each other participant can exceed the volume sent to each other participant only by a predetermined amount. Bilateral credit limits thus provide a mechanism for controlling the risk that the participants face in exchanging payments with each other participant in the arrangement. To the extent that participants agree to share losses arising from the default of one or more other participants and that these loss-sharing arrangements are tied to the bilateral credit limits, incentives are created for each participant to manage its bilateral credit positions prudently.

Credit and liquidity risks may also be controlled by imposing limits on the net debit position of each participant. Such limits reduce the risk that any one participant may impose on the group and may be related in principle to each participant's ability to fund its daily settlement obligation. Assuming that such limits, or net debit caps, are set realistically, their use reduces the potential that an individual participant will be unable to settle its position at the close of business.

To handle settlement defaults, some clearing groups rely on settlement recasts and unwinds. In a recast, all of the defaulting participant's payments are deleted from the settlement, and the net settlement positions of the remaining participants are recalculated. As a last resort, if a clearing group is unable to achieve settlement after more than one recast, then it may decide to unwind *all* transactions. This procedure essentially requires all the participants to settle independently with each other.

For small-value arrangements, settlement recasts may be able to address both liquidity and credit risk without serious systemic implications. If a participant defaults, the clearing group relies on the resources of each remaining participant to fund its adjusted settlement position on the settlement day. Further, by removing all of the transactions of the defaulting participant, a settlement recast automatically allocates the losses associated with the default to the participants that dealt with the defaulting participant. Such an approach to resolving a settlement default is viable only when the value of payments exchanged is relatively low and the potential change in participants' settlement obligations is relatively small and can be funded easily by the remaining participants.

In a large-value netting arrangement, the recast of the settlement could remove significant credits that other participants were relying on to meet their own obligations and thus cause them to be unable to settle. Therefore, recasts or unwinds can be a significant source of systemic risk.

To avoid the undesirable effects of a recast, large-value multilateral netting arrangements—such as CHIPS—may provide special "assurances" of settlement akin to "guarantees." The nondefaulting participants may, for example, agree in advance to share the burden of meeting the defaulting participant's obligation to allow settlement to occur on schedule. Lines of credit or pools of collateral may be maintained, either of which can be used for overnight borrowing to provide the funds to achieve settlement on the day of the occurrence. In such arrangements, the nondefaulting participants would share losses after the settlement had occurred, based on some method of loss allocation agreed upon in advance. Such arrangements would help prevent the sudden market disruptions that might otherwise occur with recasts or unwinds.

*Legal Basis for Netting*

Netting must have a sound legal basis for the settlement to be certain. In particular, in the event that a participant in the netting becomes insolvent, it is important that the net obligations of the participants be legally recognized so that a receiver of the insolvent participant is not able to "cherry pick," that is, accept incoming payments while voiding outgoing payments.

A variety of legal approaches may be used to net obligations. For example, netting by novation would substitute a new legal obligation each time an additional payment instruction is sent or received. Netting among several participants in an arrangement may be accomplished by placing an intermediary between the counterparties so that all obligations are due to or from this new intermediary. These approaches are applicable to the netting of financial contracts, such as foreign exchange deals, as well as to payments. Recent work by the Group of Ten central banks has emphasized the need for significant netting arrangements to have sound legal foundations.

. . .

*Payment Netting Arrangements*

At present, CHIPS is the only "pure" payment netting arrangement for large-value transfers operating in the United States. It is the largest payment netting system in the world and processes nearly $1 trillion in payments daily. It has about 130 participants, the majority of which are branches or agencies of non-U.S. banks. Only twenty U.S. participants, however, are settling participants that actually send or receive net payments to settle on behalf of themselves and other, nonsettling participants.

Since its inception in 1970, CHIPS has adopted a variety of measures to control and reduce credit and liquidity risk. Currently, it employs admission standards; bilateral credit limits, which are used by each participant to establish its maximum exposure to each other participant in the event of a default; net debit caps, which are based on all bilateral credit limits established for each participant; explicit loss-sharing rules, which are based on the bilateral limits; and collateral requirements to ensure timely settlement.

Since moving to same-day settlement in 1981, CHIPS has used a special settlement account with the Federal Reserve Bank of New York to settle each day. Immediately after the system closes for the day at 4:30 p.m. eastern time, participants are notified of their final net settlement obligations. The settlement payments for the twenty U.S. banks that settle directly for themselves and the other participants are made over Fedwire into the special settlement account at the Federal Reserve Bank of New York.

If any participant fails to settle, the loss-sharing rules are invoked. In essence, an additional settlement obligation (ASO) is calculated for each participant that dealt that day with the defaulting member to make up that member's unpaid obligation, and the participants are given a reasonable period of time to cover this ASO. If any participant failed to meet its ASO, U.S. government securities held in a special CHIPS collateral account at the Federal Reserve Bank of New York would be tapped to collateralize a loan in the market to use for ensuring timely settlement. Sufficient collateral is kept in the special CHIPS account to cover any one participant's largest potential uncovered net debit. In certain cases, there would be sufficient collateral to cover several simultaneous defaults by participants with smaller uncovered net debits.

Thus, the CHIPS collateral account ensures timely settlement for all but cataclysmic default situations.

. . .

### *Notes and Questions*

1. FedWire is a real time gross payment system. There is no netting; each transaction settles separately on the Fed's books. It is owned and operated by the 12 Federal Reserve Banks and in 1992 transferred about $850 billion per day (U.S. GNP is $4 trillion), in 270,000 transactions, with the average size of a transaction about $3 million. All depository institutions (not securities firms) may have access, including branches of foreign banks. Over 4000 do have direct access to FedWire; others have indirect access through correspondents.

CHIPS is a net settlement payment system in which transactions are settled at the end of the day. In 1992, transfers amounted to about $1.25 trillion per day (more than FedWire) in 160,000 transfers. The average transaction was about $7 million (more than FedWire). CHIPS is owned and operated by the NYCHA which is controlled by the major New York City banks. There are presently about 130 total participants, the majority of which are foreign. There are only 20 settling participants, all domestic.

2. Banks sending FedWires commonly overdraft their accounts (daylight overdrafts). The total of all banks' highest average daylight overdrafts per day were about $150 billion in 1993. If a bank fails with an overdraft outstanding, the Fed has a loss. The Fed does not take money back from the banks that received payments from the failed bank. The principal reason is that FedWires are final when sent; they are "good funds." Receiving banks need to know that the funds are good so they can allow the receivers to use them. Finality supports the high velocity of money in the economy, particularly in the financial system. Could the Fed just prohibit overdrafts? This would risk a slowdown in the economy and possible gridlock. Citibank wouldn't be able to send funds to Morgan until Chase sent them to Citibank, but Morgan can't send funds to Chase until it gets them from Citibank. Do overdrafts on FedWire cause systemic risk problems?

Overdrafts of Fed accounts can occur as a result of a variety of different transactions, including transfers of book-entry securities. When book-entry securities are bought by a dealer, such as Salomon Brothers, they are delivered electronically to its clearing bank's (CB) account with the Fed. CB's securities account is credited and its funds account is debited. CB then makes corresponding entries on its own books to the funds and securities accounts of Salomon. Deliveries of book-entry securities during the day are substantial, and cause very substantial overdrafts on the accounts of the clearing banks (there are only a handful with any volume). The overdrafts are extinguished at the end of the day when the dealer sells out or finances (for example, by repo transactions in which securities are exchanged for cash for a defined period) its position. Is there the same risk to the Fed from an overdraft caused by funds transfer as compared to book-entry deliveries?

3. Let's look at how CHIPS settlement works by examining the hypothetical example (Table 2) in the Juncker piece. What is A's situation? Bank A sent 25 to B and 50 to C: its obligations (funds owed) are 75. Bank A received 50 from B and 100 from C: its claims (funds owed to it) are 150. Thus, its net position, the net of its obligations of 75 and claims of 150, is a net claim of 75. Under a delete and unwind rule (CHIPS Rule 13) if D fails to settle, all transactions involving D would be deleted. The new settlement positions of the banks would be as follows:

| | A | B | C | D | Net |
|---|---|---|---|---|---|
| Pre | 75 | 25 | 50 | −150 | 0 |
| Post | 75 | −50 | −25 | xx | 0 |

How would A, B and C be affected? What would the Fed do in this situation?

## B. FEDWIRE AND CHIPS: RISK REDUCTION MEASURES

***FedWire***

The Fed has adopted a two-pronged strategy to control daylight overdrafts on FedWire, ceilings on and pricing of overdrafts. Pricing is effective as of April 14, 1994.

### 1. Ceilings

BOARD OF GOVERNORS OF THE FEDERAL RESERVE SYSTEM, FEDERAL RESERVE POLICY STATEMENT ON PAYMENT SYSTEM RISK

57 Fed.Reg. 40455 (September 3, 1992).

*D. Net Debit Caps*

To limit the aggregate amount of daylight credit extended by Reserve Banks, each institution that incurs daylight overdrafts in its Federal Reserve account must adopt a net debit cap, i.e., a ceiling on the aggregate net debit position that it can incur during a given interval. Alternatively, if an institution's daylight overdrafts generally do not exceed the lesser of $10 million or 20 percent of capital, the institution may qualify for the exempt-from-filing status. Subject to the provisions for special situations described below, an institution must be financially healthy and eligible to borrow from the discount window in order to adopt a cap greater than zero or qualify for the filing exemption.

Cap categories and associated cap levels, set as multiples of capital, are listed below:

An institution is expected to avoid incurring net debits that, on average over a two-week period, exceed the two-week average cap, and, on any day, exceed the single-day cap. The two-week average cap provides flexibility, in recognition that fluctuations in payments can occur from day-to-day.

Net Debit Cap Multiples

| Cap Category | Two–Week Avg. | Single Day |
|---|---|---|
| High ........................ | 1.50 | 2.25 |
| Above Avg.................... | 1.125 | 1.875 |
| Average...................... | 0.75 | 1.125 |
| *De Minimis* ................. | 0.20 | 0.20 |
| Exempt-from-filing .......... | $10 million (0.20) | $10 million (0.20) |
| Zero ........................ | 0.0 | 0.0 |

The purpose of the higher single-day cap is to limit excessive daylight overdrafts on any day and to assure that institutions develop internal controls that focus on the exposures each day, as well as over time.

The two-week average cap is measured against the average, over a two-week reserve maintenance period, of an institution's daily maximum net debit positions in its Federal Reserve account. In calculating the two-week average, individual days on which an institution is in an aggregate net credit position throughout the day are treated as if the institution was in a net position of zero. The number of days used in calculating the average is the number of business days the institution's Reserve Bank is open during the reserve maintenance period.

The Board's policy on net debit caps is based on a specific set of guidelines and some degree of examiner oversight. Under the Board's policy, a Reserve Bank may prohibit the use of Federal Reserve intraday credit if (1) an institution's use of daylight credit is deemed by the institution's supervisor to be unsafe or unsound, (2) an institution does not qualify for a cap exemption, does not perform a self-assessment, or does not file a board-of-directors-approved *de minimis* cap, and (3) an institution poses an excessive risk to a Reserve Bank.

The net debit cap provisions of this policy apply to foreign banks to the same extent as they apply to U.S. institutions. The Reserve Banks will advise home-country supervisors of banks with U.S. branches and agencies of the daylight overdraft capacity of banks under their jurisdiction, as well as of other pertinent conditions related to their caps. Home-country supervisors that request information on the overdrafts in the Federal Reserve accounts of their banks will be provided that information on a regular basis.

### 1. Cap Set Through Self–Assessment

An institution that wishes to establish a net debit cap category of high, above average, or average must perform a self-assessment of its own creditworthiness, credit policies, and operational controls, policies, and procedures. The assessment of credit worthiness should address the overall financial condition of the institution, placing emphasis on conformance of the institution's capital with supervisory standards for capital adequacy. The institution should also assess its procedures for evaluating the financial condition of its customers and should establish intraday credit limits that reflect these assessments. Finally, an institution should ensure that its operational controls permit it to contain its use of Federal Reserve intraday credit and restrict its customers' use of credit to the limits it has established. The *Users' Guide* to the Board's Payments System Risk Reduction Policy, available from any Reserve Bank, includes a detailed explanation of the steps that should be taken by a depository institution in performing a self-assessment to establish a net debit cap.

Each institution's board of directors is expected to review the self-assessment and determine the appropriate cap category. The process of self-assessment, with board-of-directors review, should be conducted at least once in each 12–month period. A cap determination may be reviewed and approved by the board of directors of a holding company parent of a depository institution, or the parent of an Edge or agreement corporation, provided that (1) the self-assessment is performed by each entity incurring daylight overdrafts, (2) the entity's cap is based on the entity's own capital (adjusted to avoid double-counting), and (3) each entity maintains for its primary supervisor's review its own file with supporting documents for its self-assessment and a record of the parent's board-of-directors review.

In applying these guidelines, each institution is expected to maintain a file for examiner review that includes (1) worksheets and supporting analysis developed in its self-assessment of its own risk category, (2) copies of senior management reports to the board of directors of the institution or its parent (as appropriate) regarding that self-assessment, and (3) copies of the minutes of the discussion at the appropriate board-of-directors meeting concerning the institution's adoption of a cap category.

As part of its normal examination, the depository institution's examiners will review the contents of the self-assessment file. The objective of this review is to assure that the institution has applied the guidelines seriously and diligently, that the underlying analysis and methodology were reasonable and that the resultant self-assessment was generally consistent with the examination findings. Examiner comments, if any, should be forwarded to the board of directors of the institution. The examiner, however, would generally not require a modification of the self-assessment cap category unless the level of daylight credit used by the institution constitutes an unsafe or unsound banking practice.

The contents of the self-assessment cap category file will be considered confidential by the institution's examiner. Similarly, the actual cap level selected by the institution will be held confidential by the Federal Reserve and the institution's examiner. (However, cap information will be shared with the home country supervisor of agencies and branches of foreign banks.)

. . .

On August 24, 1993, the Board proposed some important modifications to its methodology for determining daylight overdraft ceilings.

BOARD OF GOVERNORS OF THE FEDERAL RESERVE SYSTEM, PROPOSALS TO MODIFY THE PAYMENTS SYSTEM RISK REDUCTION PROGRAM; SELF ASSESSMENT PROCEDURES, CAPS FOR U.S. BRANCHES AND AGENCIES OF FOREIGN BANKS

58 Fed.Reg. 44677 (August 24, 1993).

. . .

**Self-Assessment Procedures**

Under the Board's policy, an institution's net debit cap (for a single day and on average over a two-week period) is based on its cap category. The three cap categories that permit the highest use of intraday credit are the Average, Above Average, and High cap categories. An institution that wishes to establish a cap in one of these categories must complete a self-assessment of its creditworthiness, intraday funds management and control, and customer credit policies and controls.

The Board is proposing to add a fourth component, operating controls and contingency procedures, to the self-assessment procedures. This component is critical to a thorough self-assessment because institutions could incur significant financial losses as a result of fraud and because operational failures at payment system participants could disrupt financial markets.

As a result of the potential added burden placed on depository institutions, the Board anticipates that implementation of this requirement, if approved, will be delayed until January 1, 1995 in order to provide institutions sufficient time to adopt procedures for evaluating this component. The Board would welcome comments on whether it is appropriate to incorporate a component on operational controls and contingency procedures into the self-assessment procedures as well as any potential administrative burden of including this additional requirement.

The Board is also proposing a change in the procedures for completing the creditworthiness component of the self-assessment. These new procedures are described fully in the draft Guide to the Federal Reserve's Payments System Risk Policy, which is available from any Reserve Bank. Since the inception of the self-assessment process for establishing net debit caps, concerns have been raised regarding the administrative burden raised by the self-assessment procedures. In an attempt to reduce burden on institutions electing to complete a self-assessment, the Board has developed a matrix that combines an institution's supervisory rating and Prompt Corrective Action capital category into a creditworthiness rating. This "Creditworthiness Matrix" is shown below.

**Creditworthiness Matrix**

| Capital level | Supervisory composite rating | | |
|---|---|---|---|
| | Strong | Satisfactory | Fair |
| Well Capitalized | Excellent | Very Good | Adequate |
| Adequately Capitalized | Very Good | Very Good | Adequate |
| Undercapitalized | Full Assessment | Full Assessment | Below Standard |

**Note:** Institutions with a capital level or supervisory rating not shown in the matrix would receive a creditworthiness rating of "below standard."

. . .

2. U.S. Agencies and Branches of Foreign Banks

For U.S. agencies and branches of foreign banks, net debit caps on daylight overdrafts in Federal Reserve accounts are calculated by applying the cap multiples for each cap category to consolidated "U.S. capital equivalency." [4]

For a foreign bank whose home-country supervisor adheres to the Basle Capital Accord, U.S. capital equivalency is equal to the greater of 10 percent of worldwide capital or 5 percent of the total liabilities of each agency or branch, including acceptances, but excluding accrued expenses and amounts due and other liabilities to offices, branches, and subsidiaries of the foreign bank. In the absence of contrary information, the Reserve Banks presume that all banks chartered in G–10 countries meet the acceptable prudential capital and supervisory standards and will consider any bank chartered in any other nation that adopts the Basle Capital Accord (or requires capital at least as great and in the same form as called for by the Accord) eligible for the Reserve Banks' review for meeting acceptable prudential capital and supervisory standards.

For all other foreign banks, U.S. capital equivalency is measured as the greater of: (1) The sum of the amount of capital (but not surplus) that would be required of a national bank being organized at each agency or branch location, or (2) the sum of 5 percent of the total liabilities of each agency or branch, including acceptances, but excluding accrued expenses and amounts due and other liabilities to offices, branches, and subsidiaries of the foreign bank.

In addition, any foreign bank may incur daylight overdrafts above its net debit cap up to a maximum amount equal to its cap multiple times 10 percent of its worldwide capital, provided that any overdrafts above its net debit cap are collateralized. This policy offers all foreign banks, under terms that reasonably limit Reserve Bank risk, a level of overdrafts based on the same proportion of worldwide capital. Conse-

4. The term "U.S. capital equivalency" is used in this context to refer to the particular capital measure used to calculate daylight overdraft net debit caps, and does not necessarily represent an appropriate capital measure for supervisory or other purposes.

quently, banks chartered in countries that follow the Basle Accord and whose net debit cap is based on 10 percent of worldwide capital are not permitted to incur overdrafts above their net debit cap. All other foreign banks may incur overdrafts to the same extent as banks from Basle Accord countries, that is, up to their cap multiple times 10 percent of their worldwide capital, provided that sufficient collateral is posted for any overdrafts in excess of their net debit cap. In addition, foreign banks may elect to collateralize all or a portion of their overdrafts related to book-entry securities activity.

. . .

***Notes and Questions***

1. Does it make sense to use capital as a base for the ceilings on daylight overdrafts? Why are ceilings generally enforced only by ex-post rather than real time monitoring?

2. Why shouldn't the capital base for foreign banks be their worldwide capital?

## 2. Pricing

In addition to ceilings, there will be a pricing of daylight overdrafts beginning in April 1994.

BOARD OF GOVERNORS OF THE FEDERAL RESERVE SYSTEM, MODIFICATION OF THE PAYMENTS SYSTEM RISK REDUCTION PROGRAM; DAYLIGHT OVERDRAFT PRICING

57 Fed.Reg. 47084 (October 14, 1992).

The overdraft fee will be 60 basis points (annual rate), quoted on the basis of a 24–hour day. To obtain the daily overdraft fee (annual rate) for the standard Fedwire operating day, the quoted 60 basis point fee will be multiplied by the fraction of a 24–hour day during which Fedwire is scheduled to operate. Under the current 10–hour Fedwire operating day, the overdraft fee will equal 25 basis points (60 basis points multiplied by 10/24/92), the same price as originally proposed by the Board. Daylight overdraft pricing is effective April 14, 1994, six months after the October 14, 1993, effective date of the Board's new overdraft measurement procedures, published elsewhere in today's Federal Register (Docket No. R–0721).

The Board plans to phase in the 60 basis point fee (times an operating hour fraction) over a three-year period. On April 14, 1994, the fee will be 24 basis points, rising to 48 basis points on April 13, 1995, and 60 basis points on April 11, 1996. Under current Fedwire operating hours, these phase-in fees are equal to the proposed phase-in fees of 10, 20, and 25 basis points. A change in the length of the scheduled Fedwire operating day would not change the effective fee because the fee is applied to average overdrafts which, in turn, would be deflated by the change in the operating day. After evaluating the market's response to pricing, the Board may slow or accelerate the phase-in, cease the phase-in at a level below 60 basis points, or increase the fee above 60 basis points at the end of the phase-in or at a later date.

The fee will apply to combined funds and book-entry securities intraday overdrafts in accounts at the Federal Reserve. The average daily overdraft will be calculated by dividing the sum of the negative reserve or clearing account balances at the end of each minute of the scheduled FedWire operating day (with credit balances set to zero) by the total number of minutes in the scheduled FedWire operating day.

. . .

### *Notes and Questions*

1. Assume a U.S. bank has $10 billion in capital and $6 billion in daily average overdrafts over the current 10 hour FedWire operating day. How much will the bank pay in daylight overdraft fees to the Fed, assuming pricing has been fully phased-in, that is after April 11, 1996, and there are no further changes to the pricing methodology?

2. Is the 60 basis point fee high or low? How could that be determined?

3. The Fed does not think substantial volume will shift to CHIPS as a result of pricing. If it did, why would this be of concern? Doesn't an important part of the answer to that question depend on the effectiveness of risk reduction techniques on CHIPS? It is interesting to note that in 1992–93 FedWire volume decreased by 4% and CHIPS volume increased by 8%. Could this have been an anticipatory reaction to the advent of pricing?

4. Can banks simply pass on to customers the costs of their daylight overdrafts?

5. The most intense controversy over pricing of daylight overdrafts had to do with the measurement of daylight overdrafts. There are many transactions other than the sending or receiving of FedWires that can affect the level of balances in Fed accounts, for example check debits and credits. The Fed has adopted a complicated measurement system, see Board of Governors of the Federal Reserve System, Modification of the Payments System Risk Reduction Program; Measurement of Daylight Overdrafts, 57 Fed.Reg. 47093 (October 14, 1992).

#### *CHIPS*

In the CHIPS system, three principal devices (apart from membership admission requirements) have been employed to minimize the probability and impact of a settlement failure: (1) ceilings in the form of bilateral and net debit caps; (2) collateralized "Additional Settlement Obligations" (ASOs); and (3) the validity of netting in bankruptcy. Each of these devices is dealt with below.

## 1. Ceilings

The Fed's Policy Statement provides that private Large–Dollar Funds Transfer Networks, of which CHIPS is by far the most important, must establish certain ceilings.

### BOARD OF GOVERNORS OF THE FEDERAL RESERVE SYSTEM, FEDERAL RESERVE POLICY STATEMENT ON PAYMENT SYSTEM RISK

57 Fed.Reg. 40455, 40461–62 (September 3, 1992).

Any large-dollar payments system obtaining net settlement services from a Federal Reserve Bank must establish liquidity and credit controls that provide a reasonable degree of assurance that settlement can be achieved on the settlement day. Under the Board's policy, no private large-dollar payments network is eligible for Reserve Bank net settlement services unless it:

(1) Requires each participant to establish bilateral net credit limits vis-a-vis each other participant on that network.

(2) Establishes a system to reject or hold any payment that would exceed such limits, and

(3) Establishes and monitors in real time network-specific net debit limits. In order that Reserve Banks may properly monitor the use of intraday credit, no future or existing large-dollar network will be permitted to settle on the books of a Reserve Bank unless its members authorize the network to provide position data to the Reserve Bank on request.

In setting bilateral net credit limits, each participant on a network must determine for itself the maximum dollar amount of net transfers (i.e., the excess of the value received over the value sent) that it is willing to accept from each other participant on that network. The Board believes that bilateral net credit limits reduce risk by enabling an institution to identify and control the exposure it could face in the event of a settlement failure. The volume of daylight exposure that each participant is willing to accept from each other participant is likely to be quite large when aggregated across the network. Moreover, participants may be unaware of the credit made available to a given sender by other potential receivers. For this reason, bilateral net credit limits should be supplemented by network-specific net debit caps, which will limit the aggregate amount of risk a participant may present to the network.

The federal bank examiners will, during regular examinations, review and comment on the procedures used by each institution in establishing, monitoring, reviewing, and modifying bilateral net credit limits, and ensure that institutions understand their potential exposures with each other participant over more than one network and in more than one market.

Avoidance of Risk Reduction Measures

The Board believes that the use of FedWire for the avoidance of Federal Reserve or private-sector risk reduction measures is not appropriate. The Board seeks to prevent institutions from participating in bilateral netting arrangements that provide only payments netting under which gross payment messages are exchanged during the day and settled at the end of the day by using FedWire to adjust net positions bilaterally. Such arrangements would be difficult for Reserve Banks to detect and would be outside of Federal Reserve and private-sector risk control measures. They still, however, present the same risks to the payments mechanism that other net settlement arrangements present because settlement failures are possible, and such failures could have deleterious consequences to the payments system.

The Board realizes, however, that certain netting arrangements are not intended to avoid risk reduction measures and can, in fact, reduce risk. For example, institutions may, by means of novation, net transactions prior to settlement, with each participant legally obligated only for the resultant net position. This arrangement reduces risk because it replaces gross transactions with the smaller net obligation, and failures to settle would almost always involve smaller exposures (and less systemic risk) than with simple bilateral net settlement. The Board's policy on limiting avoidance techniques is not intended to restrict this kind of netting arrangement.

. . .

### *Notes and Questions*

1. Can bilateral credit limits control the risk of settlement failure? Review Table 2 in the Juncker piece. The Fed policy, and CHIPS Rule 22(a), permit banks to set whatever limits they want on other participants. The CHIPS system will not permit the release of payment messages that would cause the receiving bank's bilateral credit limit to be violated. Instead, it will store the message until it is possible to release it consistent with the limits, e.g. after the receiving bank has sent a payment message to the bank whose message has been stored. Bilateral credit limits were first adopted by CHIPS in 1984.

2. How can a net debit limit control the risk of settlement failure? CHIPS Rule 23(b) sets a debit cap for each participant equal to five percent of the sum of all the bilateral credit limits that all other participants established for that participant. For example, if the sum of all participants' bilateral credit limits set for Participant N were $100 billion, its bilateral net debit limit would be $5 billion, meaning its net debit position could not exceed that amount. The CHIPS system will store and hold payment messages sent by banks which exceed net debit limits until it is possible to release them consistent with limits, e.g. after the sender has received messages. Net debit limits were first instituted by CHIPS in 1986. Are they effective in reducing risk?

## 2. Collateralized ASOs

Since October 1991, the CHIPS system has adopted a system of loss sharing—additional settlement obligations (ASOs)—to limit the systemic risk from the delete and unwind system. If a participant (F) fails, the loss is shared among the remaining participants based on their bilateral credit limits to the failed bank. The higher a particular participant's (P) bilateral credit limit to the failed bank, the higher its ASO.

$$\text{ASO} = \text{shortfall} \times \frac{\text{P's highest bilateral credit limit to F}}{\text{Total highest bilateral credit limits to F}}$$

The maximum ASO for any participant is 5% of its largest bilateral credit limit to a participant. Thus, if its largest bilateral credit limit was, in fact, to F, $100 million, its maximum ASO would be $5 million.

Total ASO obligations are clearly sufficient to support the failure of the largest net debtor in the settlement. Suppose the worst case, a net debtor incurs the maximum of its net debit position (NDP), e.g. $1 billion, and cannot settle. We know that its maximum net debit position cannot exceed 5% of the sum of its bilateral credit limits. Suppose there were four other participants and each had given the same and its highest bilateral credit limit to the participant. The ASO would be exactly sufficient to cover the shortfall.

Thus, NDP = 5% of Total bilateral credits
$1 billion = .05 bilateral credits
Bilateral credits = $20 billion
Maximum ASO of each P = .05 × $5B = $250 million
Total ASO = $1 billion

Total ASO obligations could be sufficient to cover several simultaneous failures if we relax these somewhat unrealistic assumptions, but in the worst case, the largest net debtor plus other large net debtors fail, the ASOs may not be sufficient.

Participants must pledge readily marketable collateral (treasuries) to cover their maximum ASO.

### *Notes and Questions*

1. Will this ASO system make participants set more realistic bilateral credit limits on other participants, and therefore reduce the risk of a settlement failure?

2. Will this ASO system put constraints on the willingness of banks to shift volume from FedWire to CHIPS? ASO obligations are backed up by collateral currently totaling about $3 billion. What does this collateral requirement cost the banks?

## 3. Netting Validity

The whole CHIPS system is built on multilateral netting. Each participant has a net debit or credit position vis a vis the system. If a participant fails, the collateralized ASO obligations should insure the completion of the settlement. As we have seen, these ASOs represent allocated portions of the failed bank's net debit position.

The ASO providers would then have a claim against the failed bank for their ASOs—which might be partially secured by whatever collateral the failed participant had posted with the N.Y. Federal Reserve Bank. In the United States, bank bankruptcies are not dealt with under the Bankruptcy Code; instead, almost all bank bankruptcies are handled under banking law rules by the FDIC, as a receiver.

A major issue of concern would be whether the FDIC as receiver would respect the CHIPS netting. Suppose the failed bank (FP) had a net debit position of $5 billion, which resulted from having sent out transfers of $12 billion, and having received transfers of $7 billion.

The FDIC might ignore the CHIPS netting, and the ASO arrangements based on it, and take the position that FP has not been paid for the $7 billion in funds it received, and make claims against the CHIPS participants that sent these funds to FP. This would remit the CHIPS banks to making unsecured claims for $12 billion against the FDIC. Under the netting arrangements, the maximum loss (assuming FP's assets were worth zero) of the banks would be the net debit position, $5 billion. Under a FDIC gross approach, disaggregating transfers sent from those received, the maximum loss of the banks would be $7 billion. They would pay for the $7 billion in transfers sent to FP but get nothing for the $12 billion in transfers received.

The Payments System Risk Reduction provisions of the Federal Deposit Insurance Corporation Improvement Act of 1991, 12 U.S.C. § 4401 et seq. deal with this problem. The key provision affecting CHIPS, 12 U.S.C. § 4404, provides:

### § 4404. Clearing organization netting

#### (a) General netting rule

Notwithstanding any other provision of law, the covered contractual payment obligations and covered contractual payment entitlements of a member of a clearing organization to and from all other members of a clearing organization shall be netted in accordance with and subject to the conditions of any applicable netting contract.

#### (b) Limitation of obligation to make payment

The only obligation, if any, of a member of a clearing organization to make payment with respect to covered contractual payment obligations arising under a single netting contract to any other member of a clearing organization shall be equal to its net obligation arising under that netting contract, and no such obligation shall exist if there is no net obligation.

**(c) Limitation on right to receive payment**

The only right, if any, of a member of a clearing organization to receive payment with respect to a covered contractual payment entitlement arising under a single netting contract from other members of a clearing organization shall be equal to its net entitlement arising under that netting contract, and no such right shall exist if there is no net entitlement.

**(d) Entitlement of failed members**

The net entitlement, if any, of any failed member of a clearing organization shall be paid to the failed member in accordance with, and subject to the conditions of, the applicable netting contract.

**(e) Obligations of failed members**

The net obligation, if any, of any failed member of a clearing organization shall be determined in accordance with, and subject to the conditions of, the applicable netting contract.

**(f) Limitation on claims for entitlement**

A failed member of a clearing organization shall have no recognizable claim against any member of a clearing organization for any amount based on such covered contractual payment entitlements other than its net entitlement.

**(g) Effectiveness notwithstanding status as member**

This section shall be given effect notwithstanding that a member is a failed member.

---

This statute only goes so far. Suppose a failed participant is not a U.S. bank. CHIPS participants include substantial numbers of branches of foreign banks whose bankruptcy would be handled abroad, and foreign countries may not have clear rules establishing the validity of netting in bankruptcy.

The major industrialized countries' central banks have promulgated minimum standards for "Netting Schemes" which includes the requirement that "[n]etting schemes should have a well founded legal basis under all relevant jurisdictions," Bank for International Settlements, Report of the Committee on Interbank Netting Schemes of the Central Banks of the Group of Ten Countries 5 (1990) ("Lamfalussy Report"). The New York Fed has received letters from counsel to CHIPS participants stating that their home countries would respect the netting. But these are only opinions; in many cases the law is unclear. Furthermore, it is clear that in some major countries netting would not be respected. In Italy and the Netherlands, bank liquidators employing the so-called "zero-hour clause" can revoke all payments of a failed bank on the day it becomes bankrupt. Working Group on EC Payments Systems, Report to The Committee of Governors of The Central Banks of The Member States of the European Economic Community on Minimum Common Features for Domestic Payment Systems 27 (November 1993).

The problem of the uncertainty of foreign laws may not be that serious, however, for U.S. banks. As the BCCI bankruptcy demonstrated, any foreign bank that fails will have substantial dollar balances held with U.S. banks, and U.S. authorities are likely to use these assets for the benefit of U.S. creditors, including U.S. banks. See H. Scott, Multinational Bank Insolvencies: The United States and BCCI, in *Comparative Commercial Insolvency Law*, ed. J. Ziegel (Oxford University Press, 1994).

### *Notes*

The United Kingdom currently has a version of CHIPS called CHAPS but has no equivalent to FedWire. Consider the following excerpt from P. Allsopp, Payments Systems and Risk, Banking World 22, 23–24 (May 1993). Mr. Allsopp is head of the Payments System Division of the Banking Department of the Bank of England:

"Reduction. In an end-of-day settlement system it is not possible for a bank to avoid acquiring an involuntary exposure to another bank, if it wishes to receive payments for credit to its customers. It is, however, possible to take steps to control those exposures.

One way is to place explicit limits on them: such limits have, for instance, been a feature of CHIPS, in New York, for some years, and they have successfully begun to be implemented in CHAPS from last year.

There is, however, a level below which these limits cannot be reduced, even by means of collateral, if the payment system is to continue to function efficiently, by which I mean that it will handle in a timely fashion the legitimate payment needs of the participating banks and their customers. Thus a regime of limits, however, constructed, is liable to leave some residual risk in the system.

The problem for any central banks is that, if it accepts that one of its domestic payment systems should retain a residual risk, in the event that the risk crystallizes, the central bank may find that it has inescapably picked up part, if not all, of the responsibility for covering it. It is not acceptable to have a private sector payment system relying on implicit central bank support against a risk inherent in the design of the system. Public funds cannot be used to, in effect, underwrite private sector risks. Hence the third stage, elimination of this interbank credit risk.

Risk elimination. One approach to this, which has been accepted by the members of CHAPS as an objective for 1995, and is being pursued in a number of other countries also, is to transform the end-of-day net settlement system into a real time gross settlement system, in which each payment instruction from the sending bank is settled across the accounts of the two banks in the books of the central bank before it is sent on to the beneficiary bank. Thus, the beneficiary bank receives final funds, by way of an irrevocable credit to its account with the central bank, and it can immediately pass good value to its customer, or use the funds to meet its own obligations elsewhere, without any exposure to the sending bank.

What that approach does, of course, imply is that if the payment is transferred between the accounts of the two banks before the sending bank has sufficient good funds to support the outpayment, the central bank—the Bank of England, for CHAPS—will itself acquire an exposure to the sending bank."

Do you agree with the approach being taken in the United Kingdom?

## C. HERSTATT RISK

An important feature of the international payment system is that different payment systems of different countries operate at different times. This creates "Herstatt risk" as explained below. Herstatt was a German bank that failed in 1975 with unsettled foreign exchange positions.

### K. TANIGUCHI, "HERSTATT RISK"

in Kinyuhomujijo
No. 1305 (1991)
Pp. 14–18.

*BCCI and Herstatt Risk*

1. Herstatt Risk

Herstatt risk, the risk due to the time-lag in payments for foreign exchange transactions, is a concern over the course of a transaction, and was actually manifested when BCCI became insolvent last year.

What is Herstatt risk? I will use Yen–Dollar transactions as an example. In Yen–Dollar transactions, Yen delivery takes place through either the Check Collection System or the Foreign Exchange Yen Clearing System. Suppose Bank A sells Yen against dollars to Bank B (on a spot basis) on October 1st. Bank B, payee of the Yen, brings the bill to the central Check Collection System on October 3nd. The net amount of all the checks and bills is calculated on that day and the final settlement of this net amount takes place at 10 AM on October 2nd, in the account of the Bank of Japan ("BOJ"). This is the normal settlement procedure for domestic banks.

In the case where one (or both) of the parties is a foreign bank, the Foreign Exchange Yen Clearing System operated by BOJ is usually utilized. In this system, Bank A, the payor, inputs the payment instructions into the computer terminal of the system between 9 AM and 1:45 PM on October 3rd. The settlement is simultaneous.

On the Dollar side, the payment takes place in New York by the New York branch of the bank (or a correspondent bank) using CHIPS, and is finally settled in Federal Reserve accounts. In Tokyo, however, there is a special system, called the Tokyo Dollar Clearing System, operated by Chase Manhattan Bank ("Chase"). In this system, both Bank A and Bank B have accounts at Chase's Tokyo branch and settle Dollar transactions multi-laterally by intra-branch fund transfers. The net amount of the account is settled between Chase (New York) and New York branches of other banks (correspondent banks) through CHIPS at 6 PM (New York time) on the settlement date (in the instant case, October 3rd in New York, i.e., 8 AM on October 4th in Tokyo).

2. The BCCI Case

In the BCCI case, Herstatt risk was manifested because the insolvency procedures by British and Luxembourg authorities were started at noon London time (8 PM Tokyo time) and assets were frozen by the New York authorities at 1 PM London time (9 PM Tokyo time; 8 AM New York time). Thus, BCCI became insolvent 7–8 hours after the Yen settlement (Tokyo 1 PM) and 10 hours before the Dollar settlement.

3. Preventing Herstatt Risk

There are various means by which actualization of Herstatt risk might be prevented, but each means has problems.

(1) International "Against Payment" System.

If an international "against payment" system could be established for different currencies, the risk could be eliminated. But unlike securities clearing systems (Euro–Clear and CEDEL), no such system yet exists because: i) the payment system is deeply rooted in currency sovereignty and countries are unwilling to surrender such sovereignty, and ii) such a system would be too costly.

(2) Extension of Payment System Operating Hours

The overlap of payment system operating hours among various countries would considerably reduce Herstatt risk, but not eliminate it entirely. The Federal Reserve Board is now considering the extension of FedWire operating hours by changing the starting time from 8:30 AM to 6:30 AM. In Japan, the Zengin System, the domestic fund transfer system, is considering the same-day settlement system by changing the settlement time from 1 PM of the day following input to 6 PM of the same day, but the effect of such changes would be quite limited, as long as the operating hours of CHIPS remained unchanged.

(3) The Timing of Insolvency Procedures

Herstatt risk would not have been actualized in the BCCI case if the insolvency procedures had been started after the New York settlement time and before the opening of the Tokyo market. But this solution would also be difficult in some cases. For example, in the BCCI case, local law required that the insolvency procedures take place during business hours in Luxembourg.

(4) Netting by Novation

Netting by Novations (Obligation Netting) before the settlement date is useful for reducing Herstatt risk. The BIS Basle Committee is now discussing the treatment of netting under the minimum capital requirements.

(5) Inclusion of Foreign Exchange Risk under Capital Requirements

Note that Herstatt Risk is not taken into account under the current BIS capital requirement formula because foreign exchange forward transactions with less than 14 day maturity are considered to have no credit risk. BIS is now discussing the inclusion of foreign exchange risks into the framework of the capital requirements. To account for foreign exchange risks, the so-called "BOE method" now prevails. In the BOE method, the position is defined as the summation of net short positions of currencies including domestic currency. The risk weight is 100%, i.e., a bank is required to hold capital in an amount of 8% of the position. One problem of this approach is that it does not account for differences in the volatility of currencies and currency-pairs (e.g., the DM–Pound rate is less volatile than the Yen–Dollar rate), and it may thus distort the banks' positions (holding more volatile currencies requires the same capital as holding less volatile ones).

---

In February 1994, the Federal Reserve announced that beginning in 1997 it would extend its operating hours by eight hours, opening at 12:30 a.m. eastern time and closing at 6:30 p.m. Will this reduce Herstatt risk?

## D. SOME ASPECTS OF THE INTERNATIONAL PAYMENT SYSTEM

### 1. Types of Domestic Payment Systems

CHIPS (net) and/or FedWire (gross) type systems exist in the currencies of all major countries, as indicated in the following Table from C. Borio, D. Russo and P. Van den Bergh, Payment System Arrangements and Related Policy Issues: A Cross Country Comparison in *Proceedings of the Workshop on Payment System Issues in the Perspective of European Monetary Unification,* ed. Banca D'Italia 31, 57 (1991).

Table 11

Salient features of selected large-value interbank funds transfer systems

| | Gross (G) or net (N) settlement | Underlying transactions | | | | Automated (A) or manual (M) | Installation date |
|---|---|---|---|---|---|---|---|
| | | Commercial | Money market | Foreign exchange and international | Securities market | | |
| **Belgium** | | | | | | | |
| C.E.C. | N | * | | | | A | 1986 [1] |
| **Canada** | | | | | | | |
| IIPS | G [2] | * | * | * | | A | 1976 |
| **France** | | | | | | | |
| SAGITTAIRE | N | * | * | * | | A | 1984 |
| **Germany** | | | | | | | |
| Daily Clearing | N | * | * | * | | M | 1990 |
| CB Express System | G | * | * | * | | A | 1987 |
| **Italy** | | | | | | | |
| BISS | G | * | * | | * | A | 1988 |
| ME | N | * | * | * | * | A | 1989 |
| SIPS | N | | * | * | | A | 1989 |
| **Japan** | | | | | | | |
| BOJ-NET | G | * | * | | * | A | 1988 |
| FEYSS | N | | | * | | A | 1989 |
| Zengin System | N | * | | | * | A | 1987 [3] |
| CB Cheque System | N | * | * | | * | M | |
| **Netherlands** | | | | | | | |
| CB Current Account | G | | * | | | A | 1985 |
| BCH-S.W.I.F.T. | N | * | * | * | * | A | 1982 |
| **Sweden** | | | | | | | |
| CB Clearing/Interbank | G [4] | * | * | * | * | A | 1986 |
| **Switzerland** | | | | | | | |
| SIC | G | * | * | * | | A | 1987 |
| **United Kingdom** | | | | | | | |
| CHAPS | N | * | * | * | * | A | 1984 |
| Town Clearing | N | * | * | * | * | M | 1946 |
| **United States** | | | | | | | |
| Fedwire | G | * | * | * | * | A | 1982 [5] |
| CHIPS | N | * | * | * | | A | 1970 [6] |

1. 1974–75 for the exchange of magnetic media; 1986–87 for telecommunication.
2. The receiving bank creates a paper document called an inter-member debit voucher for each credit transfer received. These vouchers are delivered to the sending bank in batches, for which value and volume counts are entered into the Automated Clearing and Settlement System (ACSS), a netting scheme operated by the Canadian Payments Association.
3. Originally 1973.
4. The system has been designed to allow participants to enter funds transfer instructions continuously. If the instructions are confirmed by the counterparty, settlement takes place on the central bank's books immediately. The system is, however, also used to settle on an overall net basis at noon all netted interbank transactions executed through the various domestic clearing systems.
5. Date of the latest upgrade of the communications system. The system was originally set up in 1914 and the first fully automated system was implemented in 1973.
6. Same-day settlement introduced in 1981, risk management measures in 1984 and 1986 and loss-sharing and collateral requirements in 1990.

The following chart shows the global time-zone relationships between various national payment systems. It is the lack of overlap that is at the heart of the Herstatt risk.

## BANK FOR INTERNATIONAL SETTLEMENTS, REPORT OF THE COMMITTEE ON PAYMENT AND SETTLEMENT SYSTEMS OF THE CENTRAL BANKS OF THE GROUP OF TEN COUNTRIES

Central Bank Payment and Settlement Services With Respect to Cross–Border and Multi–Currency Transactions 19 (September 1993).

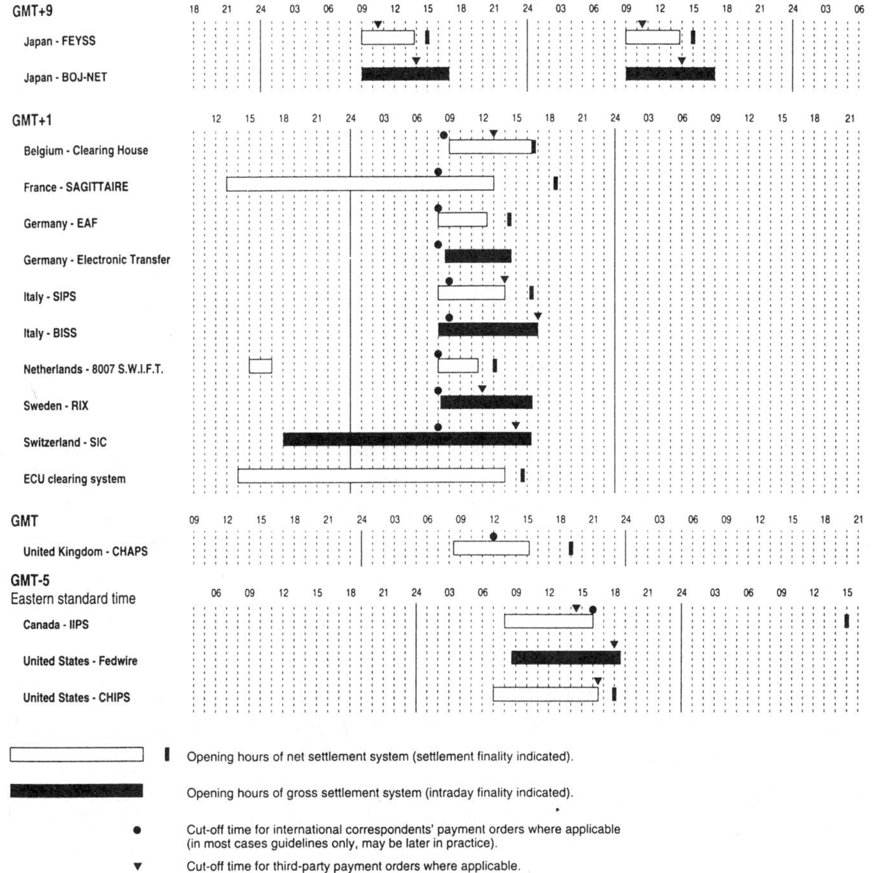


* The diagram shows the opening hours, as of August 1993, of selected interbank funds transfer systems as they relate to the same value day; some systems, including SAGITTAIRE and the ECU clearing system, may accept payment orders for a number of value days. As indicated, some systems open on the day before the value day. For Canada, settlement finality for IIPS occurs on the next business day, with retroactive value dating. Precise information on opening hours and cut-off times is provided in the table. For FEYSS, Fedwire and CHIPS, the cut-off time for third-party and international correspondents' payment orders is the same.

Note that the operating hours of the U.S. and Japanese systems have no overlap. Japan is 14 hours ahead of the U.S. so when CHIPS opens at 7:00 a.m. EST (12 noon GMT), it is 9:00 p.m. Tokyo time.

## 2. International Payment Systems

In addition to domestic systems, there are payment systems that are set up to operate on a cross-border basis.

COMMITTEE OF GOVERNORS OF THE CENTRAL BANKS OF THE MEMBER STATES OF THE EUROPEAN ECONOMIC COMMUNITY, AD HOC WORKING GROUP ON EC PAYMENT SYSTEMS

Payment Systems in EC Member States (September 1992).

## SECTION 3: NETTING SYSTEMS FOR FOREIGN EXCHANGE CONTRACTS

### 3.2. FX NET

#### *3.2.1. Netting mechanisms*

FX NET Limited is a limited partnership formed under English Law, owned by the UK subsidiaries of 12 major banks. It facilitates bilateral netting for spot and forward foreign exchange obligations between participating banks, using the concept of netting by novation. Banks are able to participate in FX NET by obtaining the necessary software package (prepared by Quotron) under license from FX NET for installation in their own in-house systems.

Through participation in FX NET, banks are able to reduce their credit and liquidity risks from gross to bilateral net positions for each of their branches which participate in the service, vis-à-vis branches of other banks.

Once a bank has installed the FX NET/Quotron software, it is then free to negotiate which other participants to net with and in which currencies. Within this process, FX NET provides well-documented model netting agreements which its participants may choose to use, though it is each participant's responsibility to obtain independent legal advice regarding the effectiveness of these agreements.

As of February 1992, 31 bank branches in London, New York, Los Angeles, Tokyo and Singapore were participating in FX NET, netting both within each centre and between different centres. In addition, a further 16 branches of existing, as well as new member banks, were preparing to join FX NET in these financial centres as well as in Hong Kong, whilst banks were also considering the establishment of FX NET in Paris and Zürich.

#### *3.2.2. Central banks oversight*

In early 1986, before FX NET was first implemented in pilot form, formal approval was sought from the Bank of England and the Federal Reserve Bank of New York (FRBNY). The Bank of England's approval was given in the following terms (similar to those of the FRBNY):

(i) each participant bank would be expected to satisfy itself as to the legal validity of netting by novation in the UK, and in the country of origin of each of its participating counterparties;

(ii) a commensurate reduction would be expected in each participant's limits on such counterparties;

(iii) these aspects of participation would be subjects for discussion during the routine prudential interviews between each participant in the UK and the Bank of England in its role of banking supervisor.

Both the Bank of England's and the FRBNY's formal responses form part of the package for legal documentation that FX NET currently provides to its participants.

## SECTION 5: THE ECU CLEARING AND SETTLEMENT SYSTEM

### 5.1. Origin of the System

The Private ECU Clearing and Settlement System was developed in order to replace a clearing scheme for the settlement of private ECU balances which had been set up in 1982 by a small group of commercial banks active in the ECU market. This original scheme, known as MESA (Mutual ECU Settlement Accounts), soon proved to be ill-suited to handling the increasing number of ECU payment orders between a growing circle of financial institutions.

The ECU clearing banks and the BIS explored the possibility of creating a system in which the BIS would act as a settling agent. The Committee of Governors was consulted prior to setting up the present system and, in March 1983, it issued certain guidelines for the operation of the system.

### 5.2. Major participants to the System

*The Association Bancaire pour l'Écu—ECU Banking Association (EBA)* is a body formed under French Law in September 1985, whose headquarters are in Paris. Membership is open to commercial banks which have their head office or branch in one of the EC countries and which demonstrate sufficient interest in the development of ECU transactions; members which meet certain criteria set forth in the EBA clearing rules, may also be designated as clearing banks.

*The Bank for International Settlements (BIS),* as agent of the individual clearing banks, acts as the settlement bank for the system. Each clearing bank agrees to maintain an account with the BIS which may only be used for settlement operations, does not bear interest and may never show a debit balance; as a result, the BIS does not take any credit risk in the ECU clearing and settlement system.

*S.W.I.F.T. Service Partners (SSP)* is a subsidiary of S.W.I.F.T. which acts as the netting centre of the System and provides the data support for the netting phase.

### 5.3. Operating rules of the System

*The netting stage* lasts until 14.00 (Brussels time) every working day. During this period, clearing banks exchange payment orders in ECUs through the netting centre. Immediately after 14.00, the netting centre determines the preliminary credit or debit balances of each clearing bank, value same day; it then reports all these balances to the BIS and notifies each clearing bank of its preliminary balance.

*The borrowing and lending stage* begins immediately after the netting phase. In this clearing system, where the sum of preliminary debit balances is equal to the sum of preliminary credit balances, those clearing banks in a debtor position must, in a second phase up to 3.15 p.m., borrow funds from creditor banks in order to reduce their preliminary debit balances to an amount not exceeding ECU 1 million.[6]

Shortly after 3.15 p.m., the netting centre determines the final netting balances, notifies each ECU clearing bank of its own balance and reports all balances to the BIS. These final balances—which take account of all bilateral operations which the clearing banks have been able to conclude with each other between 2.00 and 3.15 p.m.—must be confirmed by each bank to the BIS before 3.45 p.m.

If then, a clearing bank's netting balance remains in debit of more than ECU 1 million, the debtor clearing bank must, before 3.45 p.m., require the assistance of the BIS, with a view to borrowing ECUs from other clearing banks to permit the settlement of its final netting balance.

Any sum thus transferred constitutes a loan between the banks in question, value the same working day and repayable the following working day. All these transactions bear interest at a fixed rate which is calculated every day by the BIS according to the "tomorrow/next" ECU interest rate, reported to it by the clearing banks on the previous day.

At 3.45 p.m. the BIS is normally able to carry out *the settlement operations* by debiting or crediting the respective ECU sight accounts held in its books with the amounts necessary to square all the corresponding netting balances.

If after 3.45 p.m., owing to some incident, a clearing bank is unable to cover its debit position, the BIS may, as far as possible, proceed with the operations authorised by the risk reduction measures described below. If however, cover cannot be produced, an "unwind" procedure occurs. The entire clearing for that day is then carried over to the following working day; all payments to and by the debtor bank are withdrawn from the day's clearing transactions and new balances calculated and added to the clearing for the following settlement day. This "next day" solution means that beneficiaries of payments would not have good funds until the completion of the clearing the next day. Furthermore, the clearing may have to be cancelled if the BIS does not receive notification of all the final netting balances from the netting centre. So far, it has never been necessary to carry over or cancel any clearing.

**6.** This remaining position will be then covered during the settlement stage by the transfer of funds, up to 1 million ECU per account, that the BIS is entitled to organise under the terms of the standing transfer order it has received from each clearing bank.

### 5.4. Volume of transactions

At mid-November 1991, the System cleared about 5,600 transactions every day among the 44 clearing banks for an amount of about 38 billion ECUs.

## SECTION 6: S.W.I.F.T.

### 6.1. The Organisation

The Society for Worldwide Interbank Financial Telecommunication (S.W.I.F.T. s.c.) is a private company, created in Belgium in 1973, which engages in the transmission of financial messages for the benefit of its shareholding member banks and of other approved categories of financial institutions. The S.W.I.F.T. Group is also involved in the development and marketing of specific network applications and in research, development, marketing and sales of terminals and related software. S.W.I.F.T. s.c. is a cooperative company, owned by 1,963 banks worldwide.[7] It fully owns S.W.I.F.T. Service Partners s.a. (SSP) and S.W.I.F.T. Terminal Services s.a. (STS), two limited liability companies also incorporated in Belgium, as well as a number of subsidiaries in other countries and a re-insurance company in Luxembourg, through which part of the Group's insurance is placed.

S.W.I.F.T. transmits financial messages between the 3,648 financial institutions connected to the company's proprietary network which covers 73 countries. While access to the network has traditionally been restricted to S.W.I.F.T. s.c.'s shareholding members and their subsidiaries (sub-members)—all of whom are banks—a number of so-called participants have been allowed to use it since 1987 (at the end of 1991 there were 78). These participants include securities brokers and dealers and various other institutions, mostly in the securities business, such as Euroclear and Cedel. Participants are not shareholders in S.W.I.F.T. s.c. and their message traffic over the network is restricted. Some categories of participants may, for instance, neither send nor receive certain types of messages, while other categories may exchange specific messages with their banks (e.g. payment messages), but not with each other.

### 6.2. Basic Services

The core service offered by S.W.I.F.T. s.c. consists of operating its proprietary network (composed of computer facilities, switching equipment, leased lines and related software) to handle the exchange of financial messages. The network functions comprise of the acceptance, validation, storing and delivery of messages. The network, which is accessible 24 hours a day, seven days a week, handled a total message traffic of 365 million in 1991 or an average of about 1.5 million per business day. These messages are highly structured and cover a wide range of banking and other transactions such as payment orders, foreign

7. All figures in this section relate to the end of 1991 or to the year 1991.

exchange confirmations and securities deliveries. There are nine categories of banking messages covering more than 120 message types, each designed to meet specific data requirements of the transactions involved. S.W.I.F.T., with its members, is active in enhancing existing message text standards and developing new standards, for the benefit of all network users. Thus, for instance, S.W.I.F.T. has developed Bank Identifier Codes (BIC) which amount to a universal standard for identifying financial institutions in telecommunication messages. More recently, S.W.I.F.T. has become actively involved in drawing up EDIFACT standards.

To ensure secrecy, each message is automatically encrypted by S.W.I.F.T. when it enters the network while users have the option to encrypt the message flow between their in-house terminals and their S.W.I.F.T. access point. Each message also contains an authenticator which permits the identification of the sender and receiver and which guarantees that the message text has not been modified during transmission. Authentication is based on a common algorithm provided by S.W.I.F.T. and on bilateral keys, known only to the sending and receiving pair of users. The network's operating system generates a broad range of automatic reports on individual users' message traffic, for instance relating to undelivered messages, but users may also request special reports, such as terminal error reports, queue status reports and delivery status reports.

S.W.I.F.T. s.c. accepts a contractual responsibility, and associated financial liability in respect of the carriage and delivery of messages. The rules governing the use of the system and the company's responsibility and liability are set out in the S.W.I.F.T. users handbook, and are contractually binding on every member and participant. They spell out some of the responsibilities of the originating and receiving banks, and of S.W.I.F.T. itself, in respect of the timely transmission and handling of payment orders and other financial messages. The rules are often taken as a reference source for correspondent bank relationships.

### 6.3. Traffic size

Statistics on the geographical breakdown of S.W.I.F.T. users and of message flows over the network are shown in the tables. This shows a strong presence of EC members (especially Italy, Germany and France), sub-members (especially the United Kingdom) and participants (mainly located in the United Kingdom) in the S.W.I.F.T. user community. Banks in EC members countries also generate almost half of the traffic over the network and hold almost half of the shares in the company—with the banking community of France, Germany and the United Kingdom each holding around nine per cent.[8]

With respect to message traffic, the S.W.I.F.T. network may be used for both cross-border and internal domestic transactions involving mem-

8. The shareholdings in S.W.I.F.T. by individual members are a function of their share in message traffic over the network.

ber banks or participants. The proportion of domestic traffic in the total varies considerably from country to country, partly depending on the rules of the national telecommunication authority and partly on the types of alternative interbank telecommunication facilities available. Among EC countries, France and the United Kingdom generate the largest proportion of domestic traffic, in relation to their total traffic. In the case of France this reflects the fact that the SAGITTAIRE system uses S.W.I.F.T. as message carrier. Total intra EC traffic, including both domestic traffic within EC countries and cross-border traffic between EC countries, is around 60 per cent of the total traffic from EC countries. Reflecting the increasing diversification of the use of the network, the tables also shows that messages other than those relating to customer or bank transfers account for 45% of total S.W.I.F.T. traffic.

### 6.4. Value-added services

In addition to the basic service, S.W.I.F.T. provides application and processing services to groups of banks engaged in particular activities. One so-called value-added processing service relates to the ECU Banking Association's private *ECU Clearing and Settlement System,* described elsewhere in this chapter, for which ECU payment messages between the Association's members sent over the network are copied and forwarded to a central ECU netting computer. Another service, called *Accord,* was introduced in 1990. It is a computerised system for the automatic matching of foreign exchange and money market deal confirmations sent through the S.W.I.F.T. system. In 1991, the Accord service was extended to include an advisory bilateral foreign exchange netting service: payment information from matched confirmations are extracted to provide statements of bilateral net positions, which subscribers can use in the implementation of bilateral netting agreements. Both the ECU netting and Accord services are supplied by S.W.I.F.T. Service Partners (SSP), with the messages carried by the network.

In 1991, S.W.I.F.T. announced a new application service for its members and participants—Interbank File Transfer (IFT). This allows bulk data to be sent across the network, for example reports between branches of the same bank, or batches of low-value payment orders. For the latter application (Mass Payments Facility), a bulk payments format has been devised, generic enough to allow receiving banks to input the instructions into their domestic automated clearing house(s). In the long term, the IFT facility will also be used to exchange EDI messages, using EDIFACT standards.

Finally, through its second major subsidiary, S.W.I.F.T. Terminal Services (STS), S.W.I.F.T. supplies specialised hardware and software to its members for handling their message traffic. STS also provides computer-based training programmes for S.W.I.F.T. users.

### 6.5. Nature of S.W.I.F.T. messages

A S.W.I.F.T. message containing a payment order is different from those electronic messages passing through domestic large-value funds transfer systems because the S.W.I.F.T. payment order does not, by itself, create an irrevocable obligation on the part of the sending bank. Financial institutions exchanging S.W.I.F.T. messages have to arrange the clearing and/or settlement of the incoming payment orders themselves, either by relying on bilateral correspondent relationships which they have with one another or by forwarding incoming orders to domestic interbank funds transfer systems. However, an increasing number of major banks have introduced "straight-through processing", in which there is an automated linkage between their S.W.I.F.T. connection and their computer systems linking to the domestic payment system. Banks are also increasingly tending to treat an incoming S.W.I.F.T. payment order as authoritative, particularly if it includes the beneficiary's account number. Although these automated links will normally include, as in the case of manual procedures, internal mechanisms for controlling banks' exposures to their correspondents and customers, S.W.I.F.T. is often an integral part of interbank funds transfer systems, especially those handling internationally related payments. Furthermore, where S.W.I.F.T. messages are sent or copied to clearing houses or netting providers, as in the case of SAGITTAIRE in France or the ECU Clearing and Settlement System, they are the backbone for the particular funds transfer systems involved. The technical standards set by the S.W.I.F.T. community for international financial transaction messages—including those drawn up in cooperation with international bodies such as ISO and with EDIFACT—are increasingly used by outside organisations and also tend to set the norm for many countries' domestic financial messages.

---

This excerpt from H. Scott, A Payment System role for a European System of Central Banks, in Committee for the Monetary Union of Europe, *For a Common Currency* 77, 89–90 (1990), adds some information about Euroclear and Cedel, arrangements to clear and settle internationally traded securities.

**Euroclear**

The Euroclear is operated by the Brussels branch of Morgan Guaranty Trust Company of New York (Morgan–Brussels) under contract with Euroclear Clearance System Societe Cooperative, a Belgian cooperative corporation in which over 2200 of the 2500 participants in the Euroclear Clearance System are members. The Euroclear System clears and settles more than 33,000 different internationally-traded debt and equity instruments including domestic government debt from eleven countries. The value of securities held on behalf of Euroclear participants at the end of 1989 was approximately $782 billion, with daily instruction volume averaging over 30,000. The System cleared approximately $3.4 trillion of securities in the same year. Since 1985, the 5 year annual compound growth of turnover has been 23%.

The system permits participants to confirm, clear and settle trades by book-entry in 27 currencies. Participants maintain securities and cash accounts in these currencies with Morgan–Brussels. While the funds accounts are generally used for the settlement of securities trades, fund can be received into the System, transferred to other participants through debit and credit entries on Morgan–Brussels books, or transferred out of the system. In this sense Morgan functions as a clearing bank for funds transfers. Participants communicate through one central point in Brussels, the Euroclear Operations Centre ("EOC"), principally over EUCLID, a proprietary telecommunications system. Participants may also communicate with EOC by SWIFT or telex.

The Euroclear securities settlement process takes place during the night prior to the relevant value date for settlement. Transactions reflected in matched instructions from the buyer and seller are settled if the seller has sufficient securities in its account and if the buyer has adequate cash or credit. Once entries are made on the settlement, it is final and cannot be revoked by Morgan–Brussels. Certain settlements with external counter-parties are conditional upon acceptance of delivery, or payment, in other clearance and settlement systems.

Sellers who, either themselves prior to settlement processing or, by prior arrangement, pursuant to automatic procedures, identify a shortage in their securities positions, may borrow securities from other participants. Return of loaned securities, income payments and other entitlements are guaranteed by Morgan–Brussels.

In order to finance net purchases to be settled in the securities settlement processing for value on a settlement date, participants may "preadvise" funds for the value on a settlement date by 10:00 a.m. on the business day prior to the value date. Morgan–Brussels makes a credit decision as to whether to make credit available in respect to such preadvises in the overnight processing.

Preadvised funding requires the participant to transfer funds to Morgan–Brussels' cash correspondent, a bank designated to receive payments on Morgan's behalf in a given currency, for value the settlement date. Thus, for example, for dollar transfers, the preadvising participant arranges for delivery of funds to the dollar cash correspondent (Morgan–New York) by the close of business in New York on the settlement date. Thus generally, Morgan is at risk from the time any credit extension is used during the overnight securities settlement processing in Brussels until final credit of funds to its account at the relevant cash correspondent.

Thus, for example, US dollar transfers would become final at the time of transfer of Fed Funds over FedWire, or at the close of business for CHIPS transfers (6:00 p.m. New York time on the value date, 12 midnight in Brussels). Morgan–Brussels would then have slightly less than 24 hours credit exposure. In the event a preadvising participant fails to cover the credit extended by Morgan–Brussels, Morgan–Brussels can look to pledged securities and cash accounts of the debtor, if the credit is secured on such basis.

**Cedel**

Cedel like Euroclear, is a system which provides for the custody and transfer of internationally traded securities. Approximately 100 financial institutions from 20 countries are shareholders of Cedel, a limited liability Luxembourg company (1). Currently there are more than 2,000 participants from 66 different countries. At year end 1989, Cedel held $344.5 billion of securities, and cleared $1.8 trillion in securities during the same year (2).

Securities are held by 50 depositary banks, and funds by approximately 40 correspondent banks, located in various countries. Securities and funds are denominated in 27 different currencies. Participants hold accounts with Cedel which reflects their securities and funds balances with the depositary and correspondent banks. The major means of communicating instructions to Cedel is through CEDCOM, the Cedel Communication System. The system can be accessed through General Electric and IBM networks, SWIFT, or Telekurs, the Swiss financial information service.

Buyers and sellers of securities send trade instructions to Cedel in Luxembourg by noon of the settlement date. The processing cycle extends from noon until 4:00 p.m. Luxembourg time. Cedel calculates the net securities and funds positions of each participant, and posts the resulting entries to its books, which reflect the underlying movement of funds and securities in the banking system.

Participants may establish a 48 hour technical overdraft facility or tripartite financing agreement to cover the payment for incoming securities with the approval of the Cedel Admission and Credit Subcommittee. The technical overdraft represents a collateralized credit extended by Cedel for a short period. The Tripartite Financing Agreement, concluded between the participant and a financing bank under which Cedel monitors compliance with collateral requirements, provides longer term financing. Technical overdraft facilities are relatively small in size; fewer than half of all participants have such facilities available to them. Many of the smaller participants have guarantees from parents or third parties.

In addition to these credit arrangements, participants can use a preadvise procedure to fund securities purchases. Preadvises in same day funds (US and Canadian dollar) must be received by 11:00 a.m. of the day of the processing cycle. Other currencies must be preadvised at an earlier date. Settlement is complete at 5:00 p.m. (11:00 a.m. New York time). This exposes Cedel to a 7 hour settlement risk since CHIPS does not close until 12:00 a.m. Luxembourg time. If a participant fails to cover his preadvise or overdraft within the 48 hour period, Cedel will either block the account or take appropriate steps to liquidate collateral. The value of the collateral is marked to market with a haircut for market risk.

### *Questions*

1. For large-value payments, ECU clearing is a multilateral clearing in a "european" monetary unit, the ECU, functioning outside of any country. But since the ECU is not actually a currency of any country, no central bank can easily loan banks ECU. This greatly impedes the liquidity of the system. Net debtors in the system can only settle by borrowing from net creditors in the system. Is this a risky arrangement?

2. Could private banks devise a payments system in which payments in different currencies were netted against each other so that each bank would make one settlement for payments in all currencies at the end of the day? Does Euroclear offer something close to this? What would be the benefits of the arrangement? What would be the operating hours? How would banks borrow to meet settlements when their home currency markets were closed? What would need to be done about changes in exchange rates, if anything?

---

Consider the following alternative of a central bank provided multi-currency net settlement, as suggested in Bank for International Settlements, Report of the Committee on Payment and Settlement Systems of the central banks of the Group of Ten countries, *Central Bank Payment and Settlement Services With Respect to Cross–Border and Multi–Currency Transactions* 24–25 (September 1993).

### Multi-currency payment and settlement services

4.15 Another possible option might involve the joint offering of multi-currency payment and settlement services. Multi-currency accounts and settlement facilities might be provided by the central banks of issue through a "common agent". The rationale for developing and offering these multi-currency services would be to support the elimination of the current risks associated with non-DVP settlements by creating the technical ability to conduct a DVP settlement of all relevant currencies at one location.

4.16 In the basic model considered by the Working Group, a central bank controlled common agent could be established to accept deposits in multiple currencies and to facilitate final transfers between these accounts. The central bank common agent would accept private sector deposits denominated in the currencies of issue of the controlling central banks. Deposits with the common agent would, in turn, be fully backed by deposits at the respective central banks of issue (i.e. subject to a 100% reserve requirement); this is to ensure that central banks of issue retain full authority over the process of creating central bank money in their currencies. To guarantee that deposits at the common agent are fully backed by deposits at the central banks of issue, deposits into and withdrawals from accounts at the common agent would require corresponding final transfers between accounts on the books of the respective central banks of issue. Accordingly, the respective large-value funds transfer systems would need to offer intraday final transfer capabilities.

4.17 A variant of this model would involve one or more central banks offering settlement accounts in foreign currencies. The services offered would be similar to those envisaged for the common agent. The central bank or banks playing this role would operate the accounts in each currency in accordance with predefined authority from the central bank of issue. As in the case of the common agent, foreign currency deposits in these accounts would represent deposits at the central banks of issue.

4.18 The purpose of collectively offering multi-currency services would be similar to that of creating an overlap in the operating hours (with or without direct operational and informational links) of the major large-value funds transfer systems: to provide the private sector with the technical ability to achieve on the same value date DVP in the settlement of multi-currency obligations. With multi-currency services this would be accomplished by effecting settlement over operational accounts in each currency held either at the common agent or, in the case of the variant, at one or more individual central banks. In both cases, an important issue is whether arrangements would be in place to provide assurances that sufficient liquidity would be available to complete settlement in the relevant currencies.

4.19 Multi-currency payment and settlement services could be used by multilateral clearing houses, should they be established, and their members to settle net multi-currency obligations. Similar to the situation where an overlap exists in the operating hours of the major payments systems, the actual DVP settlement process (i.e. the debiting and crediting of the relevant accounts) could be managed either by the clearing house and its participants or by the controlling central banks through a common agent. The issues that would arise if these services were also used by the counterparties to individual or bilaterally netted transactions are discussed in Section 5.

4.20 Establishing and operating central bank multi-currency payment and settlement services would require a high degree of central bank coordination and cooperation. Integrated central bank policies and operational links would be needed to create and run a common agent. Furthermore, in setting up and operating the technical and settlement arrangements, central banks would likely need to share confidential information.

---

## 3. Off–Shore Dollar Payment Systems

Another aspect of the international payment system is offshore settlement. For example, there are various methods by which banks can clear dollar payments outside the United States through formal clearing systems. For example, there are the London Dollar Clearing Scheme (LDC) and the Tokyo Dollar Clearing system.

LDC clears United States dollar cheques and banker's drafts and payments (LDC items). Direct access to the clearing, administered by the Association for Payment Clearing Services (APACS) was limited in 1987 to seven major English banks ("Settlement Banks"), but other banks ("Agency Banks") have indirect access to the clearing through correspondent accounts with the banks that have direct access.

LDC is a net settlement system. On the basis of a day's clearing activities in London each Settlement Bank has a net position. A Settlement Bank's net positions are settled through New York on the same business day that they arise in London. Positions are determined by 4:30 p.m. London time, or 11:30 a.m. New York time. Instructions to New York correspondents must be sent out by 12 noon New York time, leaving ample time during the same business day in New York to complete the settlement.

A net debtor Settlement Bank would instruct its New York correspondent to transfer funds to the New York correspondent account of the Settlement Agent (each Settlement Bank acts in this capacity on a rotating basis). This transfer could go through CHIPS or be a book transfer on the books of a New York bank which is the correspondent for both the Settlement Agent and the net debtor Settlement Bank. Conversely, the Settlement Agent transfers funds to the New York correspondent of a net creditor Settlement Bank.

In addition to the LDC net settlement among Settlement Banks, bilateral settlements must take place between LDC Settlement Banks, e.g. Lloyd's Bank, and their Agency Banks, e.g. Bankers Trust's London branch (BTL). Thus, for a day's LDC clearing, (BTL) may be in a net credit or net debit position with Lloyd's. If BTL is in a net credit position, Lloyd's would transfer funds, through its correspondent in New York, via CHIPS, to Banker Trust's New York head office (BTNY) for the account of BTL, and if BTL were in a net debit position, BTL would transfer funds, through BTNY, via CHIPS, to Lloyd's New York correspondent, the settlement could take place by book-entries on the books of BTNY to the accounts of BTL and Lloyd's.

The Tokyo Dollar Clearing (TDC), which has existed since the occupation of Japan after World War II, is presently a clearing of all types of electronic dollar transfers among more than 180 participant banks and branches in Tokyo, operated by Chase Manhattan's Tokyo branch (Chase–Tokyo).

Participating banks send electronic transfers to each other during the Tokyo day that may represent payments for any transactions between participants, e.g. the dollar payment on a foreign exchange transaction, or payments by a customer of one participant in favor of a customer of another participant. Customers receiving payments get credit on the books of their banks in Tokyo. All payments are routed through the computer system of Chase–Tokyo.

At the end of the day's clearing (3 p.m. Tokyo time), Chase calculates the net debit and net credit positions of participants, and communicates this information to the participants and to Chase New York. Chase New York then transfers credits to net creditors, on its books, through CHIPS, or by FedWire, by 10 a.m. New York time (midnight same day in Tokyo). Net debtors must transfer credits to Chase in New York by the end of the CHIPS day. Net credit transfers by Chase are conditional on the net debtors settling with Chase by the end of the day.

As with LDC, TDC settlement takes place entirely in New York. But, also like LDC, the actual payments which underlie the TDC net calculation are made in Tokyo.

### *Notes and Questions*

1. Could offshore dollar netting systems be used to avoid U.S. regulation of on-shore netting systems like CHIPS? Can this be controlled?

2. Do these systems create risk to participants and to the U.S. payments system through which the net obligations are settled?

3. The Federal Reserve Board's September 1992 Payments System Policy Statement establishes guidance for offshore systems. They must be subject to central bank supervision, participants must identify significant risk, finality of settlement must be provided for, and settlement in the U.S. must be conducted through an identified settlement agent in a specified procedure.

---

### *Links to Other Chapters*

The payment system is the core of the financial system, and concern about its potential collapse coupled with multiple bank bankruptcies around the world, is responsible for much of the banking regulation examined in this book. The payment system is also crucial to securities markets. Settlement of securities transactions requires payments, as well as the movement of securities. A major concern for regulators is whether the failure of securities firms to settle positions could trigger failures of other securities firms, and their banks. Thus, virtually all of the Chapters in this book require a basic understanding of the payment system.

# Chapter X

# ASSET FREEZES

In this Chapter we use two cases to explore some political risks of holding eurodollar deposits. *Libyan Arab Foreign Bank v. Bankers Trust Co. (LAFB),* 1 Lloyd's Law Reports 259 [Q.B.1988], involves the attempted freeze by the United States (the country of the currency) of eurodollar accounts held in the United Kingdom, while Wells Fargo Asia Limited v. Citibank, N.A., 936 F.2d 723 (2d Cir.1991), cert. denied ___ U.S. ___, 112 S.Ct. 2990, 120 L.Ed.2d 868 (1992), on remand from 495 U.S. 660, 110 S.Ct. 2034, 109 L.Ed.2d 677 (1990), involves a freeze on repatriation of dollars by the Philippines (the country where the deposits were placed).

## A. FREEZES BY THE CURRENCY COUNTRY: *LAFB*

Mr. Justice STAUGHTON

The plaintiffs are a Libyan corporation, wholly owned by the Central Bank of Libya. They carry on what is described as an offshore banking business, in the sense that they do not engage in domestic banking within Libya. I shall call them "the Libyan Bank." The defendants are a New York corporation with their head office there. They no doubt have a number of branches in various parts of the world; but I am concerned with one in particular, their branch in London. I shall refer to them as "Bankers Trust," and when it is necessary to refer to particular offices as "Bankers Trust London" or "Bankers Trust New York."

In January 1986 the Libyan Bank had an account with Bankers Trust London, denominated in United States dollars. That was a call account, which meant that no cheque book was provided, interest was payable on the balance standing to the credit of the account at rates which varied from time to time, and some minimal period of notice might be required before instructions relating to the account had to be complied with. The suggestion in this case is that instructions would have to be given before noon if they were to be carried out that day. In English practice it would, I think be described as a species of deposit account. The amount standing to the credit of that account at the close of business on 8 January 1986 was U.S. $131,506,389.93. There may be a small element of subsequent adjustment in that figure. But the point is not material.

The Libyan Bank also had an account with Bankers Trust New York, again denominated in United States dollars. This was a demand account. No interest was paid on the balance, and no significant period of notice was required before instructions had to be complied with. But there was not, so far as I am aware, a cheque book. In England it would have been a current account. The amount standing to the credit of that account at the close of business on 8 January 1986 was U.S. $251,129,-084.53.

Relations between Libya and the United States in January 1986 were not good. At 8.06 p.m. New York time on 7 January the President of the United States of America issued an executive order, which had the force of law with immediate effect. It provided, so far as material:

> "Section 1. The following are prohibited, except to the extent provided in regulations which may hereafter be issued pursuant to this Order: ... (f) The grant or extension of credits or loans by any United States person to the Government of Libya, its instrumentalities and controlled entities."

That order did not in itself have any great effect on the events with which this case is concerned. But there followed it at 4.10 p.m. New York time on 8 January a second order, reading as follows:

> "I, Ronald Reagan, President of the United States, hereby order blocked all property and interests in property of the Government of Libya, its agencies, instrumentalities and controlled entities and the Central Bank of Libya that are in the United States that hereafter come within the United States or that are or hereafter come within the possession or control of U.S. persons including overseas branches of U.S. persons. The Secretary of the Treasury, in consultation with the Secretary of State, is authorized to employ all powers granted to me by the International Emergency Economic Powers Act 50 U.S.C. 1701 et seq. to carry out the provisions of this Order. This Order is effective immediately and shall be transmitted to the Congress and published in the Federal Register.
>
> Ronald Reagan
>
> The White House
>
> 8 January 1986"

It is not in dispute that Bankers Trust are a United States person; or that Bankers Trust London are an overseas branch of a United States person; or that the Libyan Bank are an agency, instrumentality or controlled entity of the Government of Libya. Consequently by the law of and prevailing in the State of New York (which I shall refer to as New York law for the sake of brevity) it was illegal at and after 4.10 p.m. on 8 January 1986 for Bankers Trust to make any payment or transfer of funds to or to the order of the Libyan Bank in New York, either by way of debit to the Libyan Bank's account or as the grant of credit or a loan. Similarly it was illegal, by the law of New York or of any other American state, for Bankers Trust to make any such payment or transfer of funds in London or anywhere else.

The United Kingdom Parliament did not enact any similar legislation. No doubt there were reasons of high policy for that forbearance; but with them I am not concerned. It is sufficient to say that nothing in English domestic law prohibited such a transaction. So the main issues in this case are concerned with the rules of conflict of laws, which determine when and to what extent the law of New York is given effect in our courts, and with the contractual obligations of banks. In a word, Bankers Trust say that they cannot, or at any rate are not obliged to, transfer a sum as large as U.S. $100m. or more without using the payment machinery that is available in New York; consequently they have a defence to the Libyan Bank's claim, because performance of this contract would have required them to commit an illegal act in New York. Alternatively they say that their contract with the Libyan Bank is governed by the law of New York, so that performance is for the time being illegal by the proper law of the contract.

*The Libyan Bank's claims*

These are as follows (using a slightly different system of numbering from that adopted in the pleadings and in argument):

(1) The first claim is for the balance of U.S. $131,506,389.93 standing to the credit of the London account at the close of business on 8 January 1986. It is said that this sum is due to the Libyan Bank, and can be claimed on a cause of action in debt. Alternatively it is said that Bankers Trust ought to have responded to demands for U.S. $131m. that were made by the Libyan Bank in various different ways after 8 January, and are liable in damages.

(2) If they are right on the first claim, the Libyan Bank further say that one or other of three sums ought to have been transferred from the New York account to the London account on 7 and 8 January, thus increasing the amount which they are entitled to recover. These are: (i) U.S. $165,200,000 on 7 January, *or* (ii) U.S. $6,700,000 on 8 January, *or* (iii) U.S. $161,400,000 on 8 January. Indeed it is said that the sum of U.S. $6,700,000 was in fact transferred to London on 8 January, with the consequence that the Libyan Bank are in any event entitled to recover that additional amount.

(3) Largely but not entirely as an alternative to the second claim, the Libyan Bank say that they gave a number of payment instructions to Bankers Trust New York for execution on 8 January, those instructions could and should have been executed before 4.10 p.m. on that day, but were not. Consequently the Libyan Bank claim damages in the sum of U.S. $226,147,213.88.

. . .

(6) Lastly there is a claim which is quite independent of the events of 7 and 8 January 1986 and President Reagan's executive orders. It is said that during the period from April 1984 to November 1985 Bankers Trust operated a system of transfers between the New York account and the London account, which was not in accordance with their contract

with the Libyan Bank. In consequence the Libyan Bank were deprived of interest for one day or three days on a succession of sums during that period. It is said that the loss suffered is of the order of $2m. Bankers Trust do not deny that, initially, the system of transfers which they operated during this period failed to accord with their contract. But they say that, by the doctrine of account stated or estoppel, the Libyan Bank are precluded from asserting this claim.

The issues thus raised, or at any rate those that arise under paragraph (1) above, are of great interest and some difficulty. Similar problems occurred a few years ago in connection with the freeze on Iranian assets by executive order of 14 November 1979, and litigation was commenced. But before any of those actions could come to trial the freeze was lifted. This time the problems have to be resolved.

*History of the banking relationship*

This can be considered in three stages. The first stage was from 1972 to 15 December 1980.

The Libyan Bank came into existence in June 1972. A correspondent relationship was established between the Libyan Bank and Bankers Trust. Initially an account was opened for that purpose with the Paris branch of Bankers Trust. But in April 1973 that account was closed, and an account opened with the London branch. It was described as a 7-day notice account. However, any requirement that notice of that length should be given before debits were allowed on the London account was not enforced. In this period the Libyan Bank did not wish to have any account with Bankers Trust New York. Transfers for the credit of the Libyan Bank used regularly to arrive at Bankers Trust New York, in accordance with the system most often used for transferring large dollar amounts, which I shall describe later. But they were dealt with by an instruction from Bankers Trust New York to Bankers Trust London to credit the account of the Libyan Bank there. Indeed the Libyan Bank insisted on that from time to time. Thus on 14 July 1973 they said in a telex to New York: "We also request immediate transfer of any funds you may receive in future for our favour to your London office." And on 17 July 1973 to London:

> "When we have agreed to have the account of Libyan Arab Foreign Bank with Bankers Trust I have made it very clear that no balance at all should be kept in New York and should be transferred immediately to our call account which started in Paris and now with you in London."

Certainly one motive for that attitude, and in 1973 possibly the only motive, was that dollar credit balances outside the United States earned a higher rate of interest than was obtainable in the United States. That is all that Eurodollars are—a credit in dollars outside the United States, whether in Europe or elsewhere. (It may be that one should add to this definition "at a bank" or "at an institution.") The interest rate is higher owing to the terms of the requirement imposed by the Federal

Reserve Board that banks should maintain an amount equal to a proportion of the deposits they receive on deposit interest-free with the Federal Reserve system. That requirement is less demanding in connection with deposits received by overseas branches.

In fact Bankers Trust New York had operated an account in New York, for the handling of transactions by the Libyan Bank. But that account was closed on 17 December 1973 in consequence of the above and other protests by the Libyan Bank.

There followed a long period of discussion and negotiation. Bankers Trust were dissatisfied because the London, so-called 7-days' notice, account was used as a current account. Large numbers of transactions occurred on it, but interest was paid on the balance. This was not thought to be profitable for Bankers Trust. Furthermore, transfers to or from the account would commonly be made through New York, with a risk of delay and the possibility of error. On 23 November 1977 Mr. Ronai of Bankers Trust New York wrote to the Libyan Bank as follows:

> " . . . I am writing to outline our proposal for clearing up the operational difficulties encountered in your dollar-clearing activity through Bankers Trust in New York.
>
> "I feel that the problems stem from the number of intermediate steps required to effect a large number of transfers to and from your London Call account via New York. In order to simplify this situation, my proposal is to set up a fully-managed account relationship with Libyan Arab Foreign Bank. This should provide you with several major benefits, among which are:
>
> —more timely information for yourselves
>
> —simplification of transactions
>
> —greater ease in researching possible errors
>
> —the ability to tailor the system to your requirements.
>
> "The basic elements of a managed account consist of a current account in New York and a call account in London with Bankers Trust Co. The current account will be used for your daily dollar-clearing activity; the call account should be considered as an investment of liquid funds. An explanation of the operation of your managed account follows.
>
> "On a daily basis, all transactions concerning the demand account are reviewed, and the balance is 'managed' so that it does not exceed or fall below a predetermined target or 'peg' balance. Excess funds will be credited to your call account, or your current account will be funded from your call account, as the case may be."

In 1980 that proposal was more actively pursued. At first it was suggested by Bankers Trust that the current account should be in London. But by the time of a meeting in New York on 7 July it was again proposed that there should be a demand account there. Following that meeting Bankers Trust wrote from London to the Libyan Bank with details of the proposed managed account system:

> "We will establish a 'peg' (or target) balance for the demand account of U.S. $750,000. That amount is intended to compensate Bankers Trust Co. for the services which we expect to provide, and is subject to periodic renegotiation as appropriate, for example when our costs increase, when interest rates decline significantly or when our level of servicing is materially changed. Each morning our account management team will review the demand account's closing book balance from the previous business day. If that balance is in excess of the 'peg,' they will transfer in multiples of U.S. $100,000 the excess amount to your call account in London with value the previous business day.
>
> "Similarly, if the demand account balance is below the U.S. $750,-000 peg, they will transfer funds back from your call account with value the previous business day. ... As you can appreciate, our account management team must closely follow the balance in your call account. Given time zone differences with London, all entries to your call account must be passed by that team in New York, and all your instructions to effect payments or foreign exchange settlements must be directed to our money transfer department in New York."

The figure of U.S. $750,000 as the peg balance was later agreed at U.S. $500,000.

There was some discussion of political risk at the New York meeting. I am confident that political risk was at any rate in the minds of both parties, seeing that the freeze on Iranian assets had occurred only eight months previously. Mr. Abduljawad, then deputy chairman, is recorded as saying: "Placing at call is not an effort to avoid political risk, which he believes to be unavoidable." Whilst I accept that record as accurate, I also accept Mr. Abduljawad's oral evidence that "political risk is always being taken into consideration." Mr. Van Voorhees, who was among those attending the meeting on behalf of Bankers Trust, accepted that the Iranian crisis was at the back of everyone's mind in 1980.

A further meeting took place in Paris on 28 October 1980 between Mr. Abduljawad and Mr. Van Voorhees. At that meeting too no complete agreement was reached, so there was no new agreement or variation of the existing agreement. But important progress was made. Mr. Van Voorhees explained in plain terms that all the Libyan Bank's transactions would have to pass through New York. According to Mr. Van Voorhees, Mr. Abduljawad at first objected to that requirement, but later agreed to it. Mr. Abduljawad's evidence was that he did not reject it and equally did not agree to it. I do not need to resolve that conflict. It is plain to me that one of the terms which Bankers Trust were putting forward for the new arrangement was that all transactions should pass through New York; whether or not it was accepted at that stage is immaterial.

There followed a meeting in Tripoli and correspondence between the parties, and agreement was finally reached by 11 December 1980. Thus the managed account system was agreed on Bankers Trust New York would open a demand account for the Libyan Bank, with a peg balance of U.S. $500,000. Transfers between that account and the call account in London would be made, as the need arose, in multiples of U.S. $100,000. The need for a transfer would be determined each morning by examining the closing balance of the New York account for the previous business day; if appropriate a transfer to or from London would be made with value the previous business day—in other words, it would take effect from that date for interest purposes.

It was, as I find, a term of that arrangement that all the Libyan Bank's transactions should pass through New York. Although not mentioned in the correspondence by which agreement was ultimately reached, this had plainly been a requirement of Bankers Trust throughout the later stages of the negotiations, and I conclude that it was tacitly accepted by the Libyan Bank. It was virtually an essential feature of the system: Bankers Trust New York would know about and rely on the credit balance in London in deciding what payments could be made from New York; they might be exposed to risk if the balance in London could be reduced without their knowledge. It was argued that such a term is not to be found in the pleadings of Bankers Trust; but in my judgment it is, in paragraph 3(4)(v) of the re-re-amended points of defence. There remains an important question whether the managed account arrangement was irrevocable, or whether it could be determined. I shall consider that later.

The second stage ran from December 1980 to November 1985. Before very long Bankers Trust took the view that the remuneration which they received from the relationship, in the form of an interest-free balance of between U.S. $500,000 and U.S. $599,999 in New York, was insufficient reward for their services. On 15 March 1983 they proposed an increase in the peg balance to $1.5m. Negotiations continued for a time but without success. By 15 March 1984 Bankers Trust had formed the view that the Libyan Bank would not agree to an increase in the peg balance; so, on 3 April 1984, they decided unilaterally on a different method of increasing the profitability of the relationship for Bankers Trust; and it was put into effect on 17 April.

The new method required a consideration of the balance on the New York account at 2 p.m. each day. If it exceeded the peg balance of U.S. $500,000 the excess was transferred in multiples of U.S. $100,000 to the London account with value that day. Consideration was also given on the following morning to the balance at the close of the previous day. If it was less than the peg balance, a transfer of the appropriate amount was made from London to New York on the next day, with value the previous business day; if it was more than the peg balance there was, it seems, a transfer to London with value the same day. The effect of the change was that the Libyan Bank lost one day's interest whenever (i) credits received after 2 p.m. exceeded payments made after 2 p.m., and (ii) the closing balance for the day would under the existing arrangements have required a transfer (or a further transfer if one had been made at 2 p.m.) to be made with value that day. If a weekend intervened, three days interest might be lost. I am not altogether sure that I have stated the effect of the change correctly; but precision as to the details is not essential.

Bankers Trust did not tell the Libyan Bank about this change. Indeed an internal memorandum of Bankers Trust dated 14 August 1984 wondered whether Libya (possibly referring to the Libyan Bank) would notice the drop in interest earnings. Although the effect was on any view substantial, I am satisfied that the Libyan Bank did not in fact appreciate what was happening until mid–1985; and they complained about it to Bankers Trust in October 1985. I am also satisfied that the Libyan Bank could have detected, if they had looked at their statements from Bankers Trust with a fair degree of diligence, that they were not receiving the full benefit by way of interest to which they were entitled. Indeed, they did, as I have said, eventually detect that. But I am not convinced—if it matters—that they could have divined precisely what system Bankers Trust were now operating.

The third stage began on 27 November 1985, with a telex from Bankers Trust which recorded the agreement of the Libyan Bank to a new arrangement. This telex is important, and I must set out part of it:

> "As discussed with you during our last meeting in your office in Tripoli, we have changed the method of investment from same day by means of next day back valuation, to actual same day with investment cut off time of 2 p.m. New York time. ... In this regard, those credits which are received after our 2 p.m. New York time cut off which result in excess balances are invested with next day value. This you will see from observing your account. For your information, the way our same day investment system works, is as follows: each day, at 2 p.m. the balance position of your account is determined and any credits received up to that time, less payments and less the peg balance, are immediately invested. An example of this investment system can be seen for instance by comparing both statements of your demand and call accounts for 26 and 30 September 1985 which indicate same day investment on 26 September for U.S. $33.7 million which is reflected on your London call account statement on 27 September with value 26 September and on 30 September for U.S. $181.3 million which is reflected on your London call account statement on 1 October with value 30 September."

That was not in substance any different from the system which Bankers Trust had been operating since April 1984 without informing the Libyan Bank. It was now accepted by them.

*7 and 8 January 1986*

At 2 p.m. on 7 January the balance to the credit of the New York account was U.S. $165,728,000. (For present purposes I use figures rounded down to the nearest U.S. $1,000, save where greater accuracy is desirable.) Subject to two points which I shall consider later; a transfer of $165.2m. should then have been made to London. Mr. Fabien Arnell, an account manager of Bankers Trust New York says somewhat laconically in his statement.

> "On 7 January 1986 I instructed the managed account clerk not to make a 2 p.m. investment. I cannot now recall the precise reason why I gave that instruction."

During the rest of that day there were substantial transfers out of the New York account, with the result that it would have been overdrawn to the extent of $157,925,000 if the 2 p.m. transfer had been made. There would then have had to be a recall of U.S. $158,500,000 from London on 8 January, with value the previous business day, to restore the peg balance. As no 2 p.m. transfer had been made, the closing balance was in fact U.S. $7,275,000 in credit.

On the morning of 8 January there was an amount of $6,700,000 available to transfer to London. The same amount would have been left as a net credit to the London account if $165.2m. had been transferred at 2 p.m. on 7 January and $158.5m. recalled on 8 January with value the previous day. An instruction for the transfer of U.S. $6,700,000 was prepared. But in the event the computer which kept the accounts in New York was not ordered to effect this transfer, nor was the London branch informed of it.

At 2 p.m. on 8 January the balance to the credit of the New York account was U.S. $161,997,000. After deducting the peg balance of U.S. $500,000 there was a sum of U.S. $161,400,000 available to transfer to London. No transfer was made. Those figures assume, as was the fact, that U.S. $6,700,000 had not been transferred to London in respect of the excess opening balance on that day.

Bankers Trust New York had received payment instructions totalling U.S. $347,147,213.03 for execution on 8 January. All of them had been received by 8.44 a.m. New York time. None of them were executed, for reasons which I shall later explain. (In case it is thought that not even the combined London and New York accounts could have sustained such payments, I should mention that substantial credits were received in New York during 8 January for the account of the Libyan Bank. If all the payment instructions had been implemented, there would still at the end of the day have been a net balance due to the Libyan Bank on the total of the two accounts).

In the hope of rendering those figures somewhat more intelligible, I set out a summary of the actual state of the New York account on 7 and 8 January 1986, with notes:

| | | |
|---|---|---|
| Balance at 2 p.m. 7 January | U.S. $165,728,000 | (1) |
| Post 2 p.m. operations | (158,453,000) | |
| Opening balance 8 January | 7,275,000 | (2) |
| Receipts before 2 p.m. | 154,722,000 | |
| Balance at 2 p.m. 8 January | 161,997,000 | (3) |
| Receipts after 2 p.m. | 89,132,000 | (4) |
| Closing balance 8 January | 251,129,000 | |

*Notes:*

(1) $165.2m. available for transfer to London

(2) $6.7m. available for transfer

(3) $161.4m. available for transfer

(4) This figure contains some minor adjustments of no consequence.

Next I turn to the Civil Evidence Act statement of Mr. Brittain, the chairman of Bankers Trust. Late in the afternoon of 7 January he received a telephone call from Mr. Corrigan, the president of the Federal Reserve Bank of New York. Mr. Corrigan asked that Bankers Trust should pay particular attention on the next day to movement of funds on the various Libyan accounts held by Bankers Trust, and report anything unusual to him.

Late in the morning of the next day Mr. Brittain informed the New York Fed. (as it is sometimes called) that "it looked like the Libyans were taking their money out of the various accounts." (So far as the Libyan Bank were concerned, it will be remembered that they had already given instructions for payments totalling over U.S. $347m. on that day.) Later Mr. Brittain learnt that sufficient funds were coming in to cover the payment instructions; he telephoned Mr. Corrigan and told him that the earlier report had been a false alarm. Mr. Corrigan asked Mr. Brittain not to make any payments out of the accounts for the time being, and said that he would revert later.

That assurance was repeated several times during the early afternoon. Mr. Brittain's statement continues:

> "Finally I telephoned Mr. Corrigan at about 3:30 p.m. and told him that we now had sufficient funds to cover the payments out of the various Libyan accounts and were going to make them. Mr. Corrigan's response to this was, 'You'd better call Baker' (by which he meant the Secretary of the United States Treasury, Mr. James A. Baker III). I said that I would release the payments and then speak to Mr. Baker. Mr. Corrigan's reply to this was. 'You'd better call Baker first'."

Mr. Brittain was delayed for some 20 minutes talking to Mr. Baker and to an assistant secretary of the Treasury on the telephone. Then at approximately 4.10 to 4.16 p.m. Mr. Baker said: "The President has signed the order, you can't make the transfers."

Mr. Brittain adds in his statement that this was the first occasion on which he became aware that an order freezing the assets was contemplated. In a note made a few weeks after 8 January he adds: "That is how naive I was." I am afraid that I can but agree with Mr. Brittain's description of himself. It seems to me that a reasonable banker on the afternoon of 8 January would have realised, in the light of the first executive order made on the previous day, the requests of Mr. Corrigan, and particularly his saying "You'd better call Baker first," that a ban on payments was a distinct possibility.

There is other evidence as to Mr. Brittain's telephone conversations. First, Mr. Blenk was in Mr. Brittain's office and heard what was said by him. There was not, it seems, any reference by name to Libyan Arab Foreign Bank, but merely to "the Libyans," which meant some six Libyan entities (including the Libyan Bank) which had accounts with Bankers Trust. Secondly, Mr. Sandberg, a senior vice-president of the Federal Reserve Bank of New York, heard Mr. Corrigan's end of the conversations. He accepted in evidence that the New York Fed. probably knew which Libyan banks held accounts with Bankers Trust.

*(1) The U.S. $131 million claim*

*(a) Conflict of laws—the connecting factor*

There is no dispute as to the general principles involved. Performance of a contract is excused if (i) it has become illegal by the proper law of the contract, or (ii) it necessarily involves doing an act which is unlawful by the law of the place where the act has to be done. I need cite no authority for that proposition (least of all my own decision in Euro–Diam Ltd. v. Bathurst [1987] 2 W.L.R. 1368, 1385) since it is well established and was not challenged. Equally it was not suggested that New York law is relevant because it is the national law of Bankers Trust, or because payment in London would expose Bankers Trust to sanctions under the United States legislation, save that Mr. Sumption for Bankers Trust desires to keep the point open in case this dispute reaches the House of Lords.

There may, however, be a difficulty in ascertaining when performance of the contract "necessarily involves" doing an illegal act in another country. In *Toprak Mahsullerr Ofisi v. Finagrain Compagnie Commerciale Agricole et Financière S.A.* [1979] 2 Lloyd's Rep. 98, Turkish buyers of wheat undertook to open a letter of credit "with and confirmed by a first class United States or West European bank." The buyers were unable to obtain exchange control permission from the Turkish Ministry of Finance to open a letter of credit, and maintained that it was impossible for them to open a letter of credit without exporting money from Turkey. It was held that this was no answer to a claim for damages for nonperformance of the contract. Lord Denning M.R. said, at p. 114:

> "In this particular case the place of performance was not Turkey. Illegality by the law of Turkey is no answer whatever to this claim.

The letter of credit had to be a confirmed letter of credit, confirmed by a first-class West European or U.S. bank. The sellers were not concerned with the machinery by which the Turkish state enterprise provided that letter of credit at all. The place of performance was not Turkey.

"This case is really governed by the later case of Kleinwort, Sons & Co. v. Ungarische Baumwolle Industrie Aktiengesellschaft [1939] 2 K.B. 678 where bills of exchange were to be given and cover was to be provided in London, but at the same time there was a letter saying, 'We have to get permission from Hungary.' It was said that because of the illegality by Hungarian law in obtaining it, that would be an answer to the case. But Branson J. and the Court of Appeal held that the proper law of the contract was English law; and, since the contract was to be performed in England, it was enforceable in the English courts even though its performance might involve a breach by the defendants of the law of Hungary.

"That case has been quoted in all the authorities as now settling the law. ... The only way that Mr. Johnson (for the Turkish state enterprise) could seek to escape from that principle was by saying—' ... Although there was no term, express or implied, in the contract that anything had to be done in Turkey as a term of the contract, nevertheless it was contemplated by both parties. It was contemplated by both parties that the Turkish buyers would have to go through the whole sequence in Turkey of getting exchange control permission, and all other like things: and, if the contemplated method of performance became illegal, that would be an answer. Equally, if it became impossible, that would be a frustration.'

"I am afraid that those arguments do not carry the day. It seems to me in this contract, where the letter of credit had to be a confirmed letter of credit—confirmed by a West European or U.S. bank—the sellers are not in the least concerned as to the method by which the Turkish buyers are to provide that letter of credit. Any troubles or difficulties in Turkey are extraneous to the matter and do not afford any defence to an English contract ... "

From that case I conclude that it is immaterial whether one party has to equip himself for performance by an illegal act in another country. What matters is whether performance itself necessarily involves such an act. The Turkish buyers might have had money anywhere in the world which they could use to open a letter of credit with a United States or West European bank. In fact it would seem that they only had money in Turkey, or at any rate needed to comply with Turkish exchange control regulations if they were to use any money they may have had outside Turkey. But that was no defence, as money or a permit was only needed to equip themselves for performance, and not for performance itself.

. . .

Some difficulty may still be encountered in the application of that principle. For example, if payment in dollar bills in London was required by the contract, it would very probably have been necessary for Bankers Trust to obtain such a large quantity from the Federal Reserve Bank of New York, and ship it to England. That, Mr. Sumption accepts, would not have been an act which performance necessarily involved; it would merely have been an act by Bankers Trust to equip themselves for performance as in the Toprak case. By contrast, if the contract required Bankers Trust to hand over a banker's draft to the Libyan Bank in London, Mr. Sumption argues that an illegal act in New York would necessarily be involved, since it is very likely that the obligation represented by the draft would ultimately be honoured in New York. I must return to this problem later.

*(b) The proper law of the contract*

As a general rule the contract between a bank and its customer is governed by the law of the place where the account is kept, in the absence of agreement to the contrary. Again there was no challenge to that as a general rule; the fact that no appellate decision was cited to support it may mean that it is generally accepted. However, since the point is of some importance, I list those authorities that were cited. They are X A.G. v. A Bank [1983] 2 All E.R. 464; Mackinnon v. Donaldson, Lufkin & Jenrette Securities Corporation [1986] Ch. 482, 494; Dicey & Morris, The Conflict of Laws, 11th ed. (1987), p. 1292, n. 51; Rabel, The Conflict of Laws, 2nd ed., p. 17; American Law Institute, Restatement of the Law, Conflict of Laws 2d, vol. 4 (1979), para. 622, and the Memorandum of Law in the Wells Fargo case which I have referred to, and the Lexis report of judgment in that action.

That rule accords with the principle, to be found in the judgment of Atkin L.J. in N. Joachimson v. Swiss Bank Corporation [1921] 3 K.B. 110, 127, and other authorities, that a bank's promise to repay is to repay at the branch of the bank where the account is kept.

In the age of the computer it may not be strictly accurate to speak of the branch where the account is kept. Banks no longer have books in which they write entries; they have terminals by which they give instructions; and the computer itself with its magnetic tape, floppy disc or some other device may be physically located elsewhere. Nevertheless it should not be difficult to decide where an account is kept for this purpose, and it is not in the present case. The actual entries on the London account were, as I understand it, made in London, albeit on instructions from New York after December 1980. At all events I have no doubt that the London account was at all material times "kept" in London.

. . .

In my judgment, the true view is that after December 1980 there was one contract, governed in part by the law of England and in part by the law of New York.

. . .

I hold that the rights and obligations of the parties in respect of the London account were governed by English law.

. . .

*(d) Means of transfer*

The credit balance of the Libyan Bank with Bankers Trust constituted a personal right, a chose in action. At bottom there are only two means by which the fruits of that right could have been made available to the Libyan Bank. The first is by delivery of cash, whether dollar bills or any other currency, to or to the order of the Libyan Bank. The second is the procuring of an account transfer. (I leave out of account the delivery of chattels, such as gold, silver or works of art, since nobody has suggested that Bankers Trust were obliged to adopt that method. The same applies to other kinds of property, such as land.)

An account transfer means the process by which some other person or institution comes to owe money to the Libyan Bank or their nominee, and the obligation of Bankers Trust is extinguished or reduced pro tanto. "Transfer" may be a somewhat misleading word, since the original obligation is not assigned (notwithstanding dicta in one American case which speak of assignment); a new obligation by a new debtor is created.

Any account transfer must ultimately be achieved by means of two accounts held by different beneficiaries with the same institution. In a simple case the beneficiaries can be the immediate parties to the transfer. If Bankers Trust held an account with the A bank which was in credit to the extent of at least $131m., and the Libyan Bank also held an account at the A bank, it would require only book entries to achieve an account transfer. But still no property is actually *transferred.* The obligation of Bankers Trust is extinguished, and the obligation of A bank to Bankers Trust extinguished or reduced; the obligation of A bank to the Libyan Bank is increased by the like amount.

On occasion a method of account transfer which is even simpler may be used. If X Ltd. also hold an account with Bankers Trust London, and the Libyan Bank desire to benefit X Ltd., they instruct Bankers Trust to transfer $131m. to the account of X Ltd. The obligation of Bankers Trust to the Libyan Bank is extinguished once they decide to comply with the instruction, and their obligation to X Ltd. is increased by the like amount. That method of account transfer featured in Momm v. Barclays Bank International Ltd. [1977] Q.B. 790.

In a complex transaction at the other end of the scale there may be more than one tier of intermediaries, ending with a Federal Reserve Bank in the United States. Thus the payer may have an account with B bank in London, which has an account with C bank in New York; the payee has an account with E bank in London, which has an account with D bank in New York. Both C bank and D bank have accounts with the Federal Reserve Bank in New York. When an account transfer is effected the obligations of the New York Fed. to C bank, of C bank to B bank, and of B bank to the payer are reduced; the obligations of the

New York Fed. to D bank, of D bank to E bank, and of E bank to the payee are increased. That is, in essence, how the Clearing House Interbank Payments System (C.H.I.P.S.) works, by which a large proportion of transfers of substantial dollar amounts are made.

I shall call the three methods which I have described a correspondent bank transfer, an in-house transfer and a complex account transfer. There are variations which do not precisely fit any of the three, but the principle is the same in all cases. Sooner or later, if cash is not used, there must be an in-house transfer at an institution which holds accounts for two beneficiaries, so that the credit balance of one can be increased and that of the other reduced. In the example of a complex account transfer which I have given that institution is the New York Fed., which holds accounts for C bank and D bank.

Evidence was given by Professor Scott of a method which, at first sight, did not involve an in-house transfer at any institution. That was where different Federal Reserve Banks were used. However, the Professor assured me that an in-house transfer was involved, although it was too complicated to explain. That invitation to abstain from further inquiry was gratefully accepted.

Thus far I have been assuming that only one transaction affecting any of the parties takes place on a given day. But manifestly that is unlikely to be the case; there may be thousands, or tens of thousands. One purpose of a clearing system between banks must be to set off transfers against others, not only between the same parties but also between all other parties to the clearing system. Thus C bank and D bank, in my example of a complex account transfer, may have made many transactions between themselves on the same day. Only the net balance of them all will be credited to one by the New York Fed. and debited to the other at the end. So the identity of the sum which the payer wished to pay to the payee may be entirely lost in one sense. The net balance may be the other way, and a sum be credited to C bank and debited to D bank instead of vice versa. Or, by a somewhat improbable coincidence, the net balance may be nil.

There are two further complications. The first is that set-off occurs not only between C bank and D bank, but between all other participants to the clearing system. An amount which would otherwise fall to be debited to C bank and credited to D bank may be reduced (i) because F bank has made transfers on that day to C bank, or (ii) because D bank has made transfers on that day to G bank.

Secondly, an intermediate clearing system may be used, such as London dollar clearing. If the chain of transmission on each side reaches a bank that is a member of the London dollar clearing, and if the item in question is eligible for that clearing system, it may be put through it. Then it will go to make up the net credit or debit balances that are due between all the members at the end of the day—and they in turn are settled in New York.

*(e) Particular forms of transfer*

I set out below those which have been canvassed in this case, and discuss the extent to which they involve activity in the United States.

*(i) In-house transfer at Bankers Trust London*

This is quite simple, as has been explained. It involves no action in the United States. But it cannot take place unless the Libyan Bank are able to nominate some beneficiary who also has an account with Bankers Trust London.

*(ii) Correspondent bank transfer*

Again, this is relatively simple and involves no action in the United States. But for it to be effective in this case a bank must be found outside the United States where two conditions are satisfied: the first is that Bankers Trust have a credit balance there of U.S. $131m. or more; the second, that an account is also held there for the Libyan Bank or for some beneficiary whom they nominate.

*(iii) C.H.I.P.S. or Fedwire*

These are two methods of complex account transfer which are used for a high proportion of large dollar transactions. They can only be completed in the United States.

. . .

*(vi) London dollar clearing*

It may not be right to describe this as a means of transfer in itself, but rather as a method of settling liabilities which arise when other means of transfer are used, such as a banker's draft or banker's payment, or indeed a cheque. Bankers Trust are not themselves members of London dollar clearing, but use it through Lloyds Bank Plc.

Suppose H bank, also a member of the clearing, presented a banker's draft issued by Bankers Trust to or to the order of the Libyan Bank for U.S. $131m. At the end of the day net debits and credits of all the members of the clearing would be calculated—and settled by transfers in New York. As already explained, there would not necessarily be a transfer there of U.S. $131m. or any sum by Lloyds Bank or their New York correspondent to the New York correspondent of H bank. But somewhere in the calculation of the sum that would be transferred by some bank in New York to some other bank in New York the U.S. $131m. would be found.

That is the first aspect of the transaction which requires action in New York. But thus far only the liabilities of the clearing members between themselves have been settled. What of the liabilities of the banks that have used the clearing but are not members? Bankers Trust owe Lloyds Bank U.S. $131m. That sum will go into a calculation of all the credits and debits between Bankers Trust and Lloyds Bank on that day; the net balance will be settled by a transfer in New York between

Bankers' Trust New York and Lloyds Bank or their New York correspondent.

Since I have assumed that H bank are a member of the London dollar clearing, no similar transfer is required in their case. They have already received credit for U.S. $131m. in the clearing process and the transfers which settled the balances which emerged from it.

There is another aspect of the London dollar clearing which featured a great deal in the evidence. This is that a rule, at the time unwritten, excluded from the clearing "cheques drawn for principal amounts of interbank Eurocurrency transactions." The system is described in the Child report, where it is said that "by mutual consent 'wholesale' interbank foreign exchange deals and Eurodollar settlements are excluded." That in turn raises a question as to the meaning of "wholesale." Bankers Trust argue that it includes transactions on interest-bearing call accounts between banks, at any rate if they are for large amounts. The Libyan Bank say that it refers only to transactions for time deposits traded between the dealing rooms of banks.

I prefer the evidence of Bankers Trust on this point. The reason for the exclusion appears to be that the introduction of a very large sum by one participant into the clearing system would impose an excessive credit risk. The average value of transactions passing through the system is U.S. $50,000, and the vast majority of items are of the order of U.S. $10,000. It is not normally used for transactions over U.S. $30m.; indeed, there were not many transactions in millions. I find that a transfer of U.S. $131m. by Bankers Trust to or to the order of the Libyan Bank would not, in the circumstances of this case, be eligible for London dollar clearing.

*(vii) Other clearing systems outside the United States*

Apart from the last point about eligibility, it seems to me that much the same considerations must apply to the other three systems discussed—Euroclear, Cedel and Tokyo dollar clearing. Although the identity of a particular transaction will be difficult or impossible to trace in the net credits or debits which emerge at the end of the clearing, these debits and credits must ultimately be settled in the United States. (The word "ultimately" constantly recurs and is of importance in this case, as was stressed in the course of the evidence.)

But whether that be so or not, there are other points relevant to the use of these systems. Euroclear in Brussels is a system run through Morgan Guaranty Trust Co. for clearing securities transactions and payments in respect of such transactions. If it so happened that Bankers Trust had a credit of U.S. $131m. in the system, it could arrange for that sum to be transferred to the Libyan Bank or any nominee of the Libyan Bank which had an account with Euroclear. That would be a species of correspondent transfer. Alternatively, it could order the transfer to be made anywhere else—but that would involve action in New York.

Cedel, in Luxembourg, is similar to Euroclear in all respects that are material.

The Tokyo dollar clearing system is run by Chase Manhattan Bank at its Tokyo branch. Bankers Trust did not have an account with the system. If they had done, and had used it to pay U.S. $131m. to the Libyan Bank, they would have had to reimburse Chase Manhattan via New York.

. . .

*(ix) Cash—dollar bills*

I am told that the largest notes in circulation are now for U.S. $100, those for U.S. $500 having been withdrawn. Hence there would be formidable counting and security operations involved in paying U.S. $131m. by dollar bills. Bankers Trust would not have anything like that amount in their vault in London. Nor, on balance, do I consider that they would be likely to be able to obtain such an amount in Europe. It could be obtained from a Federal Reserve Bank and sent to London by aeroplane, although several different shipments would be made to reduce the risk. The operation would take some time—up to seven days.

Banks would seek to charge for this service, as insurance and other costs would be involved, and they would suffer a loss of interest from the time when cash was withdrawn from the Federal Reserve Bank to the time when it was handed over the counter and the customer's account debited—assuming that the customer had an interest-bearing account. I cannot myself see any basis on which a bank would be entitled to charge, although there might be a right to suspend payment of interest. If a bank chooses, as all banks do for their own purposes, not to maintain a sum equal to all its liabilities in the form of cash in its vaults, it must bear the expense involved in obtaining cash when a demand is made which it is obliged to meet. If a customer demanded U.S. $1,000 or U.S. $10,000 in cash, I do not see how a charge could be made. When the sum is very much larger it is an important question—which I shall consider later—whether the bank is obliged to meet a demand for cash at all. If it is so obliged, there is not, in my opinion, any right to charge for fulfilling its obligation.

As I have already mentioned, it is accepted that there would be no breach of New York law by Bankers Trust in obtaining such an amount of cash in New York and despatching it to their London office.

*(x) Cash—sterling*

There would be no difficulty for Bankers Trust in obtaining sterling notes from the Bank of England equivalent in value to U.S. $131m., although, once again, there would be counting and security problems. Bankers Trust would have to reimburse the Bank of England, or the correspondent through whom it obtained the notes, and this would probably be done by a transfer of dollars in New York. But, again, it was not argued that such a transfer would infringe New York law.

*(f) Termination of the managed account arrangement*

Those means of transfer are all irrelevant so long as the managed account arrangement subsists; for I have found it to be a term of that arrangement that all the Libyan Bank's transactions should pass through New York. Apart from some minor teething problems at the start in 1980, that term was observed. The only entries on the London call account were credits from, or debits to, the New York demand account. It was the New York account that was used to make payments to, or receive credits from, others with whom the Libyan Bank had business relations. If the arrangement still exists, the London account can only be used to transfer a credit to New York, which would be of no benefit whatever to the Libyan Bank.

In my judgment, the Libyan Bank was entitled unilaterally to determine the managed account arrangement on reasonable notice, which did not need to be more than 24 hours (Saturdays, Sundays and non-banking days excepted). The important feature of the arrangement from the point of view of Bankers Trust was that their operators could make payments in New York, on occasion giving rise to an overdraft in New York, safe in the knowledge that there was a credit balance in London which they could call upon and which would not disappear. If it were determined, Bankers Trust New York would be entitled to refuse to make payments which would put the account there into overdraft. For the Libyan Bank an important feature was that they obtained both the speed and efficiency with which current account payments could be made in New York, and the advantage of an account in London bearing interest at Eurodollar rates. If the arrangement were determined and the Libyan Bank began once again to use the London account as if it were a current account, Bankers Trust would be entitled (again on notice) to reduce the rate of interest payable on that account, or to decline to pay interest altogether.

I find nothing surprising in the notion that one party to a banking contract should be able to alter some existing arrangement unilaterally. Some terms, such as those relating to a time deposit, cannot be altered. But the ordinary customer can alter the bank's mandate, for example by revoking the authority of signatories and substituting others, or by cancelling standing orders or direct debits; he can transfer sums between current and deposit account; and he can determine his relationship with the bank entirely. So too the bank can ask the customer to take his affairs elsewhere. In this case it does not seem to me at all plausible that each party was locked into the managed account arrangement for all time unless the other agreed to its determination, or the entire banking relationship were ended. I accept Mr. Cresswell's submission that the arrangement was in the nature of instructions or a mandate which the Libyan Bank could determine by notice. For that matter, I consider that Bankers Trust would also have been entitled to determine it on reasonable notice—which would have been somewhat longer than 24 hours in their case. I hold that the arrangement was determined, implicitly by the Libyan Bank's telex of 28 April 1986, and if that were wrong, then expressly by their solicitors' letter of 30 July 1986.

What, then, was the position after determination? The New York account remained, as it always had been, a demand account. Subject to New York law, Bankers Trust were obliged to make transfers in accordance with the Libyan Bank's instructions to the extent of the credit balance, but they were not obliged to allow an overdraft—even a daylight overdraft, as it is called when payments in the course of a day exceed the credit balance but the situation is restored by further credits before the day ends. The London account remained an interest-bearing account from which Bankers Trust were obliged to make transfers on the instructions of the Libyan Bank, provided that no infringement of United States law in the United States was involved. If Bankers Trust became dissatisfied with the frequency of such transfers, they were, as I have said, entitled on notice to reduce the rate of interest or bring the account to an end. And if I had not held that the rights and obligations of the parties in respect of the London account were governed by English law at all times, I would have been inclined to hold that they were once more governed by English law when the managed account arrangement was determined, although there is clearly some difficulty in recognising a unilateral right to change the system of law governing part of the relations between the parties.

*(g) Implied term and usage*

It is said in paragraph 4(2) of the re-re-amended points of defence that there was an implied term that transfer of funds from the London account, whether or not effected through the New York account

> "would be effected by instructing a transfer to be made by the defendants' New York Head Office through a United States clearing system to the credit of an account with a bank or a branch of a bank in the United States nominated or procured to be nominated by or on behalf of the plaintiffs for that purpose."

In other words, of the various forms of transfer which I have mentioned, only C.H.I.P.S. or Fedwire were permitted. That term is said to be implied (i) from the usage of the international market in Eurodollars, and (ii) from the course of dealing between the parties since 1980.

. . .

The high point of Bankers Trust's case on this issue lies in the expert report of Dr. Stigum from which I quote some brief extracts:

> "The usages and practices that apply to wholesale Eurodollar accounts are moreover, well understood by *all* wholesale participants in the Eurodollar market ... Cash transactions are a feature of only an insignificant portion of total Eurodollar deposits, namely those held by small retail accounts. At the wholesale level, the Eurodollar market is understood by *all* participants to be a *strictly non-cash* market. ... *All* wholesale Eurodollar transactions (these

occurring not just in London, but in other centres around the world as well) must, unless they involve a movement of funds from one account at a given bank to another account at that same bank, be cleared in the United States. The reason for this custom and usage is that the ultimate effect of the clearing of a wholesale, Eurodollar transaction is to remove dollars from the reserve account of one bank at the Fed. to the reserve account of another bank at the Fed."

Even as it stands, that passage does not support the implied term pleaded, that transfers would be made "through a United States clearing system." However, it is fair to say that in the particulars of usage there were added by amendment to the points of defence the words "save where book transfers fall to be made between accounts at the same branch"—which would allow, as Dr. Stigum apparently does, both an in-house transfer and a correspondent bank transfer.

Dr. Stigum is an economist and not a banker. I did not find her oral evidence impressive. On the other hand, Mr. Osbourne, who was until 1985 an assistant general manager of Barclays Bank, did seem to me an impressive witness, whose evidence was very sound on most points. His views were inconsistent with the usage alleged, at any risk in the case of an account such as that of the Libyan Bank with Bankers Trust London.

Furthermore, the supposed usage was inconsistent with the course of dealing between the parties, to which I now turn. It is, of course, true that from December 1980 to January 1986 all transactions by the Libyan Bank were carried out in New York. That is not in itself proof of a course of dealing, since, as I have found, there was an express term to that effect—until the managed account arrangement was brought to an end. What happened between 1973 and December 1980? Fortunately the parties agreed to treat one month as a suitable sample. That was December 1979, in which there were 497 transactions. They have been analysed as follows:

| | |
|---|---|
| "Entries generated internally by Bankers Trust London, that is to say, mostly intra-branch transfers | 15 |
| London clearable bank drafts, London dollar clearing eligible bank drafts | 8 |
| London dollar clearing bankers payments | 1 |
| Intra-branch transfers between Bankers Trust London and accounts at Bankers Trust New York | 68 |
| Intra branch transfers between Bankers Trust London and accounts at Bankers Trust Paris | 3 |
| Payments through Fedwire | 13 |
| Payments through C.H.I.P.S | 389." |

There was still a slight dispute as to how the London/Paris transfers were effected but that is not material.

The vast majority of those transactions (402) were, as the suggested implied term required, through a United States clearing system. If one adds the in-house transfers of one kind or another in Bankers Trust, as Dr. Stigum's custom permits, the total reaches 488. But there were 9 transactions in that month alone (London bank drafts and a London banker's payment) which were not permitted, either by the implied terms which Bankers Trust allege or by Dr. Stigum's custom and usage, although they may very well have been for relatively small amounts.

I find difficulty in seeing how course of dealing by itself could support a negative implied term of the kind alleged. The phrase is often used to elucidate a contract or to add a term to it. But if course of dealing is to eliminate some right which the contract would otherwise confer, I would require evidence to show, not merely that the right had never been exercised, but also that the parties recognised that as between themselves no such right existed. In other words, there must be evidence establishing as between the parties what would be a usage if it applied to the market as a whole. But whether that be so or not, I find no implied term such as Bankers Trust allege to be established either by usage, or by course of dealing, or by both.

There was a great deal of evidence as to which Eurodollar transactions could be described as "wholesale" and which as "retail." I am inclined to think that the answer depends on the purpose for which the description is used. I have found that a payment of U.S. $131m. by Bankers Trust to the Libyan Bank would be excluded from London dollar clearing. In that context it may, perhaps, be described as wholesale. But I have also found that no usage applies to the Libyan Bank's account. I do not exclude the possibility that some usage applies to time deposits traded between the dealing rooms of banks. If the word "wholesale" is applied to that class of business, the Libyan Bank's account is not within it.

*(h) Obligations in respect of the London account*

Having considered and rejected the two methods by which Bankers Trust seek to limit their obligations in respect of the London account—that is, an express term from the managed account arrangement still subsisting, or an implied term—I have to determine what those obligations were. What sort of demands were the Libyan Bank entitled to make and Bankers Trust bound to comply with? As I said, earlier, it is necessary to distinguish between services which a bank is obliged to provide if asked, and services which many bankers do provide but are not obliged to.

Dr. F.A. Mann in his book *The Legal Aspect of Money,* 4th ed. (1982), pp. 193–194, discusses this question in the context of the Eurodollar market. I have given careful attention to the whole passage. His conclusion is:

> "The banks, institutions or multinational companies which hold such deposits, frequently of enormous size, and which deal in them are said to buy and sell money such as dollars. In law it is likely, however, that they deal in credits, so that a bank which has a large

amount of dollars standing to the credit of its account with another (European) bank probably does not and cannot expect it to be 'paid' or discharged otherwise than through the medium of a credit to an account with another bank. In the case of dollars it seems to be the rule (and therefore possibly a term of the contract) that such credit should be effected through the Clearing House Interbank Payments System (C.H.I.P.S.) in New York. . . . In short, as economists have said, the Eurodollar market is a mere account market rather than a money market."

Dr. Mann cites Marcia Stigum's book, *The Money Market* (1978) and finds some support for his view—which he describes as tentative—in an English case which has not been relied on before me. The passage in question appeared for the first time in the 1982 edition of Dr. Mann's book after the litigation about the Iranian bank freeze.

I am reluctant to disagree with such a great authority on money in English law, but feel bound to do so. There is one passage, at p. 194, which appears to me to be an indication of economic rather than legal reasoning:

> "it could often be a national disaster if the creditor bank were entitled to payment, for in the last resort this might mean the sale of a vast amount of dollars and the purchase of an equally large sum of sterling so as to upset the exchange rates."

But if a person owes a large sum of money, it does not seem to me to be a sound defence in law for him to say that it will be a national disaster if he has to pay. Countries which feel that their exchange rates are at risk can resort to exchange control if they wish.

Furthermore, the term suggested by Dr. Mann—that all payments should be made through C.H.I.P.S.—is negatived by the evidence in this case. It may for all I know be the rule for time deposits traded between the dealing rooms of banks, but I am not concerned with such a case here.

R.M. Goode, in *Payment Obligations in Commercial and Financial Transactions* (1983), p. 120, writes:

> "Would an English court have declared the Executive Order effective to prevent the Iranian Government from claiming repayment in London of a dollar deposit maintained with a London bank? At first blush no, as it is unlikely that an English court would accord extra-territorial effect to the United States Executive Order. However, the argument on the United States side (which initially appeared to have claimed extra-territorial effect for the Order) was that in the Eurocurrency market it is well understood that deposits cannot be withdrawn in cash but are settled by an inter-bank transfer through the clearing system and Central Bank of the country whose currency is involved. So in the case of Eurodollar deposits payment was due in, or at any rate through, New York, and the Executive Order thereby validly prevented payment abroad of blocked Iranian depos-

> its, not because the order was extra-territorial in operation but because it prohibited the taking of steps within the United States (i.e. through C.H.I.P.S. in New York) to implement instructions for the transfer of a dollar deposit located outside the United States."

That was published in 1983. I have not accepted the argument which Professor Goode refers to, that it is well understood that deposits cannot be withdrawn in cash. I find that there was no implied term to that effect.

I now turn again to the forms of transfer discussed in subsection (e) of this judgment, in order to consider in relation to each whether it was a form of transfer which the Libyan Bank were entitled to demand, whether it has in fact been demanded, and whether it would necessarily involve any action in New York.

. . .

*(ix) Cash—dollar bills*

Of course it is highly unlikely that anyone would want to receive a sum as large as $131m in dollar bills, at all events unless they were engaged in laundering the proceeds of crime. Mr. Osbourne said in his report:

> As to the demand for payment in cash, I regard this simply as the assertion of a customer's inalienable right. In practice, of course, where such a large sum is demanded in this manner, fulfilment of the theoretical right is unlikely, in my experience, to be achieved. A sensible banker will seek to persuade his customer to accept payment in some more convenient form, and I have yet to encounter an incident of this nature where an acceptable compromise was not reached, even where the sum was demanded in sterling.

I would substitute "fundamental" for "inalienable"; but in all other respects that passage accords with what, in my judgment, is the law. One can compare operations in futures in the commodity markets; everybody knows that contracts will be settled by the payment of differences, and not by the delivery of copper, wheat or sugar as the case may be; but an obligation to deliver and accept the appropriate commodity, in the absence of settlement by some other means, remains the legal basis of these transactions. So in my view every obligation in monetary terms is to be fulfilled, either by the delivery of cash, or by some other operation which the creditor demands and which the debtor is either obliged to, or is content to, perform. There may be a term agreed that the customer is not entitled to demand cash; but I have rejected the argument that there was any subsisting express term, or any implied term, to that effect. Mr. Sumption argued that an obligation to pay on demand leaves very little time for performance, and that U.S. $131m. could not be expected to be obtainable in that interval. The answer is that either a somewhat longer period must be allowed to obtain so large a sum, or that Bankers Trust would be in breach because, like any other banker they choose, for their own purposes, not to have it readily available in London.

Demand was in fact made for cash in this case, and it was not complied with. It has not been argued that the delivery of such a sum in cash in London would involve any illegal action in New York. Accordingly I would hold Bankers Trust liable on that ground.

*(x) Cash-sterling*

*Dicey & Morris, The Conflict of Laws,* 11th ed. state in Rule 210, at p. 1453:

> "If a sum of money expressed in a foreign currency is payable in England, it may be paid either in units of the money of account or in sterling at the rate of exchange at which units of the foreign legal tender can, on the day when the money is paid, be bought in London . . . ."

See also *Chitty on Contracts,* 25th ed., para. 2105.

> "Where a debtor owes a creditor a debt expressed in foreign currency . . . the general rule is that the debtor may choose whether to pay in the foreign currency in question or in sterling."

. . .

Given that a foreign currency debtor is entitled to choose between discharging his obligations in foreign currency or sterling, I consider that he should not be entitled to choose the route which is blocked and then claim that his obligation is discharged or suspended. I prefer the view that he must perform in one way or the other; so long as both routes are available he may choose; but if one is blocked, his obligation is to perform in the other.

. . .

*(2) The claim that a further sum should have been transferred from New York*

This arises in three different ways on the facts. First it is said that U.S. $165.2m. should have been transferred to London at 2 p.m. on 7 January 1986.

Bankers Trust have two answers to this claim. First they say that instructions had been received and were pending for further payments to be made on 7 January after 2 p.m., which exceeded the amount then standing to the credit of the New York account (and, for that matter, the London account as well). It was only because further receipts also occurred after 2 p.m. that the New York account ended the day with a credit balance of U.S. $7.275m., and the London account remained untouched.

Secondly, Bankers Trust say that, if they were obliged to make a transfer to London on 7 January, they could lawfully have postponed it until after 8:06 p.m. New York time, when the first Presidential order came into force. Thereafter, they say, the transfer would have been illegal because it would have left the New York account overdrawn and would have constituted the grant of credit or a loan to the Libyan Bank.

In my judgment both those arguments fail. The telex of 27 November 1986, from which I have already quoted, contained this passage:

> Each day, at 2 p.m., the balance position of your account is determined and any credits received up to that time, less payments and less the peg balance, are immediately invested.

It is said that "payments" there are not confined to payments actually made, and include payments for which instructions were pending. In view of the precision with which the time of 2 p.m. is stated, and the word "immediately," I do not consider that to be right. Mr. Sumption argued that "immediately" is coloured (one might say contradicted) by the illustration given in the telex; but I do not agree. The argument that Bankers Trust were entitled to delay the transfer until after 8:06 p.m. also fails, for the same reason, and it is unnecessary to decide whether it would have been a breach of the first Presidential order to allow an overdraft in New York which was less than the credit balance in London. They would certainly have been entitled in any event not to make payments which exceeded the net credit balance of the two accounts. But after credits which were received during the afternoon there was no need to do that.

Mr. Sumption also argued that the passage in the telex set out above was merely an illustration of how the arrangement would work, and not part of the revised terms of the managed account arrangement. That argument I also reject.

Some attention was paid to the course of dealing on these points. Mr. Blackburn's evidence showed that there was no consistency in the treatment of unprocessed payments, sometimes they were taken into account in deciding whether a 2 p.m. transfer should be made, and at other times they were ignored. As to the actual timing of the transfer, it was always booked in New York on the same day, and in London on the following day with one day's back value. The important feature to my mind is that, so long as there was no legislative interference, it did not make any difference to the parties whether the actual transfer was made at 2 p.m. or at any time up to midnight. Banking hours in London had already ended. Nor did it necessarily make a difference whether unprocessed payments were taken into account; if they were not, and a debit balance in New York resulted at the end of the day, Bankers Trust would recall an appropriate amount next morning from London, with one day's back value. It was only when the Presidential orders came to be made that timing became important. Bankers Trust were, as I hold, in breach of contract in failing to transfer U.S. $165.2m. to London at 2 p.m. on 7 January.

If they had done so, they would have been entitled to recall U.S. $158.5m. from London next morning, so that the net loss to the London account was only U.S. $6.7m. Mr. Cresswell argues that, in practice,

Bankers Trust only recalled sums from the London account late in the day, and therefore after 4:10 p.m. when the second Presidential order came into effect; a transfer from London would thereafter have been illegal. In point of fact that may well be correct. But I have no doubt at all that, if there had been a large overdraft on the New York account on the morning of 8 January 1986, Bankers Trust would on that particular day have recalled the appropriate sum from London with the utmost despatch.

No transfer to London having in fact been made on 7 January, and no recall the next morning, U.S. $6.7m. should then have been transferred, as the amount by which the New York balance exceeded the peg of U.S. $500,000. The only issue of potential importance here is whether the transfer was actually made. Although preparations were made for effecting the transfer, I am satisfied that it was countermanded and did not take effect. There is no need for me to decide precisely when the transfer ought to have been made, since that is subsumed in the next point.

The Libyan Bank's third complaint under this head is that, no transfers between New York and London having in fact been made at 2 p.m. on 7 January or in the morning of 8 January, the balance in New York at 2 p.m. on 8 January was U.S. $161,997,000. It is said that a sum of U.S. $161.4m. should then have been transferred to London. In answer to that Bankers Trust rely on points that are the same as, or similar to, those raised in respect of 2 p.m. on 7 January: they say that they were entitled to take pending payment instructions into account; and that they were entitled to delay payment until after 4:10 p.m. when the second Presidential order had been made, which certainly prohibited such a transfer. I reject both arguments for the reasons already given, based on the telex of 27 November 1985. It is true that if the pending payment instructions were to be executed in the afternoon, there were grounds for apprehension that the New York account would become overdrawn, which might be a breach of the first Presidential order, and even that the total of both accounts would be overdrawn, which would plainly be a breach of that order. The solution for Bankers Trust was not to execute those pending instructions unless and until further credits were received in New York. Some were in fact received—the New York account ended the day in credit to the extent of U.S. $251,129,000. Payment instructions for that day totalled U.S. $347,147,213.03, and none of them were in fact executed. So on any view the New York account would have been overdrawn if all had been executed, and that much more overdrawn if in addition U.S. $161.4m. had been transferred to London at 2 p.m. But the net total of the two accounts would still have been a credit balance. If Bankers Trust took the view that an overdraft on the New York account would itself be a breach of the Presidential order, and if they were right, the solution as I have said was to execute the pending instructions only as and when credits received permitted them to do so.

Accordingly I hold that (i) Bankers Trust were in breach of contract in failing to transfer U.S. $165.2m. to London at 2 p.m. on 7 January; (ii) if they had done that, they could and would have recalled U.S. $158.5m. from London in the morning of 8 January; but, (iii) on the assumption that both those steps had been taken, there would have been a further breach in failing to transfer U.S. $154.7m. to London at 2 p.m. on 8 January. (I trust that the calculation of this last figure is not too obscure. The 2 p.m. transfer on 8 January should have been U.S. $161.4m. if *neither* of the previous transfers had been made—as in fact they were not. If they had both been made, the figure would have been reduced to U.S. $154.7m.)

The balance resulting from those three figures is a net loss to the London account of U.S. $161.4m. I hold that this must be added to the Libyan Bank's first claim, as an additional sum for which that claim would have succeeded but for breaches of contract by Bankers Trust. It is said that this loss is not recoverable, because it arose from a new intervening act and is too remote. In the circumstances as they were on 7 and 8 January I have no hesitation in rejecting that argument.

. . .

*Conclusion*

The Libyan Bank are entitled to recover U.S. $131m. on claim (1) and U.S. $161m. (the amount of their demand) on claim (2). Claims (3) and (4) fail. Claim (5) would have failed if it had been material. On claim (6) the Libyan Bank must have judgment for damages to be assessed.

*Postscript*

In August of this year there were 20 working days. Fourteen of them were entirely consumed in the preparation of this judgment. In those circumstances it is a shade disappointing to read in the press and elsewhere that High Court judges do no work at all in August or September and have excessively long holidays.

*Judgment for plaintiffs.*

### *Notes and Questions*

1. The basic features of the managed account relationship are set out below:

| New York | London |
|---|---|
| Operational Account<br>(for payments) | Investment Account<br>(Call account at Libor +) |

*Peg Arrangement*

1. NY balances in excess of $500k peg transferred daily at 2:00 p.m. NY time to London account for same day value.
2. If at 2:00 p.m. NY time, NY balance below $500k peg, transfer from London account to NY account, value previous day.

*Transfer Mechanics* (e.g. to London)

1. BTNY credits BTL branch on its books, with notice to BTL of amount.
2. BTL credits LAFB on its books.

What was the point of this arrangement for LAFB and for BT?

2. Let's look at some freeze basics. Let's start with the first freeze order of January 7, 1986. At 8:06 p.m. NY time, President Reagan signed an Executive Order prohibiting "U.S. persons", which included foreign branches but not foreign subsidiaries of U.S. banks, from extending credit to certain Libyan entities. This prohibited BTNY or BTL from extending credit to LAFB.

At 2:00 p.m. that day, the NY account had a balance of $165.7 million. Under the peg arrangement $165.2 mm (165.7 – .5) should have been transferred to London account but was not. Why wasn't this transfer made?

The second freeze order came at 4:10 p.m. on January 8, 1986. At 8:44 a.m., BTNY had on hand $347.1 million in payment instructions. Why were none of these payments ever made? At 2:00 p.m., the NY account had a balance of $161.997, but there was no transfer to the London account. Why not? How naive was Mr. Brittain?

When the freeze was imposed, there was $251.1mm in the NY account and $131.5mm in the London account.

3. The second freeze order (1) prohibited transfers or cash withdrawals from Libyan accounts; (2) applied only to foreign branches of U.S. banks, not subsidiaries; (3) applied only to dollar accounts; and (4) prohibited any transaction whose purpose or effect was to evade the freeze. Why didn't the U.S. impose the freeze order on foreign subsidiaries of U.S. bank holding companies or foreign currency accounts of foreign branches of U.S. banks?

4. There were various actors affected by the freeze: (1) the United States; (2) the United Kingdom; (3) U.S. banks (including BT); and (4) foreign banks. How did they view the benefits and costs of the freeze? Did they want it to be effective?

5. Let's turn to the issues in the lawsuit. The main claim by LAFB was for the $131mm in the U.K. account, brought as a cause of action for debt. LAFB asked that these funds be paid in cash or by any reasonable method of making a payment. It said it would accept payment in sterling, as well as dollars. In particular, it asked that the funds be transferred to its account with UBAF Bank Limited London, an arab owned consortium bank. You should focus on this claim.

LAFB also claimed funds in New York that it contended should have been in London. There were various theories about how to calculate this amount. One version was rather straightforward: BTNY should have transferred $161.4mm on January 8. This was the version the court accepted.

LAFB also claimed damages with respect to BTNY's failure to execute payment instructions to third parties on January 7. This claim was disallowed. Finally, there was a successful fraud claim for damages with respect to a unilateral change made by BT in the way interest was calculated under the peg arrangement.

6. BT contended that there was an established usage that all dollar payments had to be made through the United States (New York). Why was this an important argument in the lawsuit? Was there such a usage? Are there ways to transfer dollars abroad without going through the United States?

7. As a result of the court's decision, BT was required to pay LAFB approximately $300 million in dollar cash or sterling. How could BTL actually pay this judgment? Could the bank actually get the dollar cash? If it couldn't get dollars, why didn't BTL have a valid impossibility defense to its contractual obligation?

8. Do you think a London bank should be required to pay off dollar accounts in sterling if it can't do so with dollars?

9. Could BT pay this judgment in sterling without being subject to criminal penalties in the United States? Couldn't the United States (through a U.S. court) enjoin BT from making the sterling payment? If the United States did this, what legal remedies might LAFB pursue in the United Kingdom?

10. Judgment was given in dollars, but the statutory judgment interest rate was 15% (near the market interest rate on sterling but considerably in excess of the 7% dollar interest rate). What impact might this have had in persuading the Treasury to issue a license to BT—which Treasury, in fact, did—to enable BT to pay the judgment? Ironically, BT made the payment under the license through a CHIPS transfer.

## B. FREEZES BY THE HOST COUNTRY

There follows the Supreme Court decision in *Wells Fargo* followed by the Second Circuit's decision on remand.

Justice KENNEDY delivered the opinion of the Court.

At issue here is whether the home office of a United States bank is obligated to use its general assets to repay a Eurodollar deposit made at one of its foreign branches, after the foreign country's government has prohibited the branch from making repayment out of its own assets.

I

The case arises from a transaction in what is known in the banking and financial communities as the Eurodollar market. As the District Court defined the term, Eurodollars are United States dollars that have been deposited with a banking institution located outside the United States, with a corresponding obligation on the part of the banking institution to repay the deposit in United States dollars. See App. to

Pet. for Cert. 42a; P. Oppenheim, International Banking 243 (5th ed. 1987). The banking institution receiving the deposit can be either a foreign branch of a United States bank or a foreign bank.

A major component of the Eurodollar market is interbank trading. In a typical interbank transaction in the Eurodollar market, the depositing bank (Bank A) agrees by telephone or telex, or through a broker, to place a deposit denominated in United States dollars with a second bank (Bank X). For the deposit to be a Eurodollar deposit, Bank X must be either a foreign branch of a United States bank or a foreign bank; Bank A, however, can be any bank, including one located in the United States. To complete the transactions, most banks that participate in the interbank trading market utilize correspondent banks in New York City, with whom they maintain, directly or indirectly, accounts denominated in United States dollars. In this example, the depositor bank, Bank A, orders its correspondent bank in New York (Bank B) to transfer United States dollars from Bank A's account to Bank X's account with Bank X's New York correspondent bank (Bank Y). The transfer of funds from Bank B to Bank Y is accomplished by means of a wire transfer through a clearing mechanism located in New York City and known as the Clearing House Interbank Payments System, or "CHIPS." See Scanlon, Definitions and Mechanics of Eurodollar Transactions, in The Eurodollar 16, 24–25 (H. Prochnow ed. 1970); Brief for New York Clearing House Association et al. as *Amici Curiae* 4. Repayment of the funds at the end of the deposit term is accomplished by having Bank Y transfer funds from Bank X's account to Bank B, through the CHIPS system, for credit to Bank A's account.

The transaction at issue here follows this pattern. Respondent Wells Fargo Asia Limited (WFAL) is a Singapore-chartered bank wholly owned by Wells Fargo Bank, N.A., a bank chartered by the United States. Petitioner Citibank, N.A., (Citibank), also a United States-chartered bank, operates a branch office in Manila, Philippines (Citibank/Manila). On June 10, 1983, WFAL agreed to make two $1 million time deposits with Citibank/Manila. The rate at which the deposits would earn interest was set at 10%, and the parties agreed that the deposits would be repaid on December 9 and 10, 1983. The deposits were arranged by oral agreement through the assistance of an Asian money broker, which made a written report to the parties that stated, *inter alia:*

> " 'Pay: Citibank, N.A. New York Account Manila
>
> " 'Repay: Wells Fargo International, New York Account Wells Fargo Asia Ltd., Singapore Account # 003–023645,' " 852 F.2d 657, 658–659 (CA2 1988).

The broker also sent WFAL a telex containing the following " '[i]nstructions' ":

> " 'Settlement—Citibank NA NYC AC Manila

" 'Repayment—Wells Fargo Bk Intl NYC Ac Wells Fargo Asia Ltd Sgp No 003–023645,' " id., at 659.

That same day, the parties exchanged telexes confirming each of the two deposits. WFAL's telexes to Citibank/Manila read:

" 'We shall instruct Wells Fargo Bk Int'l New York our correspondent please pay to our a/c with Wells Fargo Bk Int'l New York to pay to Citibank NA customer's correspondent USD 1,000,000.' " Ibid.

The telexes from Citibank/Manila to WFAL read:

" 'Please remit US Dlr 1,000,000 to our account with Citibank New York. At maturity we remit US Dlr 1,049,444.44 to your account with Wells Fargo Bank Intl Corp NY through Citibank New York.' " Ibid.

A few months after the deposit was made, the Philippine government issued a Memorandum to Authorized Agent Banks (MAAB 47) which provided in relevant part:

" 'Any remittance of foreign exchange for repayment of principal on all foreign obligations due to foreign banks and/or financial institutions, irrespective of maturity, shall be submitted to the Central Bank [of the Philippines] thru the Management of External Debt and Investment Accounts Department (MEDIAD) for prior approval.' " Ibid.

According to the Court of Appeals, "[a]s interpreted by the Central Bank of the Philippines, this decree prevented Citibank/Manila, an 'authorized agent bank' under Philippine law, from repaying the WFAL deposits with its Philippine assets, i.e., those assets not either deposited in banks elsewhere or invested in non-Philippine enterprises." Ibid. As a result, Citibank/Manila refused to repay WFAL's deposits when they matured in December 1983.

WFAL commenced the present action against Citibank in the United States District Court for the Southern District of New York, claiming that Citibank in New York was liable for the funds that WFAL deposited with Citibank/Manila. While the lawsuit was pending, Citibank obtained permission from the Central Bank of the Philippines to repay its Manila depositors to the extent that it could do so with the non-Philippine assets of the Manila branch. It paid WFAL $934,000; the remainder of the deposits, $1,066,000, remains in dispute. During the course of this litigation, Citibank/Manila, with the apparent consent of the Philippine government, has continued to pay WFAL interest on the outstanding principal. See App. to Pet. for Cert. 48a.

After a bench trial on the merits, the District Court accepted Citibank's invitation to assume that Philippine law governs the action. The court saw the issue to be whether, under Philippine law, a depositor with Citibank/Manila may look to assets booked at Citibank's non-Philippine offices for repayment of the deposits. After considering affidavits from the parties, it concluded (1) that under Philippine law an obligation incurred by a branch is an obligation of the bank as a whole; (2) that repayment of WFAL's deposits with assets booked at Citibank offices other than Citibank/Manila would not contravene MAAB 47; and (3) that Citibank therefore was obligated to repay WFAL, even if it could do so only from assets not booked at Citibank/Manila. Id., at 31a–35a. It entered judgment for WFAL, and Citibank appealed.

A panel of the United States Court of Appeals for the Second Circuit remanded the case to the District Court to clarify the basis for its judgment. The Second Circuit ordered the District Court to make supplemental findings of fact and conclusions of law on the following matters:

"(a) Whether the parties agreed as to where the debt could be repaid, including whether they agreed that the deposits were collectible only in Manila.

"(b) If there was an agreement, what were its essential terms?

"(c) Whether Philippine law (other than MAAB 47) precludes or negates an agreement between the parties to have the deposits collectible outside of Manila.

"(d) If there is no controlling Philippine law referred to in (c) above, what law does control?" Id., at 26a.

In response to the first query, the District Court distinguished the concepts of repayment and collection, defining repayment as "refer[ring] to the location where the wire transfers effectuating repayment at maturity were to occur," and collection as "refer[ring] to the place or places where plaintiff was entitled to look for satisfaction of its deposits in the event that Citibank should fail to make the required wire transfers at the place of repayment." Id., at 14a. It concluded that the parties' confirmation slips established an agreement that repayment was to occur in New York, and that there was neither an express agreement nor one that could be implied from custom or usage in the Eurodollar market on the issue of where the deposits could be collected. In response to the second question, the court stated that "[t]he only agreement relating to collection or repayment was that repayment would occur in New York." Id., at 18a. As to the third query, the court stated that it knew of no provision of Philippine law that barred an agreement making WFAL's deposits collectible outside Manila. Finally, in response to the last query, the District Court restated the issue in the case as follows:

"Hence, the dispute in this case ... boils down to one question: is Citibank obligated to use its worldwide assets to satisfy plaintiff's deposits? In other words, the dispute is not so much about where repayment physically was to be made or where the deposits were collectible, but rather which assets Citibank is required to use in order to satisfy its obligation to plaintiff. As we have previously found that the contract was silent on this issue, we interpret query

> (d) as imposing upon us the task ... of deciding whether New York or Philippine law controls the answer to that question." Id. at 19a.

The District Court held that, under either New York or federal choice-of-law rules, New York law should be applied. After reviewing New York law, it held that Citibank was liable for WFAL's deposits with Citibank/Manila, and that WFAL could look to Citibank's worldwide assets for satisfaction of its deposits.

The Second Circuit affirmed, but on different grounds. Citing general banking law principles, the Court of Appeals reasoned that, in the ordinary course, a party who makes a deposit with a foreign branch of a bank can demand repayment of the deposit only at that branch. In the court's view, however, these same principles established that this "normal limitation" could be altered by an agreement between the bank and the depositor: "If the parties agree that repayment of a deposit in a foreign bank or branch may occur at another location, they authorize demand and collection at that other location." 852 F.2d, at 660. The court noted that the District Court had found that Citibank had agreed to repay WFAL's deposits in New York. It concluded that the District Court's finding was not clearly erroneous under Federal Rule of Civil Procedure 52(a), and held that, as a result, WFAL was entitled "to collect the deposits out of Citibank assets in New York." 852 F.2d, at 661.

We granted certiorari. 493 U.S. ___ (1989). We decide that the factual premise on which the Second Circuit relied in deciding the case contradicts the factual determinations made by the District Court, determinations that are not clearly erroneous. We vacate the judgment, and remand the case to the Court of Appeals for further consideration of the additional legal questions in the case.

## II

Little need be said respecting the operation or effect of the Philippine decree at this stage of the case, for no party questions the conclusion reached by both the District Court and the Court of Appeals that Philippine law does not bar the collection of WFAL's deposits from the general assets of the Citibank in the State of New York. See 852 F.2d, at 660–661; App. to Pet. for Cert. 18a. The question, rather, is whether Citibank is obligated to allow collection in New York, and on this point two principal theories must be examined. The first is that there was an agreement between the parties to permit collection in New York, or indeed at any place where Citibank has assets, an agreement implied from all the facts in the case as being within the contemplation of the parties. A second, and alternative, theory for permitting collection is that, assuming no such agreement, there is a duty to pay in New York in any event, a duty that the law creates when the parties have not contracted otherwise. See 3 A. Corbin, Contracts § 561, pp. 276–277 (1960).

The Court of Appeals appears to have relied upon the first theory we have noted, adopting the premise that the parties did contract to permit recovery from the general assets of Citibank in New York. Yet the District Court had made it clear that there is a distinction between an agreement on "repayment," which refers to the physical location for transacting discharge of the debt, and an agreement respecting "collection," which refers to the location where assets may be taken to satisfy it, and in quite specific terms, it found that the only agreement the parties made referred to repayment.

The Court of Appeals, while it said that this finding was not clearly erroneous, appears to have viewed repayment and collection as interchangeable concepts, not divisible ones. It concluded that the agreement as to where repayment could occur constituted also an agreement as to which bank assets the depositor could look to for collection. The strongest indication that the Court of Appeals was interpreting the District Court's findings in this manner is its answer to the argument, made by the United States as *amicus curiae,* that the home office of a bank should not bear the risk of foreign restrictions on the payment of assets from the foreign branch where a deposit has been placed, unless it makes an express agreement to do so. The court announced that "[o]ur affirmance in the present case is based on *the district court's finding of just such an agreement.*" 852 F.2d, at 661 (emphasis added).

That the Court of Appeals based its ruling on the premise of an agreement between the parties is apparent as well from the authorities upon which it relied to support its holding. The court cited three cases for the proposition that an agreement to repay at a particular location authorizes the depositor to collect the deposits at that location, all of which involve applications of the act of state doctrine: Allied Bank International v. Banco Credito Agricola de Cartago, 757 F.2d 516 (CA2), cert. dismissed, 473 U.S. 934 (1985); Garcia v. Chase Manhattan Bank, N.A., 735 F.2d 645, 650–651 (CA2 1984); and Braka v. Bancomer, S.N.C., 762 F.2d 222, 225 (CA2 1985). Each of these three cases turns upon the existence, or nonexistence, of an agreement for collection. In *Garcia* and *Allied Bank,* the agreement of the parties to permit collection at a location outside of the foreign country made the legal action of the foreign country irrelevant. See *Garcia,* 735 F.2d, at 646 (agreement between the parties was that "Chase's main office in New York would guarantee the certificate [of deposit] and that [the depositors] could be repaid by presenting the certificate at any Chase branch worldwide"); id., at 650 (purpose of the agreement was "to ensure that, no matter what happened in Cuba, including seizure of the debt, Chase would still have a contractual obligation to pay the depositors upon presentation of their CDs"); *Allied Bank,* supra, at 520 (agreement between the parties was that Costa Rican banks obligation to repay various loans in New York "would not be excused in the event that the Central Bank [of Costa Rica] failed to provide the necessary United States dollars for repayment"). In *Braka,* the agreement between the parties was that repayment and collection would be permitted only in the foreign country, and so the foreign law controlled. See 762 F.2d, at 224–225 (specifically distinguishing *Garcia* on the ground that the bank had not guaranteed repayment of the deposits outside of Mexico). By its reliance upon these cases, the Court of Appeals, it seems to us, must have been relying upon the existence of an agreement between Citibank and WFAL to permit collection in New York. As noted above, however, this premise contradicts the express finding of the District Court.

Under Federal Rule of Civil Procedure 52(a), the Court of Appeals is permitted to reject the District Court's findings only if those findings are clearly erroneous. As the Court of Appeals itself acknowledged, the record contains ample support for the District Court's finding that the parties agreed that repayment, defined as the wire transfers effecting the transfer of funds to WFAL when its deposits matured, would take place in New York. The confirmation slips exchanged by the parties are explicit: the transfer of funds upon maturity was to occur through wire transfers made by the parties' correspondent banks in New York. See supra, at 3.

As to collection, the District Court found that neither the parties' confirmation slips nor the evidence offered at trial with regard to whether "an agreement concerning the place of collection could be implied from custom and usage in the international banking field" established an agreement respecting collection. See App. to Pet. for Cert. 16a–17a. Upon review of the record, we hold this finding, that no such implied agreement existed based on the intent of the parties, was not clearly erroneous. The confirmation slips do not indicate an agreement that WFAL could collect its deposits from Citibank assets in New York; indeed, Citibank/Manila's confirmation slip, stating that "[a]t maturity *we* remit US Dlr 1,049,444.44 to your account with Wells Fargo Bank Intl Corp NY *through Citibank New York,*" see supra, at 3 (emphasis added), tends to negate the existence of any such agreement. The telexes from the money broker who arranged the deposits speak in terms of repayment, and indicate no more than that repayment was to be made to WFAL's account with its correspondent bank in New York; they do not indicate any agreement about where WFAL could collect its deposits in the event that Citibank/Manila failed to remit payment upon maturity to this account.

Nor does the evidence contradict the District Court's conclusion that the parties, in this particular case, failed to establish a relevant custom or practice in the international banking community from which it could be inferred that the parties had a tacit understanding on the point. Citibank's experts testified that the common understanding in the banking community was that the higher interest rates offered for Eurodollar deposits, in contrast to dollar deposits with United States banks, reflected in part the fact that the deposits were not subject to reserve and insurance requirements imposed on domestic deposits by United States banking law. This could only be the case, argues Citibank, if the deposits were "payable only" outside of the United States, as required by 38 Stat. 270, as amended, 12 U.S.C. § 461(b)(6) and 64 Stat. 873, as amended, 12 U.S.C. § 1813(*l* )(5). It argues further that higher rates reflected the depositor's assumption of foreign "sovereign risk," defined as the risk that actions by the foreign government having legal control over the foreign branch and its assets would render the branch unable to repay the deposit. See, e.g., App. at 354–367 (testimony of Ian H. Giddy).

WFAL's experts, on the other hand, testified that the identical interest rates being offered for Eurodollar deposits in both Manila and London at the time the deposits were made, despite the conceded differences in sovereign risk between the two locations, reflected an understanding that the home office of a bank was liable for repayment in the event that its foreign branch was unable to repay for any reason, including restrictions imposed by a foreign government. See, e.g., App. at 270–272 (testimony of Gunter Dufey).

A fair reading of all of the testimony supports the conclusion that, at least in this trial, on the issue of the allocation of sovereign risk there was a wide variance of opinion in the international banking community. We cannot say that we are left with "the definite and firm conviction" that the District Court's findings are erroneous. United States v. United States Gypsum Co., 333 U.S. 364, 395 (1948). Because the Court of Appeals' holding relies upon contrary factual assumptions, the judgment for WFAL cannot be affirmed under the reasoning used by that court.

Given the finding of the District Court that there was no agreement between the parties respecting collection from Citibank's general assets in New York, the question becomes whether collection is permitted nonetheless by rights and duties implied by law. As is its right, see Dandridge v. Williams, 397 U.S. 471, 475–476 and n. 6 (1970), WFAL seeks to defend the judgment below on the ground that, under principles of either New York or Philippine law, Citibank was obligated to make its general assets available for collection of WFAL's deposits. See Brief for Respondent 18, 23, 30–49. It is unclear from the opinion of the Court of Appeals which law it found to be controlling; and we decide to remand the case for the Court of Appeals to determine which law applies, and the content of that law. See Thigpen v. Roberts, 468 U.S. 27, 32 (1984); *Dandridge,* supra, at 475–476, and n. 6.

One of WFAL's contentions is that the Court of Appeals' opinion can be supported on the theory that it is based upon New York law. We do not think this is a fair or necessary construction of the opinion. The Court of Appeals placed express reliance on its own opinion in Garcia v. Chase Manhattan Bank, N.A., 735 F.2d 645 (CA2 1984), without citing or discussing Perez v. Chase Manhattan Bank, N.A., 61 N.Y.2d 460, 463 N.E.2d 5 (1984). In that case, the New York Court of Appeals was explicit in pointing out that its decision was in conflict with that reached two days earlier by the Second Circuit in *Garcia,* supra, a case that the *Perez* court deemed "similar on its facts." See 61 N.Y.2d, at 464, n. 3, 463 N.E.2d, at 9, n. 3. Given this alignment of authorities, we are reluctant to interpret the Court of Appeals' decision as resting on principles of state law. The opinion of the Court of Appeals, moreover, refers to "general banking law principles" and "United States law," 852 F.2d, at 660; whether this is the semantic or legal equivalent of the law of New York is for the Court of Appeals to say in the first instance.

Alternatively, if the Court of Appeals, based upon its particular expertise in the law of New York and commercial matters generally, is of the view that the controlling rule is supplied by Philippine law or, as Citibank would have it, by a federal common law rule respecting bank deposits, it should make that determination, subject to any further review we deem appropriate. In view of our remand, we find it premature to consider the other contentions of the parties respecting the necessity for any rule of federal common law, or the preemptive effect of federal statutes and regulations on bank deposits and reserves. See 12 U.S.C. §§ 461(b)(6), 1813(*l* )(5)(a); 12 CFR § 204.128(c) (1990). All of these matters, of course, may be addressed by the Court of Appeals if necessary for a full and correct resolution of the case.

The judgment of the Court of Appeals is vacated, and the case remanded for further proceedings consistent with this opinion.

It is so ordered.

The Second Circuit decision follows.

Before TIMBERS, KEARSE and MAHONEY, Circuit Judges.

KEARSE, Circuit Judge:

This action, brought by plaintiff Wells Fargo Asia Limited ("WFAL") to recover funds deposited with the Philippine branch of defendant Citibank, N.A. ("Citibank"), returns to us on remand from the United States Supreme Court, see Citibank, N.A. v. Wells Fargo Asia Limited, ___ U.S. ___, 110 S.Ct. 2034, 109 L.Ed.2d 677 (1990), vacating and remanding 852 F.2d 657 (2d Cir.1988), aff'g 660 F.Supp. 946 (S.D.N.Y.1987) (Knapp, J.), for a determination of what law applies to the present controversy and the content of that law, and for resolution of the controversy in light of those determinations. For the reasons below, we affirm the district court's ruling that the law of New York is applicable and its award of judgment in favor of WFAL.

## I. BACKGROUND

The background of this action has been recounted in several opinions, including Citibank, N.A. v. Wells Fargo Asia Limited, ___ U.S. ___, 110 S.Ct. 2034, 109 L.Ed.2d 677 ("WFAL IV"); Wells Fargo Asia Limited v. Citibank, N.A., 852 F.2d 657 (2d Cir.1988) ("WFAL III"), Wells Fargo Asia Limited v. Citibank, N.A., 695 F.Supp. 1450 (S.D.N.Y. 1988) ("WFAL II"), and Wells Fargo Asia Limited v. Citibank, N.A., 660 F.Supp. 946 (S.D.N.Y.1987) ("WFAL I"), familiarity with which is assumed. Briefly, in 1983, WFAL, a Singapore-chartered bank wholly owned by the United States-chartered Wells Fargo Bank, N.A., placed two six-month-nonnegotiable U.S. $1,000,000 deposits with Citibank for its branch in Manila, Philippines ("Citibank/Manila"). The deposit agreement called for WFAL to pay this amount to Citibank in New York for deposit at Citibank/Manila; it called for Citibank to repay Wells Fargo International's New York account for WFAL.

The deposits were to mature in December 1983. In October 1983, however, the Philippine government issued a Memorandum to Authorized Agent Banks ("MAAB 47"). As described in our earlier opinion, MAAB 47 provided, in pertinent part, as follows:

> Any remittance of foreign exchange for repayment of principal on all foreign obligations due to foreign banks and or financial institutions, irrespective of maturity, shall be submitted to the Central Bank [of the Philippines] thru the Management of External Debt and Investment Accounts Department (MEDIAD) for prior approval. As interpreted by the Central Bank of the Philippines, this decree prevented Citibank/Manila, an "authorized agent bank" under Philippine law, from repaying the WFAL deposits with its Philippine assets, i.e., those assets not either deposited in banks elsewhere or invested in non-Philippine enterprises. Citibank/Manila did not repay WFAL's deposits upon maturity.

*WFAL III,* 852 F.2d at 659. After WFAL commenced the present suit for repayment of the deposited amounts, Citibank/Manila sought and received permission from the Central Bank of the Philippines to repay its foreign depositors to the extent it could do so with non-Philippine assets. Citibank/Manila thereafter repaid WFAL $934,000, leaving $1,066,000 in dispute.

The district court, Honorable Whitman Knapp, *Judge,* entered judgment in favor of WFAL, rejecting Citibank's contention that MAAB 47 made it impossible to repay the WFAL deposits. Noting that MAAB 47 allows obligations to foreign banks to be repaid if the consent of the Central Bank is obtained, and further noting that Citibank had not satisfied its good faith obligation to seek that consent, the court concluded that Citibank's impossibility defense must fail. Though originally making this ruling on the hypothesis that the law of the Philippines applied, *see WFAL I,* 660 F.Supp. at 947, the district court concluded, upon request from this Court for clarification, that New York law, rather than Philippine law, governed the dispute, *WFAL II,* 695 F.Supp. at 1454. It ruled that under New York law, Citibank's worldwide assets were available for satisfaction of WFAL's claim. Id.

We affirmed. Though the district court had concluded (a) that repayment and collection are independent concepts, and (b) that the parties had not reached an agreement as to the situs of collection, and we did not disturb those rulings, we concluded that the

> authorities suggest that a debt may be collected wherever it is repayable, *unless* the parties have agreed otherwise. Since the court found here that there was no separate agreement restricting where the deposits could be collected, and we are aware of nothing in the

> record that contradicts that finding, we conclude that WFAL was entitled to collect the deposits out of Citibank assets in New York.

*WFAL III,* 852 F.2d at 661 (emphasis added).

The Supreme Court vacated our decision, stating that we appeared to have treated the concepts of repayment and collection as interchangeable rather than independent and to have "rel[ied] upon the existence of an agreement between Citibank and WFAL to permit collection in New York." *WFAL IV,* 110 S.Ct. at 2040. The Supreme Court concluded that the district court's finding that there was no agreement as to the situs of collection was not clearly erroneous; it also endorsed "the District Court's conclusion that the parties, in this particular case, failed to establish a relevant custom or practice in the international banking community from which it could be inferred that the parties had a tacit understanding on the point." Id. at 2041. Concluding that our decision could not be upheld on the theory that there was an agreement as to the place of collection, the Supreme Court remanded for a determination of whether WFAL's claim is governed by New York law, Philippine law, or federal common law, and what the content of the governing law is, and directed us to decide the appeal in light of those determinations:

> Given the finding of the District Court that there was no agreement between the parties respecting collection from Citibank's general assets in New York, the question becomes whether collection is permitted nonetheless by rights and duties implied by law. As is its right, ... WFAL seeks to defend the judgment below on the ground that, under principles of either New York or Philippine law, Citibank was obligated to make its general assets available for collection of WFAL's deposits .... It is unclear from the opinion of the Court of Appeals which law it found to be controlling; and we decide to remand the case for the Court of Appeals to determine which law applies, and the content of that law.

Id. at 2042.

Accordingly, we proceed to those questions.

## II. DISCUSSION

In response to this Court's earlier inquiry, the district court discussed the choice-of-law question as follows:

> The legal principles governing our determination are straightforward. Jurisdiction in this action is asserted both on the basis of diversity and federal question involving 12 U.S.C. § 632. In diversity cases, of course, we must apply the conflict of law doctrine of the forum state. Klaxon Co. v. Stentor Elec. Mfg. Co. (1941) 313 U.S. 487, 61 S.Ct. 1020, 85 L.Ed. 1477. In federal question cases, we are directed to apply a federal common law choice of law rule to determine which jurisdiction's substantive law should apply. Corporacion Venezolana de Fomento v. Vintero Sales Corp. (2d Cir.1980) 629 F.2d 786, 794–95, cert. denied (1981) 449 U.S. 1080, 101 S.Ct. 863, 66 L.Ed.2d 804. The rule in New York is that "the law of the

jurisdiction having the greatest interest in the litigation will be applied and that the facts or contacts which obtain significance in defining State interests are those which relate to the purpose of the particular law in conflict." Intercontinental Planning, Ltd. v. Daystrom, Inc. (1969) 24 N.Y.2d 372, 382, 300 N.Y.S.2d 817, 825, 248 N.E.2d 576, 582. Federal law invokes similar considerations, see, Corporacion Venezolana, 629 F.2d at 795, and the place of performance is considered an important factor. *Citibank, N.A. v. Benkoczy* (S.D.Fla.1983) 561 F.Supp. 184, 186 and cases cited therein.

Regardless of whether the New York or federal test is used, application of these standards leads us to the conclusion that New York law should be used to evaluate Wells Fargo's contention that Citibank's worldwide assets are available for repayment of the deposits. As the New York Court of Appeals has recognized, "New York ... is a financial capital of the world, serving as an international clearing house and market place for a plethora of international transactions ... [.] In order to maintain its preeminent financial position, it is important that the justified expectations of the parties to the contract be protected." J. Zeevi and Sons, Ltd. v. Grindlays Bank (Uganda) Ltd. (1975) 37 N.Y.2d 220, 227, 371 N.Y.S.2d 892, 898, 333 N.E.2d 168, 172. In our view, these expectations will be best promoted by applying a uniform rule of New York law where, as here, the transactions were denominated in United States dollars and settled through the parties' New York correspondent banks, and where the defendant is a United States bank with headquarters in New York. Since Eurodollar transactions denominated in U.S. dollars customarily are cleared in New York ... the rationale for application of New York law becomes even stronger. If the goal is to promote certainty in international financial markets, it makes sense to apply New York law uniformly, rather than conditioning the deposit obligations on the vagaries of local law, and requiring each player in the Eurodollar market to investigate the law of numerous foreign countries in order to ascertain which would limit repayment of deposits to the foreign branch's own assets.

*WFAL II,* 695 F.Supp. at 1453–54.

As to the content of New York law on the matter, the district court noted that the most recent pronouncement of the New York Court of Appeals, see Perez v. Chase Manhattan National Bank, N.A., 61 N.Y.2d 460, 468, 474 N.Y.S.2d 689, 691, 463 N.E.2d 5, 7, cert. denied, 469 U.S. 966, 105 S.Ct. 366, 83 L.Ed.2d 302 (1984), indicated that the parent bank is ultimately liable for the obligations of the foreign branch. Though the district court reasoned that an actual expropriation by the foreign government would be treated differently, it concluded that in the present case, there having been no expropriation and no limitation of the depositor's rights but only action affecting the assets of the branch, New York law would allow collection of the debt in New York:

[I]f the Philippines had confiscated plaintiff's deposits, New York courts would interpret the expropriation as a compulsory assignment of the depositor's rights, so that payment to the Philippine assignee would discharge the debt. A New York court would further recognize such compulsory assignment as an act of a foreign sovereign unreviewable under the Act of State doctrine. *Perez,* supra, 61 N.Y.2d 460, 474 N.Y.S.2d 689, 463 N.E.2d 5. We believe New York would take a similar approach in the situation where a foreign government had effected a partial confiscation in the form of a tax on a deposit made at a foreign branch. See, Dunn v. Bank of Nova Scotia (5th Cir.1967) 374 F.2d 876. However, we are aware of no persuasive authority to tell us to what extent, if any, a New York court would defer to local law in the situation here presented, where the foreign sovereign did not extinguish the branch's debt either in whole or in part but merely conditioned repayment on the obtaining of approval from a government agency. Fortunately, we need not resolve that troublesome question.

*WFAL II,* 695 F.Supp. at 1454–55. The court found it unnecessary to determine whether New York law would hold that a foreign government's refusal to give the prerequisite consent constitutes an excuse for refusal to make repayment, in light of its earlier finding that Citibank "had not satisfied its good faith obligation to seek the [Philippine] government's consent to use the assets booked at Citibank's non-Philippine offices." Id. at 1455. The court reaffirmed that finding.

We agree with the district court's analysis, and we conclude, substantially for the reasons that court stated; that New York law governs the present claim and that under New York law, Citibank was not excused from making repayment. In urging that we reach the contrary conclusion. Citibank argues that there is a clear federal policy placing the risk of foreign-law impediments to repayment on the depositor. In so arguing, it relies on federal banking rules such as 12 U.S.C. § 461(b)(6) (1988), which provides that banking reserve requirements "shall not apply to deposits payable only outside the States of the United States and the District of Columbia," and 12 C.F.R. § 204.128(c) (1990) (issued at 52 Fed.Reg. 47696, Dec. 16, 1987), which provides that "[a] customer who makes a deposit that is payable solely at a foreign branch of the depository institution assumes whatever risk may exist that the foreign country in which a branch is located might impose restrictions on withdrawals." Citibank's reliance on these provisions is misplaced. Federal law defines a deposit that is "payable only at an office outside the United States" as "a deposit ... as to which the depositor is entitled, *under the agreement with the institution,* to demand payment *only* outside the United States." Id. § 204.2(t) (emphasis added). The provisions relied on thus do not reveal a policy allocating the risk to depositors as a matter of law where there is no such agreement. So long as state law does not restrict a bank's freedom to enter into an agreement that allocates the risk of foreign sovereign restrictions, state law does not conflict with the federal policy reflected in current statutes or regulations. We see no such restriction in the law of New York, and hence there is no " 'significant conflict'," Mires v. DeKalb County, Georgia, 433 U.S. 25, 31, 97 S.Ct. 2490, 2494–95, 53 L.Ed.2d 557 (1977) (quoting Wallis v. Pan American Petroleum Corp., 384 U.S. 63, 68, 86 S.Ct. 1301, 1304, 16 L.Ed.2d 369 (1966)), between New York law and federal law such as would be necessary to justify the creation of a federal common law.

We conclude that under New York law, unless the parties agree to the contrary, a creditor may collect a debt at a place where the parties have agreed that it is repayable. In applying this principle to the circumstances of the present case to affirm the judgment in favor of WFAL, we do not assume the existence of an agreement between Citibank/Manila and WFAL to permit collection in New York; rather, in light of the express finding of the district court that the parties had no agreement as to permissible situses of collection, we rely on the absence of any agreement forbidding the collection in New York.

Finally, we note that on the present remand, WFAL urged us to affirm on the basis of recently submitted evidence that in fact Citibank, while refusing to use non-Manila assets to pay Citibank/Manila's debts, has received profits of at least $25 million from Citibank/Manila during the period 1984–1989. WFAL contends that it is entitled to have its deposits repaid out of these profits. Citibank does not dispute that it received these profits (see Citibank reply brief on remand at 20, n. 18, stating that these transfers "represent a small yield on capital investment that the Central Bank permits Citibank/Manila to remit to its home office") but takes the position that it is not required to use these profits to pay persons whose deposits in Citibank/Manila remain unpaid. We need not resolve this question. Suffice it to say that Citibank's acknowledged ability to obtain Philippine Central Bank approval of transfers to it of moneys as profits appears to support the district court's finding, if further support were needed, that Citibank in fact did not satisfy its good faith obligation to seek that government's approval of repayment of WFAL's deposits to WFAL.

## CONCLUSION

We have considered all of Citibank's arguments on this appeal and have found them to be without merit. The judgment of the district court is affirmed.

### *Notes and Questions*

1. Make sure you understand how this freeze affected Citibank. Wells Fargo Asia Ltd. (WFAL), a bank chartered in Singapore (a subsidiary of Wells Fargo Corp., a U.S. bank holding company), placed two $1 million 6 month time deposits with the Manila branch of Citibank–NY (Citibank/Manila), on June 10, 1983, repayable on December 9–10, 1983. After the transaction, the account entries on the Citibank's balance sheets were as follows:

| Citibank Manila (C/Manila) | | Citibank New York (C/NY) | |
|---|---|---|---|
| A | L | A | L |
| $2mm C/NY | $2mm WFAL | $2mm | $2mm C/Manila |

After the deposits had been made, the Philippines issued the "Memorandum to Authorized Agent Banks" which prevented C/Manila from repaying the WFAL deposits with its "Philippine Assets." Philippine assets were local assets, assets denominated in pesos. They did not include deposits in banks outside the Philippines or invested in non-Philippine enterprises.

The purpose of the decree was to limit the outflow of Philippine foreign exchange reserves. This would happen if Citibank Manila were to use Philippine assets, denominated in pesos, to obtain dollars from the Philippines Central Bank, and remit these dollars to foreign creditors such as Wells Fargo.

If Citibank/Manila had the full $2 million in a deposit at Citibank–NY, it could have used these funds to pay WFAL. But it did not; it had invested this money in various assets, some Philippines, some not, along with funds from other Citibank Manila depositors. It was able to pay WFAL $934K from non-Philippine assets (WFAL's pro rata share), but still owed $1,066,000.

2. Why did Wells Fargo place $2 million in time deposits with the Manila branch of Citibank rather than with Citibank's New York head office or London branch?

3. The Federal Reserve Bank of New York sided with Citibank's position that the head office should not be responsible for foreign branch liabilities. Why?

4. Under existing case law, it is clear that Head Office would be responsible if the parties had contracted to this effect—although courts have varied in how liberally contracts would be read to find such an agreement. The first decision by the Court of Appeals thought there was such a contract. Do you agree with the Supreme Court that there wasn't?

On remand, the Court of Appeals held that under applicable New York law, absent contract to the contrary, the Head Office was responsible for branch deposits, and the Supreme Court denied further review. What was the basis for this decision? How will the decision affect eurodollar interest rates? Was this the right result?

---

*Links to Other Chapters*

Obviously asset freezes are directly linked to the payment system, the details of which were examined in the prior Chapter. Control of the domestic payment system is a major weapon at the disposal of national sovereigns that may permit them—if they are willing to use it—to exert control over offshore markets. For example, the Japanese could effectively stop Euroyen transactions by not allowing them to clear through the Japanese payment system. The desire of countries to control offshore markets, particularly in their own currency, is a recurring theme in this book.

# Chapter XI

# EUROBONDS AND GLOBAL BONDS

This Chapter looks at two important international bond markets, eurobonds and global bonds. With respect to eurobonds, we first look at the development and some important characteristics of the market. We will then examine two key issues, issuing procedures and withholding taxes. As to global bonds, our focus is on what they are, how they relate to eurobonds, and what obstacles have to be overcome for further expansion.

## A. EUROBONDS

### 1. The Market

"THE INTERNATIONAL BOND MARKET"

31 Bank of England Quarterly Bulletin (November 1991), pp. 521–528.

Eurobonds are traditionally defined as bonds which are issued, and largely sold, outside the domestic market of the currency in which they are denominated. They are typically underwritten by an international syndicate of banks, are exempt from any withholding taxes (ie taxes on coupon payments deducted at source), and are bearer in nature (ie no register of ownership is maintained). Originally, investors were attracted in particular by (and thus prepared to pay a premium for) the bearer status of eurobonds and their freedom from liability to withholding tax, although it is an over-simplification to characterise all eurobonds as having such distinctive features—practices vary between currency sectors and have altered with time. Eurobonds are distinct from domestic and foreign bonds. For the purposes of this article domestic bonds can in general be taken to mean bonds issued by largely domestic borrowers through domestic syndicates of banks and securities houses to predominantly domestic investors. "Foreign" bond markets can be viewed as subsets of domestic bond markets, comprising domestic bonds issued by foreign borrowers.

#### Early development of the eurobond market

An international bond market can be traced back to the 19th century, when, for example, foreign governments launched bonds in London. However, the eurobond market developed much more recently, in the early 1960s, as an offshore market in, primarily, dollar bonds. A contributory factor to its development was the prior growth of a London eurodollar deposit market in the post-war period reflecting, *inter alia,* the emergence of a substantial US current account deficit in the early

1960s and restrictions on the maximum rate of interest which US-based banks could pay on US-held dollar deposits under Regulation Q.

Over time, eurodollar depositors diversified into the first important foreign bond sector—"Yankee" bonds (US dollar bonds issued in New York by non-US borrowers). Although Yankee bond issues were normally underwritten by US securities firms in New York, European intermediaries were often invited to help distribute the bonds abroad. As European investors and issuers became more important in the Yankee bond market, the necessary conditions were in place for European securities firms to avoid the listing and disclosure requirements of the US bond market by themselves lead managing and underwriting dollar bond issues in London.

The introduction in July 1963 of an Interest Equalisation Tax, in response to the deterioration in the US current account, gave the decisive impetus to the development of the eurobond market. The Interest Equalisation Tax was levied on US investors' purchases of foreign securities and in turn raised the cost of foreign borrowing in the US market by 1%. The effect was a sharp contraction of issuance in the Yankee bond market and, with access to a number of other foreign bond markets subject to restrictions, issuance was diverted to the emerging eurodollar bond market. Reinforcing this, in 1965 the Voluntary Restraint Program established voluntary limits on foreign direct investment out of the United States (unless matching balance of payments earnings accrued) and in 1968 the guidelines were replaced by mandatory restrictions. As a result, US multinationals had little alternative but to fund their foreign subsidiaries through the euromarkets.

Eurobond market issuance expanded rapidly in the 1960s (reaching $3 billion in 1970) and the currency base of the market broadened (in particular, markets in deutschemarks. Dutch guilders, yen and Canadian dollars became well established). In the 1970s, some of the factors which contributed to the early development of the eurobond market ceased to have effect: for instance, the Interest Equalisation Tax was abolished in 1974. Nevertheless, the eurobond market consolidated its position as a channel of intermediation for international capital flows, largely because an infrastructure for economical primary distribution and secondary trading had become well established, and because many domestic bond markets were subject to strict issuing requirements.

During these early stages of the eurobond market, London became established as the main centre for issuance and trading. Apart from the advantages possessed in terms of time zone and language, London also benefited from the international, innovative and entrepreneurial traditions of many of its institutions, as well as the relatively restrictive regulatory and fiscal regimes in other centres.

### Eurobond market: 1980–90

The past decade has seen the eurobond market evolve considerably in terms of growth of issuance, currency diversification, shifts in the patterns of instruments and borrowers, and innovation.

## Total issuance

Eurobond issuance grew very rapidly, increasing from $26 billion in 1980 to $185 billion in 1986. Subsequently, issuance has fluctuated between $142 billion in 1987 and $224 billion in 1989 (Chart 1), reflecting, inter alia, a sharp fall in issues of floating-rate notes (FRNs) and the extremely high volume of dollar equity-warrant bonds issued by Japanese borrowers in 1989, a phenomenon owing much to the buoyancy of Japanese equity prices. Straight eurobond issuance rose to record levels in the early part of 1991 as confidence returned to capital markets following the Gulf War, with investors switching into longer maturities and yields falling.

## Currency diversification

Deregulation has contributed to a widening of the range of currencies in which eurobonds are issued from 11 in 1980 to 21 in 1990. New currency sectors have included, for instance, the French and Luxembourg francs, the lira and the Swedish krona. The increased spread of currencies in the eurobond market has presented a means through which investors may diversify their portfolios without incurring the complications of investing in domestic markets (eg tax). It has also contributed to a natural widening in the investor and issuer base of the eurobond market.

As a result of the development of other currency sectors, reflecting the growing role of other currencies in international trade and capital flows, the share of the dollar in eurobond issuance has declined (from 57% in 1980 to 35% in 1990), matched by an increase in the share of the yen in the mid–1980s and more recently in the share of European currencies, notably the Ecu (Chart 1).

## Instruments

Straight fixed-rate eurobonds have been the dominant instrument in the eurobond market, although their relative importance has diminished from 72% of eurobond issuance in 1980 to 61% in 1990 (Table A). The decline reflects developments in the markets for FRNs and equity-linked bonds.

**Chart 1**
**Currency composition of eurobond issues 1980-90**

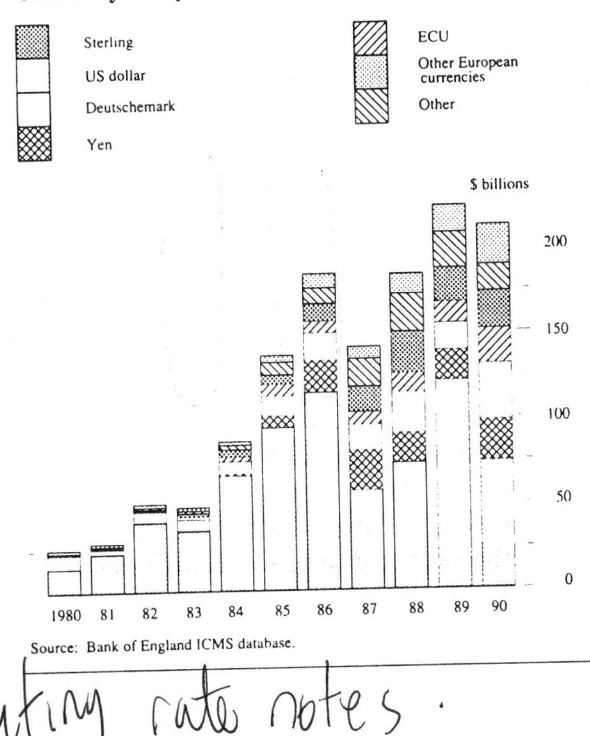


Source: Bank of England ICMS database.

FRN issuance grew rapidly until 1985, supported by issues from banks attracted by the ability to match the income from their loans with the interest expense of their FRNs. However, in 1986, investor demand for FRNs began to weaken, as concerns about oversupply heightened and as interest rates fell. Moreover, the successful introduction of asset-backed securities caused investors as well as market-makers to reassess the relative value of deeply subordinated perpetual FRN issues. This reassessment occurred at a time when perpetual FRN investors, particularly the Japanese banks, were increasingly concerned about the treatment of perpetual FRNs, in the light of new capital adequacy requirements to be imposed by the Japanese Ministry of Finance: in December 1986, the cumulation of these factors led to a sharp sell-off of perpetual FRNs and a drying-up of liquidity, which also affected the dated FRN market. Since then, the growth of the swap market has made it easier for investors and issuers to create synthetic floating-rate instruments through the fixed-rate markets, and issues of FRNs have remained relatively subdued.

**Table A**
**Eurobond issues by instrument type**

$ billions

| Year | Straight fixed-rate | Floating-rate note (FRNs) | Equity-related bonds: Equity warrant | Equity-related bonds: Convertible | Bonds with non-equity warrants(a) | **Total** |
|---|---|---|---|---|---|---|
| 1980 | 18.6 | 3.5 | — | 3.6 | — | **25.7** |
| 1981 | 18.7 | 7.6 | — | 2.6 | 0.3 | **29.2** |
| 1982 | 36.4 | 12.4 | 0.4 | 1.4 | 1.1 | **51.7** |
| 1983 | 29.1 | 14.1 | 1.6 | 3.3 | 1.3 | **49.4** |
| 1984 | 40.8 | 33.5 | 2.7 | 4.6 | 5.6 | **87.2** |
| 1985 | 73.1 | 55.0 | 2.7 | 4.8 | 1.6 | **137.2** |
| 1986 | 115.2 | 46.7 | 15.3 | 5.9 | 2.0 | **185.1** |
| 1987 | 91.7 | 11.4 | 23.0 | 13.0 | 2.5 | **141.6** |
| 1988 | 126.6 | 23.4 | 28.3 | 5.4 | 0.7 | **184.4** |
| 1989 | 125.1 | 26.8 | 67.0 | 4.6 | 0.2 | **223.7** |
| 1990 | 129.9 | 57.2 | 20.6 | 4.3 | 0.1 | **212.1** |

Source: Bank of England ICMS database.

(a) Currency, debt, gold.

. . .

## Borrowers

Eurobond market investors have typically been "name-conscious", so most issuers have been highly-rated borrowers from OECD countries. (Between 1985 and 1990, issues by non-OECD countries averaged 3.7% of total eurobond issuance.) Over the last decade (Table B), issuance of eurobonds by the US private sector, the largest national group of issuers in the early 1980s, more than halved for a variety of reasons: for example, the use of shelf registration in the United States accelerated the process of domestic bond issuance and reduced one of the competitive advantages enjoyed by the eurobond market; the abolition of withholding tax in the US domestic market also contributed to a decline in the attractiveness of the eurobond market to US borrowers; and in recent years increased corporate indebtedness, often associated with large takeover bids, has led to heightened investor awareness of the credit risk of US corporations.

**Table B**
**Gross flows in the eurobond market: borrowing by nationality**
Percentages

| | United States | Japan | United Kingdom | West Germany(a) | France | Canada | International institutions | Other |
|---|---|---|---|---|---|---|---|---|
| 1980 | 19.0 | 6.3 | 6.3 | — | 8.4 | 5.0 | 18.5 | 36.5 |
| 1981 | 22.2 | 9.9 | 4.2 | 0.2 | 7.2 | 16.8 | 13.5 | 26.0 |
| 1982 | 26.2 | 4.2 | 2.2 | 2.9 | 14.3 | 13.4 | 12.3 | 24.5 |
| 1983 | 13.2 | 9.6 | 3.4 | 4.8 | 11.5 | 7.8 | 19.9 | 29.8 |
| 1984 | 26.9 | 11.2 | 5.1 | 2.1 | 8.2 | 5.4 | 9.7 | 31.4 |
| 1985 | 27.4 | 10.2 | 10.3 | 2.0 | 7.9 | 5.3 | 8.9 | 28.0 |
| 1986 | 19.9 | 12.3 | 10.1 | 5.3 | 6.7 | 7.8 | 7.1 | 30.8 |
| 1987 | 14.1 | 23.3 | 6.9 | 5.9 | 5.0 | 4.2 | 10.4 | 30.2 |
| 1988 | 8.5 | 20.9 | 12.8 | 5.6 | 7.8 | 5.1 | 8.8 | 30.5 |
| 1989 | 6.9 | 36.7 | 10.2 | 4.1 | 5.0 | 4.3 | 7.6 | 25.2 |
| 1990 | 9.3 | 22.1 | 9.7 | 3.0 | 8.1 | 2.3 | 10.7 | 34.8 |

Source: Bank of England ICMS database.

(a) Includes borrowing by East German institutions following unification.

Japanese private sector borrowers have supplanted their US counterparts as the largest issuers in the international bond market. In most cases, Japanese corporate borrowers have issued bonds with equity-warrants in the euromarkets through syndicates led by Japanese securities houses' affiliates in London, with placement thought to be largely with Japanese investors. The sharp decline in Japanese equity prices last year led to some reduction in equity-warrant issues, although this has partly been offset by increased issuance by Japanese corporates of fixed-rate debt. Meanwhile, following authorization in July 1990, Japanese City banks have over the past year or so been heavy issuers of subordinated debt in the international markets to help bolster their balance sheets.

equity warrants work when you have a booming Stock MKT.

**Chart 2**
**Share of eurobond market by business sector**

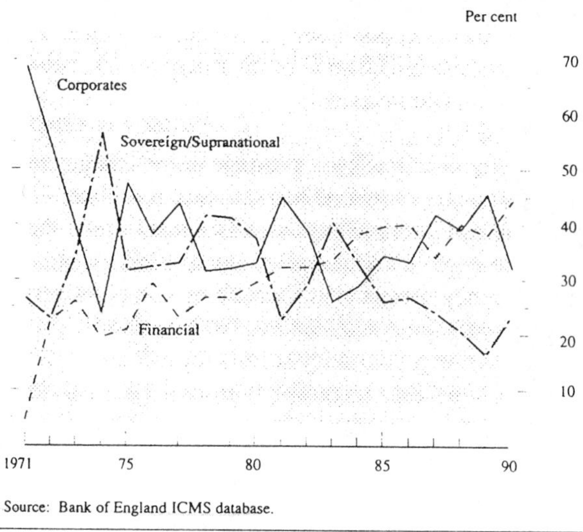


Source: Bank of England ICMS database.

Supranational organisations, such as the International Bank for Reconstruction and Development (IBRD), the European Investment Bank (EIB) and regional development banks, have been consistently important issuers in the international bond market. The larger supranational organisations have become significant issuers of large liquid bonds which, together with a few bonds by top quality sovereigns, act as benchmarks in the eurobond market.

## Investors

The bearer status of eurobonds precludes a comprehensive analysis of the investor profile, but a number of observations can be made.

UK residents' purchases of eurobonds were limited until the abolition of exchange controls in 1979, since then they have been free to purchase eurobonds without restriction. In the United States, domestic investors are inhibited from buying eurobonds through an initial public offering which has not been registered with the SEC (although they may be sold freely after an official "seasoning period" of 40 days). US investors have, in any case, ready access to large and liquid domestic capital markets. Continental European investors—traditionally "name-conscious" and placing a premium on bearer instruments and freedom from withholding tax—have been a major source of demand for eurobonds. And in recent years Japan has become a major source of demand as its external surplus has grown; in addition, equity-warrant bond issues in the eurobond market have become a significant channel of intermediation between Japanese borrowers and investors.

A separate development has been a change in the character of certain segments of the eurobond market. Small private investors ("retail" investors) were a significant feature of the early days of the market, and remain important in high interest rate currency sectors characterized by comparatively small, illiquid issues (eg Australian and New Zealand dollars). However, other currency sectors (eg US dollar, Ecu, yen, sterling) have become increasingly institutionalized (ie the proportion of funds professionally managed, rather than being managed directly by the final investor, has increased); as a result, a demand for liquidity in the secondary market, and hence for large primary issues, has been created. Nevertheless, institutional investors are usually subject to restrictions on the diversification of their investments (eg German life insurance companies may only invest a maximum of 5% of their assets in overseas securities).

**Table C**
**Distribution of eurobond bookrunners by nationality**
Percentages

| | United States | Japan | Continental Europe | United Kingdom |
|---|---|---|---|---|
| 1980 | 19.5 | 4.9 | 52.4 | 12.0 |
| 1981 | 26.9 | 10.0 | 42.2 | 11.3 |
| 1982 | 28.6 | 5.5 | 51.3 | 8.1 |
| 1983 | 16.6 | 6.3 | 59.1 | 9.4 |
| 1984 | 34.4 | 8.9 | 40.4 | 9.3 |
| 1985 | 33.6 | 12.2 | 39.5 | 10.0 |
| 1986 | 27.2 | 24.3 | 37.5 | 7.5 |
| 1987 | 18.1 | 36.9 | 33.6 | 9.8 |
| 1988 | 19.6 | 44.8 | 25.8 | 6.6 |
| 1989 | 19.7 | 44.8 | 25.8 | 6.6 |
| 1990 | 18.8 | 29.1 | 40.8 | 8.1 |

Source: Bank of England ICMS database.

The global nature of the eurobond market—intermediating between borrowers and investors throughout the developed world—is matched by the wide nationality range of bookrunners (Table C). Banks and securities houses have traditionally maintained especially close links with issuers and investors from their home country. Consequently, the market shares of bookrunners have changed to reflect the pattern of intermediation through the eurobond market (eg Japanese firms have been bookrunners for virtually all equity warrant bond issues by Japanese companies), although there remain some banks and securities houses with a significant presence in a variety of countries and currency sectors.

## Other instruments of international financial intermediation

A variety of instruments—eg syndicated credits, euro medium-term notes and eurocommercial paper—can be regarded as alternatives, in varying degrees, to eurobonds as a means of raising finance in the international capital markets. Table D shows that, in contrast to the pattern of eurobond issuance, the volume of syndicated credit announcements fell sharply in the first half of the 1980s owing partly to the international debt crisis. However, syndicated credit activity later recovered, helped by a surge in merger and acquisition financings, to reach a record level of $165 billion in 1990. Both eurobonds and syndicated credits provide long-term finance for borrowers and, although they are in certain circumstances alternative sources of finance, each has distinct characteristics: for instance, the syndicated credits market is normally open to borrowers with a lower credit-standing than the eurobond market; it can raise exceptionally large amounts for highly-rated credits (eg to finance takeover bids); and syndicated credit facilities can provide flexibility over the pace of disbursement.

**Table D**

**Gross borrowing in the international financial markets**
$ billions

| | Eurobonds | Foreign bonds | Syndicated credits | Euronotes | Total |
|---|---|---|---|---|---|
| 1980 | 25.7 | 11.3 | 82.9 | — | **119.9** |
| 1981 | 29.2 | 19.5 | 100.7 | 1.0 | **150.4** |
| 1982 | 51.7 | 22.6 | 88.2 | 2.4 | **164.9** |
| 1983 | 49.4 | 24.4 | 38.1 | 3.3 | **115.2** |
| 1984 | 87.2 | 21.5 | 30.1 | 18.8 | **157.6** |
| 1985 | 137.2 | 27.3 | 19.0 | 50.7 | **234.2** |
| 1986 | 185.1 | 36.5 | 29.9 | 75.1 | **326.6** |
| 1987 | 141.6 | 34.0 | 88.8 | 76.3 | **340.7** |
| 1988 | 184.4 | 43.1 | 111.8 | 84.2 | **423,5** |
| 1989 | 223.7 | 39.0 | 151.7 | 71.8 | **486.2** |
| 1990 | 212.1 | 50.6 | 165.0 | 70.5 | **498.2** |

Source: Bank of England ICMS database.

. . .

## Innovation

The eurobond market—just like the US domestic bond market—has traditionally been a leading channel of financial market innovation, allowing financial structures to be adapted to accommodate the requirements of issuers and investors more flexibly than has been possible in some domestic capital markets. For instance, the use of swaps in the eurobond market was a natural consequence of the increased internationalisation of bond markets, while the eurobond market also witnessed the development of the Japanese equity warrant. Other instruments, such as asset-backed securities, had earlier developed into a sizable market in the United States, and became an important part of the eurobond market (with issuance rising to $15 billion in 1990). The eurobond market is now host to a wide and diversified range of instruments, including many which have relatively complex interest-rate and redemption profiles: for example, capped FRNs, in which the coupon rate has an upper limit, and index-linked bonds, such as bull-bear bonds, in which redemption prices are linked to, say, a stock market index, with redemption proceeds on the bull portion rising as the index rises and the redemption proceeds on the bear tranche rising as the index falls. In many cases, the wider range of instruments available in the eurobond market compared with domestic markets has reflected regulatory regimes: for instance, issuance of FRNs, zero-coupon bonds and dual-currency bonds was prohibited in Germany until May 1985, although such instruments were issued in other currency sectors of the eurobond market.

## Secondary market

Investors' desire for liquidity (eg the ability to buy or sell bonds in sizable amounts before they mature without much influencing the price) has led to the development of a sizable secondary market in eurobonds.

The secondary market is primarily an over-the-counter market, even though most eurobonds are listed on the London or Luxembourg Stock Exchanges. (Listings are normally obtained because some institutional investors are not allowed to purchase unquoted securities). Secondary market trading has expanded rapidly in recent years: Table E shows the growth in secondary market trading through the international clearing systems (Euroclear and Cedel).

**Table E**
**Secondary market turnover**[(a)]
$ billions

| | |
|---|---|
| 1980 | 240 |
| 1981 | 404 |
| 1982 | 864 |
| 1983 | 896 |
| 1984 | 1,512 |
| 1985 | 2,208 |
| 1986 | 3,570 |
| 1987 | 4,666 |
| 1988 | 4,627 |
| 1989 | 5,084 |
| 1990 | 6,262 |

Source: AIBD.

(a) Comprises secondary market turnover of fixed-income bonds, floating-rate notes, certificates of deposit and short and medium-term notes in euro and domestic sectors through Euroclear and Cedel.

The rapid growth of secondary trading is closely linked to structural changes in the market, in particular the increased institutionalisation of the investor base. During the early development of the market, issues were small (particularly in relation to government bond issues in domestic markets) and the market was oriented towards retail investors who were attracted by the anonymity and perceived tax advantages of eurobonds. Institutional investment was focused on domestic capital markets, partly reflecting exchange controls, while the lack of competitive market-making, inefficient settlement systems and unsophisticated communications technology represented further disincentives to sizable institutional investment in the eurobond market. As a result, there was little secondary market trading and bid/offer spreads were wide.

. . .

## Convergence of bond markets

In recent years there has been a growing integration—in terms of increased substitutability and interactions—between the euro, domestic and foreign bond markets. Moreover, the term "eurobond" as a synonym for an international bearer bond which is exempt from withholding tax has become something of a simplification in view of both the diverse arrangements in different currency sectors, and the expansion of the number of currencies in which eurobonds are issued.

The two major differences of form which distinguished eurobonds from domestic and foreign bonds have gradually been eroded. Fiscal reforms have led to the dismantling of withholding tax regimes in a number of major OECD countries (eg in the United States in 1984, Germany in 1989 and France—for foreign investors only—in 1989); and, in those countries which retain withholding taxes, procedures often exist for the reclaiming of tax under double taxation agreements for at least some categories of investor. The bearer status of eurobonds was not at the outset a unique feature of eurobonds: bearer bonds were, and are, issued in a number of domestic markets eg Germany, Switzerland and Luxembourg. Moreover, the increasing role of institutions as eurobond investors means that the anonymity associated with bearer status is less valued. The settlement of eurobond trades through the two clearing systems (Cedel and Euroclear) is also no longer a distinguishing feature; a significant amount of domestic bonds, notably government bonds, are now settled in the same way.

The integration of euro and national bond markets has been enhanced by the "global" bond which can be readily transferred between depositories in these sectors. To facilitate this transfer links have been created between Cedel and Euroclear in Europe and Fedwire in the United States. The enhanced worldwide marketability of "global" bonds increases their liquidity and thus the attractiveness of these issues to institutional investors, enabling the borrower to launch an issue at a lower spread than would have been attained had separate tranches been issued in more than one market. The first fully fungible global issue was a US $1.5 billion issue by the IBRD in September 1989 which was distributed and settled simultaneously in North America, Europe and the Far East.

The eurobond market is no longer the only bond market which is genuinely international in character. Over the years the traditional domestic bond markets have attracted increasing international investor interest as a result of factors such as improved communications technology and dismantlement of exchange controls. At the same time, portfolio diversification across markets has become an accepted component of investment strategy: for instance, the Employee Retirement Income Security Act (ERISA) in the United States promoted overseas investment as helping to reduce risk. The process of international portfolio diversification has been further stimulated by the development of markets in swaps, futures, options, etc, which have facilitated the elimination or transformation of currency and interest rate risks.

Furthermore, eurobonds are no longer characterised by the composition of the syndicate, or by their syndication procedures. Traditionally, eurobond issues were underwritten by an international syndicate, while domestic issues were underwritten by local firms. However, domestic bond markets have been increasingly opened up to foreign-owned financial institutions (eg from May 1985, foreign-owned banks were permitted to lead-manage deutschmark domestic bond issues), while primary market syndication procedures have become increasingly similar in many domestic and eurocurrency sectors: for example, the negotiated fixed-price re-offering, a method already adopted in the US domestic market, was re-introduced in the eurodollar bond market in June 1989.

**Chart 3**
**Eurodollar/US domestic bond yield differential**[(a)]

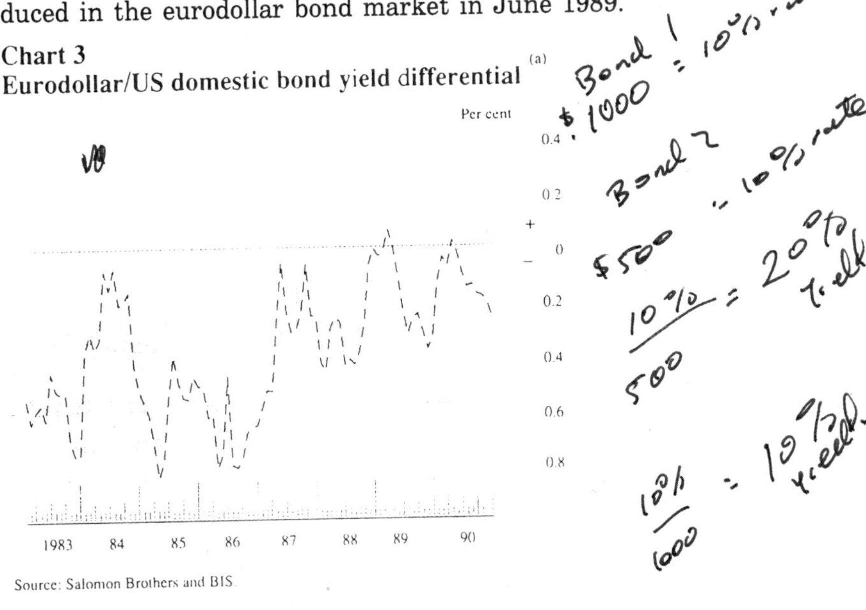


Source: Salomon Brothers and BIS.

(a) 10-year maturities. Composite of prime quality borrowers.

The effect of all these developments has been the evolution of an increasingly international bond market in which the previously rather distinct domestic, foreign and euro sectors have become more interlinked. Instruments traded in different markets are becoming more homogeneous, as is the investor base in different markets. Nevertheless, the process is far from complete: although yield differentials between domestic and eurobond markets have been substantially arbitraged away in recent years, they still exist (Chart 3). The substitutability of euro and domestic sectors of the bond market is limited by a number of factors: for example, restrictions on domestic financial institutions' investment in overseas securities and differences in the registered/bearer status of certain domestic bonds and eurobonds.

If the eurodollar bond market is set in the context of US domestic bond markets (a comparison which gains validity as a truly international bond market becomes a more relevant paradigm), it is apparent that, although the rate of growth of issuance of the euro sector of the US dollar market has outstripped the rate of growth of issuance in the domestic sector during the last ten years, the euro sector remains quite small relative to the domestic sector (Table F). The greater size of the domestic sector partly reflects government borrowing, although the domestic market is also a much larger source of finance than the euromarkets for corporate borrowers: for instance, corporate borrowing in the eurosector of the US dollar bond market is only just over a quarter of the size of corporate borrowing in the domestic sector.

**Table F**
**US dollar sector—bond issuance**
$ billions

| | Total | | | *of which:* corporate | | |
|---|---|---|---|---|---|---|
| | Domestic(a) | Foreign | Euro | Domestic | Foreign | Euro |
| 1980 | 267.8 | 1.8 | 14.5 | 42.2 | 0.5 | 4.4 |
| 1981 | 284.0 | 6.7 | 22.7 | 40.1 | 1.7 | 9.4 |
| 1982 | 392.9 | 5.9 | 40.9 | 53.0 | 0.3 | 13.8 |
| 1983 | 434.8 | 5.2 | 35.8 | 45.4 | 0.2 | 7.4 |
| 1984 | 557.8 | 1.8 | 67.3 | 66.8 | 0.1 | 16.3 |
| 1985 | 754.2 | 3.5 | 95.1 | 111.5 | — | 26.4 |
| 1986 | 819.8 | 6.1 | 115.3 | 189.7 | 0.5 | 35.0 |
| 1987 | 744.7 | 4.7 | 57.9 | 152.8 | 0.1 | 33.4 |
| 1988 | 736.2 | 9.8 | 73.4 | 169.5 | 1.7 | 39.8 |
| 1989 | 761.2 | 8.1 | 121.3 | 158.2 | 1.5 | 72.4 |
| 1990 | 831.7 | 12.8 | 74.0 | 151.0 | 3.8 | 29.0 |

Source: OECD *Financial Statistics Monthly* for domestic bond market data, and Bank of England for foreign and eurobond market data.

(a) From 1987, data exclude issues by central government agencies. (Government agencies accounted for approximately 6% of total domestic issuance, and 9% of public sector bond issuance in 1986, the last year for which these data are available.)

* * *

## *Notes and Questions*

1. What exactly is a Eurobond? Consider the following definition from F. Graaf, *Euromarket Finance: Issues of Euromarket Securities and Syndicated Eurocurrency Loans* 13–14 (1991) (Euromarket Finance).

### Definition of Eurobonds

Eurobonds, whether they be dollar instruments or denominated in another currency, can be defined as follows. They are:

(a) normally unsecured debt instruments, whereby the issuer promises to pay the amount specified on the bond at a stated future date (the *'maturity date'*) and to pay an annual rate of interest until such date to the holder of the bond; and

The trend towards asset-backed issues in the Euromarket will be discussed later (see Chapter 2 § (k)(5)); these, however, do not detract from the general rule that Eurobonds are mostly unsecured.

(b) issued by large, generally multinational corporations, sovereign states, public sector entities and supra-national institutions in order to raise large scale debt finance for a medium to long period of time; and

(c) issued simultaneously in a number of countries across the globe (other than the country in whose currency they are denominated) to a wide range of investors through a multinational syndicate of underwriting securities firms and banks and in a manner which does not subject the bonds, the issuer or the syndicate to national constraints in any of the countries; and

The crucial characteristic of Eurobonds is that they *are not issued on or into a single market* but are marketed internationally and that they are generally offered and placed in a non-public, semi-private fashion so as to avoid the securities legislation on public offerings in the various countries into which distribution takes place. These laws would otherwise impose prospectus, licence, registration or listing requirements incompatible with the nature and purpose of a Eurobond issue. Broadly speaking, syndicate members will generally make use of either a 'private placement' exemption or a 'professional-investors-only' exemption under local securities laws.

As it would be extremely difficult for the managers or the issuer to provide comprehensive guidance on compliance with all local laws which could possibly be relevant in distributing Eurobonds, it will generally be stated in the relevant contracts that each syndicate member is responsible for making certain that its distribution efforts are legal in the various jurisdictions in which it approaches investors and the issuer will normally disclaim any responsibility with respect to the qualification of the securities in any specific jurisdictions.

Obviously, for certain currencies investor demand tends to be strongest in their home country so that such issues are for a substantial part placed with end-investors from that country.

In the Eurobond market the buyers of bonds in the first instance are exclusively financial institutions. Eurobonds are never offered directly to the public, but are offered mostly to banks and other financial institutions for placing with central banks, insurance companies, investment funds, pension funds or multinational corporations.

(d) denominated, therefore, in a currency that is not necessarily native to the borrower, the investors or the syndicate members through whom the securities are sold; and

Investors in Eurobonds, therefore, take both credit and foreign exchange risks. In addition, a number of foreign jurisdictions are involved whose rules could all impact on the value of the investment while the paying agents, to whom the investors must turn for their funds, are often located in foreign jurisdictions. This and the absence of credit ratings for Eurobonds helps to explain why the market is used almost exclusively by '*prime*' issuers, i.e. top-quality international corporations and banks, international organisations and sovereign states (see § (f) below), and why the investors require the securities to be easily traded, i.e. payable to bearer.

(e) generally bearer instruments to allow negotiability (high liquidity and, therefore, easy cash convertibility) and anonymity of the ultimate investors; and

(f) either issued with the benefit of a stock exchange listing, normally in London or Luxembourg, and therefore a 'public offering' according to the laws of the country of the exchange (although still placed with investors in the various countries on an essentially private basis) or placed with such investors without a listing.

The general method of distribution discussed under (c) above should be distinguished from those Eurobond issues that are taken up entirely by a small number of institutional investors (or even by a single investor) already identified before the managers sign the subscription agreement with the issuer, and which will buy the securities directly from the managers (no syndicate being required) and hold such securities generally until their maturity. These so-called *'private-private'* placements of Eurobonds are not publicly announced and are not normally listed on a stock exchange (at least initially). This book will not deal with such private placements of Eurobonds which are, in effect, syndicated (or single lender) loans that are, for one reason or another, documented as an issue of securities.

2. As the Bank of England notes, in the early 1960's the U.S. imposed an interest equalization tax (initially 15%) on interest paid by foreign debt issuers to investors in the United States. The tax was intended to decrease U.S. investment in these securities because such transactions were putting downward pressure on the dollar. Since there were fixed exchange rates at this time, the U.S. had to offset market pressure by buying dollars with its reserves. Investments in foreign bonds denominated in dollars resulted in the issuer exchanging the dollar proceeds for local currency. The tax discouraged the investments because it increased the cost of borrowing in the U.S. market by 1%, since the issuer had to compensate investors for the tax.

So foreigners issued their dollar denominated bonds to U.S. and other investors outside the United States. Thus originally, the eurodollar bond replaced yankee bonds, bonds issued by foreigners to U.S. investors in the United States.

As Table A indicates, the eurobond market prospered even after the tax was abolished in 1974. Total eurobonds issued in 1991–1993 were:

| Total Eurobonds Issued ($ billions) | |
|---|---|
| 1991 | 277.9 |
| 1992 | 293.3 |
| 1993 | 400.0 |

Sources: Euromoney bondware, Financial Times

The 1993 $400 billion in eurobonds compares with $481 billion in international bonds, which counts foreign as well as eurobonds. To recall, foreign bonds are issues in domestic markets by foreign issuers, for example a Japanese issuer sells dollar bonds in the United States.

An important factor in the dramatic growth in 1993 was the continued expansion of eurobond issues by emerging countries, as detailed below.

"FINANCIAL MARKET DEVELOPMENTS"

Bank of England Quarterly Bulletin 469, 471 (November 1993).

### Non–OECD borrowing in the international bond markets

Non–OECD borrowers regained access to the international bond markets in 1989. Since then they have made increasing use of these markets (see the chart)—in the third quarter of 1993, $10 billion was raised by non-OECD borrowers, more than double the amount raised in the same quarter of the previous year (see the table). This rise reflects the return of investor confidence in Latin America and the increasing attraction of investment in Asian economies. Eastern European borrowers have also begun to tap the international bond markets, although on a smaller scale (the Hungarian and Czech central banks have been the only issuers from the region so far).

**International bond issues by non-OECD borrowers**

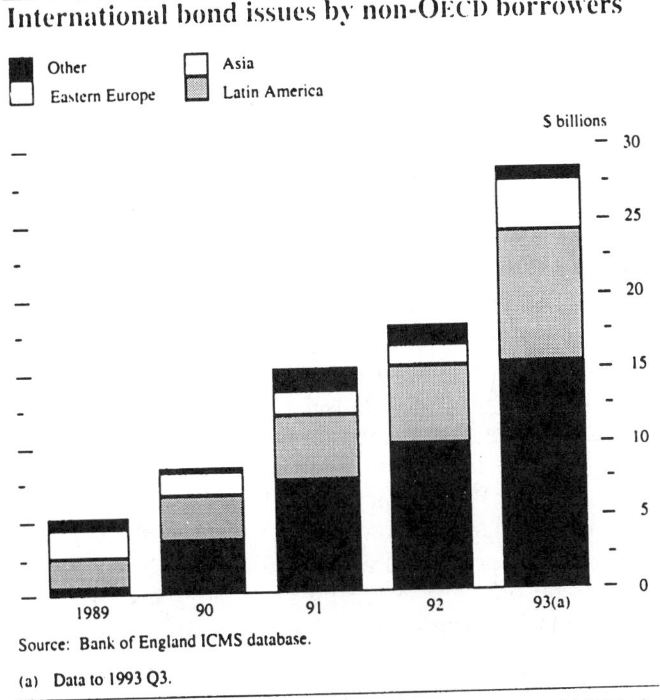


Source: Bank of England ICMS database.

(a) Data to 1993 Q3.

An important factor behind the increase in non-OECD borrowing has been the low interest rate environment in the United States and Japan over the past few years. This has led investors to search for higher yields than are available on eurobonds from high-quality borrowers from the OECD area. Latin American borrowers, as well as those from other emerging regions, particularly Asia, have taken advantage of this.

Several factors have contributed to the steady increase in non-OECD borrowing in recent years, in particular the confidence induced in foreign investors by the adoption of stability-oriented policies and the completion of debt restructurings. Latin American issues have not been confined to bonds, and issuers have diversified their range of borrowing instruments and the markets from which they borrow. Mexican, Brazilian and Argentinian borrowers have, for instance, issued euromedium-term notes and eurocommercial paper. Mexico has also issued sovereign debt in the US foreign bond market, and some Mexican borrowers have issued US domestic commercial paper.

Mexican entities have been the most active Latin American borrowers in the international bond markets (see Chart 4 in the main text), having issued $7 billion in 1993 to date compared with $4 billion in the whole of 1992. Investor perception of Mexican borrowers over the coming months could receive a further boost if the North American Free Trade Agreement is ratified. Brazilian private sector banks have also been prominent. High domestic interest rates in Brazil have allowed the banks to offer attractive yields to international investors while on-lending the proceeds domestically as wide profit margins.

The cost to Latin American entities of borrowing in the international markets varies between countries, reflecting their perceived creditworthiness. Most Latin American borrowers have seen spreads narrow since their return to the market; they have narrowed most for Mexican entities. In line with improved creditworthiness, the maturity structure of Latin American borrowing has lengthened. In 1991, maturities were generally up to three years, though the average maturity has now risen to five years and some Mexican borrowers have issued at a maturity of twelve years.

Asian borrowers have also been making increasing use of the international bond markets. The proportion of non-OECD international bonds issued by Asian borrowers has risen from one quarter in 1992 to almost one third in 1993, with Korea, Taiwan and Thailand accounting for most of the borrowing. Euroconvertible bonds have been popular instruments with international investors, since they offer the opportunity to obtain exposure to equity markets which might otherwise be restricted by shareholding limits placed on foreign investment. In the past year there have been several deregulatory initiatives and a loosening of restraints on offshore financing to encourage borrowers to tap the international capital markets, while high domestic interest rates provided an additional incentive.

## Borrowing by non-OECD entities in the international bond markets

$ billions at a quarterly rate

| | 1991 | 1992 | | | 1993 | | |
|---|---|---|---|---|---|---|---|
| | Year | Year | Q3 | Q4 | Q1 | Q2 | Q3 |
| International bond issues(a) | | | | | | | |
| Straight fixed-rate | 2.9 | 3.5 | 2.4 | 3.7 | 6.6 | 8.0 | 8.9 |
| Equity-related | 0.5 | 0.4 | 0.2 | 0.9 | 0.6 | 0.8 | 0.8 |
| FRNs | 0.4 | 0.6 | 1.0 | 0.8 | 0.7 | 1.6 | 0.5 |
| **Total** | **3.8** | **4.5** | **3.6** | **5.4** | **7.9** | **10.4** | **10.2** |
| *of which:* | | | | | | | |
| *Latin America* | *1.8* | *2.5* | *1.7* | *3.2* | *3.8* | *5.8* | *5.5* |
| *Asia* | *1.1* | *1.2* | *1.5* | *1.3* | *2.3* | *3.7* | *2.7* |
| *Eastern Europe* | *0.3* | *0.3* | *0.2* | *0.6* | *1.6* | *0.2* | *1.5* |

Source: Bank of England ICMS database.

(a) Excluding bonds issued as a result of debt rescheduling agreements.

Another factor in the growth of the market, was the continued rise of Euro-deutschmark (Euro–Dm) issues. In 1993, these issues accounted for 13 percent of new issues, surpassing both yen and sterling.

## KEVIN MUEHRING, "KING OF THE EUROPEAN BOND MARKETS"

Institutional Investor (February 1993).

The Euro–Dm market has always been considered a relative backwater in the Euromarket—a great irony considering the importance of the deutschmark as an international currency. For one thing, borrowers were never able to issue in size. The average bond issue was barely Dm262 million by the fourth quarter of 1991. Also, the market was illiquid and underwriting fees were high (as they still are in traditionally syndicated issues). The typical commission for a ten-year issue was an astounding 3 percent, versus 1.875 percent in the Eurodollar market for traditional syndications.

The reasons for these conditions lay mainly in the buy-and-hold habits of the retail investors who dominated the market. According to estimates by Moody's Investors Service, at the end of 1991, retail investors still held more than half the outstanding Dm245 billion of Euro–Dm paper. Accounting for another 13 percent of the investor base were German domestic banks, who also tend to buy and hold. That left foreign institutional investors with less than a third of the outstanding paper. "From a purely Anglo–Saxon point of view," notes Gordon Anderson, senior vice president for trading at Commerzbank in Frankfurt, the market does not work well because there is a natural tendency towards illiquidity."

Three developments helped make the market deeper and more liquid. The first was a set of legal changes that the Bundesbank announced last July, with the goal of making Euro–DM issuance more flexible. The new rules permitted listing on foreign exchanges, issuance under foreign rather than German law and clearance of bonds through Cedel or Euroclear in addition to (or instead of) the *Kassenverein,* the German bond-clearing system. The Bundesbank also removed the minimum two-year maturity for foreign issues, which should boost the Euro–Dm medium-term and commercial paper markets.

By themselves, the legal changes would probably have given the market only a minor lift. But their introduction last August came a month after the collapse of the primary market for European currency units in the aftermath of the Danish vote against the Maastricht treaty. Issuers, particularly sovereign issuers, raised some funds in Eurodollars, but had to look elsewhere for large-scale funding requirements, especially if they needed longer maturities. And the only European market open to them, given the relatively small size of the other markets, was in deutschmarks.

Finally, the withdrawal of the lira and the pound from the ERM in September and the turmoil that followed brought institutional investors running to the deutschmark. The realignment pressures within the ERM overshadowed the economic difficulties Germany was having with reunification and any doubts over the Bundesbank's success in quelling domestic inflation. The first stop for foreign investors in Germany tends to be the Dm500 billion, ultraliquid market for German government paper, especially five-year *Bundesobligationen (Bobls)* and ten-year government Bunds. Foreign purchases in the German bond market, for instance, tripled from August to September to Dm34 billion—a level that was about six times higher than in September 1991.

But with the foreign inflows depressing government yields, the spread to Euro–Dm paper widened, causing institutional funds to overflow into the Euro-sector. By then larger Euro–Dm issues were coming to market, making the sector "an attractive alternative to the Bund market, with high credit quality, liquidity and a little yield pickup to boot," says Thierry Porte, Morgan Stanley's managing director for capital markets in London. Adding to the market's attractiveness to foreign institutional investors, says Porte, has been the growing use of the fixed-price reoffer as the syndication technique best suited to tailoring a new issue for institutional demand.

. . .

3. What accounts for the continued growth of the eurobond market in general, and more specifically the DM sector? How could Germany control the issuance of Euro–DM bonds? Why has it now liberalized its restrictions?

4. In the first Bank of England reading, Chart 3 shows eurodollar bond yields as lower than U.S. domestic bond yields, with the gap narrowing. Why is this?

5. As Table A in the first Bank of England reading shows, equity warrants have been a major part of the Eurobond market since 1986; a very high percentage of these equity warrants have issued by Japanese firms. In 1992, Japanese equity warrants accounted for over 80% of the market, and it was even a higher percentage in the 1980's. As the following article indicates, major problems confronted the issuers of these instruments, when the Nikkei index began its downward ascent in 1990.

## "JAPAN'S WARRANT HANGOVER"

The Economist (September 8, 1990).

Financial instruments that claim to keep everybody happy usually end up leaving the glummest faces. During the 1980s, the favourite financial fix of many Japanese firms came from equity warrants, which offered ultra-cheap and abundant capital. That may have encouraged firms to over-borrow, and perhaps to invest some of the loot in risky investments. In any case, their borrowing costs are about to become much steeper than they thought.

The warrants are issued with bonds, but can be traded separately. The bonds usually mature in four to five years, and the warrants give the right during the bonds' life to buy new shares at 5% above what the share price was on a particular date (usually specified to be only a few days after the bond was issued). In return for this perk the bonds carry very low interest rates. The clever part is that when the warrant-holders exercise their right to buy newly-issued shares, the cash they pay covers the issuers' repayment to bond-holders.

In 1987–89 Japanese companies issued some $115 billion-worth of bonds with warrants attached, bringing the total outstanding to $140 billion. Nearly all were issued in dollars. In theory everybody won. The investors held a safe debt instrument with a jazzy equity kicker (many warrants quadrupled in value as the stockmarket soared). The dollar bonds usually carried coupons of 4% or less: by the time the Japanese companies swapped that exposure into yen (whose interest rate was then as much as five percentage points lower than the dollar's), their cost of capital was either zero or negative.

Supposedly the only losers were existing shareholders in the issuing company, whose stakes faced dilution by the warrant-exercisers. In America and Britain companies are discouraged from issuing warrants by rules that force them to account for this dilution, so the equity-warrant market was dominated by Japanese companies. Another worry for shareholders was that the proceeds from the warrant-and-bond issues were used not only to finance Japan's robust capital spending but also to bet on the country's booming stock and property markets. During the late 1980s neither of these traits bothered the Ministry of Finance.

However, like most something-for-nothing schemes, equity warrants had a hitch: what happened if the stockmarket fell and the warrants became worthless? Since the start of 1990 the Tokyo stockmarket has fallen by 38% and three-month Euroyen interest rates have risen to 8.4%. That has undermined the warrant market's *raison d'être,* since such warrants, a sort of long-dated option, work only in rising markets. The Tokyo slump has also dramatically reduced the value of the existing warrants.

Baring Securities, one of the leading market-makers in warrants, reckons that of the $140 billion-worth of outstanding warrants, $125 billion are "out of the money"—ie, the share prices are below the exercise prices (see chart on next page). Of the 500 or so most-actively traded warrants with an issue size of some $80 billion, around $60 billion-worth are out of the money. In all, over $50 billion-worth are more than 30% out of the money. This is obviously a problem for the investors that own the warrants, but it is also a time-bomb for the issuers.

Japanese borrowers have tended to view warrants they issue as money in the bank which is already paid for: a sort of rolling rights issue. But if the warrants never come into the money, investors will not exercise them and buy shares—and those proceeds will not be available to repay the bond-holders. That means that issuers will have to raise more cash to meet their obligations—around $125 billion if the market were to stay still. Bank loans currently cost over 8%—a startling increase in financing costs for companies used to almost-free money.

In other words it looks as if the warrants may be about to turn round and bite the hands of those that issued them. Investors and issuers alike are playing for time, hoping that the Tokyo stockmarket will rebound. According to Barings, only around $22 billion of warrants mature before April 1992; the biggest chunk of warrants, some $80 billion-worth, are due to expire in the financial year ending March 1993, with a further $33.8 billion the following year. Still, in many cases prices are so low that very large annual increases in a share price are needed to bring the warrant back into the money.

. . .

The following Chart from the *Financial Times* (November 9, 1992) indicates that the redemption problem continued to exist in 1992.

In 1992, the Japanese equity warrant market was all but dead; only $9 billion in new equity warrants were issued, but the market took somewhat of a rebound in 1993, with the rise of the Nikkei. The contraction of the market resulted from market conditions and regulatory factors. Beginning in 1990, MOF had a "gentleman's agreement" with issuers to restrict the maximum issues per week to $1 billion, and individual issuers had to meet certain tests, for example a 30% dividend payout ratio (dividends/earnings), and a forecast of higher earnings.

The following excerpt from Shinichi Uchida, "Japanese Equity Warrants—Interaction of Market and Regulations" (unpublished, February

1992) shows how this market developed outside Japan, and was then imported back into Japan.

Historically low interest rates generated a "stock inflation," the sharp rise in stock and real estate prices in '88 and '89. Excess liquidity ran into these two markets in which supply was limited. The investors were speculators and sought for capital gains. The warrant became popular especially for these speculators because it required little money to invest.[36] This was also a time to issue equity related bonds, because the high stock price and the anticipation of further rises made it possible to finance them cheaply. One could even observe negative-interest rates in this period.

Until 1988, issues were concentrated in foreign markets because:

(i) The liquidity of foreign issued warrants in the secondary market had been increased after JSDA abolished its self regulatory rule prohibiting the flow-back of foreign issued warrants (January 1986).

(ii) In the domestic market, it was still prohibited to sell detached warrants separately from bond portion at the time of issuance. Therefore investors had to detach the warrant after they bought BWs, which prevented small investors from buying warrants.

(iii) The after-swap cost of a Euro-dollar issue was lower than domestic issue at that time.

| | Domestic Issue | | Foreign Issue | |
|---|---|---|---|---|
| FY | # | Amount | # | Amount |
| 87 | 0 | 0 bil Yen | 223 | 3,430.0 bil Yen |
| 88 | 0 | 0 | 219 | 4,982.1 |
| 89 | 24 | 915.0 | 242 | 8,269.8 |

### (5) *Revival of domestic market and transparency of warrant price*

In 1989, domestic issue revived somewhat because

(i) JSDA allowed separate sales of detachable warrants in the domestic market.

(ii) The coupon rate in domestic issues became comparable to the rate for foreign issues.

Yet the dominance of foreign issues remained and government policy focused on the protection of domestic investors in foreign issued warrants. First, MOF abolished the "50% rule" (the domestic holdings of foreign issued BWs should be limited to 50% of total issues) in '89, acknowledging that this restriction was hard to enforce. Instead, MOF made the domestic sales of foreign issued warrants subject to the reporting requirement under the Foreign Exchange and Foreign Trade Control Act in February 1990. MOF and JSDA also took steps to improve the transparency of prices of Euro Dollar warrants in the

**36.** The warrant is the only way to speculate in such ways because there is no option market for individual stocks in Japan.

domestic secondary market. For example, Nihon Sogo Shoken (BB) started interbroker transactions of BWs. All interbroker transactions were to be done with Nihon Sogo Shoken during its operating hours. The price of customer transactions was also limited to within certain range of the price quoted by BB.

The government took another step to remove the obstacles for domestic issues in 1990. The most important obstacle was the Commercial Act § 297, which limited the issuance of corporate bonds to the amount of the issuer's net assets. Although the Temporary Measures on Corporate Bond Act liberalized this limit, raising it to twice the issuer's net assets for foreign issued bonds, secured bonds, and CBs, the Act did not apply to BWs (Temporary Measures on Corporate Bond Act § 1). The Act was amended in 1990 (enforceable from April 1991) to extend its application to BWs.

. . .

Why didn't U.S. issuers use equity warrants in 1993 to take advantage of the rising stock market in the United States? Could the Japanese authorities have prevented the development of the offshore market? If so, why didn't they? Why did the Japanese authorities decide to repatriate the market in the late 1980's and then limit both the euro and domestic markets in the 1990's?

## 2. Issuing Procedures

### a. Registration

Eurobonds do not generally have to be registered when sold in european countries. Issuers can take advantage of exemptions in local law for bonds distributed to institutional buyers. As we have seen, banks are the initial buyers of eurobonds. But note, that if a euroyen bond were sold in the United States it would have to be registered unless it met the terms for a private placement exemption. The European markets generally have a more broadly defined exemption. Also, you may recall that "eurosecurities" are exempt from the EU's POP.

The fact that eurobonds are usually exempt from registration requirements does not mean that there are no disclosures made about the issuer. If the bonds are listed in London or Luxembourg, they are subject to the exchanges' disclosure requirements and the minimum standards of the Listings Directive. In addition, since many eurobonds are sold in London, their distribution will be subject to the disclosure requirements of the International Primary Market Association (IPMA), a London-based membership group for euro-issuers.

What is the rationale for the general exemption from disclosure requirements? The idea is that this is an institutional market. There is, however, substantial argument as to whether the ultimate investors in these bonds are institutional or retail. Although securities are initially bought by banks, they may be quickly resold to retail investors. It is difficult to determine how much retail investment there is since the bonds are in bearer form. The Bank of England thinks this market has become largely institutional.

Why do issuers seek to avoid registration? Naturally, they seek to avoid the costs and potential liabilities. But perhaps most importantly bonds can be brought promptly to market based on market conditions. There is no need to wait for approval or clearance of a registration statement. Lack of registration may make it difficult for lower credit rated companies to sell eurobonds—institutional investors would want disclosure on no name companies. Eurodollar issuers have higher credit ratings than issuers in the U.S. domestic market, 47 percent of SP ratings in eurobonds are AAA, compared to 2 percent in U.S. bonds.

Can U.S. investors buy (or can issuers sell to them) eurobonds that have not been registered in the United States? This depends on the treatment of the issue under Regulation S. If there is high "substantial U.S. market interest," (SUSMI), which would certainly be the case if the bond issuer was a U.S. "reporting" company (had public issues in U.S. market), the issuer would have to comply with the Regulation S restrictions. Regulation S provides that in such case, U.S. investors cannot buy the bonds for 40 days after the initial distribution, the "seasoning" period. By this time the market has already incorporated relevant information about the issuer into the price of the bond. During this period, no bearer bonds can be issued because bearer bonds could be easily bought by U.S. investors. So, a temporary global note is used for the first 40 days, requiring investors to register—during this period investors can buy or sell interests in the note.

## b. Underwriting

### EUROMARKET FINANCE: ISSUES OF EUROMARKET SECURITIES AND SYNDICATED EUROCURRENCY LOANS

53–89 (1991) (Euromarket Finance) (excerpts).

#### (B) Eurobond Issuing Procedures

Before discussing the legal aspects of Eurobond documentation it seems practical to describe the process of making a new issue of Eurobonds or FRNs. A new issue first moves through the primary market before being traded on the secondary market.

> The IPMA Recommendations are presumed to be followed in the primary market (unless a departure is indicated in the invitation telex for a particular issue) and the AIBD's rules govern secondary market activities (including so-*called 'gray market' trading and primary settlement procedures both of which are discussed in detail below).*

The primary market starts with banks, securities houses and financial institutions competing for a new issue by a particular borrower, i.e. trying to obtain a lead management *'mandate'* or to become co-managers or underwriters. Building the contractual structure of participants together forming the *'syndicate'*, which is responsible for finding investors for the issue is the second stage of the primary market and is known as the *'syndication process'* or simply *'syndication'*. The lead manager controls it. It ends when no further indications of interest in acting as an underwriter or selling group member can be made and the final *'allotments'* of securities to the syndicate members are determined and, where necessary, accepted, meaning that all securities have been subscribed for. The primary market ends with the *'primary settlement'* when the issue proceeds are made available by the syndicate to the issuer in exchange for the delivery of the bonds. The secondary market commences immediately thereafter.

Before moving to the main stages of the issuing process, the various structures of an issue syndicate, formed in the primary market, and the respective duties and responsibilities of its members will be reviewed. Thereafter, the stages of the issuing process will be highlighted for each type of issue syndicate.

## Structure of the Issuing Syndicate

Until the early 1980s the conventional syndicate structure comprised three-tiers and the prevailing underwriting method used in this structure was *'negotiated'* or *'open priced'* underwriting.

To *'underwrite'* means to assume a contractual obligation to place a certain number of securities (this can be the entire issue or an agreed share of the issue) with investors, either as principal or as agent for the issuer, failing which one is bound to subscribe for any unsold bonds. An underwriter's success (or lack of it) in finding investors willing to purchase securities from it will thus determine its exposure vis-a-vis the issuer. The underwriting risk materialises at *'closing'* when *primary settlement* occurs and the issuer must receive the proceeds of the bonds (less certain agreed fees). The issuer is assured by the management group's underwriting commitment that any lack of demand in the market will not result in a proportional reduction of the proceeds. In essence, the underwriting commitment shifts market risk from the issuer to the syndicate (save for force majeure situations).

In *'open priced'* underwriting the bond issue was launched on tentative terms (i.e. coupon and issue price) in order to test market demand and, based upon market response, final pricing terms were then agreed with the issuer. Only then were legally binding underwriting commitments entered into. In this method the issuer takes a risk that during the period in which the market is sounded out (the *'offering period'*), market rates move against the rate it would prefer to pay on its bonds.

During the early 1980s, the speed with which an issue was brought to the market had to increase due to rapid currency and interest rate fluctuations and, as a consequence, since that time a new method of underwriting known as the *'bought deal'* (or *'pre-priced deal'*) has been used in the overwhelming majority of new euromarket issues of bonds and FRNS. It involves a greatly simplified syndicate structure.

> A further factor in the emergence of pre-priced deals is the fact that many issues are swap-driven, i.e. would not be brought to the market were it not for the opportunity, on the part of the issuer, to enter into a currency or an interest rate swap (or both). As swaps require pre-established issue and coupon prices, the issuer must ensure that these are not modified. An open-priced issue would not accomplish this.

Under this technique one or more lead managers jointly and severally agree with the issuer before and regardless of syndication to firmly underwrite the entire issue at a fixed issue price and a specific coupon, so that the issuer has certainty as to its cost of funds. Only after the issuer has agreed these fundamental terms with the lead manager does the lead manager launch the issue and invite other managers to underwrite a portion of the issue at the terms already agreed. Pre-priced issues require realism on the part of the managers, as they and the borrower may be locked into a very bad deal if interest rates fall below the agreed rate after the announcement. If these rates rise above the agreed rate, there will not be sufficient demand and underwriters will be called upon to take the securities on their books (and suffer a loss if they are unable to sell the securities profitably later on in the secondary market). To mitigate these risks somewhat, the offering period is reduced to a few days and the timetable for pre-closing events is generally accelerated. In an extreme case the management group may terminate their commitments pursuant to the *'market out clause'* commonly contained in the subscription agreement with the issuer (see § (c)).

More recently the market has witnessed a gradual retreat from bought deals and a return to open priced underwriting as a result of several developments in relation to bought deals. Firstly, in an increasingly competitive primary market, lead managers have been bidding for mandates to issue Eurobonds and FRNS on unrealistic terms that investors were unable to accept, thereby forcing co-managers to mark down their re-sale prices to such an extent that Euromarket underwriting has become increasingly unprofitable. Secondly, a further erosion of managers' commissions occurred as a result of the fact that deliberately aggressive or mispriced new issues force the lead manager to influence the market price of the paper for the first few weeks through transactions that provide price support (a practice known as *'stabilisation'* which will be discussed in greater detail below). The lead manager's stabilisation losses are traditionally deductible from the co-managers' underwriting fee (and not against the management fee), so that in essence the lead managers shift the costs of bringing mispriced issues to the market onto their syndicate. In response to these developments a reform of new issue procedures and stricter rules on stabilisation have been called for. The latter has resulted in a change in IPMA's recommendations in April 1989. The former has led several of the principal lead managers in the market to introduce new underwriting procedures derived from the 'negotiated underwriting' technique. These new procedures, known as *'fixed price reoffering'*, allow the managers to test investors' appetite and obtain commitments before the final pricing of the issue is agreed with the issuer. Accordingly, using this technique, new issues should be priced more closely to the market so that stabilisation by the lead manager and price dumping by co-managers become rare. The syndicate structure used in a fixed price reofferings is a middle ground between classic 'negotiated underwriting' and the 'bought deal'.

Although the classic Euromarket syndicate is now mainly of historical interest, it is important for an understanding of both bought deals and fixed price reofferings. On the other hand, it is not certain at this stage whether the latter will displace bought deals. Consequently, the following discussion devotes attention to all three underwriting techniques in the order of their historical development.

### Main Stages of the Issuing Process/Syndicate Participants

The following more detailed discussion of new issue procedures will first concentrate on the classic open priced underwriting method (which is by far the most elaborate procedure) and then describe bought deals and fixed price reofferings. As most of the technical terms and IPMA recommendations are explained in the discussion of open priced underwriting, they will not be reiterated in the subsequent paragraphs. Where deviations from open priced underwriting are not expressly mentioned in those paragraphs, the procedures, devices and practices used in bought deals and fixed price reofferings are broadly similar.

#### *Open priced underwriting*

The three-tier syndicate structure used in open priced underwriting is illustrated in Exhibit 1. The lead manager is a bank, financial institution or securities house selected by the issuer and given a *'mandate'* to arrange (*'lead manage'*) the issue. Generally, this will take the form of an exchange of letters (or telexes) between the issuer and the lead manager setting out the principal terms of the issue and authorising the lead manager, on the issuer's behalf, to announce the issue and invite co-managers into the management team. The principal terms of the issue would normally include: timing and size of the issue, *tentative* issue price and *approximate* interest rate (or a range for the price and the interest rate), final maturity, bullet repayment or amortization, security (if any), optional redemption (for issuer and/or bondholders) and fees and other expenses charged by the manager, the underwriters and the selling group.

Although lead management responsibility is sometimes shared between two or more firms or banks, this discussion will—for simplicity's sake—proceed on the basis that there is only one lead manager.

Exhibit 1: Three-tier Issue Syndicate

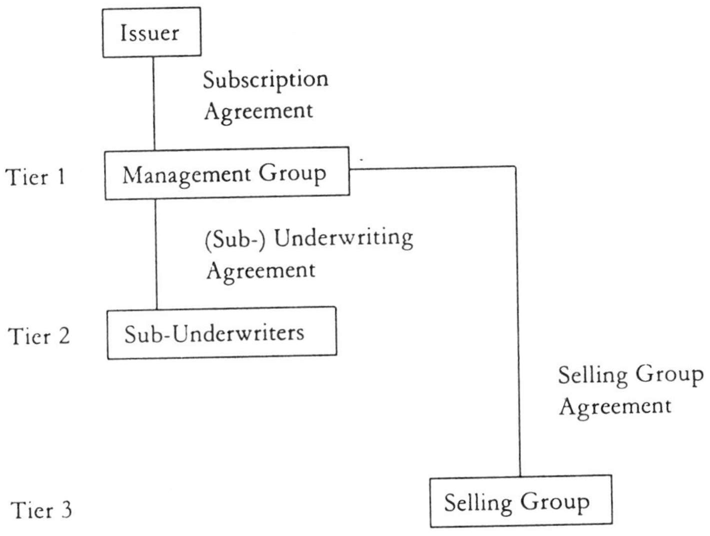


The lead manager will commit itself and invite a small group of co-managers (selected by itself although the issuer may wish certain of its relationship banks to be included) to commit themselves to the issuer to underwrite the entire issue together.

However, in open priced deals underwriting commitments are only entered into *after* the offering period, during which the syndicate invited by the lead manager approaches investors and attempts to make sales on a tentative basis (i.e. on *indicative coupon and issue price* ), has ended and the issuer and the lead manager have been able to agree the final issue terms. Before that day, known as the '*signing day* ', the issuer bears the risk of rising market rates.

> The majority of the securities will be reserved by the management group for itself for sale to investors (the co-managers being chosen primarily because they are thought to represent significant investor demand in their respective geographic areas), but they may need others to assume some responsibility for selling a certain portion of the issue. For that purpose *a selling group* is invited to purchase small portions (normally not more than 0.5% to 1%) of the offering from the managers at the issue price less a selling concession.
>
> To mitigate the risk of having to subscribe for substantial portions of the issue if demand (from investors and the selling group) is weak, the management group may also invite '*underwriters* ' to *sub-underwrite* portions of the issue. In the event that an issue is undersubscribed and the managers are held to subscribe for the remaining unplaced securities, they can require the (sub-)underwriters to buy a pro rata portion, which can be no larger than the (sub-)underwriter's total underwriting commitment (less the

amount of securities it has been allotted). To this extent the sub-underwriters effectively grant the management group a 'put-option', but by the same token they can limit their exposure as underwriters by asking for high re-sale allotments.

The selling group is invariably much larger than the group of managers and underwriters and consists of professional securities dealers and financial institutions located in various countries. Strictly speaking the selling group *includes* all the managers and underwriters, although these are under an obligation to find investors (being one element of an underwriting commitment), whereas the 'pure' selling group members simply agree to purchase a small percentage of the offering themselves.

Selling group members who are not also managers or underwriters are frequently referred to as '*selling banks*'.

Selling banks are selected by the lead manager who will enter into a '*selling group agreement*' with such banks during the offering period. This agreement sets out the procedure, whereby the final '*allotments*' are agreed between the lead manager and each selling group member and the date on which payment must be made for the bonds that have been so allotted.

Because of the structure of the syndicate, the selling group acquires the securities from the managers not the issuer. The same applies to the (sub-)underwriters, both in respect of their re-sale allotment and their underwriting liability. Only the management group '*subscribes*' in the legal sense of the word; all others '*purchase*' bonds.

This is different from the underwriting arrangements often adopted under English law where the managers offer the securities for subscription as agents *on behalf of the issuer* and where they also contract with any selling group or (sub-)underwriting group as agents for the issuer. In English-style subscription agreements, the managers' underwriting commitment to the issuer will therefore be formulated as follows: 'to procure subscribers or, failing that, to subscribe for the total principal amount of the securities from the issuer'.

All members of the selling group are granted a discount from the official issue price of the bonds known as the '*selling concession*'; this is a percentage (between 1.25 and 1.5%) of the nominal value of the bonds allotted to them.

All fees for the syndicate take the form of a deduction from the definitive issue price; the combined deduction is known as the '*spread*' which is 1.875% to 2% for intermediate term securities and 2.5% for longer term (i.e. between 5 and 10 years) securities. As a result of the spread, the effective interest rate on a Eurobond issue may be higher than the formal coupon rate; to the extent that the bonds have an issue price above par, this effect is mitigated. The composition of the spread is as follows:

| | Intermediate term: | | Long term: |
|---|---|---|---|
| Management fee | 0.250% | 0.375% | 0.5% |
| Underwriting fee | 0.375% | 0.375% | 0.5% |
| Selling concession | 1.250% | 1.250% | 1.5% |
| Gross spread: | 1.875% | 2.0% | 2.5% |

The management fee is based on the entire amount of the issue and is shared between the lead- and co-managers pro rata to their underwriting commitments as agreed in the *agreement among managers,* after deduction of a special fee for the lead manager known as the *'praecipium'*. The underwriting fee is paid in proportion to the underwriting commitments. The IPMA Recommendations prescribe uniform fee structures and payment dates.

Before the offering period commences the issuer and, mostly, the lead manager will need to make arrangements with other banks, financial or professional institutions that are to fulfil an important role in the forthcoming issue and whose responsibilities will be discussed in more detail in a separate paragraph.

These include: the trustee (or, alternatively, the fiscal agent), the paying agents (where there is no fiscal agent) and, in FRN issues, the agent bank. Also, in case listing is sought in Luxembourg, the issuer will appoint a listing broker or agent to apply for and obtain a listing. In the event that the issue is to be listed on the London stock exchange, the lead manager will generally be in a position to assume the responsibilities of sponsor in all contacts with the stock exchange.

Contact with the relevant exchange is, therefore, always through an intermediary. The Luxembourg listing agent, who deals with the Luxembourg Monetary Institute and the stock exchange, must be a Luxembourg bank which is a member of the stock exchange. Likewise, the sponsor for a London listing must be a member firm of the stock exchange or a firm authorised by The Securities Association (a self-regulatory organisation under the UK's Financial Services Act 1986). The lead manager will generally be either or both. Reference numbers from Cedel and/or Euroclear in respect of the forthcoming issue must also be applied for and obtained.

The commencement of the *'selling'* or *'offering period'* is marked by an announcement of the forthcoming offering on screens and by telephone and by the despatch of invitation telexes to potential underwriters and selling group members. These announce the issue to a large number of market participants and investors and test their demand.

During the offering period the managers and prospective underwriters and selling group members approach potential investors and attempt to commit these investors to buy portions of their prospective allotments; all purchase agreements are, of course, concluded on the basis of tentative price and coupon and subject to allotment.

The period typically lasts about up to two weeks, starting on the day of the screen announcement and the despatch of the invitation telexes (*'announcement'* or *'launch day'*) and ending on the day the subscription agreement is signed and the issue is formally offered with its final terms (*'offering'* or *'signing day'*).

The invitation telexes to underwriters give an initial indication of the issue's size, maturity, price and coupon, the fee structure, the percentage of the offering (the *'bracket'*) the underwriter is invited to underwrite, a summary of the bonds' principal commercial and non-commercial terms, a description of the issuer, a time schedule, a list of procedural matters, the applicable selling restrictions and any unusual features of the issue. The invitation telex to selling group members is virtually identical to that sent to the underwriters, save that no mention is made of underwriting commitments. All recipients are given to understand that the terms and the price are *subject to adjustment* during the course of the offering period to reflect the development of market conditions prior to final pricing.

> The IPMA Recommendations provide that the screen announcement (when used), the telephone invitation and the invitation telex should cover certain specified commercial and non-commercial terms in a recommended format. These rules aim to achieve the earliest possible disclosure to syndicate members of the basic commercial and non-commercial terms of the forthcoming issue they are invited to participate in (for which, it should be remembered, there is at such time no prospectus). If no reference is made to departures from IPMA rules, it will be presumed that they apply.

Telex recipients will be requested to notify the lead manager in writing within a fixed period (no later than a number of days prior to the *pricing meeting*) whether they accept the invitations and what their underwriting commitment and/or sales demand for securities is. The response to the invitation telexes is meant to give the management group and the issuer an indication of demand in the market. Under IPMA Recommendations the commitments given in response to the invitation telex are *'subject to documentation'* i.e. if subsequent documentation shows material changes in or additions to the invitation telex, commitments may be withdrawn.

After a short period the managers will be able to assess whether the terms of the issue (particularly coupon, maturity or issue size) or its price should be changed in view of the state of the market. The lead manager will agree the final terms with the issuer at the *'pricing meeting'*. At this stage the issuer may still cancel the issue, if it considers its borrowing costs are becoming too high.

> Because of this risk, the mandate should preferably specify how costs will be borne and what fees are to be paid if the issue is cancelled before the subscription agreement is signed by the issuer and the managers.

Revision of terms is not common practice; the conventional way to reflect changes in market conditions is through an adjustment of the issue price. If indications are that the issue will be over-subscribed, it may be decided to increase its size, to lower the coupon or to raise the issue price. If, on the other hand, it is likely that the issue would be undersubscribed in the event that the issuer's preferred terms and price are maintained, the managers will be very reluctant to give their underwriting commitment and they will argue with the issuer to lower the issue size, increase the coupon, reduce the issue price or agree to a combination of these measures. Failure to reach agreement on these matters will mean that the proposed issue is withdrawn.

Should the issue proceed, the underwriters are informed by the managers of the final terms and price of the bonds. They are given a short period to react with an adjustment to or a withdrawal of their earlier commitment and sales demand, failing which these are deemed to have been confirmed.

Once this deadline has expired the management group:

(a) can calculate the total amount of bonds (out of the total not reserved for the managers themselves) that can be allotted to the underwriters and, subject to their confirmation, the selling group; and

(b) can execute the subscription agreement with the issuer.

The execution of the *'subscription agreement'* by the issuer, the lead manager and the co-managers normally takes place the day immediately following the *'pricing day'* to await the underwriters' response. It initiates the formal offering of the securities (hence the term *'offering day'*). Under the subscription agreement the managers' obligation to underwrite the whole issue is *joint and several,* but in the *'agreement among managers',* to which the issuer is neither party or privy, the actual amounts of the individual underwriting commitments are agreed between all managers (including the lead manager).

On the offering day *'allotment telexes'* are despatched to managers, underwriters and selling group members, stating the total principal amount of bonds allotted to each of them respectively, repeating the definitive issue terms and giving directions as to the payment and transfer instructions which need to be given to Euroclear and Cedel in connection with the settlement (*'primary settlement',* which will be discussed in detail under a separate heading below) at the forthcoming closing. The allotment telexes sent to managers and underwriters, both of whom have underwriting commitments, simply give the total amount of bonds allotted rather than showing which part of the allotment is based on selling interest and which part is for the addressee's own account in fulfillment of its underwriting obligation. In case of an undersubscribed issue, the lead manager will make allotments of the unsold bonds pro rata to individual underwriting commitments. The total amount of all allotments should come to at least 100 per cent of the issue (it could exceed that limit in the event of *'over-allotment'*, a device discussed below under the heading 'price stabilization').

> IPMA Recommendations prohibit a lead manager from offering underwriting participation on the basis of a tacit or overt understanding or agreement to repurchase the commitment or restrict the allotment to a significantly reduced portion of the commitment.

Selling group members may accept their allotments either by sending confirmation telexes or by not objecting within a given time. Those who accept their allotments receive the final offering circular as a sales aid. At this time, the final offering circular will also be delivered to the stock exchange.

> In principle, the lead manager is contractually empowered to determine the allotments in its own discretion. Both underwriters and selling group members will agree with the lead manager that the latter will have authority to determine the final allotments of securities after the underwriters have agreed to the final issue price. The lead manager requires this flexibility, as it does not know the extent of investor demand until the period for sending indications of interest has expired. Underwriters and selling group members often want to be assured that they will be allotted no less than (a portion of) their sales demand; when such a commitment is given by the lead manager, this is called *'protection'*.

Immediately after the allotments have been made, all the managers, underwriters and those selling group members that have accepted allotments will make definitive sales agreements for the bonds with clients that have shown interest or entered into conditional purchase agreements with them and will try to find investors for any unplaced bonds (i.e. that portion of their allotment for which they have not yet found investors and for which they may therefore be required to pay themselves at closing—the amount that is unsold at such time is known as a *'stick position'*).

> The reason for the period between offering and closing day is primarily to allow sales proceeds to be collected from investors and for the managers, underwriters and selling group members to pay these to the lead manager to be provided to the issuer at closing.

On the *'closing day'* itself the trust deed (or fiscal agency agreement) and the paying agency agreement(s) are executed by the respective parties thereto and the issuer will execute and deposit the *'temporary global bond'* (or note), which is a type-written document executed manually on behalf of the issuer, representing the aggregate principal amount of the issue, with a common depositary (normally a bank) acting for both Euroclear and Cedel. Simultaneously, the issuer's lawyers and accountants will deliver to the trustee and the management group their legal opinions (see Annex III) and auditors comfort letters respectively and any other conditions precedent (e.g. the official listing approval obtained for the securities) will also have to be fulfilled. Only then will the subscription funds be released to the issuer.

*Pre-priced underwriting*

In a bought deal the syndicate structure is much simpler than in open priced issues. Normally, there will be no (sub-)underwriters or selling banks and the entire issue is syndicated among managers only, so that the only underwriters are the managers led by the lead manager. Consequently, the group of managers tends to be larger than in open priced underwriting. Bought deals have a short pre-launch period; immediately after the lead manager has agreed the major terms of the issue, the issue price and the fee structure with the issuer, it will announce the forthcoming issue on screen displays and commence syndication, i.e. approach co-managers informally to obtain indications as to their interest to join the syndicate. Obviously, this has priority for the lead manager: it needs to ensure that a large portion of its overall commitment to the issuer is taken over. This is then followed by invitation telexes which confirm the offering and its *fixed* terms and request the addressees whether and to what extent they would be willing to assume an underwriting commitment and to state their sales demand (i.e. the quantity of bonds or notes they actually require for sale to their customers) before a certain deadline. Within the same timeframe, underwriting acceptances are to be received from co-managers. The management group itself is responsible for placing the issue with investors although occasionally there might be a certain amount of bonds to be distributed by a selling group.

> At the same time, draft agreements (primarily the subscription agreement, the agreement among managers, the fiscal agency agreement (or trust deed)) are being prepared, discussed and distributed together with the preliminary offering circular in the event that the bonds are to be listed. Steps will be taken to agree the text of the preliminary offering circular with the stock exchange.

Simultaneously with or even prior to syndication, the lead manager will start *'pre-selling'* large portions of the issue itself on an *'if, as and when issued basis'* to institutional investors, banks and others in order to further reduce its overall exposure to the issuer. As the terms of the issue are fixed, there is no pricing or offering day in a bought deal. As soon as possible after receipt of underwriting acceptances and statements of selling interest the lead manager will therefore make the allotments to the managers and, where applicable, the selling group members by despatching allotment telexes.

> IPMA Recommendations require that in pre-priced issues that are syndicated among managers only, final allotments must be made within one business day from and including the day of the first invitation (i.e. the launch day) or as soon as practicable after the management group is formed, if earlier. Where a statutory, stock exchange or conduct of business rule prohibits allotments before a prospectus is issued, a deviation from this rule is generally agreed in advance. In these circumstances the lead manager will only give

'indications of proposed allotments' while 'formal allotment' is delayed until the time allowed under the relevant provisions.

On the signing day the subscription agreement and the agreement among managers, which should previously have been sent to and approved by the co-managers, are executed and the final offering circular is bulk printed and distributed to the managers and, where applicable, the selling group members and the stock exchange.

The procedure for primary settlement on the closing day is identical to that for open-priced bond issues. The period from the launch date to the closing is generally fixed in advance in a bought deal (often to coincide with the timing of the related swap agreement(s)). It generally takes between one to four weeks. If there should be insufficient investor demand, the shortfall is taken by the management group in proportion to the respective underwriting commitments agreed upon in the agreement among managers.

The fee structure in pre-priced issues is the same as in open priced issues and, similar to open priced issues, there is no restriction on the managers as to the price at which they should offer the issue (or at least that part of it allotted to them) to the market. Each manager may quote a different price and each is free to give up all or part of its fees by quoting discounts below the issue price. If an issue has been priced unrealistically by the lead manager and the issuer, the likelihood of such *price dumping* by the syndicate is quite high. It is this practice which fixed price reofferings intend to eliminate.

*Fixed price reofferings*

So far, fixed price reofferings have used a small syndicate of co-managers assisted occasionally by a selling group. This inevitably means that their underwriting commitments are much larger than in a bought deal where the group of managers is larger. The essence of this new syndication method, however, is that all managers agree with each other and the issuer to offer the bonds or notes only at (or, alternatively, at or above) the agreed issue price during the primary market until such time as the lead manager decides to release the syndicate from this obligation (referred to as *'breaking the syndicate'*). In return the managers are allowed to take part in agreeing the issue price with the issuer which takes place only after they have tested demand and perhaps pre-sold parts of the issue to their customers on tentative terms. Furthermore, the lead manager undertakes to stabilize the issue only in unusual circumstances and not to start its own pre-sales until some time after sending out invitation telexes. As the bonds are priced at a level where they should sell and because of the managers' pre-marketing activities, very swift placement by the syndicate in the primary market is possible so that syndicate price-discipline can normally be lifted within 24 hours from the allotments.

Because the group of managers is small, it will be easier for the lead manager to enforce this price-discipline. Those managers that do not have genuine capacity to place correctly priced paper with investors and consequently must sell below the agreed issue price to professional traders rather than investors will be identifiable. Due to a different fee structure there is no incentive for managers to ask for an allotment of bonds that is larger than they can actually place with their customers. The management and underwriting fees will be a uniform percentage (in total anywhere between 0.25% and 0.4%), the lead manager does not take a praecipium before paying out the management fee and a selling concession of 0.125% is granted. Because the syndicate is not allowed to give up its fees in the form of a discount to the issue price when offering the issue to their customers and because the lead manager rarely conducts stabilisation, underwriting fees are not lost or uncertain.

A further interesting aspect of this new type of underwriting is that the period from launch to closing is shortened substantially compared to the other syndication methods; parties will normally aim for the closing day to occur approximately 7 days from launch. The reason for this is to limit the period in which *'grey market'* is active and to start secondary market trading as soon as possible. To facilitate this sharp timing standardized documentation is necessary.

The issuer's risks in this syndication technique are the same as in classic negotiated underwriting, i.e. it assumes a certain market risk and in most cases it will not be able to launch a bond issue for the sake of an attractive swap opportunity.

---

The following excerpt from Kevin Muehring, "The Eurobond Market at 30," *Institutional Investor* 57, 60–64 (May 1993) further elaborates on the new underwriting practices.

Increasingly, underwriters won bought-deal mandates by overpricing new issues (which a bull market enabled them to do) and putting together largely meaningless syndicate groups whose members, ever keen for prestige and league-table position, would accept loss-making co-management positions in hopes of establishing client relationships—which rarely materialized.

"It was a way of transferring wealth from the weak to the strong," jokes Tikuma Shibata, now head of investment banking at Nomura International. Co-managers eventually tired of the losses, and learned to routinely sell their allotted bonds via brokers back to the lead manager. Lead managers, in turn, often withdrew the support bid during the offering period to allow the bonds to falter, or refused to allot the bonds to co-managers, forcing them to pay hefty premiums if bonds had been shorted. The resulting frenzy of syndicate shorting and squeezing and secondary ramping finally drove scores of fund managers out of the new-issue market altogether. "Investors simply got sick of it all," recalls Andrew Pisker, Lehman Brothers International's head of syndicate.

**Sanity in syndicate**

Things had to change, and they did. Tightly priced bought deals mandated through competitive bidding have given way to more negotiated mandates at prices that have attracted institutional investors back to the primary market. There is also a growing number of deals with joint-book numbers requiring a higher degree of cooperation among underwriters, albeit with the business going to a smaller bracket of firms. There is far more dialogue among syndicate members and investors on pricing, and the houses take down more realistic allotments and make firmer commitments to trading an issue in secondary. "The will to talk and to share the obligations is there much more than ever before," says UBS's Harwood. Even Goldman, Sachs & Co., considered the most aggressive of the underwriters, has now jointly run books with such rivals as Warburg, Lehman, CSFB and Banque Paribas. Among Goldman's joint-book deals: a landmark $500 million 30–year issue, done last March for the African Development Bank with Lehman.

. . .

The underlying trend here is a change in the nature of the market's liquidity. The Eurobond market's traditional liquidity—the result of multiple-market makers who quote both bids and offers—is giving way to the customer-driven, bid-side liquidity of the U.S. corporate bond market. This means that bond houses can better control their inventory and concentrate on relative-value and credit-arbitrage research for clients. "There has been a sea change in the nature of the liquidity," confirms William Watt, who heads international fixed income at Kidder Peabody. "What the investor needs to see is a reasonable, continuous bid in the paper, and the bid-side liquidity is as high as I have ever seen it."

This new cooperative spirit also has a certain balance-of-terror aspect to it. The sheer size of the deals and their attendant risks have made underwriters want to team up only with those they know well or can control reliably. Supporting an issue in the secondary market is crucial and difficult; best to put the paper in a few reliable hands, where it can be watched closely. "I screen you, and you screen me," is how Nomura's Shibata puts it. This kind of cooperation doesn't extend much beyond the narrowing universe of reciprocity-minded firms that comprise the emergent Euro-bulge bracket.

**A semblance of order**

Yet there is reason to believe that the cycle may be broken this time around. The introduction of the fixed-price reoffer—the standard Wall Street syndicate management method—by Morgan Stanley for a $500 million issue for New Zealand in mid–1989 is usually cited as the watershed. Since then almost all Eurobonds in any currency—save the most retail-driven currencies, such as the Australian dollar—are now launched as fixed-price reoffers. "There is no question that there is a semblance of order to which you have to credit the fixed-price reoffer," says Salomon's Tye.

The fixed-price reoffer—in which the bonds are reoffered, or sold, to any bank or institution outside the syndicate at a single, firm price—imposed a new discipline in several ways. It eliminated the advantage to the lead manager of pocketing the ⅛ praecipium, for instance, as well as the lead manager's nasty habit of forcing other syndicate members to pay whatever the lead decided were the stabilization costs in maintaining a support bid. Investors also took to the single price of the bonds reoffered because it removed doubt over the likely value of the bonds when they were seasoned. "Before, there was an element of uncertainty about it because you would never know how much they actually sold and how much was on their books," recalls Gordon Johns, managing director of Kemper Investment Management's $1.5 billion portfolio in London.

But the fixed-price reoffer is in fact less a cause than an effect. What lies behind its acceptance has been the preference—some would say obsession—on the part of institutional investors for valuing Eurobonds (in nearly every currency sector) in terms of the spread between them and the relevant benchmark government bonds. Retail investors were interested in the issuer's name and a bond's absolute coupon level. Institutions, by contrast, are concerned with relative performance. Institutions move in and out of currencies or sectors in search of the highest return, always with the domestic government bond markets as the investment touchstone. This style of portfolio management, together with the related growth of the swaps market and the widespread use of futures markets for hedging purposes, has produced a fundamental shift in the way Eurobonds are valued.

Eurobonds, for the most part, have evolved into a complementary asset in the institutional view. "It is governments [first, and then] everything else," remarks Kemper's Johns. "The major return is in getting the currency and market right first. Buying Eurobonds [for their relative value to governments] marginally adds to income, but it certainly comes with illiquidity and credit risk as well."

**New benchmark**

The signs are unmistakable. The Eurobond market is moving into closer alignment with domestic capital markets—especially the mammoth U.S. bond market. These days nearly all bonds are quoted in terms of their spread above governments, and one often has to check the *International Financing Review* for the coupon level. And J.P. Morgan's Gray is quite clear on who's responsible for this fundamental shift: "The really big changes in thinking have come from the investors and issuers; the latter in being much more attuned to the performance in secondary, and the former in simply being much more institutionalized, and all that goes with it."

For the bond houses it is a new mind-set. They must make realistic bids for mandates, and the lead manager must enforce syndicate discipline. "You have to support your deals ruthlessly, because otherwise the borrower will lose confidence in you," says Goldman Sachs' Sherwood. Deals are no longer judged in terms of the price on issue day but rather according to the bonds' ongoing performance—until their price rises so high that their yield crosses that of the underlying governments, indicating its passage into retail hands or asset swaps, and illiquidity.

. . .

### *Notes and Questions*

1. In a "bought deal" the underwriter buys bonds from the issuer at a fixed price, meaning with a fixed coupon and with an agreed amount of proceeds going to the issuer. Standard documentation is set by a dealers association (ISMA). Suppose the underwriter agrees to give the issuer $10 million in proceeds at a coupon rate of 8.25 percent. Further assume that each bond is $100 (there are 100,000 bonds). How does the underwriter make money? How might the underwriter lose money?

2. Will the underwriter seek to have a higher or lower coupon rate than the market demands? How can the issuer control the underwriter setting the premium too high?

3. Negotiated deals are now more typical in the United States than in the Euromarket. In these deals, the issuer retains an underwriter, who structures the terms of offering. The price of the issue is set after the prospectus is circulated to an underwriting group without a price and preliminary indications of interest are obtained; then the issue is priced. During this period, the registration can become effective, i.e. cleared by the SEC—which might take up to three weeks.

The underwriter fixes a price, usually in terms of a discount from par, to make a spread on the transaction that compensates for the service, e.g. the issuer gets 99 with 8.25 bond that the underwriter knows it can sell at par. The service is structuring the deal, a corporate finance function, as well as delivering the agreed proceeds to the issuer.

How would you compare underwriter compensation on bought and negotiated deals? What kind of deals would underwriters prefer?

4. Shelf registration was introduced in the United States in 1982. You may want to review the idea, as set forth in Chapter II. Why did shelf registration make bought deals possible for the first time in the U.S. market?

5. How does a fixed-price reoffer system of distribution work, as compared with the type of pricing that preceded its adoption? Which system would bond buyers prefer? Which system would syndicate members prefer?

---

## c. Taxation

### T. PRIME, INTERNATIONAL BONDS AND CERTIFICATES OF DEPOSIT

45–54 (1991).

**The nature of withholding taxes**

The incidence of withholding taxes or, as they are more familiar to English eyes, taxes levied at source on the payer of interest, have a very significant impact upon the structure of international bond financing. The idea behind a withholding tax is quite simple, and dictates that the payer of interest should deduct from the interest payment the tax at the appropriate rate attributable to the payment, and forward this to the relevant revenue authorities. Such taxes are well accepted revenue devices facilitating the collection of tax, and, indeed, are commonly used even where borrower and lender are resident in the same jurisdiction. They become of even more crucial importance in international transactions, since, once the interest has departed from the jurisdiction of the borrower, the revenue authorities of that jurisdiction would be left with no effective means of collection in the absence of the use of the device. It is a feature of the Eurcbond market that interest on the coupon should be paid free of tax, so that the set interest rate is actually received by the bondholder. Given this expectation of the bondholder, an issue will not be generally acceptable to the market unless the bondholder's position is secured in this respect.

**Bond terms**

The bonds themselves usually make explicit provision in their terms to cover the difficulties of the tax situation. The terms provide that payment of principal and interest will be made without deduction on account of any present, or future, taxes or duties, levied by the jurisdiction of the issuer. If, however, the matter was simply left there the issuer would be left in an unsatisfactory position, because he would be left to pay the commercial rate of interest and the tax upon it at a grossed up amount. His borrowing would, therefore, be crippling to him.

**Arrangements on issue**

Accordingly, as a matter of practice, international bonds are not issued by issuers subject to a withholding tax in their own jurisdiction at the time the issue is made. The sophistication of the techniques used in the international financial market is such that this problem can be overcome by companies incorporated in a jurisdiction which imposes a withholding tax. The means employed is the use of one of the many countries in the world, operating a tax system which looks kindly upon the tax implications of commercial transactions (and often the acquisition of wealth by individuals as well), commonly referred to as 'tax havens'. In particular, what is needed is a country which allows payment of interest to be made free of withholding tax, such as the Netherlands Antilles and the Cayman Islands.

The means employed is for the corporation wishing to undertake the loan to form a subsidiary in the tax haven, and for the issue to be made by the foreign subsidiary, which then receives the results of the issue, and lends them on to the parent company. The loan made by the subsidiary to the parent company is interest bearing, and the interest is at a rate which allows the subsidiary to finance the interest on the coupons of the bonds. In this way the parent corporation receives the required funds, and is able to undertake the issue on normal commercial terms.

### Choice of tax haven

The choice of a satisfactory tax haven depends upon two separate sets of considerations. The first of these relate to the tax haven itself. To be satisfactory as a tax haven for the location of the subsidiary in an international bond issue, the laws of the jurisdiction must be such as to allow the subsidiary to make payments of interest to the bondholders without the deduction from the agreed sum of any withholding tax. Secondly, the tax haven must either charge no local stamp or documentary taxes, or, if any are levied, they must be at such an insignificant level as not to give rise to any major cost to the issuer. Thirdly, the jurisdiction chosen must not seek to impose any capital, or inheritance, taxes upon bondholders merely because the issue was made within that jurisdiction. Fourthly, the chosen jurisdiction must be free of any local exchange control regulations, which would either prohibit or make difficult the payment of interest to bondholders, or the ultimate repayment of their capital to them, or the repatriation of the proceeds of the issue to the jurisdiction of the parent company. Fifthly, since the subsidiary is incorporated merely to raise the loan, there must be no requirements of the local corporate law that a significant proportion of share capital be subscribed in relation to the borrowing being undertaken, for the parent would find this an unacceptable burden since its interest in the subsidiary is purely for the raising of capital and not for trading purposes. Sixthly, the cost of incorporation and administration of the subsidiary under local corporate law must be inexpensive. Finally, the political complexion of the local jurisdiction must be considered, for it is important that the benign fiscal and commercial environment should continue and not be brought to an abrupt end by political developments, causing a new administration with radically opposed policies to come into power.

The second set of considerations arise from the jurisdiction of the parent company, and the relations between that jurisdiction and the tax haven itself. In particular, not only is it important that the subsidiary be able to make payments of interest without deduction of tax, but the parent must be entitled to make payments free of tax to the subsidiary without the imposition of a withholding tax, and also, in due course, be able to repatriate the funds to the subsidiary to redeem the bonds without falling foul of tax or exchange control regulations. Secondly, the subsidiary having no significant assets of its own, the issue will be made palatable to the market by the parent company guaranteeing its subsidiary's issue, thereby substituting its own credit-worthiness for that of the subsidiary.[1] If, therefore, the parent is called upon to make payment under the guarantee, it is important that these too can be made free of any tax or exchange control regulations. Finally, since in the hands of the parent the interest paid on its bonds is an operational expense for its trading purposes, it is vital that the interest should be deductible in the computation of the parent's tax liability for its trading operations in its own jurisdiction.

In evaluating the position of the parent company with regard to both the allowance of interest in the calculation of its tax liability and the impact of exchange control regulations, the law of its own jurisdiction must be considered at the time that the issue is made. If the laws of that jurisdiction prove to have insurmountable obstacles, it will not be possible to undertake an issue by the parent corporation beneficially. With regard to the impact of withholding taxes, the matter to be investigated is whether the country in which the subsidiary is to be incorporated has a sufficiently favourable double taxation treaty with the jurisdiction of the parent.

Stamp duties and other documentary taxes levied in many jurisdictions are another area of taxation which may give rise to difficulty to an issuer by increasing the cost of the issue. In international finance they can take the form of taxes imposed upon the securities which are issued, and which may be calculated by reference to a small percentage of their face value. Equally, some jurisdictions levy a straight issue tax on the value of bonds issued, or, in the case of convertible bonds, on the share capital into which the bonds may be converted. It is necessary to investigate the tax position in the jurisdiction of the issuer with regard to these matters, which can significantly increase the cost of the issue to the issuer.

A further area of difficulty in the field of taxation, which can significantly affect the attractiveness of a bond issue to the bondholders, arises from the possible extra jurisdictional impact of the capital taxation of some countries. Capital taxes comprise taxes on capital gains made by taxpayers on realisation of their investments, inheritance taxes payable on the death of a property holder, and gift taxes which are often supportive of inheritance taxes and which tax gifts made by one person to another. A particular jurisdiction may seek to levy one or all of these forms of capital taxation. So far as they affect only residents within that jurisdiction no difficulties arise, but some jurisdictions may seek to levy them on a different basis which can have the result that a bondholder, having no connection with the country of the issuer, may find himself

1. He would pay in all the notional interest which would, less the tax at the appropriate rate, give the actual interest agreed—a significantly higher figure than the appropriate rate of tax on the net agreed figure.

liable to pay the tax simply because of his holding bonds issued by an issuer resident in the jurisdiction concerned.

Of course, in any event, the mere fact that the issuer's jurisdiction passes a withholding, capital, or inheritance tax does not necessarily mean that this will necessarily be enforced except by the courts of that jurisdiction. An English court will not enforce a foreign tax where the agreement affected is governed by English law. This is probably also true of the attitude of the English courts in dealing with an agreement governed by the law of some other country, unless presumably the chosen law would give effect to the tax.

However in dealing with foreign stamp duties a further distinction must be drawn. Where the effect of the foreign law is to make the unstamped contract unenforceable and inadmissible, the English courts take the view that the failure to stamp is merely a procedural matter, and will ignore it. On the other hand, where under the foreign stamp law the agreement is void due to defective stamping, the English courts will recognise this and give effect to it.

. . .

## U.S. CORPORATIONS IN THE EUROBOND MARKET

The U.S. also operates a withholding tax. This was introduced in 1936 at a rate of 10 per cent. Slight modifications were made in the following two years, and the modified version of the tax became part of the Internal Revenue Code of 1939 at general rates of 10 per cent for individuals and 15 per cent for corporations. Subsequently, by degrees, the rates were raised to 30 per cent where they remain to this day.

Inevitably therefore, when the international bond market developed and U.S. corporations wished to participate, this tax represented a problem to be overcome. The finance subsidiary was pressed into use, but the form depended on whether or not the parent corporation's activities were almost exclusively foreign or largely domestic. If the U.S. parent corporation's activities were almost exclusively foreign, and the money raised was to be invested in foreign affiliates, the parent corporation could use a domestic international finance subsidiary (IFS). The intermediary is usually referred to as an 'eight-twenty company'. The domestic IFS would be wholly owned by the U.S. parent, issuing securities guaranteed by the parent, and lent the proceeds to the foreign affiliates. The affiliates would necessarily pay interest on the money borrowed to the affiliate and this would represent the whole, or virtually the whole, of the income of the domestic I.F.S. Since the operations of the foreign affiliates were largely, or even exclusively, overseas, the interest payments paid to the I.F.S. would be largely non-U.S. source income in its hands. Under the terms of the Internal Revenue Code a U.S. company (which includes a domestic I.F.S.), which derives less than 20 per cent of its gross income from U.S. sources, is not required to withhold tax on interest paid to foreigners.

This was an effective means of dealing with the problem of withholding tax where the parent company's interests were largely overseas, and the bond issue was made to capitalise this. Where however this was not the case, or if it was likely that its operations would not continue to be so heavily based overseas, other means had to be considered. In such circumstances the natural solution was the overseas I.F.S. Naturally, such an I.F.S. would need to be situated within a jurisdiction offering the advantages already considered, and, while a number of satisfactory locations were available, it was the Netherlands Antilles which came to be the most used.

The use of the Netherlands Antilles for this purpose depended on the terms of the tax treaty between itself and the U.S., and the local law of the Netherlands Antilles. Under local law non-residents are free of withholding tax on their income receipts, and also free of any other taxes which would adversely affect the position. Under Article VIII of the treaty, interest receipt of the Netherlands Antilles subsidiary from the U.S. are in general not subject to U.S. withholding tax. Effectively, the only real cost in respect of the borrowing were comparatively minor administrative and legal costs.

However, since 1980 the U.S. has applied deeper thought to the position of the U.S. corporation in relation to the Eurobond market. On the one hand, to have a tax system which drives its own corporations to the necessity of complex overseas arrangements to raise the capital they need to develop and expand their overseas activities, was hardly beneficial to U.S. economic (and probably political) interests. On the other hand, there was a concern that holders of bearer securities could draw income entirely anonymously from their investments, and not declare it as part of their income on their tax returns. This latter consideration was of far wider implication than the Eurobond market, since so many different forms of investment can be held in bearer form with the consequent anonymity which this brings. Having thus analysed the real issues with which it wished to deal, the U.S. passed legislation accordingly. The effect of the legislation is that U.S. issuers may now issue direct into the market without the use of an I.F.S., and will not suffer fiscally as a result, provided strict conditions are met.

In order to issue bearer securities that will be free of withholding taxes U.S. issuers must now comply with three separate, but interrelated, sets of tax rules. These are contained in or based on three separate statutes, the Tax Equity and Fiscal Responsibility Act of 1982 (TEFRA), the Tax Reform Act 1984 (the TRA), and the Interest and Dividend Tax Compliance Act of 1983 (I.D.T.C.A.).

The fundamental purpose of TEFRA was to move issuers away from the use of bearer securities to those requiring registration by means of fiscal disincentives. It achieves this with the aid of temporary regulations introduced in August 1984 by worsening the tax position of parties on the issue of bearer securities, with a view to ensuring that they would not be sold to U.S. investors in the initial distribution of the securities.

The particular fiscal disincentive applied is the imposition of an excise tax equal to 1 per cent of the face value of the securities issued multiplied by the number of years to maturity. However, since the U.S. authorities were primarily concerned with their foreign and domestic markets and not with the Eurobond market, in which they wished their corporations to be able to issue freely as desire and necessity arise, they were content to include an express 'Eurobond exception' applicable if three criteria are satisfied. First, interest must be payable on the bearer securities only outside the U.S. Secondly, the face of each security and detachable coupon must bear a legend setting out that any U.S. person holding such security or coupon will be subject to various limitations under the revenue laws of the U.S. Finally, the securities must be sold under 'arrangements reasonably designed' to ensure that the securities will not be sold or distributed to any U.S. person (other than qualified U.S. financial institutions such as banks, brokers and insurance companies).

IDTCA was introduced to build on the basis established by TEFRA. IDTCA imposed stronger information and reporting requirements than TEFRA to improve compliance with U.S. tax laws, particularly the taxation of interest and dividends. Issuers, paying agents, and brokers are all required to obtain and report the tax identification numbers of investors receiving payments of interest or dividends on, or the proceeds of sale of, securities. If this is not done a 20 per cent withholding tax must be withheld from the payments of interest, dividends, or sales proceeds.

The choice imposed by the form of the legislation is plainly unacceptable to the international bond market, which has always demanded payment of interest free of taxes, and also respect for and preservation of the traditional anonymity of the market. As a result of pressure from those who are involved in, or wish to use, the Euromarkets, temporary regulations have now been introduced to protect the needs of the market. Issues made in compliance with the TEFRA Eurobond exception are free of the information and reporting requirements if all payments of interest and principal are made outside the U.S., and neither the issuer nor the paying agent has actual knowledge that the holder is a U.S. person. Further, information and reporting requirements do not apply to sales proceeds paid to investors by non-U.S. custodians and brokers that are not controlled by a U.S. person and derive most of their income from outside the U.S. Where, however, the custodian or broker is controlled by a U.S. person, or derives most of its income from the U.S., information must be reported, unless the institution has on its files evidence of the holder's non-U.S. status.

If the thrust of these reforms were to insist on less anonymity for investors and therefore greater fiscal rectitude, at some risk to the traditions of the international bond market until specific exemptions were made for it, the thrust of the Tax Reform Act was to try to assist the market by eliminating the need for a foreign I.F.S. This it achieved by repealing the 30 per cent withholding tax on 'portfolio interest' in the case of a debt-securities issued by non-resident alien individuals and foreign corporations after 18 July 1984. Three types of debt-securities produce income qualifying as portfolio interest, two of the exceptions relating to registered debt securities in particular circumstances and the third being 'obligations in bearer form issued in compliance with the TEFRA Eurobond exception.' Coupled with the creation of this means for U.S. issuers to issue international bonds without the use of an IFS, the Inland Revenue Service took steps to clamp down on the use of the Netherlands Antilles finance subsidiary structure.

The overall effect of these provisions is, therefore, now to create a means whereby U.S. issuers can freely make use of the international bond market without the impositions of financial penalties. Indeed U.S. issues are now made direct without the use of an I.F.S.

## TRACY CORRIGAN, "ITALY'S NEW TAX REGIME TO HAVE WIDESPREAD REPERCUSSIONS"

Financial Times (September 14, 1992).

The changes to Italy's investment taxation regime, announced last week as part of the government's economic package, will not only shift patterns of investment in Italy, but will have a knock-on effect in several areas of the international capital markets.

Eurobonds issued by some supra-national agencies (the World Bank, the European Investment Bank (EIB), the European Coal and Steel Community and the European Atomic Agency) and government and state agencies (the Republic of Italy, Enel, the electricity utility, Crediop, the financial institution, and Ferrovie, the national railway) have lost their tax exemption for Italian residents, and future deals will have withholding tax levied at 12½ per cent. But existing issues remain exempt from withholding tax, even if they continue to be traded.

Prices in existing tax-exempt issues rallied on the news on Friday. The World Bank's global bond issues benefitted most, with the yield spread on its $1.5bn five-year global narrowing from 3 basis points above the five-year treasury to 10 basis points below. The bank's 10–year yen global bonds tightened from 20 basis points to 12 basis points over the 10–year Japanese government bond yield. However, there was concern that the effect of aggressive buying of these issues would "strip all our liquid benchmarks out of the market," one trader said.

Other Eurobonds did not appear to be following these deals to tighter spreads.

The tightening of existing paper should help the World Bank achieve aggressive funding when it launches its next global bond, despite its loss of tax-exempt status. The bank said it may advance its funding programme to take advantage of the shortage of paper. The bank's next offering, a yen global offering totalling at least Y200bn is scheduled for mid-October. But the next dollar global offering, expected in 1993, may be brought forward.

Although the effect will vary from one sector to another, bankers expect costs for the World Bank to rise, in the medium to long term, by around 20 basis points, to about 20 basis points under Libor.

The EIB is likely to suffer a greater increase in funding costs, since it has targetted Italian investors with issues in smaller markets such as the matador bond market. It has frequently achieved funding costs of 75 to 80 basis points under Libor, now also set to rise to around 20 basis points under Libor.

The EIB decided on Friday to pull its Pta10bn issue of floating-rate notes, launched on Wednesday, just hours ahead of the tax change announcement. Although the change did not take effect until Thursday, there was some uncertainty over whether it applied to the launch or the signing of the deal. Trades in the issue, which had been largely placed ahead of the announcement, were cancelled, according to lead manager Banco Bilbao–Vizcaya. The EIB is still considering whether to go ahead with a Y50bn deal scheduled for last Thursday. However, dealers said the planned terms of the issue would have to be changed to take account of the new tax regime.

Meanwhile, spreads of Italy's Eurobonds barely tightened on the news. Dealers said concern about Italian credit and the excess supply of Italian paper stifled any rally in Italian paper.

The sizeable repurchase agreement (repo) market is likely to suffer on several fronts. As well as the loss of tax-exempt status for supranational names, the new rules limit companies ability to deduct the repo costs as a business expense.

Also included in the package is a cut in withholding tax for Italian investors on foreign bonds from 30 per cent to 12.5 per cent, the same as for Italian government bonds. This is expected to encourage Italian institutions to diversify their investments in overseas markets.

However, the new regulations also close a loophole used by some Italian institutions. They will no longer be able to avoid paying withholding tax by "coupon-washing" farming out bonds when the coupon is due to be paid. In future, taxation will be applied to accrued interest.

Volume on Italy's new bond futures market, the Mercato Italiano Futures (MIF) reached 10,000 contracts on its first day of trading on Friday.

### *Notes and Questions*

1. Until 1984, the United States imposed a withholding tax on interest paid to foreigners. Assuming there was no way to avoid the tax, was this a good policy? How did U.S. companies, in fact, use the Eurobond market to issue debt to foreigners free of this tax? How could foreigners be sure that no tax would be imposed?

2. In June 1987, the Treasury announced that it would terminate the Netherlands Antilles tax treaty. Why was this a problem for bonds issued before 1984?

3. As the Prime article relates, U.S. withholding taxes are no longer a problem. What about the one percent excise tax on issuing bearer securities? Is this a problem?

4. Let's look at the Italian case. Until late 1992, eurolira bonds issued by supranationals, like the World Bank, to Italian investors in the euromarket—outside Italy—were not subject to the normal Italian 38% withholding tax. Italian investors in these bonds were subject to an income tax on interest earned, but given massive tax cheating in Italy, these issues were effectively tax-exempt. Italy has now made new issues of these bonds sold to Italians subject to a reduced withholding tax of 12.5%.

Before imposition of the new withholding tax a high proportion of World Bank funds were raised through eurolira bond issues. Why? What did the World Bank do with all this lira?

---

## B. GLOBAL BONDS

The eurobond market has been the heart of the international bond market. Issuers used off-shore markets to tap investors from a variety of domestic markets, including their own. Thus, a U.S. issuer might issue eurodollar bonds through London rather than U.S. or Japanese domestic bonds (subject to the market regulations of those two countries). Similarly, a Japanese issuer would issue euroyen through London rather than use the domestic markets of the U.S. or Japan. The advent of global offerings is changing this pattern. New issues of international bonds in 1993 were $481 billion, of which $35 billion represented globals.

### KEVIN MUEHRING, "THE GLOBAL COMES OF AGE"

Institutional Investor 82 (December 1983).

#### Four years old

In the four years since the World Bank launched the concept with a $1 billion issue in September 1989, there have been 61 globals, worth a total of $88.4 billion, according to IFR Securities Data. Although the World Bank still accounts for about a quarter of the outstanding volume, issuers now include several European sovereigns (Sweden, Italy, Finland and Portugal), a handful of Canadian provinces, two corporates and a string of U.S.-bank-issued credit-card-backed receivables. And though most globals have been denominated in U.S. dollars, issues have also been launched in Canadian dollars, yen, New Zealand dollars, Australian dollars and, most recently, deutsche marks.

An instrument that offers to integrate the world's bond markets by offering investors and issuers the bonds at a single price worldwide has such broad appeal that it is surprising the global took so long to come about. The structure is seemingly simple: Globals differ from Eurobonds and international bonds in being launched simultaneously in the U.S., Europe and Asia, with trading within and among all three markets.

Globals are inherently large and liquid. The issues are usually $1 billion or larger in size, which enables market makers to quote prices in secondary worldwide with a 5–to–10–cent dealing spread on lots of up to $25 million. Compared with 3 cents on on-the-run U.S. Treasuries and 15–to–50–cent dealing spreads on most Eurobonds, globals are the most liquid alternative to on-the-run government bonds. The World Bank's four yen-denominated globals, for instance, are the most actively traded paper in the yen market after the benchmark ten-year Japanese government bond, notes the World Bank's Lay.

. . .

**Ensuring liquidity**

But the biggest factor in the global's success has been the assurance of liquidity. "We take positions as an active investor," says Ian Kelson, head of fixed income at Morgan Grenfell Asset Management in London, "which means, of course, that we are looking to get out of the position as well." To Kelson, liquidity means the ability to trade in tickets of $25 million "without having a material effect on the price." Indeed, institutional investors—who are likely to be taking not long-term positions on yield but shorter-term ones on currency, spread or interest rates—are willing to pay a premium for liquidity. "The global has proved the issuer can get size without any concession on price," says John McNiven, a managing director at Merrill Lynch International in London.

. . .

In theory, the primary distribution is spread evenly throughout all three main investor markets. But in reality, the bulk of the paper is sold into the market where the bid is strongest. For instance, more than half of the 30–year tranche of Italy's $3.5 billion global in October sold into the U.S., though barely a fifth of Sweden's $1 billion three-year floater went into U.S. accounts.

The result is a uniformly lower price for issuers. Five years ago, says the World Bank's Lay, the Bank's paper was trading at 15 basis points above federal agency paper, whereas it is now trading in the U.S. at more than 10 basis points below the federal agency paper. Lay strongly believes that the global program has been instrumental in achieving this lower cost of funding.

. . .

---

The following reading discusses a major problem with the use of globals, insuring a simultaneous offer in the various countries of issue given different national market regulations. The piece first deals with global equity offerings but the same types of problems also occur with bonds.

E. GREENE, A. BELLER, G. COHEN, M. HUDSON, JR., AND E. ROSEN

U.S. Regulation of the International Securities Markets § 6.01 (1992).

## § 6.01 GLOBAL EQUITY OFFERINGS

In recent years many large multi-national companies have made "global offerings" of their shares—that is, offerings in their home country combined with offerings in other markets (e.g., the United States, Japan or Europe). This chapter focuses on the impact of U.S. rules and regulations on a global offering when a U.S. tranche is included. The extent of that impact varies depending on whether the U.S. tranche is publicly or privately sold.

### [1] The U.S. pattern

U.S. rules and regulations have imposed a standard pattern on public offerings in the United States, and much of the complexity of global offerings is generated by the way in which foreign regulatory regimes impose conflicting patterns.

The standard pattern for a U.S. public offering is as follows:

— No offer can be made in the United States until a registration statement is filed with the SEC. The registration statement includes a preliminary prospectus, which is generally printed and distributed to potential purchasers after filing. The preliminary prospectus is the only document that can be used to make offers in writing.

— After the filing is made, the SEC can be expected to comment on the registration statement, especially if it is the first offering by the company in the United States. Although it typically takes about one month to receive comments, the SEC has been very cooperative in providing comments in a shorter period of time to accommodate the timing of global offerings. It should generally be possible to respond to those comments within a week or two, and then to file an amended registration statement, including the form of amended preliminary prospectus used in roadshows or other marketing efforts, or if the offering timetable calls for it, the form of final prospectus (the final prospectus would not include pricing information if such information is to be added to the final prospectus pursuant to Rule 430A). After the amended registration statement containing the form of final prospectus is filed, the SEC will declare the registration statement effective on request.

— At about the time the amended registration statement is declared effective, the underwriting agreement is signed and the share price is set. During the period between filing and effectiveness, executive officers of the issuer will have participated in road-shows, and the underwriters will have obtained indications of interest at various prices from their customers. The lead underwriter will then negotiate the price and the ultimate size of the U.S. tranche with these indications of interest in mind. In a public offering of shares that are already listed on an exchange, pricing is usually based on the quoted share price, or a formula related to it.

— After effectiveness, and as soon as possible after pricing, the final prospectus (including the pricing information) is printed and the underwriters confirm sales to their customers. The closing typically occurs five business days later, and is subject to certain conditions being met, including the delivery of opinions and accountants' comfort letters and the absence of material adverse changes in the issuer's business or serious disruptions in the financial markets.

There is more flexibility in a U.S. private placement, since the registration requirements of the Securities Act do not apply and the SEC is not involved.

### [2] Selected foreign regulatory regimes

The pattern for a global equity offering must be determined in the context of both the U.S. rules and regulations and the regulatory regimes abroad. In many cases, the foreign component of a global offering is made in a way that is exempt from the application of most foreign regulations. The exemption typically relied on in many countries, such as the United Kingdom, is the so-called "professionals" exemption, which generally permits offers and sales of securities to be made to large institutions and other market professionals with few regulatory requirements. If the international offering includes a public offering in a national market, however, various registration and regulatory requirements of that country may apply, and these requirements will have to be integrated with the U.S. rules. In such a situation, complex issues are likely to arise that could expose the issuer or the underwriters to risks not otherwise encountered.

#### *[a] United Kingdom*

The standard U.S. pattern was modified for the privatizations in the United Kingdom in the 1980s that were combined with U.S. public offerings. In those offerings, marketing in both countries prior to pricing was done on the basis of a "pathfinder" prospectus, which took the form in the United States of a preliminary prospectus included in a registration statement filed with the SEC. Pricing took place on "impact day," which occurred about three weeks following release of the pathfinder prospectus and also marked the beginning of a one- to four-week subscription period in the United Kingdom. Although the SEC could have been asked to declare the registration statement effective on impact day, thus allowing the U.S. underwriters to confirm sales and eliminate much of their underwriting exposure, this was unacceptable to the participants in the offering in the United Kingdom. An effective registration statement would result in "grey-market" trading of the shares on a "when-issued" basis in the United States, and potentially the United Kingdom, during the U.K. subscription period; and the possibility of such trading was considered potentially disruptive. As a result, the U.S. underwriters were required to agree to purchase the shares on impact day but were not permitted to request the SEC to declare the registration statement effective or to confirm sales to their customers until "allotment day" when the U.K. subscription period ended. This extended period between pricing and confirmations of sales subjected the U.S. underwriters to risks that were not borne by their U.K. counterparts, who typically "laid off" their underwriting commitments on large U.K. institutions acting as sub-underwriters prior to impact day.[4] When this extended underwriting period was combined with the absence of a *force majeure* clause in the underwriting agreement, the underwriting disaster in the 1987 British Petroleum offering became possible.

More recent U.K. privatizations have adopted procedures that minimize the risk to underwriters and the inconsistency between U.S. and U.K. underwriting practice. In the 1991 secondary offering by the British Government of shares in British Telecommunications public limited company ("BT"), which involved a registered public offering in the United States, marketing took place on the basis of a "pathfinder" prospectus abroad and a preliminary prospectus in the United States, but pricing did not occur on impact day. Institutional U.K. offerees and offerees elsewhere around the world tendered bids for shares beginning on impact day and the British Government and the global coordinator set the final offer price for both the tender offer and retail tranches at the end of the subscription period based on those bids. The U.S. registration statement was declared effective at the end of the subscription period before the final offer price was set. This process more closely resembles pricing practices in U.S. public offerings, where the formal "tender offer" process of the BT offering is analogous to the somewhat less transparent U.S. "book-building" process.

. . .

*[v] Comparison of U.S. and U.K. rules*

It is useful to contrast the U.S. and U.K. rules on publicity and distribution of research reports in order to highlight some of the difficulties that arise in global offerings. The United Kingdom, like many other jurisdictions, permits much more publicity about an offering outside the offering document than the United States. Large global equity offerings in the United Kingdom are sometimes preceded by full-scale television and press advertising campaigns and distributions of brochures describing the issuer and the offer process. Such advertising is permitted in

4. The U.S. underwriters could not arrange for sub-underwriting in this manner, since sub-underwriting commitments, like other binding commitments to purchase securities, can only be obtained after the registration statement is declared effective.

the United Kingdom if certain procedural requirements are followed. U.K. law also would permit unlimited distribution of advertisements that do not comply with such procedural requirements so long as distribution is limited to certain professionals. Notwithstanding such permitted advertising, offers by U.K. companies technically can be made to the public in the United Kingdom, as in the United States, only on the basis of prospectuses that contain mandated disclosure.

Conflicts between the U.K. and U.S. systems arise in global offerings involving both jurisdictions because the U.K. publicity efforts must be restricted as described above to jurisdictions outside the United States. Difficulties arise, for example, when placing advertisements in newspapers such as *The Financial Times* and *The Wall Street Journal*. Such publications are distributed in the United States, and steps must be taken to prevent the publication of advertising materials in their U.S. editions. In some recent transactions, offering participants have even succeeded in getting certain newspapers to agree in writing not to publish advertisements in specified jurisdictions. The need to coordinate conflicting legal systems has led to the practice of distributing written publicity guidelines to all participants in a global offering that synthesize the legal requirements in all relevant jurisdictions. Since compromises often need to be made to place all syndicates on an equal footing, these guidelines typically reflect the most restrictive elements of the participating jurisdictions' legal systems.

. . .

The U.S. requirement that no publicity efforts begin before circulation of the preliminary prospectus led to a dilemma in the recent Wellcome offering. The offering participants felt that lengthy pre-marketing was necessary in all jurisdictions, and in the United States especially, to educate investors about a company that was not widely known outside the United Kingdom. Since this pre-marketing could begin in the United Kingdom and elsewhere before a prospectus was prepared, the original intention was to distribute the preliminary prospectus about a month before pricing, but to begin other marketing efforts (including an advertising campaign) about two months before pricing. Marketing efforts could not begin in the United States before the filing of the preliminary prospectus, so the U.S. underwriters convinced the other underwriters that it was important to file a preliminary U.S. prospectus one month early for distribution to a limited audience of key U.S. investor groups. The early filing contained the full substance of the preliminary prospectus that would be widely distributed one month before pricing, but omitted certain details about the offer structure. Since the U.S. syndicate would be circulating a preliminary prospectus, the U.K. and other syndicates decided to do the same in order to maintain a consistency of marketing efforts, so they simultaneously issued a pathfinder prospectus abroad. The preliminary prospectus that was distributed on a limited basis was referred to by the non-U.S. offering participants as a "pink herring," since it came one month earlier than the intended date of distribution of the "red herring" prospectus, and contained slightly less information than the red herring.

. . .

## § 6.02 GLOBAL DEBT OFFERINGS

. . .

The anti-bearer bond rules ("TEFRA") of the U.S. Internal Revenue Code of 1986 (the "Internal Revenue Code") add a further dimension to global offerings of debt securities. It is the custom in many foreign markets for bonds to be offered and sold in bearer form. TEFRA, however, prohibits bearer bonds from being offered or sold in the United States, whether in a public offering or a private placement, as part of their original issuance. As a result, bonds offered and sold in the United States must be in registered form and, moreover, cannot be converted into bearer form. Thus the issuer and underwriters in a global debt offering must decide either (i) to offer and sell bearer bonds outside the United States and registered bonds in the United States, with the consequent impairment of trading between markets, since investors outside the United States may be unwilling to purchase bonds in registered form in the secondary market, or (ii) to offer and sell bonds in registered form both in the United States and outside, with the consequent shrinking of the market for the bonds outside the United States, since many investors in foreign jurisdictions may only wish to purchase bonds in bearer form. What is more, if the issuer of bonds in registered form is a U.S. company, U.S. tax rules will require each foreign investor to provide an Internal Revenue Service form W–8, identifying itself, in order to receive interest payments free of U.S. withholding tax. This requirement is inconsistent with the desire of many foreign investors to remain anonymous and is likely further to reduce the attractiveness of bonds in registered form.

It is possible, through the use of global bonds registered in the name of clearing systems or their nominees, to reconcile the requirements of TEFRA with the desire of European investors to remain anonymous, at least in the case of offerings by foreign issuers to which the W–8 requirement does not apply, and at the same time to offer and sell identical securities in the United States and abroad. Because a global bond registered in the name of a clearing system or its nominee is a registered bond for purposes of TEFRA, interests in the global bond may be offered and sold in the United States, and so long as the bond remains in global form the beneficial owner can remain undisclosed. In the case of a U.S. issuer, the requirement to deliver a form W–8, which applies to the beneficial owner, in order to receive interest payments free of U.S. withholding tax, makes this less than a complete solution.

. . .

### *Notes and Questions*

1. Why are global offerings becoming more attractive than eurobonds given that issuers must comply with different national market regulations?

2. The reading excerpt gives an illustration of the coordination problem. What differences in market rules between the U.S. and the U.K. accounted for the fact that the underwriters did not want the registration statement to be effective on "impact day"? Why did the solution, delaying the U.S. effective date to the end of the U.K. subscription period, increase the risks for the U.S. underwriters? How did the 1991 BT offering reduce this risk?

3. Global offerings have generally used a negotiated or open priced style of underwriting, as opposed to a bought deal. The BT3 offer in July 1993 used "a formal bookbuilding process, in which managers are involved in the solicitation of 'non-binding indications of interest in purchasing shares' which are communicated through a formal process to the Global Co-ordinator (S.G. Warburg Securities for BT3), and which leads to a final pricing and allocation decision, following which the managers become legally bound to underwrite the offer." E. Greene and W. Underhill, "Structuring A Successful Global Offering—The BT3 Offer," *Recent Developments in International Securities Law,* ed. American Conference Institute (October 25 and 26, 1993), p. 6. Allocation decisions among bidders were based on four "quality" considerations, in addition to price: (1) price leadership (high bids early in the process); (2) after market support (bids from investors likely to hold in the immediate after market); (3) pre-sale support (bids from investors who increased their bids during the bidding period); and (4) no adverse activity (bids from investors believed not to have engaged in adverse market activity, for example, short sales). The shares are actually allocated to the underwriters who then sell the shares to the underlying bidders.

Why have globals used open priced underwriting? Why allocate shares on any basis other than price?

---

*Links to Other Chapters*

To a large extent, the success of the eurobond market has depended on onerous regulation of domestic bond markets, examined to some degree for the U.S. (Chapter II) and Japan (Chapter VIII). The development of the global bond market represents a major challenge to eurobonds, and depends on further deregulation of domestic markets. Clearance and settlement arrangements, on a coordinated global basis, may be crucial to further expansion of global markets, a matter taken up in Chapter XIV. Finally, the issue of both global and eurobonds may be driven by swap possibilities (Chapter XVI).

# CHAPTER XII

# SECURITIZATION

## A. INTRODUCTION

Securitization means many things. One expert, rather than defining it, describes three forms. It may substitute securities for loans, when borrowers shift from bank credit to commercial paper, for example. It may decompose a large standard bank loan into loan participations, as in a syndicated eurocredit. It may transfer smaller loans to a pool that issues its own securities [Frankel, Securitization (1991) 6].

Securitization by pooling is the topic of this chapter. It is "the process of converting loans or receivables into negotiable investments" [Morrissey, International Securitisation (1992) 5]. These securities are, according to the U.S. Securities and Exchange Commission, rated investment grade securities

> primarily serviced by the cash flows of a discrete pool of receivables or other financial assets, either fixed or revolving, that by their terms convert into cash within a finite time period plus any rights or other assets designed to assure the servicing or timely distribution of proceeds to the security holders [Morrison, Securitization International Guide, International Financial Law Review (August 1993) Supplement 3].

This chapter emphasizes mortgage-backed securities (MBS) for comparison across countries. Other asset-backed securities (ABS) include automobile loans, credit card receivables, home equity loans, leases of real property or equipment like airplanes, education loans, junk bonds, boat loans, and even oil or gas reserves. These ABS appear routinely in the U.S., increasingly in the U.K., and much less so in Germany or Japan, the four countries we examine here. The assets are often less standardized than mortgages and may introduce additional complexity, such as receipts in various currencies.

By 1993, MBS outstanding were estimated at between $1–1.3 trillion. Most—about 85%—had single family mortgages as assets, with the remaining 15% split almost evenly between multifamily mortgages (over 4 units) and commercial mortgages. Commercial mortgages were growing fast: 1993 saw almost $18 billion new issues, on a base of $38 billion. Of ABS, auto and credit card assets back about 75%–80%; 60% are publicly placed. Standard and Poor's reported over $140 billion in auto and credit card issues and over $65 billion of rated ABS commercial paper in the U.S., which dominates. Non-mortgage assets grew faster than MBS. Markets outside the U.S. were much smaller and grew faster than U.S. markets.

What are the key elements of the pooled form of securitization? Why is each important? Could the market create ABS that lack even one of the key elements?

## B. ELEMENTS OF A SECURITIZED TRANSACTION

A simple schematic of securitization is as follows.

### S. ALMOND AND C. HENDERSON, "ACCOUNTING FOR INTERNATIONAL SECURITISATION"

In H. Morrissey, International Securitisation 151 (1992) [hereafter Morrissey].

Assets, such as credit card, leasing and mortgage loan receivables will have been generated by an originator. The originator will segregate the assets to be securitised into relatively homogeneous pools with respect to credit quality, maturity and interest rate profile. A pool of assets is then sold to a special purpose vehicle company, set up by the originator specifically for this transaction. To meet the purchase price of the pool this company will fund itself by issuing securities backed by the pool of assets. Typically, some form of credit enhancement will be attached in order to achieve a high rating for the issue of securities. There will also be a servicer, often the originator itself, responsible for collecting interest and principal repayments on the assets in the underlying pools and making payments to investors or *a trustee* representing them.

C.A. Stone and A. Zissu, II *Global Risk Based Capital Regulations* 325 (1994).

**EXHIBIT 1**
**A Typical Mortgage-Backed Securities Transaction**

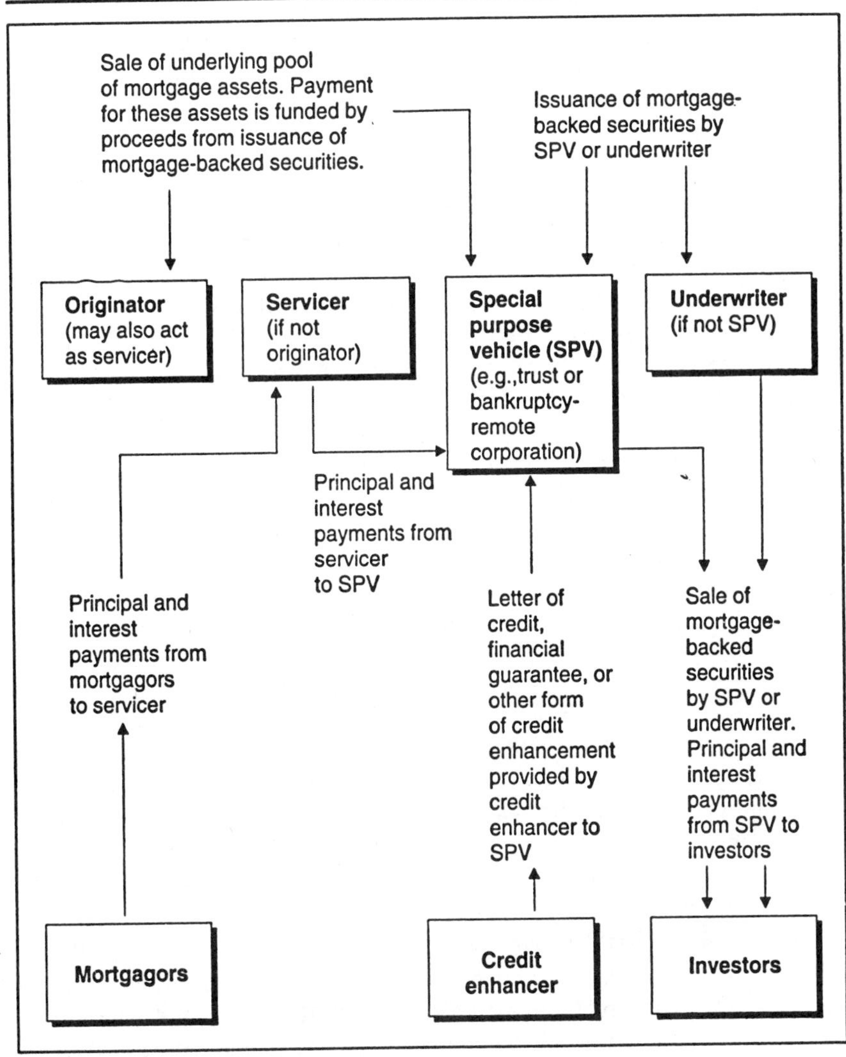


## C. THE EVOLUTION OF MORTGAGE–BACKED SECURITIES IN THE UNITED STATES

Only in the 1970s in the United States did mortgage-backed securities remove the assets from the originator's balance sheet.

Almond and Henderson, Morrissey, 6–14.

### The US Mortgage-backed Securities Market

The US mortgage-backed securities (MBS) market has undergone dramatic expansion since the first deals were made in the 1970s, and now boasts the stature of one of the most significant capital markets in the world. By the end of 1990, over US$1tr of US mortgages had been securitised, representing around a quarter of the total outstanding mortgage debt and comparing with outstanding Federal Government debt of nearly US$2.6tr. The success of the US MBS market has encouraged more widespread use of securitisation, both to embrace other assets besides mortgages, and in other countries. Some of the reasons behind its particular success are, however, attributable to specific features of the US mortgage and banking systems.

Home ownership has long been an integral part of the "American dream", and has received official encouragement in the form of various initiatives dating back as far as the early 1930s and designed in the first instance to help the economy recover from the Depression. These include the tax deductibility of mortgage interest payments; government programmes and agencies created to promote housing finance; and the structure of the "Savings and Loan" industry, traditionally the main provider of residential mortgages. The combination of these factors and rapid economic expansion led to a flourishing primary mortgage market, with the volume of outstanding mortgage debt growing from US$73.1bn in 1950 to US$3,852.0bn in 1990. This formidable total makes it the largest capital market in the world and almost as large as the US corporate, federal, state and local government markets combined.

. . .

The US government established the Federal Housing Administration (FHA) in the 1930s to insure residential mortgage loans made to lower income Americans against default. This helped to improve the level of finance available for home purchase at a time when confidence was low as a result of the Depression. Later, the Veterans Administration (VA) established a similar programme to the FHA insurance scheme, whereby it guaranteed the mortgage loans of home purchasers who had served in the US military forces.

The government also established three agencies to promote housing finance through the development of secondary debt markets. The first of these, the Federal National Mortgage Association, known as FNMA or "Fannie Mae", was founded in 1938, to buy and sell mortgage loans insured by the FHA. Fannie Mae bought these loans from their originators, boosting the lenders' capacity to make new loans. The purchases were initially funded through Fannie Mae's issuance of straight corporate debt paper, creating the first link between the US housing finance and wholesale capital markets. The second housing agency, the Government National Mortgage Association, known as GNMA or "Ginnie Mae", was established within the US Department of Housing and Urban Development ("HUD") in 1968. Its mandate was to encourage the development of the secondary market for FHA-insured or VA-guaranteed mortgages. GNMA issued the first US mortgage-backed securities in 1970. Finally, the Federal Home Loan Mortgage Corporation, FHLMC or "Freddie Mac" was established in 1970 to provide the same function for non-government, or "conventional", mortgages as Ginnie Mae provides for FHA and VA loans. Freddie Mac made its debut issues in 1971.

The early GNMA and FHLMC issues were "pass-throughs". A pass-through security is created by the issuer forming a collection or pool of mortgages with similar characteristics, and then selling shares or participations in the pool. Investors in a pass-through security own undivided interests in the pool of underlying mortgages, and receive pro rata shares of the cash flows. The mortgages continue to be serviced by the originators or other appointed servicer. The cash flows from a pass-through are similar but not identical to those on the collateral, with the differences deriving from the deduction of servicing (and guarantee or insurance fees) and a delay in the receipt of payments. There are three sources of cash flow on the mortgages which are in turn "passed through" to the investor:

- interest payments (the mortgage interest rate less expenses);
- scheduled principal repayments (the standard US residential mortgage loan involves the amortisation of principal over its term);
- unscheduled principal repayments, known as prepayments. US mortgage borrowers typically have the option to prepay their loans at any time and without penalty.

[The author notes that the possibility of prepayment "detracts from the appeal of pass-throughs ...." As a result:]

Much of the innovation within the US MBS market over the past decade has indeed been driven by the recognised need to deal with prepayment risk. Collaterlised Mortgage Obligations (CMOs), for example, consist of several tranches with differing priorities over the cash flows on the underlying collateral. Some tranches offer greater certainty of cash flows ("call protection") while supporting tranches carry the risk and are priced accordingly. The CMO structure was created by First Boston in 1983, and has become one of the most important types of US mortgage security. During the 1970s, however, the agencies continued issuing pass-throughs and the secondary mortgage market grew slowly, lacking an impetus such as strong investor demand or support from Wall Street.

The thrifts' early mortgage-related securities were mortgage-backed bonds. This third basic category of US mortgage-related securities (the others being pass-throughs and CMOs) echoes the original *Pfandbriefe* structure, being a general obligation of the issuer backed by a pool of mortgages. Mortgage-backed bonds therefore allow the issuer to access funds beyond its own deposit base but do not achieve the comprehensive transference of risks off balance sheet that is accomplished *via* the pass-through structure. The first US mortgage-backed bond issue was brought by California Federal ("Cal Fed") Savings and Loan in 1975. The mortgages collateralising this deal were FHA-insured or VA-guaranteed, with an initial collateralisation of 175% of the issue. A "maintenance level" of 135% was specified; if the value of the collateral were to fall below this threshold, Cal Fed was required to provide additional collateral to the extent of the principal payments it had received on the mortgages. Other mortgage-backed bonds were subsequently issued in the mid–1970s by thrifts, on the basis of FHA, VA and conventional mortgage loans.

[U.S. savings and loan institutions, hit by soaring deposit interest rates in the late 1970s and early 1980s and low interest on long-term mortgages, were helped by Congress in September 1981.]

On 30 September 1981, Congress passed an apparently life-saving new tax and accounting break for the thrifts: they could sell their existing portfolios of mortgage loans, amortise the realised losses over the life of the loans and offset these losses against any taxes they had paid over the previous ten years. At the same time the proceeds from the asset sales could be reinvested at current, higher rates. To take advantage of the new rules, the thrifts turned to the government housing agencies. As we have seen, Ginnie Mae, Fannie Mae and Freddie Mac are between them able to transform most types of residential mortgages into securities carrying at least an implicit government guarantee. The thrifts rushed to sell their mortgage portfolios, paying fees to the government housing agencies in exchange for their guarantees. The thrifts themselves invested in the resulting mortgage-backed securities, effectively swapping their loss-making portfolios for government-backed securities offering current market yields, while diminishing the impact of their realised losses through the new accounting and tax rules.

[But the continuing mismatch and even riskier lending forced a massive bailout of saving and loan institutions in 1989.]

At that point, there was widespread concern that the liquidation of insolvent thrifts' vast holdings of MBS would weigh heavily on the market, and the yield spreads between MBS and the "risk-free" benchmark, US Treasuries, widened sharply. In the event, this proved to be a buying opportunity. Other circumstances, such as the favourable risk-weightings applied to agency MBS for the purposes of the BIS capital adequacy requirements for banks, and growth in overseas investor interest, have contributed to healthy demand for US mortgage product.

. . .

Today's investor in the US secondary mortgage market has a choice of instruments offering fixed or floating rates, the whole spectrum of maturity structures, agency or "private label" credit status and bearing very different levels of prepayment risk. He can assess the risk and return profiles of these alternatives using sophisticated pricing models incorporating prepayment patterns observed from historical data and computer simulations of a wide range of possible market environments.

### *Questions*

1. What sort of institutions perform the various functions in a MBS? For example, who would be likely to buy the MBS? Why?

2. What benefits would each type of institution get from performing this function? For example, what factors would encourage a U.S. bank to originate mortgages for a MBS? Consider factors you have seen in earlier classes. For example, how would the way the U.S. implemented the Basle risk-weighted capital rules affect U.S. banks' interest in the MBS and ABS markets? See Attachment II in the chapter on capital adequacy.

3. What major risks would investors face? How does this structure address those risks?

4. The ABS market was an offshoot of the MBS market. Given this, how important to the evolution of markets for securitized pools was the existence of Ginnie Mae, Fanny Mae, and Freddy Mac? Would other countries need such institutions to promote their ABS markets?

---

## D. SELECTED LEGAL ISSUES IN SECURITIZATION IN THE U.S.

The readings in this section are excerpted from R. Dayan, et al., "Legal Overview of Asset–Backed Securities," in J. Lederman, ed., The Handbook of Asset–Backed Securities 41 (1990).

As you read each section, consider the role of the U.S. government in the evolution of the MBS and ABS markets. What accounts for the government's policy? Would the engineers of policy toward Ginnie Mae have been pleased by the longterm growth of these markets?

### 1. Bankruptcy and Insolvency

A primary goal of asset securitization is to obtain a credit rating for an issuance that is based primarily on the quality of the assets (and any credit enhancements) backing the obligation, without regard to the originator's own credit-worthiness. To accomplish this, the transaction must be structured so that the assets and their attendant cash flows will not be impaired by bankruptcy or insolvency of the originator of the assets.

Ordinarily, the rating of secured debt issued by a bankruptcy-eligible entity takes into account the rating of the borrower, regardless of the strength of the collateral. Thus, if a BBB-rated industrial corporation issued $1 million of debt secured by U.S. Government securities with a market value of $2 million, at first glance one might think that the debt could be rated AAA based on the collateral. However, in reality, it is unlikely that the collateral would improve the rating much beyond BBB+.

The rating of the obligation at a level substantially below the quality of the security is explained by the effect that a bankruptcy or insolvency proceeding of the originator would have on the rights of creditors.

***Bankruptcy-Eligible Entities***

Upon the filing of a petition under the federal Bankruptcy Code, 11 U.S.C. Sections 101 et seq., the rights of creditors, including secured creditors, are substantially impaired.

. . .

A secured creditor would not receive timely payments and would be unable to realize on its collateral once a petition was filed.

In addition, as long as the creditor's interest is adequately protected, a debtor may use a secured creditor's collateral under Section 363(c) and may substitute collateral for the collateral originally pledged to the creditor—even if the substitute collateral is of a different type or quality—under Sections 363(e) and 361(3).

A debtor may also restructure secured debt as part of a plan of reorganization by changing the interest rate, the amortization schedule, the type of collateral, and the maturity date under Sections 1123(a) and 1123(b). A bankruptcy court may also allow the imposition of a lien that would be senior to existing liens against the collateral under Section 364(d) and may direct a secured creditor to relinquish its lien on collateral in excess of an amount reasonably necessary to protect the creditor under Sections 363, 506, and 542.

***Banks and Thrifts***

Insolvency proceedings for banks and thrifts are governed by the statutes and regulations applicable to receiverships of the Federal Deposit Insurance Corporation (FDIC) and the Federal Savings and Loan Insurance Corporation (FSLIC) and by the policy pronouncements of governing regulatory agencies.

. . .

Generally, the impairment of creditors' rights that occurs when an entity becomes a debtor under the Bankruptcy Code does not occur upon the appointment of a receiver for a bank or thrift.

***Structuring Methods***

To achieve the goal discussed earlier—the rating of an issuance based on the quality of the collateral—the structure of the transaction must insulate payment of the obligation and the assets backing that payment from the effects of the originator's bankruptcy. If the rights of the holders of the obligations would not be impaired in a bankruptcy of the originator, the rating for financing could be based exclusively on the creditworthiness of the assets.

Two basic methods are employed to achieve this result:

. . .

**True Sale**

The insulating effect of a true sale is derived from the principle that only debts of an entity that is a debtor under the Bankruptcy Code and assets that are "property of the estate" of the bankrupt debtor are subject to the impairment of creditors' rights that occurs upon the bankruptcy of a debtor.

. . .

In addressing the true sale issue, courts generally look at the extent to which the transferor has parted with the risks and the benefits of owning the assets. Although no single factor or even group of factors is considered dispositive of the issue, the following factors are particularly relevant to the inquiry:

- The form of the transaction and the consistency of the parties' treatment of the transaction, including how the transaction is characterized in the documents, how tax and accounting disciplines treat the transaction, and whether the originator executes a promissory note to the purchasers.
- The nature and extent of the risks transferred, including whether the investor has recourse to the seller in some form, such as a guarantee or obligation to repurchase nonperforming assets and the extent of any such recourse; who is at risk if the value of the assets declines; who has the risk of reinvesting the income from the assets; and who is at risk if there is a default on the underlying assets.
- The nature and extent of the benefits transferred including who benefits from any appreciation in the value of the assets and who receives the income from the assets.
- The irrevocability of the transfer, including whether specific and identifiable assets are sold; whether and in which circumstances the transferor can reacquire the assets or substitute assets; who exercises control over and uses the assets and, if the originator services the assets, how the originator uses and accounts for the assets and their proceeds; and whether the purchaser can resell the assets without accounting to the transferor for any gain on the sale.
- The extent and timing of the purchase price, including whether the price reflects the fair market value of the assets and whether the full price is paid at the time of sale or a portion is held back, with payment subject to performance of the assets.
- The extent to which the transferor's creditors and others are provided with notice of the sale; whether the transferor retains documents related to the assets and, if so, the extent of the

purchaser's right to inspect or require delivery of the documents; how the maturity dates of the assets compare with the maturity dates of the obligations sold to investors; and whether public policy issues are implicated by recharacterization—for example, if the sale were recharacterized as a loan, would applicable usury law be violated?

**Bankruptcy–Remote Entities**

A second method of insulating an obligation and the related assets and cash flows from the originator's bankruptcy is to have the obligation incurred and the assets owned by an issuer that is bankruptcy remote—usually a special-purpose corporation.

. . .

To forestall the likelihood that the special-purpose corporation would itself become the subject of bankruptcy proceedings, its business activities are severely limited by its charter. The charter limits its activities to the purchase of assets and the issuance of rated obligations. The charter also prohibits it from incurring any additional debt that would impair the rating of its rated obligations. Thus, restrictions on the special-purpose corporation virtually eliminate the possibility that it would incur debt that it could not pay and, accordingly, make it bankruptcy remote. In addition, banks and thrifts are regarded as bankruptcy remote because they are not eligible for relief under the Bankruptcy Code.

The bankruptcy remoteness of a special-purpose corporation would not protect the holders of its debt, however, if its separateness from its parent could be disregarded by a court. If this were to occur, the special-purpose corporation's assets, including those pledged for the debt, would become subject to the bankruptcy proceedings of the parent.

The general rule is that a corporation is a distinct legal entity separate from its shareholders, and, therefore, its assets are not directly available to satisfy the claims of its shareholders' creditors. However, exceptions exist to this general rule when the subsidiary corporation has failed to maintain its separate identity and when prejudice would result from giving effect to the separateness of the corporation. Exceptions are generally given effect under the doctrines of "piercing the corporate veil" or substantive consolidation.

Piercing the corporate veil is an equitable doctrine that typically arises under common law at the request of a creditor of an affiliated entity. In determining whether to pierce the corporate veil, courts have generally focused on three principal elements necessary to find a person, corporation, or other entity responsible for the obligations of a different, legally distinct entity: (1) complete domination and control of the corporation by the entity on which liability is sought to be imposed; (2) the use of such control to commit a fraud or other wrong, to violate a statutory or other duty, or to engage in unjust conduct; and (3) proximate causation of the movant's injury by such wrongdoing.

Substantive consolidation, a doctrine that arises under federal bankruptcy law, could be applicable if the parent were to become a debtor under the Bankruptcy Code.

. . .

The cases suggest, however, that the elements considered by the courts to be the most significant are (1) hopeless confusion of assets and liabilities and (2) substantial integration of operations. However, more recent cases have stressed an approach that gives substantial weight to a balancing of prejudices—whether the prejudice for creditors that would result from ordering substantive consolidation would outweigh the prejudice of respecting the separate corporate existence of the subsidiary.

. . .

## 2. Federal Income Tax

From a tax viewpoint, two basic questions should be considered in structuring asset-backed security transactions: (1) How is the entity or arrangement that holds the assets taxed? Is it a flow-through vehicle that is not taxable separately or is it treated as an association that is taxable as a corporation? (2) Who is the owner of the assets for tax purposes? Have they been sold to investors or pledged by the insurer as collateral for a debt issued to investors? The answers to these questions determine the nature and timing of taxation of the sponsor or servicer, the issuing entity, and investors.

### *Taxation of the Issuing Entity*

Arrangements in which property is beneficially owned through an entity are classified under applicable Treasury regulations as trusts, partnerships, or corporations (including associations taxable as corporations). Owners of a trust must be passive investors that are not jointly engaged in business activity, whereas investors in a partnership or corporation are viewed as so engaged. Corporations have the characteristics of continuity of life separate from their investors, centralization of management, liability limited to corporate assets, and free transferability of ownership, while partnerships lack these characteristics. However, an entity with no more than two of these factors will generally be classified as a partnership instead of a corporation.

### Grantor Trusts and the Sears Regulations

In a sale of assets, the vehicle used to hold legal title to the assets is most commonly structured as a grantor trust, in which the investors' ownership interests are represented by pass-through certificates that evidence fractional undivided interests in the pool of assets. Grantor trusts are structured as passive vehicles to hold assets and are self-liquidating; the trustee cannot reinvest the proceeds of the assets beyond distribution dates and must pass them through to the investors, usually monthly. Grantor trusts are not taxed at the entity level; instead, investors report their share of gross income (interest and, if applicable, original-issue discount or market discount) and expenses (servicing or other administrative fees and, if applicable, amortization of purchase premium) with respect to the assets.

Grantor trusts are treated as "fixed investment trusts" under regulations that were amended in 1986 to forestall offerings of multiple classes of pass-through certificates made by Sears Mortgage Securities Corporation (hence the name Sears Regulations). In general, grantor trust pass-through certificates may only be issued in one class, with exceptions for certain transactions, including stripped bonds, stripped coupons, and senior/subordinated offerings (in which a senior class is sold to investors and a subordinated class, typically representing up to 10 percent of the undivided interests in the trust, functions as a support for payments to the senior class). Failure to comply with the Sears Regulations results in classification of the entity either as a partnership or, more likely for a pooled investment vehicle of this type, as an association taxable as a corporation (with a resulting entity-level tax on net income).

### REMICs

The Tax Reform Act of 1986 introduced a new vehicle for issuing mortgage-backed securities that is generally not subject to tax at the entity level: the real estate mortgage investment conduit (REMIC). REMICs may issue two types of securities: regular interests (that is, one or more classes of debt or pass-through instruments) and a single class of residual interests (which may be in any form, but is taxed similarly to interests in a partnership that owns the mortgages and has issued debt secured by the mortgages). REMICs can hold any mortgages secured by real property, including commercial mortgages. The advantage of REMICs is that they offer specific tax accounting rules for treating multi-class securities that could otherwise have been addressed only by using less cost effective structures to overcome tax problems by ensuring debt classification.

### Vehicles for Offering Asset–Backed Debt

As the typical corporate debt issuer is a special-purpose finance subsidiary within a corporate group, earnings are generally subject to only one level of tax. An alternative structure uses an owner trust, which is structured under state law as a trust whose equity owners beneficially own the assets and finance them by issuing secured debt. The organizational documents of an owner trust should be drafted so that the issuer will not be treated as an association taxable as a corporation but as either a grantor trust or a partnership—without an entity-level tax. The owner-trust structure was developed so that the sponsor could sell off residual interests in the assets to investors by using a vehicle that would not be subject to an entity-level tax.

#### *Sale versus Debt Treatment*

Characterization of the transaction as a sale for federal income tax purposes requires that the seller transfer the economic ownership of the assets, including the risks and benefits of ownership.

. . .

It is critical that the securities be treated as the issuer's indebtedness (generating deductible interest expense) instead of as an equity interest in the issuer (generating dividends that are not deductible by the issuer and, thus, resulting in taxable income at the issuer's level).

## 3. Federal Securities Law

### *The Investment Company Act of 1940*

Statutory exemptions from the requirements of the 1940 Act exist for banks, insurance companies, savings and loan associations, and similar institutions, as well as for issuers not making a public offering of their securities and whose outstanding securities (other than short-term paper) are held by no more than 100 persons. Nevertheless, the most frequently used statutory exemption from the 1940 Act is Section 3(c)(5), which exempts issuers that are not issuing redeemable securities and that are primarily engaged in purchasing certain assets. Section 3(c)(5)(C) exempts issuers that are primarily engaged in purchasing mortgages and other liens on or interests in real estate. Qualifying investments for purposes of Section 3(c)(5)(C) include (1) whole loan mortgages; (2) whole pool Government National Mortgage Association (GNMA), Federal National Mortgage Association (FNMA), and Federal Home Loan Mortgage Corporation (FHLMC) mortgage pass-through certificates (GNMAs, FNMAs, and FHLMCs, respectively); and (3) whole pool private label pass-throughs, although the SEC has not taken a position. With respect to nonmortgage assets, Sections 3(c)(5)(A) and 3(c)(5)(B) of the 1940 Act exempt issuers primarily engaged in purchasing "notes, drafts, acceptances, open accounts receivable, and other obligations representing part or all of the sales price of merchandise, insurance and services" or "making loans to manufacturers, wholesalers, and retailers of, and to prospective purchasers of, specified merchandise, insurance, and services."

### *The Securities Act of 1933*

The offer and sale of securities must be registered under the Securities Act of 1933, as amended (1933 Act), unless an exemption from registration is available. To be exempt from registration, a security must either be an exempt security or be sold in an exempt transaction. Securities issued or guaranteed by a bank or issued by a savings and loan association are exempt securities. However, securities offered by a subsidiary of a bank or savings and loan association are not entitled to the bank or savings and loan exemption, although other exemptions may be available.

Securities offered and sold in "transactions by an issuer not involving a public offering" (private placements) are sold in exempt transactions. However, a private placement under Section 4(2) of the 1933 Act will limit the number of potential investors in an issue and will result in restrictions on the resale of securities. Although there are other types of exempt transactions, they are generally not appropriate for securitizations.

If a security is neither an exempt security nor sold in an exempt transaction, three possible forms of registration are generally used. Public offerings of mortgage securities are registered pursuant to a registration statement on Form S–11 or Form S–3. Form S–11 is prescribed for registration of securities issued by real estate investment trusts and issuers whose primary business is acquiring and holding for investment real estate or interests in real estate. Form S–3 is generally available for the issuance of both mortgage and nonmortgage asset-backed debt securities if the issuer is a majority-owned subsidiary of an established company that is obligated to file periodic reports under the Securities Exchange Act of 1934 (1934 Act). The primary advantage of Form S–3 is that it expedites SEC review of the registration statement. Public offerings of nonmortgage asset-backed securities issued in pass-through form or cases in which an S–3–qualified parent is not involved are generally registered on Form S–1, which is to be used when no other forms are available.

Rule 415 of the 1933 Act permits an issuer to register a large amount in one "shelf" filing and to make periodic offerings thereunder on a delayed or continuous basis after the effective date of the registration statement. Availability of shelf registration is limited to certain types of securities, including mortgage-related securities (which include both debt and pass-through securities registered on any registration form) and debt securities registered on Form S–3. Accordingly, Rule 415 is generally unavailable for the issuance of nonmortgage asset-backed securities in pass-through form.

## 4. Bank and Thrift Regulations

***Authority to Issue Asset–Backed Securities***

. . .

### National Banks

In recent years, the Office of the Comptroller of the Currency (OCC) has consistently maintained that national banks are authorized to issue securities backed by or representing interests in mortgages and other assets. Depending on the accounting, tax, and other structural aspects, securitization activities of national banks have been justified as a means of either borrowing funds or selling assets. In both cases, securitization of bank assets is perceived as a way to enhance liquidity; manage capital and other balance sheet ratios, as well as interest rate exposure; reduce asset concentrations; and diversify income sources.

Under 12 C.F.R. Section 5.34, national banks also have the authority to establish operating subsidiaries to issue any securities that the bank could have issued directly. The authority of national banks' subsidiaries to issue securities collateralized by mortgages or securities backed by pools of mortgages was established by the OCC in a May 22, 1986, letter regarding Liberty Norstar Bank, N.A., in Buffalo, New York.

### Federally Chartered Thrift Institutions

Federally chartered savings and loan associations and savings banks (federal associations) are statutorily authorized to borrow, to pledge assets as security therefor, and to issue notes, bonds, and other securities under 12 U.S.C. Section 5(b)(2). This statutory provision has been interpreted to permit the issuance of securities backed by or representing interests in mortgages or other receivables.

Moreover, under 12 C.F.R. Section 545.82, federal associations may establish single-purpose finance subsidiaries to issue any securities that the parent could issue directly.

. . .

***Securities Offering Registration with Federal Banking Agencies***

### Bank Regulatory Requirements

. . .

OCC regulations [12 C.F.R. Section 16.3(a) ] require a national bank that issues securities to file an offering circular with the OCC's Securities Disclosure Division and to have that offering circular declared effective by the OCC prior to any offers or sales of securities, unless an exemption applies. The only exemption from the offering requirements that is relevant in most asset-backed security offerings applies to transactions that do not involve any public offering under 12 C.F.R. Section 16.5. Pass-through securities supported by cash flows on collateral that is sold by a bank to a trust formed by the bank are deemed to be issued by the trust—not by the bank—for purposes of the offering circular requirements. Hence, they must be registered under the 1933 Act.

. . .

### Thrift Regulatory Requirements

Under 12 C.F.R. Section 563g.2(a), federal associations and state-chartered institutions that are insured by the FSLIC are required to file an offering circular on Form OC with the Corporate and Securities Division of the Office of the General Counsel of the FHLBB and to have that offering circular declared effective by the FHLBB prior to any offers or sales of securities. Exemptions from this offering circular requirement are afforded to nonpublic offerings under 12 C.F.R. Section 563g.4 and to offerings of debt securities that are issued in denominations of $100,000 or more and that are fully collateralized by cash; by any security issued or guaranteed by the United States, the FNMA, the FHLMC, or the GNMA; or by interests in mortgage notes secured by real property under 12 C.F.R. Section 563g.3.

. . .

## Sales of Assets Using Participation Certificates

Under both GAAP and RAP, the transfer of mortgage or other assets entirely without recourse to the transferor is normally treated as a sale.

The manner in which federal associations and state-chartered, FSLIC-insured institutions account for transfers with recourse is governed by Financial Accounting Standards Board (FASB) Statement of Financial Accounting Standards (SFAS) No. 77, *Reporting by Transferors for Transfers of Receivables with Recourse.* Under SFAS No. 77, a transfer of receivables with recourse will be treated as a sale if:

- The transferor has surrendered control of the future economic benefits embodied in the receivables
- The transferor's obligation under any recourse provisions can be reasonably estimated
- The transferee cannot require the transferor to repurchase the receivables, other than pursuant to the recourse provisions

Thus, conceivably, transactions may be structured with significant recourse to the thrift, provided that the above conditions are met.

By contrast, under RAP, a transfer of mortgages on one- to four-family residences (including loans on cooperative apartments) will be deemed a sale only if the transferor's retained risk is not significant. (The level of recourse that is deemed significant is not well defined and appears to be the subject of divergent regulatory views.) The transfer of mortgages on multifamily property (that is, greater than four families) or other commercial real estate or the transfer of nonmortgage assets, such as automobile or credit card receivables, will be treated as a sale only if the transferor retains "no risk of loss ... from any cause" on the assets.

. . .

### *FSLIC and FDIC Receivership Considerations*

## Bonds Issued Directly by Banks or Thrifts

When a financial institution directly issues pay-through bonds, such as CMOs, in an offering that is not required to be registered under the 1933 Act and is not subject to the 1939 Act, the indenture ordinarily provides that, in the event of insolvency, the trustee is precluded from liquidating the collateral in circumstances in which cash flows available under the indenture would be sufficient to make timely payments of principal and interest on the bonds.

. . .

Both the FSLIC and the FDIC, respectively, indicated that neither would seek acceleration of the debt and liquidation of the collateral if the market value of the collateral was insufficient to pay principal and accrued interest on the bonds. In such circumstances, acceleration and liquidation would not produce any excess collateral for the benefit of the insolvent thrift or bank or their creditors.

**Special–Purpose Subsidiary**

. . .

As a result, pay-through bonds issued by a special purpose subsidiary would be insulated from the insolvency of a parent thrift or bank and would have "call protection" from a FSLIC or FDIC receiver's attempt to accelerate the bonds and liquidate the collateral.

***Glass–Steagall Act Considerations Applicable to National Banks***

In the case of security activities by financial institutions, the most relevant provisions of the Glass–Steagall Act are Section 16 and Section 21 [12 U.S.C. Section 24 (seventh) and 12 U.S.C. Section 378, respectively]. Section 16 prohibits national banks from engaging in the business of dealing or underwriting in securities, other than certain bank-eligible instruments. 12 U.S.C. Section 355 applied this provision to FRB member banks. Section 21 prohibits depository institutions from being "engaged in the business of issuing, underwriting, selling or distributing securities" other than bank-eligible instruments. However, Section 21 states that its restrictions will not affect any right that "any bank ... may otherwise possess to sell, without recourse or agreement to repurchase, obligations evidencing loans on real estate."

***Notes and Questions***

1. The authors note that while a deposit is a liability that includes mortgage-backed bonds, the definition "excludes sales of one- to four-family mortgages when no more than a 10 percent interest is retained by the selling depository institution. The 10 percent exclusion permits the use of senior/subordinated structures and other forms of self-insurance in mortgage securitizations, but is not available for automobile-, credit card-, and other non-mortgage-backed asset sales."

2. What is the combined effect of these rules on the structure of the SPC? Are the effects of each set of rules consistent? What would explain this?

3. To what extent would these rules encourage U.S. originators of MBS or ABS to go offshore, either in structuring the transaction of financing it? What would explain the underlying policy?

---

## E. COUNTRIES WITH LIMITED MARKETS FOR SECURITIZATION

Outside the U.S., the markets for securitization are much smaller and until recently have not grown very fast. In 1990, for example, new ABS issues were $45 billion in the U.S., only $19 billion in Europe, and minimal in Japan. But the reasons for limited growth differ greatly, as the following material about Germany and Japan demonstrates.

As you read this material, contrast the laws in both countries with those of the United States and with each other. Specifically, consider the following:

[1] The U.S. market vastly overshadows MBS markets elsewhere. Is this just a matter of evolution or does government policy play a role?

[2] Should either Germany and Japan be concerned about U.S. government policy toward the growth of its MBS market?

## 1. Germany

Securitisation in Germany, in Morrissey, 405.

### The Market Environment

Asset-backed securitisation has begun only recently in Germany and has achieved moderate success so far.

This relatively slow development is not, however, attributable to a lack of knowledge amongst German financial institutions regarding securitisation. On the contrary, asset-backed and cash flow-based financing techniques have been understood as funding possibilities for Germany banks for quite some time. Furthermore, the existing accounting rules in Germany could be regarded as fostering securitisation rather than hindering it. For example, our civil law allows for the establishment of special purpose companies owned by charitable trusts. It also sets out a framework for the creation of a type of trust, which differs somewhat from the concept as it is used in the US and UK, for example, but which has nevertheless been found to be suitable for bestowing trust-type security. Moreover, loans (as well as any other payment claim, right or obligation) can be assigned easily without additional formalities.

Asset-backed products in Germany do, however, face an obstacle in the form of the structure of the local primary lending markets. These are dominated by credit institutions offering the full range of financial products including loans, deposit-taking, and securities trading. This makes the lending markets very efficient in Germany, and credit margins are accordingly considerably lower than typically found in those markets where more asset-backed securities have been originated. The low margins make it difficult to cover the additional costs of structuring associated with securitisation (such as legal and documentation fees) so that securitisation is often not an attractive option for the originator unless it can achieve other objectives by using the technique.

Part of the appeal of asset-backed financing lies in the possibilities it offers for structuring risk. For example, the credit quality of senior tranches of asset-backed securities can be supported by mezzanine and subordinated tranches, and the different pieces sold to investors with varying appetites for risk. Such risk structuring is quite familiar to investors participating in project financing and cash flow-based financing deals offered by German banks, but capital market investors in Germany generally prefer simpler and more straightforward instruments. These investors are typically wary of complex structures and as a group have not yet adopted the risk/reward evaluation techniques employed by US investors, who appreciate that various degrees of credit risk—monitored by rating agencies—can be scaled, made transparent and priced accordingly in the public capital markets.

Despite these obstacles, the market for asset-backed securities in Germany is picking up. A few German companies have already securitised auto loans in the US market. Some months ago the first Deutsche mark-denominated deal was launched, which involved the securitisation of consumer loans. The increasing number of seminars, workshops and presentations covering asset-backed securities reflects the growing interest of investors as well as potential originators.

### The Various Sectors

The examples set by the US and UK markets would suggest that the assets which might offer the most potential for securitisation are mortgage loans, credit card receivables, auto loans and consumer loans.

#### *Mortgage Loans*

For over two hundred years, German mortgage banks have funded themselves by issuing *Pfandbriefe,* making these one of the earliest kind of mortgage-backed securities. In contrast with US asset-backed techniques, however, the underlying loans stay on the balance sheet of the mortgage bank. Should the bank default, the holder of the Pfandbriefe has an additional direct claim on the mortgage payments. Another difference from the US and UK situations is that a German mortgage bank may exclude the prepayment of a loan secured by a mortgage. Unlike US and UK mortgage-backed bonds, therefore, German *Hypothekenbankpfandbriefe* have no prepayment risk.

The outstanding Pfandbriefe market currently stands at approximately DM140.2bn. Spreads between mortgage loans and rates on Pfandbriefe are very tight. Mortgage banks have always been very well capitalised and even the new BIS requirements will not cause a substantial problem for these institutions. One reason for this is the *Deckungsstock–Fähigkeit* governing securities offered by German mortgage banks. Since German mortgage banks are subject to very strict and conservative governmental lending regulations, securities issued by them can be bought by insurance companies, which also have very strict governmental investment regulations.

This combination of a highly efficient existing funding system and the strong capitalisation of the mortgage banks suggests that the development of an off-balance sheet mortgage-backed security market is unlikely in Germany.

### *Credit Card Receivables*

In the last few years credit cards have become popular in Germany and there has been an immense increase in the size of the market. Despite this favourable development, credit cards are unlikely to be securitised in the near future because most German "credit" cards are in fact charge cards, which either debit directly from consumer's current accounts or require payment in full each month. Nonetheless, there might be some potential in future for securitising department store credit card receivables, to the extent that such receivables are interest-bearing assets, although most department stores' credit cards only charge interest if payments are delayed. However, it should be pointed out that interest charges on these cards comparable to those in the US (around 20%) and in the UK (around 30%) would not be acceptable to German consumers. Moreover, consumer loans offered by department stores specifically for the purchase of merchandise are subject to the borrower's right to refuse to repay if the merchandise does not reach acceptable standards of quality. These loans are therefore unsuitable for securitisation.

### *Auto Loans*

As mentioned previously, auto loans made by German companies have already been securitised in the US market. Auto loans in Germany are usually granted by finance companies of car manufacturers ("auto banks") and not by "universal" banks, as is the practice in several other markets. If cars were to be financed by "universal" banks they would qualify as normal consumer loans and thus would simply become part of a bank's large portfolio of consumer loans. The interest rates charged by the auto banks are very competitive since they are used as a marketing device.

The potential for the securitisation of auto loans will depend on each company's specific situation. Questions arise such as: Does the company have other funding sources? Can it lower its funding costs? Are there any specific balance sheet considerations? All of these companies do have one thing in common, however—by taking their assets off-balance sheet and selling them to an offshore special purpose vehicle, they can repay outstanding debt and thus reduce their trade tax liability (*Gewerbesteuer*).

### *Consumer Loans*

German "universal" banks have large pools of consumer loans. The banks' servicing capabilities are typically good, and they have the technology to pool loans, but there are several reasons why large-scale securitisation of consumer loans is unlikely in the near future. Most German banks are well prepared to meet the BIS requirements since their own banking supervisory agency's capital requirements have already been quite comprehensive in the past. Another reason is that the banks place a high priority on maintaining confidential and close relationships with their retail customers, which is reinforced by strict rules in Germany concerning banking confidentiality. Furthermore, even with clear non-recourse transactions, the federal supervisory agency is not sympathetic to the concept of selling assets to try to decrease a bank's capital adequacy requirements. It takes the view that over and above a mere technical solvency ratio calculation, the banks' own funds should cover, and limit, its operations. This would be jeopardised if part of such activities were transferred off-balance sheet by way of securitisation. Finally, as described above, the competitive environment means that the spreads on consumer loans make it difficult to cover the costs associated with securitisation.

. . .

**Investor Demand**

An increasing number of German investors have begun to show their interest in asset-backed securities. This trend is likely to gain momentum, helped by the liberalisation of the regulatory framework for institutional investors (such as insurance companies and mutual funds) in the context of EC-harmonisation.

Banks have a particular interest in this market both in their role as potential originators and in the context of using the securities as interesting investment alternatives. It could even be argued that banks should buy securitised consumer loan portfolios instead of implementing a vast overseas branch network. In general, however, investors are still reluctant to consider asset-backed securities since it will take some time to get used to the complex mechanics of these structures.

**Outlook**

To summarise, a German securitised asset market is likely to continue to develop slowly and the investor potential is probably higher than the originator potential. Fields in which German banks can be expected to play an increasing role internationally include underwriting, credit enhancement (by writing letters of credit), trustee services and, eventually, servicing of assets.

Securitisation in Germany: Legal Framework Overview

The securitisation of most kinds of financial assets that have been securitised in other jurisdictions is legally feasible in Germany. One asset securitisation transaction has been done thus far, and the German asset repackaging transactions effected during recent years provide useful precedents for the securitisation of assets.

. . .

**The Issuer**

The issuer of the asset-backed securities would be a special purpose company whose sole function would be to issue the new securities, to hold the underlying assets and to engage in related activities. Experience with repackaging and securitising assets in the Euromarkets suggests that the most suitable location for such a company would be the

Cayman Islands, or, to a lesser extent, the Channel Islands or the Netherlands. The jurisdiction chosen would have to offer a liberal regulatory environment, virtually tax-free status of the company and of payments in respect of the securities, and a financial infrastructure able to provide a bank or trust company for the administration of the company, lawyers and accountants. A possible disadvantage of the Cayman Islands (as well as of any other tax-free jurisdiction) is the lack of double tax treaties with Germany. This point may become important if the proposed new German withholding tax applies to payments to the special purpose company in respect of the underlying assets (see "Taxation" below). In such a case, the Netherlands might be a possible alternative because the Dutch–German tax treaty exempts interest payments from domestic withholding tax.

The company would generally have little paid-up capital, and its shares would be held by a bank or trust company for the benefit of a charitable organisation or the investors of the securities issued by the company. The same or another local bank or trust company would manage the company, subject to the supervision of the trustee for the holders of the securities.

**The Assets**

Most of the assets that have been securitised in other jurisdictions are also suitable for securitisation in Germany. These include loans, credit card receivables (should this market reach a more advanced stage of development in Germany) and other receivables. Mortgage loans are less likely to be the subject of securitisation in Germany because of the efficiency of the statutory mortgage bank system. Loans and receivables are assignable by a simple contract of assignment between the seller of the assets and the special purpose company, unless the terms of the agreement governing the assets exclude or restrict the assignment. To be valid, the assignment does not require notification of the account debtor, although in the absence of notification the account debtor can continue to make payments to the assignor. The seller of the assets could continue to act as the servicer of the assets. For customer relationship reasons, notification of the assignment would presumably only be given in the event that the seller of the assets were to find itself in financial difficulties. Under German law, the assignee of contract rights (which would include payment rights under a loan of receivables) is subject to defences that the account debtor has against the assignor, including any right of set-off or counterclaim. Such defences may not be precluded by notification of the assignment to the account debtor. An express waiver of the defences by the account debtor would be necessary, but would presumably not be feasible as a practical matter. Since under German law, the seller of contract rights is under an obligation to assign the rights free from defences of third parties, the buyer of the rights would have a claim for breach of contract against the seller in the event that the account debtor exercised any defences. The risk of the assertion by the account debtor of any defences available to it would be particularly relevant in securitisations of receivables or other assets arising under contracts that create on-going obligations of the seller of the assets, such as lease agreements.

**The Securities**

The securities issued by the special purpose company should be limited recourse obligations, payable only if and to the extent that the company receives funds on the underlying assets. If the securities are denominated in Deutsche marks, the issuing procedures and the terms of the securities would have to comply with the 1989 guidelines of the Bundesbank for the issuance of Deutsche mark-denominated securities by foreign issuers. The principal objective of the guidelines is to ensure that the Deutsche mark securities market is based in Germany. Among other things, the guidelines require that the terms of the securities be governed by German law, that a German bank act as the lead manager, that the German clearing system be used and that the minimum maturity of the securities not be less than two years. The minimum maturity requirement could be problematical for asset-backed securities if and to the extent that the amortisation of the principal of the underlying assets begins prior to the end of the two-year period. Instead of passing the amortised principal through as a partial prepayment of the securities, the issuer (or the trustee) would have to reinvest the amortised amounts at least until the end of two years from the issue date. The minimum maturity requirement would not apply to an issue of asset-backed securities through a German special purpose company, but a domestic structure would raise other complex regulatory and tax issues, including the question of the liability of the company under corporate income tax and trade tax laws.

If and to the extent that the asset-backed securities are placed in Germany, the new German Prospectus Law would apply. Under this law, the primary distribution of debt securities in Germany requires the preparation of a prospectus at the time the offering commences, unless an exemption is available.

**The Collateralisation**

The special purpose company would assign the underlying assets to a trustee as security for the holders of the securities. The assignment would involve the same steps as the original sale and assignment of the assets by the originator to the special purpose company. The Bundesbank guidelines for the issuance of Deutsche mark-denominated securities by foreign issuers do not expressly require the use of a German trustee, but in light of the general requirement that the Deutsche mark securities market be based in Germany, it may be advisable for the trustee to be a German institution unless there are legal or practical obstacles.

**Regulatory Issues**

There is no government approval or notification requirement for the securitisation of financial assets in Germany. Special considerations apply, however, to banks that wish to securitise loans or similar assets held on their books. Although there is no express prohibition on the sale of such assets, the Federal Banking Supervisory Authority has expressed some concern about such transactions, presumably on the theory that the borrowers' interests may be better served if their counterparty is a German bank. A bank considering the securitisation of assets should therefore discuss the transaction with the Federal Banking Supervisory Authority at an early stage.

Another bank regulatory issue is the treatment of the transaction for accounting and balance sheet ratio purposes. If the bank does not retain any obligations in respect of the assets except for the obligation to ensure that the assets are not subject to defences (see "The Assets" above), it should be possible to conclude that the assets will be removed from the bank's balance sheet. On the other hand, if the bank retains other obligations, such as a partial retention of the credit risk, a careful analysis of the accounting and bank regulatory consequences would be necessary.

**Taxation**

The principal tax issue would be the impact of the proposed German withholding tax on payments in respect of the underlying assets. In November 1991, the Federal Government announced its intention to introduce a German withholding tax of 25% on all payments on loans and similar obligations in Germany, effective from 1 January 1993. It is unclear at this stage what, if any, exceptions to this basic rule will apply (for example, whether creditors that are not resident in Germany for tax purposes will be exempt from the tax). Pending clarification of the withholding tax legislation, it would be difficult to securitise loans to German borrowers and similar assets.

**Other Issues**

Other legal questions that arise in connection with the securitisation of financial assets in Germany include the impact of data protection laws and bank secrecy rules on the transfer of the assets and the effect of bankruptcy of the originator. While these questions should be carefully considered, it is unlikely that they would be legal obstacles to the securitisation of assets in Germany.

**Credit Support**

Customary credit support techniques, such as use of a letter of credit or a bank guarantee, over-collateralisation or creation of senior and subordinated tranches, would be possible alternatives for enhancing the creditworthiness of the asset-backed securities.

***Notes and Questions***

1. The antecedents of securitisation lie in Silesia some two centuries ago:

Morrissey, 6.

> Silesia was financially devastated following the Seven Years' War between Austria and Prussia. Landowners needed credit but lacked access to funds. To pool their resources effectively, the Prussian government organised the landowners into the *Landschaft.* A member could issue a mortgage bond representing up to half of the value of his estate. He was responsible for selling the bond, but it was collateralised by both his own land and the estates of all *Landschaft* members. The borrower paid a fixed rate of interest to the *Landschaft,* which in turn remitted payments to the bondholders. The first such mortgage-backed bond issues, known as *Pfandbriefe,* date back to 1769. The mortgage bond system still flourishes as a principal source of housing finance in many Continental European countries.

2. For years, universal banks dominated German financial markets. Most corporate finance took the form of loans and capital markets were weak compared to those in the U.K. or the U.S. How would this affect the MBS and ABS markets?

3. "Many Europeans believe, with some justification, that securitization is what banks do when they are in trouble," according to M. Popper in "The asset-based culture clash." Institutional Investor (1994) 135. How does culture affect the German MBS and ABS markets?

4. Why does the author (above) say "Although it may be possible to use other structures, such as a domestic special purpose vehicle or a German bank that issues participation certificates on a fiduciary basis, the least complex structure for the securitisation of financial assets in Germany from a regulatory and tax perspective would probably involve the use of a foreign special purpose vehicle that issues securities secured by, and serviced from, the underlying assets."

5. German tax rules are important. Two sources explain:

a. C. von Dryander, "Legal aspects of asset securitisation in Germany," in C. Stone et al., Asset Securitisation: Theory and Practice in Europe (1991) 379.

> Questions arise about taxation of the issuer of the securities in the event that the issuer is organised in Germany or resident in Germany for tax purposes. In the case of a German SPV issuer, the transaction needs to be structured to avoid both corporate income and trade taxes payable by the issuer. The trade tax is a local tax based on income and net assets. Its amount varies, depending on the location, but the net cost is in any event considerably more than 10 per cent of 'taxable income'. A peculiarity of the German trade tax system is that the tax is levied not only on actual taxable income but also, *inter alia,* on 50 per cent of the amount of interest payments on long-term debt (that is, generally, debt exceeding a term of one year), including debt in the form of bonds or notes. The rationale for this is that leveraging should not result in trade tax

benefits. To avoid trade tax in an asset securitisation transaction using a domestic SPV as issuer of the asset-backed securities, an argument could be made that 'non-recourse' obligations should not constitute debt for trade tax purposes, but the arranger of an asset-backed issue would be well advised to confirm this view with the tax authorities and may want to seek a ruling to this effect. The trade tax issue may be of lesser concern in the case of a domestic structure using a bank issuer, because there are special trade tax exemptions for banks and, more specifically, for the treatment of 'pass-through' credits. No trade tax or other German tax issues should arise if a foreign issuer is used. Care should, however, be taken to ensure that the issuer is managed outside Germany.

According to a recent tax ruling, the sale of assets in connection with an asset-backed financing does not give rise to VAT.

b. Dr. U. Koch, "Germany," in Securitization: An International Guide, International Financial Law Review (August 1993), 12 [IFLR Guide hereafter].

ABS investment funds are probably not being established in Germany because of high German tax rates. It is vital for the structure of ABS that the investment funds is a separate legal entity from the transferring company and that the payment of interest to the investors must be deductible for tax purposes. The latter is only partly possible in Germany because the bonds issued by the investment company are subject to additional tax ... on trade capital.

6. Restrictions on institutional investors persist, according to Koch:

Institutional investors/investment companies are subject to the restrictions on investment contained in the Law governing Investment Companies ... and may only invest in specified assets. This poses a practical problem for ABS in Germany, although these restrictions were relaxed when the German law on investment was amended. It is noticeable that there are no rating agents in Europe comparable with Moody's or Fitch which examine the securities and how they are issued within the ABS financing system and which provide a reliable rating. It is extremely difficult for investment companies to invest in issues of securities by ABS investment funds without having such a rating.

Why would rating agencies be less prevalent in Germany than the U.K. or the U.S.?

---

## 2. Japan

The following two pieces describe policy toward the MBS/ABS markets in Japan.

## "SECURITISATION IN JAPAN: OVERVIEW"

In Morrissey, 452–6.

Over the two years beginning March 1988, subcommittees of the Ministry of Finance's System Reform Committee discussed the issuance of subordinated debt and preferred stock, and the securitisation of loans (including housing loans, loans to government and public corporations, and other loans, which we shall refer to as "general loans"). New measures were passed over this period to help facilitate each of these alternatives.

More recent discussions over other measures needed to further improve the BIS capital adequacy positions of the Japanese banks have concentrated on subordinated bonds and convertible bonds and the changes required to improve the framework for securitisation.

. . .

By March 1991, a year after measures were taken to supposedly facilitate asset securitisation, just Y390.1bn of housing loans, Y3.6bn of loans made to government and public corporations, and Y953.7bn of general loans had been securitised. These figures represent tiny proportions of the total loans outstanding in each category: for example, Y953.7bn is only 0.3% of the total volume of general loans, standing at over Y300tr.

This slow start to securitisation can be attributed to the still significant obstacles and constraints remaining. The measures passed in March 1990 permitted only very restricted "securitisation" of Japanese banks' portfolios. The banks are allowed to sell parts of their loans to other financial institutions, but the new purchasers are not permitted to sell them on. This rule, effectively forbidding a secondary market, avoids potential conflict with the provisions of Article 65 of the Securities and Exchange Law (SEL), Japan's version of Glass–Steagall, which prevents commercial banks from being involved in securities dealing. Other constraints include limiting securitisation to fixed-rate loans, making it impossible to securitise most new housing loans, which are variable rate.

Besides these specific restrictions contained within the new rules to facilitate securitisation, there are many other features of the Japanese financial system which present the nascent securitised market with difficulties. One very fundamental problem arises because Paragraph 1 of Article 2 of the existing SEL contains specific definitions of instruments which qualify as "securities", such as government bonds, corporate stocks and bonds etc., delineated according to their legal status. As the subcommittees studying the problem concede, this approach excludes those securities, such as mortgage and asset-backed securities, which might serve a similar purpose as permitted instruments but which have a different legal nature. Furthermore, the current wording of the law makes it difficult to enlarge its scope to apply more broadly.

. . .

The definition of "security" is of vital importance to the development of the securitised asset markets because non-qualifying instruments have a very restricted investor universe (only financial institutions may invest in them) and they cannot be traded on a secondary market (this explains the restriction contained within MOF's March 1990 guidelines for securitisation).

Other basic difficulties include a very complex system of borrower notification which must be undertaken by creditors before they may reassign and transfer debt, if they are to achieve a "true sale". This requirement, which is also found in several other countries, places an enormous, if not prohibitive, administrative burden on a "true" securitisation programme involving many small loans. In attempting to address this particular problem, the Financial System Reform Committee is considering adopting the loan participation method used in the US and the UK. Under the US and UK systems, creditors are not obliged to seek debtor permission before loans can be transferred and creditors do not guarantee the credit risk of the loans to third party investors.

Another problem is that at present special purpose vehicles cannot be established in Japan. Changes to the 1947 anti-monopoly law (prohibiting holding companies) are required in order to overcome this particular difficulty. Existing rules stipulate that an instrument must take the complex form of a trust or partnership. Operations must therefore be consigned to the trust banks, which charge a 25 basis point fee. This extra cost obviously lowers the potential profitability of securitised transactions.

Perhaps one of the most fundamental albeit less specific hindrances, however, is the lack of a long-established sensitivity to credit risk amongst Japanese investors. The investment community is only now beginning to appreciate the value of credit ratings on bonds. There has been little incentive to date, therefore, for Japanese banks and corporations to seek to improve their balance sheets via securitisation, which in the US, for example, would help them achieve better access to cheaper funds.

Other issues still requiring attention include the practical difficulties associated with the collection of data on a large number of small loans, and investor education. These matters, like the others cited above, are also being addressed by various subcommittees. Formal criteria for establishing whether an asset is on- or off-balance sheet have yet to be decided upon, but for now as long as credit risk is passed on to third party investors, it can be excluded from risk-weighted assets.

Citibank has spearheaded a major effort to bring the concept of securitisation closer to the forefront of attention in Japan. One Citibank deal which received particular international attention and which has encouraged those who expect significant issuance of asset-backed securities over the next few years, involved the securitisation of the Japanese trade receivables of Kawasaki Steel, the third-largest crude steel producer in Japan. Brought in August 1990, the transaction was a US$500m US commercial paper (CP) programme, launched *via* a special purpose vehicle ("APRECO", set up in November 1988). The deal was purportedly well received by traditional US CP investors, and Citibank has continued to actively market the structure to Japanese corporates as a means of enhancing balance sheet management. However, this particular deal was only practicable in the context of the restrictions described above because it was brought and distributed outside Japan.

. . .

Citibank also secured a concession from MOF, in September 1990, to issue and arrange for the distribution of its own "global" credit card-backed deals in the Japanese market. The concession was achieved after intense discussion beginning early the same year, and took advantage of certain "grey areas" within the existing regulations. Specifically, as we discussed above, under the terms of the SEL, a securities company may not be principally engaged in any business outside the securities arena. Of course, as asset-backed instruments fail to meet the criteria of "securities", this would normally prohibit securities firms from trading and distributing them. However, a securities company may be engaged in a "side business" (*Kengyo* ), subject to MOF approval. On 28 September 1990, MOF formally approved Citibank's *Kengyo* application (made through Citicorp Scrimgeour Vickers) relating to its "global" credit card-backed deals.

As far as the small number of domestic Japanese asset-backed deals are concerned, IBJ and Fuji Bank are amongst those leading the initiatives at present. Many Japanese banks appear keen to consider using securitisation to control their asset base, and to reduce their exposure to, say, property loans. As the purpose of asset reduction by banks is primarily to achieve a higher capital adequacy ratio, with the BIS deadlines looming it is important that effective changes to enhance securitisation are made shortly. New achievements are being recorded; for example, in November 1991 the city banks reached an agreement with the Federation of Economic Organisations (*Keidanren* ) to sell corporate loan receivables without the prior approval of the firms involved. Previously, Japanese corporations had opposed the securitisation of their debt, concerned that such transfers could be detrimental since they would have no control over the identity of the purchaser. Japanese city banks could only sell the loans to a small group of regional and foreign banks, often at a loss.

. . .

D. ROSSNER AND Y. SHIMADA, "JAPAN"

In IFLR Guide (1993) 15.

"JURISDICTIONAL BATTLE" BETWEEN MOF AND MITI

The Ministry of International Trade and Industry ("MITI") has sought to encourage the non-bank companies under its jurisdiction (such as leasing and finance companies) to diversify their funding sources through securitization so as to lessen their dependence on bank borrowings, and such companies have been major proponents of asset securitization. The Ministry of Finance ("MOF"), in an effort to bring the securitization business under its own regulatory jurisdiction, has generally opposed efforts which would allow non-bank companies to bypass banks and securities companies (which are regulated by the MOF) and finance themselves directly through securitization structures which are not subject to MOF regulation. This has resulted in an ongoing jurisdictional battle between the MOF and MITI which has been, and is likely to remain, a significant impediment to the rapid development of asset securitization in Japan.

Despite this jurisdictional battle, some preliminary steps toward the development of a framework for asset securitization in Japan have been taken, including the passage of several laws which open up the possibility of working with the MOF, MITI and other regulatory authorities to structure asset-backed financings in Japan.

. . .

Effective April 1, 1993, The Law Concerning the Realignment of Relevant Laws for the Reform of the Financial System and Securities Trading System (Law N°87 of 1992) amends Article 2 [of the Securities and Exchange Law of 1948 (Law N°25 of 1948, the "SEL").] to add to the list of instruments which qualify as "securities" under the SEL certain additional financial instruments. The MOF had initially pushed to amend Article 2 in a manner which would have added a broad array of asset-backed instruments to the definition of "security" therein, thereby bringing the issuance of such instruments under the MOF's jurisdiction. However, as a result of a MOF and MITI compromise, the instruments added to the definition of "security" in Article 2 have been limited to:

- promissory notes issued by a corporation to raise funds necessary for its business, as prescribed by MOF ordinance;
- instruments or certificates issued by foreign corporations which represent beneficiary trust interests, or similar interests, in loans by a bank or other lending institution, as prescribed by MOF ordinance; and
- other instruments or certificates which may be prescribed by Cabinet order as necessary to protect the public interest and investors in light of their liquidity and other characteristics.

. . .

To date, the SEL amendments have been interpreted as adding the following to the list of instruments which qualify as "securities": commercial paper issued by Japanese and foreign legal entities, certificates representing beneficial interests in residential long-term mortgage trusts, certificates issued by foreign legal entities representing beneficial interests in trusts consisting of loans, and negotiable certificates of deposit issued by foreign legal entities. (Having been designated as "securities" under the SEL, these instruments are now subject to certain disclosure requirements pursuant to MOF ordinance.)

The amendments to Article 2's definition of "security" have generally disappointed proponents of asset securitization. The instruments designated thus far do not specifically include most asset-backed instruments. Notably, they do not include asset-backed instruments such as lease- and credit-card-backed instruments issued by Japanese leasing and finance companies (i.e. asset-backed instruments authorized by the MITI Law discussed below). In addition, ... no instrument was ever designated a "security" under a similar previous catch-all provision in the SEL.

. . .

As a result of the problems involved in perfecting assignments of assets in Japan (and also because Japan lacks a tradition of asset-based lending), proposed securitization structures in Japan have tended to rely primarily on the creditworthiness of the seller/servicer of the assets to be securitized (rather than on providing investors with a perfected ownership interest in such assets) to assure the repayment of the resulting asset-backed instruments. This contrasts with the general approach to asset securitization in the United States where the creditworthiness of the seller/servicer in an asset securitization transaction is generally considered to be of limited importance and primary reliance for assuring repayment on asset-backed instruments is placed on the assets being securitized, the perfection of the assignment of such assets and other structural elements.

On June 1, 1993, The Law Relating to the Regulation of the Business of Specified Claims (Law N°77 of 1992, the "MITI Law") became effective. The MITI Law (which like the SEL amendments discussed above, was a result of a MOF and MITI compromise) provides certain eligible transferors, including leasing and finance companies (but excluding banks and other originators of securitizable receivables), a less cumbersome method for perfecting asset transfers with respect to certain eligible assets. The new procedure consists of public notice to the relevant obligors in a newspaper or official publication of record instead of individual written notices and official certification.

In order to use this procedure, an eligible transferor and the assignee to whom the eligible assignment plan to MITI. MITI has 60 days to review the plan and may request modification. An entity that is in the business of having assets assigned to it or in the business of selling interests in pools of assigned assets is required to be licensed by the MOF and MITI. Certain limitations are placed on the investment of excess funds by the vehicles to which assets are assigned, and such vehicles are made subject to certain disclosure requirements.

Specified assets eligible to be securitized are limited to:

the right to receive money ("monetary credit") pursuant to contractual agreements for the lease of machinery and goods, the term of which exceeds one year;

monetary credit arising out of agreements pursuant to which purchasers of goods promise to make payments in three or more installments for two or more months;

monetary credit arising out of the purchase of merchandise where the purchaser promises to pay in pre-determined installments; and

monetary credit similar to the types specified above as designated by Cabinet order.

The methods of securitization are limited to:

sales by an eligible transferor which has assigned eligible monetary credits to a special purpose vehicle ("SPV") of divided portions of payables owed by the SPV to the transferor as consideration for the assignment of the eligible monetary credits;

sales of beneficial interests in a trust under which eligible monetary credits are transferred to a trust company (including trust banks) from the eligible transferor;

sales of interests in a partnership which purchases the eligible monetary credits from the eligible transferor and distributes the interest paid on, and the principal amount of, such eligible monetary credits pursuant to the partnership agreement; and

such other arrangements designated by Cabinet order as protecting investors and assuring the fairness of the asset assignment.

(It should be noted that these methods do not, in effect, allow for subsequent assignments of rights in the securitized assets from the initial investor to others, thereby limiting the liquidity of the instruments or certificates evidencing such rights.)

. . .

[The amendment to the SEL [and] the MITI Laws do provide:]

. . .

a possible basis for the further evolution of asset-backed structures in cooperation with Japanese regulatory authorities. Given the nature of capital markets regulation in Japan, the type of free-market conversion of assets and instruments into securities which generally exists in the United States may never be fully possible. However, the potential benefits of asset securitization for both bank and non-bank issuers make it likely that pressure will continue to be exerted for the development of a regulatory framework for securitization which adequately meets the financing needs of these entities.

### *Questions*

1. According to Rossner and Shimada, "In order for a special purpose issuer of asset-backed securities to be 'bankruptcy remote', it must not be able to be consolidated with any other entity (including the seller/servicer of the assets being securitized) in the event of such entity's bankruptcy. Although the doctrine of 'consolidation' is not entirely recognized in Japan, the extent to which legal entities may be consolidated in bankruptcy remains uncertain."

2. To what extent do the 1993 amendments resolve the legal problems identified in the preceding article from Morrissey? Would you expect to see a stronger MBS market now, in Japan?

3. Bureaucratic politics seem to explain much of the Japanese policy. What other forces are at work? Refer to the material in the earlier chapter about Japan.

## F. CROSS-BORDER SECURITIZATION

Little systematic data describe cross-border securitization and flows into and out of domestic markets. Much of the preceding material suggests that those structuring MBS and ABS should carefully choose the jurisdiction whose law will govern the transaction. Euromarkets are sometimes home to securitizations. Investors in domestic and euro-MBS and ABS come from all over the world. The following sections describe this.

As you read this, consider the following hypothetical:

> Assume a major German bank, with a merchant bank subsidiary in London, made many mortgage loans for residences in Germany. Assume that, before tax issues are considered, an MBS makes financial sense for the bank. What factors would guide your advice about the jurisdictions in which it should consider locating the main components of an MBS issue? How many jurisdictions could be involved in the transaction?

### 1. Selecting a Jurisdiction

R. Palache and I. Bell, "Legal and tax issues"
In Morrissey 91, 117–29.

If you have a jurisdiction where taking security or issuing bonds is difficult or where the tax treatment of a securitisation transaction is unfavourable (see below), you will want to shift the financing aspects of the structure to another jurisdiction where these matters are dealt with in a way felt to be more amenable. Clearly, such jurisdictions exist. Whether you can make use of them will usually depend on the answers that can be provided to two questions:

- Can a transfer of, and creation of security over, the receivables in that jurisdiction be achieved which will also be effective in the original jurisdiction of the deal?
- Since, in the event of difficulties with the deal, the investors will need to enforce rights directly against the debtor in the original jurisdiction of the deal, will the courts in that jurisdiction recognise the investors' rights if they are held pursuant to the laws of another jurisdiction?

In any jurisdiction where the issue of transferring financial assets abroad is raised, the first question that must be dealt with is whether such transfer (bringing with it, as it necessarily must, a flow of cash outside of the jurisdiction) is lawful under the exchange control regime then existing in the country. Over the last few years we have seen a very large degree of liberalisation in this respect. In particular, within the European Community most countries have abandoned exchange controls. Spain committing to do so most recently. However, in many jurisdictions this remains an issue and, since in most cases breaches of exchange control regulations are criminal offences, it should remain an item that is high on the check list of any would-be securitiser.

With respect to other barriers to transferring receivables off-shore, the liberalisation regarding exchange controls has usually done away with most difficulties. Certainly in jurisdictions such as England and Wales, Italy, the Netherlands or Germany there are no impediments to selling receivables to foreign entities. It must be noted, however, that in Italy it remains unclear, because the relevant legislation is so recent, whether factoring can be done by non-Italian companies.

. . .

Turning now to the enforcement by the local courts of off-shore security structures, the main problem tends to be whether or not the local jurisdiction will enforce the trust pursuant to which the securities are held. This trust is obviously important as it is the usual way in which security is held in the bond market and therefore corresponds to the investor base's expectation. One must therefore ensure that the local courts will recognise the trustee as a proper person entitled to enforce the investors' rights under the security.

Usually, jurisdictions which recognise trusts such as England and Wales would have no difficulties accepting the trusts of other jurisdictions. In some other jurisdictions, although foreign trusts may not be accepted by the local courts, alternative means may exist whereby the same commercial result can be obtained. This, for example, is the case in Germany.

. . .

The use of an appropriate jurisdiction other than the "natural" jurisdiction of the deal is one of the most complex and uncertain matters which legal advisers to securitisations must deal with. It involves complex issues of conflicts of law. However, such a choice, driven either by the difficulties that we have already encountered in the natural jurisdiction of the deal or by the tax issues that we will deal with below, is often an absolute necessity if the deal is to be done. It is, therefore, an area where international co-operation between legal advisers and creative lawyering is essential.

. . .

The ideal jurisdiction for an SPV is, of course, a tax haven where no tax will be collected more or less regardless of how the inflow and outflow of cash generated by the receivables is structured. However, two issues tend to arise when trying to situate an SPV in a tax-free area.

First, many jurisdictions have anti-avoidance provisions designed for tax entities which, although incorporated or resident in a foreign jurisdiction, are nevertheless set up to do business in their own country.

In Germany, foreign companies will be taxed if they are held to have "permanent establishment" in the jurisdiction. In Germany, an SPV could be held to have such a permanent establishment through its link to and the presence within the jurisdiction of the servicer. It is therefore important to show that the servicer is not an "agent" of the SPV for tax purposes. This can be done by a variety of means.

Also, it may be possible for the SPV to be situated in a jurisdiction which, although friendlier from the tax perspective, has a double-tax treaty with the relevant jurisdiction, thus preventing the fiscal authorities in that jurisdiction from claiming the existence of a permanent establishment within their borders. Unfortunately for those structuring securitisation transactions, and for reasons which are not difficult to fathom, most western countries do not have double-tax treaties with tax havens.

The other difficulty in situating the SPV in a tax-friendly jurisdiction is that in many cases this will lead to the imposition of withholding tax.

Such imposition is usually felt to be sufficiently nefarious to the cash flows in the transaction to make the deal uneconomic. Again, in those jurisdictions where withholding tax will be imposed on flows to an SPV outside the jurisdiction and where no other exemptions are available, it will be necessary to situate the SPV in a jurisdiction which has an appropriate double tax treaty with the jurisdiction of the originator whilst still furnishing some tax advantages. The Netherlands will often provide such a location for the SPV. The Netherlands has a wide network of double-tax treaties but also has a tax regime which makes it easier than in many other places to generate near fiscal transparency for the SPV. The Netherlands has been canvassed as a provider of a suitable jurisdiction for SPVs in relation to actual or potential deals in Germany, Spain and Belgium, for example. However, one small downside of situating the SPV in the Netherlands is the requirement of the Netherlands tax authorities that the SPV is not a complete conduit.

This means that the Netherlands tax authorities will require the SPV to generate a certain amount of profit, which will of course be subject to Dutch corporation tax. The amount of profit that needs to be kept in the vehicle, however, is usually felt to be quite manageable. In one deal the authors have been involved in, it was reckoned to be 12.5 basis points of the principal amount outstanding of the receivables.

## 2. Offshore Securities

Asset-backed Eurobonds have been sold since the mid–1980s. In 1988, most were sterling Collateralized Mortgage Obligations, for example. In 1989, most were ex-warrant bonds, World Bank bonds, and credit-card receivables. Overall, Euro-securitization is not large, but by 1990, Simon Brady could write of "The Year of the Asset–Backed Eurobond" in Euromoney (February 1990):

This is the year in which asset securitisation in the Euromarkets will come of age. That's the prediction of Jonathan Hakim, a director at UBS Phillips and Drew. Two ground-breaking deals in December and January bear him out.

The deal even his competitors concede is crucial was a $750 million issue of bonds backed by credit-card receivables brought by UBS Phillips and Drew in January. "The deal represented a significant leap in size and was the most ambitious deal of its type done in the Eurodollar bond market," says Hakim. There had been just two such issues previously, worth only $625 million combined.

The issue is secured on credit-card receivables originated by Citibank South Dakota and Citibank Nevada, further protection of investors being provided by a letter of credit from UBS. The latter also provided a guarantee that at least 46% of the principal amount would still be outstanding at maturity.

An important point, according to Hakim, is that "as in our previous deal [a $325 million credit card receivable-backed issue launched in September] we showed a quantum leap in the investor base. There was real global distribution." A significant shift in the investor pattern lay in the extent of demand from the Far East—not only Japan—in addition to that already seen from continental Europe, the UK and the Middle East.

A year of educating investors has clearly paid off. Syndication, by the fixed-price re-offering method, went smoothly and the issue was trading at 100.18 bid, 84 basis points over equivalent US Treasuries, the day after the offering. The pricing of the issue at this spread over Treasuries raised questions about the pricing of the whole triple-A corporate and sovereign sector. How long will investors continue to buy lower-yielding corporate and sovereign paper, subject to event risk and possible downgrading, when asset-backed securities offer a safer, better return?

Confirming this, syndicate members report that a number of investors switched out of sovereign triple-A paper to buy the new issue, which they put in the same category as the benchmark issues of the Republic of Italy and the Province of Alberta.

The asset-backed departments at the major banks expect more deals. Says one syndicate chief: "You can't expect a $750 million deal every two weeks: that would clearly saturate the market pretty quickly. But there is scope for further carefully priced and timed issues."

The market is less optimistic, though, about using European credit-card receivables. In a number of the major European countries, West Germany and Switzerland, for example, the only credit cards are charge cards. Even the UK market is not yet considered large enough. "We see this as a medium-term objective," says one market participant.

## 3. The International Investor Base

### I. MACKINTOSH, "THE INTERNATIONAL INVESTOR BASE FOR MORTGAGE AND ASSET–BACKED SECURITIES," PAPER DELIVERED AT CONFERENCE ON THE EVOLVING WORLDWIDE LEGAL AND REGULATORY CLIMATE FOR SECURITIZATION"

ABA Section of Real Property, Probate and Trust Law, (April 1993).

The constant education and information process involving visits and other communications with investors throughout Europe, the Middle East and the Far East has resulted in truly investor-driven structural changes as various series of offerings have evolved. This process of adaptation is a healthy one and is an example of classic investment banking in action. The asset-backed market, to the extent that the collateral can be moulded to create different classes of securities, lends itself to investor-driven structures. Examples of investor-driven, investor-friendly modifications include:

- bearer bond tranches;
- bullet-style maturities;
- linkage of the CEDEL/EUROCLEAR settlement systems with Depository Trust Company (DTC) in New York;
- creation of Eurocommercial Paper (ECP)/Euro medium-term note (EMTN) tranches of domestic CP/MTN programmes;
- improved investor communication procedures (both written and screen-based);
- global syndicates with discrete allocations of risk and paper for foreign dealers;
- listing (even of SEC-registered issues) on recognised European exchanges such as Luxembourg.

These features, sponsored and funded by some of the larger US securitisers, have to varying degrees all been designed to accommodate local investor preferences. There can be little doubt that such initiatives have not only expanded the investor universe for US securitised products, but have also paved the way for the anticipated flow of European issues. The GPA aircraft leasing securitisation in 1992, for example, structured as a US$ Eurobond, can no doubt claim many investors in common with earlier US-based asset-backed offerings.

It should be noted that in their first attempts to distribute internationally, some major US securitisers failed to make the structural adaptations desired by Euromarket investors and accordingly experienced difficulties selling paper overseas. They missed substantial rewards; it is believed that around 30% of Citibank's credit card asset-backed offerings (as much as US$8bn over three to four years) was sold to non-US investors, and while it is difficult to quantify the benefits, such wide, indeed global, distribution has clearly contributed to the overall success of this programme.

## Importance of Disclosure and Information

A leading US securitiser was asked for a definition of securitisation at a domestic investor conference and instead of the conventional 're-packaging' recitation replied simply 'securitisation is information'. He was making the point that transparency of structure in ABS and MBS relies on sufficient and timely communication of collateral performance to maintain investor confidence. The most successful issuance programmes have been those featuring regular and full market communications, not only through road-shows and visits but also through publishing and distributing investor handbooks and through screen-based information.

The US rating agency Fitch was quick to perceive this particular investor need and successfully introduced its asset-backed securities screen service about a year ago. Primarily addressing credit quality control, the Fitch 'surveillance service' covers over 200 mortgage and asset-backed securities and discloses details of most published collateral loss and delinquency information. International investors regard this as a step in the right direction and also recognise the merits of other services such as the Goldman Liquid Asset–Backed Index. However, they still feel that in Europe there is not enough ongoing and objective performance discussion on the price and spread history and market behaviour of structured securities in general.

Investors in Europe rely heavily on American rating agencies (Moody's, Standard & Poor's, Fitch and Duff & Phelps) for initial credit ratings of asset and mortgage-backed issues, and for ongoing monitoring not only of collateral performance but also of structural risk. To some extent the rating agencies are supplementing bond analyst research into these instruments, research which is not consistently sponsored in Europe. Investors certainly appreciate having access to rating agencies and other professionals to discuss matters relating to the creditworthiness and structure of asset-backed securities. Special structured finance topic papers presented by the agencies have been very well received, which suggests that more broker-dealer research will be demanded by the structured investor community, especially research covering new issues which tend to be sprung suddenly upon the market.

### Contrasts Between US and Non–US Investors

In reviewing the evolution of international investment in securitised products, some relevant distinctions between US and non-US investor bases should be noted. The universe of European and Asian investors generally differs from the domestic US investor base in being:

- multi-currency oriented;
- multi-currency based;
- geographically fragmented;
- differentiated by local law, regulation, tax and accounting;
- often without the support of life insurance and pension institutions (which need local currency assets);
- sometimes irrationally sceptical about 'complex story paper'.

Euromarket New Asset Backed and Structured Securities Sales
(Excluding Stering MBS)

Estimated Investor Geographic Mix, 1990–92

| Country | Share of Total |
|---|---|
| United Kingdom based | 34% |
| | |
| Germany | 8 |
| Switzerland | 6 |
| France | 5 |
| Ireland | 4 |
| Benelux | 5 |
| Italy/Portugal/Spain | 4 |
| Scandinavia | 4 |
| | |
| Japan | 8 |
| Pacific Basin | 5 |
| Australia | 2 |
| | |
| Middle East | 15 |

[Note: the information contained in this table is taken from the original chart in the text.]

International investors' gradual acceptance of asset and mortgage-backed securities as key sectors of the investment grade bond universe has at times been a laborious process. Initially, only a few sophisticated fund managers and some large 'nostro account' investors, such as Abbey National Treasury Services, were involved. Momentum has picked up in the 1990s, particularly across Europe, returning good dividends on the efforts of dealers promoting asset-backed securities. Even so, relatively few international fixed income managers appear to be aware of the sheer size of the US securitised asset market. Most recent data shows that mortgage and asset-backed securities represent almost a third of all outstanding components of the Lehman Brothers Aggregate Bond Index (which contains all domestic US$ public issues of reasonable size rated BBB or better and having maturities of at least one year). The US Government and Agency component stands at over 52% but corporates are now less than 17% of the total—down from about 30% a decade ago. In contrast, over the past six years, asset- and mortgage-backed securities have increased their weighting from 24% to more than 31%, and currently offer the investment grade bond investor tailored choices of product from over a trillion dollars of structured securities.

**Lehman Brothers Aggregate Bond Index Weightings by Sector**

Lehman Brothers Aggregate Bond Index Weightings by Sector

| Type of instrument | Share of Index |
|---|---|
| Corporate bonds | 16.9% |
| MBS & ABS | 31.0 |
| U.S. Government and agency bonds and notes | 52.1 |

[Note: the information contained in this table is taken from the original chart in the text.]

**Dominance of London-based Investors**

London is, in most respects, the acknowledged centre of both the international capital market and fund management industries, and also the geographic focus for structured product sales to investors outside the US. It is likely that UK-based asset and mortgage-backed investment has in most years to date exceeded the aggregate involvement from the rest of Europe. The Middle East and Far East rank next in terms of volume of investor participation.

**Group 'A' and Group 'B' Investors**

Outside the US, where a third category consisting of pension and life insurance funds is involved, the MBS/ABS investor universe can simplistically be divided into two distinct groups, referred to as 'A' (for Asset Managers) and 'B' (for Balance Sheet Investors). Group 'A' investors are typically managers of third party assets, the fund managers and private portfolio managers throughout Europe, as well as selected large insurance and reinsurance entities. Group 'B' investors, on the other hand, can be described collectively as mostly floating rate investors, and this category includes commercial and money centre banks, regional banks and corporate and finance company-style investors who obtain their funding in the interbank or CP markets. 'B' investors also include some 'unfunded' corporate treasuries in both public and private sectors which seek performance versus low risk benchmarks such as local currency or Eurodollar Libor. The 'A's will tend to have greater appetite for interest rate and currency risk than the 'B's, who tend to rely for their returns on credit spreads accruing on duration and currency-neutral assets.

## Risk Tolerances of Investor Groups

The risk appetites of the 'A' and 'B' investor types can be represented in a matrix diagram. Clearly the table below is a simplified picture and ignores the incidence of swaps and other derivative contracts which can transmute basis, currency and duration risk. Nevertheless a risk tolerance pattern emerges.

A typical 'A' investor, such as the fixed income desk of a major international wholesale fund manager, would tend to be attracted by large, liquid, fixed rate AAA rated issues of, say, credit card asset-backed securities, provided that the investor perceives:

- the spread outlook as stable to narrowing;
- the outlook for the currency as positive (or is prepared to currency-hedge);
- early amortisation risk (the possibility of early principal repayment) and therefore interest risk arising from duration shortening as low.

Tolerance of risk

| Risk category | Group A | Group B |
|---|---|---|
| Credit | low | moderate to high |
| Liquidity | low | moderate to high |
| Credit premium/spread | moderate | high |
| Currency | high | low to moderate |
| Interest | high | low |

At the other end of the spectrum, a typical 'B' investor might simultaneously be giving positive consideration to a medium-sized, privately placed, floating rate, A-rated subordinated instrument with a much higher equivalent Libor spread and be planning to match-fund this instrument in respect of interest basis and periodicity, currency and possibly also final maturity.

## The current outlook

Greed appears nevertheless to have been ascendant over fear in the early 1990s for investors in securitised product. Asset allocations by investors in at least 21 countries and regions outside the US now routinely include mortgage and asset-backed securities, suggesting significant progress since the pioneering days of the 1980s.

At present, the securitised market is actually benefiting from being mostly dollar-denominated since the consensus expectation is for a cyclical dollar recovery as the US leads the world out of recession. Meanwhile, owing to their 'negative convexity', mortgage and asset-backed securities tend to underperform US Treasuries in periods of rapidly falling bond yields, as witnessed in recent years. However, now that yields are generally expected to be relatively stable with a tendency to increase, these same securities appear in a more favourable light. Structured US dollar securities, particularly those with short or neutral duration, may be useful investment vehicles in what may prove to be a bear market in dollar bonds but possibly a strong market for the dollar itself.

Internationally, American MBS and ABS are generally suitable for managers of 'natural' dollar assets: large fund managers running yield conscious dollar portfolios, private banks and central bank reserve asset managers. In addition, there now appears to be widely based European, Middle East and Pacific Basin support for these securities, spanning a broad spectrum of financial industries and including commercial banks, private banks, mutual funds, building societies, corporations and reinsurance reserve asset managers. This healthy investor base can be expected to expand further as and when more non-dollar asset-backed transactions emerge from Europe, Japan and elsewhere.

## 4. The U.K. as an Offshore Center

Mackintosh sees London as the natural euro-center for securitization. The U.K. MBS and ABS markets are second only to the U.S. markets. The U.K. MBS market thrived in the late 1980s and ABS have developed there as well. The U.K. Government did not set up analogues to Ginnie Mae, Fannie Mae, or Freddie Mac. It is responsive, however, to concerns of its financial institutions. The legal infrastructure in the U.K. resolves the legal problems securitization poses to its parties. The major issues concern the treatment of bank capital, as the following article describes. As you read it, consider the ways in which the U.K. would attract originators from Japan and Germany.

### J. MAY, ET AL., "UNITED KINGDOM"

In IFLR Guide 20.

The capital adequacy treatment of securitizations is important to banks both as Investors in asset-backed securities and as potential Originators themselves. Looking at these different aspects in turn:

**Banks as Investors**

Not surprisingly because of the fact that the great majority of outstanding UK asset-backed issues are mortgage-backed securities, the main concern for banks has been how the holding of this type of security is treated. The position was set out by the Bank of England in 1990 to the effect that, broadly, first mortgages to individuals on residential property which were at the outset of the securitization fully performing are subject to a 50% risk-weighting. The Bank of England announced in 1992 a change in the regime so that a 100% risk-weighting would apply from January 1, 1993 but relented late in 1992 when new provisions were announced to the effect that, from January 1, 1993, mortgage-backed securities would be subject to 100% risk-weighting unless various conditions are satisfied. The conditions should be capable of being met in most cases although they will prevent 50% risk-weighting where, for instance, the pool assets include second mortgages or mortgages which are in default at the time that they are transferred to the SPV.

**Banks as Originators**

The Bank of England issued a Notice in 1989 (entitled Loan Transfers and Securitization (BSD/1989/1)) setting out the criteria determining whether a bank as an Originator can exclude securitized assets from its capital adequacy calculations.

In order to achieve a clean break so far as the bank Originator is concerned:

the Originator must not own any share capital in the Issuer nor otherwise control it;

the Issuer's name must not include the name of the Originator or imply any connection with it;

the Originator must not bear any recurring expenses of the Issuer although it may make a one-off contribution to enhance the creditworthiness of the Issuer and lend on a long-term subordinated basis (although such amounts will be deducted from capital for capital adequacy purposes);

the Originator may not retain an option to repurchase loans except where the loan portfolio has fallen to less than 10% of its maximum value and the option extends to only fully-performing loans.

On the whole, the criteria have not been seen as constituting an insurmountable barrier to securitization by banks; it should be entirely possible to structure a securitization within this framework which involves an assignment of loan assets without giving notice to the debtors (generally the desired approach).

---

*Links to Other Chapters*

Securitized instruments, one type of financial innovation, are derivatives like swaps (Chapter XVI) and futures and options (Chapter XV) in that their values reflect the values of underlying assets. This derivative nature means that MBS and ABS integrate the banking and securities markets (Chapters II, III, V, and VII). In this function, they take the link forged by syndicated eurocredits (Chapter VIII) a step further.

The offshore markets for securitized instruments are still young. The more mature markets are those for eurobonds (Chapter XI) and eurocredits (Chapter VIII).

National policies have played an important role in the development of markets for MBS and ABS around the world. We saw the different approaches of major governments in Chapters II, III, V and VII. The promotional role of the U.S. government contrasts with the more protective role of the Japanese government.

# Chapter XIII

# STOCK MARKET COMPETITION

One important feature of the world's financial system is increased competition between stock markets both within and among countries. This Chapter examines the terms and consequences of this competition. It begins by looking at competition in the U.S. market, and then turns to comparative material about other major markets.

## A. U.S. MARKET

In 1994, the Securities and Exchange Commission issued a long awaited study of the U.S. securities markets, *Market 2000, An Examination of Current Equity Market Developments.* Some excerpts from the study follow.

### A. The Users of the Markets

The predominant trend of the past 20 years has been the growth in size and diversity of users of the equity markets. Current market participants include numerous large entities, representing both retail customers and professionals. In the Securities and Exchange Commission's ("Commission") 1971 Institutional Investor Study, this trend was described as the "institutionalization" of the market. The institutional presence in the markets has continued to grow. For example, in 1975, institutions owned 30% of U.S. equities, but by 1992 they owned slightly more than 50% (Exhibit 1).* The following summaries describe the various users of the markets.

### 1. The Public Investor

Although the level of individual investor activity has fluctuated with various market cycles, the importance of the individual investor has never been questioned. Indeed, in the 1950s, the New York Stock Exchange ("NYSE") encouraged investors to "own your share in America" by buying equities. Individual investors have always been considered the cornerstone of U.S. equity markets.

The number of shareholder accounts increased from 25 million in 1975 to 51 million in 1990 and is still growing. A typical individual account averages approximately $14,000, generates several hundred dollars per year in brokerage commissions, and places orders that average approximately 300 shares per order. Over two-thirds of these accounts, however, effect no more than two transactions per year. Many retail investors use a discount broker for execution.

* Exhibits are omitted.

The absolute amount of retail investor activity is greater than in years past, but the *percentage* of market activity attributable to direct individual investor participation in the market has declined. In 1992, block trades, which are effected almost exclusively by institutions, accounted for 50% of NYSE volume, an increase from 16% in 1975. Program trades, negligible in 1975, accounted for another 11% of NYSE volume in 1992. Activity by market professionals, such as options market makers and equity trading desks, accounted for an additional significant portion of NYSE volume. Thus, of the total volume on the NYSE, a minority results from the direct activity of individual investors. This trend is not as pronounced for the OTC market, but there is increasing institutional activity in that market as well, especially for OTC stocks included in the major market indexes.

Although there has been a decline in the percentage of *direct* individual participation, there actually has been an increase in *indirect* participation in the equity securities market. Individual investors are more likely to participate through institutions, such as mutual funds, public pension plans, private pension plans, or insurance companies. Together with the endowment funds of colleges and religious organizations, these entities now own over $2.3 trillion of U.S. equities.

. . .

### 3. Market Professionals

**a. Broker–Dealer Trading Desks.** The equity trading activity of larger broker-dealers has expanded significantly in terms of size and investment alternatives over the past 20 years. For example, in 1975, the amount of revenue that broker-dealers derived from trading amounted to $1.3 billion. By 1991, this amount had grown to $22.5 billion. Aided by advances in telecommunications and computer technology, the introduction of derivatives, and the growth of buy-side assets, the equity trading desks of the larger broker-dealers are significant forces in the equity markets. Moreover, they have fueled the growth in program trading and, together with pension funds, have sparked the growth in index derivatives. The Commission's Division of Market Regulation ("Division") understands that, although the October 1987 market break and lower agency commissions have reduced the willingness of the larger firms to commit capital for block positioning, equity trading desks remain important providers of liquidity to the institutional customer.

The derivatives trading desks of the large broker-dealers are among the most significant professional participants in the equity markets. For example, in 1992, program trades in NYSE stocks accounted for 27.6 million shares per day (11% of reported volume). During one week in 1992, these trades averaged 68.4 million shares per day. The firms engaging in these trades also effected other types of derivatives related trades. In addition, the derivatives trading desks of large broker-dealers are among the major dealers in the growing OTC derivatives business.

The large broker-dealers also are a primary factor in the rise of global trading. They have established trading desks in the major market centers around the world. Some of these broker-dealers pass their trading books from the Far East to Europe to the United States as the major markets open and close.

**b. Retail Brokers.** The equity operations of retail firms have changed dramatically over the past 20 years. The automation of broker-dealer order handling and processing technology, as well as the automation of the order routing, execution, and reporting services of the equity markets, have enabled broker-dealers and the markets to handle an exponentially greater order flow; they do so in a time frame that was unimaginable 20 years ago. For example, a customer's order to buy 100 shares of a listed stock at the market in 1975 would have taken from several minutes to an hour to travel from the branch office that accepted the order to the firm's trading desk, and finally to the firm's broker on the floor of the exchange, who transmitted the order to the specialist post. Between the time that the customer entered the order and the time it was executed, it was possible for the market in the stock to change. An additional delay would occur before the trade was confirmed to the customer. Today, the entire process—from the entry of the order to its confirmation to the customer—can take less than a minute, often while the customer is still on the telephone with a sales representative.

The automation of the order handling process also includes the order routing decision. Rather than evaluate the best possible market or market maker among competing markets or market makers for every individual order, most retail firms automatically route their small-size order flow (e.g., all orders under 3,000 shares) to a specified market or market maker, based on the characteristics of the stock and the order. Many factors determine where a small order is routed. For example, broker-dealers will route orders to an affiliated specialist unit on a regional exchange or, for stocks quoted on the National Association of Securities Dealers Automated Quotation ("NASDAQ") system, to their OTC market making desks. Some order flow is routed based on payment for order flow or reciprocal order flow arrangements. Some firms will route orders only to the primary market. A few large broker-dealers internally cross their order flow and then route these orders to regional exchanges. Regardless of the method selected, retail firms generally consider individual order routing decisions to be unduly expensive or inefficient. Whether handled by a discount or a full-service broker, an individual customer's order typically is routed to a specific market or market maker through a predetermined routing algorithm employed by the broker-dealer. The customer's order is viewed by the broker-dealer as part of its overall order flow, which is packaged and distributed to specific locations.

. . .

**c. Specialists and Market Makers.** Traditionally, the specialists and floor brokers on the exchanges and the market makers on

NASDAQ have played an important role in providing liquidity, depth, and price continuity. Because of their physical presence on the exchange floor or their display of quotations on NASDAQ, it is tempting to view these participants as constituting "the market." This view is no longer accurate because of the participation of institutional investors and equity trading desks in the market and the availability of derivative products. Nevertheless, specialists and market makers still perform an important role in the operation of the markets. On the exchanges, specialists direct the auction on the exchange floor, handle limit orders, and ensure accurate quotations. In the OTC market, NASDAQ market makers establish quotations and execute most orders. Both specialists and market makers are responsible for maintaining markets and, in return, receive certain privileges. Because of their order handling and market maintenance roles, specialists and market makers are subject to special regulatory scrutiny.

. . .

### B. Structure of the Equity Markets

. . .

#### 1. Primary Exchanges (NYSE and Amex)

There are seven registered stock exchanges in the United States. The two primary exchanges—the NYSE and the Amex—list most of the stocks traded on an exchange. The five U.S. regional stock exchanges include: the Boston Stock Exchange ("BSE"), the Philadelphia Stock Exchange ("Phlx"), the Cincinnati Stock Exchange ("CSE"), the Chicago Stock Exchange ("CHX"), and the Pacific Stock Exchange ("PSE"). These exchanges primarily trade securities that also are listed on the primary markets.

The primary exchanges operate as modified auction markets. In the exchange auction all order flow for a stock is directed to a central location, the trading post for the specialist in the stock, and orders interact to the maximum extent possible. A specialist acts as a market maker by trading for its own account to ameliorate temporary disparities in supply and demand for the stock and also acts as the agent for orders left on the limit order book. This structure proved inadequate to accommodate large block orders in the late 1960s and early 1970s. The NYSE and the Amex responded by modifying their auction rules to enable block orders to be negotiated by the trading desks of member firms off the floor of the exchange. The trading desk would find a customer to take the other side of the block, acting as an agent for both sides in the transaction, or would commit its capital by taking the other side of the block itself. In either event, a negotiated price for the block would be established off the exchange (i.e., upstairs), and the transaction would then be brought down to the trading post and exposed to the trading crowd and to any limit order book interest.

The modified auction structure served the NYSE well when it was practically the sole price discovery mechanism for stock. In 1975, the

NYSE captured approximately 86% of the volume in NYSE-listed stocks. This concentration of volume allowed the NYSE to operate as a self-contained auction, albeit modified for block trading, which at the time accounted for only 16.6% of NYSE volume. Third market makers (discussed shortly) garnered a modest share of small customer orders.

In contrast, in the first six months of 1993, the NYSE accounted for only 70% of the total orders and 79% of the volume in NYSE-listed stocks. Moreover, block transactions, which often are negotiated off the floor of an exchange, accounted for half of the NYSE volume. Some blocks are sent to regional exchanges for execution, whereas blocks accounting for over 2 million shares per day are executed off the exchange after the close of regular trading hours. A substantial portion of small orders for public customers (i.e., orders for 3,000 shares or less) is sent to the regional exchanges or third market dealers for execution (Exhibit 11). Proprietary trading systems handle 1.4% of the volume in NYSE stocks, usually in the form of portfolio trades or block trades. Several large institutions or money managers cross portfolio orders internally between accounts. These crosses account for up to 1 million shares on any given day.

Almost 200 NYSE stocks are traded on foreign exchanges. Foreign trading accounts for several million shares per day in these stocks. Ten million shares per day are executed as program trades after the NYSE closes, either on the NYSE's after-hours crossing session or through the foreign desks of U.S. broker-dealers. Perhaps most importantly, active options and index futures markets provide an alternative means of trading NYSE stocks. The aggregate dollar value of trading in these markets far surpasses the dollar value of trading on the NYSE.

Although order flow is dispersed, the NYSE still receives the majority of small orders. Its market share in these orders, however, has eroded steadily over the past decade. The NYSE generally has retained the 3,000 to 25,000 share trades, which are too large for the small order systems of the regional exchanges and third market and too small to be handled by block positioners. These orders benefit from the liquidity provided by the NYSE floor, but they are also often difficult for the NYSE specialists to handle because the orders require capital commitment and trading acumen. In addition, the NYSE attracts orders that need special handling as well as trades for which the institutional customer wants to "see a NYSE print."

Despite the fact that it has lost some volume, the NYSE still plays an important price discovery function as does the Amex. Most securities markets set prices equal to or based on the primary market prices. For example, the regional exchanges and third market makers usually base their quotations on the primary market quote, and many of them simply autoquote the primary markets. Block positioners use the NYSE price as the reference point for negotiating block prices. Much after-hours trading is executed at NYSE closing prices. Similarly, proprietary trading systems often use the NYSE quotes as a pricing reference. The derivatives markets obviously rely on NYSE (as well as Amex and NASDAQ) prices to price options and futures. There are also numerous transactions involving equities that use NYSE prices.

The NYSE also serves as the market of last resort during times of market stress. During volatile market conditions, when normal liquidity is unavailable in the index-derivatives markets, market participants channel their stock orders to the NYSE. Moreover, supplemental sources of liquidity to the floor, such as block positioners, are less active during such periods. The NYSE has attempted to accommodate periodic surges of demand by upgrading the capacity of its automated floor systems and by increasing the amount of capital that specialists are required to have available. At the same time, the NYSE has adopted certain circuit breaker provisions, such as NYSE Rules 80A and 80B, which are designed to dampen these surges. Users of the market must understand that, if the NYSE is to perform the role of market of last resort, they will have to pay for this service in some manner.

### 2. Regional Exchanges

At an earlier point in their history, the regional exchanges served as "incubator" markets for small, local companies. For the past 20 years, however, the overwhelming percentage of regional stock exchange business has been in the stocks of NYSE- and Amex-listed companies that the regional exchanges trade pursuant to grants of unlisted trading privileges ("UTP"). In 1992, over 97% of the regional stock exchanges' volume derived from issues traded pursuant to UTP. Because all of the regional exchanges have UTP in most NYSE and many Amex issues, for the majority of NYSE- and Amex-listed stocks there are five exchanges competing with the primary market. The regional exchanges are linked with the primary markets in UTP issues through ITS, the Consolidated Quotation System ("CQS"), and the consolidated tape.

The regional exchanges captured 20% of the orders in NYSE issues in the first six months of 1993. Most of this market share derives from small orders from individual customers. During the 1970s and 1980s, the regional exchanges built automated systems that enabled member firms to route small customer orders to their specialist posts. Orders routed over these systems generally are executed automatically at the ITS best bid or offer, regardless of the quote of the particular regional specialist. Because of the speed and efficiency of these systems, lower transaction fees, and the guarantee of the ITS best bid or offer, many retail broker-dealers send some of their small order flow to the regional exchanges.

. . .

### 3. Third Market

OTC trading of exchange-listed securities is commonly known as "third market" trading. Third market dealers handle order flow sent to them by other broker-dealers. At the time of the Institutional Investor Study, third market volume derived principally from two sources. First, institutional investors desiring to avoid the NYSE fixed commission schedule entered into various order flow arrangements with third market dealers and regional exchange members. The unfixing of commission rates in 1975 caused this business to decline. Second, a few third market dealers acted as block positioners; the services of these firms were especially in demand when the NYSE was closed. Some third market firms continue to act as block positioners, but their role has been partially undercut as NYSE member firms have developed the ability to effect transactions in blocks at their foreign desks.

The past few years have seen third market trading increase, principally from operations established by a few third market makers to handle small customer order flow. The third market makers act much like NASDAQ market makers in that they accept orders of up to a few thousand shares in the most active listed stocks from retail firms or discount brokers. Market orders are executed against the best bid or offer on ITS, and limit orders are handled according to preestablished execution parameters.

Third market makers offer three advantages to firms with large retail order flow. First, third market makers have automated their operations so that they provide virtually instantaneous executions and reports. Second, they do not charge transaction fees, membership fees, or limit order commissions. Third, they usually pay $0.01 to $0.02 per share for order flow.

Third market activity is concentrated in the 400 most active NYSE stocks and a much smaller number of Amex stocks. The remaining NYSE- and Amex-listed stocks are not sufficiently active for third market operations. In 1989, the third market garnered 3.2% of reported NYSE volume and 5% of the reported trades; in 1993, this percentage had increased to 7.4% of reported NYSE volume and 9.3% of the reported trades.

## 4. NASDAQ

NASDAQ is an interdealer quotation system operated by the National Association of Securities Dealers ("NASD"), which is registered as a national securities association under Section 15A of the Securities Exchange Act of 1934 ("Exchange Act"). NASDAQ consists of competing market makers for each security. Customer orders are not normally reflected in the market makers' quotes. Unlike the exchange market, limit orders are handled individually by each market maker.

At the time of the Securities Acts Amendments of 1975, Congress and the Commission found it unnecessary to regulate NASDAQ as an exchange. Although certain trading characteristics of NASDAQ are functionally similar to those of the traditional exchanges, the Commission believed that these similarities did not transform NASDAQ into an exchange. Nevertheless, the NASD is subject to regulation under Section 15A of the Exchange Act that is substantively similar to the regulation for national securities exchanges under Section 6 of the Exchange Act.

At its inception in 1971, NASDAQ publicly displayed only representative bids or offers; nevertheless, it revolutionized OTC trading by increasing the availability of quotes for OTC securities. As a result, spreads for these stocks narrowed, volume increased, and liquidity improved. In addition, NASDAQ led to greater visibility for its issues and expanded coverage in the media. NASDAQ also reduced dealers' reliance on the telephone and enabled integrated firms to compete as market makers with wholesale firms.

NASDAQ has made tremendous strides in automating OTC market making and increasing the efficiency and transparency of the OTC market, including: (1) the display of all market makers' quotes; (2) the implementation of real-time trade reporting for NASDAQ/NMS securities in 1982 and NASDAQ Small–Cap stocks in 1992; (3) the display of market maker quote size; (4) the introduction of its Automated Confirmation Transaction Service; and (5) the development of SelectNet. In addition, all NASDAQ/NMS securities have been marginable pursuant to Federal Reserve Board guidelines since 1984. They also are exempt from state blue-sky registration provisions in most states.

Initially, NASDAQ was considered primarily an "incubator" market. When its companies matured financially, they usually became listed on exchange markets. NASDAQ now is a major market in its own right. Based on volume, it is the second largest securities market in the world after the NYSE. Its dollar volume of trading is 43% of the NYSE's dollar volume. Its NMS market trades 3,104 companies, many of which qualify for listing on the primary exchanges but choose to remain on NASDAQ. Although most of the most highly capitalized companies are listed on the NYSE, a significant portion of the younger, widely held companies are quoted on NASDAQ. The three primary markets compete aggressively for listings.

NASDAQ is not a completely automated market. With the exception of its Small Order Execution System ("SOES") and SelectNet features, order entry and execution for NASDAQ stocks still occur by telephone. Moreover, it is difficult for a customer to have a limit order exposed on NASDAQ. As a result, proprietary trading systems, which offer both automation and limit order exposure, have been able to capture 13% of the volume in NASDAQ/NMS stocks.

NASDAQ now is linked with the exchanges through the interface between ITS and the NASDAQ's Computer Assisted Execution System ("CAES"). Through this linkage, NASDAQ market makers are linked to ITS for listed stocks that are not subject to off-board trading restrictions. The NASD has proposed to expand the linkage to all NYSE and Amex stocks.

### 5. Automated Trading Systems

Several types of automated trading systems offer institutions and broker-dealers the opportunity to trade off the exchanges and NASDAQ.

The first are proprietary trading Systems ("PTSs"), screen-based automated trading systems typically sponsored by broker-dealers. PTSs are not operated as or affiliated with self-regulatory organizations ("SROs") but instead are operated as independent businesses. PTSs currently permit trading in equities, government securities, corporate debt, and options. As a practical matter, participation in these systems is limited to institutional investors, broker-dealers, specialists, and other market professionals.

Advancements in telecommunications and trading technology over the past decade have fostered the growth of PTSs. They have been used by institutional investors to reduce execution costs, avoid the market maker spread, and trade in size without incurring the market impact costs that could result if orders were handled on the organized markets. The popularity of PTSs has been fueled by two phenomena. For listed securities, they are attractive to passive managers or other patient investors who are sensitive to transaction costs, but do not need the instant liquidity that the exchanges provide and do not want to pay the market spread. For NASDAQ securities, they are used by institutional investors who do not want to go through NASDAQ market makers to enter an order or who want to avoid paying the bid-ask spread, but instead prefer to seek liquidity through interaction with other institutional investors.

PTSs have combined technology with features attractive to institutional investors to gain an increasing share of volume in the past few years. For the first half of 1993, the total share volume on PTSs was 4.7 billion shares, which was almost equal to their entire volume in 1992. The total share volume for 1992 was nearly 4.9 billion, an increase of more than 60% from the 1991 volume of 2.9 billion. Trading in NASDAQ stocks represented 87% of PTS volume in the first half of 1993. During this same period, listed stocks were only 13% of PTS volume.

Even though PTS volume is growing rapidly, it is important to keep these numbers in perspective. First, the rising trend in PTS volume is consistent with the increasing volume occurring in the equity markets as a whole. Second, these systems represent only a small segment of primary market activity. The PTS volume in exchange-listed securities represents only 1.4% of the volume in the NYSE stocks. PTS volume in NASDAQ stocks, however, has grown to 13% of the total volume in NASDAQ/NMS stocks. Third, many institutional investors still consider these systems to be experimental and have not sought access to PTSs.

The second type of automated trading systems are, as described above, internal crossing systems operated by several large broker-dealers. These systems cross orders submitted by the broker-dealer's customers and, in some cases, orders from other broker-dealers. The systems route crosses in listed stocks to exchanges for execution. Crosses in NASDAQ stocks are submitted to NASDAQ for trade reporting.

### 6. Fourth Market

The fourth market refers to the trading of shares directly between institutional investors without the intermediation of a broker-dealer. This type of trading differs from the trading done through PTSs because the latter must either register as broker-dealers or secure the services of a registered broker-dealer in order to process and guarantee the trades. The distinction is important because trades effected through PTSs are, for the most part, subject to transparency rules, and they are subject to oversight by the NASD.

The Division requested data on the extent of fourth market trading, but commentators did not submit any information on this market. The Division understands, however, that the fourth market consists of internal crosses of orders between different accounts of the same institution or money manager. A few large institutions or money managers use this technique to avoid brokerage commissions and to limit the search for alternative sources of liquidity. Internal crossing of orders is used primarily for passively managed accounts that are cost-sensitive but do not need immediate liquidity. Although it is impossible to quantify the amount of fourth market trading, the Division estimates that such trading averages several million shares per day. In addition, some trading may be conducted in a "rolodex market" of institutions that call one another to solicit contra-side interest to an order, but this activity does not appear to involve significant volume.

### 7. Foreign Markets

Over the past 20 years it has become easy to trade securities around the world because of advances in telecommunications. Hundreds of U.S. equities are traded on foreign stock exchanges by the larger U.S., Japanese, and European broker-dealers, which have established trading desks at the major securities markets around the world.

The trading of U.S. equities by U.S. broker-dealers on foreign exchanges amounts to several million shares per day. Most of this trading is done abroad because of time zone differences between the major markets in New York, Tokyo, and London. Institutional investors that wish to trade when U.S. markets are closed seek the markets open at the time. By and large, this trading is concentrated on the London Stock Exchange ("LSE") and occurs shortly before the opening of the NYSE. Most additional trading abroad is not done on foreign markets but results from orders faxed by U.S. broker-dealers to their foreign desks. These orders usually involve a large block in a single stock or a large basket of multiple stocks. Currently, this "fax" trading amounts to approximately 7 million shares per day in NYSE stocks.

### 8. Block Positioning

Most transactions involving block trades over 50,000 shares (and many from 25,000 to 50,000 shares) are effected with block positioning firms. Block prices are negotiated based on current prices disseminated from the exchange floor or NASDAQ, with a block premium added or subtracted. Block positioners supplement the liquidity of the NYSE and NASDAQ by "shopping" their customer's block order upstairs to find a contra-side. They also take the other side of the transaction, keeping the block as a proprietary position.

Once price is negotiated for a block of NYSE stock, the transaction is executed on the exchange floor. Block positioners who are not members of the NYSE are not required to execute the block transaction on the exchange. When a block transaction is executed on the NYSE floor, it is subject to special auction market procedures designed to allow the limit order book or the trading crowd to participate. Block positioners prefer not to have the block broken up by the trading crowd or the limit order book. In some cases they use a regional exchange to execute the transaction (i.e., "print the block"). Because some institutions request an NYSE execution for their trade, block positioners can wait for a trade to clear the auction on the NYSE floor and then invoke precedence based on size under NYSE rules if the block is larger than the interest on the limit order book. In other cases, block positioners work part of a block on the NYSE floor if contra interest upstairs is insufficient and the firm does not want to take the other side of the block trade.

Until the October 1987 market break, upstairs firms often would commit capital to position a block. The market break and volatility that followed dampened the enthusiasm to commit capital. In addition, some commentators have suggested that the shrinking level of commission dollars and the rise in soft dollar practices have further reduced block positioning liquidity. Block positioners today are more likely to attempt to find contra-side interest for the block order, execute the cross, and collect agency commissions than to position the block.

Most blocks in NYSE stocks are negotiated off the exchange (i.e., "upstairs") but are executed on the exchange. A small percentage is executed on the regional exchanges. Indeed, the NYSE captures over 90% of the blocks in its stocks during regular trading hours. Some blocks, comprising approximately 2 million shares per day, are faxed by NYSE member firms to their foreign desks, where they are executed nominally in a foreign OTC market in order to comply with the NYSE's off-board trading restrictions. Because these trades are not reported to the consolidated tape, they avoid U.S. transparency requirements.

. . .

## B. Off–Shore Trading

Overseas markets generally compete for volume in U.S. stocks after regular U.S. business hours. This competition has arisen partly from the practice of U.S. broker-dealers "booking" trades through their foreign desks or foreign affiliates to avoid U.S. transparency requirements, off-board trading restrictions, transaction fees, or limits on short sales. In what is commonly referred to as the "fax market," for instance, a U.S. broker-dealer acting as principal for its customer negotiates and agrees to the terms of a trade in the United States, but transmits or faxes the terms overseas to be "printed" on the books of a foreign office without reporting the trade in compliance with U.S. requirements. The Division estimates that approximately 7 million shares a day in New York Stock Exchange ("NYSE") stocks are faxed overseas. Many of these trades are nominally "executed" in the London over-the-counter market. Transparency standards in overseas markets are often much weaker than in the United States, thus, off-shore trades generally are not reported publicly. Rather, they are reported weekly for regulatory purposes only to the NYSE pursuant to NYSE Rule 410B or to the National Association of Securities Dealers ("NASD") on Form T.

Fairness and efficiency in U.S. secondary markets is directly related to the public availability of current transaction and quotation information. Transparency is weakened when trades in U.S. securities are negotiated and arranged in the United States, but sent off-shore for nominal execution. Due to the absence of an international consensus on adequate transparency standards, the Division believes it is necessary to examine which off-shore trades should be included in U.S. transaction reporting mechanisms.

The Division notes that the United Kingdom's Securities Investments Board ("SIB") takes a different approach toward off-shore transactions. In SIB's view, the issue with respect to off-shore transactions is not whether there is public reporting, but whether there is regulatory reporting. The Division disagrees with this viewpoint: regulatory reporting cannot substitute for transparency and its benefits of fair and accurate price discovery.

Thus, the Division is of the view that the U.S. transaction reporting system should capture trades in reported securities when the price discovery occurs in the United States, but the trades are nominally booked overseas for execution. For example, a U.S. money manager decides to sell a block of 500,000 shares in an NYSE security. The money manager negotiates a price with a U.S. broker-dealer, who sends the order ticket to its foreign trading desk for execution. The price discovery for this trade occurred in the United States as much as if the trade had been executed by the broker-dealer's U.S. trading desk.

To capture these trades, the Division believes that self-regulatory organizations ("SROs"), in developing an after-hours transaction reporting mechanism, should require that their members publicly report these types of off-shore trades. At a minimum, the SRO reporting mechanism should include trades where the material terms are negotiated and arranged in the United States, but the trade is: (1) transmitted overseas to be entered into the books of an overseas branch office or affiliate of the U.S. broker-dealer; or (2) reflected in the books of a U.S. broker-dealer or affiliate, but is effected overseas—either on an overseas exchange or through a broker-dealer in a foreign over-the-counter transaction. A transaction would be deemed negotiated and arranged in the United States if the essential terms of the transaction, such as price and quantity, were agreed upon in the United States.

SROs also must address other issues in defining the off-shore trades to be captured. First, should the trades include only those transactions negotiated between a U.S. registered broker-dealer and a U.S. customer, or should they extend to transactions negotiated directly between an affiliate of the registered broker-dealer and a U.S. customer? Suppose, for example, that the U.S. money manager calls a broker-dealer's foreign desk directly and negotiates a block transaction. It would be difficult to determine where the terms of this transaction were arranged. Second, should the reporting system capture only those trades that involve a U.S. resident customer? Third, should off-shore trades that are subject to comparable public reporting in a foreign jurisdiction be exempted from the reporting system?

In answering these questions, the overriding goal of the SROs should be to capture trades where price discovery occurred in the United States. The Division's recommended approach will increase the transparency of off-shore trades that are virtually indistinguishable from U.S. over-the-counter transactions while recognizing that some off-shore trades will be beyond the purview of U.S. transparency standards.

The Division believes that the cost to market participants for reporting these off-shore trades will be small. The most immediate cost will be to SROs that must establish procedures to report the trades. Even so, the Division expects this cost will be low, because SROs have trade reporting systems in place for trading during regular hours. As mentioned in Study IV, the existing reporting mechanism could be extended for the entire day, or alternatively, after-hours trades (including off-shore trades) could be reported hourly, or batched for dissemination before the opening of the regular trading day.

In arguing against this position, dealers have suggested that transparency of large off-shore trades will increase their position risk and result in wider spreads and less liquid markets. They argue further that if a block must be disclosed on a real-time basis, dealers could be "picked-off" by their competitors (who might guess their position in the security), and the dealers generally would receive lower prices on the sale of those securities to investors; therefore, dealers would be less willing to risk their capital, would widen their spreads for block trades, or would stop making markets altogether. As discussed in Study IV, this is the same argument dealers used against the Commission's initiatives to improve transparency in the 1970s. The evidence, however, shows that transparency has improved the liquidity of the equity markets in the United States, and that it has not led to an exodus of large traders to alternative markets. Thus, the Division believes increased transparency is warranted for off-shore trades.

## C. U.S. Activity by Foreign Exchanges

As interest in trading foreign equities grows, U.S. investors are seeking more direct, efficient, and economical means of executing cross-border trades in foreign markets. Assisted by rapid technological advances in data processing and telecommunications, foreign exchanges now are able to provide U.S. investors with direct access to their quotation and execution capabilities. It is technologically possible for a foreign, non-U.S. registered exchange and its facilities (including specialists and market makers) to reach U.S. investors without intercession by a U.S. exchange or a foreign entity ("cross-border exchange access"). When a foreign exchange provides this kind of direct access to U.S. investors and broker-dealers, whether through exchange-owned terminals located in the United States, software that permits a U.S. investor's own computer system to gain access to the foreign exchange, or any other mechanism using U.S. jurisdictional means, the foreign exchange conducts activity and establishes a presence in the United States that is subject to the Commission's jurisdiction.

In this context, the Division has two concerns: (1) that U.S. investors executing a trade through a foreign exchange facility located in the United States should be afforded the same or similar protection that U.S. investors who execute trades on domestic exchanges in the United States receive; and (2) that the proper level of U.S. regulation for foreign exchanges with a limited presence in the United States be determined.

The Commission has a significant regulatory interest in trades that are made by U.S. customers through foreign exchange facilities located in the United States, based on quotes displayed in the United States. For example, the Commission seeks to prevent the use of foreign exchange facilities for the perpetration of fraud and manipulation in the United States and must also ensure that these facilities are not being used by U.S. broker-dealers to avoid U.S. regulatory requirements. Also, the direct dissemination of a foreign market maker's quotes in the United States would typically require broker-dealer registration.

At the same time, the limited presence of a foreign exchange that is adequately regulated abroad may not warrant the full application of rules designed to regulate U.S. exchanges. The Exchange Act, however, does not specifically identify the presence of a foreign regulatory scheme as a factor to consider when devising solutions to these issues.

The Division believes that the issues facing the Commission as a result of cross-border exchange access are harbingers of future cross-border trading issues. In this regard, the Commission will need to consider whether the placement of foreign exchange terminals in the United States and other means of cross-border exchange access may trigger exchange registration requirements, regardless of the adequacy of home country regulation.

Although such issues may be raised in different forms as innovations in cross-border trading occur, the issues themselves will stem from fundamental jurisdictional and regulatory concerns endemic to a highly automated global trading environment. As competition in the securities industry increases and communications between jurisdictions improve, reconciling the competitive and regulatory issues inherent in cross-border trading with the existing U.S. regulatory structure will be necessary. With this in mind, the Division is examining what regulatory changes or legislative amendments may be necessary to accommodate the jurisdictional and regulatory dilemmas raised by cross-border exchange access and other innovative cross-border trading mechanisms. The Division expects to produce recommendations for Commission consideration on these issues.

## D. After–Hours Trading

### 1. Introduction

Over the past few years, after-hours trading has been the subject of much discussion. Some market participants are of the view that after-hours trading will increase as a result of four factors: (1) advances in telecommunications and computer technology; (2) the development of a global economy with multinational corporations demanding both international communication and international sources of capital; (3) the emergency of huge institutional investment funds that require cross-border diversification; (4) and regulatory changes such as those that open stock exchanges to foreign membership. These factors are also contributing to an increase in international trading.

To date, volume of after-hours trading in U.S. equities is modest. Most customers and broker-dealers prefer to trade during primary market hours, when liquidity is greater, spreads are narrower, and information is more current. As a consequence, an active 24–hour market in U.S. equities has not developed. For instance, during the first six months of 1993, NYSE members executed after-hours trades involving only several million shares per day in NYSE stocks, with most of this nominally executed overseas; proprietary trading systems ("PTSs") that operate after-hours captured only one million shares per day in NYSE stocks; and broker-dealers averaged slightly over one million shares of after-hours trading in stocks quoted on the National Association of Securities Dealers Automated Quotation ("NASDAQ") system.

Given existing capabilities to trade on a 24–hour basis and the expansion of global securities trading, however, after-hours trading may develop further in the future. To attract order flow associated with certain trading strategies, several U.S. markets have already taken steps toward 24–hour trading. The NYSE, for example, has developed a multi-phase plan to respond to the evolving demand among NYSE members and customers to trade outside the 9:30 a.m. to 4:00 p.m. trading session. Phase one consists of revisions to its market-on-close procedures, discussed below, that permit firms to enter orders for guaranteed execution at the closing price, including matched buy and sell orders. Phase two, also discussed below, is an "Off–Hours Trading" ("OHT") facility that operates after the close of the regular NYSE trading day. (The OHT permits NYSE members to enter orders on closing-price, single-sided, and coupled orders from 4:00 p.m. until 5:00 p.m., and to enter orders for program trades from 4:00 p.m. until 5:15 p.m.)

. . .

## EXHIBIT 11

1993 MARKET SHARE DATA: NYSE STOCKS*

| | Average Shares Per Day (In Millions) | Average Shares Per Day (%) | Average Transactions Per Day | Average Transactions Per Day (%) |
|---|---|---|---|---|
| *NYSE* | | | | |
| Regular Hours | 264.8 | 78.53% | 186,410 | 70.48% |
| Crossing Session I | 0.2 | 0.06% | | |
| Crossing Session II | 4.4 | 1.30% | | |
| *ALL REGIONALS* | 34.3 | 10.17% | 52,699 | 19.92% |
| BSE | 4.2 | 1.25% | 6,941 | 2.62% |
| CHX | 13.1 | 3.88% | 16,202 | 6.13% |
| PHLX | 4.8 | 1.42% | 7,609 | 2.88% |
| PSE | 8.4 | 2.49% | 15,602 | 5.90% |
| CSE | 3.8 | 1.13% | 6,345 | 2.40% |
| All Regionals Excluding CSE | 30.5 | 9.05% | 46,354 | 17.53% |
| *THIRD MARKET* | | | | |
| Regular Hours ** | 19.6 | 5.81% | 24,847 | 9.39% |
| After Hours | 0.9 | 0.27% | | |
| *PTS* | | | | |
| Regular Hours | 3.6 | 1.07% | 543 | 0.21% |
| PTS After Hours | 1.1 | 0.33% | | |
| *OVERSEAS BY NYSE FIRMS* | | | | |
| Program Trades | 5.9 | 1.75% | | |
| OTC (non-program) | 1.7 | 0.50% | | |
| Foreign Exchanges (non-program) | 0.7 | 0.21% | | |
| TOTAL | 337.2 | 100.00% | 264,499 | 100.00% |

* These figures are for the first six months of 1993 (125 trading days), except for non-program foreign data, which uses a daily average from May, June, and July 1993. The figures do not include trades executed in the fourth market, such as trades directly between institutions without using an exchange or a broker-dealer.

** Regular hours refers to the operating hours of the NYSE. After hours trades are trades executed outside of the operating hours of the NYSE.

EXHIBIT 42

# NEW YORK STOCK EXCHANGE

## DISTRIBUTION OF REVENUE BY SOURCE

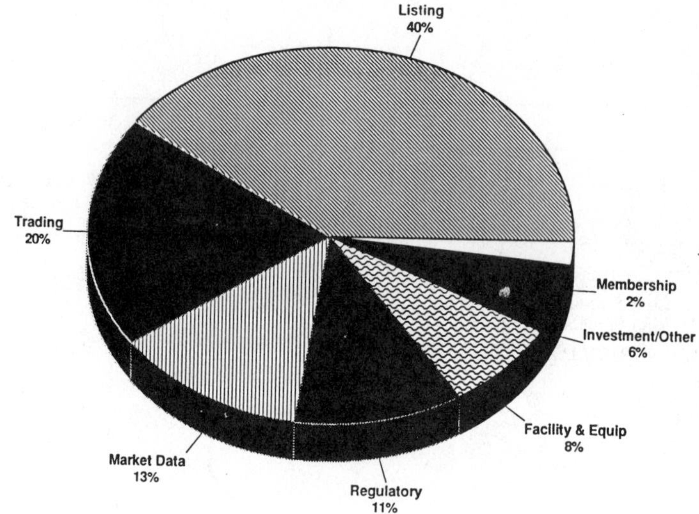


CALENDAR YEAR 1992

Data Source: NYSE Annual Report

---

NASDAQ International represents an attempt to keep off-hours NASDAQ trading in the United States.

### "NASDAQ INTERNATIONAL STAGGERS OPENING"

20 Securities Week 1 (November 8, 1993).

The pre-dawn stock market of Nasdaq International will campaign to revive flagging trading volume by launching staggered opening hours, adding 5.30 a.m. and 7.30 a.m. (EST) slots to the current 3.30 a.m. opening, sources said. The market also has studied the feasibility of extending the reach of Nasdaq International outside Europe to include the Pacific Rim, sources said.

Nasdaq International allows trading in securities listed on the Nasdaq Stock Market to take place in London for most of London's trading day (8.30 a.m. to 2 p.m., London time). Traders use the same screen-based technology as the Nasdaq Stock market.

Buoyed by SEC approval for a second two-year pilot program for the market and staggered opening hours, the NASD, which regulates Nasdaq International, hopes to turn around the market's paltry performance since it was launched with much fanfare two years ago.

Current daily trading volume averages 20,000–25,000 shares and there are only three participating market makers, Goldman Sachs & Co., Morgan Stanley and Madoff Securities, dealing in about 25 equity issues, sources said. On opening day two years ago about 10 market makers and 1,500 securities were registered.

"We are anticipating more market makers to participate as a result of staggered hours. Some of our conversations indicate that there will be an increase in market making. We hope to add the staggered hours in a few months. This is a step towards 24 hour global trading," Gary Guinn, director of Nasdaq International, said.

Guinn attributed the small trading volume in part to the SEC's refusal to allow Nasdaq International to trade NYSE listings and the fact that some European investors execute securities orders "off the formal markets." But he was upbeat about the future, stressing that Nasdaq International had looked "in an informal basis" at doing business in the Pacific Rim and in other regions.

"The NYSE is looking at us with concern," Guinn claimed. "We are their competitor. The NYSE is not a computer-driven building. We tend to be a bit more progressive with the style of markets we have developed. This is different from having to centralize your operations in an old building."

Guinn added that the NASD didn't know what to expect when it launched Nasdaq International. "The market was ahead of its time, as it were," he said.

While the SEC material gives an overview of participants and markets, the following excerpt from Office of Technology Assessment, *Electronic Bulls and Bears: U.S. Securities Markets and Information Technology* 44–45 (1990) (Bulls and Bears) gives the mechanics of a stock transaction by a small investor.

What happens when you visit or call a stock broker to buy or sell stock? The following description traces the chain of events that results in a transaction by a small investor.

A. When you decide to buy or sell stock, an Account Executive writes an order ticket, filling in the details—whether to buy or sell, the name of the security, how many shares, whether the order is to be executed at the market price or is a limit order (an order to buy or sell when the price reaches a specified level). The market order is passed to a teletype operator who keyboards the information and sends it immediately to an electronic system linking the broker to the various exchanges and over-the-counter dealers.

B. If the order involves an exchange-listed stock and there are no special instructions routing it to another market center, the order will enter the Common Message Switch, an electronic pathway linking brokerage firms and trading floors. This is the beginning of a journey that could carry the order to several alternative destinations.

C. Most orders in NYSE-listed stocks are routed to the NYSE's SuperDOT 250 system, where orders of fewer than 2,000 shares are executed. These orders can go either to the specialist's post on the floor of the exchange, or to the brokerage firm's floor booth (although with a small order, that is unlikely).

What happens next depends on the timing. On a typical day, between 15 and 20 percent of all orders are executed at the market opening. Through SuperDOT, *market orders* to buy or sell, routed to the specialist post prior to the market opening, are automatically paired with opposing orders. The specialist, after matching buy and sell market orders and checking outstanding *limit orders* and larger opening orders, sets an opening price for the stock. The specialist then executes all paired orders at one price and sends confirmation notices to originating brokers within seconds of the market opening, through the Opening Automated Reporting System (OARS).

Orders that arrive at the specialist's post through SuperDOT after the opening can be filled in several ways. Orders of up to 2,099 shares are usually filled at the best quoted price or better in the Intermarket Trading System (ITS). This system connects NYSE, AMEX, five regional exchanges, and NASD's Computer Assisted Execution System (CAES). ITS quotes are displayed at the NYSE specialist's post for all floor traders to see. An order sent to ITS will be filled within 1 or 2 minutes at the best price among any of these markets.

For larger orders, or when a wide spread exists between bid and asked prices, the specialist will execute a SuperDOT order in the traditional way (see D). He can also execute the trades from limit orders in his "book." The specialist is obligated to get the best price available at that moment for the client.

D. Some orders are not handled electronically but rather by the broker firm's floor broker. Wire orders reach floor brokers when they are too large for SuperDOT (see C above) or are larger than the broker's chosen parameters for direct routing through SuperDOT.

At the broker's floor booth, these orders are translated into floor tickets containing the essential buy/sell information necessary to make the trade. Floor clerks pass the details to floor brokers by hard copy (or through hand signals at the AMEX). The floor broker then presents the order at the specialist's post. There the stock is traded with another brokerage firm, or with the specialist, who may be acting as agent for a client on his books, or who may be acting for his own account. Or the floor broker may execute the trade on another exchange, if there is a better price posted on the ITS screen over the specialist's post. The above applies to exchange-traded stock.

E. If the stock is traded over the counter, and the quantity is more than 1,000 shares, the wire order goes to one of the broker's OTC traders at its main office. There, a computer on the OTC trader's desk displays the identities of all market-makers for that stock and their current bids and asked prices. The trader telephones the market-maker with the best price, and executes the trade.

If the brokerage firm itself makes a market in that stock, and the broker's OTC trader is willing to match the best price shown on NASDAQ, the trader can buy or sell it as principal. In either case, at the press of a button on the trader's keyboard, the trade is executed and a confirmation notice is sent to the originating office.

If the OTC order is for 1,000 shares or less, and the stock is listed on NASD's "National Market System," it will be automatically routed via NASDAQ's Small Order Executive System (SOES) to the market-maker with the best price at the time of order. (If the stock is not on the National Market System, it must be for 500 shares maximum to go through this system.) Trades executed through SOES take less than 90 seconds from order wire to confirmation.

. . .

### *Notes and Questions*

1. Stock markets compete over trading volume in securities. Trading increases the commissions for firms that are members of the market. An important element of trading volume is listings. Listings also produce revenue in their own right; listings can cost as high as $500 and $50 thousand per year, respectively on the NYSE and NASDAQ. The amount of listing revenue reduces transaction fees charged to firms and thus increases their net profit per trade.

2. Why would a broker-dealer care whether an order for a stock traded on both NASDAQ and SEAQ (the London Stock Exchange) was executed on one or the other market?

3. The NYSE is principally an order market in which brokers bring customer orders to a central point to be matched. On the NYSE this matching is not automatic, it is done through the specialist. Bulls and Bears, at 42, describes the role.

> Stock exchange specialists act as both brokers and dealers. As brokers, specialists buy and sell for the public, by executing limit orders that are brought to them on behalf of customers by floor brokers; they also execute market orders that reach them through the automated order routing system, SuperDOT. (A limit order specifies the price at which an investor is willing to buy or sell. Limit orders are put in the specialist's "book" until they can be executed at the designated price or a better price. A market order is an order to buy or sell immediately, at the prevailing price.) Specialists are prohibited by law from handling customer orders other than limit orders. The specialist's book was once a looseleaf notebook but now it is, for most NYSE stocks, a computer screen. The specialist is not, with some exceptions, required to show this screen to other traders, exchange members, or the public, although he must disclose aggregate price information.
>
> As dealers, specialists buy and sell for their own account. They have an "affirmative obligation" to do so when it is necessary to provide liquidity. Specialists provide liquidity by buying or selling

> when there are no other bidders or offerers at or near the market price. The specialist tries to keep prices from making big jumps, by making a bid or offer that acts as a bridge when there is a wide gap between bids and offers. The specialist also has a "negative obligation," *not* to trade for his own account when there are already customers wanting to trade at or near the market price.

NYSE figures in 1990 show that specialists' purchases and sales as dealers accounted for 19 percent of all sales on the exchange. Id.

In a quote market, like NASDAQ, dealers quote bid and offer prices to other dealers. On NASDAQ, many dealers make markets in the same stock. Their inventory consists of their own positions and those of their customers. For example, a dealer may quote a bid of 95 (the price at which she will buy) and an offer of 98 (the price at which she will sell). The bid-offer spread compensates the dealer for the risk of taking positions in a stock (which decreases as the trading depth and volume increases).

In share of U.S. equity trading volume, NASDAQ's is gaining on the NYSE. In 1992, NASDAQ average dollar daily trading volume was approximately $3.5 billion as compared with approximately $7 billion on the NYSE, Market 2000, Exhibit 13. This can be compared to 1982, when NASDAQ was at approximately $.3 billion compared with the NYSE at approximately $2 billion. NASDAQ gained market share over this period despite the fact that from May 1989 to May 1983 the trade-weighted average spread on NASDAQ's National Market increased from 43 cents to 59 cents while the spread on NYSE held steady at 21. Does this mean customers are getting a raw deal on NASDAQ trades?

Why aren't competitive market makers in the same stock operating over a screen, better than a live auction market in which a specialist is given a monopoly in making a market in a stock? Consider the following justification from L. Benveniste, A. Marcus and W. Wilhelm, "What's Special About the Specialist," 32 J. of Financial Economics 61 (1992).

The chairman of the New York Stock Exchange, William Donaldson, recently asserted:

> When you have a human being in the middle of a trade working for you and a crowd of other buyers and sellers you can get the benefits of better bids and offers. (*Business Week,* November 5, 1990, p. 121)

This claim is representative of the widely-held belief among exchange members that the professional relationships that evolve on exchange floors yield benefits not easily duplicated by an anonymous exchange mechanism.

. . .

Floor brokers are easily identified and trade repeatedly with the specialist. We contend that this previously ignored layer of intermediation on exchange floors offers an opportunity for the specialist to reduce the costs of asymmetric information.

The second element of our argument is that asymmetric information imposes a burden on the exchange as well as on uninformed traders if the volume of uninformed (liquidity) trading is sensitive to the bid-ask spread. Brokers representing information trades may reap private benefits while sharing the costs of a lower volume of liquidity trading with the remainder of the exchange membership. In our model, the specialist, acting for the exchange membership, enforces sanctions that focus the burden of this externality on the offending broker. The exchange membership willingly subjects itself to this discipline because it recognizes that the long-term benefits of doing so outweigh the short-term private benefits of exploiting private information. Although each broker would find it privately beneficial to conceal the informational motivation for a trade, each is willing to be bound to a system that punishes such behavior. The specialist in our model acts as an enforcer of the agreement that protects the common good.

Although it may be relatively difficult for specialists to identify in advance floor brokers exploiting information on behalf of their principals, the stability and relatively small size of the trading community limit brokers' ability to systematically exploit private information by increasing the probability that those doing so will be identified after the fact.

. . .

An anonymous trading environment necessarily implies pooling of liquidity traders and information traders. As does earlier work, we find that in a pooling equilibrium, the specialist's inability to distinguish between members of the two classes of traders leads to a positive bid-ask spread (reflecting a transfer from uninformed to informed traders) that increases with the expected value of such information.

Identification and sanctioning of information traders provides the leverage necessary for the specialist to improve on the terms of trade that would result from pooling informed and uninformed traders. If the specialist can impose sanctions on a broker discovered to have exploited private information, he or she can always charge brokers representing uninformed traders a smaller bid-ask spread than they would face when pooled with informed traders. The threat of sanctions induces informed brokers to reveal their private information and allows the specialist to reduce losses by imposing an explicit or implicit charge on the informed traders. Since the specialist passes losses on to uninformed liquidity traders through the bid-ask spread, lower losses permit a reduction in the spread faced by uninformed traders.

Less obvious and more important is that under certain circumstances the specialist's leverage over informed brokers can actually lead to improvement in their terms of trade as well. The intuition behind this result rests on an assumption similar to that used by Admati and

Pfleiderer (1988), that uninformed trading demand is discretionary. If the reduction in the bid-ask spread charged to uninformed brokers swells the volume of liquidity trading (and thus specialist revenues) sufficiently, the specialist will be able to charge informed brokers a lower spread than would be possible in the pooling equilibrium. Thus the specialist's ability to improve the terms of trade for informed traders is contingent on the elasticity of liquidity volume with respect to transaction costs as well as on the value of private information.

4. Why is the NYSE losing market share to other domestic markets?

5. NYSE Rule 390 has been extensively debated over the years. J. Hasbrouck, G. Sofianos, and D. Sosebee, "New York Stock Exchange Systems and Trading Procedures," NYSE Working Paper # 93–01 (April 27, 1993), pp. 19–20, describes the Rule.

> The purpose of NYSE Rule 390 is to encourage order flow concentration and to discourage member firms from matching orders internally without exposing them to the auction process. Rule 390 prohibits, with certain exemptions, member firms from effecting proprietary trades and in-house agency crosses in NYSE-listed securities off an organized exchange. In 1976, the SEC limited the scope of Rule 390 by exempting agency transactions, provided the same member firm does not represent both sides of the trade (in-house agency crosses): *member firms may effect one-sided agency trades anywhere, anytime.*[56] In addition, SEC Rule 19c–3 exempts from Rule 390 securities *initially* listed on a U.S. exchange after April 26, 1979.[57] Member firms may trade, at any time, NYSE-listed securities on any organized domestic exchange where the securities are cross-listed or have unlisted trading privileges (see page 20) as well as on organized foreign exchanges.[58] Outside of Exchange business hours, member firms may also trade NYSE-listed securities in *foreign* over-the-counter markets. Broker-dealers that are not members of the NYSE are not subject to Rule 390.

*Examples* Broker-dealer John is a NYSE member and stock XYZ is listed on the NYSE since 1968 (XYZ is a "Rule 390 stock"). John cannot buy or sell XYZ for his own account in the U.S. over-the-counter market even outside NYSE trading hours. John has a 1,000–share customer buy order in XYZ and a 1,000–share customer sell order also in XYZ. During NYSE trading hours, John must cross the two orders (agency cross) on an organized (domestic or foreign) exchange. Outside NYSE trading hours, John may cross them in a foreign over-the-counter market.

**56.** In-house (two-sided) agency crosses remain subject to Rule 390.

**57.** A security initially listed on another exchange that subsequently transferred to the NYSE is subject to Rule 390 if the initial listing day (on the other exchange) was before April 26, 1979. Such a security is subject to Rule 390 even if the transfer to the NYSE occurred after April 26, 1979 (see example 6).

**58.** Trading of U.S. securities on foreign exchanges is subject to the registration and listing requirements of those exchanges.

John, however, can buy or sell XYZ for a customer (a one-sided agency trade) in the U.S. (or in a foreign) over-the-counter market during NYSE trading hours.

John can buy XYZ for his own account in a foreign over-the-counter market outside NYSE trading hours.

Stock ABC was initially listed on the NYSE in 1992; it is therefore a "19c–3 stock" and is not subject to Rule 390. John can buy or sell ABC for his own account in the U.S. over-the-counter market even during NYSE trading hours.

Stock CBA was initially listed on the Amex in 1983. In 1992 the stock moved to the NYSE. Stock CBA is subject to Rule 390.

Broker-dealer Mary is not a member of the NYSE and therefore is not subject to Rule 390. Provided Mary is not restricted by the rules of other U.S. exchanges she is a member of, she may buy and sell XYZ in the U.S. over-the-counter market even during NYSE trading hours.

At the end of 1992, 54 percent of NYSE-listed stocks were classified as 19c–3 stocks and were not subject to Rule 390.[59] In December 1992, 19c–3 stocks accounted for 40 percent of NYSE share volume and 31 percent of NYSE dollar volume. The Exchange accounts for 82 percent of the share volume in 19c–3 stocks and 83.2 percent of the share volume in Rule 390 stocks.[60]

Is Rule 390 anticompetitive? Can member firms of the NYSE trade NYSE listed stocks on SEAQ during NYSE trading hours?

6. Following the market break of 1987, the NYSE adopted certain circuit breakers, as described below, id., at 62.

NYSE Circuit Breakers
March 31, 1993

At current levels, eight points on the Dow Jones Industrial Average are equivalent to approximately one point on the S & P 500 Index.

| Event | Rule |
|---|---|
| The Dow Jones Industrial Average moves 50 points up or down from the previous day's close. (Approximately 6 S & P 500 points.) | In an up market, index arbitrage program buys in S & P 500 stocks must be executed on a minus or a zero-minus tick. In a down market, index arbitrage program sells (including short sales) in S & P 500 stocks must be executed on a plus or zero-plus tick. Applies for the remainder of the day, unless the DJIA moves back to within 25 points of the previous day's close. (Since 8/1/90, now has permanent approval) On expiration Fridays market-on- |

**59.** Of 2,678 issues (including common stocks, preferred stocks, warrants and rights), 1,457 were not subject to Rule 390.

**60.** Common stocks and warrants only. The market share figures are for the first six months of 1992.

| Event | Rule |
|---|---|
| | close orders to liquidate previously established stock positions against expiring derivative products are exempt from the index arbitrage restrictions. (Since 10/18/90) |
| The primary S & P 500 futures contract declines 12 points from the previous day's close. (Approximately 100 DJIA points.) | 5-minute sidecar.* New stop and stop limit orders in all stocks are banned for the rest of the day, except for those orders from individuals for 2,099 shares or less. Does not apply in the last 35 minutes of trading. (Since 10/19/88.) |
| The Dow Jones Industrial Average declines by 250 points from the previous day's close. (Approximately 30 S & P 500 points.) | Trading in all stocks is halted for one hour. (Since 10/19/88.) |
| The Dow Jones Industrial Average declines by 400 points from the previous day's close. (Approximately 50 S & P 500 points.) | Trading in all stocks is halted for two hours. (Since 10/19/88.) |

* In the sidecar procedure, all program trading market orders entered in SuperDot for NYSE-listed component stocks of the S & P 500 are diverted to a separate blind file. After the sidecar period ends, buy and sell orders are paired off and become eligible for execution. If there is an order imbalance, the specialist may make up the difference and/or adjust the price and resume trading. Alternatively, if the imbalance is large, the specialist with Floor Official permission may halt trading and publicly disseminate the imbalance information. If the imbalance is greater than 50,000 shares and if the stock is a "pilot" stock, then the imbalance information is publicly disseminated immediately after the sidecar period ends even if orderly trading has resumed. The pilot stocks consist of the 50 NYSE S & P 500 stocks with the highest market capitalizations plus any other component stocks of the Major Market Index.

Does the presence of such circuit breakers make it more or less attractive to trade on the NYSE?

## B. FOREIGN MARKETS

We turn now to the characteristics of two important foreign exchanges, London's SEAQ International and the Tokyo Stock Exchange (TSE).

R. Huang and H. Stoll, Major World Equity Markets: Current Structure and Prospects for Change

Monograph Series in Finance and Economics, pp. 2–20, 43–47 (N.Y.U.1991).

### II. London: Back to the Future

In the early 1970s, predictions in the United States of the demise of stock exchanges as then organized were commonplace. The Securities Acts Amendments of 1975 called for a National Market System in which the computer would make possible efficient trading of securities without the need for face-to-face contact on an exchange floor. Trading on the New York Stock Exchange (NYSE) has continued to flourish, albeit its market share has declined. But in the United Kingdom, the predicted future has arrived. Along with a variety of other significant changes, the "big bang" of October 1986 shifted trading to upstairs computer screens. In the wake of the "big bang" have come a variety of dislocations and problems, leading some observers to suggest that London's dramatic step into the future has been a backward step; but others argue that the changes in London are a vast improvement over the preceding antiquated system.

## A. The Changes of October 1986

On October 27, 1986, major changes in rules and operating procedures dramatically altered the London stock market.

### 1. Single Capacity Abolished

Before October 1986, members of the London Stock Exchange could act either as brokers or dealers (jobbers), but not both. Under this single capacity system, jobbers traded only for their own accounts on the exchange floor and could not trade with the public except through brokers. Brokers acted only as agents for public customers and could not take positions for their own accounts. The jobber was similar to the specialist on U.S. markets without the specialist's brokerage function of representing orders on the book of limit orders. The London market did not, and does not now, have a central book of limit orders.

Despite the fact that the London exchange had 4,300 individual members before the "big bang," restrictions on entry into various parts of the business and by certain types of firms had seriously impaired competition.[1] In addition to the fact that brokers could not act as jobbers, stock exchange rules made it difficult for brokers to establish an agency market in competition with jobbers. While two customer orders could be matched by a broker, the trade was subject to "put-through" rules that required disclosure to the jobber and the sharing of part of the order with the jobber.

The "big bang" abolished the single capacity system, allowing firms to act as both dealers and brokers. The potential conflicts of interest inherent in dual trading (that are currently attracting a great deal of attention in U.S. futures markets) were judged to be less important than the beneficial effects of increased competition in jobbing. The move to dual capacity increased the number of market-makers from the previous eight jobbers to about 35 firms, as firms previously restricted to brokerage entered market making. The amount of capital available for market making increased even more dramatically. The "big bang" gave firms

1. In 1981, there were 17 jobber firms and 234 broker firms. This and other details of the pre–1986 London Stock Exchange are taken from an unpublished "Observation Report" prepared by David Whitcomb in 1981.

greater flexibility in meeting trading needs of their customers since firms could act either as broker or principal vis-à-vis customers.

## 2. Fixed Brokerage Commissions Abolished

The abolition of fixed commissions occurred in London more than ten years after the United States' "May Day," 1975, but the delay was more than made up by wholesale changes in all aspects of the London market. As in the U.S., commission rates dropped and trading volume increased.

## 3. Removal of Entry Restrictions

Before the "big bang," member firms were organized as partnerships with unlimited liability, an organizational form that deterred the entry of other firms. Foreign firms were limited to a stake of 29.9 percent in any British firm. After the "big bang," membership was opened to corporate members, and foreign firms were allowed to purchase 100% of existing firms. Membership is open to any firm that meets capitalization and certain other requirements.

At the time of the "big bang," the London Stock Exchange merged with the International Securities Regulatory Organization (ISRO), the members of which consisted of the London branches of the largest foreign banks and securities houses that had previously traded in curobonds and non-UK equities. The entry of these firms greatly increased competition and market-making capacity.

## 4. International Focus

An impetus for the "big bang" was the recognition that the international competition could threaten London's historical role as a world financial center. At the same time, London observed opportunities to attract listings and trading activity from the continental markets. The London Stock Exchange changed its name to the International Stock Exchange for a time, and evidence indicates that London has attracted business from the continent, particularly Paris. London has the most extensive listing of foreign securities and the largest number of foreign member firms of any market in the world.

## 5. Regulatory Changes

The Financial Services Act of 1986 sets out the regulatory structure for securities and commodities. General oversight for these instruments lies in the Department of Trade and Industry. The Securities Investment Board (SIB) has regulatory authority over the London Stock Exchange. The SIB is a private organization, but the members are appointed by the government. Its rules have statutory force, but its powers are more limited than those of the Securities and Exchange Commission in the United States. The SIB oversees the self-regulatory organizations (SROs), such as the London Stock Exchange.

## 6. New Technology

The rule changes implemented in October 1986 were accompanied by the introduction of a new automated dealer quotation system—Stock Exchange Automated Quotation (SEAQ) system—modeled after the NASDAQ system. Within weeks of SEAQ's introduction, trading entirely migrated from the exchange floor to upstairs offices in which the SEAQ terminals were located. Since the London Exchange had operated as a continuous dealer market without a limit order book, the adoption of SEAQ was consistent with existing trading procedures and not as dramatic a change as is sometimes claimed.

More significant than the technology itself was the increased competition and increased disclosure made possible by rules changes and by the automated system. The entry of additional market-makers dramatically increased dealer capacity. SEAQ also required the public disclosure of bids and offers by all market-makers and the immediate reporting of transaction prices and quantities, something that had not previously been the case. Before the "big bang," jobbers posted only the midpoint price and disclosed the bid and ask prices only upon request from individual brokers. The disclosure provisions have caused some consternation among market-makers. Furthermore, it became possible for institutional investors to trade directly with dealers over the SEAQ system without the intervention of a broker, something that was not possible under the old rules.

## 7. Market Integrity

The admission of corporations to the London Stock Exchange changed the financial obligations of principals of firms from the unlimited liability under the old rules of organization. As a result other methods for insuring financial integrity of the market had to be implemented. These include capital requirements and guarantee funds along the lines implemented by U.S. securities markets. Still undergoing change are clearing and settlement arrangements, which are old-fashioned and slow. The London Stock Exchange runs a trade comparison system, TALISMAN, which validates trades of its members. While TALISMAN is computerized, settlement is still paper-based and takes place in two week rolling intervals.

. . .

## 8. Stock Classifications

With the introduction of SEAQ, the London Stock Exchange began to classify stocks according to market value and trading activity. The alpha category contains about 160 of the most active securities, the beta category, about 610 of the next most active, and the gamma category, the approximately 1450 least actively traded SEAQ securities. The delta category includes those securities not traded on SEAQ. In 1990, the classification system was again modified to reflect solely a stock's liquidity.

## B. The Functioning of the London Securities Market

### 1. The Trading System

The trading system of the London Stock Exchange is a competing dealer market in which dealers display quotes over computer terminals. The system is essentially the same as the NASDAQ system. The heart of the London market is the SEAQ system, which allows registered market-makers to change quotes and report transactions, but several different systems constitute the London market. The "big bang" brought major improvements in the *information system.* Data on transaction volumes, prices and bid-ask quotations received by SEAQ computers from dealers is disseminated over TOPIC, the London Stock Exchange's viewdata system. As in NASDAQ, a level one display gives the inside quote for any stock on the system, and a level two display gives the quotes of all dealers making a market in the stock. Prior to the "big bang" neither the inside quote nor the individual quotes of dealers were available to the public. Computer readable information on transactions and quotes is provided over the CRS–Lynx system to interested firms who wish to use the data to support internal trading systems.

. . .

### 2. Dimensions of the Market

#### (a) Volume of Trading

The dollar volume of trading in stocks in all UK exchanges in 1989 was approximately 663,000 million dollars, which compares with 431,000 million dollars for NASDAQ and about 1,240,000 million dollars for the NYSE. Table 1 shows the dramatic increase in volume in London, particularly around the "big bang." The value of volume in 1987 increased 113 percent over 1986, which compares with an increase of 32 percent for NASDAQ and an increase of 36 percent for the NYSE in that year. London share prices are low, averaging about £3 per share. A round lot is 1000 shares, or a total value of £3,000, which is $4,800 at an exchange rate of $1.6 per pound.

**Table 1. Volume in Listed Shares, All U.K. exchanges**

| Year | Annual Volume (million pounds) | Share volume (million shares) | Number of trades (thousands) | Average trade size (pounds) | Average price of share (pounds) | Percent change in volume |
|---|---|---|---|---|---|---|
| 1981 | 32387 | 24260 | 3944 | 8212 | 1.33 | |
| 1982 | 37414 | 26379 | 3883 | 9635 | 1.42 | 15.52 |
| 1983 | 56121 | 35314 | 4726 | 11875 | 1.59 | 50.00 |
| 1984 | 73119 | 42163 | 4849 | 15079 | 1.73 | 30.29 |
| 1985 | 105554 | 53655 | 5568 | 18957 | 1.97 | 44.36 |
| 1986 | 181211 | 77901 | 7638 | 23725 | 2.33 | 71.68 |
| 1987 | 386518 | 150420 | 13021 | 29684 | 2.57 | 113.30 |
| 1988 | 266024 | 103351 | 6717 | 39605 | 2.57 | – 31.17 |
| 1989 | 409273 | 131843 | 8505 | 48121 | 3.10 | 53.85 |

Source: ISE, *Quality of Markets Quarterly Review,* October/December, 1989.

### (b) Listed Equities

The London Stock Exchange equities are grouped into domestic equities and into foreign equities. At the end of 1989, 2,041 equity securities of U.K. and Irish companies were listed on the London Stock Exchange, and 680 overseas equities were listed. These constitute the "Official List." Less stringent listing requirements apply to the USM (Unlisted Securities Market) and the Third Market, both of which are intended for smaller and newer companies. In comparison, the total number of equity securities on NASDAQ is in excess of 5,000.

### (c) Market-makers

While the number of market-makers increased significantly as compared with the number of jobbers before the "big bang," the number is not large in comparison to the number of market-makers on NASDAQ. In December 1986, 33 market-makers were registered. That number increased slightly until the end of 1988, and by 1990 declined to 28 market-makers. The number is small in comparison to the over 500 different market-makers in NASDAQ. As in NASDAQ, stocks in the London Stock Exchange differ according to the number of market-makers posting quotes in the stocks. Table 2 indicates that NASDAQ issues tend to have more market-makers.

**Table 2. Distribution of Number of Issues by Number of Market-makers, London Stock Exchange and NASDAQ**

| Market-makers | Number of Issues London (1989) | Number of Issues Nasdaq (1988) |
|---|---|---|
| 18 or more | 14 | 223 |
| 10–17 | 177 | 615 |
| 6–9 | 273 | 1113 |
| 1–5 | 1907 | 1090 |

Source: ISE, *Quality of Markets Quarterly Review*, October/December, 1989.

In both London and NASDAQ, business in a particular stock tends to concentrate in a few market-makers. The Quality of Markets Unit of the London Stock Exchange estimates that 8 market-makers are responsible for more than 85 percent of the volume in alpha stocks.

## 3. Cost of Trading

The London Stock Exchange's Quality of Markets Unit carries out surveys of commission cost and tracks bid-ask quotes of dealers.

. . .

### (b) Bid–Ask Spread

Much attention has focused on the problems of competing market-makers in the London market, the presence of aggressive quote setting and the resultant lack of profitability. Table 4 provides information on average inside quoted bid-ask spreads for standard transaction sizes (the so-called "touch at yellow strip") by stock category. These spreads are not low by NYSE standards. According to data from McInish and Wood (1989) shown in Table 5, the average spread for the most active twenty percent of NYSE stocks (about 280 stocks) was 0.62 percent in 1987.

**Table 4. Inside Quotes by Stock Category and Time Period, International Stock Exchange, In percent**

| Time period | Alpha stocks | Beta stocks | Gamma stocks |
|---|---|---|---|
| Pre-crash | 0.83 | 1.76 | 3.00 |
| December, 1987 | 1.52 | 3.82 | 6.12 |
| December, 1988 | 0.85 | 3.20 | 5.30 |
| December, 1989 | 1.20 | 3.40 | 6.30 |

Source: ISE, *Quality of Markets Quarterly Review,* October/December, 1989.

**Table 5. Bid–Ask Spreads for NYSE Stocks Classified into Quintiles According to Trading Frequency, Calendar Year 1987**

| | Percentage spread |
|---|---|
| Most active | 0.62 |
| 2 | 0.99 |
| 3 | 1.38 |
| 4 | 1.59 |
| Least active | 2.06 |

Source: McInish and Wood (1989), Table 1. The spreads are those prevailing at the end of the day.

The spread on the London Stock Exchange is comparable to the spread on NASDAQ, perhaps somewhat lower. Stoll (1989, p. 128) reports spreads for 820 NASDAQ/NMS stocks in December 1984. Spreads range from 1.16 percent for the 10 percent of most actively traded stocks to 6.87 percent for the 10 percent of least actively traded stocks. While these spreads in 1984 are somewhat higher than London Stock Exchange spreads in 1989, they are not markedly different. Furthermore, no attempt has been made to control for differences in volume, risk and other factors. It is difficult to say that London Stock Exchange spreads are too high or too low.

Differences in reported spreads are to be expected between the NYSE and either the NASDAQ market or the London Stock Exchange even when comparable stocks are examined. First, the limit order book on the NYSE tends to narrow spreads, as Stoll (1985) notes. Limit orders act like a competing dealer and thereby reduce spreads just as competing dealers reduce spreads. Probably more important is the fact that public limit orders offer free trading options to the rest of the market. When market prices changes slightly and limit orders are not adjusted, spreads will be smaller than the inside spread of competing dealers who adjust quotes quickly to reflect current market conditions.

Second, spreads also tend to be larger in a competing dealer market because it is more difficult to guard against informational trading. A trader with information can "hit" each of fifteen dealers in a stock with 1000 shares, thereby disposing of 15,000 shares at the current quote. Each of the 15 dealers must set a quote that provides protection against this possibility and against the greater difficulty of liquidating his position when all other dealers acquire similar positions. If there is only one dealer, he can trade the first 1000 shares (or even a larger amount) at a narrow spread and then adjust the price as additional orders arrive. The final effect is the same, but the spread is greater in the multiple dealer market.

. . .

### (c) Disclosure of Transaction Prices

One of the most controversial accommodations to market-makers was the London Stock Exchange ruling in February 1989 permitting the delayed publication of the transaction size and price until the following day for transactions exceeding 100,000 pounds. The argument for such delay was that market-makers disclosing such a large trade would cause prices to move against them and make it difficult to unwind their position. The Elwes committee brought this argument and recommended a smaller delay of up to 90 minutes (now implemented) in the publication of price information for transactions more than three times NMS (£750,000).*

The failure to disclose block trades disadvantages public investors who trade at unfair prices. Indeed, the argument that disclosure must be postponed to give the market-maker time to dispose of the block is based on the proposition that market-makers have a right to trade on inside market information, something that would not be permitted in the United States. The predicament of the market-maker who must dispose of a block is understandable, but if the block is fairly priced, disclosure of that price might encourage traders to buy. In U.S. markets, prices tend to rebound from the block price, thereby giving buyers of blocks a positive return and an incentive to participate.

Immediate disclosure of block prices might alter the procedures by which blocks are traded in the U.K. For example, a market-maker might try to find the other side of a block before executing the trade (as is often the case in the U.S.). Under current and proposed arrangements, the block is traded by the dealer at the wrong price and then sold to the unsuspecting public at the wrong price. It would be preferable to negotiate before the block and determine a fair price that could immediately be disclosed to the public. If the risk is great, the price of the block can incorporate a discount for that risk.

. . .

M. Sato, "The Tokyo Equity Market: Its Structure and Policies," in Japan Securities Research Institute
Capital Markets and Financial Services in Japan, pp. 40–55 (1992).

## 1. Introduction

Tokyo equity market has drawn much attention from the international community in the recent past. Yet, despite many talks, it still

* NMS means normal market size.

appears not to have been very well understood by foreigners due partly to its recent emergence as a major equity market and partly to the linguistic and cultural differences between Japan and Western countries.

This paper, not intended to provide a highly analytical discussion nor an empirical study, simply attempts to help understand the Tokyo equity market. It covers two major areas: One is its structural characteristics, or, what features the Tokyo market in comparison with other markets in the world; the other is its major policies, or, how the market is undertaking to further develop in the future. Discussion of these two aspects is expected to make the market clearer to those who are interested.

## 2. Mechanism/Structure

Structurally, or in terms of trading mechanism, the Tokyo market is characterized by three major elements: a continuous auction market based on order-book system; a high degree of automation; and integration of cash and derivative markets.

### (1) Continuous Auction Market

First of all, the Tokyo market is a continuous public auction market based on an order-book system. All orders, either limited or at market, are placed by member broker/dealer firms with what we call "Saitori" members who are solely in charge of matching these orders in their order-books in accordance with the auction principles, i.e., price priority and time precedence. The Saitori members are not allowed to trade any listed stocks for their own accounts. Thus, the Tokyo market is a pure "order-driven" market without any responsible market-makers.

From the international perspective, the market differs from some European markets in that it adopts a "continuous", as against "call" method of trading, meaning that any listed stocks are available for trading during the entire trading hours. It is also different from a "dealer" market in that it is "order-driven" rather than "quote-driven". A typical dealer market exists in London and over-the-counter market in the United States, known as NASDAQ, where market-makers competitively indicate their asks and bids on screen to which brokers and public investors react. Further, within the family of order-driven market, it is unlike some Asian exchanges or derivative markets in the United States in that it uses an order-book system rather than "board" or "open-outcry" system to match buy and sell orders continuously. Finally, even within the group of order-driven market based on order-book system, the market is not perfectly the same as others in that it is without any help of responsible market-makers such as "specialists" on the New York Stock Exchange and elsewhere.

Rationales behind the features are several. First, need for providing immediacy of trading has commanded the adoption of a continuous rather than call method of trading, although a batch trading is used at the opening of trading session since the market does not trade for 24 hours. The method also permits to provide market information on a continuous basis, of course. Indeed, the immediacy requirement has caused many markets in the world to shift from a call to continuous method of trading, most notably in France in 1986.

Second, an order-book system is preferred to a board or open-outcry system chiefly because of fairness consideration. An open order-book permits the fairest treatment of all orders, large and small, by matching them in strict compliance with the auction principle and making the matching process visible to all concerned. A board system seems to favor floor traders and investors represented by them as against those not represented because of the absence of an order-book widely publicized. An open-outcry system may not achieve time precedence, since all orders must be handled as "discretionary" orders. In addition, the Tokyo market trades too many shares to be handled by bilateral bargains in a crowd, and too heavily to permit brokers/dealers themselves to write offers on the trading board; hence a middleman specialized in matching operation is needed and can be afforded by the market.

Third and more importantly perhaps, there are several reasons why the Tokyo market adopts an order-driven rather than quote-driven system. Historically, Japan has no tradition of dealers' quoting asks and bids to make markets for brokers and public investors. More essentially, Japan, as a matter of capital market policy, emphasizes the importance of concentrating all orders into a single market in order to provide best prices to investors. Given this policy, public limit orders, which are not allowed to compete with market maker asks and bids under a quote-driven system, must be fully provided for. If not, there will be an incentive for brokerage firms handling public orders to create in-house limit-order books and order matching systems or to act as dealers, resulting in fragmentation of market to the detriment of investors' interests. Further, admitting that a quote-driven system can maximize market liquidity by providing immediacy of trading, an order-driven system may achieve the same goal by strengthening investor confidence in fairness of the market and providing maximum opportunity for orders to meet with counter-orders. While actual quote-driven markets are said to be less transparent in actual trade consummation than they first appear, an order-driven market with open order-book permits maximum transparency to ensure the fairest price formation. Finally, advantages of quote-driven market would not be too great and disadvantages rather pronounced in the particular circumstances of Japan. Generally, a quote-driven system can take care of "block" orders better than an order-driven one, given sufficient capital base of market makers, but competition among market makers is crucial to successful working of the entire system. In Japan, while block orders are being taken care of by so-called "crossing" technique, proper competition among market makers would not be too easy to achieve, given the industrial structure of securities business in Japan.

Thus, the Tokyo market is purely of public auction type. Then, the question may be, "How can the market be stable without any market makers responsible for the stabilization?"

Both phenomenal and institutional factors may answer the question. Phenomenally, there is active private, or individual, participation in the market, tending to stabilize stock prices with diverse investment judgements. Of a total turnover of 190 trillion yen (or US $1.3 trillion) and total 29 million trades in 1990, roughly one third is accounted for by individual investors. Numbering approximately 10 million, they act as stabilizer, as shown by the fact that they bought massively immediately after stock falls like 1987 October crash and recent plunges. Institutional traders appear to behave more on a "herd instinct" due perhaps to their concern about self-protection. Also, phenomenon of cross-holding of shares within the corporate sector, unique to Japan, may provide a sort of "downward rigidity" in critical times.

Institutionally, member broker/dealer firms, especially the big-sized, can and do act as de facto market makers since they are allowed to trade on their own accounts, though on certain conditions. Also, "crossing" of orders substantially mitigates the impact of block trading upon stock prices, under which a broker finds counterparty to large orders beforehand or he himself becomes counterparty if he finds no one to counter, with actual crossing being effected in the order book in accordance with the auction principle. Further, a so-called "circuit-breaker", i.e., price limit and trading halt, does work to stabilize the market especially when investors behave rather irrationally.

**(2) Highly Computerized Market**

The Tokyo equity market is also characterized by a high degree of automation of exchange operations.

In the Exchange, there are two different kinds of trading facilities. One is a trading floor where people meet to trade stocks in a traditional manner, the other a totally computerized trading system called "Computer-assisted Order Routing and Execution System" ("CORES"), introduced in 1982. More than 1,400 of all domestic stocks and all foreign stocks are at present traded by CORES, leaving most active 150 stocks to the floor trading.

CORES is believed to have performed quite well. Operational efficiency has been enhanced mainly through elimination of data reentries which had been necessary before in the sequential process of order collection, routing, matching, trade confirmation and clearing and settlements. Accuracy of trading has been achieved because of the avoidance of errors in such processes that are inherent in manual works. Also, cost-savings have taken place on the members' side in the form of elimination of traders on the floor, and the market as a whole has enjoyed an increased capacity to handle trades thanks to greatly reduced burdens of trade comparison.

Regarding the quality of market, visibility has been enhanced by duplicating the order-book on screens at members' headquarters and information dissemination quickened and improved, both of which, together with speedier order routing and matching, are believed to have contributed to more liquidity of the market.

Then, the question may be, "Why not go to entire automation to cover all the trades on the Exchange?" The issue has been considered in light of the advantages of modern technology on one hand and those of traditional physical floor on the other. True, CORES has proved efficiency, accuracy and speediness of trading. However, liquidity of the market might suffer from entire automation, since order flows are generated, to some extent at least, by subtle interactions of human activities on the floor, including general atmosphere at the floor, facial expression of rivals, so-called "floor gossips", and so on, all of which can hardly be computerized. Also, volatility of the market might be enhanced, were it not for the physical floor where information behind price moves can be quickly exchanged among traders. In other words, prices might be "over-shooting" or "under-shooting" if traders are just reacting to price moves on screen without well understanding the reasons for the moves. Difficulty might be compounded by less easy crossing of orders on the screen than on the floor due to the "mechanical" nature of screen trading. All these, together with costs involved in an entire automation, not to speak of nostalgia of older generations and tourist consideration, have led the Exchange to a new system which maintains but restructures the floor by using the modern technology.

The system is essentially to combine the advantages of the technology, efficiency and accuracy, with those of trading floor, intimacy and visibility. While small orders, up to 3,000 shares, are routed, matched and reported back all electronically, larger orders are routed through members' booths located on the floor down to the trading posts where the orders are merged with the small orders by key operation of Saitori members. The new system, fully operative since this March, enables us to smoothly handle a trading volume of 5 billion shares a day, instead of 2 billion shares under the old system.

Besides, all the derivative markets on the Exchange have been computerized in the same fashion as CORES, futures on Japanese government bonds, options on the futures, futures and options on "TOPIX" ("Tokyo Stock Price Index") and futures on U.S. Treasury bonds.

. . .

Broadly, there appear to be four alternative patterns of providing investors with a global market. One is an exchange market which is open for 24 hours a day and hence accessible from any part of the world through computer terminals. A sort of international division of labor exists under this approach, with a "home" market being in charge of trading its own stocks exclusively. Second is to link different exchanges in different time zones to permit investors to trade stocks whenever they want to do so. Multiple listing is essential to this approach, and the market in effect goes around the world as foreign exchange market currently does. Third is defactor global market run by broker/dealer firms, especially the big sized. Such firms may wish to actively make market for 24 hours through their international communication networks, using in-house, exchange or off-exchange market, or combination of these. Last is to use communication networks held by a third party, most notably information vendors. Some of them now appear to be capable of providing trading facilities by combining electronic terminals located over the world with an automated order matching center, which may work for 24 hours.

Now, which is the most desirable? In our view, the second alternative should be adopted in light of two normative criteria, i.e., investor protection and inter-market competition.

Judging from the investor protection criterion, a global market to be created by information vendors is least satisfactory in the absence of effective means to prevent defaults and fraudulent activities from occurring, not to speak of other regulatory requirements. The same will apply, though to a lesser extent, to the concept of global market to be run by broker/dealer firms. On the other hand, the idea of an exclusive exchange market operating for 24 hours, while satisfying the investor protection criterion, falls short of the inter-market competition norm, since it means a monopoly of equity trading. These have brought us to the conclusion that the exchange-linkage alternative is the best to serve the interests of investors worldwide.

While we are aware that the discussion is more theoretical than practical at the moment, given most exchanges behaving independently of each other with sporadic and unsystematic linkages between them, we believe that for that very reason it is important for major marketplaces to have a clear perspective toward a truly global market. Once the notion of linking exchanges in different time zones is accepted, efforts should be made to harmonize rules and practices between the exchanges in order to prevent so-called "regulatory arbitrage" or "race to the bottom" from arising and to enable investors to enjoy the benefits of inter-market competition in its true sense.

### (4) Brokerage Commissions: Fixed vs. Negotiable

Finally, we are to maintain the present fixed brokerage commissions but to review and revise them flexibly.

We are fully aware that the Tokyo's is the only major market that still maintains fixed brokerage commissions, and that "financial deregulation" is the word of the day. Nevertheless, any financial system is facing trade-off between stability and efficiency, as discussed earlier in connection with "circuit-breaker". If one stresses financial efficiency, he must do it at the cost of more systemic instabilities, and financial stability at the cost of more competitive inefficiencies. The choice between them depends upon the circumstances in which a financial system is situated, and eventually upon the value judgment of a society.

Tokyo has a high degree of concentration of equity trading in the exchange market, with no substantial outflows of trading to off-exchange or overseas market. Experiences abroad tell us that such outflows have often triggered deregulation of brokerage commissions. Meanwhile,

Japan's securities industry is characterized by high concentration of market shares in a limited number of large broker/dealer firms. Given an economy of scale inherent in securities business, drastic deregulation will lead to serious financial turbulences which not only severely hit smaller firms but also render the whole system quite unstable to the ultimate detriment of benefits of investors in general. Also, substantial decline in commission rates due to severe competition among securities firms may well discourage them from functioning as block positioners and market makers who provide additional liquidity to the market in exchange of commission revenues. Investors may face higher liquidity costs in return for lower direct trading costs, as a result. Further, deregulation of brokerage commissions would surely hit small investors by raising their trading costs in light of experiences in many countries, running counter to our policy to call them back to the market.

These considerations have led us to maintaining the present fixed commission system. But this by no means, means that we need not pay attention to the interests of public investors. Frequent and flexible review of commission rates will be made in future, as we did in the past.

. . .

### *Question*

1. How would you compare the trading and price reporting systems of SEAQ and TSE to the NYSE and NASDAQ?

2. Which market has the best system?

---

## C. WORLDWIDE COMPETITION BETWEEN STOCK MARKETS

The following pieces examine some important aspects of the competition between stock markets worldwide.

### AILSA RÖELL, "COMPARING THE PERFORMANCE OF STOCK EXCHANGE TRADING SYSTEMS"

In The Internationalization of Capital Markets and The Regulatory Response, ed. J. Fingleton, pp. 167–177 (1992)

#### 8.1 INTRODUCTION

The past few years have seen an unprecedented increase in international competition for stock trading business among European stock exchanges. In particular, London's SEAQ International market has rapidly captured a large share of trading in blue-chip foreign equities. This has fuelled policymakers' interest in the organisation and regulation of stock exchange trading. Is it possible to recapture trading volume that has moved abroad? What determines the success or failure of a stock trading system? How do investors, listed companies and market professionals fare when rules and regulations are changed? These are some of the issues that are central to the policy debate.

In this chapter I would like to describe first a few stylised facts concerning the liquidity of the markets in French cross-listed equities. This will set the stage for a more theoretical discussion of the relative merits of the market institutions used for trading in Paris (and many other European centres) and in London. This includes some comments about market transparency, a very contentious issue in the EC at present.

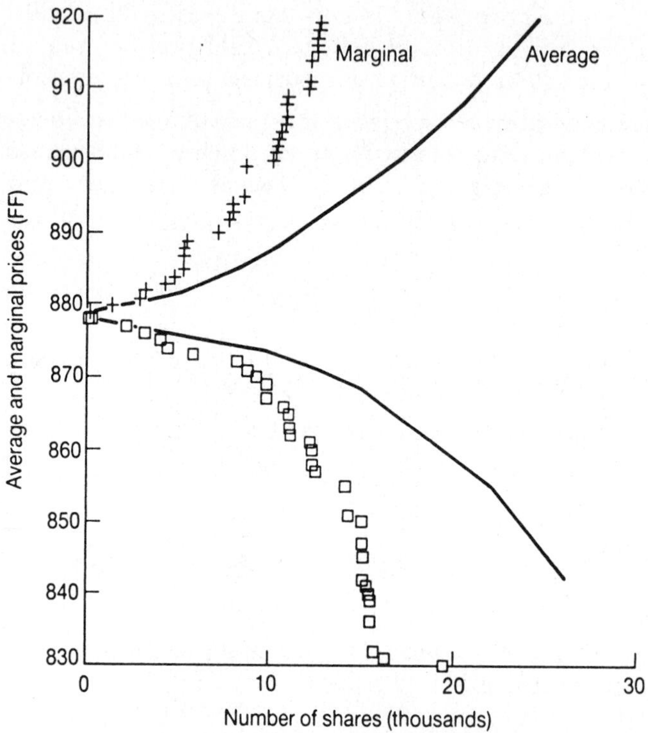


**Fig. 1.** Paris Limit orders, BSN, 24 June 1991.

## 8.2 THE MARKETS IN CROSS–LISTED FRENCH EQUITIES

It is not easy to compare the liquidity of the Paris Bourse and London's SEAQ International. The reason is that the trading systems are so different that one invariably finds oneself comparing apples with pears.

Measuring liquidity in Paris is relatively easy. The CAC (Cotation Assistée en Continu) electronic auction system provides a continuous picture of the reigning limit order book. Any trader who requires *immediacy* (trading without any delay to search for, or simply hope for, better terms of trade) need only hit these limit-orders to obtain a deal.

Thus, with a picture of the limit order book in hand, it is simple to compute the cost of trading for any given deal size.

Figures 1 and 2 show typical examples of the Paris limit order book. Figure 1 plots the average price a broker looking at the limit order book knows that he can obtain (pay) for sell (buy) orders of different size, for shares in a major French company (BSN). Note that the market is very *tight:* the 'fourchette', or bid-ask spread for minimal size deals, is very small indeed (less than 0.5%). On the other hand the market is not very *deep.* For larger deals, say of size 20,000 shares or more (about FF 20 million or more in value), the effective spread is quite wide: the average price obtained when selling a block this size would be more than 5% below the price paid when buying it. And beyond this size the limit order book soon runs out altogether. Figure 2 rounds out the picture by giving an impression of the extra liquidity supplied to the market by 'hidden orders': that is, portions of limit orders that are there to be executed against but invisible to the users of the system. Agents like to hide part of their larger orders in this way so as not to alarm market participants. In any case these 'hidden orders' do not seem to be overwhelming in relative size: in Figure 2, a typical case, they enhance the depth of the market by increasing the size one can trade at any given bid-ask spread by roughly ⅓ to ½.

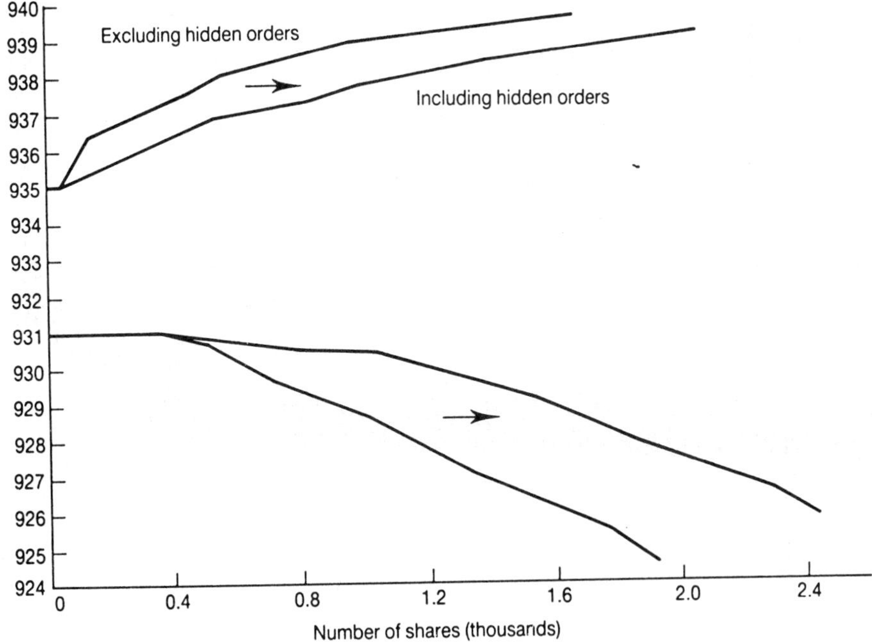


**Fig. 2.** Axa–Midi, 22 July 1991, best few limit orders in Paris.

If you are contemplating a trade in Paris, what you see is what you get (apart from the hidden orders). Measuring the liquidity of the London market is more difficult, because prices are often negotiated to yield a better deal than is quoted onscreen. Market makers display bid and ask prices onscreen, together with the quantity for which they undertake to guarantee these prices to all customers (i.e. the trade size for which their price is 'firm'. This quantity must equal at least the NMS—Normal Market Size—for the security in question, set by the Stock Exchange at roughly the median trade size). But in practice customers who telephone a market maker to execute a deal can generally negotiate a better price or a larger quantity than quoted, especially if the deal is of substantial size.

As shown by the 'single market maker' prices in Figure 3, the London market in French equities is not very tight. The market touch (the difference between the best bid and ask quotes) at minimum trade sizes generally exceeds that in Paris by a factor of about 2. If it were the case that traders could only rely on the firm quotes of single market makers, the market would not be very deep either. Figures 1 and 3 concern the same security (BSN) at the same moment of time, and are drawn to the same scale. Based on these figures one would conclude that the cost of immediacy in French equities is lower in Paris over the entire range of trade sizes.

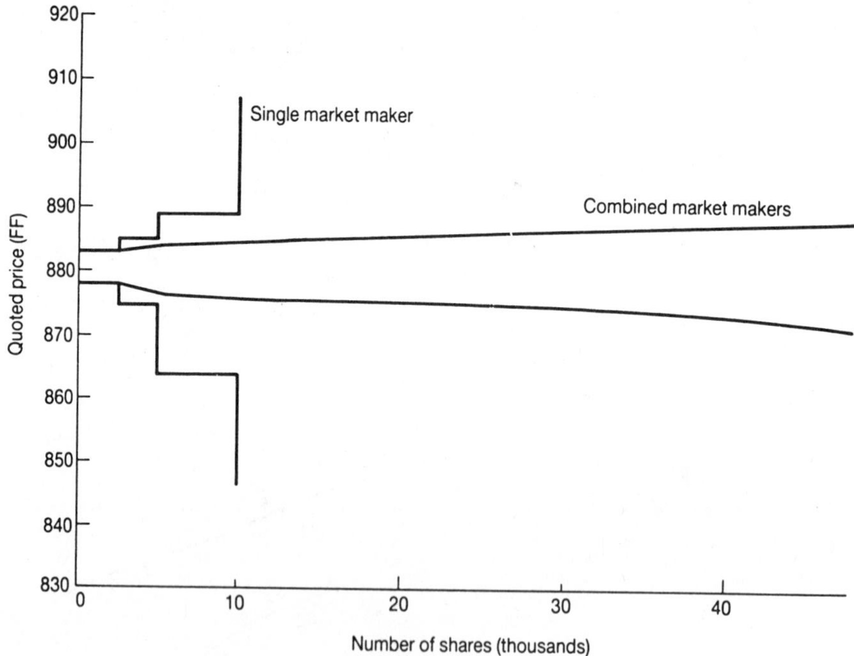


**Fig. 3.** SEAQ quotes for BSN, 24 June 1991.

Realised transaction prices present a rather different picture from market makers' quotes. Table 1 displays the average deviation between the transaction price and the quoted market mid-price for a selection of French equities on SEAQ International. This measure roughly represents half the realised bid-ask spread (but note that inaccurate reporting of deal times leads the transaction price to stray away from the presumed contemporaneous mid-price, so that this measure may be an overestimate). In Table 1, average realised spreads *decrease* with transaction size. Moreover, trade sizes far exceeding NMS and market makers' quoted sizes are commonplace. Thus the market is rather deeper than one would infer by looking at market makers' quotes.

**Table 1 Average percentage deviation of transaction price from market mid-price on SEAQ International, May-July 1991, for selected French equities**

| *Stock* | *Normal market size (NMS)* | *Median trade size* | *Price deviation for trade size ranges:* | | | |
|---|---|---|---|---|---|---|
| | | | *All* | *1/10 NMS and below* | *1/10 NMS to NMS* | *Above NMS* |
| *Axa-Midi* | *1000* | *1000* | *0.823* | *1.522 (30)* | *0.736 (183)* | *0.794 (177)* |
| *B.S.N.* | *2500* | *1000* | *0.565* | *0.693 (202)* | *0.498 (659)* | *0.[illegible]52 ([illegible]14)* |
| *Carrefour* | *500* | *500* | *0.690* | *0.939 (73)* | *0.704 (428)* | *[illegible] 611 (456)* |
| *Elf Aquitaine* | *5000* | *4800* | *0.670* | *0.860 (138)* | *0.659 (703)* | *0.639 (588)* |
| *Gen. des Eaux* | *500* | *500* | *0.572* | *0.726 (102)* | *0.549 (497)* | *0.563 (505)* |
| *L'Oreal* | *2500* | *1500* | *0.687* | *1.031 (52)* | *0.638 (353)* | *0.686 (198)* |
| *Pernod-Ricard* | *1000* | *615* | *0.673* | *1.084 (37)* | *0.597 (152)* | *0.685 (106)* |
| *Schneider* | *2000* | *1500* | *0.852* | *1.291 (37)* | *0.872 (157)* | *0.640 (91)* |
| *Un Ass Paris* | *2000* | *3000* | *0.659* | *0.824 (19)* | *0.600 (264)* | *0.693 (369)* |

*Number of transactions in parentheses.*

It is not clear, however, whether Table 1 really represents the price immediacy. Did the larger deals require extensive negotiation or delay before the price could be agreed? The data do not provide this information.

To summarise the facts: there has been considerable migration of trading volume, and in particular of larger deals, towards SEAQ International. Indeed, on occasion the day's trading volume in a blue-chip continental European equity on SEAQ international can exceed that on the domestic market, though on average the domestic market trading volume remains considerably higher (by a factor of about 3 in the case of France). The data on trading costs and liquidity suggest that Paris's electronic auction market provides tighter spreads for small deals but that the limit order book is not deep enough to accommodate large deals at prices that are competitive with those obtained from London's market makers. The London market makers' firm quotes are not particularly tight or deep; but the transaction data suggest that when asked to improve upon their firm quotes, they routinely do so; especially for large deals.

## 8.3 DISCUSSION OF TRADING STRUCTURE AND POLICY ISSUES

It is not just for French equities that large deals have migrated to London following their introduction onto the SEAQ International system. There is the same pattern in the trading of blue-chip equities from many other European countries such as Spain, Italy and Sweden. One can think of a number of different reasons why this might be so. Some are inherent in the trading systems used. Some concern additional specifications not inextricably tied to the trading system used. And some have nothing to do with the methods and regulation of trading at all.

In Paris, Madrid, Stockholm and now Milan also, shares are traded on a continuous electronic auction, using variants of a system developed by the Toronto stock exchange. This system differs from London's SEAQ system along a number of different dimensions.

### *Public Limit Order Exposure*

One important difference lies in the way entry into market making is regulated. In Paris, any member of the general public is free to 'make' the market by instructing a broker to input limit orders into the system on his behalf. Thus in theory everyone can come in and provide liquidity on the spur of the moment. In London, only registered market makers can display their limit orders on the screen: there is no 'public limit order exposure' (PLOE). While there is no great barrier to entry into market making (any stock exchange member who passes minimum competence and capital adequacy standards qualifies), day-to-day liquidity provision by members of the public is ruled out. Thus ordinary members of the public cannot trade directly with each other as in Paris; all trading must go via the market makers (unless one has access to a network of potential counterparties to trade with, and that is not worth building up except for large institutional investors who trade regularly and in size).

It is a common perception that this lack of PLOE alone increases transaction costs in London because ordinary traders cannot avoid giving a cut to the intermediary, namely the market maker's spread ('jobber's turn'), even when willing counterparties are available. But would not competition among market makers eliminate such an opportunity for excessive profit? Figure 4 shows the number of market makers per share for the French equities traded on SEAQ International. Securities with less than 10 registered market makers are rare. It seems unlikely that there are substantial opportunities for oligopoly profit.

More prosaically, the high spread in London for smaller deals may simply reflect the order processing costs involved. The process of trading by telephoning a market maker and the paperwork involved are costly in terms of time and trouble. Paris's automatic system, where trades are executed directly and electronically at the touch of a button, is simply less costly. And even with automatic execution of small orders in London, a trade between two final customers would still tend to be more costly as it necessarily involves intervention of a market maker, i.e. two separate transactions. Such order processing cost differentials clearly loom larger for smaller deals, explaining why London is less competitive in that category of trades.

**Fig. 4.** SEAQ market makers per security.

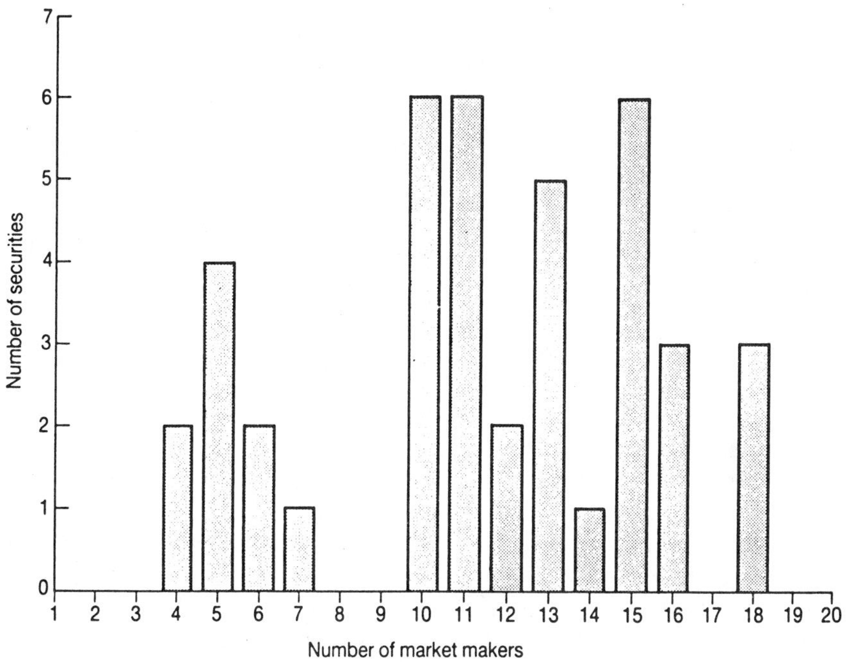

### *Transparency and Last Trade Publication*

A second important difference, and the focus of the current debate about EC regulatory policy, is the *transparency* of the two types of market. Can all participants see the order flow promptly and simultaneously? On the electronic auction markets, all trades are necessarily inputted into the system at the moment they are executed. It is thus relatively simple for the exchange authorities to publish a wide range of information about recent deals: their size and price, and even the identities of the brokers involved. On a telephone dealing market accurate and prompt publication of trading information is harder to achieve. Traders have to be explicitly required to report their trades promptly and accurately. And traders who do not wish to reveal information about their current deals can easily evade such requirements and delay their trade reports, for instance by entering into provisional agreements to trade that are not officially finalised until some time later. In short, the London system is inherently less transparent.

In addition, the exchange authorities in London have deliberately chosen not to try to enforce immediate trade reporting and publication. In the international equity section of the market exchange the authorities have not imposed any trade publication requirements at all, while for domestic equities (in response to pressure from market makers) publication of large deals is quite slow. The justification for this is that market makers can quote a better price if they are able to lay off a position they take on before it becomes publicly known that the deal is overhanging the market, moving the market price adversely.

It should be emphasized that there is a pure redistribution of trading costs from large and informed traders to small traders at work here. Why would a market maker offer a better price for large deals that are not published? Precisely because large deals in particular convey information; the market maker can take advantage of the fact that others do not have this information by trading at a price that does not reflect it yet, after compieting the initial deal. So the initial trader's gain is the rest of the market's loss. In equilibrium, market spreads for all deals (in particular those that are too small to convey much information) will widen, as market makers need to protect themselves against competitors who have superior order flow information, as well as against traders with superior information.

Clearly, a market maker who is not subject to immediate trade publication can outcompete those who are, who have no window of time before everyone else knows about a trade. Thus it is not surprising that large trades gravitate towards the market with the slowest publication of trades: large institutional traders, and the market makers who vie for their business, prefer a market with slower trade publication. This point has been recognised by policy-makers. Thus in the debate about EC regulations, continental exchange authorities have tended to push for the imposition of greater transparency across the board, and in particular, for faster trade publication in London. Meanwhile London authorities argue that the current system is very successful and that prompt trade publication would drive away business (not just back to continental Europe, but also back to the USA and other countries whose shares are traded on SEAQ International). If it ain't broke, why fix it?

In this context it is interesting to note the new Paris proposals for reporting of block trades. Up to now, stock exchange member firms who arrange negotiated block deals have been required to report them promptly as a 'cross transaction' on the CAC system, where the information is displayed to all participants. The new proposals delay the publication of this information. It is hoped that this will increase the volume of block deals done in Paris and within exchange trading hours.

This tendency towards reduced market transparency as a result of competition among exchanges has a beggar-thy-neighbour ring to it. Why not have the EC impose greater transparency, a principle that has long guided US policy-making. Or would the damage to London's position as an international marketplace for large transactions be too great?

*Negotiating Deals*

Both the limit order book in Paris and the firm quotes of the market makers in London are generally not deep enough to accommodate most of the transactions exceeding the median trade size in London. This is not surprising. Any agent who places a limit order (or displays a firm quote) is in effect giving an option to trade at a fixed price to counterparties. If a counterparty trades just as the market price moves through the limit order, or if he trades on superior information, the placer of the limit order loses out.

**Table 2. Market makers in French sector of SEAQ International, June 1991.**

| | | |
|---|---|---|
| BZW | Barclays de Zoete Wedd | 41 |
| CCF | CCF | 9 |
| CSFB | Credit Suisse First Boston | 3 |
| CNW | County NatWest | 31 |
| LYON | Credit Lyonnais | 41 |
| ENSK | Enskilda Sec | 33 |
| GOL | Goldman Sachs | 31 |
| JCAP | James Capel | 32 |
| KLWT | Kleinwort Benson | 19 |
| LEHM | Lehman Brothers | 14 |
| MER | Merrill Lynch | 17 |
| MSI | Morgan Stanley | 28 |
| NOR | Nomura International | 9 |
| UBS | Phillips & Drew | 41 |
| RFS | Robert Fleming | 28 |
| WBG | SG Warburg | 41 |
| SAL | Salomon Brothers International | 6 |
| SNC | Smith New Court | 17 |
| SGDA | Soc Gen S.T. | 27 |

The last column gives the number of French SEAQ International equities in which the market maker is registered.

Thus it is not surprising to see a reluctance to provide continuous liquidity. Telephone negotiation of large deals (for smaller deals, negotiation is not worth the time and trouble) allows the market maker to check whether there is anything untoward going on at the instant of trading, and also to form an opinion about the possible trading motives of the counterparty: (Can he give a convincing reason for needing to trade that is not based on superior information? Is he a trusted repeat customer with a good reputation? etc.) This means that the transaction prices that can be obtained through negotiation are typically better than the electronically displayed quotes or limit orders. And in equilibrium, the latter are likely to be wider apart than they would be in a market where there is no scope for negotiation.

This explains why even in Paris, very large deals must be arranged outside the electronic limit order book. It does not explain why large deals gravitate to London. There is no fundamental reason for there not to be well-known large institutions in the home markets, who are prepared to trade blocks upon inquiry, effectively acting as market makers for large deals.

*Other Factors*

Finally, there are a number of other factors, unrelated to stock exchange trading systems, that may explain London's advantage in large-scale dealing even though company information and customers tend to be concentrated in the home countries.

One contributing factor is high home-country turnover taxes, which drive business abroad. This explains some but not all of the migration of trading reduced or eliminated their turnover taxes. There is again a beggar-thy-neighbour element to this which could be remedied by supra-national policies. For reasons that are not entirely clear to me, the relevant EC directive is aimed at harmonising these taxes down to zero. There has been no discussion of whether a turnover tax might not be a relatively attractive source of government revenue.

Some have argued that in London there is a 'culture' of taking risks and making markets, while continental financial market participants are cautious and not used to large-scale speculation. But Table 2 lists the market makers involved in French equity market making on SEAQ International: hardly an all-British collection! And similarly, in the Italian sector of SEAQ International the largest market maker is Italian (IMI). Even so, most of the skilled individuals employed in market making may well be Anglophone and unwilling to move to the Continent.

Others have argued that it is the presence of a large concentration of large financial players in London that keeps the trading business there. Still, the explosive growth of European equity trading in London is a fairly recent phenomenon. Moreover, many trades involve home-country institutions trading with home-country market makers on SEAQ International. Why go to London?

## 8.4 CONCLUDING COMMENTS

How and why has London's SEAQ International been able to capture such a large share of trading volume in European equities? The data on dealing spreads in this paper agree with the actual patterns of trading volume: London's advantage is confined to larger sized deals. Why is this so? Apart from London's pre-eminent position as an international centre, there are a number of innate features of the market maker based dealing system which makes it suitable for large scale deals.

Amongst these, slower trade reporting seems to be a significant factor in its attractiveness to large-scale dealers. One would expect harmonisation of trade publication speeds—either through stricter EC rules or through laxer rules on the Continent—to lead to some repatriation of trading activity to the domestic stock exchanges.

## "EUROPEAN STOCK MARKETS, TOO MANY TRADING PLACES"

The Economist (June 19, 1993).

How many stock exchanges does Europe with a single capital market need? Nobody knows. But a part-answer is clear: fewer than it has today. America has eight stock exchanges, and seven futures and options exchanges. Of these only the New York Stock Exchange, the American Stock Exchange, NASDAQ (the over-the-counter market), and the two Chicago futures exchanges have substantial turnover and nationwide pretensions.

The 12 member countries of the European Community (EC), in contrast, boast 32 stock exchanges and 23 futures and options exchanges. Of these, the markets in London, Frankfurt, Paris, Amsterdam, Milan and Madrid—at least—aspire to significant roles on the European and world stages. And the number of exchanges is growing. Recent arrivals include futures exchanges in Italy and Spain. In eastern Germany, Leipzig wants to reopen the stock exchange that the Russians closed in 1945.

. . .

Today the London exchange reckons to handle around 95% of all European cross-border share-trading. It claims to handle three-quarters of the trading in blue-chip shares based in Holland, half of those in France and Italy and a quarter of those in Germany—though, as will become clear, there is some dispute about these figures.

London's market-making tradition and the presence of many international fund managers helped it to win this business. So did three other factors. One was stamp duties on share deals done in their home countries, which SEAQ usually avoided. Another was the shortness of trading hours on continental bourses. The third was the ability of SEAQ, with market-makers quoting two-way prices for business in large amounts, to handle trades in big blocks of stock that can be fed through order-driven markets only when they find counterparties.

A similar tussle for business has been seen among the exchanges that trade futures and options. Here, the market which first trades a given product tends to corner the business in it. The European Options Exchange (EOE) in Amsterdam was the first derivatives exchange in Europe; today it is the only one to trade a European equity-index option. London's LIFFE, which opened in 1982 and is now Europe's biggest derivatives exchange, has kept a two-to-one lead in German government-bond futures (its most active contract) over Frankfurt's DTB, which opened only in 1990. LIFFE competes with several other European exchanges, not always successfully: it lost the market in ecu-bond futures to Paris's MATIF.

European exchanges armoured themselves for this battle in three ways. The first was to fend off foreign competition with rules. In three years of wrangling over the EC's investment-services directive, several member-countries pushed for rules that would require securities to be traded only on a recognised exchange. They also demanded rules for the disclosure of trades and prices that would have hamstrung SEAQ's quote-driven trading system. They were beaten off in the eventual compromise, partly because governments realised they risked driving business outside the EC. But residual attempts to stifle competition remain. Italy passed a law in 1991 requiring trades in Italian shares to be conducted through a firm based in Italy. Under pressure from the European Commission, it may have to repeal it.

## New ways for old

The second response to competition has been frantic efforts by bourses to modernise systems, improve services and cut costs. This has meant investing in new trading systems, improving the way deals are settled, and pressing governments to scrap stamp duties. It has also increasingly meant trying to beat London at its own game, for instance by searching for ways of matching London's prowess in block trading.

Paris, which galvanised itself in 1988, is a good example. Its bourse is now open to outsiders. It has a computerised trading system based on continuous auctions, and settlement of most of its deals is computerised. Efforts to set up a block-trading mechanism continue, although slowly. Meanwhile, MATIF, the French futures exchange, has become the continent's biggest. It is especially proud of its ecu-bond contract, which should grow in importance if and when monetary union looms.

Frankfurt, the continent's biggest stockmarket, has moved more ponderously, partly because Germany's federal system has kept regional stock exchanges in being, and left much of the regulation of its markets at Land (state) level. Since January 1st 1993 all German exchanges (including the DTB) have been grouped under a firm called Deutsche Börse AG, chaired by Rolf Breuer, a member of Deutsche Bank's board. But there is still some way to go in centralising German share-trading. German floor brokers continue to resist the inroads made by the banks' screen-based IBIS trading system. A law to set up a federal securities regulator (and make insider-dealing illegal) still lies becalmed in Bonn.

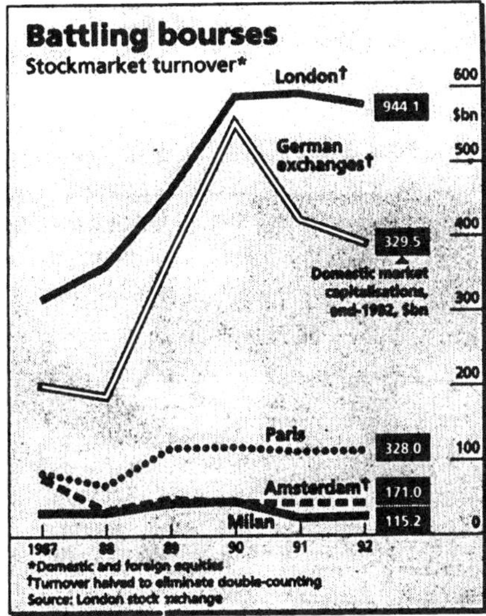


Other bourses are moving too. Milan is pushing forward with screen-based trading and speeding up its settlement. Spain and Belgium are reforming their stockmarkets and launching new futures exchanges. Amsterdam plans an especially determined attack on SEAQ. It is implementing a McKinsey report that recommended a screen-based system for wholesale deals, a special mechanism for big block trades and a bigger market-making role for brokers.

Ironically, London now finds itself a laggard in some respects. Its share settlement remains prehistoric; the computerised project to modernise it has just been scrapped. The SEAQ trading system is falling apart; only recently has the exchange, belatedly, approved plans drawn up by Arthur Andersen for a replacement, and there is plenty of scepticism in the City about its ability to deliver. Yet the exchange's claimed figures for its share of trading in continental equities suggest that London is holding up well against its competition.

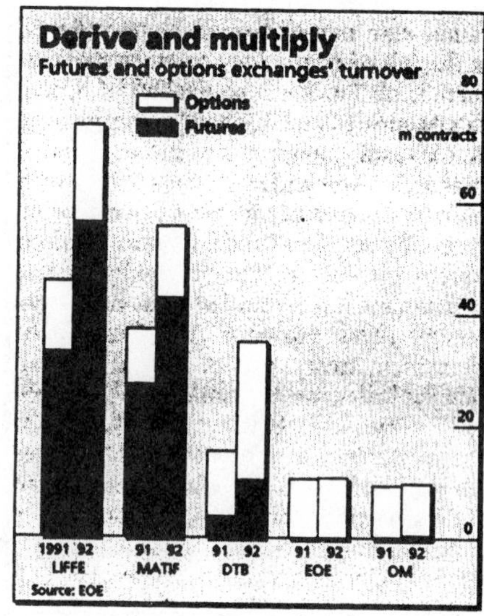


Are these figures correct? Not necessarily: deals done through an agent based in London often get counted as SEAQ business even when the counterparty is based elsewhere and the order has been executed through a continental bourse. In today's electronic age, with many firms members of most European exchanges, the true location of a deal can be impossible to pin down. Continental bourses claim, anyway, to be winning back business lost to London.

Financiers in London agree that the glory-days of SEAQ's international arm, when other European exchanges were moribund, are gone. Dealing in London is now more often a complement to, rather than a substitute for, dealing at home. Big blocks of stock may be bought or sold through London, but broken apart or assembled through local bourses. Prices tend to be derived from the domestic exchanges; it is notable that trading on SEAQ drops when they are closed. Baron van Ittersum, chairman of the Amsterdam exchange, calls this the "queen's birthday effect": trading in Dutch equities in London slows to a trickle on Dutch public holidays.

## Co-operate or die

Such competition-through-diversity has encouraged European exchanges to cut out the red tape that protected their members from outside competition, to embrace electronics, and to adapt themselves to the wishes of investors and issuers. Yet the diversity may also have had a cost in lower liquidity. Investors, especially from outside Europe, are deterred if liquidity remains divided among different exchanges. Companies suffer too: they grumble about the costs of listing on several different markets.

So the third response of Europe's bourses to their battle has been pan-European co-operative ventures that could anticipate a bigger European market. There are more wishful words here than deeds. Work on two joint EC projects to pool market information, Pipe and Euroquote, was abandoned, thanks mainly to hostility from Frankfurt and London. Eurolist, under which a company meeting the listing requirements for one stock exchange will be entitled to a listing on all, is going forward—but this is hardly a single market. As Paris's Mr. Théodore puts it, "there is a compelling business case for the big European exchanges building the European-regulated market of tomorrow". Sir Andrew Hugh–Smith, chairman of the London exchange, has also long advocated one European market for professional investors.

One reason little has been done is that bourses have been coping with so many reforms at home. Many wanted to push these through before thinking about Europe. But there is also atavistic nationalism. London, for example, is unwilling to give up the leading role it has acquired in cross-border trading between institutions; and other exchanges are unwilling to accept that it keeps it. Mr. Théodore says there is no future for the European bourses if they are forced to row in a boat with one helmsman. Amsterdam's Baron van Ittersum also emphasises that a joint European market must not be one under London's control.

Hence the latest, lesser notion gripping Europe's exchanges: bilateral or multilateral links. The futures exchanges have shown the way. Last year four smaller exchanges led by Amsterdam's EOE and OM, an options exchange based in Sweden and London, joined together in a federation called FEX. In January of this year the continent's two biggest exchanges, MATIF and the DTB, announced a link-up that was clearly aimed at toppling London's LIFFE from its dominant position. Gérard Pfauwadel, MATIF's chairman, trumpets the deal as a precedent for other European exchanges. Mr. Breuer, the Deutsche Börse's chairman, reckons that a network of European exchanges is the way forward, though he concedes that London will not warm to the idea. The bourses of France and Germany can be expected to follow the MATIFF/DTB lead.

It remains unclear how such link-ups will work, however. The notion is that members of one exchange should be able to trade products listed on another. So a Frenchman wanting to buy German government-bond futures could do so through a dealer on MATIF, even though the contract is actually traded in Frankfurt. That is easy to arrange via screen-based trading: all that are needed are local terminals. But linking an electronic market such as the DTB to a floor-based market with open-outcry trading such as MATIF is harder. Nor have any exchanges thought through an efficient way of pooling their settlement systems.

In any case, linkages and networks will do nothing to reduce the plethora of European exchanges, or to build a single market for the main European blue-chip stocks. For that a bigger joint effort is needed. It would not mean the death of national exchanges, for there will always be business for individual investors, and in securities issued locally. Mr.

Breuer observes that ultimately all business is local. Small investors will no doubt go on worrying about currency risk unless and until monetary union happens. Yet large wholesale investors are already used to hedging against it. For them, investment in big European blue-chip securities would be much simpler on a single wholesale European market, probably subject to a single regulator.

More to the point, if investors and issuers want such a market, it will emerge—whether today's exchanges provide it or not. What, after all, is an exchange? It is no more than a system to bring together as many buyers and sellers as possible, preferably under an agreed set of rules. That used to mean a physically supervised trading floor. But computers have made it possible to replicate the features of a physical exchange electronically. And they make the dissemination of prices and the job of applying rules to a market easier.

Most users of exchanges do not know or care which exchange they are using: they deal through brokers or dealers. Their concern is to deal with a reputable firm such as S.G. Warburg, Goldman Sachs or Deutsche Bank, not a reputable exchange. Since big firms are now members of most exchanges, they can choose where to trade and where to resort to off-exchange deals—which is why there is so much dispute over market shares within Europe. This fluidity creates much scope for new rivals to undercut established stock exchanges.

. . .

### *Notes and Questions*

1. Roell finds that bid-offer spreads on CAC (Paris order market) are narrower on small trades but larger on big trades than SEAQ (quote market). Why might narrow spreads be an indication of market efficiency? Should brokers execute all small trades on CAC rather than SEAQ?

2. Why might a quote market be more efficient for large trades?

3. Review the arguments over the EU's Investment Services Directive in Chapter V. What was the competitive strategy of the Club Med countries?

4. Do you think we will have cooperation and/or merger of various European stock exchanges in the next five years? What kind of cooperation might there be? With respect to merger possibilities, note that in November 1993, the Chicago Board of Options Exchange made an offer to buy the Philadelphia Stock Exchange through making an offer for each of the Philadelphia's 505 memberships. The Board of the Philadelphia Exchange rejected the offer, however. Chapter XV deals more generally with the issue of competition between derivatives exchanges. In April 1994, the members of New York's two major futures exchanges, the New York Commodity Exchange and the New York Mercantile Exchange, approved a merger. Do you think there is a relationship between competition for trading in derivatives and stocks, given modern trading strategies?

5. How will the increasing use of ADRs affect competition between stock markets? Note that the problems of competition between some derivative markets may be different in one important respect from trading in stocks. The market that first designs some derivative products may have a proprietary right that requires its consent before the product is traded elsewhere. Thus, the Chicago Mercantile Exchange and the Chicago Board of Trade have competed for the right to make a market in the Major Market Index (a stock index future). The rights to trade in the index are licensed by the American Stock Exchange.

6. Recall the Daimler Benz case discussed in Chapter II. This case indicates that government policy can heavily affect the competition between stock markets. If the United States were to liberalize its disclosure rules—particularly the requirement of U.S. GAAP reconciliation for publicly traded stocks, foreign listings and, therefore, trading in foreign stocks would increase.

---

*Links to Other Chapters*

Competition among stock markets depends on some understanding of domestic securities markets. We have already looked at the U.S. (Chapter II), Europe (Chapters VIII and XI), and Japan (Chapter VII). Domestic considerations and regulation have a significant impact on the ability of domestic markets to compete for international business. The next Chapter focuses on a very important term of competition, clearance and settlement, and Chapter XV on Futures and Options looks at some issues affecting competition between derivatives exchanges. Finally, Chapter XVII on emerging markets, looks at competition for listings of emerging market companies between emerging markets and developed exchanges.

# Chapter XIV

# CLEARANCE AND SETTLEMENT

This Chapter examines the clearance and settlement of securities. Efficient and reliable systems are a necessity for domestic and cross-border portfolio investment. First, we will look at the basic elements and mechanics of the clearing and settlement process, with emphasis on the clearing and settlement of U.S. equities through the National Securities Clearing Corporation (NSCC).

Second, we will explore the risks, systemic and nonsystemic, of clearing and settlement, and the Group of 30 recommendations to reduce them.

Third, we shall explore the mechanisms through which securities traded in one market can be cleared and settled in another market. The focus will be on inter-market linkages and international systems such as Euroclear.

Finally, we will look at how clearing and settlement systems may evolve in the future.

## A. THE BASIC ELEMENTS

### U.S. CONGRESS, OFFICE OF TECHNOLOGY ASSESSMENT

Trading Around the Clock (1990), Ch. 5.

"Clearing and settlement" is the processing of transactions on stock, futures, and options markets. It is what happens after the trade. "Clearing" confirms the identity and quantity of the financial instrument or contract being bought and sold, the transaction price and date, and the identity of the buyer and seller. It also sometimes includes the netting of trades, or the offsetting of buy orders and sell orders. "Settlement" is the fulfillment, by the parties to the transaction, of the obligations of the trade; in equities and bond trades, "settlement" means payment to the seller and delivery of the stock certificate or transferring its ownership to the buyer. Settlement in futures and options takes on different meanings according to the type of contract.

Trades are processed differently depending on the type of financial instrument being traded, the market or exchange on which it is traded, and the institutions involved in the processing of the trade (i.e., an exchange, a clearinghouse, a depository, or some combination). The clearing and settlement mechanisms and institutions in the United States, the United Kingdom, and Japan are described in the appendix. The differences in countries' clearing and settlement are important because clearing and settlement systems used for domestic trading are now being called on to accommodate international participants. The integrity and efficiency of a nation's clearing and settlement systems are important to both its internal financial and economic stability and its ability to compete with other nations.

Many markets have "clearinghouses" that handle both the clearing process and some of the settlement process. This is the most common system in the United States for exchange-traded financial products. Many markets, including the U.S. markets, have "depositories," that hold stocks and bonds for safekeeping on behalf of their owners.

Where clearinghouses do not exist (e.g., in some European markets), depositories may take on functions of clearinghouses. Depositories may transfer ownership of stocks and bonds by "book entry" (a computer entry in the depository's record books) instead of physical delivery of certificates to the buyer, which saves time and money. There are also markets in which exchanges perform some of the clearing and settlement functions (e.g., London's International Stock Exchange), and markets in which neither clearinghouses nor depositories exist (e.g., until very recently, foreign exchange, or "forex," markets).

## THE GOALS OF CLEARING AND SETTLEMENT

Differences in the clearing and settlement process among countries are often linked to historical, economic, and cultural factors in their laws and customs. These differences can expose international investors to extra risk in some instances. Perceptions of the purposes of the clearing and settlement process vary widely among countries. In the United States and Canada, where public policy supports broad public access to the markets, the reduction of risk, through the clearinghouse as an intermediary, is a major goal of clearing and settlement. These policies are reflected in a hierarchy of protections for the clearinghouse, including minimum capital requirements for clearinghouse members.

In many other countries, risk reduction is imposed before trading takes place, by controls on who is allowed to participate, or by the participants "knowing their trading partners," and, in equities, by reducing the time allowed to settle a transition. In these markets, clearinghouse guarantee funds are generally small or nonexistent, and settlement is seen merely as a delivery function, rather than as a mechanism for risk reduction.

These different views of the purpose of clearing and settlement have become significant as more investors begin trading in markets other than their domestic markets. U.S. investors, accustomed to domestic markets where safeguards are in place, may assume that the clearing and settlement of their trades in a foreign market has risks comparable to those in the United States, where there are guarantees provided by clearing and settlement organizations.

The chief aims of clearing and settlement in the United States and some other countries are efficiency and safety. The faster and more accurately a trade can be processed, the sooner the same capital can be reinvested, and at less cost and risk to investors. Therefore, as markets become global, one could expect that investment capital will flow toward markets that are most attractive on a risk-return basis, and that also have efficient and reliable clearing and settlement systems.

The soundness of clearing and settlement systems in one nation can also impact other nations. The failure of a clearing member at a foreign clearinghouse could affect a U.S. clearinghouse through the impact on a common clearing member. To reduce the risk of such an occurrence, different countries' clearing and settlement systems must be coordinated with each other, for example, by sharing risk information and harmonizing trade settlement dates. Both the private sector and Federal regulators have begun to take steps in this direction. It is doubtful that the private sector can achieve the needed changes without national governments taking a prominent and concerted role.

## HOW CLEARING AND SETTLEMENT WORKS

Many kinds of organizations are involved in clearing and settlement. Their functions vary from market to market, and not all of these organizations exist in every country. For instance, clearinghouses play a key role in the United States and some Asian markets; but in many European markets, depositories are more important.

A key role of a clearinghouse is to assist in the comparison of trades and sometimes, as in the United States, also to remove counterparty risk from the settlement process. Clearinghouses can provide the buyer with a guarantee that he will receive the securities—or other interest—he purchased, and provide the seller with a guarantee that the payment will be received.

In the United States, the clearinghouse has a number of working relationships, or interfaces, with other institutions (figure 5–1). A trade in the United States (as well as in Japan, Canada, and some other countries) cannot settle through the central systems until it has been matched, i.e., buyers' and sellers' records of the trade are compared and reconciled. A clearinghouse has an interface with a market in which trades are executed and from which the clearinghouse receives information on the trades. The clearinghouse may receive previously "locked-in" trades (trades which have already been matched), or it may match the trades itself.

A second interface is with its clearing members, i.e., the member firms of an exchange or market. A clearing member delivers trade information to the clearinghouse and may hold positions both for itself (proprietary positions) and on behalf of its customers. Other traders in a market, who are not clearing members, must clear their trades through a member of a clearinghouse for that market. A clearinghouse controls the risks of the clearing and settlement process through its relationships with its clearing members. For example, it may have minimum capital requirements for clearing members, use margins or mark-to-market procedures, and require that its clearing members place collateral in a guarantee fund as protection against default by other clearing members. In the event of the failure of a clearing member, the clearinghouse may also have the ability to assess all other clearing members. It may also provide its clearing members with a trade-matching service and notify members about the way a trade is to be settled (the settlement date, and the way payment and delivery or transfer of ownership will be accomplished).

**Figure 5-1—Interfaces Among Clearing Participants**

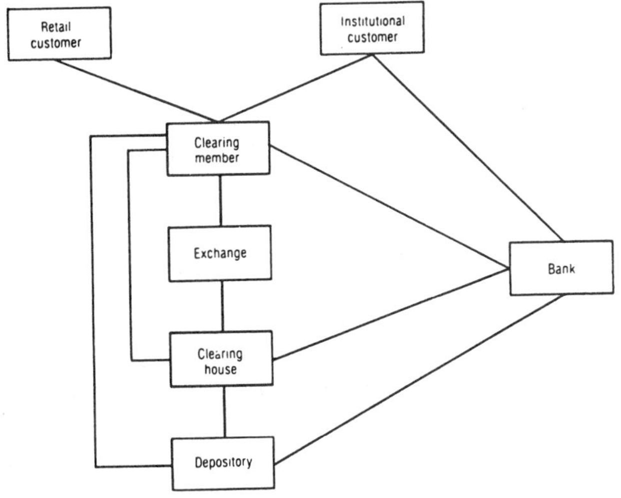


SOURCE: Office of Technology Assessment, 1990.

A third interface is with clearing and credit banks. The clearinghouse and the banks work together in the payment and collection process, since clearinghouses today do not have direct access to the payment system, e.g., FedWire in the United States. The banks also provide credit to clearing members.

In the securities markets—but not typically in futures and options markets—there is often a fourth interface with the depository. The depository records and arranges the legal transfer of ownership of securities, and holds securities for safekeeping. The clearinghouse instructs the depository on how the transaction is to be settled. The depository may act as an agent, on behalf of the clearinghouse, to receive funds to settle the transaction.

In addition to the relationships between clearinghouses, markets, depositories, and banks, these organizations also have relationships with each other. Clearing members of a designated market deal with the banks to settle with the clearinghouse and to obtain credit. There is an important relationship between the banks and the depository. When a bank acts in a custodial role, e.g., delivering securities and receiving payments in behalf of its customers, instructions on payment and title transfer are sent to the bank by the customer. The depository, in turn, as an accounting system for immobilized or dematerialized instruments, and/or as a central vault for the physical instruments themselves, interfaces with the banks as custodian. It may also, as custodian, have an interface with the banks for payment.

## RISKS FROM DIFFERENCES IN CLEARING AND SETTLEMENT MECHANISMS

These differences—the use of guarantee funds, the time allowed to settle a trade, etc.—in countries' clearing and settlement systems are a major constraint on global trading and may impose risks on traders and investors. Defaults in a national clearing and settlement process can propagate through other national systems, since multinational financial institutions may be active in several national markets. Collapse of a major settlement system could endanger financial systems in both its own and other countries.

Even in day-to-day operations, differences in clearing and settlement systems and in their performances constrain some kinds of trading. For example, in Japan, settlement in equities and bonds is normally on the third day after a trade (T+3) and in the United States it is normally on the fifth day (T+5). An investor trading General Motors (GM) stock on both the New York Stock Exchange (NYSE) and the Tokyo Stock Exchange (TSE) would have trouble perfectly arbitraging his holdings. If the investor were to buy GM shares on the NYSE and simultaneously sell them on the TSE, because the U.S. settlement period is 2 days longer, the GM shares would be delayed by 2 business days for the Japanese settlement. If the investor were to buy GM stock on the TSE and sell GM stock that same day on the NYSE, the shares could be available for the NYSE settlement because that is 2 days later than Tokyo's. The Japan Securities Clearing Corp. (JSCC)—through its link with International Securities Clearing Corp. (ISCC) in the United States—holds the U.S. shares at The Depository Trust Co. (DTC); therefore instead of physical movement of certificates there simply would be a book entry delivery at DTC. The average number of days for settlement of various financial instruments in different countries differs widely (figure 5–2). The number of days for settlement varies widely among countries in each geographical region. As a result, harmonized clearing and settlement is needed.

**Figure 5-2—Settlement Date: T+?**

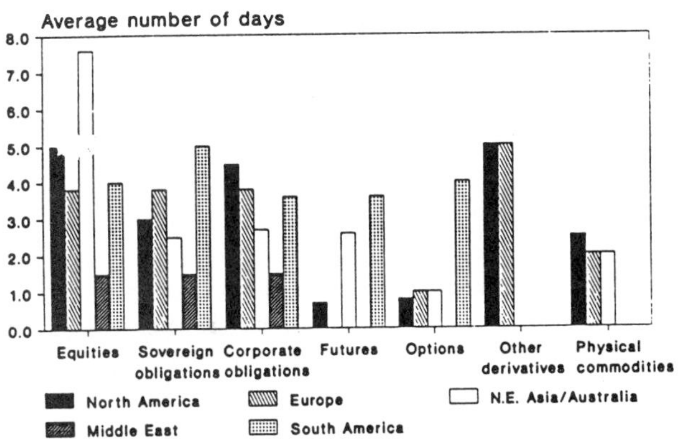


SOURCE: Bankers Trust Co., "Study of International Clearing and Settlement," OTA contractor report, October 1989.

Trading in European markets, unlike in the United States, mostly does not rely only on stock exchanges. In Japan, there is as yet no central depository, but there is a clearing and custody system at TSE. Many European countries have depositories, but their functions vary from country to country, and are often different from U.S. depositories.

There are three principal models for clearing and settlement in the world's major stock markets. The first model has no centralized depository or independent clearinghouse beyond the stock exchange. The exchanges usually perform as many of the clearing and settlement functions as are feasible. These include trade matching, confirmation, and some type of settlement facility—usually a central location where market participants can deliver and receive securities and payments. The equities market in the United Kingdom is an example.

The second model of clearing and settlement is one in which there is a central depository structure, with trade matching and confirmation services provided by the exchanges. Once trades have been matched and confirmed, the trade data are sent to the depository for settlement. There are variations on this model with differing degrees of settlement services provided by the depository. The depository may offer book-entry transfer of ownership of immobilized securities, with limited provisions for varying payment methods. Or the depository may provide book-entry transfer of dematerialized securities and the ability, through direct links to local payment systems, to simultaneously and irrevocably transfer funds for each settlement. An example is West Germany and its Deutscher Kassenverein (KV) depository system.

The third model has not only a stock market and a central depository, but also a clearinghouse that stands between the stock market and depository to reduce risk. The stock market, along with the clearinghouse, provides trade matching and confirmation services. A trade is confirmed by the market participants and is then passed to the clearinghouses which substitutes itself as the counterparty to each trade. This gives a degree of financial assurance to the markets since the clearinghouse will honor the obligations of a clearing member if necessary. The clearinghouse then passes the trade information to the depository for delivery versus payment on the settlement date. An example is the United States equities market.

In most European equities markets, there are no central clearing organizations that assume the role of counterparty to every trade or provide other kinds of mechanisms to ensure the financial integrity of all market participants in the clearing and settlement phase. Where there is no third-party guarantee mechanism for trade settlement, market participants are forced to choose their counterparties based on their own credit assessment.

. . .

## Appendix

## Clearing and Settlement in Major Market Countries

*Clearing and Settlement in the United States*

Three clearinghouses and three depositories serve the Nation's 7 stock exchanges, NASDAQ, and other over-the-counter dealers; 9 clearinghouses serve the 14 futures exchanges; and 1 clearinghouse serves all the equities options markets. The major clearing members, who also clear for non-clearing members of a clearinghouse, tend to be highly automated for lower costs and greater operating efficiency. For safety purposes, U.S. clearinghouses also tend to be financially structured such that a failing clearing member can be isolated quickly and its problems resolved without a ripple effect.

While arrangements between clearinghouses and their clearing firms vary, the general goal is that the clearinghouse maintain adequate resources and commitments to assure settlement if a clearing firm or its non-clearing firm customer defaults. These include capital requirements for members, claims on items in process, if any, as well as claims on the defaulting member's remaining assets on deposit with the clearinghouse (e.g., cash, letters of credit, Treasuries, or securities posted as collateral for margin). The clearinghouse also has claims on other assets of the failed clearing member. The clearinghouse's guarantee fund is another resource. Finally, the clearinghouse can make assessments against other clearing member firms. This succession of fallbacks is a buffer against shocks ranging from sudden large drops in the prices of securities and futures to defaults by members. As a result, there have been few cases of a failure of a clearing member in the United States, and no instances of a failure of a clearinghouse.

### Equities Clearing Organizations

*The National Securities Clearing Corp.*—NSCC processes 95 percent of all equities trades in the United States. It is jointly owned by the principal equities markets: the New York Stock Exchange (NYSE), American Stock Exchange (AMEX), and National Association of Securities Dealers (NASD). It serves 1,800 brokers, dealers, banks, and other financial institutions, through about 400 direct participants.

NSCC's clearance and settlement process normally requires five business days. Trade information is received either in the form of locked-in trades already matched by the computer systems of the exchange or market; or, as buy and sell data reported by market participants. The latter still must be compared and buy and sell orders matched. Locked-in trades are entered directly in the NSCC computer system on the same day as the trade. This sharply reduces the need for the matching of buy and sell orders at the clearinghouse level. On a typical day, about 75 percent of the trades on the NYSE are locked-in (a smaller proportion by dollar value). Figures A–1 and A–2 illustrate the steps in the NSCC's clearing and settlement of retail and institutional customers' trades, respectively.

Securities which are held for NSCC members by The Depository Trust Co. (DTC), and whose ownership can therefore be transferred within DTC via its computer book-entry system, are also eligible for settlement through the Continuous Net Settlement (CNS) computer system. This includes the preponderance of trades settled through the NSCC. NSCC becomes the counterparty to each trade; it guarantees that the settlement obligations of the trade will be met—both the obligation to deliver securities and the obligation to make payment. For locked-in trades, NSCC's guarantee takes effect at midnight on the day (T+1) that the counterparties to the trade have been notified that the trades matched.

Trades that do not match begin a reconciliation process that is being shortened and by the end of 1990 will occur on the day following the trade (T+1). Those that remain unmatched by T+3 are returned to their originating marketplace for face-to-face negotiation. With the increasing number of trades locked-in at the marketplaces, and with the availability of on-line reconciliation systems at these marketplaces, the need for this process is being eliminated.

**Figure A-1—Clearance and Settlement of Retail Customer Trades**

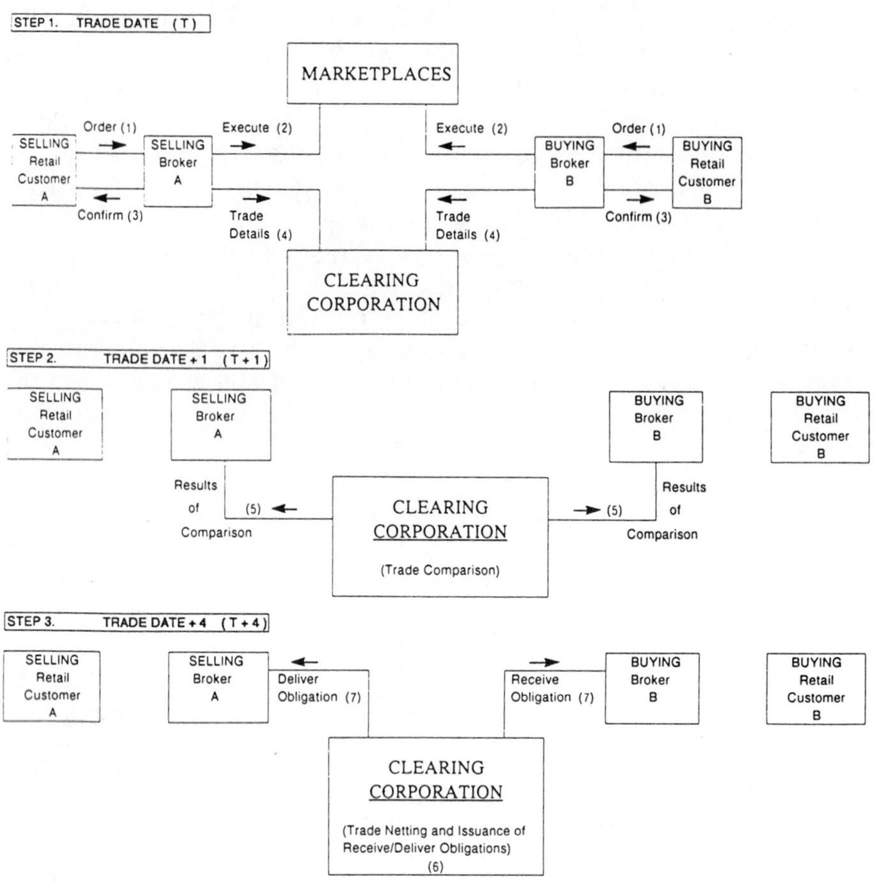


(1) Retail Customers give orders to buy and sell stock to their respective Brokers.
(2) Brokers execute Retail Customers orders in the Marketplaces.
(3) Brokers confirm back to their respective Retail Customers that the trades were executed.
(4) Brokers submit details of trades executed in the Marketplaces to the Clearing Corporation.
(5) Clearing Corporation generates reports back to the Brokers indicating the results of comparison.
(6) Clearing Corporation nets the trades.
(7) Clearing Corporation issues projection reports indicating net receive/deliver obligations to the buying and selling Brokers.

SOURCE: NSCC, 1990.

**Figure A-1—Clearance and Settlement of Retail Customer Trades—Continued**

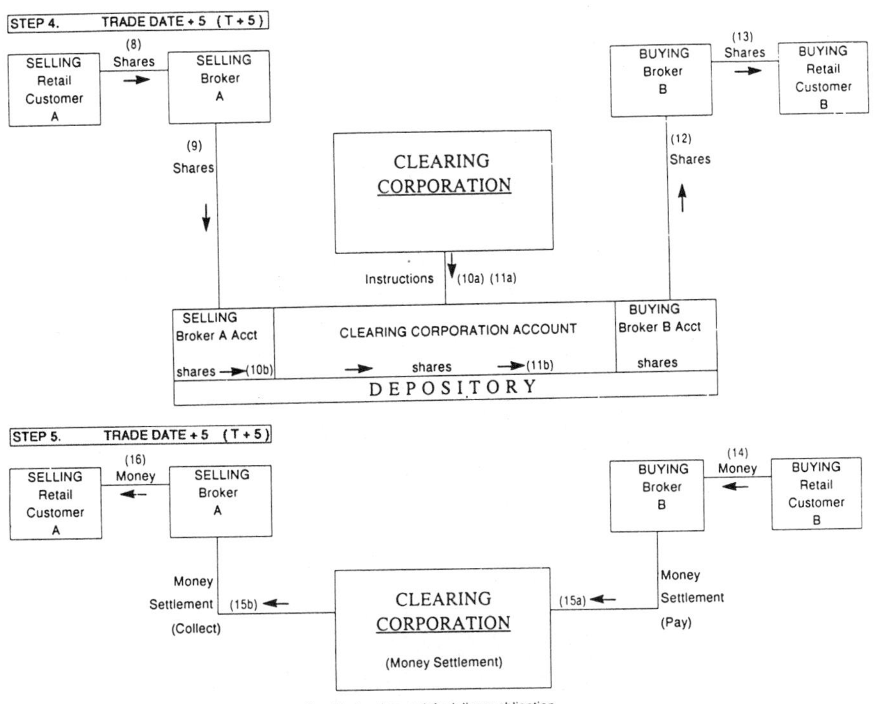

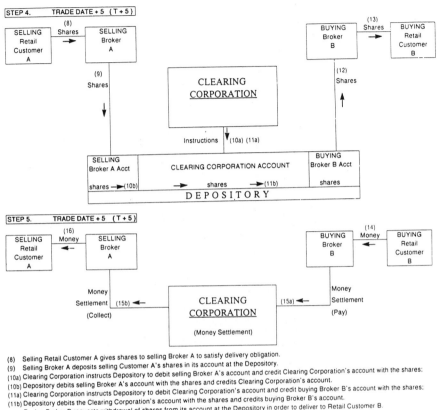

(8) Selling Retail Customer A gives shares to selling Broker A to satisfy delivery obligation.
(9) Selling Broker A deposits selling Customer A's shares in its account at the Depository.
(10a) Clearing Corporation instructs Depository to debit selling Broker A's account and credit Clearing Corporation's account with the shares;
(10b) Depository debits selling Broker A's account with the shares and credits Clearing Corporation's account.
(11a) Clearing Corporation instructs Depository to debit Clearing Corporation's account and credit buying Broker B's account with the shares;
(11b) Depository debits the Clearing Corporation's account with the shares and credits buying Broker B's account.
(12) Buying Broker B requests withdrawal of shares from its account at the Depository in order to deliver to Retail Customer B.
(13) Buying Broker B delivers the shares to its buying Retail Customer B.
(14) Buying Retail Customer B pays buying Broker B for shares received.
(15a) Clearing Corporation advises buying Broker B of net pay amount for shares received;
Buying Broker B delivers a check to Clearing Corporation for the requested amount.
(15b) Clearing Corporation advises selling Broker A of net collect amount for shares delivered;
Clearing Corporation issues check to selling Broker A for the specified amount.
(16) Selling Broker A pays selling Retail Customer A for shares delivered.

SOURCE: NSCC, 1990.

**Figure A-2—Clearance and Settlement of Institutional Customer Trades**

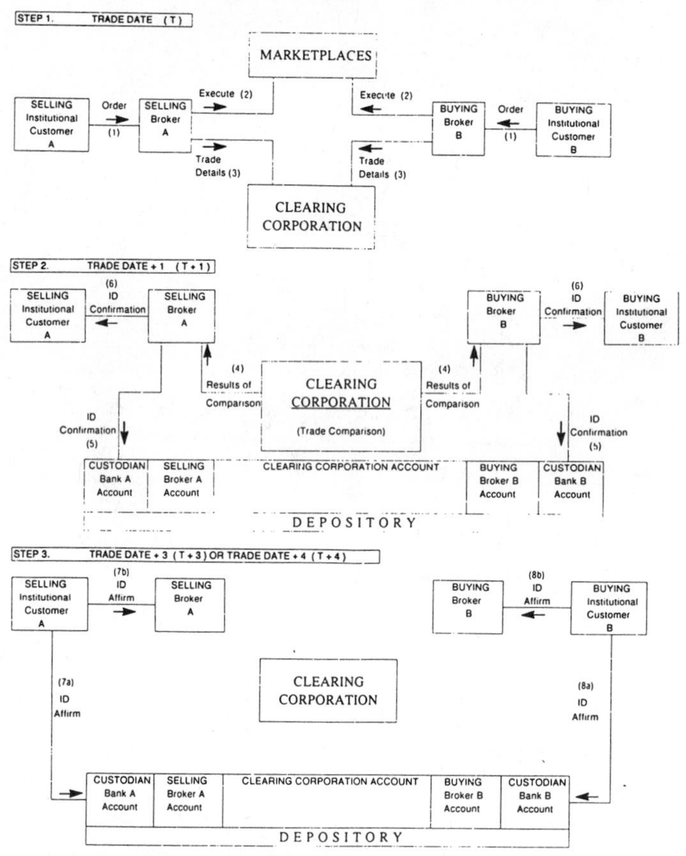


(1) Institutional Customers give orders to buy and sell stock to their respective Brokers.
(2) Brokers execute Institutional Customers orders in the Marketplaces.
(3) Brokers submit details of trades executed in the Marketplaces to the Clearing Corporation.
(4) Clearing Corporation generates reports back to the Brokers indicating the results of comparison.
(5) Brokers send ID confirmation to the Custodian Banks of their Customers.
(6) Brokers send ID confirmation to their respective Institutional Customers.
(7a) Selling Institutional Customer A sends ID affirmation to Custodian Bank A to deliver securities on settlement day (T+5) to its' Broker (A).
(7b) Selling Institutional Customer A sends ID affirmation to selling Broker A indicating that Custodian Bank A will deliver the securities to it on settlement day.
(8a) Buying Institutional Customer B sends ID affirmation to Custodian Bank B, notifying it to receive securities on settlement day from its' Broker (B).
(8b) Buying Institutional Customer B sends ID affirmation to Broker B, instructing it to deliver securities to its' Custodian Bank (B) on settlement day.

SOURCE: NSCC, 1990.

**Figure A-2—Clearance and Settlement of Institutional Customer Trades—Continued**

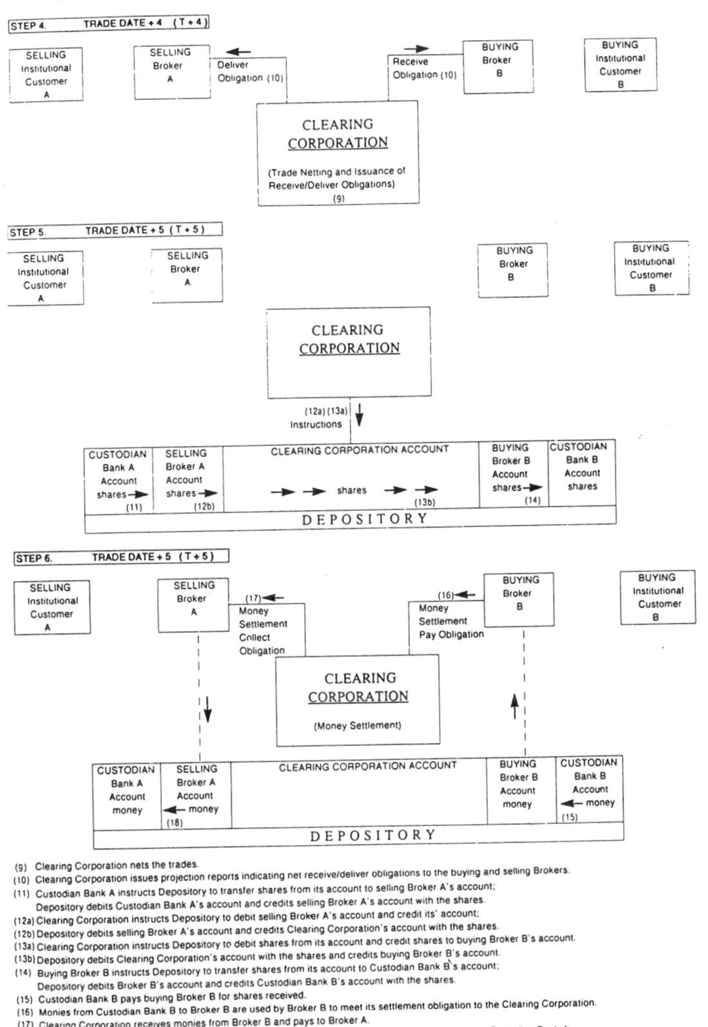


SOURCE: NSCC, 1990.

Using the CNS system, the NSCC calculates each day a net long or short securities position for each CNS-eligible security that was traded by the clearing member on that day. The number of settlement transactions and the gross amount of the clearing member's obligation either to deliver securities or to make payment is adjusted by the amount of any securities or payments that it would receive as a result of other trades of the same security. This type of calculation process is known as netting. It reduces the total number of securities to be delivered or received, and the number and size of aggregate cash payments. As a result of this process of offsetting obligations, the NSCC estimates that movement of about five-sixths of the total daily transactional volume of owed securities and cash payments otherwise required on the settlement date is eliminated. Netting may indirectly increase market liquidity by reducing the gross amount of funds necessary to meet settlement obligations. After netting through CNS, the NSCC then informs the DTC of the net amount that each counterparty owes in securities on the settlement date. T+5. The DTC, using its book entry system, records the transfer of ownership by debiting the securities account of the delivering counterparty and crediting the account of the receiving counterparty. Payment on the settlement date is in the form of a certified check, payable to the NSCC. When settlement cannot be made on the settlement date—e.g., when the securities are not available in the participant's DTC account—these obligations remain in the CNS system and are carried forward and netted with the next day's obligations.

Securities that are not eligible for the CNS system may be settled either through balance order accounting or on a trade-for-trade basis. These other forms of settlement comprise a very small percentage of trades settled through NSCC.

In 1989, the fail rate—the percentage of trades which do not settle on the settlement date—in trades cleared through CNS was 8.13 percent of the total net dollar value of cash and securities due on the settlement date. Since the NSCC takes the counterparty position and guarantees the settlement of all CNS-matched trades, NSCC is exposed to various credit, market, and non-market risks. The ways in which clearinghouses protect themselves against such risks are critically important.

NSCC protects against credit risk, first of all, by retaining a lien over securities which the receiving participant has not paid for. For trades not settled by T+5, NSCC uses a mark-to-market procedure to limit its market risk until settlement does occur. Market risk is kept to 1–day's market movement by adjusting members' settlement obligations to current market prices. Members pay or are paid at settlement based on the current value of their open positions on and after T+5, rather than their value when they made the trade. In the interim, until the position settles, members pay or receive the net difference in market price movement. NSCC's guarantee fund for CNS takes account of potentially adverse movements on trades which have not settled before T+5. It is based on the total size of all positions open. These include those pending (before settlement); trades settling on T+5; and trades for which T+5 has passed and settlement has not occurred. In addition, a percentage of the market value of securities for next-day (T+1) delivery must be deposited in order to protect the NSCC in the event the member defaults. This calculation is done daily for all members and can be collected more frequently than the monthly norm. All NSCC clearing members are required to contribute to the guarantee fund. NSCC's total funds on deposit, not including lines of credit, totaled over $400 million in 1989 and 1990.

The NSCC also maintains a full compliance-monitoring system to ensure its continuing ability to judge the creditworthiness of its participants. It shares risk information with other SEC-registered clearinghouses, both through the SEC's Monitoring Coordination Group and the Securities Clearing Group. NSCC and a number of futures clearinghouses are now discussing proposals for increasing the sharing of risk information; e.g., data on market participants' holdings on various exchanges.

The NSCC is linked to its clearing members by means of the Securities Industry Automation Corp. (SIAC), which operates NSCC's technology base. Most participants now have direct computer links; only about 1 percent of the full-service members continue to report trades via computer tape.

All payments to NSCC are on a net basis; i.e., the NSCC calculates each clearing member's total credit and debit positions and nets to a single figure that is either owed to NSCC or is owed by NSCC. Payment to NSCC is by certified check. Funds are concentrated in one central clearing bank. If a certified check is not received on the settlement date, then payment via FedWire is required the next morning. NSCC pays selling members with regular bank checks, but intends to move towards the increased use of electronic payments as one way to improve the settlement process.

*The International Securities Clearing Corp.*—ISCC is a subsidiary of the NSCC and is an SEC-registered clearinghouse. It was founded in 1985 to assist in clearing and settlement and to provide custody services for securities traded among American brokers and banks and their counterparties across national borders. It has links with clearinghouses and depositories in foreign markets, including:

- the International Stock Exchange (ISE), in London;
- the Centrale de Livraison de Valeurs Mobilieres (CEDEL), in Luxembourg;
- 20 depositories and custodians in Europe and Asia, indirectly linked by means of a conduit provided by CEDEL;
- the Japan Securities Clearing Corp. (JSCC), the Tokyo Stock Exchange's clearing and custody organization;
- the Central Depository subsidiary of the Stock Exchange of Singapore; and
- the Canadian Depository for Securities (CDS), in Toronto, linked through NSCC.

ISCC also serves as the clearing system for the NASD's PORTAL market for foreign private placements exempt from SEC registration by virtue of Rule 144A.

---

### *Note on the NSCC Fail Process*

When trades are matched, NSCC becomes the counterparty to the trades. This occurs at T+1 for locked-in trades and T+4 for others. Suppose A sells B 100 IBM at $100 per share, and the trade is locked-in at T+1. What is the risk for NSCC? First, there is the risk that B may fail to pay NSCC. If this occurs, NSCC must still pay A $10K on the settlement date, T+5. If the price of IBM has gone down, the IBM shares NSCC gets from A may be worth less than $10K. If they were worth only $5K, because they are now selling at $50 per share, NSCC has a $5K loss.

It is also possible that A may not deliver the shares to NSCC on T+5, even though NSCC must deliver the shares to B on the same date. If the price of IBM shares has gone up, NSCC must buy the shares at a higher price than $10K, the funds it gets from B. If the shares were worth $15K, because they are now selling at $150 per share, NSCC has a $5K loss.

How does NSCC protect itself against these risks? There are two periods of concern, the interim period (between the trade and settlement), T to T+5, and the period after settlement, T+5 and after. Settlement is actually supposed to take place before 1:30 p.m. on T+5.

In the interim period, the clearing fund for each member is supposed to cover potential losses, based on a 20 day rolling average of a participants' portfolio value away from the stock price. Participants pay in on sells where the stock rises, and on buys where the stock falls. But the 20 day average measures positions and market risk in the past; this could have already changed as of today, and could further change in the future. Also, the money due is only actually collected once a month.

After the interim period, if the party does not settle a trade on T+5, NSCC must perform as counterparty. Failures to pay can result in NSCC closing out the position of the failing party. Failures to deliver usually result in a mark-to-market procedure. These procedures are further elaborated below.

## Failure to Pay

Failure to pay usually means insolvency. However, there can be unusual situations, floods, riots etc. They can be handled by requiring settlement at T+6 in same day funds (e.g. by wire), the equivalent to a normal T+5 settlement in next day funds (e.g. by check).

In case of insolvency, NSCC closes out the failing broker's (FB) positions on T+5. It will pay for/deliver securities according to FB's contracts. NSCC has a 5 day market risk on FB's positions. It loses on price decreases on long positions (NSCC must pay the delivering broker the contract price in exchange for securities worth less than the contract price) and price increases on short positions (NSCC must pay for securities at the T+5 price and only gets back the lower contract price).

## Failure to Deliver

(a) The routine case

A failure to deliver occurs routinely when the delivering broker (DB) does not have the required securities. DB may not, for example, have received them from the customer and is unwilling to borrow them.

If DB fails to deliver on T+5, it must pay NSCC any positive difference between the T+4 price (the last closing market price) and contract price. Thus, if the trade was at $100 and the price at T+4 was $150, DB must pay NSCC $50 on T+5. The $50 is passed on to the receiving broker (RB) on the same date. NSCC has no loss, because it has taken no position in the stock. DB has paid over its $50 loss, as of T+4, to RB which had a corresponding $50 gain.

If DB delivers on T+6, RB would pay the T+4 closing price, $150 to NSCC (the mark-to-market price), and NSCC would pay DB $150. In effect, the deal is still done at the $100 contract price. RB has paid $150 on T+6, but had previously received the $50 mark payment on T+5; net payments are $100. DB gets $100 net, $150 from NSCC minus its previous mark payment of $50.

(b) Insolvency

We set out below what happens when DB declares insolvency on either T+5 or T+6. Chart I below shows how the mark-to-market system works, assuming the market prices in the left column.

CHART I

| Contract/Market Price | | Mark-to-Market Price | Mark |
|---|---|---|---|
| Contract = | 100 | N.A | N.A. |
| T+4 | 150 | N.A. | N.A. |
| T+5 | 190 | 150 | 50 |
| T+6 | 220 | 190 | 40 |
| T+7 | 250 | 220 | 30 |

The mark-to-market price is the price RB pays for the delivery of stock and the mark is the amount the DB must pay if delivery is not made on the indicated date.

Chart II below shows NSCC's exposure on T+5 and T+6 depending on whether or not NSCC can purchase the stock on the date of insolvency before the market closes, and whether or not DB has paid the mark due on the date of insolvency.

CHART II

T+5 INSOLVENCY

| After Market Close | | Before Market Close | |
|---|---|---|---|
| Before Mark | After Mark | Before Mark | After Mark |
| T+6p−Kp(1) | T+6p−T+4p(2) | T+5p−Kp(3) | T+5p−T+4p(4) |

T+6 INSOLVENCY

| After Market Close | | Before Market Close | |
|---|---|---|---|
| Before Mark | After Mark | Before Mark | After Mark |
| T+7p−T+4p(5) | T+7p−T+5p(6) | T+6p−T+4p(7) | T+6p−T+5p(8) |

Lets go through each of these cases (case number in parenthesis).

**Case 1**

NSCC must purchase the stock at the T+6 price (p) because DB became insolvent after the market closed. NSCC receives the contract price (Kp) from RB. NSCC thus loses 120 (220–100).

**Case 2**

NSCC must again purchase the stock for T+6p. Since the stock has been marked to market, and RB has already received a $50 mark, RB pays NSCC the T+5 mark-to-market price (which is the actual T+4p) of 150. NSCC thus loses 70 (220–150).

**Case 3**

NSCC can purchase the stock at T+5 since the insolvency occurs before the market closes, and pays RB the Kp. NSCC thus loses 90 (190–100).

**Case 4**

NSCC can again purchase the stock at T+5, but here RB has received the 50 mark, and the stock is marked to market on T+5 to the T+4 price, 150. NSCC loses 40 (190–150).

**Case 5**

NSCC purchases the stock for T+7p. We assume no T+6 mark has been paid and thus the stock has not been marked-to-market on T+6. B pays the T+4 price (the T+5 mark-to-market price)—150 (the 100 contract price plus the T+5 50 mark). NSCC loses 100 (250–100).

**Case 6**

NSCC again purchases the stock for T+7p. RB has received two marks, 50 on T+5 and 40 on T+6, and pays 190, the T+6 mark-to-market price which is actually the T+5 market price. DB has paid the contract price plus the two marks. NSCC loses 60 (250–190).

**Case 7**

NSCC purchases the stock before the market closes for T+6p. Since no T+6 mark has been paid, and the stock has not been marked-to-market at T+6, DB pays 150, the T+5 mark-to-market price and the T+4 market price. NSCC loses 70 (220–150).

**Case 8**

NSCC again purchases the stock for T+6p. As in Case 6, RB pays 190, the T+5 market price and the T+6 mark-to-market price. NSCC loses 30 (220–190).

STAFFS OF BOARD OF GOVERNORS OF THE FEDERAL RESERVE SYSTEM AND THE FEDERAL RESERVE BANK OF NEW YORK

Clearance and Settlement in U.S. Securities Markets 1–20 (1992).

. . .

## 2. Overview of Clearance and Settlement in U.S. Securities Markets

U.S. securities markets are notable for their large size, the diversity of instruments traded, and the complexity of the clearing arrangements. Table 1 lists the most significant instruments, the markets in which they are traded, and the principal clearinghouses and depositories for the instruments. Further information is provided in the remainder of this section and in the appendixes.

### Size, Turnover, and Trading Volume

Approximately $9.5 trillion of marketable U.S. government and agency securities, mortgage-backed securities, equities, and corporate and municipal bonds were outstanding at the end of 1990 (table 2). The various markets have grown at different rates: among the most notable developments in the 1980s was the emergence of mortgage-backed securities (MBSs) and futures based on equity indexes (charts 1 and 2).

Turnover varies widely among the markets. U.S. government and federal agency securities are by far the most actively traded, with an annual turnover in 1990 of nearly nine times the amount of securities outstanding, counting only nonfinancing trades by primary government securities dealers. U.S. government securities underlying traded futures contracts and options on futures contracts were equivalent to an additional five times the amount of U.S. securities outstanding. MBSs, most of which are guaranteed by a federal agency, turned over approximately four times in 1990. Trading in government and non-MBS agency securities grew nearly 440 percent between 1980 and 1990. Trading in MBSs grew even faster, as is often the case in a relatively new market.

Turnover in the equities market (about 0.6 times annually) is smaller than in the government bond market. Derivatives (futures and options) are relatively more important where equities are concerned: The underlying value of the derivative instruments traded in 1990 was more than three times that in the cash market. Trading in equities, measured by the value of the underlying securities, grew 290 percent between 1980 and 1990. Trading in equity derivatives, originally just options on individual stocks, grew phenomenally when futures contracts based on equity indexes were introduced in 1982, followed by equity index options in 1983. Turnover in the markets for corporate bonds and state and local government (or municipal) bonds is also smaller than turnover in U.S. government securities. The value of municipal bonds that changed hands in 1990 was approximately 0.9 times of the amount outstanding. Annual turnover in corporate bonds was approximately 2.8 times (if only publicly issued bonds were included in the base of corporate bonds, the turnover rate would be higher).

## Investors

Investors differ from market to market. The main investors in U.S. government and federal agency issues are households, state and local governments, foreign investors, commercial banks, pension funds, and insurance companies. Corporate equities and bonds are traded by both individuals and institutions (insurance companies, bank trust departments, mutual funds, and pension funds). MBSs have attracted an increasingly diversified group of investors, as the relative importance of thrift institutions as investors has diminished considerably.

## Marketplaces and Clearing Organizations

Some instruments are traded on established exchanges, some over the counter, and some in both places (table 1). The mechanisms for clearance and settlement vary not only across markets, but also, in some cases, within markets.

Corporate equities and bonds are traded on seven stock exchanges and over the counter. Initially, each exchange operated its own clearinghouse. In 1977, the clearinghouses for the New York and American Stock Exchanges and the over-the-counter market merged to form the National Securities Clearing Corporation (NSCC). Since then, the Boston Stock Exchange, the Cincinnati Stock Exchange, and the Pacific Stock Exchange have transferred their clearing work to NSCC. In 1991 NSCC cleared more than 90 percent of the equity shares traded in the United States. Most corporate and municipal bonds and equities are immobilized at the Depository Trust Company, which works closely with NSCC; others are immobilized at affiliates of the Midwest Clearing Corporation (Midwest Securities Trust Company) and the Stock Clearing Corporation of Philadelphia (Philadelphia Depository Trust Company).

1. Principal securities, options, and financial futures markets in the United States, 1991

| Type of instrument | Where traded | Principal clearinghouse | Depository |
|---|---|---|---|
| U.S. government bonds [1] | Over the counter | Government Securities Clearing Corp. | Federal Reserve Banks |
| Mortgage-backed securities | Over the counter | MBS Clearing Corp. | Participants Trust Co., Federal Reserve Banks, and Depository Trust Co. |
| Equities [2] | New York Stock Exchange<br>Over the counter<br>American Stock Exchange | National Securities Clearing Corp. | Depository Trust Co. |
| Corporate bonds [3] | Over the counter<br>New York Stock Exchange | National Securities Clearing Corp. | Depository Trust Co. |
| Municipal bonds | Over the counter | National Securities Clearing Corp. | Depository Trust Co. |
| Options [4] | Chicago Board Options Exchange<br>American Stock Exchange<br>Philadelphia Stock Exchange | Options Clearing Corp. | Not applicable |
| Financial futures and futures options [5] | Chicago Board of Trade<br>Chicago Mercantile Exchange | Board of Trade Clearing Corp.<br>Chicago Mercantile Exchange | Not applicable |

1. Also traded on the New York Stock Exchange (cleared by National Securities Clearing Corp. (NSCC)).
2. Also traded on the Midwest Stock Exchange (cleared by Midwest Clearing Corp.; depository is Midwest Securities Trust Co.), the Philadelphia Stock Exchange (cleared by the Stock Clearing Corp. of Philadelphia; depository is Philadelphia Depository Trust Co.), and the Boston Stock Exchange, the Cincinnati Stock Exchange, and the Pacific Stock Exchange (all cleared by NSCC; depository is Depository Trust Co. (DTC)).
3. Also traded on the American Stock Exchange (cleared by NSCC; depository is DTC).
4. Also traded on the Pacific Stock Exchange and the New York Stock Exchange (both cleared by Options Clearing Corp.).
5. Also traded on the Mid-America Commodity Exchange (cleared by Board of Trade Clearing Corp.), the New York Cotton Exchange (cleared by Commodity Clearing Corp.), the Kansas City Board of Trade (cleared by Kansas City Board of Trade Clearing Corp.), and the New York Futures Exchange and the Philadelphia Board of Trade (both cleared by Intermarket Clearing Corp.). Additionally, the AMEX Commodities Corp. plans to start operations as an exchange in 1992; its trades will be cleared by Intermarket Clearing Corp.

U.S. government and federal agency securities and MBSs are traded over the counter. The Government Securities Clearing Corporation (GSCC) was formed in 1986 to compare, net, and settle trades in U.S. government securities. Same-day trades and repurchase agreements, however, clear and settle directly between broker-dealer counterparties. Although the business of GSCC has grown, the par value of same-day trades and repurchase agreements still exceeds the volume of transactions cleared by that organization. The MBS Clearing Corporation (MBSCC), formed in 1979, compares and nets the vast majority of broker-dealer MBS trades. (MBS transactions also may be cleared directly between counterparties.) The Federal Reserve is the depository for virtually all U.S. government securities, many federal agency securities, and MBSs guaranteed by the Federal National Mortgage Association and the Federal Home Loan Mortgage Corporation. In 1989, the Participants Trust Company commenced operations as a depository for MBSs guaranteed by the Government National Mortgage Association. Settlement of MBSs not guaranteed by a government agency (private MBSs) continues to be in physical form.

. . .

2. Key figures for U.S. securities, options, and financial futures markets, 1990

| Type of security | Amount outstanding at year-end | Average daily volume (value) | Annual turnover (percent) [1] |
|---|---|---|---|
| U.S. government and federal agency securities [2] | $2.589 billion [3] | $83.5 billion [4] | 860 |
| Mortgage-backed securities (MBSs) | $1.020 billion [5] | $16.4 billion [4] | 440 |
| Equities | $3.408 billion | 326 million shares ($7.9 billion) | 60 |
| Corporate bonds | $1.640 billion | $17.1 billion [6] | 280 |
| Municipal bonds | $840 billion | $3.0 billion [7] | 90 |
| Options | | | |
| Interest rate | Not significant | 300 contracts ($5 million underlying) | nil |
| Equity and equity index | 7.0 million contracts ($65 billion underlying) | 789.000 contracts ($13.2 billion underlying) | 90 [8] |
| Foreign currency | 575,000 contracts ($26 billion underlying) | 40,000 contracts ($1.7 billion underlying) | ... |
| Financial futures and futures options | | | |
| Interest rates | 2.0 million contracts ($1.071 billion underlying) [9] | 627,000 contracts ($218.7 billion underlying) [10] | 490 [11] |
| Equity index | 233,000 contracts ($35 billion underlying) | 65,000 contracts ($11.0 billion underlying) | 80 [12] |
| Foreign currency | 434,000 contracts ($40 billion underlying) | 148,000 contracts ($12.6 billion underlying) | ... |

1. Based on average amount outstanding during the year.
2. Excluding mortgage-backed securities.
3. Marketable issues only.
4. Primary dealers only.
5. Issues backed by a U.S. government agency.
6. Includes $1.9 billion cleared by NSCC.
7. Includes $2.2 billion cleared by NSCC.
8. Securities underlying options traded as a percentage of all equities outstanding.
9. Includes 1.0 million contracts on U.S. government securities ($155 billion), 874,000 contracts on Eurodollar deposits ($874 billion), and 53,000 other contracts ($42 billion).
10. Includes 460,000 contracts on U.S. government securities ($52.4 billion), 164,000 contracts on Eurodollar deposits ($164.3 billion), and 3,000 other contracts ($1.9 billion).
11. Securities underlying futures and futures options on U.S. government securities traded as a percentage of all marketable U.S. government and non-MBS agency securities.
12. Securities underlying futures and futures options traded as a percentage of all equities outstanding.

SOURCES: *Federal Reserve Bulletin,* National Securities Clearing Corporation (NSCC), Options Clearing Corporation, Futures Industry Association, Public Securities Association, Securities Industry Association, and Federal Reserve staff estimates.

### 3. Credit, Liquidity, and Operational Risks in Clearance and Settlement

#### Definitions

At the outset, the terms *credit risk, liquidity risk,* and *operational risk* must be defined precisely. The definitions of credit risk and liquidity risk used in this paper are those used by the Committee on Payment and Settlement Systems (formerly the Group of Experts on Payment Systems) and the Committee on Interbank Netting Schemes in analyzing interbank systems for clearance and settlement of payment orders and foreign exchange obligations. *Credit risk* is the risk that a trade will not settle for full value, either when due or at any time thereafter. *Liquidity risk* is the risk that settlement will be made not at the appointed time, but at some unspecified time thereafter. Although the distinction between credit and liquidity risks is important, it is worth noting that at the time a settlement failure is detected, the counterparties of the participant that failed to settle may not know whether a credit problem or a liquidity problem is involved.

*Operational risk* is the risk of a breakdown of some component of the hardware, software, or communications systems that are critical to settlement of financial transactions. Such breakdowns clearly could create serious liquidity problems by delaying settlement of transactions. Breakdown of a key operational component also could heighten credit risks in at least two ways. First, it could hamper the ability of participants in the settlement process to monitor and control their credit exposures. Second, as is discussed below, any development that increases the time between a trade and its settlement increases credit risk.

As noted in section 1, policymakers have been especially concerned about the potential for clearance and settlement arrangements to create systemic risks. Here again, a precise definition of systemic risk is needed. In previous work by various Group of Ten groups, systemic risk was defined as the risk that the inability of one counterparty to meet its obligations when due (for either financial or operational reasons) will cause other counterparties also to be unable to meet their obligations when due. If the obligation were met at a later time, the systemic risk in question would be a liquidity risk; if not, it would be a credit risk. Defined this way, systemic liquidity risks are commonplace; for example, failure of one counterparty to make timely delivery of a security frequently causes the receiver to fail to make timely redelivery. Private market participants have developed banking and other contractual arrangements that allow them to manage such routine liquidity pressures.

Thus, although this definition of systemic risk is precise, it covers events that most central bankers probably would not include in their definition of systemic risk. From a central banker's perspective, *systemic risk* is the risk that credit losses and liquidity pressures arising from financial or operational problems (of a clearing organization, a participant, or a settlement bank) could be sufficiently large that they cannot be managed and contained using the established banking and contractual arrangements and that, as a result, the stability of financial markets could be jeopardized.

## Credit Risk

The counterparties to a financial transaction are exposed to credit losses in the course of clearing and settling the transaction because (1) the price of the security involved can change between the time the trade is initiated and the time it is settled and (2) delivery of the security and payment in many cases are not synchronized. Credit risk that stems from changes in security prices is often called market risk. However, to avoid confusion with the risk of capital loss (absent a default by a trading counterparty), it seems appropriate to adopt the terminology used by the Committee on Interbank Netting Schemes and refer to such credit risk as *replacement-cost risk.* (This terminology reflects an assumption that if a counterparty defaults prior to settlement, the nondefaulting counterparty would not complete its settlement obligation, but instead would promptly replace its obligation to deliver or receive the security with a new contract with a third party.) Credit risk that stems from gaps in the timing of payments and receipts on the settlement date is termed *principal risk.*

At the time a transaction is initiated, it generally can be replaced at virtually no cost, because the market price of the security—the price at which the replacement transaction would be consummated—presumably would be quite close to the original contract price. As time passes, however, the market price may move away from the contract price. Depending on the direction of the price change, one of the counterparties would suffer a loss in replacing the transaction—the buyer if the price had increased, the seller if the price had decreased. Because the direction of change in market price is uncertain, both parties to the transaction are exposed to replacement-cost risk. The magnitude of the risk depends on the volatility of the security price and the length of time between the transaction and its settlement.

Even so-called cash or spot market transactions can involve significant replacement-cost risk. Relatively few transactions are settled on a same-day, much less a real-time, basis. In U.S. securities markets, the lag between trade and settlement typically is one day for U.S. government securities, five days for equities and most corporate and municipal bonds, and as much as thirty days for certain mortgage-backed securities. To cite an extreme example of replacement-cost risk, the prices of ten of the thirty stocks making up the Dow Jones Industrial Average declined 35 percent or more over five-day intervals in October 1987. A default by a buyer of one of the stocks during that period would have exposed the seller to losses of that magnitude. Forward contracts can entail quite substantial replacement-cost risk. In fact, if the seller defaults and the market price of the security has more than doubled since the transaction, the added cost to the buyer would exceed the value of the security at the time of the original trade. However, such extreme movements in security prices are the exception rather than the rule.

The largest credit exposures in clearance and settlement typically occur on settlement day, when the full principal value of the security can be at risk. In some markets, delivery of the security and delivery of the payment often are not synchronized. If the security is delivered prior to receipt of payment, the deliverer risks losing the full value of the security. If payment is made prior to delivery, the payor risks losing the full value of the payment. In some cases, the sequence in which deliveries and payments will occur is known in advance and principal risk is clearly asymmetric. In other cases, the sequence is not known in advance; indeed, even on settlement day the counterparties may lack real-time information on the status of deliveries and payments.

**Liquidity Risk**

Both counterparties to a financial transaction are exposed to liquidity risk on settlement day. The seller has an incentive to minimize its holdings of relatively low yield transactions balances. Consequently, if its counterparty does not pay on settlement day, the seller generally must borrow funds or liquidate assets to offset the resulting shortfall in its transactions account. The cost to the seller of covering the shortfall depends on the time of day the payment is due; because access to sources of liquidity often becomes limited as the end of the business day approaches, payment failure late in the day can be especially costly.

On the other side of a transaction, the buyer may have engaged in subsequent transactions that require it to deliver the security in question. If the seller defaults, the buyer must either borrow the security from a third party or fail to complete its delivery obligation. The liquidity of markets for borrowing and lending securities varies widely. Moreover, borrowing and lending securities in turn involve credit, liquidity, and operational risks.

## 4. Potential Benefits of Clearing Organizations

### Types and Functions of Clearing Organizations

Two types of specialized financial intermediaries (or *clearing organizations* ) have been developed to reduce credit and liquidity risks (as well as transactions costs) to participants in securities clearance and settlement. *Clearinghouses* perform multilateral netting of securities transactions among their participants; many also provide trade comparison (confirmation and matching) services. *Depositories* immobilize or dematerialize securities and typically integrate a book-entry securities transfer system with a money transfer system to achieve delivery against payment.

### Trade Comparison

*Trade comparison* is the process of confirming and matching the terms of a securities transaction (the issue, price, quantity, and counterparties). This function may be performed by the clearinghouse or, in the case of securities traded on an exchange, by the exchange itself. By speeding up the matching of trades, a trade comparison system reduces credit risk in several important ways. First, it provides a clearing organization and its participants with more timely information on the magnitude of unsettled positions and associated risks. Some clearinghouses have moved to replace batch, end-of-day comparison systems with on-line systems, thereby making it possible to monitor and control intraday exposures. Second, by decreasing the time between trade and settlement, a trade comparison system generally reduces replacement-cost risk, both because potential changes in securities prices between trade and settlement are smaller and because the number of unsettled trades tends to decrease. Finally, a trade comparison system, with its quicker matching of trades, allows trades to be netted more promptly.

### Multilateral Netting

Both the legal foundations and the economics of multilateral netting of securities transactions closely parallel those for the netting of payment orders and foreign exchange transactions, which have been studied in detail by the Committee on Interbank Netting Schemes. In securities markets, *multilateral netting* is achieved in several ways. In some cases, the clearinghouse acts as a central counterparty. Participants enter into a transaction bilaterally. If certain conditions are met, the clearinghouse subsequently is substituted as the buyer to the seller and the seller to the buyer, and any obligations between the participants pursuant to the original transaction are discharged. The clearinghouse keeps a running record of its net position vis-á-vis each participant for each security and each settlement date. For a given set of transactions, this process leaves each participant with net obligations to deliver to, or receive from, the clearinghouse amounts of securities equal to its multilateral net position vis-á-vis other participants in the clearinghouse. For each settlement date, each participant's payment obligations are settled by a single payment to, or from, the clearinghouse.

In other multilateral netting schemes, the clearinghouse guarantees completion of all matched, unsettled transactions among its participants. In still other arrangements, the clearinghouse calculates a multilateral net position for each participant vis-á-vis other participants but neither substitutes itself as central counterparty nor guarantees completion of transactions. The latter arrangements are what the Committee on Interbank Netting Schemes called "position netting"; obligations are routinely settled by delivery and payment of the net amounts, but in the event of a default, the multilateral net positions are not legally binding on participants.

Legally binding multilateral netting has the potential to reduce both principal risk and replacement-cost risk. Principal risk can be reduced because the value of the securities that must be delivered to settle a given value of trades typically is far smaller than the gross value of the securities traded. Replacement-cost risk can be reduced because potential losses from replacing some trades are offset by gains from replacing other trades. The magnitude of potential risk reductions depends on trading patterns. Principal risks can be reduced dramatically when participants both buy and sell substantial amounts of the same securities. Assuming that securities prices are positively correlated, smaller but still significant reductions in replacement-cost risk can be achieved if participants are buyers of some securities and sellers of others.

Regardless of the pattern of trading, multilateral netting by a clearinghouse can reduce replacement-cost risk by facilitating prompt closeout and replacement of unsettled transactions. Because a single counterparty or guarantor replaces multiple counterparties, there is no need for multiple negotiations to close out unsettled transactions. Also, multilateral netting arrangements generally specify procedures for determining the value of unsettled positions and for allocating losses to surviving participants.

Netting arrangements also are designed to reduce liquidity risk. In a multilateral netting system, all of a participant's obligations to deliver or receive a *particular* security on a specific settlement day are discharged through making or receiving a single delivery. In addition, *all* of a participant's obligations to make or receive payment on settlement day are discharged through making or receiving a single payment. If a security is to be received, the amount to be received is no larger, and generally is considerably smaller, than the sum of the amounts that would be delivered in the absence of netting. Likewise, if a cash payment is to be received, the amount to be received is reduced by netting. Consequently, the liquidity pressures arising from unanticipated failures to receive securities or payments can be greatly diminished by legally binding multilateral netting. Clearinghouses in the United States typically report that multilateral netting reduces the value of deliveries by 70 percent to 90 percent, implying potential reductions of that magnitude in both principal and liquidity risks.

**Delivery Against Payment**

Credit and liquidity risks can also be reduced through creation of a depository. A depository immobilizes or dematerializes securities and uses a computerized accounting system to record and transfer ownership of securities. By integrating a book-entry system with a money transfer system, a depository can substantially reduce or even eliminate principal risk. Elimination of principal risk requires a *delivery-against-payment* system, which provides assurances to participants that final securities transfers (deliveries) will occur if, and only if, final money transfers (payments) occur. In such a system, when instructed to transfer ownership of a security from one participant to another, the depository debits the security account and credits the money account of the first participant, and simultaneously credits the security account and debits the money account of the second participant for the same amounts.

In the United States, debits and credits to securities and money accounts in the Federal Reserve's book-entry system for U.S. government securities are final (irrevocable and unconditional) as soon as they are posted; both the securities and funds transfer systems are gross, real-time systems. In contrast, at private depositories, both the money and securities transfers in these systems initially are provisional. Participants receive final payment in the form of a claim on the Federal Reserve or on a settlement bank. Payment typically must be made by the end of the day. Throughout the day, debits and credits to money accounts are netted. At the end of the day, participants in a net debit position make final payment to the depository, and participants in a net credit position receive final payment from the depository. Securities transfers in the system become final only when all participants in a net debit position have completed final payment. Private depositories typically employ a variety of safeguards (discussed in section 6) designed to assure participants that the net settlements will be completed on schedule.

. . .

## 6. Risk Management by Individual Clearing Organizations

**Key Issues**

To ensure that they realize their potential benefits, U.S. securities clearing organizations have established risk-management systems designed to limit potential credit losses and liquidity pressures from participant defaults and to ensure that even if defaults occur, settlement can be completed on schedule and losses recovered from surviving participants. They also have sought to ensure the operational reliability of all the hardware, software, and communications systems that are critical to the completion of settlements. Although the approaches to achieving these objectives vary from clearing organization to clearing organization, all well-designed systems have addressed several key issues: responsibilities and incentives for risk management; standards for membership; safeguards against credit and liquidity risks; and operational safeguards. Table 3 summarizes safeguards at selected U.S. clearing organizations.

**Responsibility for Risk Management**

The most basic issue in risk management is the division of responsibility for risk management between the clearing organization and its participants. A clearing organization may seek to preserve incentives to manage risks bilaterally (a decentralized approach to risk management), or it may itself assume primary responsibility for risk management (a centralized approach). Either approach can prove effective in limiting risks; what is critical is that participants understand clearly where the responsibility rests.

Many U.S. clearing organizations assume total responsibility for risk management. They typically employ a full-time staff that reviews membership applications and continually monitors member compliance with financial and operational requirements. Participants are not expected to manage their counterparty exposures and have little or no incentive to do so. Participants in a clearinghouse, for example, might be expected to be responsible for losses from their bilateral dealings with a defaulting counterparty if the default occurred before the substitution of the clearinghouse as counterparty (or prior to the time when its guarantee became effective). However, when defaults have occurred, clearinghouses sometimes have accepted responsibility for all matched trades, even if the substitution (or guarantee) had not taken effect prior to the default. In such instances, the extent of participants' bilateral dealings have had no effect on their losses from a default. Consequently, participants in such systems may perceive the clearing organization to have assumed complete responsibility for risk management and may differentiate among trade counterparties only on the basis of their reliability in reporting terms of transactions promptly and accurately, if at all.

Although assumption of complete responsibility for risk management by the clearing organization is common in U.S. markets, several recently established organizations for clearing and settling over-the-counter transactions have been structured to encourage participants to manage credit risks bilaterally. These organizations (Participants Trust Company (PTC), the Government Securities Clearing Corporation (GSCC), the Depository Trust Company's (DTC) same-day funds settlement (SDFS) system, and the MBS Clearing Corporation (MBSCC)) have, for example, instituted loss-sharing rules that allocate credit losses to surviving participants on the basis of their bilateral dealings with the defaulting participant.

Even though they require loss sharing, however, most of these clearing organizations have retained substantial responsibility for risk management.

None has adopted an approach as highly decentralized as that of the Clearing House Interbank Payment System (CHIPS), in which limits on a participant's activity are based solely on bilateral credit decisions by other participants.

. . .

3. Key features of risk-management systems at selected U.S. clearing organizations, 1991

| Feature | U.S. government securities | | Mortgage-backed securities | | Corporate and municipal securities | | Options | Futures |
|---|---|---|---|---|---|---|---|---|
| | Book-entry | | | | | DTC | | BOTCC, |
| | GSCC | Fedwire | MBSCC | PTC | NSCC | (NDFS) | OCC | CME |
| Monitoring of participants' financial condition | Yes | Yes | Yes | Yes | Yes | Yes | Yes | Yes |
| Incentives for bilateral risk management (loss-sharing agreements) | Yes | No | Yes | Yes | No | No | No | No |
| Membership standards | Yes | Yes | Yes | Yes | Yes | Yes | Yes | Yes |
| Net debit caps (or position limits) | No | Yes | No | Yes | No | No | Yes | Yes |
| Marking-to-market | Yes[2] | No | Yes | No | Yes[3] | No | Yes | Yes |
| Collateral requirements | | | | | | | | |
| On direct obligations | Yes | Yes[4] | Yes | Yes | No | No | Yes | Yes |
| On contingent obligations | Yes | n.a. | n.a. | Yes | Yes | Yes | Yes | Yes |
| Bank credit lines | Yes | n.a. | No | Yes | Yes | No | Yes | Yes |

2. Forward-settling trades and trades that failed to settle on the customary settlement day are subject to variation margin.
3. Trades that failed to settle on the customary settlement day are subject to variation margin.
4. Since January 10, 1991, the Federal Reserve has required account holders that incur material and frequent funds overdrafts related to book-entry activity to pledge collateral.
n.a. Not applicable.

## *Notes and Questions*

1. The clearing of securities involves two basic functions, matching of trades and the net position calculation. Trade matching requires confirming the identity and quantity of the security being traded, the transaction price and date, and the identity of the buyer and seller. This is often referred to as the trade comparison process. The net position calculation involves calculating the net position of the participants in terms of securities that must be delivered and funds that must be paid. How does trade matching occur when securities are traded on an exchange. How are the trade facts captured?

2. Net position calculation can be on a bilateral or multilateral basis. If A buys from B 100 shares of IBM at $1 per share and sells to B 50 shares of IBM at $3 per share, what are their net securities and cash positions? If A buys 100 IBM from B at $1, B buys 50 IBM from C at $3, and C buys 40 IBM from A at $2, what are the net securities and cash positions of the three parties if there is a multilateral netting?

3. The settlement of the securities and cash positions may take place through a variety of mechanisms. The actual transfer of the securities may occur by physical delivery of certificates or by book entries denoting a change of ownership. Where transfer is by book

entries, the securities may be held by a central depository which will make the appropriate debit or credit entries to the appropriate parties. Cash payments are usually by cashiers checks or wire transfers. For exchange trades, who has the obligation to deliver the securities and pay the funds? How does this affect the risk of trading?

4. It is quite important whether or not the delivery of securities and the payments occur relatively simultaneously. If securities are delivered before funds, the party that has delivered the securities is out the cash, and is at risk for a failure to pay. Conversely if funds are paid out before securities are received, the party that has paid the funds is at risk for the failure to deliver the securities. This is why some systems have a delivery versus payment (DvP) requirement.

5. Note that settlement occurs at two levels: between the parties to the trade, e.g. two broker-dealers (b/d), and between the b/ds and their customers. The timing between these two levels may be important. If a b/d must settle with another b/d before settlement occurs between the b/d and the customer, the b/d may have risk, e.g. b/d purchases the security, it goes down in value and the customer does not pay.

6. Let's now look specifically at the NSCC process. NSCC is owned by the major U.S. stock exchanges and NASD, and has 400 direct participants. NSCC effects clearing and settlement of 95% of all equity trades in the United States, and also clears corporate bonds, as well as some other securities, e.g. municipal bonds. NSCC does not clear all securities or derivatives. U.S. treasuries are cleared by the Federal Reserve and other clearing corporations clear commercial paper, options, and futures.

DTC is a New York limited purpose trust company, a quasi-bank, which is the world's largest securities depository. It is owned by bank and securities firm participants. DTC holds securities (individual or global certificates) and accounts for the ownership interests of its participants in the form of book-entries, e.g. A +100 IBM. It also has funds accounts in connection with institutional settlement. It holds some securities that are not cleared by NSCC, e.g. commercial paper.

DTC apart from accounting for the ownership of securities and funds, also performs other functions, e.g. it collects and distributes dividends and interest.

Look at Figure A–1, in the Office of Technology Assessment piece, that details the NSCC–DTC process for retail trades. The process begins on T, and is completed with settlement on T+5. Why does this take so long?

8. The NSCC system to deal with fails does not eliminate all of NSCC's risk. How would you summarize its maximum risk in the interim and later periods? What can NSCC do to protect itself against these remaining risks?

9. Lets look at T+5 on Figure A–1. How are the securities delivered and how are the funds paid? Is this a DvP system?

10. Lets now look at Figure A–2 for institutional trades. How do the procedures differ from those used on retail trades? What explains the differences?

---

## B. GROUP OF THIRTY PROPOSALS

Trading Around the Clock, pp. 59–61.

### EFFORTS TO REDUCE THE DIFFERENCES

Improvement of clearing and settlement for global or cross-border trading in equities is being addressed by the Group of Thirty, an independent, non-profit organization of businesspersons, bankers, and representatives of financial institutions from 30 developed nations. The Group of Thirty addresses multi-national financial and economic issues, including Third World debt. The Group's recommendations for the world's securities markets are aimed at "maximizing the efficiency and reducing the cost of clearance and settlement," and thereby reducing risk. They set target timetables of 1990 for some objectives and 1992 for others. In a report released in 1989, the Group concluded that:

> While the development of a single global clearing facility was not practical, agreement on a set of practices and standards that could be embraced by each of the many markets that make up the world's securities system was highly desirable, . . . and (reached) agreement that the present standards were not acceptable.

Their recommendations are:

1. By 1990, all comparisons of trades between direct market participants (i.e., brokers, dealers, and other exchange members) should be compared within 1 day after a trade is executed, or "T+1."
2. Indirect market participants—institutional investors, or any trading counterparties which are not broker/dealers—should be members of a trade comparison system which achieves positive affirmation of trade details.
3. Each country should have an effective and fully developed central securities depository, organized and managed to encourage the broadest possible industry participation.
4. Each country should study its market volumes and participation to determine whether a trade netting system would be beneficial in terms of reducing risk and promoting efficiency.
5. Delivery versus payment should be the method for settling all securities transactions.
6. Payments associated with the settlement of securities transactions and the servicing of securities portfolios should be made consistent across all instruments and markets by adopting the

"same day" convention. (No date has been set for achieving this objective.)

7. A "rolling settlement" system should be adopted by all markets. Final settlement should occur on T+3 by 1992. As an interim target, final settlement should occur on T+5 by 1990 at the latest, except where it hinders the achievement of T+3 by 1992.
8. Securities lending and borrowing should be encouraged as a method of expediting the settlement of securities transactions. Existing regulatory and taxation barriers that inhibit the practice of lending securities should be removed in 1990.
9. Each country should adopt the technical standard for securities messages developed by the International Organization for Standardization (ISO Standards 7775 and 6166).

Table 5–1 compares nine of the Group of Thirty recommendations with the present status of clearing and settlement procedures in 21 countries, including the United States. Major changes will be required by many countries in order to meet these recommendations by 1992. In the United States, which is well-positioned relative to other countries, automated systems will facilitate trade matching on the trade date and settlement of all trades within 3 days. But, in the United States, there are non-technological barriers to fully achieving the accelerated trade and settlement objectives, some of which have been acted on recently. For example:

- More stocks must be immobilized in book entry form; this means that retail customers may have to abandon their pattern of receiving certificates of ownership for their stock shares.
- The pattern of mailing personal checks to pay for stock purchases will have to change to a more rapid payment method such as electronic bank-to-bank transfer of guaranteed funds.

**Table 5–1**

**Group of Thirty: Current Status of International Settlement Recommendations—Equities***

| Recommendation No.<br>Country: | 1<br>Institutional Comparison on T+1 | 2<br>Central Comparison System | 3<br>Securities Depository | 4<br>Securities Netting | 5<br>DVP | 6<br>Same-Day Funds | 7<br>Rolling Settlement on T+3 | 8<br>Securities Lending | 9<br>ISO/ ISIM |
|---|---|---|---|---|---|---|---|---|---|
| Australia | Yes | No | No | Yes | Yes | No | T+5 | Yes | No |
| Austria | Yes | No | Yes | Yes | Yes | Yes | Weekly | Yes | Yes |
| Belgium | Yes | No | Yes | No | Yes | Yes | T+3 | No | Yes |
| Canada | Yes | Yes | Yes | Yes | Yes | No | T+5 | Yes | No |
| France | Yes | Yes | Yes | Yes | Yes | Yes | T+3 | Yes | Yes |
| Germany | Yes | No | Yes | No | Yes | Yes | T+2 | No | No |
| Hong Kong | Yes | No | Yes | Yes | Yes | No | T+2 | Yes | No |
| Italy | Yes | Yes | Yes | Yes | Yes | Yes | T+3 | Limited | No |
| Japan | Yes | No | Yes | Yes | Yes | No | T+3 | Yes | No |
| Singapore | Yes | Yes | Yes | No | No | No | T+5 | Yes | No |
| Spain | Yes | No | No | No | No | No | Weekly | Limited | No |
| Switzerland | Yes | No | Yes | No | Yes | Yes | T+3 | Yes | No |
| United Kingdom | Yes | Yes | No | Yes | No | Yes | Fortnightly | Yes | Yes |
| United States | Yes | Yes | Yes | Yes | Yes | No | T+5 | Yes | No |

* The editors have updated this chart through mid-1992.

# GROUP OF THIRTY, CLEARANCE AND SETTLEMENT STATUS REPORTS

*Autumn 1992* (United States).

## I. DEVELOPMENTS TO 1992

How close is the U.S. to implementing the Group of Thirty recommendations? Specifically, how close is the U.S. to a T+3 settlement period and a same day funds payment convention, the two recommendations with which the U.S. market system is not in compliance? Neither of the recommendations will be implemented in 1992, the year targeted by the Group of Thirty for implementation of most of the nine recommendations, including settlement on T+3. However, the U.S. Working Committee has identified the specific issues involved in implementing the recommendations and has made progress in addressing those issues.

### A. Overview of the U.S. Clearance and Settlement Project

The U.S. securities industry initially viewed the goal of the Group of Thirty recommendations to harmonize clearance and settlement practices among developed securities markets as worthwhile. However, complete, unquestioned acceptance of any change is rare. As the U.S. securities industry evaluated the two recommendations applicable to the U.S. in terms of existing operations, systems and business practices, and the possible changes their implementation represented, over time the recommendations came to mean different things to industry participants.

By 1990 both the T+3 settlement and same day funds recommendations were thought by some to represent significant operational and technological changes as well as change to long-standing, well-established business practices in the U.S. corporate and municipal securities markets. Therefore, throughout 1990 and 1991, the U.S. Working Committee focused on identifying and evaluating the specific issues involved in shortening the settlement cycle and adopting a same day funds payment mechanism. Early on in this evaluation, the Working Committee recognized that the T+3 settlement recommendation provided an opportunity to accelerate the current trend toward book entry settlement and, therefore, expanded the scope of the clearance and settlement project to include recommendations for street-side book entry only settlement and depository eligibility for new issues (see the section on The Group of Thirty Recommendations in the U.S. for the specific wording of these recommendations).

The Working Committee, after extensive review of the specific issues and concerns raised by the book entry only settlement, depository eligibility, and same day funds recommendations, concluded in 1992 that all of these issues are solvable by modifying systems, changing settlement practices, and educating investors and are not impediments to implementing the recommendations.

The Working Committee's evaluation of the T+3 settlement recommendation, however, was more complicated because of the retail component of the securities markets and the potential impact this recommendation might have on that segment of the market. As a result, this recommendation was the source of considerable discussion. Some participants viewed shortening the settlement period as an opportunity for substantial benefit at a small cost while others viewed it as representing a major change to existing systems and practices requiring great sacrifice with little to gain. In light of the complex economic and operational issues affecting retail firms, the chairman of the U.S. Securities and Exchange Commission formed a small, independent task force to facilitate the discussion and evaluation of changes to the U.S. securities clearance and settlement system. Following the formation in November 1991 of the Task Force, chaired by John W. Bachmann, Managing Principal of Edward D. Jones & Co., the U.S. Working Committee suspended its evaluation of T+3 settlement pending the release of the Task Force's findings.

The U.S. Working Committee reviewed the recommendation and built its discussions around global competitiveness and efficiency. The Bachmann Task Force, whose specific charter was to evaluate the safety and soundness of the clearance and settlement system in the U.S. securities markets and to determine changes necessary to achieve a safer and more efficient system, analyzed the recommendation from a risk perspective. The Task Force's quantitative risk analysis of shortening the settlement cycle supported, from the standpoint of reducing risk, the original Group of Thirty recommendation to adopt a T+3 settlement cycle. In addition, the Task Force's review of the practicality and potential obstacles to shortening the settlement period confirmed the Working Committee's conclusion that the lack of an electronic retail payment mechanism and the existing affirmation process for institutional transactions are solvable problems rather than obstacles to moving to settlement on T+3. The Working Committee fully supports the findings of the Task Force, including its recommendation to move quickly to shorten the settlement period to T+3 in the interest of increasing the safety and soundness of the clearance and settlement system. The Task Force's findings were formally presented in a report to the chairman of the U.S. Securities and Exchange Commission in May 1992.

### B. The Group of Thirty Recommendations in the U.S.—The Final Form

The U.S. Working Committee, as a result of preliminary fact gathering and analysis of the recommendations, further defined the same day funds and T+3 settlement recommendations for the U.S. corporate and municipal securities markets. As stated earlier, the Working Committee also expanded the scope of the clearance and settlement project to include recommendations for book entry settlement among financial intermediaries and their institutional customers and depository eligibility for all new issues. The Committee believes the recommendations, as follows, are the most effective and practical method for reducing risk in the national market system:

- Settlements and other movements of corporate and municipal securities must be effected only by book entry movements within a depository for transactions among financial intermediaries (brokers, dealers, and banks) and between financial intermediaries and their institutional clients.
- All new corporate or municipal securities issued must be eligible for depository processing, and procedures have to be developed to monitor inappropriate sale transactions during new issue stabilization periods.
- Payments for settlements among financial intermediaries, and between financial intermediaries and their institutional customers, should be made using same day funds. This recommendation would also apply to payments associated with dividends, interest, redemptions, and reorganizations. The Committee does not recommend, at this time, the use of same day funds for settlement payments between financial intermediaries and their retail customers.

While the Working Committee set 1992 as the target date for implementing these recommendations, its primary focus was on achieving implementation at the earliest possible date with minimal disruption to the industry; therefore, the Working Committee recognized that the goal of implementing the recommendations in 1992 was optimistic.

The Working Committee, as noted before, put aside its discussions of the recommendation to shorten the settlement cycle to T+3 when the chairman of the U.S. Securities and Exchange Commission chartered the Bachmann Task Force to explore that recommendation as part of its study of improving the safety and soundness of the U.S. securities clearance and settlement system.

. . .

### F. T+3 Settlement

In its discussions of shortening the settlement cycle, the Working Committee initially identified several issues that needed to be addressed to move T+3. These included the receipt of a written confirmation by the retail customer as a trigger for payment, the lack of an electronic payment system for retail transactions, and the current affirmation process for institutional trades. Of equal importance was the issue of changing customer behavior regarding long-standing business practices. Each of these issues was discussed at length by the Working Committee and later by the Bachmann Task Force.

### Receipt of Confirmations

- The Legal and Regulatory Subgroup quickly dismissed the significance of the confirmation issue by determining that the receipt of the confirmation is not legally required for the settlement of an equities transaction, although there is a legal requirement to send a confirmation. However, since many customers are accustomed to receiving a confirmation before paying for their transactions, the confirmation issue becomes one of modifying customer behavior. The Working Committee concluded that modifying customer behavior can be achieved through industry-wide information and education efforts.

**Electronic Retail Payment System**

- Many firms rely on checks to send and receive customer funds. The current mail delivery time frames in many cases would not accommodate payment by check in a T+3 settlement period. Recognizing that collection of funds from customers was a major issue in moving to T+3, the Working Committee determined that some type of electronic retail payment system was necessary.

One such payment mechanism already in use by some in the securities industry is the Automated Clearing House (ACH), a domestic electronic payment system used by over 22,000 banks, thrifts, and other depository financial institutions on behalf of corporations and individuals. The diverse body of regulations governing ACH, however, do not mesh smoothly with the conventions in place in the securities industry to permit widespread use. Specifically, these regulations, which were designed to protect retail users of electronic funds transfer systems, allow retail users to rescind payment for unauthorized transactions for a lengthy period of time. After reviewing ACH as a payment alternative to checks, the Working Committee determined that the use of ACH is a step toward achieving safer and sounder markets and that the removal of these rescission rights for retail securities transactions would permit more widespread use of ACH as a payment mechanism, thereby further increasing the safety and soundness of the markets.

The National Automated Clearing House Association (NACHA), whose rules govern the use of ACH, initiated rule changes in 1992 that would eliminate the rescission rights for securities transactions. In May 1992 the Rules and Operations Committee of NACHA approved the proposed amendment to its Operating Rules and Guidelines which would add a new Standard Entry Class Code for the purchase of retail securities and commodities. The new Standard Entry Class Code would eliminate the current 60–day rescission rights for payments. In June NACHA's Executive Committee recommended approval of the rule change and put it out to the associations for vote. It is unfortunate that the member associations of NACHA voted against the proposed rule change. While this rule change is not critical to the adoption of the T+3 recommendation since ACH can be used without the rule change, it would make the use of ACH for retail securities transactions more practical. Because the Working Committee views this rule change as part of the drive toward safer and sounder markets, it will work with NACHA to develop a strategy to bring the issue to another vote.

Federal Reserve Regulation E, which was also designed to protect retail users of electronic funds transfer systems, must also be amended to exempt securities transactions from rescission rights. A formal request to amend Regulation E was drafted and presented to the Board of Governors of the Federal Reserve which has expressed an interest in amending Regulation E; however, the Board of Governors of the Federal Reserve has not indicated a time frame for doing so.

The Working Committee recognizes that changing customer behavior about payment practices is perhaps the most significant issue involved in moving to T+3. This represents a cultural change for retail investors and may require broker/dealers to adjust well-established, settled customer relationships. The Working Committee believes that just as banking customers accepted Automated Teller Machines, retail investors will accept an electronic payment mechanism if properly educated and informed by the industry about the advantages of such a system.

## III. DEVELOPMENTS AFTER 1992

The Working Committee has finished its evaluation and analysis of the issues involved in implementing the two recommendations that affect the U.S. The exploratory phase of the clearance and settlement project has been completed. What remains is the development of the systems that are required to address the issues raised during the analysis of the recommendations and finally, the implementation of those systems.

In the next year, the SROs will distribute the proposed uniform book entry rule to their individual memberships for comment. While some changes to the rule may be necessary to accommodate exceptions to the book entry settlement requirement, the Working Committee envisions that the implementation of book entry settlement among financial intermediaries and their institutional customers will occur in 1993 following membership approval of the rule. The Working Committee also anticipates that depository eligibility for new issues will occur in 1993 through the adoption of a uniform rule by the membership of the SROs.

As stated earlier, the DTC already anticipates the implementation of an initial interactive ID system by the end of 1993 with full implementation in 1994.

The recent defeat of the proposed rule change to eliminate rescission rights for ACH payments for securities transactions will delay the use of ACH as a practical electronic payment alternative to checks. NACHA expects to revise the rule further to address the concerns expressed in the recently completed voting process and distribute the rule change to the NACHA associations for vote in 1993. However, NACHA generally implements new rules once a year in April. Therefore, if accepted, this rule would most likely not become effective until April 1994.

While both the T+3 and same day funds have targeted implementation dates of 1994, these dates are dependent on favorable responses to their respective public comment periods.

What is the role of the Working Committee over the next two years? Now that the project is in the systems development phase, the Working Committee believes these efforts are best left to the focus groups and other organizations that participated in the detailed analyses of the recommendations. The actual implementation of the recommendations is best left to the appropriate industry organizations and regulatory agencies. The Working Committee will continue to meet to review the development efforts and to provide ongoing oversight of the implementation of the recommendations.

The Working Committee acknowledges that there is a limit to what private-sector initiatives such as this one can accomplish, particularly in terms of timing. However, the Working Committee is optimistic that, working with the regulatory organizations, it can effectively oversee the implementation of the recommendations in a timely manner.

### *Notes and Questions*

1. The G–30 has made a number of recommendations to standardize clearing and settlement in different countries. Is standardization a desirable objective? If so, why?

2. What changes will NSCC have to make to comply with the G–30 recommendations? And what are the costs and benefits of making those changes? It is important to note that the SEC adopted a new Rule 15c6–1 on October 6, 1993, requiring T+3 settlement by June 1, 1995.

3. As one can see from Table 5–1, in the excerpt from *Trading Around the Clock,* the LSE in the United Kingdom has a fortnightly settlement (once every two weeks). They also have a paper based settlement system with no central depository. The following pieces describe some of their difficulties in changing the present system. What does the sorry state of the LSE settlement system say about the importance of such systems in competition between stock exchanges?

## RICHARD WATERS, "THE PLAN THAT FELL TO EARTH"

Financial Times (March 12, 1993).

The City yesterday turned its back on a complicated and expensive stock market settlement system in favour of a "quick fix". Hundreds of millions of pounds of development costs, incurred by more than 150 financial institutions in the City and many more listed companies, were formally abandoned at 3 pm, when news of the decision was announced.

The London Stock Exchange board's decision to drop its blighted Taurus project has shaken the confidence of the City establishment. It was planned by a wide range of institutions with interests in the securities industry to be an electronic system of ownership and transfer of shareholdings.

City leaders had always stressed that it was an essential part of the infrastructure needed to underpin London's stock market and reinforce its claim to being Europe's leading financial centre. In the event, it proved only that the City establishment is incapable of overcoming the conflicting self-interests of its members to put London as a financial centre first.

Mr. Peter Rawlins, chief executive of the Stock Exchange, yesterday resigned, to take responsibility for the failure of the project. But Sir Andrew Hugh Smith, exchange chairman and chief executive for the moment, pinned the blame largely on the fact that the early design for Taurus, developed by the exchange, was rejected in 1989. Service registrars, who maintain share registers for listed companies, voted down the idea because it could have put them out of business. "It wasn't surprising—after all, turkeys don't vote for Christmas."

Yesterday's move also raises serious questions about the future of the Stock Exchange, which has been traumatised by its failure to complete Taurus. Settlement is one of the exchange's core services, providing £47.5m of its £194m of income last year.

Yesterday, it was effectively shunted aside by the Bank of England, which stepped forward to take over responsibility for over-hauling stock market settlement in London. The exchange will continue to run the current system, and may eventually have a role in whatever new arrangements the Bank proposes—though Sir Andrew said he had urged the Bank to consider an independent clearing house to run whatever system it comes up with. "If you're providing an industry-wide service, it should be done by an industry-wide utility," he said.

City-wide projects such as Taurus have been tried and failed before. They have also relied on leadership from the Bank of England to pull them through. In the early 1980s, the Bank and the Stock Exchange spent three years trying to build an automated settlement system for the gilts market before the Bank took over sole responsibility in 1985. The Central Gilts Office is now an effective and widely admired part of the gilts market.

Also in the mid–1980s, the Bank was forced to step in when a City-wide grouping of banks and discount houses failed to complete London Clear, a project to automate settlement of transactions in the money markets. The result was the Central Money Markets Office, which is also now run by the Bank.

The Bank has no plans to take stock market settlement under its wing in this way—but it believes it knows enough about clearing and settlement to take a lead. Inevitably, the banking industry will be asked to play a stronger role.

The Stock Exchange itself toyed with the idea of hiving off settlement to the banking industry in the late 1980s. A committee under the chairmanship of Sir Geoffrey Littler, a former Treasury official, was set up to plan an independent clearing house. It was never formally closed, but ceased to meet more than two years ago as the banks and the exchange lost interest.

For at least two reasons, the UK clearing banks are now likely to find themselves thrust into a central role, whether or not they want it. First, they play a central role in the securities markets.

Barclays, for instance, operates the UK's largest share registration service, maintaining share registers for listed companies. It is a custodian, providing administrative services to institutional shareholders, and runs a retail stockbroking service through its branches. In Barclays de Zoete Wedd, its securities subsidiary, it also owns one of the country's largest institutional stockbrokers and an investment management company.

Second, the banks are likely to be forced into a central role because they control the cash clearing system, Apacs. Cash and securities settlement will need to be meshed together under whatever system is developed—and would have been necessary under Taurus—to achieve "delivery versus payment", the automatic exchange of shares for cash after a stock market transaction has taken place. This was one of the objectives laid down by the Group of 30, the Washington-based think-tank whose initiative on the subject four years ago helped to stimulate the modernisation of settlement systems in most leading financial centres.

Also, banks will play an important role in any move away from the current "account" arrangements on the stock market, under which all the share transactions which take place over a two-week period are settled on a single day, a week later. This will be replaced by rolling settlements—another G30 initiative—under which bargains are settled a set number of days after they take place.

A stock market based on such a short settlement cycle can only function when control of shares and cash is centralised. Germany has achieved this partly because the securities business has always been the domain of the banks.

The London Stock Exchange, meanwhile, has been left to pick up the pieces from the unfortunate episode. Mr. Rawlins had been brought in three years ago—with the Bank of England's backing—to give a new direction to a venerable City institution which had lost its way.

Costs were rising at a time when profits in the securities industry were being squeezed as never before. The exchange's technology base, pulled together piecemeal over a number of years, needed replacing. The exchange had lost one of its central roles—regulation—to the Securities and Futures Authority, set up under the Financial Services Act of 1986. Mr. Rawlins was to bring it a new sense of purpose.

Three years later, costs have fallen but the technology base remains the same. Of two grand technology plans, one—Taurus—has now been scrapped. The other could now prove to be still-born.

This is the proposed new electronic trading system, viewed in some parts of the City as a white elephant on a par with Taurus. Under review ever since Mr. Rawlins arrived at the exchange, it was meant to replace the system put together hastily in the run-up to the Big Bang reforms of 1986.

The exchange has never publicly divulged its plans. However, brokers in the City say that the proposed system is too complex and expensive. Eighteen months ago, the estimated cost of building the system was £40m. Recent indications of the cost given to securities houses put it at more than £70m.

"Clearly, we will have to go over it with the board and assure them that this is not another can of worms," Sir Andrew said. "I'm convinced we can do that."

In the stock market's current straitened circumstances, such projects look too expensive. That was certainly the mood yesterday, with the new emphasis on reducing the cost and time it takes to bring in a new settlement system.

The exchange's existing technology base, discounted by Mr. Rawlins, may yet be pressed into service for a little longer.

## RODNEY SMYTH, "BANK OF ENGLAND BLUEPRINT FOR LSE SETTLEMENT SYSTEM"

International Financial Law Review (October 1993), pp. 21–23.

The Bank of England's task force on securities settlement, set up in March this year when the London Stock Exchange (LSE) abandoned Taurus, has pronounced. Its report, dated June 30, recommends a new LSE UK equity settlement system code-named (not acronymed) CREST to replace Talisman.

CREST will:

- save time and money by eliminating stock transfer forms and share certificates ie, paper; it will substitute electronic transfers and evidence legal title by register (book) entries alone, and not also certificates;
- limit counterparty risk through closer delivery-against-payment (DVP);
- remove post-settlement market risk through irreversible DVP; and
- accelerate registration and settlement through registration on the same day as settlement ie, closer DVP, and, in time, settlement in under T + 5.

This will make the LSE a more attractive market, although only for UK equities at first because, initially, CREST will not cover other securities. The LSE is already the principal market for UK equities and there seems to be no sign of this changing. CREST should therefore increase LSE UK equity trade volume rather than stop the trades going elsewhere.

The UK equity limit should be noted. CREST may eventually include, albeit with difficulty, non-UK ('international') equities. Without them, roughly half LSE equity trading value on recent figures will be outside it—and at a time when international is growing faster.

**Simpler and Cheaper**

Will it be better than Taurus would have been? Yes. Mercifully, it will be simpler and cheaper. There will be no off-market transactions, few private investors, no 'entitlement' and its offspring ie, account controllers, accountholders and statements of account (and so no new paper), and no yawning settlement/registration gap (of up to five weeks four days).

Although the verdict is favourable, CREST is at this stage only a project and uncosted. Looking to the future, its electronic stock and corresponding money transfers should enable same day LSE trade, settlement and registration ie, T+0, although there is no schedule for this. Simultaneous trade, settlement and registration require automated LSE dealing, eliminating the need for telephone deals ('first the floor went, then the 'phone. . . .') and, presumably, leading to fewer salespeople and market makers. This may be nearer than thought because buying, paying for and getting securities at the same time is surely what most market users want.

CREST will be 'members (participants) only'. Membership will in principle be voluntary, but the LSE will have to require its UK equity market makers to join. Probably only they, and broker principals, major institutional investors and brokers' nominees—in short, market (ie, LSE) players—will do so.

UK equity market maker membership will have to be compulsory because almost all LSE trades have a market maker on one side or both. So, if some UK equity market makers were not participants, some non-market maker participants' LSE UK equity trades would be in CREST and some outside. This would be impractical. Institutional investors will join for the advantages of cheaper (no paper and rolling) and, ultimately, much faster settlement. The private investor's only route to CREST will be through registering shares in the name of his broker's nominee (if he has one). Membership charges, and the eventual need to fund purchases in under T+5, will keep out other private investors, ie, the vast majority who hold their shares in their own name.

**Only LSE Trades**

CREST will exclude off-market ie, off-LSE transfers, and therefore will apply only to LSE trades. Taurus, on the other hand, would have covered all transfers, both on- and off-market. This savagely complicated it because many transfers of shares in UK companies with large registers are off-market. They include, for instance, transfers between relatives and on death, and all gifts.

CREST will not cover securities not traded on the LSE. Initially, it will include only LSE-traded UK equities ie, shares, not debt securities, issued by UK-incorporated companies. Therefore, at first, it will exclude all non-UK company securities and all UK company debt securities, even if LSE-traded. LSE-traded UK company debt securities will probably join later (it is not clear why not initially). Unlike Taurus, even LSE-traded non-UK company securities may do. The difficulty here is linking settlement with legal ownership, since what constitutes legal ownership will depend on local, not UK, law. A solution may be to include UK depositary receipts for these securities. UK government securities, or gilts, will continue to have a separate settlement system outside CREST.

**CREST—key points**

- Simpler and cheaper than Taurus

- London Stock Exchange (LSE) players only
- Company securities only (initially, just UK equities)
- Closer delivery-against-payment (DVP)
- Same day settlement and registration
- Payment through settlement banks
- Registration intact
- Continuous register updates
- Less new law than Taurus

- LSE trades only
- No paper—electronic stock and money transfers
- Irreversible DVP
- No netting
- No central nominee shareholder
- No central register
- Bank of England-operated
- Rolling short settlement (T + 5) pre-CREST

**Timetable (provisional)**

T + 10 – July 1994
T + 5 – January 1995
CREST – March 1997 or earlier
Under T + 5 – post-CREST

## Paperless back office

There will be no paper to transfer or evidence legal title. Electronic messages effecting register entries will replace stock transfer forms (paper) for UK equity trades between CREST participants. The only written part of this transfer process will be the register entries—book-entry transfers or BETs—which will remain *prima facie* evidence of legal title to the corresponding shares. Share certificates will go and nothing will replace them. It should be noted that even investors outside CREST may be able to choose not to have them for CREST shares. Even now there is no paper to transfer title to UK equities between LSE market makers or certificates to evidence their title. SEPON is the legal owner of all their UK shares and therefore UK share transfers between them do not affect legal title. The UK Companies Act 1985 does not require companies to issue share certificates to SEPON, and as a result they do not.

CREST will involve closer, and irreversible, DVP, and, potentially, real, irreversible, DVP. Real DVP is simultaneous delivery and payment ie, you get the shares (delivery) when you pay for them, like goods you buy for cash in a shop. You still do not necessarily get them when you order them ie, when you deal (trade). Closer DVP will be same day delivery and payment. If delivery and payment are irreversible, so that, unlike now, completed LSE UK equity deals cannot be unwound, DVP removes:

- counterparty risk, since delivery and payment are simultaneous, the risk your counterparty fails to pay or fails to deliver and leaves you without the stock and without the money because you have already delivered or paid, respectively; and
- post-settlement market risk, since delivery and payment (together, settlement) are irreversible, the risk that if your trade is unwound, you can replace it only at a worse price.

Closer DVP and, potentially, real DVP will come through (i) treating delivery of UK equities as the transfer of their legal ownership ie, as registration in the buyer's name, and (ii) electronically linking this, with the transfer of money the other way, therefore from the buyer's bank to the seller's. Closer DVP will mean same day settlement and registration, and real DVP, simultaneous settlement and registration.

Irreversible DVP will come by legal means alone, by a stipulation in CREST's rules, which will bind participants contractually or as the law of the land. As stated, UK share transfers between LSE market makers do not affect legal as distinct from beneficial title. If closer and irreversible DVP will apply here (which is unclear), it will probably come through electronic links between SEPON account entries, which transfer the beneficial title, and payment.

### No netting

Curiously, it seems impractical to combine irreversible share DVP with the netting of settlement payments with the market as a whole, with a system where each participant makes or receives a single payment for each settlement period. Instead, CREST settlement will be trade-by-trade. In contrast, under the Talisman system, the LSE nets payments due between market makers, brokers and Institutional Net Settlement Participants (INSPs), a blessing given the number of trades in each two- or three-week settlement period.

Why no netting? It would require either (1) a guarantee by the CREST operator, the entity effecting the netting (the 'central counterparty'), against the default of any of the original parties to the various deals being netted or (2) a facility, as is the case now, to unwind completed deals. They are alternatives because a guarantee preserves the market chain whereas unwinding breaks it.

The difficulties with the alternatives are: (1) the operator would require security for its guarantee from the potential beneficiaries, all the CREST participants, and only their shares passing though the CREST system could provide it in practice. The operator would dislike this because share prices are volatile. Margining to preserve its value would be impractical because a rapid fall would require repeated margin calls; and (2) unwinding completed deals defeats irreversibility, and so the point of DVP.

Closer DVP will involve electronic cash transfers between banks admitted to the CREST system ie, settlement banks because only electronics will be able eventually to make the cash and share transfers simultaneously, and so achieve real DVP. The only other route is the impractical goods-in-shop approach ie, manual amendment of the share register at the same time as manual delivery of cash (not even of a cheque, because it is a mere promise of cash!).

A settlement bank will have to be a direct member of the CHAPS network. Payment will operate through two tiers of accounts. Both the purchaser and seller of shares will have an account with a settlement bank (tier one) and each settlement bank will in turn have one with the CREST system's bank, the Bank of England (tier two). To enable even trade-by-trade as distinct from netted settlement without the CREST operator's guarantee, the purchaser's settlement bank will have to have sufficient funds in its account with the Bank for the Bank to be able to transfer the purchase price to the seller's settlement bank's account with the Bank at the settlement time ('pre-funding'). It will, of course, be up to the purchaser's settlement bank whether it requires funds from the purchaser or gives him credit.

There will be no central nominee shareholder. A central nominee shareholder would be the nominee on registers for all CREST participants' CREST shares, and, as such, the sole legal owner of them, as SEPON is now for all LSE market makers' UK shares. The participants or their clients would be the beneficial owners. The advantage would be that a deal in CREST shares between CREST participants would not result in alteration of a register because the central nominee would be the registered holder both before and after the deal. Only amendment of the central nominee's own stock accounts would be necessary. The disadvantages the report identifies are (1) the legal uncertainty of an interest in a pool of shares—here, a pool of all the shares of a particular type held (through the nominee) by CREST participants; (2) the nominee's custody functions; and (3) the reduction in shareholder visibility to the companies in which the nominee held shares—which would, of course, be, at a minimum, all UK companies with LSE-traded shares.

Legal uncertainty and visibility are unconvincing. Admittedly, pooling in practice means pool members are tenants in common. So, if there are 1,000,000 shares in a pool and you have ten of them, you have a 100,000th interest in each, not ten particular ones. This is hard to explain to private investors, but not legally uncertain. For instance, the LSE has operated its Talisman pools in this way since 1979 without no apparent hitch. As for general visibility, a central CREST nominee would only add a further nominee layer to an existing registration in the name of a nominee—for an INSP, brokers' clients or LSE market makers. Custody is a fair objection. There would have to be electronic facilities for participants to instruct the central nominee on stock situations, and at the right time, as well as for the nominee to relay them to the intended recipient, again at the right time. This is fiendish to devise, as Taurus proved.

The UK share registration system will remain intact. The task force rejects as unnecessary a central share register ie, a single registrar for all UK companies with LSE-traded shares. Each UK company now has one register for each class of its shares, and this would continue. The centralisation would therefore reduce, pace, its name, the number of registrars (to one), not registers. The fragmented UK registration industry might find this unattractive.

CREST will require continuous register updates, as is the case now, for LSE UK equity trades ie, an update for every settlement day. Rolling settlement, with each working day a settlement day, will therefore mean daily updates, although it is not yet clear how up to date ie, how long after settlement they will be. For instance, a daily update to a date six weeks previously is less informative than one to yesterday. Continuous is in contrast to periodic. A periodic update is only once in a period covering more than one settlement day, and is confusing. For instance, Taurus could have combined rolling settlement with five-weekly updates! Currently, for LSE UK equity trades, there are continuous updates, once an account, and so every two or three weeks, depending on whether it is a two-or three-week account. The importance of continuous updates is to open the way to real DVP, since real DVP means updating at the same time as settlement.

Rolling on

You may be wondering what has become of rolling short LSE UK equity settlement, one of Taurus' principal, and simpler, benefits. Rolling means settling a fixed number of days after a trade so that every working day is a settlement day. This is unlike the current LSE system of account settlement for UK equities, where all deals within the two- or three-weekly account settle on the same day, six working days, the second Monday, after the end of it. Whilst an interesting City relic of pre-railway communications, this is slow, creates spasmodic two or three weekly workloads, and puzzles the private investor—at least if he is selling, and so waiting for money.

Short means shorter than now, which is therefore a minimum of six, and a maximum of 15 or 20, working days after a trade. The task force has decided, as many thought, that rolling short LSE UK equity settlement is practical without dematerialisation, and so with paper and without Taurus or CREST. So, the LSE should introduce settlement 10 working days after a UK equity trade (T + 10) in July 1994, and T + 5 in January 1995. Further reductions will be post-CREST, which should itself arrive by March 1997. They will probably apply only to CREST trades, unlike T + 10 and T + 5, because of the difficulty of achieving paper (non-CREST) settlement (stock transfer forms one way, cheques the other) in under five working days.

The Bank of England will probably operate CREST. Probably, because it will consider it only if no private sector interests want to. They are unlikely to, because, apart from anything else, few will now be credible for the task post-Taurus. If the Bank does, it will be on a fully commercial basis and so it will aim to make a profit out of it.

**Less New Law**

CREST will mean less new law than Taurus because it will be simpler. Obvious changes will be removing stock transfer forms and share certificates for CREST trades and holdings. The legal delivery mechanism will probably be the same as for Taurus, a statutory instrument under section 207 of the Companies Act 1989, supported by rules made by the CREST operator. Again as for Taurus, the rules will probably have the force of law, like the statutory instrument, rather than being just a private contract between CREST participants. Assuming it is made under section 207, the instrument will have to 'secure that the rights and obligations in relation to securities dealt with under the new procedures correspond, so far as practicable, with those which would arise apart from any regulations under this section' ie, make as few changes as possible to the existing law. Be warned—despite this injunction, Taurus managed to produce over 1,000 pages of regulations and draft rules and procedures.

How much of an improvement will CREST be over Talisman?

4. In the past, there have been problems with stock lending in the United Kingdom. The availability of stock lending is important in avoiding failures to deliver. If a party does not have the security, and has sold it (has shorted the stock), it can borrow it from another party. This has raised tax problems for the Inland Revenue. Prior to July 1, 1991, a 15% withholding tax was imposed on the lender on dividends paid on shares which were part of a borrowing arrangement. The concern was that "stock lending" might be used as a device by which domestic "borrowers" that really bought the stock would escape the withholding tax. The lender recovered the tax from a charge to the borrower, thus raising the cost of stock borrowing. Many of these lenders were foreign institutions, who would normally not have a withholding tax imposed on dividends under various U.K. tax treaties. After July 1, no withholding tax will be imposed on qualified "pool" foreign lenders.

## C. INTERNATIONAL DIMENSIONS

We now turn to some international aspects of clearing and settlement. One important aspect of the international system is linkage between settlement systems. Suppose an investor buys IBM shares on the Tokyo Stock Exchange (TSE). How would the transaction be cleared and settled. The Japanese Securities Clearing Corporation (JSCC), which is the Japanese version of NSCC, holds an account at DTC that contains securities deposited into JSCC by traders in Japan. If the selling party had securities held by JSCC, JSCC accounts for securities transferred on its books, e.g. debit A and credit B, and JSCC's DTC account would be unaffected. If the selling party did not have securities deposited with JSCC, it would have to deliver these securities to DTC for the account of JSCC, before JSCC could account for the trade. It would typically do so through its custodian bank. Payment for the shares would be in Yen transferred through the Japanese payment system. Many of these kinds of linkages exist.

What is the purpose of such links? Investors typically hold securities in custody in the home country of the traded security. This is because this is where most of the trades with respect to that security occur. Without the linkage, the selling party's custodian would physically have to move the security to Japan where it would be received by the buyer. The buyer, in turn, even if Japanese might want to move the security back to the U.S. Securities would constantly be moved in and out of the trading country with the attendant expense.

We now turn to a truly international clearing and settlement system, Euroclear.

Euroclear (February 1992).

## THE EUROCLEAR SYSTEM

### Profile and History

The Euroclear System is the larger of the two clearance and settlement systems for internationally traded securities. Since its inception in 1968, it has been a catalyst for change and growth, and it has been instrumental in the development of the international securities markets.

The Euroclear System has more than 2,600 Participants worldwide, all of which are banks, broker-dealers and other institutions professionally engaged in managing new issues of securities, market-making, trading or holding the wide variety of securities accepted in the System.

Euroclear Participants can confirm, clear and settle trades by book-entry in any of 30 currencies on a simultaneous delivery versus payment basis. Once securities are delivered versus payment in the Euroclear System, settlement is final. Delivery against simultaneous payment limits risks to Participants.

The markets served by the Euroclear System are diverse. The System accepts over 40,000 different securities, covering a broad range of internationally traded fixed and floating rate debt instruments, convertibles, warrants and equities. This includes domestic debt instruments from sixteen countries and more than 4,400 equity securities from seventeen markets.

Immobilization of securities is achieved through an extensive network of depositary banks, national clearing systems and central banks. The network also facilitates links with domestic markets to effect external deliveries and receipts of securities, thereby reducing the risk involved in cross-border settlement.

The efficiency of the settlement process in the Euroclear System is enhanced by an automated securities borrowing and lending facility and a multi-currency money transfer service. Extensive custody services are also provided through a centralized custody management facility.

Participants communicate through one central point in Brussels, the Euroclear Operations Centre ("EOC"). EUCLID and EUCLID 90, the proprietary telecommunication systems, provide efficient, secure and reliable input and reporting for securities transactions. Computer communication via the EUCLID system began in 1979. EUCLID 90 is a major revision of this communication structure and was launched in September 1991. EUCLID 90 provides timely and comprehensive input of trade and settlement data for confirmation, as well as reporting of matching and settlement data for confirmation, as well as reporting of matching and settlement information and access to Euroclear information databases. In addition, EUCLID PC, a personal computer software application available in early 1992, offers an efficient and economical access mechanism for EUCLID 90. Participants may also communicate with EOC by S.W.I.F.T. and telex.

For the market, the System's success is measured by its growing volumes and multiplying services. The value of securities held on behalf of Euroclear Participants was $1,120 billion at the end of 1991. The System settled transactions valued at approximately $5.74 trillion in 1991, with daily instruction volume averaging over 30,000 and peaks exceeding 40,000. Average daily securities loans outstanding were $2.8 billion in 1991.

A high priority on investment in research and development and in advanced technology is maintained to meet the constantly changing and complex requirements of Euroclear Participants. The System is operated by a highly skilled, multilingual staff, trained and dedicated to the standards of excellence associated with its contract operator, Morgan Guaranty Trust Company of New York, Brussels office ("Morgan Guaranty Brussels".)

Securities deposits and the operations of the System are governed by Belgian law, including special provisions regulating deposits of securities on a fungible basis.

Morgan Guaranty Brussels is fully regulated by the Belgian Banking Commission, the Federal Reserve Board and the State of New York Banking Department. In its capacity as Operator of the Euroclear System, Morgan Guaranty Brussels is also authorized as a Service Company by the Securities and Investments Board under the U.K. Financial Services Act (1986). Service Company status recognizes that Euroclear services are provided exclusively to market professionals.

. . .

**Growth of the Euroclear System**

The key statistics of the Euroclear System are securities turnover, value of securities held, average daily value of securities loans, number of transactions settled and number of Participants. The table below shows the trend in these figures over the past five years:

| | 1987 | 1988 | 1989 | 1990 | 1991 |
|---|---|---|---|---|---|
| **Turnover** *(USD trillions)* | 3.08 | 3.03 | 3.57 | 4.09 | **5.74** |
| **Value of Securities Held for Participants** * *(USD billions)* | 527 | 610 | 782 | 937 | **1,120** |
| **Average Daily Value of Securities Loans** *(USD billions)* | 3.1 | 2.4 | 2.3 | 2.6 | **2.8** |
| **Participants** * | 2,248 | 2,456 | 2,528 | 2,621 | **2,646** |
| **Loaded Instructions** *(daily average)* | 35,531 | 30,649 | 36,586 | 32,658 | **33,263** |

* *As of December 31*

## Description of Euroclear Services

Participants in the Euroclear System are able to make use of the following four basic services through one central point at EOC in Brussels: (i) multi-currency securities clearance and settlement, (ii) securities lending and borrowing, (iii) custody and (iv) money transfer.

### *Securities Clearance and Settlement*

Before considering the settlement process, it is important to understand the daily processing cycle and the matching of trade information.

Participants provide EOC with instructions to receive securities if they are purchasers or to deliver securities if they are sellers. Such instructions are validated automatically for processing. Invalid instructions are rejected immediately. EOC attempts to match a Participant's valid receipt instruction with a counterparty Participant's delivery instruction to ensure that the terms of the trade are identical. Matching is done continuously through the day; valid instructions are matched as they are received. Information required for matching includes (1) account numbers, (2) settlement date, (3) nominal amount, (4) the security code number of the issue traded, and (5) currency and cash countervalue.

Unmatched instructions remain in an inventory of valid instructions and continue to be put through the matching process until they either match or are cancelled. Participants can obtain daily reports of matched and unmatched instructions via ACE, which is a trade confirmation and matching service developed in 1987 in cooperation with Cedel and with the support of the International Securities Market Association ("ISMA"). ACE was designed to meet the market's need for a simple, secure and fast confirmation and matching system for international securities transactions.

ACE allows confirmation and matching of trades between Participants as early as trade date. Euroclear Participants can obtain reports showing the status of their transactions four times a day starting on trade date. ACE delivers more than just trade confirmation: matched trades can, if so designated, enter the settlement processing without any additional input. Furthermore, contract notes, if needed, can be produced from ACE directly, substantially reducing the costs of communications and reconciliation for Participants. Almost all settlement instructions sent to EOC now contain the requisite ACE trade date.

EOC takes matched instructions for a given settlement date along with any unsettled transactions from previous days and passes them into the next step, settlement.

The Euroclear securities settlement computer processing takes place during the night prior to the relevant value date for settlement. Transactions may be settled against payment in any of 30 currencies. Transactions reflected in matched instructions having reached their settlement dates settle overnight, if the seller has sufficient securities in its account and if the buyer has adequate cash or credit. Overnight processing results in final positions at the opening of business in Europe, in order to facilitate subsequent transactions by Participants. Delivery versus payment is assured by the fact that settlement cannot occur unless the seller has securities and the buyer has cash available to exchange.

In the Euroclear System, there is no separate cash payment cycle and, in part because the risks that a separate payment cycle would represent are absent, no netting of transactions; rather the System operates through simultaneous book-entry movement of cash and securities through a transaction-by-transaction program that recycles cash and securities received during the securities settlement processing in order to enable Participants to settle as many matched transactions as possible with the resources available to it. Participants may specify the priority in which their trades are cleared in the processing cycle.

Interest payments and redemption proceeds are also credited during the overnight processing cycle. Generally, where the issuer is creditworthy, such payments are credited on the scheduled payment date without requiring prior receipt of funds from the issuer. The value dates of cash and securities debits and credits are directly related to type of instrument and whether or not the instrument must be delivered outside the Euroclear System. The most notable cases where the value date is not that of the settlement day for the processing cycle are transactions involving transfers to and from domestic markets and distributions of new issues. Cash and securities positions resulting from the overnight settlement are reported to the Participants in the early morning (Brussels time). At the end of the securities processing cycle, at the beginning of each business day, EOC provides each Participant with reports listing which securities transactions settled and which did not, and resulting cash and securities positions. An important advantage of overnight processing is that it gives Participants effective cash management capabilities in same-day currencies.

U.K. Participants which are members of The Securities and Futures Association ("SFA") are required to comply with SFA's rules under the U.K. Financial Services Act and are able to use the EUCLID communications system, described above, to report trades to SFA.

***Securities Lending and Borrowing***

The Euroclear securities lending and borrowing program was designed in 1975 to improve the efficiency of securities settlement and increase market liquidity. The service allows Participants with stable portfolios of securities to increase overall yield (without loss of ownership benefits) by lending securities to other Participants who seek to avoid fails because of lack of inventory.

Borrowers in the program are usually active traders such as market-makers or dealers. Participants may be either Automatic Borrowers, which provide standing instructions to EOC both to identify and, if possible, meet their borrowing needs following the well documented rules of the program, or Opportunity Borrowers, which retain the responsibility for submitting their own borrowing requests. Borrowers also benefit from the automatic reimbursement program, in which borrowings are automatically reimbursed as soon as sufficient securities are credited to the account of the Borrower. All Borrowers may choose the classes of securities, currencies and specific issues for which they wish to borrow.

Lenders in the program are mainly portfolio managers and custodians who are not active traders. These Participants may become either Automatic Lenders or Opportunity Lenders. Automatic Lenders provide standing instructions to EOC to lend certain portions of their portfolios when opportunities arise and authorize EOC to determine the securities available for lending under program rules. Lenders may also exclude certain securities, types of instruments or currencies. Opportunity Lenders may be requested by EOC to lend securities whenever the supply of securities from Automatic Lenders appears inadequate to meet all borrowing needs.

The integration of securities lending and borrowing into the securities settlement processing in June 1991 greatly simplified Participants' management and administration of settlement-related securities borrowing and improved settlement efficiency. Thanks to the direct linkage of securities settlement with lending and borrowing, borrowings correspond directly to Participants' actual needs, thereby eliminating the risk of over- and under-borrowing. Settlement efficiency was further enhanced by the addition of Dutch, German, French and Swiss equities in the borrowing program.

To protect against concentrated borrowings either in a single issue or by a single Participant, aggregate borrowings are limited to specified percentages of the outstanding issue. In addition, no Participant may borrow more than a percentage of an entire issue that varies depending on the trading characteristics of the particular type of issue.

Morgan Guaranty Brussels guarantees the return of securities lent (or the cash equivalent) if a borrower fails to return the securities. Lenders are automatically credited with interest proceeds as if they still held such securities, and may recall any loan on ten days' notice.

Lenders retain the collateral value of securities loaned out in order to secure their own borrowings through the System.

EOC provides Participants with comprehensive reports in respect of their lending and borrowing activity. Reports are available through EUCLID, EUCLID 90, telex and mail.

***Custody***

Euroclear Participants have access to extensive custody-related services, including safekeeping, administration of coupon, dividend and redemption payments, related tax services, exercise of warrants, conversions and other options and assistance with corporate actions.

The entire custody operation of the Euroclear System is designed to minimize the need to move physical securities. Securities are immobilized in the Euroclear depositary network, which includes major depositary banks, national clearing systems and central banks in 22 countries around the world. The network is managed centrally by EOC, which includes effecting and monitoring external receipts and deliveries of securities.

Securities accepted into the Euroclear System are assigned to the most conveniently located depositary (specialized depositary) and subdeposited by EOC with such depositaries. Once deposited into the System, all securities are held on a fungible basis.

If a depositary accepts the delivery of a physical security for which it is not the specialized depositary, its ability to authenticate that security may be limited. For that reason, the particular security is "frozen" until it is authenticated by the specialized depositary. In addition, the number of entry points where particular types of securities can be accepted is limited. These rules help determine clear responsibility for deposited securities and, by enhancing controls, protect both the System and its Participants.

Virtually all new issues of internationally traded securities and eurocommercial paper, and many important international equity distributions are closed and distributed on a same-day against payment basis through the two international clearance and settlement systems. Distribution of securities either against payment or free of payment facilitates centralized control of allotment payments from Participants to the lead manager. Approximately 70% of all primary distributions of securities issued in the euromarkets are through the Euroclear System. Assistance in connection with the administration of the exchange of global certificates for definitive certificates is also provided.

Morgan Guaranty maintains a number of insurance policies with respect to securities held in the Euroclear System. A $500 million transit and location policy provides protection against all risk of physical loss or damage from whatever cause including but not limited to negotiable and non-negotiable securities held on the premises of Morgan Guaranty or any depositary or subdepositary. Coverage applies anywhere in the world in transit or at rest.

On behalf of the Participants of the Euroclear System, a $15 million policy covers securities sent by any depositary of the Euroclear System by registered mail. Morgan Guaranty also maintains $105 million fidelity coverage under a separate bankers' blanket bond which covers losses from dishonest or fraudulent acts of an employee.

### *Money Transfer*

In order to support their securities settlement processing, Participants also open a Cash Account with Morgan Guaranty Brussels. This Cash Account is subdivided into 30 sub-accounts, one for each of the 30 currencies accepted in the Euroclear System.

The Cash Account is used primarily for settlement of securities transactions. In addition, money transfer transactions can be executed in respect of Participants' Cash Accounts: book transfers of funds between Participants, wire transfers by the debit of a cash account for payment out of the System, preadvices of funds to be received, foreign exchange conversions, aggregation or disaggregation of special drawing rights, and crediting of funds received by a correspondent.

Participants are able to use S.W.I.F.T., telex or mail for sending money transfer instructions; EUCLID 90 will be enhanced to include money transfer services and as a result provide a single access to all Euroclear services.

### Computer Systems and Back-up Facilities

The EOC computer center in Brussels normally handles between 35,000 and 45,000 loaded securities instructions per day. There have been no large volume fluctuations for the past two years, but the October 1987 peak of about 162% of average volume was handled without difficulty.

The EOC computer center includes a back-to-back pair of powerful IBM 9000 mainframe computers providing substantially more processing power and disc capacity than is anticipated to be required for foreseeable peak demand settlement days (a doubling of average volume could be accommodated without difficulty). Separate pairs of fault-tolerant Tandem computers control communications and other functions. All significant systems include 100% back-up within the computer center (in addition to full duplication at the separate back-up center). Emergency back-up power sources assure complete, uninterrupted independence in the event of interruption of external supplies.

Substantial ongoing investments are made in systems, software and systems maintenance and development staff to maintain the highest possible standards of performance and to meet the rapidly evolving needs of a demanding professional client group.

The Euroclear operator also maintains a full back-up computer center at a location separate from EOC, to prevent interruption of services in the event of serious malfunctions at the EOC computer center. Every major piece of equipment is duplicated at the back-up center to assure uninterrupted essential processing and communications capabilities. The back-up center is frequently tested and is subject to an annual simulation of a transfer of operations from EOC.

In addition to computer capacity, the back-up center includes facilities for essential staff to perform their functions.

## HOW EUROCLEAR MEETS GROUP OF THIRTY STANDARDS

The Euroclear System compares favorably with the international clearance and settlement standards established by the Group of Thirty, a private sector group concerned with international financial issues.

The nine Group of Thirty recommendations are quoted verbatim below. Following each recommendation is an analysis showing how the Euroclear System meets each recommendation.

- ***By 1990, all comparisons of trades between direct market Participants (i.e., brokers, broker/dealers and other exchange members) should be accomplished by T+1.***

"ACE", a comparison service developed by the Euroclear Operations Centre (EOC) in cooperation with Cedel and the International Securities Market Association was introduced in September 1987. ACE allows confirmation and matching of trades among Participants as early as trade date (T).

Euroclear Participants can obtain transaction status reports four times a day starting on trade date and into the morning of trade date plus one (T+1). ACE delivers more than just trade confirmations: these same matched trades can, if so designated, enter the settlement processing without any additional input. Furthermore, contract notes, if needed, can be produced from ACE directly, substantially reducing the costs of communications and reconciliation.

In connection with a phased development program designed to enhance efficiency and expand services, ACE and other Euroclear communication services are planned to be moved progressively toward a real-time environment.

- ***Indirect market participants (such as institutional investors, or any trading counterparties which are not broker/dealers) should, by 1992, be members of a trade comparison system which achieves positive affirmation of trade details.***

The Euroclear trade comparison system (ACE) is currently available only to Participants of the Euroclear System to confirm and match trade details with other Euroclear Participants or Cedel members. However, it could certainly be adapted to include an affirmation service for indirect market participants if market demand develops.

Custodians can confirm trades through ACE and use their own communication systems to relay timely transaction information to their clients.

■ ***Each country should have an effective and fully developed central securities depository, organised and managed to encourage the broadest possible industry participation (directly and indirectly), in place by 1992.***

The Euroclear System has performed the role of a central securities depositary for international securities since its founding in 1968.

The System includes centralized custody, clearance and book-entry settlement for a wide range of internationally traded fixed and floating rate debt and money market instruments, convertibles, warrants and equities. It includes extensive custody related services, including safekeeping; administration of interest, dividend and redemption payments and corporate actions; exercise of warrants and other options and conversions; and tax services.

Securities are immobilized in the Euroclear depositary network, which includes major custodian banks, national clearing systems and central banks. The network is managed centrally by EOC in Brussels. Central management includes effecting and monitoring external receipts and deliveries of securities.

■ ***Each country should study its market volumes and participation to determine whether a trade netting system would be beneficial in terms of reducing risk and promoting efficiency. If a netting system would be appropriate, it should be implemented by 1992.***

The Euroclear System has already achieved a low risk and high efficiency environment with its simultaneous delivery versus payment settlement method.

The Euroclear settlement method has been designed to maximize the number of trades that can be settled on the basis of each Participant's cash and securities positions. Cash proceeds of a sale of securities can be immediately recycled to pay for the purchase of other securities. A number of settlement options are available to enable Participants to optimize use of their resources. In addition, simultaneous delivery versus payment eliminates many of the counterparty risks that netting is intended to control in other systems.

Other settlement methods have been studied at EOC in detail, including various forms of netting. These studies concluded that the present method is the most effective for the type of businesses and markets supported by the Euroclear System. The efficiency of Euroclear settlement has been increased substantially and development programs are focused on enhancing settlement efficiency.

■ ***Delivery versus payment (DVP) should be employed as the method for settling all securities transactions. A DVP system should be in place by 1992.***

The Euroclear System provides the facility for automated, simultaneous DVP settlement of transactions between Euroclear Participants in any of 30 currencies including gold or composite currencies. Once securities are delivered versus payment in the Euroclear System, settlement is final and irrevocable.

EOC has also established DVP links with domestic markets such as Australia, Austria, Belgium, Canada, Denmark, Finland, France, Germany, Italy, Japan, Malaysia, the Netherlands, Norway, Singapore, Spain, Sweden, Switzerland and New Zealand, reducing substantially the risk involved in cross-border settlement.

■ ***Payments associated with the settlement of securities transactions and the servicing of securities portfolios should be made consistent across all instruments and markets by adopting the 'same-day' funds convention.***

Settlement within the Euroclear System is accomplished by simultaneous exchange of cash and securities. The settlement process not only provides the facility for simultaneous DVP settlement, it also allows the cash proceeds of a sale of securities to be recycled immediately for the purchase of other securities.

In addition, net proceeds from sales, interest payments, dividends and redemptions, can be withdrawn the same day for five currencies (US Dollar, Canadian Dollar, Pound Sterling, Belgian Franc and ECU). External funding of purchases can also be provided the same day in these same currencies plus French Francs, Deutsche Mark and Dutch Guilder. The feasibility of providing the same facility for other currencies depends on the cash clearing deadlines in the relevant countries, the operational ability of cash correspondents to meet those deadlines and the impact of time zone differences.

■ ***A 'Rolling Settlement' system should be adopted by all markets. Final settlement should occur on T+3 by 1992. As an interim target, final settlement should occur on T+5 by 1990 at the latest, save only where it hinders the achievement of T+3 by 1992.***

The Euroclear System is technically capable of providing settlement as early as T+1. Transaction instructions received at EOC before 7:45 p.m. Brussels time on trade date can be settled on T+1 provided the settlement conditions are met. These conditions require that the trade be matched, the seller have sufficient securities and the buyer have sufficient funds (or credit available).

The Euroclear System provides settlement facilities with a range of settlement periods, including instruments which settle on T+2, such as German domestic securities and eurocommercial paper.

■ ***Securities lending and borrowing should be encouraged as a method of expediting the settlement of securities transactions. Existing regulatory and taxation barriers that inhibit the practice of lending securities should be removed by 1990.***

EOC introduced a securities borrowing and lending program in 1975; it was the first such facility made widely available in the international securities market.

The present securities lending program is highly automated and includes a broad range of instruments. Daily average loan volume of USD 2.8 billion in 1991 (with peaks of up to USD 2.9 billion) attests to the market demand for this service.

The Euroclear securities lending and borrowing program has enhanced market liquidity and maximized usage of resources for borrowers and lenders alike, thereby supporting the recommendation to reduce existing local barriers to securities lending and borrowing.

■ ***Each country should adopt the standard for securities messages developed by the International Organisation for Standardisation (ISO Standard 7775). In particular, countries should adopt the ISIN numbering system for securities issues as defined in the ISO Standard 6166, at least for cross-border transactions. These standards should be universally applied by 1992.***

EOC is actively participating in these two ISO projects and supports further international standardization.

Morgan Guaranty Brussels, in its capacity as operator of the Euroclear System, is a member of the ISO Standard 7775 working group which is responsible for establishing a standard format for securities messages. It is also one of two ISIN numbering agents responsible for allocating ISINs for Eurobonds and has agreed to move to a common numbering system with Cedel effective as from July 1990. ISINs have been accepted in securities messages sent to or received from all Euroclear Participants since January 1991.

### *Notes and Questions*

1. Could Euroclear clear and settle a trade in IBM on the NYSE? How would this work? Would parties want to use Euroclear rather than NSCC?

2. Euroclear and other international clearing mechanisms may rightly be seen as competing with domestic arrangements. These international mechanisms may eventually make domestic systems obsolete. One might question the need to improve these systems, with the attendant expense, when an international alternative exists. This also calls into question the entire effort of the G–30.

---

Where will we go in the future? The following report, Morgan Guaranty Trust Company of New York, Brussels office as Operator of Euroclear, *Cross–Border Clearance, Settlement and Custody: Beyond the G30 Recommendations* (June 1993), sets out some basic criteria for evaluating future changes and then sets forth some possible infrastructure models for the future. The excerpt describes three models: (1) Worldclear; (2) Global Hub; and (3) Bilateral Links. Would you prefer any of these models to our existing system? Which one is the best?

---

The G30 Report concluded that "the development of a single global clearing facility was not practicable," but determined that "agreement on a set of practices and standards that could be embraced by each of the many markets that make up the world's securities system was highly desirable." It therefore made nine recommendations designed to improve the quality and standardize the practices of *national* clearance and settlement systems. These recommendations were centered around the establishment of one or more central securities depositories ("CSDs") in each market.

The Group of Thirty focused on the efficiency of individual national systems; it did not conduct an analysis of the specific costs and risks that impede the efficiency of *cross-border* settlement when these systems operate together. It therefore did not analyze the complexities of settling transactions in a *multi-currency, multi-time-zone* environment, or identify the conditions that must be satisfied to maximize cross-border efficiency.

. . .

**Friction Costs**

The unrealized benefits of international portfolio diversification give a sense of urgency to minimizing an important category of *friction costs* in international financial markets—those associated with cross-border securities clearance, settlement, and custody. These can be explicit (e.g., fees) or implicit (e.g., risks). They can arise in connection with a securities transaction or over the life of a security (e.g., settlement or custody fees). They can be borne by market participants or absorbed by CSDs, the banking sector, central banks, or other financial intermediaries (e.g., credit exposure of a seller to its buyer between trade execution and settlement or the credit exposure of a bank to a seller who is allowed to send a wire transfer in anticipation of confirmation of the final settlement of a buyer's payment).

The friction costs associated with cross-border clearance, settlement, and custody are readily identifiable when examined in the context of the *life cycle of a securities transaction.* Such a life cycle begins when market participants make decisions about whether to hold, buy, or sell a particular security and ends with investment management decisions about maximizing the risk-adjusted returns on the resulting portfolio of securities or cash. A decision to buy or sell a security requires the use of a settlement system to process the resulting transaction.

## Settlement Pipeline

Settlement systems can be compared to factories. They take an array of inputs and transform them into an array of outputs. The clearance and settlement process itself, like a high-velocity manufacturing process, can be pictured as a *pipeline*. Work enters the pipeline at one end, and finished products flow out the other. Efficient processing reduces the time between when inputs are acquired from suppliers and finished products are delivered to consumers.

Similarly, an efficient clearance and settlement process reduces the time between when market participants must position their securities or cash for settlement and when their new securities or cash positions are available for redeployment. In other words, market participants wish to retain injecting them into the settlement pipeline, and to assert control over their proceeds (new securities or cash) as soon as possible after they emerge from the pipeline.

## Pipeline Liquidity Risk

The G30 Report and other studies identified some of the major costs and risks associated with clearance and settlement. These studies did not focus, however, on what this paper calls *pipeline liquidity risk* —risk associated with delays in a settlement pipeline arising primarily from gaps in time between the processing cycles of various CSDs and between the processing cycles of CSDs and national payment systems. There was no need to focus on this risk because previous studies concentrated on domestic rather than cross-border transactions. Pipeline liquidity risk is less pronounced in domestic markets. Moreover, it has typically been absorbed on both the payment and delivery sides of purely domestic transactions by domestic banks, the relevant central bank, or other financial intermediaries.

These institutions absorb pipeline liquidity risk in the domestic context by providing intra-day or other *uncompensated* credit. For example, in domestic markets where a CSD achieves DvP at the end of the business day and the deadline for same-day payments through the national payment system occurs earlier in the day, pipeline liquidity risk arises on the payment side of a transaction. The banking sector typically provides intra-day cash advances to permit sellers to execute wire transfers so the anticipated proceeds from the buyer can be redeployed on the *same* day, before the payment system closes. If banks were not willing to make intra-day cash advances for this purpose, sellers could not use the proceeds until at least the *next* business day, resulting in at least one day's interest cost at market rates. Credit is also extended in real-time systems where DvP is achieved throughout the day. For example, the Federal Reserve currently absorbs the pipeline liquidity risk on the cash side of transactions in U.S. government securities that settle through the Fedwire system by extending intra-day overdrafts to buyers' banks that are short of cash at the time settlement occurs.

Pipeline liquidity risk also arises on the securities side of *back-to-back transactions* undertaken by customers of local custodians, and is typically bridged in domestic markets by extensions of intra-day credit by bank custodians. A simple back-to-back transaction consists of a pair of purchase and sale transactions in which a party agrees to purchase securities from one counterparty and sell them to another. Such a transaction creates a classic chicken-and-egg problem. The customer wants to use the securities from the purchase transaction to settle the sale transaction, and it also wants to use the proceeds from the sale transaction to settle the purchase transaction. However, because CSDs typically have only one processing cycle, the sale transaction cannot be settled on the same day as the purchase transaction, unless the customer prepositions the securities to be sold or the custodian arranges an intra-day securities loan to the underlying customer. If custodians cannot arrange intra-day securities loans, customers will incur the cost of borrowing securities for at least one day.

Pipeline liquidity risk can no longer be ignored in the cross-border environment. As recognized by the Committee on Payment and Settlement Systems of the central banks of the Group of Ten countries (the "G10 Committee"), credit and liquidity risks tend to be more complex and last longer in a cross-border environment. The number and size of *gaps in time* between the processing cycles of the various CSDs and between those of CSDs and national payment systems are greater. These gaps are the result of multiple currencies, localization of national payment systems, localization of CSDs, time-zone differences, and certain customs and traditions that complicate cross-border settlement.

It is difficult for domestic CSDs to shift this risk to the international banking sector because of the number of jurisdictions involved and the lack of financial incentive. If domestic CSDs or the international banking sector were not willing to supply the necessary credit, a participant could be forced to incur or forego one (or more) day's interest or securities borrowing fees on its daily purchase and sale transactions in different securities. For a trader with an average net daily volume of, for example, USD 500 million, this can generate annual interest expenses or foregone interest income of USD 25 million or more at current interest rates—a substantial friction cost.

If a CSD of one country establishes a bilateral link with that of another, pipeline liquidity risk can arise with respect to cross-market buyers, cross-market sellers, back-to-back traders, and the other CSD. Because CSDs have generally been unable or unwilling to assume the pipeline liquidity *risks* associated with settling transactions, their participants have faced the risk of incurring significant *costs* if they used the link to settle cross-border transactions. The existence of pipeline liquidity risks—and the failure of any intermediary to absorb them—results in friction costs that may explain why many of the existing bilateral links between domestic CSDs have yet to attract much traffic.

Although pipeline liquidity risks cannot be eliminated altogether, this paper recommends that steps be taken to reduce their duration and the probability that they will result in credit losses. This should help CSDs absorb risk, or assemble international banks to do so, to eliminate the pipeline liquidity friction costs otherwise associated with bilateral links or other cross-border settlement structures.

## Legal Risk

National securities ownership, transfer, and pledging laws generally reflect a different era—when individual securities were held directly by owners in physical form. Instead, securities today are generally held indirectly through multiple tiers of intermediaries. Cross-border investment requires not only tiering of intermediaries, but also involvement by intermediaries in different countries, with each tier being subject to a different country's laws. Existing national laws contain unnecessary ambiguities when applied to such multi-tiered securities holding systems.

## Basic Custody Services

Previous studies also have not concentrated on the friction costs associated with holding and maximizing the value of a security over its life. The life of a security begins with its issuance and, in the case of debt, ends with its maturity or redemption. The life of an equity security theoretically continues into perpetuity, although it can end with the repurchase of the security by, or the bankruptcy or merger of, the issuer. Along the way, market participants must engage in *income collection* and *withholding tax reclamation,* and react to any number of *corporate events.*

Most market participants today hold their securities positions through multiple tiers of local or global custodians, CSDs or other intermediaries, in what can be called a *multi-tiered securities holding system.* This reduces the cost and risk of holding securities and makes it easier for market participants to transfer them, thus increasing the liquidity of securities positions. ... Market participants rely on such intermediaries to collect dividends and interest, process withholding tax reclamations, transmit notices from issuers about corporate events, carry out instructions from customers, and perform other *basic custody services.*

The costs and risks associated with basic custody services vary greatly depending on the nature of the service. Income collection and withholding tax reclamation services are relatively low-risk activities. Other services, such as transmitting notices and instructions with respect to corporate events, can create more substantial costs and risks, if they involve delays or if inaccurate information is transmitted.

The business of supplying basic custody services to the market is becoming more standardized and, as a result, commoditized. Local and global custodians increasingly try to differentiate their services either by subsidizing basic custody services with revenues from more profitable *value-added services* or by assuming greater risks in their provision. For example, some global custodians now offer "contractual" settlement and "guaranteed" income and tax reclamation services. They may also offer sophisticated analytical and portfolio management services.

This paper recommends that CSDs be encouraged to develop the capacity to provide basic custody services so that the market can benefit from their economies of scale and scope. Measures should also be taken to reduce the costs of collecting corporate events information from different jurisdictions; acting on client instructions as to elected options, proxy voting, and the like; and of processing tax reclamation entitlements.

**Progressive Displacement**

The current status of basic custody services is reminiscent of the situation of safekeeping and settlement services a number of years ago. Local custodians historically maintained physical possession of securities in almost all domestic markets. They settled customer transactions through physical delivery of securities against cash. Over time, competition to supply these services became intense, and the services became standardized and commoditized. With settlement delays, the rate of failed transactions grew.

In many markets, the growing trading volumes, cumbersome nature of physical settlement, and lack of clear financial incentives to develop a commoditized service led to the back-office paperwork crisis of the 1960s. The response was to establish CSDs to perform the safekeeping and settlement functions on behalf of custodians or other market participants. CSDs achieved immobilization of securities and exploited economies of scale and scope in supplying safekeeping and settlement services. CSDs thus allow custodians to subcontract an otherwise low-margin service and focus on supplying more profitable custody services, sparing the industry the deficiencies of physical settlement.

The process by which CSDs displaced local custodians as the primary suppliers of safekeeping and settlement services occurred over a period of years. A similar process of *progressive displacement* seems now to be occurring with respect to basic custody services because of the economies of scale and scope that CSDs have in supplying these services. This paper recommends that CSDs develop the capacity to supply basic custody so that custodians will be able to subcontract aspects of their businesses with rapidly-deteriorating margins and focus on supplying more profitable, value-added custody services to their customers.

**Regulatory Costs**

Previous studies have also tended not to address the friction costs associated with regulating CSDs. CSDs generally provide clearance, settlement, and custody services only to wholesale market participants. This is particularly true with respect to cross-border transactions because retail investors hold and transfer securities through professional brokers and fund managers.

Regulatory burdens on innovation or intersystem linkages can substantially increase the costs and risks of clearance, settlement, and custody. It is essential that national regulators resist the temptation to assert extraterritorial jurisdiction over CSDs based in other countries, as they establish links with domestic CSDs. Otherwise, such other CSDs, which already have primary regulators, could become subject to overlapping and even conflicting regulation, which could substantially increase the costs and risks of cross-border settlement and the time required to implement improvements. To the extent local regulators have concerns about the local effects of cross-border links, their attention should be focused on the home-country CSD that is linked to the foreign CSD, and encourage international convergence of regulatory standards.

. . .

### *Multiple–Access Model*

### Description

The multiple-access model consists of one or more CSDs in each country, local custodians, ICSDs, global custodians, and market participants. The multiple-access model enables market participants to settle transactions in domestic, foreign, or international securities through a variety of channels.

Figure 3 on the next page shows *some* of the possibilities; many more channels exist. For example, the solid arrows from "international investors" show how investors can settle cross-border transactions in domestic securities in any market in the world through a global custodian that gains access to local CSDs through a network of local custodians. The global custodian could also obtain access to certain local CSDs through membership in an ICSD. ICSDs can obtain access to local CSDs either through their own networks of local custodians or by establishing direct links with local CSDs. Similarly, the solid arrows from banks or brokers trading for their own accounts show how traders can settle cross-border transactions through an ICSD, and the dotted arrows show the alternative of establishing a network of direct relationships with local custodians.

. . .

**Figure 3. Multiple-Access Model**

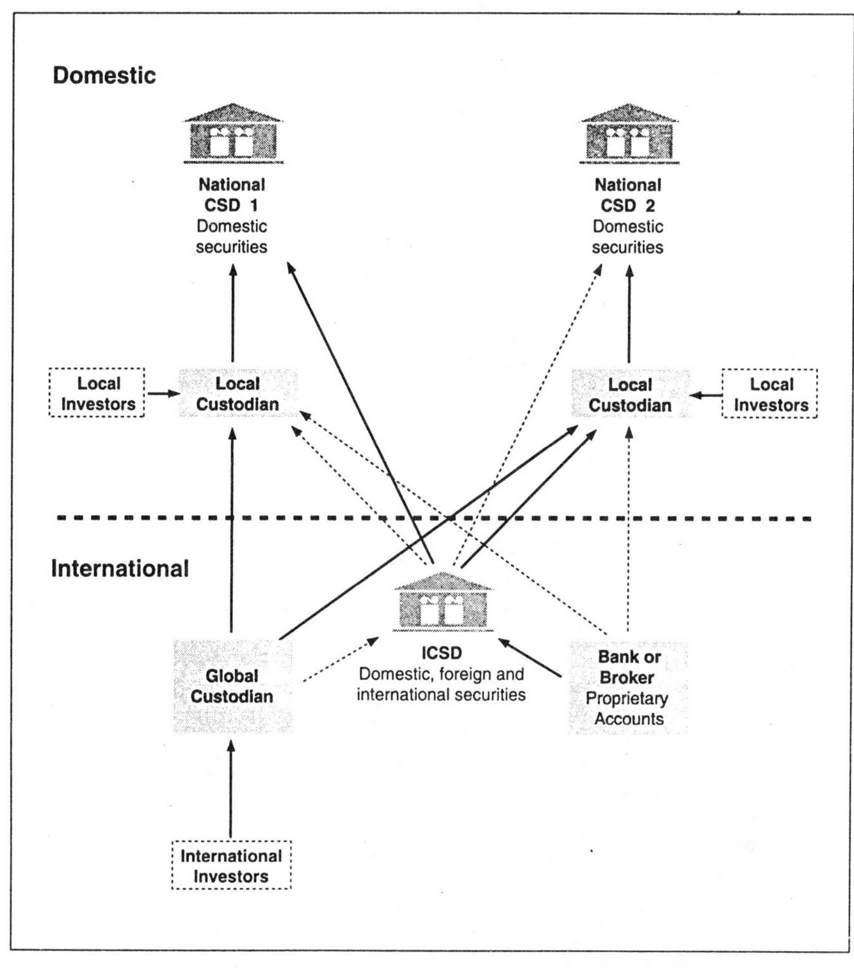


Signifies the access option selected for cost or efficiency reasons by each player (bank, broker, custodian or ICSD).

Signifies an alternative option that might be selected on the basis of competitive analysis.

## *Alternative Models*

### Worldclear

### Description

The worldclear model is the most radical model for restructuring the cross-border settlement infrastructure. It assumes the establishment of a single, global CSD to perform the safekeeping, clearance, and settlement functions for all securities—domestic, foreign, and international. (See Figure 4). Worldclear would replace national and international CSDs with a single, centralized, global CSD. All participants of existing CSDs would become participants of worldclear. It would maintain the cash and securities accounts for all wholesale market participants, and effect all transfers in its own electronic files. Worldclear nevertheless assumes that multiple national currencies and payment systems continue to exist.

**Figure 4. Worldclear Model**

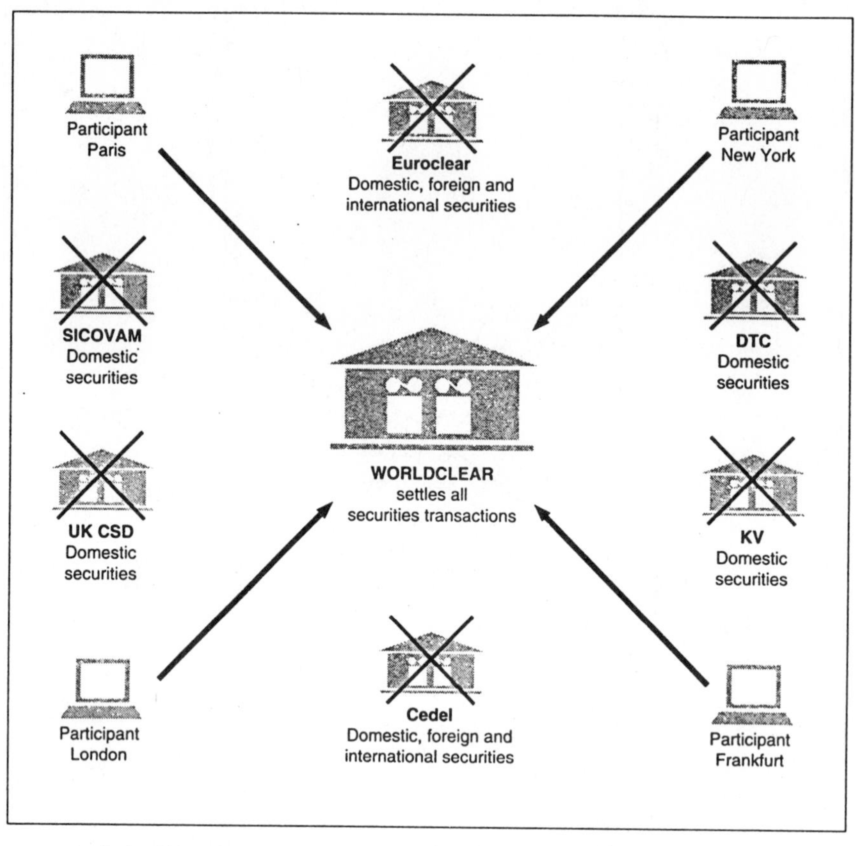


Each participant has a securities account with Worldclear for all securities.

[39] The recent difficulties with achieving European monetary union suggest that world monetary union is not imminent.

## Global Hub

### Description

The global hub model assumes the establishment of a single, global CSD with both "home-market securities" and "other-market securities" links with each national and international CSD for settling cross-market transactions in all securities. A "home-market securities link" is a bilateral link in which the global hub essentially acts as a participant of a national or international CSD. It would permit transactions to be settled between the global hub and any of the participants of the CSD with respect to securities held by such CSD ("home-market securities").

An "other-market securities link" is a bilateral link in which a CSD acts as a participant of the global hub. It would permit transactions to be settled between any pair of CSDs with respect to securities that are not held by either CSD ("other-market securities"). (See Figure 5).

Each CSD would continue to perform the safekeeping function for all home-market securities. Its securities accounts would reflect the positions both of its participants and of the global hub in its home-market securities. Its securities accounts would also reflect the positions of its participants in all other securities. It would perform the clearance and settlement function for all transactions in its home-market securities when at least one of the counterparties is a participant in its system. It would perform the same function for transactions between two of its participants in all other securities.

The global hub would perform all clearance and settlement functions for all transactions between the various CSDs and ICSDs. It would maintain cash and securities accounts for each CSD (but not their participants), and effect transfers in all securities through its own electronic records.

In contrast to an ICSD, the global hub would not have any participants except for other CSDs.

. . .

**Figure 5. Global Hub Model**

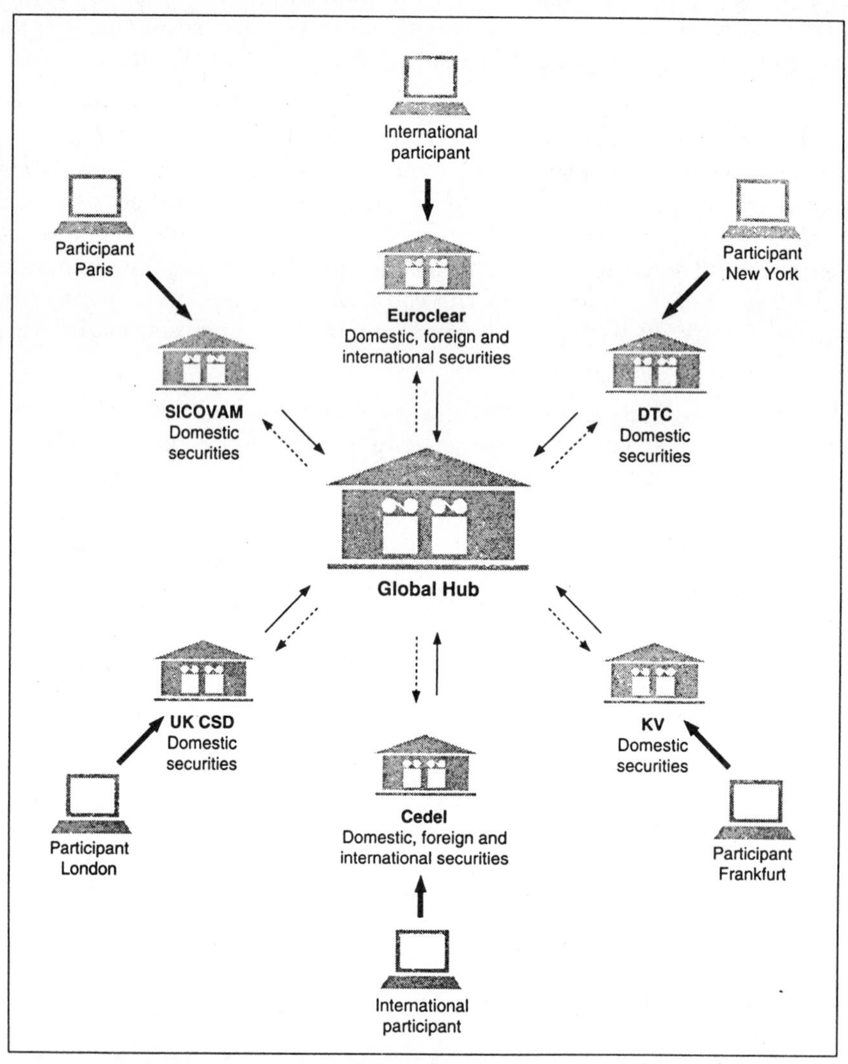


Each participant has a securities account with its home CSD for all home-market securities and all other-market securities accessible through the Global Hub.

Home-market Link: Global Hub has securities accounts with the home CSD reflecting its positions in home-market securities held for other CSDs. This allows the Global Hub to settle transactions between participants of the home CSD and other CSDs.

Other-market Link: home CSD has securities accounts with the Global Hub reflecting its positions in other-market securities. This allows its participants to settle transactions with participants of all other CSDs.

## Bilateral Links

### Description

The bilateral links model assumes the establishment of both "home-market" and "other-market" links between each pair of existing national or international CSDs. (See Figure 7). Each CSD would continue to perform the safekeeping functions for all home securities, maintain cash and securities accounts for each of its participants (including each other), and perform the clearance and settlement functions for all transactions in its home securities, as well as in all other securities.

**Figure 7. Bilateral Links Model**

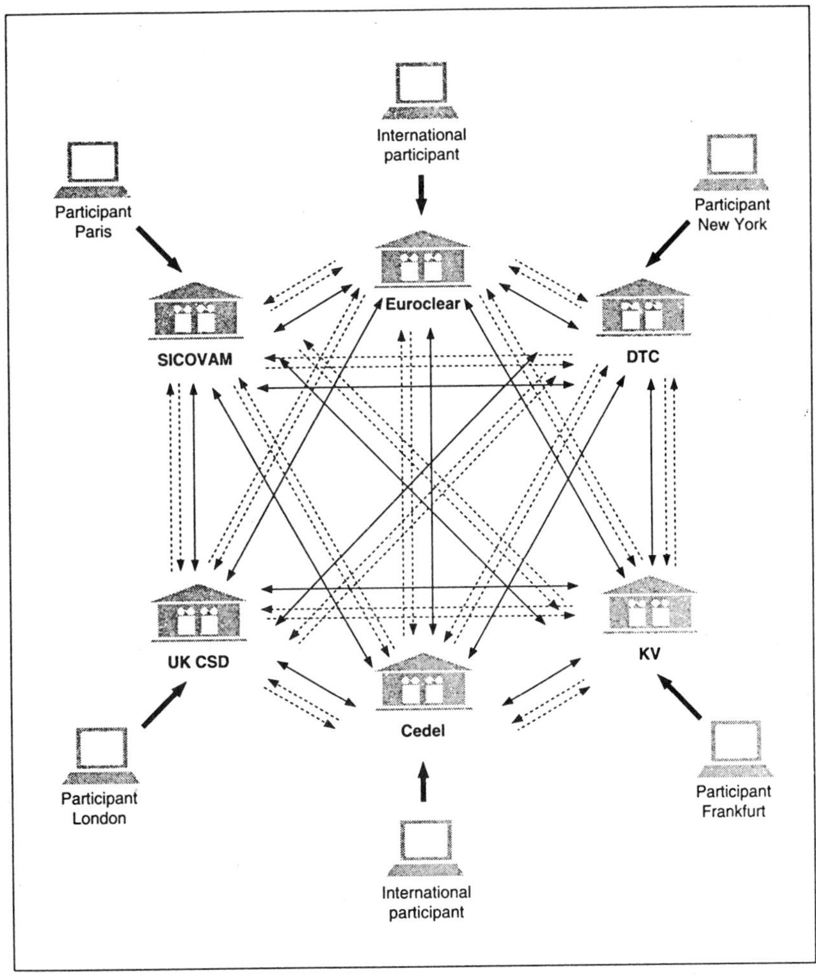


Each participant has a securities account with its home CSD for both home-market securities and all other securities accessible through its bilateral links.

Home-market Links: each CSD has securities accounts with each other CSD reflecting its positions in the other's home-market securities. These links allow each CSD to settle transactions between participants and those of the other CSD in the home-market securities of each CSD.

Other-market Link: each CSD has securities accounts with each other CSD reflecting its positions in third-market securities. This allows each CSD's participants to settle transactions with those of the other CSD in third-market securities.

. . .

### *Notes and Questions*

1. How is Worldclear different than Euroclear? How would we get from Euroclear to Worldclear if we wanted to?

2. Could clearinghouses in different countries coordinate their activities to reduce risk? Could they share information? Could they establish a common collateral pool? Is there any way they could work together to net off transactions in one clearinghouse against those in another? This would probably be difficult given different time zones.

Within the same time zone, there are moves one can make, as illustrated by current DTC–NSCC arrangements. DTC settles institutional trades and NSCC settles retail trades from the same exchange. There are two parts to the process: (1) 2:45 p.m. NSCC pays DTC on behalf of common clearing members that are owed a payment by NSCC and owe a payment to DTC, and (2) 4:00 p.m. DTC pays NSCC on behalf of common clearing members that are owed a payment by DTC and owe a payment to NSCC.

An Example: Participants' Net Positions

| | **DTC** | **NSCC** | **Net** |
|---|---|---|---|
| Salomon | −100 | +400 | +300 |
| Goldman | −200 | +100 | −100 |
| Morgan | +100 | −300 | −200 |
| Merrill | +600 | −200 | +400 |

(1) NSCC pays off DTC positions of Solly and Goldman: (−300); pays Solly 300, gets 100 from Goldman.

(2) DTC pays off NSCC positions of Morgan and Merrill: (−500); gets 200 from Morgan and pays Merrill 400.

(3) The NSCC and DTC positions do not net to zero because there are additional transactors.

---

*Links to Other Chapters*

Clearance and settlement is an important aspect of all domestic securities markets (see Chapters II and VII), and is a key term of competition among those markets, as we saw in Chapter XIII on Stock Market Competition, and as we shall see again in Chapter XVII on Emerging Markets. A clearance and settlement system (for example, Euroclear) is also necessary for Eurosecurities like Eurobonds (Chapter XI). It must work hand in hand with national payments systems (Chapter IX). We will also see that the clearance and settlement systems for exchange traded derivatives (Chapter XV) are different in important respects from those for the underlying securities.

# Chapter XV

# DERIVATIVES: FUTURES AND OPTIONS

## A. INTRODUCTION

Derivatives are financial instruments whose value is based on or derived from other assets or variables. Futures and options are among the best known. A futures contract is an agreement to buy or sell an asset at a set time in the future for a set price. Two types of options exist. A call option gives the holder the right to buy an asset by a set date for a set price. A put option gives the holder the right to sell an asset by a set date for a set price.

Today financial futures and options markets span the globe. The underlying asset may be a deposit in a major currency, a bond issued by a major government, equity in a firm, or an index of a leading stock market. The exchanges that create and trade the contracts are scattered about the world. The players hale from many countries.

The markets have a long pedigree. Futures markets began hundreds of years ago, giving farmers and traders firm prices for crops well before harvest. U.S. futures exchanges opened during the mid–1800s. Options markets appeared in Europe and America in the 1700s, but not until the early 1900s was an exchange-like association set up. The Chicago Board of Exchange opened the first options exchange in 1973.

This Chapter examines the international financial futures and options markets. It uses money market contracts designed by the Chicago Mercantile Exchange, notably the three-month euroyen time deposit futures contract and options on it. Many other types of futures and options exist. It sketches the risks users encounter and the tools available to governments and exchanges to manage the risks. As you read the Chapter, be sure you understand the risks and ask which the regulators can curtail.

## B. INTEREST-RATE FUTURES AND OPTIONS BASED ON THEM

The Chicago Mercantile Exchange ("CME") is one of about 62 futures and options exchanges around the world. One-third are in the U.S. Many are in other industrial countries: the U.K. (8, including the London International Financial Futures Exchange—LIFFE), Japan (5, including the Tokyo International Financial Futures Exchange—TIFFE), Canada (5), Germany (the Deutsche Terminborse—DTB), France (the Marche a Terme International de France—MATIF), and 10 other European countries. Exchanges exist in a few financial centers: the Hong Kong Futures Exchange Ltd and Singapore International Futures Exchange Ltd (SIMEX). A handful of developing countries have exchanges: Brazil (3), Malaysia, and Philippines. [See K. Park and S. Schoenfeld, The Pacific Rim Futures and Options Markets (1992).]

As the second largest exchange ranked by trading volume, CME and the leader, Chicago Board of Trade, accounted for 38% of all trading in 1992 and 49% of trades on the 10 largest exchanges worldwide. [See Philip McBride Johnson, "Cooperation and competition between futures exchanges," paper given at a seminar in Harvard Law School, fall semester, 1992) ("Johnson").]

CME formed in 1919 to trade futures, emerging from an exchange for agricultural commodities founded in 1874. It set up the International Monetary Market (IMM) in 1972 to trade foreign currency futures. Now it has over 600 general members and over 1000 IMM division members. Today, chicken and live hog futures and options trade alongside those in Yen and Swiss Franc, London's FT–SE 100 share index, Japan's Nikkei Stock average, and the S & P 500 index, among others.

Clearing mechanisms vary across countries. In Japan and France, for example, clearing is within the exchange. Most British exchanges use a separate entity, such as the London Clearing House Limited. In the U.S., futures clearing is closely associated with the exchange, either as a separate clearing house or, as for the CME, a department of the exchange. The clearing house monitors all transactions during a day to determine the net position of each member broker. Non-member brokers do business through members. In the U.S., the Options Clearing Corporation ("OCC") issues and clears publicly offered options traded on the exchanges. The OCC is owned by five stock exchanges, including the New York Stock Exchange and the Chicago Board Options Exchange.

Exchanges attract potential investors by describing their contracts. A CME brochure "Using Interest Rate Futures and Options" follows. As you read it, remember it is a marketing tool. Identify the risks in these markets.

## INTRODUCTION

The Chicago Mercantile Exchange (CME) introduced the trading of financial futures in 1972. Since then the value of futures in transferring financial risk has been widely recognized and financial futures trading has experienced explosive growth.

The first financial futures were currency contracts. In 1976 the CME introduced the 13–week Treasury bill futures contract, the first interest rate futures contract based on a money-market instrument. Its success indicated the need to transfer short-term interest rate risk. In 1981 the CME initiated trading in another futures contract, based on three-month Eurodollar time deposits. In 1990, a contract based on one-month Eurodollar time deposits was introduced, the One–Month LIBOR futures contract.

In 1984, Eurodollar futures contracts, identical to those traded on the CME, began trading at the Singapore International Monetary Exchange (SIMEX). Under a linked clearing program, the Mutual Offset System, Eurodollar futures can be traded on one exchange and held or liquidated at the other. Since SIMEX is open when the CME is closed, this allows traders to have access to an extended trading day.

Options on Eurodollar futures were introduced in 1985, and options on Treasury bill futures were opened in 1986. Options, used separately or in combination with the futures, offer additional trading flexibilities and positioning choices.

### What Are Interest Rate Futures?

The 13–week U.S. Treasury bill futures contract is an agreement to buy or sell, at a given time in the future, a U.S. Treasury bill with 13 weeks to maturity and a face value of $1,000,000. The 3–month Eurodollar Time Deposit futures contract implies an agreement to place a deposit (lend) or to take a deposit (borrow), at a given time in the future, of $1,000,000 in Eurodollars for 3 months in the London Interbank Market. The One–Month LIBOR futures contract implies an agreement to place a deposit or to take a deposit of $3,000,000 in Eurodollars for one month in the London Interbank Market.

The CME's three-month Euro Deutsche mark (also known as Euromark) futures and options are the Exchange's first non-dollar denominated short-term interest rate contracts. The Euromark futures contract calls for a 3–month deposit of Deutsche marks. The contract size is DM 1,000,000. With the addition of Euromark contracts, the CME's interest rate complex offers investors a way to utilize short-term interest rate markets on both sides of the Atlantic.

All of these contracts are traded using a price index, which is derived by subtracting the interest rate from 100.00. For instance, an interest rate of 10.00 percent translates to an index price of 90.00. If interest rates move higher, the price of the contract falls; if rates move lower, the contract price rises.

### What Are Options on Interest Rate Futures?

A futures option contract confers the right from seller to buyer to take a futures position at a stated price. Two types of options are traded on the CME's Index and Option Market: calls and puts. Calls are the right to buy the futures at a predetermined "exercise" price. If the futures price rises above the exercise price, the calls will represent a bargain to the holder. Puts are the right to sell at that fixed price. If the futures price falls below the fixed exercise price, the puts give the holder the opportunity to sell the futures at an above-market price.

### Who Should Consider Interest Rate Contracts?

Banks, security dealers and other financial firms were the early users of financial futures and options for managing their interest rate exposures. Interest rate contracts are an obvious and effective risk management tool where uncertain interest income and expense are integral parts of a business.

Interest expense is, in fact, an important expense component in nearly any type of business. Interest rate volatility can have a major impact on any company's earnings and cash flows. Any firm with a substantial interest rate exposure—temporary or permanent—should investigate the risk-minimizing benefits financial futures and options can provide.

. . .

## THE MONEY MARKET

. . .

Since the Eurodollar futures contract was introduced by the Chicago Mercantile Exchange in 1981, joining the Treasury bill futures contract, spreading between these two (the simultaneous purchase of one contract and sale of the other) has become increasingly popular. The basic reason for trading the "TED" spread is to take action based upon an opinion of what will happen to the rate differential between the two instruments.

The TED spread represents a "quality play." One takes action on an opinion that, all else being equal, the gap between rates required for U.S. Treasury bills and rates required for Eurodollar time deposits will widen or narrow. As the gap in rates moves, so will the gap in the prices of the respective futures instruments. If the gap in rates widens, then the gap in prices will widen, and vice versa.

The LIBOR futures contract is identical to the Eurodollar contract except that it represents a one-month (versus three-month) London Interbank Offer Rate (LIBOR) on a $3,000,000 (versus $1,000,000) Eurodollar time deposit and settles monthly (versus quarterly).

In addition to providing more flexibility for financial managers, the LIBOR futures contract allows spreading against the Eurodollar futures (the "LED" spread) for a yield curve play and spreading against the T-bill futures (the "TEL" spread) for a combination quality and yield curve play.

Euromark futures and options offer the hedging, trading and arbitrage opportunities in Deutsche mark-denominated deposits (such as swaps, FRAs, caps, floors, etc.) that have been enjoyed for so long in dollar-based deposits by users of the CME's Eurodollar contracts. Among the many uses of the Euromark contracts are: hedging Euromark loans and deposits; hedging Euromark forward foreign exchange exposures and FRAs during U.S. trading hours; creating synthetic term rates for mark-denominated investments and borrowings; arbitraging with interbank deposits; and spreading with other CME futures contracts, such as Eurodollars and Deutsche marks.

## THE MECHANICS OF FUTURES TRADING

Whereas trading in the money markets takes place over the telephone between dealers, interest rate futures trading occurs in an open outcry auction market, where all traders have equal access to the best price at the time of the trade. If interest rates move higher, the price of the contract falls; if rates move lower, the contract price rises. To protect against a rising interest rate, sell the futures contract (go short). If rates rise and the futures price falls, you can buy back the contract at a lower price, producing a profit on the transaction. Likewise, to protect against falling rates, buy the futures contract (go long). If rates fall and the futures price rises, you will be able to sell the contract at a higher price, producing a profit on the transaction.

### Add–On Yield and the IMM Index

. . .

Eurodollar futures are also traded by index price. 100 percent minus the add-on (or interest-bearing) yield determines the index price. Eurodollars are quoted on the basis of this add-on yield over a 360–day year. The add-on yield is the interest to be earned divided by the purchase price, rather than by the maturity value which is used with T-bills.

. . .

### Longs and Shorts

Before buying or selling a futures contract, you must open a trading account, depositing "initial margin" with a broker—either a cash deposit or another form of collateral. This margin serves as a good-faith deposit, guaranteeing performance. The price at which a buy or sell order is executed becomes the "entry" price, and at the end of trading on that day, the contract value is "marked-to-market." Your account balance is adjusted, reflecting the profit or loss based on the difference between the entry price and the "settlement" (or closing) price. This process continues for each day your position is open.

Because each futures contract covers $1 million face amount of three-month securities, each "basis point" (0.01) of price change is worth $25 (.01% × $1,000,000 × ¼ year = $25). Thus, if you took a long position, buying the contract at 91.05, and it settles at 91.20, you would be credited with a profit of 15 basis points × $25 per point, or $375. If the price falls on the next day by 10 basis points, from 91.20 to 91.10, your account would then be debited with a loss of $250 for that day's trading. In other words, each day your contract position is marked to the new settlement price until you sell the same contract to close the position. At that time your position will be marked to the sale price.

If you sell a contract to open a short position, it works the same way, in reverse. If you short the contract at 91.05, and it settles at 91.20, your position would be debited with a loss of 15 basis points, or

$375. The position would be "marked to market" daily until it is closed by buying an identical contract.

Profits that bring the brokerage account above the initial margin requirement can be withdrawn while a contract position is still open; but if daily losses cause the trading account to fall below a certain level (the "maintenance margin" level), further funds will be required to bring this account back to the initial margin level.

### Futures Pricing

Although the cash and futures prices of a three-month security generally move in tandem, the price relationship between them, called the "basis," is affected by changes in the shape of the yield curve.

The futures price is directly related to the cash price of the *deliverable* security (for example, an already-issued one-year or six-month T-bill that will mature 91 days after the T-bill futures' first delivery day).[1] On the futures' delivery date, the futures contract becomes a cash position, so that the two prices are the same at that point. Prior to contract delivery, the futures price (yield) reflects the market price (yield) of the deliverable security, as well as the financing rate associated with holding the deliverable security until the contract delivery date.

If the short date financing rate is higher than the yield on the deliverable security, there is a cost of carrying the deliverable; and the yield implied by the futures price would tend to be lower than the deliverable's yield. Conversely, if the financing rate is lower than the deliverable's yield, there is a profit from carrying the deliverable, and the futures yield will have to be higher.

As the futures' delivery date approaches, the effects of yield curve changes on the futures price become smaller, until the futures, the deliverable and the current three-month security all become identical and thus assume the same price on the futures' expiration day.

### Delivery

Although relatively few contract position holders ever take or make actual delivery of securities, the integrity of the contracts rests heavily on the Exchange's ability to provide an accurate, timely transfer when called upon to do so.

The CME's interest rate contracts have distinct delivery procedures:

- Treasury bills—the futures settlement price on the last contract trading day determines the purchase price to be paid by the long to the short for the delivery of new 91-day or aged 6-month or one-year bills with 91 days left to maturity.
- Eurodollar Time Deposits—since time deposits are not transferable, "delivery" is actually a cash settlement. The full contract

1. Although Eurodollar Time Deposits are not transferable, market participants can generally place or take deposits for any date, so that the same pricing mechanism is in place.

value is not exchanged; rather, the long and short positions are simply marked to a price dictated by the cash market. More precisely, the settlement price of the futures is determined by an authoritative Exchange poll on the final contract trading day. The cash market offered rate for 3-month Eurodollar Time Deposits (the London Interbank Offered Rate, or LIBOR) is deducted from 100 to determine the final contract settlement price.

- Euromarks—cash settled in the same way as Eurodollars, but based on a survey, conducted by Telerate, of the British Bankers' Association Interest Settlement Rate for 3-month Euro Deutsche marks.
- One-Month LIBOR—also cash settled, in the same way as the Eurodollar time deposit. The only difference is that the cash market for One-Month Eurodollar time deposits is deducted from 100.

## THE MECHANICS OF OPTIONS TRADING

Taking a position on a T-Bill or Eurodollar rate by buying a call or a put option requires no margin. The price paid for the option is the absolute limit of the buyer's risk; margin security is therefore unnecessary.

As an option buyer, you have the right, but not the obligation, to take a position in the underlying futures contract.[1] The decision whether to enter the futures market is entirely up to you, the option holder. Rather than "exercising" the option, you may re-sell it in the market, or simply let the option expire if it has no value.

Buying a call option gives you the right to take a long position in the underlying (same contract month as the option) futures at a specific price—the strike or exercise price. If the futures price rises (interest rate falls), the price of the call will tend to rise. The call's *likelihood* of profit increases, and therefore its price rises.

Buying a put option gives you the right to take a short futures position at a specific strike price. If the futures price falls (the interest rate rises), the price of the put will tend to rise. As the futures price falls, the probability increases that the put will bring a short futures position at a profit.

The option "writer," who sells the option to *open* a position, assumes the obligation of taking a futures position opposite to the option holder, if the option is exercised. The call writer stands ready to take a short futures position. The put writer stands ready to take a long futures position.[2]

1. Upon taking a futures position, a margin deposit will be required.

2. The writer of an option is required to post a margin deposit when the position is opened. The amount of margin required is recalculated daily until the option position is closed. The writer of an option must post margin because it is the writer who must stand ready to take a futures position at an unfavorable price at any time before the position is closed.

The option writer sells the right to exercise in order to earn the option price with the passage of time and no movement or adverse movement in the futures price. Such a position carries unlimited risk, but can be liquidated at any time before expiration by buying the same option. Many option writers limit their risks by writing the option against an opposite futures, cash or option position. This enables any loss on the written option to be offset by profit from the other position.

### Strike Prices

The strike price of an interest rate option is the price at which you would take a futures position upon exercise. The strike prices that currently are listed for trading are at every 25 basis points for the options on T-bills and Eurodollars.

As is the case with the futures contracts, trading for option contracts is on the March–June–September–December cycle. On the first day of trading for options in a new contract month, exercise prices for puts and calls will be listed above and below the settlement price of the underlying futures contract.

Each strike price and month represents a distinct option contract, just as puts and calls are distinct. For example, to offset a long March T-bill 93.00 call position, only the *sale* of that same call will do.

After the first day of trading, new exercise prices for puts and calls will be created based on the upward and downward movement of the underlying futures contract.

### Option Prices

To simplify trading, option prices (or premiums) are quoted in terms of index points rather than a dollar value. Since the futures price, the option price and the strike price are quoted in the same terms, the price relationships are very evident. The dollar value of a T-bill or Eurodollar option price is equal to the quoted index price times $2,500. For example, an option quoted at 1.23 would cost $3,075 (1.23 × $2500). One option covers one futures contract and, like the futures contract, has a minimum price change of .01 index points, equal to $25.

The price of an interest rate option is directly related to the underlying futures price, rather than to the current cash market interest rate. The option price is shaped by the following three factors.

### 1. Relationship of the Strike Price of the Option to the Current Underlying Futures Price

If the current futures price is higher than a call's strike price, the call is said to be "in-the-money." If the call holder exercises it today, he takes a long futures position at the strike price. The difference between the futures price and the strike price is the amount he will be credited, and is termed the option's "intrinsic value."

Similarly, if the futures price is lower than the strike price of a put, that put is "in-the-money." The exercise of an in-the-money put results in a sale of the futures at an above-market price.

In general, the greater an option's intrinsic value, the higher that option's price. If the option is "out-of-the-money" (currently has no intrinsic value because the futures price is lower than the call's strike or higher than the put's strike), the more out-of-the-money it is, the lower the option price.

## 2. Time

The more time that remains until an option's expiration, the higher the premium tends to be. The longer time period provides more opportunity for the underlying futures price to move to a point where the purchase or sale of the futures at the strike price becomes profitable. Therefore, an option with six months remaining until expiration will have a higher price than an option with the same strike price/futures price relationship and with only three months until expiration. The time component of an option's value tends to be largest when the underlying futures contract is trading near the exercise price of the option—that is, when an option is "at-the-money."

An option is a wasting asset. As the option approaches its maturity, the time value declines to zero. At expiration, the option's value is only its in-the-money amount.

## 3. Volatility

The more the futures price tends to fluctuate, the higher the potential profit on the option. *Volatility* is a measure of the degree of fluctuation in the futures price. More specifically in the case of options on the T-bill and Eurodollar futures, volatility is a measure of the degree of fluctuation in the *rate implied* by the futures contract price. If volatility increases, with all else remaining the same, the option price will rise; and if it declines, the option price will fall.

There are a number of different measures of volatility. The following exhibit, for instance, illustrates the two most common measures: historical volatility is based on the *futures* contracts' price movements over a specific time period in the past. In contrast, the implied volatility is a measure of variability "implied" by a given option's price. It is the volatility underlying each of the options prices determined by the marketplace.

## The "Delta Factor"

How will the changing price of an option relate to changes in the price of the underlying futures contract? The relationship is usually not one-for-one. A price change in the futures will usually result in a smaller change in the option's price. The option's potential is related to the time remaining and to the futures' volatility, as well as to the futures price.

The option's price consists of intrinsic value, if any, and time value. The greater the intrinsic value portion of the option price, the more responsive it will be to a changing futures price. On the other hand, the more time value makes up the option price, the less responsive it will be to a changing futures price. The price-change relationship between the option and the underlying futures is summarized in what option theorists call the "delta factor."

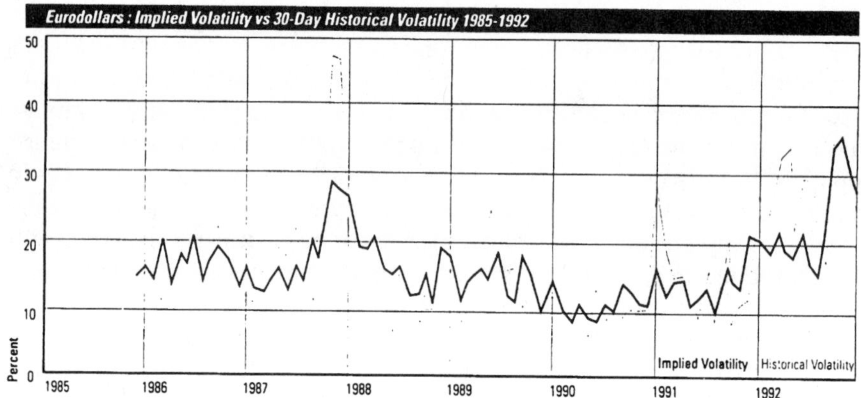


The delta factor is a measurement drawn from the mathematical option pricing formula, and serves several purposes. Basically, it can be used to gauge the change in the option price for a given change in the futures price. For instance, if a call's delta is 50 percent, and the futures price rises quickly by 25 basis points, the call's price should rise by 12 or 13 basis points. If the futures fall, the delta will predict the loss in option value of similar magnitude.

The table below lists hypothetical details for some calls with the futures price at 91.50, and with various lengths of time remaining until expiration. Notice the symmetry represented. Put deltas would have a very similar distribution if the strike prices across the top were reversed in order.

**Hypothetical Call Deltas (with the futures price at 91.50)**

| call strikes: | 90.50 | 91.25 | 91.50 | 91.75 | 92.50 |
|---|---|---|---|---|---|
| time remaining: | | | | | |
| 1 day | 100% | 96% | 50% | 4% | — |
| 1 week | 100% | 75% | 50% | 25% | — |
| 1 month | 90% | 62% | 50% | 38% | 10% |
| 3 months | 77% | 57% | 50% | 43% | 23% |
| 6 months | 70% | 55% | 50% | 45% | 30% |
| 1 year | 64% | 54% | 51% | 47% | 36% |

The deltas can also be considered ratings of the probability that the option will expire in-the-money. If the 92.50–strike call is far out-of-the-money with the futures price at 91.50, it makes sense that as time to expiration diminishes, so does the delta. With only a week to expiration, a small futures price move would not attract many buyers to the call, so that call's price will not react. On the other hand, the 90.50–strike call is very likely to finish in-the-money with only a week to expiration. Even a small futures price change would reflect a change in the potential in-the-money amount at expiration, and, thus, the call's price varies nearly one-to-one with the futures.

The preceding table illustrates that deltas will vary with both changing futures prices and the passage of time. Deltas are also affected by changes in volatility. An increase in the futures' volatility would drive up the time value of the options, and consequently their prices. Higher time value would tend to drive up the out-of-the-money option deltas, and diminish the in-the-money deltas, leaving the at-the-money deltas nearly unaffected. A decrease in volatility would decrease the out-of-the-money deltas and increase the in-the-money deltas. The longer the time until expiration, the more effect a volatility change would have on the option prices and deltas.

### Exercising Your Options

You may exercise an option on any business day the option is open for trading, including the day on which it is purchased. Exercise of a call results in a long futures contract at the call's exercise price, effective on the next trading day. Exercise of a put option results in a short futures contract at the put's exercise price. Your account would be credited the difference between the exercise price and the closing futures price, and you would be required to post futures margin. You could hold the futures position, or liquidate it immediately with an offsetting transaction.

You would want to exercise the call only if the current futures price is higher than the call's exercise price, and exercise the put only if the current futures price is lower than the put's exercise price. Further, you would normally exercise an option prior to the expiration day only if it is very deep in-the-money. If the option carries any time value in addition to its intrinsic value, you could profit more by selling the option and directly entering a futures position.

At expiration, an option has no remaining time value, so you probably would exercise any open in-the-money option contracts. Exercise of a T-bill option on expiration day results in a futures position that will have two to four weeks of trading life remaining. On the other hand, Eurodollar option exercise on expiration day results in a cash settlement instead of a futures position. Since the Eurodollar options and futures expire on the same day and the futures are settled in cash, exercise of expiring in-the-money options results in a cash payment to the option holder of the final in-the-money amount. The CME Clearing House automatically exercises expiring in-the-money Eurodollar options. However, the T-bill option is not automatically exercised, since it involves depositing margin and taking a futures position.

When an option is exercised, a writer of that same option is randomly chosen and assigned for exercise. The assigned option writer's position is transferred into the futures contract on the next trading day. A written call results in a short futures position; a written put results in a long futures position. The futures position can, of course, be offset or held. If offset on the assignment day, the writer's position account is marked from the exercise price to the exit price. If held, the futures position is marked from the exercise price to the daily settlement, and futures margin is required.

Expiration day exercise of T-bill options results in the assignment of futures positions to the option writers. Exercise of Eurodollar options on the expiration day, including automatic exercises, results in cash debits charged to the option writers. The relationship of the Eurodollar futures final settlement price (since the futures contract expires simultaneously) to the exercise price determines the debit amount.

## HEDGING WITH INTEREST RATE FUTURES

The idea behind hedging with interest rate futures is to offset an existing interest rate risk. This offset is accomplished by maintaining an appropriate futures position that will generate profits to cover the losses associated with an adverse interest rate move. You should note that a properly constructed futures hedge will also generate losses that will offset the effects of a beneficial interest rate move. Consider these hedge examples:

### Hedging a Forward Borrowing Rate

In late September, a corporate treasurer projects that cash flows will require a $1 million bank loan on December 15. The contractual loan rate will be 1 percent over the three-month Eurodollar rate (LIBOR) on that date. LIBOR is currently 9.25 percent. The December Eurodollar futures, which can be used to lock in the forward borrowing rate, are trading at 90.45, implying a forward Eurodollar rate of 9.55 percent (100.00–90.45). By selling one December Eurodollar futures contract, the corporate treasurer hopes to ensure a borrowing rate of 10.55 percent for the three-month period beginning December 15. This rate reflects the bank's 1 percent spread above the rate implied by the futures contract.

By December 15, the existing Eurodollar rate rises to 11.10 percent, and the December futures price declines to 89.00 (reflecting an 11 percent rate). As a result, the treasurer's interest payment to the bank is $30,250 for the quarter ($1,000,000 × 12.10 percent × ¼ year). However, the decline in the futures price produces a profit on the short futures of $3,625 (that is, 90.45–89.00 × $2,500 or, more simply, 145 × $25). Thus, the net interest expense for this quarter is $26,625 for an effective annual rate of 10.65 percent.

This example illustrates that the realized cost of funds may differ somewhat from the cost of funds anticipated at the time the hedge is initiated. The difference can be accounted for by the difference between the spot market LIBOR rate and the rate implied by the futures contract at the time the hedge is liquidated. The LIBOR rate was 10 basis points higher than the rate implied by the December futures contract on December 15, accounting for the 10 basis point differential between the anticipated and realized cost of funds. In this case, the difference worked against the hedger; but in other situations the difference may prove beneficial. In general, this hedging inaccuracy, called "basis risk," is minimized the closer the loan-pricing date is to the delivery date of the futures contract.

**Modifying Maturities**

Asset managers can lengthen the effective maturity of short-term investment assets by buying futures contracts, and shorten the effective maturity of those assets by selling futures contracts. Liability managers can achieve the same effects by doing the opposite, i.e., selling futures to lengthen their liabilities and buying futures to shorten them.

For either assets or liabilities, hedging serves as an alternative to restructuring the portfolio in the cash markets. The use of futures may be attractive when physical restructuring is not possible (e.g., term deposits cannot be bought back prior to their maturity dates). It may also be cheaper to use futures because (a) transaction costs in the futures market may be lower than those in cash markets, or (b) liquidity conditions in the cash market would result in substantial market penalties.

. . .

**Cross Hedging to Establish Yields or Costs**

The asset manager who knows that funds will be available for investment beginning on some forward date may buy futures to establish a rate of return for this investment. Also, the liability manager who plans for a forthcoming debt issuance can prearrange funding costs by selling interest rate futures. In either case, the manager may hedge even if his risk does not involve precisely the same instrument that underlies a futures contract.

. . .

**Locking in a Funding Rate**

Consider the case of a bank that funds itself with three-month Eurodollar Time Deposits at the London Interbank Offered Rate (LIBOR). This bank has a customer who wants a one-year fixed-rate loan of $10 million, with interest to be paid quarterly. At the time of the loan disbursement, the banker raises three-month funds at 12.55 percent; but he has to roll over this funding in three successive quarters. If he does not lock in a funding rate and interest rates rise, the loan could prove to be unprofitable.

The three quarterly refunding dates fall shortly before the next three Eurodollar futures contract expirations in March, June, and September. At the time the loan is taken down, the prices of these contracts are 86.81, 86.45, and 86.20, respectively. These prices correspond to yields of 13.19 percent, 13.55 percent and 13.80 percent. Coupled with the initial funding rate of 12.55 percent, the banker could lock in a cost of funds for the year equal to the average of these four rates (13.27 percent). He would sell 10 contracts for each expiration, reflecting the funding need of $10 million per quarter. Then, on the refinancing dates, the banker would take in three-month Eurodeposits and simultaneously liquidate the appropriate hedging contracts by buying them back. With the March refunding, the March contracts would be liquidated; June contracts would be liquidated in June; and September contracts would be liquidated in September.

As it turns out, the banker is able to re-fund at 14.55 percent, 14.30 percent and 11.30 percent for the respective quarters. The corresponding futures are liquidated at 85.42 (14.58 percent), 85.73 (14.27 percent), and 88.92 (11.08 percent). The overall results are presented in Exhibit 3.

**Exhibit 3**

| | | |
|---|---|---|
| Quarterly Eurodeposit costs | | |
| Qtr 1: $10 million × .1255 × ¼ = $313,750 | | |
| Qtr 2: $10 million × .1455 × ¼ = $363,750 | | |
| Qtr 3: $10 million × .1430 × ¼ = $357,500 | | |
| Qtr 4: $10 million × .1130 × ¼ = $282,500 | | $1,317,500 |
| Less the futures profits | | |
| Mar : 10 contracts × (8681 − 8542) × $25 = | $34,750 | |
| June: 10 contracts × (8645 − 8573) × $25 = | $18,000 | |
| Sep : 10 contracts × (8620 − 8892) × $25 = | −$68,000 | $ 15,250 |
| Net Interest Expense | | $1,332,750 |
| Effective rate | | 13.33% |

(Note that the September futures contracts resulted in a loss of $68,000. This caused the overall hedge to produce a net loss of $15,250, which must be added to the Euro-deposit costs to result in the net interest expense.)

The unhedged interest expense over the four quarters would have been 13.18 percent, lower, in fact, than the hedged expense. However, the funding rate was quite volatile over the period and could have easily resulted in a loss on the loan program. It should be recognized that effective futures hedges materially lock in an interest rate, precluding both advantage and loss from rate movement.

Recall that the banker had expected to lock up funding at 13.27 percent. In fact, funds actually were acquired at 13.33 percent, or 6 basis points higher. This discrepancy occurred because of less-than-perfect convergence between the cash refunding rates and the futures liquidation rates. If the bank had funded at exactly the same rate as the futures liquidation rate, the target would have been achieved. In this case, however, the actual funding over the term of the loan was, on average, six basis points higher than the futures liquidation rates. Put another way, these basis adjustments adversely affected the performance.

The minimal difference between the target rate and the effective funding rate can be attributed to the fact that the refunding dates were quite close to the futures expiration dates. If the respective dates were further apart, the funding rates and the futures rates would not necessarily converge so closely.

This example of a one-year loan funded with three-month deposits is an example of a negative interest rate "gap"—that is, where shorter-term liabilities are funding a longer-term asset and rising interest rates will have an adverse impact. The same basic hedging approach can be followed to remedy an overall balance sheet maturity mismatch.

## HEDGING WITH OPTIONS ON INTEREST RATE FUTURES

Whenever T-bill or Eurodollar futures can be used to lock-in a rate, options on futures can be substituted to guarantee a rate floor or ceiling. As an alternative to a long futures position, which predetermines a forward investment return for an asset, a call can be substituted. The call gives the right to buy the futures contract at a stated price. This provides a floor for the asset return while preserving the opportunity for better performance. On the other hand, instead of taking a short futures position to predetermine a liability rate, a put option can provide protection. The put gives the right to sell the futures at a stated price, providing a ceiling for the liability rate, while preserving the opportunity for a lower cost of funds.

The floor or ceiling rate provided by the option is determined by its strike price and the premium paid. The "strike yield" (simply 100 minus the option strike price) is adjusted to reflect the cost of the option. For example, suppose the following prices were observed:

| | |
|---|---|
| Sep Eurodollar futures | 91.74 |
| Sep 91.50–strike call | .43 |
| Sep 92.00–strike call | .18 |
| Sep 91.50–strike put | .18 |
| Sep 92.00–strike put | .42 |

Under these conditions, the user of the futures contract could lock-in a target rate of 8.26 percent (100.00–91.74)—an asset return if long or a liability cost if short. Subject to basis risk, this yield would be locked up regardless of whether market rates rise or fall over the hedge period.

Using the 91.50–strike call to hedge a floating-rate investment, a hedger could guarantee a minimum return of 8.50 percent for a cost of 43 basis points. In other words, the realized minimum return would be 8.07 percent as a worst case (8.50–.43).

If the rate falls below 8.50 percent, futures prices would rise and the call option would increase in value. The fallen investment rate on the asset would be supplemented by the profit on the call to ensure a minimum net return of 8.07 percent. On the other hand, if the rate rises above 8.50 percent, the option would be worthless at expiration, and the investor would simply lose the cost of the option and receive the higher market rate on the asset.

Using the 92.00–strike call, the investment hedger would establish a minimum return of 7.82 percent (100.00–92.00–.18). Why would someone use the 92.00–strike call rather than the 91.50 strike call, when the 91.50–strike call offers a higher minimum return? The question goes to an important tradeoff consideration.

While it is true that the 91.50–strike call provides a more attractive worst-case scenario, it does so for a larger up-front cost. The purchaser of the 91.50–strike call pays $1,075 for this protection ($25 × 43 basis points), while the cost of the 92.00–strike call is only $450 ($25 × 18 basis points).

. . .

Options offer a special advantage for hedging contingent liabilities or investments. If it is not certain whether funds will be needed or available, interest rate options can secure a rate at the least risk. If the contingency is eventually not realized, forward or futures hedging commitments could present sizable losses. The potential loss on long puts or calls, on the other hand, is limited to their purchase price, known in advance.

**Creating a Cap–Rate Loan**

Suppose a financial manager has access to funding at three-month LIBOR plus ¼ percent, and he wants to put a limit on how high this rate could rise by the time he will borrow in September. In effect, he wants insurance that will pay off if rates increase, but will not generate losses if rates fall. A Eurodollar put will serve this purpose.

At the time of the decision (July 1), three-month LIBOR is 8¾ percent, the September Eurodollar futures are trading at 90.60 (9.40 percent), and the 91.00–strike put is trading at .72. At these prices, this put provides a maximum cost of funds equal to 9.97 percent (100.00 − 91.00 + .72 + .25—where .25 reflects the ¼ percent spread above LIBOR).

When the put is purchased in July, the manager knows what he can expect in September. If LIBOR at that time were less than 9 percent, the put would expire worthless, and the manager would simply borrow at LIBOR plus ¼ percent. Of course, he would have to add the initial .72 cost of the put option to his total cost, but even with that expense it would never be higher than 9.97 percent (9.00 + .25 + .72).

In the event that LIBOR were to rise above 9 percent, the price of the futures contract would decline, and the put would have intrinsic value at its expiration equal to LIBOR minus 9.00 percent. Suppose for example, LIBOR were to rise to 11.50 percent at the expiration of this option contract. In this case, the cost of funds from the bank would be 11.75 percent (reflecting the ¼ percent spread) for an interest cost of $29,375 per million for the quarter ($1,000,000 × .1175 × ¼ year). The final value of the 91.00–strike put would be $6,250 ((91.00 − 88.50) × $25). The profit on the put, $6,250 less its initial cost (72 bps. × $25 = $1,800), would be deducted from the interest expense. Net interest expense would thus be $24,925 per million for the quarter (29,375 − 6,250 + 1,800). On an annualized basis, the effective rate is calculated:

$$\frac{24{,}925}{1{,}000{,}000} \times \frac{360}{90} = 9.97\%$$

Importantly, this same rate would result, regardless of how high market rates rise.

. . .

The combination of calls and puts can take any form to suit any set of expectations and hedging goals. The choice of strike prices for calls and puts allows the manager to tighten or expand the re-investment range, or to tilt it in one direction or the other.

The preceding examples are based on the simplest buy-and-hold strategy in order to keep the exposition simple. Delta and other option-pricing parameters can be used to weight option positions and manage them. Further study also will yield several other option combinations that can be useful to the sophisticated trader.

## CONCLUSION

Determining which hedging strategy is best—using futures or options—depends on the goals of the hedger. A futures contract essentially locks in a rate, making the holder indifferent to the way interest rates move. On the other hand, the hedger who buys an option is purchasing one-way protection with upside potential. In return for the price of the option, he receives compensation if adverse conditions evolve; but if good news develops, he is able to reap the benefits.

The choice of which instrument to use is really a judgement call, reflecting the probability of an adverse interest rate change, the potential damage of such a rate adjustment, and the cost of protection. In all likelihood, different choices will be made at different times, as conditions change. For that reason an understanding of both futures and options will provide managers with the greatest opportunity for effective risk management.

. . .

| Three–Month Eurodollar Time Deposit Futures | |
|---|---|
| **Ticker Symbol** | ED |
| **Trading Unit** | $1,000,000 |
| **Price Quote** | IMM Index points |
| **Minimum Price Fluctuation (Tick)** | US $25.00 = 1 IMM Index point = 0.01 or 1 basis point (e.g., from 93.00 to 93.01) (.0001 × $1,000,000 × 90/360 = $25) |
| **Daily Price Limit** | None |
| **Contract Months** | Mar, Jun, Sep, Dec |
| **Trading Hours** [1, 2] **(Chicago Time)** | 7:20 am–2:00 pm<br>Last day: 7:20 am–9:30 am |
| **Last Day of Trading** | Second London business day immediately preceding the third Wednesday of the contract month |
| **Delivery Date** | Last day of trading—cash settled |

1 Trading will end at 12:00 noon on the business day before a CME holiday and on any U.S. bank holiday that the CME is open.
2 This contract also is traded on the GLOBEX system. Contact your broker or the CME for specific GLOBEX trading hours.

| Options on Three–Month Eurodollar Futures | |
|---|---|
| **Ticker Symbols** | Calls: CE Puts: PE |
| **Underlying Contract** | One ED futures contract |
| **Strike Prices** | $.25 intervals, e.g., 92.25, 92.50, 92.75 |
| **Premium Quotations** | Total IMM Index points, e.g., 0.34 quoted as "34 Index points" or "34 basis points" |
| **Minimum Price Fluctuation (Tick)**[1] | US $25.00 = 1 IMM Index point = 0.01 or 1 basis point, e.g., from 0.34 to 0.35 (cabinet = $12.50) |
| **Daily Price Limit** | None |
| **Contract Months** | Mar, Jun, Sep, Dec & 2 serial months[2] |
| **Trading Hours** [3, 4] **(Chicago Time)** | 7:20 am–2:00 pm<br>Last day March-quarterly expirations:<br>7:20 am–9:30 am |
| **Last Day of Trading** | March quarterly cycle: Second London business day immediately preceding the 3rd Wednesday of the contract month; Serial options (Jan, Feb, Apr, May, Jul, Aug, Oct, & Nov): Friday immediately preceding 3rd Wednesday of contract month. |

| Options on Three–Month Eurodollar Futures | |
|---|---|
| **Minimum Performance Bond** | No performance bond required for put or call option buyers, but the premium must be paid in full; option sellers must meet additional performance bond requirements as determined by the Standard Portfolio Analysis of Risk (SPAN[3]) performance bond system. |
| **Exercise Procedure** [5] | An option may be exercised by the buyer up to and including last day of trading. To exercise, the clearing member representing the buyer submits an Exercise Notice to the Clearing House by 7:00 p.m. on the day of exercise. Any long in-the-money option position not liquidated or exercised prior to termination of trading will be automatically exercised. |

1 A trade may occur at the value of a half-tick (cabinet).

2 Options on ED futures are listed for all 12 calendar months, with each exercisable into the March-quarterly, quarter-end futures contract. For example, Jan, Feb and Mar options are exercisable into the March futures contract, and the March futures price is relevant for the pricing of the 3 sets of options. At any point in time, you can choose from options that expire in the next three calendar months, plus five March-quarterly expirations.

3 Trading will end at 12:00 noon on the business day before a CME holiday and on any U.S. bank holiday that the CME is open.

4 This contract also is traded on the GLOBEX system. Contact your broker or the CME for specific GLOBEX trading hours.

5 Consult your broker for specific requirements.

### *Questions*

1. Be sure you understand the basic terms.

(a) What is a future? What is a long position? A short position? What is a three-month Eurodollar time deposit futures contract? Who benefits if the contract price rises in the future? What is the effect of this contract if LIBOR rises or falls in the future?

(b) What is an option? What is the difference between a call and a put? What is a writer of a put or call? What is the holder? Buyers take long positions. Sellers take short positions.

(c) How is an option different from a future on the same instrument?

2. Who designs future and option contracts? What factors would shape the design?

3. Notional principal amounts outstanding at year-end 1991, according to the Bank of England (Quarterly Bulletin, November 1992, 402), were (in U.S. $ billions):

| | |
|---|---|
| Exchange traded instruments | $3,518 |
| Interest rate futures | 2,159 |
| Interest rate options (calls, puts) | 1,072 |
| Currency futures | 18 |
| Currency options | 59 |
| Stock market index futures | 77 |
| Options on stock market indices | 132 |
| Over the counter instruments | $4,449 |

(a) OTC data exclude forward rate agreements, OTC currency options, forward foreign exchange positions, equity swaps and warrants on equity. The CFTC estimates that at the end of 1991 OTC interest rate options (such as caps, floors, collar, and swaptions) had a notional value worldwide of $577 billion [OTC Derivative Markets and Their Regulation (October 1993) ].

(b) Actual exposures are far less than the notional amounts. "The amount at risk through counterparty default, for example, represented on average on conventional assumptions between 2% and 4% of the contracts notional value." Bank of England Quarterly Bulletin (November 1992) 402. For example, the 50 largest U.S. Bank Holding Companies reported a total notional value of $6.3 trillion at the end of December 1992. The replacement cost, called credit exposure, was merely 2.30% gross and 1.46% net, according to a report by the House Banking Committee minority staff on Financial Derivatives (November 1993).

4. In the U.S., futures and options trading grew exponentially in the 1980s. From 10 million contracts in 1968 to 100 million in 1981, trading reached 360 million in 1992. Options only started to trade in 1982; since 1987, they accounted for about one-seventh of all trading. Non–U.S. trading rose from less than half the U.S. volume in 1986 to almost equal the U.S. in 1993 [Johnson], most as interest rate contracts [CFTC, October 1993]. The CME's 3–month eurodollar future contract won the largest volume gains and was among the most traded contracts in the world during 1992.

5. The following tables are from the International Monetary Fund, International Capital Markets, Part II (August 1993). Note the role of banks in Table 9. In the U.S., the 10 largest BHCs held 95% of all BHC futures (and forwards), which had a notional value of $5.8 trillion on June 30, 1993, according to the Federal Reserve Board. They held 94% of the $2.2 trillion in options.

## Table 8. Annual Turnover in Derivative Financial Instruments Traded on Organized Exchanges Worldwide

*(In millions of contracts traded)*

| | 1986 | 1987 | 1988 | 1989 | 1990 | 1991 |
|---|---|---|---|---|---|---|
| Futures on short-term interest rate instruments of which: | 16.4 | 29.4 | 33.7 | 70.2 | 75.8 | 84.8 |
| Three-month Eurodollar [1] | 12.4 | 23.7 | 25.2 | 46.8 | 39.4 | 41.7 |
| Futures on long-term interest rate instruments of which: | 74.6 | 116.3 | 122.6 | 130.8 | 143.3 | 149.7 |
| U.S. Treasury bond [2] | 54.6 | 69.4 | 73.8 | 72.8 | 78.2 | 69.9 |
| Notional French Government bond [3] | 1.1 | 11.9 | 12.4 | 15.0 | 16.0 | 21.1 |
| Ten-year Japanese Government bond [4] | 9.4 | 18.4 | 18.8 | 19.1 | 16.4 | 12.9 |
| German Government bond [5] | — | — | 0.3 | 5.3 | 9.6 | 12.4 |
| Currency futures | 19.7 | 20.8 | 22.1 | 27.5 | 29.1 | 29.2 |
| Interest rate options and options on interest rate futures | 22.2 | 29.3 | 30.5 | 39.5 | 52.0 | 50.8 |
| Currency options and options on currency futures | 13.0 | 18.2 | 18.2 | 20.7 | 18.8 | 21.5 |
| Total | 145.9 | 214.0 | 227.1 | 288.6 | 319.1 | 336.0 |
| of which: | | | | | | |
| in the United States | 122.9 | 161.4 | 165.3 | 198.1 | 205.7 | 199.7 |
| in Europe | 9.8 | 27.2 | 32.6 | 49.0 | 61.0 | 84.2 |
| in Japan | 9.4 | 18.3 | 18.8 | 23.7 | 33.6 | 30.0 |

Source: Adapted from Bank for International Settlements (1992b), p. 55.

1 Traded on the Chicago Mercantile Exchange–International Monetary Market (CME–IMM), Singapore Mercantile Exchange (SIMEX), London International Financial Futures Exchange (LIFFE), Tokyo International Financial Futures Exchange (TIFFE), and Sydney Futures Exchange (SFE).

2 Traded on the Chicago Board of Trade (CBOT), LIFFE, Mid-America Commodity Exchange (Midam), New York Futures Exchange (NYFE), and Tokyo Stock Exchange (FSE).

3 Traded on the Marché à Terme International de France (MATIF).

4 Traded on TSE, LIFFE, and CBOT.

5 Traded on LIFFE and the Deutsche Terminbörse (DTB).

## Table 9. Open Positions in Financial Futures and Options on Financial Futures Contracts Traded on U.S. Exchanges, 1992

*(In percent of total, end-year data)*

| | Distribution of Positions | | | | | |
|---|---|---|---|---|---|---|
| | Purchases (Long) | | | Sales (Short) | | |
| | Banks | | | Banks | | |
| Types of Contract | U.S. | Non–U.S. | Other | U.S. | Non–U.S. | Other |
| | | | *Futures* | | | |
| Short-term interest rate [1] | 23.56 | 11.71 | 64.73 | 11.06 | 26.96 | 61.97 |
| Long-term interest rate [2] | 4.30 | 7.32 | 88.37 | 8.19 | 16.35 | 75.47 |
| Currency [3] | 11.24 | 12.18 | 76.58 | 2.13 | 18.20 | 79.67 |
| Stock market index [4] | 26.57 | 0.50 | 72.93 | 11.78 | 10.29 | 77.94 |
| | | | *Options* | | | |
| Call options | | | | | | |
| Short-term interest rate [1] | 14.83 | 28.85 | 56.32 | 17.46 | 26.08 | 56.46 |
| Long-term interest rate [2] | 17.78 | 15.46 | 66.76 | 7.09 | 18.86 | 74.05 |
| Currency [3] | 15.48 | 39.17 | 45.34 | 6.43 | 47.38 | 46.19 |
| Stock market index [4] | 0.29 | 0.34 | 99.37 | 1.16 | 10.77 | 88.07 |
| Put options | | | | | | |
| Short-term interest rate [1] | 23.17 | 25.08 | 51.75 | 16.71 | 31.83 | 51.46 |
| Long-term interest rate [2] | 3.56 | 18.48 | 77.95 | 7.60 | 19.52 | 72.89 |
| Currency [3] | 7.55 | 30.57 | 61.89 | 5.77 | 46.42 | 47.81 |
| Stock market index [4] | 2.94 | 2.17 | 94.89 | 1.34 | 1.01 | 97.65 |

Source: Commodity Futures Trading Commission (CFTC).

1 Chicago Mercantile Exchange–International Monetary Market (CME–IMM) one-month LIBOR, CME–IMM Treasury bills, Chicago Board of Trade (CBOT) 30–day interest rate, and CME–IMM Eurodollars.

2 CBOT Treasury bonds, CBOT 2–year and 6.5 10–year Treasury notes, and CBOT municipal bonds.

3 CME–IMM Canadian dollar, deutsche mark, Japanese yen, pound sterling, and Swiss franc.

4 CME–IMM Nikkei, Standard & Poor's (S & P) 500, and S & P 400.

6. What factors shape the pricing of a 3 month eurodollar future contract and an option on this contract? How is a $1 million futures contract priced?

(a) If LIBOR was 7% on the expiration date, what would be the price of the contract then?

(b) Assume that at the time a contract was purchased, the market expected LIBOR to be 5% two months later when the contract expired. What would the price of the contract have been at purchase?

(c) On the facts in (a) and (b), what would be the dollar value of the change from purchase to expiration? Which party pays, buyer or seller? If a player expects interest rates to rise, does it want a long or short position?

(d) How much is at risk with a $1 million eurodollar contract? How would operations in the eurodollar futures market affect the underlying cash market?

7. Who would buy or sell futures generally and the 3 month eurodollar contract specifically? Give examples of hedgers, arbitragers, and speculators using the eurodollar contracts.

8. Who would buy or write options on futures generally and on the 3 month eurodollar contract specifically? Give examples of hedgers, arbitragers, and speculators using the eurodollar contracts. How would a call buyer and a call writer react to the following:

(a) Whether the strike price should be set high or low?

(b) Whether the exercise date is set sooner or later in the future?

(c) Whether the underlying value of the future rises or falls? Whether it is volatile?

(d) Whether interest rates rise or fall?

9. Option positions and investment strategies can become quite complex. For simplicity, we draw on examples of stock options (not complicated by interest payments). American options can be exercised at any point. European options cannot be exercised before the expiration date. The following material is from J. Hull, Introduction to Futures and Options Markets (1991), 213–20 ("Hull"). As you read it, consider its implications for determining the riskiness of individual options and managing that risk.

(a) Hull describes profit and loss opportunities available to parties to option contracts. "On one side is the investor who has taken the long position (i.e., has bought the option). On the other side is the investor who has taken a short position (i.e., has sold or written the option). The writer of an option receives cash up front but has potential liabilities later. His or her profit/loss is the reverse of that for the purchaser of the option." The following figures show the profit and loss to buyers (figures 7.1 and 7.2) and writers (Figures 7.3 and 7.4) of a call and put option.

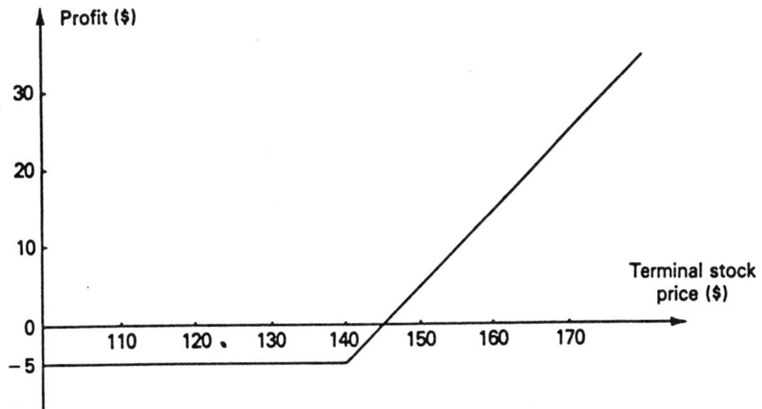


**FIGURE 7.1** Profit from buying a European call option on one IBM share. Option price = $5, strike price = $140.

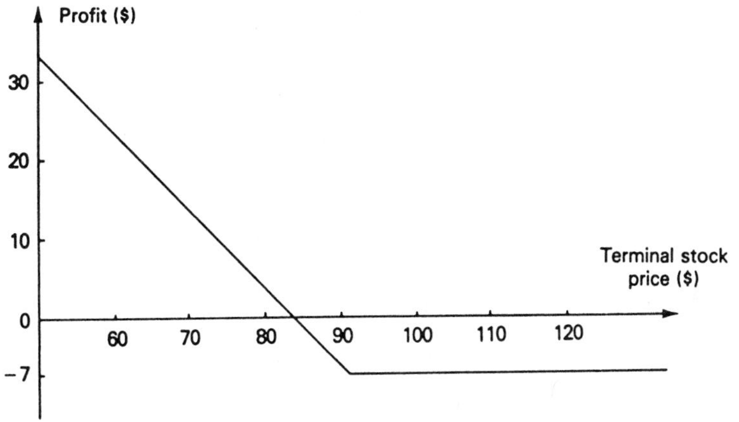


**FIGURE 7.2** Profit from buying a European put option on one Exxon share. Option price = $7, strike price = $90.

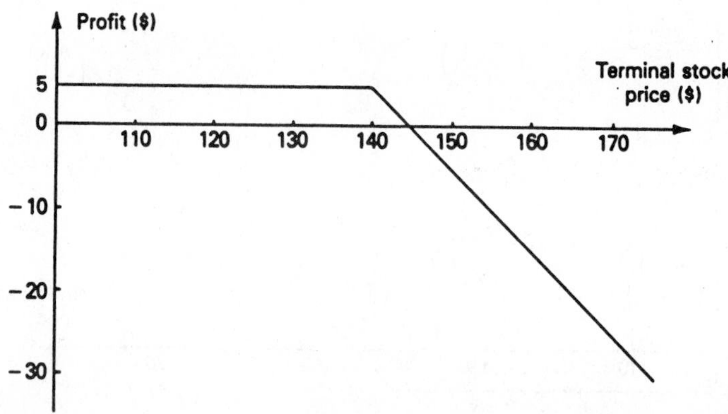


**FIGURE 7.3** Profit from writing a European call option on one IBM share. Option price = $5, strike price = $140.

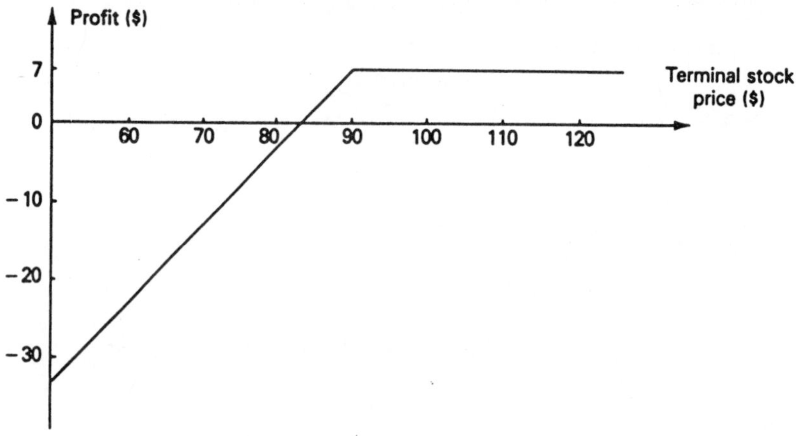


**FIGURE 7.4** Profit from writing a European put option on one Exxon share. Option price = $7, strike price = $90.

(b) Hull then describes four strategies involving a single option and the underlying stock. Focus on the protective put strategy (chart c and the elaborated version following this note). What is it? How do you interpret its profit curve? How does it compare to the normal long put curve? What happens with the protected put if at strike time the stock price is below the put strike price? Above the strike price? What does this profit curve resemble? Hull says:

There are a number of different trading strategies involving a single option on a stock and the stock itself. The profits from these are illustrated in Figure 9.1. In this figure, and in other figures throughout this chapter, the dashed line shows the relationship between profit and stock price for the individual securities constituting the portfolio, while the solid line shows the relationship between profit and stock price for the whole portfolio.

In Figure 9.1a the portfolio consists of a long position in a stock plus a short position in a call option. The investment strategy represented by this portfolio is known as *writing a covered call.* This is because the long stock position "covers" or protects the investor from the possibility of a sharp rise in the stock price. In Figure 9.1b a short position in a stock is combined with a long position in a call option. This is the reverse of writing a covered call. In Figure 9.1c the investment strategy involves buying a put option on a stock and the stock itself. This is sometimes referred to as a *protective put* strategy. In Figure 9.1d a short position in a put option is combined with a short position in the stock. This is the reverse of a protective put.

The alert reader will notice that the profit patterns in Figure 9.1a, b, c, and d have the same general shape as the profit patterns discussed in Chapter 7 for short put, long put, long call, and short call, respectively. Put-call parity provides a way of understanding why this is so.

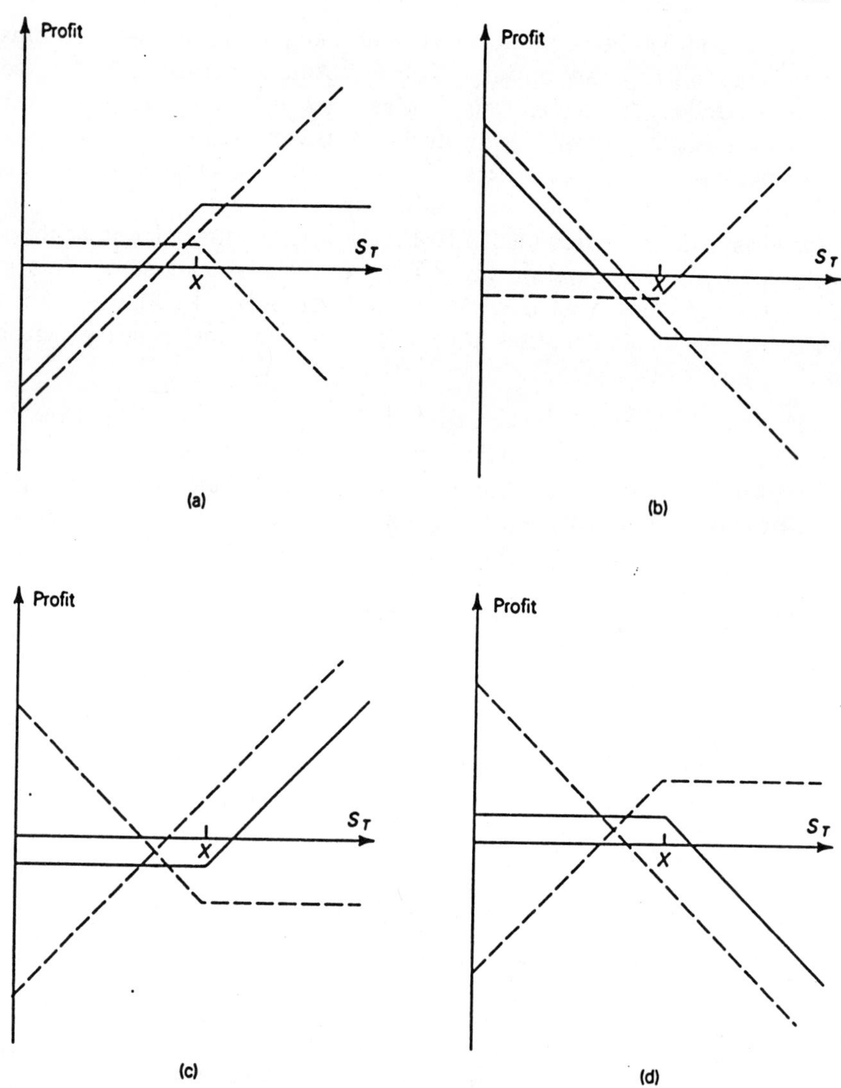


**FIGURE 9.1** Profit from (a) a long position in a stock combined with a short position in a call, (b) a short position in a stock combined with a long position in a call, (c) a long position in a put combined with a long position in a stock, (d) a short position in a put combined with a short position in a stock.

The following chart elaborates the protective put in chart (c) above.

The vertical axis is the profit on a position. Above point (b) the position runs a profit, below is a loss. The horizontal axis is the stock price, which increases to the right. The (x) represents the strike price. The (w) is basically the price at which the long stock was bought. The (z) is the cost of the put.

The dotted lines represent the profit and loss on two long positions. The straight diagonal sloping up to the right is the long stock, which becomes profitable when its market price exceeds the price at which it was bought, point (w). Two other items affect (w) (neither is separately calculated on the chart): any cost of funding the purchase of the stock reduces profit and any dividend received on the stock while it is held increases profit.

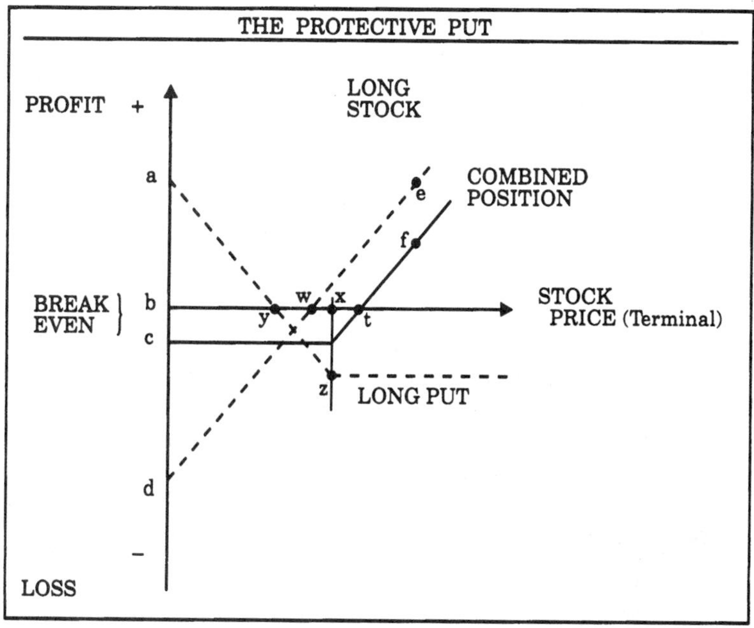


HOLD LONG STOCK AND LONG PUT IN THE STOCK

X = STRIKE PRICE

W = LONG STOCK PURCHASE PRICE

(X -> Y) = (X -> Z) = LONG PUT COST = (E -> F)

(B -> C) = (W -> Y) = LOSS ON LONG STOCK (B -> D) <u>LESS</u>

PROFIT ON PUT (B -> A)

(c) Put-call parity says that the current value of a call on a stock equals the current value of an associated put plus the current market price of the stock less the present value of the strike price.

The relationship is most easily demonstrated with a European put and call on a stock that does not pay dividends, ignoring transactions costs, margins, and taxes. The idea is that if put and call prices are not in this parity, arbitrage is possible. One "could make a certain profit on zero investment by selling the relatively overpriced option and using the proceeds to buy the relatively underpriced option, together with an appropriate position in the stock and borrowing or lending .... The portfolio would require no cash outflow (or inflow) on the expiration date of the options." J.C. Cox and M. Rubenstein, Options Markets (1985) 39–44.

---

## C. THE CME's THREE–MONTH EUROYEN TIME DEPOSIT FUTURES CONTRACT AND OPTIONS ON IT

When U.S. exchanges design a new future or option contract, they apply for approval to the Commodity Futures Trading Commission, a federal agency. The following memorandum sets out the CFTC staff's reasoning and proposals to the Commission for the CME's proposed Three-month Euroyen Time Deposit futures contract and options on the future. The memorandum is dated November 20, 1992.

As you read the memorandum, consider these questions. What do you learn from it about the way the U.S. government and the exchange regulate futures and options markets? How do they share responsibility? What are the regulators' major concerns and what standards or criteria are used to resolve them? Specifically, for a proposed contract based on a foreign instrument, what international factors play a role in the proposal from the CME and the recommendations of the CFTC staff?

### I. Introduction

In separate submissions dated July 15, 1992, the Chicago Mercantile Exchange (CME or Exchange) applied to the Commission for designation as a contract market in the Three–Month Euroyen Time Deposit (Euroyen) futures contract and options on that futures contract.

. . .

The Division recommends that the Commission designate the CME as a contract market in the Three–Month Euroyen Time Deposit futures contract pursuant to Section 5 of the Act and as a contract market in options on that futures contract pursuant to Sections 4c and 5 of the Act and that the Commission approve proposed CME rules, as listed above, pursuant to Section 5a(12) of the Act. Copies of the proposed approval letter and orders of designation are included as Attachments D and E, respectively. Since many of the terms and conditions of the subject contracts are substantially identical to those of the CME Three–Month

Eurodollar Time Deposit Rate (Eurodollar) futures and option contracts, the following discussion has been abbreviated, where appropriate.

## II. Cash Market Overview

The cash market underlying the proposed futures contract, the Tokyo interbank market, is extremely large. According to *Institutional Investor,* as of December 31, 1991, Japanese banks accounted for 14 of the 25 largest banks in the world, with those 14 banks alone accounting for over $3 trillion in deposits. In terms of deposits, the six largest banks in the world were Japanese.

Trade sources indicated that the Tokyo interbank market exhibits the highest degree of breadth and liquidity, and is characterized by a tight bid-ask spread and extensive arbitrage. Deposits in the Tokyo interbank market may be referred to by market participants as Euroyen deposits.[3] The interest rate on these deposits often is referred to as the Tokyo Interbank Offered Rate (TIBOR). Real-time TIBOR quotes are publicly available on electronic quote screens.

The Tokyo International Financial Futures Exchange (TIFFE) lists for trading a Euroyen futures contract. Based on the volume of trading and open interest, the TIFFE contract is one of the ten leading futures contracts in the world.[4] Trade sources have indicated that there is extensive arbitrage between the TIFFE Euroyen futures contract and TIBOR cash markets.

## III. Analysis of Proposed Futures Contract

### A. *Summary of Proposed Terms and Conditions*

The unit of trading for the proposed futures contract is the interest on a three-month time deposit in the Tokyo interbank market with a principal value of 100,000,000 Japanese yen (¥100,000,000, i.e., approximately $833,000).[5]

Future prices for the proposed contract will be quoted on an index basis; that is, 100.00 minus the annual yield in percentage points on a three-month Euroyen time deposit. The minimum price fluctuation will be 0.01 index point (equal to ¥2,500, i.e., approximately $20.85 per contract).

The CME proposes to trade the subject contract during both Regular Trading Hours (RTH) in the open outcry environment and Electronic Trading Hours (ETH) on the Globex system. During RTH, the proposed

**3.** Eurocurrencies (such as Eurodollars, Euromarks, and Euroyen) are generally defined as deposits denominated in a particular currency outside that currency's home country. The yen-denominated deposits underlying the proposed futures contract may be located in Japan and may not technically meet this definition.

**4.** During the one year period ending July 31, 1992, 15.75 million TIFFE Euroyen futures contracts were traded (average daily volume of approximately 65,000 contracts). The open interest as of month-end June 1992 was 333,000 contracts.

**5.** The exchange rate used in this memorandum is based on the September 30, 1992 spot rates published in the October 1, 1992 *Wall Street Journal.* At that time, $1.00 was equal to ¥120.00 and ¥1 was equal to $.008333.

futures contract will not be subject to a maximum price fluctuation limit. However, there will be a maximum price fluctuation limit of 1.00 index points above or below the previous day's settlement price during ETH.[6]

The proposed contract is to be cash settled using normal variation margin procedures based on the final settlement price established by TIFFE for its corresponding Euroyen futures contract.[7] To determine the final settlement price for its Euroyen futures contract, TIFFE performs two surveys of banks, one at the close of trading in the expiring futures contract—11:00 a.m. Tokyo time—and one at a randomly selected time in the 90 minute period preceding that close—between 9:30 a.m. and 11:00 a.m. Tokyo time.[8] In each survey, TIFFE randomly selects 12 banks from a TIFFE-created list of major banks active in the Tokyo interbank market. Each participating bank is asked to state its perception of the prevailing rate for three-month Euroyen deposits. TIFFE eliminates the two highest and two lowest quotes that it receives in each survey and computes the mean of the remaining eight quotes. The average of the results of the two surveys is used as the final settlement price. This procedure is similar to the CME's procedures for determining the final settlement prices of its Eurodollar futures contract.

The last day of trading for the subject contract will be the same as the last day of trading in the TIFFE Euroyen futures contract.[10] The TIFFE contract generally expires on the second Japanese bank business day immediately preceding the third Wednesday of the contract month.

The Exchange has proposed a speculative position limit of 5,000 contracts in all months combined. Exemptions from this limit may be granted on a case-by-case basis for hedging and for certain other positions that meet existing CME requirements. The reportable level will be 25 contracts.

B. *Justification of Contract Terms and Conditions*

1. *Par Contract Unit*

Exchange Proposal: The proposed contract unit is the interest on a ¥100,000,000 three-month Euroyen time deposit. As noted, delivery on the proposed contract is by cash settlement based on the final settlement

**6.** The opening of the CME Globex trading session is defined as the start of a trading day. The CME defines the end of a trading day as the close of RTH.

**7.** The CME has stated that it is negotiating with TIFFE to purchase the TIFFE's settlement price directly from TIFFE, in addition to relying on wire services for that price.

**8.** As noted, the close of trading in expiring TIFFE Euroyen futures contracts is 11:00 a.m. Tokyo time. Currently, Japan does not utilize a daylight savings time convention. Thus, 11:00 a.m. Tokyo time is equal to 9:00 p.m. Central Daylight Time (in Chicago), or 8:00 p.m. Central Standard Time (CST). The current trading day for the TIFFE Euroyen futures contract is divided into three sessions: 9:00 a.m. to noon Tokyo time (6:00 p.m. to 9:00 p.m. CST), 1:30 p.m. to 3:30 p.m. (10:30 p.m. to 12:30 a.m. CST), and 4:00 p.m. to 6:00 p.m. (1:00 a.m. to 3:00 a.m. CST).

**10.** Trading in the expiring CME contract will cease at the same time as in the expiring TIFFE contract, 11:00 a.m. Tokyo time, which is in the evening on the prior calendar day in Chicago and is during ETH. However, as noted in footnote 6, the CME considers an ETH session to be part of the same trading day as the RTH session which begins the next morning.

price established by TIFFE for its corresponding Euroyen futures contract, which TIFFE determines by cash market surveys on the last day of trading of the TIFFE Euroyen futures contract, generally the second Japan bank business day immediately preceding the third Wednesday of the contract month.

The CME previously has conducted surveys of the London Interbank Offered Rate for yen deposits, in conjunction with its now dormant Japanese Yen Euro–Rate Differential futures contract. Rather than conduct such surveys as a basis for cash settlement of the proposed contract, the CME proposes to utilize the TIFFE settlement price. As noted above, the TIFFE Euroyen contract is very actively traded. The CME's proposal is intended to minimize any pricing difference and facilitate arbitrage between the two contracts.[12]

Analysis: For cash settled futures contracts, Section (a)(2)(iii) of Commission Guideline No. 1 states that a board of trade must submit evidence that (1) the cash settlement of the contract is at a price reflecting the underlying cash market, (2) the cash settlement of the contract will not be subject to manipulation or distortion, and (3) the price series upon which the settlement price is based is reliable, acceptable, publicly available, and timely.

As discussed in detail below, the Division believes that the proposed contract meets each of the Guideline No. 1 requirements for cash-settled futures contracts.

a. *Price Reflects Underlying Cash Market and is Reliable, Acceptable, Publicly Available, and Timely:*

As noted above, the proposed cash settlement price is currently used by TIFFE as the basis for cash settlement of its very actively traded Euroyen futures contract. TIFFE surveys major banks active in the Tokyo interbank market, which is a deep and liquid cash market. Trade sources confirmed that the TIFFE survey price is reliable and accurately reflects prices in the underlying cash market. Further, as noted above, TIBOR quotes are publicly available on a timely basis.

Division staff spoke to trade sources concerning the acceptability of the proposed cash settlement price series for hedging purposes. These sources indicated that the series adequately reflects the Tokyo interbank deposit rate market for that purpose and noted that the TIFFE Euroyen contract is widely used for hedging purposes.

b. *Susceptibility to Manipulation:*

As noted, the TIFFE settlement price determination procedure is substantially identical to a procedure that the Commission previously has approved for the CME's Eurodollar futures contract and other

**12.** The Singapore International Monetary Exchange (SIMEX) also lists a Euroyen futures contract for trading. The SIMEX contract, like the proposed CME contract, settles to the TIFFE final settlement price. According to CME staff, SIMEX and TIFFE have entered into an agreement for TIFFE to supply SIMEX with the final settlement price (see footnote 7).

futures contracts. The Division notes that there have been no apparent problems related to the CME's procedure. It is reasonable to expect that the TIFFE final settlement price determination procedure, as described above, also would be effective in minimizing the susceptibility of the proposed contract to manipulation and price distortion.

Trade sources interviewed by Division staff indicated that the cash settlement price calculated by TIFFE is not readily susceptible to manipulation. As discussed above, the underlying cash market is very liquid, with a tight bid-ask spread and continuous, public reporting of cash market values. Therefore, an attempt to manipulate the final settlement price is likely to be detectable by TIFFE, the CME, and cash market participants.

An unusual feature of the proposed cash settlement procedures is that TIFFE's primary activities, including the cash settlement price determination of its Euroyen futures contract, take place outside the United States, specifically in Tokyo, Japan.[13] In addition, TIFFE has indicated that it will not reveal the identities of the banks it surveys nor the actual data received from survey participants to either the CME or the Commission.[14]

In view of these unusual features, the CME has undertaken to conduct special surveillance procedures during the period in which the cash settlement value is being derived. In order to verify that the TIFFE settlement price is reflective of the cash market, CME staff will monitor, using electronic quote screens, the three-month TIBOR for yen-denominated deposits during the 90 minute period prior to 11:00 a.m. Tokyo time and for the following 10 minute period, when TIFFE is performing its surveys. The CME has indicated that it would take appropriate action in the event of an apparent price distortion or manipulation. The CME has represented that such appropriate action could include direct discussions and information gathering, to the extent possible, with (1) TIFFE,[16] (2) cash market participants and (3) large position holders in the CME contract. The Exchange retains self-regulatory authority to address possible manipulation attempts and to take appropriate action to prevent artificial prices from influencing the final settlement value of the contract.[17]

**13.** The CME Eurodollar futures contract, by contrast, is based on offering prices of firms located outside the United States, but the data are collected, and the final cash settlement value is calculated, by CME staff.

**14.** The CME currently is negotiating with TIFFE to obtain a surveillance sharing agreement (SSA). The Commission also is negotiating with Japanese regulatory authorities to obtain a memorandum of understanding regarding the sharing of market information by officials representing the two governments.

**16.** The CME has indicated that, in the event of an apparent manipulation or price distortion, it would discuss the matter with TIFFE, if appropriate, even in the absence of an SSA (see footnote 14).

**17.** For example, the Exchange has the authority to adopt an emergency rule suspending the proposed final settlement price calculation procedure and to establish an alternative final settlement price. The CME has confirmed that such action would be taken, if deemed appropriate.

Conclusion: In view of (1) the high level of breadth and liquidity in the Tokyo interbank market in yen-denominated deposits and in the TIFFE Euroyen futures market, (2) TIFFE's status as a regulated exchange under Japanese law, (3) the procedures used by TIFFE to derive the cash settlement price, and (4) the CME's special surveillance program regarding the monitoring of the TIFFE settlement price determination, the cash settlement price for the TIFFE Euroyen futures contract is acceptable as a basis of cash settlement for the proposed CME Euroyen futures contract. It is reasonable to expect that the proposed CME contract should not be readily susceptible to manipulation or price distortion.

2. *Trading Months and Hours*

The Exchange has stated that its regular trading hours typically will be from 7:20 a.m. to 2:00 p.m. Chicago time, which are the same as the trading hours for the CME Eurodollar futures contract. The CME also proposes to list the subject contract for trading during ETH through the Globex system. The Exchange intends to list contract months in the March quarterly cycle for up to five years in the future.

Since delivery will employ cash settlement and since there is active trading in Euroyen every month of the year, the relationship of the delivery month cycle to available supplies is not a concern. Thus, any months chosen by the CME would be acceptable from an economic standpoint.

The Exchange intends to list a subset of the RTH contract months for trading through Globex. Regarding the initial determinations of and subsequent changes in this subset, the Division recommends that the Commission establish the same standards under the expedited procedures of Commission Regulation 1.41(n) as have been established previously by the Commission for other futures contracts.

3. *Contract Size*

Exchange Proposal: The Exchange is proposing as a trading unit the interest on a ¥100,000,000 (i.e., approximately $833,000) three-month Euroyen time deposit. For comparison, the size of the CME Eurodollar contract is $1,000,000.

Analysis: Yen-denominated deposits held by institutional investors typically exceed the size of the proposed contract. However, this should not interfere with the proposed contract's commercial utility since traders can trade in multiple contracts.

Conclusion: The proposed contract size is acceptable.

4. *Minimum Price Fluctuation*

The futures contract will be quoted on an index basis, i.e., 100.00 minus the three-month interbank yen time deposit interest rate on an annualized basis for a 360-day year (*e.g.*, a price of 96.00 would imply a 3-month rate of 4.00% per annum). The Exchange proposes a minimum price fluctuation of 0.01 index point (valued at ¥2,500 or approximately $20.85 per contract).

The proposed minimum price fluctuation (i.e., 0.01 percent in yield or one basis point) is the same as that of the CME Eurodollar contract and is not inconsistent with cash market practices. The proposed minimum price fluctuation is acceptable.

5. *Position Limits*

Exchange Proposal: Proposed rule ___ 02.D would establish a position limit of 5,000 contracts net long or net short in all contract months combined. Proposed rule ___ 02.E would provide standards for aggregation of accounts. The position limits would not apply to bona fide hedge or other positions exempted pursuant to existing rules 543 and 4006. In accordance with existing rule 817, the Exchange proposes to establish a reporting level of 25 contracts for a single contract month in connection with its large-trader reporting system.

Analysis: The proposed speculative limit level appears appropriate for the proposed Euroyen futures contract. The Commission originally approved a similar speculative position limit for the CME's Eurodollar futures contract. Subsequently, the Commission approved a position accountability rule for the CME Eurodollar futures contract. In view of the extremely high degree of liquidity in the underlying cash market, and since the proposed contract also could be readily arbitraged with the cash market, the Division believes that the proposed speculative position limit level is acceptable and meets the requirements of Commission Regulation 1.61.

Further, as with other cash-settled contracts, the Division believes that the proposal of only a net position limit for all futures combined, with no spot month limit and an implied spread exemption, is acceptable. The proposed aggregation standard and position limit exemption provisions are identical to those approved by the Commission for other CME contracts. The proposed reporting level of 25 contracts is acceptable.

Conclusion: The proposed speculative limit provisions meet the requirements under Section 1.61 of the Commission's regulations and, therefore, are acceptable.

C. *Public Interest Considerations*

The Division, based upon its analysis, is of the opinion that the proposed contract potentially could, or would, be used for hedging or price basing. Moreover, the Division is of the opinion that the contract does not appear to be readily susceptible to price manipulation or other distortion and, based upon its economic review, is otherwise consistent with Section 5(g) of the Act, which requires that designation of a contract market not be contrary to the public interest. Finally, the Division notes that the Commission has received no adverse comments indicating that trading in the proposed contract would be contrary to the public interest.

## IV. Analysis of Proposed Option Contract

### A. *Summary of Proposed Terms and Conditions*

One Euroyen futures option contract will give the holder the right to buy or sell one Euroyen futures contract at a specified price by a certain expiration date. As noted above, the unit of trading for the CME's underlying Euroyen futures contract is the interest on a ¥100,000,000 (i.e., approximately $833,000) three-month Euroyen time deposit.

Option premiums will be quoted in terms of index points. The minimum premium fluctuation will be 0.01 index point, equal to ¥2,500 (i.e., approximately $20.85) per contract. However, trades may occur at a price of 0.005 index point (¥1,250, i.e., approximately $10.42 per contract) if such transactions result in the liquidation of positions for both sides of the trade. Further, on the Globex system, prices of options and combinations involving Euroyen futures option contracts may be quoted in terms of the annualized implied price volatility of the underlying futures contract. The minimum fluctuation for such quotes will be 0.01 percent.

There is no maximum premium fluctuation limit on the proposed option contract. However, during ETH, option trading will be halted when the underlying futures contract is bid or offered at its ETH price limit.

Strike price intervals will be in increments of 0.25 index points for all option contract months. For each contract month with twelve months or less to expiration, the Exchange will list initially and maintain strike prices in a range of 1.50 index points above and 1.50 index points below the previous day's settlement price in the underlying futures contract. For each contract month with more than twelve months but less than 15 months to expiration, the Exchange will list initially and maintain strike prices in a range of 1.75 index points above and 1.75 index points below the previous day's settlement price in the underlying futures contract. For each contract month with more than 15 months to expiration, the Exchange will list initially and maintain strike prices in a range of 2.25 index points above and 2.25 index points below the previous day's settlement price in the underlying futures contract. New strike prices may be added up to the last day of trading in the option.

Proposed Exchange rules authorize trading in options on the Euroyen futures contract in the March quarterly cycle months and in serial months. The last day of trading in an expiring option in the March quarterly cycle will be the same day as the last trading day for the underlying Euroyen futures contract—typically the second business day preceding the third Wednesday of the contract month. Options in serial months generally will terminate on the Friday before the third Wednesday of the contract month that is not an Exchange holiday.

The proposed option is American style; that is, it may be exercised on any CME business day prior to expiration. Any options that are in-the-money and not exercised by the close of trading on the last day of trading will be exercised automatically, unless instructions to the contrary are received at the clearing house before 7:00 p.m. on the last day of trading.[24]

The CME's Euroyen futures contract and options on that futures contract will be subject to a joint speculative limit of 5,000 futures-equivalent contracts net on the same side of the market in all months combined, which is the same speculative limit level applicable to positions in the underlying futures contract. Exemptions from the limit for bona fide hedging and certain other positions meeting CME requirements may be granted on a case-by-case basis pursuant to existing rules. A reporting level of 25 contracts will apply to Euroyen option positions held in any contract month.

B. *Option Designation Criteria*

The Division is of the opinion that the terms and conditions of the proposed option contract meet all of the standards for designation found in the Act and regulations thereunder, including Part 33.

. . .

C. *Commercial Categories*

Regarding commercial user categories for potential participants in the proposed Euroyen option contract, the Division believes that the Commission's existing list of categories for financial instrument options (57 *Fed.Reg.* 40645) is appropriate for the proposed option contract.

## V. Rule Enforcement Program

As noted, T&M believes that designation of the CME as a contract market in the subject futures and option contracts would not be inconsistent with the Act. T&M's most recent review of the CME's rule enforcement program was presented to the Commission in a memorandum dated September 29, 1992.

### *Questions and Notes*

1. Compare this euroyen future to the CME's 3 month eurodollar contract. What are the similarities? What accounts for the differences? Is this really a euroyen contract? What might explain its name?

2. Buyers and sellers pay in yen. Variation payments on margin accounts must be in yen (although performance bonds can be in any of several currencies or government securities). CME took advantage of a change in the law in January 1990 allowing banks in the U.S. to hold foreign currency deposits. CME has yen accounts in its settlement banks and next day payment through them is possible in yen. Finality is through the Japanese banking system. According to CFTC rules governing the treatment of customer funds, the foreign currency ac-

**24.** Since the Globex trading session is considered by the CME to be part of the same trading day as the following RTH session, the last day of trading for March-quarterly-cycle options is interpreted by the CME, for this purpose, as being the calendar day after the calendar day on which trading is terminated. See footnote 10.

counts would be subordinate to U.S. dollar claims in bankruptcy. More generally, Chemical Bank lets CME clearing firms buy or sell foreign exchange through it, making funds available the next day rather than on the second day, which is the normal settlement day in foreign exchange transactions.

3. A contract such as this can be coordinated more or less closely with almost identical contracts on other exchanges, such as TIFFE or SIMEX. How willing would TIFFE be to help CME develop this contract?

(a) Exchanges do not have identical rules. TIFFE's margin rules differ from those in the U.S., described below. TIFFE requires customers to close their position if they want to withdraw any equity (or surplus over the maintenance level) from their margin account. TIFFE's brokers charge fixed commissions at least twice as high as commissions for trading on SIMEX or CME. How would these rules affect the willingness of TIFFE to cooperate with CME on this contract?

(b) TIFFE and SIMEX have locked horns over several SIMEX contracts on Japanese instruments. What would account for this?

(c) Exchanges in various countries are just starting to cooperate. As you read the following, ask what forces would push for cooperation and what would hinder it.

## TRACY CORRIGAN, "QUIRKY OFFSHOOTS GAIN RESPECT"

Financial Times (October 20, 1993).

Exchanges have also been trying to prepare themselves for a potentially more difficult environment by creating cross-trading agreements, linkages and even partnerships. One example is a grouping of smaller European exchanges, known as First European Exchanges (Fex). The only linkage currently in place is between OM London, the Swedish-owned electronic exchange, and the European Options Exchange in Amsterdam. Under that agreement, EOE members have OM screens on their desks in Amsterdam. However, OM members are linked to the EOE only by telephone. Not surprisingly, the flow of business from EOE members to OM has been the more significant.

Fex's other plans have already faltered. In July, Switzerland's Soffex was forced to pull back from its linkage plans under pressure from Swiss banks which want to get their own electronic stock trading system in place first.

Still in the early stages is a linkage of France's Matif and Germany's Deutsche Terminbörse, using DTB screens. As these exchanges command some of the most actively traded contracts in Europe, this alliance could become a powerful force.

The development of these linkages has fueled discussion of technological developments. Such linkages only really function efficiently for products traded on a screen. Most large exchanges still trade using the traditional open-outcry method, which involves grouping traders in a large pit. Proponents of open-outcry trading claim that screen systems cannot cope with heavy volume.

The success of the DTB has shown that screen trading does not necessarily mean illiquid trading. Nevertheless, most traders familiar with both methods prefer trading using the open-outcry method. Some, though, say that it is only a matter of time before the technology of screen-trading is sufficiently advanced to be able to simulate pit-trading.

Despite its shaky start, the most important development in exchange trading so far this decade was the launch last year of Globex, the international after-hours screen trading system jointly developed by Reuters and the Chicago Mercantile Exchange and the Chicago Board of Trade. Volume on the system jumped when France's Matif, the only exchange to join the system so far, added its products earlier this year; but much of the volume was a direct shift of business from the Matif's over-the-counter after-hours market, which closed at the same time as Matif products moved on to Globex. Globex has also been dogged by squabbles between the two exchanges, and failure to reach agreement with other potential members of the system, particularly Liffe.

Nevertheless, the description of the system at its launch by Mr. Leo Melamed, then head of Globex, as "the dawn of a new era", could still prove true. The Chicago exchanges point out that the system cannot be judged to have failed until it has screens all over the world, as envisaged in their original vision of a global trading village. "How do you sell hot dogs in Japan when you don't even have a hot dog stand there?" asks Mr. Jack Sandner, head of the CME. Globex has only recently received regulatory approval to install screens in Asia, which is potentially the key time-zone for the after-hours market, and is starting a marketing thrust in the region.

Nevertheless, the success of the system will also depend on attracting other exchanges to list their products. The recent reopening of talks between Liffe and Globex is clearly a hopeful sign, but the battle for a critical mass of volume on the system has yet to be won.

---

4. Would the Japanese finance ministry support or oppose this proposed contract? Suppose the government believed that options trading in Japan contributed to the stock market collapse over the last few years and had instituted policies to limit price movements on Japanese futures and options markets. How much leverage would the Japanese government have to affect the CME's decision about whether to list this contract?

5. How would the CME euroyen futures contract look to potential investors in it? Who would be likely to use it?

---

## D. THE REGULATION OF FUTURES AND OPTIONS MARKETS

Countries regulate their futures and options markets in many ways. Regulators, such as the CFTC, generally must recognize contracts and clearing houses, setting minimum standards that include the public interest; foreign contracts and clearing houses may come under special scrutiny. To promote financial safety, regulators require adequate capital for intermediaries like clearing members and brokers, though many major countries do not set specific capital rules for exchanges or clearing houses. Clearing houses may set capital requirements for their members. Regulators expect exchanges to set margin rules, keep the markets under surveillance, and require customer funds to be segregated from the broker's own accounts. Supervision of records varies across countries. Regulators protect customers through rules about brokers' fitness, order execution, sales practices, and records. Market efficiency is the goal of rules about product design and market disruption. Manipulation is forbidden, though its definition varies. See CFTC, International Regulation of Derivative Markets, Products, and Financial Intermediaries (1993). Regulation of futures and options differs from that of securities. The CFTC explained in its October 1993 study:

> The futures exchange markets do not exist to facilitate the transfer of ownership of a cash commodity. Futures markets developed to reallocate the risk in commercial transactions and facilitate discovery of the efficient price for commodities in general commerce. Unlike the federal securities regulatory framework, the main focus of futures transaction regulation was on transactions in the "secondary" exchange market reflecting that all futures transactions were required to be effected on a centralized exchange and that there is considered to be no "issuer" of futures contracts and thus no offering process comparable to that for securities. All futures transactions were required to be conducted in the public marketplace and thus included in the auction price. This centralization was considered important for the effective functioning of the markets as a price discovery mechanism, and much of the regulatory scheme was directed at the proper reflection of price. In general, subject to certain financial protections, futures markets were not required to be "continuous" and until recently, affirmative market-making obligations to maintain liquidity were foreign to such markets. Although all large market participants were required to report their positions, regulatory financial requirements were directed solely to agents (brokers) transacting on behalf of customers.
>
> Exchange-traded stock and stock index options did not exist until the 1970's. At that time, options on individual equities were listed and in subsequent years significant regulatory and legislative attention was directed to the appropriate regulation of such products. Unlike futures regulators, domestic securities regulators deem the clearing entity to be the issuer of exchange traded options.

Exchange markets, both securities and futures, characteristically have had regulatory or self-regulatory criteria relating to the financial capacity and accountability of members entering into transactions for themselves or for others. These were necessary because transactions in such markets are concluded anonymously, without the benefit of individual credit judgments concerning counterparties. In exchange markets for securities, the clearing agency assures delivery of an asset against payment; in most derivative markets, the clearing system guarantees the obligation to make daily payments of losses.

Regulatory overlap exists in the options market in the U.S. Registered broker-dealers may engage in OTC option transactions, subject to NASD rules, position limits, SEC capital and fraud rules. If they are also members of options exchanges, some margin rules extend to their OTC transactions.

### *Questions and Notes*

1. **Margin rules generally.** A key tool to affect trading and reduce risk is the margin rules and marking-to-market. Futures and options exchanges, supervised by their regulators, usually set margin rules for their brokers' transactions with them or with their clearinghouse and for the brokers' customers. The rules vary by country. Paragraphs 2–6, which follow, describe margin rules mainly in the U.S.

2. **Margin rules for positions in stock.** Suppose someone buys equity on the New York Stock Exchange. The Federal Reserve Board sets initial margin requirements. The buyer pays for part of the stock and gets a loan from the broker for the remainder of the cost until full payment is made. The broker holds the stock as security for the loan. The initial margin rules determine the amount of the loan by requiring a down payment as a percent of the stock's current market value. Some stock exchanges require adjustments after the initial margin; this is called a variation or maintenance margin. The Fed does not require it. The NYSE sets a minimum maintenance margin of 25% of the stock's current market value. If the customer's margin falls below that level as the stock price drops, the broker gives the customer a margin call to bring the margin up to the minimum. The purchased securities secure the loan, but since their value is volatile, they are marked to market daily.

(a) If the initial margin were 50% and the stock's current market value were $5000, the customer must pay $2500 at purchase and the broker can only lend $2500. If the stock then fell in value to $2800, since the broker's loan was still $2500, the customer margin account would be only $300. But the maintenance margin is 25% of $2800 or $700. The customer pays the broker $400 on margin call to raise the margin account to $700.

(b) Why would the Fed have such rules?

(c) Why would the NYSE impose maintenance margin requirements since the Fed has not seen the need to do so?

(d) Why are brokers not required to have margin accounts with their clearinghouses for stock operations, considering that they do need such accounts for futures and options?

3. **Margin rules for customers' futures contracts.** For customers' futures contracts, long and short positions are subject to margin rules in the U.S. At the time of purchase, a customer buying a position pays an initial margin that is a share of today's cash future price. The amount is usually a small percentage and it varies depending on whether the position is a hedge or speculative and on the contract's variability. The customer may give cash or securities. No loan is made, since futures contracts take no initial payment. The maintenance margin is set daily against the current market value of the contract, which is marked to market daily. Any loss in value is deducted entirely from the margin account and any gain is added. This is called the variation. The broker passes the variation to the exchange, which in turn passes it to the broker on the other side of such a transaction, for the customer. The customer, who also has a margin account, can withdraw any amount above the initial margin. So any shift raises one margin account and lowers the other. Whenever a customer's margin account falls below the minimum maintenance level, the broker makes a margin call and the customer must return the margin deposit to its initial level.

(a) Why use the futures' current market value? Why not use the current market value of the underlying stock?

(b) Work through the following example. Long Customer buys a long futures contract for $5000. The exchange sets the initial margin at 5% or $250. The maintenance level is 75% of the initial margin. If on the following day the current market value of the contract is $4900, the margin account of the Long Customer is only $150, below the maintenance level of $188. The broker gives a margin call for $100 to return the margin to its initial $250 level. The margin account of a Short Customer is increased by $100. If the current market value had fallen only $50, the margin account of the Long Customer would be reduced by that $50 but there would be no margin call. The Short Customer would receive $50 more in its margin account as a variation payment, which it could withdraw. The exchange is not exposed; the debit to the Long Customer's account funds the credit to the Short Customer's account.

(1) What is the role of the brokers for each customer?

(2) What is the role of the exchange?

(c) How do margin rules for futures differ from the margin rules for someone who buys stock long? Does the initial margin have the same function? What would explain why the maintenance margins are treated differently?

4. **Margin rules for brokers' futures contracts.** A member broker (or clearing member) has many customer accounts as well as its own proprietary accounts. Futures exchange clearing houses set mar-

gins for member brokers' futures contracts. The clearing house usually calculates gains or losses on each broker's total long positions and on its total short positions in each contract at the end of the trading day. Some net the sums, offsetting gains in short (or long) against losses in long (or short). Some rules gross them, adding both. The clearing house then adjusts the broker's clearing margin account for each contract by the gain or loss and the broker tops up or withdraws funds as appropriate.

(a) Which is more important to mitigate systemic risk, individual customer margins with the broker or member margins with the exchange?

(b) Is it good policy to calculate positions and margin requirements at the end of the day? LIFFE, through the London Clearing House, CBOT, and CME make at least one intra-day assessment.

(c) Rules governing the treatment of a broker's proprietary accounts and its customers' accounts vary. Most exchanges require the broker to differentiate between them. For example, LIFFE requires differentiation if the broker itself segregates the customers. Germany's DTB requires differentiation. If the broker defaults, LIFFE prohibits set-off between proprietary and customer accounts, while DTB merges all accounts. Why would LIFFE and DTB differ as to set-off between customer and proprietary accounts?

(d) Clearing houses protect themselves with more elaborate use of margin rules. U.S. futures clearing houses use "simulation analysis and . . . pricing theory to measure the potential risk of one-day price moves to a specified level of probability." They adjust the methodologies "periodically to reflect changes in implied volatility." This form of risk simulation extends to surveillance [see CFTC October 1993]. Clearing houses make "super" margin calls if a customer or proprietary position could endanger a member's capital and the member must post it within one hour. They require members to use settlement banks to make margin payments; if the settlement banks cannot advance the payment needed, the member will fall back on prearranged credit from other banks. So banks do their own credit check on members.

(e) In addition are other ways to defend the exchange/clearing house and the system. The Clearing House can:

— set net capital rules for each member;

— if a member defaults, transfer the customer accounts to other members.

— if a member defaults, "liquidate the member's positions and original margins, sell his exchange membership, use his contributions to the clearinghouse guarantee fund and its committed lines of credit, assess all clearing members, where permissible, and finally, use the clearinghouse's capital."

[Office of Technology Assessment, "Electronic Bulls and Bears (1990) ].

(f) How are the many different types of margin rules that one finds on exchanges likely to affect cooperative ventures among exchanges?

(g) Overall, what is the purpose of the margin rules for futures contracts?

5. **Margin rules for options.** Margining for calls is described in the following excerpt from Hull, 179–81.

When call and put options are purchased, the option price must be paid in full. Investors are not allowed to buy options on margin. This is because options already contain substantial leverage. Buying on margin would raise this leverage to an unacceptable level.

When an investor writes options, he or she is required to maintain funds in a margin account. This is because the investor's broker and the exchange want to be satisfied that the investor will not default if the option is exercised. The size of the margin required depends on the circumstances.

Writing Naked Options

Consider first the situation where the option is naked. This means that the option position is not combined with an offsetting position in the underlying stock. If the option is in the money, the initial margin is 30% of the value of the stocks underlying the option plus the amount by which the option is in the money. If the option is out of the money, the initial margin is 30% of the value of the stocks underlying the option minus the amount by which the option is out of the money. The option price received by the writer can be used to partially fulfill this margin requirement.

Example

An investor writes four naked call option contracts. The option price is \$5, the strike price is \$40 and the stock price is \$42. The first part of the margin requirement is 30% of \$42 × 400 or \$5,040. The option is \$2 in the money. The second part of the margin requirement is therefore \$2 × 400 or \$800. The price received for the option contracts is \$5 × 400 or \$2,000. The additional margin required is therefore

$$\$5{,}040 + \$800 - \$2{,}000 = \$3{,}840$$

Note that if the option had been a put, it would be \$2 out of the money and the additional margin requirement would be

$$\$5{,}040 - \$800 - \$2{,}000 = \$2{,}240$$

A calculation similar to the initial margin calculation is repeated every day. Funds can be withdrawn from the margin account when the calculation indicates that the margin required is less than the current balance in the margin account. When the calculation indicates that a significantly greater margin is required, a margin call will be made.

### Writing Covered Calls

Writing covered calls involves writing call options when the shares that might have to be delivered are already owned. Covered calls are far less risky than naked calls since the worst that can happen is that the investor is required to sell shares already owned at below their market value. If covered call options are out of the money, no margin is required. The shares owned can be purchased using a margin account as described above, and the price received for the option can be used to partially fulfill this margin requirement. If the options are in the money, no margin is required for the options. However, the extent to which the shares can be margined is reduced by the extent to which the option is in the money.

### Example

An investor decides to buy 200 shares of a certain stock on margin and to write 2 call option contracts on the stock. The stock price is \$63, the strike price is \$60 and the price of the option is \$7. The margin account allows the investor to borrow 50% of the price of the stock less the amount by which the option is in the money. In this case, the option is \$3 in the money so that the investor is able to borrow

$$0.5 \times \$63 \times 200 - \$3 \times 200 = \$5{,}700$$

The investor is also able to use the price received for the option, \$7 × 200 or \$1,400, to finance the purchase of the shares. The shares cost \$63 × 200 = \$12,600. The minimum cash initially required from the investor for his or her trades is therefore

$$\$12{,}600 - \$5{,}700 - \$1{,}400 = \$5{,}500$$

The Options Clearing Corporation (OCC) performs much the same sort of function for options markets as the Clearinghouse does for futures markets

It guarantees that the option writer will fulfill his or her obligations under the terms of the option contract and keeps a record of all long and short positions. The OCC has a number of members, and all option trades must be cleared through a member. If a brokerage house is not itself a member of an exchange's OCC, it must arrange to clear its trades with a member. Members are required to have a certain minimum amount of capital and to contribute to a special fund that can be used if any member defaults on an option obligation.

When purchasing an option, the buyer must pay for it in full by the morning of the next business day. These funds are deposited with the OCC. The writer of the option maintains a margin account with his or her broker as described earlier. The broker maintains a margin account with the OCC member that clears its trades. The OCC member, in turn, maintains a margin account with the OCC. The margin requirements described in the previous section are the margin requirements imposed by the OCC on its members. A brokerage house may require higher margins from its clients. However, it cannot require lower margins.

Exercising an Option

When an investor wishes to exercise an option, the investor notifies his or her broker. The broker in turn notifies the OCC member that clears its trades. This member then places an exercise order with the OCC. The OCC randomly selects a member with an outstanding short position in the same option. The member using a procedure established in advance selects a particular investor who has written the option. If the option is a call, this investor is required to sell stock at the strike price. If it is a put, the investor is required to buy stock at the strike price. The investor is said to be *assigned*. When an option is exercised, the open interest goes down by one.

At the expiration of the option, all in-the-money options should be exercised unless the transactions costs are so high as to wipe out the payoff from the option. Some brokerage firms will automatically exercise options for their clients at expiration when it is in their clients' interest to do so. The OCC automatically exercises stock options owned by individuals that are in the money by more than $0.75 and stock options owned by institutions that are in the money by more than $0.25.

---

(a) What is the rule for buyers of calls? What protects against the risk that the buyer cannot come up with the strike price when it exercises the call? Note that not all exchanges follow this practice. LIFFE options buyers do not have to pay up front, but must hold margin accounts. Why would LIFFE have such a rule?

(b) For a seller of a naked call that is out of the money, assume a stock price of $5000, a strike price of $5500, an option price of $600, and a 30% initial margin requirement. The margin would be $400. What is the rationale?

(c) For a seller of a naked call that is in the money, assume a stock price of $6000, a strike price of $5500, an option price of $600, and a 30% initial margin requirement. The margin owed is $1700. What is the rationale for treating this transaction differently from the out of the money option?

(d) What is the rationale for the margin rules governing sellers of covered calls?

6. **Margin rules based on forecast price movements.** When LIFFE and the London Traded Options Market merged in March 1992, the LIFFE margining rules extended to options as described below.

R. WATERS, "OPTIONS MARKET ADOPTS REVISED MARGINING REGIME"

Financial Times (March 24, 1992) 28.

A REVISED margining regime came into force in the UK options market yesterday which, some traders claim, will have a significant impact on the way options are traded.

. . .

The new method of assessing margining for options is one which has been in use for some time on the futures market. It is based on the "Span" method for calculating margins, developed by the Chicago Mercantile Exchange and used in London by Liffe and other derivatives markets. Liffe claims the system is more sensitive to risk than its previous version, or that used by the traded options market.

"The intention is to assess risk more accurately. There are particular situations where it will result in an increase in margin, but they are very few," Liffe said. The Span method assesses margin requirements by taking an overall view of a trader's portfolio. Factors which determine margin levels include market volatility over the past six months. One result of this has been to push up margining for stocks which have fallen in recent months, in some cases substantially. Previously, the traded options market applied only a nominal margining requirement for options which are substantially "out of the money" (where the exercise price and current market price are far apart, making exercise unlikely).

The implications of this for the market are only just beginning to sink in. As one trader said: "Before, you tried to get spreads as wide apart as possible. Now, the aim will be to get them as close to the money as possible."

7. **Margining for futures and options.** Why do margin rules for options differ from those for futures?

---

## E. RISKS POSED BY THE USE OF FUTURES AND OPTIONS MARKETS

Stories of disaster due to derivatives pepper the financial press. In October 1993, for example, the Financial Times reported that the Bundesbank warned "that the growth of derivatives markets could endanger the stability of the world financial system." The German central bank argued, said the reporter, "that the increase in the use of options, futures, and other complex derivative instruments has led to an interlinking of the world's financial markets that makes them more vulnerable to crisis" [Financial Times (October 20 1993) ]. In fact, the Bundesbank report noted that German banks' exposure to exchange based derivatives was rather small; the OTC markets were the source of the greatest concern. The news report got the concern wrong. One question is whether futures and options pose a major threat. The following article argues that they do.

## TRACY CORRIGAN, "ON TRIAL FOR DANGEROUS DEALING"

Financial Times (March 21, 1994).

There is a new breed of bogeymen in the financial markets—hedge fund managers, who make large bets on price movements using private clients' money.

They have been demonised, in particular, for driving bond prices down sharply last month by suddenly withdrawing bets on European bond markets. They had taken fright at the US Federal Reserve's decision to raise interest rates for the first time in five years.

The Bank of England is now investigating the activities of hedge funds—pools of money which are switched between financial markets to exploit short-term opportunities. Regulators worry that excessive lending to hedge funds could leave banks vulnerable to heavy losses.

But there is an aspect of the hedge fund industry that strikes greater fear into the hearts of regulators: their heavy use of derivatives.

. . .

Derivatives are already widely used by banks and securities houses; but the emergence of hedge funds—most of them unregulated—as significant players in the derivatives market worries market supervisors.

. . .

One aspect of derivatives is that, for a small downpayment, the purchaser can control a larger portion of the market. For example, $10,000 could buy a contract to purchase $100,000 worth of bonds later. Such leverage means potential gains or losses are magnified.

To address their concerns about these instruments, US and UK securities regulators last week agreed to share information on derivatives trading. The move reflects an awareness that derivatives regulation is outdated—and possibly ineffective.

In most countries, regulators supervise specific types of companies—banks, insurers and securities houses, for example. But the derivatives market spans a range of financial institutions and national borders.

Regulators have two main concerns about derivatives. The first is that poor management or a lack of understanding of these complicated financial instruments could cause companies to incur heavy losses. For example, a trading subsidiary of Metallgesellschaft, the German oil and metals company, faces final losses of $1bn on dealings in the oil derivatives market last year. The second is the broader impact on other financial markets, particularly whether derivatives increase price swings and have a destabilising influence.

Banks and securities houses welcome volatility as it increases their opportunities to make money, either through trading their own capital or by charging fees to buy and sell on behalf of clients. But non-financial companies—and less sophisticated investors—do not like large price swings which could leave them facing losses. Central banks want to pull all the levers and do not like to feel that they are losing control of monetary policy.

Evidence that derivatives destabilise markets is, however, far from conclusive. No empirical study over the past 20 years has yet shown that derivatives increase volatility, and some have concluded they may even reduce it.

Most recently, in December a study of the effect of derivatives on the London stock market by Mr. Gary Robinson of the Bank of England concluded that "futures trading has been associated with a significant reduction in volatility of around 17 per cent".

Other observers agree that derivatives markets may dampen volatility. During the sharp bond price falls in February market participants were able to trade bonds via the futures market when dealers became unwilling to quote prices in the underlying bond market. Mr. Fred Stambaugh, a vice-president of Chase Manhattan Bank, says: "If there were no derivative markets, and traders had those heavy positions on their books, you would have seen greater movement in the [conventional] physical instruments, because a lot of what happens in the derivative markets is designed to diffuse risk."

But the academic evidence does not always impress market participants. "Various studies say there is a benign relationship between the two markets, but it certainly doesn't feel like that some days," observes one UK fund manager. It is not just a gut feeling of traders. There is a case for arguing academic studies have asked the wrong questions, or focused on excessively long time periods, which iron out glitches. "The sort of tests that have been conducted do not determine whether in abnormal conditions derivatives create volatility," says one regulator. One theory is that, in periods of volatility, because market participants holding futures have to provide for potential losses, they may have to sell other holdings to generate the extra cash needed.

A likely explanation for the divergence of views is that derivatives produce different effects depending on market conditions. Moreover, their impact could vary according to whether they are used mainly to hedge risks, or to speculate on markets. The worrying feature about hedge funds is that—despite their name—the latter is more usually the case.

One problem in isolating the effects of derivatives is that they have become an integral part of a fast-evolving world financial system. A decade ago fund managers were concerned mainly with their own domestic stock or bond markets. But the dismantling of regulatory barriers and improvements in the infrastructure of financial markets have allowed investors to gain access to a wider range of products.

Derivatives have heightened that trend. Because transaction costs are lower and derivatives are often more actively traded than conventional instruments, it is easier, for example, to switch from the German to the Japanese stock market by using futures rather than by selling a portfolio of individual stocks.

"Derivatives have created much greater linkage between markets, and the leverage involved means that positions can turn much quicker," said Mr. Carter Beese, a commissioner at the Securities and Exchange Commission, which regulates the U.S. securities industry.

---

Hedge funds started in the late 1940s. They hedged by picking an industry (like pharmaceuticals), holding long positions in stocks of a few strong firms, holding short positions in the weaker firms, and making money on the relative volatility of the various securities. This conservative strategy dominated until recently. In the last few years, many different specialized types emerged (Institutional Investor, April 1994):

— arbitrage between securities

— hold emerging markets securities

— directional (eg., bet yen appreciates against $)

— short selling

— invest in bankrupt firms

— yield-curve arbitrage

Recent commentators in the press talk mainly about the directional funds.

### *Notes and Questions*

1. **Market risk.** The risk of a wrong bet is that the value of the futures or options contract will fall because of adverse changes in the underlying security. This is market risk. Two elements are at work: the volatility of the underlying asset's value and the sensitivity of the futures or options contract to changes in the underlying asset value. For options, volatility and sensitivity are not likely to be constant. When an option is deep out of the market, even a big change in the value of the underlying asset is not likely to affect the contract value as much as if the option was near the strike price. Since volatility and sensitivity can vary over the life of the contract, calculation of market risk is difficult.

(a) How important is market risk likely to be for investors in futures and options?

(b) An important question is whether to calculate a player's market risk by individual instrument (gross) or across the portfolio (net). A strong argument can be made to net offsetting positions.

(c) Margining and marking to market are the major tools to manage market risk now. How effective is this? What are the limits, if any?

(d) What other tools can address market risk? How effective would they be?

(e) In May 1993, the U.S. Securities and Exchange Commission issued a concept release (No. 34–32256) suggesting capital standards for broker-dealers participating in derivatives markets. For listed options, Rule 15c3–1 now requires haircuts "based on the market value of the option, not the underlying security" and so does not take into account potential price movements. For futures and options on futures, the haircut is "based on the margin requirement of the applicable" clearinghouse. The Options Clearing Corporation has asked the SEC to use the OCC's theoretical pricing model system to determine haircuts on options:

> The capital charges associated with a portfolio of options on a given underlying instrument would be the difference between the closing market prices and the option's theoretical price after applying assumed adverse market movements. In addition, if the portfolio contains related underlying instruments, the charge for those positions would be equal to the market movement assumed for purposes of calculating the option's theoretical price.
>
> The SEC observed that "reliance on a financial model that incorrectly predicts future volatility of the underlying instrument may lead to financial distress" and that "the difficulty of estimating future volatility is well recognized although difficult to resolve." It called for comments. It also acknowledged that different capital requirements for broker-dealers and futures commission merchants (regulated by the CFTC) could pose problems for firms registered as both.

(f) The Tokyo Stock Exchange drafted rules that would allow circuit breakers when "extraordinary price distortions ... may be caused by derivatives products trading and index arbitrage." The rule would suspend index futures and options trading, not trading on the cash markets (as occurs on the New York Stock Exchange) (6 International Securities Regulation Report 18 (August 10, 1993). TSE limits the daily price movement of securities traded on the exchange.

When the active month futures price moves more than two-thirds of the contract's daily limit against the "base price" and, simultaneously, its spread against the futures theoretical value exceeds one-third of the daily limit, the exchanges will suspend futures and options trading for 15 minutes. ... When the futures price reaches its allowable fluctuation limit, the exchanges will cease trading of physical stocks used for index arbitrage executed for securities houses' own positions.

2. **Market liquidity risk.** A liquidity drought can hurt investors.

(a) How does an option holder convert to cash or close out its position on an exchange? In an over-the-counter transaction, the holder tries to write an offsetting OTC transaction with another party or to negotiate with the writer. Is liquidity likely to be greater for an exchange or OTC transaction? Are there plausible conditions under which exchange backed futures and options might lack adequate liquidity?

(b) How effectively do margining and marking to market manage market liquidity risk now? What other solutions might exist?

3. **Counterparty risk.** Since the vast majority of futures and options are listed on exchanges, the counterparty risk for an investor is that of the exchange. In the OTC markets, the buyer and seller are counterparties. The CFTC explains the role of the exchange and its members [CFTC October 199–3]:

Obligations of end-users of exchange-traded instruments, engaging in regulated transactions through regulated intermediaries, are effectively guaranteed by the clearing member which carries them. These end-users receive the benefit of creditworthiness protections applicable to the intermediary, such as minimum capital requirements, audit requirements, and customer funds protections.

Exchange regulatory and self-regulatory structures also address the risk that the default or failure of one firm, whether through failure to manage risk or otherwise, will adversely affect others in the market. These safeguards include mechanisms, in addition to clearing house guarantees of positions, that localize the consequences of such failures, including procedures for the transfer of positions to financially stable firms or prompt liquidation of positions to minimize losses if such transfers cannot be effected. Further, end-users in the market are subject to reporting requirements, if they are large traders, and to speculative position limits or position accountability standards. These requirements facilitate third-party surveillance of concentration risk and impose some limitations upon the size of the outstanding market exposure of individual market users.

(a) An exchange protects itself against its many counterparties by assuring that it can fund any default it encounters. Funding sources include the defaulting member's capital, a guaranty fund subscribed by members (up to a limit), the members' own capital, and insurance. LIFFE and the London Clearing House make clear that members do not guarantee each other and have no risk exposure. In the U.S., according to the CFTC in an undated memorandum:

An exchange clearing house guarantees the payment of variation margin to clearing members with net gains on positions in their accounts at the clearing house even if it is unable to collect the variation margin owed to it by clearing members with net losses on their positions. A clearing house, however, does not guarantee the obligations of clearing members to their customers, nor does it guarantee any obligations of brokers or traders who are not clearing members. At all U.S. clearing houses the clearing guarantee attaches when the trade matches and is accepted for clearance. Most clearing houses do not guarantee delivery or acceptance of delivery on futures contracts that have reached the delivery stage, although some clearing houses do guarantee to their members payment of damages for default on deliveries.

The rules of most clearing houses provide that upon default of a clearing member, the clearing house must close out or transfer to other members all of the positions carried by the defaulting member. Positions are immediately liquidated if they cannot be transferred. If a member defaults and his margin deposits and available liquid assets are insufficient to cover the amounts owing to the clearing house, the deficit is covered first by available assets of the clearing member at the exchange and clearing house and then by the guaranty fund deposits of non-defaulting members. If there is still a deficiency, most clearing houses are then required by their rules to assess their members to cover the balance.

(b) Capital adequacy is another line of defense. The Basle Accord sets capital adequacy rules for banks, which are major players. The SEC, in its concept release cited above, says it is concerned about counterparty risk for OTC transactions but not for "centrally-cleared, exchange transactions." Do you agree?

(c) Position limits are used. How effective is the position limit rule in the CME euro-yen future likely to be?

(d) OTC market players protect themselves by only making options with AAA/AA rated counterparties.

4. **Operating risk.** A big fear is that inadequate internal controls, error, system failure (like the flawed hedging model), or fraud lead to unexpected losses. A bank, for example, may not even know it exceeds its position limits.

(a) Concern about most futures and options transactions does not appear to fall into the headline grabbing events that other kinds of derivatives generate. The most spectacular recent disaster involving the futures market was in commodities rather than financial instruments. The question is whether a similar loss could hit players in financial futures markets. In late 1993, the German firm Metallgesellschaft A.G. admitted to more than $1 billion in losses when an American subsidiary bet wrong in the commodity futures markets and slid deeper into loss trying to recoup. Much of the trading was on the New York Mercantile Exchange, which also offers financial futures. A smaller loss involved financial futures. In fall 1992, Sumitomo Finance International lost $2–3 million on interest rate options when one of its traders lied about his position. From your reading, would you be surprised to learn that a large U.S. multinational company lost over $1 billion on financial futures markets? How could it happen? How seriously could it affect financial stability?

(b) The U.S. Comptroller of the Currency has proposed many ways to strengthen the way national banks manage their derivatives risks. One proposal is to have a unit, independent of the traders, that carefully monitors the traders' investments. The Comptroller acknowledges that the internal systems used by the biggest banks are more sophisticated than those it is considering. [See Banking Circular BC 277, "Risk Management of Financial Derivatives" (October 27, 1993).]

5. **Hedge Funds and threats to international financial stability.** During 1993–4, hedge funds caught the spotlight of public anxiety about derivatives markets. Hedge funds are investment partnerships with fewer than 100 limited partners and so are unregulated. Rich individuals invest a minimum of $1 million each, which the fund leverages by borrowing primarily from banks. Without hard numbers, observers estimate leveraging ranges from 2 to 20 times, with an average of about 10. The numbers and size of hedge funds is also slippery. One service tracks over 200 funds. One estimate put the assets of all U.S. hedge funds at about $50 billion, while another said the 10 largest held about $30 billion.

Hedge funds came under attack in 1992–3 for betting big against the European Monetary Union and the narrow Exchange Rate Mechanism, and winning. In early 1994, they were badly hit by betting wrong on interest rate movements. The following article describes how they used the futures markets in these bets.

## THOMAS FRIEDMAN, "SOROS GIVES HOUSE PANEL HEDGE FUND LESSON"

The New York Times (April 14, 1994) ["Friedman"].

The hedge funds ... take their multibillion-dollar pools of money and make a bet. For instance, they might bet that over a certain period of time the Japanese yen is going to lose value against the dollar. So they enter into a futures contract in which they agree to sell yen at a certain set rate six months from today.

Bet Can Be Wrong

If in six months the yen does fall in value, the fund can reap a huge profit. But if the bet is wrong, and the yen increases in value against the dollar, the fund can suffer a huge loss.

That is what happened last fall. Several huge hedge funds, including Mr. Soros's, bet that the Japanese yen was going to fall in value. They made that bet because they believed that President Clinton and Japan's former Prime Minister, Morihiro Hosokawa were going to reach a settlement of their trade dispute last February and that such a settlement would lead the American Government to let the yen fall.

The American Government had previously been encouraging the yen to rise in value as a tactic to put pressure on Japan in the trade negotiations, because if the yen is rising it makes Japanese exports more expensive and harder to sell around the world.

But Mr. Soros bet wrong. The talks between Mr. Clinton and Mr. Hosokawa collapsed, and instead of the yen falling in value, it rose. Those losses were destabilizing because as banks demanded more collateral on the money they lent to the hedge funds—a practice known as a "margin call"—some of the hedge funds had to sell part of their holdings to raise the cash.

In this case, to cover their bad debt, many hedge fund dealers had to sell not only some of their Japanese securities but also some of their European positions. Hedge funds make dozens of simultaneous currency bets around the world, hoping that the winners will outnumber the losers. They are "hedging their bets," hence the name hedge funds.

Effect Felt in Europe

But in this case, the forced selloffs by some dealers who had stocked up on yen caused a chain reaction on the other side of the world. Some other hedge fund dealers, who were not involved in Japan at all, had been betting that German and other European interest rates were going to fall, since the high unemployment there required these European governments to stimulate their economies. So they had stocked up on European bonds, assuming that as European interest rates went down the value of their European bonds would go up.

But when the hedge funds that lost money on the yen started selling some of their European bonds, it drove down the price of bonds all across Europe as well. This forced bond issuers in Europe to effectively raise their interest rates to keep attracting buyers.

That surprise move caught more hedge fund investors. Many of them had nothing to do with speculating in Japan but had been making what they saw as a sound fundamental long-term bet that trends in European economies were toward lower interest rates. Nevertheless, they, too, then had to sell some of their European bonds to cover their own margin calls. This, in turn, caused a rush to the door all at once that ravaged European bond markets and caused even worse losses for some hedge fund dealers.

---

Soros acknowledged losing $600 million in two days gambling against the Yen. His $10 billion under management, when leveraged, gave him between $75 billion and $150 billion, according to one estimate [Michael Sesit and Laura Jereski, "Hedge Funds Face Review of Practices," The Wall Street Journal (February 28, 1994) ["Sesit"]. The same article said:

> Behind the central banks' latest concern lie the huge losses that investors have suffered in global bond markets over the past month and a half, and especially last week when French, German and British government bond prices fell 1.4% to 2.2%. Much of the decline in prices—and rise in bond yields—has been attributed to forced selling by highly leveraged hedge funds that bet wrongly that European and Japanese bond yields would fall.
>
> In mid-January, one hedge fund asked Goldman, Sachs & Co. to unload $2.5 billion of 20-year Japanese government bonds. By the time the U.S. investment bank completed the trade, the bonds' yield had jumped to 4.30% from 3.70%. Goldman officials said they don't comment on clients' activities.

The question was whether governments should act. In March, central bankers ruled out coordinated action now. On the other hand [Sesit]:

> Several bankers felt that central banks would try to jawbone banks into cutting back their lending to hedge funds.
>
> However, "from a practical point of view, the ability of banks to lend against collateral is impossible to control," said Mr. Golden of Lehman Brothers. "In the futures market, there is absolutely no ability to control hedge funds' activities."
>
> "The authorities are bound to be upset with anything that has the potential to be so destabilizing," said Mr. Golden. "But at the same time, the hedge funds can say: 'Everything we are doing is legitimate, aboveboard, and in the final analysis, we're the ones that are taking the losses.'"

And even Mr. Soros had suggestions about appropriate government action [Friedman]:

> Mr. Soros said that if there were to be any new Government regulation of hedge funds it should be focused on leveraging.
>
> "We do use borrowed money and we could cause trouble if we failed to meet a margin call," he said. But, he added, "If regulations are to be introduced, they ought to apply to all market participants equally."
>
> Mr. Soros said it would be wrong to single out hedge funds when many investment banks, like Bankers Trust or Goldman, Sachs & Company, engage in the same sort of speculative trading for their own accounts as hedge funds do.
>
> He pointed a finger at mutual funds, and those who trade in financial instruments known as derivatives—investments that are linked to interest rates, currency rates, stock prices and commodity prices—as the real culprits in the market instabilities. He said they magnified market volatility by engaging in "trend-following behavior"—buying in response to a rise in prices, which would tend to push prices even higher, or selling in response to a drop in prices,

which would tend to push prices still lower, reinforcing whatever trend is dominant in the market.

Eugene A. Ludwig, the Comptroller of the Currency, told Mr. Gonzalez's committee that in his view, hedge funds do not pose a significant risk to the nation's banking system. Mr. Ludwig said that only eight national banks and nine national banking companies have a total of only $1.04 billion in credit exposure through loans or lines of credit to the funds. "Our examiners report that those banks are adequately controlling those risks," Mr. Ludwig said.

Nevertheless, he added, no one should ignore the potential the hedge funds have for destabilizing the markets when they make the wrong investment. The combination of their leveraged positions, complex trading strategies and instantaneous, 24–hour, global trading networks "has increased the rate at which shocks spread throughout the financial system," he said.

---

(a) The reading suggests hedge funds use the organized futures and options markets to hedge. Do they use these markets in ways that would increase systemic risk?

(b) Debate rages between those worried about the systemic dangers posed by the derivatives markets and those who deride the worriers. Many people, including U.S. Congressmen, believe the problem is big, though they often are speaking of the OTC markets. The enormous notional growth implies that operations outstrip systems. The complexity eludes the senior managers who are supposed to evaluate the systems and the risks, but must instead rely on the traders themselves, exposing the firm to possible fraud. The many imponderables cripple efforts to calculate exposures. Intra-day swings may be large. The industry responds that the risk is vastly overstated. Nothing has happened yet, say supporters. From the perspective of a U.S. bank regulator looking at the futures and options markets, how serious would you find these concerns?

---

*Links To Other Chapters*

In earlier chapters we saw many of the instruments that make up the assets underlying futures and options: the bonds traded on domestic and offshore markets (Chapters II, V, VII and XI), the eurocurrency deposits (Chapter VIII), and the foreign exchange instruments traded around the world (Chapter VI).

Futures and options are part of the wave of innovation that swept international finance beginning in the 1980s. Securitization (Chapter XII) and swaps (Chapter XVI) are other examples. Motivating much of the innovation is the investors' desire to reduce risk. The same motive propels many institutional investors to diversify their portfolios internationally (Chapter XVII).

The futures and options markets further integrate domestic financial markets. This tendency is also at work in the global offerings of bonds (Chapter XI) and equities (XVII) and in the competition and cooperation among exchanges, whether for futures and options or for stocks and bonds (Chapter XIII).

The major tool to protect the futures and options markets, margining, supplements the capital adequacy rules seen earlier for banks and securities firms in these markets (Chapter IV). Many basic rules governing these markets appear in the readings about major countries (Chapters II, III, V, and VII). The payments system, a possible tool of national control over the development of futures and options markets outside the country, is examined in detail in Chapter IX.

Finally, the still very limited use of futures and options on organized exchanges in developing countries contrasts with the dynamism of securities markets in emerging markets (Chapter XVII).

# Chapter XVI
# SWAPS

In this Chapter, we look at the most important OTC derivative, swaps.[1] Unlike futures and options, this market is not based on an exchange. Instead, like the foreign exchange market, it consists of specific contracts negotiated and settled by individual parties (counterparties).

We begin the Chapter with a description of the two most widely used swaps, interest rate and currency swaps, an examination of why parties use them, and some characteristics of the overall market. We then turn to the risk of swaps. A key question is whether swap risks are different and greater than risks involved in traditional banking activity, deposit-taking and lending. Our examination of risk concentrates on credit risk and market risk. We conclude this discussion with an examination of capital requirements for swap transactions (mainly focusing on the Basle Accord). The Chapter concludes with material regarding netting arrangements.

## A. SWAP TRANSACTIONS AND MARKETS

We start with a description of some standard swap transactions.

### 1. Swap Transactions

#### S. HENDERSON, "SWAP CREDIT RISK: A MULTI–PERSPECTIVE ANALYSIS" IN INTERNATIONAL BANKING AND CORPORATE FINANCIAL OPERATIONS

K. Lian, H. Kee, C. Cheong, and B. Ong., eds. (1989)
(Henderson), pp. 41–47.

#### I. Description of Swaps

Regardless of form, the underlying principle of a swap is the agreement of each of two parties to provide the other with a series of cash flows, based on fixed or floating interest rates and in the same or different currencies. At the outset, the parties view the respective values of the two streams as equal. In other words, when the agreement is formed, the present values of the respective cash flows at the current prevailing interest rates and, if applicable, exchange rates are equal. Virtually all common interest rate indices are regularly used in swaps:

1. We would like to thank Bruce Darringer whose 1994 third year paper was of great help in writing this chapter.

US dollar fixed, prime, London interbank offered rate (LIBOR), bankers' acceptance, treasury bill, certificate of deposit, commercial paper and zero coupon rate, and a further variety of rate indices for other currencies. All major convertible currencies are swapped.

A typical interest rate swap agreement obligates the first party to pay an amount equal to the interest which would accrue on an agreed amount during a given period at one type of interest rate and obligates the second party to pay an amount equal to the interest which would accrue on that agreed amount during the period at another type of interest rate. To the extent that payment dates are simultaneous, the parties typically would net the payments, with the party owing the larger amount paying the difference to the other party. The economic relationship of the parties under a simple interest swap agreement is illustrated in the following diagram of a swap between Party X, in this instance a company which is about to incur a LIBOR-based debt but which would prefer a long-term fixed rate financing at a favourable rate, and Party A, a bank which is about to incur a fixed rate debt but which would prefer financing on a LIBOR basis:

**Figure 1***

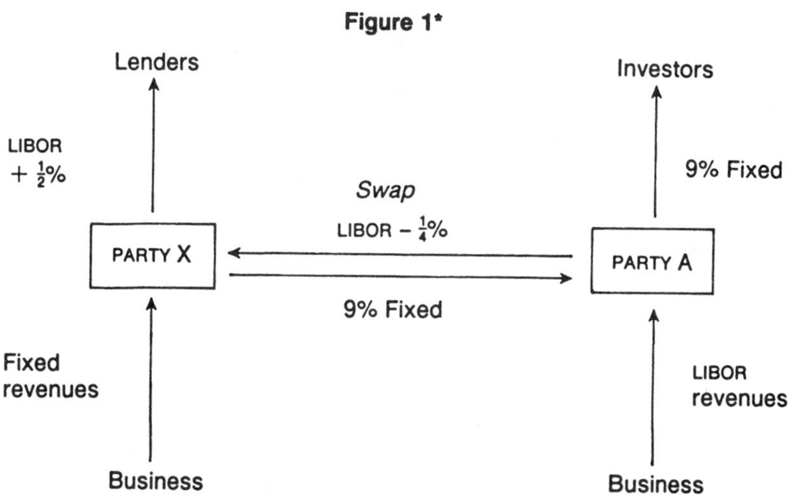


[2] Some swaps (termed 'off-market' swaps) do have unequal cash flows, usually in consideration of a front-end payment by one of the parties. The statement in the text holds true if that front-end payment is included in the cash flows.

* For illustration purposes all numbers and percentages herein are based on hypothetical figures and are not meant to imply that the rates are current market rates.

A typical currency swap involves an agreement under which the first party agrees to pay an amount in one currency, usually at periodic intervals, and the second party agrees to pay an amount in a different currency at the same or different intervals. These amounts may be expressed as either stated amounts due at stated times (in which case the interest rate and principal components are implicit in the specified amounts) or in terms of interest accruing on principal amounts in different currencies plus payment of those principal amounts at maturity. It is not uncommon to have the notional interest rates in a currency swap calculated on different bases so that effectively the interest rate swap and the currency swap are combined. Payments, even if due on the same date, are usually not netted but are paid gross. The economic relationship of the parties in a combined currency and interest rate swap agreement is illustrated in the following diagram of a swap between Party C, a company with LIBOR dollar liabilities and Swiss franc revenues, and Party X, in this instance a company with fixed rate Swiss franc liabilities and dollar revenues.

**Figure 2**

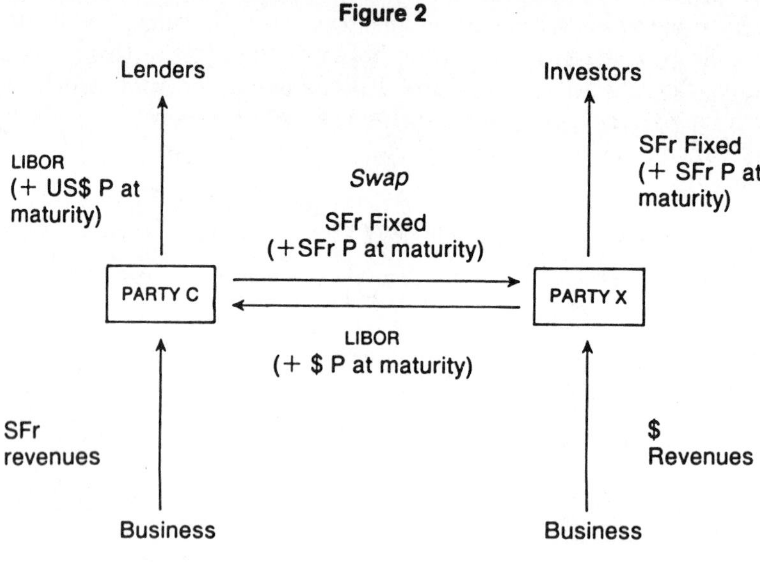


. . .

Parties entering into swaps for the above reasons are termed 'end-users', ie parties using the swap for direct financing, asset and liability management or investment purpose. In fact, parties desiring a swap on similar terms, but from reverse perspectives, may not have a commercial relationship with each other, may not be in the business of making credit decisions or may not be able to find counterparties directly. Each would prefer to deal with a strong credit financial institution acting as an intermediary. The intermediary financial institution would, in effect, stand in the middle by entering into matching reverse agreements with each party, thereby bearing the credit risk of each and retaining a spread in the transaction. Each agreement would normally be independent of, and not even refer to, the other. Indeed, the end-users would normally not know of the existence of the other counterparty. Thus, the typical swap is not one illustrated in Figure 1 or 2, but a swap in which one or more financial institutions act as intermediary between end-users.

**Figure 4**

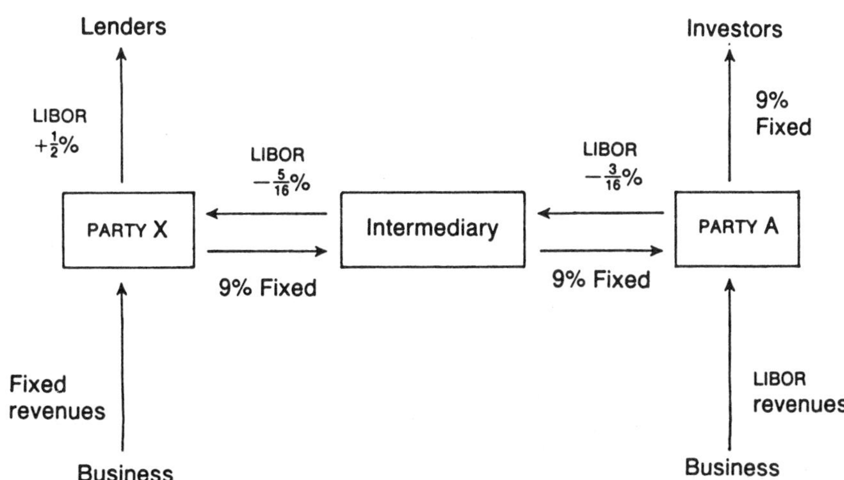


As intermediaries refined their swap funding capabilities, the critical mass of swaps developed to the point that these swaps themselves became an instrument which, while not tradeable, developed many indicia of tradeability. An early swap innovation was the termination of swaps for a fee. Intermediaries noted that termination was often more profitable than the intermediated swap spread itself had been. As it was logical to view a termination as if it were a sale and a realization on the value intrinsic in the swap, swap specialists began to think in terms of trading, particularly as competition drove down swap margins. Also as a result of increased competition for swap-related financings, intermediaries began to commit to swaps prior to obtaining hedging swaps. Delay while a hedging swap was sought would mean loss of the desired swap and related financial services, such as an underwriting position. The risk posed by the absence of a hedging swap focused attention on the means of temporarily hedging swap risk, or 'warehousing' a swap, until the match could be found. Once these temporary hedging techniques were developed, swap institutions were able and began to quote swap prices on a regular basis.

Trading indicia were simulated through the entering into, terminating and assigning of swaps and the quoting of swap prices, coupled with the use of sophisticated portfolio hedging activities.[3] Many swap institu-

**3.** If Party X wishes to terminate a swap with a dealer, a typical dealer would agree to do so on payment of a fee to or by Party X, depending on rates at the time. An 'assignment' by a dealer of its swap with Party X to another dealer is accomplished through:

(1) termination of the dealer's swap with Party X,

(2) Party X entering into a swap on similar terms with the 'assignee' and

(3) the 'assignee' paying a fee to, or receiving a fee from, the 'assignor'.

This requires the consent of all parties, including Party X, and two-step documentation, and is thus obviously not as smooth a process as selling a negotiable instrument which does not have mutual payment oblitions began to view themselves as 'dealers' in swaps, rather than as extenders of corporate financial services or credit. The swap market began to take coherent form with the creation of the International Swap Dealers Association Inc (ISDA), now composed of more than 90 major financial institutions.

The vast majority of swaps written therefore represent, at least from one of the party's point of view, a financial service or a dealing function of a financial institution which enters into swaps in the ordinary course of its business in order to earn either spreads between matching swaps, a profit on their swaps portfolio on an aggregate basis or a combination thereof. Some (but by no means all) commercial banks view their swap activity primarily as part of their business in providing financial services to their customers. Even if these banks often do not enter into exactly matching swaps (at least for interest rate swaps), and hedge their risk on a portfolio basis, they may still view their primary function as one of providing a financial accommodation. Most investment banks (and many commercial banks), on the other hand, view their swap activity primarily as part of their dealing activities. Their profit is perceived as deriving from the entry, transfer and termination of swaps on a portfolio basis.

. . .

The interest rate swap in Figure 1 only involves an exchange of interest payments, not of principal (the notional amount). The only relevance of the notional amount is for the calculation of the interest payments. The maturity of the swap (the time period over which interest payments will be exchanged) is typically 3–10 years, much longer than forward interest rate contracts.

## 2. Why Parties Do Swaps

The following excerpt looks at why parties enter into swap transactions.

### GROUP OF THIRTY, DERIVATIVES: PRACTICES AND PRINCIPLES

34–43 (July 1993) (G–30 Derivatives Study).

### II. Who Uses Derivatives and Why?

The participants in derivatives activity can be divided into two groups—end-users and dealers. End-users consist of corporations, governmental entities, institutional investors, and financial institutions. Dealers consist mainly of banks and securities firms, with a few insurance companies and highly rated corporations (mainly energy firms) having recently joined the ranks. An institution may participate in

gations. In a termination or assignment, the fee payable is roughly the Agreement Value of the swap, described below.

derivatives activity both as an end-user and a dealer. For example, a money-center bank acts as an end-user when it uses derivatives to take positions as part of its proprietary trading or for hedging as part of its asset and liability management. It acts as a dealer when it quotes bids and offers and commits capital to satisfying customers' demands for derivatives.

Derivatives permit end-users and dealers to identify, isolate, and manage separately the fundamental risks and other characteristics that are bound together in traditional financial instruments. Desired combinations of cash flow, interest rate, currency, liquidity, and market source characteristics can be achieved largely by separable choices, each independent of the underlying cash market instrument. As a result, management is able to think and act in terms of fundamental risks.

The next section describes specific uses of derivatives by different groups of end-users.

**End–Users**

Derivatives are used by end-users to lower funding costs, enhance yields, diversify sources of funding, hedge, and express market views through position taking.

*Corporations* According to the Survey of Industry Practice, over 80% of the private sector corporations consider derivatives either very important (44%) or imperative (37%) for controlling risk. Roughly 87% of the reporting private sector corporations use interest rate swaps, while 64% use currency swaps and 78% use forward foreign exchange contracts. For option-based derivatives, 40% use interest rate options and 31% use currency options.

Different uses of derivatives by corporations are discussed in more detail below.

*Lowering Funding Costs through Arbitrage Opportunities or Issuance of Customized Instruments* Derivatives allow corporations to lower funding costs by taking advantage of differences that exist between capital markets. They allow the principle of comparative advantage to be applied to financing. Where financial markets are segmented nationally or internationally, whether due to market or regulatory barriers or to different perceptions of credit qualities in various markets, the use of derivatives has delivered unambiguous cost savings for borrowers and higher yields for investors.

For example, a borrower may issue debt where it has a comparative advantage, and use a currency swap to achieve funding in its desired currency at a lower funding cost than a direct financing. A borrower generating savings in this way is, in effect, using a swap to exploit an arbitrage between the financial markets involved. Similarly, borrowers are able to achieve savings by issuing structured securities tailored to meet specific investor requirements. Then, the borrowers use swaps to achieve the borrowing currency and structure they need.[9]

**The Connection Between Swaps and Financing:** *In light of the significant reductions in funding costs that swap arbitrage can achieve, evaluating swap opportunities has become a crucial consideration in issuing bonds. That is, the choice of market and timing of issuance is driven by relative swap opportunities. It has been estimated that from 1985 to 1989, the volume of international new issues that were swap driven increased steadily, reaching 70% of international U.S. dollar new issue volume and 53% of total international new issue volume. Today all major borrowers monitor their funding opportunities regularly by evaluating the relative pricings for new issues and swaps across markets worldwide. See* Global Swap Markets *(IFR Publishing, 1991), Table 3.*

*Diversifying Funding Sources* By obtaining financing from one market and then swapping all or part of the cash flows into the desired currency denominations and rate indices, issuers can diversify their funding activities across global markets. Placing debt with new investors may increase liquidity and reduce funding costs for the issuer.

*Funding Operations in Multiple Countries at Lowest Cost* For international corporations, borrowing needs in a particular country or countries may be too small to be funded cost effectively through the local capital markets. It may be cost effective, however, to borrow more than they need in those capital markets and swap excess debt into the other needed currencies.

*Hedging the Cost of Anticipated Issuance of Fixed–Rate Debt* Volatile interest rates create uncertainty about the future cost of issuing fixed-rate debt. Delayed start swaps, or forward swaps, can be used to "lock in" the general level of interest rates that exists at the time the funding decision is made. Such hedging eliminates general market risk. It does not eliminate, however, specific risk—the risk that an issuer's funding cost may move out of line with the funding cost of other borrowers, due to factors related principally to the issuer.

. . .

*Managing Existing Debt or Asset Portfolios* As its assessment of economic prospects changes, a company may want to change the characteristics of its existing debt portfolio—either the mix of fixed- and floating-rate debt or the mix of currency denominations. Interest rate swaps can be used to adjust the ratio of fixed- to floating-rate debt, while currency swaps can be used to transform an obligation in one currency into an obligation in another currency, changing the currency mix of the debt portfolio.

**9.** In the early days of the swap market, funding could be obtained at savings of as much as 50 basis points (0.50%) given the significant arbitrage opportunities that then were available. Today arbitrage savings are more likely to be in the range of 10 to 25 basis points (0.10% to 0.25%).

**Making Small Business Loans and Adding Lending Capacity Using Interest Rate Swaps:** *Two of the primary lenders to McDonald's U.S. franchisees use swaps to better accommodate franchisees' needs for financing. One of these lenders had accumulated a large portfolio of fixed-rate loans to the franchisees. It sold participations in these loans in the secondary market to investors who were willing to buy a portion of the portfolio if they could receive a floating-rate return. Interest rate swaps were used to convert the fixed-interest payment stream on the participations to the floating rate that investors desired. This freed lending capacity so the bank could make additional loans to franchisees. Another lender manages a special purpose corporation which issues commercial paper to fund franchisee loans. It uses interest rate swaps to offer McDonald's franchisees either floating- or fixed-rate funding.*

Volatile interest rates may affect the value of a firm's assets as well as its liabilities. To protect the firm's net worth from interest rate risk, corporate treasurers increasingly take account of the interest rate sensitivity of both assets and liabilities in designing hedges. Interest rate swaps can be used to adjust the average maturity or interest rate sensitivity of a company's debt portfolio so that it more closely matches the interest rate sensitivity of the asset side of the balance sheet, reducing the exposure of the company's net worth or market value to interest rate risk.

Roughly 78% of the private sector corporations responding to the Survey indicate that they use derivatives to manage or modify the characteristics of their existing liabilities and assets.

*Managing Foreign Exchange Exposures* Both importers and exporters are exposed to exchange rate risk. As a result of this transactional exposure, an importer's profit margin can, and often does, evaporate if its domestic currency weakens sharply before purchases have been paid for. International firms with overseas operations also face translation exposure as the values of their overseas assets and liabilities are translated into domestic currency for accounting purposes. The competitive position of many domestic producers also is subject to change with major movements in foreign exchange rates. Currency swaps and foreign exchange forwards and options can be used to create hedges of those future cash flows and reduce the risk from currency fluctuations.

. . .

**Managing Sovereign Debt with Currency Swaps:** *Finland is a highly rated sovereign and an active borrower in the international capital markets. The government of Finland, through the Ministry of Finance, has actively used swaps to lower its effective cost of debt and manage the currency composition of its foreign liabilities to hedge foreign exchange risks. During the period 1987–1990, Finland entered into approximately 50 swaps with notional principal equivalent to U.S. $50–200 million at a time. Roughly 30% of the government's total outstanding foreign debt* *was swapped, with most swaps being related to newly issued debt. Swaps were used in 1990 to achieve funding costs of 30–50 basis points below LIBOR. They were also used to configure the currency composition of Finland's foreign liabilities in the direction of its official currency basket. The Finnish mark was pegged to the value of the currency basket. The Ministry used currency swaps to access the lowest-cost offshore debt markets, while translating the currency composition of the debt portfolio to the desired mix. Substantial changes in the debt composition were achieved through swaps. For example, although the actual share of the Japanese yen in the external debt was 23% in 1989, currency swaps were used to reduce the effective share to 12% in 1989 and 5% in 1990. See "Government Use of Cross Currency Swaps" in* Cross Currency Swaps *(Business One Irwin, 1992) edited by Carl Beidleman.*

. . .

*Institutional Investors*

*Enhancing Yields Through Arbitrage Opportunities* The earliest use of swaps by institutional investors involved asset swaps, in which the cash flows from a particular asset are swapped for other cash flows, possibly denominated in another currency or based on a different interest rate. Institutional investors use derivatives to create investments with a higher yield than corresponding traditional investments. They might do this when securities trade poorly because of some unattractive feature. In such a case, an investor may purchase the securities, neutralize the undesirable feature with a suitable derivatives transaction, and create, for example, a synthetic fixed-rate investment with a higher yield than comparable fixed-rate instruments of the same credit quality.

*Managing Exposures to Alternative Assets* Institutional investors have recently begun to use derivatives, especially interest rate and equity swaps, to manage their exposure to debt and equity markets, both domestic and international. The immediate appeal is the ability to quickly and effectively adjust exposures—between debt and equity or among different equity classes—without incurring substantial transaction and custodial costs. There is also potential to enhance yields. The availability of equity swaps on the major international equity indices allows investors to diversify globally and adjust their portfolios in a cost-effective manner.

*Eliminating Currency Risk* Some institutional investors wish to benefit from investment in or exposure to foreign debt or equity markets without necessarily incurring foreign exchange risk. For instance, a Japanese investor might want to earn a return based on the S & P 500 Index but payable in yen at a predetermined exchange rate. A family of swaps called "quanto" swaps have been designed to meet the growing demands of investors for investment diversification without currency risk.

Global derivatives are now used widely by financial institutions to manage the interest rate and foreign exchange risk arising from a variety of activities. Eighty-four percent of the financial institutions responding to the Survey indicate that they use derivatives for hedging market risks arising from new financings, 77% use them to manage their existing assets and liabilities, 39% use them to offset option positions embedded in the institution's assets and liabilities, 39% use them to hedge transaction exposures, and 46% use them to hedge translation exposures.

## Dealers

*The Function of Dealers* Early in the evolution of OTC derivatives, financial institutions—including investment banks, commercial banks, merchant banks, and independent broker/dealers—acted for the most part as brokers finding counterparties with offsetting requirements with regard to notional amount, currencies, type of interest to be paid, frequency of payments, and maturity. They then negotiated on behalf of the two parties. Acting as agent or broker for a fee, the institutions took no principal position in the transactions and, hence, were not exposed to credit or market risk.

Most financial institutions found their role soon evolved beyond brokering to acting as dealers, offering themselves as counterparties or principals to intermediate customers' requirements. Transactions, however, were immediately matched or hedged by entering into an opposing transaction such as a "matched swap." Each pair of transactions was dealt with separately and discretely. As a result, the dealer's book of business was relatively simple to monitor and manage. This new role, however, required a commitment of capital since dealers now faced credit risk and some limited market risk.

The next step in the evolution of dealer activities was the "warehousing" of derivatives transactions. Dealers would temporarily hedge a swap—typically with a cash security or futures position—until a matched transaction could be found to replace the temporary hedge. This advance in risk management practice increased the ability of dealers to accommodate customer needs.

Today, major dealers have moved from the "warehouse" approach to a "portfolio" approach, wherein the dealer simply takes the customer's transaction into its portfolio or book of derivatives and manages the net or residual risk of its overall position. Each new transaction is decomposed into its component cash flows and risk factors and aggregated with all previous transactions. The focus of risk management changes from individual transactions to portfolio exposures. This has led to a marked improvement in the ability of dealers to accommodate a broad spectrum of customer transactions, and has improved their ability to monitor and manage the various components of market risk, regardless of the transactions from which the risks derive.

By quoting bid and offer prices, dealers provide liquidity and continuous availability of derivatives transactions. To supply the immediacy demanded by end-users, dealers use their own inventory, or establish new positions, and manage the resulting risk. They are compensated by earning a return from a bid-ask spread. In addition, dealers can take market risk positions to express market views in the expectation of profiting from favorable movements in prices or rates.

Dealers also provide an arbitrage function, identifying and exploiting anomalies between derivatives and underlying cash market instruments, thereby enhancing market liquidity and pricing efficiency. Finally, dealers earn a return for the amount of financial engineering that goes into developing customized and structured transactions that meet specific customer needs.

*Types of Dealers* Dealing in derivatives has tended to concentrate among principals possessing not only the requisite technology and know-how but also ample capital and credit appraisal experience. Banks have become the dominant derivatives players, but they hold no monopoly.[11] Securities firms, insurance companies, and high-rated corporates (especially in the energy area) are deploying capital and credit experience to run swap books to profit from both dealing and position-taking activity.

The credit standing of the dealer is very important. Several dealers have created special purpose derivatives product companies which benefit from the support of a strong parent or shareholder. Some dealers have established separately capitalized, triple-A rated, derivatives vehicles.

## 3. Overall Markets

The G–30 Derivatives Study, pp. 54–58, also contains some International Swaps and Derivatives Association (ISDA) data on the size of the swaps market.

---

### The Level, Growth, and Composition of Derivatives Activity

ISDA survey data provides the most comprehensive and consistent data set for measuring the level, growth, and composition of derivatives activity. The survey data is based on the responses of ISDA's members, capturing the vast bulk of activity in most sectors, and is adjusted for doublecounting.

*Interest Rate and Currency Swaps* As indicated in Table 2, the notional principal of interest rate plus currency swaps written in 1991

11. Based on a ranking in *The World's Major Swap Dealers* (Swaps Monitor Publications, Inc., November 1992) for year-end 1991, 19 of the top 25 dealers in interest rate and currency swaps were banks; four were securities firms; and two were insurance companies. Out of the 25 dealers from around the world, 14 were U.S. based. Of the top 25 dealers in foreign exchange forwards, 24 were banks, while one was a securities firm.

was $1.95 trillion, 32% more than in 1990 and a three-fold increase over 1987. Likewise, the notional principal of interest rate swaps written during 1991 was $1.62 trillion, four times the amount written in 1987. Currency swaps written during 1991 were $328 billion, somewhat less than three times the amount written in 1987. Table 2 also shows that, for year-end 1991, the notional principal outstanding of interest rate plus currency swaps was $3.87 trillion, or three and a half times the year-end 1987 outstanding of $867 billion.

Table 3 provides information on the composition of swap activity by type of counterparty. Of the $1.95 trillion in interest rate and currency swaps written in 1991, $866 billion in notional principal or 44% involved transactions between dealers; $591 billion or 30% was between dealers and other financial institutions; $362 billion or 18.6% was between dealers and corporations; while $132 billion or 6.8% was between dealers and governments or other entities.

**Table 2**
**Interest Rate and Currency Swaps Written Annually by Underlying and Outstanding**
(Notional Principal in Billions of U.S. Dollars: 1987–91)

| Type of Swap | 1987 | 1988 | 1989 | 1990 | 1991 |
|---|---|---|---|---|---|
| *Interest Rate Swaps* | | | | | |
| US$ | 287 | 366 | 545 | 676 | 926 |
| DM | 22 | 33 | 41 | 106 | 103 |
| Yen | 32 | 43 | 62 | 137 | 194 |
| Others | 47 | 126 | 185 | 345 | 399 |
| Subtotal | 388 | 568 | 833 | 1,264 | 1,622 |
| *Currency Swaps* | | | | | |
| Yen–Dollar | 24 | 35 | 53 | 48 | 80 |
| Others–Dollar | 30 | 35 | 40 | 33 | 60 |
| Non–Dollar | 32 | 54 | 86 | 132 | 188 |
| Subtotal | 86 | 124 | 179 | 213 | 328 |
| Total Swaps Written | 474 | 692 | 1,012 | 1,477 | 1,950 |
| Total Swaps Outstanding (at Year–End) | 867 | 1,328 | 1,952 | 2,890 | 3,872 |

Source: International Swaps and Derivatives Association

**Table 3**
**Interest Rate and Currency Swaps Written Annually by Type of Counterparty and Outstanding**
(Notional Principal in Billions of U.S. Dollars: 1987–91)

| Counterparty | 1987 | 1988 | 1989 | 1990 | 1991 |
|---|---|---|---|---|---|
| Transactions Between Dealers | 144 | 222 | 368 | 546 | 865 |
| Transactions With End–Users | | | | | |
| Financial Institutions | 203 | 282 | 370 | 472 | 591 |
| Corporations | 86 | 127 | 186 | 286 | 362 |
| Governments | 35 | 52 | 63 | 98 | 111 |

| Counterparty | 1987 | 1988 | 1989 | 1990 | 1991 |
|---|---|---|---|---|---|
| Others | 6 | 9 | 25 | 75 | 21 |
| Subtotal | 330 | 470 | 644 | 931 | 1,085 |
| Total Swaps Written | 474 | 692 | 1,012 | 1,477 | 1,950 |
| Total Swaps Outstanding (at Year–End) | 867 | 1,328 | 1,952 | 2,890 | 3,872 |

Source: International Swaps and Derivatives Association

. . .

*Comparison to Other Financial Activities* While the numbers on new swaps written and swaps outstanding shown in Table 2 indicate a significant growth in overall swaps activity from 1987 to 1991, it is important to put these numbers in perspective. One obvious comparison is with the trading or turnover in exchange-traded markets for futures and options and the foreign exchange markets. In 1991, ISDA dealers reported writing 74,340 swaps with a notional principal of $1.95 trillion. In contrast, in 1992, more than 600 million futures and options contracts were traded on organized exchanges, representing a face value or notional amount exceeding $140 trillion. Global net turnover in the foreign exchange markets, in April 1992, was estimated to have totalled $880 billion per day, or roughly $220 trillion on an annual basis.

The size of OTC derivatives activity can be put into further perspective by comparing it with the activity in other selected global financial markets. This is done in Table 6 for year-end 1991. Swaps outstanding of $4.5 trillion (including caps, floors, collars, and swaptions, along with interest rates and currency swaps) is compared to bonds (domestic and cross-border) outstanding of $14.4 trillion and equities (domestic and cross-border) outstanding of $10.1 trillion.

**Table 6**
**Global Financial Activity**
(Outstandings in Trillions of U.S. Dollars: Year–End 1991)

| Selected Markets | Outstanding |
|---|---|
| Swaps | 4.5 |
| Bonds (Domestic and Cross-border) | 14.4 |
| Equities (Domestic and Cross-border) | 10.1 |

The amount for swaps includes interest rate and currency swaps plus caps, floors, collars, and swaptions outstanding for year-end 1991. Equity, commodity, and multi-asset derivatives are not included. They totalled $131 billion year-end 1992.

Source: J.P. Morgan

---

By 1992, total swaps outstanding had risen to $4.7 trillion. Swaps activity is somewhat concentrated. As of 1991, the top eight dealers accounted for 58 percent of the worldwide notional interest rate and currency swaps. G–30 Study, at 61. The GAO has viewed the market as highly concentrated. GAO, *Financial Derivatives* (May 1994), (hereinafter GAO Report), p. 36. The GAO study included a survey of the notional amount of swaps outstanding of 14 major dealers in 1993. They reported $7.6 trillion, an increase of over 60% since 1992!

### *Notes and Questions*

1. Consider the following two $100 million 5 year interest rate matched swaps entered into between Bank A (AAA credit rating) and Company B (BBB credit rating) with Swap Bank, when the yield on the 5 year treasury bond was 9%:

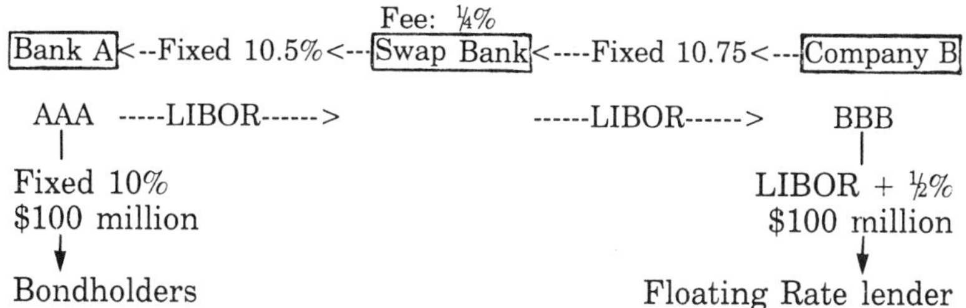


Assume Bank A's cost of floating rate funding would be LIBOR and Company B's cost of fixed rate funding would be 11¾. Is Bank A at risk if Company B fails to pay Swap Bank?

Why would Company B enter into this transaction? Has Company B hedged or reduced its interest rate risk? Would Company B be better off, post-swap, if interest rates increased or decreased. How about Bank A?

2. Did Company B reduce its pre-swap floating rate funding cost by entering into the transaction described in note 1? This would be determined by the following calculation:

<u>Analysis of Company B's Savings</u>

| | | |
|---|---|---|
| 1. | Direct Cost (to floating lender): | (LIBOR + 2/4%) |
| 2. | Swap Cost (to Swap Bank): | (10¾%) |
| 3. | Swap Revenue (from Swap Bank): | LIBOR |
| 4. | Net Cost (3 − (1 + 2)) | 11¼% |
| 5. | Cost Savings: | ½% (11¾ − 11¼) |

In this transaction Company B saved ½% by entering into this transaction. Did Bank A reduce its funding cost by entering into this transaction? What was the total funding cost savings of entering into this transaction? What are the essential conditions for having funding cost savings in this transaction? Does it follow from the fact that there are funding cost savings for Bank A that Bank A has reduced its risk by entering into this transaction?

3. Let's assume Bank A wants to hedge or speculate on interest rates. Why not use interest rate futures/options rather than swaps? How would these alternatives compare with respect to liquidity, maturities, credit risk and nature of participants.

4. The Swap Bank earns a bid-asked spread of 25 basis points in the transaction described in note 1. The bank has bid 10.5% fixed to buy LIBOR, but offers to sell LIBOR for 10.75% fixed. Swap dealers regularly quote bid and ask prices on fixed-floating swaps. Does the Swap Bank have any risk in this transaction? How would the Swap Bank determine its bid-ask prices?

5. Consider (and diagram) the two following 5 year currency swaps. Issuer A swaps $40 million for ¥5 billion with Swap Dealer, and pays Swap Dealer 5.10% fixed on ¥5 billion in return for 9.40% fixed on $40 million. Issuer B swaps ¥5 billion with Swap Dealer for $40 million and pays Swap Dealer 9.90% fixed on $40 million in exchange for 5.50% fixed on ¥5 billion. Issuer A has raised the $40 million by issuing bonds paying 9.40% fixed, and Issuer B has raised the ¥5 billion by issuing bonds paying 5.50% fixed. The current spot foreign exchange rate between the dollar and yen is assumed to be US $1.00 = ¥125 ($40 million = ¥5 billion).

How are the fixed interest rate payments on these currencies determined. Do you think they are the current interest rates on the dollar and the yen? Why would these two issuers enter into these swaps? Suppose issuer A, a Japanese company, issued a dollar equity warrant (bond cum warrant) instead of a straight bond, with an interest rate of 2%. The lower rate is due to the warrant feature. What is the impact on the issuer?

6. Consider the FX risk on the currency swap described in note 5. Assume that the dollar-yen rate changes to $1 = ¥100 during the life of the swap. What is the FX risk for A and B?

7. What role do you think regulatory and tax factors play in parties entering into swap transactions? Consider the following: "A case of tax and regulatory arbitrage through swaps occurred in 1984, when Japan still treated interest 'income' on zero-coupon bonds as nontaxable capital gain, whereas accruing interest 'payments' on zeros were tax deductible by U.S. borrowers. Financing packages utilizing swaps were devised in the market to exploit the discrepancy, enabling a number of U.S. borrowers to procure cheap dollar funding, effectively at the expense of the Japanese taxpayer." JP Morgan, "Swaps: Versatility at Controlled Risk," *World Financial Markets* (April 1991), p. 17. U.S. borrowers could issue zero-coupon yen denominated bonds to Japanese investors and swap the proceeds for dollars.

8. Does the Japanese zero coupon case indicate that swaps are an important tool for regulatory and tax arbitrage? Were the Japanese powerless to stop this? If swaps are an important tool, then they may play an important role in liberalizing domestic capital markets.

9. A recent study has shown that changes in commercial and industrial loans are positively related to banks' participation in interest rate swaps. This suggests that swaps allow banks to better manage the interest rate exposure of their loan portfolios, and that regulatory restraints on swaps could result in lower lending growth. E. Brewer III,

B. Milton and J. Moser, The Effect of Bank–Held Derivatives on Credit Accessibility, Federal Reserve Bank of Chicago, Working Paper Series, Issues in Financial Regulation (April 1994).

# B. CREDIT AND MARKET RISKS IN SWAPS

While we have already touched upon risks in swaps, we now turn to a more focused examination of credit and market risks.

Henderson, pp. 49–65.

. . .

## A. DEFINITION OF CREDIT RISK

The risk incurred by a counterparty entering into a swap with Party X can be analysed as consisting of two parts: the rate risk and the credit risk of Party X. The rate risk (including currency risk if applicable as well as interest rate risk) is that, based on movement of rates in the future, the counterparty will be the net payor under the swap. Worded another way, after all payments have been made, the payments made by the counterparty will turn out to have been more valuable than those received by it. This is the risk that the swap becomes unfavourable to it. This risk can be and is hedged, as illustrated in all the examples above.[5]

It should be noted that the swap is almost always independent of the position which it is hedging or which is hedging it. Whether the swap is viewed as hedged by other positions or as itself hedging those positions, the result is the same: if the swap terminates, the counterparty is then exposed because of the continued existence of those positions. As swaps are hedged either explicitly or implicitly, the counterparty has no rate risk as long as Party X performs.

Thus, exposure arises if rates have moved in such a way that the swap is favourable to the counterparty (which means that the corresponding hedge is unfavourable) and Party X does not perform. Swap credit risk is this risk of the failure of Party X to perform under those circumstances.

## B. QUANTIFICATION OF CREDIT RISK

The sensible means of quantifying that risk is through measuring the cost of replacing the cash flows under the swap if Party X defaults and the swap terminates. Since swaps involve reciprocal obligations and the possibility of bilateral cash flows, depending on rate movements there will almost certainly be a gain or loss to the counterparty if the

5. A party which hedges itself through general asset and liability management techniques may have no direct hedge in place and, in fact, may have an open position. The party may be taking a view on rates. Indeed, every party that incurs a loan takes a view on rates when it determines whether or not it wishes to borrow at fixed or floating rates. This position represents as real a hedge as does a specific, matching hedge. For the balance of this chapter, it will be assumed that a swap is hedged even if only through the taking of a managed open position for which it has bargained in the swap.

swap terminates: a gain if, in recreating the future cash flows, the value of the termination of the counterparty's liability to pay under the swap exceeds its cost of replacing its income under the swap; and a loss, if termination of its liability is worth less than its cost of replacing its income under the swap.

This quantification cannot be precisely calculated in advance, that is to say prior to an actual default, since the counterparty does not know how rates will move and what their level will be at an indefinite time in the future. At best, when entering into the swap a rough estimate can be made of the range of exposures depending on theoretical rate movements. At the time of Party X's default, however, the measurement of the counterparty's gain or loss on replacement can be calculated precisely through the cost of one or a combination of several alternative transactions: a replacement swap on similar terms but commencing on the date the original swap is terminated and running through the original term; a combination of borrowing and investing in order to recreate the remaining cash flows under the swap agreement; or the use of forward rate agreements, futures, options, caps, floors and other instruments to recreate the hedge which the swap was serving.

Replacement of the cash flows of an interest rate swap through a combination of borrowing and investment can be illustrated as follows:

**Figure 5**

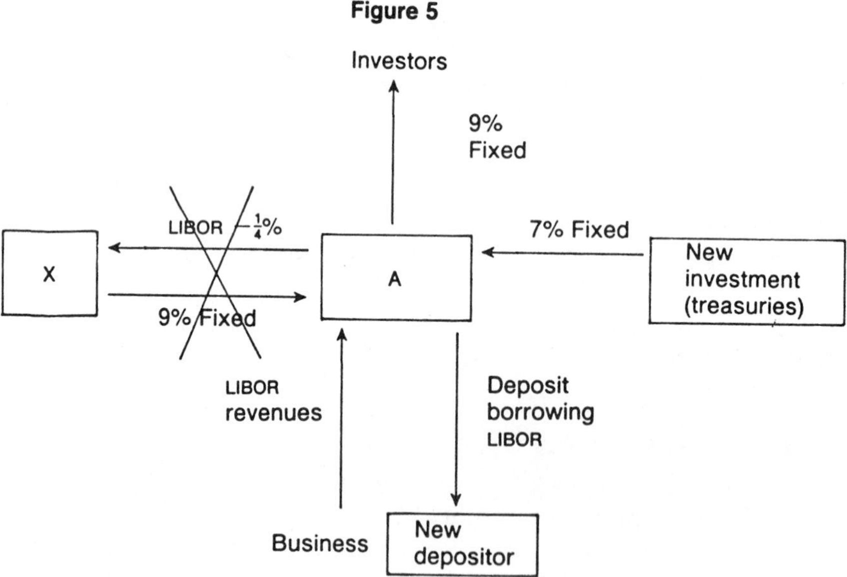


(A's loss = Present value of $2\frac{1}{4}$% pa over the remaining term.)

The basic financial gain or loss at a given time is equal to the then present value of the difference for each future payment date between the fixed rate on the investment or borrowing (depending on whether the gain or loss is viewed from the perspective of the fixed rate recipient or payor) and the rate on the swap.

Replacement of the cash flows through a new swap can be illustrated as follows:

**Figure 6**

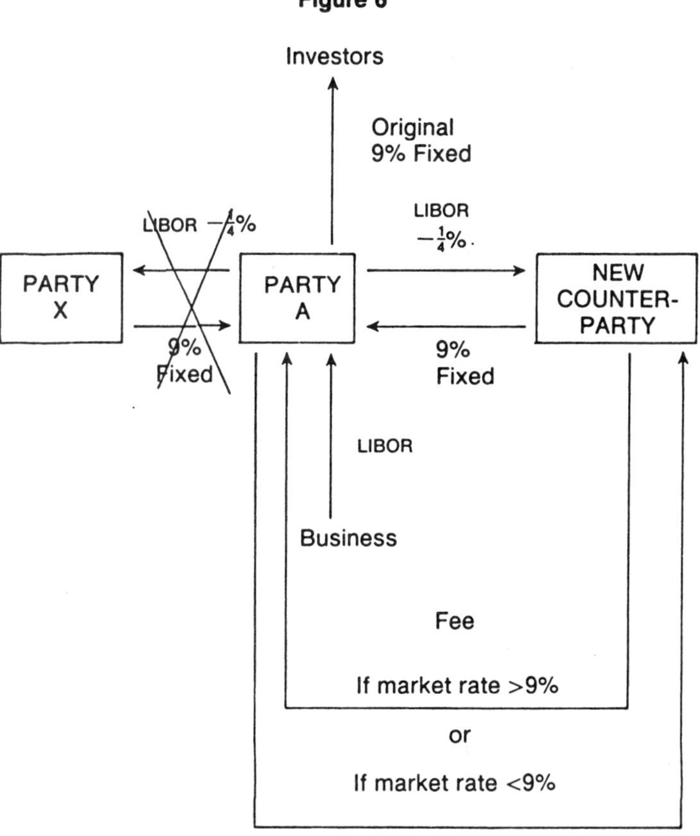


The basic financial gain or loss of a party at a given time is equal to the front-end fee which the party could receive or would have to pay to a third party in consideration of the third party entering into the replacement swap given rates current in the swap market at the time of replacement.

The right to terminate, calculate gain or loss in each swap, and claim for losses is set forth in the lengthy but standardized swap agreements on the forms published by the ISDA. These agreements are described below, but it may be useful at this point to describe several elements which will be necessary for the balance of this chapter.

## C. DETERMINATION OF GAINS AND LOSSES: AGGREGATION

Each ISDA agreement is a master agreement which provides that all swaps done between Party X and the counterparty under the master shall be regarded as integral parts of a single agreement. This being the case, if Party X defaults generally or on one swap, the agreement provides that the counterparty may terminate all (but not less than all) swaps with Party X. The measure of damages, the counterparty's gain or loss, is calculated through reference to the average cost of a replacement swap with respect to each swap (the mark-to-market value, the Agreement Value, at the time of each terminated swap). The gains and losses of all swaps are then netted, with one resulting figure being used as the counterparty's gain or loss on termination. This termination of all swaps and netting of gains and losses on termination is generally termed 'aggregation'.

. . .

## IV. Perspective of counterparty

What does the foregoing mean for the counterparty? A counterparty, which we will assume is a financial institution, would analyse its credit exposure to Party X in several contexts: its initial credit approvals; pricing; its view on documentation; means of reducing credit risk through security or guarantees; and, if it is also a lender to Party X, practical enforcement restraints which may result.

It should first be noted that the evolution of a dealing market in swaps has had an effect on the way financial institutions deal with credit exposure. Market competitiveness requires accelerated responsiveness of a sort which traditionally has been regarded as appropriate for truly liquid instruments but perhaps less appropriate for intrinsically illiquid instruments such as swaps. Swaps are entered into over the phone and promptly confirmed by telex (with the parties generally viewing themselves as being bound from that point). Thus, ultimate credit decisions are made quickly, sometimes without the detailed analysis customary in the past, and formal documentation is left for future discussion. The bankers on the front-line in many instances are now dealers rather than credit officers. Their training is in market pricing, not credit analysis. An approach which is appropriate for trading listed securities, outstanding in established markets and already fully documented, may not be fully appropriate for incurring commitments for term exposure on a less-than-fully-documented basis. Due to the potentially large exposure in swaps, financial institutions have created systems which will permit the dealers to operate, but on a basis consistent with their credit standards and the traditional framework of their operations.

### A. APPROVALS

Prudence dictates that a financial institution carefully monitor its credit exposure to its individual customers. The first decision which the counterparty must make with respect to Party X is an estimation of Party X's ability to perform, ie whether it has assets to pay its debts as they fall due. This is the analysis of the general creditworthiness of Party X, which analysis should theoretically be the same as for any other financial transaction in which the counterparty incurs exposure to Party X. Swap credit risk is therefore generally included in overall controls which an institution places on the aggregate credit risk it wishes to incur with respect to Party X. These controls are in part maintained through a dealer having a preapproved swap line for each of its likely swap counterparties, each line forming a part of the overall credit lines for that customer.

However, allocating usage under the swap credit line requires the risk to be quantified. In this sense, determination of general credit lines in the swap context differs from determinations in other financial relationships such as direct lending. In a loan, the principal amount can simply be applied against the credit line and the loan's outstanding balance can be monitored to control credit line availability over future periods. In a swap the issue is more complicated in two respects.

First, at the inception of the typical swap (assuming no special circumstances, such as a front-end fee or prepayment), the immediate exposure, assuming a default then, is generally zero: if the swap was done at market rates, obtaining a replacement swap would generally incur little cost. Intuitively, given the potential for future exposure arising from movements in rates, some amount must nonetheless be allocated since there is a realistic possibility that exposure will arise in the future. Second, once the initial credit allocation for a swap is made, another distinction arises: the amount of actual exposure does not, as with a loan, stay constant. Actual exposure can rise and fall as rates move in an unpredictable way.

Proper allocation of credit line utilization under a swap thus requires a cushion to provide for unpredictable rate movements. Most financial institutions use rough estimates for credit line utilization based on broad historical rate estimates, which generally are conservative in the sense that they often allocate higher credit exposure than might be expected. The amount may amortize over time in a fashion predetermined by the formula, but due to administrative necessity would generally not change with actual rate movements. Some banks, however, in managing their credit lines, will adjust credit usage for purposes of determining available credit if the mark-to-market exposure in a given swap exceeds the formula-based level.

Conceptual difficulties also arise in formula-based credit quantification which does not distinguish between different structural situations. First, it may not pick up quirks in the swap which may in fact increase or decrease credit risk. For instance, assume the following in which the counterparty makes payments prior to those of Party X:

(1) a swap in which the counterparty pays semi-annual LIBOR against Party X's annual fixed payments;

(2) a swap in which the counterparty pays semi-annual LIBOR against a 'zero-coupon' payment at maturity by Party X; and

(3) a swap in which the counterparty makes a front-end payment to Party X in return for receiving above-market payments from Party X, or making below-market payments to Party X, going forward.

In each case the counterparty is at risk with respect to each of its payments made in gross or with respect to the front-end payment, as the case may be, until it receives the corresponding payment from Party X in respect of which the early payment was made. Conversely, in swaps which are the reverse of the above swaps, the counterparty's risk is reduced.

Second, allocation of credit exposure for each swap on a formula basis does not differentiate between swaps with the same party which run generally in the same direction and swaps with the same party which run in off-setting directions. Assume that Party X is a LIBOR borrower, entering into a series of swaps with the counterparty where it pays fixed. All of its swaps are running in the same direction. A precipitous decline in interest rates will result in the counterparty having a greater credit exposure to Party X than if its swaps were multi-directional. For example, assume that the counterparty has two swaps with Party X, in each of which Party X is paying fixed, at 8% and 9% respectively. If rates drop, the counterparty has a direct exposure on both swaps. If, however, the counterparty is paying fixed at 8% on one swap and Party X is paying fixed at 9% on the other swap, a drop in rates means that the counterparty has exposure only on one and no exposure on the other.[20] On the other hand, this off-setting risk means that the counterparty will almost always have exposure on at least one and, if it cannot aggregate with the other on termination, is almost certain to be at risk.

This leads to the difficulty of factoring in the legal risk of uncertainty of enforcement. For instance, should the counterparty quantify the exposure in each swap with Party X on an individual basis or should it quantify exposure in all swaps with Party X on an aggregate basis, given the absence of complete certainty as to whether or not aggregation would be permitted? If the counterparty could aggregate, a new reverse swap could in fact decrease the credit risk it bears to Party X. If the counterparty is uncertain of aggregation, each swap carries with it a potential exposure regardless of other positions.

Finally, given the vast number of swaps, it is not clear how many institutions factor into their initial credit analysis the fact that the agreements with Party X may be on a non-standard form or, if on a standard form, may not include provisions which they would customarily require in extensions of credit to Party X (see below).

## B. PRICING

Evolution of a dealing market has also affected the pricing of swaps. The tendency in the market, which is competitive and dealer-oriented, is

**20.** The 1% difference in this example does present a band in which there could be exposure in both swaps (eg if rates are at 8% to 8½%). In addition, if rates drop to 7%, the gain on termination of the first swap (counterparty paying 8%) would be somewhat less than the loss on termination of the second swap (counterparty receiving 9%). The larger the difference between the two off-setting swaps, the greater the risk, though the risk is never as great as would exist if there were no off-setting swap.

for there to be an accepted and quoted swap rate. While this may be based on a bench-mark (eg treasuries for US dollar fixed rates), the swap spread over the bench-mark is market-driven. If a party is an approved credit risk, the market tendency (but certainly not the invariable case) is for it to get that swap rate. If its credit is not approved, the market tendency is for it to get no swap. A high degree of competitiveness and the high volume of swaps in the dealing market thus discourage credit-sensitive pricing which would permit finer gradations based on credit analysis and encourage the use of an 'all or nothing' approach in which the decision is often just whether or not to do the swap. This result is generally justified on the basis of the high creditworthiness of most swap counterparties.

## C. DOCUMENTATION

Once the initial credit analysis is satisfactorily completed and allocation is made against credit lines, the counterparty will control its swap credit risk with Party X on an ongoing basis through contractual provisions in the swap agreement. A party's ongoing commercial concerns about the creditworthiness of its counterparty will be most directly reflected in its attitude towards the substantive credit controls in the document: the requirement for closing documents, representations and warranties, covenants and events of default. Warranties and closing documents lend assurance to each party at the commencement of the transaction as to the other party's requisite legal, tax and commercial status and the absence of certain credit-sensitive events. Covenants and events of default set forth the commercial and credit standards with which each party must comply on an ongoing basis failing which the other party will no longer wish to maintain its credit exposure to that party. The key enforcement provisions of a swap agreement, those which provide the remedy for breach of the substantive credit controls, are found in the clauses which entitle the non-defaulting party to terminate the swap agreement and recover its losses resulting from termination or to exercise any other remedies produced by law, as discussed above.

Documentation controls can be analysed in the context of the form of documentation and of the ongoing policing of compliance with its provisions.

### 1. Form of documentation

Early swap documentation involved individualized agreements which were somewhat reduced versions of each bank intermediary's lending documents. However, swap practice evolved in such a way that financial institutions generally required less stringent documentary controls in swaps than in the provision of other financial services. This practice was based on several factors:

(1) the evolution of swaps from back-to-back loans and the reduction of credit concerns because of the off-setting nature of those obligations;

(2) the generally high credit-standing of most swap counterparties;

(3) increased competition in the swap market, which resulted in a marginal advantage for the dealer which required the shorter, less onerous agreement; and

(4) the general decline in the credit ratings of many banks in comparison to many corporate counterparties, which meant that what a bank required it would have to give, thereby discouraging the tendency to require.

However, market attention became focused on documentation for other reasons:

(1) the growing delays, or backlogs, in executing swap agreements after confirmation and the risks arising from undocumented swaps, which delays were perceived as resulting from the need to negotiate each agreement separately and in detail;

(2) the desire to encourage a trading market in swaps, which was deemed to be hindered in part by the necessity to review and approve widely divergent documentation; and

(3) the declining margins in swaps, which heightened sensitivity to the cost of negotiating documentation.

These concerns led to publication by the British Bankers' Association of the Recommended Terms for Interest Rate Swaps (BBAIRS) in 1985, which set forth both financial and credit provisions to be used as the basis of the parties' agreement. The use of BBAIRS was intended for, and did expedite, the completion of short-term interbank transactions in the London market, but most institutions chose not to base their general forms on BBAIRS.

The ISDA was initially formed to expedite documentation through the development of standard terms. The first step was publication of the ISDA's 1985 and 1986 Editions of the Code of Standard Wording, Assumptions and Provisions for Swaps (Swaps Code). The 1985 edition was primarily concerned with financial provisions and provisions relating to compensation on early termination. The 1986 edition of the Swaps Code reiterated the existing provisions of the 1985 edition and added more extensive credit related provisions. Each edition together with minor amendments is a compendium of standard terms from which the parties to a swap may freely choose in a separately drafted, negotiated and executed agreement.

Finally, in 1987 the ISDA published two master agreements, presented on printed forms. The first master, prepared by an ISDA working group in New York (the Rate Swap Master), is for US dollar interest rate swaps only, incorporates terms from the 1986 edition of the Swaps Code and is governed by New York law. The second, prepared by an ISDA working group in London (the Rate and Currency Swap Master), is for rate swaps in any currency as well as currency swaps, does not incorporate Swaps Code terms (since the Swaps Code contemplates only dollar rate swaps), and has been drafted to be governed by either New York or English law. However, the provisions in the two agreements are nearly identical in substance, except to the extent necessary for the London agreement to accommodate currency transactions and non-dollar rate swaps. In addition, a pamphlet, ISDA's 1987 Interest Rate and Currency Exchange Definitions, has been prepared for optional use as a companion to the Rate and Currency Swap Master in the same way that the 1986 Swaps Code is a companion (albeit required) for the Rate Swap Master. Indeed, these 1987 Definitions are patterned after the financial provisions of the Swaps Code, setting forth definitions of rates and related terms for swaps involving 15 currencies.

Each of the agreements consists of two parts, the first of which sets forth the basic terms of the master and the second of which is a Schedule on which some of those terms may be completed, supplemented or varied. Specially tailored cross-default provisions, additional covenants to be complied with by certain kinds of counterparties, and special clauses relating to credit support, such as guarantees and collateral, must be added to the Schedule under 'Other Provisions'. Another provision, to be completed in the Schedule, facilitates the designation of the third parties that will be providing credit support (eg a guarantee or a letter of credit) or that will be relevant for purposes of the cross-default clause, if appropriate. The ISDA has published a User's Guide to assist in the process of 'customization'.

Existence of the ISDA agreements has had a strong effect on bringing documentation into a 'market acceptable' form and has greatly facilitated the growth of the swap market on the basis of prudent documentation and reduced backlogs. However, standardization discourages provisions which may be desired by a particular institution either for credit purposes or because of the unique character of the counterparty (such as UK local councils) or its jurisdiction. Dealers are increasingly reluctant to require provisions which, while perhaps desirable in principle, meet market resistance, require the sort of negotiation which the Swaps Code and master agreements were intended to avoid and which could result in the deal being lost. This reluctance even exists where the forms provide for insertion of various types of clauses or for modifications which are readily visible. For instance, the agreements provide space for insertion of a description of financial information required on execution, but this is often not utilized (particularly outside of the USA) and, indeed, often meets market resistance when a party attempts to utilize it. Credit terms which would be regarded as mandatory in more traditional credits are thus often not required in swaps.

. . .

## D. CONTROL THROUGH SECURITY, GUARANTEES AND SUBORDINATION

The counterparty may wish further to control its credit exposure to Party X through guarantees, collateral or the existence of a protective cushion of subordinated debt, as in other financial transactions.

1. *Guarantees and security*

Subject to the general legal uncertainties with respect to swaps described above, the general terms of guarantees and security for swaps are similar to those for other serial financial transactions. The dealing market in swaps, however, creates a different environment in which this support is obtained.

As noted above, swaps are generally committed over the telephone and confirmed through an initial exchange of telexes, by which the parties generally view themselves as bound. If the counterparty intends to obtain security, it should be specified in the phone conversation and confirmation telex. Failure so to specify credit support in adequate detail may result in the counterparty becoming bound and incurring the credit risk of Party X without having the *right* to obtain the security. Even if specified in the confirmation telex and the counterparty has the *right* to obtain security, there is no actual security or guarantee in place until it is actually given. The fact that the confirmation telex recites that the parent of Party X is to give a guarantee or that Party X is to deliver security is a simple statement to that effect. That statement, if properly drafted, might well be construed as an obligation to provide the support so that the counterparty could claim breach of the agreement. This, however, does not give the counterparty the guarantee or security; it gives the counterparty the right to claim damages for breach on an unsecured, unguaranteed basis. Even if Party X performs and delivers collateral, but the delivery of the collateral occurs after the effectiveness of the agreement (arguably the date of the confirmation telex), the pledged collateral would be likely to be avoided as a preference if it was delivered within 90 days before Party X's bankruptcy petition was filed and, if the counterparty is an 'insider' of Party X, if it was delivered within one year prior to the bankruptcy filing, in either case if Party X was insolvent at the time when the collateral was delivered. Finally, if the counterparty entered into a swap with Party X hoping for a share in already existing collateral, the collateral documents must be amended to provide for the security to extend to the swap obligations of Party X and, before the telex is issued, the counterparty should ensure that amendments in the desired form are acceptable to the existing lenders.

Proper attention to drafting and structuring can eliminate or substantially mitigate these problems in the context of the confirmation telex. However, the fact that swap exposure may vary over time may also create enforcement difficulties where a counterparty wishes to have security from Party X if the mark-to-market value of the swap is in the counterparty's favour beyond certain pre-agreed levels of tolerance. The obligation of Party X to deliver guarantees or other collateral in the future is subject to the same legal complexities described above with respect to its obligations under the confirmation telex. Failure to provide the security may be a breach of an obligation, but the security is not automatically in place; and actual delivery of collateral in the future may be a voidable preference.

2. *Subordinated debt*

If Party X has subordinated debt, the counterparty should be aware that the subordination cushion may well not apply to swap liabilities. The terms of subordinated debt often provide that the debt is subordinated only to (1) indebtedness in respect of borrowed money which is either not expressed to be subordinated or is expressed to be senior or (2) specifically described debt. In this case, the protection afforded by the subordination provisions would probably not be available to a swap counterparty. In particular, on an insolvency of Party X, the counterparty may not have a claim that is senior to the subordinated debt even if the debt in respect of which Party X had entered the swap was senior debt. The counterparty would therefore wish to assure itself in advance that the provisions governing the subordinated debt expressly state that obligations under swap agreements constitute senior debt.

. . .

---

As the Henderson piece explains, a counterparty is only exposed to credit risk when the swap is in the money, i.e. has a positive value. The value of a swap, referred to as its mark-to-market value, can be calculated as the present value of the net payments the holder expects to receive over the life of the contract. An alternative expression of the same value is replacement cost, the cost of obtaining a replacement swap on the same terms and for the time remaining on the initial swap should the counterparty default.

As an example, consider the interest rate swap in note 1 above. Assume that at the end of the third year of the swap, the market rate for the five year swap is 12.75% fixed for LIBOR. This means the swap is in the money (a good deal) for Company B, since it would now cost Company B 12.75% rather than 10.75% to get LIBOR. The replacement cost is the present discounted value of this two percent differential (multiplied by the notional amount of the swap) over the remaining 2 year life of the swap. Company B would have to pay $2,000,000 ($100,000,000 × .02) more in each interest period to obtain LIBOR. Using the current 2 year swap rate (12.75) as the discount rate, the replacement cost would be $2{,}000{,}000/1.1275 + 2{,}000{,}000/(1.1275)^2 =$ $3,347,081. This cost would only be incurred if Company B's counterparty, Swap Bank, defaulted.

Consider the position of Company A under the same scenario of a 2% rise in interest rates. It is out of the money; it has made a bad deal. In the market, it could get 12.75% for LIBOR, while under its contract it is only getting 10.50%. The loss in the value of its contract is the present discounted value of the 2.25 percent differential in fixed rates (12.75 − 10.50) over the remaining 2 year life of the swap. Company A will be receiving $2,250,000 ($100,000,000 × .0225) less than the market would pay in each interest period. Using the current market rate

(10.50) as the discount rate, the loss would be 2,250,000/1.1050 + 2,250,000/(1.1050) $^2$ = $3,878,913. This is a market loss for Company A, assuming A's fixed rate exposure is not hedged.

Finally, consider the position of Swap Bank. It is in the money on its contract with Company A (it would have to pay more now to get LIBOR) and out of the money on its contract with Company B (it could now get more for LIBOR in the market). Swap Bank does have a credit risk on its contract with Company B, but absent default, its market loss on its contract with B is offset by its market gain on its contract with A.

This analysis of risk looks at gains or losses on the contract at a fixed point in time, two years into the contract. Suppose we want to predict the risk of the contract over the life of the swap. Let's go back to credit risk and Company B's position. We know that Company B stands to lose about $3.3 million if Swap Bank were to default at the end of two years. This is referred to as current exposure. But B might stand to lose even more money if interest rates further increased and Swap Bank then defaulted. This is referred to as future or potential exposure.

The usual methodology used to estimate potential exposure over the remaining life of a swap is the Monte Carlo simulation. The remaining life of the swap is analyzed on the basis of simulations which model movements in swap rates based on different assumptions of interest rate volatility.

A recent study by K. Simons, "Interest Rate Structure and the Credit Risk of Swaps," *New England Economic Review* (July/August 1993), performed a Monte Carlo simulation for interest rate swaps of various maturities. The study used matched pairs of swaps to control for market risk, i.e. gain on one swap would be exactly offset by loss on the other. This approach allows for isolation of credit risk. Interest rate predictions were based on two scenarios. The first assumed that interest rates follow a random walk in accordance with historical volatility and further assumes that changes are lognormally distributed around a mean corresponding to historical volatility. The second used the forward interest rates implied by the shape of the swap yield curve (maturity on horizontal axis, percentage yields on vertical axis) as a forecast of expected future swap interest rates. The results were as follows:

Table 2: Exposure on a Matched Pair of Swaps as a Percentage of Notional Principal

| | 10–Year | | 7–Year | | 5–Year | | 3–Year | | 1–Year | |
|---|---|---|---|---|---|---|---|---|---|---|
| Swap Maturity | Flat Rate | Rising Rate | Flat Rate | Rising Rate | Flat Rate | Rising Rate | Flat Rate | Rising Rate | Flat Rate | Rising Rate |
| Confidence Interval | | | | | | | | | | |
| 99% | 11.22 | 13.07 | 7.78 | 9.49 | 5.12 | 6.44 | 2.25 | 2.79 | .34 | .36 |
| 95% | 8.28 | 9.24 | 5.67 | 6.79 | 3.59 | 4.64 | 1.63 | 2.02 | .24 | .25 |
| 90% | 6.93 | 7.57 | 4.71 | 5.54 | 3.06 | 3.75 | 1.37 | 1.66 | .20 | .21 |
| 75% | 5.12 | 5.33 | 3.37 | 3.75 | 2.22 | 2.54 | .98 | 1.13 | .14 | .14 |
| Mean Expected Lifetime Exposure | 4.03 | 4.27 | 2.68 | 2.97 | 1.74 | 2.00 | .77 | .87 | .10 | .10 |

The values in the Table indicate the expected replacement costs over the lifetime of the swap. The "flat rate" is based on the random walk methodology, while the "rising rate" is based on the shape of the swap yield curve. The results are interpreted as follows. For a swap with a remaining life of 10 years, the flat rate exposure will be no more than 8.28 and the rising rate exposure will be no more than 9.24 percent of the notional amount in 95% of the cases, while the mean expected lifetime exposure is 4.03 and 4.27 percent under the two respective methodologies. The mean expected lifetime exposure is calculated by averaging the expected exposure for each period. The lower mean expected lifetime exposures take into account the fact that the risk reduces as the swap approaches maturity since fewer periods remain in which the difference between the initial and the current rate can accumulate.

### *Notes and Questions*

1. The G–30 Derivatives Study, p. 59, gave the following estimates for the gross replacement costs of the derivatives portfolio of the 50 largest U.S. bank holding companies.

**Table 7**
**Derivatives Exposure by Lead Banks of 50 Largest U.S. Bank Holding Companies**
(Year–End 1990–1992)

| | Gross Replacement Costs | | | | |
|---|---|---|---|---|---|
| | *Interest Rate Contracts* | | *Currency Contracts* | | *Combined Exposure* |
| Year | $ Billion | Percent of Notional Principal | $ Billion | Percent of Notional Principal | $ Billion |
| 1990 | 26.2 | 1.15 | 76.3 | 2.82 | 102.5 |
| 1991 | 47.8 | 1.61 | 99.4 | 3.70 | 147.2 |
| 1992 | 49.7 | 1.61 | 94.3 | 2.98 | 144.0 |

The gross replacement cost is the mark-to-market value for OTC derivatives contracts with positive replacement cost, including swaps, forwards, purchased options, when-issued securities, and forward deposits accepted. Exchange-traded contracts and foreign exchange contracts with less than 14 days maturity are excluded.

Source: Consolidated Reports of Condition and Income.

Can these results for interest rate contracts (which include futures/options and swaps) be squared with the Simons study? Why would exposure on currency contracts be higher than on interest rate contracts. The G–30 Study stated that the "total replacement cost of $144.0 billion represents less than 11% of the market value of the assets of these banks and 120% of their total capital." id. This was at year-end 1992. On the other hand, a 1992 study by the International Monetary Fund (IMF), *International Capital Markets Part 2: Systemic Issues in International Finance.* p. 27, reports that replacement cost was $170 billion for the 10 largest U.S. banks, or 17.3% of their assets, as of September 1992 (U.S. banks must report replacement cost to the Federal Reserve Board). What do you think replacement cost was in the spring of 1994, after the U.S. experienced a sudden surge in interest rates?

2. How would you compare the credit and market risks to a bank on an interest rate swap with those from lending. Banks that lend typically have exposure to interest rate risk, for example if they have a mismatch between long-term fixed rate assets and short-term floating rate liabilities. Is this just like entering a swap in which a bank pays a fixed rate and receives a floating rate?

The actual credit risks on swaps, like loans, not only depend on the credit rating of the counterparty, but also on security provisions. Some swap arrangements require the out-of-the money participant to provide collateral or "mark-to-market" payments to the in-the-money participant.

In 1992, Citicorp had $135 billion in loans compared to $217 billion in interest rate swaps. Does this mean it has more total risk from swaps than loans?

3. How can a Swap Dealer deal with market risk? One possibility, as in our paradigm interest rate swap, is to enter into a matched swap with another counterparty. In practice, however, it is very difficult to run a swaps portfolio that is entirely matched. One way to deal with this is to use non-swap interest rate contracts, futures, forwards or options, to hedge swap exposure. However, these hedges are "dynamic" since they need to be adjusted over time due to the fact that non-swap interest rate contracts have a shorter maturity than swaps. Indeed, a major problem in estimating the market risk to a particular institution from swaps is deciding to what extent swap risks are offset or hedged by positions in other instruments. It should be noted that dealers mark-to-market their derivatives portfolio daily in order to assess their value.

4. Dealing in swaps is a very competitive business, reflected in the narrowing of dealer spreads over time. Does the competitiveness of a dealer depend on having a low credit risk? Consider the following excerpt from M. Peltz, "Wall Street's Triple–A For Effort," *Institutional Investor* (May 1993), pp. 93–98.

Investors in the derivatives markets have discovered a fundamental law of risk that's similar to the first law of thermodynamics governing conservation of energy. Risk never disappears, it just changes form. "Over-the-counter derivatives allow investors to lay off market risk very accurately," Securities and Exchange Commissioner J. Carter Beese Jr. noted last March. But hedging, he continued, "certainly has its own price tag. [Customers] are, in effect, trading market risk for credit risk."

Not if they can help it, however. When several financial institutions were down-graded during the recession to humble single-A status, many users of interest rate and currency swaps shifted business to the highest-rated banks and firms or demanded that counterparties put up collateral. Now, says attorney Kenneth Raisler, co-head of Sullivan & Cromwell's commodities, futures and derivatives group, "if you don't have the credit rating, people won't deal with you."

Single–A doesn't cut it. Most swappers insist on double-A or better. So to counter the advantage of triple-A banks like swaps powerhouse J.P. Morgan & Co., investment banks have cobbled together "credit-enhanced" derivatives subsidiaries. (The Comptroller of the Currency has informally dissuaded commercial banks from forming such units.) The first triple–A sub, Merrill Lynch Derivative Products, was separately capitalized upon its debut in November 1991 so that it would survive even if parent Merrill Lynch were to go bankrupt. To guarantee a top rating (see box, page 92), MLDP was endowed with a cool $350 million, or about $117 million per "A."

**Collateral vs. credit**

Since MLDP's debut, only two other firms—Goldman, Sachs & Co. and Salomon Brothers—have formed special-purpose triple-A derivatives subs. The process is exacting, requires large dollops of capital and relies on elaborate and expensive technology to ensure that all transactions are properly hedged and collateralized. In essence, it involves all the complexity of setting up a separate company with its own changing liabilities. And all this trouble produces a less-than-breathtaking return on equity, though MLDP claims that its own earnings, plus the ancillary business it generates, enable it to meet its 15 percent ROE target.

Yet with the growing importance of swaps in underwriting and risk management—swaps volume was up 44 percent from the last half of '91 to the first half of '92 (the latest figures available)—Wall Street firms and any other less-than-gilt-edged credits that want to partake of this business have scant choice but to form credit-enhanced subsidiaries. "Everybody has gotten much more cognizant of the credit risk, the dealers as well as the end users," says Benjamin Weston, a managing director of Credit Suisse Financial Products.

To some derivatives investors, however, what counts is not a credit rating but collateral. They insist that they can best protect themselves by persuading a counterparty to regularly mark its portfolio to market and post collateral to cover the exposure. "All else being equal," says a credit officer of the Federal National Mortgage Association, "we think that our agreements are more conservative than doing something uncollateralized with a triple-A."

Most swaps users, though, take the less time-consuming route of dealing with a highly rated institution in the first place. "Most of our counterparties in currency and interest rate swaps are commercial banks that are at least double-A," says World Bank chief commercial-credit-risk officer Samir El Daher. "For non-commercial banks we require triple–A."

The catch is that, what with recent downgradings, there are fewer and fewer commercial banks worldwide that are double- or triple-A. And a triple-A investment bank—if there were such a thing—would have to make a wide detour of Wall Street. "Very honestly, you're not going to find a lot of true triple-A's," says Sprint Corp. treasurer M. Jeannine Strandjord. "Domestically I think it's just J.P. Morgan."

**Morganesque?**

Merrill's MLDP and the other triple-A subsidiaries would dearly like the swaps market to accept them as little synthetic Morgans. MLDP is the brain-child of Conrad Voldstad, who himself left Morgan to join the then-double-A Merrill Lynch in London five years ago. "Connie had talked about improving Merrill's credit in swaps, but this wasn't really an issue until 1990, when we were downgraded to single-A and the business took a hit," says managing director Flavio Bartmann, who followed his swaps boss from Morgan to Merrill. "The reason we set up MLDP was because our credit was not accepted by a large segment of the market here in Europe."

. . .

Basically, MLDP is a swaps intermediary. When a counterparty enters into a contract with it, the transaction is offset by a corresponding swap with Merrill Lynch Capital Services, Merrill's single-A traditional derivatives operation. Thus does MLDP transfer the market risk to MLCS, which then posts collateral to MLDP to cover its exposure. "We showed that market risks could be separated from credit risks very efficiently," says Bartmann. "It took a long time for us to convince the rating agencies that was possible."

MLDP's $350 million stash is a hefty sum for any investment bank to devote exclusively to one business line, but Merrill contends that the swaps market wouldn't have taken it seriously if it had put up anything less. A triple-A sub was, after all, a radical new idea. "Merrill was the first, so to satisfy the ratings agencies they grossly overcapitalized MLDP," says a rival banker. According to Merrill, at the end of last year, MLDP had more than 32 times the equity needed to meet Bank for International Settlements capital requirements for its $26 billion swaps book. The cushion, Merrill reasons, will allow MLDP to grow without a capital infusion anytime soon.

. . .

Salomon Swapco is intended to compete with MLDP but without the same capital outlay. The subsidiary, which did its first swap only two months ago, has a rating-agency-agreed-upon minimum capital requirement of $175 million, but that can be increased as the need arises. "What Swapco has effectively done is become a booking center through which Salomon will generate more business flow," says Swapco co-CEO Anil Narang. Unlike MLDP, Swapco has the flexibility to do swaps with all investment-grade counterparties, not just double- and triple-A's.

(Both MLDP and Swapco do collateralized transactions with their single-A and single-A-minus parents, respectively.) Swapco also offers a larger menu of swaps than MLDP, which is limited to mostly plain-vanilla fare.

**To Be or Not to Be**

An even bigger difference between MLDP and Swapco is what happens if their parents default. MLDP lives on if Merrill's capital services unit can't meet its obligations. Although it couldn't enter into any new swaps, MLDP would be able to continue to hedge those in its book until they matured, at which point the remaining capital would be distributed among its shareholders.

Swapco, however, would terminate right away. "If in the remote event that [Salomon defaults or goes bankrupt and] Swapco gets downgraded below single-A, then the company will liquidate its contracts across the board and pay back at fair market value," says Narang. "The rationale is that while you're triple-B-plus, you're still strong enough to pay everyone back."

Not all Swapco clients would be thrilled with this outcome. Many would be getting paid at midmarket (by averaging prices from several dealers), and would most likely have to go through the difficult process of replacing a swap in a market that's changed significantly since the swap was put in place. And a market that has just witnessed a Salomon default is going to be anything but stable.

Hence, a swap user who didn't want to lose a strategic hedge already in place would probably prefer MLDP's continuation structure. But a counterparty that's a large dealer or a sovereign borrower with a sizable swap book—making it easier to replace its position—might prefer Swapco's termination feature because it would be assured of getting out with its money.

Swappers might also be concerned that MLDP and Swapco offset all their swaps through less-than-double-A companies: Merrill Lynch Capital Services (A+) and Salomon Brothers Holding Co. (A−), respectively. Half of MLDP's swaps are with MLCS.

. . .

Ironically, being triple-A affords only a token advantage in swap pricing, if that. Fierce competitive bidding essentially means that the swaps market doesn't price credit. "Credit is an absolute," explains CSFP's Weston. "A counterparty either will deal with you or it won't."

Although some credit sensitivity has emerged lately, it mostly shows up as one-or-two basis-point variations. "Some end users are formally restricted from using less than a double-A, but for many it is a question of the trade-off of the risk of bankruptcy or downgrading against the improvement in price you could get," says W.H. Bruce Brittain, managing director of capital markets at Swiss Bank Corp. Investment Banking in New York. All else being equal, of course, a user would prefer a higher credit.

As the above article recounts, U.S. bank regulators have not allowed banks (Citibank and Continental Illinois were denied permission in 1992) to set up AAA subsidiaries. Why would they be against this? Should banks be concerned about the competitive impact?

This article suggests that pricing in the swaps market does not materially take counterparty creditworthiness into account. Why would that be? Is the following explanation from R. Litzenberger, "Swaps: Plain and Fanciful," XLVII *J. of Finance* 831, 836–838 (1992) persuasive?

There are four reasons why swap rates are not credit sensitive. First, an initial exchange of fixed and floating rate notes which allows either counterparty to sell the other counterparty's note in the secondary market is not identical to the same initial exchange which requires each counterparty to hold the other counterparty's note until maturity. Pricing the notes as stand alone obligations implicitly assumes the former. While swaps may be assigned to acceptable credits, the receive side of a swap cannot be bifurcated and separately sold in the secondary markets. Thus the latter is more analogous to an interest rate swap. In the United States the value of a note is determined in bankruptcy by accelerating the claim, which in effect sets value at the note's face amount (accreted value for a zero coupon note) no matter how much interest rates have changed since the note was originally issued. Of course, the actual value received could be a small fraction of that amount. Merton (1976) and Geske (1978) view corporate note spreads as compensation for the implicit compound put option that noteholders are writing. Consider a single class of debt and assume that the rule of absolute priority is followed in bankruptcy. If the value of the firm as a going concern exceeds its current interest or principal payment obligation, the payment will be made, otherwise the firm will be put to noteholders. Thus, the firm's note spread is an increasing function of both the debt equity ratio and the variance of the rate of return on total market value.

Now consider an exchange of two debt instruments that cannot be separately sold in the secondary market. In the United States bankruptcy results in a netting of the accelerated claims associated with the floating and the fixed rate notes. The net claim based on offsetting equal face amounts of fixed and floating rate notes is zero and does not depend upon changes in interest rates from the time the transaction was initiated. In our example, if Firm A1 were to go bankrupt and term interest rates have risen since the swap was initiated, AAA Agency would benefit from the resulting netting of the notes. Conversely, if Firm A1 were to go bankrupt and interest rates have fallen since the swap was initiated, AAA Agency would lose from the resulting netting of the claims. However, in either case the net claim in bankruptcy is zero. In effect, AAA Agency's net position is analogous to an exchange of default-free notes combined with holding a put swaption (the option to pay fixed and receive floating on a swap) conditional on Firm A1 going bankrupt and writing a call swaption (an option to receive fixed and pay floating on a swap) conditional on Firm A1 going bankrupt. If bankruptcy is independent of interest rate levels, the market values of the conditional put and call swaptions will be equal and the swap rate will be dependent on neither the debt equity ratio nor volatility of the return on total market value. However, if low interest rates and bankruptcies are associated with recessionary conditions then the market value of the conditional put swaption will exceed the market value of the conditional call swaption and the initial swap rate will be an increasing function of both the debt equity ratio and the volatility of the return on total market value.

Second, the treatment of swaps in the event of bankruptcy is asymmetric and differs from the treatment of offsetting fixed and floating debt obligations. In contrast to the netting of the face value of offsetting notes, for an interest rate swap the bankruptcy code supports the industry practice of determining the settlement amount for early termination. Under standard swap documentation supported by the International Swap Dealers Association (ISDA), bankruptcy is an automatic default event. The payment due the solvent party is the higher of the market value of its position based on prevailing swap rates or zero. That is, if the market value of the position of the insolvent party is positive its claim is zero. If the market value of the position of the insolvent party is negative, that amount represents the claim of the solvent firm in the bankruptcy proceeding or the claim against which any collateral may be netted. The ISDA provision permitting termination without payment if the market value of the solvent counterparty's position is negative has not been subject to a court challenge. In practice, most solvent counterparties have either voluntarily made the payments or settled out of court. Stronger corporate credits frequently negotiated the removal of this provision from their master swap agreements with swap dealers.

If swap rates have risen, the market value of the swap is positive to the fixed rate payer and negative to the floating rate payer and vice versa. Most swap dealers value a simple fixed/floating swap by: (1) assuming that a LIBOR flat floater sells for par, (2) assuming that a bond having a coupon equal to the swap rate also sells for par, and (3) valuing the difference from the current swap rate as an annuity. The valuation of this annuity for our example requires an estimate of the ten-year zero swap rate, which in turn requires a term structure model to interpolate zero swap rates that are not actively quoted from quoted par swap rates.

While the determination of the value of the swap is based on direct market determination, the actual quotes provided by dealers are based on their proprietary term structure models as well as their existing swap positions. Under standard International Swap Dealers Association (ISDA) swap documentation, the "market quotation" is determined by the solvent counterparty obtaining the market quotes from swap dealers for replacing the insolvent swap counterparty. The solvent swap counterparty obtains three or more market quotes and the "market quotation" is the truncated average disregarding the highest and lowest quotes. The "settlement amount" is the higher of the market quotation or zero. In Appendix A, the relevant sections of the standard ISDA swap documentation are quoted. These sections describe the procedure for obtaining the market quotations and for calculating the settlement amount.

The asymmetric treatment of the solvent and the insolvent parties under a default event partially offsets the need for credit-sensitive swap spreads. The asymmetric determination of the settlement amount is favorable to the stronger counterparty. However, the impact of this provision is diluted by three factors: (1) the ability of a counterparty to assign a profitable swap prior to a default event, (2) the realization of only a fraction of any positive ISDA settlement amount in a bankruptcy proceedings, and (3) the tendency of solvent counterparties to make at least partial payment for any negative market quotation to avoid litigation.

Third, long-term swaps with maturities in excess of ten years generally contain credit triggers. A typical credit trigger specifies that if either counterparty falls below investment grade (BBB), the other counterparty has the right to have the swap cash-settled at the settlement amount based on the market quotation obtained by the investment grade credit to take the place of the "fallen angel." Investment grade credits very rarely go bankrupt prior to being downgraded. Thus, credit triggers offer substantial protection to both swap counterparties. However, if the investment grade credit's position has a negative value, it may choose not to terminate the swap, because in the event of a subsequent default it may terminate the swap without payment. Credit triggers, combined with the asymmetric treatment of swaps in bankruptcy, substantially mitigate the potential for large credit losses and, under certain conditions, the expected value of the swap may actually increase to a AAA-rated credit if its swap counterparty were downgraded below investment grade.

Fourth, weaker credits are either simply rejected or required to collateralize swaps, rather than be quoted higher swap spreads. Unlike a collateralized loan where the lender is automatically stayed from liquidating the collateral by the filing of a bankruptcy petition, the collateral supporting a swap may be liquidated and applied by the solvent counterparty to offset a positive settlement amount.

To recapitulate, the unique treatment of swaps under default events is the primary reason why swap rates do not depend on credit ratings and do not display the cyclical behaviors evidenced by single A corporate bond spreads. It is incorrect to view a swap as a exchange of fixed and floating rate bonds. The next section motivates the existence of an active swap market with rational value maximizing participants.

6. The material has focused on plain vanilla swaps. While these constitute a very substantial percentage of all swaps outstanding there are others. One important variation is the "Diff" swap, as described in

the following piece by Tracy Corrigan, "Borrowers Take A Chance on Diffs as Swaps' Allure Dims," *Financial Times* (November 23, 1992).

Falling US interest rates have squeezed the availability of swaps in the dollar market. Borrowers have been unwilling to lock themselves into fixed-rate interest costs, while rates are expected to ease further. The result: fewer people willing to pay the fixed-rate leg of a swap agreement.

Other factors have also contributed to the decline in the swap market's attractions. The growing sophistication of investors and intermediaries and a breakdown of the barriers between domestic markets have eroded the opportunities for arbitrage between markets. At the same time, bond and swap markets have become tightly linked, so that price movements in one are quickly transmitted into the other.

"Swaps and bonds have become much more closely correlated. Those who want cheap funding are now having to take risks to get it," said Mr Nick Burge, executive director at Nomura International.

The most successful product this year has been the differential or "diff" swap, also known as the "quanto" swap, which allows a borrower to separate currency and interest rate exposure, by paying interest rates based on one currency while taking the currency risk of another.

For example, a company with D–Mark liabilities, paying say 8 per cent interest, may look enviously at dollar rates of 3½ per cent. Under a differential swap agreement, the company agrees to receive D–Mark Libor in D–Marks, and to pay a margin over dollar Libor in D–Marks.

The structure takes advantage of different-shaped yield curves to create immediate cost savings for the borrower. Such an agreement typically runs from three to five years, so the borrower is essentially betting that the shift in interest rates will be slower than the yield curve suggests.

"There are monetary policy pressures to keep short-term interest rates low, and supply fears to keep rates high at the long end [of the dollar market]," says Mr. Ron Tanemura, head of fixed-income derivatives products at Salomon Brothers.

The risk for the company is that if US interest rates rise or D–Mark interest rates fall more quickly than expected, planned cost savings could soon be replaced by losses. Because it is more complicated than a conventional swap, a diff swap is also more difficult to unwind.

The financial intermediary assumes substantially greater risk than in a normal swap. Currency risk, artificially separated from interest rate risk in this way, is very difficult to hedge, since there is no direct correlation between currency and interest rate movements.

"Diff swaps are more difficult to manage than a straightforward swap," says Mr. Malcolm Basing, who heads the International Swaps

Dealers Association. "It's not something you can put into the top drawer and forget about."

Diff swaps require what is known as dynamic hedging, which means that hedges must be constantly adjusted in line with the latest market moves.

Even then, there is the risk that assumed correlation between interest rates and currencies will suddenly disappear.

According to swap specialists, the structure of differential swaps is now widely understood, but the methods of hedging residual exposure remain proprietary.

Diff swap technology has also been applied to suit investors' requirements. Credit for the concept is claimed by Credit Suisse Financial Products, which began marketing diff swaps to Japanese investors in early 1991.

There could be room for further product expansion. According to Mr. Chris Goekjian, head of risk management at CSFP, it may be that "not all the applications [of diff swap technology] have been developed yet."

---

A Diff is an exchange of interest payments calculated with respect to different currencies but payable in one currency. Let's take a specific example. Assume we have a 5 year Diff for DM 100 million in which Company A agrees to receive DM LIBOR (currently 8%) from Company B in exchange for paying B $ LIBOR + 50 basis points ($ LIBOR currently being 3%).

A's current cashflow on the swap is positive, A pays B DM 3.5 million (100 million × .035) and receives DM 8 million (100 million × .08). This looks like a great deal for A, but is it? What would you expect the yield curves for German and U.S. interest rates to look like?

The first reported diff was done by Sallie Mae arranged by Credit Suisse. Sallie Mae issued a $105 million 3 yr floating note in July 1991 with a coupon of DM Libor -160 BP, with all payments in dollars. The initial coupon was 7.90% which was equivalent to U.S. Libor plus 128 bp. Sallie Mae then did a Swap with CS in which Sallie Mae paid CS U.S. Libor—for DM Libor -160 BP. What was Sallie Mae trying to accomplish?

Is a Diff more or less risky than the plain vanilla swaps? Consider the problems that a dealer in diffs might have in hedging its exposure, as described in Mark Palsey, "The Last Piece of the Jigsaw," Euromoney (November 1993), pp. 29–31.

. . .

Diffs are easy to describe and almost impossible to hedge. The swap writer undertakes to receive Libor in one currency, usually dollars, and to pay Libor in another currency with that payment stream denominated in dollars. This creates two correlation problems.

First, the dealer is exposed to the correlation between the two Libors. This can be avoided relatively easily using a pair of interest rate swaps, by buying bonds or using futures or FRAS.

Second, there is the correlation between interest rates and FX rates. Suppose the swap writer is paying Deutschmark Libor in dollars and receiving dollar Libor. He is funding the Deutschmark Libor payout through the Deutschmark swap market, so even if interest rates remain the same he is exposed to the risk that the dollar will strengthen leaving him short of Deutschmarks to pay off the dollar liability. Hedging this risk means taking a view on the correlation between interest rates and FX rates.

Does the bank believe that a rise in Deutschmark interest rates will affect the $/Dm rate? If so, exactly how strong is the correlation effect—to what extent does the bank believe that any rise in Deutschmark rates (and so in the amount of money it must pay out to the counterparty) will be compensated for by a strengthening of the Deutschmark against the dollar?

"Customers are basically getting the bank to remove the uncertainty between the relationship of interest rates and currency values, that is to guarantee that movements in European interest rates will have no impact on the value of the currency. The problem we have is that if we take a position to hedge against the most likely scenario, that is that when European rates fall European currencies will weaken, and it doesn't happen, then we lose money," says Ronald Tanemura, a director at Salomon Brothers.

The correlation problem in the case of diffs is particularly acute. A corporate hedger's rationale for using one shows why. Before the ERM meltdown, a corporation with Libor-based sterling liabilities found itself paying interest rates that bore no relationship to the economic environment in which it operated. Treasurers saw that US rates were more obviously tied to the real economy and decided to take advantage of this by opting to swap dollar Libor for sterling Libor in dollars. If the US recession were prolonged, dollar Libor would remain low, while levels of political support for high European interest rates looked strong. The political and economic factors that drive FX and interest rate correlations make those correlations difficult to predict and subject to sudden, extreme movements.

### Need to Quantify

So how do dealers hedge the risk? The simple answer is that they don't. "Correlation risk is essentially unhedgeable," says one trader. "Providers of these products are taking correlation views, over- or under-hedging and basically being optimistic that what is unhedgeable today will be hedgeable in a couple of years." They can overhedge with expensive foreign exchange options, desirable because diff pricing is related to FX volatility and is therefore option-like, or in the interest rate futures markets.

. . .

Further consider the problems of Proctor & Gamble which recently lost $102 million on a diff swap.

## "CORPORATE HEDGING, HARD SOAP"

The Economist (April 16, 1994).

When things go wrong, the first instinct of Americans is often to phone their lawyer. The same holds for American corporations. On April 12th Proctor & Gamble, a consumer-goods maker, grimly announced that it had lost $102m, after tax, on two interest-rate swaps. Edwin Artzt, P & G's chairman, said he was considering suing Bankers Trust (BT), the bank that had sold it the loss-making swaps, on the ground that these instruments were inappropriate for managing his firm's interest-rate risk.

They were: the swaps bought by P & G about a year ago ("diff" swaps in traders' jargon) are complex even by the standards of that most arcane of markets. They were based on the hope that German and American three-year interest rates would converge more slowly than the market thought they would. If so, P & G would cash in, having leveraged its bet by as much as ten times. But the bet started to go badly wrong towards the end of 1993. German and American interest rates converged. Every hundredth of a percentage point of that convergence cost P & G about $400,000. Since three-year rates have converged by 2.5%, it is easy to see how P & G lost about $100m.

Whose fault? Certainly diff swaps are inappropriate for most corporations: they are splendid speculations but have nothing to do with hedging. Yet the fault appears to lie with P & G, not the bank which sold it the swaps. P & G has a sophisticated treasury operation and ought to have understood the risks it ran by buying these products. BT claims that it warned P & G to close these positions when they began to sour. On April 12th P & G announced that it had moved its treasurer to pastures new, which suggests that it accepts part of the blame.

Still, BT and other firms that sold these products (among them J.P. Morgan, Swiss Bank Corporation, Merrill Lynch and Credit Suisse Financial Products) may fear that others will have better reason to sue. P & G was not the only company using such products. Less sophisticated companies have also used them, some with exposures leveraged by 20 or even 50 times. A few have used still racier swaps. One ex-BT swapper claims that some companies were foolish enough to use what the market dubs Libor-squared or even Libor-cubed swaps. These pay buyers a lot if interest rates stay low, but bring exponential losses as rates rise. Though BT argues that it carefully explains the risks of such products in advance, few corporate treasurers understand them. And Wall Street firms have earned fat fees pushing such products.

America's companies stand to lose less than the mutual-fund industry from using such products. Although mutual funds are not allowed to leverage the money they have under management, some fund managers have bent this rule by using swaps to try to boost their returns. What would happen to nerves on Wall Street if they were to start calling their lawyers?

---

A new developing area of swaps is credit derivatives. These allow a party to swap LIBOR for LIBOR plus a substantial premium, on a basket of bank loans to single-to-triple B companies (borrowers). The investor gets higher LIBOR, but assumes an increased credit risk. This would be an alternative to selling existing assets generating LIBOR, for a higher yielding portfolio. If a borrower defaults, the investor can either sell the loan in the market, or purchase it from the counterparty, and restructure it. Either way, the swap is terminated. J. Schultz, "Empowering Portfolio Managers," Institutional Investor 143 (February 1994).

7. As of April 1994, generally accepted accounting principles (GAAP) did not directly address accounting issues for swaps. Industry practice is to record the net difference in interest payments on interest rate swaps, and for dealers to mark their positions to market on the balance sheet, and to record changes in market value on the income statement. GAO Report, at 96.

8. The G–30 Derivatives Study, pp. 60–64, concluded that there should not be a lot of concern over the systemic risk that might arise from derivatives activity (including swaps). In particular, it noted that the notional amounts of derivatives overstate the size of the market (only replacement value should be relevant), that the participants understand the complexities, that the markets are not highly concentrated, and that credit risks are less in derivatives than traditional lending (because swap counterparties are generally more creditworthy). Nonetheless, there has been an outcry for more regulation by congressional committees and some regulators. Should we be worried about the risks of swaps? A 1992 ISDA Default Survey, which surveyed swap dealers accounting for over 70% of the market, found that the cumulative losses over the history of the involvement of these firms with swaps was \$358.36 million, or about .011% of the notional amount of swaps outstanding as of December 31, 1991.

## C. CAPITAL REQUIREMENTS FOR SWAPS

A principal way of dealing with the risks of swaps to financial institutions is through capital requirements.

### 1. The Basle Accord: Credit risk

Under the Basle Accord capital rules for credit risk, which we covered in Chapter IV, swaps are dealt with as a special type of off-balance sheet asset. Swaps must first be converted into asset equivalents and are then risk weighted under the normal Basle risk-weight categories, subject to a maximum risk weight of 50%. Thus, a swap with an OECD sovereign would have a 0 percent risk weight, whereas a swap with a private obligor would have a 50 percent risk weight.

The following excerpt describes how the Accord handles the conversion of swaps into asset equivalents.

## H. SCOTT AND S. IWAHARA, IN SEARCH OF A LEVEL PLAYING FIELD: THE IMPLEMENTATION OF THE BASLE ACCORD IN JAPAN AND THE UNITED STATES

49–54 (Group of Thirty, 1994).

The Basle Accord permits countries to use one of two methods in calculating the asset equivalents of these contracts, the original exposure or current exposure method. At the Basle conference Japan strongly pushed to permit countries to use either method. The United States has required banks to use the current exposure method.

Japan, on the other hand, has allowed banks to choose the method if their transaction volume of foreign exchange and interest rate contracts is not large or if they do not have the administrative ability to use the current exposure method. Once a bank has chosen the current exposure method, it cannot switch back to the original exposure method. Only one Japanese bank has chosen the current exposure method in full, and three have chosen it with respect to some kinds of contracts and will choose it in full in the near future. Other Japanese banks, however, have chosen the original exposure method.

We will examine how each of these methods works by using a simple fixed-floating interest rate swap as an example.

Suppose Company A and Company C seek to enter into a fixed-floating rate swap through Intermediary Bank B on the following terms:

| | |
|---|---|
| Notional principal .......... | $10 million |
| Maturity .................. | 3 years |
| Floating index .............. | 6 months LIBOR (currently 8.5%) |
| Floating reset period ........ | Every 6 months |
| Fixed rate .................. | T bill rate + 70 basis points<br>(current T bill rate = 8%) |
| B's profit (spread) .......... | 10 basis points |

This transaction can be diagrammed as follows:

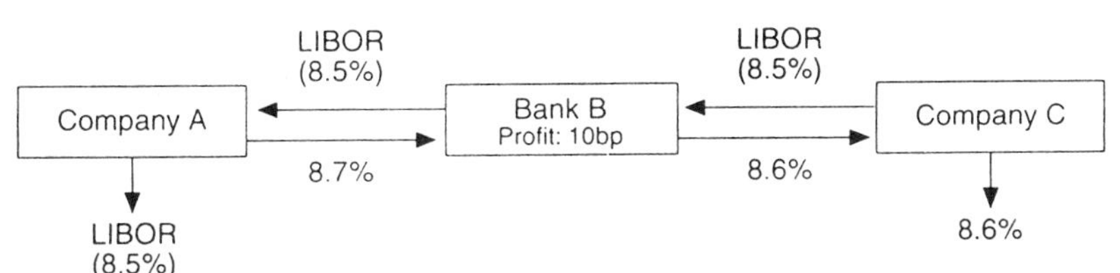


Note that Intermediary Bank B has entered into two independent contracts. Under its contract with Company A, it pays A a floating rate of 8.5 percent and receives a fixed rate of 8.7 percent. Under its contract with Company C, it pays C a fixed rate of 8.6 percent (8.7 – profit of 0.1) and receives a floating rate of 8.5 percent.

Under the Basle original exposure method, a bank must apply the following conversion factors to the notional principal amounts of interest rate contracts (including swaps) to determine their asset equivalents:

| **Maturity** | **Factor** (percent)* |
|---|---|
| Less than one year | 0.5 |
| One year and less than two years | 1.0 |
| Each additional year | 1.0 |

On the date on which these contracts are entered into, each has three years to run. The asset equivalent amount of the two contracts is, thus, \$10,000,000 × .03 × 2, or \$600,000. As prescribed by Basle, and as implemented in both the United States and Japan, this asset equivalent is then risk-weighted according to the appropriate risk-weight category, but with a weight no greater than 50 percent. Since these swaps are with private companies, the risk-weight would be 50 percent (the normal risk-weight for private sector credit is 100 percent). Thus, these two contracts would generate risk-weighted assets of \$300,000, or a capital requirement of \$24,000 (\$300,000 × .08). After the contracts have been held for a year, regardless of changes in the market rates of interest, the capital requirement in Japan remains the same because original maturities must be used.

Under the current exposure method, the conversion process has two steps. First, a bank marks to market the replacement cost of contracts with a positive value (in the money). This reflects the cost the bank

* The Basle Committee on Banking Supervision has proposed a new matrix, Basle Capital Accord, the Treatment of the Credit Risks associated with Certain Off–Balance–Sheet Items, Annex 3 (1994), for interest rate and other swaps, as follows:

| **Maturity** | **Interest rate contracts** | **Exchange rate contracts** |
|---|---|---|
| Less than one year | 0.3B% | 1.5% |
| One year and less than two years | 0.75% | 3.75% (i.e. 1.5% + 2.25%) |
| For each additional year | 0.75% | 2.25% |

would incur if it entered into a new swap on the same terms. Second, the bank calculates the potential future credit exposure on the contract based on its residual maturity. This calculation reflects the potential risk of loss from counterparty default. Contracts with a residual maturity of less than one year are deemed to have no future exposure; contracts with one year and over are deemed to have 0.5 percent risk. The asset equivalent amount is the sum of these two calculations: replacement cost plus future exposure.

On the date on which these contracts are entered into, there is no replacement cost—they are entered into at market prices. Since both contracts are for one year and over, the asset equivalent amount of the two contracts is \$10,000,000 × .005 × 2, or \$100,000. The two contracts would generate risk-weighted assets of \$50,000 (\$100,000 × .50), and a capital requirement of \$4,000 (\$50,000 × .08).

Suppose that at the end of one year, interest rates have increased so that Bank B would now have to pay Company D a fixed rate of 8.95 percent to get a six-month LIBOR floating rate, if Company C defaulted.

. . .

In this situation, Bank B would have a loss of 0.25 percent of \$10,000,000, or \$25,000 for each of the two remaining years on the two contracts, the difference between receiving a fixed rate from A of 8.70 percent and paying a fixed rate to D of 8.95 percent. This loss would be discounted to present value using an appropriate discount rate derived from interest rate yield curves for each of the two one-year periods remaining on the contract. If one assumed a flat yield curve at 9 percent for each period, the replacement cost would be \$43,978. The potential future exposure, \$100,000, would be unchanged since the two contracts have two years to run. The credit equivalent amount would be the sum of replacement cost and future exposure, \$143,978, and the cost of capital would be \$5,759 (\$143,978 × .50 × .08).

The comparative cost of capital under the two methods is as follows:

| | **Original exposure** | **Future exposure** |
|---|---|---|
| Contract date | \$24,000 | \$4,000 |
| One year later | \$24,000 | \$5,759 |

Some general points can be made about the two methods. First, the original exposure method is always more expensive than the current exposure method on the swap contract date for swaps with a maturity of over one year, given the original exposure conversion rate of 1 percent compared with the future exposure conversion rate of 0.5 percent. For swaps of one year or less, the cost is the same, given the same 0.5 percent conversion rate. Second, under the current exposure method no capital is required against replacement value when the swap has a negative value (out of the money); only 0.5 percent capital is required for future exposure. However, under the original exposure method, more than 0.5 percent capital is always required, regardless of whether the swap is in or out of the money.

Over the life of the swap, the comparison between the two methods depends on the maturities of the swap portfolio and possible changes in interest rates. Table 9 compares the capital cost of a matched $10 million notional amount swap at an original fixed rate of 8 percent, under the two methods, with various assumptions about original and remaining maturities, and about changes in interest rates at the end of one year. Present value calculations are made by discounting all future losses at either 5 percent or 10 percent.

**Table 9. Capital Required for Swap Contracts, Original and Current Exposure**

Dollars

| Change and original maturity (years) | Original exposure | Current exposure: Remaining maturity (years) 1 | 2 | 3 | 4 |
|---|---|---|---|---|---|
| | | **5 percent discount rate** | | | |
| **1 percent** | | | | | |
| 2 | 16,000 | 7,810 | .. | .. | .. |
| 3 | 24,000 | 7,810 | 11,438 | .. | .. |
| 4 | 32,000 | 7,810 | 11,438 | 14,893 | .. |
| 5 | 40,000 | 7,810 | 11,438 | 14,893 | 18,194 |
| **2 percent** | | | | | |
| 2 | 16,000 | 11,619 | .. | .. | .. |
| 3 | 24,000 | 11,619 | 18,875 | .. | .. |
| 4 | 32,000 | 11,619 | 18,875 | 25,875 | .. |
| 5 | 40,000 | 11,619 | 18,875 | 25,875 | 32,368 |
| **3 percent** | | | | | |
| 2 | 16,000 | 15,429 | .. | .. | .. |
| 3 | 24,000 | 15,429 | [26,313] | .. | .. |
| 4 | 32,000 | 15,429 | 26,313 | [36,679] | .. |
| 5 | 40,000 | 15,429 | 26,313 | 36,679 | [46,551] |
| | | **10 percent discount rate** | | | |
| **1 percent** | | | | | |
| 2 | 16,000 | 7,636 | .. | .. | .. |
| 3 | 24,000 | 7,636 | 10,942 | .. | .. |
| 4 | 32,000 | 7,636 | 10,942 | 13,947 | .. |
| 5 | 40,000 | 7,636 | 10,942 | 13,947 | 16,679 |
| **2 percent** | | | | | |
| 2 | 16,000 | 11,273 | .. | .. | .. |
| 3 | 24,000 | 11,273 | 17,884 | .. | .. |
| 4 | 32,000 | 11,273 | 17,884 | 23,895 | .. |
| 5 | 40,000 | 11,273 | 17,884 | 23,895 | 29,359 |
| **3 percent** | | | | | |
| 2 | 16,000 | 14,909 | .. | .. | .. |
| 3 | 24,000 | 14,909 | [24,826] | .. | .. |
| 4 | 32,000 | 14,909 | 24,826 | [33,842] | .. |
| 5 | 40,000 | 14,909 | 24,826 | 33,842 | [42,038] |

**Note**: Highlight indicates current exposure is larger than original exposure.

Table 9 shows that the original exposure method would be less expensive, in terms of capital, when the change in interest rates after one year of a contract is 3 percentage points or more, for contracts with remaining maturities of two years or more, assuming a discount rate of either 5 percent or 10 percent.

. . .

---

Looking at our interest rate swap paradigm (first note 1 above), the capital requirements for Bank A under the current exposure method (assuming the notional amount was 1000), at inception, would be (1000 x .005) x .50 = 2.5, or .25% of the notional amount. Of course, if the swap went into the money the capital charge would increase by the amount of the positive value times the 50% risk weight.

## 2. Basle Accord: Market Risk Proposals

Under the new Basle market risk proposals, *The Prudential Supervision of Netting, Market Risks and Interest Rate Risk* (1993), capital will be required for the market risk on interest rate and currency swaps as part of the general capital requirements for market risk.

### a. Debt Securities and Interest Rate Swaps

Interest rate swaps are dealt with in connection with market risk for debt securities. The requirements only apply to debt securities (including interest rate swaps) on a bank's trading book. These are a bank's proprietary positions "which are taken on with the intention of benefiting in the short term from actual or expected differences between their buying and selling prices or hedging other elements of the trading book, or which are held for short-term resale, or in order to execute a trade with a customer." Consultative proposal by the Basle Committee on Banking Supervision, *The Supervisory Treatment of Market Risks* 6 (1993) (Market Risk Proposal). The proposal would, nonetheless, "allow banks to exclude from their trading books derivative products which are taken on explicitly to hedge positions on the banking book." *Id.* To the extent swaps were considered to be on the trading book, the market risk capital requirements would replace the current Basle requirements for credit risk. Swaps on the banking book would continue to be governed by the current requirements and would not be subject to an additional charge for market risk.

The proposals for debt securities are, like the proposals for equities examined in Chapter IV, based on a building block approach, in which the specific risk of the instrument (related to the issuer) and the general risk of the market (movement of interest rates) are separately taken into account. However, interest rate swaps would not be subject to a specific risk charge. The proposal states that "the majority of interest-rate sensitive off-balance-sheet instruments relate to an underlying or notional underlying security which does not bear an identifiable specific risk, e.g. currencies or market interest rates." Id., at 25. Thus, swaps would be treated like government securities, as having no specific market risk.

The capital requirements for debt securities depend on the maturities of the obligation and the coupon rate. Swaps would be treated as two notional positions with the relevant maturities. "Fixed-rate instruments would be allocated according to the residual term to maturity and floating-rate instruments according to the next repricing date." Id., at 17. Go back to our interest rate swap paradigm (the transaction in the first note in this Chapter) and assume that the LIBOR swap rate reset every 3 months. At the outset, Bank A would be considered to have a short position (the position it had to pay) in a three month security and a 5 year long position in the fixed rate swap (the position it is paid). Over the 5 years, the fixed rate leg of the swap would decrease in maturity, and the floating rate swap would decrease in maturity every three months, e.g. after the elapse of one month of time, it would be a two-month security, and at the end of three months would again revert to a three-month security.

Swap Bank would not have any position because of its exactly matched book (Swap bank is completely hedged). Close matches might also not require capital, e.g. if the coupons on offsetting fixed rate swaps were within 10–15 basis points of each other, and the maturities of the swaps were close.

Annex 4 of the Market Risk Proposal is set out below:

Debt securities

Sample market risk calculation

| | | | Specific risk | | General market risk | |
|---|---|---|---|---|---|---|
| Time-band | Issuer | Position | Weight (%) | Charge | Weight (%) | Charge |
| 0– 1 mo. | Treasury | 5,000 | 0.00 | 0.00 | 0.00 | 0.00 |
| 1– 3 mos | Treasury | 5,000 | 0.00 | 0.00 | 0.20 | 10.00 |
| 3– 6 mos | Qual Corp | 4,000 | 0.25 | 10.00 | 0.40 | 16.00 |
| 6–12 mos | Qual Corp | (7,500) | 1.00 | 75.00 | 0.70 | (52.50) |
| 1– 2 yrs | Treasury | (2,500) | 0.00 | 0.00 | 1.25 | (31.25) |
| 2– 3 yrs | Treasury | 2,500 | 0.00 | 0.00 | 1.75 | 43.75 |
| 3– 4 yrs | Treasury | 2,500 | 0.00 | 0.00 | 2.25 | 56.25 |
| 3– 4 yrs | Qual Corp | (2,000) | 1.60 | 32.00 | 2.25 | (45.00) |
| 4– 5 yrs | Treasury | 1,500 | 0.00 | 0.00 | 2.75 | 41.25 |
| 5– 7 yrs | Qual Corp | (1,000) | 1.60 | 16.00 | 3.25 | (32.50) |
| 7–10 yrs | Treasury | (1,500) | 0.00 | 0.00 | 3.75 | (56.25) |
| 10–15 yrs | Treasury | (1,500) | 0.00 | 0.00 | 4.50 | (67.50) |
| 10–15 yrs | Non Qual | 1,000 | 8.00 | 80.00 | 4.50 | 45.00 |
| 15–20 yrs | Treasury | 1,500 | 0.00 | 0.00 | 5.25 | 78.75 |
| > 20 yrs | Qual Corp | 1,000 | 1.60 | 16.00 | 6.00 | 60.00 |
| Specific risk | | | | 229.00 | | |
| Residual general market risk | | | | | | 66.00 |

How would the paradigm swap be dealt with (assuming it was on the trading book)? The 100 million fixed rate 5 year leg would at the outset be like a 4–5 year Treasury security with a market risk weight of 2.75. This risk weight is generated from the Annex 2 risk weight table below:

## ANNEX 2

Debt securities: risk weights

The table below sets out the general risk weights which are proposed for the net open positions (long or short) in each time-band under the standard method described in paragraphs 13 to 19 of Section 2.

| Coupon 3% or more | Coupon less than 3% | Duration weight (A) | Assumed change in yields (B) | Risk weight (A) × (B) |
|---|---|---|---|---|
| up to 1 mo. | up to 1 mo. | 0.00 | 1.00 | 0.00% |
| 1 to 3 mos | 1 to 3 mos | 0.20 | 1.00 | 0.20% |
| 3 to 6 mos | 3 to 6 mos | 0.40 | 1.00 | 0.40% |
| 6 to 12 mos | 6 to 12 mos | 0.70 | 1.00 | 0.70% |
| 1 to 2 yrs | 1.0 to 1.9 yrs | 1.40 | 0.90 | 1.25% |
| 2 to 3 yrs | 1.9 to 2.8 yrs | 2.20 | 0.80 | 1.75% |
| 3 to 4 yrs | 2.8 to 3.6 yrs | 3.00 | 0.75 | 2.25% |
| 4 to 5 yrs | 3.6 to 4.3 yrs | 3.65 | 0.75 | 2.75% |
| 5 to 7 yrs | 4.3 to 5.7 yrs | 4.65 | 0.70 | 3.25% |
| 7 to 10 yrs | 5.7 to 7.3 yrs | 5.80 | 0.65 | 3.75% |
| 10 to 15 yrs | 7.3 to 9.3 yrs | 7.50 | 0.60 | 4.50% |
| 15 to 20 yrs | 9.3 to 10.6 yrs | 8.75 | 0.60 | 5.25% |
| over 20 yrs | 10.6 to 12 yrs | 10.00 | 0.60 | 6.00% |
| | 12 to 20 yrs | 13.50 | 0.60 | 8.00% |
| | over 20 yrs | 21.00 | 0.60 | 12.50% |

| Calculation of capital charge | Charge |
|---|---|
| 1. Specific Risk | 229.00 |

2. Vertical offsets WITHIN SAME TIME-BANDS

| Time-band | Longs | Shorts | Residual * | Offset | Disallowance | Charge |
|---|---|---|---|---|---|---|
| 3–4 yrs | 56.25 | (45.00) | 11.25 | 45.00 | 10.00% | 4.50 |
| 10–15 yrs | 45.00 | (67.50) | (22.50) | 45.00 | 10.00% | 4.50 |

3. Horizontal offsets WITHIN SAME TIME-ZONES

| | Longs | Shorts | Residual * | Offset | Disallowance | Charge |
|---|---|---|---|---|---|---|
| Zone 1 | | | | | | |
| 0–1 mo. | 0.00 | | | | | |
| 1–3 mos | 10.00 | | | | | |
| 3–6 mos | 16.00 | | | | | |
| 6–12 mos | | (52.50) | | | | |
| Total Zone 1 | 26.00 | (52.50) | (26.50) | 26.00 | 40.00% | 10.40 |
| Zone 2 | | | | | | |
| 1–2 yrs | | (31.25) | | | | |
| 2–3 yrs | 43.75 | | | | | |
| 3–4 yrs | 11.25 | | | | | |
| Total Zone 2 | 55.00 | (31.25) | 23.75 | 31.25 | 30.00% | 9.38 |

| | Longs | Shorts | Residual * | Offset | Disallowance | Charge |
|---|---|---|---|---|---|---|
| Zone 3 | | | | | | |
| 4–5 yrs | 41.25 | | | | | |
| 5–7 yrs | | (32.50) | | | | |
| 7–10 yrs | | (56.25) | | | | |
| 10–15 yrs | | (22.50) | | | | |
| 15–20 yrs | 78.75 | | | | | |
| > 20 yrs | 60.00 | | | | | |
| Total Zone 3 | 180.00 | (111.25) | 68.75 | 111.25 | 30.00% | 33.38 |

4. Horizontal offsets BETWEEN TIME–ZONES

| | Longs | Shorts | Residual * | Offset | Disallowance | Charge |
|---|---|---|---|---|---|---|
| Zone 1 & Zone 2 | 23.75 | (26.50) | (2.75) | 23.75 | 40.00% | 9.50 |
| Zone 1 & Zone 3 | 68.75 | (2.75) | 66.00 | 2.75 | 150.00% | 4.12 |

5. Total capital charge

| | |
|---|---|
| Specific risk | 229.00 |
| Vertical disallowances | 9.00 |
| Horizontal disallowances | |
| (offsets within same time-zones) | 53.16 |
| (offsets between time-zones) | 13.62 |
| Residual general market risk after all offsets | 66.00 |
| Total | 370.78 |

* Residual amount carried forward for additional offsetting as appropriate.

## Risk–Weights

The proposal describes the derivation of these weights as follows: "The first stage in the proposed calculation would be to weight the positions in each time-band by a factor designed to reflect the price sensitivity of those positions to changes in interest rates. The weights proposed have two components: the modified duration [duration divided by a factor of one plus the interest rate] of a bond with a maturity equal to the mid-point of the respective time band, assuming an 8% interest rate environment and an 8% coupon [2]; and an assumed change in yield which is designed to cover about two standard deviations of one month's yield volatility in most major markets." Id., at 17. A footnote explains that since in most countries long-term rates are less volatile than short-term rates, the volatility protection sought diminishes progressively with lengthening maturities. Thus, short-term instruments assume a volatility of one percent, while long-term instruments assume a volatility of .60 percent. On the other hand, longer term maturities have a higher duration risk, since a given change in interest rates has more impact on the price of a longer term instrument, due to the need to discount a longer period of cash flows. These duration weights range from 0 to 21.[3]

**2.** The assumption of an 8% interest rate environment only appears important to dealing with zero-coupon or deep-discount bonds, column 2 in Annex 2. The proposal generally treats these kinds of instruments as having more market risk. Obviously in a lower rate environment, this added risk would have to be recalculated.

**3.** The Committee entertained the possibility that sophisticated institutions could use a more accurate measure of measuring duration by calculating the price sensitivity of each position separately if those who use it "demonstrate that it produces results which are consistently equivalent with the standard method." Id., at 20. However,

Notice that one set of volatility weights is used for interest rates on instruments denominated in different currencies, even though separate charge calculations ("reporting ladders") must be made for instruments in different currencies. With respect to the latter requirement, the proposal states: "It is recognized that such treatment would be rather harsh since it assumes a worst-case scenario in the movement of interest rates in different currencies. On the other hand, the purpose of the proposals is to provide protection against movements in interest rates over relatively short periods and while some correlation across currencies is observable circumstances quite frequently occur in which interest rates in different countries move in opposite directions." Id., at 20.

In our paradigm example, let's look at Bank A's position, assuming that the swap was for 1000 rather than for $100 million. In the calculation of residual market risk in Annex 4, the fixed rate swap leg (the long) would generate a charge of 27.50, 2.75% of the notional amount, and the floating rate swap leg (the short) would generate a charge of (2.00), .20% of the notional amount. The overall net charge (before offsets) for the swap position would be 25.50 (netting the long position against the short one), or 2.55% of the notional amount. In the Annex 4 example, it would increase the Residual general market risk from 66.00 to 91.50.

The next step of the analysis, as reflected in Annex 4, is vertical and horizontal offsets. Let's start with vertical offsets.

## Vertical Offsets

The idea behind vertical offsets is to deal with the problem that the calculation of residual market risk assumed that the interest rate sensitivity of every instrument within one of the 13 time bands was the same, even though different instruments within the same time band will not react uniformly to changes in interest rates. For this reason, the Committee did not want to fully allow longs to offset shorts, and therefore applies a "vertical disallowance factor" of 10% to the smaller of the long or short position.

In Annex 4, this disallowance is applied to both the 3–4 and 10–15 year time bands where there are both long and short positions. Thus, for the 3–4 year time band, where the charge for the short position of (45.00) is smaller than the charge for the long position, 56.25, it becomes the offset, and generates an additional charge of 4.50, 10% of 45. Our swap has just increased the charge for the long positions in the 4–5 time band and therefore requires no vertical offset. However, in the 1–3 months time band, we now have a short position charge of (2.00) generated by the swap to go along with the existing 10 charge on the long. Since (2.00) is the smaller, there would be an additional vertical offset of .20, 10% of 2.

this latitude is limited only to the duration weights.

**Horizontal Offsets**

The idea behind horizontal offsets is to limit the netting between time zones in the calculation of residual market risk (the first calculation). In getting the 66 residual general market risk charge, shorts in one time band were netted off against longs in another time band. The Market Risk Proposal, id. at 19, handles that problem, as follows:

. . .

Observed correlations suggest that the likelihood of divergent movements is lower for nearer segments of the yield curve and higher for more distant segments. It is therefore proposed that there should be two rounds of partial "horizontal" offsetting, first between the net positions in each of the three zones (zero to one year, one year to four years and over four years), and subsequently between the net positions in the different zones. At each stage, the offsetting of opposite positions would be subject to a disallowance (expressed, in the same way as the vertical disallowance, as a fraction of the smaller of the offsetting positions), based on observed correlations of interest rate movements. The disallowances proposed ... would result in a greater recognition of hedging for offsets taking place within the same zone than for offsets between different zones. The resulting disallowances would be added to the disallowances for vertical offsetting referred to above, and to the absolute amount of the residual net short or long position within the whole book.

---

Let's take the first offset, horizontal offsets within the same time zones. Our swap has increased the shorts in Zone 1 to (54.50) but does not lead to any additional charge, because the longs are less than the shorts. Our swap has increased the longs in Zone 3 by 27.50 to 207.50, but again there is no impact because the disallowance is applied to the smaller short position. Notice that the disallowance factor is higher in Zone 1 (40%) than in Zones 2 or 3. This seems to be because rates are believed to be more volatile, or rates on different instruments within the Zone are believed to be less correlated, in the shorter Zone 1 maturities.

Let's now take the second offset, horizontal offsets between time zones. Before taking the swap into account, Zone 1 has an overall short position of (26.50) (also the Zone 1 residual) and Zone 2 has an overall long position of 23.75 (also the Zone 2 residual). This produces an offset of 23.75, the smaller long position, and a charge of 9.50 (40% of 23.75). The same type of calculation is performed for Zones 1 and 3. Zone 3 has an overall 68.75 long. Zone 2's position is now considered net of the offset against Zone 1, or short (2.75). This is the residual produced by the first offset between Zones 1 and 2. The offset is 2.75, the smaller position, and the charge is 4.12 (150% of 2.75). Larger disallowances are set where positions between more distant time zones have been offset, 1 and 3 (150%) compared to 1 and 2 (40%).

The short leg of our swap with a charge of (2.00) will increase the Zone 1 residual to (28.50) and the long leg of our swap with a charge of 27.50 will increase the Zone 3 residual to 96.25 (68.75 + 27.50). This will not result in any increased charge in the Zone 1 and 2 calculation since the long position is still the smallest, but it does increase the Zone 1 and 2 residual to short (4.75)—(23.75 − (28.50)).

There will be an increase in the Zone 1 and 3 calculation. The Zone 3 residual or longs (its the same) is increased to 96.25 as against the Zone 1 residual of (4.75). The disallowance is applied against the smaller (4.75) to produce a charge of 7.13, as compared with the original charge of 4.12. The swaps thus increase the offset charge by 3.01.

The total capital charge, taking account of the swap, is therefore:

| | Swaps | All Debt Securities |
|---|---|---|
| Specific Risk | 0.00 | 229.00 |
| Vertical disallowances | .20 | 9.20 |
| Horizontal disallowances | | |
| (offsets within same time zones) | 0.00 | 53.16 |
| (offsets between time zones) | 3.01 | 16.63 |
| Residual general market risk | 25.50 | 91.50 |
| Total | 28.71 | 399.49 |

The 28.71 swap charge represents about 2.9% of the 1000 notional amount of the swap. Recall that under the existing credit risk approach the charge for the swap would have been .25%. This comparison only holds true at the inception of the swap. The .25% credit risk charge can increase if the swap has positive value, and the market risk charge will decrease over the life of the fixed rate swap leg. Nonetheless, it would appear that the market risk requirements are significantly more onerous than the credit risk ones.

(b) Foreign Exchange Positions and Currency Swaps

Happily, the approach to capital for foreign exchange positions is less complicated. The bank first calculates its net open currency position in each currency. On a currency swap, the bank would be short on the currency it must deliver and long on the currency it will receive at the end of the swap. Thus, a U.S. bank that had swapped $40 million for ¥5 billion would be long the dollars and short the yen.

The amount of the bank's net position in each currency is then converted at current spot rates into the bank's reporting currency, i.e. dollars for a U.S. bank. Under the "shorthand" method, the capital charge would be 8% of the higher of its long or short positions. Alternatively, a bank can use a simulation method—"actual exchange rates experienced in a defined past observation period would be used to revalue the bank's present foreign exchange positions and—from those revaluations—to calculate 'simulated' profits and/or losses which would have arisen if those positions had remained fixed for a defined holding period. The capital requirement would be set in relation to the worst or near to the worst simulated loss which would have arisen during that period." Id., at 40.

The Committee points out that policy decisions by national supervisors would have to be taken with respect to four parameters in any simulation: (1) the defined holding period (two weeks is proposed); (2) period of past observation necessary to capture sufficient evidence of currency volatility (five years is proposed); (3) the confidence level required for prediction (95% is proposed); and (4) the "scaling factor." As to the latter, the Committee states, id. at 42:

. . .

The final step is to select the *scaling factor* which determines the toughness of the capital requirement. The first three parameters having been fixed, adding to the 95% quantile a scaling factor of somewhere between 2% and 4% of the overall net open position as measured under the shorthand method, would deliver approximate equivalence in terms of toughness of the capital requirement for a portfolio of average riskiness between the shorthand and the simulation methods. The Committee is continuing to test bank portfolios to help it come to a final view, but at present inclines towards 3%. Setting the scaling factor in this way would mean that the minimum capital requirement would never be less than 3%.

---

Note that the bank would have to have adequate capital to cover any losses predicted by its model *plus* 3%.

### *Notes and Questions*

1. Assuming the market proposals are implemented, how will a bank know whether a swap is subject to the credit risk or market risk rules? Does it make sense to talk about swaps being part of a bank's trading book?

2. How would you evaluate the credit rules for capital?

(a) The rules for future exposure use a coefficient of 0.5 for all interest rate swaps without regard to the currency of the notional amount (the same is true for volatilities for debt securities under the market risk proposal). Does this make sense?

(b) In the example used from the Scott and Iwahara article, Swap Bank is considered to have two separate swap positions, each generating a capital charge. Does that make sense?

(c) As Table 2 from the Simons study shows, the timing of the peak exposure for different swaps varies with their maturities. Do the credit rules take this into account?

(d) Should the credit rules for diff swaps be the same as for other interest rate swaps?

3. How would you evaluate the market rules for capital?

(a) The market rules for debt securities appear to generate higher capital requirements than do the credit rules. Does this make sense?

(b) Will it be difficult to tell whether a swap on the trading book is hedging a position on the banking book? How would one go about figuring this out?

(c) Various parameters are used by the Committee with respect to debt securities (including interest rate swaps) to calculate risk-weights and disallowances. How would we decide whether they were correct? Would it be better to follow the approach the Committee has taken with respect to foreign exchange risk—allow the banks to use their own models subject to supervisory approval? Would a more discretionary approach raise competitive problems? Mr. William McDonough, president of the New York Federal Reserve Bank, has stated that a "models-based approach" would be "a major step for the international supervisory community." Tracy Corrigan, Searching For Consensus on Risk Assessment, Financial Times (June 23, 1994). Part of the problem of using this approach is the need to evaluate models, and the limited ability of regulators to do so. One difficulty in using outside expertise is the fact that market participants consider such models as proprietary, viewing their ability to measure and control risk as part of their overall competitive capacity.

(d) Why should there be a 3% add-on for foreign exchange risk?

4. Should market risk capital requirements focus on the risk of specific instruments, like debt securities or swaps, or instead look at the portfolio risk of all of a bank's assets? How would these two approaches be different?

5. If swap capital requirements become too onerous for banks, won't the business just go elsewhere, e.g., insurance companies or industrial companies' subsidiaries. Note that the European Union's Capital Adequacy Directive (CAD) applies methodology similar to Basle to European banks (and their securities affiliates) but that U.S. and Japanese securities firms, not affiliated with banks, are not covered by Basle or CAD.

---

## D. ENFORCEABILITY ISSUES

The following excerpt from the G–30 Derivatives Study, pp. 45–48, discusses major issues regarding the enforceability of swap contracts.

## Five Main Enforceability Risks

Five main enforceability risks can occur at different stages of an OTC derivatives transaction.

## Contract Formation: The Statute of Frauds

*Background* Due to the growth over the last 10 years in derivatives activity, documentation often was delayed—a problem that dealers identified as documentation "backlog." In the early days of derivatives, documentation backlog became commonplace. Some transactions went undocumented for long periods of time. The issue thus arose whether an oral agreement made prior to a signed writing represented a binding contract. This created a legal risk that a counterparty with unrealized losses could disaffirm the transaction before a writing was executed.

. . .

*Survey Results* It is reassuring to learn from the Survey that documentation backlog is not nearly as severe a problem as it once was. Among dealers, the most common area of "little concern" (as compared to "some concern" or "serious concern") is the risk of undertaking transactions without subsequently being able to complete documentation. Dealers and end-users also were asked to characterize documentation backlog. Among dealers, 5% say *severe* backlog is getting better, 4% say it has stayed the same and none says it has become worse; 49% say *moderate* backlog is getting better, 19% say it has stayed the same and 4% say it has become worse. Among end-users, 6% say *severe* backlog is getting better, 1% say it has stayed the same and 3% say it has become worse; 22% say *moderate* backlog is getting better, 14% say it has stayed the same and none says it has become worse.

## Capacity

*Background* Major corporations, financial institutions, governmental entities, insurance companies, pension funds, and others use derivatives transactions to manage financial risk. Transactions with major corporations and financial institutions do not create capacity issues as frequently as do transactions with the other entities named above. Specifically, the issue that may arise in relation to agreements with a governmental entity, for example, is whether that entity has the capacity to enter into such a transaction or whether the transaction is beyond its capacity (*i.e., ultra vires* ).

The concerns revealed by the Survey with respect to municipalities and sovereigns are undoubtedly the result of the decision of the U.K. House of Lords in the *Hammersmith and Fulham* case decided in January 1991. In that case, the House of Lords restored the judgment of the first instance court, ruling that the London Borough of Hammersmith and Fulham, a local government authority in the United Kingdom that had been an active participant in the market for sterling interest rate derivatives during the mid–1980s, lacked the capacity to enter into those transactions. Therefore, the many swap and related transactions it had entered into were ruled void.

The effect of the ruling of the House of Lords was to render void agreements between over 130 councils and over 75 of the world's largest banks. It involved more than 600 business relationships stretching back as far as 1981.

. . .

*Survey Results* The third most commonly cited serious concern among all dealer respondents is uncertainty over the legal status of transactions with certain counterparties. Dealers also were asked the extent of their concern with respect to various counterparties. The entities causing "serious concern" are municipalities (41%), followed by sovereigns (10%), and pension funds (9%). The three entities most commonly causing "some concern" are unit trusts, pension funds, and insurance companies.

## Early Termination: Bankruptcy/Insolvency/Liquidation

*Background* Another area presenting major enforceability concerns is early termination. The specific issue is whether the nondefaulting party to a derivatives master agreement would be able to enforce the provisions entitling it to terminate the agreement and net out or offset termination values and payment amounts (*i.e.,* close-out netting) upon the bankruptcy/insolvency/liquidation of its counterparty. In dealing with a counterparty organized in the United States, participants in the derivatives market once faced an element of uncertainty in assessing the bankruptcy and insolvency risks involved. The risks could vary depending upon the type of counterparty—bank, savings institution, or corporation—with which one was dealing, since each was subject to a separate set of laws and regulations.

The most significant area of concern was that, in a proceeding under the U.S. Bankruptcy Code, termination rights under master swap agreements were subject to an automatic stay. Thus the ability to terminate the master agreement and enforce the close-out netting provisions could be delayed for a long time. Moreover, although it generally was believed that a U.S. bankruptcy court should give effect to essential elements of a master agreement, such as netting of transaction values upon early termination, there was no guarantee that this would be the result. The considerable degree of legal certainty, however, that can be achieved in this area is illustrated by legislative amendments and new legislation that have been adopted in certain jurisdictions, including the United States.

*Survey Results* Netting remains a persistent concern among derivatives dealers as illustrated by the Survey. Both areas of serious concern receiving the greatest response rate involve netting: 43% of all dealers state that the enforceability of netting provisions in the jurisdiction(s) of the counterparty in the event of default caused them "serious concern," and 19% state that the difficulty in achieving a high degree of cross-product counterparty exposure netting through master agreements causes such concern.

Close-out netting is the most common form of netting (as opposed to netting by novation) for various derivatives transactions. The Survey asked dealers for what products they use close-out netting. In response, 80% say interest rate derivatives (excluding FRAs) (compared with 30% of dealers using netting by novation), 68% say currency derivatives (excluding foreign exchange forwards and options) (compared with 18% of dealers using netting by novation), and 34% say forward rate agreements (compared with 15% of dealers using netting by novation).

### Multibranch Netting Arrangements

Banks use multibranch master agreements to "book" individual derivatives transactions through any branch designated in the agreement. The use of such master agreements involves a netting issue that has not received sufficient attention from participants and regulators: whether upon the insolvency of a counterparty, parties to a multibranch master agreement can terminate that agreement and net across branches to achieve one net amount owed by or to a counterparty.

The Survey asked dealers and end-users if they typically allow their counterparties to contract as a multibranch party. In response, 88% of all dealers and 38% of all end-users say they are open-minded about this issue; 5% of dealers and 22% of end-users say only if their counterparties insist; and 5% of dealers and 35% of end-users say they do not allow this. This suggests that multibranch master agreements may be used more than occasionally.

### Legality/Enforceability of Derivatives Transactions

In some jurisdictions, issues exist relating to the legality or enforceability of derivatives transactions generally. Brazil, Canada, Japan, and Singapore each indicates that issues exist whether swaps or other derivatives transactions could be deemed gambling contracts, and thus illegal or unenforceable. In Australia, it is a recognized concern that a derivatives contract may be classified as a gaming or wagering contract and thus invalid, because the state and territory legislation does not define the terms "gaming" or "wagering."

. . .

---

In the United States, all "futures contracts" must be executed on an exchange designated by the Commodities Futures Trading Commission (CFTC). Recently, the CFTC, using authority given to it under the Futures Trading Practices Act of 1992, exempted swaps from the exchange trading requirement. CFTC, Exemption for Certain Swap Agreements, 58 Fed.Reg. 5587 (January 22, 1993).

The remainder of the material focuses on the validity of netting, the most important of the enforceability issues.

## 1. Netting and Bankruptcy

### a. Cherry Picking

The following Memorandum describes how the U.S. has handled the bankruptcy issue.

Cravath, Swaine & Moore, Memorandum for the International Swaps and Derivatives Association, Inc., "Over-the-Counter Derivatives Transactions: Netting Under the U.S. Bankruptcy Code, FIRREA and FDICIA" (December 20, 1993).

This memorandum examines the treatment under the United States Bankruptcy Code (the "Bankruptcy Code"),[1] the Financial Institutions Reform, Recovery, and Enforcement Act of 1989 ("FIRREA")[2] and the Federal Deposit Insurance Corporation Improvement Act of 1991 ("FDICIA")[3] of over-the-counter derivatives transactions ("Transactions") that are documented under an ISDA Master Agreement.

. . .

**B. Background**

In structuring a contractual relationship, parties will often negotiate an ISDA Master Agreement that is structured as a complete contract containing payment provisions, representations, agreements, events of default, termination events, provisions for early termination, methods for calculating termination payments and other provisions. An ISDA Master Agreement may cover multiple Transactions, the economic terms of which are documented in separate confirmations exchanged between the parties and which each constitutes a supplement or amendment to the relevant ISDA Master Agreement. Accordingly, participants in the derivatives markets might include within one ISDA Master Agreement, for example, interest rate swaps, currency swaps, equity index swaps, as well as Physically Settled Transactions.

. . .

The ISDA Master Agreements provide that on each payment date all amounts otherwise owing in the same currency under the same Transaction are netted so that only a single amount is owed in that currency. The ISDA Master Agreements also provide, if the parties so elect, for such netting of amounts in the same currency among all Transactions identified as being subject to such election that have common payment dates and booking offices. *See* Section 2 of the ISDA Master Agreements. The obligation of each party to make scheduled payments or deliveries with respect to the Transactions is subject to the conditions that (i) no event of default in respect of the other party (including,

**1.** 11 U.S.C. § 101 *et seq.*

**2.** Pub.L. No. 101–73, 103 Stat. 183 (1989).

**3.** Pub.L. No. 102–242, 105 Stat. 2236 (1991).

without limitation, a payment or delivery default) has occurred and continues and (ii) no early termination date has occurred or been designated. *See* Section 2(a) of the ISDA Master Agreements. The failure by a party to make a payment or delivery with respect to any Transaction or the insolvency of that party constitutes an event of default under the ISDA Master Agreements as it relates to all Transactions. *See* Sections 5(a)(i) and (vii) of the ISDA Master Agreements. Finally, the default-based termination of any other specified derivatives transactions between the parties constitutes an event of default under the ISDA Master Agreements. *See* Section 5(a)(v) of the ISDA Master Agreements.

. . .

In the event of a default-based termination, the ISDA Master Agreements provide for a lump-sum amount (reflecting the positive or negative values of all Transactions) to be calculated on the early termination date (commonly referred to as "close-out netting").

. . .

The ISDA Master Agreements also require the parties to elect between the "First Method" of calculating termination payments and the "Second Method". Under the First Method, in the case of an event of default, if the lump-sum termination amount is positive, it is paid by the defaulting party to the nondefaulting party, but, if it is negative, no payment is due; the nondefaulting party is not required to make a termination payment to the defaulting party after an event of default. Under the Second Method, if the lump-sum termination amount is a positive number, the defaulting party will pay it to the nondefaulting party; if that amount is a negative number, the nondefaulting party will pay the absolute value of that number to the defaulting party.

. . .

On November 9, 1992, in the case of Drexel Burnham Lambert Products Corp. v. Midland Bank, PLC,[7] Judge Pollack of the U.S. District Court for the Southern District of New York held that "[t]he so-called 'Limited Two–Way Payments Clause' ... is enforceable". This memorandum, however, does not address the enforceability of the First Method (formerly called limited two way payments) or the Second Method (formerly called full two way payments), because resolution of this issue would have no impact upon the conclusions reached herein.

. . .

## IV. "SWAP AGREEMENT" UNDER THE BANKRUPTCY CODE AND FIRREA

### A. Bankruptcy Code

1. ***Background; Definitions.*** On June 25, 1990, legislation amending the Bankruptcy Code to deal expressly with a "swap agreement" was signed into law. The Bankruptcy Code now provides:

7. No. 92 Civ. 3098 (S.D.N.Y. Nov. 9, 1992).

(i) an express exemption from the automatic stay contained in Section 362 to allow non-bankrupt parties to set off any mutual obligations arising under or in connection with any "swap agreement" following a bankruptcy filing and to use any collateral held to satisfy amounts due from the bankrupt party;

(ii) express recognition that parties will be entitled to exercise contractual rights to terminate a "swap agreement" and net or offset termination values and payment amounts under such "swap agreement"; and

(iii) express protection for transfers in good faith under a "swap agreement" against a trustee's power to avoid payments and other transfers made within 90 days (or in some cases one year) prior to a bankruptcy filing.

Under Section 101(56) of the Bankruptcy Code, 11 U.S.C. § 101(56), a "swap participant" is defined as "an entity that, at any time before the filing of the petition, has an outstanding swap agreement with the debtor". Under Section 101(55) of the Bankruptcy Code, 11 U.S.C. § 101(55), "swap agreement" is defined as:

"(A) an agreement (including terms and conditions incorporated by reference therein) which is a rate swap agreement, basis swap, forward rate agreement, commodity swap, interest rate option, forward foreign exchange agreement, rate cap agreement, rate floor agreement, rate collar agreement, currency swap agreement, cross-currency rate swap agreement, currency option, any other similar agreement (including any option to enter into any of the foregoing);

(B) any combination of the foregoing; or

(C) a master agreement for any of the foregoing together with all supplements".

. . .

The definition of "swap agreement" also contemplates that more than one "swap agreement" may be effected under a master agreement such as an ISDA Master Agreement, and clarifies that in such a case, all such agreements taken together will constitute a single "swap agreement". This provision, together with Section 560 of the Bankruptcy Code, 11 U.S.C. § 560, discussed below, should bar any efforts by a trustee to "cherry-pick" among Transactions advantageous to the trustee that fall within the definition of "swap agreement" and that are documented under an ISDA Master Agreement.

**2. *Automatic Stay.*** Section 362(b)(14) of the Bankruptcy Code, 11 U.S.C. § 362(b)(14), creates an exception to the scope of the automatic stay set forth in Section 362(a) of the Bankruptcy Code, 11 U.S.C. § 362(a). This exception permits a swap participant to set off any mutual obligations arising under or in connection with any "swap agreement" or to apply to the satisfaction of such obligations any cash, securities or other property held as collateral or margin. This permits netting of payment amounts at any time, including obligations arising after the filing of the bankruptcy petition. This provision also allows parties holding collateral or margin, or entitled to the benefits of a guarantee, to utilize such credit support, notwithstanding the bankruptcy filing.

In the case of a *conservatorship,* the above applies except that a party to a qualified financial contract will be able to exercise any contractual right to terminate *other than* one based *solely* on the appointment of the conservator (i.e., a "bankruptcy" default provision).

Another important feature of FIRREA is that it expressly provides that neither payments made nor collateral transferred by a depository institution prior to its insolvency, nor any legally enforceable or perfected security interest in any of the assets of the institution, may be avoided by the FDIC (subject to certain exceptions), except where the transferee intended to "hinder, delay, or defraud" the creditors or the receiver or conservator of the institution.

FIRREA distinguishes between the FDIC's power as an insolvency receiver and as a conservator. As receiver, the FDIC has the power to liquidate and wind up the affairs of an institution, while as a conservator, the FDIC has the power to operate the insolvent institution as a going concern. When acting in either capacity, the FDIC generally will have many of the powers of a bankruptcy trustee under the Bankruptcy Code, including the right to repudiate burdensome contracts, to enforce contracts and to assign contracts to another party. FIRREA, however, contains significant limitations on the FDIC's powers with respect to financial contracts meeting the definition of "qualified financial contract".

"Qualified financial contract" is defined to include securities contracts, commodity contracts, forward contracts, repurchase agreements and swap agreements. "Swap agreement" is defined to include rate swap agreements, basis swaps, commodity swaps, forward rate agreements, interest rate futures, interest rate options purchased, forward foreign exchange agreements, rate cap, floor and collar agreements, currency swap agreements, cross-currency rate swap agreements, currency futures, or currency options purchased, or any other similar agreements and any options on the foregoing.

In a manner nearly identical to the definition of "swap agreement" under the Bankruptcy Code, the definition of "swap agreement" under FIRREA includes "any other similar agreement", indicating that it is intended to cover both current and newly developed Transactions that, while not specifically enumerated, share fundamental characteristics with those specified. FIRREA also specifies that a master agreement such as an ISDA Master Agreement that documents Transactions falling within the definition of "swap agreement" together with its supplements will be treated as one "swap agreement".

**2. *Right to Terminate.*** In the case of receivership, FIRREA and the FDIC Statement of Policy on Qualified Financial Contracts (the

"FDIC Policy Statement") provide that a party to a qualified financial contract will be entitled to enforce any contractual right to terminate or liquidate such a contract as a result of the appointment of the receiver one day after such appointment. Again, in the case of a conservatorship, a party to a qualified financial contract may enforce any contractual right to terminate or liquidate, other than one based *solely* on the appointment of the conservator (i.e., a "bankruptcy" default provision).

Where the FDIC is acting as the conservator for a bank or savings institution, the qualified financial contract will continue in effect in accordance with its terms. The FDIC or the Resolution Trust Corporation, a legal entity created by FIRREA and managed by the FDIC, will succeed to the rights and obligations of the bank or savings institution. A party to a qualified financial contract will not be able to terminate the contract as a result of the appointment of the FDIC as conservator, but any default subsequent to this succession, such as failure to make a payment, may result in termination of the contract.

As discussed below, the limitations described above on the ability of a party to utilize a bankruptcy or insolvency default provision do not affect the rights of parties to enforce contractual rights to net out or set off payment values or termination amounts upon any termination of an ISDA Master Agreement. Therefore, these limitations on the right to terminate under FIRREA should not affect the basic evaluation of the credit exposure that exists under a swap agreement or other qualified financial contract.

In addition, Section 553(b)(1) of the Bankruptcy Code, 11 U.S.C. § 553(b)(1), protects the right of a swap participant to exercise rights of set-off by exempting them from a trustee's power to readjust any set-off that takes place during the 90–day period prior to the filing of a petition.

**3. *Right to Terminate and Exercise Netting Provisions.*** Section 560 of the Bankruptcy Code, 11 U.S.C. § 560, preserves a swap participant's contractual right to terminate a "swap agreement" and offset or net out any termination or payment amounts owed under it in the event that the other party to the agreement files a bankruptcy petition or becomes insolvent, or in the event that a trustee or custodian is appointed for the party. A contractual right is defined to include a right arising under common law, under law merchant, or by reason of normal business practice, whether or not the right is evidenced in writing.

One principal effect of this provision is to override Section 365(e) of the Bankruptcy Code, 11 U.S.C. § 365(c), which otherwise generally would prevent a nonbankrupt party from using the bankruptcy filing as a basis for exercising a typical bankruptcy default provision in order to terminate a "swap agreement". Equally important, by permitting a party to "net out any termination values", Section 560 of the Bankruptcy Code, 11 U.S.C. § 560, makes clear that the provisions contained in an ISDA Master Agreement for close-out netting will be enforceable upon termination of a "swap agreement".

**4. *Limitation on Avoiding Powers.*** Section 546(g) of the Bankruptcy Code, 11 U.S.C. § 546(g), limits certain powers of a bankruptcy trustee to reclaim property previously transferred by the debtor. For example, a trustee can ordinarily reclaim property transferred within the 90 days prior to the bankruptcy filing if such transfer constituted a "preference" (*i.e.,* if it enabled a creditor to receive more than it would have been entitled to receive in a liquidation proceeding), Section 546(g) of the Bankruptcy Code, 11 U.S.C. § 546(g), provides that transfers "under a swap agreement, made by or to a swap participant, in connection with a swap agreement", cannot be reclaimed by a bankruptcy trustee, unless such transfer is made with actual intent to hinder or defraud creditors.

Section 548(d)(2) of the Bankruptcy Code, 11 U.S.C. § 548(d)(2), protects transfers of property made in connection with a "swap agreement" from avoidance as fraudulent transfers. The amendment provides that such transfers are deemed to be transfers "for value". As long as such transfers also are made "in good faith", as provided in Section 548(c) of the Bankruptcy Code, 11 U.S.C. § 548(c), they will be exempt from challenge as fraudulent transfers.

## B. FIRREA

On August 9, 1989, FIRREA was signed into law. Among other things, FIRREA significantly revised the powers of the FDIC as the receiver or conservator for an insolvent financial institution and extended its powers to cover almost all banks and savings institutions in the United States.

**1. *Background: Definitions.*** FIRREA provides that, in the case of *receivership,* subject to certain limitations, a party to a qualified financial contract will be entitled to:

(i) exercise any contractual right to terminate or liquidate a qualified financial contract as a result of the appointment of the receiver;

(ii) exercise any rights under any security arrangement relating to any qualified financial contract; and

(iii) exercise any right to "offset or net out any termination value, payment amount or other transfer obligation arising under or in connection with [one] or more [qualified financial contracts]".

. . .

**3. *Netting.*** A key provision of FIRREA expressly addresses the concerns of swap participants over whether netting provisions will be enforced. It protects the rights of parties to swap agreements and other qualified financial contracts to "offset or net out any termination value, payment amount, or other transfer obligation arising under or in connection with [one] or more [qualified financial contracts]". This provision, together with the anti-cherry-picking provisions described below, should ensure that credit exposures to an insolvent institution can be calculated fairly on a net basis as long as the "swap agreement" so provides—an ISDA Master Agreement does so provide.

**4. *Selective Repudiation.*** FIRREA provides that, in any *transfer* of assets of an insolvent institution, the receiver or conservator may not "cherry-pick" among qualified financial contracts between the insolvent institution and any particular counterparty. Instead, if any qualified financial contract with a given counterparty is transferred, all qualified financial contracts with that counterparty must be transferred to the same party (together with all claims relating thereto).

In some circumstances with several separate agreements for qualified financial contracts, there is a risk that a receiver or conservator could (without effecting any transfer of assets) "cherry-pick" by selectively repudiating only disadvantageous qualified financial contracts. If, however, all the Transactions documented under an ISDA Master Agreement fall within the definition of "swap agreement", then selective repudiation will not pose a problem because there is only *one* agreement to repudiate or honor. Under FIRREA, the treatment of a master agreement as one "swap agreement" is specifically addressed as follows:

> "(vii) TREATMENT OF MASTER AGREEMENT AS 1 SWAP AGREEMENT.—Any master agreement for any agreements described in clause (vi)(I) together with all supplements to such master agreement shall be treated as 1 swap agreement."

## V. FDICIA

. . .

In the event a court did not treat an ISDA Master Agreement as one agreement or did not (or could not) apply the analysis concerning the Bankruptcy Code and FIRREA set forth in Section IV above,[30] a counterparty still may be able to rely on FDICIA to enforce the close-out netting provisions in an ISDA Master Agreement with certain U.S. entities. Congress recently enacted FDICIA, which recognizes the enforceability of the netting of payment obligations between two "financial institution[s]" under a "netting contract", "notwithstanding any other provision of law" and notwithstanding any "stay, injunction, avoidance, moratorium or similar proceeding or order, whether issued or granted by a court, administrative agency, or otherwise".

---

France passed a similar law in December of 1993, but one major issue remains:

"THE HOLES IN NETTING"

Euromoney (April 1994), p. 54.

**The Holes in the Netting**

It took the French parliament more than five years to adopt the Group of 12's 1988 recommendation that netting be recognized in bankruptcy.

When it finally did, on December 31 last year, French bankers were delighted because the move reduced their obligation to cover risk. "The new provisions for netting will enable French banks to balance their total exposure," says Patrick Stevenson, a managing director at Banque Paribas.

Unfortunately, that may not be true if the banks work with foreigners.

When netting is in place, bankruptcy administrators, which normally have broad freedom to decide what debts are paid when a company goes bankrupt, must take account of offsetting payment obligations. This is particularly important when companies trade derivatives such as swaps, where each counterparty owes the other a sum of money.

The new law permits netting for French banks and similar institutions that operate in the credit markets, including insurance companies—but foreign institutions are eligible only if they have "similar status".

Financial lawyers complain that the law does not explain this term. "The definition of the foreign institutions which may benefit from the new rules relating to netting is unclear," says Pierre Chabert, a lawyer with Cleary, Gottlieb, Steen & Hamilton in Paris. "An unregulated affiliate of a US bank, a broker-dealer, a fund manager or a foreign investment advisor would probably not qualify under these new rules."

Notably unprotected are the foreign derivative product companies that banks have set up to handle their trading. "It is not clear that special-purpose derivative units organized outside France would have the benefits of the legislation available to them," complains Ed Nalbantian, of Watson, Filey, Williams. Also unprotected, he says, are foreign insurance companies.

In theory, the Bank of France or the treasury could approve netting for these institutions. But since the law does not provide for such approvals, lawyers point out, the courts might not recognize them.

This seems to be one area where neither the Bank of France nor the ministry of the economy has the power to intervene. Either parliamentary action will be required to make the law clearer, or a lot of cases will have to go through the courts.

The next piece deals with a more narrow but important remaining issue, the enforceability of one-way payments.

## b. One-Way Payments

Schuyler K. Henderson of Baker & McKenzie, London, explores the relative merits of the two approaches to the termination of swap transactions where one party to the agreement is in default.

### S. HENDERSON, "SHOULD SWAP TERMINATION PAYMENTS BE ONE-WAY OR TWO-WAY"

International Financial Law Review (October 1990), pp. 27–32.

The 1987 ISDA Interest Rate and Currency Exchange Agreement and the 1987 ISDA Interest Rate Swap Agreement (collectively referred to as the ISDA Agreements, using the same defined terms) provide that a defaulting party will never receive payment of its net value, if any, in terminated swap transactions. An alternative approach, which is beginning to be used by some major swap dealers, is for the non-defaulting party to pay over its gain resulting from termination. The gain would approximate, but be somewhat less than, a defaulting party's loss of its net value on termination.

**Termination**

A swap transaction can be terminated on a date (the early termination date) before its scheduled termination date by one party acting alone on either of two bases: a termination event with respect to itself or, in some cases, the other party (generally a 'no fault' event beyond the control of the parties, such as supervening illegality or change in tax law but also including certain merger events); or an event of default with respect to the other party.

Because of the movement of rates since inception of the swap, and also at times because of the mismatch of payments made prior to the early termination date, a termination of the swap transactions and their future cash flows without a cash settlement will generally favour one party at the expense of the other. If a swap transaction has become 'out-of-the money' or unfavourable for a party, it has a negative value, and termination results in a gain to it. If the swap transaction is 'in-the-money' or favourable for a party, it has a positive value for the party, and termination results in a loss to it.

On termination, the amount of gain or loss under the ISDA Agreements is determined by first calculating two components: unpaid amounts and settlement amounts.

A party's unpaid amounts are payments (plus interest) which were scheduled to be, but were not, made before the early termination date. These payments may not have been made because either the payer defaulted or the payment was deferred because the payee was in default.

**Market quotations**

The settlement amount is the gain or loss to a party resulting from the termination of the future cash flows, that is, the aggregate of market quotations for the individual terminated swap transactions. The ISDA Agreements provide for the non-defaulting party or the non-affected party to calculate a market quotation for each terminated swap. Quotations are taken from four leading swap dealers as to the amount each dealer would require from (a positive amount)—or would pay to (a negative amount)—the non-defaulting or non-affected party for the dealer to enter into a replacement swap with that party on substantially the same economic terms as those of each terminated transaction. The highest and lowest quotations are disregarded and the market quotation for the terminated swap is the average of the remaining quotations. Where there are two affected parties, both parties go to the market and their respective market quotations are averaged.

The market quotation for a given swap transaction will differ depending on which party obtains the market quotation for two main reasons. First, due to the bid-offered spread, the party obtaining the quote will, other things being equal, always show a gain less than the other party's loss, or a loss greater than the other party's gain. The procedure is therefore advantageous to the party obtaining the quote. Second, the quotes will differ depending on the credit-worthiness of the parties. If the party obtaining the quote is a better credit than the other, it would have to pay less or would receive more from a dealer than would the other party. If termination is a result of an event of default, the non-defaulting party will in most circumstances be the better credit and therefore get a better replacement quote. If termination is a result of a termination event, there is no structural reason (unless, perhaps, the relevant event is a merger) why one party's quote would necessarily be more favourable than the other's, other than by reason of the bid-offered spread.

**Settlement provisions**

Counterparties invariably provide in their agreements that, where early termination is based on a termination event, two-way payments applies. Under this method, the non-affected party's settlement amount (positive or negative) is aggregated with any unpaid amounts (always positive) owing to the non-affected party and, from this sum (which may be positive or negative), any unpaid amounts owing to the affected party are subtracted. The resulting amount, if positive, is paid over by the affected party. If the amount is negative, the non-affected party would pay the absolute value of that amount to the affected party.

Where early termination is based on an event of default, most dealers generally provide in their agreement that one way payments applies. The non-defaulting party would calculate the aggregate of its settlement amount and unpaid amounts owing it and subtract unpaid amounts owing to the defaulting party, as above. If the resulting amount is positive, the defaulting party is obliged to pay that amount to the non-defaulting party. If the resulting amount is negative, there is no obligation imposed on the non-defaulting party to make any payment to the defaulting party. This method is referred to as 'one-way payments'.

There is concern that there may be a penalty aspect with respect to forfeiture of unpaid amounts otherwise owing to a defaulting party. If the settlement amount was zero and there were unpaid amounts owing to the defaulting party (for instance, as the result of deferral by reason of a potential event of default with respect to the defaulting party at the time payment was due to it), no payment of those unpaid amounts would be made. Some dealers modify one-way payments so that the settlement amount, if it is a negative number, will be treated as equalling zero and the two unpaid amounts will be compared. If the unpaid amounts owing to the defaulting party exceed those owing to the non-defaulting party, the non-defaulting party would in this situation, and this situation alone, pay the excess to the defaulting party. This method of settlement is referred to as 'modified one-way payments'. A variation is 'two pool damages'. Here, if a party has fully performed some transactions (eg, purchased caps), the market quotations for these transactions are not included in the settlement amount, but are included as an unpaid amount owing to the party, and modified one-way payments is applied.

However, in modified one-way payments a negative settlement amount cannot be used to reduce unpaid amounts owing to the non-defaulting party. For instance, if the settlement amount was negative, unpaid amounts owing to the non-defaulting party were positive and unpaid amounts owing to the defaulting party were zero, under one-way payments the defaulting party would effectively be able to reduce unpaid amounts owing to the non-defaulting party by the amount of the negative settlement amount. Under modified one-way payments, the settlement amount would be deemed to be zero and the defaulting party would not be able to reduce its payment. Although it eliminates the forfeiture issue as to unpaid amounts, modified one-way payments may create a greater risk of being regarded as an unenforceable penalty, since it may impose a payment obligation on the defaulting party in excess of the non-defaulting party's loss.

## Safeguards

Some end-users and a small but growing number of dealers also use two-way payments in default terminations. The non-defaulting party would make the above calculations and would be entitled to claim from the defaulting party any resulting positive amount or be obligated to pay to the defaulting party any negative amount. Because of concerns that payments to a defaulting party might be made under circumstances where the non-defaulting party would be at further risk, parties include a provision (referred to as 'conditional two-way payments') which contains important safeguards for the non-defaulting party. The obligation to make any payment to the defaulting party is subject to the conditions that: the non-defaulting party receive confirmation (including an unqualified opinion of counsel, if desired) that all swap transactions between the parties under their ISDA Agreement and all other swap transactions between the parties or their affiliates have been effectively terminated; no other obligation (contingent or absolute, matured or unmatured) owed by either the defaulting party or any of its affiliates to the non-defaulting party or any of its affiliates is outstanding; and all costs of enforcement not otherwise paid are deducted from the payment.

To summarise, in either one-way payments or modified one-way payments the defaulting party does not receive any net value which it had in the terminated swap transactions except to the extent, in one-way payments, it reduces any net unpaid amounts otherwise payable to the non-defaulting party. In conditional two-way payments, the defaulting party would receive the non-defaulting party's gain on termination after assurance that all other liabilities and costs have been satisfied.

### Calculating termination payments

($000's)
*Non-defaulting party's loss or gain from termination*

| | | |
|---|---|---|
| Settlement amount | = | −1,000 |
| + Unpaid amounts owing non-defaulting party | = | 100 |
| − Unpaid amounts owing defaulting party | = | 50 |
| Net loss (gain) of non-defaulting party | = | (950) |

*Calculation of termination payments*

| | *Limited two-way payments* | *Modified limited two-way payments* | *Two-way payments* |
|---|---|---|---|
| | −1,000 | 0 | −1,000 |
| | +100 | +100 | +100 |
| | −50 | −50 | −50 |
| | −950 | 50 | −950 |
| Amount owing by: | | | |
| Defaulting party = | 0 | 50 | 0 |
| Non-defaulting party = | 0 | 0 | 950 |

($000's)
*Non-defaulting party's loss or gain from termination*

| | | |
|---|---|---|
| Settlement amount | = | 1,000 |
| + Unpaid amounts owing non-defaulting party | = | 100 |
| − Unpaid amounts owing defaulting party | = | 50 |
| Net loss (gain) of non-defaulting party | = | 1,050 |

*Calculation of termination payments*

| | *Limited two-way payments* | *Modified limited two-way payments* | *Two-way payments* |
|---|---|---|---|
| | +1,000 | +1,000 | +1,000 |
| | +100 | +100 | +100 |
| | −50 | −50 | −50 |
| | 1,050 | 1,050 | 1,050 |
| Amount owing by: | | | |
| Defaulting party = | 1,050 | 1,050 | 1,050 |
| Non-defaulting party = | 0 | 0 | 0 |

## One-way payments: the arguments for

**Avoiding rewarding a defaulting party:** in principle, a party should not be able to benefit from its wrongful act or event of default. Many institutions oppose, on an emotional level, making payments to a defaulting party.

**Inducement not to breach:** one-way payments creates a powerful incentive for a counterparty to honour its obligations and not default. Two-way payments creates an incentive to breach.

**Bargaining leverage:** one-way payments strengthens the non-defaulting party's bargaining position in negotiating with an in-the-money defaulting party which is resisting termination. At the time of desired termination, if it appears prudent to do so, the non-defaulting party could waive the right not to make payment and agree to pay, perhaps a reduced amount, on conditions similar to those set out in conditional two-way payments. In several default situations, defaulting parties have been able to negotiate either orderly payouts on, effectively, a two-way payment basis or agreed novations of their swap portfolios.

**Windfall:** with one-way payments, a non-defaulting party might obtain a gain, a 'windfall', through the cancellation without cost of a disadvantageous contract (and, if hedged, continue to benefit from a corresponding advantageous contract or contracts). The active market participant should anticipate that at some times it will be the losing, in-the-money counterparty and unable to recover its loss. At other times it will be an out-of-the-money counterparty and be entitled to retain its gain. The windfalls would balance the losses.

**Enforceable:** in the most active swap jurisdiction (the United States), the risk of inability to terminate has been greatly diminished and the risk of 'cherry-picking' has apparently been eliminated. This results from the Financial Institutions Reform, Recovery and Enforcement Act, 1989 (FIRREA) with respect to banks and savings and loan institutions and as a result of recent legislation with respect to corporations subject to the US Bankruptcy Code (Bankruptcy Swap Amendment). Enforcement risks presented by one-way payments in the context of a US bankruptcy, referred to below, have therefore been substantially reduced.

**Market practice:** most dealers use one-way payments as a matter of policy and completion of documentation will be expedited through use of that settlement method.

**Payment where affiliate in default:** if two-way payments are used, a payment could be made to a defaulting party only to have it or an affiliate not make a payment under another agreement with the non-defaulting party or one of its affiliates. While conditional two-way payments may substantially reduce this risk, as a practical matter it cannot eliminate the further risk that a payment made by the defaulting party or its affiliate under another agreement might be recaptured as a preference.

**Are conditional two-way payments unenforceable?** Conditional two-way payments may be unenforceable or unauthorised in several situations. Since a defaulting party which gives up a right to receive a payment to the extent an affiliate has not made a payment could arguably be viewed as giving, in effect, a guarantee of that affiliate, questions as to the power and authorisation of the defaulting party to agree to such a provision must be addressed. In particular, some entities, such as US banks, may be expressly prohibited from giving guarantees of the obligations of certain affiliates.

### Arguments against one-way payments

**Status as a dealer:** a dealer holds itself out as a market-maker and generally is expected to and does offer quotes for terminating a swap transaction. Exercise of one-way payments by a dealer is inconsistent with this role and expectation. This has a number of ramifications discussed below.

**No "reward" to defaulting party in two-way payments:** there is no net benefit or reward to a defaulting party receiving a payment on termination. The value the defaulting party had in the agreement, which is now lost, will exceed any payment it receives on default. In addition, payments are often made to defaulting parties in bilateral financial arrangements such as repos, exchange-traded futures and FX netting agreements. The purpose of two-way payments in these situations is to provide greater certainty of enforcement and to preserve the soundness of the dealing market (including orderly distribution of assets to creditors), not to be generous to defaulters. It is consistent with the orderly settlement of the defaulting parties' swap portfolios referred to in Bargaining leverage above (but would not present the risks to orderly settlement posed by actions which were taken by a few non-defaulting parties in each of those situations which refused to co-operate and attempted to retain their windfall).

**One-way payments will not reduce defaults:** the event of default may be involuntary and unintentional (such as a bankruptcy or an event of default relating to an affiliate). Onerous contractual provisions, such as one-way payments, will not affect the defaulting party's actions relating to those defaults. In fact, to the extent a reorganisation proceeding is voluntary, the existence of one-way payments could be a marginal incentive for a party to enter bankruptcy proceedings to obtain the protection of the courts (see below). The covenants in the ISDA Agreements which are realistically subject to voluntary breach are generally not of great significance, with the exception of payment obligations. A counterparty, particularly if it is in-the-money (is the only circumstance in which it would receive a payment on termination), should not be influenced by two-way payments in determining whether or not to breach its payment obligations for several reasons:

- As noted in No "reward" to defaulting party above, the settlement amount it receives under two-way payments is the gain of its counterparty on termination. At best the defaulting party receives less than full payment for loss of a valuable asset.
- Given the liquidity of the swap market and the readiness of a dealer to quote for termination or to approve transfers, the value in swaps is best realised by the counterparty through transfer or agreed termination. In a transfer, the transferring party could realise its value in the swap transactions based on the creditworthiness of the remaining party. The dealer counterparty would normally consent to a transfer to another dealer, particularly if the transferring party is in credit difficulties (see Lender liability below).
- The consequential effects of a breach are serious. It would possibly trigger default provisions in other swap or credit agreements (such as cross default) and, at a minimum, the defaulting

party would no longer be able to deal in the swap market and its ability to obtain credit would be substantially impaired.

— The non-defaulting party does not have to terminate. If the defaulting party breached while in-the-money and solvent (ie an intended breach), the non-defaulting party could withhold payments, sue for any scheduled payments due from the defaulting party, and recover these payments, all costs of enforcement and default interest. While this may not be a desirable course of action viewed prospectively, the existence of remedies other than termination makes a voluntary breach a highly uncertain and risky action, particularly in the context of factors described above.

**Unenforceable forfeiture in one-way payments:** the counter arguments above are each a euphemistic expression of the basic purpose of one-way payments, in effect to pressure a party to perform obligations to which it has already agreed. This is the usual definition of a penalty or forfeiture. The denial of payment to the defaulting party may thus be an unenforceable forfeiture provision.

— In some jurisdictions, the penalty/forfeiture nature could adversely affect the right to terminate, thereby creating uncertainty.

— In some jurisdictions, the defaulting party or its representative in bankruptcy might be able to recover the forfeited value (probably being the non-defaulting party's gain but, perhaps, more). Neither FIRREA nor the Bankruptcy Swap Amendment addresses the issue of the right of a non-defaulting party to retain a windfall.

Conditional two-way payments retains many of the legitimate 'coercive' advantages of one-way payments but without the penalty element.

### Cherry picking

**Bankruptcy—questionable enforceability of one-way payments:** despite the improved situation in the United States following the Bankruptcy Swap Amendment, insolvency laws in some other jurisdictions provide that the non-defaulting party will not be able to terminate after formal insolvency proceedings have commenced, regardless of whether one-way payments or two-way payments are used. In addition, one-way payments could in these jurisdictions draw the attention of the bankruptcy representative to related legal issues. For instance, the representative might challenge the "single agreement" concept and attempt to 'cherry-pick' among the swap transactions, ie assuming (or assuming and assigning) those swaps where the insolvent party is in-the-money and rejecting those where it is out-of-the-money (leaving the solvent party obligated on the former with only a claim for damages on the latter).

**Windfall not always realised in one-way payments:** for reasons discussed above there are strong possibilities that, if challenged, the non-defaulting party might not be able to obtain the windfall or, once obtained, to retain it.

**Uncertainty as to when to cover with one-way payments:** to the extent that one-way payments creates uncertainty as to the right of the non-defaulting party to terminate (either prior to or after bankruptcy), the non-defaulting party does not know if and when it should go to the market to replace the cash flows under the terminated swaps. Two-way payments provides greater certainty and is likely to encourage a counterparty or its representative, in need of cash, to accede to termination for approximately fair value in accordance with the terms of the agreement rather than engage in protracted litigation. To the extent uncertainty is reduced, as it is with two-way payments, the risk on redeployment is reduced.

**"Lender liability"—improper termination:** Exercise of the right to terminate, coupled with the forfeiture of value to the defaulting party, at a time when (perhaps viewed with hindsight) the non-defaulting party was not at risk could expose the non-defaulting party to liability in some jurisdictions for consequential damages on a "lender liability" theory. If the non-defaulting party had previously refused to agree to a voluntary termination for value or to a transfer, possible exposure would be increased. This risk would be largely avoided (of course it can never be totally avoided) by using a fair settlement procedure in which the defaulting party is not penalised.

. . .

Just to be clearer with respect to Henderson's Chart, focus on the left hand side example. For ease of reference let's refer to Party A as the non-defaulting party and Party B as the defaulting party. As shown on the top of the Chart, Party A owes B 1000. This means the swap is in the money for B, not A (based on replacement value quotes). Party A also owes 50 to B in "unpaid amounts". These are payments which were scheduled to be made but which have not been made. Also, B owes 100 in "unpaid amounts" to A. Thus, B has a gain of 950.

Column 1 shows the result under the earlier swap documentation rules if Party B defaulted. All payments are netted. Since A owes B a settlement amount of 1000, but is on net owed 50 in unpaid amounts (is owed 100, but owes only 50), the net of all payments is -950. The standard swap rule was that the non-defaulting party makes no net payments to the defaulting party; thus A makes no payments to B.

How did that compare with the normal termination rule, e.g. where the contract was at an end, or the parties mutually agreed to terminate? Column 3 shows this. Here the rule is two-way payments, the party out of the money, A, pays the party in the money, B, 950, the net of all payments.

How would a modified limited two-way payment rule change this? This is shown in Column 2. The issue of the payment of the settlement amount is separated from that of the payment of unpaid amounts. A does not pay B the settlement amount since B has defaulted. But since, on net, B owes A 50 in unpaid amounts, B pays A 50.

The right hand example deals with the situation where the non-defaulting party has a gain. Here the result is always the same. B must always pay A the net amount, 1000 + 50 (net of unpaid amounts). This is the asymmetry which Listenberger was referring to.

### *Notes and Questions*

1. Assume Party A and Party X have three swap contracts between them, and that marking each contract to market, and calculating replacement value, there are some contracts favorable to Party A, but others that are favorable to Party X.

| | X | A | |
|---|---|---|---|
| 1. | +200,000 | −200,000 | (A owes X) |
| 2. | +500,000 | −500,000 | (A owes X) |
| 3. | −800,000 | + 800,000 | (X owes A) |

So, in this example, on net, X owes A 100,000. Before the U.S. passed the new law what was X's risk if A were to go bankrupt?

2. Does the new U.S. law protect A against the cherry-picking risk? Would it depend on whether X was a U.S. company or a foreign company? The ISDA 1992 Master Swap Agreement provides that the governing law is either English or New York. Assuming netting is valid in England, does this choice of law provision protect swap parties against cherry-picking risk?

3. Given the new French law, and the netting hole it creates, what would you advise a special-purpose derivative unit organized outside of France to do?

4. What would you advise a client to do with respect to one-way or two-way payments in a swap contract?

## 2. Netting and Capital Requirements

We turn again to capital requirements. The issue here is how the capital requirements deal with the netting issue. The credit rules of the Basle Accord do not permit swaps to be netted among the same counter-parties. Thus, in the example in Note 1, the values of the contracts could not be netted for capital purposes.

Under the new Basle proposals, Consultative Proposal by the Basle Committee on Banking Supervision, *The Supervisory Recognition of Netting for Capital Adequacy Purposes* (April 1993) (The Netting Proposal), the Committee would permit bilateral netting of swaps (those between the same counter-parties) with respect to replacement values but not future exposure values. This proposal was adopted by the Committee in July 1994. Basle Capital Accord: The Treatment of the Credit Risk Associated with Certain Off-Balance-Sheet Items ("Basle Committee 1994"). Thus suppose Banks A and B have entered into two swap contracts which have the following values to Bank A:

| | Replacement Value | Future Exposure |
|---|---|---|
| #1 | 1000 | 3000 |
| #2 | −500 | 700 |

A is in the money on # 1 and out of the money on # 2. Thus, if the swap were to terminate today due to B's default A would have a claim in B's bankruptcy of 500 after the swaps were netted. The asset equivalent amounts for Bank A of these two swaps will be: 500 [net replacement value] + (3700 × .005) [future exposure] = 518.50, whereas under the old Accord, it would be 1018.50.

The permissibility of bilateral netting is subject to certain requirements. The netting contract must be enforceable as stated below, *Netting Proposal,* Annex 2, p. 2. Supervisors must be assured that a bank has:

(1) a netting contract or agreement with the counterparty which creates a single legal obligation, covering all included transactions, such that the bank would have either a claim to receive or obligation to pay only the net sum of the positive and negative mark-to-market values of included individual transactions in the event a counterparty fails to perform due to any of the following: default, bankruptcy, liquidation or similar circumstances;

(2) written and reasoned legal opinions that, in the event of a legal challenge, the relevant courts and administrative authorities would find the bank's exposure to be such a net amount under:

— the law of the jurisdiction in which the counterparty is chartered and, if the foreign branch of a counterparty is involved, then also under the law of the jurisdiction in which the branch is located;

— the law that governs the individual transactions; and

— the law that governs any contract or agreement necessary to effect the netting.

The national supervisor, after consultation when necessary with other relevant supervisors, must be satisfied that the netting is enforceable under the laws of each of the relevant jurisdictions;[8]

(3) procedures in place to ensure that the legal characteristics of netting arrangements are kept under review in the light of possible changes in relevant law.

Contracts containing walkaway clauses will not be eligible for netting for the purpose of calculating capital requirements pursuant to this Accord. A walkaway clause is a provision which permits a non-defaulting counterparty to make only limited payments, or no payment at all, to the estate of a defaulter, even if the defaulter is a net creditor.

**8.** Thus, if any of these supervisors is dissatisfied about enforceability under its laws, the netting contract or agreement will not meet this condition and neither counterparty could obtain supervisory benefit.

### Notes and Questions

1. Should we permit netting of future exposures as well as replacement values? The Basle Committee has made the following proposals in this regard:

1. In the April 1993 proposal the Committee favoured retaining the present approach in the Capital Accord to calculating add-ons for potential future credit exposure (i.e. multiplying the notional principal amounts of transactions by the appropriate add-on factors found in Annex 3). This was the Committee's view in the absence of a compelling case having been made for any of the alternative approaches put forward up to that time.

2. Some industry participants and supervisory authorities took the opportunity of the comment process to provide the results of empirical research on the effects of netting on potential future credit exposure and to submit alternative formulae for recognising netting effects in the calculation of add-ons. The Committee also has conducted further research in this area and now sees merit in incorporating into the add-ons methodology a formula for recognising netting effects on potential future exposure.

3. The Committee proposes the formula below to reduce the add-ons for transactions subject to legally enforceable netting agreements consistent with the requirements set out in the attached amendment to the Capital Accord on bilateral netting. Under the proposal the add-on for netted transactions ($A_{Net}$) would equal the average of the add-on as presently calculated ($A_{Gross}$),[3] reduced by the ratio of net current replacement cost to gross current replacement cost (NGR), and the $A_{Gross}$.

$$A_{Net} = 0.5 * A_{Gross} + 0.5 * NGR * A_{Gross}$$

where

NGR = level of net replacement cost/level of gross replacement cost for transactions subject to legally enforceable netting agreements

4. The advantage of the formula from a supervisory perspective is that it uses bank-specific information (i.e. the NGR) but imposes greater stability over time and across banks than a formula giving full weight to the NGR. Moreover, using this formula banks will always hold capital against potential exposure as the net add-on can never be zero. In this context, the NGR can be seen as somewhat of a proxy for the impact of netting on potential future exposure but not as a precise indicator of future changes in net exposure relative to gross exposure, reflecting the fact that the NGR and potential exposure can be influenced by many idiosyncratic properties of individual portfolios. With the weight at 0.5 the reduction in add-on, assuming an NGR of 0.5, would be 25%.

3. $A_{Gross}$ equals the sum of notional principal amounts of all transactions subject to legally enforceable netting agreements times the appropriate add-on factors from Annex 3 of the Capital Accord.

5. In presenting the formula above the Committee has not specified whether the calculation of NGR should be made on a counterparty by counterparty basis or on an aggregate basis for all transactions subject to legally enforceable netting agreements which meet the Committee's requirements. The Committee invites specific comment on this issue, in particular whether the choice of method could bias the results, and whether there is a significant difference in calculation burden between the two. A highly simplified example of calculating the NGR in both ways is presented in Annex 2.

6. As a result of the comment process on the April 1993 netting proposal the Committee is aware of the view that internal simulation models may be useful in the calculation of add-ons for potential future credit exposure. The Committee believes this is an interesting approach and worthy of further consideration at some future date. However, for the time being the Committee wishes to enhance prudential coverage of derivatives under the existing methodology.

. . .

**Annex 2**

**Simple example of calculating the net to gross ratio**

| Transaction | Counterparty 1 | | Counterparty 2 | | Counterparty 3 | |
|---|---|---|---|---|---|---|
| | Notional amount | Mark to market value | Notional amount | Mark to market value | Notional amount | Mark to market value |
| Transaction 1 | 100 | 10 | 50 | 8 | 30 | −3 |
| Transaction 2 | 100 | −5 | 50 | 2 | 30 | 1 |
| Gross replacement cost (GR) | | 10 | | 10 | | 1 |
| Net replacement cost (NR) | | 5 | | 10 | | 0 |
| NGR (per counterparty) | 0.5 | | 1 | | 0 | |
| NGR (aggregate) | $\Sigma NR/\Sigma GR = 15/21 = 0.71$ | | | | | |

2. Do you think the proposal has tough enough standards for determining the enforceability of netting? Why are we worried about swap enforceability in three possible jurisdictions?

3. U.S. bank regulators have proposed to allow bilateral netting on much the same terms as proposed by the Basle Supervisors' Committee. Office of the Comptroller of the Currency and Board of Governors of the Federal Reserve System, Risk–Based Capital Standards: Bilateral Netting Requirements, Notice of Proposed Rulemaking, 59 Fed.Reg. 26456 (May 20, 1994).

## E. FUTURE REGULATION

The G–30 Derivatives Study basically concluded that sophisticated companies had derivatives risk under control, and that known management techniques could adequately deal with the problems. This conclusion has not convinced the regulators or legislators. They continue to call for strict capital requirements. Some have called for more disclosure of swap risks, and accounting requirements are sharply moving in that direction. More recently, some have questioned whether banks should be permitted to offer "designer" swaps.

The GAO Report released in May 1994 concluded that Congress should require federal regulation of the safety and soundness of all major U.S. OTC derivatives dealers, particularly currently unregulated securities firm and insurance company affiliates, principally on the grounds of concern with systemic. It also called on FASB to develop and adopt more consistent accounting rules, and for the SEC to make sure major end-users of complex derivatives products establish adequate internal controls. GAO Report, at pp. 126–129.

## KEITH BRADSHER, "BANKS' SECURITIES TRADING MAKES COMPTROLLER FEARFUL"

New York Times (April 21, 1994), p. D1.

WASHINGTON, April 20—In a sharp policy shift, the Clinton Administration's top bank regulator expressed alarm today that the nation's biggest commercial banks were taking too many risks in trading stocks, bonds, foreign currencies and other financial instruments. He said new regulatory limits might be needed.

The official, Eugene A. Ludwig, the Comptroller of the Currency, criticized two related but distinct approaches banks have taken to expand their securities trading as traditional corporate lending operations have withered. One approach involves increasingly speculative trading operations; the other involves derivatives, which are complicated contracts that allow traders to bet on the direction of future price changes in stocks, bonds, currencies and other financial instruments.

Banks have bought and sold bonds and currencies for years to limit their losses if interest rates or exchange rates suddenly move in an unexpected direction, or to help customers find scarce bonds and currencies. But in recent years they have used more complicated financial instruments like derivatives for these purposes and have increasingly sought profits from trades unrelated to reducing risks or serving customers.

Mr. Ludwig, who oversees more than 3,000 federally chartered banks—three-fifths of the banking industry—expressed his worries today in a speech to the Exchequer Club, a group of economic policy makers, financial lobbyists and wealthy investors.

Until now, Administration and Federal Reserve officials have tended to play down Congressional concerns about bank trading practices and derivatives. It was unclear whether Mr. Ludwig was simply responding to Congressional pressures or actually intended to take quick action on banks. He would not elaborate on his speech.

Douglas E. Harris, a senior policy adviser to Mr. Ludwig, said that the Comptroller's office had become more worried about banks' trading risks after reviewing information the agency gathered in preparation for a House Banking Committee hearing last week.

Edward L. Yingling, the chief lobbyist for the American Bankers Association, said the industry trade group would oppose any move by the

Comptroller's office or by Congress that would impose tougher limits on commercial banks than on insurance companies, securities firms and other financial services businesses that engage in securities trading. Special limits on commercial banks would put them at a competitive disadvantage, he said.

Mr. Ludwig said he was concerned about federally insured institutions whose failure might cost taxpayers money.

Mr. Ludwig said in his speech that limits might be needed on the size of bank trading desks that operate independently of such traditional bank operations as buying and selling for customers and reducing risk. He compared these trading desks to hedge funds, which are investment partnerships, usually of fewer than 100 wealthy investors, that borrow heavily to take highly speculative positions in securities and commodities.

### Concern About 6 Banks

Mr. Ludwig had mentioned last week that six nationally chartered banks had trading desks that he considered speculative, but he refused then and today to identify them. Many banks have trading desks.

He also warned today that banks might not belong in the derivatives market at all, adding that banks accounted for $12 trillion of the $14 trillion market for derivatives in the United States.

"Because of our increasing concern about the risks posed by exotic and complex derivative instruments, we are looking at whether they are appropriate for national banks—and, if so, to what extent they are appropriate, and whether we need to take further regulatory action on these instruments," Mr. Ludwig said.

Mr. Ludwig's comments today coincide with growing enthusiasm in the House Banking Committee for legislation concerning bank trading of derivatives. The committee's Democratic and Republican leaders have introduced separate bills requiring extensive bank disclosure to regulators of derivatives holdings, and raising the threat of barring from the banking industry any bank executives who fail to supervise derivatives trading adequately.

Mr. Ludwig said today that while he perceived no immediate threat to the financial soundness of big banks, his agency would nonetheless send out 20 pages of policy guidance to senior bankers next week and would consider drafting new regulations.

The guidance would consist of answers to commonly asked questions about the agency's position on derivatives, he said. Mr. Harris said that the new guidance would expand and elaborate on existing policy, but would not represent a change in direction.

### "Still Not Comfortable"

The office of the Comptroller first issued guidance on derivatives trading to banks in October. But Mr. Ludwig said today that after subsequent Federal examinations of large banks, "We are still not comfortable with the extent of senior management and board knowledge and oversight of bank derivative instruments."

Mr. Ludwig's speech came a day after Citicorp and Bankers Trust announced that they had suffered heavy trading losses in the first quarter, although Mr. Ludwig did not mention either institution by name. Bankers Trust said it had made money trading derivatives but lost money trading stocks and bonds.

---

*Links to Other Chapters*

Swaps, as well as futures and options (Chapter XV) and securitized instruments (Ch. XII) raise crucial problems of dealing with financial innovation. From a regulatory point of view, the focus has been on capital (generally reviewed in Ch. IV) and netting. Netting issues are crucial not only for swaps, but with respect to the payment system (Ch. IX) and clearance and settlement (Ch. XIV). The development of swaps, like other euromarket products, has in part responded to the inefficiencies or regulatory restrictions in national markets, which we have reviewed for the U.S. (Chapter II and III) and Japan (Ch. 7).

# Chapter XVII

# EMERGING MARKETS: PRIVATIZATION AND INSTITUTIONAL INVESTORS

## A. INTRODUCTION

The growth of stock markets in many developing countries outstripped that in industrial countries since the mid–1980s. Fueling this growth was an almost insatiable appetite for emerging market securities on the part of investors worldwide. Apparently radical change in the countries' economic policies attracted the investors. A key change was privatization, as governments sold state owned enterprises to the private sector.

In 1989, the new president of Mexico, Carlos Salinas de Gortari, announced that the government would divest itself of its controlling interest in Telefonos de Mexico, S.A. de C.V. ("Telmex"). A Harvard trained economist, he took office in a close and bitter election in which he had promised to reform the country's economy. In his first year, he started with banks nationalized in late 1982. Then he looked beyond the financial sector. Telmex was the third largest company in Mexico, ranked by assets.

This Chapter describes the steps taken by the government to sell its shares in Telmex. It starts with background about privatization worldwide. It describes circumstances in Mexico that prompted the government's action and Telmex during the period before 1989/90. Two options were to divest only on the Mexican stock exchange and to sell the Government's full share in a block to foreign investors; both routes are explored.

The actual privatization had two stages. The first, in 1990, transferred voting control (but not all of the government's portion of the capital) to a private consortium of Mexicans and foreign investors. The second stage, in 1991, sold much of the government's remaining stake in Telmex on equity markets in Mexico, the U.S., Japan, and Europe. Institutional investors, such as pension funds, were major buyers. The Chapter gives information about them and factors that propelled them on emerging markets.

As you read the Chapter, consider why the government would privatize Telmex as it did. Were there reasonable alternatives? What were the risks for the parties? Why did the investors show such interest in the company's 1991 offering?

## B. PRIVATIZATION IN THE 1980s AND 1990s

Government control of business seemed to be a permanent feature of the landscape in almost every country well into the 1970s. When Margaret Thatcher became U.K. prime minister in 1979, she set out to reverse this trend in her country and soon officials were devising ways the government could divest itself of productive firms. Momentum picked up as other industrial and developing countries saw benefits for themselves in the early and mid–1980s. Then communist countries across Eastern Europe and Asia shifted toward market economics and the prospect of the largest asset transfer in the history of the world raised dazzling prospects.

In 1994, the U.S. Congress, as overseer of foreign aid programs funding private investment in Eastern Europe and elsewhere, requested an explanation of the privatization process. The executive director of Price Waterhouse's international privatization group gave the following description.

### TESTIMONY OF JAMES A. WADDELL BEFORE THE SMALL BUSINESS COMMITTEE OF THE U.S. HOUSE OF CONGRESS

(April 14, 1994).

**What is Privatization?**

Privatization is the process of transferring productive operations and assets from the public sector to the private sector. Broadly defined in this fashion, privatization is much more than selling an enterprise to the highest bidder, as it includes contracting out, leasing, private sector financing of infrastructure projects, liquidation, mass privatization, etc. My testimony will argue that there is no single "best" approach to privatization; the appropriate privatization path depends on the goals that the government is seeking to attain, the individual circumstances facing the enterprise and the economic and political context of the country.

It should be noted that privatization is fundamentally a political process as well as a commercial and economic process. Privatization changes the distribution of power within a society, as it diminishes control of the economy by the state and government-appointed managers. Workers often feel threatened by the potential changes inherent in privatization, although employees frequently benefit from the process. As a result, public support is a major consideration in any privatization program and many of the choices made in designing and implementing transactions reflect the need for such support. Two consequences flow from this factor: 1) choices of approaches are sometimes altered due to "political" considerations, meaning that equity must be promoted in the privatization strategy, and 2) program implementation must be objective and fair to avoid adverse publicity.

**What are the Goals of Privatization?**

Many, varied goals are often pursued through privatization programs. These goals often fall along two principal dimensions: 1) broad social or macroeconomic goals, and 2) enterprise specific or macroeconomic goals.

Macroeconomic goals are numerous. Fundamentally, privatization is advocated as a means to reduce the government's role in the economy, partly as a philosophical matter (as in the UK) but principally because governments have performed badly in that role. Many countries can attribute substantial portions of their external debt to liabilities of state-owned enterprises and significant portions of government budgets are devoted to paying subsidies or otherwise assisting loss-making state-owned enterprises. Government's objectives in these situations is often simply to extricate themselves from these financial commitments, and focus scarce resources instead on education, infrastructure, and social welfare.

A second macroeconomic goal of privatization is to promote the development of the private sector by "levelling the playing field" and ending subsidized competition from state-owned enterprises. There is a danger in some countries that emerging private businesses face unfair competition from state enterprises that have access to credit and other inputs at below market rates and better access to government distribution channels. In order to give the private sector a fair opportunity to compete and thrive, state-owned enterprises are privatized.

A third goal of privatization, is to obtain the sales proceeds and use them to finance shortfalls in the government's budget or retire some of the public sector debt. While it is widely recognized that focusing on sales proceeds may be short-sighted and ignore other important outcomes of privatization, it is a fact that many governments are strongly influenced by the availability of funds from privatization.

A fourth goal is to broaden share ownership so that the public has mechanisms for saving money and participating in the economies of their countries.

The macroeconomic goals of privatization focus mostly on the potential improvements that private sector operators will bring to an enterprise to improve this performance and increase chances of survival. These goals recognize the need to improve enterprise efficiency by introducing new technology and financing sources, improving the quality of the product, enhancing marketing-especially in the international market, providing information systems, and generally improving the management of the enterprise. Obviously successful changes of this nature, when applied to a number of individual enterprises, will have significant macroeconomic implications as well.

A final comment on the goals of privatization is to note that in most countries privatization is but one part of a broad program of structural reform. This is most evident in former Communist countries, where privatization is an element of the process of developing a market economy and its associated financial institutions. In such cases, the privatization program designed should take into account the broader economic goals that are being pursued, as well as the goals specific to the enterprise.

### What Types of Privatization Techniques Can Be Used?

There are a variety of techniques that can be selected to use in privatizing state-owned enterprises of activities. These techniques include the following:

Small business auctions—A normal procedure for privatizing small businesses is to auction them to the highest bidder. Especially when dealing with truly small businesses, such as sole proprietorships and small partnerships, it is advantageous to sell to a single bidder. Given the size of the enterprises, elaborate bid evaluations and valuations are not appropriate and will only serve to delay the process. Auctions also create a dramatic setting to promote the visibility of privatization and allow for broad participation, and they are truly transparent, in the sense that all participants can see for themselves how the process was conducted and identify the high bidder.

Auctions are generally not appropriate for larger enterprises because the bids will not be as readily comparable: the quality of the new ownership group becomes important—what technology will it bring, is it well-financed, what investments will it commit to making, where will it market the product, will it close the business to limit competition, etc.?

Strategic investors—Larger enterprises are often sold on a case-by-case basis, by soliciting technically and financially capable investors to acquire the enterprise. In soliciting the investors, the seller normally conducts a thorough review of the business and prepares material describing the business and its equipment, workforce, financial condition, markets, and prospects. This information is circulated to a group of candidate investors that express initial interest in the business. These investors then submit bids outlining the terms under which they would purchase shares of the enterprise. The offers will discuss the percentage of shares to be purchased, what debts will be assumed, future investment plans and the financing associated with the expansion, any anticipated changes to the underlying business or the workforce, actions required by the government (sometimes requesting measures such as tariff protection), and other significant factors. Because bids received in this fashion are not readily comparable, the seller must prepare a valuation of the enterprise and the bids received, analyze the strengths and weaknesses of the bidding groups, and then engage in a significant amount of negotiation with the highest ranked bidder. This process is often lengthy, as there are significant but difficult issues at stake.

Trade sales have significant disadvantages in that they can take a long period of time and substantial expense to conduct. Because of the substantial amount of negotiation often involved, they also have the aura

of "back room deals" being conducted and are susceptible to complaints from bidders that the decision process was unfair—particularly when the bids are structured very differently.

Initial Public Offerings (IPOs)—Initial Public Offerings are the sale of shares directly to the public. Most of the privatizations conducted in the United Kingdom during the 1980's were done through IPOs. Because the potential buying public includes a large number of unsophisticated investors, relatively more information and higher quality information needs to be prepared to conduct an IPO. A valuation of the enterprise is prepared and a pricing strategy is developed that reflects the valuation, but seeks to ensure that the offer is sufficiently attractive that the shares available can be sold. IPOs have the virtue of stimulating interest among the general public in financial markets and increasing share ownership in society. They are also less subject to negotiated agreements than trade sales, although the negotiations between the selling government and its agent, the underwriter, may be elaborate.

The disadvantages of IPOs are that they do not bring new capital to the enterprise and do not bring in new managerial talent or resources. As a result, IPOs should only be used if the performance of existing management is satisfactory. In addition, IPOs are very time consuming and expensive to conduct, and they generally require the existence of a formal stock exchange and broker network or other distribution mechanism to be implemented effectively.

Joint Ventures—A common form of privatization in some parts of the world—especially China—is the joint venture. Under a typical joint venture, an investor approaches the government and offers to contribute something of value to an enterprise, such as capital, management, or technology, and in return receives a share of the ownership of the newly constituted business. Joint ventures are often attractive to governments that are not fully supportive of privatization because the government does not relinquish all control of the enterprise. Over time, and with new investments, it may be possible to minimize government control by diluting its ownership interest.

There are several significant disadvantages to joint ventures as a form of privatization. Because of the government's continued involvement, many of the goals of privatization set forth at the outset of my testimony are not met: the government remains involved in management and its liability for poor performance is retained. In addition, joint ventures are subject to the same complaints about lack of transparency and participation as trade sales—sometimes even more so due to the fact that joint ventures are often proposed by the investor on an exclusive basis and are less subject to standardization than trade sales.

Mass Privatization Programs—One of the significant innovations in privatization techniques during the last few years is the development of mass privatization programs. In concept, mass privatization programs avoid the time and expense of case-by-case transactions and involve the general public by distributing shares for free or in exchange for specially

created privatization vouchers. The mechanics of mass privatization programs are similar to IPOs, except that vouchers are used to purchase shares, rather than cash. As a result, significantly less analytical time is required and disclosure requirements are greatly reduced. The virtues of a speedy process, which I discuss in the next section, cannot he overestimated, particularly in the transitional economies of the former Communist world.

The disadvantages of the mass privatization programs lie principally in the diffusion of ownership across broad groups and in the critical role that management is able to play in the privatization process. It is argued that subsequent restructuring of enterprises will be more difficult due to these factors. Offsetting this argument to some degree is the fact that potential investors in these enterprises can negotiate with the new owners—rather than the government—and can make investments into the enterprise in return for shares, rather than have their funds go into the state treasury. Both of these factors are valued by investors.

Build–Own–Operate/Build–Own–Transfer Programs—Governments facing severe needs for infrastructure investments increasingly turn to the private sector to finance, build, and operate the needed facilities. In return, the government gives certain assurances to the investor and pays fees for the services provided. This technique has proved useful in attracting additional capital into infrastructure investments and alleviating critical shortages of power and transportation, especially in Asia.

The disadvantages of these programs are that they are often very difficult and time consuming to negotiate and structure. Because these programs are relatively new and involve financing of new projects—not assets that are already existing—many difficult issues emerge that have not previously been confronted.

Liquidation—State-owned enterprises with very limited prospects for survival are sometimes liquidated and their assets auctioned to the private sector. Sometimes these "liquidated" enterprises continue as going concerns; in other cases their assets are sold separately, liquidation ends the government's commitment to support an enterprise and lays the groundwork for private sector investment—if the product has a market and it can be manufactured efficiently.

Liquidation is normally a last resort, used when the government has no realistic alternatives. In this sense, it is applicable only in a limited set of circumstances.

### *Questions*

1. The author describes several options available to governments wishing to privatize. Consider which of these options would be most appropriate to each of two countries with large state owned enterprises, one fitting profile (a) and the other profile (b):

a. A leading industrial country with a deep and broad stock market, large banks, sophisticated accounting systems and investors,

moderate domestic savings, no exchange controls, good pools of managers, and a legal system that resolves commercial disputes quickly and predictably.

b. A former Communist country with no working financial system, a small inactive stock market, banks with minimal capital and bad debts equalling at least 30% of all loans, government officials and a population with limited understanding of how a market economy works, a legal system unequipped to resolve private commercial disputes, minimal domestic savings eroded by serious inflation, and a private sector consisting of only small family owned firms.

---

## C. MEXICO'S EVOLVING ECONOMY

In the 1970s and early 1980s, the growth of the Mexican economy depended on production and export of its massive petroleum reserves, among the largest in the world. The quadrupling of the oil price in 1973–4 and doubling in 1979 made Mexico appear to be one of the strongest developing economies. The country also exported agricultural products mainly to the United States, where its goods encountered protective barriers. These farm goods came from northern Mexico, which boasted a modern agricultural technology. Most of the population, however, were peasant farmers on small subsistence plots. The manufacturing sector, itself protected by high tariffs and quotas, was weak. Its workforce was almost entirely in Mexico City. The government fixed the cost of many domestic goods. The peso was fixed to the dollar although inflation rates were much higher in Mexico than in the U.S. Mexican state owned enterprises had borrowed more than any other developing country from foreign banks. U.S. banks dominated, but banks from Japan and Europe actively competed. In late 1979, the government encouraged private sector firms and individuals to borrow on the eurocurrency market as well. By 1981, many in Mexico realized that as the price of oil weakened, the country's economic strategy would founder. Along with sophisticated foreign investors and financial institutions, they began to shift their assets out of pesos and mainly into dollars, in the form of real estate investments and bank deposits in the United States. Flight capital reached billions of dollars.

In August 1982, the government of Mexico shocked the international financial world by declaring a moratorium on servicing the country's foreign debt, imposing exchange controls, and massively devaluing the peso. Inflows of foreign private capital stopped abruptly.

## STEVEN BAVARIA, "MEXICO COMES BACK TO MARKET: THE MIRACLE RECOVERY"

Investment Dealer's Digest Inc. (December 10, 1990) [Bavaria].

The nation's foreign debt then was over $100 billion and virtually unserviceable. In just a few years newly oil-rich Mexico had borrowed its way into bankruptcy, with the eager assistance of the world's leading commercial banks. Falling oil prices brought a heady—but bogus—prosperity to a brutal halt. A country that for years had enjoyed solid growth and low inflation faced punishing recession, with triple-digit inflation threatening to soar completely out of control.

The business community was reeling from major shocks: massive currency devaluation, the freezing of dollar bank accounts, the nationalization of the mighty private banks. As much as $20 billion in flight capital had left a gaping hole in the balance of payments. Exchange controls, long the ultimate taboo, were imposed in a desperate attempt to conserve foreign exchange.

Outgoing President Jose Lopez Portillo was openly reviled, while blatant corruption among government officials became the stuff of outrage. Things were bad and destined to get still worse.

---

Mexico's creditors, led by then Federal Reserve governor Paul Volcker, rallied. Rather than declaring default, they restructured the outstanding loans several times. Foreign governments, also led by the U.S., increased aid to Mexico. The peso was linked to the dollar and devalued in small steps to adjust for inflation differentials. Over the years, the trade balance improved, the country returned to servicing its debt, and the banks' relative exposure in Mexico fell.

Much of the credit for this recovery went to President Salinas' predecessor, President Miguel de la Madrid. For sixty years, a party known as the PRI dominated Mexican politics. Every six years the outgoing president would nominate his successor after Byzantine negotiations in secret within the PRI. Some noted a tendency to alternate between spokesmen for the more liberal and more conservative wings of the PRI. The party's grip on the electoral process had assured an overwhelming majority at the polls. President Salinas' predecessor adopted the austerity programs urged on him by foreign governments and the International Monetary Fund. When Salinas took office in 1989, public discontent with the economic crisis translated into a very close call at the polls; many PRI opponents accused it of fraud as Salinas barely slipped by. It looked as though the PRI was about to lose control of the government. Salinas pledged to reform not only the economy but the political system. Neither promised to be easy.

In 1990, the country had a population of 81 million. The government budget deficit was Pesos 23 trillion (or $7.7 billion at Pesos 3000 to $1). Balance of payments reserves had grown $3.4 billion. Gross domestic product, or total annual output, was Pesos 669 trillion ($223 billion). By 1990, according to Bavaria,

> With the strong support of the US, his government has decreased external debt from $100 billion to $80 billion. Economic growth has finally regained its momentum, with GDP growing at 3% in 1989 and a projected 4% in 1990.
>
> . . .
>
> Salinas has encouraged unprecedented liberalization of Mexico's xenophobic foreign investment regulations. And he is now pushing the heretofore unthinkable; a free trade agreement with the gringos. With Presidents Bush and Salinas engaged in what has been described as a "love fest" as they lay plans for a North American free trade agreement, Mexico enjoys the best relations it has ever had with its northern neighbor.

## "THE NEW MODEL DEBTOR," THE ECONOMIST

(October 6, 1990).

- The government kept its promise to cut public spending. In 1986 and 1987 the budget deficit was 16% of GDP; in 1988 it fell to 12.3%, in 1989 to 5.8%. This year the deficit will be about 3% of GDP, according to CIEMEX–Wharton, Mexico's leading private forecaster. As Mr. Pedro Aspe, Mexico's finance minister, proudly points out, the cut in the deficit is equivalent to that envisaged by America's Gramm–Rudman act several times over—except that it happened.
- After an initial devaluation of 20%, the government fixed the peso's exchange rate against the dollar in February 1988. Later it began to devalue daily, but at a rate equivalent to only 14% a year—well below the country's inflation rate of 60%. Since May the rate of devaluation has been even slower. This strong-peso policy has its risks (principally of declining competitiveness); but it has helped to anchor domestic prices and reduce inflationary expectations.
- Latin America's other governments froze prices and wages more or less indiscriminately and all at once. Mexico's plan, unlike the others, was supported by business and the unions. It let prices adjust before the plan took effect, and called on a few big firms to keep prices down, but only for one or two months at a time. Prices and wages could adjust somewhat between periods, preventing relative costs from moving too far out of line.
- Mexico opened its economy to imports. First, tariffs replaced import quotas. Then the tariffs were steadily reduced. The free flow of

imports, together with the frequent adjustment of relative prices, ensured that shortages (with some exceptions, such as meat) were rare, and never threatened to destroy the programme. Since 1987 the "shortage ratio" (the proportion of shops that were out of stock of a product they normally sold) has wavered around 10%. Shortages in Argentina during the Austral plan and Brazil during its Cruzado plan have been much worse—60% and 25% respectively.

- The government negotiated a deal on foreign debt in March 1990.

. . .

The cut in debt-service payments was no more than $4 billion a year—smaller than originally hoped for. But the deal has boosted private-sector and foreign confidence in the economy, and interest rates have now fallen to their lowest levels since 1981.

Inflation remains the country's biggest macroeconomic worry. Mr. Aspe says he will reduce the inflation rate by buying up the government's domestic debt with money earned from privatisation sales. But few if any countries have cut inflation from three digits to one without suffering a fearsome recession. Mexico will not be the exception.

Underlying inflation may be lower than the official 30%, because the government has raised public-sector prices much more than other prices in order to cut subsidies to state-owned industries. In December 1989 subway fares rose 30%, which by itself added four percentage points to the inflation rate. Since then the government has raised electricity prices by 300%, telephone charges by 400%, and so on. Mr. Salinas therefore argues that the current inflation rate does not reflect "macroeconomic imbalances". Unfortunately, these once-and-for-all rises will fuel inflation by pushing up wage demands and encouraging businesses, when they can, to raise their own prices. There is evidence that this is already happening.

. . .

Most Mexicans, mind you, must be disappointed with the results so far. Real wages have fallen for eight consecutive years; they are barely half what they were in 1982. Some 30% of Mexicans live in poverty, roughly the same proportion as in 1980. This year the economy will grow by 2–3%, half what it achieved in the 1960s and 1970s. Inflation will be close to 30% this year, ten percentage points higher than last year. The trade balance has suffered from the country's open-door policies. In 1985 Mexico ran a trade surplus of $8 billion; this year, despite the influence of Mr. Saddam Hussein on oil prices, the country may run a deficit.

Before you call that a failure, look at Latin America's other big debtors. It is more than likely that, if Mexico had failed to reform its economy, its people would already have suffered even more. The real test, however, will come in the next few years. Wages and economic growth seem likely to pick up; inflation, though high, should remain manageable. Crucially, the government is now in a position to tackle Mexico's appalling social problems, and to improve the country's deteriorating infrastructure. In the mid–1980s such ambitions would have been dismissed out of hand.

### *Questions and Notes*

1. General purpose syndicated eurocredits, studied in Chapter VIII, were the form of many of the bank loans to Mexico in the 1970s and early 1980s. What seems to have prompted Mexico to rely on this source of funds? If banks had made substantial loans to Mexico and then begun to realize that the economy was weakening in the early 1980s, how easily could they stop lending and reduce their exposure? To determine the weakness of these loans to Mexico before August 1982, how readily could their real value be fixed? As you read this Chapter, compare syndicated loans as a source of foreign capital for Mexico with the foreign funding for Telmex.

2. Consider the management of Mexico's 1982 debt crisis. For the next 6 years, Mexico got prompter treatment and more funds from the U.S. and other governments than other large debtor countries. Part of the reason was that the Mexican government's economic policy seemed to address the country's macroeconomic problems. What other factors do you think might have prompted the U.S. to play an active role resolving the crisis? As you read this Chapter, ask if these other reasons would affect investors in Telmex equity instruments.

3. From the sketch of Mexico, would you say it more closely resembles country (a) or country (b) in the question at the end of the previous section?

---

## D. TELMEX UNDER GOVERNMENT CONTROL

Telmex did not start as a government-owned firm. In 1947, foreign investors set it up to buy a Swedish firm's telephone business in Mexico. Three years later, Telmex acquired its only national competitor from International Telephone and Telegraph Company. Independent local companies ceased to exist in 1981. From then, Telmex became "the only licensed supplier of fixed link public telecommunications services in Mexico." By 1990, Telmex owned "all public exchanges, the nationwide network of local telephone lines and the principal public long-distance telephone transmission facilities." The prospectus continues:

### TELEPHONOS DE MEXICO, S.A. DE C.V., PROSPECTUS

(May 13, 1991) [Prospectus].

A group of Mexican investors acquired the Company in 1953, but from the 1950s onward the Government was closely involved in the Company's strategic and financial planning. In 1972 the Government acquired the majority of the Company's capital stock, and in 1976 a new concession was granted to serve as a general framework for the Company's activities. In 1989 Telmex decentralized its internal organization, creating five operational divisions and four administrative divisions.

At December 31, 1990, the Mexican telephone system comprised 5.4 million lines in service, or 6.6 lines in service per 100 inhabitants, and 10.3 million telephone sets. It was the eighteenth-largest national telephone system in the world based on the number of lines in service at year-end 1988.

The business of the Company and the rates it charges for telephone services are subject to comprehensive regulation by the Communications Ministry under the Communications Law, the Telecommunications Regulations and the Concession. The regulatory regime applicable to the Company changed substantially in 1990.

Telmex provides basic telephone services, consisting of international long-distance, domestic long-distance and local telephone service. Of the consolidated revenues of the Company in 1990, approximately 29.1% was attributable to international long-distance service, approximately 35.5% to domestic long-distance service and approximately 31.6% to local service.

---

Rates, through 1989, were below cost for local service and far above cost for international service, 90% of which was with the United States and Canada. New customers had to buy Telmex shares or bonds at a premium over their market value to have new lines installed. Problems were rife, according to Bruce Wasserstein, whose firm advised a foreign investor during privatization.

## BRUCE WASSERSTEIN, "REALITIES OF CROSS-BORDER FINANCE"

A talk Given at Harvard Law School, October 25, 1993 ["Wasserstein"].

In 1990, Mexico, the 13th largest world economy, ranked 83rd in phone line per capita. The average waiting period for a new line was three years. Mexico's access to capital markets had been restricted throughout the 1980's, and *Telmex* was constrained in its ability to make necessary investments in equipment and technology. This resulted in a telephone system in which completed calls were the exceptions rather than the norm. Lines were so often crossed that dialers commonly opened a conversation by asking "*A donde hablo?*" *Where* am I speaking?

The Company had been managed with little emphasis on operating efficiency. An audit after the sale found $300 million of equipment scattered in 105 *Telmex* warehouses throughout the country. The Consortium found the opposite problem with maintenance centers: They were too centralized. All of the repair crews in Mexico City, which has 20 million residents, were crammed into 11 buildings. In one center there were 300 repair trucks—and one exit. It took an hour and a half each morning simply to roll all of the trucks onto the street.

*Telmex* has nearly twice as many employees per line as the average Bell company. Accordingly, productivity was always substandard. Repair crews traditionally sold their services to the highest bidder. For example, *Telmex* linemen for years refused to use rain-proof cable, complaining it was too slippery to handle. Similarly, operators for years labored at 1940s vintage switchboards.

---

In 1990, Telmex had assets of $9.6 billion, total long-term debt of $2.7 billion, and total stockholders' equity of $5.3 billion. Its operating income was $1.05 billion. Its workforce of 65,200 was one of the largest in Mexico aside from the government.

The Telmex capital structure was relatively straight-forward at this point. There were two classes of stock, AA and A shares. They had identical rights except for voting. AA shares could only be owned by Mexican citizens because Mexican law, described shortly below, required that Telmex be controlled by Mexicans. The A shares could be owned by anyone. The distribution of voting rights and the capital stock was as follows:

| | Distribution of voting rights | Distribution of capital stock |
|---|---|---|
| Class AA: | 51% | 51% |
| Class A: | 49 | 49 |

The Government owned 55.9% of Telmex capital stock, the AA shares and a small portion of the A shares. The public owned 44.1% of Telmex stock, the majority of the A shares. The A shares were traded on the Mexican Stock Exchange. Mexico's government-owned banks took positions in A Shares and Nacional Financiera (Nafin), a government owned bank, accounted for on average 10% of all A share trades on the Mexican exchange and on some occasions even 35%.

About 60% of the A shares were held as A Share American Depositary Shares (ADSs) quoted on NASDAQ. Prices of the A shares moved in tandem on the Mexican stock exchange and NASDAQ, although they were not exactly equal. On the Mexican stock exchange trading in A shares was in pesos; the U.S. dollar value of A shares moved steadily up from $0.34 in early 1989 to $3.35 on May 9, 1991. Trading was in dollars on NASDAQ. Before 1990, shares of two other Mexican companies also had ADRs. During 1990, five more Mexican companies joined them.

### *Questions and Notes*

1. From 1970–76, Mexico's president enforced a nationalistic policy that relied on direct government intervention in the economy. This general strategy would encourage the government to take control of Telmex in 1972. What else might explain why the government acquired control of Telmex then?

2. The reading in Section B above lists several goals of privatization. Which of these goals would be likely to motivate President Salinas' decision to sell most of the government's stake in Telmex? How would these goals affect the privatization option he might choose?

3. How might the fact that the public already owned 44.1% of Telmex shares and that 60% of this was already traded on NASDAQ affect the options open to President Salinas?

---

## E. TRADITIONAL OPTIONS THE GOVERNMENT COULD USE TO SELL ITS TELMEX STAKE

Among the ways to privatize described in Section B are what might be called two traditional options: a sale on the national stock exchange and a sale to a small group of foreigners who would take full control of the company. This section describes the Mexican stock exchange and the laws governing foreign investment in Mexico. As you read it, consider the extent to which these two traditional options were available to President Salinas for the sale of the government's Telmex stock.

### 1. The Mexican Stock Exchange

**a. Background information.** The following paragraphs from the prospectus describes the exchange:

The Mexican Stock Exchange, located in Mexico City, is the only stock exchange in Mexico. Founded in 1907, it is organized as a corporation whose shares are held by 26 brokerage firms, which are exclusively authorized to trade on the floor of the Exchange. Trading on the Mexican Stock Exchange takes place principally on the floor of the Exchange, which is open between the hours of 10:30 a.m. and 1:30 p.m., Mexico City time, each business day. The Mexican Stock Exchange operates a system of automatic suspension of trading in shares of a particular issuer as a means of controlling excessive price volatility. Each day a price band is established, with the upper and lower limits being a specified percentage above and below a reference price, which is initially the day's opening price. For Telmex the specified percentage is 15%. If during the day a bid or offer is accepted at a price outside this band, trading in the shares is automatically suspended for one hour. When trading resumes, the high point of the previous band becomes the new reference price in the event of a rise in the price of a security and the low point of the previous band becomes the new reference price in the event of a fall in the price of a security. If it becomes necessary to suspend trading on a subsequent occasion on the same day, the suspension period lasts one and a half hours. Suspension periods in effect at the close of trading are not carried over to the next trading day.

. . .

In 1990, the ten most actively traded equity issues represented 66.6% of the total volume of equity issues traded on the Exchange. A Shares of the Company were the most actively traded equity issue in 1990, accounting for 17.6% of total shares traded on the Exchange.

**b. Government policy toward the stock market.** The government had started developing its capital markets in the mid–1970s. Mexico adopted a Securities Market Law in 1975. Institutional development followed the law. The country opened a central depository institution for shares in 1978, a Stock Market Law Academy in 1979, a Mexican Brokerage Houses Association, a Mexican Capital Markets' Institute, and a Contingency Fund in 1980. The debt crisis plunged the stock market index to below its level in 1975, but it more than recovered by 1985.

The National Securities Commission (the "CNV"), which reports to the Ministry of Finance and Public Credit, regulates the stock market. According to Guillermo Barnes Garcia, a finance ministry official who spoke at a Seminar on Financial Sector Liberalization and Regulation at Harvard Law School in June 1990.

The Securities Market Law issued in 1975 substantially improved the structure and efficiency of securities markets. This law has been updated several times, the most recent in December 1989. As previously mentioned, the law passed in 1975 introduced two important changes for the financial system: the operation of brokerage houses instead of individual brokers and a far more active role of the National Securities Commission in supervision and promotion.

In 1978 the law was reformed to include the centralized depository institution for shares (INDEVAL). In 1980, the law was complemented in order to take into account the requirements to public offers of shares, bonds or other obligations to be previously approved by the National Securities Commission. In 1983 the concept "insider information" was defined and incorporated in the law, with sanctions to be applied to those who profited from it. In 1985, the Contingency Fund was created with the full participation of the stock exchange and the brokerage houses. Several additions in the law were included, to require the formal approval of the National Securities Commission of the corporation's balance sheets previous to dividend payments. In 1986 branches of INDEVAL where approved within the country.

In December 1989, Congress passed a new legislation which is having a significant impact on the structure of the financial system. The main objectives of the reform were (1) enlarge competition and efficiency within the financial system (2) allow an expansion in the amount of private investment, both domestic and foreign (3) increase the operation autonomy of the banks, allowing an addition in the amount of private investment (restricted by law to 34% until May 1990), and giving private sector investors a greater role managing the banks.

. . .

The Securities Market Law was also reformed to correct abuses in the securities industry and to encourage increased competition. The main amendments include:

— authorization of shelf registration for companies that meet listing and quarterly reporting requirements;

— authorization of Mexican brokerages to open branches abroad;

— authorization of arbitrage operations in Mexican stocks traded in New York;

— authorization for firms to invest in money market accounts at banks and brokerage firms (previously limited to individuals);

— authorization of foreign investment in Mexican stock without voting rights through the national financial global trust mechanism;

— the introduction of stronger penalties for investors found to have used insider information;

— promotion of a securities rating agency, on the model of Moody's and Standard & Poor's.

c. **Comparisons with other stock markets.** Mexico's exchange was among the largest in emerging markets and it equaled the combined volume of the four other leading Latin American exchanges. The following tables show the size and growth of the Mexican stock market and compare the number of its listed companies to those on other exchanges. For reference, 1990 market capitalization in some other countries was (in billions): U.S.—$3,090, Japan—$2,918, France—$342, and Canada—$242.

# INTERNATIONAL FINANCE CORPORATION, EMERGING STOCK MARKETS

Factbook 1992.

Mexico, 1982–1991

(Currency amounts in millions)

| | 1982 | 1983 | 1984 | 1985 | 1986 | 1987 | 1988 | 1989 | 1990 | 1991 |
|---|---|---|---|---|---|---|---|---|---|---|
| *A. Number of listed companies* | | | | | | | | | | |
| Bolsa Mexicana de Valores | 206 | 163 | 160 | 157 | 155 | 190 | 203 | 203 | 199 | 209 |
| *B. Market capitalization* | | | | | | | | | | |
| 1) In pesos | 165,826 | 432,435 | 423,009 | 1,418,168 | 5,496,862 | 18,415,504 | 31,977,806 | 60,514,035 | 96,472,097 | 303,271,345 |
| 2) In U.S. dollars | 1,719 | 3,004 | 2,197 | 3,815 | 5,952 | 8,371 | 13,784 | 22,550 | 32,725 | 98,178 |
| *C. Trading value* | | | | | | | | | | |
| 1) In pesos | 44,071 | 133,505 | 362,491 | 606,106 | 2,349,694 | 21,436,504 | 13,026,825 | 15,421,436 | 34,574,647 | 95,724,515 |
| 2) In U.S. dollars | 781 | 1,112 | 2,160 | 2,360 | 3,841 | 15,554 | 5,732 | 6,232 | 12,212 | 31,723 |
| 3) Turnover ratio | 20.5 | 44.6 | 84.8 | 65.8 | 68.0 | 179.3 | 51.7 | 33.3 | 44.0 | 47.9 |
| *D. Local index* | | | | | | | | | | |
| 1) BMV General Index (Nov 1978=0.7816)[a] | 0.7 | 2.5 | 4.0 | 11.2 | 47.1 | 105.7 | 211.5 | 418.9 | 628.8 | 1,431.5 |
| 2) Change in index (%) | -28.5 | 261.8 | 64.7 | 177.3 | 320.6 | 124.3 | 100.2 | 98.0 | 50.1 | 127.6 |
| *E. IFC Emerging Markets Data Base* | | | | | | | | | | |
| 1) Number of stocks | 21 | 21 | 22 | 26 | 26 | 26 | 52 | 52 | 54 | 56 |
| 2) Share of market cap. (%) | 35.4 | 38.4 | 62.6 | 36.6 | 56.3 | 36.9 | 64.1 | 65.5 | 62.5 | 51.6 |
| 3) P/E ratio | - | - | - | - | 10.5 | 6.2 | 5.0 | 10.7 | 13.2 | 14.6 |
| 4) P/BV ratio | - | - | - | - | 1.0 | 0.8 | 0.7 | 1.0 | 1.3 | 2.6 |
| 5) Dividend yield (%) | 21.9 | 7.6 | 4.3 | 6.5 | 2.6 | 3.9 | 3.0 | 2.1 | 3.4 | 0.8 |
| 6) Total return index (Dec 84=100) | 43.8 | 88.4 | 100.0 | 118.5 | 236.4 | 215.8 | 448.3 | 770.9 | 1,002.8 | 2,048.7 |
| 7) Change in index (%) | -75.0 | 101.6 | 13.1 | 18.5 | 99.6 | -8.7 | 107.7 | 71.9 | 30.1 | 104.3 |
| *F. Economic data* | | | | | | | | | | |
| 1) Gross domestic product (US$) | 166,965 | 142,736 | 171,300 | 177,476 | 129,858 | 140,375 | 174,201 | 199,662 | 237,748 | - |
| 2) Change in consumer price index (%) | 58.9 | 101.8 | 65.5 | 57.7 | 86.2 | 131.8 | 114.2 | 20.0 | 26.7 | 18.8 |
| 3) Exchange rates (end of period) | 96.4800 | 143.9299 | 192.5599 | 371.6997 | 923.5000 | 2,200.0000 | 2,320.0000 | 2,683.5000 | 2,948.0000 | 3,089.0000 |
| 4) Exchange rates (average of period) | 56.4017 | 120.0935 | 167.8275 | 256.8713 | 611.7698 | 1,378.1800 | 2,272.5660 | 2,474.4609 | 2,831.1166 | 3,017.5194 |

[a] The BMV General Index was divided by 1,000 in May 1991. This series reflects that division.
- Not available.

## Number of Listed Companies, End 1991

| Country | Number | Country | Number |
|---|---|---|---|
| Brazil | 570 | Mexico | 209 |
| Chile | 221 | Taiwan | 221 |
| France | 839 | Thailand | 276 |
| Greece | 126 | UK | 1,915 |
| India | 6,500* | USA | 6,742 |
| Japan | 2,107 | Venezuela | 66 |
| Korea | 686 | | |

* Estimated

### *Notes and Questions*

1. All told, the Telmex privatization in 1990–1 raised over $3 billion. Could the Mexican government have done this through an offer on the Mexican stock exchange?

---

## 2. Foreign Investment in Mexico and Policy Toward It

For over 50 years, Mexico had rules containing or prohibiting the ability of foreigners to control Mexican business. About the time of World War II, foreign control of the country's oil industry was ended by fiat. Soon after, foreigners were prohibited from owning banks in

Mexico. Mexicans wanted to assure the country's independence from economic as well as political domination.

Mexico's foreign investment law was designed to protect the country from foreign control. The prospectus explained the policy and its effect:

> Ownership by non-Mexicans of shares of Mexican enterprises in certain economic sectors, including telephone services, is regulated by the 1973 Law to Promote Mexican Investment and Regulate Foreign Investment (the "Foreign Investment Law") and the 1989 Regulations thereunder (the "Foreign Investment Regulations"). The National Commission on Foreign Investment (the "Foreign Investment Commission") is responsible for administration of the Foreign Investment Law and Regulations. In order to comply with restrictions on the percentage of their capital stock that may be owned by non-Mexican investors, Mexican companies typically limit particular classes of their stock to Mexican ownership. Under the administrative practice of the Foreign Investment Commission, a trust for the benefit of one or more non-Mexican investors may qualify as Mexican if the trust meets certain conditions that will generally ensure that the non-Mexican investors do not determine how the shares are voted.
>
> Non–Mexicans may not own more than 49% of the capital stock of a Mexican corporation in the telephone business. No foreign state may own shares directly or indirectly in it.
>
> A Mexican company with foreign owners of its shares must register those owners, including a depositary for ADSs, with the National Registry of Foreign Investment. No unregistered foreign owner may vote its shares or receive dividends for those shares.

### *Questions*

1. Many countries have had rules to limit foreign investment. Many of these countries have been removing or reducing those limits through formal changes in the laws. Mexico has been reluctant to do so. What might account for Mexico's concern about foreign domination of its economy?

2. How does this law affect the ability of the Mexican government to sell its shares in Telmex? Is it a serious obstacle?

## F. THE TRANSFER OF CONTROL OVER TELMEX TO THE CONSORTIUM

### 1. The Winning Bidders

The government decided to sell its control to a private group. Three groups bid initially.

- Southwestern Bell, with France Telecom and Grupo Carso as partners. Salomon Brothers advised Southwestern Bell. Wasserstein, Perella advised France Telecom.

- GTE Corp., Telefonica de Espana, and Acciones y Valores (a Mexican securities firm).
- NYNEX, BCE, and Casa de Bolsa Inverlat Associates.

The winner, the Southwestern Bell consortium, paid $1.8 billion for the shares. Of this, the Mexican partner, Grupo Carso, provided 51%. Bell effectively beat the GTE group. The NYNEX group had withdrawn shortly before the bids were submitted. Wasserstein described the members of the winning group:

> GRUPO CARSO—led by Mexican industrialist Carlos Slim is an entrepreneurial organization with a splendid track record in running diverse enterprises. Mr. Slim's partners have included such impressive multi-nationals as Philip Morris and Michelin. Grupo Carso has had experience in basic industry, finance, retailing and real estate, all of which had application in making *Telmex* a world class provider of telecom services. Carlos Slim's personal knowledge, credibility and project management expertise made him the leading contender in the fight for *Telmex.*
>
> SOUTHWESTERN BELL—was and continues to be one of the most highly regarded U.S. telecommunications companies with a reputation for particular excellence in cellular communications, telephone directories, general marketing and customer service skills. Furthermore, 2000 miles of common border made for significant interest in *Telmex.*
>
> FRANCE TELECOM—has substantial experience in rapid modernization, having built up the French network from 4 million access lines in 1971 to approximately 28 million lines today, a compound annual growth rate of almost 11% sustained over two decades. This achievement is particularly relevant given the government's requirement that access lines growth in Mexico be no less that 12% a year for five years, more than double *Telmex's* historical growth level. A fully integrated telephone company, FRANCE TELECOM enjoys expertise in long distance telephony, satellite and network administration, and most other aspects of telecommunications.

## 2. The New Capital Structure

The government transferred to the winning consortium all of the AA stock in Telmex and with it 51% of the votes. But at the same time Telmex's capital stock was increased 1.5 times by the addition of a new type of share, the L share. The L share effectively had no voting power. This remained with the AA and A shares, which now accounted for 40% of Telmex's total capital stock and 100% of its voting stock. As a result, the consortium received only 20.4% of the company's entire capital stock because the new non-voting share was added.

All AA and A shareholders were entitled to 1.5 L shares for each AA or A share they held. The government had held all AA shares and some A shares, amounting for 55.9% of Telmex capital, as described above.

When it transferred the AA shares to the winning consortium, it was still entitled to receive the L shares for the AA shares it transferred. It also held Telmex shares subject to an option by the consortium to buy them later. And some shares were set aside for Telmex employees. Each A share in the hands of the public or the government also entitled its holder to 1.5 L shares, so the public's share of the total capital remained unchanged. The table shows the shift in ownership.

| Owner groups | Before sale to winning consortium | After sale to winning consortium |
|---|---|---|
| Government | 55.9% | 26.0% |
| Government subject to option of controlling shareholders | | 5.1 |
| Consortium | | 20.4 |
| Employees of Telmex | | 4.4 |
| Public | 44.1 | 44.1 |

The impact of these changes on voting rights was different. The AA shares could still be owned only by Mexicans, while anyone could own A shares. Only the AA and A shares had voting power. The following table compares changes in the distribution of shares by voting rights and by class. The L shareholders could only elect 2 of the board's 19 directors, so they were treated as having no vote.

| | Distribution by class of stock | | | | |
|---|---|---|---|---|---|
| | of voting rights | | of capital stock | | |
| | AA | A | AA | A | L |
| Before the L share dividend | 51% | 49% | 51% | 49% | |
| At the L share dividend (12/20/91) | 51 | 49 | 20.4 | 19.6 | 60.0 |

The consortium received the AA shares in trust, which gave it 20.4% of all shares and 51% of voting rights. Among members of the consortium, beneficial ownership in the trust was distributed to Grupo Carso (28% itself and 23% through 50 other Mexican investors), and 25% to each of the two foreign members. Grupo Carso had 51% of the vote to control the trust.

Mexican laws were interpreted in a way that allowed this arrangement. The prospectus explained:

> Pursuant to a decision dated August 10, 1990 of the Foreign Investment Commission, the L Shares, because of their limited voting rights, are not taken into account in determining compliance with this restriction. Accordingly, the L Shares are not restricted to Mexican ownership. The A Shares, which represent approximately 49% of the combined AA Shares and A Shares, are also unrestricted. The AA Shares, however, which must always represent at least 51% of the combined AA Shares and A Shares, may be owned only by holders that qualify as Mexican investors as defined in the Compa-

ny's by-laws. The criteria for an investor to qualify as Mexican under the by-laws are stricter than those generally applicable under the Foreign Investment Law and Regulations. A holder that acquires AA Shares in violation of the restrictions on non-Mexican ownership will have none of the rights of a shareholder with respect to those AA Shares.

As a consequence of these limitations, non-Mexican investors cannot under Mexican law own a majority of the Company's voting stock except through trusts that effectively neutralize the votes of non-Mexican investors. The Controlling Shareholders, which include non-Mexican corporations as beneficial owners of 49% of the AA Shares, own the AA Shares through a trust that has been approved by the Foreign Investment Commission for this purpose.

In addition to the limitations on share ownership, the Foreign Investment Law and Regulations and the Concession require that Mexican shareholders retain the power to determine the administrative control and the management of the Company. Violation of this prohibition may render the Concession void.

Foreign states are prohibited under the by-laws and the Communications Law from directly or indirectly owning shares of the Company. The Telecommunications Regulations and the Concession provide, however, that foreign state-owned enterprises organized as separate entities with their own assets may own minority interests in the Company or any number of shares with limited voting rights. In the opinion of Santamarina y Steta, the Company's Mexican counsel, ownership of A Shares or L Shares by such foreign state-owned companies, or by pension or retirement funds organized for the benefit of employees of state, municipal or other governmental agencies, will not be considered direct or indirect ownership by foreign states for the purposes of the by-laws or the Communications Law.

## 3. The Modified Concession

Mexican laws were modified to embody the government's new policies. Some new rules set standards that Telmex would have to meet. Others provided incentives to the new owners to meet these standards. The prospectus explained. As you read it, identify incentives and performance standards.

### General

The Communications Law, adopted in 1940, and the Telecommunications Regulations, adopted in October 1990, provide the general legal framework for the regulation of telecommunications services in Mexico. Under the Communications Law and the Telecommunications Regulations, a provider of public telecommunications services, such as Telmex, must operate under a concession granted by the Communications Ministry. Such a concession may only be granted to a Mexican citizen or corporation and may not be transferred or assigned without the approval of the Communications Ministry. Telmex's current Concession was granted in 1976 and amended in August 1990.

Substantial changes in the regulatory regime applicable to the Company occurred in 1990, including the amendment of the Concession, the adoption of the Telecommunications Regulations and the elimination of excise taxes on telephone services.

**Supervision**

The Communications Ministry is the government agency principally responsible for regulating telecommunications services. The Ministry's approval is required for any change in the by-laws of the Company and for any issuance of debt or equity securities to finance construction of the telecommunications network. It also has broad powers to monitor the Company's compliance with the Concession, and it can require the Company to supply it with such technical, administrative and financial information as it may request. The Company must submit its service expansion plans to the Ministry for publication, and the Ministry is authorized to require the Company to modify certain technical plans in response to objections from other interested parties. The Company must also advise the Ministry quarterly of the progress of its expansion program. Finally, under the Company's by-laws the Communications Ministry may appoint one member and one alternate member of the Company's Board of Directors, and the Concession requires such a provision through August 1993.

Until 1990, the annual budget of the Company required approval by the Ministry of Budget and Planning; and until December 1990, when the Government ceased to own a majority of the full voting stock of the Company, the Company's rates were subject to the approval of the Ministry of Finance and Public Credit.

The Communications Law gives certain rights to the Government in its relations with concessionaires. For example, it provides that the Government may require a 50% discount on services provided by the Company to the Government. The federal judiciary currently receives such a discount. The legislative branch and the executive branch of the Government do not currently receive such a discount, although they have exercised their right to do so in the past. If they were to receive such a discount, the Company does not expect that its revenues would be materially affected. The Government also has the right to take over the management of the Company in cases of imminent danger to internal security or the national economy. The Government has used this power, most recently in 1986, to ensure continued service during labor disputes. The Communications Law also provides that the Company may not sell or transfer any of its assets unless it gives the Government a right of first refusal. If the Government declines to exercise its right, the Company's unions also have a right of first refusal.

**Rates**

The Communications Law and the Telecommunications Regulations provide that the basis for setting rates of a telecommunications concessionaire is set forth in its concession.

Through 1990, the Company's rates were established separately for each category of service by the Communications Ministry, upon application by the Company. Under the 1990 amendment to the Concession, beginning in 1991 the Company's rates for basic telephone services, including installation, monthly rent, measured local service and long-distance service, are subject to a ceiling on the price of a "basket" of such services weighted to reflect actual volume of each service during the preceding period. Within this aggregate "price cap", the Company is free to determine the structure of its own rates. Approval of the Communications Ministry is not required for rates to take effect, although the Company must publish its rates and register them with the Ministry. The Communications Ministry also has the power, subject to the basis set forth in the Concession for determining rates, to modify rates when required in the public interest.

The price cap varies directly with the NCPI, permitting the Company to raise nominal rates to keep pace with inflation. The Concession also provides that, beginning on January 1, 1997, the price cap will be adjusted downward periodically to pass on the benefits of increased productivity to the Company's customers. The adjustment will be 3% per year for 1997 and 1998. Beginning on January 1, 1999 and every four years thereafter, the Communications Ministry will set the amount of the periodic adjustment of the price cap, following administrative proceedings, to permit the Company to maintain an internal rate of return equal to the Company's weighted average cost of capital.

A principal goal of the Government in establishing the price cap system was to permit the Company to increase local service rates to meet its costs and to reduce long-distance rates in anticipation of possible competition beginning in August 1996. The Company is required under the Concession and the Telecommunications Regulations to eliminate cross subsidies between different categories of services, subject to specified exemptions such as rural telephone services. In order to further this and other public policy objectives, several provisions of the Concession modify the application of the price cap in the initial years of its application. These include mandatory reductions in installation charges for new telephone lines, a mandatory increase in domestic long-distance rates that took effect on January 1, 1991, and permitted increases in basic monthly rent in 1991 that are partially excluded from the calculation of the price cap.

The Company is currently free to set its prices free of rate regulation for "value-added" services extending beyond basic telephone services. These services include the Integrated Digital Network, private circuits, directory services and new services based on digital technology such as call waiting, speed calling and automatic re-dialling. The

Company is required to register the rates it charges for value-added services, and the Communications Ministry has power under the Telecommunications Regulations to begin regulating rates for such services if it determines that there is no effective competition and that the Company is abusing monopoly power in pricing such services. Rates for cellular mobile telephone services are regulated under separate concessions.

### Taxation of Telephone Services

Through 1989 the Government imposed a high level of taxation of telephone use. In 1989, for example, telephone charges were subject to an excise tax that ranged from 22% on international long-distance calls to 72% on local commercial service charges, and to a value added tax of 15% calculated on the aggregate of the charges plus the excise tax. Beginning on January 1, 1990, excise taxes no longer apply to telephone charges. Also beginning on January 1, 1990, the Company is subject to a tax on revenues from telephone services.

### Expansion and Modernization Requirements

As amended in 1990, the Concession requires the Company to expand, improve and modernize its telephone network. In particular, the Company must (i) during the period between August 10, 1990 and December 31, 1994, expand the number of lines in service by an average minimum annual rate of 12%; (ii) expand its services to rural areas, and in particular provide each town in Mexico with more than 500 inhabitants (as determined by the 1990 Census) with at least one public telephone booth or agency for providing long-distance services by December 31, 1994; (iii) expand the number of public telephone booths from a current density of 0.8 booths per 1,000 inhabitants to 2 booths per 1,000 inhabitants by the end of 1994 and 5 booths per 1,000 inhabitants by the end of 1998; and (iv) reduce the maximum waiting time for installation of telephone service (in cities with automatic exchanges) to six months by 1995 and to one month by the year 2000.

The amended Concession also sets forth extensive goals for the quality of the Company's services, including reductions in line failures, reductions in repair time, reductions in the time required to obtain a dial tone, improvements in the percentage of calls completed on the first attempt, and reductions in installation time.

### Competition

The Telecommunications Regulations and the 1990 amendment to the Concession contain various provisions designed to introduce competition in the provision of communications services. In general, the Communications Ministry is authorized to grant concessions to other parties for the provision of any of the services provided by the Company under the Concession, except that, as long as the Company is in compliance with the Concession, no competing provider of domestic or international long-distance services may operate before August 1996. After August

1996 the Communications Ministry may grant concessions to other long-distance carriers. The Company is required to permit any other concessionaire to connect to its network and, after December 31, 1996, it must permit other long-distance telephone networks to be connected in a manner that enables customers to choose the network by which their calls are carried. The Company is also required to permit users of its telephone network to resell excess capacity, except that until August 1996 it is not required to permit the resale of any excess capacity for use in providing long-distance services. Concessions are not required to operate certain private local telecommunications networks or to provide value-added services, although other authorizations may be required.

**Termination of the Concession**

The Concession provides that it will remain in force until 2026, and that it may be renewed by the Company for an additional fifteen years subject to additional requirements the Communications Ministry may impose.

The Concession provides that upon its expiration the Government is entitled to purchase the telecommunications assets of the Company at a price determined on the basis of an appraisal by a public official, and the Telecommunications Regulations provide that upon expiration of the Concession the Government has a right of first refusal to acquire the telecommunications assets of the Company. The Communications Law, however, provides that upon expiration of the Concession the telecommunications assets of Telmex will revert to the Government free of charge. There is substantial doubt as to whether the provisions of the Concession and the Telecommunications Regulations would prevail, and accordingly there can be no assurance that upon expiration of the Concession the telecommunications assets of the Company would not revert to the Government free of charge.

The Communications Law and the Concession include various provisions under which the Concession may be terminated before its scheduled expiration date. Under the Communications Law, the Communications Ministry may cause early termination of the Concession in certain cases, including (i) failure to expand telephone services at the rate specified in the Concession; (ii) interruption of all or a material part of the services provided by Telmex; (iii) transfer or assignment without Ministry approval of the Concession or any asset used to provide telephone service; (iv) violation of the prohibition against ownership of Telmex shares by foreign states; (v) any material modification of the nature of the Company's services without prior Ministry approval; and (vi) breach of certain other obligations under the Communications Law. In addition, the Concession provides for early termination by the Communications Ministry following administrative proceedings in the event of (i) a material and continuing violation of any of the conditions set forth in the Concession; (ii) material failure to meet any of the service expansion requirements under the Concession; (iii) material failure to meet any of the requirements under the Concession for improvement in the quality of service; (iv) engagement in any telecommunications business not covered by the Concession and requiring prior approval of the Communications Ministry; (v) following notice and a cure period, failure without just cause to allow other concessionaires to interconnect their telephone networks to the Company's telephone network; or (vi) bankruptcy of the Company.

The Communications Law provides that in the event of early termination of the Concession for specified causes, including violation of the prohibition on ownership of the Company's shares by foreign states, the Company would forfeit all of its telecommunications assets to the Government. In the event of early termination of the Concession for any other cause, the Communications Law provides that a portion of the Company's telecommunications assets would revert to the Government free of charge, and that the Company may be required to dismantle the remaining portion. There is substantial doubt as to whether the provisions of the Concession and the Telecommunications Regulations regarding the consequences of expiration of the Concession would apply to mitigate the provisions of the Communications Law in the event of early termination.

### *Questions and Notes*

1. Be sure you understand this transfer of ownership and the reasons for it. Compare it to the privatization options in Section B above. Which does it resemble? Why? What would the consortium members bring in addition to money?

2. Compare the old and new capital structures. What accounts for the added complexity? Does the new capital structure reflect the spirit of the foreign investment laws?

3. How does the modified concession protect Mexico now that the government no longer controls Telmex? Compare the performance requirements with the incentives given to the restructured company. How complete is this privatization?

4. Why would the consortium want to enter this transaction? What incentives are given to them?

5. Suppose the consortium manages Telmex successfully and the company is very profitable. Should the consortium be concerned about anything? Evaluate the rules governing the termination of the Concession from the perspective of members of the winning group.

---

## G. THE OFFER OF TELMEX SHARES IN WORLD MARKETS

In May 1991, the government sold another 14% of its Telmex shares in a $2.17 billion global public offering. The funds went to the government. The offering consisted of 100 million L shares offered in Mexico and 70 million American Depositary Shares (ADSs), each representing 20 L shares. At the time, about 2.2 billion AA shares, 2.1 billion A shares, and 6.4 billion L shares were outstanding.

## 1. The evolution of the Telmex capital structure

Although the L shares had been issued in 1991 as a stock dividend to all Telmex shareholders, they were not to be distributed until the closing of the May 1991 combined share offer. The government, which had held the AA shares, had been able to separate and hold its rights to the L shares when it delivered the AA shares to the trust for the consortium. The trust, therefore, held no L shares. In effect, at the time of the offering, only A shares had associated L shares, each A carrying the right to 1.5 L shares. The A shareholders, however, were not allowed to deliver the L shares separately from the A shares until after the May closing. When the A shares (or the ADSs for them on NASDAQ) were traded before the May closing, their L shares were traded with them.

After the May closing, L shares would be listed on the Mexican Stock Exchange. The A shares remained listed on the exchange and the A ADSs remained on NASDAQ.

Also after the May closing, any AA or A share could be exchanged for one L share, subject to limits to protect the integrity of the overall allocation of voting power among AA, A, and L shares. The AA or A shareholder make the exchange as long as all AA shares would not represent less than 20% of the Company's outstanding stock or 51% of the combined AA and A shares.

From January 1, 2001, each L share could be exchanged for an AA share, provided the AA and A shares together never exceeded 51% of Telmex outstanding stock and AA shares continued to be subject to limits on non-Mexican ownership.

After the privatization, ownership of Telmex had been distributed among several groups, including the government. The government's ownership of all shares had fallen from almost 56% before the sale to the consortium to just under 10% after the public offering.

| Owner groups | Before sale to winning consortium | After sale to winning consortium | After May 1991 offering |
|---|---|---|---|
| Government | 55.9% | 26.0% | 9.5% |
| Government subject to option of controlling shareholders | | 5.1 | 5.1 |
| Consortium | | 20.4 | 20.4 |
| Employees of Telmex | | 4.4 | 5.8 |
| Public | 44.1 | 44.1 | 59.2 |

The offering would shift voting rights and the distribution of the stock among the three categories of shares in the following ways:

| | Distribution by class of stock | | | | |
|---|---|---|---|---|---|
| | of voting rights | | of capital stock | | |
| | AA | A | AA | A | L |
| Before the L share dividend | 51% | 49% | 51% | 49% | |
| At the L share dividend (12/20/91) | 51 | 49 | 20.4 | 19.6 | 60.0 |
| After the combined public offering and A to L exchanges | 64 | 36 | 20.4 | 11.5 | 68.1 |

## 2. The American Depositary Receipts

The ADSs on the L shares would be listed on the New York Stock Exchange. Morgan Guaranty Trust Company was to serve as the depositary for the L Shares. The depositary would issue American Depositary Receipts evidencing American Depositary Shares. Each ADS would represent 20 L Shares. The Banco Nacional de Mexico, as custodian, would hold the L shares. Any L shareholder could place the shares with the custodian and receive ADSs from the depositary. Any ADS holder could surrender the ADSs to the depositary and receive L shares. Cash payments of dividends on L shares would be converted promptly by the depositary into U.S. dollars and distributed to ADS holders. Mexico would impose no taxes on any distribution or on capital gains.

### *Questions and Notes*

1. Why would an A shareholder, after the May 1991 closing, want to exchange its shares for L shares? In the first two months after the May closing, about 70% of all A ADR holders converted into L shares in ADR form, one-for-one. Only 1.2% of A shareholders in Mexico opted to convert into L shares. Moreover, in the U.S. market, the L ADSs never traded at a discount to the A ADSs. Why would investors trading ADSs in Telmex A shares on NASDAQ want to switch to L shares? What do they gain and what do they lose? Why would investors trading Telmex A shares in Mexico not want to switch to L shares?

2. Which privatization option, described in Section B above, does this offer resemble? What would have motivated the government to take this route? How does this offer benefit privatization in Mexico? How would it benefit Telmex?

3. What accounts for the complex nature of this offer? Is the offer and its structure consistent with the spirit of the Mexican foreign investment law?

4. What is likely to be the relation between the L shares traded on the Mexican Stock Exchange and the L ADSs traded on the New York Stock Exchange? Would you expect pricing in one market to lead the other? If so, what are the implications for the country whose exchange follows the other?

## H. DEMAND FOR THE TELMEX OFFER

The market for the Telmex offer was institutional investors in the U.S., Europe, and Japan. Less than a decade earlier, pension funds, insurance companies, and mutual funds showed little interest in foreign equities, particularly in developing countries. Regulations that limited their freedom to invest were sometimes said to be the reason: a U.S. insurance company might be allowed to invest no more than 5% of its assets in foreign securities. A German pension fund would be limited to investing only 30% of its funds in equity. But these rules were not so binding, since few funds pushed against the regulatory ceilings. German pension funds, for example, invested barely 3% of their funds in equity.

This section describes pension funds, an increasingly major force in international markets, and their role in emerging markets. It then sketches the way the Telmex offer was marketed around the world and reports the buyers by region. As you read it, consider why pension funds would be attracted to the Telmex offer.

### 1. Pension Funds as Institutional Investors

Pension funds are among the largest sets of investors in the world. At the end of 1993, U.S. pension fund assets were $3.65 trillion, just over half the total worldwide of 86.9 trillion. Their assets exceeded the total output of any country in the world except the U.S. Among major industrial countries, pension funds' assets as a percentage of GDP ranged in 1993 from a high of 84% in Holland and Switzerland, 76% in the U.K., 60% in the U.S., and 45% in Canada, down to 28% in Japan and a mere 7% in Germany. So in many countries pension funds were extraordinarily powerful investors. U.S. funds held over one-third of all equity of U.S. listed companies, a share that grew steadily from 19% in 1980 (see Research and Information Center, State Street Bank and Trust Company ("State Street"), "The Impact of Pension Investments on the World's Financial Market Structure," August 3, 1994).

OECD pension assets have grown 3.5 times faster than personal income in those countries over the last 25 years, so fund managers face growing pressure to deploy their assets productively. State Street explains the funds' investment style:

#### Pension Investment Styles

Pension funds have a voracious appetite for investments that satisfy a unique set of investment styles and characteristics. Their investments are distinguished from corporate or individual investments by a particular set of rules and preferences. While maximizing returns and reducing risk are the predominant considerations in all financial investments, a more systematic approach is taken by pension investors:

— Pension investment must be "prudent," barring highly risky and irrational investment decisions.

— Pension fund sponsors are particularly concerned with the need to match assets with liabilities, the future payouts of the plans.

— Pension investments are professionally managed, guided by modern portfolio management theories regarding asset allocation and risk control. A diversified, balanced portfolio is a trademark of pension funds.

— Pension investment is more strongly inclined to quantitative methods, including indexing and passive investments, and portfolio performance is analyzed and benchmarked carefully.

— Pension investments are long-term, designed to provide funding for long-term liabilities. Long investment horizons and aggressive yield assumptions attract many pension funds to high-yield investments and newly developed investment instruments. One of the keys to managing a pension fund is viewing asset allocation and targets in terms of decades rather than quarters.

— Meeting aggressive yield targets requires careful analysis and quantification of risk. Risk, whether it pertains to emerging market investment or derivative instruments, has become a commodity that can be bought and sold.

This systematic approach contrasts with that of individual investors, many of whom are either excessively risk-averse or dangerously speculative. Sometimes, individual investors combine the two ends of the spectrum to develop a "balanced" portfolio, half of which is CDs and half is highly speculative instruments. Pension funds tend to have a different idea of diversification.

The structures, assumptions and theories intrinsic to pension investment are transforming the financial services industry drastically and permanently.

## 2. Pension Funds in International Financial Markets

The funds moved into international financial markets rather recently. State Street describes the situation today:

Let's look at some statistics. The InterSec Research Corporation estimates that total cross-border investment by pension funds reached $725 billion in 1993. The U.K., Germany, Netherlands, Japan and the U.S. are among the most aggressive international investors.

**Exhibit 3** shows the top seven countries in terms of pension asset accumulation for 1993. Note that U.S. pension funds invest a substantially lower percentage of their assets overseas than do other major international investors. Since total U.S. pension assets dwarf those of other countries, however, U.S. pension funds rank among the leaders in global investment.

Although total U.S. cross-border investment is substantial and U.S. pensions are the most globally active of all U.S. investor groups, cross-border assets as a percentage of total assets is a relatively small 7%. That is far below the conservative recommendation of 15%, the progressive recommendation of 20% and the U.K. pension industry practice of 26%. This leaves room for substantial growth in the dollar value of U.S. pension funds' international holdings. ... Since 1987, U.S. pension investment overseas has grown at an annual rate of 25%, dramatically higher than the 6% growth for U.S. pension assets as a whole.

The flow of cross-border investing has greatly accelerated in 1993. Many pension funds have made their first international forays this year; others, particularly the largest ones, have aggressively increased their foreign exposure. The California Public Employees' Retirement System, which manages $78 billion of assets, began to invest overseas only about five years ago and now has about 15.5% of its assets—some $12 billion—invested in foreign markets. Overseas investments of U.S. pension funds are expected to grow at a slightly reduced pace of 23% per year over the next five years, reaching 10% of total assets by 1997.

The scale of investment flows indicates a structural shift in pension investment strategy. The quests for diversification and higher returns are the two driving forces behind globalization. When U.S. pension funds began to invest in foreign equities a dozen years ago, a key reason was diversification—other markets would not move in sync with the U.S. domestic market. Although the globalization of financial markets is increasing the correlation among world markets, advantages can still be gained from diversification.

The globalization of pension investments is breaking down financial barriers. According to a recent study by the International Monetary Fund, home-country bias (an unjustified preference for the domestic securities market) caused U.S. institutional investors to earn 2% less in annual return than global investment would have produced. In Germany, the cost of home-country bias is 9%. Globalized pension investments, for both traditional pensions and 401(k)-type plans, are clearly in the best interest of both pension sponsors and beneficiaries.

In October, the European Community voted to limit cross-border investments by pensions to 20% of total assets in the unified Europe. Some member countries want to use the restriction to limit capital outflows. The proposed 20% limit is already high compared with the current U.S. level of 7% of international investment and with European practices in general, except the U.K., Ireland and the Netherlands.

These three countries, however, account for 83% of current European assets and appear to be completely uninterested in the 20% cap. It remains to be seen how this issue will be resolved.

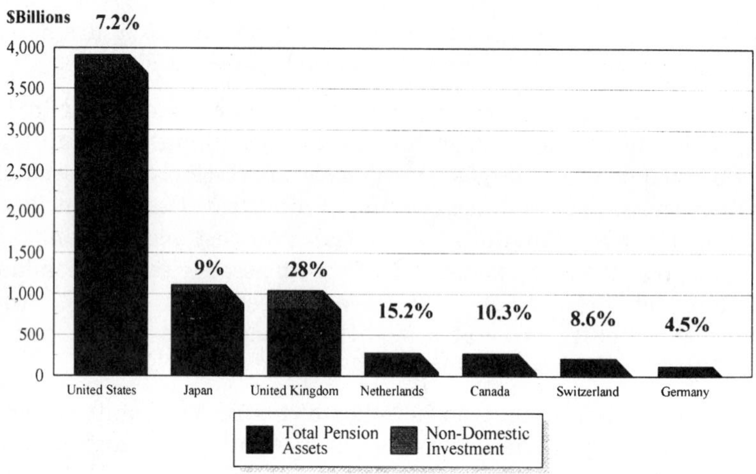


STATE STREET BANK AND TRUST COMPANY

## 3. Pension Funds in Emerging Markets

Pension funds still invest only a very small portion of their assets in emerging markets. In the following articles, State Street gives some broadbrush comparisons, while Faber portrays the thinking of individual fund managers. State Street:

Emerging markets have become one of the fastest growing areas of international investment. In the U.K., one survey estimates that $1 of every $3 of new investment is channeled into emerging markets.

Much of the increased demand for emerging market securities comes from pension investors. Among the most aggressive are U.K. funds, which have allocated 5.5% of their total assets to emerging markets, an allocation almost equal to their U.S. investment. By comparison, U.S. pension investments are still heavily biased toward Europe and Japan, although a process of asset allocation restructuring is well underway. In the past three years, U.S. pension sponsors have dramatically increased their exposure to these markets. At the end of 1992, they had invested approximately US $8.5 billion in emerging markets. Although this still represents little more than 0.2% of total assets, it reflects an average growth rate of 50% during 1991 and 1992. Emerging market investments jumped an additional 35% in the first six months of 1993.

The potential for further emerging market investment is tremendous, considering that these markets represent 20% of global GDP and 12% of the capitalization of the world's equity markets .... Their economies are estimated to grow at about 2.5 times the rate of those of industrialized countries. Some financial consultants recommend a 3% to 6% asset allocation to emerging markets.

### DAVID FABER, "U.S. PENSIONS EXPLORE EMERGING MARKETS"

Institutional Investor (April 1993).

U.S. pension funds—even a few public plans—have become the newest, and still somewhat tentative, explorers of third-world markets. The main attraction is the prospect of spectacular riches, but growing liquidity and the proliferation of vehicles for, and guides to, investing in emerging markets have helped to overcome lingering reservations.

. . .

Pension funds of multinational companies and the bolder foundations and endowments formed the early expeditionary party, investing modest sums in third-world markets in their modern-day infancy in the mid–1980s. Since then these institutions have by and large become more aggressive in allocating funds to the developing world.

. . .

Public funds, many of which didn't get into international investing of any sort until three to five years ago, are also beginning to set aside a small portion of their assets for emerging markets. No one, however, seems precisely sure how much U.S. pension money has flowed into emerging markets, in part because it has happened so quickly. But a sophisticated guess is one half of one percent of total pension assets, or around $18 billion. The potential for further investments is thus considerable: Emerging markets represent 13 percent of global GNP and 6 percent of the capitalization of all equity markets.

. . .

The U.S. institutions with the most experience in third-world investments tend to be the pension funds of top 50 companies and the largest endowments. Antoine van Agtmael, president of Emerging Markets Management, one of the largest of the emerging-markets specialist firms, ... says he's seeing interest both from smaller corporate pension funds and from the larger ones that just hadn't gotten around to investing before.

. . .

The largest, and by far the most important, prospective emerging-markets investors, however, are public funds.

. . .

The larger the fund, whether public, private or endowment, the more likely it is to invest in emerging markets. Twenty-eight percent of foundations and endowments with more than $1 billion in assets use an emerging-markets specialist. For equivalent corporate and public funds, the comparable proportions are 15 percent and 10 percent, respectively. Moreover, 5 percent of the large public funds and 13 percent of the corporate ones expect to hire a specialist this year.

. . .

**The Dictator Drawback**

Those that do commit tend to be timid about it. Douglas Lemon Jr., chief investment officer for the $10 billion Arizona State Retirement System, has adopted a deliberate approach typical of plan sponsors. Arizona has allocated $50 million to emerging markets. ... "A lot of toe dipping will go on until people become a lot more comfortable," says Lemon. Many funds, he notes, took a bath investing directly in South America during the 1960s: "Every time you thought you had something good, a new dictator took over and nationalized the industries."

Arizona's 0.5 percent emerging-markets allocation is smaller than most, even for a public fund. Nevertheless, few plan sponsors are expected to reach the 3 percent to 6 percent allocation recommended by consultants for another two years. Their initial allocations will be on the order of 1 percent, say plan sponsors, and after they gain some experience, they may move up to the recommended zones.

Even for plans that have been in emerging markets for a number of years, though, allocations typically comprise no more than 3 percent of assets and 10 to 15 percent of international exposure. Frank Russell's Castelin notes that a 3 percent allocation is close to the true investable market capitalization of emerging markets as a proportion of all the world's stock markets.

. . .

Lawrence Speidell is international portfolio manager at Batterymarch Financial Management, which runs $500 million in emerging-market equities through various regional funds. He confides that he's often asked, "Why should we invest in countries that oppress their people, ravage their environment and take jobs away from American workers?" His answer: Economics is more important than politics; a rising standard of living is the best protection for the people and the resources of nations; investment in support of free trade is important for world growth; and economic reforms need the early support of foreign investors.

. . .

**Patience Needed**

Experts advise wide geographical diversification for an initial exposure to emerging markets, which have low relative correlations. PGGM's Keijzer suggests a two-tiered approach: Go with a global mandate first, then move to a smaller allocation for regional managers. Unless a country fund is the only way to play a market, stay away from it, most plan sponsors counsel. Devoting too much cash to one market undermines the benefits to be gained by diversifying. "We considered going with country funds, but quickly dropped that idea in favor of letting a manager decide where we should be," says Scott Malpass, the University of Notre Dame's investment officer.

. . .

To truly benefit from emerging markets, investors must reconcile themselves to being in for the long haul. "This is the growth area for the next ten to twenty years," states Wilshire's Nesbitt. A long-term mindset can also help console plan sponsors when emerging markets suffer a setback, as they inevitably will from time to time. A disruption in a country with putative political stability, like Mexico, would undoubtedly slow the stream of funds into emerging markets. But Fisher and many other managers and consultants now feel certain that the markets are sufficiently well established to surmount their own vulnerability to volatility.

As for the danger that emerging markets will prove so popular that too much money will end up chasing too few stocks, the massive privatization of government-owned assets, such as telephone companies, should assure an adequate supply of shares indefinitely. Add to that the possibility that China, Brazil or India will blossom in the same way Mexico has, and liquidity should be no problem, experts say.

The beauty of emerging markets is precisely that—that new ones are *always* emerging. As a Mexico or a Thailand develops beyond the parameters that define "emerging," another country is certain to take its place. This process has been going on for a long time, notes Genesis' Paulson–Ellis: "In the nineteenth century I think [the emerging market] was called America."

A simple explanation for the relative lack of pension fund investment in emerging markets is their small relative size. The following table compares the market capitalization of the Group of 7 countries with some leading emerging stock markets over a decade. Their growth suggests where emerging markets got their name.

## JOHN MULLIN, "EMERGING EQUITY MARKETS IN THE GLOBAL ECONOMY"

Federal Reserve Bank of New York Quarterly Review (Summer 1993).

### Table 7

### Total Market Capitalization: 1981–91

| | 1981 | | 1986 | | 1991 | |
|---|---|---|---|---|---|---|
| | Billions of U.S. Dollars | Percent of GDP | Billions of U.S. Dollars | Percent of GDP | Billions of U.S. Dollars | Percent of GDP |
| Canada | 106 | 36 | 166 | 46 | 267 | 45 |
| France | 38 | 7 | 150 | 20 | 374 | 31 |
| Germany | 63 | 9 | 258 | 29 | 394 | 25 |
| Italy | 24 | 6 | 140 | 23 | 154 | 13 |
| Japan | 431 | 37 | 1,842 | 93 | 3,131 | 93 |
| United Kingdom | 181 | 35 | 440 | 78 | 1,003 | 99 |
| United States | 1,333 | 44 | 2,637 | 62 | 4,180 | 74 |
| Group of Seven markets | 2,176 | 33 | 5,632 | 60 | 9,503 | 65 |
| All developed markets | 2,502 | — | 6,367 | — | 10,760 | — |
| Argentina | 2 | 2 | 2 | 2 | 19 | 17 |
| Brazil † | 13 | 5 | 42 | 16 | 43 | 9 |
| Chile | 7 | 22 | 4 | 24 | 28 | 93 |
| Mexico | 10 | 4 | 6 | 5 | 98 | 40 |
| India | 7 | 4 | 14 | 6 | 48 | 16 |
| Korea | 4 | 6 | 14 | 13 | 96 | 37 |
| Thailand | 1 | 3 | 3 | 7 | 36 | 41 |
| Malaysia | 15 | 61 | 15 | 54 | 59 | 127 |
| Taiwan | 5 | 11 | 15 | 19 | 125 | 74 |
| Nine emerging markets | 64 | 6 | 115 | 12 | 551 | 32 |
| All emerging markets tracked by International Finance Corporation | 83 | — | 145 | — | 643 | — |

Sources: International Finance Corporation, *Emerging Stock Markets Factbook*, various issues; and International Monetary Fund, International Financial Statistics.
Note: Capitalization data refer to the market value of shares listed on domestic exchanges, including shares associated with international placements and those used to back American depository receipts.
† Sao Paulo only.

## 4. The Telmex offer: Marketing to Institutional Investors

Goldman Sachs lead managed the global offering. In the following material, Goldman summarizes the marketing and its results. The first chart lists the places Goldman's roadshow team went to sell the offer to investors. The second shows the results of the offering: how much was sold in four different areas, the fee distribution, and the lead managers.

The third chart gives more information about the international part of the offering. The final chart shows allocation relative to demand, by region. The offer was oversubscribed in every region, but more in some than others. As you read these, consider why demand might have been so relatively strong in some regions and not in others.

**Marketing**

Summary of Roadshow Attendance

| City | | Total No. Attendees | No. Institutions Represented |
|---|---|---|---|
| Tokyo | | 145 | 106 |
| Paris | | 92 | 78 |
| Copenhagen | | 27 | 17 |
| Frankfurt | | 51 | 38 |
| Edinburgh | | 14 | 13 |
| Zurich | | 14 | 13 |
| Geneva | | 68 | 61 |
| London | | 68 | 61 |
| Houston | | 44 | 21 |
| Denver | | 24 | 12 |
| Baltimore | | 19 | 13 |
| Philadelphia | | 21 | 17 |
| San Francisco | | 47 | 36 |
| Los Angeles | | 45 | 20 |
| Montreal | | 50 | 13 |
| Toronto | | 160 | 52 |
| Minneapolis | | 16 | 11 |
| Chicago | | 62 | 32 |
| New York | —Breakfast | 24 | 18 |
| | —Lunch | 224 | 157 |
| Boston | | 70 | 48 |
| Total | | 1,285 | 837 |

*The Telmex international Roadshow had an unprecedented attendance of almost 1,300 investors representing over 800 institutions worldwide*

## Syndication

### Structure of the Global Offering

| | Combined Offering | Mexico | United States | International[(a)] | Japan |
|---|---|---|---|---|---|
| Type of Security Sold[(b)] | Ordinary Shares/ADRs | Ordinary Shares | ADRs | ADRs | ADRs |
| Size of Tranche | | | | | |
| —Shares or ADRs | 79,750,000 | 115,000,000[(c)] | 44,000,000[(d)] | 25,000,000 | 5,000,000 |
| —Dollars (millions) | $2,173.2 | $156.7 | $1,199.0 | $681.3 | $136.3 |
| Percent of Offering | 100.0% | 7.2% | 55.2% | 31.3% | 6.3% |
| Percent of Govt. Ownership | 57.9 | 4.2 | 32.0 | 18.2 | 3.6 |
| Percent of Total Equity | 15.0 | 1.1 | 8.3 | 4.7 | 0.9 |
| Offer Price | $27.25/ADR | 4,090 pesos/share | $27.25/ADR | $27.25/ADR | $27.25/ADR |
| Gross Spread per ADR | $1.22(4.5%) | | | | |
| —Underwriting | 27¢ | | | | |
| —Management | 25¢ | | | | |
| —Selling | 70¢ | | | | |
| Lead Manager(s) | | Acciones y Valores Invetsora Bursal: | Goldman Sachs (Co-lead Managers: Bear Stearns, Merrill Lynch) | CSFB Deutsche Bank Goldman Sachs Paribas S.G. Warburg Wood Gundy | Nomura |
| Goldman Sachs' Role | Global Coordinator | | Lead Manager | Co–Lead Manager (Lead Manager of ROW) | Co–Lead Manager |
| Banco Internacional • ISEFI | Global Agent of the Mexican Government | | | | |

(a) Includes offerings in Canada, France, Germany, Switzerland, the U.K. and the rest of the world.
(b) Banamex is the custodian for all the ordinary shares and Morgan Guaranty is the ADR Depositary Bank.
(c) Equal to 5,750,000 ADRs; includes overallotment option exercised in Mexico for 15,000,000 L shares on May 13, 1991.
(d) Includes overallotment option exercised in the US market for 4,000,000 L ADRs on June 5, 1991.

*The Telmex offering constitutes the first simultaneous offering of shares in the Mexican, US and international markets*

## Syndication

### Breakdown of the International Offering

| | Total International Offering | Canada | France Belgium and Luxembourg | Germany and Austria | Switzerland and Liechtenstein | United Kingdom | Rest of World |
|---|---|---|---|---|---|---|---|
| Size of Tranche | | | | | | | |
| —ADRs | 25,000,000 | 2,760,000 | 3,000,000 | 2,040,000 | 3,000,000 | 11,000,000 | 3,200,000 |
| —Dollars (millions) | $681.3 | $75.2 | $81.8 | $55.6 | $81.8 | $299.8 | $87.2 |
| Percent of Offering | 31.3% | 3.5% | 3.8% | 2.6% | 3.8% | 13.8% | 4.0% |
| Percent of Govt. Ownership | 18.2 | 2.0 | 2.2 | 1.5 | 2.2 | 8.0 | 2.3 |
| Percent of Total Equity | 4.7 | 0.5 | 0.6 | 0.4 | 0.6 | 2.1 | 0.6 |
| Syndicate Managers | | | | | | | |
| —Lead Manager | | Wood Gundy | Paribas | Deutsche | CSFB | S.G. Warburg | Goldman Sachs |
| —Co-lead Managers | | Goldman Sachs Scotia McLeod | Banque Indosuez Goldman Sachs | Dresdner Goldman Sachs | Goldman Sachs Swiss Bank Corp. | Baring Brothers Goldman Sachs | S.G. Warburg |

*Regional syndicates were essential to ensure focussed marketing and depth of distribution*

## Allocation

*Telmex shares were oversubcribed in all the regional markets and unsatisfied demand helped strengthen the after-market*

**Regional Allocations Relative to Demand (a)**

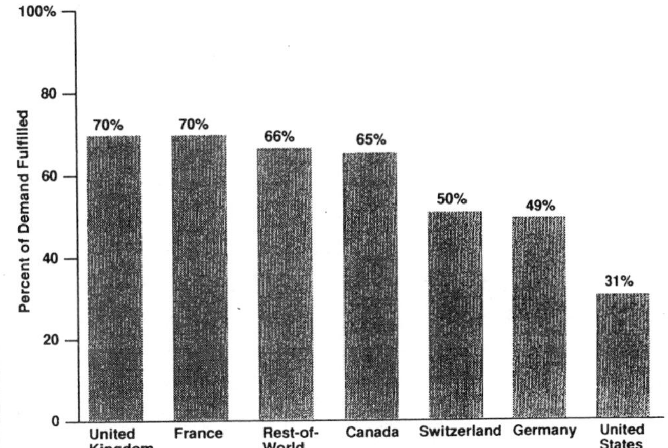


(a) These figures are based on regional demand estimates. Estimates were not available for Mexico and Japan syndicates

### *Questions and Notes*

1. What would account for the relative distribution of the tranches among the four regions: Mexico, U.S., International, and Japan? What explains Japan's share?

2. What might account for the regional allocations relative to demand? Specifically, what might explain the U.S. share?

3. How important is control over Telmex likely to be to institutional investors like the pension funds? Why? What other factors are likely to be more important to them?

4. The following items are said to affect institutional investors' interest in emerging markets. How did Mexico deal with these potential problems, in the Telmex offer and in its development of its stock market? Would the investors in the Telmex ADSs care much about these items?

a. restrictions on capital inflows;

b. restrictions on repatriation of dividends and capital;

c. limited market transparency;

d. illiquid and shallow stock markets;

e. unreliable broker networks; and

f. limited financial instruments.

5. How would institutional investors who held Telmex L share ADSs react to the news in early 1994 of:

a. a backlash in Mexico against the privatization and combined offer, due in part to the news of very high profits for the concession in the first year?

b. slower economic growth accompanied by growing inflation that the slow devaluation of the peso against the U.S. dollar was not offsetting?

c. insurgency in southern Mexico and the assassination of the PRI's candidate to succeed Salinas as president?

d. assistance from the U.S. government enabling the Mexican government to intervene in foreign exchange markets in order to support the peso?

6. According to Goldman Sachs, in the first two months after the offer, the New York Stock Exchange was the home market for Telmex. Trading on peak days is "as much as 85% of all trading activity in Telmex." The L shares trading on the Mexican stock exchange represented up to 40% of all Telmex trading on peak days.

7. Since the ADSs are traded on the NYSE, does the Mexican government not need to worry about a weakening of investors' demand? Is the institutional investors' behavior in a crisis likely to be similar to that of the banks in 1981 that had loaned to Mexico? Would the effect of the institutional investors' behavior on Mexico be the same as that of the banks?

---

*Links To Other Chapters*

The Telmex offering raises issues that appear throughout the book. This is a global offering, like those discussed in Chapter IX. Some of the syndication techniques used to market the security worldwide remind one of those described in Chapter VIII. Capital adequacy rules affect the capabilities of the underwriters to do their job (Chapter IV).

Access to the major national markets was very important. The choice of ADRs as a vehicle to reach the American investors and the factors that influence decisions to make a public or private offer, or both, appear as topics in Chapter II. The problems faced by Japanese equity investors are described in Chapter VII.

The relationship of the ADS and its underlying stock are vitally affected by exchange rates (Chapter VI) and clearing and settlement (Chapter XIV). The exchanges in Mexico and the U.S. cooperate as well as compete (Chapter XIII).

The offering suggests important trends in the relative importance of the debt and equity markets (Chapter I). The ADR is a type of derivative (Chapters XV and XVI) that is found increasingly in international markets.

†

Julie from Mckenna + Cuneo

213 - 243 - 6148

~~Susan Mitchell~~

Barbara Bacon 29

Susan Myers 34